German-American Relations and German Culture in America: A Subject Bibliography, 1941–1980

German-American Relations and German Culture in America: A Subject Bibliography, 1941–1980

Arthur R. Schultz

VOLUME 1

KRAUS INTERNATIONAL PUBLICATIONS
Millwood, New York

A Division of Kraus-Thomson Organization Limited

Copyright © 1984 Arthur R. Schultz

All rights reserved.
No part of this work covered by the copyright hereon may be reproduced or used in any form or by any means—graphic, electronic, or mechanical, including photocopying, recording, or taping, or information storage and retrieval system—without written permission of the publisher.

First printing 1984

Printed in the United States of America

Material in the Appendix is adapted from the work by Margaret Hobbie: *Museums, Sites, and Collections of Germanic Culture in North America: An Annotated Directory of German Immigrant Culture in the United States and Canada*. Westport, Conn.: Greenwood, Press, 1980. Reprinted by permission of the publisher.

Library of Congress Cataloging in Publication Data
Schultz, Arthur R.
German-American relations and German culture in America.

Includes bibliographies and index.
1. German Americans—Bibliography. 2. United States—Relations—German—Bibliography. 3. Germany—Relations—United States—Bibliography. 4. United States—Civilization—German influences—Bibliography. 5. Germans—Canada—Bibliography. I. Title.
Z1361.G37S38   1984   [E184.G3]   016.3058'31'073   82-48987
ISBN 0-527-71572-7

Contents

VOLUME 1

Preface i
Introduction ii
A Note to the User iii
Acknowledgments iv

A

German Americana and the German Element in General   1

AA
America and Germany/General German-American Relations   3
  General   3
  The Image of America in German-Speaking Europe   5
  Germany and American Popular Culture   7
  America and German School Texts   8

AB
Culture and History of the German Element—General   8

AC
General Bibliographies of German Americana   11

AD
Libraries and Archives/General Repositories of National Scope   14
  General   14
  Specific Institutions   16

AE
German Americana as a Field of Study and Research   17

AF
Societies/Organizations/Publications in Support of German American Interests   19
  General   19
  Specific Societies and Organizations   19

AG
Handbooks/Directories/Guides for German-American Interests — 24

AH
Promotion of Friendship and Goodwill Between Germany and America — 25
- Agencies — 25
- Exchanges of Persons/Academic Exchange — 27
- City Partnerships — 29

AI
Opinion and Views on America — 29
- German Visitors and Guests in America — 29
- German Opinion on America and the Americans — 30

AJ
Opinion and Views on Germany — 31
- American Visitors/Students in Germany — 31
- American Views of Germany and the Germans — 34

AK
German-American Commemorations/Festivals/Celebrations — 36
- Commemorations—General — 36
- Goethe — 37
- Schiller — 38
- Carl Schurz — 38
- Steuben — 38
- Weiser — 39
- Festivals/Celebrations — 39
- Exhibitions — 39
- Symposia/Conferences/Lecture Programs — 40

AL
The German Language in American Life — 42
- General — 42
- In the Cities and Regions — 45

AM
German Language Instruction — 47
- Enrollments and Curricula — 47
- Readers and Texts on Subjects of German American Interest — 48
- Textbooks for Language Instruction — 49

AN
German-Language Newspapers and Periodicals — 49
- General — 49
- Refugee Press in America, 1933–1945 — 52
- Publishing and the Book Trade — 53
- Radio and Television — 54

B

Ethnic Subgroups in German America 55

BA
Austrian Americana — 57
- Austrian-American Relations — 57
- Austrian and East European Peoples in America — 58

BB
Canadian Germans/German Life and Culture in Canada — 59
- Canadian Bibliography and Sources — 59
- Ethnic Germans in Canada—General — 61
- Churches and Religious History — 64
- The German Language in Canada — 68
- The German Press and the Media — 69
- The Arts/Music/Literary Life — 71
- Canadian German History—Revolutionary Era — 72
- Canadian German History—World War I — 72
- German Canadian Biography — 73
- Local History — 75

BC
Germans from Russia — 84
- Bibliography/Sources/Journals — 84
- History and Description — 86

BD
German Jews/German Jewish Life and Culture in America — 90
- General Sources and Bibliography — 90
- German Jewry in America/History and General Studies — 92

Jewish Life and Culture/Judaism 95
Local Jewish History 97
German Jewish Biography 101

BE
Hutterite Communities in the United States and Canada 109

BF
Mennonite Communities in the United States 110
   General 110
   Mennonite Biography 113

BG
Amish-Mennonite People and Culture 120

BH
The Pennsylvania Germans 124
   Bibliography/Sources/Historiography 124
   Historical Societies/Archives/Study Programs 125
   Museums/Restorations/Festivals/Tour Guides 129
   Pennsylvania German History and Culture 130
   German Language in Pennsylvania/ Bilingualism 143
   Agriculture and Industry 144
   The Press and the Schools 146

BI
Pennsylvania Local History 150
   Berks County 150
   Central Region 155
   Lancaster County 158
   Lebanon County 162
   Lehigh County and Region 163
   Montgomery County 165
   Northeastern Region 167
   Philadelphia—Germantown 168
   Southeast—Bucks County, Chester County 170
   Western Counties 171
   Pennsylvania Germans in Other States and Canada 172
   Pennsylvania Biographies and Memoirs 173

BJ
Refugees from National-Socialist Germany 178
   General 178
   Memoirs/Refugee Experiences 180

BK
Switzerland-American Relations/Swiss-Americans in General 183
   General 183
   Swiss-American Historical Society 184

C

Philosophical, Intellectual, and Literary Relations 187

CA
Philosophical and Theological Relations 189
   General 189
   Theological Interrelations/Biblical Criticism/Unitarianism 189
   The Eighteenth Century and Before 192
   Early Nineteenth-Century Intellectual Relations 196
   Kant and Kantianism 197
   Samuel Taylor Coleridge 198
   Ralph Waldo Emerson 199
   The Transcendentalist Movement 200
   Hegel and Hegelianism 205
   Francis Lieber 206
   Friedrich List 207
   Marxism and Socialist Thought 207
   Later Nineteenth Century Figures 209
   Friedrich Nietzsche 210
   H. L. Mencken 211
   Die Freie Gemeinde/Free Thought Movement 212
   Twentieth Century Figures 212
   Freud and Psychoanalysis 214
   Paul Tillich 215

CB
Elementary and Secondary Schools—Educational Theory 217
   General 217
   The Kindergarten 218
   Secondary Schooling/Teacher Training 219

CC
Germanic Influences in American Higher Learning — 220
- Educational Theory/Reform/Philosophy of Education — 220
- History of American Higher Education — 221
- Development of the Graduate Disciplines in America — 223
- Refugee Scholars in America — 229

CD
Germanistic Study in the United States and Canada — 232
- General — 232
- Germanistic Scholars and Teachers in America — 234

CE
German-American Literary Relations—General — 245
- Library Holdings and Special Collections — 245
- Bibliographies and Sources — 248
- Translation: Issues and Problems — 250
- Comparative Literature/Mutual Interactions between German and American Literatures — 254

CF
Vogue and Reception of German Literature in America — 259
- General — 259
- German and German-American Themes and Motifs in American Literature — 262
- American Writings on German and German-American Themes and Subjects — 265
- American Authors: Their Germanic Interests and Influences — 268
- Reception and Influence of German Authors in America — 287

CG
Reception of American Literature in Germany — 302
- American Studies in Europe — 302
- American Literature in German Translation—General — 304
- American Drama and Film in Germany — 304
- American Themes and Settings in German Literature — 305
- The Image of America in German Literature — 306
- Vogue and Influence of American Literature in Germany—General — 308
- Influence and Reception of American Authors in Germany — 312
- American Influences on German Authors — 318

CH
Emigré Authors/Refugees from Nazi Germany — 327

CI
German-American Literature — 335
- German American (U.S.A.) Writers, Including Writers in Exile — 335
- Canadian-German Literature — 341
- Specific Canadian- and American-German Authors, Including Writers in Exile — 342

CJ
Pennsylvania German Dialect Literature — 375
- Collections and Monographs — 375
- Pennsylvania German Wit and Humor — 379
- Pennsylvania German Dialect Writers — 380

D
Linguistics, Dialectology, and Sociology of Language — 391

DA
General Studies — 393
- Demographics/Geography of Language — 393
- Theoretical and General Studies — 394
- Multilingualism and Bilingualism — 396
- Law of Language Rights — 399

DB
English and German Languages—Interactions — 400
- The German Language in America—Impact of English — 400
- The German Language in America—German Influence on English — 405

Anglo-American Influences on Standard
German ... 408

DC
Dialects of German—United States and
Canada ... 412
   General ... 412
   The Pennsylvania German Dialect ... 415
   Swiss Dialect—Schwyzerdütsch ... 422
   Low German Dialects—"Platt" ... 423
   Yiddish Language in America ... 424

DD
Dictionaries of "American" for German
Speakers ... 426

DE
Names and Nicknames ... 427
   Family Names ... 427
   Nicknames ... 428
   Place Names ... 428
   Other ... 430

E

Folklore and Material Culture of the German-Americans   433

EA
General Works—Backgrounds ... 435
   Bibliography/Sources/Background
    Studies ... 435
   General ... 437

EB
Sayings and Stories ... 440
   Tale and Story ... 440
   Riddles/Proverbs/Inscriptions ... 442

EC
Folk Music ... 443
   Folk Song ... 443
   Dance/Folk Music ... 445
   Fiddle and Dulcimer ... 446

ED
Folklore ... 446
   Folk Customs—General ... 446
   Superstitions, Beliefs, the Occult ... 447
   Folk Medicine and Healing ... 449
   Religious Lore ... 452
   Weather, Nature, and Calendar Lore ... 452
   Weddings and Marriage Customs ... 453
   Death and Funeral Lore ... 455
   Games and Amusements ... 455
   Christmas Customs/Christmas Lore ... 456
   New Year's Lore ... 458
   Easter ... 458

EE
Folk Arts/Material Culture ... 459
   General ... 459
   Exhibitions/Museums/Collections ... 462
   Antiques/Collecting/Auctions ... 463

EF
Motifs and Symbols in Folk Art ... 464
   General ... 464
   The "Hex Sign" as Barn Symbol ... 465

EG
Fraktur—Illuminating Writing ... 466
   Collections and Exhibits ... 466
   Frakturs—General ... 467

EH
Folk Traditions in Building ... 473

EI
Other Folk Arts ... 477
   Furniture ... 477
   Pottery ... 479
   Glass ... 482
   Wrought and Cast Iron ... 483
   Basketry ... 484
   Stonecutting ... 484
   Metal Work—Copper, Brass, Tin,
    Pewter ... 485
   Woodcarving ... 486
   Clock Making ... 486
   Gunsmithing ... 487
   Wagon Building ... 488
   Weaving/Stitchery/Embroidery ... 489
   Clothing ... 491
   Paper Cutting ... 491
   Other ... 492

EJ
Cookery and Food — 493

EK
Gardening/Husbandry/Horticulture — 498

F

Fine Arts, Architecture, and Decorative Arts — 501

FA
Arts in America: Background — 503
  General — 503
  Reception of German Art and Artists in America — 506
  Holdings of German and German-American Art in America — 507
  Exhibitions of German and German-American Art — 508
  The Düsseldorf Academy and Its Influence in America — 510

FB
German-American Painters — 512
  Individual Artists — 512
  Artists of German Origin Listed in the Censuses of 1850 and 1860 — 532

FC
Sculptors — 534
  Individual Sculptors — 534

FD
Graphic Artists/Printmakers and Engravers — 537
  General — 537
  Engravers of German Origin Listed in the Censuses of 1850 and 1860 — 538

FE
Lithographers — 540
  General — 540
  Individual Lithographers — 540
  Lithographers of German Origin Listed in the Censuses of 1850 and 1860 — 543

FF
Architecture and Architects — 545
  General — 545
  Individual Architects — 546

FG
Other Arts — 548
  Book Arts — 548
  Cartography and Topographical Drafting — 548
  Ceramics/Art Pottery — 549
  Furniture Design — 551
  Photography — 553
  Goldsmithing, Jewelry, and Silver — 553
  Medals/Die Sinking — 554
  Pewter — 554
  Glass/Porcelain/Silhouettes/Wax Portraiture — 555

G

Music and the Performing Arts — 557

GA
Music — 559
  Bibliography and Sources — 559
  German Music in American Life—General — 560
  Reception of German Musical Culture in the Cities and Regions — 564
  Performers/Virtuosi/Teachers of Music — 566
  Instruments — 570

GB
Secular Song — 572

GC
Sacred Music	574
General	574
Spirituals and Hymns	575
Music of the Moravian Church	577
Music of the Ephrata Community	579
Hutterite Music	579
Lutheran and Reformed Hymnology	580
Mennonite and Amish Mennonite Hymnology	581
Music of the Evangelical Church and Evangelical Association	582

GD
Theater and Stage	582
German and German-American Theater in the United States	582
Opera and the Musical Stage	589
Other Stage Entertainments	591

GE
Cinema and Film	592

VOLUME 2

H

America: Travel and Description 595

HA
Bibliography and Sources	597

HB
To 1800	601

HC
In the Nineteenth Century	605

HD
From 1901 to 1940	610

HE
From 1941 to 1980	612

I

Historical Perspectives, Immigration, and Church History 619

IA
General	621
Bibliography and Sources in General History	621
General Studies/Historiography	622

IB
Colonial Era	626
General Studies	626
Salzburger Exiles	629
Some Leading Figures in Colonial History	630

IC
Revolutionary War Era	641
Sources/Archives/Bibliography	641
General Studies	643
Prominent German and German-American Figures	647
German Auxiliaries ("Hessians") in British Service	650
The German Reaction to Revolution in America	652

ID
1800–1865 655
   The Nativist Movement—Know-Nothing
     Party 655
   The Forty-Eighters 656
   Carl Schurz 660
   The U.S. Civil War 663

IE
Latter Nineteenth Century Society and
Politics 670
   American Influences in German Political
     Life 670
   Ethnic Politics—German Ethnic Vote   670
   Radicalism/Socialism/Labor Movement 671
   American Turners/Turnverein
     Movement 677
   Haymarket Incident 677
   Wilhelm Weitling 678
   Communal and Utopian Societies . . 679

IF
German-Americans in Nineteenth and
Twentieth Century Agriculture, Science,
Trade and Industry 686
   Agriculture and Foresty 686
   Trade and Industry 689
   Science and Medicine 692

IG
Nineteenth Century Trade and Diplomatic
Relations Between Germany and the
United States 694
   Diplomatic Relations to 1914 694
   Trade Relations 697

IH
The Twentieth Century 699
   1900–1920: The Era of World War I 699
   Weimer Era 706
   George Sylvester Viereck 708
   National Socialism—1933 to 1945 . . 708
   World War II 713
   Postwar Era From 1945/American
     Occupation of Germany 720

II
Immigration/Acculturation/Ethnic
History 728
   Sources and Archives/Historiography of
     Immigration 728
   Demographics/Geographical and
     Statistical Aspects of Immigration   731
   Immigration Law and United States
     Immigration Policy 734
   Migration of Germans to the United
     States—General 736
   Emigration from German-Speaking
     Lands—General 738
   Emigrant Aid 740
   Immigrant Experiences/Letters from
     America 741
   Emigration Projects: Promotion and
     Subsidy of Migration 743
   Emigrant Guides 745
   Emigration from Austria and the Former
     Habsburg Empire 747
   Emigration from Northern Germany
     (Northeast) 749
   Emigration of Germans from Russia   751
   Emigration from Hesse and the Middle
     Rhein area 752
   Emigration from Northern Germany
     (Northwest) 752
   Emigration from Southern Germany
     (Excluding the Pfalz) 754
   Emigration from the Pfalz 756
   Emigration from Switzerland and
     Alsatia 760
   Ethnicity: The Ethnic Factor in American
     Life 762

IJ
Religion and Church History 773
   Bibliography and General History . 773
   The Sects/Pietism/Mysticism 776
   Revivalism 777
   Anabaptism—General 778
   Mennonites 779
   Hutterites 793
   German Quakers 798
   Church of the True Inspiration—
     Amana 799
   Seventh Day Baptists—Ephrata
     Community 800
   Church of the Brethren (Dunkers) . 802
   Brethren in Christ/River Brethren . 804
   German Baptist Brethren/German
     Baptists 805

IK
Lutherans and the Lutheran Church   805
   Lutheran Bibliography and Publications 805

Contents

Lutheran Church History	809
Doctrine/Theology/Confessional History	814
Lutheran Schools	815
Lutheran Biography	816

IL
Other Denominations	825
German Reformed	825
Schwenkfelders	827
Moravian Church/Church of the Brethren	829
German Methodist Episcopal Church	834
German Presbyterians	835
Evangelical Church and Evangelical Association	835
United Brethren	837
Church of God	838
Roman Catholic Church	839

J
German-American Local History 849

JA
General/Alabama–Maine	851
General	851
Alabama	851
Alaska	851
Arizona	851
Arkansas	852
California	853
The Carolinas	855
Colorado	855
Connecticut	858
Dakota Territory	858
Delaware	858
District of Columbia	859
Florida	859
Georgia	859
Hawaii	860
Idaho	860
Illinois	861
Indiana	865
Iowa	868
Kansas	871
Kentucky	877
Louisiana	878
Maine	879

JB
Maryland–New Mexico	880
Maryland	880
Massachusetts	886
Michigan	886
Minnesota	889
Mississippi	894
Missouri	894
Montana	900
Nebraska	900
Nevada	904
New Hampshire	904
New Jersey	904
New Mexico	905

JC
New York–Tennessee	906
New York	906
North Carolina	911
North Dakota	913
Ohio	916
Oklahoma	926
Oregon	927
Pennsylvania—*see* Section BH (p. 124) *and* Section BI (p. 150)	
South Carolina	928
South Dakota	929
Tennessee	931

JD
Texas–Wyoming	934
Texas	934
Utah	942
Vermont	942
Virginia	943
Washington	946
West Virginia	947
Wisconsin	948
Wyoming	956

K
Biography: Prominent Americans of German Descent 957

KA
Biography—Collective 959

KB
Biography—Individual 959

L
Genealogy and Family History 1009

LA
Guides and Aids to Genealogical Research 1011

LB
Family Histories, A through C 1014

LC
Family Histories, D through G 1037

LD
Family Histories, H through K 1060

LE
Family Histories, L through R 1086

LF
Family Histories, S 1112

LG
Family Histories T through Z 1135

APP
Appendix 1151

Index 1171

Preface

History

On the initiative of Germanists in the late nineteenth century, certain long-range projects of research were launched with the aim of clearing the ground for future studies in German-American history. We recall the important efforts of Marion Dexter Learned at the University of Pennsylvania in the 1890's to extend and continue the output of historical studies by such pioneers as Rattermann and Kapp. In the 1930's, Alexander Hohlfeld began the Wisconsin Project, which aimed to investigate the history of American interest in German literature as recorded in the journals and periodicals of the late eighteenth and nineteenth centuries. By the 1950's, the Wisconsin Project had borne fruit: the studies of Henry A. Pochmann in the fields of German-American literary–historical and philosophical relations, as well as in broader bibliographic studies.

A decade later, Karl J. R. Arndt and May E. Olson completed their massive survey of the newspaper press, and Harold Jantz published his studies on the intellectual exchanges between New England divines and German students of theology. Since 1960 a number of contributions by academic historians, as distinguished from Germanists, have notably expanded the range of our knowledge: the names of Carl Wittke, Oscar Handlin, Clifton J. Child, Joseph Schafer, Frederick Luebke, Philip Gleason, John A. Hawgood, and Mack Walker come readily to mind. The impetus toward the sociological study of ethnic groups came in the wake of *Beyond the Melting Pot* (1960) by Nathan Glazer and Daniel Patrick Moynihan. This line of research has led to important sociological analyses of groups such as the Amish, Hutterites, Russian Germans, German Catholics, and others.

German-American Relations and German Culture in America: A Subject Bibliography, 1941–1980 brings to completion a private project envisioned in the 1930's by Henry Pochmann, in connection with his research in American history. The publication of his *German Culture in America to 1940* (1953) was the initial stage of this comprehensive work; in 1982 Pochmann's work was reissued in a revised, enlarged, and corrected edition, as prepared by the editor of the present work and published by Kraus International Publications.

The two volumes of the present publication continue in the tradition of Pochmann's bibliography, and cover materials published from 1941 to 1980. This Bibliography provides a comprehensive and often annotated guide to works on German ethnic culture and history in America, as well as sources dealing with German-American literary, philosophical, and cultural relations. Included here are books, monographs, articles, and dissertations from the past forty years, and the reviews thereof. Also cited are appropriate manuscript collections and various unpublished works that discuss some aspect of German-American culture and relations.

In part, the titles collected in the present work are based on the annual bibliographies of Americana Germanica published in the *American-German Review* and later in the *German Quarterly* (1942 to 1971). In addition, the editor has searched and researched the sources in history, literature, American studies, folklore, and the like, to round out and complete the entries to 1980. For the preparation of the final text, entries were corroborated, verified, collated, and revised as necessary, with recourse to authoritative references such as the National Union Catalog and the OCLC data base.

German Ethnic Culture in America

The theme of "German ethnic culture" embraces the following topics in the history of the "German element" in what is now the continental United States and Canada:

- general cultural history;
- German writings;
- newspapers, press and publishing;
- folklore, customs, and art;
- societies and organizations;
- German ethnic and religious communities;
- refugees from Nazi Germany;
- the German language and its history in the New World;
- the life of the German-Americans seen in terms of regional, state, and local history;
- genealogy and biography;
- immigration history, demographics, acculturation and Americanization;
- German-American involvement in politics, the professions, industry and trade.

The term "German-American" refers to anyone who speaks (or spoke) German or a dialect of German as his or her mother tongue and who came to America with the purpose of settling. The term "German" as used in the works here cited refers to anyone who partakes of some variant of German-speaking culture in Europe; it is not used in a political, governmental, tribal, or racial sense. The term "America," as it has been used by Europeans since the beginnings of New World exploration, is unavoidably ambiguous. It frequently signifies the United States or the thirteen original British colonies with the exclusion of Canada, but in other contexts it refers to the entire North American continent.

German-American Relations

The field of German-American relations includes the following:

- exchanges of people;
- travel in America;
- diplomatic and political relations between the United States and German governmental entities;
- interrelations in the area of intellectual history (e.g., Freudianism, theological and philosophical exchanges, the Transcendentalist movement, or the philosophy and reform of education);
- the vogue, influence, and reception of German literature in America;
- translation of German works into English;
- the image of Germany in America and public opinion about the Germans and the German-Americans;
- the image of America in Germany;
- American settings and themes in German literature;
- Austrian-American relations;
- Swiss-American relations.

The present Bibliography adds an increment of well over 20,000 new titles. Thus in bulk it matches the accumulation of entries prepared and published during the entire span from the beginning of the Colonial era to 1940. The nearly geometric annual increase in the number of contributions in the field testifies to the reality and impressive scope of the "information explosion" affecting all branches of knowledge.

Introduction

The Invisible Ethnics

> *Let immigrants come.*
> *The Energy of Irish, Germans, Swedes, Poles, and Cossacks, and all the European tribes—and of the Africans, and of the Polynesians...will construct a new race, a new religion, a new state, a new literature....*[1]

From as early as the mid-nineteenth century and as recently as the United States Census of 1980, the German-speaking lands of Europe have provided more immigrants to America than any other national group except the British. A recent report cites the following figures for 1980: 49,224,000 Americans, or 26.14% of the total U.S. population, stated that their ancestry was fully or partly German. In contrast, 49,598,000 Americans stated their ancestry was English; 40,165,000 Irish; 20,964,000 Afro-American, 12,892,000 French; 12,183,000 Italian; 10,048,000 Scottish, 8,228,000 Polish, and 7,692,000 Mexican.[2]

This preponderance of the German "element" alongside the British among the national stocks in the American population is a fact seldom remarked upon and often ignored in the annals of popular American history. The *Concord* of 1683 is by no means comparable with the *Mayflower* of 1620 in legend or story, and there are few folk heroes among the prominent German-Americans of the past. In recent days, the American Bicentennial and Tercentenary of German immigration (1983) have attracted some attention to some aspects of German-American history which previously had not been prominent. The art and culture of the Pennsylvania Germans has long attracted widespread interest, and public attention has often been drawn to such conspicuous phenomena as the Amish Mennonites, the Hutterites, the Germans from Russia, and the like. The Roebling family has received acclaim as builders of our most famous bridge. Yet the upshot of these developments is to leave much of the story of German-Americana as little known as before. For the greater part of this century, in contrast to the period from 1880 to 1914, the German element remains invisible, a featureless part of the general landscape.

---

1. R. W. Emerson, quoted in *Essays and Poems of Emerson*, ed. Stuart P. Sherman (New York, 1921), p. xxxiv.
2. U.S. Bureau of the Census. See also "American Residents of German Ancestry Lead Census Survey," *New York Times*, 16 May 1982, Sec. 1, p. 17, 32; and "English Top Germans in Report on US Ancestry," *ibid*., 5 June 1983, Sec. 1, p. 10, 23.

Reasons are not far to seek. Without doubt, one reason is that many Americans of German background are now contained in that large middle-class group of erstwhile "ethnics" who are so thoroughly assimilated into the majority that they have slipped wholly into the category of White Anglo-Saxon Protestants. By virtue of the length of their presence on American soil and the similarity in ethos and outlook they bear to that of their Anglo-Saxon neighbors, these German-Americans have taken on a "general American" coloration. In their relationships of language, culture, work patterns, and social relations, they no longer occasion any questions as to ethnic identity.

In a recent edition of an authoritative reference work on American history, for instance, the statement is made with reference to the Pennsylvania Germans, that they are "a distinctive people with a history all their own and should not be confused with the general mass of German-Americans."[3] The work, however, offers no further explanation as to exactly who the Pennsylvania Germans might be and why they must not be counted in the body of German-Americans in the land.

A further reason for the German "invisibility" lies in the fact that the German element in America has never been a unitary bloc; it has been pluralistic, split, even splintered along various lines, such as the time of migration, religious differences, the length of stay in America, differences of *Land* (region of origin), occupation, social status, and class. In central and eastern Europe in the modern era, cultural, tribal, religious, and political demarcations have been the rule; German *Kleinstaaterei* was both a political and a social reality. The allegiances of American "Germans" have been to specific European hometowns (*Heimat*) or regions (*Land*) and the dialect indigenous to that region. In America they have held fast to the local cultural patterns of their settlements, rural or urban, Midwestern, Texan, Southern, as the case might be. The westward migrations of the Germans extended over a full nine or ten generations, and this alone has resulted in every possible degree and kind of differential adaptation to American styles. Germans lack the profile (apart from TV stereotypes) and the recognition factor that comes of social homogeneity. Many German-Americans themselves, let alone their non-German neighbors, are but dimly aware of the involvement of their countrymen as immigrants and settlers in the life and growth of the nation.

German-American Studies

In recent years historians and sociologists have joined forces in the field of ethnic studies to produce pioneering investigations of cross-cultural sociological analyses, social and demographic history, and local history based on econometric and statistical analysis. In such ventures, German-American studies are being integrated into the larger program of American studies and American social history.

It is the job of German-American studies to address the problems of historical perspective and understanding. It should aid the student, especially one who is of German-American background, to identify and recognize the particular strand of emigrant and settlement history which pertains to his or her life and community experience. German-American studies will enable students of general American history to discover the point of juncture at which German-American history enters into the broader American experience, and it will illuminate aspects of the past which heretofore have not been fully understood. In all of this, close attention to the European backgrounds of local American traditions is crucial.

> *The value of additional consideration of foreign contributions is clear, not only to give greater substance to writings and teaching but also to provide a better perspective....More needs to be known about the conditions which immigrants left (and to which a considerable number returned)....Greater sophistication is required in ana-*

---

3. *Dictionary of American History,* rev. ed. (New York, 1976), vol. 5, p. 251.

> *lyzing immigrant views both of the new land and the old country, for many historians have taken too literally their complaints or paeans.*
>
> *...no single nation served as a model for or forced its customs on the United States; constitutionally, socially, and in religious variety it has been sui generis. Consequently, Americans have paid little heed to the currents of thought and patterns of life in other lands, of their similarity to and influence on America, and of their contribution to the diversity of its people and customs....*[4]

American social history is the record of the changes, interchanges, dilutions, reinterpretations, and "adjustments" of groups and communities within society as a whole. History in this sense focuses on aspects of cultural development that show how "American" values and mores emerge from the mutual accommodations between groups.

The logical end of Americanization, nowhere yet manifest, (i.e., the emergence of the uniform "American" type) would be to cause all ethnics, including the German-Americans, to disappear. However, and in spite of the factor of invisibility mentioned above, there is little prospect that the absorption of the ethnics will proceed more rapidly in the future than it moved in the past. Beneath the appearance of accommodation in manners, speech, and social forms, there remains in a number of German communities a bedrock resistance to certain central "American" values. Thus the momentum of Americanization varies as between the newer immigration and the older, between Roman Catholics and Protestants, between sectarians and church people, and between rural communities and urban. The lively interest of the present time in family histories, restorations, and antiquarian researches points to a search for group identity within the society at large. Distinctive German ethnic colorations in culture, expressed in terms of distinct regional patterns (Upper Midwestern, Texan, Carolinian, and the like), are not likely to fade away.

A historian of a generation ago observed:

> *Today only in Pennsylvania is there any considerable group of the German colonial stock which remains...German in speech and culture; most of the old culture has been thoroughly merged in what we call American culture. Where could one find more typical American careers than those suggested by the names of Wanamaker and Rockefeller?*
>
> *Instead of this being a reason for neglecting the peculiarly German elements in our colonial life, it is a reason for studying them with increasing thoroughness. If the culture which they represented has lost its clear identity, if it is hidden in the general mass, its contribution has been more essential. If the Germans have become somewhat English in social habits, then the Engish have become somewhat German. All this is a factor in making the American temper what it is.*[5]

---

4. Donald R. McCoy, "Underdeveloped Sources of Understanding in American History," *Jour. of Amer. Hist.*, vol. 54, no. 2 (September 1967), p. 257–59.
5. Dixon Ryan Fox, Introd., *Early 18th Century Palatine Emigration*, by Walter A. Knittle (Philadelphia, 1937), p. vi.

A Note to the User

Arrangement and Entry Forms

The present work is organized by subject. Materials are grouped under twelve main sections in the body of the work, with appropriate subdivisions and subtopics within each main subject.

Each section is assigned a two-letter designation, and entries are numbered consecutively within each section. This subject code system was designed to facilitate referrals from the Index to the main body of the text, and to allow for cross-referencing between sections.

Practical considerations dictated a judicious selectivity and limitation in the number of items which could be included. Experts in one or another of the specialties here dealt with will recognize that the treatment of principal subjects concentrates on the more pertinent, useful, scholarly, or authoritative works on a given subject. The purpose of the work is above all to orient the researcher and student in the main lines of a topic and to enable him or her to identify and locate leads to materials bearing on specific subjects of interest. The Bibliography as a whole reflects the current state of research in German-Americana: while many topics have been intensively cultivated and as a consequence are represented by a multitude of titles, others have remained relatively dormant and await their fuller treatment at a latter time.

Entries render the titles of books and articles in a standard format. In the case of books and monographs, the entry includes the name of the author or authors; title of the work; name of an editor, if any; name of translator; place of publication and publisher's name; year of publication; and number of pages. Entries for articles in journals and serial publications include the author or authors; title of the article; title of the journal in which it appeared; and publication data (volume number, date, and inclusive pages). Dissertations are listed by author, and include the author, title of the work, the designation "diss.," the institution at which the work was submitted, year, and number of pages. Manuscript collections include the name of the person or organization whose papers are collected, the amount of material, the manuscript number as listed in *The National Union Catalog of Manuscript Collections* (if available), and a short annotation.

Editorial annotation and comment and/or lists of reviews are placed at the end of the entries. The annotations have been supplied to assist the user in interpreting the significance of bearing of a particular title. In the case of reviews, the name of the reviewer is given when known, along with precise data on the location of the review.

Standard abbreviations have been used, including shortened forms of publishers' names, state names, and standard publishing terms. Full titles of books, monographs, and articles are cited. English-language journal titles have been abbreviated, but foreign-language journal titles are cited in full.

Under main topics and subtopics, a number of cross-references have been employed to call attention to closely allied headings and to make note of relevant supplementary materials listed in other subject areas.

Scope of the Bibliography

The materials in this Bibliography are items that first appeared in the years 1941 to 1980. Reprints of works whose original publication fell prior to 1941 have been included when known, but it cannot be assumed that the absence of information about reprinting means that a work has not been reissued. Works are usually cited for the year of their first appearance; in some cases, as indicated, later editions have been separately listed if they have been significantly enlarged or revised. In general, we have followed the policy of not repeating a title already adequately described in *German Culture in America to 1940*.

This Bibliography focuses on the history and acculturation of German groups and individuals resident in the Western Hemisphere. It seeks out those influences that came from Europe to America and deals with the ideas, population movements, and cultural features that moved westward across the Atlantic from Europe. This work is not designed to provide a comprehensive guide to the reception and influence of American civilization in Europe.

In geographical terms, the work is concerned with North America exclusive of Mexico and the Caribbean, but fully inclusive of Canada.

Areas of inquiry which have been omitted from full treatment in the present work are to be noted. This Bibliography was not designed to provide a checklist of primary German-American literary writings. Similarly, to attempt to make this work a catalogue of German imprints in America would have swelled its volume beyond all practicable size. We have included secondary studies about German-American authors and writers, but have not attempted to list the thousands of separate poems, stories, novels, articles, and tracts which were carried by the German-American press. Detailed information on newspapers and the periodical press is so fully covered in *German-American Newspapers and Periodicals 1732–1955* by Karl J. R. Arndt and May E. Olson (Heidelberg, 1961) as to stand in no need of repetition here. Translations of German literary writings into English have not been systematically included, inasmuch as the standard reference bibliography by Bayard Q. Morgan, and later supplements, provide excellent coverage.

Finally, we have not attempted to detail foreign relations and German-American diplomatic history; we do not recapitulate the vast numbers of historical studies dealing with international diplomatic exchanges, foreign relations, or the economic and political aspects of German-American involvement within the larger movements of modern European history. Materials here included on World Wars I and II are limited to the repercussions, effects, and local experiences of the German-American communities caught in the midst of these conflicts.

Appendix and Index

The Appendix provides information on some aspects of German-American culture which are not directly reflected through publications or printed documents: exhibits, museum displays, historic sites, academic programs and symposia, festivals and celebrations, library collections and archives.

Access to works by author, editor, or reviewer is afforded in the Index. It is a single-alphabet list of names of authors, translators, co-authors, editors, etc., as well as of secondary subjects, geographical units of the regions covered by the material, and other topics of potential significance to the user not identifiable from the arrangement of the main list alone.

Acknowledgments

The editor is indebted to the reference staff of Olin Memorial Library of Wesleyan University for patient assistance through the years of research on particular problems encountered in the preparation of this work: Joan Jurale, Erhard Konerding, Documents, Susanne M. Javorski, Edmund A. Rubacha, and Alan J. Nathanson, Bibliographer.

Since 1956 the compiler served as contributing member, and since 1959, as editor of the Bibliography Committee sponsored by Group VI, Comparative Literature, of the Modern Language Association. This committee had been established for the purpose of studying the literary currents and influences flowing between England and America on the one hand and between America and Germany on the other. The continuing work of this committee from 1934 to 1971 resulted in the publication of two series of annual bibliographies in the field of Americana Germanica. These have served as an invaluable resource in the compilation of the present work.

The editor wishes to acknowledge (and put on record) the indispensable assistance afforded by the devoted and extended labors of the following scholars of older, as well as of more recent, generations. All these served either as contributing members or editors of the committee which supported the project through the years: Bayard Q. Morgan, Stanford University, co-chairman of the Bibliography Committee from 1934; Henry A. Pochmann, University of Wisconsin, co-chairman from 1934; Lawrence M. Price, University of California, Berkeley, Walter A. Reichert, University of Michigan, Harry R. Warfel, University of Maryland, William L. Werner, Pennsylvania State College, and Adolf E. Zucker, Carl Schurz Memorial Foundation (editor of the Bibliography in 1942), from 1942; Dieter Cunz, University of Maryland (editor of the Bibliography in 1944), Eugene E. Doll, Carl Schurz Memorial Foundation, Augustus J. Prahl, University of Maryland, Felix Reichmann, Carl Schurz Memorial Foundation and Cornell University, and Philip A. Shelley, Pennsylvania State University, from 1943; John W. Frey, Franklin & Marshall College, from 1944; Oskar Seidlin, Smith College, Charlotte Weiss, University of Maryland, and Ralph C. Wood, Muhlenberg College, from 1945; Hildegard Binder Johnson, Macalester College, from 1946; Otto Springer, University of Pennsylvania, from 1947; Albert B. Buffington, Pennsylvania State University, Elisabeth K. Gudde, University of California, Berkeley, from 1950; Carroll E. Reed, University of Washington, from 1955; Ernest Reinhold, University of Alberta, and Klaus G. Wust, Alexandria, Virginia, from 1956; Gerhard Baumgaertel, University of Pennsylvania, from 1960; Lucille Pinto, Pennsylvania State University, from 1961; August R. Suelflow, Concordia Historical Institute, St. Louis, from 1962; K. W.

Maurer, University of Manitoba, from 1963; Guy T. Hollyday, Clark University, from 1964; Erich Albrecht, University of Kansas, and Glenn G. Gilbert, University of Texas, from 1965; Morton Nirenberg, University of New York at Stony Brook, Walter Schatzberg, Clark University, and Brigitte Schludermann, University of Manitoba, from 1967; W. LaMarr Kopp, Pennsylvania State University, Cornelius Krahn, Bethel College, Robert E. Ward, Youngstown State University, and Wolfgang Viereck, Seminar für Englische Sprache und Literatur, Universität Hamburg, from 1968; and Thomas Kennedy, Holy Cross College, from 1969.

The editor wishes also to express his appreciation for the patient care and guidance given him in the furtherance of this project by Barry Katzen, Managing Editor, and Marion Sader, Editor-in-Chief, Kraus International Publications.

Middletown, Connecticut
12 December 1983

German-American Relations and German Culture in America: A Subject Bibliography, 1941–1980

A

German Americana and the German Element in General

AA
America and Germany/General German-American Relations

General

AA1 Adams, Henry Nason. *Prussian-American Relations, 1775–1871.* Cleveland, n.p., 1960.

AA2 Baumgarten, Eduard. *Von der Kunst des Kompromisses. Studie über den Unterschied zwischen Amerikanern und Deutschen.* Stuttgart: S. Hirzel, 1949. 85p.

AA3 Eisenstadt, Michael G., and Dieter Oberdörfer, eds. *200 Jahre deutsch-amerikanische Beziehungen: The Bicentennial of American-German Relations.* Bonn: Eichholz, 1976. Rev. by R. R. Doerries, *Amerikastudien*, vol. 24 (1979), 167–68.

AA4 Engelsing, Rolf. "Deutschland und die Vereinigten Staaten im 19. Jahrhundert." *Die Welt als Geschichte*, vol. 17 (1958), 138–56.

AA5 Epstein, Fritz T. "Germany and the United States: Basic Patterns of Conflict and Understanding." In: *Issues and Conflicts: Studies in Twentieth Century American Diplomacy.* By George L. Anderson. Lawrence, Kans: n.p., 1959, p.284–314.

AA6 *Europa und Amerika in der Welt von morgen.* Hrsg. von Atlantica e. V., Vereinigung zur Förderung der atlantischen Zusammenarbeit. Freiburg: Rombach, 1964. 132p. Rev. by E. Kessel, *Jahrbuch für Amerikastudien*, vol. 13 (1968), 274.

AA7 Firda, Richard A. "The *North American Review*, 1815–1860: A. Study in the Reception of German-American Cultural Influences." Diss., Harvard, 1966–1967.

AA8 Gatzke, Hans W. *Germany and the United States. A Special Relationship?* Cambridge, Mass., and London: Harvard Univ. Pr., 1980. 314p. Rev. in *German Quar.*, vol. 53 (1980), 508–09. Historical survey of relations between Germany and the United States from the beginning, with emphasis on the twentieth century.

AA9 Haselier, Günther. "Aspekte der geschichtlichen Verbindungen zwischen den U S A und der vormaligen Ländern Baden, Württemberg und Hohenzollern." In *U S A und Baden-Württemberg in ihren geschichtlichen Beziehungen.* Ed. G. Haselier. Stuttgart, n.p., 1976, p.9–14.

AA10 Henningsen, Manfred. "Das Amerika von Hegel, Marx und Engels: zur Genealogie des europäischen Anti-Amerikanismus." *Zeitschrift für Politik*, vol. 20 (September 1973), 224–51.

AA11 Höfer, Werner, ed. *Favored—Forever? Werner Höfer Presents Twenty Journalists from Two Countries/A Critical Dialogue on America and Germany Today and Tomorrow.* Wien, Düsseldorf: Econ Vlg., 1976. 284p. Exchanges pro and con on politics, economics, society, science, literature, TV, film, art, music and sports.

AA12 Holthusen, Hans E. *Amerikaner und Deutsche. Dialog zweier Kulturen.* München: Callwey, 1977. 39p. From an address before the Bayerische Akademie der schönen Künste, 1 July 1976.

AA13 Holthusen, Hans Egon. "America Mediatrix." *Merkur*, vol. 11 (1957), 698–702. Concerning the magazine *Perspektiven*.

AA14 Holthusen, Hans Egon. "Deutsch-amerikanische Wechselwirkungen." In: *Jahresring 66/67.* Stuttgart: Deutsche Verlagsanstalt, 1966, p.277–90.

AA15 Institut für Auslandsbeziehungen (Stuttgart). *Zeitschrift für Kulturaustausch* Vol. 17, nos. 3–4, (July–December 1967). These issues are devoted to current German-American relations, marking the 20th anniversary of the inception of the Marshall Plan. Greetings and messages by Wernher von Braun, Willy Brandt, Sen. Ful-

General *(cont.)*

bright, George McGhee, Heinrich Knappstein, Erik Blumenfeld, Norbert Muehlen, and many more.

AA16 Jantz, Harold. "The Myths About America: Origins and Extensions." *Jahrbuch für Amerikastudien*, vol. 7 (1962), 6–18.

AA17 Kaiser, Karl, and Hans-Peter Schwarz. *Amerika und Westeuropa, Gegenwarts- und Zukunftsprobleme des amerikanisch-westeuropäischen Verhältnisses.* Stuttgart: Belser, 1977. 480p.

AA18 Knapp, Manfred. "Das deutsch-amerikanische Verhältnis im Spannungsfeld zwischen Politik und Wirtschaft." *Amerikastudien*, vol. 24 (1979), 21–33.

AA19 Knapp, Manfred, ed. *Die deutsch-amerikanischen Beziehungen nach 1945.* Frankfurt/New York: n.p., 1975. A collection of essays on the subject of German-American interdependence in political and economic life.

AA20 Leppmann, Wolfgang. "Vermisst wird das deutsche Kulturwunder: Warum der deutsche Einfluss in den Vereinigten Staaten nach wie vor weit hinter dem Frankreichs zurücksteht." *Die Zeit*, 31 May 1963.

AA21 Lohr, Otto. *Deutschland und Übersee. Zur Geschichte deutscher Kulturbeiträge im Ausland.* Herrenalb: Erdmann, 1963. 213p.

AA22 "Matthew T. Mellon Honored." *Amer.-German Rev.*, vol. 24, no. 3 (1958), 21–22. The Federal Republic of Germany presents Dr. Mellon the Commander's Cross of the Order of Merit in recognition of his support of American-German cultural relations.

AA23 McClelland, David G. "The United States and Germany: A Comparative Study of National Character." In: *The Roots of National Consciousness*. Princeton: D. Van Nostrand, 1964. American concern with achievement and self-actualization is kept in check by other-direction, here declared to be "the psychological precondition of a democratic political system."

AA24 McGhee, George C. "Cultural Relations Between the United States and Germany." *Amer.-German Rev.*, vol. 35, no. 2 (1968), 16–18.

AA25 Meyer, Heinrich. "Some Remarks about German-American Relations." In: *The German Contribution to the Building of the Americas: Studies in Honor of Karl J. R. Arndt.* Ed. G. K. Friesen and W. Schatzberg. Hanover, N.H.: Univ. Pr. of New England, 1977, p.359–72.

AA26 Morris, Brewster H. "Grundlagen, Wege und Ziele der deutsch-amerikanischen Zusammenarbeit." *Auslandskurier*, vol. 3 (1962), 2–3.

AA27 Muehlen, Norbert. *The Return of Germany: A Tale of Two Countries.* Chicago: Regnery, 1953. 310p. Rev. by R. G. L. Waite, *Amer. Hist. Rev.*, vol. 59 (1953), 204–06. Insists that the *N.Y. Times* and American social psychologists have misrepresented and misunderstood Germany.

AA28 Ottnad, Bernd. "Geschichtliche Beziehungen zwischen Baden-Württemberg und den Vereinigten Staaten." *Ruperto-Carola. Vereinigung der Freunde der Studentenschaft der Universität Heidelberg, e.V.*, vol. 18 (1966).

AA29 Paulsen, Wolfgang, ed. *Die USA und Deutschland: Wechselseitige Spiegelungen in der Literatur der Gegenwart. Achter Amherster Kolloquium . . . .* Bern: Francke, 1976.

AA30 Piltz, Thomas, ed. *Die Deutschen und die Amerikaner. The Americans and the Germans. Eine Dokumentation mit 349 Abbildungen im Text und auf Tafeln. A Documentary . . . .* München: Heinz Moos Vlg., 1977, 244p. German and English texts in parallel columns.

AA31 Piltz, Thomas, ed. *Zweihundert Jahre deutsch-amerikanische Beziehungen/Two Hundred Years of German-American Relations 1776–1976. Eine Dokumentation mit 391 Abbildungen im Text und auf Tafeln/A Documentary with 391 Illustrations and Plates.* München: Heinz Moos Verlag, 1975. 188p. See also *The Americans and the Germans. Die Deutschen und die Amerikaner.* Ed. Thomas Piltz. Identical with the above (in soft cover) but lacking the 32 colored plates. Rev. by J. Eichhoff, *Monatshefte*, vol. 70 (1978), 313.

AA32 Rein, Gustav Adolf. *Europa und Übersee. Gesammelte Aufsätze.* Göttingen: Musterschmidt, 1961. 347p. Collected essays on Steuben, Geo. Washington, the U.S. party system, Germany and the United States, the Versailles Treaty, etc.

AA33 Schwelien, Joachim H. *Encounter and Encouragement: A Bicentennial Review of German-American Relations.* Bonn: Bonner Universitäts-Buchdruckerei, 1976. 143p. Sponsored by the West German government.

AA34 Taubert, Sigfried. "Deutsche Bücher in den USA/Nordamerikanische Bücher in Deutschland." *Zeitschrift für Kulturaustausch,* vol. 17 (1967), 213–16.

AA35 *U S A und Baden-Württemberg in ihren geschichtlichen Beziehungen. Beiträge und Bilddokumente anlässlich der von den Staatlichen Archiven Baden-Württembergs und dem Institut für Auslandsbeziehungen in Stuttgart veranstalteten Ausstellung zur 200-Jahr-Feier der Unabhängigkeitserklärung der U S von A.* Ed. Günther Haselier et al. Stuttgart: n.p., 1976. Issued as catalogue for the exhibit shown at the headquarters of the Institut für Auslandsbeziehungen, Stuttgart, Charlottenplatz 17. The work includes essays by Bernd Ottnad: "Die politischen Beziehungen;" "Die kulturellen Beziehungen;" "Die wirtschaftlichen Beziehungen," p.99–113.

AA36 *U S A und Deutschland. Zeitgeschichtliche Fragen. Referate und Gutachten der 3. amerikanisch-deutschen Historikertagung 1960.* Braunschweig: n.p., 1962. 92p.

AA37 Ziemke, Earl F. "Edwin L. Hunt, Henry J. Morgenthau, Jr., and German-American Relations after Two Wars." In: *Germany and America: Essays on Problems of International Relations and Immigration.* Ed. Hans L. Trefousse. New York: Columbia Univ. Pr., 1980.

AA38 *Zwei Völker im Gespraech.* Aus der Vortragsreihe der Amerika-Häuser in Deutschland. Speeches—Essays. Frankfurt: n.p. 1961. 216p.

The Image of America in German-Speaking Europe

See also Section IA: General *in* Part I: Historical Perspectives, Immigration History, and Church History.

AA39 Appel, Benjamin. *With Many Voices. Europe Talks about America.* New York: Morrow, 1963. 417p. A writer gathers opinion about the U.S. in eastern and western Europe.

AA40 Baudet, Henri. *Paradise on Earth: Some Thoughts on European Images of Non-European Man.* Trans. by Eliz. Wentholt. Forew. by F. L. Baumer. New Haven: Yale Univ. Pr., 1965. 87p.

AA41 Beate-Schilling, Hanna. "Rediscovering America. J. F. K.'s Legacy in Berlin." *Amer.-German Rev.,* vol. 33, no. 6 (1966), 14–16. The John F. Kennedy Institute for American Studies, Freie Universität, Berlin.

AA42 Beck, Earl R. "German Views of Negro Life in the United States (1919–1933)." *Jour. of Negro Hist.,* vol. 48 (January 1963), 22–32.

AA43 Berg, Peter. *Deutschland und Amerika 1918–1929. Über das deutsche Amerikabild der zwanziger Jahre.* Lübeck: Matthiesen, 1963. 163p.

AA44 Bergstraesser, Arnold. "Zum Problem der sogenannten Amerikanisierung Deutschlands." *Jahrbuch für Amerikastudien,* vol. 8 (1963), 13–23.

AA45 Borch, Herbert von. *The Unfinished Society.* Trans. by Mary Ilford. New York: Hawthorn Books, 1962. 253p. American society examined by a German writer.

AA46 Brumm, Ursula. "Amerika in deutscher Sicht." *Neue deutsche Hefte,* vol. 6 (1959), 636–39.

AA47 Buchwald, Manfred. "Das Kulturbild Amerikas im Spiegel deutscher Zeitungen und Zeitschriften, 1919–1932." Diss., Kiel, 1964.

AA48 Burnham, James, ed. "What Europe Thinks of America." New York: John Day, 1953. 222p.

AA49 Chester, Edward W. *Europe Views America—A Critical Evaluation.* Forew. by Mark A. May. Washington, D.C.: Public Affairs Pr., 1962. 182p. Observations by some seventy European writers concerning the U.S. since 1920.

AA50 Chiappelli, Fred, Michael J. B. Allen, and Robert L. Benson, eds. *First Images of America: The Impact of the New World on the Old.* Berkeley: Univ. of Calif. Pr., 1976. 2 vols. 515, 442p.

General *(cont.)*

Incl. the essay by Harold Jantz: "Images of America in the German Renaissance," p. 91–106.

AA51 Eckert, Georg, and Otto-Ernst Schüddekopf, eds. *Die USA im deutschen Schulbuch.* Schriftenreihe des Internationalen Schulbuchinstituts, no. 3. Braunschweig: Internationales Schulbuchinstitut, 1958.

AA52 *European Beliefs Regarding the United States.* New York: Common Council for American Unity, 1949. 134p.

AA53 Fabian, Bernhard. *Alexis de Tocquevilles Amerikabild. Genetische Untersuchungen über Zusammenhänge mit der zeitgenössischen, insbesondere der englischen Amerika-Interpretation.* Beihefte zum Jahrbuch für Amerikastudien, no. 1. Heidelberg: Winter, 1957. 158p.

AA54 Feiler, Arthur. *America Seen through German Eyes.* Trans. by Margaret L. Goldsmith. Repr. New York: Arno Pr., 1974. 284p.

AA55 Gabrielson, A. "Die Behandlung Amerikas im Englischunterricht." *Die Neueren Sprachen,* N.F., vol. 6 (1957), 325–32.

AA56 Hartig, Paul. "Das Amerika-Bild der Deutschen." In: *Politik und Bildung* (Braunschweig), 2. Aufl. 1964, p. 166–72.

AA57 Herm, Gerhard. *Amerika erobert Europa.* Düsseldorf: Econ Vlg., 1964. 470p. Survey of four centuries of the Americanizing of Old Europe.

AA58 Ingrim, Robert. "Das verzerrte Amerikabild." *Neues Abendland* (München), vol. 8, no. 7 (1953), 421–24.

AA59 Jantz, Harold. "The Myths about America: Origins and Extensions." *Jahrbuch für Amerikastudien,* vol. 7 (1962), 6–18. Myths and Utopian dreams in the history of European interest in the New World.

AA60 Jones, Howard Mumford. *O Strange New World: American Culture: The Formative Years.* New York: Viking Pr., 1964. 464p. European ideas of what the Americas were and should be; what European settlers who became Americans thought America meant—from the age of Columbus to the age of Jackson. Rev. by C. Bridenbaugh, *Amer. Hist. Rev.,* vol. 70, no. 3 (April 1965), 796–97.

AA61 Kaufmann, Walter. *Begegnung mit Amerika heute.* Trans. from the English by Helga Zimmik. Rostock: Hinstorff VEB, 1965. 178p.

AA62 Koht, Halvdan. *The American Spirit in Europe.* Philadelphia: Univ. of Pa. Pr., 1949. 289p. Rev. by W. E. Rappard, *Annals of the Amer. Academy of Political and Social Science,* vol. 266 (1949), 218–19. A Norwegian historian interprets the impact of America since World War II on Scandinavia, Great Britain and Germany.

AA63 Lasky, Melvin J. "America and Europe: Trans-Atlantic Images." *Encounter,* vol. 18 (January 1962), 66–78.

AA64 McCreary, Edward A. *The Americanization of Europe.* New York: Doubleday, 1964. 295p. Rev. by M. Hoffman, *N.Y. Times Book Rev.,* 13 December 1964, p. 3, 19.

AA65 Mann, Golo. *Vom Geist Amerikas. Eine Einführung in amerikanisches Denken und Handeln im zwanzigsten Jahrhundert.* 3rd ed. Stuttgart: n.p., 1961.

AA66 Moltmann, Günter. "Anti-Americanism in Germany: Historical Perspectives." *Australian Jour. of Politics and Hist.,* vol. 21, no. 2 (August 1975), 13–26. For the entire period from 1776.

AA67 Moltmann, Günter. "U S A. Eine Bilanz Deutsch-Amerikanischer Beziehungen." *Geschichte in Wissenschaft und Unterricht,* vol. 27, no. 7 (1976), 393–408. Survey of economic relations since 1800; the influence of German immigrants; U.S.-Germany cooperation since 1945.

AA68 Schlegelmilch, Wolfgang. "Zum Amerikabild von Haupt- und Realschülern. Teilergebnisse einer Befragung." *Jahrbuch für Amerikastudien,* vol. 13 (1968), 158–73.

AA69 Skard, Sigmund, ed. *USA in Focus: Recent Re-Interpretations.* Oslo/Copenhagen/Stockholm: Scandinavian Univ. Books, 1966. 200p. Rev. by H. Petter, *Jahrbuch für Amerikastudien,* vol. 13 (1968), 275–76.

AA70 Smith, Duncan. "'...beschreibung eyner Landtschaft der Wilden/Nacketen/Grimmigen Menschfresser Leuthen': The German Image of America in the Sixteenth Century." In: *The German Contribution to the Building of the Americas: Studies in Honor of Karl J. R. Arndt.* Eds. G. K.

Friesen and W. Schatzberg Hanover, N.H.: Univ. Pr. of New England, 1977, p.1–19.

AA71 Spencer, Thomas E. "Hegel on America." *Ball State Univ. Forum*, vol. 12, no. 3 (1971), 31–43.

AA72 Stratowa, Wulf, ed. *Spektrum Amerika*. Wien: Manutius, 1964. 452p. Rev. by H. A. Walbruck, *Monatshefte*, vol. 57 (1965), 263–64. Commentary on America from the writings of 141 European authors and thinkers.

Germany and American Popular Culture

AA73 *Das Amerika-Buch für die Jugend; die U.S. von A. in Berichten, Erzählungen, Aufsätzen, Versen und Briefen*. Frankfurt: Hirschgraben Verlag, 1951. 494p.

AA74 "Das amerikanische Buch im Nachkriegsdeutschland." *Welt und Wort*, vol. 5 (1950), 404f.

AA75 Anderson, Dennis. "Bob Dylan's Reception in Germany." *Negatief* (Rotterdam), vol. 3 (1980).

AA76 Anderson, Dennis. *The Hollow Morn: Bob Dylan's Reception in the U.S. and Germany*. Heidelberg: Carl Winter, 1981.

AA77 Burridge, E., and G. Sandy. *Die echte amerikanische Küche*. Berlin: Mary Hahns Kochbuchverlag, 1968. 207p.

AA78 Commeret, Lorraine M. "Edwin Booth's German Tour." Diss., Illinois, 1980. 327p. The American tragedian toured Germany and Austria in 1883.

AA79 Helt, Richard C. "'Country-Musik?': Some Notes on the Popular Music of Texas and the Gulf Coast in West Germany." In: *Texas and Germany: Crosscurrents*. Ed. Joseph Wilson. Houston: Rice University, 1977, p.111–18.

AA80 Hetman, Frederick. *Amerika singt. 70 Lieder aus den USA*. Frankfurt: Europäische Verlag-Anstalt, 1966. 155p. With one record.

AA81 Hewett-Thayer, Harvey W. "Yankee Doodle in Germany." *Amer.-German Rev.*, vol. 16, no. 3 (1950), 27–29. Tracing the knowledge of the song in Germany from the first reference in 1839.

AA82 Huyssen, Andreas. "The Cultural Politics of Pop: Reception and Critique of U.S. Pop Art in the Federal Republic of Germany." *New German Critique*, vol. 4 (1975), 77–97.

AA83 Kristensson, Göran. *Angloamerikanische Einflüsse in DDR—Zeitungstexten unter Berücksichtigung semantischer, pragmatischer, gesellschaftlich-ideologischer entlehnungsprozessualer und quantitativer Aspekte*. Stockholmer Germanistische Forschungen, vol. 23. Stockholm: Almqvist & Wiksell, 1977. 365p.

AA84 McMahon, Virginia, and Ruth Phelps. *Das Bristoler Tanzbuch*. Middlebury, Vt.: n.p., 1950. Rev. by P. Dunsing, *Amer.-German Rev.*, vol. 17, no. 3 (1951), 36.

AA85 Marjasch, Sonja. *Der amerikanische Bestseller, Sein Wesen, seine Verbreitung unter besonderer Berücksichtigung der Schweiz*. Bern: Francke, 1946. 176p.

AA86 *Okay. The American Language Magazine for Study and Entertainment*. Ed. Bernhard E. Müller, Wilhelm Hesse, and Karl Wittmann. Göppingen: Müller and Hesse, 1950f.; Stuttgart: Klett, 1949f.

AA87 Palm, Franz, ed. *Tänze aus Amerika: Play Parties, Mixers, Couples, Contra Dances, Square Dances*. Im Auftrag des Arbeitskreises für Tanz im Bundesgebiet hrsg. Regensburg: Bosse, 1961. 60p.

AA88 Schmiedt, Helmut. "No Satisfaction oder keiner weiss mehr: Rockmusik und Gegenwartsliteratur." *Zeitschrift für Literaturwissenschaft und Linguistik*, vol. 9, no. 34 (1979), 11–24.

AA89 Stammel, Heinz J. *Der Cowboy: Legende und Wirklichkeit von A–Z: Ein Lexikon der amerikanischen Pioniergeschichte*. Gütersloh/Berlin/München/Wien: Bertelsmann Lexikon-Vlg., 1972. 416p.

America and German School Texts

AA90 Lang, Hans-Joachim. "Amerikakunde im deutschen Schulbuch." *Jahrbuch für Amerikastudien*, vol. 8 (1963), 75–83.

AA91 Lewis, Ralph. "Books that Germans are Reading about America." *Library Quar.*, vol. 29 (1959), 246–50.

AA92 Reisige, Wilhelm. "Amerikakunde in der Schule." *Praxis des neusprachl. Unterrichts*, vol. 4 (1957), 97–99.

AA93 Schneider, Rolf. "Amerika in Unterricht und Schulbuch der höheren Schulen. Ein Überblick vom Standpunkt des Verlegers." *Jahrbuch für Amerikastudien*, vol. 8 (1964), 56–68.

AB

Culture and History of the German Element — General

AB1 Adamic, Louis. "Americans from Germany." In: *A Nation of Nations*, by L. Adamic. New York: Harper, 1945, p. 167–95.

AB2 Billigmeier, Robert Henry. *Americans from Germany: A Study of Cultural Diversity*. Belmont, Calif.: Wadsworth Publ., 1974. 189p.

AB3 Bode, Emil. *Deutsche Kämpfer in Nordamerika*. Deutschlands Werden, Heft 23–24. Leipzig: Schloessmann, 1934. 31p.

AB4 Bruncken, Ernst. "Deutsches Wesen in der amerikanischen Volksentwicklung." *Die Glocke*, vol. 1 (1906), 262–63.

AB5 Conzen, Kathleen N. "Germans." In: *Encyclopedia of American Ethnic Groups*. Ed. Stephan Thernstrom. Cambridge: Harvard Univ. Pr., 1980, 405–25.

AB6 Cunz, Dieter. "The German Americans." In: *One America. The History, Contributions, and Present Problems of Our Racial and National Minorities*. Eds. Francis Brown and Joseph Roucek, New York: Prentice-Hall, rev. ed., 1945, p. 104–20.

AB7 Deeken, Hans Werner. "Erbe und Aufgabe der Deutsch-Amerikaner." *IFA-Korrespondent* (Stuttgart), vol. 4 (1964), 1–3; *Auslandskurier*, vol. 5, no. 1 (1964), 27.

AB8 Dubois, Rachel D., and Emma Schweppe, eds. *The Germans in American Life*. New York: Nelson, 1936. Repr. Freeport, N.Y.: Books for Libraries, 1972. 180p.

AB9 Faust, Albert B. "German-Americans." In: *One America*... Ed. Francis Brown and Joseph Roucek. New York: Prentice-Hall, 1945, p. 101–13.

AB10 "Foreign Language Press Discusses Prejudice: Results in Prize Contest." *Common Ground*, vol. 8, no. 2 (1948), 77–83.

AB11 Friesen, Gerhard K., and Walter Schatzberg, eds. *The German Contribution to the Building of the Americas: Studies in Honor of Karl J. R. Arndt*. Worcester: Clark Univ. Pr., 1977. Rev. by Don H. Tolzmann, *Jour. of Ethnic Studies*, vol. 7 (1979), 117–18; J. L. Sammons, *Unterrichtspraxis*, vol. 10, no. 2 (1977), 171; W. Lagerwey, *German Quar.*, vol. 51 (1978), 267–69; and S. Mews, *Mod. Lang. Notes*, vol. 93 (1978), 551–53.

AB12 Furer, Howard B., comp. and ed. *The Germans in America, 1607–1970. A Chronology and Fact Book*. Dobbs Ferry: Oceana Publs., 1973. 156p. Rev. by Robert E. Ward, *German-Amer. Studies*, vol. 7 (1974), 134–35.

AB13 Gay, Kathlyn. *Germans Helped Build America*. New York: Messner, 1971. Juvenile work.

AB14 *The Germans in America.* Chicago: Claretian Publications. Paperback. An article, "Germans in the United States" in *Rundschau, an American German Review*, vol. 3, no. 7 (October 1973), 1–3, is based on the paperback publication.

AB15 "Germans in the United States." In: *New Catholic Encyclopedia*. Washington, 1967, p.425–28.

AB16 Haack, Hanns-Erich. "Germany's Contribution to American Civilization." *Amer.-German Rev.*, vol. 31 (1964), no. 2, p.24–27.

AB17 Handlin, Oscar. *America: A History.* New York: Holt, Rinehart and Winston, 1968. 1069p. Textbook.

AB18 Hannemann, Max. "Das Deutschtum in den Vereinigten Staaten. Seine Verbreitung und Entwicklung seit der Mitte des 19. Jahrhunderts." *Petermanns Mitteilungen, Ergänzungsheft* Nr. 224. Gotha: Perthes, 1936. With more than a dozen good maps.

AB19 Herr, Christ. "Sturmgeläute: Rettet das Deutsch-amerikanertum." *Der Deutsch-Amerikaner*, vol. 15 (July 1973).

AB20 Hobbie, Margaret, ed. *Museums, Sites and Collections of Germanic Culture in North America: An Annotated Directory of German Immigrant Culture in the United States and Canada.* Westport, Conn.: Greenwood, 1980. 184p. A well-organized handbook of (1) collections and repositories of material culture and (2) National Register Sites, as of 1976.

AB21 Huebener, Theodore. *Germans Helped Build America.* New York: Literary Soc. Foundation, 1980. Pamphlet.

AB22 Huebener, Theodore. *The Germans in America.* Philadelphia: Chilton, 1962. 168p. Rev. by D. Cunz, *German Quar.*, vol. 36 (1963), 491–93; G. Moltmann, *Jahrbuch für Amerikastudien*, vol. 9 (1964), 348–49; R. E. Ward, *German-Amer. Studies*, vol. 1, no. 2 (1969), 101–02; vol. 2, no. 2 (1970), 67–68.

AB23 Institut für Auslandsbeziehungen. Stuttgart. "Chronik deutschen Kulturlebens im Ausland. Kanada. Vereinigten Staaten von Amerika." *Zeitschrift für Kulturaustausch.* Regular column of two to four pages reporting news of German-Americans and their cultural endeavors in the United States and Canada. Started in the *Mitteilungen* of the Institut, vol. 11 (1961) and continued in the *Zeitschrift für Kulturaustausch.*

AB24 Kunze, Wolfgang. "A National Videotheque as a Means of Information and Communication in the Field of German-American Literature and Culture." In: *Germanica Americana 1976 Symposium on German-American Literature and Culture.* Ed. E. A. Albrecht and J. A. Burzle. Lawrence, Kans: Max Kade Document and Research Center, Univ. of Kansas, 1977, p.7–11.

AB25 Maisel, Albert Q. "The Germans Among Us." *Reader's Digest*, March 1955, 97–101.

AB26 Marx, Karl T. *Deutsch-Amerikanische Aphorismen.* München: n.p., 1956. 56p.

AB27 Marx, Karl T. "Second-Class Citizens." *Steuben News*, May 1973.

AB28 Moquin, Wayne, comp. *Makers of America.* 10 vols. Chicago: Encyclopedia Britannica Educational Corp., 1971. Rev. in *Amer. Notes and Queries*, vol. 9 (1971), 141. For a bibliography of the German Americans, see vol. 10, p.189–97. The encyclopedia brings good coverage of the German element for the period 1536–1970.

AB29 O'Connor, Richard. *Die Deutsch-Amerikaner. So wurden es 33 Millionen.* Aus dem Amerikanischen von Uwe Bahnsen. Hamburg: Hoffmann & Campe, 1970. 504p.

AB30 O'Connor, Richard. *The German-Americans; an Informal History.* Boston: Little, Brown & Co., 1968. 484p. Rev. by Russell W. Gilbert, *Pa. History*, vol. 37, no. 1 (January 1970), 106–07; T. Saloutos, *Pacific Hist. Rev.*, vol. 39 (1970), 240–41; J. M. Bergquist, *Internat. Migration Rev.*, vol. 4, no. 1 (Fall 1969), 119–121; Thomas Weyr, *Amer.-German Rev.*, vol. 35, no. 4 (1969), 28–30; Karl J. R. Arndt, *German Quar.*, vol. 42 (1969), 750–53; Irving Katz, *Civil War Hist.*, vol. 16, no. 3 (1970), 275–76; C. Wittke, *Amer. Hist. Rev.*, vol. 74 (1969), 1367–68; W. A. Swanberg, *N.Y. Times Book Rev.*, 8 September 1969, p.8. A lively and popular once-over of the subject in its broader aspects.

AB31 Reeves, Dona B., and Glen E. Lich, eds. *Retrospect and Retrieval: The German Element in Review, Essays on Cultural Preservation*. Ann Arbor: Univ. Microfilms, 1979.

AB32 Rippley, La Vern J. *The German Americans. The Immigrant Heritage of America*. Boston: Twayne, 1976. 271p. Index and Bibliography. Rev. by E. A. Albrecht, *German Quar.*, vol. 50, no. 3 (May 1977), 384; Marc Lee Raphael, *Jour. of Amer. Hist.*, vol. 63, no. 4 (March 1977), 1044; D. H. Tolzmann, *German-Amer. Studies*, vol. 11 (1976), 98; Karl J. R. Arndt, *Ohio Hist.*, vol. 86 (1977), 220–21; G. H. Weiss, *Die Unterrichtspraxis*, vol. 9, no. 2 (Fall 1976), 137.

AB33 Rippley, LaVern J. "The German-Speaking." In: *Language and Culture: Heritage and Horizons*. Ed. Warren C. Born. Montpelier, Vt.: Northeast Conference Reports, 1976, p.42f., 64f., 89f.

AB34 Rippley, LaVern J. "A Look at Americans of German Descent." In: *The Cultural Revolution in Foreign Language Teaching*. Ed. Robert C. Lafayette. Skokie, Ill.: National Textbook, 1975, p.72–90.

AB35 Rippley, La Vern J. *Of German Ways*. Minneapolis: Dillon Pr., Inc., 1970. 301p. A thoughtful book about German life and character in the Old and New Worlds.

AB36 Rosenberger, Homer T. "The Germans in America." In: *The Pennsylvania-Germans, 1891–1965*. Ed. H. T. Rosenberger. Lancaster: Pa. German Society, 1966, p.24–52.

AB37 Sammons, Jeffrey. "Some Considerations on Our Invisibility." In: *German Studies in the United States: Assessment and Outlook*. Eds. Walter F. W. Lohnes and Valters Nollendorfs. Monatshefte Occasional Vol. 1. Madison: Univ. of Wisconsin Pr., 1976, p.17–23.

AB38 Schlesinger, Arthur R. "Biography of a Nation of Joiners." *Amer. Hist. Rev.*, vol. 50 (1944), 1–25. On some prominent traits and characteristics of the Germans in America.

AB39 Starck, Taylor. "Der deutsche Anteil an der Entwicklung der Vereinigten Staaten von Nordamerika." In: *Jahrbuch 1960* (Deutsche Akademie für Sprache und Dichtung, Darmstadt) (1961), 61–63. From a paper read at the conference held in Darmstadt, October 1960.

AB40 Tolzmann, Don H. *Handbuch eines Deutschamerikaners*. Gordonville, Pa.: Andrew S. Kinsinger, 1973.

AB41 Tolzmann, Don H. "Was ist des Deutschamerikaners Vaterland?" *Der Milwaukee Herold*, 29 November 1973.

AB42 Von Hagen, Viktor W. *The Germanic People in America*. Norman: Univ. of Oklahoma Pr., 1976. 404p. Rev. by F. R. DeFederico, *Smithsonian*, vol. 7 (1976), 162, 164–166; J. R. Dukes, *Wis. Mag. of Hist.*, vol. 61 (1978), 325–26; and Glen E. Lich, *German Studies Rev.*, vol. 1 (October 1978), 364–65. Germanic culture in North and South America to 1871; stresses the figures of von Steuben, Astor, von Humboldt, and Carl Schurz.

AB43 Von Hagen, Victor W. *Der Ruf der Neuen Welt. Deutsche bauen Amerika*. München: Droemersche Verlagsanstalt, 1970. 368p. Rev. *Wächter und Anzeiger*, 12 March 1971, 4; and L. Rippley, *German-Amer. Studies*, vol. 5 (1972), 186–88. The larger part of this work is a vivid account of German participation in the European conquest of South and Central America. Well illustrated.

AB44 Wächtler, Fritz. *Deutsche fern der Heimat*. Ed. Friedrich Wilh. Brepohl. 2nd ed. München: Deutscher Volksvlg., 1949. 200p.

AB45 Wagner, Fritz. "Deutsche Kultureinflüsse in Amerika." Sonntagsblatt, *New Yorker Staatszeitung und Herold*, 11 December 1966, Unterhaltungsbeilage, 4, 22.

AB46 Walter, Hilde. "Die Deutschamerikaner." *Der Monat*, vol. 4 (1952), 478–85. Attempt to characterize psychologically and politically the present generation of the German Americans.

AB47 Wandel, Joseph. *The German Dimension of American History*. Chicago: Nelson-Hall Publs., ca. 1978.

AB48 Ward, Robert E. "Biographical Notes on German-American Culture." In: *Symposium on German Culture in America and Ohio* (Festschrift). Cleveland: German-American National Congress, [October 13,] 1973.

AB49 Ward, Robert E. "Deutschamerikanische Kulturecke." *Wächter und Anzeiger*, 2 April 1971–. Weekly series of articles on German-American literature.

AB50 Ward, Robert E. *General Proposal for the Creation of an American Foundation for the Preservation of German Culture in America.* Parma, Ohio: Soc. for German-Amer. Studies, 1973.

AB51 Ward, Robert E. "Symposium über deutsche Kultur in den Vereinigten Staaten." *Der Deutsch-Amerikaner,* vol. 15 (December 1973).

AB52 Wiley, Marion E. "Exploring German-American Culture in the Community." *Die Unterrichtspraxis,* vol. 11 (1978), 48–52.

AB53 Wittke, Carl. "The German Americans." *Common Ground,* vol. 1, no. 4 (1941), 8–16.

AB54 Wittke, Carl. *The Germans in America.* New York: Teachers Coll. Pr., Columbia Univ., 1967. 26p. A handbook for high school and college students.

AB55 Wust, Klaus G. "Deutschamerikanische Geschichte auf Briefmarken." *Deutsche Zeitschrift für Briefmarkenkunde,* vol. 30 (1955), 868–69.

AB56 Wust, Klaus, and Norbert Muehlen. *Span 200. A Companion Piece to the Span 200 Exhibit. The Story of German-American Involvement in the Founding and Development of America. Who They Were, Where They Came From, Why They Came, What They Accomplished.* Philadelphia: Publ. in Behalf of the Institut für Auslandsbeziehungen, Stuttgart, by the National Carl Schurz Association, 1976. 95p.

AB57 Wust, Klaus, and Heinz Moos, eds. *300 Years of Germans in America/300 Jahre Deutsche in Amerika.* 1683–1983. Baltimore and Gräfelfing: Heinz Moos Publishing, 1982. 208p. Over 700 illus. Engl. and German text.

AB58 Yoder, Don. "Palatine, Hessian, Dutchman: Three Images of the German in America." In: *Ebbes fer alle—ebber ebbes fer dich: Essays in Memoriam Albert Franklin Buffington.* Breinigsville, Pa.: The Pa. German Soc., vol. 14, 1980, p.107–29.

AB59 Zeydel, Edwin H. "German Culture in America, Past and Present." *Hartwick Rev.,* vol. 3, no. 1 (1967), 80–83.

AB60 Zucker, Adolf E. "Natural Selection and German Americans." *Report, Soc. for the Hist. of the Germans in Md.,* vol. 25 (1942), 7–12. Argues that the love of freedom was a characteristic of the German-American through the centuries.

AC
General Bibliographies of German Americana

AC1 "Articles in American Studies." Annually in the *Amer. Quar.,* Supplement issue. An interdisciplinary bibliography, published since 1955 (for 1954).

AC2 Benjamin, Steven M. "The Annual German-American Bibliography of the Society for German-American Studies: Organization in a New Vein: Resources and Possibilities." *Die Unterrichtspraxis,* vol. 9, no. 2 (1976), 3–18. See also the *Newsletter of the Soc. for German-Amer. Studies,* vol. 1, no. 2 (1979–1980), 6–8; and no. 4, 15.

AC3 Benjamin, Steven M. "The Major Sources for German-American Bibliography." *Newsletter of the Soc. for German-Amer. Studies,* vol. 2, no. 1 (1980–1981), 10–11.

AC4 Benjamin, Steven M., and Renate L. Benjamin. "Bibliography of German-Americana Published in 1979 and 1980. Articles, Books, and Dissertations." *Yearbook of German-American Studies,* vol. 16 (1981), 161–95. With subject index.

AC5 Benjamin, Steven M., et al. *German-American Bibliography for 1979 with Supplements for 1971–1978.* Occasional Papers of the Soc. for Ger.-Amer. Studies, No. 9. Morgantown, W. Va.: Dept. of Foreign Langs., West Va. Univ., 1980. 106p.

AC6 Berquist, James M. *Germans in North America.* Philadelphia: Balch Institute, 1975. An annotated bibliography of works in English for use at the secondary- and college-level of study.

AC7 *Bibliographie fremdsprachiger Germanica.* Ed. Erika Jesche. Publ. Deutschen Bücherei. Jahrgang 1. 1972. Leipzig: Verlag für Buch- und Bibliothekswesen, 1972. Quarterly.

AC8 "Bibliography Americana Germanica." Annually in the April (later the June–July) issue of the *Amer.-German Rev.* in the years 1942–1967 (for 1941–1966). Commenced as part of the "Anglo-German Bibliography" in the *Jour. of Engl. and Germanic Philology* as ed. by Henry A. Pochmann. Since 1942 ed. by A. E. Zucker, L. M. Price, Dieter Cunz, and A. R. Schultz. For the years 1967, 1968, 1969, and 1970 it was carried in *German Quar.*, vols. 41–44. After a hiatus of four years, the project was resumed in *German-Amer. Studies*, vol. 4, no. 4 (1979), 153–84 for 1978, under the editorship of Arthur R. Schultz.

AC9 Bowers, David F., ed. *Foreign Influences in American Life.* Princeton: Princeton Univ. Pr., 1944. 254p. Includes good bibliographies for various aspects of the field. Rev. by A. Johnson, *Amer.-German Rev.*, vol. 11, no. 3 (1945), 38. See also *ibid.*, vol. 11, no. 4 (1945), 27.

AC10 Bristol, Robert P. *Supplement to Charles Evans's "American Bibliography."* Charlottesville: Univ. of Virginia Pr., 1970. Bringing over 11,000 new items.

AC11 "Deutsche amerikakundliche Veröffentlichungen, 1945–1954." *Jahrbuch für Amerikastudien*, vol. 1 (1956). Ed. W. Fischer, B. Fabian, and U. Sassen (Fabian). Continued annually through vol. 18 (1973), ed. Ursula Fabian and Ilse Wodke-Repplinger. With vol. 19 (1974) the publication changed to *Amerikastudien/American Studies*, but continued the bibliography under its original title.

AC12 European Association for American Studies. "Current Bibliography, 1950–56." *Newsletter*, vol. 3 (1957), 25–36. Continued after 1957 at irregular intervals.

AC13 Fittbogen, Gottfried. *Wie lerne ich die Grenz- und Auslandsdeutschen kennen? Einführung in die Literatur über die Grenz- und Auslandsdeutschen.* Im Auftrage des Vereins für das Deutschtum im Ausland. Dessau: Dünnhaupt, 1923. 2nd ed. München/Berlin: n.p., 1927.

AC14 Friedrich, Gerhard. "A New Supplement to Seidensticker's American-German Bibliography." *Pa. Hist.*, vol. 7 (1941), 213–24.

AC15 Froeschle, Hartmut. "Neuere deutschamerikanische Literatur." *German-Canad. Yearbook*, vol. 4 (1978), 331–42. Extended review article; guide to current developments in the field.

AC16 Gieselberg, Margarita. "Beiträge zum Thema 'Deutsche im Ausland' in der *Zeitschrift für Kulturaustausch* 1951–1967 (1951–1961 unter dem Titel: *Mitteilungen des Instituts für Auslandsbeziehungen*)—Bibliographie." *Zeitschrift für Kulturaustausch*, vol. 18, no. 1 (1968), 41–46.

AC17 Haase, Yorck Alexander, and Harold Jantz, eds. *Die neue Welt in den Schätzen einer alten europäischen Bibliothek: Ausstellung der Herzog August Bibliothek Wolfenbüttel.* [German/English.] Ausstellungskatalog no. 17. Braunschweig: Waisenhausdruckerei, 1976. Rev. by T. R. Adams, Albert R. Schmitt, *The Book Collector*, vol. 27 (Spring 1978), 116–20.

AC18 Keresztesi, Michael, and Gary U. Cocozzoli. *German-American History and Life. A Guide to Information Sources.* Detroit: Gale, 1980: 372p.

AC19 Kloss, Heinz. "Forschung im Dienst der Sprachen und Schulen. Bibliographie." Sonderdruck aus *Europa-Ethnica*, vol. 28, no. 2 (1971). Incl. a valuable bibliography of Americana-Germanica.

AC20 Koster, Donald, ed. "Articles on American Studies, 1957." *Amer. Quar.*, vol. 10 (1958), 225–62.

AC21 Merrill, Peter C. "Recent Doctoral Dissertations in German-American Studies." *Newsletter, Soc. for German-Amer. Studies*, vol. 1, no. 3 (1980), 7–9.

AC22 Miller, Wayne Charles, comp. *A Comprehensive Bibliography for the Study of American Minorities.* 2 vols. New York: New York Univ. Pr., 1976. 1380p. The German-American ethnics are treated in the bibliographies, p. 279–349. A basic reference tool with full author and title indexes.

AC23 Mönnig, Richard. *Amerika und England im deutschen, österreichischen und schweizerischen Schrifttum 1945–1949.* Stuttgart: Kohlhammer, 1951. Rev. T. O. Brandt, *Monatshefte*, vol. 44 (1952), 426–27; W. P. Friedrich, *Amer.-German Rev.*, vol. 18, no. 4 (1952), 32; H. F. Peters, *Mod. Lang. Quar.*, vol. 13 (1952), 113–14; L. M. Price, *Comparative Lit*, vol. 5 (1953), 179–80. A list of 4,400 items.

AC24 Mönnig, Richard. *Deutschland und die Deutschen im englischsprachigen Schrifttum, 1948-1955; eine Bibliographie.* Göttingen: Vandenhoeck and Ruprecht, 1957. 147p.

AC25 Mönnig, Richard, ed. and comp. *Bibliography of Paperbound Books Translated from the German and of Works on Germany.* 2nd ed. Born, 1965. 61p.; 4th ed. Bad Godesberg: Inter Nationes, 1967.

AC26 Pochmann, Henry A., comp., and Arthur R. Schultz, ed. *Bibliography of German Culture in America to 1940.* Madison; Univ. of Wisconsin Pr., 1953. 483p.; 2nd printing, rev., 1954. Rev. by A. E. Zucker, *Monatshefte*, vol. 45 (1953), 443; B. Q. Morgan, *Amer.-German Rev.*, vol. 20, no. 3 (1954), 36f.; D. Cunz, *Germanic Rev.*, vol. 29 (1954), 158-59; W. A. Reichert, *German Quar.*, vol. 27 (1954), 277f.; C. G. Loomis, *Jour. of Engl. and Germanic Philology*, vol. 53 (1954), 677-78; J. W. Thomas, *Amer. Lit.*, vol. 26 (1954), 107-08; E. Doll, *Pa. Mag. of Hist. and Biography*, vol. 78 (1954), 384-86; N.P. Springer, *Mennonite Quar. Rev.*, vol. 28 (1954), 155-57; F. Reichmann, *Mod. Lang. Quar.*, vol. 16 (1955), 88-89; P. A. Barba, "'S Pennsylfawnisch Deitsch Eck." Allentown *Morning Call*, March 26 (1955); H. J. Stucky, *Menn. Life*, vol. 10 (1955) 94; J. P. Donnelly, *Hist. Bull.*, vol. 33 (1956), 47; H. R. Stevens, *South Atlantic Quar.*, vol. 53 (1956) 604; P. Levy, *Etudes Germaniques*, vol. 9 (1956), 328; R. Glanz, *Jewish Social Studies*, vol. 17 (1956), 360; L. A. Willoughby, *German Life and Letters*, vol. 9 (1956), 80; *Yearbook of Comparative and General Lit.*, vol. 5 (1956), 73-74. [See also *U.S. Quar. Book Rev.*, vol. 10 (1956), 135; *Regesten* (Utrecht), vol. 1, no. 3 (1956); *Börsenblatt für den deut. Buchhandel*, 23 Aug. 1956.] C. J. Barry, *Catholic Hist. Rev.*, vol. 43 (1957), 84-86; H. Closs, *Mitteilungen des Instituts für Auslandsbeziehungen*, vol. 7 (1957), 79-80.

AC27 Pochmann, Henry A., comp., and Arthur R. Schultz, ed. *Bibliography of German Culture in America to 1940.* Rev. and Corr. by Arthur R. Schultz. With Addenda, Errata, and Expanded Index. Millwood, N.Y.: Kraus International Publications, 1982. 775p.

AC28 Price, Arnold H. *The Federal Republic of Germany. A Selected Bibliography of English-Language Publications.* 2nd ed. Washington, D.C.: Library of Congress. 116p. Address: Superintendent of Documents, Govt. Printing Office, Washington, D.C. 20402.

AC29 Rippley, LaVern J. "Selected Publications on German-Americana since the Completion of the 'Report' in the Year 1937." In: *Research Possibilities in the German-American Field.* By Heinz Kloss. Ed. L. J. Rippley. Hamburg: Buske, 1980, p.231-41.

AC30 Tolzmann, Don Heinrich. *German-Americana: A Bibliography.* D. H. Tolzmann, comp. Metuchen, N.J.: Scarecrow, 1975. 384p. Rev. by K.J.R. Arndt, *German Quar.*, vol. 49 (1976), 549-50.

AC31 *Übersetzungen deutscher Bücher in fremde Sprachen 1941. Bibliographisches Verzeichnis.* Leipzig: Börsenverein, 1944. 110p.

AC32 United States. Library of Congress. *List of Newspapers Principally Representative of German Groups Outside of Germany.* Collated by the Deutsches Ausland-Institut. Received through American Military Documents Section. Camp Ritchie, Md., 1946. On film.

AC33 United States Information Agency. *Verzeichnis amerikanischer Bücher in deutscher Übersetzung, erschienen seit 1945, nebst Nachtrag.* Bonn/Washington: n.p., 1954. 294p.

AC34 United States Information Agency. *Verzeichnis amerikanischer Bücher in deutscher Übersetzung. Nachtrag Sept. 1954-August 1956.* Bonn, 1956. 108p. *Nachtrag 2 (Sept. 1956-Aug. 1958). Nachtrag 3 (Sept. 1958-Sept. 1960).* Bad Godesberg-Plittersdorf: Office of Public Affairs, American Embassy, 1958, 1961. 93, 144p.

AC35 Ward, Robert E. "Bibliographical Notes on German-American Culture." In: *Symposium über deutsche Kultur in America und Ohio.* Cleveland: Classic Printing, 1973, p.6-8.

AC36 Ward, Robert E. "Deutschamerikanische Kulturecke: neuere deutschamerikanische Publikationen." *Wissenschaftliche Annalen*, 26 January 1973.

AC37 Ward, Robert E. "Englischsprachige Literatur über Deutsche in Amerika." *German-Amer. Studies*, vol. 3, no. 2 (1971), p.46-47.

AC38 Wassermann, Paul, and Jean Morgan, eds. *Ethnic Information Sources of the United States.*

A Guide to Organizations, Agencies, Foundations, Institutions, Media, ... Government Programs, Research Institutes, Libraries and Museums, Religious Organizations, ... Festivals and Fairs, ...Bookdealers, ...and Books Pamphlets and Audiovisuals on Specific Ethnic Groups. Detroit: Gale Research Co., 1976. 751p. For data on the German-Americans, *see* p.181–213.

AC39 Wynar, Lubomyr R., and Lois Buttlar. *Ethnic Film and Filmstrip Guide for Libraries and Media Centers: A Selective Filmography.* Littleton, Colo.: Libraries Unlimited, 1980. 277p.

AD

Libraries and Archives/General Repositories of National Scope

See also Section CD: Germanistic Study in the United States and Canada *and* General Studies/Historiography *under* Section IA: General [Historical Perspectives].

General

AD1 Alden, John E. "Out of the Ashes, A Young Phoenix. Early Americana in the Harvard College Library." *William and Mary Quar.*, 3rd ser., vol. 3, no. 4 (1946), 487–98. Library of C. D. Ebeling, German geographer and historian; acquired by Harvard in 1818.

AD2 American Philosophical Society of Philadelphia. *Manuscript Catalogue of the Library, 1768–.* Incl. the papers of many distinguished American figures, e.g., Louis Agassiz, David Rittenhouse, Davis Zeisberger; also such foreign authors as Alexander von Humboldt.

AD3 *Catalogue of the Manuscripts, Maps, Medals, Coins, Statuary, Portraits and Pictures; and an Account of the Library of the Maryland Hist. Society, Made in 1854 ....* By Lewis Mayer, Assistant Librarian. Baltimore: n.p., 1854. 51p.

AD4 "Collection of German-Americana Established." *Candid Campus* (Univ. of Cincinnati), 29 May 1974.

AD5 Dennis, Rodney G. "The Ebeling Purchase." In: *John Quincy Adams: Pioneer of German-American Literary Studies.* Ed. Anneliese Harding. Boston: Harvard Univ. Printing Office, 1979, p.63–67.

AD6 Downs, Robert B. "Wartime Co-operative Acquisitions." *Library Quar.*, vol. 19, no. 3 (1949), 157–66. Incl. a statement of the Library of Congress's policy regarding the acquisition in time of war of materials for research libraries in the United States.

AD7 Epstein, Fritz T. *German Source Materials in American Libraries.* Milwaukee: Marquette Univ. Pr., 1958. 20p.

AD8 Epstein, Fritz T. "The Growth of the German-Language Collections." *Library of Congress Quar. Jour. of Current Acquisitions*, vol. 16, no. 3 (May 1959), 123–30.

AD9 Fink, Albert F. "A Bibliography of German-Language and Related Items in the Rare Book Collection of Beeghly Library, Heidelberg College, Tiffin, Ohio." *German-Amer. Studies*, vol. 7 (1974), 50–67. The collection is predominantly of a theological nature but includes some secular works on history, languages, natural science and practical medicine. Heidelberg College was founded in 1850 by the Reformed Church in the United States.

AD10 Gass, Brigitte. "Deutschsprachige Literatur über die USA seit 1945 aus den Beständen der Bibliothek des Instituts für Auslandsbeziehungen." *Zeitschrift für Kulturaustausch*, vol. 17 (1967), 235–42. Approx. 400 items arranged by topics.

AD11 Gerhard, Dietrich et al., eds. *Americana in deutschen Sammlungen (ADS); Ein Verzeichnis von Materialien zur Geschichte der Vereinigten Staaten von Amerika in Archiven und Bibliotheken der Bundesrepublik Deutschland und West-Berlins.* Comp. under the auspices of the Deutsche Gesellschaft für Amerikastudien [by D. Gerhard, E. Zechlin, and E. Angermann.] 6 vols. Köln: n.p., 1967. Microfilm ed. avail. through Omnia K.G., Kraus, Weiss & Co., Münich. A monumental guide to archival resources for U.S. history in the Federal Republic of Germany. Embraces approx. 200,000 entries on a wide range of subjects. Entries are arranged by the physical location of the records.

AD12 Gerhard, Elmer Schultz. "Library of the Davenport Turngemeinde." *Amer.-German Rev.*, vol. 12, no. 5 (1946), 33–35, 37. A book collection acquired by the Carl Schurz Memorial Foundation in 1946.

AD13 Gerhard, Elmer Schultz. "The Research Library and Literary Notes." *Amer.-German Rev.*, vol. 12, no. 1 (1945), 24–25; *ibid.*, vol. 12, no. 2 (1945), 34; *ibid.*, vol. 13, no. 3 (1946), 36. Notes on the library of the Carl Schurz Memorial Foundation.

AD14 Hamer, Philip M., ed. *A Guide to Archives and Manuscripts in the United States.* New Haven: Yale Univ. Pr., 1961. 775p. Rev. by L. J. Cappon, *Library Quar.*, vol. 31, no. 4 (1961), 410–11. A guide to the holdings of 1300 depositories, arranged by the geographical location of the collection.

AD15 Hintz, Carl W. "Notable Materials Added to North American Libraries, 1943–47." *Library Quar.*, vol. 19, no. 2 (1949), 105–18; *ibid.*, vol. 19, no. 3 (1949), 186–200. Incl. material relating to German culture.

AD16 Hoyt, William D., Jr. "The Warden Papers." *Md. Hist. Mag.*, vol. 36 (1943), 69–85. Incl. materials pertinent to Nicholas H. Julius, Francis Lieber, William P. C. Barton, F. Wurdemann, Gen. Walterstorff, Robert Mohl of Tübingen, and others.

AD17 Jones, George F. "A New Source of German American History." *Report, Soc. for the Hist. of the Germans in Md.*, vol. 32 (1966), 64–65. On the London archives of the Society for Propagating Christian Knowledge (SPCK).

AD18 Kielman, Chester V., comp. and ed. *A Guide to the Historical Manuscript Collections in the University of Texas Library.* Austin: Univ. of Texas Pr., 1967–.

AD19 Klett, Ada M. "The Jesse Isidor Straus Manuscripts in the Vassar College Library." *Amer.-German Rev.*, vol. 8, no. 1 (1941), 16–18, 36; *ibid.*, vol. 8, no. 2 (1941), 8–10, 39.

AD20 Kraus, Joe W. "Book Collections of Five Colonial College Libraries: A Subject Analysis." Diss., Univ. of Illinois, 1961.

AD21 *The Leiter Library. A Catalogue of the Books, Manuscripts and Maps Relating Principally to America, Collected by the Late Levi Ziegler Leiter.* With Collations and Bibliographical Notes . . . . Washington: Priv. Printed, 1907. Levi Ziegler Leiter, 1834–1904.

AD22 [Lich, Glen E.] "Notes on German-American Studies at Southwest Texas State University." *Jour. of German-American Studies*, vol. 12, no. 2 (1977), 47. The university has acquired a research collection (15,000 items) of German-Americana in the Southwest: the Brinkmann-Ransleben library. It consists of books, documents, maps, and photographs assembled by the bibliophiles Mrs. Otto Brinkmann, Alexander Brinkmann, and Guido Ernst Ransleben.

AD23 Loacker, Elso. "The Germanic Libraries at the University of California in Los Angeles." *Mod. Lang. Forum*, vol. 25 (1941), 82–84.

AD24 Martin, Horst, comp. *A Reference Guide to Germany. A Selective Checklist of Printed Materials Relating to Germany, Listing the Holdings of the Public Libraries of Greater Vancouver.* Vancouver: The German-Canadian Cultural Soc., 1976. 104p.

AD25 North Carolina Historical Records Survey. *Guide to the Manuscript Collections in the Archives of the North Carolina Historical Commission.* Prep. by the N. Car. Hist. Records Survey Project, Div. of Community Service Programs, Works Project Administration . . . Raleigh: N. Car. Hist. Commission, 1942. 216p. Rev. by L. J. Cappon, *N. Car. Hist. Rev.*, vol. 20, no. 1 (January 1943), 83–84.

AD26 Peckham, Howard H. *Guide to the Manuscript Collections in the William L. Clements Li-*

General *(cont.)*

brary. Ann Arbor: Univ. of Michigan Pr., 1942. 403p.

AD27 Ratterman, Heinrich A. Papers. 55 items. In the Illinois Hist. Survey collections, Univ. of Ill. at Urbana-Champaign (MS 69-1615; 72-1531). Chiefly biographical, published articles and poems, photos, clippings, ca. 1862–1875. See *Jour. of Amer. Hist.*, vol. 61, no. 2 (September 1974). *See also*: Sell, Donna-Christine, and Dennis Walle. *Guide to the Heinrich A. Rattermann Collection of German-American Manuscripts*. Champaign: Graduate School of Library Science, Univ. of Illinois, 1979. 215p. Rev. by D. H. Tolzmann, *Unterrichtspraxis*, vol. 13, no. 1 (1980), 123–24. Rattermann (1832–1923), editor, historian, and German-American man of letters, devoted his life and energies to the history of the German Americans.

AD28 Schweizerische Landesbibliothek, Bern. *Katalog der amerikanischen Büchersammlung*. Bern: n.p., 1947. 55p.

AD29 Stilwell, Mary B., ed. *Incunabula in American Libraries: A Second Census of Fifteenth Century Books Owned in the United States*. New York: Bibliographical Soc. of America, 1940. 619p. Rev. by L. Thorndike, *Amer. Hist. Rev.*, vol. 47, no. 1 (1941), 104–05.

AD30 Stevens, B. F., ed. *Facsimiles of MSS in European Archives Relating to America, 1773–1783*... London: n.p., 1889–1895. A collection of 2107 facsimiles in 24 portfolios.

AD31 Syracuse University. Ranke Bibliography Committee. *The Leopold von Ranke Manuscripts of Syracuse University*. Ed. Howard A. Brogan. Syracuse: Syracuse Univ. Pr., 1952. 150p. Rev. by Dieter Cunz, *Amer.-German Rev.*, vol. 20, no. 2 (1953), 35. Titles dealing primarily with the Republic of Venice in the 16th to 18th centuries.

AD32 United States. Department of State. American Legation, Bern, Switzerland. Press Department. *Library Catalog*. N.p., 1945. 52p.

AD33 Viereck, Louis. "The Need of a Germanic Museum." *The Harvard Graduates Mag.*, vol. 5 (1896–1897), 356–60. Repr. in "German Instruction in American Schools." *U.S. Bureau of Education. Report of the Commissioner of Education for the Year 1900–01*. Washington, D.C.: Govt. Printing Office, 1902, p.679–81.

AD34 Ward, Robert E. "Address to the Participants of the German Day Program Sponsored by the Western Reserve Historical Society on November 26, 1975." *German-Amer. Studies*, vol. 10 (1975), 20–24. On Ward's collection of German-Americana.

AD35 Ward, Robert E. "Bibliographical and Genealogical Data in the Publications of the German Pioneer Society of Cincinnati." *Jour. of German-Amer. Studies*, vol. 13 (1978), 113–16.

AD36 Weinberg, Gerhard L. "Zu den deutschen Akten in den Vereinigten Staaten." *Historische Zeitschrift*, vol. 194 (April 1962), 519–26.

AD37 Wolfe, Robert, ed. *Captured German and Related Records: A National Archives Conference*. Athens: Ohio Univ. Pr., 1974. 279p.

AD38 Wynar, Lubomyr, and Lois Buttlar. *Guide to Ethnic Museums, Libraries, and Archives in the United States*. Kent, Ohio: Kent State Univ., 1978. 378p.

Specific Institutions

MAX KADE GERMAN-AMERICAN DOCUMENT AND RESEARCH CENTER

AD39 Albrecht, Erich A., and J. Anthony Burzle. "Bericht über die Gründung und Tätigkeit des Max Kade German-American Document and Research Centers." *German-Amer. Studies*, vol. 3, no. 1 (1971), 4–6.

AD40 Burzle, J. Anthony. "Max Kade and Kansas University." *German-Amer. Studies*, vol. 3, no. 1 (1971), 3.

AD41 Max Kade German-American Document and Research Center. *Catalogue*. Lawrence: Univ. of Kansas, October 1976. 204p. A preliminary checklist to provide an overview of the holdings of this research center. Index, p.177–205. Mimeogr.

AD42 "Want-List/*Such-Liste*." *German-Amer. Studies*, vol. 3, no. 1 (1971), 22–23. A list of German-American writers whose works are sought for the archives of the center.

UNITED STATES. LIBRARY OF CONGRESS

AD43 *German Imprints. Part 2: European Imprints for the War Years Received in the Library of Congress and Other Federal Libraries, 1940–1945.* Washington, D.C.: Library of Congress; New York: Stechert, 1946. 315p. A list of 11,000 titles.

AD44 Lederer, Max. "Deutsche Bücher in der Library of Congress." *German Quar.*, vol. 22, no. 3 (1949), 152–58. Acquisitions of the years 1947–1948.

AD45 O'Neill, James E. "European Sources for American History in the Library of Congress." *Quar. Jour. of the Lib. of Congress*, vol. 24 (July 1967), 152–57. Outlines a program for the copying of materials carrying information on America.

STATE HISTORICAL SOCIETY OF WISCONSIN

AD46 *Index to vols. 1–20 of the Wisconsin Historical Collections.* Wisconsin Historical Publications Collection, vol. 21 Madison, 1965. 573p. Repr. of edition of 1915.

AD47 Thwaites, Reuben G. *Descriptive List of MSS Collections of the State Historical Society of Wisconsin.* Madison: n.p., 1906.

AE

German Americana as a Field of Study and Research

AE1 Albrecht, Erich A., and J. Anthony Burzle. "Panel Discussion, German-American Literature and Culture 1976: Where Do We Go from Here?" In: *Germanica Americana 1976: Symposium on German-American Literature and Culture.* Ed. E. A. Albrecht and J. A. Burzle. Lawrence: Max Kade Document and Research Center, Univ. of Kansas, 1977, p. 127–29.

AE2 Appel, John J. "Marion Dexter Learned and the German American Historical Society." *Pa. Mag. of Hist. and Biography*, vol. 86 (1962), 287–318. On German-American historiography in the era of the *Annals* and *Geschichtsblätter*. Professor Learned's "ideals of culture and historical method were largely beyond the ken of the leaders as well as the members of the Alliance."

AE3 Benjamin, Steven M. "Roundtable Discussion on German-American Studies." *Newsletter, Soc. for German-Amer. Studies*, vol. 1, no. 1 (1979–1980), 5–10; "1980 Roundtable Discussion: Proposals." *Ibid.*, vol. 2, no. 1 (1980–1981), 14.

AE4 Benjamin, Steven M. "The Society for German-American Studies: Its History and Present Activities." In: *Papers from the Conference on German-Americana in the Eastern United States.* Occasional Papers of the Soc. for German-Amer. Studies, no. 8. Ed. S. M. Benjamin. Morgantown: Dept. of Foreign Langs., West Va. Univ., 1980, p. 197–201.

AE5 Brister, Louis E. "Exploring German-American Culture in the Community." *Die Unterrichtspraxis*, vol. 11, no. 2 (1978), 48–52.

AE6 Busse, Adolf. "Rubbish and Relics." *Amer.-German Rev.*, vol. 9, no. 1 (1942), 39–40. On collecting German-Americana.

AE7 Cunz, Dieter. "Twenty Years of German-American Studies." *Report, Soc. for the Hist. of the Germans in Md.*, vol. 30 (1959), 9–28. An excellent survey of research and publication.

AE8 El-Beheri, Mary M., and Susan Clayton. "High School Students Research History of German-English School in San Antonio." *Die Unterrichtspraxis*, vol. 8, no. 2 (1975), 62–66.

AE9 Ferrell, Jack L. "German Literature in Context: A Case Study for German Studies at the United States Air Force Academy." Diss., Univ. of Washington, 1975–1976.

AE10 Galinsky, Hans. "Annual Conferences of the German Association for American Studies;" and "American Studies in the Federal Republic of Germany." *EAAS. American Studies: An International Newsletter*, vol. 14 (1971), 14–16, 28–32; *ibid.*, vol. 15 (1973), 17–18, 23–26. See also *ibid.*, vol. 12 (1973), 25–28.

AE11 Galinsky, Hans. "Vom 'Boppard-Ausschuß' bis zur Gegenwart: Ein Rückblick auf zwanzig Jahre Deutsche Gesellschaft für Amerikastudien (1953–73)." *Mitteilungsblatt der Deutschen Gesellschaft für Amerikastudien*, vol. 20 (1973), 4–12.

AE12 "German Culture Studies: Courses, Programs, Staff." *Monatshefte*, vol. 68, no. 3 (Fall 1976), 303f. A survey by the editors of the *Monatshefte*.

AE13 Herminghouse, Patricia. "German-American Studies in a New Vein: Resources and Possibilities." *Die Unterrichtspraxis*, vol. 9, no. 2 (1976), 3–18.

AE14 Keel, William D., and Barbara A. Bopp. "Some Suggestions for a Course on the German Heritage of America." *Die Unterrichtspraxis*, vol. 9, no. 2 (Fall 1976), 18–23.

AE15 Kloss, Heinz. "Grenzen des auslandsdeutschen Schrifttums und von der Sammelarbeit der Bücherei des Deutschen Ausland-Instituts." *Der Auslandsdeutsche*, vol. 19 (1936), 188–93.

AE16 Kloss, Heinz. *Research Possibilities in the German-American Field*. Ed. L. J. Rippley. Hamburg: Buske, 1980. 242p. With an addendum by La Vern J. Rippley, "Selected Publications on German-Americana since the Completion of the 'Report' in the Year 1937," p.231–41.

AE17 Knowlton, James. "Charles Evans' *American Bibliography* as a Research Tool for German-American Studies." In: *Papers from the St. Olaf Symposium on German-Americana*. Ed. L. J. Rippley and S. M. Benjamin. Morgantown: Dept. of Foreign Langs., W. Va. Univ., 1980, p.70–78.

AE18 Lange, Victor. "Thoughts in Season." In: *German Studies in the United States: Assessment and Outlook*. Ed. W. Lohnes and V. Nollendorfs. Madison, Wis.: n.p. 1976, p.5–16.

AE19 Reichmann, Felix. "The Subject Union Catalogue 'Americana Germanica'." *School and Society*, vol. 58 November 1943), 372–74.

AE20 Rippley, La Vern J. "The German-Americans: A Course Proposal." *Die Unterrichtspraxis*, vol. 9 (1976), 24–30.

AE21 Rippley, La Vern J. "Introduction 1980." In: Heinz Kloss. *Research Possibilities in the German-American Field*. Ed. L. J. Rippley. Hamburg: Buske, 1980, p.v–ix.

AE22 Schultz, Arthur R. "Notes on German-Americana and the Discipline of History." In: *Germanica Americana 1976: Symposium on German-American Literature and Culture*. Ed. E. A. Albrecht and J. A. Burzle. Lawrence: Max Kade Document and Research Center, Univ. of Kansas, 1977, p.21–28.

AE23 Spiller, Robert E. "American Studies Abroad: Culture and Foreign Policy." *Annals of the Amer. Academy of Political and Social Science*, vol. 366 (July 1966), 1–16. Notes the establishment of chairs, courses, degrees and societies devoted to American dies in foreign countries.

AE24 Tolzmann, Don H. "Dr. Robert Ward-Leyerle und das Deutsch-Amerikanertum." *Der Milwaukee Herold*, 1 November 1973.

AE25 Tolzmann, Don H. "History of the Society for German-American Studies." *Newsletter of the Soc. for German-Amer. Studies*, vol. 2, no. 2 (1980–1981), 1–2.

AE26 Tolzmann, Don H. "Teaching German-Americana." *Die Unterrichtspraxis*, vol. 9, no. 2 (1976), 16–17.

AE27 Viereck, Wolfgang. "Volkstums-Forscher in Chicago gesucht." *Abendpost/Sonntagspost* (Chicago), 8 January 1967.

AE28 Von Hofe, Harold. "German Culture in English Lecture Courses." *German Quar.*, vol. 21 (1948), 158–62.

AE29 Zucker, Adolf E. "On Collecting [German-American] Historical Data." *Amer.-German Rev.*, vol. 7, no. 3 (1941), 39–40.

AE30 Zucker, Adolf E., and Felix Reichmann. *Subject-Approach to Americana-Germanica*. Philadelphia: Carl Schurz Memorial Foundation, 1943. 50p. Subject classification adopted for the Union Catalogue of the Foundation.

AF
Societies/Organizations/Publications in Support of German American Interests

General

See also Section AG: Handbooks/Directories/Guides for German-American Interests; *and* Agencies *under* Section AH: Promotion of Friendship and Goodwill Between Germany and America.

AF1 Bahr, Gisela E. "Deutsche Vereine in Amerika." *German Quar.*, vol. 37, no. 2 (1964), 189–92. Current statistics on German clubs of all kinds.

AF2 "Deutsch-amerikanischer Vereins-Wegweiser 1980: Guide to German-Speaking Clubs and Societies in the United States in 1980." *New Yorker Staats-Zeitung und Herold*, vol. 146, no. 21 (1980), Sect. C, 64p. Guide for 1981: *ibid.*, vol. 147, no. 21 (1981), Sec. C, p.1, 64.

AF3 Faust, Albert B. "German-American Historical Societies: Their Achievements and Limitations." *Report, Soc. for the Hist. of the Germans in Md.*, vol. 28 (1953), 21–28. From a lecture given in 1946.

AF4 Hexamer, C. J. "Deutschamerikanische Institutionen." *Jahrbuch der Deutschamerikaner für das Jahr 1918.* Ed. Michael Singer. Chicago: German Yearbook Publ. Co., 1918.

AF5 Single, Erwin. "Deutsch-Amerikanische Vereine: Teil unseres Lebens." *New Yorker Staats-Zeitung und Herold*, 13 May 1973.

AF6 Tolzmann, Don H. "Encyclopedia of German-American Voluntary Organizations." *Newsletter of the Soc. for German-Amer. Studies*, vol. 2, no. 2 (1980–1981), 15.

Specific Societies and Organizations

See also under Section BH: The Pennsylvania Germans.

AMERICAN ASSOCIATION OF THE TEACHERS OF GERMAN (AATG)

AF7 "Deutsche Kultur blüht in Atlanta." *New Yorker Staats-Zeitung und Herold*, vol. 145, no. 50 (1979), Sec. A, 5. Report on the national meeting of the AATG.

AF8 *German Quarterly.* Vol. 1—, 1928—. Appleton, Wis.: AATG.

AF9 *Newsletter* of the American Association of the Teachers of German. Quarterly. 1954–1965. Ed. Glenn Waas and others. Philadelphia: AATG.

AF10 *Outlines of Programs for the Teaching of German by Television.* N.p.: n.p., 1955. 24p.

AF11 Reports and Minutes of Annual Meetings, 1928—. Publ. annually in *German Quarterly.*

AF12 Stephenson, Herta M. "AATG National High School Contest 1968–69." *Die Unterrichtspraxis*, vol. 2, no. 1 (1969), 86–90.

AF13 *Teaching Aid Project (T.A.P.)*, vol. 1–, 1966–. Philadelphia: AATG.

AF14 *Die Unterrichtspraxis for the Teaching of German.* Twice a year. Vol. 1–, Spring 1968–. Ed.

Eberhard Reichmann. Publ. under the auspices of the AATG by the Teaching Aid Project at Philadelphia.

AMERICAN COUNCIL FOR THE TEACHING OF FOREIGN LANGUAGES (ACTFL)

AF15 "Annual ACTFL Bibliography." Ed. John T. Harmon (1967–1968); Dale L. Lange (1969–). In *Foreign Language Annals*, annually.

AF16 *Foreign Language Annals. A Review of Current Progress in Teaching Foreign Languages.* Quarterly. Vol. 1–, 1967–. New York: ACTFL.

AMERICAN GOETHE SOCIETY

AF17 Prahl, Augustus "American Goethe Society." *Monatshefte*, vol. 51 (1959), 248. Chapters in Baltimore and Washington.

AMERICAN TURNERS

AF18 *American Turner Topics.* Bimonthly featuring recreational and sports articles and general news. Ed. E. A. Eklund. 1550 Clinton Ave. North, Rochester, N.Y. 14621.

CURRICULUMGRUPPE AMERIKAKUNDE HAMBURG

AF19 Curriculumgruppe Amerikakunde Hamburg. *Arbeitsbuch Amerikakunde: Studienband I.* Stuttgart: Metzler, 1976. 241p. An association for American studies organized at the University of Hamburg.

DEUTSCHE GESELLSCHAFT FÜR AMERIKASTUDIEN

AF20 Deutsche Gesellschaft für Amerikastudien. *Jahrbuch für Amerikastudien.* Eds. Walther Fischer, Ernst Fraenkel, Hans Galinsky, Dietrich Gerhard, Hans-Joachim Lang et al. Heidelberg: Winter, vol. 1–, 1955–. *Register zu Band 1–10 (1955–65).* Heidelberg, 1966. 64p. *Register zu den Bänden 11 bis 20 (1966–1975).* Miriam Hansen, comp. Stuttgart: Metzler, 1977. 55p. Title changed to *Amerikastudien/American Studies (Amst.)*

AF21 Deutsche Gesellschaft für Amerikastudien. *Mitteilungsblatt.* Im Auftrage der Gesellschaft hrsg. von Teut Andreas Riese. Ed. Ernst Fraenkel and Ursula Müller-Richter. Marburg/Lahn/Berlin/Heidelberg. Vol. 1–, 1954–. Annual.

DEUTSCHE IN DER WELT

AF22 *Deutsche in der Welt: Deutsche Zeitschrift für Kulturelle und wirtschaftliche Auslandarbeit in Europa und Übersee.* Baden-Baden. 1960–. Succeeded by *Auslands-Kurier. Deutsche Zeitschrift für wirtschaftliche und kulturelle Tätigkeit in Europa und Übersee.* Frankfurt a.M. 6 issues per year. 1960–.

GERMAN AMERICAN LEAGUE, INC.

AF23 *Neue Zeitung.* 1966–. Ed. H. Jurisch. German language. American European Weekly. Sponsored by the German American League, Inc. 9471 Hidden Valley Place, Beverly Hills, Calif. 90210. Emphasizes European politics; articles on commerce and travel, local club activities.

GERMAN-AMERICAN NATIONAL CONGRESS/DEUTSCH-AMERIKANISCHER NATIONAL-BUND

AF24 *Der Deutsch-Amerikaner. Offizielles Organ des Deutsch-Amerikanischen National-Kongresses* formerly *Deutschamerikanische National Kongress (D.A.N.K.).* Monthly. In English and German. Vol. 1–, ,1961–. Ed. Werner Barari. The Congress also publishes its *Mitteilungen.* 4740 N. Western Ave., Chicago, Ill 60625.

AF25 Kollacks, Walter. "Bericht des Hauptvorstandes." *Der Deutsch-Amerikaner*, October 1973, 1. Report on German-American National Congress/Deutsch-Amerikanischer National-Bund (D.A.N.K.).

AF26 *Der Landsmann.* Vol. 1–, 1970–. Journal. Rockville, Md. D.A.N.K. (Deutsch-Amerikanischer National Bund). Gruppe Washington D.C. "Landsmannschaft Ost."

GERMAN INFORMATION CENTER

AF27 *The Week in Germany.* Vol. 1–, 1969–. Ed. C. Hausmann, D. Willinger, P. Freedman. Weekly newsletter of the German Information Center, 410 Park Ave., New York. Six pages of news and notes about current events, in German.

GERMAN MASONIC HOME CORPORATION

AF28 *Nine Manhattan Masonic News.* 1937–. Ed. Marvin Goldsmith. Semi-monthly; English-language fraternal magazine; German Masonic Home Corporation, Ninth Manhattan District.

GERMAN SOCIETY OF MARYLAND

AF29 Wust, Klaus G. *Pioneers in Service. The German Society of Maryland, 1783–1958.* Baltimore: the Society, 1958. 53p. Rev. in *Amer.-German Rev.*, vol. 24, no. 6 (1958) 40. Supplements Hennighausen's history of 1909.

AF30 Wust, Klaus G. "A Proud Record of Service: The German Society of Maryland, 1783–1958." *Amer.-German Rev.*, vol. 24, no. 3 (1958), 29–30, 39. Its record of 175 years of service to immigrants.

GERMAN SOCIETY OF PENNSYLVANIA/ DEUTSCHE GESELLSCHAFT VON PENNSYLVANIEN

AF31 Pfund, Harry W. *A History of the German Society of Pennsylvania*. Philadelphia: The Society, 1944. 38p. Bicentenary ed., 1764–1964: 2nd rev. ed., 1964. 129p.

GERMAN SOCIETY OF THE CITY OF NEW YORK

AF32 *Annual Reports, The German Society of the City of New York*. Founded 1784. 150 Fifth Ave., New York 10011. Exec. Director, Wolfgang Hamel.

GERMANISTIC SOCIETY OF AMERICA

AF33 *Annual Report*, Germanistic Society of America, Inc. 548 W. 113th St., New York 10025. Sponsors lectures and receptions; organized shipment of books and journals to university libraries in Germany in the post-War period; supports fellowships in aid of university study.

GOETHE INSTITUT, MUNICH

AF34 Bruggan, M.F.E van. "Die Arbeit des Goethe Instituts zur Pflege der deutschen Sprache und Kultur im Ausland." *Levende Talen*, no. 224 (1964), 239–41.

GOETHE SOCIETY OF NEW ENGLAND

AF35 Greenberg, Valerie. "The Goethe Society of New England." *Amer.-German Rev.*, vol. 32, no. 4 (April–May 1966), 38. On the current programs of the society.

GOETHEAN LITERARY SOCIETY

AF36 Prahl, Augustus J. "The Goethean Literary Society of Franklin and Marshall College." *Amer.-German Rev.*, vol. 16, no. 1 (1949), 29–30. The oldest Goethe Society in the world.

INSTITUT FÜR AUSLANDSBEZIEHUNGEN

AF37 *Zeitschrift für Kulturaustausch*. Started in 1950 as *Mitteilungen des Instituts für Auslandsbeziehungen*. Six times annually. (Scheduled to be discontinued.) Inst., located in Stuttgart, was founded in 1917 as the Deutsches Auslands-Institut. Maintains library and information service about Germans in all parts of the world.

INTER NATIONES

AF38 "Portrait. Inter Nationes." *Die Unterrichtspraxis*, vol. 9, no. 2 (Fall 1976), 121–23. Located in Bonn.

JUGENDPOST

AF39 Hanhardt, Arthur M. "Jugendpost." *Amer.-German Review*, vol. 21, no. 4 (1955), 22, 31. Periodical for students of German in the United States, publ. since 1938.

LITERARY SOCIETY FOUNDATION, INC./ LITERARISCHER VEREIN

AF40 Flacke, Lieselotte. "Literary Society Foundation, Inc. New York." *Zeitschrift für Kulturaustausch*, vol. 12, no. 4 (1962), 332.

AF41 "Literarischer Verein bespricht das Deutsche in den U S A." *New Yorker Staats-Zeitung und Herold*, vol. 146, no. 2 (1980), Sec. B, 11. Announcement of talks for 18 January 1980 by Doris Guilloton, Margaret Sander, and Volkmar Sander. For summaries, see *ibid.*, vol. 146, no. 4 (1980), Sec. A, 6.

AF42 Meier, Henry. "Forty Years of the Literarischer Verein." *Amer.-German Rev.*, vol. 12, no. 5 (1946), 20–21. "Fifty Years of Literarischer Verein." *Ibid.*, vol. 22, no. 3 (1956), 13–14.

AF43 Reiter, Wilhelm. "Der literarische Verein in New York—ein Hort deutscher Sprachpflege in Amerika." *Auslandskurier*, vol. 8 (1967), no. 2, 19.

LUXEMBOURGERS OF AMERICA

AF44 *Luxembourg News of America*. 1967–. E. Victor Jacoby. 201 Sunset Drive, Wilmette, Ill. 60091. English-language papers, sponsored by the Luxembourgers of America.

NATIONAL CARL SCHURZ ASSOCIATION (NCSA) [CARL SCHURZ MEMORIAL FOUNDATION (CSMF)]

AF45 *Amer.-German Rev.* Vol. 1, 1932—Vol. 35, 1969. Bi-Monthly. Wilbur K. Thomas, Managing Ed. Philadelphia, The Association.

AF46 Carl Schurz Memorial Foundation. *Research Department Bulletin*. Vol. 2. Ed. Felix Reichmann and Eugene Doll. Philadelphia: n.p., 1943–1944.

AF47 Cunz, Dieter. "Die wissenschaftliche Arbeit der Carl Schurz Foundation." *Schweizer Bei-*

Specific Societies and Organizations *(cont.)*
träge zur Allgemeinen Geschichte (Bern), vol. 7 (1949), 206–12.

AF48 Deeken, Hans. "1968 Report of the Executive Director." *Amer.-German Rev.*, vol. 35, no. 5 (1969), 30–32.

AF49 Deeken, Hans Werner. "Living Ties." *Amer.-German Rev.*, vol. 34, no. 1 (1967–1968), 2–5. Also publ. in the *Zeitschrift für Kulturaustausch*. The NCSA and other organizations as mediators between the United States and Germany.

AF50 Doll, Eugene E. "The Basis for a Rare Book Collection at the Carl Schurz Memorial Foundation." *Amer.-German Rev.*, vol. 18, no. 1 (1951), 7–10, 34. Reviewing some of the rare and early imprints in the possession of the Foundation.

AF51 Doll, Eugene E. *Twenty-Five Years of Service, 1930–1955*. Philadelphia: CSMF, 1955. 28p. History of the Foundation.

AF52 Elkinton, Howard. "Immortal Values." *Amer.-German Rev.*, vol. 19, no. 5 (1953), 20–21. Obituary of Wilbur K. Thomas, director of the CSMF 1930–1946.

AF53 Gilchrist, Agnes Addison. "Before Our Time." *Amer.-German Rev.*, vol. 17, no. 5 (1951), 22–23. History of the building of the Second Bank of the U.S. in Philadelphia, used by the CSMF in the 1950's. See also, the article on the same subject by Charles E. Peterson, *ibid.*, vol. 18, no. 1 (1951), 11–12.

AF54 Graeff, Arthur D. "As Shadows Lengthen, 1930–1950." *Amer.-German Rev.*, vol. 16, no. 5 (1950), 4–6, 33. Backward glance at the first 20 years of the CSMF.

AF55 "Hanns Gramm." *Amer.-German Rev.*, 32, no. 2 (1965), 40; "In Memoriam, Hanns Gramm." *Hist. Rev. of Berks Co.*, vol. 31 no. 2 (1965), 41. Co-founder of the CSMF and prominent German-American spokesman (1887–1965).

AF56 Gramm, Hanns. *The Oberländer Trust 1931–1953*. Philadelphia: CSMF, 1956. 132p. Rev. by E. E. Doll, *Hist. Rev. of Berks Co.*, vol. 22, no. 1 (1956), 23–24; in *Amer.-German Rev.*, vol. 22, no. 6 (1956), 38–39.

AF57 Hogue, Arthur R. "The Carl Schurz Memorial Foundation: The First Twenty-Five Years." *Ind. Mag. of History*, vol. 51 (1955), 335–39.

AF58 Jones, Elsa L. "CSMF Library Development." *Amer.-German Rev.*, vol. 25, no. 2 (1959), 40. Progress report on the Union Catalogue of American-Germanica, a major library project of the Foundation.

AF59 National Carl Schurz Association. *Thirty-Fifth Anniversary May 7, 1965. Down Town Club, Philadelphia*. Philadelphia: n.p., 1965. Program. 4p.

AF60 Peterson, Charles E. "Before Our Time." *Amer.-German Rev.*, vol. 18, no. 1 (1951), 11–12. The building of the Second Bank of the United States (Philadelphia), home of the Carl Schurz Memorial Foundation.

AF61 Pfatteicher, Carl F. "Music and the Carl Schurz Foundation." *Amer.-German Rev.*, vol. 13, no. 3 (1947), 40–41.

AF62 Reichmann, Felix. "The Library of the Carl Schurz Memorial Foundation." *Bull. of the Special Libraries Assoc. of Philadelphia*, vol. 10, no. 1 (September 1943).

AF63 "Report" (later titled "CSMF Condensed Annual Report," etc.). *Amer.-German Rev.*, vols. 2–35, 1935–1968. Annually in issue no. 5. In addition, the Foundation published an annual chronicle of activities and events: "The CSMF Year." In issue no. 2, 1953 (vol. 20) to 1961 (vol. 28).

AF64 *Teaching Aid Project (TAP). Teachers' Guide—The TAP Guide*. Comp. by Eberhard Reichmann. Vol. 1–, 1966–. Quarterly. National Carl Schurz Association; newsletter of discussion of language pedagogy for secondary and college-level teachers of German.

AF65 Thomas, Wilbur K. "The Foundation." *Amer.-German Rev.*, vol. 11, no. 5 (1945), 30–31; vol. 11, no. 6 (1945), 30–31; vol. 12, no. 2 (1945), 37. Reports of progress and plans.

AF66 [Thomas, Wilbur K.] *Immortal Values*. Philadelphia: The Carl Schurz Memorial Foundation, 1943. 24p. Editorial discussion of the German-American war crisis.

AF67 Thomas, Wilbur Kelsey. [Editorials and Reports.] *Amer.-German Rev.* (1942): "An Early Effort in the Cultural Field," vol. 9, no. 2, 36–37; "Americans All," vol. 8, no. 6, 3; (1944): "The Home Front," vol. 10, no. 3, 3; "Education, For What and by Whom?" vol. 10, no. 4, 3; "Free-Born," vol. 10, no. 5, 3; "Facing the Immediate Future," vol. 10, no. 6, 3; (1945): "Turn On the Lights," vol. 11, no. 1, 3; "The Star of Hope," vol. 11, no. 2, 3; "Personal Leadership," vol. 11, no. 3, 3; "Faith in the Future," vol. 11, no. 4, 3; "Peace—Hard or Soft," vol. 11, no. 5, 3; "Thrift," vol. 11, no. 6, 3; "Demobilization—To What," vol. 12, no. 1, 3; "The New Beginning or the Beginning of the End," vol. 12, no. 2, 3.

AF68 "A Unique Reference Source." *Amer.-German Review*, vol. 28 (1962), no. 5, 28, 36. The Union Catalogue housed at the NCSA headquarters, Philadelphia.

AF69 Zucker, Adolf E. "The Foundation. Notes on the Research Library." *Amer.-German Rev.*, vol. 8, no. 5 (1942), 40. See also "The Foundation's Library—A Unique Aid to Scholars." *Amer.-German Rev.*, vol. 13, no. 2 (1946), 39–40.

NATIONAL FEDERATION OF STUDENTS OF GERMAN

AF70 *N.F.S.G. News*. A Rundschau Supplement. Ed. Maria Conway. Monthly. Publ. by Federation. Sponsor: National Carl Schurz Association, Philadelphia. National organization for students of German at the secondary level. *See*: "National Federation of Students of German: Portrait of a German Club." *Amer.-German Rev.*, vol. 35, no. 1 (1968), 55–56. The German club under the direction of Sister Marie Genevieve at Little Flower Catholic High School for Girls, Philadelphia, predated the club of the same name organized by the National Carl Schurz Association. Starting in 1969, the *Amer.-German Rev.* carried a bi-monthly department entitled "National Federation of Students of German."

DIE SCHLARAFFIA

AF71 Polt, N. K. "Die Schlaraffia." *Amer.-German Rev.*, vol. 20, no. 2 (1953–54), 16–19. History and list of local chapters of a social organization.

SOCIETY FOR GERMAN-AMERICAN STUDIES

AF72 Benjamin, Steven M. "The Society for German-American Studies: Its History and Present Activities." In: *Papers from the Conference on German-Americana in the Eastern United States*. Ed. S. M. Benjamin. Morgantown: Dept. of Foreign Langs., West Va. Univ., 1980, p.197–201.

AF73 *Journal of German-American Studies. A Journal of History, Literature, Biography and Genealogy*. Vol. 1–, 1969–. (To 1976 entitled *German-American Studies*.) Quarterly. Cleveland: German-American Publishing Co., in collaboration with the Soc. for German-American Studies.

AF74 *Newsletter of the Society for German-American Studies*. Vol. 1–, 1969–. (4156 Claridge Drive, Youngstown, Ohio 44511.) Resumed under the editorship of LaVern J. Rippley, Northfield, Minn.: Vol. 1–, 1980–.

AF75 Tolzmann, Don Heinrich. "History of the Society for German-American Studies." *Newsletter of the Soc. for German-Amer. Studies*, vol. 2, no. 2 (1980–1981), 1–3.

AF76 Tolzmann, Don Heinrich, comp. "The *Journal of German-American Studies*, 1969–80: An Index." *Jour. of German-Amer. Studies*, vol. 15, nos. 3–4 (1980), 75–94.

SOCIETY FOR THE HISTORY OF THE GERMANS IN MARYLAND

AF77 Becker, Ernest J. "The Society for the History of the Germans in Maryland: A Chronicle." *Report, Soc. for the Hist. of the Germans in Md.*, vol. 28 (1953), 9–20. History of the Society from its founding in 1886.

AF78 *Report of the Society for the History of the Germans in Maryland*. (After 1969: *The Report. A Journal of German-American History*.) Vol. 1–, 1887–. Ed. D. Cunz (to 1956) and Klaus G. Wust. Publ. by the Soc. in Baltimore. Rev. (vol. XXV): A. E. Zucker, *Germanic Rev.*, vol. 18 (1943), 310–11; (XXVI): E. J. Becker, *Md. Hist. Mag.*, vol. 40 (1945), 169; C. F. Kramer, *Amer.-German Rev.*, vol. 11, no. 5 (1945), 28; Vol. XXVI: E. E. Doll, *Pa. Mag. of Hist. and Biography*, vol. 71 (1947), 94–95; R. C. Wood, *Monatshefte*, vol. 38 (1946), 121; XXVII: E. E. Doll, *Amer.-German Rev.*, vol. 16, no. 6 (1950), 36; A. C. Repp, *Concordia Hist. Inst. Quar.*, vol. 23 (1950), 161–62; (Vol. XXVIII): E. E. Doll, *Amer.-German Rev.*, vol. 20, no. 2 (1954), 34–35; P. A. Barba, "'S Pennsylfawnisch Deitsch Eck," Allentown *Morning Call*, 9 May 1954; R. King, *German Quar.*, vol. 26 (1954), 219; W. D. Hoyt, *Md. Hist. Mag.*, vol. 48 (1954), 244; E. Lang, *Ind. Mag. of Hist.*, vol. 49 (1954), 433–35; in *Va. Mag. of Hist. and Biography*, vol. 61 (1954), 197; in *Amer. Genealogist*, vol. 29 (1954), 171; in *Histor. Zeitschrift*, vol. 176 (1954), 433; (Vol. XXIX): by C. Wittke, *Ohio Hist. Quar.*, vol. 65 (1956), 425–27; in *Md. Hist. Mag.*, vol. 51 (1956), 365; (Vol. XXX): by W. Fischer, *Jahrbuch für*

Specific Societies and Organizations *(cont.)*

Amerikastudien, vol. 4 (1959), 287; C. Wittke, *Amer.-German Rev.*, vol. 26, no. 3 (1960); Arthur R. Schultz, *Ohio Hist. Quar.*, vol. 70 (1961), 83–84; (Vol. XXXI): in *Mod. Lang. Quar.*, vol. 24 (1963), 319; Karl Arndt, *German Quar.*, vol. 38 (1965), 113–14.

STEUBEN SOCIETY OF AMERICA

AF79 *The Steuben News: A Newspaper for Americans.* Vol. 1–, 1928–. English-language monthly. Ed. Edward J. Sussmann. Publ. by National Council of the Soc.

AG
Handbooks/Directories/Guides for German-American Interests

AG1 Ahn, F. *Amerikanischer Dolmetscher für Deutsche, zum Erlernen der englischen Sprache ohne Lehrer.* New York: Steiger, ca. 1870.

AG2 American Chamber of Commerce in Germany. "65 Years in the Service of German-American Relations: The American Chamber of Commerce in Germany." *Gazette*, vol. 9, no. 5 (September–October 1968), 15–17.

AG3 Deubel, Stefan. *Der Deutsch-Amerikaner von Heute. Deutsch-Amerikanisches Adressbuch für die USA und Westdeutschland.* Cleveland: Wächter und Anzeiger, 1963. 464p. Directory of societies, church organizations, business firms, and newspapers, with biographical sketches of German-American personalities in the business world.

AG4 *Deutsch-Amerika Almanach 1958.* New York: Verlag Plattdütsche Post, 1958. 160p.

AG5 Friederice, George. *Amerikanistisches Wörterbuch mit Hilfswörterbuch für den Amerikanisten.* 2nd ed. Hamburg: Cram, de Gruyter & Co., 1959. ca. 840p.

AG6 Galinsky, Hans. "Das amerikanische Englisch in sprachwissenschaftlicher und schulpraktischer Sicht." *Die neueren Sprachen*, N.F. vol. 12 (1963), 1–18.

AG7 *Hamburgischer Auslandkalender. Ein Taschenbuch für Auslanddeutschtum.* Vol. 1–, 1920/21–. Ed. Wilhelm Herkenroth. Hamburg.

AG8 Handler, Beulah. *English the American Way for German-Speaking Adults.* 2nd ed. New York: Barnes and Noble, 1961. 294p.

AG9 Herman, Lewis, and Marguerite Shalett Herman. *Talk American. A Practical Guide for Eliminating a German Accent.* Chicago N.Y.: Ziff-Davis, 1944. 129p.

AG10 Institut für Auslandsbeziehungen, Stuttgart. Amerika-Referat. *Transatlantischer Austausch: Ein Führer durch die am Kulturaustausch zwischen Deutschland und den Vereinigten Staaten beteiligten Organisationen, Institute, Verbände, Behörden.* München: Hueber, 1958. 172p. New ed. München, 1965. 168p. Rev. in *Zeitschrift für Kulturaustausch*, vol. 15 (1965), 100–01.

AG11 *Jahrbuch der auswärtigen Kulturbeziehungen* 1964. Ed. Berthold Martin. Bonn: Akademischer Verlag, 1964. 291p. Essays and discussions of current questions at the diplomatic level; treaties relating to cultural interchange; agencies active in cultural work.

AG12 Mayer, Arthur, ed. *Junckers Wörterbuch: Amerikanisch.* 4th ed. Berlin: Juncker, 1965. 487p. "Amerikanisch-deutsch" and "Deutsch-amerikanisch".

AG13 Räber, Ben J., ed. *Der Neue Amerikanische Calendar.* Baltic, Ohio: Räber's Bookstore, 1979. Also available in an English language edition.

AG14 *1776–1976.* [Calendar.] *Two Hundred Years of German-American Relations.* München: Heinz

Moos Verlag, 1975. Publ. in cooperation with Inter Nationes, Bonn/Bad Godesberg. 30 l. Richly illustrated to mark the Bicentennial. Essays and sketches on topics associated with German-American relations.

AG15 Steiner, Arthur. *Amerikanisch wie es nicht im Wörterbuch steht.* Frankfurt a.M.: Scheffler, 1966. 157p.

AG16 Straube, Max. *Die Aussprache englischer Wörter. Ein kurze Anleitung zum schnellen Erlernen der englischen Aussprache.* Philadelphia: N.Y. International News Co., 1885. 68p.

AG17 *300 Years of German Immigrants in North America. A Calendar for 1983.* Baltimore/Gräfelfing vor München: Heinz Moos Publishing, 1982. 112p.

AG18 Whyte, John. *American Words and Ways: Especially for German Americans.* New York: Viking, 1943. 184p. Rev. by E. W. Stoetzner, *Amer.-German Rev.*, vol. 10, no. 1 (October 1943), 37; Edwin Roedder, *Monatshefte für deut. Unterricht*, vol. 35, no. 8 (December 1943), 444–46; C. B. Palmer, *N.Y. Times Book Rev.*, 4 July 1943, 8.

AH

Promotion of Friendship and Goodwill Between Germany and America

Agencies

AH1 Adam, Robert. "Die Bundeshilfe für Studenten, Colleges und Universitäten in U.S.A." *Deutsche Universitätszeitung*, vol. 21, no. 2 (1966), 35–36.

AH2 "American Institute in Berlin." *American Studies News* (Washington, D.C.), vol. 1 (April 1963), 1–3. Ernst Fraenkel here outlines plans for an enlarged American institute and American studies research center.

AH3 Amerika-Gesellschaft e. V., Hamburg. *Germany: Facts, Figures, Features.* Trans. by Helen Streit. Hamburg: Vlg. Transport-Orientierung St. Annen, ca. 1950. 176p.

AH4 *Amerikakunde; zwölf Beiträge von E. Baumgarten, M. Biehl, W. Fischer u.a.* 2nd rev. and expanded ed. Frankfurt a.M.: Diesterweg, 1952. 461p. In the series Handbücher der Auslandskunde.

AH5 Andrews, Hal J. *Geschichte des Verbands deutschamerikanischer Klubs 1947–1958. Westdeutschland. History, Federation of German-American Clubs.* Trans. into German by Erika Schwarz. Heidelberg: Neumann, 1958. 53p.

AH6 *Aus Geschichte und Geistesleben der Vereinigten Staaten von Amerika.* Ausstellungskatalog. Dortmund: Stadt- und Landesbibliothek, 1962. 62p.

AH7 "Das Austauschprogramm Deutschland—U S A seit 1947." *Amerika-Dienst, Allgemeines* (Bad Godesberg), vol. 6 no. 39 (1953), 1–3.

AH8 Brause, Herman F. "Handbuch eines Deutsch-Amerikaners." *Deutscher Wochenspiegel*, 28 March 1973.

AH9 Brunner, Emil. "Geistige Hindernisse und Brücken zwischen Amerika und Europa." *Neue Schweizer Rundschau*, vol. 8 (1951), 482–95.

AH10 Brunner, Otto, and Dietrich Gerhard, eds. *Europa und Übersee. Festschrift für Egmont Zechlin.* Hamburg: Hans Bredow-Institut, 1961. 267p.

AH11 Burmeister, Irmgard. "International Understanding Begins at School. American and German Historians Discuss each Other's Textbooks."

Agencies *(cont.)*

Amer.-German Rev., vol. 39, no. 4 (1964), 15–17, 37.

AH12 "Carl Schurz Gesellschaft, Bremen." *Amer.-German Rev.*, vol. 25, no. 4 (1959), 40. The tenth anniversary celebration of the society.

AH13 "Columbus Medal for the American Field Service and the Work of the Columbus Society, Munich." *Gazette*, vol. 9, no. 6 (1968), 5–6.

AH14 Dash, Emma. "Sharing American Knowledge." *Amer.-German Rev.*, vol. 20, no. 2 (1953), 28–29. The German book plan of the CARE organization.

AH15 "Deutsche-amerikanische Freundschaftswoche." *New Yorker Staats-Zeitung und Herold*, vol. 146, no. 19 (1980), Sec. A, 1. Celebration held in Germany.

AH16 Easum, Chester V. "Zur Einweihung des Carl Schurz-Hauses, Bonn." *Amer.-German Rev.*, vol. 21, no. 3 (1955), 20–22. Student community house at Bonn University.

AH17 Flacke, Lieselotte. "Washington International Center—Besucherdienst und Stätte der Begegnung." *Transatlantische Austausch-Nachrichten* (Stuttgart), vol. 6, no. 1 (1964), 1–3.

AH18 *Gazette*. Vol. 1–, 1960–. Bi-monthly. Oficial Publication of the Federation of German-American Clubs/Verband der Deutsch-Amerikanischen Klubs e.V. München.

AH19 Genzel, Fritz. "Vier Jahre Goethe-Haus Montreal." *Der Auslandskurier*, vol. 7, no. 6 (1966), 13–14.

AH20 "German-American Clubs in Germany." *Amer.-German Review*, vol. 20, no. 1 (1953), 31.

AH21 "Gruppe '47 at Princeton University, April 21–25, 1966." *Amer.-German Review. Special Supplement*, April 1966. 24p.

AH22 Guild, Hazel. "German-American Friendship Week." *Amer.-German Rev.*, vol. 29, no. 6 (1963), 22, 34. The tenth annual "week" celebrated by German hosts and United States military and embassy personnel in May 1963.

AH23 Gurlitt, Willibald. "The Praetorius Organ in Freiburg." *Amer.-German Review*, vol. 22, no. 4 (1956), 7–9. Freiburg Univ. organ project made possible through the generosity of its Honorary Senator, Dr. Matthew T. Mellon.

AH24 Heintges, John A. "Let Us Think of Lasting Friendship." *Gazette*, vol. 9, no. 5 (1968), 2. Address before the Darmstadt convention by Lt. Gen. J. A. Heintges, Dep. Commander-in-Chief for the Seventh Army.

AH25 Helbig, Louis F., and Eberhard Reichmann, eds. *Teaching Postwar Germany in America: Papers and Discussions, German Studies Conference 1972*. Bloomington: Institute of German Studies, Indiana University, 1972. 244p. Rev. by E. Helms, *Amerikastudien*, vol. 19, no. 2 (1974), 370–71.

AH26 Holthusen, Hans Egon. "Eine deutsche Schaubude in Amerika: Theorie und Praxis des 'Goethe House'." *Der Monat*, vol. 15, no. 172 (1962–1963), 24–33.

AH27 Isaak, Suse. "Kulturerbe als Brücke." *Zeitschrift für Kulturaustausch*, vol. 16 (1965), 81–82.

AH28 Kahn, Sy M., and Martha Raetz, eds. *Interculture: A Collection of Essays and Creative Writing Commemorating the Twentieth Anniversary of the Fulbright Program at the Institute of Translation and Interpretation, Univ. of Vienna (1955–1974)*. Wien/Stuttgart: W. Braumiller, 1975. 298p. Rev. by J. B. Hubbell, *Amer. Lit.*, vol. 48, no. 2 (November 1976), 414–16. Incl. art. by E. Klambauer: "U.S. Authors in the Program of *Donauland*, Austria's Largest Book Club."

AH29 Kellerman, Henry J. *Cultural Relations as an Instrument of U.S. Foreign Policy: The Educational Exchange Program between the United States and Germany, 1945–1954*. Washington, D.C.: Government Printing Office, 1978. 290p.

AH30 König, Rene, et al. *Geist einer Freien Gesellschaft/Spirit of a Free Society*. Essays in Honor of Senator James William Fulbright on the Occasion of the Tenth Anniversary of the German Fulbright Program. Heidelberg: Quelle & Meyer, 1962. 392p.

AH31 "Mission to Germany. Interview with Dr. Hertha Kraus." *Amer.-German Rev.*, vol. 30, no. 2 (1964), 14–17. Representatives of the American Friends Service Committee on a mission through the Germanies, September 1963.

AH32 "New Yorker Turnverein leistet Entwicklungshilfe." *Der Milwaukee Herold,* 30 August 1973.

AH33 Paetel, Karl O. "Das Goethe-Haus in New York." *Der Auslandskurier,* vol. 3, no. 3 (1962), 6–7.

AH34 Rauch, Malte J. "Joint American-German Literature Seminar." *Amer.-German Rev.,* vol. 27, no. 1 (1960), 12. Report on an experiment in teaching.

AH35 Rieser, Max. "Deutsche Kultur in Amerika." *Transatlantische Austauschnachrichten* (Stuttgart), vol. 3, no. 1 (1961), 17–20.

AH36 Rippley, La Vern J. "Gift Cows for Germany." *N. Dak. Hist.* vol. 40 (Summer 1973), 4–15. Also: "American Milk Cows for Germany: A Sequel." *Ibid.,* vol. 44 (1977), 15–23.

AH37 Röder, Rudolf. "Amerikahaus und Volksbücherei." *Bücherei und Bildung,* vol. 3 (1951), 245–47. See also: "Die Büchereien der Amerikahäuser." *Ibid.,* vol. 1 (1949), 275.

AH38 Sahl, Hans. "Brücke über den Atlantik. Deutsche Kultur in America—Die Arbeit des Goethe-Hauses." *Zeitschrift für Kulturaustausch,* vol. 13, no. 1 (1963), 14–15. On the Goethe House in New York.

AH39 Schuh, Oscar Fritz. *Zwei Völker in Gespräch; Aus der Vortragsarbeit der Amerika-Häuser in Deutschland,* "res novae," vol. 11. Frankfurt a. M.: Europäische Verlags-Anstalt, 1961. 216p.

AH40 "Steuben-Schurz Gesellschaft, Frankfurt a. M." *Amer.-German Rev.,* vol. 31, no. 6 (1965), 18.

AH41 United States. Office of the Military Government. *Cultural Exchange Program for the Period 1948–49.* OMGUS, Cultural Affairs Division, 1948. 64p.

AH42 Van der Smissen, Nina. "Amerika-Gesellschaft, Hamburg." *Amer.-German Rev.,* vol. 24, no. 5 (1958), 36. Report on ongoing projects of the society.

AH43 Werner, Alfred. "Goethe Lives Here." *Amer.-German Rev.,* vol. 23, no. 5 (1957), 20–21. On the Goethe House in New York City.

AH44 Werner. Bürgermeister. "Busenbach ehrt einen G. I." *Amer.-German Rev.,* vol. 22, no. 3 (1956), 25–26. Busenbach (Baden) honors the memory of Roy L. Mattson, who lost his life while performing voluntary service for the community.

AH45 Whitney, Craig. "Age Seen Eroding German-U.S. Ties." *N.Y. Times,* 24 November 1974. On private and government-sponsored efforts to stimulate friendship and exchanges between West Germany and the United States.

AH46 *Yearbooks,* Federation of German-American Clubs/Verband der Deutsch-Amerikanischen Klubs e.V. Stuttgart: The Federation, 1951–1952. 54, 36, 24p.

AH47 Zohn, Harry. "American-European Friendship Week." *Books Abroad,* vol. 28 (1954), 28–29. Lectures at Stamford, Conn., under the auspices of the American-European Friendship Association.

Exchange of Persons/Academic Exchange

AH48 Balis, Tony. "Three Little Manhattans." *Wesleyan University Alumnus,* vol. 60, no. 4 (Summer 1976), 22–23. The Expansion Committee of the German-American Football Association approves the formation of a soccer team "Little Three Manhattan" drawn from alumni of Amherst, Williams, and Wesleyan.

AH49 *Begegnung mit dem Erziehungswesen der USA. Erfahrungsbericht über den deutsch-amerikanischen Lehreraustausch 1952–1959.* Ed. Gerhard Neumann and Gerhard Schellenberg. München: Hueber, 1961. 283p.

AH50 Brandt, Thomas O. "Student Broadcast to Europe." *German Quar.,* vol. 24, no. 4 (1951), 250–55. Students of German in the U.S. transmitting over the Voice of America.

AH51 Cox, Henry B. "Mutual Understanding through Exchange." *Amer.-German Rev.,* vol. 23, no. 6 (1957), 4–8. Two-way United States-Germany exchanges under the Fulbright Act.

AH52 Döhring, C. "Friedliche Brücken von Volk zu Volk." *German Canad. Rev.,* vol. 10, no. 1 (1957), 21–23. See also: *Mitteilungen des Instituts*

Exchange of Persons/Academic Exchange *(cont.)*
für Auslandsbeziehungen, vol. 7 (1957), 215–16. Five years of German-Canadian association in Hannover.

AH53 *Freunde hüben und drüben. Schulverbindungsdienst.* Darmstadt: n.p., n.d. American Friends Service Committee.

AH54 Gariss, Philip, and Helen Ott. "The American German Teacher Exchange." *German Quar.*, vol. 27 (1954), 104–09.

AH55 *German and Austrian Teacher-Education Project.* N.p.: Illinois State Normal University, 1949. 30p.

AH56 Hettich, L. "Die höhere Schule in den Vereinigten Staaten." *Der deutsche Lehrer im Ausland* (München, Düsseldorf), vol. 7 no. 3 (1960), 59–62.

AH57 Institute of International Education. *Open Doors.* N.p.: n.p., 1966. Handbook of information and statistics on the student exchanges facilitated by the Institute: 22,000 Americans who went abroad and 92,000 foreign citizens who came to United States colleges and universities. Address: 809 United Nations Plaza, New York 10017.

AH58 Kahn, S. M., and M. Raetz, eds. *Interculture: A Collection of Essays and Creative Writing Commemorating the Twentieth Anniversary of the Fulbright Program at the Institute of Translation and Interpretation, University of Vienna (1955–1975).* Wien: Braumüller, 1974. 298p.

AH59 Kline, James D. "German Exchanges, Before and After Fulbright." *News Bull.*, vol. 28, no. 5 (1953), 23–27.

AH60 Krippendorf, Herbert. "1926–1962: zwei Generationen Amerika-Praktikanten." *Der Auslandskurier*, vol. 3, no. 3 (1962), 9–10.

AH61 Linke, Willy. "International Ties between Elementary Schools." *Amer.-German Rev.*, vol. 23, no. 4 (1957), 18–19. Links between German and U.S. schools.

AH62 Lochner, Louis P. "The Letter Writingest Youngsters on Earth." *Amer.-German Rev.*, vol. 23, no. 2 (1956), 27–30. On a letter exchange program with German youth launched by Clara Leiser.

AH63 Neumann, Gerhard, and Bernard Schellenberg, eds. *Begegnung mit dem Erziehungswesen der U S A; Erfahrungsbericht über den deutsch-amerikanischen Lehreraustausch, 1952–1959.* München: Hueber, 1961. 283p.

AH64 *Open Gate.* At irregular intervals, 1950–1951. English, German, French. Viersen (Rheinl.): Internationale Gesellschaft zur Förderung des Jugendaustausches; Rheinland Vlg.

AH65 Russel, Howard H. "Der Anteil der Bundesrepublik am amerikanischen Austauschprogramm." *Der Auslandskurier*, vol. 3, no. 3 (1962), 8.

AH66 Sack, Marion G. "Bridges of Friendship." *Amer.-German Rev.*, vol. 23, no. 6 (1957), 9–10, 17. Exchange of elementary school principals between the U.S. and Germany.

AH67 Schneider, Dieter. "Umfang und Wege des deutsch-amerikanischen Studentenaustausches." *Der Auslandskurier*, vol. 3, no. 3 (1962), 10–11.

AH68 *Das Schüleraustauschprogramm zwischen den Vereinigten Staaten von Amerika und der Bundesrepublik Deutschland, durchgeführt von privaten amerikanischen Organisationen.* N.p.: n.p., 1959. 36p.

AH69 "Student-Exchange." *Gazette* (Federation of German-American Clubs), vol. 9, no. 5 (September–October 1968), 10–12; no. 6 (November–December 1968), 12–16. Reports by R. de Clerck (Florida South. Coll.), A. Czerkas (Bowling Green State); R. Eck (Delaware); W. McNabb (Würzburg); W. Montgomery (Marburg), B. Rode (Bowling Green.)

AH70 Vent, Myron H. "Teacher Exchange with Germany." *Amer.-German Rev.*, vol. 24, no. 2 (1957), 24–26.

AH71 Wessling, Wolfgang. "Zehn Jahre deutsch-amerikanischer Lehreraustausch." *Bildung und Erziehung*, vol. 15 (1962), 30–37.

AH72 Winterscheidt, Friedrich, and Jörg Frey. "German-American Partnership Program. Exchange Program for German and American High School Students." *Zielsprache Deutsch* (München: Hueber), no. 3 (1974), 137–39. Program conducted by the Goethe Institute, Boston, since 1972.

City Partnerships

AH73 Breuer, Willi. "Seit 13 Jahren: Wesel-Hagerstown/U S A." *Zeitschrift für Kulturaustausch*, vol. 15, nos. 1–2 (1965), 55. A city partnership.

AH74 Flacke, Lieselotte. "Aus der Praxis deutschamerikanischer Partnerschaften." *Zeitschrift für Kulturaustausch*, vol. 15, nos. 1–2 (1965), 17–19. The "People to People" Program and city-to-city partnerships.

AH75 Flacke, Lieselotte. "Die deutsch-amerikanischen Städtepartnerschaften." *Der Auslandskurier*, vol. 3, no. 3 (1962), 4–5.

AH76 Institut für Auslandsbeziehungen, Stuttgart. "Drittes deutsch-amerikanisches Schwesterstadttreffen in Stuttgart." *Zeitschrift für Kulturaustausch*, vol. 13, no. 4 (1963), 325–26.

AH77 Kreutner, Robert. "Von Breisach am Rhein nach Frankreich und U S A." *Zeitschrift für Kulturaustausch*, vol. 15, nos. 1–2 (1965), 37–38. Citypartners Breisach–Locust Valley, N.Y., and Saint-Louis (Haut-Rhin), France.

AH78 Meyer, Ursula. "Goethe House. Headquarters for German American Partnership Program." *Rundschau—An Amer.-German Rev.*, vol. 5, no. 5 (May 1975), 11. On the Goethe House, Fifth Avenue, New York City.

AH79 *O.T.A.—Nachrichten*. (Formerly: *Neues von der Aktion für Gemeindeverschwisterung*). German ed. by the Institut für Auslandsbeziehungen, Stuttgart. Mimeogr. News of the sister cities program.

AH80 *Protokoll der Arbeitsbesprechung westdeutscher Schwestergemeinden amerikanischer Städte in Wesel am 8.9.1955*. Wesel: n.p., 1955. 35p. Mimeogr. Sister-city program.

AH81 Schnelle, Hans H. "538 Partnerschaften in 26 Ländern." *Zeitschrift für Kulturaustausch*, vol. 15, nos. 1–2 (1965), 72–80. List of city partnerships.

AH82 *Städte-Partnerschaften, Anregungen für die Ausgestaltung der Zusammenarbeit zwischen deutschen und amerikanischen Schwesterstädten*. Stuttgart: Institut für Auslandsbeziehungen, 1957. 16p.

AH83 "Zur Städtepartnerschaft Stuttgart-St. Louis." *Zeitschrift für Kulturaustausch*, vol. 15, no. 3 (1965), 174.

AI
Opinion and Views on America

German Visitors and Guests in America

AI1 Deurr, Erich. "Kanada mit den Augen eines jungen Dichters gesehen." *Der Nordwesten*, 11 October 1966. The comments of an exchange student.

AI2 Ehmcke, Heidi, and Burkhard von Hausen. "Bericht... aus Ohio Wesleyan University ...German Exchange Student on Scholarship Study..." and "Report of a German Exchange Student... at Bowling Green University." *Gazette*, vol. 8, no. 3 (1967), 17–18; *ibid*., vol. 8, no. 4 (1967), 9–10; *ibid*., vol. 8, no. 5 (1967), 14.

AI3 Faherty, W. B. "John Hagen. Eminent European Astronomer Sojourns in Wisconsin (1880–1888)." *Wis. Mag. of Hist.*, vol. 25, no. 2 (1941), 178–86.

AI4 Gundermann, Hans-Peter. "Erziehung in Harvard. Eindrücke eines deutschen Austauschstudenten." *Deutsche Universitätszeitung* (Göttingen), vol. 9, no. 13 (1954), 10–12.

AI5 Holthusen, Hans E. *Indiana Campus. Ein amerikanisches Tagebuch.* 2nd ed. N.p.: Piper Vlg, 1969. 78p. Impressions of a writer on an American college campus.

AI6 International Public Opinion Research Associates. *German Exchangees: A Study in Attitude Change.* Prepared for the Educational Exchange Service, International Information Administration, Dept. of State & Office of Public Affairs, Office of the U.S. High Commissioner of Germany. New York: n.p., 1953.

AI7 Rissler, Howard F. "The Sesquicentennial of Lincoln's Birth." *Annals of Iowa,* vol. 52 (1959), 291–306. Pictures and descriptions of Mayor Willy Brandt's visit and address, Springfield, Ill., 12 February 1959.

AI8 United States. Department of State. *Preparation for Tomorrow. A German Boy's Year in America.* Washington, D.C.: U.S. Govt-Printing Office, 1951. 54p.

AI9 Watson, Jeanne, and Ronald Lippitt. *Learning Across Cultures: A Study of Germans Visiting America.* Ann Arbor: Univ. of Michigan Institute for Social Research, 1955. 205p.

German Opinion on America and the Americans

AI10 Barraclough, Geoffrey. "Europa, Amerika und Russland in Vorstellung und Denken des 19. Jahrhunderts." *Historische Zeitschrift,* vol. 203 (1966), 280–315.

AI11 Baumgarten, Eduard. *Von der Kunst des Kompromisses. Eine Studie über den Unterschied zwischen Amerikanern und Deutschen.* Stuttgart: Hirzel, 1949. 35p.

AI12 Behrendt, Richard F. "Deutscher Geist and American Way of Life. Gemeinsames und Unterschiedliches." In: *Vorträge anlässlich der Hessischen Hochschulwochen für staatswissenschaftliche Fortbilding* (Bad Homburg v. d. Höhe), vol. 23 (1959), 206–26.

AI13 Billington, Ray Allen. *Land of Savagery, Land of Promise. The European Image of the American Frontier in the Nineteenth Century.* New York: W. W. Norton & Co., ca. 1980. 364p. Rev. in *N.Y. Times Book Review,* 25 January 1981. On the mythology of the American West as popularized in Europe.

AI14 Bock, Hellmut. "Anglo-American Common Sense and German Geist." *Amer. Quar.,* vol. 8 (1956), 155–65.

AI15 Brettauer, Alfred E. "Amerikanische Geschichte in der Sicht deutscher Historiker der zweiten Hälfte des neunzehnten Jahrhunderts." Diss., München, 1962. 195p.

AI16 Doll, Eugene E. "American History as Interpreted by German Historians from 1770–1817." *Transactions, Amer. Philosophical Soc.,* vol. 38, part 5 (1949), 421–534. Rev. by E. Kraehe, *Jour. of Southern Hist.,* vol. 15 (1949), 529–30; A. E. Zucker, *Amer.-German Rev.,* vol. 16, no. 2 (1949), 33; C. R. Lovell, *Miss. Valley Hist. Rev.,* 37 (1950), 696–97; M. Kraus, *Amer. Hist. Rev.,* vol. 55 (1950), 435–36; D. E. Emerson, *Pa. Mag. of Hist. and Biography,* vol. 74 (1950), 421–22; Oscar Handlin, *William and Mary Quar.,* vol. 7 (1950), 323–24. (Ph. D. diss., Univ. of Pennsylvania, 1947.)

AI17 Fraenkel, Ernst. *Amerika im Spiegel des deutschen politischen Denkens.* Köln: n.p., 1959. 333p. Based on interviews with eighty political scientists, poets, thinkers, and statesmen, from Christian Schubart to Theodor Heuss. Rev. C. V. Easum, *Amer. Hist. Rev.,* vol. 65 (1959), 158; B. Fabian, *Hist. Zeitschrift,* vol. 191 (1960), 410–11; E. Fraenkel, "Selbstanzeige," *Jahrbuch für Amerikastudien,* vol. 7 (1962), 348–49.

AI18 Fraenkel, Ernst. "Die U S A in deutscher Sicht: die politischen Parteien." In: *Hessische Hochschulwochen für staatswissenschaftliche Fortbildung* (Bad Homburg), vol. 43 (1964), 32–45.

AI19 Freund, Ludwig. *Zum Verständnis des amerikanischen Menschentypus: Schnittpunkte und Verschiedenartigkeiten der amerikanischen und deutschen Lebensgewohnheiten und politischen Grundsätze.* Würzburg: Holzner, 1964. 74p.

AI20 Frisch, Max. "Unsere Arroganz gegenüber Amerika." In: *Öffentlichkeit als Partner.* Frankfurt a.m.: Suhrkamp, 1967. 152p. The contribution of Frisch is dated 1952.

AI21 Heller, Peter. "Unterschiede in der Denkart amerikanischer und deutscher Intellektueller." *Neue deutsche Hefte*, vol. 5 (1958), 620-32.

AI22 Hermand, Jost. "Die falsche Alternative: Zum Verhältnis von E- und U-Kultur in der BRD und den USA." *Zeitschrift für Volkskunde*, vol. 76 (1980), 234-50.

AI23 Koht, Halvdan. *The American Spirit in Europe. A Survey of Transatlantic Influences*. New York: Octagon Books, 1970 [ca. 1949]. 289p.

AI24 Loch, Theo. "A German View: Estrangement between America and Europe." *Amer.-German Rev.*, vol. 34, no. 4 (1968), 14-18.

AI25 Lütkens, Charlotte, and Walther Karbe, eds. *Das Bild vom Ausland: Fremdsprachliche Lektüre an höheren Schulen in Deutschland, England und Frankreich*. München/Oldenbourg: n.p., 1959. 182p. Rev. by H. Kirchhoff, *German Quar.*, vol. 34 (1961), 208-09.

AI26 Sideman, B. B., and L. Friedman, eds. *Europe Looks at the Civil War*. New York: Orion, 1960. 323p. Views and reports by more than a hundred contemporary European observers.

AJ
Opinion and Views on Germany

American Visitors/Students in Germany

AJ1 Beam, Jacob N. "Charles Hodge's Student Years in Germany." *Princeton Univ. Library Chronicle*, vol. 8 (1947), 103-14.

AJ2 Beardsley, Edward H. "The Making of a Scientist: Harry L. Russell in Europe." *Wis. Mag. of Hist.*, vol. 49, no. 1 (1965), 3-15. On his studies in bacteriology in Berlin in the late 1890's.

AJ3 Bell, Whitefield J. "Philadelphia Medical Students in Europe, 1750-1800." *Pa. Mag. of Hist. and Biography*, vol. 67 (1943), 1-29. Williamson at Utrecht, Barton at Göttingen, Foulke at Leipzig; only those studying in Britain are treated in detail.

AJ4 Bonner, Thomas Neville. *American Doctors and German Universities. A Chapter in International Intellectual Relations, 1870-1914*. Lincoln: Univ. of Nebraska Pr. 210p. Rev. by Fred B. Rogers, *Amer.-German Rev.*, vol. 29, no. 6 (1963), 39; by D. Fleming, *Miss. Valley Hist. Rev.*, vol. 50, no. 3 (1963), 521-22.

AJ5 Brown, Cynthia Stokes. "American Discovery of the German University: Four Students at Göttingen, 1815-1822." Diss., The Johns Hopkins Univ., 1964.

AJ6 Buchloh, Paul G., and Walter T. Rix, eds. *American Colony of Göttingen. Historical and Other Data Collected between the Years 1855 and 1888*. Arbeiten aus der Niedersächsischen Staats- und Universitäts-Bibliothek Göttingen, vol. 15. Forew. and commentary by Paul G. Buchloh and Walter T. Rix. Göttingen: Vandenhoeck & Ruprecht, 1976. 169p. Constitutes a critical ed. of the MS. chronicle and record of American students in Göttingen, 1855-1888.

AJ7 Buerk, A., and Wilhelm Wille. *Die Matrikeln der Universität Tübingen*. Tübingen: n.p., 1953.

AJ8 Colwell, James L. "The American Expatriate Experience in Berlin during the Weimar Republic." Diss., Yale, 1961. On the Americans resident in Berlin.

AJ9 Crenshaw, Ollinger, and William W. Pusey, III. "An American Classical Scholar in Germany, 1874." *Amer.-German Rev.*, vol. 22, no. 6 (1955), 30-33. Milton Wylie Humphreys of Virginia was granted a Ph. D. degree at Leipzig when few other Americans had the degree. University life of the time described.

AJ10 Diehl, Carl. "Innocents Abroad: American Students in German Universities, 1810–1870." *Hist. of Educ. Quar.*, vol. 16 (Fall 1976), 321–41.

AJ11 Dulles, Foster Rhea. *Americans Abroad. Two Centuries of European Travel*. Ann Arbor: Univ. of Michigan Pr., 1964. 212p.

AJ12 Dulles, Foster Rhea. "A Historical View of Americans Abroad." *Annals of the Amer. Academy of Political and Social Science*, vol. 368 (November 1966), 11–20.

AJ13 Earnest, Ernest. *Expatriates and Patriots: American Artists, Scholars and Writers in Europe*. Durham; Duke Univ. Pr., 1968. 310p. Scholars, artists, and writers who sojourned in Europe: Irving, Cooper, Margaret Fuller, Hawthorne, Henry James to Harold Frederic, Edith Wharton and the expatriates of the '20s. Rev. by W. Thorp, *Amer. Lit.*, vol. 41, no. 2 (May 1969), 305–07.

AJ14 Ehmcke, Heidi. "*Bericht...aus Ohio Wesleyan University*... Report of a German Exchange Student..." *Gazette*, vol. 8, no. 3 (1967), 17–18; ibid., vol. 8 no. 4 (1967), 9–10.

AJ15 Fallon, Jean. "The Lamp of Learning... and the Stove. An American Co-ed in Tübingen." *Amer.-German Rev.*, vol. 30, no. 5 (1964), 12–14.

AJ16 "Frankfurt hat grösste US-Kolonie der Welt." *New Yorker Staats-Zeitung und Herold*, vol. 146, no. 16 (1980), Sec. B, 9.

AJ17 Gariss, Philip J. "An American Teacher in West Berlin." *Amer.-German Rev.*, vol. 20, no. 3 (1954), 11–13. Experience of an exchange teacher.

AJ18 Gordon, Nancy M. "A Fulbright Couple's Year in Munich." *Amer.-German Rev.*, vol. 33, no. 3 (1967), 36–37.

AJ19 Göttingen. Staats- und Universitätsbibliothek. MS. sources on the America colony in Göttingen. See Cod. MS. Hist. Lit. 108, (Dippel, p. 372.)

AJ20 Haenicke, Diether. "Zum Ausländerstudium in Deutschland." *German Quar.*, vol. 38, no. 4 (1965), 660–70. Statistical-historical survey and commentary on foreign students in Germany.

AJ21 Herbst, Jurgen. "American Students in German Universities." In: *The German Historical School in American Scholarship. A Study in the Transfer of Culture*. Ithaca: Cornell Univ. Pr., 1965, p.1–22.

AJ22 Johnson, Walter, and Francis J. Colligan. *The Fulbright Program: A History*. Forew. by Senator Fulbright. Chicago: Univ. of Chicago Pr., 1965. 380p. Rev. by H. R. Guggisberg, *Jahrbuch für Amerikastudien*, vol. 12 (1967), 283–85.

AJ23 Jordan, E. L. "American Students Meet German Students." *German Quar.*, vol. 23, no. 3 (1950), 168–72. Impressions of Rutgers Univ. students attending summer courses at German universities.

AJ24 Joynes, Edward Southey. *Old Letters of a Student in Germany, 1856–1857*. Columbia, S. C.: Univ. of South Carolina Pr., 1916. Later J. (1834–1917) served as professor of German language and literature at the University of South Carolina.

AJ25 Kahn, S.M., and Martha Raetz, eds. *Interculture: A Collection of Essays and Creative Writing Commemorating the Twentieth Anniversary of the Fulbright Program at the Institute of Translation and Interpretation, Univ. of Vienna (1955–1975)*. Wien: Braumüller, 1974. 298p.

AJ26 Knab, Carl. Notes, 1889–1891. 10 vols. In the New York Public Library (MS 71-1244). Notes by K. as a student of theology in Bonn, Berlin, and Halle. From lectures by his professors at the German universities; in German, Greek and Hebrew.

AJ27 Koegler, Horst. "Der Besuch der Alten Dame: Martha Graham gastierte in Deutschland." *Theater heute*, vol. 4, no. 1 (1963), 29–32.

AJ28 Krumpelmann, John T. "The American Students of Heidelberg University 1830–1870." *Jahrbuch für Amerikastudien*, vol. 14 (1969), 167–84. Tabulated lists of 322 foreign students.

AJ29 Krumpelmann, John T. "Maryland Scholars at German Universities 1824–1910." *The Report of the Soc. for the Hist. of the Germans in Md.*, vol. 34 (ca. 1970), 40–47.

AJ30 Krumpelmann, John T. *Southern Scholars in Goethe's Germany*. Studies in Germanic Langs. and Literatures, No. 51. Chapel Hill: Univ. of N. Car. Pr., 1965. 200p. Legaré, Harris, Calvert, Reynolds, Gildersleeve and others, in their contacts with German literary life. Rev. by C. Eaton,

Jour. of Southern Hist., vol. 32, no. 3 (August 1966), 389–90; A. E. Zucker, *German Quar.*, vol. 40, no. 2 (March 1966), 279–80.

AJ31 Krumpelmann, John T. "Young Southern Scholars in Goethe's Germany." *Jahrbuch für Amerikastudien*, vol. 4 (1959), 220–35.

AJ32 "Many Fulbright Lecturers will Teach American Subject Overseas in 1967–68." *Amer. Studies News*, vol. 6 (Autumn 1967), 1–2. Use of the seminar in the manner of the Salzburg program in teaching American studies abroad.

AJ33 Marquardt, Hertha. "Die ersten amerikanischen Studenten an der Universität Göttingen." *Göttinger Jahrbuch*, 1955/56. Supplement. 16p. Ticknor, Everett, Cogswell, Bancroft, Patton and others, at Göttingen before 1824.

AJ34 Merz, Ludwig. "Mir wird ein Schloß geschenkt." *Gazette*, vol. 9, no. 5 (1968), 6. Recollections of a visit to Heidelberg and castle.

AJ35 Miller, Alamby M. Papers, 1866–1871. 11 vols. In Univ. of Virginia Library (MS 62-3250). Diaries and student notebooks. The diary, written in German, records the experiences of M. (b. 1848) at Heidelberg as a student in 1868–1869. See also "Annual Report of the Archivist, University of Virginia Library, 1933–1934," p.5.

AJ36 Phelps, Reginald A. "The Idea of the Modern University—Göttingen and America." *Germanic Rev.*, vol. 29 (1954), 175–90. Göttingen as a favored place of study for the Americans Everett, Ticknor, Cogswell, Bancroft, Longfellow, and William Emerson.

AJ37 Pusey, William W. "Edward Southey Joyne's 'Old Letters' from Germany." In: *Studies in Nineteenth Century and Early Twentieth Century German Literature: Essays in Honor of Paul K. Whitaker*. Ed. N. H. Binger and A. Wayne Wonderley. Lexington: ApraPress, 1964, p.138–58. A former student in Germany who taught German language and literature in the United States.

AJ38 Rie, Robert. "Ein amerikanischer Professor in der Zone." *German Quar.*, vol. 39 (1966), 267–70.

AJ39 Rogers, L. H. "Medical Memories of Berlin and Vienna." *Amer.-German Rev.*, vol. 26 (October–November 1959), 12–14. A student of medicine in Vienna, 1908.

AJ40 Rossler, Herman. "Three Americans in Berlin." *Amer.-German Rev.*, vol. 25, no. 2 (1958), 26–27. Prof. C. E. Stangeland, the California-born writer H. G. Scheffauer, and Sinclair Lewis.

AJ41 Scholz, A. H. *Amerikaner in Berlin. Americans in Berlin*. Trans. from the German by Dieter Claus. Berlin-Grunewald: Arani, 1963.

AJ42 Smith, Alson J. *A View of the Spree*. New York: John Day, 1962. 305p. Rev. by N. Rich, *Amer. Hist. Rev.*, vol. 68, no. 1 (1962), 214. Biography of Mary Esther Lee, daughter of a New York grocer, who married Duke Frederick of Augustenburg and moved in high political circles in late 19th-century Germany.

AJ43 Smith, Shirley W. *James Burrill Angell, an American Influence*. Ann Arbor: Univ. of Michigan Pr., 1954. 380p. As American student in München.

AJ44 Stowe, Calvin E. [Letters from Germany (on which Stowe's *Report* was based).] Cincinnati *Journal*, in the late 1830's.

AJ45 *Studying in Germany*. Rev. ed. Frankfurt: Deutsche Zentrale für Fremdenverkehr, 1955. 44p.

AJ46 Thilly, Frank. Papers, 1889–1935. Ca. 3 ft. In the Cornell Univ. Library collection of Regional History and University Archives (MS 70-1132.) Notes and papers, incl. notes in German ca. 1889–1890 made by Thilly while studying at Berlin and Heidelberg, under Profs. Kuno Fischer, Friedrich Paulsen, and others. Became professor of philosophy at Cornell University.

AJ47 United States. Education Commission in the Federal Republic of Germany. *Fulbright Program. American Fulbright Grantee in Germany*. Bad Godesberg: n.p., 1955. 26p.

AJ48 United States Education Office. *American Students and Teachers Abroad: Sources of Information about Overseas Study, Teaching, Work and Travel*. N.p.: n.p., 1972.

AJ49 Weiker, Walter. "An American Works at Vulkan." *Amer.-German Rev.*, vol. 18, no. 2 (1951), 10–11, 35. An Antioch College student at Vulkan shipyards.

AJ50 Weisert, John J. "A Young American Visits von Humboldt." *Amer.-German Rev.*, vol. 28, no. 3 (1962), 27–28. Samuel A. Cassaday, amateur geologist of Louisville.

AJ51 *Zehn Jahre Fulbright-Program in Deutschland: Reden in der Rheinischen Friedrich-Wilhelms-Universität Bonn am 19. November 1962 bei der Fulbright-Gedenkfeier von Hans Welzel u.a.* Bonn: Hanstein, 1964. 39p.

AJ52 Zucker, A. E. "American Professors Visit Germany." *German Quar.*, vol. 28 (1955), 96–100. Nine professors visit schools, theaters, etc.

American Views of Germany and the Germans

AJ53 Alexis, Joseph Emanuel Alexander, and William Karl Pfeiler. *In der deutschen Republik.* 2nd ed. Lincoln, Neb.: Midwest Book Co., 1943. 321p.

AJ54 Baecker, Thomas. "Das deutsche Feindbild in der amerikanischen Marine 1900–1914." *Marine-Rundschau*, vol. 70 (February 1973).

AJ55 Bahe, Barbara. "Cultural Material in First Year College German Texts in the United States, 1915–59." Diss., Columbia Univ., 1960.

AJ56 Bailey, George. *Germans. The Biography of an Obsession.* New York: World Publ. Times Mirror, 1972. The Germans examined; their soul; their behavior. Germans seen "as they are."

AJ57 Becker, Howard. "Das Deutschlandbild in Amerika." *Politische Studien* (München), vol. 10 (1959), 737–47.

AJ58 Boorstin, Daniel J. *America and the Image of Europe.* New York: Meridian, 1961.

AJ59 Breitenstein, Rolf. *Der häßliche Deutsche? Wir im Spiegel der Welt.* München: Desch 1968. 165p. Rev. by M. R., *Zeitschrift für Kulturaustausch*, vol. 19, no. 1 (January–March 1969), 61.

AJ60 Burmeister, Irmgard. "Germans—The American View. 'These Krauts Ain't So Bad'." *Rundschau. An Amer.-German Rev.*, vol. 4, no. 8 (November 1974), 1–2.

AJ61 Eich, Hermann. *The Unloved Germans.* Trans. by Michael Glenny from the German *Die unheimlichen Deutschen.* New York: Stein & Day, 1965. Rev. by J. P. Bauke, *N.Y. Times Book Rev.*, 2 January 1966. The image of Germans in the world at large and a delineation of their character.

AJ62 Elson, Ruth Miller. "Deutschland und die Deutschen in amerikanischen Schulbüchern des 19. Jahrhunderts." *Internationales Jahrbuch für Geschichtsunterricht*, vol. 7 (1959–1960), 51–57.

AJ63 "Germans as Bad Guys on T.V." *Amer.-German Rev.*, vol. 34, no. 5 (1968), 35. Repr. of an editorial in the Poughkeepsie, N.Y. *Journal*.

AJ64 Haeseler, Charles H. *Across the Atlantic. Letters from France, Switzerland, Germany, Italy and England.* Philadelphia. T. B. Peterson, 1868. 397p. Originally publ. in the *Miner's Journal* (Pottsville, Pa.)

AJ65 Hauser, Heinrich. *The German Talks Back.* New York: Holt, 1945. 215p. Issued as "representative of a dominant state of mind" in the Germany of 1945.

AJ66 Knobel, Dale T. "'Hans' and the Historian: Ethnic Stereotypes and American Popular Culture, 1820–1860." In: *Papers from the St. Olaf Symposium on German-Americana.* Eds. L. J. Rippley and S. M. Benjamin. Morgantown: Dept. of Foreign Langs., West Virginia Univ., 1980, p.55–69.

AJ67 Krodel, Gerhard. "CBS TV and the Germans." *Amer.-German Rev.*, vol. 34, no. 5 (1968), 30–35.

AJ68 Kröger, Franz. "Das Deutschlandbild der Engländer und Amerikaner in der Vergangenheit." *Die neueren Sprachen*, vol. 69, N.F. 19, (1970), 91–102.

AJ69 Kuehnelt-Leddihn, Erik von. "America's Myths of Europe." *Southwest Rev.*, vol. 40, no. 2 (1955), 170–79.

AJ70 Lange, Victor. "Probleme der deutschen Kulturpolitik in den Vereinigten Staaten." *Der Auslandskurier*, vol. 9, no. 2 (1968), 20–23.

AJ71 Löwe, Rüdiger. "Besuch aus einem fernen Land. Notizen zum Deutschlandbild von Amerikanern." *Süddeutsche Zeitung. Süddeut. Zeitung am Wochenende.* 8/9 January 1977, Supplement, 73–74. A journalistic feature of one full page on the attitudes and reactions of American students to the German milieu.

AJ72 Marcus, Eric. "Deutsche Kultur in der Meinung Amerikas," *Deutsche Rundschau*, vol. 83 (1957), 142–49.

AJ73 Meyer, Henry Cord. *Five Images of Germany. Half a Century of American Views on German History*. Publ. no. 27, Service Center for Teachers of History. Washington, D.C., 1960. 56p. Rev. by C. V. Easum, *Monatshefte*, vol. 53, no. 1 (1961), 40–41.

AJ74 Mordecai, Alfred. "Observations of European Life. Ed. by James A. Padgett." *N. Car. Hist. Rev.*, vol. 24, no. 3 (1947), 367–402. Comments on life in Germany in the 1840's.

AJ75 Mühlen, Norbert. "Deutsche, wie sie im Buche stehen. Das amerikanische Deutschlandbild im Spiegel." *Der Monat*, vol. 15, no. 171 (1962), 38–45.

AJ76 Mürbe, Hans Joachim. "The American Image of Germany Set Forth in Nineteenth-Century Travel Books." Diss., Ohio State, 1964. 259p.

AJ77 Multhoff, Robert F. "Das amerikanische Bild der deutschen Geschichte." *Aussenpolitik*, vol. 10 (1959), 570–76.

AJ78 Nelson, John. "Das Bild des Deutschen im amerikanischen Fernsehen." In: *Die USA und Deutschland. Wechselseitige Spiegelungen in der Literatur der Gegenwart. Zum 200 jährigen Bestehen der Vereinigten Staaten von Amerika.* Ed. W. Paulsen. Achtes Amherster Kolloquium zur modernen deutschen Literatur. Bern/München: Francke, 1976, p. 174–86.

AJ79 Raschen, J.F.L. "Gleanings From a Travel Book." *Amer.-German Rev.*, vol. 12, no. 1 (October 1945), 15–18; no. 2 (December 1945), 11–13. From the notes of an American traveler in Europe.

AJ80 Russell, John. *A Tour of Germany in 1820–22 ... Review. Southern Rev.*, vol. 4 (1829), 86–112.

AJ81 Schelbert, Leo. "An American Glances at Switzerland: Horace Greeley's Swiss Journal 1851." *Swiss Amer. Hist. Soc. Newsletter*, 10 July 1974, 13–22.

AJ82 Scherer, George A. C. "The German National Mind and Character in Representative American Periodicals, 1933–1939." Diss., Univ. of Iowa, 1944.

AJ83 Schoenthal, Klaus F. "American Attitudes Toward Germany, 1918–1932." Diss., Ohio State, 1959.

AJ84 Seger, Gerhart H. *Come Along to Germany*. Minneapolis: T. S. Denison, 1966. A description of German life and civilization.

AJ85 Small, Melvin. "The American Image of Germany 1906–1914." Diss., Michigan, 1965. 518p.

AJ86 Strout, Cushing. *The American Image of the Old World*. New York: Harper and Row, 1963. 288p. Rev. by J. W. Ward, *Miss. Valley Hist Rev.*, vol. 50, no. 2 (1963), 293–94; R. H. Heindel, *Annals of the Amer. Academy of Soc. and Polit. Science*, vol. 352 (1964), 217–28. Narrative history of Europe's "image" in the 19th and 20th centuries.

AJ87 Tor, Regina. *Getting to Know Germany*. New York: Coward-McCann, 1954. 64p. Rev. by E. Rose, *Monatshefte*, vol. 46 (1954), 286–87. School textbook.

AJ88 Totten, Christine M. *Deutschland—Soll and Haben. Amerikas Deutschlandbild*. München: Rütten & Loening, 1964. 480p. Rev. by J. L. Colwell, *Amer.-German Rev.*, vol. 31 (1965), no. 4, 38.

AJ89 Wead, Eunice, ed. "Kasson Letters—Austria and Germany." *Annals of Iowa*, vol. 30 (1950), 260–68. Letters to and from an Iowan giving very personal observations on German and Austrian royalty.

AJ90 "Wie neun Amerikaner Deutschland sehen." *Die Zeit*, vol. 22 (1967), 18–21. Interviews with Robert Manning, editor of the *Atlantic*, and Daniel P. Moynihan, among others.

AJ91 "Willy Brandt und das Zeichen des Kain. Spiegel-Report über das Deutschland-Bild der Amerikaner." *Der Spiegel*, vol. 24, no. 15, (6 April 1970), 132–40. Journalistic survey of image and public-opinion poll reactions, newspaper editorial views, the man in the street, etc.

AJ92 Ziock, Hermann, comp. and introd. *Sind die Deutschen wirklich so? Meinungen aus Europa,*

American Views of Germany *(cont.)*
Asien, Afrika und Amerika. Schriftenreihe des Instituts für Auslandsbeziehungen, Reihe Deutsch-Ausländische Beziehungen, no. 7. Herrenalb/Schwarzw.: Erdmann, 1965. 363p. Rev. by S. Kahle, *Zeitschrift für Kulturaustausch*, vol. 16, no. 1 (1966), 70–71.

AK
German-American Commemorations/Festivals/Celebrations

Commemorations—General

AK1 "A Commemorative Postcard and Several New Stamps Honor German-American Contributions to American Culture." *Newsletter of the Soc. for German-Amer. Studies*, vol. 1, no. 2 (1979–1980), 9.

AK2 Fritsch, Ludwig A. "Ein Deutschamerikaner zur 200-Jahr-Feier der USA." *Deutschland in Geschichte und Gegenwart. Zeitschrift für historische Wahrheitsforschung* (Tübingen), vol. 25, no. 2 (1977), 5–8.

AK3 [German-American National Congress, Cleveland, Ohio.] *The American Bicentennial German Scroll.* 1976. 27012 Hilliard Rd., Cleveland 44145.

AK4 Harris, Chauncey D. "The Von Humboldt Commemoration and Associated Meetings in Germany." *Geographical Rev.*, vol. 49 (1959), 585–88. Report on celebrations and scholarly conferences in West and East Germany.

AK5 Kaiser, Leo Max. "Granite, Bronze, and Letters." *Zeitschrift für Kulturaustausch*, vol. 13, no. 1 (1963), 15–16. On the obelisk placed in St. Louis to commemorate Friedrich Hecker, 1881; with a reprinting of the verse tribute by Caspar Butz: "Zur Enthüllung des Hecker-Denkmals."

AK6 Liebenow, Peter K., ed. *25 Jahre Amerika-Gedenkbibliothek/Berliner Zentralbibliothek. Zum 25jährigen Bestehen der Amerika-Gedenkbibliothek.* München: K. G. Saur, 1979. 304p. 18p. of illus.

AK7 Lohr, Otto. "Deutschamerikanische Jubiläen." *Mitteilungen des Instituts für Auslandsbeziehungen*, vol. 10 (1960), 141–42. Remembering Jacob Leisler, Count Zinzendorf, Conrad Weiser, and C. F. Post.

AK8 Moser, Fritz. *Die Amerika-Gedenkbibliothek Berlin. Entstehung, Gestalt und Wirken einer öffentlichen Zentralbibliothek.* Ed. Carl Wehmer. Beiträge zum Buch- und Bibliothekswesen, vol. 13. Wiesbaden: Harrassowitz, 1964. 161p. See also his pamphlet: *Die Amerika-Gedenkbibliothek als Idee und Erfahrung.* Berlin: n.p., 1956. 12p.

AK9 Overvold, Lieselotte Z. "Wagner's American Centennial March: Genesis and Reception." *Monatshefte*, vol. 68 (1976), 179–87. *See also* the note in the *Monatshefte*, vol. 68, no. 4, 435. The recording of this march as played by the London Symphony under Marek Janowski is available on Angel record No. S36879.

AK10 Reichart, Walter A. "Two Continents Commemorate a Centenary. The Gerhart Hauptmann Celebrations Abroad." *Amer.-German Rev.*, vol. 29, no. 4 (1963), 9–11.

AK11 Salzman, Patricia. "*Heinrich Vonflie*—Texas Freighter." *Amer.-German Rev.*, vol. 11, no. 2 (1944), 35–36.

AK12 Schubert, Lieselotte von. "An American Gift to Berlin." *Amer.-German Rev.*, vol. 19, no. 4 (1953), 5–6. $1,200,000 for the American Memorial Library in Berlin.

AK13 Shoemaker, Floyd C. "Hermann: A Bit of the Old World in the Heart of the New." *Mo. Hist.*

Rev., vol. 51 (1957), 235–44. The highway historical marker for the city of Hermann was dedicated 19 May 1956.

AK14 Tolzmann, Don Heinrich. *America's German Heritage. Bicentennial Minutes.* Cleveland: German-Amer. National Congress, 1976. 3rd printing. 1979. 128p.

AK15 "United States Stamp Commemorating 300 years of German Immigration in the United States." *Newsletter, Soc. for German-Amer. Studies*, vol. 2, no. 2 (1980–1981), 8. Proposal for a stamp commemorative of German-American history from 1683 to 1983. *See also* the article in the *Wash. Jour.*, vol. 121, no. 26 (1980), 6: "Wird 300 Jahre deutsche Einwanderung mit US-Briefmarke 1983 geehrt?"

AK16 Weisert, John J. "The Hauptmann Centenary in America." *Amer.-German Rev.*, vol. 29, no. 4 (1963), 11–12.

AK17 Zucker, A. E. "The Centennial of the Forty-Eighters." *Amer.-German Rev.*, vol. 14, no. 2 (1947), 22–24. On plans for the commemoration of the Forty-Eighters with a comprehensive anniversary volume.

Goethe

AK18 Bergstraesser, Arnold, ed. *Goethe and the Modern Age: The International Convocation at Aspen, Colorado.* Chicago: Regnerg, 1950.

AK19 Browne, Richard J., and Harry Zohn. "The Goethe Year in American Public Libraries." *German Quar.*, vol. 23, no. 1 (1950), 1–8. On the number of Goethe volumes in twenty public libraries and their circulation during the Goethe year of 1949.

AK20 Funke, Erich. "The Goethe Year in USA." *German Quar.*, vol. 24, no. 1 (1951), 23–31.

AK21 *Goethe Bicentennial, San Francisco, 1749–1949. Souvenir Program.* German-American Societies of San Francisco, 1949. 64p. On publications and programs of Goethe celebrations.

AK22 *Goethe. UNESCO's Homage on the Occasion of the Two Hundredth Anniversary of His Birth.* New York: Columbia Univ. Pr., 1949. 179p.

AK23 *Goethe-Year. Das Goethejahr. An International Bilingual Publication.* Ed. W. Unger. 12 parts. N.p.: Maxton, 1952. 643p.

AK24 Gudde, E. K. "The Goethe Festival in San Francisco." *Amer.-German Rev.*, vol. 16, no. 3 (1950), 20–21.

AK25 Hammer, Carl J., ed. *Goethe after Two Centuries.* Baton Rouge, La.: State Univ. Pr., 1952. 118p. A cooperative volume of lectures and papers presented during the Goethe festivals in Louisiana 1949–1950.

AK26 Hartwig, Hellmut Arthur, ed. *Southern Illinois Goethe Celebration.* Carbondale: n.p., 1951. 55p.

AK27 Hauptmann, Gerhart. "Goethe as an Educator." Addr. delivered at the Goethe celebration, Baltimore, 1936. See his *Gesammeltes Werk*. Berlin: n.p., 1942, vol. 17, p.207–33.

AK28 Henel, Heinrich. "The Goethe Bicentennial Convocation at Aspen." *Monatshefte*, vol. 41, no. 6 (1949), 295–302.

AK29 Jordan, Gilbert J., ed. *Southwest Goethe Festival.* Dallas: Southern Methodist Univ. Pr., 1949. 128p. A collection of 9 papers.

AK30 King, Rolf, et al., eds. *Goethe on Human Creativeness and Other Goethe Essays.* Athens: Univ. of Georgia Pr., 1950. 252p.

AK31 Meesen, Hubert J., ed. *Goethe Bicentennial Studies by Members of the Faculty of Indiana University.* Bloomington: Indiana Univ. Pr., 1950. 325p. Rev. by A. M. Sauerlander, *Mod. Lang. Quar.*, vol. 13 (1952), 115–17.

AK32 Nägele, Rainer. "Die Goethefeiern von 1932 und 1949." In: *Deutsche Feiern*. Eds. Reinhold Grimm and Jost Hermand. Athenaion Literaturwissenschaft, no. 5. Wiesbaden: Athenaion, 1977, p.97–122.

AK33 Werbow, Stanley N. "Goethe Celebrations in Maryland, 1949." *Report of the Soc. for the*

Goethe *(cont.)*
History of the Germans in Md., vol. 27 (1950), 71–73.

Schiller

AK34 Broadbent, Thomas L. "The Schiller Centennial in Columbia: California Germans in a Gold-Rush Town." *Amer.-German Rev.*, vol. 29, no. 6 (1963), 7–13. Social and cultural activities in November 1859, in a small town of Tuolumne County, Cal.

AK35 Frey, John R., ed. *Schiller 1759/1959. Commemorative American Studies.* Ill. Studies in Language and Literature, no. 46. Urbana: Univ. of Illinois Pr., 1959. 213p. Incl. "American Schiller Bibliography," p.203–13. Rev. by J. T. Krumpelmann, *Mod. Lang. Quar.*, vol. 21 (1960), 188–89; F. Martini, *Jour. of Engl. and Germanic Philol.*, vol. 59 (1960), 793–800.

AK36 Groen, Henry J. "How New Orleans Celebrated the 100th Anniversary of Schiller's Birth." *American-German Rev.*, vol. 9, no. 1 (1942), 29–30.

AK37 Spuler, Richard C. "*Wilhelm Tell* as American Myth." *Yearbook of German-Amer. Studies*, vol. 17 (1982), 89–98.

Carl Schurz

AK38 "Carl Schurz Centennial Observances." *Amer.-German Rev.*, vol. 18 (1952), no. 4, 3–5. In New York and in Bremen, Germany.

AK39 Kissinger, Henry. *On the One-Hundred-Fiftieth Anniversary of Carl Schurz.* Address held 8 March 1979, in the Carl Schurz Auditorium of the Embassy of the Federal Republic of Germany, Washington, D.C. 2p.

AK40 Sauer, Georg. "Die 'Carl Schurz' Brücke vor der Verkehrsübergabe." *Amer.-German Rev.*, vol. 13, nos. 5–6 (1947), 12, 41. Account of a bridge rebuilt by American soldiers and named in honor of Carl Schurz.

Steuben

See also Festivals/Celebrations *under* Section AK: German-American Commemorations *and under* Steuben *in* Section IC: Revolutionary War Era.

AK41 Baroni, Werner. "Zur 8. Steubenparade das Verdienstkreuz." *Die Amerika-Woche*, 9 September 1973. In New York City.

AK42 "Die Parade des Deutschamerikanertums: Streiflichter von und Gedanken zu der Steuben-Parade 1980." *New Yorker Staats-Zeitung und Herold*, vol. 146, no. 40 (1980), Sec. B, 5–12.

AK43 "Die Steubenparade und was sie bedeutet." *New Yorker Staats-Zeitung und Herold*, vol. 146, no. 38 (1980), Sec. B, 1.

AK44 "Steubenparade 1973." *New Yorker Staats-Zeitung und Herold* 15–16 September 1973, 1–28. Information about the Germans of New York City. See also: "22 September: Steubenparade in New York." *Aufbau*, 14 September 1973.

AK45 "Steuben-Parade 1972." *New Yorker Staats-Zeitung und Herold*, Supplement, 16–17 September 1972. Parade of Saturday, 23 September 1972.

AK46 Wilk, Gerard. "The 200th Anniversary of von Steuben's Arrival in the United States." *Rundschau*, vol. 8, no. 1 (1978), 8–9. Steuben Day is celebrated annually in September in New York City. See also "A Traveling Exhibition Commemorates the Birth of Friedrich Wilhelm von Steuben." *Newsletter, Soc. for German-Amer. Studies*, vol. 2, no. 3 (1980–1981), 13.

Conrad Weiser

AK47 "Conrad Weiser Day—July Fourth, 1942." *Hist. Rev. of Berks Co.*, vol. 8 (1942–1943), 24–25. A celebration under the direction of Arthur D. Graeff.

AK48 Graeff, Arthur D. "Conrad Weiser Day, July 4, 1942." *Amer.-German Rev.*, vol. 8, no. 6 (1942), 36–37.

AK49 Graeff, Arthur D. "Weiser Family Celebration 1710–1960." *Amer.-German Rev.*, vol. 26, no. 6 (1960), 5, 38.

AK50 "S. S. Conrad Weiser." *Hist. Rev. of Berks Co.*, vol. 8 (1942–1943), 121. A liberty ship launched at the Bethlehem-Fairfield Shipyards.

Festivals/Celebrations

See also Museums/Restorations/Festivals/Tour Guides *under* Section BH: The Pennsylvania Germans.

AK51 "Deutsche Woche 1980." *New Yorker Staats-Zeitung und Herold*, vol. 146, no. 10 (1980), Sec. A, 2. Celebration of National Foreign Language Week.

AK52 Federation of American Citizens of German Descent, Inc. *20th German-American Day. Schuetzenpark, Newark, New Jersey, June 4, 1972.* N.p.: n.p., 1972.

AK53 *Fest-Programm für das Diamantene Schwaben Volksfest Old Heidelberg Park. Veranstaltet vom Milwaukee Schwaben Unterstützungs-Verein 1957. 1882–1957.* Milwaukee: n.p. 1957. 40p.

AK54 "German Heritage Week in New Yorker Schulen." *N. Yorker Staats-Zeitung und Herold*, vol. 146, no. 45 (1980), Sec. B, 5.

AK55 "Grossveranstaltung am 6. Oktober 1973 in der Eagle Halle." *Der Milwaukee Herold*, 18 October 1973. On Dora Grunewald.

AK56 Grunewald, Dora. "Vom Deutschen Tag und von der Deutschen Sprachschule (Milwaukee)." *Der Milwaukee Herold*, 23 August 1973.

AK57 "Historical Notes and Comments." *Mo. Hist. Rev.*, vol. 46, no. 3; vol. 47, no. 1 and no. 2, 296, 77, and 178, 1952. Description and notes on the annual *Maifest* in Hermann, Missouri.

AK58 Kötting, Egon. "Dortmunds Kulturwoche im Dienste deutsch-amerikanischer Verständigung." *Der Auslandskurier*, vol. 3, no. 3 (1962), 11–12.

AK59 "Plattdeutsche Feiern in Amerika." *Europa und die Niederdeutsche Welt*, vol. 19 (1955), 131–36. Celebrations held by Low-German groups in New York, New Jersey and Pennsylvania.

AK60 *Veritas-Justitia-Libertas: Festschrift zur 200-Jahrfeier der Columbia Universität.* Berlin: n.p., 1954. 347p. Rev. by F. M. Wassermann, *Books Abroad*, vol. 28 (1954), 464.

Exhibitions

AK61 Arndt, Karl J. R. "Bicentennial Exhibitions and Publications in Germany." *Pa. Folklife*, vol. 27, no. 2 (1977–1978), 42–48.

AK62 *Bayern und die USA. Ausstellung des Bayerischen Hauptstaatarchivs München aus Anlass der 200. Wiederkehr der Unabhängigkeitserklärung der Vereinigten Staaten von Amerika.* München: n.p., 1976.

AK63 Bonn. Städtische Kunstsammlungen. *Amerikanische Zeichnungen 1942–1961.* Bonn: Städtische Kunstsammlungen, 1962. 6p. Illus. In cooperation with the Museum of Modern Art, New York, and the International Council of the Museum... 28 August–30 September, 1962.

AK64 "Deutschamerikanische Kunstgegenstände gesucht." *New Yorker Staats Zeitung und Herold*, vol. 145, no. 43 (1979), Sec. A, 2. For a planned exhibition "Die Deutschen von New Jersey."

AK65 *The German Book 1948–1956. An Exhibition Arranged by the German Publishers. Catalogue*. Frankfurt a. M.: Börsenverein des Deutschen Buchhandels, 1957. 94p. Exhibited in Washington, Chicago, New York, and Boston, January–April 1957.

AK66 Giesbrecht, Werner. *Die Gründung der Vereinigten Staaten von Amerika 1774–1789: Ausstellung der Universität Würzburg aus Anlass der 200-Jahrfeier der amerikanischen Unabhängigkeit*. Würzburg: n.p., 1976. Exhibition Catalogue.

AK67 Gittler, Lewis F. "A Happening in Montreal. The German Pavilion at Expo 67." *Amer.-German Rev.*, vol. 33, no. 3 (1967), 20–24.

AK68 Gittler, Lewis F. "Vierhundertmal 'Schau' im Jahr. Ausstellungen als Vermittler kulturellen Austauschs zwischen U S A und Deutschland." *Zeitschrift für Kulturaustausch*, vol. 17 (1967), 203–07.

AK69 Hayes, Bartlett J., Jr. "American Art in Germany." *Amer.-German Rev.*, vol. 18, no. 2 (1951), 4–9. On the exhibits at the 1951 American Cultural Festival in Berlin.

AK70 *The Imperial Style: Fashions of the Hapsburg Era*. New York: The Metropolitan Museum of Art, 1980. 166p. With essays by Joseph Wechsberg, Ursula Kehlmann and others. On "Hapsburg Splendor at the Met." Exhibit of Costume Art: "Fashions of the Hapsburg Era: Austria-Hungary." December 3, 1979–August 1980.

AK71 *Johannes Kepler, 1571–1630. An Exhibit of Books, Manuscripts, and Related Materials*. Catalogue, Austin: University of Texas at Austin, 1972. 52p.

AK72 Mozart Manuscripts. Exhibit. Pierpont Morgan Library, New York, N.Y. Summer 1976. Rev. in *N.Y. Times*, 20 June 1976, Arts and Leisure Sec., p. 28.

AK73 Pierpont Morgan Library. *Children's Literature. Books and Manuscripts. An Exhibition, November 19, 1954 through February 8, 1955*. New York: n.p., 1954. 80p. Rev. in *Publs. of the Bibliographical Soc. of America*, vol. 49 (1955), 80–82. Incl. first American editions of well-known German children's stories.

AK74 Raabe, Paul, and Harold Jantz. *The New World in the Treasures of an Old European Library: Exhibition of the Duke August Library Wolfenbüttel*. Wolfenbüttel: n.p., 1976. In German and English.

AK75 Robertson, Elizabeth H. "Singing Wood—Moennig Violins." *Amer.-German Review*, vol. 21, no. 3 (1955), 18–19. Exhibit of a famous violin collection at the Old Customs House, Philadelphia.

AK76 Shelley, Philip Allison. *A Token of the Season, Being the Headlight on Books at Penn State*, vol. 14, no. 2. State College: The Pa. State Univ. Library, 1944. 35p. Guide to an exhibit of literary almanacs, gift books and annuals in the Penn. State library.

AK77 "A Traveling Exhibition Commemorates Birth of Friedrich Wilhelm von Steuben." *Newsletter of the Soc. for German-Amer. Studies*, vol. 2, no. 3 (1980–1981), 13.

AK78 Werner, Alfred. "Masters in Black and White." *Amer.-German Rev.*, vol. 22, no. 4 (1956), 14–17. On three exhibits of German graphic art in Washington and New York, 1955.

Symposia/Conferences/Lecture Programs

See also Appendix.

AK79 Ash, Adrienne. "The Great American Windfall, Illustrious Austrian Emigres to the U.S.A." Austrian Institute, New York City. 13 April 1976.

AK80 Symposium. German-American National Congress/Deutsch-Amerikanischer National Kongress (D.A.N.K.). 13 October 1973. "Symposium über deutsche Kultur in Amerika und Ohio." With papers by William I. Schreiber, John R. Sinnema, L. J. Rippley, and Robert E. Ward. Cleveland: Classic Printing, 1973. See: "Deutsch-amerikanisches Symposium für deutsche Kultur in Amerika." Herman Brause. *Deutscher Wochenspiegel*, 31 October 1973.

AK81 Indiana University, Bloomington. *West Germany and the United States. A Systems Comparison Analysis*. Second German Studies Conference, Indiana Univ., Bloomington. 12–17 April, 1977. Papers and discussions. Incl. sessions on German-American relations; "What History Means to Us: A Comparison of American and German Attitudes toward History;" and "The Image of Germany: Constancy and Change."

AK82 Max Kade German-American Document and Research Center, University of Kansas. "Symposium on German-American Literature and Culture." Papers publ. in: *Germanica Americana 1976. Symposium on German-American Literature and Culture*. Ed. Erich A. Albrecht and J. Anthony Burzle. Lawrence: Max Kade Document and Research Center, Univ. of Kansas, 1977. 129p. Lawrence, The University of Kansas. 8–9 October 1976. Sponsored by the Center, in cooperation with the Department of Germanic Languages and Literatures and the Division of Continuing Education.

AK83 Miami University, Oxford Ohio. "The German Heritage in the Opening of the West." Miami University. 7 and 8 May 1976. Addresses and papers by P. R. Shriver, Lothar Madeheim, W. I. Schreiber, J. R. Sinnema, L. J. Rippley, R. E. Ward and others.

AK84 Modern Language Association. Special Group Meeting: "The German-American Literary Heritage." Chicago. 29 December 1977. Papers by Lisa Kahn, Allen Viehmeyer, Jacob Erhardt, Gerhard Friesen, and Alexander Waldenrath.

AK85 Modern Language Association. "German-American Studies: Post-Bicentennial Prospects." Annual meeting of the Modern Language Association. 28 December 1978. Sponsored by Maria Wagner, Rutgers, and Patricia Herminghouse, Washington University.

AK86 Society for German-American Studies. [Annual Meetings and Symposia.] First meeting, 1977. See *Bull. Soc. for German-Amer. Studies*, vol. 12, no. 1 (1977).

AK87 Society for German-American Studies. [Annual Meetings and Symposia.] Second meeting, Baldwin-Wallace College, Berea, Ohio, 12–13 May 1978. Unpublished. Papers presented by Christopher Dolmetsch, Lawrence Hartzell, LaVern J. Rippley, Martha Wallach, Peter C. Merrill, Robert Ebert, Gerhard Friesen, Robert E. Ward, Wolfgang Natter, and Clifford Scott. Erich Albrecht and J. Anthony Burzle were honored for their contributions to the field of German-American studies.

AK88 Society for German-American Studies. [Annual Meetings and Symposia.] Third meeting. St. Olaf College, Northfield, Minn., 27–28 April 1979. Papers publ. in: *Papers from the St. Olaf Symposium on German-Americana*. Eds. L. J. Rippley and S. M. Benjamin. Occasional Papers of the Soc. for German-Amer. Studies, no. 10. Morgantown: Dept. of Foreign Langs., West Va. Univ., 1980. 169p. Papers read by Frederick C. Luebke, Kathleen N. Conzen, Paul Schach, Leo Schelbert, Gerhard Friesen, Maria Wagner and others.

AK89 Society for German-American Studies. [Annual Meetings and Symposia.] Fourth meeting, Univ. of Missouri, Columbia, 18–19 April 1980. Unpublished. Topics incl.: "The Immigrant Experience," "German Settlement in America," and "Life in Missouri."

AK90 Society for German-American Studies. *Papers from the Conference on German-Americana in the Eastern United States*. Ed. Steven M. Benjamin. Occasional Papers of the Society for German-American Studies, no. 8. Morgantown: Dept. of Foreign Lang., W. Va. Univ., 1980. 206p.

AK91 Society for German-American Studies. *Papers from the Conference on German-Americana in the Eastern United States. Millersville State College, Nov. 9–10, 1979*. Ed. Steven M. Benjamin. Occasional Papers of the Soc. for German-American Studies, no. 9. Morgantown: Dept. of Foreign Langs., W. Va. Univ., 1981. See "The Millersville Conference on German-Americana." S. M. Benjamin. *Newsletter of the Soc. for German-Amer. Studies*, vol. 1, no. 2 (1979), 3–5.

AL
The German Language in American Life

General

See also The German Language in Canada *under* Section BB: Canadian Germans/German Life and Culture in Canada; *and* Part D: Linguistics/Dialectology/Sociology of Language; *and* 1910–1920: The Era of World War I *under* Section IH: The Twentieth Century; *and* Part J: German-American Local History.

AL1 American Council of Learned Societies Devoted to Humanistic Studies. *Conference on Non-English Speech in the United States. 1942*. Washington, D.C., 1942. 89p. Also publ. as the *Bull. of the Amer. Council of Learned Societies*, no. 34 (March 1942). Papers read at a conference held at Ann Arbor, Mich., 2–3 August 1940.

AL2 Arndt, Karl J. R. "German as the Official Language of the United States of America." *Monatshefte*, vol. 68, no. 2 (1968), 129–50.

AL3 Beerbaum, Alfred. "German in Our American Elementary Schools." *German Quar.*, vol. 27 (1954), 150–158. On the experience of the dependents' schools in Germany.

AL4 Deeken, Hans W. *The Advancement of the Teaching of German in the United States*. Philadelphia: National Carl Schurz Assoc., 1968. 22p.

AL5 *Deutsch oder Englisch: Ein Gespräch zwischen zwei Nachbarn, Sebastian und Jacob, über die deutsche Sprache in Nordamerika*. Allentown: n.p., 1862.

AL6 Fahrenkrog-Clay, Gudrun. "Neuere Versuche der Sprachpflege in den deutschsprachigen Ländern mit historischem Rückblick." Diss., Univ. of Colorado, 1980–1981.

AL7 Ferren, H. M. "Die nationale Aufgabe des Deutsch-Amerikanischen Lehrerbundes." *Pädagogische Monatshefte*, vol. 2, no. 1 (1900–1901), 7–10.

AL8 Flexner, Stuart B. *I Hear America Talking*. New York: Van Nostrand Reinhold, 1976. See p.163–71, 267–69 on the use of the German language in America.

AL9 "Foster-Mother Tongue: A Symposium." *Books Abroad*, vol. 23, no. 2 (1949), 129–33; vol. 23, no. 2 (1949), 237–42.

AL10 Gaarder, A. Bruce. "Conserving our Linguistic Resources." *PMLA*, vol. 80 (1964), 19–23.

AL11 Galinsky, Hans. "E pluribus unum? Die Antwort der Sprache." *Jahrbuch für Amerikastudien*, vol. 17 (1972), 9–55.

AL12 "German in the Secondary School." *German Quar.*, vol. 33 (1960), 299–352.

AL13 Grunewald, Dora. "Von der Sprache." *Der Milwaukee Herold*, 13 September 1973.

AL14 Harris, William Torrey. *German Instruction in American Schools and the National Idiosyncrasies of the Anglo-Saxons and the Germans*. Chicago: n.p., 1890. 16p. From an address delivered before the National German-American Teachers Association, Cleveland, 16 July 1890.

AL15 Heald, David. "'Deutschlisch' or 'Engleutsch': Has German a Future?" *Mod. Lang.: Jour. of the Modern Lang. Assoc.* (London), vol. 59 (1978), 139–42.

AL16 Heath, Shirley B. "Our Language Heritage: A Historical Perspective." In: *The Language Connection: From the Classroom to the World*. Ed. June K. Phillips. Skokie, Ill.: National Textbook, 1977, p.23–51.

AL17 Heckmann-French, Hannelore, and Donna Diekman Bond. "German Total-Immersion Summer Schools in the U.S." *Die Unterrichtspraxis*, vol. 12, no. 1 (1979), 87–90.

AL18 Hofman, John E. "The Language Transition in Some Lutheran Denominations." In: *Readings* in the *Sociology of Language.* Ed. J. A. Fishman. The Hague: Mouton, 1968, p. 620–38. Repr. from J. A. Fishman et al. *Language Loyalty in the United States* (1966). Deals with Midwestern churches: the Missouri Synod, the Wisconsin Synod, and the Norwegian Lutherans.

AL19 Hofman, John E. "Mother Tongue Retentiveness in Ethnic Parishes." In: *Language Loyalty in the United States.* Joshua A. Fishman et al. The Hague: Mouton, 1966, p. 127–55.

AL20 Hofmann, Margret S. "Can the Mother Tongue be Retained for Children of German Immigrants?" *Amer.-German Rev.*, vol. 23, no. 6 (1957), 15–17. See also the reply by W. F. Leopold: "American Children Can Learn Their German Mother Tongue." *Amer.-German Rev.*, vol. 24, no. 2 (1957), 4–6; and remarks by Henriette Vent and Thomas O. Brandt, *ibid.*, 39–40.

AL21 Holl, Oskar. *Fremdsprache: Deutsch; Deutschunterricht, Germanistik und deutsches Image in den U. S. A.: Ein Erfahrungsbericht.* Pullach bei München: Verlag Dokumentation, 1974. Rev. by D. H. Tolzmann, *German-Amer. Studies*, vol. 9 (Spring 1975), 61–63. If German descent is a major factor in causing young Americans to study German, then increased attention to German-Americana is indispensable. Work with and within the ethnic community is needed.

AL22 Huebener, Theodore. "The First German Grammar and Reader for American Schools." *German Quar.*, vol. 22, no. 2 (1949), 95–101. On Charles Follen's grammar.

AL23 Huebener, Theodore. "Private German Language Schools." *German Quar.*, vol. 23, no. 4 (1950), 221–22. New York schools prior to World War I as sponsored by the Turnvereine and Arbeitervereine.

AL24 Jackson, Gregory L. "Bi-Lingual German Churches in the Lutheran Church in America." *German-Amer. Studies*, vol. 9 (Spring 1975), 11–15.

AL25 Jacquith, James R. "Multilingualism Among the Old Colony Mennonites." *Mennonite Life*, vol. 24, no. iii (July, 1969), 137–42.

AL26 Kaulfers, Walter Vincent et al., eds. *Foreign Languages and Cultures in American Education.* New York: McGraw Hill, 1942. 417p. Reports on experimental programs at the Stanford Language Arts Investigation, 1937–1940.

AL27 Kloss, Heinz. *The American Bilingual Tradition in Education and Administration.* Rowley, Mass.: Newbury House, 1976. 347p.; Rowley, Mass., 1977. Rev. by LaVern J. Rippley, *Die Unterrichtspraxis*, vol. 10, no. 2 (1977), 179–81. A compilation of materials gathered from earlier publications by the same author.

AL28 Kloss, Heinz. "Die deutschamerikanische Schule." *Jahrbuch für Amerikastudien*, vol. 7 (1962), 141–75. A comprehensive survey.

AL29 Kloss, Heinz. "Die deutsche Sprache in der U S Volksschule." In *Staats-Herold Almanach 1958*, 66 Jahrgang. New York: Staats-Herold Corp., 1957, p. 88–102.

AL30 Kloss, Heinz. "Deutscher Sprachunterricht im Grundschulalter in den Vereinigten Staaten." *Der Auslandskurier*, vol. 8, no. 4 (1967), 22–24.

AL31 Kloss, Heinz. *FLES* [Foreign Languages in Elementary Schools]; *zum Problem der Fremdsprachenunterrichts an Grundschulen Amerikas und Europas.* Bad Godesberg: Verlag Wissenschaftliches Archiv, 1967. Rev. by K. Brobst, *Der Auslandskurier*, vol. 9, no. 6 (1968), 5; C. R. Beam, *German Quar.*, vol. 42, no. 3 (May 1969), 478–79.

AL32 Kloss, Heinz. "German as an Immigrant, Indigenous, Foreign, and Second Language in the United States." In: *The German Language in America. Papers Presented at the Germanic Languages Symposium November 1968, Austin, Texas.* Ed. G. G. Gilbert. Austin: Univ. of Texas Pr., 1971, p. 106–27.

AL33 Kloss, Heinz. "German Pedagogy and the Survival of German in America: Discussion." In: *The German Language in America. A Symposium.* Ed. G. G. Gilbert. Austin: Univ. of Texas Pr., 1971, p. 164–78.

AL34 Kloss, Heinz. "German-American Language Maintenance Efforts." In: *Language Loyalty in the United States.* Joshua A. Fishman et al. The Hague: Mouton, 1966, p. 206–52.

AL35 Kloss, Heinz. "Vom Lohr-Archiv und anderen Dokumenten zur Geschichte der deutschen Sprache in Übersee." *German-Amer. Studies*, vol. 9 (Spring 1975), 75–79. On the Institut für Deutsche Sprache, Mannheim.

AL36 Kluwin, Mary B. "Coping with Language and Cultural Diversity: A Study of Changing Lan-

General *(cont.)*
guage Instruction Policy from 1860 to 1930 in Three American Cities." Diss., Stanford Univ., 1977.

AL37 Kreider, Harry J. "The English Language Schism in the Lutheran Church in New York, 1794–1810." *Lutheran Church Quar.*, vol. 21, no. 1 (1948), 50–60. The struggle to achieve predominance of the English over the German language.

AL38 Krumpelmann, John T. *Mark Twain and the German Language*. Baton Rouge: Louisiana State Univ. Pr., 1953. 21p. Rev. by W. A. Willibrand, *Books Abroad*, vol. 28 (1954), 350; *Monatshefte*, vol. 46 (1954), 155; H. Heuer, *Archiv für das Studium der neueren Sprachen*, vol. 192 (1956), 71–72.

AL39 Leamon, Philip et al. "Indiana in Krefeld." *Amer.-German Rev.*, vol. 32, no. 6 (1966), 23–24. An honors programs in foreign languages for high school students; conducted in Krefeld by Indiana University.

AL40 Maurer, Karl Werner. "Lob der deutschen Sprache." *Zeitschrift für Kulturaustausch*, vol. 12 (1962), 330.

AL41 Migus, Paul M., ed. *Sounds Canadian: Languages and Cultures in a Multi-Ethnic Society*. Toronto: Peter Martin, 1975. 255p.

AL42 Nelson, Vernon H. "German Script Course, 1974." *Pa. Folklife*, vol. 24, no. 3 (1975), 15–16. A course offered as a summer seminar by the Moravian Archives, Bethlehem, Pa.

AL43 Pentlin, Susan Lee. "Effect of the Third Reich on the Teaching of German in the United States: A Historical Study." Diss., Kansas, 1977. 409p.

AL44 Rudnyćkyj, J. B. "Immigrant Languages, Language Contact, and Bilingualism in Canada." In: *Current Trends in Linguistics*. Vol. 10: *Linguistics in North America*. Ed. Thomas A. Sebeok. The Hague: Mouton, 1973, p.592–652.

AL45 Scheidt, David Lee. "Linguistic Transition in the Muhlenberg Tradition of American Lutheranism." S.T.D. Diss., Temple Univ., 1963.

AL46 Schober, Hans. "Fortschritt der deutschen Sprache in den Vereinigten Staaten." *Deutschunterricht für Ausländer* (München), vol. 9 (1959), nos. 5–6, p.178–79.

AL47 Scholz, Albert. "Why German in the Grades?" *Mod. Lang. Jour.*, vol. 38 (1954), 241–43.

AL48 Schurz, Carl. "Die deutsche Sprache in Amerika." Repr. in *German-Canad. Yearbook*, vol. 1 (1973), 87–89.

AL49 Seiler, Christiane. "Warum denn nicht eine Fremdsprache schon in der Volksschule?" *New Yorker Staats-Zeitung und Herold*, 19–20 March 1977, Sec. 1, 6.

AL50 Sell, Rainer. "The German Language—Mirror of the German-American Struggle for Identity as Reflected in *Der Deutsche Pionier* (1869–1887) and the Activities of der Deutsche Pionier-Verein von Cincinnati." *Jour. of German-Amer. Studies*, vol. 11, nos. 3–4 (Winter 1976), 71–81.

AL51 Spaeth, Adolf. "Der deutsche Pädagog in Amerika." *Pädagogische Monatshefte*, vol. 1, no. 8 (1900), 17.

AL52 "Sprach Jefferson deutsch?" *Die Zeit*, 23 March 1971. Newspaper article by "Kj" inquiring into the truth of the claim that America in 1796 came within one vote in Congress of adopting German as the official language of the nation. The reply by Prof. Heinz Kloss (*Die Zeit*, 20 April 1971) explains the origin of this legend. Germans in Virginia urged two committees of the Congress to authorize the publishing of Federal laws and enactments in German as well as in English. On 13 January 1795 this bill was rejected by the Congress by a vote of 42 to 41.

AL53 Spuler, Linus. [Remarks on the Study of the German Language in the United States.] *Sprachspiegel. Mitteilungen des Deutschschweizerischen Sprachvereins*, vol. 12, no. 4 (ca. 1956), 70–71.

AL54 Stephan, Hugo. "Warum lernen unsere Kinder Deutsch?" *Der Nordwesten* (Winnipeg), 30 August 1966.

AL55 Strasheim, Lorraine A. "We're *All* Ethnics: Hyphenated Americans, Professional Ethnics, and Ethnics by Attraction." In: *The Cultural Revolution in Foreign Language Teaching*. Skokie, Ill.: National Textbook Co., 1975, p.1–18.

AL56 Tessier, Christine. "Die erste deutsche Sommerschule in Kanada." *Die Unterrichtspraxis*, vol. 12, no. 1 (1979), 91–92.

AL57 Thierfelder, Franz. *Die deutsche Sprache im Ausland*. Hamburg: R. v. Decker Vlg., 1956–1957. 2 vols. 196, 402p. On the German language in the United States and Canada, cf. vol. 2, p.345–402. Rev. by Werner Neuse, *German Quar.*, vol. 31 (1958), 250–51; T. O. Brandt, *Amer.-German Rev.*, vol. 24, no. 3 (1958), 37; A. Closs, *Mod. Lang. Quar.*, vol. 20 (1959), 107–09.

AL58 Toepper, Robert M. "Rationale for Preservation of the German Language in the Missouri Synod of the Nineteenth Century." *Concordia Hist. Inst. Quar.*, vol. 41 (November 1968), 156–67.

AL59 Tolzmann, Don H. "Deutsch in den Kirchen." *Die Amerika-Woche*, 9 September 1973.

AL60 Tolzmann, Don H. "Deutsche Gottesdienste in Nordamerika." *Der Lutheraner*, March–April 1973, 15–16.

AL61 Tolzmann, Don H. "German Language Services in the Thirty-Fourth Season." *Lutheran Standard*, 1 May 1973.

AL62 Van Dusen, Jack. "Canadians Learn German the Right Way." *Canad. Geographical Jour.*, vol. 69, no. 2 (1964), 57–59.

AL63 Werner, William L. "The 'Official German Language' Legend." *Amer. Speech*, vol. 17 (1942), 246.

AL64 Wiebe, H. "Der deutsche Sprachunterricht unter den Mennoniten Kanadas." *Der Auslandskurier*, vol. 8, no. 3 (1967), 21–22.

AL65 Wood, Ralph Charles. "Zur Problematik der deutschen Volkssprache in Nordamerika." In: *Weltweite Wissenschaft vom Volke; Festgabe für J. W. Mannhardt*. Wien: R. M. Rohrer, 1958, p.185–89.

AL66 Zeydel, Edwin H. "The ASTP Courses in Area and Language Study." *Mod. Lang. Jour.*, vol. 27 (1943), 459; vol. 28 (1944), 383–84.

AL67 Zeydel, Edwin H. *Foreign Languages in School and Life*. Washington, D. C.: The National Educ. Assoc., 1940. 16p. Rev. by J. B. Tharp, *Mod. Lang. Jour.*, vol. 25, no. 6 (1941), 503.

AL68 Zeydel, Edwin H. "The Modern Language Teachers of America and Inter-Cultural Cooperation." *Mod. Lang. Jour.*, vol. 25 (1941), 755–56.

AL69 Zeydel, Edwin H. "A Platform for the Modern Foreign Languages." *School and Soc.*, vol. 51, no. 1329 (15 June 1940), 748–49.

In the Cities and Regions

AL70 Albrecht, Erich A. "Deutsche Sprache, Deutsche Literatur und Deutschunterricht in New Orleans, La." *German-Amer. Studies*, vol. 3, no. 1 (1971), 18–21.

AL71 Albrecht, Erich A. "Deutsche Sprache in Kansas." In: *Deutsch als Muttersprache in den Vereinigten Staaten, Teil 1: Der Mittelwesten*. Ed. L. Auburger et al. Wiesbaden: Steiner, 1979, p.161–70.

AL72 Baroni, Werner. "Deutsche Sprache in Chicago." In *Deutsch als Muttersprache in den Vereinigten Staaten, Teil 1: Der Mittelwesten*. Ed. L. Auburger et al. Wiesbaden: Steiner, 1979, p.35–39.

AL73 Becker, Ernest J. "History of the English-German Schools in Baltimore." *Report of the Soc. for the Hist. of the Germans in Md.*, vol. 25 (1942), 13–17. For the period 1873 to 1904.

AL74 Becker, Ernest J. *Western High School [Baltimore], Past and Present, 1844–1944*. Baltimore: n.p., 1944.

AL75 Domroese, Fred C. "The Indiana Teachers of German." *Amer.-German Rev.*, vol. 8, no. 5 (1942), 25–26.

AL76 Ellert, Ernst F. "The Foreign Language Program in the Holland [Mich.] Public Schools." *Mod. Lang. Jour.*, vol. 38 (1954), 416–19. Teaching of German in the fourth grade.

AL77 Ellert, Ernst F. "The Grade School German Program in Holland, Michigan." *Monatshefte*, vol. 46 (1954), 51–52.

AL78 Ellis, Frances H. "Aufschwung und Ende des Deutschunterrichts in den öffentlichen Schulen von Indianapolis." *Bildung und Erziehung*, vol. 10 (1957), 291–307.

AL79 Ellis, Frances H. "Historical Account of German Instruction in the Public Schools of Indianapolis: 1869–1919." *Ind. Mag. of Hist.*, vol. 50 (1954), 119–38, 251–76, 357–80.

AL80 "The German-English Bilingual Program in Cincinnati." *Newsletter of the Soc. for German-Amer. Studies*, vol. 1, no. 3 (1979–1980), 12.

AL81 Gohla, Kurt B. "Die Schultätigkeit des Deutsch-Amerikanischen Schulvereins von New York." *Zeitschrift für Kulturaustausch*, vol. 14, no. 2 (1964), 79–83.

AL82 Harris, William Torrey. *Reasons for the Retention of German-English Instruction in the St. Louis Public Schools*. St. Louis: n.p., 1877. 15p. In: *23rd Annual Report for the Year Ending August 1, 1877*. St. Louis Board of Education, p. 164–77.

AL83 Huebener, Theodore. "The German School of the New York Turn-Verein." *Amer.-German Rev.*, vol. 16, no. 6 (1950), 14–15.

AL84 Kreye, George W. "German Instruction in Kansas." *Amer.-German Rev.*, vol. 27 (April–May 1961), 9–11.

AL85 Lehman, Winfred. "Lone Star German." *Rice Univ. Studies*, vol. 63, no. 3 (1977), 73–81. On the language of German writers Hoffmann v. Fallersleben, P. Hörmann, and F. Goldbeck.

AL86 Liedtke, Kurt E. H. "Introducing German in a San Francisco Elementary School." *Gazette*, vol. 9, no. 6 (1968), 10–11. From an article originally appearing in *Die Unterrichtspraxis*.

AL87 McClain, William H. "The Julius K. Hofmann Memorial Fund in Baltimore." *Amer.-German Rev.*, vol. 26, no. 1 (1959), 7–9. A fund set up to encourage the study of German in Maryland schools.

AL88 Martens, Hedda. "Language Attitudes of German Immigrants and Their Families Observed in Rochester, New York." Diss., Rochester, 1973.

AL89 Martin, Horst. "Der fremdsprachliche Unterricht: Ein Überblick." In: *Deutsch als Muttersprache in Kanada: Berichte zur Gegenwartslage*. Ed. L. Auburger et al. Wiesbaden: Steiner, 1977, p. 99–102.

AL90 Moore, J. Michael. "Deutschunterricht in San Diego?—Why of Course! Nach ganz modernen Methoden." *Zeitschrift für Kulturaustausch*, vol. 16 (1966), 247–59.

AL91 Münnich, U. A. "Der Deutschunterricht in Fort Wayne, Indiana, U S A." *Muttersprache*, vol. 79 (1969), 20–25.

AL92 Odwarka, Karl. "German in the Iowa Schools." *Die Unterrichtspraxis*, vol. 10, no. 1 (Spring 1977), 85–90. Statistics of enrollments in the high schools.

AL93 Reimer, Gerhard. "Deutsche als Muttersprache unter den Mennoniten in Indiana." In: *Deutsch als Muttersprache in den Vereinigten Staaten. Teil 1: Der Mittelwesten*. Ed. L. Auburger et al. Wiesbaden: Steiner, 1979, p. 17–22.

AL94 Reimer, Gerhard. "Deutsche Sprache unter den Amischen des Mittelwesten." In: *Deutsch als Muttersprache in den Vereinigten Staaten. Teil 1: Der Mittelwesten*. Ed. L. Auburger et al. Wiesbaden: Steiner, 1979, p. 191–98.

AL95 Richter, Anton. "Gebt ihr den Vorzug: The German-Language Press of North and South Dakota." *S. Dak. Hist.*, vol. 10 (1980), 189–209.

AL96 Rodgers, Jack W. "The Foreign Language Issue in Nebraska, 1918–1923." *Nebr. Hist.*, vol. 39 (1958), 1–22. An organized anti-German movement to repress use of the language at a time when of 1,296,372 Nebraskans 149,652 were foreign-born, and of those 27.4 per cent were born in Germany.

AL97 Rohrbach, Heinrich. "Lawrence's German School." *Amer.-German Rev.*, vol. 24, no. 4 (1958), 26–27. In Lawrence, Mass.

AL98 Scheer, Herfried W. "Der Fremdsprachliche Unterricht: Quebec." In: *Deutsch als Muttersprache in Kanada: Berichte zur Gegenwartslage*. Ed. L. Auburger et al. Wiesbaden: Steiner, 1977, p. 103–06.

AL99 Tolzmann, Don H. "Deutschsprachige Gottesdienste in Minnesota." *Der Milwaukee Herold*, 5 July 1973.

AL100 Vardeman, Hazel Clare. "German in Our Schools." *Amer.-German Rev.*, vol. 20, no. 1 (1953), 19, 28. Work of the Chicago Chapter, Amer. Assoc. of Teachers of German.

AL101 Veidt, Frederick P. "Cincinnati's German English Bilingual Alternate School: An Update." *Die Unterrichtspraxis*, vol. 14, no. 1 (1981), 98–104.

AL102 Veidt, Frederick P. "German-English Bilingual Education: The Cincinnati Innovation." *Die Unterrichtspraxis*, vol. 9, no. 2 (1976), 45–50.

AL103 Voigt, Frieda. "The National Teacher's Seminary (1878–1919)." *Hist. Messenger of the Milwaukee Co. Hist. Soc.*, vol. 25, no. 4 (December 1969), 137–39.

AL104 Voigt, Frieda Meyer et al. *The Engelmann Heritage*. Milwaukee: Milwaukee Alumni Assoc. of the National Teachers' Seminary, 1951. 105p. Rev. by R. D. Owen, *Amer.-German Rev.*, vol. 18, no. 2 (1951), 37; W. F. Leopold, *Mod. Lang. Jour.*, vol. 36 (1952), no. 3, 153. Sketch of the Deutschamerikanisches Lehrerseminar and associated institutions founded by Peter Engelmann in Milwaukee.

AL105 Weiss, James. "The Problem of Language Transition Among Lutherans in Ohio, 1836–1858." *Concordia Hist. Institute Quar.*, vol. 39 (1966), 5–19. On the discussions regarding the use of German and English in worship services and seminaries.

AL106 Willibrand, W. A. "When German Was King." *German Quar.*, vol. 30 (1957), 254–61. German in the elementary schools of Westphalia, Missouri, 1864–1887.

AL107 Wilson, Joseph. "The German Language in Central Texas Today." In *Texas and Germany: Crosscurrents*. Ed. Joseph B. Wilson. Houston: Rice Univ. Pr., 1977, p.47–58.

AL108 Wilson, Joseph. "The German Language in Texas." *Schatzkammer*, vol. 2, no. 1 (1976), 43–49.

AL109 Zeydel, Edwin H. "New Light on the Early Teaching of German in Cincinnati." *Bull. of the Cincinnati Hist. Soc.*, vol. 22, no. 4 (1964), 257–58. Instruction at the school of the German Lutheran Reformed Church from 1824 on.

AL110 Zeydel, Edwin H. "The Teaching of German in Cincinnati: An Historical Survey." *Bull., Hist. 2nd Philosophical Soc. of Ohio*, vol. 20 (1962), 22–37.

AL111 Zimmermann, Gustav A. "Manual of Instruction in German for the Chicago Public Schools." Chicago: n.p., 1886. 20p.

AM
German Language Instruction

Enrollments and Curricula

AM1 Breunig, Marjorie. "Foreign Languages in the Elementary Schools of the United States, 1959–60." *Mod. Lang. Assoc. Report*, 1961, p.1–14.

AM2 Brod, Richard I. "German Studies in United States Colleges: Status and Outlook." *Die Unterrichtspraxis*, vol. 7, no. 2 (1974), 1–6.

AM3 Childers, J. Wesley. "Foreign Language Offerings and Enrollments in Public Secondary Schools, Fall 1959." *Mod. Lang. Assoc. Report*, 1961, p.15–34. For statistics for 1960 see "Fall 1960." *PMLA*, vol. 77, no. 4, Part 2 (1962), 11–30.

AM4 Childers, J. Wesley, and Barbara Bates Bell. "Modern Foreign Language Teaching in Junior Colleges, Fall 1960." *Mod. Lang. Assoc. Report 1961*, p.43–48.

AM5 Eshelman, James N. "Secondary School Foreign-Language Enrollments and Offerings,

Enrollments and Curricula (cont.)

1958–62." *PMLA*, vol. 79, no. 4, Part 2 (1964), 107–12.

AM6 Harmon, John. "Foreign Languages in Independent Secondary Schools, Fall, 1959." *Mod. Lang. Assoc. Report* 1961, p. 35–42.

AM7 Lich, Glen E. "Ethnic History: A Tool for Teaching Languages and Methods of Research." *Jour. of German-Amer. Studies*, vol. 14 (1979), 36–45.

AM8 Lohnes, Walter F. W. "The Training of German Teachers in the United States." *Die Unterrichtspraxis*, vol. 2, no. 2 (Fall 1969), 69–76.

AM9 Modern Language Association of America. *Reports of Surveys and Studies in the Teaching of Modern Foreign Languages*. New York: Mod. Lang. Assoc., 1961. 326p.

AM10 Mustard, Helen M. "A Survey of Language Schools Not under Academic Auspices." *Mod. Lang. Assoc. Report*. New York, n.p., 1961, p. 187–96.

AM11 Parker, William R. "German in American Schools Today." *Amer.-German Rev.*, vol. 22, no. 2 (1955), 11–14, 37.

AM12 Reid, J. Richard. "An Exploratory Survey of Foreign Language Teaching by Television in the United States." *Mod. Lang. Assoc. Report for 1961*, p. 197–212.

AM13 Vamos, Mara, John Harmon, Frank White, and Hannelore Fischer-Lorenz. [Modern Foreign Language Enrollments in the United States.] See *Mod. Lang. Assoc. Report*, 1961. Contents: "Language Learning in American Colleges and Universities: Data on Degrees, Majors and Teaching Practices," p. 127–34; "Modern Foreign Language Enrollments in Four-Year Accredited Colleges and Universities, Fall 1958 and Fall 1959," p. 49–90; "Modern Foreign Language Enrollments in Four-Year Colleges and Universities, Fall, 1960," p. 91–126; "Modern Foreign Language Faculties in Colleges and Universities," p. 135–52.

AM14 White, Margaret et al. "Report on the Status of and Practices in the Teaching of Foreign Languages in the Elementary Schools of the United States." *Mod. Lang. Jour.*, vol. 37 (1953), 123–27.

AM15 Zeydel, Edwin H. "The Teaching of German in 1948." *Mod. Lang. Jour.*, vol. 32 (1948), 145–49.

AM16 Zeydel, Edwin H. "The Teaching of German in the United States from Colonial Times to the Present." *German Quar.*, vol. 37 (1964), 315–92. Also in *Reports of Surveys and Studies in the Teaching of Modern Foreign Languages*. New York: Mod. Lang. Assoc., 1961, p. 285–308.

AM17 Zeydel, Edwin H. et al. *Language Study in American Education: The Report of a Special Committee*. Prepared for the Modern Language Assoc. of America. New York: Commission on Trends in Education, 1940.

Readers and Texts on Subjects of German American Interest

AM18 Alexander, Lloyd. *Border Hawk: August Bondi*. New York: n.p., 1958. Children's reader based on the life of August Bondi, Kansas Forty-Eighter and supporter of John Brown.

AM19 Apsler, Alfred. *Northwest Pioneer: The Story of Louis Fleischer*. New York: Farrar, Straus & Cudahy, 1960. 180p. Biography for juvenile readers.

AM20 Apsler, Alfred. *Sie kamen aus deutschen Landen*. New York: Irvington Publs., Inc., ca. 1960. Prose sketches about contributions of German immigrants to American life. A college text.

AM21 Arndt, Karl J. R. *Early German-American Narratives*. Selected and edited by K. J. R. Arndt. New York: American Book Co., 1941. 358p. A college reader with texts from Sealsfield and Gerstäcker.

AM22 Cunz, Dieter. *They Came from Germany. The Stories of Famous German Americans*. New York: Dodd, Mead Co., 1966. 176p. Biographies of well known German-American figures collected in a textbook reader.

AM23 Gay, Kathlyn. *The Germans Helped Build America*. New York: J. Messner, 1971. 96p. Reader for juveniles.

AM24 Goedsche, Curt R., and W. E. Glaettli. *Cultural Graded Readers, German Ser. no. 3: Carl Schurz.* New York: American Book Co., 1953–1956.

AM25 Kraft, Wolfgang S. "German Influence in the U.S." A unit in the textbook *Deutsch Aktuell 2.* St. Paul: EMC Corp., 1980, p.122–23.

AM26 Kunz, Virginia G. *Germans in America.* In America Books, Grade 5–11. Minneapolis: Lerner Publications, 1966.

AM27 Moeller, Jack, Jermaine Arendt, Manfred Heuser, and Lieselotte Schachner. "Die Deutschen in America." In: *Blickpunkt Deutschland.* Boston: Houghton Mifflin Co., 1973, p.285–310. Incl. readings on "Die ersten deutschen Einwanderer," "*Dodge County Pionier*—Einführende Bemerkungen über diese Zeitung in Wisconsin. Beispiele von Notizen and Artikeln;" and selections from *Einwanderung*, by Alice Herdan-Zuckmayer.

AM28 Walbruck, Büser, and Paul Walbruck, eds. *Besuch im Schweizer Mittelwesten. A Tour of New Glarus, Wisconsin, the Switzerland of the United States.* Ser.: "Wir Sprechen Deutsch." Skokie, Ill.: National Textbook Co., ca.1972. With illus. and tapes.

AM29 Zucker, Adolf E. *Amerika und Deutschland.* New York: Appleton-Century-Crofts, 1953. 247p. Rev. by J.D.W., *Monatshefte*, vol. 45 (1953), 329; A.H.F., *Amer.-German Rev.*, vol. 19, no. 5 (1953), 36; A. von Gronicka, *German Quar.*, vol. 26 (1953), 290–91. Textbook of readings in the parallel lives of great Americans and Germans.

Textbooks for Language Instruction

AM30 Alker, Marietta Alice. "Cultural Distortions and Biases in Level One and Two German Textbooks in Selected Florida High Schools, Community Colleges and Universities," Diss., Florida Atlantic Univ., 1977.

AM31 Buck, Kathryn, and Arthur Haase, comps. *Textbooks in German 1942–1973: A Descriptive Bibliography.* New York: Mod. Lang. Assoc. Publ. Center, ca. 1975. 162p. Classified inventory of works used in German classes and published in the United States.

AM32 Hahn, Paul T. *Survey of German Textbooks Used in Ohio High Schools, 1965–66.* Delaware: Ohio Wesleyan Univ., 1966.

AN
German-Language Newspapers and Periodicals

General

AN1 Agostan, Gerty. "Mit weit über hundert Jahren viele neue Ideen. Ein Blick auf die deutschsprachige Presse in den U S A." *Zeitschrift für Kulturaustausch*, vol. 17 (1967), 227–28.

AN2 App, Austin J. "The German Language Press in America." In: *German Society of Pennsylvania. Yearbook.* Vol. 2 (1951). Philadelphia: The Society, 1951.

AN3 Arndt, Karl J. R. *The Annotated and Enlarged Edition of Ernst Steiger's Precentennial Bibliography "The Periodical Literature of the United States of America."* Millwood, N.Y.: Kraus International Publs., 1980. Incl. a biography of Ernst Steiger; a statement on media coverage and awards to Steiger for his American newspaper exhibit; a reprint of the original book, annotated, revised, and correlated with the collection at the Austrian National Library; with a bibliography and microfilm guide to a second Steiger collection of

General *(cont.)*

American German-language newspapers and periodicals at the University of Heidelberg Library.

AN4 Arndt, Karl J. R. *Deutsche Zeitungen und Zeitschriften, welche in den Vereinigten Staaten von Amerika im Jahre 1874 erschienen, gesammelt von E. Steiger.* Heidelberg: n.p., n.d.

AN5 Arndt, Karl J. R. *The Ernst Steiger Collection of German-American Newspapers and Periodicals in Heidelberg and Vienna Diligently Compared and Catalogued for Cooperating Libraries as a Guide to Microfilm Copies of the Heidelberg Collection.* Worcester, Mass.: n.p., 1964. 51 l., reproduced from typescript. Also: *Steiger Collection of German-American Newspapers and Periodicals.* 4 reels of microfilm. Available from Karl J. R. Arndt, Clark University, Worcester. Issues of 363 serials, all stemming from the years 1872–1874, arranged by states and cities, in alphabetical order.

AN6 Arndt, Karl J. R. "Microfilm Preservation of the German Language Press of the Americas." In: *Germanica Americana 1976: Symposium on German-American Literature and Culture.* Ed. Erich A. Albrecht and J. Anthony Burzle. Lawrence, Kans.: Max Kade Document and Research Center, Univ. of Kansas, 1977, p.13–20.

AN7 Arndt, Karl J. R., and May E. Olson. *Deutsch-Amerikanische Zeitungen und Zeitschriften 1732–1968.* München-Pullach: Verlag Dokumentation, 1971.

AN8 Arndt, Karl J. R. and May E. Olson. *Die deutschsprachige Presse der Amerikas/The German-Language Press of the Americas.* Vol. 1. *Geschichte und Bibliographie 1732 bis 1955: Vereinigte Staaten von Amerika./History and Bibliography 1732 to 1955: U S A 1976.* 3rd. rev. and enl. ed. München-Pullach: Vlg. Dokumentation, 1976. 845p. Vol. 2. *Geschichte und Bibliographie 1732 bis 1968: Argentinien, Bolivien, Brasilien, Kanada, Chile, Kolumbien, Costa Rica, Kuba, Dominikanische Republik, Ekuador, Guatemala, Guayana, Mexiko, Paraguay, USA (Addenda), Uruguay, Venezuela/History and Bibliography 1732 to 1968.* München-Pullach: Verlag Dokumentation, 1973. 709p. Rev. of Vol. 2 by Hartmut Froeschle, *German-Canad. Yearbook*, vol. 1 (1973), 314. Vol. 3. *Deutsch-amerikanische Presseforschung von der amerikanischen Revolution bis 1976/German American Press Research from the American Revolution to the Bicentennial.* München: K. G. Saur, 1980. 848p.

AN9 Arndt, Karl J. R., and May E. Olson. *German-American Newspapers and Periodicals 1732–1955. History and Bibliography.* Heidelberg: Quelle and Meyer, 1961. 794p. Rev. by D. Cunz, *Amer.-German Rev.*, vol. 28, no. 6 (1962), 36–38; J. T. Krumpelmann, *La. Quar.*, vol. 32 (1962), 255.

AN10 Arndt, Karl J. R., and May E. Olson. *Microfilm Guide and Index to the Library of Congress Collection of German Prisoners of War Camp Papers Published in the United States of North America from 1943 to 1946.* Worcester: n.p. 1965.

AN11 [Ayer, N. W.] *N. W. Ayer and Sons Directory of Newspapers and Periodicals.* Philadelphia: n.p., 1960.

AN12 Benjamin, Steven M. "A Survey of German-American Newspapers and Periodicals Currently in Print." *Newsletter, Soc. for Ger.-Amer. Studies*, Vol. 1 no. 4 (1979–1980), 8–10.

AN13 Cunz, Dieter. "Die historische Rolle der deutschen Presse in Amerika." *Wash. Jour.*, 17 April 1959.

AN14 Deutsches Ausland-Institut, Stuttgart. *A List of Newspapers Principally Representative of German Groups outside of Germany, Collected by the Deutsches Ausland-Institut,* Received from Acting Chief of Staff, G–2 (Docs) U S F E T, Frankfurt, through the German Military Documents Section, Camp Ritchie, Md. Washington, D.C.: 1946. 29 l. Photocopy (neg.) of the original card record. Ca. 30 cards to a leaf.

AN15 Dolmetsch, Christopher. "Locations of German Language Newspaper and Periodical Printing in the United States: 1732–1976." *Monatshefte*, vol. 68 (1976), 188–95. Map.

AN16 Eggers, Johann. "German Publishing in the United States." *Univ. of Kentucky Libraries. Margaret I. King Library, Lexington.* Occasional Contributions no. 53. 15p. Translation of an article in *Der deutsche Pionier*, vol. 2 (1870).

AN17 Fishman, Joshua A., Esther G. Lowy, Michael H. Gertner, and William G. Milan. *Language Resources in the United States. I: Guide to Non-English Language Print Media.* Rosslyn, Va.:

National Clearinghouse for Bilingual Education, 1981. 51p.

AN18 *Handbuch der deutschsprachigen Presse ausserhalb Deutschlands*: Herausgegeben im Auftrage des "Göttinger Arbeitskreises" von Karl O. Kurth. Würzburg: Holzner-Vlg., 1946. 399p. Current German-language serials published outside Germany; chiefly concerned with manufacturing and trade.

AN19 *Handbuch für Auslandspresse*: Herausgeben vom Institut für Publizistik der Freien Universität Berlin, unter Leitung von Emil Dovifat. Bonn: Athenäum-Vlg.; Köln/Opladen: Westdeutscher Vlg., 1960. 907p.

AN20 Heide, W. *Handbuch der deutschsprachigen Zeitungen im Ausland*. Essen: n.p., 1940.

AN21 Hirseland, Gerhard. "Die deutschsprachige Presse in U. S. A." *New Yorker Staats-Zeitung und Herold*, 28 December 1969, Supplement for 135th anniversary of the paper, 2, 8, 10, 12, 14.

AN22 Hunter, Edward. *In Many Voices—Our Fabulous Foreign Language Press*. Norman Park, Ga.: Norman Coll., 1960. 190p.

AN23 Jones, Robert W. *Journalism in the United States*. New York: Dutton, 1947. 728p. Rev. by F. B. Marbut, *Amer. Hist. Rev.*, vol. 53, no. 2 (1948), 347–48.

AN24 Koszyk, Kurt. *Deutsche Presse im 19. Jahrhundert. Geschichte der Deutschen Presse*. Part 2. Berlin: Colloquium Vlg. Otto H. Hess, 1966. 372p.

AN25 Levy, Leonard W. *Freedom of the Press from Zenger to Jefferson: Early American Libertarian Theories*. Indianapolis: Bobbs-Merrill, 1966. 409p.

AN26 Marty, Martin E., John G. Deedy, Jr., et al. *The Religious Press in America*. New York: Holt, Rinehart & Winston, 1963. 184p. History and analysis of church-related journalism.

AN27 Norton, Wesley. *Religious Newspapers in the Old Northwest to 1861: A History, Bibliography, and Record of Opinion*. Athens: Ohio Univ. Pr., 1977. 196p. Rev. by J. B. Gidney, *Civil War Hist.*, vol. 24, no. 2 (1978), 161–64. Incl. the press of all denominations.

AN28 Olson, May E. "American Newspapers and Journals Printed in the German Language in America: A Checklist." Diss., Louisiana State, 1942.

AN29 Ostdeutscher Kulturrat. *Deutsche Presse im Ausland*, Düsseldorf: n.p., 1972.

AN30 Raschen, J. F. L. "American-German Journalism a Century Ago." *Amer.-German Rev.*, Vol. 12, no. 5 (June 1946), 13–15.

AN31 Reiter, Wilhelm. "Die deutschsprachige Presse der U S A. Ihre Entwicklung und gegenwärtige Lage." *IFA-Korrespondent* (Stuttgart), vol. 4, no. 11 (1964), 1–3.

AN32 Rothfuss, Herman E. "Westward with the News." *Amer.-German Rev.*, vol. 20 (February–March 1965), 22–25.

AN33 Steiger, Ernst. *Deutsch-amerikanische Zeitungen welche im Jahre 1874 erschienen*. Stuttgart: Heydt, Engesser, ca.1965. 4 reels of microfilm, 35 mm.

AN34 Ward, Robert E. "A Partial List of German Periodicals in the U S A." *German-Amer. Studies*, vol. 5 (1972), 5–6.

AN35 Wittke, Carl. "Die deutschsprachige Presse in den U S A." *New Yorker Staats-Zeitung und Herold*, 125th Anniversary ed., December 1959.

AN36 Wittke, Carl F. *The German Language Press in America*. Lexington: Univ. of Kentucky Pr., 1957. 311p. New York: Haskell House, 1973. Rev. by H. A. Pochmann, *Miss. Valley Hist. Rev.*, vol. 44 (1957), 336–37; A. E. Zucker, *Md. Hist. Mag.*, vol. 52 (1957), 159–61; D. Cunz, *Ohio Hist. Quar.*, vol. 66 (1957), 424–27; H. Groen, *Amer.-German Rev.*, vol. 23, no. 5 (1957), 39; B. J. Blied, *Canad. Hist. Rev.*, vol. 43 (1957), 353–54; G. Korman, *Wis. Mag. of Hist.*, vol. 41 (1957), 142–43; L. Koester, *Ky. Hist. Soc. Register*, vol. 55 (1957), 286–88; F. S. Siebert, *Library Quar.*, vol. 27 (1957), 216–18; M. Wachman, *Amer. Hist. Rev.*, vol. 62 (1957), 929–30; L. G. Downs, *Minn. Hist.*, vol. 35 (1957), 328–29; E. Lang, *Ind. Mag. of Hist.*, vol. 53 (1957), 462–63; S. Kobre, *Journalism Quar.*, vol. 34 (1957), 391–93; A. Werner, *Congress Weekly*, 28 October, 1957; M. Heald, *Cleveland Plain Dealer*, 12 May 1957. K. Liedtke,

General *(cont.)*

German Quar., vol. 31 (1958), 252–53; H. W. Pfund, *Pa. Mag. of Hist. and Biography*, vol. 82 (1958), 132–33; H. J. Johnson, *Manuscripta*, vol. 2 (1958), 120–21; H. P. Prentiss, *Hist. Rev. of Berks Co.*, vol. 22 (1958), 60–64; G. F. Merkel, *Bull. Hist. and Philosophical Soc. of Ohio*, vol. 67 (1958), 165–67; K. Wust, *Books Abroad*, vol. 32 (1958), 454; A. H. Marks, *Amer. Quar.*, vol. 10 (1958), 494–95; R. C. Wood, *Pa.*, vol. 25 (1959), 193–96. Comprehensive history of German-American journalism from 1732 to the present.

AN37 Wust, Klaus G. "The English and German Printing Office: Bilingual Printers in Maryland and Virginia." *Report, Soc. for the Hist. of the Germans in Md.*, vol. 32 (1966), 24–37. Incl. discussion of Jacob D. Dietrick (1788–1838), Republican newspaperman in Lancaster, Ohio.

AN38 Wynar, Lubomyr R. *Encyclopedic Directory of Ethnic Newspapers and Periodicals in the United States*. Littleton, Colo.: Libraries Unlimited, Inc., 1972. 260p. Lists 903 publications from 53 ethnic presses. These incl. 66 publications in the German language with a circulation totalling 449,666. The Jewish, Spanish, and Polish papers are the only ones that exceed the German in total circulation.

AN39 *Zeitungen und Zeitschriften deutscher Sprache im Ausland.* 4th ed. Berlin: Zentralverlag, 1934. 24p. The 1st ed., 1927, was titled *Merkblatt der Reischsstelle für das Auswanderungswesen*, no. 42.

Refugee Press in America 1933–1945

GENERAL

AN40 "Bookdealers' and Publishers' Catalogs [Listed]" In: *German Exile Literature in America 1933–1950*. Robert E. Cazden. Chicago: Amer. Library Assoc., 1970), p.232–33.

AN41 Cazden, Robert E. "The Free German and Free Austrian Press and Book Trade in the United States 1933–50, in the Context of German-American History." Diss., Chicago, 1966. p. See also "The Free German Book Trade in the United States, 1933–45." *Library Quar.*, vol. 37, no. 4 (1967), 348–65. Analysis of anti-Nazi groups outside Germany. There were three distinct networks of production and distribution: Communist, Social Democratic, and independent.

AN42 Cazden, Robert E. "Free German and Free Austrian Newspapers and Periodicals in the United States 1933–1950—A Checklist." Appendix II in his *German Exile Literature in America 1933–1950*. Chicago: Amer. Library Assoc., 1970, p.178–89. Periodicals in English and German; the German-Jewish press; the Austrian Emigre Press; the Free German Socialist Press, and the German-American Communist Press.

AN43 Cazden, Robert E. "Free German Books and Pamphlets Published in the United States 1933–1954—A Checklist." In Robert E. Czaden. *German Exile Literature in America 1933–1950*. Chicago: Amer. Library Assoc., 1970, p.190–215, Appendix III.

AN44 George, Manfred. "Die Stimme der Immigration: Notizen über den 'Aufbau'." In: *Twenty Years...1940–1960*. American Federation of Jews from Central Europe. New York: n.p., 1961, p.77–85.

AN45 George, Manfred. "Über den Aufbau." *Aufbau Almanach* (New York), 1941, p.6–9.

AN46 *Homage to a Bookman. Essays on Manuscripts, Books and Printing Written for Hans P. Kraus on His 60th Birthday, October 12, 1967.* Ed. Hellmut Lehmann-Haupt. Berlin: Gebr. Mann Vlg., 1967. Incl. many contributions by Americans.

AN47 Krause, Friedrich. "Das freie deutsche Buch in U.S.A." *Aufbau* (New York), 5 December 1941.

AN48 "Ein Loblied auf den Aufbau: Kölner Stadt-Anzeiger über die deutsche Presse in den USA." *Aufbau*, 25 May 1973.

AN49 Mack, Gerhard. "German Exile Authors and the Spanish Civil War." *Procs. of the Pacific Northwest Conf. on Foreign Langs.*, vol. 30, nos. 1–2 (1979), 64–67.

AN50 Niers, Gerd. "Einstein bei Freunden des "Aufbau": Aus den Materialien Fred J. Herrmanns." *Aufbau*, 16 March 1979.

AN51 Paetel, Karl O. "Bibliographie der Zeitschriften und Zeitungen des deutschen politischen

Exils 1933–1945." *Politische Studien*, vol. 9 (June 1958), 425–31.

AN52 Paetel, Karl O. "'Deutsche Gegenwart' in den U.S.A." *Börsenblatt für den deutschen Buchhandel* (Frankfurt a.M.), vol. 15 (25 August 1959), 1007–11.

AN53 Paetel, Karl O. "Die Presse des deutschen Exils 1933–1945." *Publizistik* no. 4 (June–August 1959), 241–53.

AN54 Schocken, Selmar. "Fünfzig Jahre Solidarität." *Solidarity*, vol. 51 (April 1956), 60–61, 91.

AN55 Sternfeld, Wilhelm. "Die Emigrantenpresse." *Deutsche Rundschau*, vol. 76 (April 1950), 250–59.

AN56 Sternfeld, Wilhelm. "Press in Exile: German Anti-Nazi Periodicals 1933–1945." *Wiener Library Bull.*, vol. 12 (1949), 31f.; vol. 14 (1950), 5f.

AN57 Walter, Hans-Albert. "Die Helfer im Hintergrund: Zur Situation der deutschen Exilverlage 1933–1945." *Frankfurter Hefte*, vol. 20 (February 1965), 121–32.

AN58 Walter, Hans-Albert. "Klaus Mann and 'Die Sammlung,' Portrait (II)." *Frankfurter Hefte*, vol. 22 (January 1967), 49–58.

AN59 Walter, Hans-Albert. "Der Streit um die 'Sammlung,' Portrait einer Literaturzeitschrift im Exil (I)." *Frankfurter Hefte*, vol. 21 (December 1966), 850–60.

AN60 White, Marjorie Taggert. "Europe's Press in Exile." *Saturday Rev. of Lit.*, 17 July 1943. 3–5.

WOLFF, KURT

AN61 Jonas, Klaus W. "Kurt Wolff. Notes on a Creative Publisher." *Amer.-German Rev.*, vol. 31, no. 5 (1965), 11–14. Publisher of distinguished authors in Germany and America.

AN62 Salzmann, Karl H. "Kurt Wolff, der Verleger." *Börsenblatt für den deutschen Buchhandel* (Frankfurt a.M.) vol. 14 (22 December 1958), 1729–49.

AN63 Scheffler, Heinrich, and Günther Neske. *Kurt Wolff: 1887–1963*. Frankfurt a.M.: Ludwig Oehms, 1963.

AN64 Wolff, Kurt. *Autoren/Bücher/Abenteuer. Erinnerungen eines Verlegers*. Berlin: Wagenbach, 1965. 120p.

AN65 Zeller, Bernard von, and Ellen Otten, eds., in collaboration with Helen Wolff. *Kurt Wolff— Briefwechsel eines Verlegers*. Frankfurt a.M.: Heinnich Scheffler, 1966. 509p.

Publishing and the Book Trade

AN66 "Book Publishers and Publishing." In: *Cambridge History of American Literature*. New York: Macmillan, 1933, esp. p.535–36. German book publishing in America.

AN67 Cazden, Robert E. "Johann Georg Wesselhöft and the German Book Trade in America." In: *The German Contribution to the Building of the Americas: Studies in Honor of Karl J. R. Arndt*. Ed. Gerhard K. Friesen and Walter Schatzberg. Hanover, N. H.: Clark Univ. Pr. and Univ. Pr. of New England, 1977, p.217–34. On the publishing and bookselling enterprises of the firm established in Philadelphia in 1834.

AN68 "Common Council for American Unity: German Publications in the United States." TS. 1950.

AN69 Eisele, Ernst. "Der deutsche Buchhandel in Amerika." *German-American Conference. Sitzungsberichte und Erläuterungen*. New York: n.p., 1932, p.29–31.

AN70 Finckh, Alice H. "A Year is Born; A Calendar is Made." *Amer.-German Review*, vol. 15, no. 2 (1948), 26–27. On the firms engaged in calendar printing.

AN71 Grothe, Sr. Justina. "German Catholic Publishing and Book Distribution within the United States from 1865 to 1880." M. A. Thesis, Catholic Univ. of America, 1950.

AN72 Heaney, Howell J. "A Century of Early American Children's Books in German, 1738–1837." *Phaedrus*, vol. 6, no. 1 (1979), 22–26; repr. in *Pa. Folklife*, vol. 29, no. 2 (1979), 75–79.

AN73 Madison, Charles A. *Book Publishing in America*. New York: n.p., 1966. Background on publishers.

AN74 Oda, Wilbur H. "A Check List of the German-Language Imprints of America through 1830." *The Pa. Dutchman*, vol. 4, no. 1 (1952), 12–14; no. 2, 12–14; no. 3, 12–14; no. 5, 6–7, 13; no. 8, 12–13. Exclusive of newspapers and New Year's wishes. For newspapers, see A. L. Shoemaker's checklists published in the *Pa. Dutchman*.

AN75 Oda, Wilbur H. "Ephrata German Imprints." *The Pa. Dutchman*, vol. 4, no. 9 (1953), 10–12; "German-Language Imprints of Harrisburg." *Ibid.*, no. 14, 12–14; "Gettysburg German Imprints." *Ibid.*, no. 10, 13; "Greensburg German Imprints." *Ibid.*, no. 11, 14; "Hanover German Imprints." *Ibid.*, no. 12, 14–15; "New Berlin German Imprints." *Ibid.*, no. 13, 13, 15.

AN76 Schoenberg, Wilfred P. *Jesuit Mission Presses in the Pacific Northwest: A History and Bibliography of Imprints 1876–1899*. Portland, Ore.: n.p., 1957. 77p.

AN77 Stapleton, Ammon. "Early German Printing in America: A Resume." *The Pa. German*, vol. 5, no. 4 (October 1904), 183; "Early German Printing in America: Supplement no. 2." *Ibid.*, vol. 6, no. 2 (April 1905), 262–63.

AN78 Steiger, Ernst. *Deutscher Buchhandel und Presse, und der Nachdruck deutscher Bücher in Nord-Amerika*. New York: Steiger, 1869. 45p. A protest against the pirating of German books in the United States.

AN79 Taubert, Sigfred. "Zur Geschichte des deutschen und deutschsprachigen Buchdrucks und Buchhandels im Ausland: Johann Gruber, Hagerstown, Maryland." *Börsenblatt für den deutschen Buchhandel*, vol. 9, no. 36 (5 May 1953); "Matthias Bartgis, Frederick, Maryland." *Ibid.*, no. 60 (28 July 1953); "Samuel Sauer, Baltimore, Maryland," *Ibid.*, no. 97 (4 December 1953).

AN80 Thompson, D. W. "Oldest American Printing Press." *The Dutchman*, vol. 6, no. 3 (Winter 1954–1955), 28–33. Incl. the making of printed frakturs.

AN81 Tolzmann, Don H. "Deutschamerikanische Buchhandlungen." *Der Milwaukee Herold*, 6 December 1973.

AN82 Weisert, John J. "The Limping Messenger." *Amer. German Review*, vol. 27, no. 3 (1961), 8–10. History in the United States of *Der hinkende Bote*, a 19th-century almanac.

AN83 Wust, Klaus G. "Jacob D. Dietrich (1778–1838)—Publisher and Bookseller in Four States." "'S Pennsylfawnisch Deitsch Eck," Allentown *Morning Call*, 15 June 1957.

Radio and Television

AN84 Berger, David. "Music from Germany: Birth and Justification of a Radio Program." *Amer. German Rev.*, vol. 35, no. 5 (June–July 1969), 11–13.

AN85 Lazenby, M. Candler. "German Class on TV," *Amer.-German Rev.*, vol. 21 (1955), no. 6, 30–31. Prof. R. C. Wood's program over WGLV, Easton, Pa.

AN86 Lindt, Peter M. *Schriftsteller im Exil: Zwei Jahre deutsche literarische Sendung am Rundfunk in New York*. New York: Willard Publ. Co., 1944. 192p.

AN87 "Organisator, Veranstalter und Rundfunksprecher Ted Hierl widmet den grössten Teil seiner Freizeit dem Deutschtum." *New Yorker Staats-Zeitung und Herold*, vol. 146, no. 40 (1980), Sec. B, 3. German-language radio program.

AN88 Shoemaker, Ted. "Broadcasting to the U.S." *Amer.-German Rev.*, vo. 33, no. 3 (1967), 25. On the Deutsche Welle.

AN89 Tolzmann, Don Heinrich. "German-Language Radio [Worship] Service." WCAL—AM Northfield, Minn. 17 October 1971 and 17 May 1972.

AN90 "Willy Seuren." *Amer.-German Rev.*, vol. 22, no. 2 (1955), 31. "Uncle Willy" of the German Hour on Radio Station WTEL, Philadelphia.

B

Ethnic Subgroups in German America

BA
Austrian Americana

Austrian-American Relations

BA1 *Amerikanische Künstler in Österreich. American Artists in Austria.* Catalogue. Trans. by Anthony Niehoff. Linz: Club der Begegnung, 1972. 48p. An exchange exhibit sponsored by the California Arts Council through the Fresno Arts Center and the Club der Begegnung, Linz.

BA2 Austria. Commerzkammer, Commerzkommission—Litorale—Prasidialakten, 1764-1830. In MS Div., Library of Congress (MS 64-147), photocopied from originals in the Public Archives of Austria concerning American commercial and consular relations, navigation, etc. *See* A. B. Faust's *Guide to the Materials of American History in Swiss and Austrian Archives.* Washington, D.C.: n.p., 1916, p.252-55.

BA3 *Austrian History Yearbook.* Vol. 1–, 1965—. Ed. John Rath. Houston: Rice Univ. An annual including indexes of American and Austrian doctoral dissertations, books and articles on Austrian history published throughout the world, and research projects in the U.S. and Canada; honors, grants, study programs, conferences, library collections, etc.

BA4 *Austrian Information.* vol. 1–, 1948–. Publ. by the Austrian Information Service, 31 E. 69th St., N.Y. Six-page weekly of news and information about Austria.

BA5 "Austrian Institute Dedicated in New York City." *Amer.-German Rev.*, vol. 29, no. 4 (1963), 26-27. Located at 11 E. 52nd St., N.Y. 10022, the institute sponsors a program of public lectures, exhibits, forums, and musical events, as well as tours of visiting Austrian artists.

BA6 Berlin, Jon D. "The United States and the Burgenland 1918-1920." *Austrian Hist. Yearbook*, vol. 8 (1972), 39-59; 84-96.

BA7 Chaffee, Marie Kreutz. "The Austro-American Institute of Education (Vienna)." *Amer.-German Rev.*, vol. 29, no. 4 (1963), 31-32.

BA8 *Der Donauschwabe. Bundesorgan der Heimatvertriebenen aus Jugoslawien, Rumänien und Ungarn.* 1951–. Ed. Franz Schuttack. Weekly publ. by Konrad Theis Vlg., Aalen, W. Germany.

BA9 *Eintracht/Harmony.* 1923–. Ed. Gottlieb Juengling. German-language weekly, official organ of the German-Austro-Hungarian Societies, 9456 N. Lawler St., Skokie, Ill. 60076. Carries news of club events, with emphasis on soccer.

BA10 Frank, Peter R. "Narrative on a Good Meal: A Collection of Austriaca at Stanford University Libraries." In: *Americana-Austriaca: Beiträge zur Amerikakunde.* Ed. Klaus Lanzinger, vol. 3. Wien, Stuttgart: Braumüller, 1974, p.236-48.

BA11 Luebke, Frederick C. "Austrians." In: *Encyclopedia of American Ethnic Groups.* Ed. Stephan Thernstrom. Cambridge: Harvard Univ. Pr., 1980, 164-71.

BA12 *Österreichische Nachrichten.* Feb. 1963–. Publ. by the Austrian American Federation, 55 W. 42nd St., N.Y. (founded 1957).

BA13 Payne, Raymond. "Annals of the Leopoldine Association." *Catholic Hist. Rev.*, vol. 50 (1964). Extracts from the *Berichte der Leopoldinen-Stiftung im Kaiserthume Österreich*, with notes on the work and origin of the association.

BA14 Pivec, Karl. "Das Amerika-Institut der Universität Innsbruck." In: *Americana-Austriaca: Festschrift des Amerika-Instituts der Univ. Innsbruck anläßlich seines zehnjährigen Bestehens.* Vol. 1. Ed. Klaus Lanzinger. Wien: Braumüller, 1966, p.1-16.

BA15 Roemer, Theodor. *Ten Decades of Alms.* St. Louis and London: Herder, 1942. On the Leopoldinen-Stiftung the Society for the Propagation of the Faith, and the Ludwigs Verein, sources of aid for American Catholic missions.

BA16 Schlag, Wilhelm. "Austro-American Cultural Relations." *Amer.-German Rev.*, vol. 25, no. 6 (1959), 12–14. Cultural contacts between the two countries.

Austrian and East European Peoples in America

BA17 [Austrian natives of the Burgenland.] *Burgenländische Gemeinschaft*, March 1964, publ. by the Burgenländische Gemeinschaft—Burgenland Society, Mogersdorf 178, A 7540 Guessing, Austria, Ed. Julius Gmoser. Article deals with Burgenland natives in the United States and other foreign countries.

BA18 Bergel, Egon. "Die Eigenart der österreichischen Einwanderung nach Amerika." In: *Americana-Austriaca: Beiträge zur Amerikakunde*. Vol. 2. Ed. Klaus Lanzinger. Wien: Braumüller, 1969, p.93–130.

BA19 Blied, Benjamin J. *Austrian Aid to American Catholics 1830–1860*. Milwaukee: n.p., 1944. 205p. Prominent Austrian church leaders were recruited for service in the United States by the Leopoldinen Stiftung: Bishop John Neumann of Philadelphia, Bishop Frederic Barago, missionary to the Indians and historian, Fr. Jos. Salzmann, founder of the St. Francis Seminary, Milwaukee, Fr. John S. Raffeiner of New York, and others.

BA20 Breycha-Vauthier, Arthur C. *Sie trugen Österreich mit sich in die Welt*. Wien: Österr. Staatsdruckerei, 1962. 173p. On emigration from Austria.

BA21 Dujmovits, Walter. "46 Burgenländer-Vereine." *New Yorker Staats-Zeitung und Herold*, vol. 147, no. 1 (1981), Sec. A, p.6. On the origin of the organizations and a list of local clubs.

BA22 Govorchin, Gerald Gilbert. *Americans from Yugoslavia*. Gainesville: Univ. of Fla. Pr., 1961. 352p.

BA23 Gundolf, Herbert. *Tiroler in aller Welt*. Innsbruck, Wien, München: Tyrolia-Vlg., 1972. 365p. Incl. bibliography.

BA24 Hietsch, Otto, ed. *Österreich und die angelsächsische Welt. Kulturbegegnungen und Vergleiche*. Wien, Stuttgart: Braumüller. 2 vol. 1961, 1968. 620, 498p. Index. Vol. 2 incl. contributions by Ernst Waldinger ("Betrachtungen eines amerikanischen Collegeprofessors"); Kurt Paümann ("Der Einfluß österreichischer Einwanderer auf das Kulturleben in Kanada"); Arthur Burkhard ("An American Family Savours Vienna, 1881–1882: Excerpts from the Diary of Mrs. John Crosby Brown"); Robert Kurz ("Salzburg und die englischsprachigen Länder"); Erich Zauner ("Kärnten und die englischsprachigen Länder"); Hans Paul ("Das Burgenland und die englischsprachigen Länder"); Paul A. Pisk ("Die Mozartforschung in den Vereinigten Staaten"); Paul Nettl ("Beethoven's American Connections"); Donald G. Daviau ("Hermann Bahr's Cultural Relations with America"); Leroy R. Shaw ("Modern Austrian Dramatists on the New York Stage"); Kurt Riegl ("Max Reinhardt, Thornton Wilder und *The Merchant of Yonkers* (1938)"); A. Burkhard ("Elizabeth Dowden's Grillparzer Translations"); and Friedrich Wild ("Arthur Burkhards neue Grillparzerüber setzungen"). Vol. 1 rev. in *Amer.-German Rev.*, vol. 28, no. 3 (1962), 37–38.; H. Petter, *Jahrbuch für Amerikastudien*, vol. 12 (1967), 285–88.

BA25 Koppensteiner, Jürgen. "'Land der Berge, Land der Seen'; Zum Österreichbild in amerikanischen Deutsch-Lehrbüchern." *Die Unterrichtspraxis*, vol. 11 (1978) 20–26.

BA26 Lanzinger, Klaus, ed. *Americana-Austriaca: Festschrift des Amerika-Instituts der Universität Innsbruck anläßlich seines zehnjährigen Bestehens. Beiträge zur Amerikakunde*, vol. 1. Wien: Braumüller, 1966. 301p. Rev. by D.M. Fox, *Amer. Hist. Rev.*, vol. 72, no. 3 (April 1967), 934–35. Vol. 2. 1969. Vol. 3. 1974. 250p. Vol. 4 (Bicentennial issue). 1978. 118p. Collections of essays on American history, political science, literature and language, with some reference to Austrian-American relations.

BA27 Lengyel, Emil. *Americans from Hungary*. Philadelphia and New York: Lippincott, 1948. 319p.

BA28 *Nachrichten der Donauschwaben in Amerika/News of the Danube Swabians in America*. 1955–. German-language quar. Ed. Jacob Awender. Sponsored by the Society of Danube Swabians, 4219 N. Lincoln Ave., Chicago.

BA29 Rie, Robert. "Austrians in the United States." *Amer.-German Rev.*, vol. 29, no. 1 (1962), 30–31.

BA30 Schlag, Wilhelm. *Österreichische Pioniere und Forscher in Nordamerika*. Pamphlet available at the Austrian Institute, 11 E. 52nd St. N.Y. 10022.

BA31 Schlag, Wilhelm. Supplement, *Wiener Zeitung*, 30 August 1959. A statistical analysis of Austrian emigration to the U.S. based on official sources.

BA32 Schlag, Wilhelm. "A Survey of Austrian Emigration to the United States." In: *Österreich und die angelsächsische Welt*. Ed. Otto Hietsch, Wien, Stuttgart: Braumüller, 1961, p.139–96.

BA33 *Siebenbürgisch-Amerikanisches Volksblatt (Transylvania-American People's Letter)*. 1905–. German-language weekly. Publ. by the Central Verband der Siebenbürger Sachsen of the United States. Ed. Knuth Beth. 1436 Brush St., Detroit.

BA34 Spaulding, E. Wilder. *The Quiet Invaders. The Story of the Austrian Impact upon America*. Forew. by Josef Stummvoll. Wien: Österr. Landesvlag für Unterricht, Wissenschaft und Kunst, 1968. 423p. Incl. a thorough survey and analysis of Austrian immigration, index of persons, Jewish emigration, and music, contemporary arts and professions.

BA35 Steigerwald, Jacob. "Zur Herkunft der Donauschwaben." *Nachrichten der Donauschwaben in Chicago*, February 1981, 5–7.

BA36 Winkler, Wilhelm. *Die Österreicher im Ausland; im Einvernehmen mit dem Weltbund der Österreicher im Auslande und mit Unterstützung des Bundeskanzleramtes, Auswärtige Angelegenheiten*. Wien: Wien Universität, Institut für Statistik, 1955. 32p.

BB

Canadian Germans/German Life and Culture in Canada

See also Part H: America. Travel and Description.

Canadian Bibliography and Sources

BB1 Arndt, Karl J. R., ed. "Halifax and Lunenburg in 1782, or Halle and London as Sources for German-Canadian Research. (With Pastor Schmeisser's Report of 1782 from Nova Scotia)." Introd. by Karl J. R. Arndt. *German-Canad. Yearbook*, vol. 4 (1978), 114–21.

BB2 Baumhard, Hans J. "Lokale Initiative im Dienst der deutschkanadischen Geschichtsforschung." *German-Canad. Yearbook*, vol. 1 (1973), 309–11.

BB3 Benjamin, Steven M. "Deutschkanadisches Jahrbuch." *Germanistische Mitteilungen* (Brussels), Heft 12 (1980), 61–65. Review of the *German-Canad. Yearbook*, vols. 1–3. See also Newsletter of the Soc. for Ger.-Amer. Studies, vol. 2, no. 3 (1980–1981), 5.

BB4 Benjamin, Steven M. *The German Canadians: A Working Bibliography*. Occasional Papers of the Soc. for German-Amer. Studies, no. 1. Morgantown: Dept. of For. Langs., West Va. Univ., 1979. 41p. Supplement to the bibliographies publ. in the *German-Canad. Yearbook*.

BB5 *Canadian Almanac*. Toronto: Copp, Clark Co., Ltd., 1911–1919.

BB6 Cardinal, C. H. von, and A. Malycky. "University Research in German-Canadians: A Preliminary Check List of Dissertations and Theses." *Canad. Ethnic St.*, vol. 1, no. 1 (April 1969).

BB7 Froeschle, Hartmut. "Deutschkanadische Bibliographie." *German-Canad. Yearbook*, vol. 1 (1973), 327–44.

BB8 Froeschle, Hartmut. "Deutschkanadische Studien: Aufgaben und Möglichkeiten." *German-Canad. Yearbook*, vol. 2 (1975), 6–23.

BB9 Froeschle, Hartmut. "The *German-Canadian Yearbook*: Its Content and Purpose." *German-Canad. Yearbook*, vol. 1 (1973), 1–4.

BB10 Froeschle, Hartmut. "Two German Recorders of Canadian Pioneer Life." *German-Canad. Yearbook*, vol. 1 (1973), 161–66. On Johann Gottfried Seume (b. 1763) and John Grossman (b. 1888).

BB11 Froeschle, Hartmut. "Der 'Verband für deutschkanadische Geschichtsforschung' (German-Canadian Historical Association)." *German-Canad. Yearbook*, vol. 2 (1975), 271–75.

BB12 Froeschle, Hartmut. "Eine Zentralstelle zur Erforschung deutschkanadischer Geschichte: Die 'Historical Society of Mecklenburg Upper Canada Inc.'." *German-Canad. Yearbook*, vol. 1 (1973), 275–85.

BB13 *German-Canadian Review.* 1948–. Irregular. Winnipeg, Man.: Canadian Soc. for German Relief, 37 King's Drive, King's Park.

BB14 *German-Canadian Yearbook/Deutsch-Kanadisches Jahrbuch.* vol. 1–, 1973–. Ed. Hartmut Froeschle. Toronto: Hist. Soc. of Mecklenburg Upper Canada. At intervals of one or two years.

BB15 Gregorovich, Andrew. *Canadian Ethnic Groups Bibliography: A Selected Bibliography of Ethno-Cultural Groups in Canada and the Province of Ontario.* Toronto: Dept. of the Provincial Secretary and Citizenship, 1972. 208p.

BB16 Gürttler, Karin and Friedhelm Lach, eds. *Annalen des 1. Montrealer Symposiums Deutschkanadische Studien. 25–27 March 1976.* Montreal: n.p., 1976. 85p.

BB17 Hänisch, W. "Die Canada-Bibliothek in Marburg." *Canad.-German Rev.*, vol. 10, no. 1 (1957), 11–13. A Canadian reference library attached to the Marburg University Library.

BB18 Haldimand, *General Sir Frederick. Papers. In the Public Archives of Canada. Transcripts of originals in the British Museum, London.*

BB19 Hess, Anna K. "Remarks on Historical Research with Special Consideration of the History of German Settlers in Canada." *Canad.-German Rev.* (1958); repr. in *German-Canad. Yearbook*, vol. 1 (1973), 25–29.

BB20 Jürgensen, Kurt. "Im Grundsatz beschlossen: Gesellschaft für Kanada-Studien." *German-Canad. Yearbook*, vol. 5 (1979), 240–41. On the formation of a new society for Canadian studies in Europe.

BB21 *Kontakt.* Vol. 1–, May 1968–. Toronto: n.p. Publ. six times a year. German-language cultural-political journal.

BB22 Leibbrandt, Gottlieb. "Canadian-German Society." *German-Canad. Yearbook*, vol. 1 (1973), 225–62.

BB23 Lohr, Otto. "Kanadisch-deutsche Kulturbeziehungen—eine bibliographische Auslese." *Mitteilungen des Instituts für Auslandsbeziehungen*, vol. 7 (1957), 216–20.

BB24 Mahne, Karl. "Informator—Mittler—Wegbereiter: Die 'Deutsch-Kanadische Industrie- und Handelskammer'." *German-Canad. Yearbook*, vol. 1 (1973), 305–08.

BB25 Mallea, J. R. "Canadian Cultural Pluralism and Education: A Select Bibliography." *Canad. Ethnic St.*, vol. 8, no. 1 (1976).

BB26 Malycky, A., and C.H. von Cardinal. "German-Canadian Periodical Publications: First Supplement." *Canad. Ethnic St.*, vol. 2, no. 1 (June 1970).

BB27 Malycky, A., and C. H. von Cardinal. "German-Canadian Periodical Publications: A Preliminary Check List." *Canad. Ethnic St.*, vol. 1, no. 1 (April 1969).

BB28 Malycky, A., and R. Goertz. "German-Canadian Periodical Publications: Second Supplement." *Canad. Ethnic St.*, vol. 5, nos. 1–2 (1973), 67–84.

BB29 Malycky, Alexander. "University Research on German-Canadians." *Canad. Ethnic St.*, vol. 5, nos. 1–2 (1973), 63–65.

BB30 Malycky, Alexander, ed. "Bibliographic Issue." *Canad. Ethnic St.*, vol. 5, nos. 1–2 (1973), 426p.

BB31 Markotte, V., comp. and ed. *Ethnic Directory of Canada*. Calgary: n.p., 1976. 119p.

BB32 Martin, Horst, comp. *A Reference Guide to Germany. A Selective Checklist of Printed Materials Relating to Germany, Listing the Holdings of the Public Libraries in Greater Vancouver*. Vancouver: The German Canadian Cultural Soc., 1976. 104p.

BB33 *Mitchell's Canada Gazetteer and Business Directory for 1864–65*. Toronto: Chewett, 1864.

BB34 Morley, William F. E. *The Atlantic Provinces: Canadian Local Histories to 1950, A Bibliography*. Toronto: Univ. of Toronto Pr., 1980.

BB35 Morley, William F. E. *Ontario and the Canadian North. Canadian Local Histories to 1950: a Bibliography*. Toronto: University of Toronto Pr., 1978.

BB36 *Pazifische Rundschau/Pacific Review*. (Formerly *Dies und Das*.) 1965–. Fortnightly. Ed. Baldwin Ackermann. Vancouver, B.C.: Ackermann Advertising. In German.

BB37 Peel, Bruce Braden, comp. *A Bibliography of the Prairie Provinces to 1953: With Biographical Index*. Toronto: Univ. of Toronto Pr., ca. 1955. 808p.

BB38 Phillips, Paul A. "Structural Change and Population Distribution in the Prairie Region, 1911 to 1961." M.A. thesis, Univ. of Saskatchewan, 1963.

BB39 Tanghe, Raymond. *Bibliography of Canadian Bibliographies*. Toronto: Univ. of Toronto Pr., in Assoc. with the Bibliographical Soc. of Canada, 1960. 206p. See also *Supplement: 1960–61; 1962–63*.

BB40 Toronto. Public Libraries. *A Bibliography of Canadiana: Being Items in the Public Library Relating to the Early History and Development of Canada*. Ed. Frances M. Staton and Marie Tremaine. Toronto: n.p., 1934. 828p. See also *First Supplement*. 1959. 333p.

BB41 Wertheimer, L. "Multiculturalism and Public Libraries." *German-Canad. Yearbook*, vol. 3 (1976), 42–45.

Ethnic Germans in Canada— General

BB42 Allen, A. R. "Untroublesome Canadians." *Maclean's* (Toronto), vol. 77 (7 March 1964), 19–21.

BB43 Amstatter, Andrew. *Tomslake: History of the Sudeten Germans in Canada*. Soonichton, B.C.: Hancock House, 1978. Rev. by Fritz Wieden, *Canad. Ethnic St.*, vol. 11 (1979), 180–82.

BB44 Barth-Flacke, Lieslotte. "Kanada und seine deutschen Einwanderer." *Globus*, (1972) Heft 3, 18–19.

BB45 Belkin, Simon. *Through Narrow Gates: A Review of Jewish Immigration, Colonization and Immigrant Aid Work in Canada (1840–1940)*. N.p.: Canadian Jewish Congress and the Jewish Colonization Assoc., 1966. 235p.

BB46 Boeschenstein, Hermann. *Unter Schweizern in Kanada*. Bern: n.p., 1974.

BB47 Bongart, Klaus H. "The Canadian Consultative Council on Multiculturalism and the Interests of the German-Canadian Community." *German-Canad. Yearbook*, vol. 1 (1973), 17–23.

BB48 Bovay, E. H. *Le Canada et les Suisses 1604–1974*. Fribourg: n.p., 1974.

BB49 Braedt, Andreas. "Die Gemeinschaft der Siebenbürger Sachsen in Kanada." In: *Siebenbürger Sachsen heute*. "Der Wegweiser" Schriftenreihe für die Ost–West-Begegnung, Kulturheft no. 60. [Troisdorf]: n.p., 1967, p.51–64.

BB50 Byerly, A. E. "The Peterson Diary—About Pennsylvania German Pioneers in Canada." "'S Pennsylfawnisch Deitsch Eck," Allentown (Pa.) *Morning Call*, 22 May, 1954.

BB51 Canada. Ministry of Agriculture. *Auskunft über den Staat Canada für deutsche Ansiedler*. Ottawa: n.p., 1882.

BB52 Cardinal, Clive H. von. "Mosaik und Doppelkultur in der Kanadischen Identität." *Der Nordwesten*, 1 February 1966.

BB53 Cardinal, Clive H. von. "Ein Ueberblick über die deutsche Einwanderung." *Mitteilungen des Instituts für Auslandsbeziehungen*, vol. 7 (1957), 168f. Emigration to Canada 1750–1950.

BB54 Cooper, John Irwin. "Canada and Germany, 1847–1848." *Amer.-German Rev.*, vol. 14, no. 5 (1948), 6–7.

BB55 Crowley, Terence A. "Mackenzie King and the 1911 Election." *Ontario Hist.*, vol. 61, no. 4 (December 1969), 181–96. References to the part new German-Canadians played during World War I in Canadian politics.

BB56 Dawson, C. A. "Group Settlement: Ethnic Communities in Western Canada." In: *Canadian Frontiers of Settlement*. Vol. 7. Ed. W. A. Mackintosh. Toronto: n.p., 1936.

BB57 Debor, H. W. "Die Baltendeutschen in Kanada." *Der Nordwesten*, 29 March 1966.

BB58 Debor, H. W. "Das deutsche Element in Kanada und seine siedlungsgeschichtlichen Leistungen." *Auslands-Kurier*, vol. 8, no. 6 (1967), 13–15.

BB59 Debor, H. W. "Deutsche Jäger in Kanada (ein Kapitel kanadischer Geschichte)." *Der Nordwesten*, 17 May 1966.

BB60 Debor, H. W. "Deutsche Standen an Kanadas Wiege." *Auslands-Kurier*, vol. 7 (1966), 1–2.

BB61 Debor, H. W. "Eine Million Kanadier ohne Vergangenheit?" *Der Nordwesten*, 13 December 1966. On the lack of sources of information about the "third group" of Canadian peoples.

BB62 Debor, H. W. "Die Österreicher in Kanada." *Der Nordwesten*, 25 April 1967.

BB63 Debor, H. W. "Die wirtschaftlichen und kulturellen Leistungen der Deutschkanadier." *Auslands-Kurier*, vol. 7, no. 6 (1966), 6–10.

BB64 "Deutschkanadische Freundschaftskarawane (Anthropologie der deutschen Sprache—Beiträge deutscher Einwanderer zur Hundertjahrfeier Kanadas)." *Der Nordwesten*, 6 December 1966.

BB65 Doughty, Howard A. and Darrel R. Skidmore. "The Germans." In: *Canadian Studies. Culture and Country*. Eds. H. A. Doughty and D. R. Skidmore. Toronto: Wiley, 1976, p.169–86.

BB66 Driedger, Leo, ed. *The Canadian Mosaic: A Quest for Identity*. Toronto: McClelland & Stewart, 1978. 352p.

BB67 Elliot, Jean L., ed. *Minority Canadians*. Vol. 2. *Immigrant Groups*. Scarborough, Ont.: Prentice-Hall of Canada, 1971. 215p. Rev. in *Canad. Hist. Rev.*, vol. 53 (1972), 443.

BB68 Elliot, Jean L., ed. *Two Nations, Many Cultures: Ethnic Groups in Canada*. Scarborough, Ont.: Prentice-Hall of Canada, 1979.

BB69 Frey, Katherine S. "The Danube Swabians in Canada: They Call It Their Land Too." *German-Canad. Yearbook*, vol. 6 (1981), 78–83.

BB70 Friedmann, Wolfgang G. *German Immigration into Canada*. Toronto: Ryerson Pr., 1952. 63p. Rev. by G. W. Simpson, *Canad. Hist. Rev.*, vol. 34, no. 2 (1953), 188. On problems of German immigration since 1945.

BB71 Froeschle, Hartmut. "Friedrich Schiller Foundation for German-Canadian Culture." *Canadiana Germanica*, vol. 32 (1981), 1–2.

BB72 Froeschle, Hartmut. "German Immigration into Canada: A Survey." Trans. by Werner Bausenhart. *German-Canad. Yearbook*, vol. 6 (1981), 16–27.

BB73 Froeschle, Hartmut. "Neuere Canadiana Germanica." *German-Canad. Yearbook*, vol. 4 (1978), 343–55. Examination and critique of some 36 publications appearing since 1972.

BB74 *German-Canadian Club Harmonie, 1921–1971: Festschrift*. Toronto: n.p., 1971.

BB75 Gürttler, Karin R., and Herfried Scheer, eds. *Annalen III: Kontakte—Konflikte—Konzepte, Deutsch-kanadische Beziehungen, Symposium 1980*. Montreal: Univ. of Montreal, 1981. 195p.

BB76 "Hand in Hand mit Indianern und Eskimos: Vor Trudeaus Reformausschuß melden Deutsch-

Kanadier ihre Rechte als 'Gründervolk' an." *Süddeutsche Zeitung*, 11 January 1981. Repr. *Canadiana Germanica*, vol. 29 (1981), 16.

BB77 Heeb, Karl. "Die Trans-Kanada Vereinigung der Deutschkanadier." *Auslands-Kurier*, vol. 7, no. 6 (1966), 14–15.

BB78 Heier, Edmund. "The Immigration of Russo-German Catholics and Lutherans into Canada." *Canad. Slavonic Papers*, vol. 4 (1960), 160–75.

BB79 Hiller, J. K. "The Moravians in Labrador, 1771–1805." *Polar Record*, vol. 15, no. 99 (September 1971), 839–54.

BB80 Jeness, R. A. "Canadian Migration and Immigration Patterns and Public Policy." *Internat. Migration Rev.*, vol. 8 (Spring 1974), 5–22.

BB81 Kage, Joseph. *Studies and Documents on Immigration and Integration in Canada*. Jewish Immigrant Aid Services of Canada. Montreal: n.p., 1968. 53p.

BB82 Kage, Joseph. *With Faith and Thanksgiving: The Story of 200 Years of Jewish Immigration and Immigrant Aid Effort in Canada (1760–1960)*. Montreal: Eagle Publ. Co., 1960. 231p.

BB83 "Die Kanada-Deutschen unter fragwürdiger Obhut Ostberlins: Stiefkinder der Bonner Aussenpolitik?" *Washington Jour.*, vol. 121, no. 3 (1980), 4. The Harmonie Klub of Toronto seeks funding from Germany.

BB84 Kastens, Eva. "Botschafter im Arbeitskleid: Aus der Geschichte der Sudetendeutschen in Kanada." *German-Canad, Yearbook*, vol. 3 (1976), 120–28.

BB85 Keyfitz, Nathan. "Ethnic Groups and Their Behaviour." *Annals of the Amer. Academy of Social and Political Science*, vol. 253 (September 1947), 158–63. Some discussion of German groups in Canada: their number, occupations, and assimilation.

BB86 Kinnear, Michael. "The Problems of Cultural Regionalism in Canada." *Mosaic*, vol. 1, no. 3 (April 1968), 58–69.

BB87 Kirkconnell, Watson. *Canadians All: A Primer of Canadian National Unity*. 2nd ed. Ottawa: Director of Public Information, 1941. 48p. On the nationality groups in Canada.

BB88 Kliem, Ottmar. "Brücken in die Zukunft—zur Bedeutung deutscher Klubs in Kanada." *Zeitschrift für Kulturaustausch*, vol. 22, no. 1 (1972), 21–24. Analysis of attitudes based on a questionnaire answered by members of the German Club in Calgary.

BB89 Küster, Mathias. "Die Baltendeutschen in Kanada." *German-Canad. Yearbook*, vol. 5 (1979), 55–65.

BB90 Kutscha, Emil. "Fünfundzwanzig Jahre gemeinsamer Arbeit—Treffen der Sudetendeutschen in Hamilton [Ont.]." *Der Nordwesten*, 28 June 1966.

BB91 Kutscha, Emil. "Sudetendeutsche in Kanada." *Mitteilungen des Instituts für Auslandsbeziehungen*, vol. 7 (1957), 208–09. See also *Amer.-German Rev.*, vol. 23, no. 3 (1957), 30–31. Cultivating over 6,600 acres since 1939, mostly in Saskatchewan and British Columbia.

BB92 Lehmann, Heinz. *Zur Geschichte des Deutschtums in Kanada*. Stuttgart: n.p., 1931.

BB93 Lower, Arthur R. M. "Canada at the Turn of the Century, 1900." *Canad. Geographical Jour.*, vol. 71, no. 1 (1965), 2–13. Incl. references to German immigration.

BB94 Lützkendorf, Hans. "'Im Herzen deutsch geblieben'. Begegnungen mit Auswanderern in Kanada." *Globus*, (1971) Heft 1, 21f.; (1972) Heft 2, 22f.

BB95 Marbach, Norbert. "Zur Lage der Deutschkanadier." In: *Deutsche Annalen*. Ed. Gerd Sudholt. N.p.: n.p., 1973, p.179–93.

BB96 Maurer, K. W. "Die Deutschen in Kanada." *Auslandswarte*, vol. 32, no. 8 (1953), 6–10.

BB97 Multiculturalism Directorate. *The Canadian Family Tree*. N.p.: Corpus, 1979. 250p. Accounts of various ethnocultural groups.

BB98 Obstfeld, Christel. "Neue Heimat Kanada." *German-Canad. Yearbook*, vol. 3 (1976), 237–43.

BB99 "People of German Origin." *Encyclopedia Canadiana*. Ottawa, 1958. Vol. 4 p.353f.

BB100 Piro, Rolf A. "German-Speaking Missionaries and Soldiers among the Indians of Upper and Lower Canada." *German-Canad. Yearbook*, vol. 5 (1979), 25–34.

BB101 Reiter, Wilhelm. "Ein deutschkanadischer Verband bewährt sich (TCV 20 Jahre alt)." *Ifa-Korrespondenz* (1971) Heft 4, 1–4.

BB102 Richmond, Anthony H. *Post-War Immigrants in Canada.* Canad. St. in Sociology, no. 2. Toronto: Univ. of Toronto Pr., 1967. 320p. Comparing the socio-economic integration of the British element with that of immigrants from other countries.

BB103 Rosenberg, Louis. "Some Aspects of the Historical Development of the Canadian Jewish Community." *Publs., Amer. Jewish Hist. Soc.*, vol. 50 (1960), 121–42. A broad survey of two hundred years of history.

BB104 Sautter, Udo. *Die Geschichte Kanadas: Das Werden einer Nation.* Stuttgart: n.p., 1972.

BB105 Schilling, Edith von. "Deutsche Siedler im kanadischen Busch." *Der Auslandsdeutsche* (August 1938), 496f.

BB106 Schmidt, Herminio. "Die deutschen Sonnabendschulen in Kanada: Entwicklung und Prognose." *German-Canad. Yearbook*, 6 (1981), 183–98.

BB107 Shoemaker, Alfred L. "Pennsylvania Dutch Canada." *The Dutchman*, vol. 7, no. 4 (Spring 1956), 8–14.

BB108 Shultz, Harold J. "Search for Utopia: the Exodus of Russian Mennonites to Canada, 1917–1927." *Jour. of Church and State*, vol. 11, no. 3 (Autumn 1969), 487–512.

BB109 Smith, Elmer L. "The New Amish Settlement in Canada—1960." "'S Pennsylfawnisch Deitsch Eck," Allentown (Pa.) *Morning Call*, 9 April 1960.

BB110 Stoll, Joseph. *Recent Amish Immigration to Ontario.* Aylmer, Ont.: n.p., 1966. 28p.

BB111 Stumpp, Karl. *German-Russian Settlements in Canada.* Lincoln, Neb.: Amer. Hist. Soc. of Germans from Russia, n.d. Map.

BB112 Sturhahn, William J. H. *They Came from East and West. A History of Immigration to Canada.* Winnipeg, Man.: n.p., 1976. 328p.

BB113 Thiessen, Jack. "Der deutsche Beitrag zur Entwicklung Kanadas." *Zeitschrift für Kulturaustausch*, vol. 20, no. 1 (January–March 1970), 28–32.

BB114 Veiter, Theodor. "Nationalitätenkonflikt und interethnische Beziehungen im ausgehenden 20. Jahrhundert." *German-Canad. Yearbook*, vol. 4 (1978), 1–19.

BB115 Weissenborn, Georg. "The Germans in Canada: A Chronological Survey of Canada's Third Oldest European Ethnic Group from 1664 to 1977." *German-Canad. Yearbook*, vol. 4 (1978), 22–56.

BB116 West, Roxroy. "Swiss Guides and the Village of Edelweiss (Canada)." *Beaver* (Summer 1979), 50–53.

BB117 Wieden, Fritz. *The Sudeten Canadians.* Toronto: Sudetenklub Vorwärts, c. 1979. Rev. in *New Yorker Staats-Zeitung und Herold*, vol. 145, no. 49 (1979), Sec. B, p.5.

BB118 Wieden, Fritz. "Überörtliche weltliche Vereine (Stand 1975)," In: *Deutsch als Muttersprache in Kanada: Berichte zur Gegenwartslage.* Eds. L. Auburger, H. Kloss and H. Rupp. Wiesbaden: Steiner, 1977, p.115–17.

BB119 Williams, William D. "The Germans." In: *Many Cultures Many Heritages.* Ed. Norman Sheffe. Toronto: McGraw Hill Ryerson, 1975, p.185–237.

BB120 Yuzik, P. "The True Canadian Identity: Its Recognition and Development." *German-Canad. Yearbook*, vol. 3 (1976), 23–38.

Churches and Religious History

See also Section IJ: Religion and Church History.

GENERAL

BB121 Barbier, Louis P. *Die Geschichte der Ersten Ev. Lutherischen Kirche Toronto, 1851–1976. The Story of the First Lutheran Church, Toronto, 1851–1976.* Toronto: n.p., 1976. 2 vols. 37, 32p.

BB122 [Bethlehem Lutheran Church, Drumheller.] *The History of Dalum.* Drumheller, Alb.: Big Country News, 1968. 226p.

BB123 Cronmiller, Carl Raymond. *A History of the Lutheran Church in Canada.* Prep. at the Request of the Evangelical Lutheran Synod of Canada to Mark Its Centennial, July 1961. Kitchener, Ont.: n.p., 1961.

BB124 Crysdale, Stewart, and Jean-Paul Montimy. *Religion in Canada: An Annotated Inventory of Scientific Studies in Religion, 1945-1972.* Quebec: Laval Univ. Pr., 1974. 189p.

BB125 Drewitz, Arthur. *Die Geschichte des Deutschen Zweigs der Pentecostal Assemblies of Canada: 40. Jubiläum, 1940-1980.* Kitchener, Ont.: German Branch, Pentecostal Assemblies of Canada, 1981.

BB126 *Der Deutsche Katholik in Kanada.* Vol. 1–, 1964–. German-language monthly. 131 McCaul St., Toronto.

BB127 Eylands, Valdimar Jónsson. *Lutherans in Canada.* Winnipeg: Icelandic Evangelical Lutheran Synod in North America, 1945. 326p. Rev. by J. T. Oleson, *Canad. Hist. Rev.*, vol. 27, no. 1 (1946), 71–72.

BB128 Goegginger, W. "Deutschsprachige religiöse Arbeit in evangelischen Gemeinden Kanadas." *German-Canad. Yearbook*, vol. 3 (1976), 273–78.

BB129 Goertz, Richard O., and Alexander Malycky. "German-Canadian Church History. Part 2: Individual Congregations, a Preliminary Bibliography." *Canad. Ethnic St.*, vol. 5, nos. 1-2 (1973), 95–123.

BB130 Holst, Wayne A. "Ethnic Identity and Mission in a Canadian Lutheran Context." *Consensus*, vol. 1, no. 2 (1975). Repr. *German-Canad. Yearbook* vol. 5 (1979), 20–24.

BB131 Kloss, Heinz. "Das Luthertum in Kanada." *Mitteilungen des Instituts für Auslandsbeziehungen*, vol. 7 (1957), 211.

BB132 Mann, William Edward. *Sect, Cult, and Church in Alberta.* Toronto: Univ. of Toronto Pr., 1955.

BB133 Schindler, Karl J. "Die deutschsprachigen katholischen Kirchengemeinden in Kanada." *German-Canad. Yearbook*, vol. 1 (1973), 291–95; vol. 2 (1975), 276–84.

BB134 Slater, Peter, ed. *Religion and Culture in Canada: Essays by Members of the Canadian Society for the Study of Religion.* N.p.: Canadian Corporation for Studies in Religion, 1977.

BB135 Swalm, E. J. *"My Beloved Brethren..." Personal Memoirs and Recollections of the Canadian Brethren in Christ Church.* Nappanee, Ind.: Evangelical Pr., 1969. 156p.

BB136 Threinen, Norman. "Early Lutheranism in Western Canada." *Concordia Hist. Inst. Quar.*, vol. 47, no. 3 (Fall 1974), 110–17. The role of William Wagner, a German immigrant, in establishing Berlin Township, Manitoba, ca. 1870; his relation to the Lutheran Church, Missouri Synod.

BB137 Threinen, Norman J. "Lutherans in Canada." *German-Canad. Yearbook*, vol. 5 (1979), 13–19.

BB138 Weiler, P. A. "Katholische Deutschenseelsorge." *Mitteilungen des Instituts für Auslandsbeziehungen*, vol. 7 (1957), 212–13. Catholic-German congregations and their priests in Canada.

MENNONITES AND AMISH MENNONITES

See also Manitoba under Local History, this section; and under Indiana, Kansas, Ohio, North Dakota in Part J: German-American Local History.

BB139 Aucléres, Dominique, and Nicolas Châtelain. "'Amish' verachten Soldaten und Autos." *Die Zeit*, 8 March 1966, 20. See also Winnipeg *Manitoba-Courier*, 17 March 1966, p.4.

BB140 Bauman, P. S. "The Unchanging Old Order Mennonites." *German-Canad. Yearbook*, vol. 3 (1976), 97–105.

BB141 Burkhalter, L. J. *A Brief History of the Mennonites in Ontario, 100 Pictures of Men and Churches.* Markham, Ont.: n.p., 1935. 358p. Illus. and maps. Rev. by Harold S. Bender, *Mennonite Quar. Rev.*, vol. 25, no. 3 (1951), 228.

BB142 Crysdale, Stewart, and Les Wheatcroft, eds. *Religion in Canadian Society.* Toronto: Macmillan, 1976. 498p. Incl. essays on the Amish, Hutterites, and Mennonites.

BB143 Davies, Blodwen. *A String of Amber: The Heritage of the Mennonites.* Vancouver, B. C.: Mitchell Pr., 1973.

BB144 Derksen, Eugene. "Steinbach: Cradle of the Mennonites in Western Canada." *Mennonite Life*, vol. 12 (1957), 72–83.

BB145 Doerksen, John Georg. "History of Education of the Mennonite Brethren of Canada." M. Ed. thesis, Univ. of Manitoba, 1963.

BB146 Driedger, Leo. "A Tale of Two Strategies: Mennonites in Chicago and Winnipeg." *Mennonite Quar. Rev.*, vol. 52 (October 1978).

BB147 Ens, Adolf. "The Relations of the Western Canadian Mennonites to the Government." Diss., Univ. of Ottawa, 1975.

BB148 Epp, Frank H. "An Analysis of Germanism and National Socialism in the Immigrant Newspaper of a Canadian Minority Group, the Mennonites, in the 1930's." Diss., Univ. of Minnesota School of Journalism, 1965.

BB149 Epp, Frank H. *Mennonite Exodus. The Rescue and Resettlement of the Russian Mennonites since the Communist Revolution.* Manitoba: J. W. Friesen & Sons, Ltd., Canad. Mennonite Relief and Immigration Council, 1962. 572p.

BB150 Epp, Frank H. "The Mennonite Experience in Canada." In: *Religion and Ethnicity.* Ed. Harold Coward and Leslie Kawamura. Waterloo, Ont.: Wilfrid Laurier Univ. Pr., for Calgary Inst. for the Humanities, 1978, p.21–36.

BB151 Epp, Frank H. "Mennonites in Canada." *German-Canad. Yearbook*, vol. 1 (1973), 141–43.

BB152 Epp, Frank H. *Mennonites in Canada, 1786–1920: The History of a Separate People.* Toronto: Macmillan, 1974. Rev. by J. S. Moir, *Church History*, vol. 44 (1975), 540; N. K. Clifford, *Mennonite Quar. Rev.*, vol. 49 (1975), 242–45; P. Yuzyk, *ibid.*, vol. 49 (1975), 246–47; A. Lapp, *ibid.*, vol. 49 (1975), 247–49; G. Friesen, *ibid.*, vol. 49 (1975), 249–50; V. C. Peters, *Canad. Hist. Rev.*, vol. 57 (1976), 198–99; J. C. Wenger, *Ind. Mag. of Hist.*, vol. 72 (1976), 168–70; by James C. Juhnke, *Jour. of Amer. Hist.*, vol. 63 (1976), 202–03; P. A. Conkin, *Amer. Hist. Rev.*, vol. 81, no. 5 (December 1976), 1282–83. In the main a chronicle and institutional history.

BB153 Epp, Frank H. "The Struggle for Recognition." In: Henry Poettcker and Rudy A. Regehr, eds. *Call to Faithfulness: Essays in Canadian Mennonite Studies.* Winnipeg, Man.: Canad. Mennonite Bible College, 1972.

BB154 Epp, Georg K. "Mennonitischer Sprachverein." *German-Canad. Yearbook*, vol. 3 (1976), 271–72.

BB155 Flint, Joanne. *The Mennonite Canadians.* Toronto: Van Nostrand-Reinhold, 1980. 64p.

BB156 "Förderung des deutschen Sprachgutes." *Der Nordwesten*, 15 November 1966. On the Mennonitischer Verein zur Pflege der deutschen Sprache.

BB157 Francis, E. K. "Mennonite Contributions to Canada's Middle West." *Mennonite Life*, vol. 4, no. 2 (1949), 21–23, 41.

BB158 Fretz, J. Winfield. *The Mennonites in Ontario.* 2nd ed., Waterloo, Ont.: Mennonite Hist. Soc. of Ontario, 1974. 43p.

BB159 Fretz, J. Winfield. "The Plain and Not-So-Plain Mennonites in Waterloo County, Ontario." *Mennonite Quar. Rev.*, vol. 51 (1977), 377–85.

BB160 Fretz, J. Winfield. "Recent Mennonite Community Buildings in Canada." *Mennonite Quar. Rev.*, vol. 18, no. 2 (1944), 5–21. Communities established by emigrants from Russia, 1923–1930.

BB161 Friesen, John W. "Characteristics of Mennonite Identity: A Survey of Mennonite and Non-Mennonite Views." *Canad. Ethnic St.*, vol. 3 (1971), 25–41.

BB162 Gingerich, Orland. *The Amish of Canada.* Waterloo: Conrad Pr., 1972. Rev. by Melvin Gingerich, *Mennonite Quar. Rev.*, vol. 49 (1975), 71–72.

BB163 Hege, Christian. "Die Anfänge unserer Ansiedlungen in Kanada: Vor 153 Jahren wanderten die ersten Mennoniten in Kanada ein." *Mennonitische Geschichtsblätter* (Weierhof, Pfalz), vol. 4 (1943), 54f.

BB164 Hildebrand, J. J. *Aus der Vorgeschichte der Einwanderung der Mennoniten aus Russland nach Manitoba.* Winnipeg, Man.: n.p., 1949. 136p.

BB165 Hildebrand, J. J. *Chronologische Zeittafel*. Winnipeg, Man.: n.p., 1945. Mennonites in Canada.

BB166 Janzen, Waldemar. *A Basic Educational Philosophy for Canadian Mennonite Bible College*. Winnipeg, Man.: Canad. Mennonite Bible College, 1966. 15p.

BB167 Klassen, Abram J., ed. *The Bible School Story: 1913–1963*. N.p.: Board of Education of the Canad. Conference of the Mennonite Brethren Church, n.d. 19p.

BB168 Klassen, Isaak. *Dem Herrn die Ehre; Schönwieser Mennoniten-Gemeinde von Manitoba, 1924–1968*. Altona, Man.: D. W. Friesen & Sons, 1969. 150p. First Mennonite Church, Winnipeg.

BB169 Klippenstein, Lawrence, ed. *In Quest of Brothers: A Yearbook Commemorating 25 Years of Life Together in the Conference of Mennonites in Manitoba, 1946–1971*. Winnipeg, Man.: Conference of Mennonites in Manitoba, 1971.

BB170 Klippenstein, Lawrence, ed. *That There Be Peace: Mennonites in Canada and World War II*. Winnipeg, Man.: Mennonite Heritage Center, 1979. 104p.

BB171 Klippenstein, Lawrence, and Julius G. Toews, eds. *Manitoba Mennonite Memories*. Altona/Steinbach, Man.: Centennial Committee, 1974. 335p.

BB172 Krahn, Cornelius. "From Bergthal to Manitoba." *Mennonite Life*, vol. 12 (1957), 84–85. Migration of a Mennonite colony from the Black Sea to Canada.

BB173 Lohrenz, Gerhard. *Heritage Remembered*. Winnipeg, Man.: CMBC Publications, 1974.

BB174 Lohrenz, Gerhard. "The Johann Bartsch Monument: From Russia to Canada." *Mennonite Life*, vol. 24, no. 1 (January 1969), 29–30.

BB175 Mage, Julius, and Robert Murdie. "The Mennonites of Waterloo County." *Canad. Geographical Jour.*, vol. 80, no. 1 (January 1970), 10–17.

BB176 Martens, Hildegard M. *Mennonites from Mexico: Their Immigration and Settlement in Canada*. Ottawa: Canada Manpower and Immigration, 1975. 134p. Old Colony Mennonites who left Canada in 1922 and returned recently.

BB177 Moyer, Bill. *This Unique Heritage*. Kitchener, Ont.: CHYM Radio, 1971. On the Mennonites.

BB178 Murdie, R. A. "The Mennonite Communities of Waterloo County." In: *The Waterloo County Area: Selected Geographical Essays*. Ed. A. G. McLelland. Waterloo: Univ. of Waterloo, 1971, p.21–30.

BB179 Oberholz, Vera. "Westgate Mennonite Collegiate—Eine Schule mit besonderer Mission." *Der Nordwesten*, 28 June 1966.

BB180 Patterson, Nancy-Lou G. "The Dutch–German Mennonite Tradition in Waterloo County, Ontario." *Canad. Antiques*, vol. 2, no. 14 (1980–81), 29–32.

BB181 Patterson, Nancy-Lou G. "Green Santas, Plum Pudding and 'Spritzen'." *Canad. Collector*, vol. 16, no. 6 (1981), 29–33.

BB182 Patterson, Nancy-Lou G. "A Laboratory of Tradition: A Visit to an Old Order Mennonite Home in Waterloo County." *Canad. Collector*, vol. 16, no. 1 (1981), 32–34.

BB183 Peters, Victor. "Mennonitisches Schrifttum und Zeitungswesen in deutscher Sprache." *Mitteilungen des Instituts für Auslandsbeziehungen*, vol. 7 (1957), 183–84. Survey of publications in Canada.

BB184 Peters, Victor. "Schicksal und Leistung der Mennoniten in Kanada." *Mitteilungen des Instituts für Auslandsbeziehungen*, vol. 7 (1957), 165–68.

BB185 Poettcker, Henry, and Rudy A. Regehr. *Call to Faithfulness: Essays in Canadian Mennonite Studies*. Winnipeg, Man.: Canadian Mennonite Bible College, 1972.

BB186 Quiring, Walter, and Helen Bartel. *Mennonites in Canada. A Pictorial Review*. Altona, Man.: D. W. Friesen & Sons, 1961. 208p.

BB187 Regehr, Ted D. "Mennonites in Saskatoon: Some Early Occurrences." *Saskatoon Hist.*, vol. 2 (1981–82), 24–32.

BB188 Reimer, David P., ed. *Erfahrungen der Mennoniten in Canada während des Zweiten Weltkrieges*. Steinbach, Man.: Derksen Printers, 1947. 177p. Rev. by Harold S. Bender, *Mennonite Quar. Rev.*, vol. 25, no. 4 (1951), 323–24.

BB189 Rempel, J. G. *Jubiläums-Album der Konferenz der Mennoniten in Canada 1902–1952*. Rosthern, Sask.: n.p., 1952, 78p.

BB190 *The Sesquicentennial Jubilee (of the) Evangelical Mennonite Conference, 1812–1962*. Steinbach, Man.: The Evangelical Mennonite Conference, 1962. 194p.

BB191 Shelly, Andrew R. "The Mennonites of Ontario Today." *Mennonite Life*, vol. 5, no. 4 (1950), 17–26.

BB192 Shultz, Harold J. "Search for Utopia: The Exodus of Russian Mennonites to Canada, 1917–1927." *Jour. of Church and State*, vol. 11 (1969), 487–512.

BB193 Snyder, Peter. *Mennonite Country*. St. Jacobs, Ont.: Sand Hill Pr., 1978.

BB194 Stucky, Solomon. *The Heritage of the Swiss Volhynian Mennonites*. Waterloo, Ont.: Conrad Pr., 1981.

BB195 Thielman, George G. "Mennonites as an Ethnic Group in Relation to the Canadian State and Society." Diss., Western Reserve, 1954.

BB196 Thiessen, J. J. "Present Mennonite Immigration to Canada." *Mennonite Life*, vol. 4, no. 3 (1949), 33–36.

BB197 Thiessen, Paul, David Hunsberger et al. *People Apart: Portrait of a Mennonite World in Waterloo County*, Ontario. St. Jacobs: Sand Hill Pr., 1977.

BB198 Thiessen, Peter. "The Mennonites and Participation in Politics." M. A. thesis, Univ. of Manitoba, 1963.

BB199 Toews, A. P. *The Mennonite Church of Manitoba*. Rosenort, Man: Lark Printing, 1974.

BB200 Toews, John. "Russian Mennonites in Canada: Some Background Aspects." *Canad. Ethnic St.*, vol. 2, no. 2 (December 1970), 117–46.

BB201 Wagner, Jonathan F. "Transferred Crisis: German Volkish Thought among Russian Mennonite Immigrants to Western Canada." *Canad. Rev. of Studies in Nationalism*, vol. 1, no. 1 (1973).

The German Language in Canada

BB202 Auburger, Leopold. "Zur Sprache kanadadeutscher Zeitungstexte: Zusammenfassung der Forschungsergebnisse von Helga Wacker." In: *Deutsch als Muttersprache in Kanada: Berichte zur Gegenwartslage*. Ed. L. Auburger, H. Kloss, and H. Rupp. Wiesbaden: Steiner, 1977, p. 149–56.

BB203 Auburger, Leopold, Heinz Kloss, and Heinz Rupp, eds. *Deutsch als Muttersprache in Kanada. Berichte zur Gegenwartslage*. Wiesbaden: Steiner, 1977. 175p. Contributions by W. Bausenhart, K. H. Bongart, C. von Cardinal et al.

BB204 Barz, Sabine. "Viele Deutsche sind ihrer Sprache untreu." *Zeitschrift für Kulturaustausch*, vol. 16 (1966): 51f. Repr. from the Winnipeg *Courier*, 3 December 1964.

BB205 Bausenhart, Werner A. "The Attitudes and Motivation of German Language School Children in Canada." *Word*, vol. 27 (1971), 342–52.

BB206 Bausenhart, Werner A. "Deutsch in Ontario, I. Toronto and Ottawa, Deutsch bei den Mennoniten." In: *Deutsch als Muttersprache in Kanada: Berichte zur Gegenwartslage*. Ed. Leopold Auburger, H. Kloss, and H. Rupp. Wiesbaden: Steiner, 1977, p. 15–24.

BB207 Bausenhart, Werner A. "Lehrfach Deutsch an Ontarios Oberschulen." *Canad.-German Yearbook*, vol. 6 (1981), 178–82.

BB208 Bongart, Klaus. "Deutsch in Ontario. II. Deutsche Sprache und Kultur in Kitchener-Waterloo." In: *Deutsch als Muttersprache in Kanada: Berichte zur Gegenwartslage*. Ed. Leopold Auburger, H. Kloss and H. Rupp. Wiesbaden: Steiner, 1977, p. 25–32.

BB209 Chambers, J. K., ed. *The Languages of Canada*. Montreal: Didier, 1979. 263p.

BB210 Hadley, Michael L. "Die deutsche Sprache in Britisch-Kolumbien." In: *Deutsch als Muttersprache in Kanada: Berichte zur Gegenwartslage.* Ed. Leopold Auburger, H. Kloss and H. Rupp. Wiesbaden: Steiner, 1977, p.47–49.

BB211 Heeb, K. "Deutsche Sprachschulen in Kanada." *Der Nordwesten* (Winnipeg), 28 October 1969, 8.

BB212 Kloss, Heinz. "Deutsche katholische Kirchengemeinden." In: *Deutsch als Muttersprache in Kanada: Berichte zur Gegenwartslage.* Ed. Leopold Auburger, H. Kloss and H. Rupp. Wiesbaden: Steiner, 1977, p.121–23.

BB213 Lermer, Artur. "Yiddish in Canada." *Zukunft*, vol. 78 (1972), 177–81. In Yiddish.

BB214 Nabert, Kurt. "Deutsch in Ontario. III: Über einige deutsche Dialekte." In: *Deutsch als Muttersprache in Kanada: Berichte zur Gegenwartslage.* Ed. Leopold Auburger, H. Kloss and H. Rupp. Wiesbaden Steiner, 1977, p.33–37.

BB215 O'Bryan, K. G., J. G. Reitz, and O. M. Kuplowska. *Non-Official Languages: A Study in Canadian Multiculturalism.* Ottawa: Secretary of State, 1977.

BB216 Oesen, Anna von. "Sprache und Heimat." *German-Canad. Yearbook*, vol. 3 (1976), 66–70.

BB217 Peters, G. H. "Mennonitischer Verein deutscher Sprache." *Mitteilungen des Instituts für Auslandsbeziehungen*, vol. 7 (1957), 187. An organization for the preservation of the German language in Winnipeg.

BB218 Peters, Victor. "Die Hutterer." In: *Deutsch als Muttersprache in Kanada: Berichte zur Gegenwartslage.* Ed. Leopold Auburger, H. Kloss and H. Rupp. Wiesbaden: Steiner, 1977, p.125–28.

BB219 Scheer, Herfried W. "Deutsche Sprache und deutsche Kultur in der Provinz Quebec: Ein Überblick über die Geschichte des Deutschtums in Quebec." In: *Deutsch als Muttersprache in Kanada: Berichte zur Gegenwartslage.* Ed. Leopold Auburger, H. Kloss and H. Rupp. Wiesbaden: Steiner, 1977, p.7–13.

BB220 Scheer, Herfried W. "Der Fremdsprachliche Unterricht: Quebec." In: *Deutsch als Muttersprache in Kanada: Berichte zur Gegenwartslage.* Ed. Leopold Auburger, H. Kloss and H. Rupp. Wiesbaden: Steiner, 1977, p.103–06.

BB221 Scheer, Herfried W. "Die Mundart der hutterischen Brüder: Ein sprachgeschichtliches Denkmal aus dem 16. und 18. Jahrhundert." In: *Deutsch als Muttersprache in Kanada: Berichte zur Gegenwartslage.* Ed. Leopold Auburger, H. Kloss and H. Rupp. Wiesbaden: Steiner, 1977, p.133–37.

BB222 Skeries, F. W. "Deutsche Kultur- und Sprachpolitik in Kanada, aus der Sicht eines davon Betroffenen." *Auslands-Kurier*, vol. 10 (1969), 12.

BB223 Skeries F. W. "Deutsche Sprachschulen in Kanada." *Torontoer Zeitung*, 5 January 1968, 9.

BB224 Thiessen, John. "Deutsch in den Prärieprovinzen." In: *Deutsch als Muttersprache in Kanada: Berichte zur Gegenwartslage.* Ed. Leopold Auburger, H. Kloss and H. Rupp. Wiesbaden: Steiner, 1977, p.39–46.

BB225 Thiessen, John. "Deutschunterricht in den Prärieprovinzen." In: *Deutsch als Muttersprache in Kanada: Berichte zur Gegenwartslage.* Ed. Leopold Auburger, H. Kloss and H. Rupp. Wiesbaden: Steiner, 1977, p.93–96.

BB226 Thiessen, John. *Yiddish in Kanada.* Bochum: Leer, 1973.

BB227 Wiebe, H. "Der deutsche Sprachunterricht unter den Mennoniten Kanadas." *Auslands-Kurier*, vol. 8, no. 3 (1967), 21f.

BB228 Wieden, Fritz. "Der muttersprachliche Deutschunterricht." In: *Deutsch als Muttersprache in Kanada: Berichte zur Gegenwartslage.* Ed. Leopold Auburger, H. Kloss and H. Rupp. Wiesbaden: Steiner, 1977, p.91–92.

The German Press and the Media

BB229 Bell, F. "Canada's Foreign Language Press Bridges the Old World and the New." *Canadian*

The German Press and the Media *(cont.)*

Business (Montreal), vol. 31 (April 1958), 130–34, 136.

BB230 "Bibliography of the History of the Canadian Press." *Canad. Hist. Rev.* (Toronto), vol. 22 (December 1941), 416–33.

BB231 Boeschenstein, Hermann. "Das Studium der deutschkanadischen Presse: Ein fruchtbares Arbeitsfeld." *German-Canad. Yearbook*, vol. 1 (1973), 41–46.

BB232 Bowling, Joyce, and M. H. Hykawy, eds. *The Multilingual Press in Manitoba.* Forew. by H. H. Roeder. Winnipeg: Canada Press Club, 1974. 248p.

BB233 The Canadian Newspaper Directory. *A Complete List of Newspapers and Periodicals Published in the Dominion of Canada....* Montreal: A. McKim & Co., Ltd. no. 1, 1892–. (Title varies: *McKim's Directory of Canadian Publications*, 1929–.)

BB234 Central Press Agency, Ltd., Toronto. *Directory of Canadian Newspapers for 1900: Being a Catalogue of all Newspapers and Periodicals Published in Canada and Newfoundland.* Toronto: The Central Press Agency, Ltd., 1900. 290p.

BB235 Debor, H. W. "Die erste deutschsprachige Zeitschrift in Kanada." *Der Nordwesten* (Winnipeg), 22 November 1966.

BB236 Drake, E. G. "Pioneer Journalism in Saskatchewan." *Saskatchewan Hist.*, vol. 5 (1952–53), 17–27, 41–54.

BB237 Duff, Louis Blake. "The Journey of the Printing Press across Canada." *Gutenberg-Jahrbuch* (Leipzig), 1937, 228–38.

BB238 Entz, Werner. "Die deutschsprachige Presse Westkanadas: Ihr Inhalt und ihre Sprache." *Seminar*, vol. 3, no. 1 (1967), 37–52.

BB239 Entz, Werner. "Der Einfluss der deutschsprachigen Presse Westkanadas auf die Organisationsbestrebungen des dortigen Deutschtums 1889–1939." *German-Canad. Yearbook*, vol. 2 (1975), 92–138.

BB240 Entz, Werner. "German Language Newspapers of Manitoba before World War I." *Canad. Ethnic St.*, vol. 2, no. 2 (December 1970), 59–66.

BB241 Entz, Werner. "120 Jahre Deutschkanadische Presse." *Mitteilungen des Instituts für Auslandsbeziehungen*, vol. 7 (1957), 175–82. Historical account covering the period from 1835 to the present.

BB242 Kalbfleisch, Herbert Karl. "Among the Editors of Ontario German Newspapers, 1835–1918." *Canad.-German Folklore*, vol. 1 (1961), 78–85.

BB243 Kalbfleisch, Herbert Karl. "The Early German Newspapers of Eastern Canada." *Seminar*, vol. 3, no. 1 (Spring 1967), 21–36.

BB244 Kalbfleisch, Herbert Karl. "German Literature as Represented in Two German Newspapers of Ontario, Canada." *Ky. For. Lang. Quar.*, vol. 3 (1956), 184–91.

BB245 Kalbfleisch, Herbert Karl. *The History of the German Language Press of Ontario, 1835–1918.* Toronto: Univ. of Toronto Pr.; Münster, 1968. 133p. Cf. his "The History of the German Newspapers of Ontario, Canada, 1835–1918." Diss., Michigan 1953. Rev. by W. Bausenhart, *Seminar*, vol. 6, no. 2 (1969), 182–83. On the rise and eventual disappearance of approximately thirty German-language weekly newspapers.

BB246 Kalbfleisch, Herbert Karl. "Kanadische Zeitungen und Zeitschriften in deutscher Sprache." *Mitteilungen des Instituts für Auslandsbeziehungen*, vol. 7 (1957), 183.

BB247 Kirschbaum, J. M. et al., eds. *Twenty Years of the Ethnic Press Association of Ontario.* Toronto: n.p., 1971.

BB248 Leibbrandt, Gottlieb. "Deutschsprachiges Fernsehen in Kitchener-Waterloo." *German-Canad. Yearbook*, vol. 2 (1975), 287–89.

BB249 MacDonald, Christine. *Historical Directory of Saskatchewan Newspapers, 1878–1950.* Saskatoon Sas.: Office of Univ. of Saskatchewan Archives Division, 1951.

BB250 McLaren, Duncan, comp. *Ontario Ethno-Cultural Newspapers, 1835–1972.* Toronto: Univ. of Toronto Pr., 1974. 256p.

BB251 Robert, M. "Everything that's Fit to Print in Every Language Fit to Read." *Maclean's Mag.* (Toronto), vol. 73 (18 June 1960), 24–25, 54–57.

BB252 Rojek, Hans-Jürgen. "Die deutschsprachige Presse in Kanada." In: *Deutsche Presse im Ausland*. Düsseldorf: Ostdeutscher Kulturrat, 1972, p.10–12.

BB253 "Role of the Ethnic Press." *Canadian Business* (Montreal), vol. 33 (1960), 35.

BB254 Serge, Joe. "A German Paper, 20, Fights for Life." *Toronto Star*, 22 August 1973.

BB255 Taubert, Sigfred. "Die frühesten deutschen Drucker in Kanada." *Imprimatur*, vol. 12 (1954–55), 223–25; also *Börsenblatt für den deutschen Buchhandel*, Frankfurter Ausgabe, no. 382 (1956), 649–50. Trans. in *German-Canad. Yearbook*, vol. 1 (1973), 71–75.

BB256 Tremaine, Marie. *Bibliography of Canadian Imprints*. Toronto: n.p., 1952.

BB257 Wieden, Fritz. "Die deutschkanadische Presse seit dem Ende des zweiten Weltkriegs." In: *Deutsch als Muttersprache in Kanada: Berichte zur Gegenwartslage*. Ed. Leopold Auburger, H. Kloss and H. Rupp. Wiesbaden: Steiner, 1977, p.59–64.

BB258 Wieden, Fritz. "Deutschsprachige Rundfunk- und Fernsehsendungen in Kanada." In *Deutsch als Muttersprache in Kanada: Berichte zur Gegenwartslage*. Ed. Leopold Auburger, H. Kloss and H. Rupp. Wiesbaden: Steiner, 1977, p.65–67.

The Arts/Music/Literary Life

See also Part F: Fine Arts, Architecture and Decorative Arts *and* Part G: Music and the Performing Arts.

BB259 Beaudoin, Emile. "Cercle Goethe, Inc., Québec: 25 Ans Rétrospection 1946–1971." *German-Canad. Yearbook*, vol. 5 (1979), 242–45.

BB260 Cardinal, Clive H. von. "Begegnung mit dem deutschen Gedicht." In *Deutsch als Muttersprache in Kanada: Berichte zur Gegenwartslage*. Ed. Leopold Auburger, H. Kloss and H. Rupp. Wiesbaden: Steiner, 1977, p.77–82.

BB261 Cardinal, Clive H. von. "A German-Canadian Painter of Eskimo Life." *Canad. Ethnic St.*, vol. 1, no. 2 (1969). Repr. *German-Canad. Yearbook*, vol. 2 (1975), 181–84. On Mario von Brentani.

BB262 Cardinal, Clive H. von. "Das kulturelle Leben der Kanadier deutscher und ukrainischer Herkunft." *German-Canad. Yearbook*, vol. 1 (1973), 53–66.

BB263 Epp, Georg K., ed. *Harvest: Anthology of Mennonite Writing in Canada, 1874–1974*. Altona, Man.: Centennial Committee of the Mennonite Hist. Soc. of the Midwest, 1974.

BB264 Epp, Georg K., ed. "Unter dem Nordlicht." *Anthologie des deutschen Schrifttums der Mennoniten in Kanada*. Winnipeg: Mennonite German Soc. of Canada, 1977. 292p. Also as: *Unter dem Nordlicht: Anthology of German Mennonite Writing in Canada*. Altona, Man.: D. W. Friesen, 1977.

BB265 Froeschle, Hartmut. "Gibt es eine deutschkanadische Literatur?" *German-Canad. Yearbook*, vol. 3 (1976), 174–87.

BB266 Geiger-Torel, Hermann. "Canada—An Operatic Desert?" *German-Canad. Yearbook*, vol. 2 (1975), 145–51. Brief mention of leading Germans.

BB267 Junker, Wolfgang. "Kulturarbeit ohne Maske und Make-Up: Der 'Deutsch-Kanadische Kulturkreis' unter der Leitung von Eva Kastens." *German-Canad. Yearbook*, vol. 2 (1975), 265–70.

BB268 Kallmann, Helmut. "Der deutsche Beitrag zum Musikleben Kanadas." *Mitteilungen des Instituts für Auslandsbeziehungen*, vol. 7, no. 3 (1957). Trans. as "The German Contribution to Music in Canada." *German-Canad. Yearbook*, vol. 2 (1975), 152–66.

BB269 Priestly, Tom M. S., ed. *Proceedings of the First Banff Conference on Central and East European Studies*. Edmonton: CEESAA, 1977. 40+523p. On the role of Germanistic studies in Canada.

BB270 Riedel, Walter, ed. *Kanada*. Introd. by Walter Riedel. Stuttgart: Erdmann, 1976. 416p. In the series *Moderne Erzähler der Welt*, pub-

The Arts/Music/Literary Life *(cont.)*
lished by the Institut für Auslandsbeziehungen, Stuttgart. Anthology of Canadian writings.

BB271 Rinck, Daniel A. "The 'German-Canadian Council for the Arts'." *German-Canad. Yearbook*, vol. 1 (1973), 287–90.

BB272 Scheer, Herfried W. et al. "Deutschsprachige Theatergruppen in Kanada." In: *Deutsch als Muttersprache in Kanada: Berichte zur Gegenwartslage*. Ed. Leopold Auburger, H. Kloss and H. Rupp. Wiesbaden: Steiner, 1977 p.85–90.

BB273 Sturm, E. "Toronto und das deutsche Theaterleben der Nachkriegsjahre." *German-Canad. Yearbook*, vol. 3 (1976), 225–33.

BB274 Thiessen, Jack. *Es war einmal...Once Upon a Time....* Manitoba: German-Canad. Centennial Committee, 1967. 24p. A work for juveniles on the subject of the *Märchen*; in two languages. Incl. etchings by J. W. Grimm.

Canadian German History— Revolutionary Era

See also Section IC: Revolutionary War Era.

BB275 Canada. Loyalist Claims. *Second Report of the Bureau of Archives for the Province of Ontario*. Toronto, 1904. References to Barbara Heck, Methodist leader.

BB276 Cooper, John Irwin. "Three German Military Officers and Canada." *German-Canad. Yearbook*, vol. 4 (1978), 57–62. Baron Jean-Armand Dieskau, in French service on the New York frontier in 1755; Baron Francis de Rottenburg, an officer in King George's "Foreign Regiment" and Commander in Chief in Upper Canada in 1813; and George de Rottenburg, in service with the militia in the mid-nineteenth century.

BB277 Debor, Herbert Wilhelm. "German Soldiers of the American War of Independence as Settlers in Canada." *German-Canad. Yearbook*, vol. 3 (1976), 71–93.

BB278 Fryer, Mary Beacock. *Loyalist Spy. Brockville*. N.p.: Besancourt Publs., 1974.

BB279 Gradish, Stephen. "The German Mercenaries in Canada, 1776–1791." M.A. thesis, Univ. of Western Ontario, 1960.

BB280 Grimsby Hist. Soc., Grimsby, Ont. *Annals of the Forty No. 3. Loyalist and Pioneer Family of West Lincoln 1783–1833*. Comp. by R. Janet Powell. Grimsby: Grimsby Hist. Soc., 1952. Repr. 1963.

BB281 Larter, Harry C., Jr. "German Troops with Burgoyne, 1776–1777." *Bull. of the Fort Ticonderoga Museum*, vol. 9, no. 1 (1952), 13–24. German units operating from Canada early in the Revolutionary War.

BB282 Parkman, F. "Dieskau." In: *Montcalm and Wolfe*, by F. Parkman. Boston: n.p., 1925, vol. 1, chap. 9. On Baron Ludwig August Dieskau, British commander in Lake George engagement, French and Indian War, 1755.

BB283 Riedesel, Fritz, Frhr. zu Eisenbach. "Message to all People of German Descent in Canada—September 1974." *German-Canad. Yearbook*, vol. 2 (1975), 2–5.

BB284 Seume, Johann G. "Der Wilde." *German-Canad. Yearbook*, vol. 1 (1973), 183–85.

BB285 Seume, Johann G. "Mein Aufenthalt in Kanada." *German-Canad. Yearbook*, vol. 1 (1973), 167–81.

Canadian German History— World War I

See also 1900–1920: The Era of World War I *under* Section IH: The Twentieth Century.

BB286 Boudreau, Joseph Amedée. "The Enemy Alien Problem in Canada, 1914–1921." Diss., Univ. Calif. at Los Angeles, 1965. 218p.

BB287 Heick, Wolf H. "The Lutherans of Waterloo County during World War I." In: *Waterloo Historical Society. 50th Annual Volume, 1962*. Waterloo: the Soc., 1963, p.23–32. Discussion of the tensions caused by German ancestry.

BB288 Hertzman, Lewis. "'A Kind of Hungary': The Kaiser Looks at Canada." *German-Canad. Yearbook*, vol. 5 (1979), 66–76. German views of Canada's role in the British defense system.

BB289 Lefcourt, Charles R. "A Rose by Any Other Name: Ethnic Conflict in Berlin, Ontario." *Keystone Folklore Quar.*, vol. 12, no. 2 (Summer 1967), 119–26. Antagonism toward Germans during World War I.

BB290 Teichroew, Allen. "World War I and the Mennonite Migration to Canada to Avoid the Draft." *Mennonite Quar. Rev.*, vol. 45 (1971), 219–49.

BB291 "War and Patriotism: The Lusitania Riot." *British Columbia Hist. News*, vol. 5, no. 1 (1971), 15–23. In Victoria, B.C., May 1915.

German Canadian Biography

ALVENSLEBEN, GUSTAV K. A. VON

BB292 Laue, Ingrid E. "Gustav Konstantin Alvo von Alvensleben (1879–1965): Ein Lebensbild." *German-Canad. Yearbook*, vol. 5 (1979), 154–73. Immigrant businessman and speculator in Vancouver.

ARNOLDI, JOHANN DANIEL

BB293 Weissenborn, Georg K. "Johann Daniel Arnoldi. The Pioneer Doctor of Lower Canada (1774–1849)." *German-Canad. Yearbook*, vol. 4 (1978), 254–56.

BECK, ADAM

BB294 Weissenborn, Georg K. "Adam Beck: The Human Dynamo (1857–1925)." *German-Canad. Yearbook*, vol. 3 (1976), 234–36. Founder of the Ontario Hydro.

BERCZY, WILLIAM BENT

BB295 Andre, John. "William Bent Berczy (1791–1873)." *German-Canad. Yearbook*, vol. 2 (1975), 167–80.

BB296 Andre, John. *William Berczy, Co-Founder of Toronto*. Toronto: Borough of York, 1967. 168p.

BB297 Burns, Florence M. *William Berczy*. Toronto: Fitzhenry and Whiteside, 1977. 64p.

BB298 Lawrence, A. B. *German-Canad. Yearbook*, vol. 2 (1976), 1–8. Speech delivered at the ceremony attendant on the unveiling of a plaque in commemoration of William Berczy.

BB299 Reaman, G. Elmore. "The Diary of a German on His Way to Upper Canada." *Amer.-German Rev.*, vol. 19, no. 5 (1953), 27–29. Germans under the leadership of a Saxon, William Berczy, settled near Toronto in 1792.

BOESCHENSTEIN, HERMANN

BB300 Boeschenstein, Hermann. *Im Roten Ochsen. Geschichte einer Heimkehr*. Schaffhausen: Meier, 1977. 231p.

DIESKAU, JEAN-ARMAND

BB301 Turnbull, J. R. "Dieskau, Jean-Armand (Ludwig August), baron de." *Dict. of Canad. Biography*, vol. 3, 185–86. On D. (1701–1767).

DYCK, ANNA R.

BB302 Dyck, Anna R. *Anna from the Caucasus to Canada*. Trans. by Peter J. Klassen. Hillsboro, Kan.: Mennonite Brethren Publ. House, 1979. 216p.

EISENHAUER FAMILY

BB303 Macdonald, Elizabeth. "The Three Brothers." *Atlantic Advocate*, vol. 59, no. 12 (August 1969), 42–53. On the Eisenhauers of Lunenburg, N.S.

FERNOW, BERNHARD EDOUARD

BB304 Stuart, E. R. "Bernhard Fernow, First Forestry Dean, Left Lasting Legacy." *Forest Scene* (Toronto), vol. 10, no. 1 (1979). Repr. *German-Canad. Yearbook*, vol. 5 (1979), 174–76. F. (1851–1923) was a native of Posen, Prussia; educated at Königsberg. He emigrated to the U.S. in 1876 and served from 1886 to 1898 as chief of the Div. of Forestry, U.S. Department of Agriculture. Moved to the Univ. of Toronto in 1907.

FUNCKEN, EUGEN

BB305 Spetz, Theobald. In: *The Catholic Church in Waterloo County*. Hamilton: The Catholic Register and Extension, 1916, p. 26–35. Biography of Eugen Funcken.

HALDIMAND, GEN. SIR FREDERICK

BB306 Luethy, Ivor C. E. "General Sir Frederick Haldimand: A Swiss Governor-General of Canada (1777–1786)." *Canad. Ethnic St.*, vol. 3 (June 1971), 63–75.

HAMM, MARTIN

BB307 Hamm, Martin. *Aus der alten in die neue Heimat: Lebensgeschichte eines schlichten Mennoniten.* Winnipeg: Christian Pr., 1971.

HARTZSCH, BERNHARD

BB308 Neatby, Leslie. "Hartzsch of Baffin Island." *Beaver.* Winter 1975, 4–13. Bernhard Hartzsch, German scientist and arctic explorer.

HECK, BARBARA

BB309 Lapp, Eula C. *To Their Heirs Forever.* Picton: Picton Gazette Publ. Co., Ltd., 1970. Incl. information on Barbara Heck (b. 1744).

BB310 Leavitt, Thad, and W. H. Leavitt. *History of Leeds and Grenville.* Brockville: Recorder Pr., 1879. Also in: *Canadiana.* Repr. no. 14. Belleville: n.p., 1972. Deals with Barbara Heck, Methodist leader.

HELLMUTH, ISAAC

BB311 Crowfoot, A. H. *This Dreamer: Life of Isaac Hellmuth, Second Bishop of Huron.* Toronto: Copp Clark Publ. Co., 1963. 86p. H. (1817–1901) was bishop of the Anglican Church; b. near Warsaw, Poland, of Jewish parents; educated at Breslau; ordained at Quebec.

HELMCKEN, JOHN SEBASTIAN

BB312 Helmcken, John Sebastian. *The Reminiscences of Doctor John Sebastian Helmcken.* Ed. by Dorothy Blakey Smith. Vancouver: Univ. of British Columbia Pr., 1975. Rev. by W. Riedel, *German-Canad. Yearbook*, vol. 4 (1978), 363–64. Surgeon and legislator in British Columbia, born in England of parents of German descent.

BB313 Riedel, Walter E. "John Sebastian Helmcken: Pioneer Surgeon and Legislator (1824–1920)." *German-Canad. Yearbook*, vol. 4 (1978), 250–53.

HERZBERG, GERHARD

BB314 Stokes, Lawrence D. "Canada and an Academic Refugee from Nazi Germany: The Case of Gerhard Herzberg." *Canad. Hist. Rev.*, vol. 57 (June 1976), 150–70.

HESPELER, WILHELM

BB315 Entz, Werner. "Wilhelm Hespeler, Britischer Parlamentarier aus Baden." *Mitteilungen des Instituts für Auslandsbeziehungen*, vol. 7 (1957), 171–72. William Hespeler, speaker of the Manitoba Parliament from 1900–1904.

BB316 Entz, Werner. "William Hespeler: Manitoba's First German Consul." Trans. by Daniel A. Rinck. *German-Canad. Yearbook*, vol. 1 (1973), 149–52.

JACOBS, SAMUEL

BB317 Jacobs, Samuel. Papers, 1759–1786. 8 reels. In American Jewish Archives, Cincinnati, copied from originals in the Public Archives of Canada, Ottawa (MS 65-1727). J. was a merchant of Montreal, Quebec, and St. Denis. Microfilmed accounts, business papers, diary, correspondence.

LAND, ROBERT

BB318 Gruppe, H.R.G. "War Robert Land ein Deutscher?" *Der Nordwesten*, 29 November 1966. Reply to statements printed in the *Nordwesten*, 8 November.

BB319 "Rätsel um Robert Land, Hamiltons ersten Siedler." *Der Nordwesten*, 8 November 1966.

LOHRENZ, GERHARD

BB320 Lohrenz, Gerhard. *Lose Blätter. 3. Teil.* Winnipeg, Man.: n.p., 1976. 168p. Memoirs and experiences; descriptions of events in the Soviet Union and World War II. Parts 1 and 2 appeared in 1974.

BB321 Lohrenz, Gerhard. *Storm Tossed: The Personal Story of a Canadian Mennonite from Russia.* Winnipeg, Man.: n.p., 1976.

MEYER, AUGUST FREDERICK

BB322 Croil, James Dundas. In: *A Sketch of Canadian History.* Montreal: n.p., 1861, p. 252–253. Repr. Belleville, Ont.: n.p., 1972.

MOSCHELL, JOHANN ADAM

BB323 Sautter, Udo. "Ein deutscher Geistlicher in Neuschottland: Johann Adam Moschell (1795–

1849)." *German-Canad. Yearbook*, vol. 1 (1973), 153–59.

NORDEGG, MARTIN

BB324 Cardinal, Clive H. von. "A Note on Martin Nordegg (1868–1948)." *German-Canad. Yearbook*, vol. 4 (1978), 246–49.

POHLE FAMILY

BB325 Pohle, Adella. *Pioneering in Two Worlds: The Life of Carl and Adella Pohle*. Vancouver, B.C.: n.p., 1974. 236p.

REESOR, THOMAS

BB326 Burkholder, Paul H. "Thomas Reesor (1867–1954)." *Canad.-German Folklore* (Pa. Folklore Soc. of Ontario), vol. 1 (1961), 137–38.

RITTINGER, JOHN A.

BB327 Kalbfleisch, Herbert Karl. "John A. Rittinger." *Amer.-German Rev.*, vol. 23, no. 6 (1957), 18–20. German-Canadian newspaperman of the Ontario *Glocke*, 1844–1915.

SCHILLING, EDITH VON

BB328 Wagner, Jonathan, ed. and introd. "Baronin Dr. Edith von Schilling. 'Deutsche Siedler in Nord-Saskatchewan'." *German-Canad. Yearbook*, vol. 4 (1978), 257–65. Dr. von Schilling emigrated to Canada in 1929. This essay relates the experiences of a group of 19 German families of the Loon River settlement, Saskatchewan, as they returned to Nazi Germany in 1939.

SCHWERDTFEGER, SAMUEL

BB329 Weissenborn, Georg K. "Samuel Schwerdtfeger: The Saint of the St. Lawrence Seaway (1734–1803)." *German-Canad. Yearbook*, vol. 2 (1975), 189–92. First Lutheran minister in Ontario.

SHANTZ, JACOB F.

BB330 Gingerich, Melvin. "Jacob F. Shantz, 1822–1909, Promoter of the Mennonite Settlements in Manitoba." *Mennonite Quar. Rev.*, vol. 24, no. 3 (1950), 230–47.

STEEVE/STIEF FAMILY

BB331 Wright, Esther Clark. *Samphire Greens*. Ottawa: n.p., 1961. 109p. The Steeves, or Stiefs, in New Brunswick history. Heinrich Stief, settler from Pennsylvania, came with seven sons to the Peticodiac River in 1766.

TOEWS, DAVID

BB332 Schellenberg, D. J. "A Moses of Our Day—David Toews." *Mennonite Life*, vol. 5, no. 3 (1950), 6–9. Life of a Mennonite in Canada.

UNRUH, A. H.

BB333 Ewert, David. *Stalwart for the Truth: The Life and Legacy of A. H. Unruh*. Winnipeg, Man.: Mennonite Central Committee, 1974.

BB334 Toews, H. P. *A. H. Unruhs Lebensgeschichte*. Winnipeg, Man.: The Christian Pr., 1961. 110p.

ZIMMERMANN, SAMUEL

BB335 Geary, R. W. "Samuel Zimmermann 1815–1857." *Welland Co. Hist. Soc. Papers*, vol. 3 (1927), 47–57. Railroad entrepreneur.

BB336 Weissenborn, Georg K. "Samuel Zimmerman (1815–1857): The Foremost Man in the Niagara Peninsula." *German-Canad. Yearbook*, vol. 5 (1979), 177–80.

Local History

ALBERTA

BB337 Badke, Robert. Alte und neue deutsche Siedlungen um und in Edmonton." *Mitteilungen des Instituts für Auslandsbeziehungen*, vol. 7 (1957), 170–71.

BB338 Bargen, Peter F. "Mennonites Settle in Alberta: Mennonite Land Settlement Policies." *Mennonite Life*, vol. 15 (1960), 187–90.

BB339 Eberhardt, Elvire. "The Area of Origin of the Bessarabian Germans in Medicine Hat, Alberta." *German-Canad. Yearbook*, vol. 3 (1976), 207–10.

BB340 Eberhardt, Elvire. "The Growth of the German Population in Medicine Hat, Alberta from

Local History *(cont.)*
1884 to the Present." *German-Canad. Yearbook*, vol. 6 (1981), 62–65.

BB341 Evans, Simon M. "The Dispersal of Hutterite Colonies in Alberta, 1918–1976." M. A. Thesis, Univ. of Calgary, 1973.

BB342 Evans, Simon M. "Spatial Bias in the Incidence of Nativism: Opposition to Hutterite Expansion in Alberta." *Canad. Ethnic St.*, vol. 6 (1974), 1–16.

BB343 Hilda Town and Country Ladies Club. *Hilda's Golden Heritage*. Hilda, Alb.: n.p., 1974.

BB344 Kleim, Ottmar. *Deutsche in Kanada; eine empirische Orientierungsstudie über den Integrationsprozess der Mitglieder des deutschen Klubs in Calgary/Alta. im Vergleich zu den Führern der deutschen Klubs in ganz Kanada*. Diss. [Erlangen-Nürnberg]: n.p., ca. 1969. 434p.

BB345 Küster, Mathias. "Die Geschichte der 'Central and Eastern European Studies Society of Alberta (CEESSA)'." *German-Canad. Yearbook*, vol. 6 (1981), 264–73.

BB346 Laatsch, William G. "Hutterite Colonization in Alberta." *Jour. of Geography*, vol. 70 (1971), 347–59.

BB347 Levy, Joanne. "In Search of Isolation: The Holdeman Mennonites of Linder, Alberta and Their School." *Canad. Ethnic St.*, vol. 11 (1979), 115–30.

BB348 Macdonald, R. J. "Hutterite Education in Alberta: A Test Case in Assimilation, 1920–1970." In: *Western Canada: Past and Present*. Ed. A. W. Rasporovich. Calgary: McClelland & Stewart, 1975, p.133–99. Repr. *Canad. Ethnic St.*, vol. 3, no. 1 (1976), 9–21.

BB349 MacGregor, J. G. *A History of Alberta*. Edmonton: n.p., 1972.

BB350 Mackie, Marlene. "Ethnic Stereotypes and Prejudice—Alberta Indians, Hutterites and Ukrainians." *Canad. Ethnic St.*, vol. 1, nos. 1–2 (1974), 39–52.

BB351 Malycky, Alexander. "German-Albertans: A Bibliography, Part I." *German-Canad. Yearbook*, vol. 6 (1981), 311–44.

BB352 Palmer, Howard. "The Hutterite Land Expansion Controversy in Alberta." *Western Canad. Jour. of Anthropology*, vol. 2, no. 2 (1971), 18–46.

BB353 Palmer, Howard. *Land of the Second Chance: A History of Ethnic Groups in Southern Alberta*. Lethbridge, Alb.: Lethbridge Herald, 1972.

BB354 Palmer, Howard. "Responses to Foreign Immigration: Nativism and Ethnic Tolerance in Alberta, 1880–1920." M.A. thesis, Univ. of Alberta, 1971.

BB355 Sawatzky, Aron. "The Mennonite Community in Alberta." M.A. thesis, Univ. of Alberta, 1962.

BB356 Schultz, Earl L. "Education in the Bruderheim Area." *Alberta Hist.*, vol. 20, no. 4 (1972), 21–27.

BB357 Tierney, Ben. "Hutterites Uneasy: Alberta May Provoke Exodus." In: *Critical Issues in Canadian Society*. Ed. Craig Boydell, Carl Grindstaff and Paul Whitehead. Toronto: Holt, Rinehart & Winston, 1971.

BB358 Van Dyke, Edward W. "Blumenort: A Study of Persistence in a Sect." Diss., Univ. of Alberta, 1972. On the Mennonites.

BB359 Wekherlien, R.P., and P.G. Otke. "Position Paper of the German-Canadian Association of Alberta." *German-Canad. Yearbook*, vol. 3 (1976), 39–41.

BB360 Wekherlien, Robert P. "The German-Canadian Association of Alberta, Past and Present." *German-Canad. Yearbook*, vol. 4 (1978), 295–311.

BRITISH COLUMBIA

BB361 "Deutsche Kulturarbeit an der Kanadischen Westküste." *Zeitschrift für Kulturaustausch*, vol. 17 no. 2 (1967), 112f. Music, theater, and cultural organizations.

BB362 Friesach, Carl. "Ein Ausflug nach Britisch-Columbien im Jahre 1858." *Mitteilungen der Philosophischen Gesellschaft Gratz* (sic), 1875. Trans. by R.L. Reid: "Two Narratives of the Fraser River Gold Rush." *British Columbia Hist. Quar.*, vol. 5 (1941), 221–28.

BB363 Goerz, H. "Russian-Germans in British Columbia, Canada." Trans. by Theodor Bauer. *Heritage Review*, vol. 15 (1976), 19-21.

BB364 Goerz, H. "Russlanddeutsche in Britisch Columbien, Kanada." *Heimatbuch* 1963, 84-86.

BB365 Janzen, Adina, and Winnie Dueck, eds. *History of the British Columbia Mennonite Women in Mission, 1939-1976*. Chilliwack, B. C.: Mennonite Women in Mission, 1976.

BB366 Klippenstein, Lawrence. "Early Mennonites in British Columbia: Renata, 1907-1965." *Mennonite Historian*, vol. 7, no. 3 (1981), 1-2.

BB367 Krahn, John Jacob. "A History of the Mennonites in British Columbia." M. A. Thesis, Univ. of British Columbia, Vancouver, 1955.

BB368 Liddell, Peter. "The First Germans in British Columbia?" *German-Canad. Yearbook*, vol. 6 (1981), 74-77.

BB369 Liddell, Peter G. "Germans on Canada's Pacific Slopes: A Brief Survey of German Discovery, Settlement and Culture in British Columbia, 1778 to the Present." *Yearbook of German Amer. St.*, vol. 16 (1981), 51-58.

BB370 Martin, Horst. "The German Contribution to B.C. Culture: Tagung in Vancouver, B.C., März 1981." *Canadiana Germanica*, vol. 30 (1981), 11-13.

BB371 Norris, John. *Strangers Entertained: A History of the Ethnic Groups of British Columbia*. Vancouver: Evergreen Pr., 1971.

BB372 Peters, Gerhard I. *A History of the First Mennonite Church, Greendale, British Columbia*. Greendale, B.C.: First Mennonite Church, 1976, 93p.

BB373 Ramsey, Bruce. *A History of the Germans in British Columbia*. Winnipeg, Man. National Publs., Ltd., 1958. 69p. Contribution of the Vancouver Alpen Club towards British Columbia's Centennial Year.

BB374 Ramsey, Bruce. [Chapters on the Germans, Austrians and Swiss in western Canada.] In: *Strangers Entertained*. Ed. John Norris. Vancouver: n.p., 1971, p.98-110.

BB375 Ray, Margaret V. "Sudeten Settlements in Western Canada." M. A. Thesis, Toronto, 1949.

BB376 Schwermann, Albert H. "Life and Times of Emil E. Eberhardt, Pioneer Missionary of Alberta and British Columbia, 1870-1957." *Concordia Hist. Inst. Quar.*, vol. 34 (January 1961), 97f.

BB377 Siemens, Alfred. "Mennonite Settlement in the Lower Fraser Valley, British Columbia." M.A. thesis, British Columbia, 1961.

BB378 Siemens, Alfred. "Mennonites in the Fraser Valley." *Mennonite Life*, vol. 15 (1960), 102-06. Russian-German Mennonites in British Columbia since 1928.

MANITOBA

See also Mennonites and Amish Mennonites *under* Churches and Religious History, this section.

BB379 Arnaud Historical Committee. *Arnaud Through the Years*. Arnaud, Man.: n.p., 1974.

BB380 Brado, Edward. "Mennonites Enrich the Life of Manitoba." *Canad. Geographic Rev.*, vol. 99 (1979), 48-51.

BB381 Brown, Dorine, ed. *Pembina County*. Miami: Manitoba Museum, Inc., 1974.

BB382 Brown, Frank. *A History of Winkler*. Winkler, Man.: n.p., 1973.

BB383 Carlyle, William J. "Mennonite Agriculture in Manitoba." *Canad. Ethnic St.*, vol. 13 (1981), 73-97.

BB384 Chiel, Arthur A. *The Jews in Manitoba. A Social History*. Toronto: Univ. of Toronto Pr., 1961. 203p. Rev. by N. F. Cantor, *Publs., Amer. Jewish Hist. Soc.*, vol. 51, no. 2 (1961), 143-44.

BB385 Debor, H. W. "Deutsche an der Wiege Manitobas." *Der Nordwesten* 30 August 1966.

BB386 De Fehr, C. A. *Memories of My Life*. Altona, Man.: D. W. Friesen & Sons, 1967. 231p.

BB387 Deutsche Vereinigung von Winnipeg. *Mitteilungen*, 1968, 1971, etc. Ten issues a year. Publ. by Hansa Credit Union, Ltd., Winnipeg.

BB388 Evers, Fritz O. "Unterwegs." *Kirchliches Monatsblatt*, vol. 13 (1956), 42-43. On St. Peter's Church (German Lutheran) of Winnipeg.

BB389 Francis, E. K. *In Search of Utopia: the Mennonites in Manitoba.* Glencoe, Ill: Free Press, 1956. 294p. Rev. by W. Kirkconnell, *Canad. Hist. Rev.*, vol. 38 (1957), 60–61; J. W. Eaton, *Annals of the Amer. Acad. of Social and Political Science*, vol. 312 (1957), 170. Well-documented socio-historical study.

BB390 Francis, E. K. "Mennonite Institutions in Early Manitoba: A Study of Their Origins." *Agricultural Hist.*, vol. 22 (1948), 144–55.

BB391 Friesen, Abram. "Die Mennoniten Manitobas." *German-Canad. Yearbook*, vol. 3 (1976), 94–96.

BB392 Friesen, J. "Expansion of Settlement in Manitoba, 1870–1900." *Papers Read Before the Hist. and Scientific Soc. of Manitoba.* Series III, no. 20 (1963–1964), 35–47.

BB393 Friesen, Jim, and Reinhard Vogt. "The Mennonite Community in Winnipeg." *Mennonite Life*, vol. 19, no. 1 (1964), 13–15.

BB394 Friesen, W. *A Mennonite Community in the East Reserve—Its Origin and Growth.* Winnipeg, Man.: The Historical and Scientific Study of Manitoba, 1964.

BB395 *Fünfundzwanzig Jahre der mennonitischen Ansiedlung zu Nord-Kildonan 1928–1953.* North Kildonan, Man.: n.p., 1953, 71p.

BB396 Grenke, Arthur. "The Formation and Early Development of an Early Ethnic Community: A Case Study of the Germans in Winnipeg, 1872–1919." Diss., Manitoba, 1975.

BB397 Hildebrand, Menno. "The Sommerfeld Mennonites of Manitoba." *Mennonite Life*, vol. 25, no. 3 (July 1970). German and Russian settlements in Manitoba.

BB398 Hoeppner, J. N. "Early Days in Manitoba." *Mennonite Life*, vol. 6, no. 2 (1951), 11–15. Mennonites arriving from Russia in 1874.

BB399 Kidd, Honor M. "Pioneer Doctor John Sebastian Helmcken." *Bull. of the Hist. of Medicine*, vol. 21 (1947).

BB400 Klippenstein, LaVerna. *The Growing Years.* Book Two of *Rosenort, a Mennonite Community.* Morris, Man.: Morris-Macdonald School Division, 1975.

BB401 Klippenstein, LaVerna. *The People Now.* Book 3 of *Rosenort, a Mennonite Community.* Morris, Man.: Morris-Macdonald School Division, 1976.

BB402 Klippenstein, Lawrence. "Manitoba Métis and Mennonite Immigrants: First Contacts." *Mennonite Quar. Rev.*, vol. 48 (October 1974), 476–88.

BB403 Klippenstein, Lawrence. "Manitoba Settlement and the Mennonite West Reserve (1875–1876)." *Manitoba Pageant*, vol. 21, no. 1 (Autumn 1975), 13–18.

BB404 Klippenstein, Lawrence. "The Mennonite Heritage Centre in Winnipeg." *Jour. of the Amer. Hist. Soc. of Germans from Russia*, vol. 4, no. 3 (1981), 42–43.

BB405 Klippenstein, Lawrence. *Mennonites in Manitoba: Their Background and Early Settlement.* Morris, Man.: Morris-Macdonald School Division, 1976.

BB406 Klippenstein, Lawrence, and Julius G. Toews, eds. *Mennonite Memories: Settling in Western Canada.* Winnipeg, Man.: Centennial Publications, 1977. Rev. by Frank H. Epp, *Canad. Hist. Rev.*, vol. 60 (1979), 365–66.

BB407 "Eine Kolonie der Schwarzwälder und Westphalen." *Manitoba-Courier* (Winnipeg), 1 September 1966, p.15. Settlement at Little Britain, near Winnipeg.

BB408 Lohrenz, G. *The Mennonites in Western Canada.* Steinbach, Man.: Derksen Printers, 1974.

BB409 Lohrenz, G. "The Mennonites in Winnipeg." *Mennonite Life*, vol. 6, no. 1 (1951), 16–25.

BB410 Neufeld, G. G. *Die Geschichte der Whitewater Mennoniten Gemeinde in Manitoba, Canada, 1925–1965.* Altona, Man.: D. W. Friesen & Sons, 1967. 242p.

BB411 *Die Post* (Steinbach, Man.), 1913–. Esp. the 50th anniversary issue (31 December 1963) which traces the history of the Mennonites in southern Manitoba.

BB412 Richmond Historical Society. *Richmond's Heritage: A History of Richmond and District, 1910–1978.* Altona, Man.: Friesen Printers, 1978.

BB413 *Der Rundschau-Kalender.* Vol. 1–, 1927–. Rundschau-Publishing House, Winnipeg.

BB414 Sawatzky, Heinrich. *Templer mennonitischer Herkunft.* Vol. 2. Historical Series of the Echo-Verlag. Winnipeg, Man.: Echo-Verlag and Karl Fast, 1956. 69p. Rev. by W. Kirkconnell, *Utah Hist. Quar.*, vol. 26 (1957), 410.

BB415 Schroeder, William. *The Bergthal Colony.* Winnipeg: Canadian Mennonite Bible College, 1974. Rev. by W. Klaassen, *Mennonite Quar. Rev.*, vol. 50 (1976), 68–69.

BB416 Schwartz, Delores. "A Visit to Steinbach." *Workpapers of the Amer. Hist. Soc. of Germans from Russia*, vol. 17 (1975), 43–46.

BB417 Suderman, Leonhard. *From Russia to America: In Search of Freedom.* Trans. by Elmer R. Suderman. Steinbach, Man.: Derksen Printers, 1974.

BB418 Toews, Julius G., and Lawrence Klippenstein, eds. *Manitoba Mennonite Memories. A Century Past But Not Forgotten.* Altona, Steinbach: Mennonite Centennial Committee, 1976. 354p.

BB419 Totten, Don E. "Agriculture of Manitoba Mennonites." *Mennonite Life*, vol. 4, no. 3 (1949), 24–27.

BB420 Warkentin, Abraham. *Reflections on Our Heritage: A History of Steinbach and the Rim of Hanover from 1874.* Steinbach, Man.: Derksen Printers, 1971. 371p.

BB421 Warkentin, John. "Mennonite Agricultural Settlements of Southern Manitoba." *Geographical Rev.*, vol. 49 (1959), 342–68. Study of cultural, economic and dispersion aspects of the Mennonite settlements, with illus. and maps.

BB422 Warkentin, John. "Mennonite Settlements in Manitoba: A Study in Historical Geography." Diss., Toronto, 1959. Abstracted in *Mennonite Quar. Rev.*, vol. 36, no. 4 (1962), 354–55.

BB423 Weir, T.R. "Pioneer Settlement in Southwest Manitoba, 1879 to 1901." *Canad. Geographer*, vol. 8, no. 2 (1964), 64–71.

BB424 Weir, T.R. "Settlement in Southwest Manitoba, 1870–1891." *Papers Read Before the Hist. and Scientific Soc. of Manitoba.* Series 3, no. 17 (1960–61), 54–64.

BB425 Wiseman, Nelson, and K. Wayne Taylor. "Class and Ethnic Voting in Winnipeg during the Cold War." *Canad. Rev. of Sociology and Anthropology*, vol. 16 (1979), 60–76.

BB426 Zacharias, Peter D. *Reinland.* Reinland, Man.: Reinland Centennial Committee, 1976.

NOVA SCOTIA

BB427 Barss, Peter, ed. *Images of Lunenburg County.* Transcribed by Myra Barss and Peter Barss. Forew. by Helen Creighton. Toronto: McClelland and Stewart. 163p. Reminiscences of fishermen of Nova Scotia.

BB428 Bell, Winthrop. *The "Foreign Protestants" and the Settlement of Nova Scotia: The History of a Piece of Arrested British Colonial Policy in the Eighteenth Century.* Toronto: Univ. of Toronto Pr., 1961. 673p. Involving settlements in Lunenburg County, 1749–1752.

BB429 Burrows, Mildred P. *The History of Wittenberg, Colchester County, Nova Scotia.* Truro: Colchester Historical Museum, 1978. 92p.

BB430 Cooper, John I. "The Germans in Nova Scotia. The Bi-Centenary of the Halifax Community." *Amer.-German Rev.*, vol. 16, no. 3 (1950), 22–24.

BB431 Cooper, John I. "Lunenburg, Nova Scotia, Bicentenary." *Amer.-German Rev.*, vol. 19, no. 5 (1953), 7–9.

BB432 Cooper, John I. "The S.P.G. Missionaries in Lunenburg." *Amer.-German Rev.*, vol. 19, no. 6 (1953), 12–14. German missionaries of the Anglican Society for the Propagation of the Gospel; present in Lunenburg since 1761.

BB433 Debor, Herbert W. "Early German Immigration in Nova Scotia." Trans. Andrew Teller." *German-Canad. Yearbook*, vol. 1 (1973), 67–70.

BB434 Des Brisay, M.B. *History of the County of Lunenburg (Nova Scotia).* Toronto: n.p., 1870.

BB435 Harper, J. Russell. *Historical Directory of New Brunswick Newspapers and Periodicals.* Fredericton: Univ. of New Brunswick, 1961, 121p.

BB436 Knopf, Friedrich. "Als die Pfälzer vor 200 Jahren nach Lunenburg zogen." *Mitteilungen des Instituts für Auslandsbeziehungen*, vol. 7 (1957), 170f. Palatine emigration to Nova Scotia in 1750.

BB437 Lacey, Laurie, ed. *Lunenberg County Folklore and Oral History Project '77.* Ottawa: National Museums of Canada, 1979.

BB438 Sautter, Udo. "Die Lunenburg-Deutschen." In *Annalen des 1. Symposiums Deutschkanadische Studien.* Montreal: n.p., 1976, p.82–84. On the German schools of Lunenburg.

BB439 Sutherland, Maxwell. "Case History of a Settlement (Nova Scotia)." *Dalhousie Review*, vol. 40, no. 1 (Spring 1961), 65–74. The settlement of German auxiliaries after the Revolution.

BB440 Waseem, Gertrud. "Die Fahrt nach Nova Scotia: Zur Vorgeschichte der Gründung Lunenburgs, N.S." *German-Canad. Yearbook*, vol. 3 (1976), 140–59. See also: "Neue Heimat in fremdem Land." *Ibid.*, vol. 4 (1978), 74–92.

ONTARIO

BB441 Andre, John. *Infant Toronto as Simcoe's Folly.* Toronto: n.p., 1971. Rev. by G. K. Weissenborn, *German-Canad. Yearbook*, vol. 1 (1973), 316–19.

BB442 Baird, K.A. "Kitchener—Waterloo, Ontario." *Canad. Geographical Jour.*, vol. 78, no. 9 (1969), 90–99.

BB443 Barbier, Louis P. *Die Geschichte der Ersten Ev.-Luth. Kirche Toronto, 1851–1976. The Story of the First Lutheran Church, Toronto, 1851–1976.* Toronto: n.p., 1976. 37, 32p.

BB444 Bauman, Salome. *150 Years First Mennonite Church.* Kitchener, Ont.: n.p., 1963. 24p.

BB445 Burghardt, Andrew F. "The Settling of Southern Ontario: An Appreciation of the Work of Carl Schott." *Canad. Geographer*, vol. 25 (1981), 75–76. With an excerpt from Schott's work in trans. by Burghardt, p.77–93.

BB446 Cannif, W. *History of the Settlement of Upper Canada, with Specific Reference to the Bay of Quinte.* Toronto: n.p., 1869.

BB447 Caplan, Gerald L. "The Ontario 'Gestapo Affair'," 1943–1945." *Canad. Jour. of Economic and Political Science*, vol. 30, no. 3 (August 1964), 343–59.

BB448 Coumans, C.C. "Ornamental Iron Grave Markers." In: *Waterloo Historical Soc. 49th Annual Volume 1961.* (Waterloo 1962), p.72–75. Iron markers used in German Catholic communities.

BB449 "'Czar's Germans' is Real Experience to Many Windsorites." *Windsor (CO) Beacon*, 25 March, 1976.

BB450 "Eine deutsche Siedlung in Nordwest Ontario." *Der Nordwesten*, 21 February, 1967.

BB451 Dunham, B. Mabel. "Beginnings in Ontario." *Mennonite Life*, vol. 5, no. 4 (1950), 14–16. Mennonite pioneers.

BB452 Eby, Ezra E. *A Biographical History of Waterloo Township and Other Townships of the County, Being a History of the Early Settlers and Their Descendants.* Berlin, Ont.: n.p., 1895. Repr. Berlin, Ont.: Eldon Weber, 1974.

BB453 Fritz, J.C. "The Early History of the Mennonites in Welland County, Ontario." *Mennonite Quar. Rev.*, vol. 27 (1953), 55–75.

BB454 *German Pioneers of Toronto and Markham Township.* Toronto: Hist. Soc. of Mecklenburg Upper Canada, Inc., 1976.

BB455 Germania Club of Hamilton, Ont. *100 Jahre Germania.* Ed. Eugene Rapp. Hamilton, Ont.: n.p., 1969. 216p.

BB456 "German-Russian Heritage Preserved." *Windsor (CO) Beacon*, 2 December 1976.

BB457 Goegginger, W. "Deutsche Kirche and Schule in Ontario." *Mitteilungen des Instituts für Auslandsbeziehungen*, vol. 7 (1957), 211–12.

BB458 Gray, Leslie R. "From Fairfield to Schonbrun, 1798: Diary of Br. and Sr. Zeisberger and Br. Benj. Mortimer." *Ontario History*, vol. 49 (Spring 1957). Cf. *Amer. Hist. Rev.*, vol. 63 (1957), 248.

BB459 Harney, R.F. "The New Canadians and Their Life in Toronto." *Canad. Geographical Jour.*, vol. 96 (1978), 20–27. Recent immigrants and the Canadian policy of multiculturalism.

BB460 Heick, Wolf H. "Becoming an Indigenous Church: The Lutheran Church in Waterloo County, Ontario." *Ontario Hist.*, vol. 56, no. 4 (1964), 249–60.

BB461 Heick, Wolf H. "A Sociological and Historical Study of the Lutherans of Waterloo County." M.A. thesis, Queen's Univ., 1959.

BB462 Herrfort, A.K., and P. E. Snyder. *Mennonite Country: Waterloo County Drawings.* St. Jacobs, Ont.: Sand Hill Pr., 1978.

BB463 Hess, Albert. "I Found Waterloo County in Hesse." *Annual Report of the Waterloo Hist. Soc.*, vol. 60 (1972), 63–65.

BB464 Home, Ruth M. "Jordan Museum of the Twenty." *Pa. Folklife*, vol. 16 (1967), no. 3, 24–27. Museum of the Twenty Mile Creek, Jordan, Ont.; a community settled in part by Pennsylvania Mennonites.

BB465 Horn, Dieter. "Die deutschen Siedlungen im County Waterloo, Ontario." *Zeitschrift für Kulturaustausch*, vol. 18, no. 4 (1968), 302–05.

BB466 Huck, Marilyn Glynn. "Early Settlement in Waterloo County (Upper Canada)." M.A. thesis, Univ. of Toronto, 1965.

B467 *Informationsblatt für die Deutsche Kanadier in Hamilton....* N.p.: n.p. September, 1970. Pamphlet for immigrants, specifically dealing with Hamilton, Ontario.

BB468 Janzen, Jacob H. *Die Geschichte der Grafschaft Ebenfeld, 3. und 4. Buch.* Waterloo, Ont.: n.p., 1944. 192, 194p. Rev. by Jacob Sudermann, *Mennonite Quar. Rev.*, vol. 19, no. 1 (1945), 70–72.

BB469 Jelen, Walter. "German Speaking People in Ontario." *Amer.-German Rev.*, vol. 30, no. 5 (1963), 13–14.

BB470 Katz, Michael B. *The People of Hamilton, Canada West: Family and Class in a Mid-Nineteenth-Century City.* Cambridge, Mass.: Harvard Univ. Pr., 1975. 381p. Study of social groupings, transciency, social mobility from 1851 to 1860's. Rev. by Edward Pessen, *Jour. of Amer. Hist.*, vol. 63, no. 2 (September 1976), 472–74.

BB471 Katz, Michael B. "Who Went to School [in Hamilton, Ontario, 1851–1861]?" *Hist. of Education Quar.*, vol. 12 (Fall 1972).

BB472 Katz, Michael B., Michael J. Doucet, and Mark J. Stern. "Population Persistence and Early Industrialization in a Canadian City: Hamilton, Ontario." *Social Science Hist.*, vol. 2 (Winter 1978).

BB473 Kluchert, Richard W. "14 Jahre 'Verein deutscher Ingenieure' in Toronto." *German-Canad. Yearbook*, vol. 2 (1975), 285–86.

BB474 Lee-Whiting, Brenda B. "Doddy-House Duties Outlined in 1912: How a German Farmer in Eastern Ontario Worked and Enjoyed a Secure Old Age." *German-Canad. Yearbook*, vol. 6 (1981), 89–102.

BB475 Leibbrandt, Gottlieb. "Deutsche Ortsgründungen und Ortsnamen in der Grafschaft Waterloo." *German-Canad. Yearbook*, vol. 1 (1973), 119–29.

BB476 Leibbrandt, Gottlieb. *25 Jahre caritative und kulturelle Arbeit des Hilfwerkes der Deutschkanadier: Festschrift zum 25-jährigen Bestehen der Canadian Society for German Relief.* Waterloo, Ont.: n.p., 1972.

BB477 Leibbrandt, Gottlieb. "100 Jahre Concordia in Kitchener." *German-Canad. Yearbook*, vol. 1 (1973), 263–74.

BB478 Leibbrandt, Gottlieb. *Little Paradise: Aus Geschichte und Leben der Deutschkanadier in der County Waterloo, Ontario, 1800–1975.* Toronto: German-Canad. Hist. Assoc., 1977. 413p. Also as: *Little Paradise: The Saga of the Germans in Waterloo County, Ontario.* Kitchener, Ont.: Allprint, 1980. 384p. Rev. by G. Moltmann, *Amerikastudien*, vol. 23 (1978), 358–59. One hundred seventy-five years' history of the German settlement at Grand River.

BB479 Lichti, Fred. *A History of the East Zorra (Amish) Mennonite Church, 1837–1977.* Tavistock, Ont.: East Zorra Mennonite Church, 1979. 132p.

BB480 McCartney, James. "Sectarian Strife in Dundas County: A Lutheran–Episcopalian Land Endowment Controversy 1784–1846." *Ontario Hist.*, vol. 54, no. 2 (June 1962), 69–86. Religious and social history of the "Royal Yorkers," loyalist participants in the American Revolution.

BB481 Mautner, Lorenz. "Die Kanadisch-österreichische Gesellschaft (Canadian Austrian Society) von Toronto." *German-Canad. Yearbook*, vol. 6 (1981), 258–60.

BB482 Mickegney, P. "The German Schools of Waterloo County, 1851–1913." *Waterloo Hist. Soc., Report*, vol. 58 (1970), 56–67.

BB483 *More Than a Century in Wilmot Township*. New Hamburg: Hist. Committee of the New Hamburg-Wilmot Township Centennial Committee, 1967. 123p.

BB484 Moyer, William G. "The Early Days in Waterloo County." *German-Canad. Yearbook*, vol. 1 (1973), 113–17.

BB485 Neufeld, J.A., and Isaak Loewen, eds. *Gedenkbüchlein des Dankfestes der neueingewanderten Mennoniten in Ontario am 2/3 Juni 1951*. Virgil, Ont.: n.p., 1952. 131p. Thanksgiving festival of recent Mennonite immigrants from Russia.

BB486 Officer, E. R. "Waterloo County: Some Aspects of Settlement and Economy before 1900." In: *The Waterloo County Area: Selected Geographical Essays*. Ed. A. G. McLelland. Waterloo: Univ. of Waterloo, 1971, p.11–20.

BB487 *Ontario Historic Sites, Museums, and Plaques*. Toronto: Dept. of Tourism and Information, Province of Ontario, n.d.

BB488 Petrie, Francis J. *Ball's Falls Conservation Area: Scenic and Historic Heritage*. Fonthill, Ont.: Niagara Peninsula Conservation Authority, 1972.

BB489 Plewman, W. R. *Adam Beck and the Ontario Hydro*. Toronto: n.p., 1947. 494p. Rev. by J. A. Stevenson, *Canad. Hist. Rev.*, vol. 28, no. 4 (1947), 443.

BB490 Reaman, George Elmore. *The Trail of the Black Walnut*. Scottdale, Pa.: Herald Pr., 1957; Publs., Pa. German Soc., vol. 57. 256p.; Toronto: McClelland and Stewart (1957). 256p. Rev. by A. W. Brink, *Utah Hist. Quar.*, vol. 27 (1958), 528; J. A. Hostetler, *Amer.-German Rev.*, vol. 24, no. 3 (1958), 36–37; W. A. Russ, Jr., *Pa. Hist.*, vol. 26 (1959), 190–91; J. J. Stoudt, "'S Pennsylfawnisch Deitsch Eck," Allentown *Morning Call*, 25 January 1958. A study of the Pennsylvania German influence upon the settlement and development of Ontario.

BB491 St. Matthews Lutheran Church [Kitchener, Ont.]. *Souvenir of the Golden Jubilee*. Kitchener, Ont.: n.p., 1954. 44p.

BB492 Sauder, Dorothy. "Sesquicentennial of Amish Settlement in Ontario." *Mennonite Life*, vol. 27 (1972), 91–92. In Wilmot Township, Waterloo County.

BB493 Schaus, Lloyd H. "German Settlers in Ontario." *Amer.-German Rev.*, vol. 20, no. 1 (1953), 9–12. After 1830 Germans arrived in Ontario directly from Europe and not, as before, via Pennsylvania.

BB494 Speisman, Stephen A. "The Jews of Toronto: A History to 1937." Diss., Toronto, 1975.

BB495 Toronto City Planning Board. *A Report on the Ethnic Origins of the Population of Toronto, 1960*. Toronto: n.p., 1961. Excellent maps showing location and movements of ethnic groups.

BB496 Trabold, Karl J. "Altenbetreuung in der Muttersprache." *German-Canad. Yearbook*, vol. 1 (1973), 297–303. The rest home "Heidehof," St. Catherines, Ont.

BB497 *The Union Publishing Co.'s Farmers' and Business Directory for the Counties of Halton, Waterloo and Wellington*. Ingersoll, Ont.: Union Publ. Co., n.d.

BB498 *Union Publishing Company's Windsor (Ont.) Directory, Including Walkerville and Sandwich*. No. 1. Ingersoll, Ont.: Union Publ. Co., 1905.

BB499 Uttley, W. V. *A History of Kitchener*. Waterloo: Wilfrid Laurier Univ. Pr., 1975.

BB500 Vincent, Dorothea. "Deutschkanadisches Geschäftsleben in Toronto am Anfang der siebziger Jahre: Ein Überblick." *German-Canad. Yearbook*, vol. 2 (1975), 83–87.

BB501 Welch, Robert. "German Heritage in Ontario." *German-Canad. Yearbook*, vol. 1 (1973), 15–16.

BB502 Witmer, Lesly D. *Pioneers of Christendom of Waterloo County, 1800–1967. History of the Hague-Preston Mennonite Church, Ontario*. N.p.: n.p., ca. 1967. 64p.

QUEBEC

BB503 Bausenhart, Werner. "The German Settlement of Ladysmith, Quebec, and the Dialect Spoken by Its Settlers." *German-Canad. Yearbook*, vol. 4 (1978), 234–45.

BB504 Beutler, Bernard A. H. "Deutschkanadischer Monat in Montreal." *German-Canad. Yearbook*, vol. 4 (1978), 312–14.

BB505 Caux, Arthur. "Les colons allemands de Saint-Gilles et leur descendants dans Lotbinière." *Bulletin des recherches historiques*, vol. 57, no. 1 (1951), 50–60.

BB506 Cooper, J. L. "German Seigneur of a Canadian Manor." *Amer.-German Rev.*, vol. 18, no. 3 (1952), 13–14. German immigrant John G. Pozer's (1752–1848) settlement in Québec.

BB507 Debor, H. W. *Die Deutschen in der Provinz Quebec 1664–1964*. Montreal: n.p., 1963. 56p. Rev. in *Zeitschrift für Kulturaustausch*, vol. 16, nos. 2–3 (1966), 197–98. See also his article "Die Deutschen in der Provinz Quebec 1664–1964." *Der Nordwesten*, 25 January 1966, and "Deutsche in der Stadt und Festung Quebec." *Ibid.*, 23 August 1966.

BB508 *Das Goethe-Haus Montreal 1962–1970*. Festschrift zu Ehren von Fritz Genzel. Ed. A. Arnold and M. Ott. Bonn: Bouvier, 1970. 80p.

BB509 Lach, Friedhelm. "L'allemand québecois." *German-Canad. Yearbook*, vol. 2 (1975), 28–33. Germans in the province of Quebec.

BB510 Saint John's Lutheran Church. Thorne Center, Québec. *The History of the Founding and Continuation of St. John's Ev. Lutheran Church, Thorne Center, Québec*. Quebec: n.p., 1912.

BB511 Scheer, Herfried W. "Deutsche Sprache und deutsche Kultur in der Provinz Quebec: Ein Überblick über die Geschichte des Deutschtums in Quebec." In *Deutsch als Muttersprache in Kanada: Berichte zur Gegenwartslage*. Ed. Leopold Auburger, H. Kloss and H. Rupp. Wiesbaden: Steiner, 1977, p.7–13.

SASKATCHEWAN AND THE WEST

BB512 Becker, A. "St. Joseph's Colony, Balgonie." *Saskatchewan Hist.*, vol. 20 (Winter 1967), 1–18. German Catholics who emigrated from Josephstal, a settlement near Odessa, Russia.

BB513 Becker, Anthony. "The Germans from Russia in Saskatchewan and Alberta." *German-Canad. Yearbook*, vol. 3 (1976), 106–19.

BB514 Becker, Anthony. "The Germans in Western Canada: A Vanishing People." *Heritage Rev.*, vol. 15 (1976), 3–12.

BB515 Bicha, Karel Denis. "The Plains Farmer and the Prairie Province Frontier, 1897–1914." *Papers, Amer. Philosophical Soc.*, vol. 109, no. 6 (10 December 1965), 398–440. Incl. discussion of movement of German-speaking groups into Saskatchewan and Alberta after 1896.

BB516 Cardinal, Clive H. von. "Some German Cultural Contributions to Canada's West." *German-Canad. Business Rev.*, Winter 1970. Repr. *German-Canad. Yearbook*, vol. 1 (1973), 47–51.

BB517 Cohnstaedt, Wilhelm. *Western Canada, 1909: Travel Letters by Wilhelm Cohnstaedt*. Ed. Klaus H. Burmeister. Canad. Plains Studies, vol. 7. Regina: Canad. Plains Research Center, Univ. of Regina, 1976. 77p. Repr. of a 1909 publication by the correspondent for the *Frankfurter Zeitung* who traveled in the region in 1907.

BB518 Dawson, C. A. *Group Settlement—Ethnic Communities in Western Canada*. Canadian Frontiers of Settlement, vol. 7. Toronto: Macmillan Co. of Canada, Ltd., 1936. See esp. p.271–91.

BB519 Dawson, Carl A., and Robert W. Murchie. *The Settlement of the Peace River Country*. Canadian Frontiers of Settlement, vol. 6. Toronto: Macmillan Co. of Canada, Ltd., 1934. 284p.

BB520 Driedger, Leo. "Early Mennonite Settlement in Saskatchewan: Hague-Osler Settlement." *Mennonite Life*, vol. 13 (1958), 13–17, 63–66.

BB521 Epp, Frank H. *Education with a Plus: The Story of Rosthern Junior College*. Waterloo, Ont.: Conrad Pr., 1975. 460p. A Mennonite parochial school in Saskatchewan which had formerly been known as the German-English Academy.

BB522 Giesinger, Adam. "Germans from Russia in Western Canada." *Work Papers of the Amer. Hist. Soc. of Germans from Russia*, vol. 7 (1971), 37–42.

BB523 Heinrichs, Margaret. "Hague in Saskatchewan." *Mennonite Life*, vol. 13, no. 1 (1958), 18–19. The village of Hague, Sask., was founded by Russo-German Mennonites in 1895.

BB524 Hoffer, Israel. "Reminiscences." *Saskatchewan Hist.*, vol. 5, no. 1 (1952), 28–32. Recollections of pioneering at Hirsch, Sask., 1905.

BB525 Johnson, Gilbert. "The Germania Mutual Fire Insurance Company of Langenburg." *Saskatchewan Hist.*, vol. 14, no. 1 (Winter 1961), 27–29.

BB526 Keller, P. Conrad. *The German Colonies in South Russia, 1804–1904*. Trans. by Dr. A. Becker. North Saskatoon, Sask.: A. Becker, n.d. Early pre-Canadian history of groups which came to Saskatchewan.

BB527 Klassen, H. T. *Birth and Growth of Eigenheim Mennonite Church, 1892–1974*. Rosthern, Sask.: n.p., 1974.

BB528 Lehmann, Heinz. "Aus der Frühzeit Westkanadas: Deutschschweizer Soldaten als Siedler." *German-Canad. Yearbook*, vol. 1 (1973), 107–11.

BB529 Metzger, H. "Historical Sketch of St. Peter's Parish and the Founding of the Colonies of Rastadt, Katharinental and Speyer." Trans. by Anthony Becker and Bernadine Kletzel. *Bull., Saskatchewan Geneal. Soc.*, vol. 5, no. 4 (1974), 7–29. Repr. in *Heritage Rev.*, vol. 15 (1976), 31–45.

BB530 Pätkau, Esther, ed. *Nordheimer Mennonite Church of Saskatchewan, 1925–1975*. Hanley, Sask.: n.p., 1975.

BB531 Peter, Karl, and Franziska Peter, trans. and eds. "The Ethnic Voice, Eyewitness Accounts: The Kurtenbach Letters, an Autobiographical Description of Pioneer Life in Saskatchewan around the Turn of the Century." *Canad. Ethnic St.*, vol. 11, no. 2 (1979), 88–96.

BB532 Rempel, J. G. *Die Rosenorter Gemeinde in Saskatchewan in Wort und Bild*. Rosthern: D. H. Epp, 1950. 183p. Rev. by Harold S. Bender, *Mennonite Quar. Rev.*, vol. 25, no. 4 (1951), 327–28.

BB533 Rodwell, Lloyd. "Saskatchewan Homestead Records." *Saskatchewan Hist.*, vol. 18, no. 1 (Winter 1965), 10–29.

BB534 Schilling, Edith von. "Deutsche Siedler in Nord-Saskatchewan." *German-Canad. Yearbook*, vol. 4 (1978), 260–65. Introd. and notes by Jonathan F. Wagner. From a MS. located in the Bundesarchiv Koblenz (BA) R57/474/44.

BB535 Schulte, W., ed. *St. Joseph's Colony, 1905–1930*. Trans. by Lambert Schneider and Tillie Schneider. Battleford, Sask.: Marian Pr., ca. 1976.

BB536 Tischler, Kurt G. "The Efforts of the Germans in Saskatchewan to Retain Their Language Before 1914." *German-Canad. Yearbook*, vol. 6 (1981), 42–61.

BB537 Wagner, Jonathan. "The Deutscher Bund in Saskatchewan." *Saskatchewan Hist.*, vol. 31 (1978), 41–50. Local activities of a pro-Nazi group, 1934–1939.

BB538 "Wolhyniendeutsche im Westen Kanadas." *Heimatbuch*, 1963, 87–91.

BC
Germans from Russia

Bibliography/Sources/Journals

See also Colorado, Nebraska, *and* Kansas *under* Part J: German-American Local History.

BC1 American Historical Society of Germans from Russia. *Journal*. 1978–. Ed. Adam Giesinger. Quarterly published in Lincoln, Neb.; supersedes the *Work Papers of the Amer. Hist. Soc. of Germans from Russia*.

BC2 Becker, Anthony. "The Book Entitled *Die deutschen Kolonien in Südrussland* by Rev. Konrad Keller: A Rare Find." *Jour. of the Amer. Hist.*

Soc. of Germans from Russia, vol. 3, no. 2 (1980), 9–12.

BC3 Bye, John E. "Germans from Russia Heritage Collection Established at North Dakota State University." *Heritage Rev.*, vol. 22 (December 1978), 3–4; vol. 23 (1979), 7.

BC4 Essig, Walter, comp. *Index I: Workpaper, Heritage Review, Stammbaum, 1971 through 1978.* Bismarck, N. Dak.: N. Dak. Hist. Soc. of Germans from Russia, 1979.

BC5 Essig, Walter, comp. *Index to Germans from Russia Heritage Society Publications, 1979.* Bismarck, N. Dak.: Germans from Russia Heritage Soc., 1980.

BC6 Fromm, Esther. *Bibliography of the Materials in the Collection of the American Historical Society of Germans from Russia: Supplement to the 1973 Edition.* Greeley, Colo.: Public Library, 1974.

BC7 Fromm, Esther. "Greeley Publication Library Archives." *Work Paper II, Amer. Hist. Soc. of Germans from Russia* (July 1969), 38–41.

BC8 Giesinger, Adam. "The Origins of the American Historical Society of Germans from Russia: A History Based on Documents in the Society Files." *Jour. of the Amer. Hist. Soc. of Germans from Russia*, vol. 3, no. 3 (1980), 11–18.

BC9 Giesinger, Adam, Emma S. Haynes, Marie M. Olson, and Esther Fromm. *Bibliography of the AHSGR Archives and Historical Library, Greeley, Colorado, 1976.* Lincoln, Neb.: Amer. Hist. Soc. of Germans from Russia, 1976.

BC10 Haynes, Emma S. "The American Historical Soc. of Germans from Russia: Its Goals and History." In: *Papers from the Conference on German-Americana in the Eastern United States.* Ed. S. M. Benjamin. Morgantown, W. Va.: Dept. of For. Langs., West Va. Univ., 1980, p.55–60.

BC11 Haynes, Emma S. "Fresno State College Library Bibliography." *Work Paper II, Amer. Hist. Soc. of Germans from Russia* (July 1969), 15–17.

BC12 Haynes, Emma S. "Researching in the National Archives." *Jour. of the Amer. Hist. Soc. of Germans from Russia*, vol. 2, no. 1 (1979), 1–6.

BC13 Haynes, Emma S. "Stuttgart—An Information Center for Germans from Russia." *Work Paper II, Amer. Hist. Soc. of Germans from Russia* (July 1969), 1–13.

BC14 Haynes, Emma S. "Treasures in Our Archives." *Jour. of the Amer. Hist. Soc. of Germans from Russia*, vol. 3, no. 3 (1980), 37–48.

BC15 "Hoover Institute Library Bibliography." *Work Paper II, Amer. Hist. Soc. of Germans from Russia* (July 1969), 18–28.

BC16 Kliewer, Victor D. "The German Literature of the Russian Mennonites: A Critical Bibliography of Writings Located in Manitoba Libraries." M. A. thesis, Univ. of Manitoba, 1972.

BC17 Klingelhoefer, Andreas, comp., John Newman, ed. *An Annotated Bibliography of General Works on the Germans from Russia.* Fort Collins: Germans from Russia in Colorado Study Project, Colorado State Univ., 1979.

BC18 Long, James W. *The German-Russians: A Bibliography.* Santa Barbara, Calif.: Clio Pr., 1978.

BC19 Long, James W., and William L. Virden. *Russian Language Sources Relating to the Germans from Russia.* Fort Collins: Germans from Russia in Colorado Study Project, Colorado State Univ., 1976. 47p.

BC20 Miller, Michael J. "Germans from Russia Class at North Dakota State University." *Heritage Rev.*, no. 22 (December 1978).

BC21 Olson, Marie M. *A Bibliography on the Germans from Russia: Materials Found in the New York Public Library.* Lincoln, Neb.: Amer. Hist. Soc. of Germans from Russia, 1976.

BC22 Olson, Marie M. *An Index to the Work Papers: Numbers 1 through 25, 1969–1977.* Lincoln, Neb.: Amer. Hist. Soc. of Germans from Russia, 1978.

BC23 Olson, Marie M., and Emma S. Haynes. *Bibliography of Materials in the Collection of the American Historical Society of Germans from Russia.* 2nd ed. Greeley, Colo.: Public Library, 1973.

BC24 Rippley, LaVern J. "Germans from Russia." In: *Encyclopedia of American Ethnic Groups.* Ed. Stephan Thernstrom. Cambridge: Harvard Univ. Pr., 1980, 425–30.

BC25 Rock, Kenneth W. "The Colorado Germans from Russia Study Project." *Social Science Jour.*, vol. 13 (April 1976).

BC26 Schmeller, Helmut J. *The Germans from Russia: A Bibliography of Materials in the Ethnic Heritage Collection at Fort Hays State University.* Hays, Kansas: Fort Hays St. Univ., 1980.

BC27 Sroka, Barbara A. *Annotated Bibliography of Materials Available for Purchase.* Lincoln, Neb.: Amer. Hist. Soc. of Germans from Russia, 1979.

BC28 Stumpp, Karl. *Ostwanderung. Akten über die Auswanderung der Württemberger nach Russland, 1816–1822.* Leipzig: 1941. Reproduces many documents from the Württemberg archives.

BC29 Stumpp, Karl. *Das Schrifttum über das Deutschtum in Russland. Eine Bibliographie.* 3rd updated and enl. ed. Tübingen: privately printed, 1971. Address Autenriethstr. 16, Tübingen.

History and Description

BC30 Anuta, Michael J. *East Prussians from Russia.* Menominee, Michigan: n.p., 1979. On a settlement of Germans from Russia.

BC31 Bischoff, G. August. "A 1909 Report on Russian-German Settlements in South Dakota." Trans. and ed. by Anton H. Richter. *South Dakota Hist.*, vol. 11 (1981), 185–98.

BC32 Bonekemper, Carl. "Johannes Bonekemper and His Family: Immanuel! Eine Hütte Gottes bei den Menschen." Trans. Theodore C. Wenzlaff. *Heritage Rev.*, vol. 24 (1979), 14–21. From an original ca. 1868.

BC33 Correll, Ernst. "The Congressional Debates on the Mennonite Immigration from Russia 1873–74." *Mennonite Quar. Rev.*, vol. 20, no. 3 (1946), 221; no. 4, 255–75.

BC34 Eisenach, George J. *Das religiöse Leben unter den Russlanddeutschen in Russland und Amerika.* Marburg/Lahn: H. Rathmann, 1950. 216p. Trans. of his *Pietism and the Russian Germans in the United States.* Berne, Ind./Yankton, N. Dak.: Berne Publ., 1948–49. 218p.

BC35 Eisenach, George J. "The Volga Germans." *Amer.-German Rev.*, vol. 10, no. 4 (1944), 4–7; vol. 10, no. 5 (1944), 24–27.

BC36 Epp, Johann. "The Coming of the Russian Mennonites to America: An Analysis by Johann Epp, Mennonite Minister in Russia, 1875." *Mennonite Quar. Rev.*, vol. 48 (October 1974).

BC37 Giesinger, Adam. "An Appraisal of Our Future." *Jour. of the Amer. Hist. Soc. of Germans from Russia*, vol. 3, no. 2 (1980), 6–7.

BC38 Giesinger, Adam. *From Catherine to Krushchev: The Story of Russia's Germans.* Battleford, Sask.: Marian Pr., 1974. Repr. Lincoln, Neb.: American Hist. Soc. of Germans from Russia, 1981.

BC39 Giesinger, Adam. "The Migrations of Germans from Russia to the Americas." *Work Papers of the Amer. Hist. Soc. of Germans from Russia*, vol. 9 (1972), 33–39. Repr. in *Heritage Rev.*, vol. 7 (1973), 21–25.

BC40 Gingerich, Melvin. "Russian Mennonites React to Their New Environment." *Mennonite Life*, vol. 15 (1960), 175–80. Gathered from letters and reports about German-speaking Mennonites from Russia.

BC41 Goertz, Reuben. "German Russian Homes: Here and There, Now and Then." *Clues 1976*, 31–50.

BC42 Griess, James R. "The German-Russians: Pioneers on Two Continents." *Heritage Rev.*, vol. 9 (1974), 21–25.

BC43 Hall, Helen L. *Grandfather's Story.* Trans. by Louise Rylko. Carthagena, Ohio: n.p., 1962. 46p. Excerpts from J. M. Linenberger's *Die Deutschen am Karman.*

BC44 Hamil, Harold. "Lesson for Others in Their Hard-Work Heritage: The German-Russians, III." *Work Papers of the Amer. Hist. Soc. of Germans from Russia*, vol. 11 (1973), 39–41.

BC45 Harwood, W. S. "A Bit of Europe in Dakota: The German Russian Colony at Eureka."

Harper's Weekly, 11 July 1898. Repr. *Work Papers of the Amer. Hist. Soc. of Germans from Russia*, no. 25 (1977), 17–20; also *Heritage Rev.*, vol. 11, no. 4 (1981), 32–35.

BC46 Haynes, Emma S. "By What Name Should We Be Called?" *Work Papers of the Amer. Hist. Soc. of Germans from Russia*, vol. 16 (1974), 33–34.

BC47 Haynes, Emma S. "Germans from Russia in American History and Literature." *Work Papers of the Amer. Hist. Soc. of Germans from Russia*, vol. 15 (1974), 4–20.

BC48 Haynes, Emma S. "The Life of Pastor Thomas Schöck Who May Be the Last Russian German to Come to America in a Sailing Ship." *Clues 1981*, Part I, 73–78.

BC49 Haynes, Emma S. "Progress Report on the Coming of Volga German Protestants to the United States." *Jour. of the Amer. Hist. Soc. of Germans from Russia*, vol. 1, no. 1 (1978), 73–75.

BC50 Haynes, Emma Schwabenland. *A History of the Volga Relief Society*. Portland, Ore.: A. E. Kern, 1941. 130p. On the activities of the Portland Volga Relief Society in assisting the American relief administration to aid Germans on the Volga during the Russian famine, August 1921–November 1922.

BC51 Height, Joseph S. *Memories of the Black Sea Germans*. Chelsea, Mich.: Lithocrafters, Inc., 1979.

BC52 Holland, Nancy B. "Our Ancestors and Their Books." *Jour. of the Amer. Hist. Soc. of Germans from Russia*, vol. 3, no. 2 (1980), 19–27.

BC53 Horst, John C. *Real Life*. Denver: n.p., 1972. The autobiography of a German-Russian.

BC54 Joachim, S. "Toward an Understanding of the Russian Germans." *Concordia College Occasional Papers* (Moorhead, Minn.), August 1939. 32p.

BC55 Kaufman, P. R. *Our People and Their History*. Trans. by Reuben Peterson. Sioux Falls, S. Dak.: Augustana College Pr., 1979. On the German Russians.

BC56 Kehrer, Andrew. "A Voice from the Past: Remembering Eighty Years." As told to Joyce K. Roether. *Jour. of the Amer. Hist. Soc. of Germans from Russia*, vol. 1, no. 1 (1978), 60–66.

BC57 Keller, P. Conrad. *The German Colonies in South Russia, 1804–1904*. Trans. by A. Becker. Saskatoon, Sask.: n.p., n.d. Background and history of some of the German colonies which eventually removed to Saskatchewan.

BC58 Kloberdanz, Timothy J. "Treasured Traditions of 'Our People': From the Cradle to the Grave." *Work Papers of the Amer. Hist. Soc. of Germans from Russia*, vol. 18 (1975), 12–18.

BC59 Kloberdanz, Timothy J. "The Volga German Life Cycle: An Ethnographic Reconstruction." M. A. Thesis, Colorado State Univ., 1974.

BC60 Kloberdanz, Timothy J. "The Volga Germans in Old Russia and in Western North America: Their Changing World View." *Anthropological Quar.*, vol. 48 (1975), 209–22.

BC61 Koch, Fred C. *The Volga Germans in Russia and the Americas, from 1763 to the Present*. University Park and London: The Pa. State Univ. Pr., 1977. 365p. Rev. by Albert R. Schmitt, *German Quar.*, vol. 52 (1979), 278–80.

BC62 Koop, P. Albert. "Some Economic Aspects of Mennonite Migration with Special Emphasis on the 1870's Migration from Russia to North America." *Mennonite Quar. Rev.*, vol. 55 (1981), 143–56.

BC63 Lindsay, Mela M. "Seventy Cents for a Lifetime of Freedom." *Work Papers of the Amer. Hist. Soc. of Germans from Russia*, vol. 13 (1973), 40–41.

BC64 Lineberry, Paul. "Community Integration and Change." Ph.D. diss., Colorado State Univ., 1975. On the German-Russians.

BC65 Loewen, Abraham J. *Immer weiter nach Osten: Russland–China–Kanada*. Ed. Gerhard Ens. Winnipeg, Man.: CMBC Publications, 1981.

BC66 Miller, David J. "Past Achievements and Future Opportunities." *Work Papers of the Amer. Hist. Soc. of Germans from Russia*, vol. 12 (1973), 1–6. On the genesis of the historical society.

BC67 Petersen, Albert J. "German-Russian Catholic Social Organization." *Plains Anthropologist*, vol. 18, no. 59 (1973), 27–32.

BC68 Petersen, Albert J. "The German-Russian House in Kansas: A Study of Persistence in Form." *Pioneer America*, vol. 8, no. 1 (1976), 19–27.

BC69 Postma, Johan S. *Das niederländische Erbe der Preussisch-Russländischen in Europa, Asien und America*. Emmen: n.p., 1959. 187p.

BC70 Rath, George. "Die Russlanddeutschen in den Vereinigten Staaten von Nordamerika." In: *Heimatbuch der Deutschen aus Russland*. Stuttgart: Die Landmannsschaft der Deutschen aus Russland, 1963, p.22–55. From an article about Peter H. Griess (1851–1917), son of Heinrich G. (1819–1885), leader of an emigrating group. See article in *Nebraska Hist.*, vol. 49 (1968), 393–99.

BC71 Redekop, Calvin. "Religion and Society: A State within a Church." *Mennonite Quar. Rev.*, vol. 47 (1973), 339–57. On the German-Russian Mennonites.

BC72 Reeb, Paul E. "Hope Valley Church. German Free Church 1907–1939." *Work Paper III, Amer. Hist. Soc. of Germans from Russia* (February 1970), 49–60.

BC73 Reeb, Paul E. "So It Was with Our German-Russians." *Heritage Rev.*, vol. 23 (1979), 40–43.

BC74 Reimer, Gustav E., and G. R. Gaeddert. *Exiled by the Czar: Cornelius Jansen and the Great Mennonite Migration, 1874*. Newton, Kan.: Mennonite Publ. Office, 1956. 205p. Rev. by Guy F. Herschberger, *Mennonite Quar. Rev.*, vol. 32 (1958), 164–65; O. H. Zabelmeier, *Nebraska Hist.*, vol. 38 (1957), 76–78.

BC75 Reitzer, Paul G. "Germans from Russia in America, 1920." *Work Papers of the Amer. Hist. Soc. of Germans from Russia*, vol. 5 (1971), 14. Population statistics of German Russians in the several states.

BC76 Rimland, Ingrid. "Roots of the Wanderers." *Heritage Rev.*, vol. 23 (1979), 37–39.

BC77 Rippley, LaVern J. "Black Sea and Volga Germans in 1763, 1804 and 1910." *Heritage Rev.*, vol. 24 (1979), 3–9.

BC78 Rippley, LaVern J. "Jacob (Jake) Klotzbeacher." *Heritage Rev.*, 25 (1979), 29–31.

BC79 Rippley, LaVern J. "Soviet-German Citizens, Now You May Come Over!" *Work Papers of the Amer. Hist. Soc. of Germans from Russia*, vol. 11 (1973), 1–5. Translation of an article in *Der Spiegel* (1972).

BC80 Rippley, LaVern J. "Xenophobia and the Russian-German Experience." *Work Papers of the Amer. Hist. Soc. of Germans from Russia*, vol. 18 (1975), 6–11.

BC81 Rippley, LaVern J. "Zur sprachlichen Situation der Russlanddeutschen in den USA." In: *Deutsch als Muttersprache in den Vereinigten Staaten. Teil I. Der Mittelwesten*. Ed. Leopold Auburger, Heinz Kloss and Heinz Rupp. Wiesbaden: Steiner, 1979, p.211–22.

BC82 Rock, Kenneth W. *Germans from Russia in America: The First Hundred Years*. Fort Collins: Germans from Russia in Colorado Study Project, Colorado State Univ., ca. 1976. 16 leaves.

BC83 Sallet, F. W., ed. "Contributions Toward a History of the German-Russian Settlements in North America." Trans. by LaVern J. Rippley. *Heritage Rev.*, vol. 12 (1975), 30–40; vol. 13–14 (1976), 14, 28; vol. 15 (1976), 46; vol. 16 (1976), 27–31; vol. 17 (1977), 11–14; vol. 18 (1977), 25–27; vol. 19 (1977), 20–24; vol. 20 (1978), 20–24; vol. 21 (1978), 20–23; vol. 22 (1978), 5–7. From the *Dakota Freie Presse*, 1909–1910.

BC84 Sallet, Richard. *The Russian-German Settlements in the United States of America*. Trans. by LaVern J. Rippley and Armand Bauer. Fargo: Institute for Regional Studies, N. Dak. State Univ., 1974. Rev. by Victor Peters, *German-Canad. Yearbook*, vol. 3 (1976); J. H. Nottage, *Jour. of the West*, vol. 14 (1975), 156; James C. Juhnke, *Jour. of Amer. Hist.*, vol. 62 (1975), 718; J. Massman, *Minn. History*, vol. 94 (1975), 273–74; Frederick C. Luebke, *Pacific Hist. Rev.*, vol. 44 (1975), 567–68; Anton Richter, *Newsletter of the Soc. for German-Amer. St.*, vol. 2, no. 3 (1980–1981), 3.

BC85 Scheuerman, Richard D. *Pilgrims on the Earth: A German Russian Chronicle*. Fairfield, Wash.: Ye Galleon Pr., 1974.

BC86 Scheuerman, Richard D., and Clifford E. Trafzer. *The Volga Germans: Pioneers of the Northwest*. Moscow: Univ. of Idaho Pr., 1981. 245p.

BC87 Schock, Adolph. *In Quest of Free Land*. Assen, Neth., and San Jose, Calif.: n.p., 1965.

192p. Account of the 300,000 Germans from Russia of the Mennonite faith who migrated from the Volga to North America.

BC88 Schreiber, William I. *The Fate of the Prussian Mennonites.* Göttingen: Göttingen Research Committee, 1955. 47p. Rev. by R. H. Phelps, *German Quar.*, vol. 29 (1956), 285.

BC89 Schroeter, Elizabeth A. *From Here to the Pinnacles: Memories of Mennonite Life in the Ukraine and in America.* New York: Exposition Pr., 1956. 320p.

BC90 Steen, Herman. "Large Part of U.S. Wheat Now Going to Russia Descendants of Turkey Red that Mennonites of Czar's Crimea Brought to Great Plains." *The Southwestern Miller*, vol. 42, no. 2 (21 January 1964).

BC91 Stumpp, Karl. *The German-Russians: Two Centuries of Pioneering.* Trans. by Joseph S. Height. Bonn, Brussels, New York: Atlantic-Forum, 1967. 139p.

BC92 Stumpp, Karl. "Reise durch die russlanddeutschen Siedlungen in Nordamerika." *Südostdeutsche Vierteljahresblätter*, 1973, Heft 1.

BC93 Stumpp, Karl, ed. *Heimatbuch der Deutschen aus Russland 1962. Heimatbuch . . . 1963. Heimatbuch . . . 1964.* Stuttgart: Landsmannschaft der Deutschen aus Russland. Annual, 1962, 1963, 1964. Much of the material in these volumes deals directly with Germans from Russia in North America. *See* Götz, Karl. "Auf den Wanderwegen russlanddeutscher Mennoniten in America." *Heimatbuch 1963*, p. 67–75.

BC94 Vogt, Esther L. *Turkey Red.* Elgin, Ill.: David C. Cook, 1975. On the German-Russian Mennonites.

BC95 Vossler, Ron. "Child (Reflections)." *Heritage Rev.*, vol. 22 (1979), 25.

BC96 Weiss, Oscar. "Aus alten Zeiten (Of Olden Times)." Trans. by William H. Simpfenderfer. *Heritage Rev.*, vol. 25 (1979), 22–24. From the *Bessarabischer Heimatkalender*, 1955.

BC97 Welsch, Roger L. "The German-Russians: Two Centuries of Submergence and Resurgence." *Work Papers of the Amer. Hist. Soc. of Germans from Russia*, vol. 19 (1975), 25–29.

BC98 Wenzlaff, Theodore C. "Causes of German Migrations to Russia and to the New World." *Heritage Rev.*, vol. 11 (1975), 9–14.

BC99 Wenzlaff, Theodor C. "Important Dates in the History of the German Colonists in Russia." *Work Papers of the Amer. Hist. Soc. of Germans from Russia.*, vol. 5 (1971), 47–50; repr. *Heritage Rev.*, vol. 19 (1977), 36–38.

BC100 Wiebe, Raymond F. "Commemorative Stamp Recognizes Hard Red Winter Wheat." *Work Papers of the Amer. Hist. Soc. of Germans from Russia*, vol. 16 (1974), 25–27.

BC101 Williams, Hattie P. *The Czar's Germans, with Particular Reference to Volga Germans.* Ed. Emma S. Haynes, Philip B. Legler and Gerda S. Walker. Lincoln, Neb.: Amer. Hist. Soc. of Germans from Russia, 1975. Rev. by L. J. Rippley, *North Dakota Hist.*, vol. 43 (1976), 43–44.

BD
German Jews/German Jewish Life and Culture in America

General Sources and Bibliography

BD1 American Jewish Archives. "Jews in the Western Hemisphere." 9 pages of photostats, 1920–1944, from materials in the Foreign Ministry Archives, Bonn, Germany. Photocopying project completed at the Research Center of the Jewish Inst. of Religion, Hebrew Union College, Cincinnati, in 1968, under the direction of Jacob R. Marcus.

BD2 *American Jewish Historical Quarterly*. Vols. 1–66 and Index 1–20. (Formerly: *American Jewish Hist. Soc. Publications*.) Waltham, Mass.; Baltimore; etc., 1893–1977. Reissued by Kraus Microform, 1978–. 12 reels, 35 mm.

BD3 American Jewish Historical Society. *First Catalogue of the Manuscript Collection*. New York: Amer. Jewish Hist. Soc., n.d. Incl. papers of prominent 18th- and 19th-century Americans.

BD4 American Jewish Historical Society. *A Preliminary Survey of the Manuscript Collections Found in the American Jewish Historical Society*. Part 1. New York: n.p., 1967. 30p. Rev. by S. M. Dubow, *American Archivist*, vol. 32 (January 1969), 35–36. Comp. by the Library Staff under the direction of Nathan Kaganoff. Entries arranged alphabetically by name of individual, family or institution, *e.g.* Haym Salomon, Mordecai Sheftall, Rebecca Gratz, Emma Lazarus, Isaac Leeser, Cyrus Adler, Louis Marshall, Simon Wolf, and Molly Picon.

BD5 *American Jewish Year Book*. Philadelphia: The Jewish Publ. Soc. of America. Vol. 1–, 1899/1900–. Each volume contains a list of Jewish periodical publications and indexes.

BD6 Appel, John J. "Hansen's Third Generation Law and the Origins of the American Jewish Historical Society." *Jewish Social St.*, vol. 23 (1961), 3–20.

BD7 Baron, Salo W. "American Jewish History: Problems and Methods." *Publs., Amer. Jewish Hist. Soc.*, vol. 29 (1950), 207–66.

BD8 Brickman, William W. *The Jewish Community in America: An Annotated and Classified Bibliographical Guide*. New York: Burt Franklin & Co., 1977. 396p.

BD9 *Canadian Jewish Historical Society. Journal*. 1977–. Formerly: *Jewish Historical Society of Canada. Journal*. Ed. Jonathan V. Plaut. Publ. in Montreal.

BD10 Cohen, Martin A. "Structuring American Jewish History." *Amer. Jewish Hist. Quar.*, vol. 57 (December 1967), 137–52. The challenge is to study the tensions between the lures of assimilation and the values of Jewish identification.

BD11 Dubow, Sylvan M. "The Jewish Historical Society of Greater Washington: Its Archival Program." *American Archivist*, vol. 30 (October 1967).

BD12 Endelman, Judith E. "Judaica Americana." *Amer. Jewish Hist. Quar.*, vol. 64 (June 1975). An annotated bibliography.

BD13 Glanz, Rudolph. *The German Jew in America: An Annotated Bibliography Including Books, Pamphlets, and Articles of Special Interest*. Cincinnati: Hebrew Union College Pr.; New York: Ktav Publ. House, 1969. 192p. Rev. in *Histor. Zeitschrift*, vol. 210 (1970), 753; B. Korn, *N.Y. Hist. Soc. Quar.*, vol. 55 (1971), 97; E. V. Toy, *Amer. Quar.*, vol. 22, no. 2, part 2 (Summer 1970), 280. A compilation of over 2500 entries.

BD14 Goertz, R. O. W. "University Research on Jewish-Canadians: First Supplement." *Canad. Ethnic St.*, vol. 2, no. 1 (June 1970).

BD15 Handlin, Oscar. "A Twenty Year Retrospect of American Jewish Historiography." *Amer. Jewish Hist. Quar.*, vol. 65 (June 1976), 295–309.

BD16 *Jewish Encyclopedia: A Descriptive Record of the History, Religion, Literature, and Customs of the Jewish People from the Earliest Times to the*

Present. 12 vols. New York: Funk & Wagnalls, 1901–1906.

BD17 *Jewish Way.* 1941–. Ed. Mrs. Alice Oppenheimer. Monthly; in English and German languages. Publ. from 870 Riverside Drive, New York, N.Y. 10032.

BD18 Kaganoff, Benzion C. *A Dictionary of Jewish Names and Their History.* New York: Schocken Books, 1977. 250p. Rev. by Elsdon C. Smith, *Names*, vol. 26, no. 3 (September 1978), 205–07.

BD19 Kaganoff, Nathan M., Judith E. Endelmann, and Martha B. Katz-Hyman. "Judaica Americana [Bibliography]." *Amer. Jewish Hist. Quar.* (after 1968 *Amer. Jewish History*), continuously from vol. 52, no. 1 (1962–1963) through vol. 70, no. 4 (1980–81). In vol. 52 there were articles in each of the four quarterly issues; from vol. 53 through vol. 70 they appeared in issues nos. 2 and 4 of each successive volume.

BD20 Kloss, Heinz. *Statistik, Presse und Organisationen des Judentums in den Vereinigten Staaten und Kanada: Ein Handbuch in Zusammenarbeit mit Edith Pütter bearb. von Heinz Kloss.* Vertrauliche Schriftenreihe Übersee, Nr. 4. Stuttgart: Selbstverlag der Publikationsstelle, 1944. 137p. Film reproduction, ca. 1955, New York Public Library. Listed in National Union Catalogue.

BD21 [Leo Baeck Institute.] *Libraries and Archives News.* Ed. Gabrielle Bamberger. Semiannual publication of the Leo Baeck Institute, New York City.

BD22 Malycky, A. "University Research on Jewish-Canadians: A Preliminary Check List of Dissertations and Theses." *Canad. Ethnic St.*, vol. 1, no. 1 (April 1969).

BD23 Malycky, A., and R. Pearlman. "Jewish-Canadian Periodical Publications: First Supplement." *Canad. Ethnic St.*, vol. 2, no. 1 (June 1970).

BD24 Marcus, Jacob Rader. *A Brief Bibliography of American Jewish History.* New York: The American Jewish Tercentenary Committee and Jewish Book Council of America, 1954. 16p.

BD25 Marcus, Jacob Rader. *An Index to Scientific Articles on American Jewish History.* Amer. Jewish Archives publ. no. 7. Cincinnati: Amer. Jewish Archives, 1971. 240p.

BD26 Marcus, Jacob Rader. "Major Trends in American Jewish Historical Research." *Amer. Jewish Archives*, vol. 16 (1964), 9–21. Points out the continuing interest in German-Jewish immigration.

BD27 Marcus, Jacob Rader. "A Selected Bibliography of American Jewish History." *Publs., Amer. Jewish Hist. Soc.*, vol. 51 (1961), 97–134.

BD28 Marcus, Jacob Rader, ed. *American Jewry: Documents—Eighteenth Century, Primarily Hitherto Unpublished Manuscripts.* Cincinnati: n.p., 1959. Rev. by G. S. May, *Michigan Hist.*, vol. 44 (1960), 114–17; E. F. Romig, *N.Y. Hist. Soc. Quar.*, vol. 44 (1960), 228–29.

BD29 Marcus, Jacob Rader, ed. *Jewish Americana. A Catalog of Books and Articles by Jews or Relating to Them Published in the United States from the Earliest Days to 1850 and Found in the Library of the Hebrew Union College–Jewish Institute of Religion in Cincinnati. A Supplement to A. S. W. Rosenbach's An American Jewish Bibliography.* Cincinnati: Amer. Jewish Archives, 1954. 115p.

BD30 Melzer, Joseph, ed. *Deutsch-Jüdisches Schicksal: Wegweiser durch das Schrifttum der letzten 15 Jahre, 1945–1960.* Köln: Jos. Melzer, 1960. See also *Nachtrag*, 1960–61. Köln: Melzer, 1961.

BD31 Pearlman, R., and A. Malycky. "Jewish-Canadian Periodical Publications: A Preliminary Check List." *Canad. Ethnic St.*, vol. 1, no. 1 (April 1969).

BD32 *Poale Zion.* Records, 1906–1960. ca. 275,000 items in American Jewish Archives, Cincinnati (MS 65-1735). Received from the Labor Zionist Organization of America, New York.

BD33 Rappaport, Ruth. "A Selective Guide to Source Materials on German Jews in the United States from 1933 to the Present Time." Unpubl. report dated 19 May 1958, Univ. of California School of Librarianship.

BD34 Rosenwaike, Ira. "An Estimate and Analysis of the Jewish Population of the United States in 1790." *Publs., Amer. Jewish Hist. Soc.*, vol. 50, no. 1 (1960), 23–67. Data tabulated by states, cities, country of origin, etc.

BD35 Rosenwaike, Ira. "The Jewish Population of the United States as Estimated from the Census

General Sources and Bibliography *(cont.)*
of 1820." *Amer. Jewish Hist. Quar.*, vol. 53, no. 2 (1963), 131–78. Analysis by country of origin and place of settlement in the United States.

BD36 Stern, Norton B., comp. and annotator. *California Jewish History. A Descriptive Bibliography: Over Five Hundred Fifty Works for the Period Gold Rush to Post-World War I.* Glendale, Calif.: Arthur H. Clark, 1967. 175p.

BD37 Tobias, Henry. "Der Bund-Archiv in die Fareinigte Shtaten." Bund Archives *Bulletin* no. 7 (April 1966), 1–2.

BD38 Weinryb, Bernard D. "Jewish Immigration and Accommodation to America: Research, Trends, Problems." *Publs., Amer. Jewish Hist. Soc.*, vol. 46 (1957), 366–403.

BD39 "Wissenschaftliche Forschung auf dem Gebiet der Geschichte der Juden in Deutschland und in der Welt." *Veröffentlichungen des Leo-Baeck Institut*. London, N.Y.: n.p., ca. 1965. Rev. in *Historische Zeitschrift*, vol. 202 (1966), 518–28.

German Jewry in America/ History and General Studies

BD40 Altmann, Alexander. *Studies in Nineteenth-Century Jewish History*. Cambridge: Harvard Univ. Pr., 1964.

BD41 Appel, John J. "Jews in American Caricature." *Amer. Jewish Hist.*, vol. 70 (1981), 103–33.

BD42 Berman, Myron. "The Attitude of American Jewry towards East European Jewish Immigration, 1881–1914." Diss., Columbia, 1963.

BD43 Bez, Khaim. "One Hundred Years of the Yiddish Press in the United States." *Zukunft*, vol. 75 (1970), 273–79. In Yiddish.

BD44 Blau, Joseph L., and Salo W. Baron, eds. *The Jews of the United States, 1790–1840: A Documentary History*. 3 vols. New York: Columbia Univ. Pr., 1963. 1034p. Rev. by K. Mellon, Jr., *Catholic Hist. Rev.*, vol. 51 (1965), 223–25.

BD45 Bolkosky, Sidney. *The Distorted Image. German Jewish Perceptions of Germans and Germany, 1918–1935.* New York: Elsevier, 1975. 224p. German Jews accepted too readily that "true Germanism" was the *Klassik* of Lessing, Goethe, and Kant.

BD46 Bush, Isidore. "The Task of the Jews in the United States—1851." *Amer. Jewish Archives*, vol. 18, no. 2 (November 1966), 155–59. Repr. in English of an address delivered by Isidore Bush, a recent immigrant from Prague, in 1851.

BD47 Dimont, Max. *The Jews in America: The Roots and Destiny of American Jews*. New York: Simon & Schuster, 1978. 286p. Argues against the "European-centered" views of 19th-century Jewish history.

BD48 Dinnerstein, Leonard, and Mary Dale Palsson, eds. *Jews in the South*. Baton Rouge: La. State Univ. Pr., 1973. 392p.

BD49 DuBois, Rachel Davis. *The Jews in American Life*. Ed. Rachel Davis-DuBois and Emma Schweppe. New York: Thomas Nelson, 1935. 130p.

BD50 Duker, Abraham G. "Emerging Culture Patterns in American Jewish Life." *Publs., Amer. Jewish Hist. Soc.*, vol. 39 (1950), 351–88.

BD51 Eisenberg, Azriel, and Hannah G. Goodman, eds. *Eyewitnesses to American Jewish History: A History of American Jewry*. Part 2. *The German Immigration, 1800–1875*. New York: Union of American Hebrew Congregations, 1977. 148p.

BD52 Feingold, Henry L. *Zion in America: The Jewish Experience from Colonial Times to the Present*. New York: Twayne, 1974. 357p. Rev. by R. A. Rockaway, *Jour. of Amer. Hist.*, vol. 62, no. 4 (March 1976), 958–59.

BD53 Feldman, Egal. *Sources of Jewish Education in America Prior to 1881*. El Paso: n.p., 1960, p.114–243. Statistical tables and quoted sources.

BD54 Friedman, Lee M. "The Problems of Nineteenth Century American Jewish Peddlers." *Publs., Amer. Jewish Hist. Soc.*, vol. 44 (1954), 1–7.

BD55 Gay, Ruth. *Jews in America: A Short History*. New York: Basic Books, 1965. Rev. by C. E. Stipe, *Rev. of Religious Research*, vol. 13 (1971), 83–84.

BD56 Glanz, Rudolf. *The German Jew in America*. Bibliographica Judaica, no. 1. Cincinnati: Hebrew Union College Pr., 1969. 192p. Rev. by R. E. Cazden, *German-Amer. St.*, vol. 5 (1972), 181–83.

BD57 Glanz, Rudolf. "The German Jewish Mass Emigration: 1820–1880." *Amer. Jewish Archives*, vol. 22, no. 1 (1970), 49–66. A rationally planned transplantation of young Jews in search of economic opportunities.

BD58 Glanz, Rudolf. *Jew and Irish: Historic Group Relations and Immigration*. New York: n.p., 1966. 159p.

BD59 Glanz, Rudolf. *Studies in Judaica Americana*. New York: Ktav Publ. House, 1970. 407p. Rev. by J. Brandes, *Internat. Migration Rev.*, vol. 7 (1973), 93–94. A significant collection of essays on the German-Jewish body in the United States and their monumental work of community building.

BD60 Goldberg, B. Z. "The American Yiddish Press at Its Centennial." *Judaism*, vol. 20 (1971), 223–28.

BD61 Golden, Harry L., and Martin Rywell. *Jews in American History, 1492–1950*. Charlotte, N.C.: n.p., 1950.

BD62 Goodman, Abram Vossen. "A German Mercenary Observes American Jews during the Revolution." *Amer. Jewish Hist. Quar.*, vol. 59, no. 2 (December 1969), 227. Observations recorded in J. C. Döhla's *Tagebuch eines Bayreuther Soldaten* (Bayreuth, 1913).

BD63 Greenberg, Gershon, ed. "A German-Jewish Immigrant's Perception of America, 1853–54." *Amer. Jewish Hist. Quar.*, vol. 67 (1978), 307–41. A translation of *Deutsch-Amerikanische Skizzen für jüdische Auswanderer und Nichtauswanderer*.

BD64 Grobman, Alex. "What Did They Know? The American Jewish Press and the Holocaust, 1 September 1939–17 December 1942." *Amer. Jewish Hist.*, vol. 68 (March 1979).

BD65 Handlin, Oscar. *Adventure in Freedom: Three Hundred Years of Jewish Life in America*. New York: n.p., 1954.

BD66 Handlin, Oscar. "American Views of the Jew at the Opening of the 20th Century." *Publs., Amer. Jewish Hist. Soc.*, vol. 40 (1951), 323–44. A characteristic of the stereotype immigrant Jew was his German accent.

BD67 Harap, Lewis. "Socialism, Anti-Semitism, and Jewish Ethnicity." *Jour. of Ethnic St.*, vol. 6, no. 4 (1979), 65–84.

BD68 Higham, John. "Social Discrimination Against the Jews in America, 1830–1930." *Publs., Amer. Jewish Hist. Soc.*, vol. 47 (September 1957), 1–33.

BD69 Hirschler, Eric E., ed. *Jews from Germany in the United States*. Introd. by Max Gruenewald. New York: Farrar, Straus and Cudahy, 1955. 182p. Rev. by L. M. Friedman, *Amer. Jewish Hist. Soc. Publs.* vol. 46, no. 1 (1955), 59–60.

BD70 Janowsky, Oscar I., ed. *The American Jews: A Composite Picture*. New York: n.p., 1942. A history of the Jews in America.

BD71 Jick, Leon A. *The Americanization of the Synagogue, 1820–1870*. Hanover, N.H.: Univ. Pr. of New England, ca. 1978. Rev. by S. D. Temkin, *Amer. Jewish Hist.*, vol. 68 (1979), 556–58.

BD72 Jonas, Harold J. "American Jewish History as Reflected in General American History." *Publs., Amer. Jewish Hist. Soc.*, vol. 39, no. 2 (1950), 283–90. Observations on how German Jews in America assimilate in contrast to other Jews.

BD73 Kisch, Guido. *In Search of Freedom. A History of American Jews from Czechoslovakia*. London: Edward Goldston & Son, 1949. 373p. Incl. a great number of German-speaking Jewish immigrants.

BD74 Kligsberg, Moses. "Jewish Immigrants in Business: A Sociological Study." *Amer. Jewish Hist. Quar.*, vol. 56 (March 1967).

BD75 Korn, Bertram Wallace. *American Jewry and the Civil War*. Philadelphia: Jewish Publ. Soc., 1952. 331p. Rev. by R. R. Levy, *N.Y. Hist.*, vol. 34 (1953), 97–99.

BD76 Korn, Bertram Wallace. *Eventful Years and Experiences: Studies in Nineteenth Century American Jewish History*. Amer. Jewish Archives Publs., no. 1. Cincinnati: Amer. Jewish Archives, 1954. 248p. Chap. I deals with the German Jews.

BD77 Lavender, Abraham D. *A Coat of Many Colors: Jewish Subcommunities in the United States.* Westport, Conn.: n.p., 1977.

BD78 Learsi, Rufus (Israel Goldberg). *The Jews in America: A History.* New York: Ktav Publ., 1972. *See* esp. "American Jewry, 1954–1971," an epilogue by Abraham J. Karp.

BD79 Levinson, Daniel J. "The Study of Ethnocentric Ideology." In: *The Authoritarian Personality.* Ed. Theodor W. Adorno et al. Series in Prejudice of the American Jewish Committee. New York: Harper, 1950, p.102–50.

BD80 Lifschutz, Ezekiel. "Jacob Gordin's Proposal to Establish an Agricultural Colony." *Amer. Jewish Hist. Quar.*, vol. 56, no. 2 (December 1966), 151–62. A Yiddish playwright who came to the United States with the intention of establishing a communal agricultural colony.

BD81 Mandel, Irving Aaron. "Attitude of the American Jewish Community toward East-European Immigration." *Amer. Jewish Archives*, vol. 3, no. 1 (1950), 11–34.

BD82 Marks, Harry H. "Down with the Jews!" *Amer. Jewish Archives*, vol. 16, no. 1 (1964), 3–8. Reprint of a 19th-century attack on anti-Semitism.

BD83 Marmer, Kalman. "The American Yiddish Press in the 1870's." *Yidishe Kultur*, vol. 32 (May 1970), 4–12. In Yiddish.

BD84 Mayo, Louise A. "The Ambivalent Image: The Perception of the Jew in Nineteenth Century America." Diss., City Univ. of New York, 1977.

BD85 Morgenthau, Hans J. *The Tragedy of German-Jewish Liberalism.* The Leo Baeck Memorial Lectures, no. 4. New York: Leo Baeck Institute, 1961.

BD86 Panitz, Esther L. "The Polarity of American Jewish Attitudes towards Immigration (1870–1891). A Chapter in American Socio-Economic History." *Amer. Jewish Hist. Quar.*, vol. 53, no. 2 (1963), 99–130. The coming of the East European Jews.

BD87 Petuchowski, Jacob J. "Abraham Geiger and Samuel Holdheim—Their Differences in Germany and Repercussions in America." *Yearbook of the Leo Baeck Institute*, vol. 22 (1977), 139–59.

BD88 Reissner, Hanns G. "'Ganstown, U.S.A.'—A German-Jewish Dream." *Amer. Jewish Archives*, vol. 16, no. 1 (1962), 20–31. The "Verein für Cultur und Wissenschaft der Juden" led by Eduard Gans, Gerson Adersbach and others, 1815–1820.

BD89 Reissner, Hanns G. "The German-American Jews (1800–1850)." *Yearbook of the Leo Baeck Institute*, vol. 10 (1965), 57–116. Substantial study of the immigration and acculturation of German-speaking Jews.

BD90 Rothstein, Jacob. "Reactions of the American Yiddish Press to the Tshernovits Language Conference of 1908 as a Reflection of the American Jewish Scene." *Internat. Jour. of the Sociology of Language*, vol. 13 (1977), 103–20.

BD91 Sarna, Jonathan D. "A German-Jewish Immigrant's Perception of America, 1953–54; Some Further Notes on Mordecai M. Noah, a Jewel Robbery, and Isaac M. Wise." *Amer. Jewish Hist.*, vol. 68 (1978), 206–12. Remarks in extension of the article by G. Greenberg listed above.

BD92 Schappes, Morris. *Documentary History of the Jews in the United States.* New York: n.p., 1950.

BD93 Schorsch, Ismar. *Jewish Reaction to German Anti-Semitism 1870–1914.* New York: Columbia Univ. Pr., 1972. 291p.

BD94 Sharfman, I. Harold. *Jews on the Frontier.* Chicago: Henry Regnery Co., 1977. 337p.

BD95 Shipton, Clifford K. "An Americanist Looks at American Jewish History." *Amer. Jewish Hist. Quar.*, vol. 56 (March 1967).

BD96 Singer, David G. "The Prelude to Nazism: The German-American Press and the Jews 1919–1933." *Amer. Jewish Hist. Quar.*, vol. 66 (March 1977).

BD97 Sklare, Marshall. *America's Jews.* New York: Random House, 1971. Rev. by M. Richman, *Rev. of Religious Research*, vol. 14 (1973), 196–97.

BD98 Sloan, Irving J., ed. *The Jews in America 1621–1977: A Chronology and Fact Book.* 2nd ed. Dobbs Ferry: Oceana Publs., 1978. 150p.

BD99 Szajkowski, Zosa. "The Attitude of American Jews to East European Jewish Immigration (1881–1893)." *Publs., Amer. Jewish Hist. Soc.*, vol. 40 (1951), 221–80.

BD100 Tcherikower, Elias, ed. *The Early Jewish Labor Movement in the United States*. New York: YIVO Institute for Jewish Research, 1961. 379p.

BD101 Teller, Judd L. *Strangers and Natives: The Evolution of the American Jew from 1921 to the Present*. New York: Delacorte Pr., 1968. 308p. Rev. by M. Rosenstock, *Amer. Jewish Hist.*, vol. 59, no. 2 (December 1969), 241–43.

BD102 Thorwald, Jürgen. *Das Gewürz. Die Saga der Juden in Amerika*. Zürich: Droemersche Buchhandlung, 1978. A "Sachbuch" or popular history of the Jews in America.

BD103 "Trail Blazers of the Trans-Mississippi West." *Amer. Jewish Archives*, vol. 8 (1956), 59–130. German Jews in the expansion of the United States beyond the Mississippi.

BD104 Vagts, Alfred. "Die Juden im amerikanisch-deutschen imperialistischen Konflikt vor 1917." *Amerikastudien*, vol. 24 (1979), 56–71.

BD105 Wilhelm, Kurt. "Die deutsch-jüdische Presse in den Vereinigten Staaten." *MB—Mitteilungsblatt* (Tel Aviv), vol. 30, no. 34 (1962), 4.

BD106 Zielonka, David, and Robert J. Wechman. *The Eager Immigrants: A Survey of the Life and Americanization of Jewish Immigrants to the United States*. Champaign, Ill.: Stipes Publ. Co., 1972. 103p.

Jewish Life and Culture/Judaism

BD107 Cohn, Bernhard N. "Early German Preaching in America." *Historia Judaica*, vol. 15 (1953), 86–134. Rabbis preach in German, 1840–1879.

BD108 Cohon, Samuel S. "The History of the Hebrew Union College." *Publs., Amer. Jewish Hist. Soc.*, vol. 40, no. 1 (1950), 17–55. Founded by I. M. Wise, native of Germany.

BD109 Cronbach, Abraham. "American Synagogues: The Lessons of the Names." *Amer. Jewish Archives*, vol. 16, no. 2 (1964), 124–34. Synagogues named after prominent leaders of Central-European origins.

BD110 Davis, Moshe. *Yahadut Amerika Be-Hitpathutah (The Shaping of American Judaism)*. New York: The Jewish Theolog. Seminary of America, 1951. 406p. In Hebrew. Rev. by O. Handlin, *Harv. Theol. Rev.*, vol. 14, no. 2 (1952), 165–66; J. Bloch, *Publs., Amer. Jewish Hist. Soc.*, vol. 42, no. 1 (1952), 91–107.

BD111 De Sola Pool, D. "Religious and Cultural Phases of American Jewish History." *Publs., Amer. Jewish Hist. Soc.*, vol. 39, no. 3 (1950), 291–301.

BD112 Frank, Helmut. "As a German Rabbi to America." In: *Paul Lazarus Gedenkbuch*. Jerusalem: n.p., 1961, p.135–42. Religious adjustment of the German-Jewish immigrant.

BD113 Gittlen, Arthur Joseph. "Political and Social Thought Contained in the Jewish-American Novel (1867–1927.)" Diss., Michigan State, 1969. 211p. A study of 13 works in English dealing with the experiences of Jewish-Americans.

BD114 Glanz, Rudolf. *The Jew in Early American Wit and Graphic Humor*. New York: Ktav Publ. House, 1973. 269p. On the new role played by the Jew in the American milieu, using social criticism humorously expressed.

BD115 Glanz, Rudolf. *The Jewish Woman in America: Two Female Immigrant Generations, 1820–1929. Vol. 2. The German Jewish Woman*. New York: Ktav Publ. House, 1976. 213p. Rev. *Jour. of Amer. Hist.*, vol. 64, no. 3 (December 1977), 794–95. Domestic, social, economic, and cultural aspects of women's lives.

BD116 Glanz, Rudolf. *Jews in Relation to the Cultural Milieu of the Germans in America up to the Eighteen Eighties*. New York: Yiddish Scientific Institute, 1947. 55p. Rev. by E. G. Hartmann, *Pa. Hist.*, vol. 16 (1949), 160; C. Hammond, *Ind. Mag. of Hist.*, vol. 45 (1949), 310. Repr. in Glanz's *Studies in Judaica Americana*. New York: Ktav Publ., 1970.

BD117 Glanz, Rudolf. "Notes on Early Jewish Peddling in America." In: *Studies in Judaica Americana*. New York: Ktav Publ., 1970. The Jewish

Jewish Life and Culture/Judaism *(cont.)*

peddler served a particular clientele: the German immigrant.

BD118 Glanz, Rudolf. "The Rise of the Jewish Club in America." *Jewish Social St.*, vol. 31 (April 1969), 82–99.

BD119 Glanz, Rudolf. "Where the Jewish Press was Distributed in Pre-Civil War America." *Western States Jewish Hist. Quar.*, vol. 5 (October 1972).

BD120 Glazer, Nathan. *American Judaism. A Historical Survey of the Jewish Religion in America.* Chicago: Univ. of Chicago Pr., 1957. 176p. See esp. chap. 3: "The German Immigration and the Shaping of Reform, 1825–94," p.22–42.

BD121 Gordon, Albert I. *Jews in Transition.* Minneapolis: Univ. of Minn. Pr., 1949. 331p. Rev. by I. Meyer, *Historia Judaica*, vol. 11, no. 2 (1949), 167.

BD122 Karp, Abraham J., ed. *The Jewish Experience in America: Selected Studies from the Publications of the American Jewish Historical Society.* Vol. 1. *The Colonial Period.* Vol. 2. *In the Early Republic.* Vol. 3. *The Emerging Community.* Vol. 4. *The Era of Immigration.* Vol. 5. *At Home in America.* New York: Ktav Publ., 1969. 2,133p. Rev. by L. Dinnerstein, *Internat. Migration Rev.*, vol. 5 (Spring 1971), 99–100; M. Freiberg, *New Eng. Quar.*, vol. 43, no. 3 (September 1970), 502–04; E. S. Shapiro, *Amer. Quar.*, vol. 22, no. 2, part 2 (Summer 1970), 291.

BD123 Kaul, Leo. *The Story of Radical Reform Judaism.* Los Angeles: n.p., 1951. 52p. On the reformer Emil G. Hirsch.

BD124 Kober, Adolf. "Jewish Preaching and Preachers in Germany and America." *Historia Judaica*, vol. 7, no. 2 (1945), 103–34.

BD125 Kober, Adolf. "Jewish Religious and Cultural Life in America as Reflected in the [Bernhard] Felsenthal Collection." *Publs., Amer. Jewish Hist. Soc.*, vol. 45, no. 2 (1955), 93–127. B. in the Pfalz in 1822, died in 1908. Article reproduces many letters, mostly in German.

BD126 Korn, Bertram W. "American Jewish Life a Century Ago." *Yearbook of the Central Conference of American Rabbis* (Philadelphia), vol. 59 (1949), 3–32.

BD127 Korn, Bertram W. *German-Jewish Intellectual Influences on American Jewish Life, 1824–1972.* Syracuse: Syracuse Univ. Pr., 1972. 25p. Traces the influence of seminal German thinkers on evolving American Judaism.

BD128 Lowi, Theodore. "Southern Jews: The Two Communities." *Jewish Jour. of Sociology*, vol. 6 (July 1964), 103–17. Discovers two groups distinct in social standing and ideology.

BD129 Lurie, Harry L. *A Heritage Affirmed: The Jewish Federation Movement in America.* Philadelphia: Jewish Publ. Soc. of America, 1961. 490p. Rev. by B. B. Rosenberg, *Amer. Jewish Archives*, vol. 16, no. 2 (1964), 166–67.

BD130 Philipson, David. *The Reform Movement in Judaism.* New York: Ktav Publ. Co. 1967. Repr. 503p. Rev. by M. A. Meyer, *Amer. Jewish Hist. Quar.*, vol. 67, no. 3 (March 1968), 439–40. Europe and Germany as the cradle of Reform Judaism.

BD131 Plaut, W. Gunther. *The Rise of Reform Judaism: A Sourcebook of Its European Origins.* New York: Union of Amer. Hebrew Congregations, ca. 1964. Rev. by L. P. Gartner, *Amer. Jewish Hist. Quar.*, vol. 53, no. 3 (1964), 301–02. The relation of Reform Judaism, which gained most strength in America, to German philosophical idealism.

BD132 Rosenberg, Stuart E. "Some Sermons in the Spirit of the Pittsburgh Platform." *Historia Judaica*, vol. 17 (1956), 59–76. With interesting sidelights on German preaching and the fight of the first-generation rabbis to abolish it.

BD133 Roth, Cecil. *The Great Synagogue.* London: Edw. Goldston. Son, 1950. 311p. Rev. by Jacob R. Marcus, *Amer. Jewish Archives*, vol. 3, no. 3 (1951), 112–16. History of the first German rite congregation in 17th-century England, which influenced American Jewry.

BD134 Rothkoff, Aaron. "The American Sojourns of Ridbas [Rabbi Jacob David Wilowski, 1845–1913]: Religious Problems within the Immigrant Community." *Amer. Jewish Hist. Quar.*, vol. 57 (June 1968), 557f.

BD135 Ryback, Martin B. "The East-West Conflict in American Reform Judaism." *Amer. Jewish Archives*, vol. 4, no. 1 (1952), 3–25. On the contending reform movements led by David Einhorn and Isaac M. Wise.

BD136 Sanders, Marion K. "The Several Worlds of American Jews." *Harper's Mag.*, April 1966.

BD137 Sherman, C. Bezalel. *The Jew Within American Society. A Study in Ethnic Individuality.* Detroit: Wayne St. Univ. Pr., 1965. 260p. Rev. by J. J. Diamond, *Internat. Migration Rev.*, vol. 1, no. 1 (Fall 1966), 65–66.

BD138 Stern, Malcolm H. "Jewish Marriage and Intermarriage in the Federal Period (1776–1840)." *Amer. Jewish Archives*, vol. 19, no. 2 (November 1967).

BD139 Whiteman, Maxwell. "The Colonial Jewish Peddler." In: *Neuman Studies.* Philadelphia: Saifert, 1966, p.503–515.

Local Jewish History

See also Local History under Section BB: Canadian Germans.

ALABAMA

BD140 Elovitz, H. *A Century of Jewish Life in Dixie: The Birmingham Experience.* Univ. of Ala. Pr., 1974. 258p.

ARIZONA

BD141 Glanz, Rudolf. "Notes on the Early Jews in Arizona." *Western States Jewish Hist. Quar.*, vol. 5 (July 1973), 243f.

BD142 Lamb, Blaine. "Jews in Early Phoenix, 1870–1920." *Jour. of Ariz. Hist.*, vol. 18 (Autumn 1977), 299–318. Phoenix's Jewish merchants of German, French, and Polish extraction.

CALIFORNIA

BD143 Cogan, Sara G., comp. *Pioneer Jews of the California Mother Lode, 1849–1880: An Annotated Bibliography.* Berkeley: Western Jewish Hist. Center, Judah L. Magnes Memorial Museum, 1968. 54p. Materials from various languages presented in translation.

BD144 Decker, Peter R. "Jewish Merchants in San Francisco: Social Mobility on the Urban Frontier." *Amer. Jewish Hist.*, vol. 68 (1979), 396–407.

BD145 Gelfand, Mitchell. "Progress and Prosperity: Jewish Social Mobility in Los Angeles in the Booming Eighties." *Amer. Jewish Hist.*, vol. 68 (1979), 408–33.

BD146 Glanz, Rudolf. *The Jews of California: From the Discovery of Gold until 1880.* New York: Waldon Pr., 1960. 188p. Rev. by S. Adler, *Jewish Social St.*, vol. 26, no. 2 (April 1964), 116–17.

BD147 Levinson, Robert E. *The Jews in the California Gold Rush.* New York: Ktav Publ. House, 1978. 232p. Rev. by Gerald Staley, *Jour. of the West*, vol. 22 (1980), 69–70.

BD148 Turner, Justin T. "The First Decade of Los Angeles Jewry: A Pioneer History (1850–1860)." *Amer. Jewish Hist. Quar.*, vol. 54 (December 1964), 123–64.

BD149 Wilson, Don W. "Pioneer Jews in California and Arizona, 1849–1875." *Jour. of the West*, vol. 6 (April 1967), 226–36.

COLORADO

BD150 Uchill, Ida Libert. Papers. 1913–1950. In American Jewish Archives (MS 68-106). Sources on Jewish settlers in Denver and Colorado.

CONNECTICUT

BD151 Kisch, Guido. "Two American Jewish Pioneers of New Haven." *Historia Judaica*, vol. 4, no. 1 (1942), 16–37. On Sigmund and Leopold Wassermann-Waterman. Sigmund was instructor in German in Yale College, 1844–1847, and first Jewish candidate to receive a degree (Doctor of Medicine) from Yale in 1848.

GEORGIA

BD152 Hertzberg, Steven. *Strangers Within the City: The Jews of Atlanta, 1845–1915.* Philadelphia: The Jewish Publ. Soc. of America, 1978. 352p. Rev. by Eli N. Evans, *Amer. Jewish Hist.*, vol. 68 (1978), 100–05. Data on individual Jewish residents, 1870–1900.

BD153 Rothschild, Janice O. "Pre-1867 Atlanta Jewry." *Amer. Jewish Hist. Quar.*, vol. 42 (March 1973), 242f.

ILLINOIS

BD154 Berkow, Ira. *Maxwell Street: Survival in a Bazaar.* Garden City, N.Y.: Doubleday, 1977. 532p. Rev. by Elinor Grumet, *Amer. Jewish Archives*, vol. 30, no. 1 (1978), 82–84.

BD155 Fleishaker, Oscar. "The Illinois-Iowa Jewish Community on the Banks of the Mississippi River." D.H.L. diss., Yeshiva Univ., 1957. 450p.

BD156 *The Sentinel's History of Chicago Jewry: 1911–1961.* Chicago: Sentinel Publ. Co., 1961. 256p.

KENTUCKY

BD157 Rosenwaike, Ira. "The First Jewish Settlers in Louisville." *Filson Club Hist. Quar.*, vol. 53 (January 1979), 37–44.

LOUISIANA

BD158 Korn, Bertram Wallace. *The Early Jews of New Orleans.* Waltham, Mass.: Amer. Jewish Hist. Soc., 1969. 382p. Rev. by A. L. Jamison, *Internat. Migration Rev.*, vol. 7 (1973), 94–95; M. Rischin, *Jour. of Amer. Hist.*, vol. 57, no. 1 (June 1970), 152–53; M. H. Stern, *Jewish Social St.*, vol. 32, no. 2 (April 1970), 168–69; T. H. Williams, *Amer. Jewish Hist. Quar.*, vol. 60, no. 2 (December 1970), 200–02.

BD159 Proctor, Samuel. "Jewish Life in New Orleans, 1718–1860." *La. Hist. Quar.*, vol. 40 (1957), 110–32.

MARYLAND

BD160 Aberbach, Moses. "The Early German Jews of Baltimore." *Report of the Soc. for the Hist. of the Germans in Maryland*, vol. 35 (1972), 27–36.

BD161 Dobert, Eitel Wolf. "Einhorn and Szold: Two Liberal German Rabbis in Baltimore." *Report of the Soc. for the Hist. of Germans in Maryland*, vol. 29 (1956), 51–57. German Reform Judaism in Baltimore.

BD162 Fein, Isaac M. *The Making of an American Jewish Community: The History of Baltimore Jewry from 1773 to 1920.* Philadelphia: Jewish Publ. Soc. of America, 1970. 368p. Rev. by L. S. Levy, *Md. Hist. Mag.*, vol. 66, no. 2 (1970), 214–16. Chap. titled "The Formative Years: 1830 to 1855" deals in particular with the period of German immigration.

BD163 Levin, Alexander Lee. *The Szolds of Lombard Street. A Baltimore Family, 1859–1909.* Philadelphia: Jewish Publ. Soc. of America, 1960. 418p. A fictionalized family history.

BD164 Rosenwaike, Ira. "The Jews of Baltimore: 1810 to 1820;" "The Jews of Baltimore: 1820 to 1830." *Amer. Jewish Hist. Quar.*, vol. 67, nos. 2 and 3 (December 1977, March 1978), 101–24, 246–59.

MICHIGAN

BD165 "A Call to Detroit." *Amer. Jewish Archives*, vol. 19, no. 1 (April 1967), 34–40. Translation from the German of a letter sent in 1869 by members of the Beth El Congregation, Detroit, to the Reform rabbi, Dr. Kaufmann Kohler, a call inviting him to assume leadership of the Detroit synagogue.

BD166 Rockaway, Robert. "Ethnic Conflict in an Urban Environment: The German and Russian Jew in Detroit, 1881–1914." *Amer. Jewish Hist. Quar.*, vol. 60, no. 2 (December 1970), 133–50.

BD167 Rockaway, Robert Allen. "From Americanization to Jewish Americanism. The Jews of Detroit, 1850–1914." Diss., Michigan, 1970. 258p.

MINNESOTA

BD168 Plaut, W. Gunther. "Jewish Colonies at Painted Woods and Devil's Lake." *N. Dak. Hist.*, vol. 32, no. 1 (January 1965), 59–70. Confrontation between Jewish settlers of German origin and the new arrivals from Russia in the 1880's. Repr. from *Jews in Minnesota*, publ. by the Amer. Jewish Hist. Soc. in 1959.

BD169 Plaut, W. Gunther. *The Jews in Minnesota. The First Seventy-Five Years.* New York: Amer. Jewish Hist. Soc., 1959. 347p. Rev. by S. H. Bederman, *Amer.-German Rev.*, vol. 26, no. 6 (1960), 36; H. B. Johnson, *Ind. Mag. of Hist.*, vol. 56 (1960), 189–90.

MISSOURI

BD170 Sachs, Howard P. "Development of the Jewish Community of Kansas City, 1864–1908."

Mo. Hist. Rev., vol. 60, no. 3 (April 1966), 350–60.

MONTANA

BD171 Levinson, Robert E. "Julius Basinski: Jewish Merchant in Montana." *Mont.: The Magazine of Western Hist.*, vol. 22 (January 1977), 60–68.

NEW JERSEY

BD172 Brandes, Joseph. *Immigrants to Freedom. Jewish Communities in Rural New Jersey since 1882*. Philadelphia: Univ. of Pa. Press, 1970. 424p.

NEW MEXICO

BD173 Parish, William J. "The German Jew and the Commercial Revolution in Territorial New Mexico, 1850–1900." *N. Mex. Quar.*, vol. 29, no. 3 (1960), 307–332. See also *N. Mex. Hist. Rev.*, vol. 35 (1959), 1–23; and issues for January and April 1960.

NEW YORK

BD174 Adler, Della Rubenstein. "Immigrants in Buffalo." *Amer. Jewish Archives*, vol. 18 (April 1966), 20–28.

BD175 Adler, Selig, and Thomas E. Connolly. *From Ararat to Suburbia: The History of the Jewish Community of Buffalo*. Philadelphia: Jewish Publ. Soc. of America, 1960. 498p. Rev. by L. R. Harlan, *Amer. Jewish Archives*, vol. 14 (1962), 177–78; S. J. Kohn, *N.Y. Hist. Soc. Quar.*, vol. 45 (1961), 322–23; B. McKelvey, *Miss. Valley Hist. Rev.*, vol. 48 (1962), 145–47; L. J. Swichkow, *Publs., of the Amer. Jewish Hist. Soc.*, vol. 51 (1962), 58–62.

BD176 Birmingham, Stephen. *"Our Crowd": The Great Jewish Families of New York*. New York: Harper & Row, 1967. 404p. Rev. by D. Cort, *N.Y. Times Book Rev.*, 2 July 1967; E. Wolf, *N.Y. Hist. Soc. Quar.*, vol. 52 (1968), 103–05; B. Supple, *Amer. Jewish Hist. Quar.*, vol. 57, no. 3 (March 1968), 442–43. Financial and social history of leading 19th-century German-Jewish families: Lehmans, Seligers, Guggenheims, Sachs, Goldmans, etc.

BD177 Boroff, David. "A Little Milk, a Little Honey." *Amer. Heritage*, vol. 17, no. 6 (1966), 12–14, 74–81. Jewish immigrants from Germany and Eastern Europe to New York's Lower East Side.

BD178 Dawidowicz, Lucy S. "Louis Marshall's Yiddish Newspaper, *The Jewish World*: A Study in Contrasts." *Jewish Social St.*, vol. 25, no. 2 (April 1963), 102–32. Marshall was of German-Jewish parentage. The paper failed as a result of differences between Russian- and German-origin American readership.

BD179 Gartner, Lloyd P. "The Jews of New York's East Side, 1890–1893." *Amer. Jewish Hist. Quar.*, vol. 53 (March 1964), 264–84. Two contemporary surveys of the community analyze population, occupation, nationality, backgrounds and schools.

BD180 Glanz, Rudolf. "German Jews in New York City in the 19th Century." *YIVO Annual of Jewish Social Science*, vol. 11 (1956–1957), 9–38.

BD181 Goldberg, Reuben. "The Rise and Decline of the NuYorker yidishe ilustrirte tsaytung, 1887–1888." *YIVO Bleter*, vol. 44 (1973), 171–86. In Yiddish.

BD182 Grinstein, Hyman B. "The Minute Book of Lilienthal's Union of German Synagogues in New York." *Hebrew Union College Annual*, vol. 18 (1944), 321–52.

BD183 Grinstein, Hyman B. "The Rise of the Jewish Community of New York, 1654–1860." Diss., Pennsylvania, 1945. Philadelphia: n.p., 1947. 645p.

BD184 Hershkowitz, Leo. *The Wills of Early New York Jews (1704–1799)*. Forew., by Isidore S. Meyer. New York: Amer. Jewish Hist. Soc., 1967. 229p. Rev. by J. Gregory, *N.Y. Hist. Soc. Quar.*, vol. 53, no. 2 (April 1969), 195.

BD185 Kaganoff, Nathan M. "Organized Jewish Welfare Activity in New York City (1848–1960)." *Amer. Jewish Hist. Quar.*, vol. 56 (September 1966), 27–61. Establishes that there were 93 Jewish charitable agencies—equal to the total number for the rest of the community.

BD186 Kohn, S. Joshua. *The Jewish Community of Utica, New York, 1847–1948*. New York: Amer. Jewish Hist. Soc., 1959. 221p. Rev. by C. E. Baker, *N.Y. Hist. Soc. Quar.*, vol. 43 (1959), 265–66.

BD187 McKelvey, Blake. "The Jews of Rochester: A Contribution of Their History during the Nine-

Local Jewish History *(cont.)*

teenth Century." *Publs., Amer. Jewish Hist. Soc.,* vol. 40 (1950), 57–73. Mire Greentree, born in Bavaria in 1819, was considered the father of the Rochester Jewish community.

BD188 New York. Congregation Shearith Israel. Records, 1706–1946. 3 ft. and 9 reels of microfilm. In American Jewish Archives, Cincinnati (MS 65-1732). Record and account books, register of births, deaths and marriages, congregational minutes, miscellaneous papers.

BD189 Provol, William Lee. "Growing Up in Syracuse." *Amer. Jewish Archives,* vol. 16 (1964), 22–40.

BD190 Rischin, Moses. *The Promised City. New York's Jews, 1870–1914.* Cambridge: Harvard Univ. Pr., 1962.

BD191 Rosenberg, Stuart E. *The Jewish Community in Rochester, 1843–1925.* New York: Columbia Univ. Pr., 1954. 325p. Rev. by M. U. Schappes, *N.Y. Hist.,* vol. 35, no. 3 (1954), 319–21.

BD192 Rudolph, B. G. *From a Minyan to a Community. A History of the Jews of Syracuse.* Syracuse: Syracuse Univ., 1970. Rev. by Lloyd P. Gartner, *Jewish Social St.,* vol. 32, no. 3 (July 1970), 225; J. S. Kohn, *Church Hist.,* vol. 40 (1971), 245.

NORTH CAROLINA

BD193 Speizman, Morris. *The Jews of Charlotte: A Chronicle with Commentary and Conjectures.* Charlotte: McNally & Loftin, ca. 1978. 246p. Rev. in *N. Car. Hist. Rev.,* vol. 56 (1979), 338.

NORTH DAKOTA

BD194 Lazar, Robert Jordan. "From Ethnic Minority to Socio-Economic Elite: A Study of the Jewish Community of Fargo, North Dakota." Diss., Minnesota, 1968. 329p.

BD195 Lazar, Robert Jordan. "Jewish Communal Life in Fargo, North Dakota: The Formative Years." *N. Dak. Hist.,* vol. 36, no. 4 (Fall 1969), 347–55.

BD196 Schwartz, Lois Fields. "Early Jewish Agricultural Colonies in North Dakota, 1882." *N. Dak. Hist.,* vol. 32, no. 4 (October 1965), 217–32. Jews from Germany and Russia, 1815–1890.

OHIO

BD197 Chyet, Stanley F. "Ohio Valley Jewry during the Civil War." *Bulletin, Hist. and Philos. Soc. of Ohio,* vol. 21, no. 3 (1963), 179–87.

BD198 Gartner, Lloyd P. *History of the Jews in Cleveland.* Cleveland: Western Reserve Hist. Soc., ca. 1978. 385p. Rev. by Joseph Brandes, *Amer. Hist. Rev.,* vol. 84 (1979), 863.

BD199 Michael, Deborah A. "The Cincinnati Jewish Community before 1860." M.A. thesis, Univ. of Cincinnati, 1970.

BD200 Philipson, David. "Strangers to a Strange Land." *Amer. Jewish Archives,* vol. 18 (1966), 133–38. From the diaries of a rabbi in Cincinnati, 1888–1948.

BD201 Raphael, Marc Lee. "The Utilization of Public, Local, and Federal Sources for Reconstructing American Jewish Local History: the Jews of Columbus, Ohio (ca. 1880)." *Amer. Jewish Hist. Quar.,* vol. 65 (September 1975), 10–36.

BD202 Whiteman, Maxwell. "Notions, Dry Goods and Clothing: An Introduction to the Study of the Cincinnati Peddler." *Jewish Quar. Rev.,* vol. 53 (1962), 306–21.

OKLAHOMA

BD203 Tobias, Henry J. *The Jews in Oklahoma.* Norman: Univ. of Oklahoma Pr., 1980. 78p.

OREGON

BD204 Nodel, Julius. *The Ties Between: A Century of Judaism on America's Last Frontier, 1858–1958.* In assoc. with Alfred Apsler. Portland, Ore.: n.p., 1959. 194p.

BD205 Toll, William. "Fraternalism and Community Structure on the Urban Frontier: The Jews of Portland, Oregon—A Case Study." *Pacific Hist. Rev.,* vol. 57 (1978), 369–403.

SOUTH CAROLINA

BD206 Reznikoff, Charles, with the collab. of Uriah Z. Engelmann. *The Jews of Charleston.* Philadelphia: Jewish Publ. Soc. of America, 1950. 343p. Rev. by J. Trachtenberg, *Publs., Amer. Jewish Hist. Soc.,* vol. 40 (1951), 398–401. Many were of German origin.

TENNESSEE

BD207 Frank, Fedora A. *Five Families and Eight Young Men. Nashville and Her Jewry, 1850–1861.* Nashville: Tennessee Book Co., 1962. 184p.

UTAH

BD208 Watters, Leon L. *The Pioneer Jews of Utah.* St. in Amer. Jewish Hist., no. 2. New York: Amer. Jewish Hist. Soc., 1952. 199p. Bambergers, Auerbachs, Siegels, Watters (Wasser): all emigrants from Germany.

VIRGINIA

BD209 Ginsberg, Louis. *Chapters on the Jews of Virginia: 1658–1900.* Petersburg, Va.: Cavalier Pr., 1969. 108p. Rev. by L. Dinnerstein, *Jewish Social St.*, vol. 32, no. 3 (July 1970), 225–26.

BD210 Ginsberg, Louis. *History of the Jews of Petersburg.* Richmond: Williams, 1959. 118p. Rev. by S. Viener, *Va. Mag. of Hist. and Biogophy*, vol. 62, no. 4 (1959), 516.

BD211 Ginsberg, Louis. "Two Streams Become One." *Va. Cavalcade*, vol. 7, no. 6 (1958), 23–29. Illustrated account of the German Jewish congregations of Richmond.

WASHINGTON, D.C.

BD212 Shosteck, Robert. "The Jewish Community of Washington, D.C., during the Civil War." *Amer. Jewish Hist. Quar.*, vol. 56 (March 1967), 319–47.

WISCONSIN

BD213 Madison, Wisconsin. Hebrew Congregation. Records 1856–1922. In American Jewish Hist. Soc. collections (MS 68-153). Incl. minute book, committees and activities from 1856.

BD214 Swichkow, Louis J., and Lloyd P. Gartner. *The History of the Jews of Milwaukee.* Philadelphia: Jewish Publ. Soc. of America, 1963. 533p. Rev. by Baird Still, *Amer. Jewish Hist. Quar.*, vol. 53 (1964), 443–45; B. Still, *Amer. Hist. Rev.*, vol. 70, no. 1 (October 1964), 269–70; J. Weinberg, *Wis. Mag. of History*, vol. 47, no. 3 (1964), 268–69.

German Jewish Biography

GENERAL

BD215 Berger, Milton, Joel S. Giffen, and M. David Hoffman, eds. *Roads to Jewish Survival: Essays, Biographies, and Articles Selected from "The Torch" on Its 25th Anniversary.* New York: National Federation of Jewish Men's Clubs and Bloch Publ. Co., 1967. 414p. Rev. by A. H. Lovins, *Amer. Jewish Hist. Quar.*, vol. 59, no. 2 (December 1969), 234–35. Incl. short biographies of famous American Jewish figures.

BD216 Fierman, Floyd S. "Jewish Pioneering in the Southwest. A Record of the Freudenthal-Lesinsky-Solomon Families." *Ariz. and the West*, vol. 2, no. 2 (Spring 1960), 54–72. German-Jews in commerce in New Mexico 1850–1900.

BD217 Fierman, Floyd S. *Some Early Jewish Settlers on the Southwestern Frontier.* El Paso, Tex.: Texas Western Pr., 1960. 58p. The Lesinsky, Solomon and Freudenthal families.

BD218 Friedman, Lee M. *Jewish Pioneers and Patriots.* New York: Macmillan, 1943. Rev. by F. Reichmann, *Amer.-German Rev.*, vol. 10, no. 1 (October 1943), 36–37.

BD219 Goldhammer, Leo. "Jewish Emigration." *YIVO Annual* (1954). On Gentile and Jewish emigration of Forty-eighters: some 300 Jews from "Austria" and a like number from Bohemia.

BD220 Goldstein, Sidney, and Calvin Goldscheider. *Jewish Americans. Three Generations in a Jewish Community.* New York: Prentice-Hall, 1968. 274p.

BD221 Grollman, Earl A. "Dictionary of American Jewish Biography in the Seventeenth Century." *Amer. Jewish Archives*, vol. 3, no. 1 (1950), 3–10. Incl. Asser Levy, the most prominent German Jew in America in his day.

BD222 Madison, Charles A. *Eminent American Jews: 1776 to the Present.* Cambridge: Ungar, ca.

German Jewish Biography *(cont.)*

1970. 400p. This work emphasizes the German-Jewish element and those with business and legal backgrounds.

BD223 Marcus, Jacob Rader. *Memoirs of American Jews, 1775–1865.* 3 vols. Philadelphia: Jewish Publ. Soc. of America, 1955–56. 387, 375, 440p.

BD224 Meissner, Frank. "German Jews of Prague: A Quest for Self-Realization." *Amer. Jewish Hist. Soc., Publs.*, vol. 50, no. 2 (1960), 98–120. Enumerates members of the Prague Jewish community who emigrated and distinguished themselves in careers in America.

BD225 Raisin, Max. *Great Jews I Have Known.* New York: Philosophical Library, 1952. 249p. Rev. by E. W. Leipziger, *Amer. Jewish Archives*, vol. 5 (1953), 37–39.

BD226 Rosenbloom, Joseph R. *A Biographical Dictionary of Early American Jews: Colonial Times through 1800.* Lexington: Univ. of Ky. Pr., 1960. 175p.

BD227 Simonhoff, Harry. *Jewish Notables in America 1776–1865: Links of an Endless Chain.* New York: Greenberg, 1956. 402p.

BD228 Simonhoff, Harry. *Saga of American Jewry 1865–1914. Links of an Endless Chain. Sequel to Jewish Notables in America, 1776–1865.* New York: n.p., 1959. 403p.

BD229 Stern, Malcolm. *Americans of Jewish Descent.* Repr. from the *National Genealogical Soc. Quar.*, 1958. 10p.

BD230 Supplee, Barry E. "A Business Elite: German-Jewish Financiers in Nineteenth Century New York." *The Business Hist. Rev.*, vol. 31 (1957), 143–78.

AARONSOHN, AARON

BD231 Levin, Alexandra Lee. "Aaron Aaronsohn: Pioneer Scientist, Spy and Friend of Henrietta Szold." *Hadassah Mag.*, March 1977, 16–17, 38–42.

ADLER, CYRUS

BD232 Adler, Cyrus. *I Have Considered the Days.* Philadelphia: Jewish Publ. Soc. of America, 1941. 429p. Memoirs of a scientist and college president.

BD233 Adler, Cyrus. Papers, 1887–1934. 3 ft. In collections of American Jewish Historical Society (MS 68-117). Materials bearing on American Jewish history. *See also his* Papers, in American Jewish Archives (MS 68-6).

BD234 Neuman, Abraham Aaron. *Cyrus Adler: A Biographical Sketch.* Philadelphia: Jewish Publ. Soc. of America, 1942. 236p.

ADLER, LIEBMANN

BD235 Adler, Liebmann. Papers. In the American Jewish Archives (MS 68-7). Letters by Adler to members of his family, 1846–66; bibliography and biography of A., prepared by Rachel Baron, 1963; MSS. of essays in English and German.

ALEXANDER, SAMUEL OSCAR

BD236 Leeser, Isaac "Samuel Oscar Alexander." *Amer. Jewish Archives*, vol. 7 (1955), 85–89.

ANGERSTEIN, ERNEST

BD237 Fierman, Floyd S. "Ernest Angerstein: Soldier, Merchant, Accused Secessionist and Post Trader." *Password*, April 1962, 42–62. German-Jewish merchant in the Southwest.

BARTH, SOL

BD238 Greenwood, N. H. "Sol Barth: A Jewish Settler on the Arizona Frontier." *Jour. of Ariz. Hist.*, vol. 14 (Winter 1973), 363–78.

BARUCH, MARCUS M.

BD239 Kahn, Edgar M. "In Memoriam Marcus M. Baruch, 1866–1942." *Calif. Hist. Soc. Quar.*, vol. 21, no. 2 (1942), 189. Baruch's parents came to California by way of the Isthmus of Panama in the early 1850's.

BELMONT, AUGUST

BD240 [Biographical sketch.] *Yearbook of the Leo Baeck Institute*, vol. 12 (1967), 227–55.

BERMAN, HAROLD

BD241 Berman, Harold. Papers, 1929–1947. 7 boxes. In American Jewish Archives (MS 66-1017). Journalist and author.

BLUM, ABRAHAM

BD242 Kramer, William M., and Reva Clar., "Rabbi Abraham Blum: From Alsace to New York by Way of Texas and California." *Western States Jewish Hist. Quar.*, vol. 12 (Fall 1979; January 1980; April 1980).

BUSH, ISIDOR

BD243 Wax, James A. "Isidor Bush, American Patriot and Abolitionist." *Historia Judaica*, vol. 5, no. 2 (1943), 183–203. Native of Prague, 1822.

COWEN, PHILIP

BD244 Cowen, Philip. Papers. Ca. 1,500 items. In American Jewish Historical Society (MS 68-124). Correspondence. C. (1876–1934) was a journalist and inspector, U.S. Immigration Service. In English, German and Russian, concerning anti-Semitism and immigration from Eastern Europe.

DRACHMAN, BERNARD

BD245 Drachman, Bernard. *The Unfailing Light: Memoirs of an American Rabbi*. New York: The Rabbinical Council of America, 1948. 456p. Rev. by J. H. Greenstone, *Publs., Amer. Jewish Hist. Soc.*, vol. 40, no. 3 (1951), 311–13. Rabbi D.'s visits to his mother's birthplace in Germany show the life of the Jewish community in Germany and Austria at the end of the 19th century.

EINHORN, DAVID

BD246 Einhorn, David. Papers, 1831–1879. 76 items. In American Jewish Archives (MS 66-1541). E. (1809–1879) was a reform rabbi; papers in German. See Adolf Brull, *Dr. David Einhorn und seine Bedeutung für das Judentum*. Frankfurt: n.p., 1882.

FELSENTHAL, BERNHARD

BD247 Felsenthal, Bernard. Papers, 1854–1921. In American Jewish Archives (MS 67-987). Letters on religious, educational, and literary subjects; journal, 1854–1857. *Also*: Papers, in American Jewish Historical Society collections. Correspondence in English, German, Hebrew, and French on Judaism, Zionism, social questions. F. (1822–1908) was a rabbi of Chicago.

FRANK, HENRY

BD248 Stern, Madeleine. "Henry Frank: Pioneer American Hebrew Publisher." *Amer. Jewish Archives*, vol. 20 (November 1968), 163–68. Arrived in America from Bavaria in 1848 to become a leading printer and publisher in the American Hebrew book trade.

FRANK, LEO

BD249 Dinnerstein, Leonard. "Leo M. Frank and the American Jewish Community." *Amer. Jewish Archives*, vol. 20 (November 1968).

FRANK, NATHAN

BD250 Boxerman, Burton Alan. "The Honorable Nathan Frank [of St. Louis]." *Amer. Jewish Hist. Quar.*, vol. 61 (September 1971), 33f. Also printed in the *Mo. Hist. Rev.*, vol. 67 (1972), 52f.

FRANKS FAMILY

BD251 Hershkowitz, Leo, and Isidore S. Meyer, eds. *The Lee Max Friedman Collection of American Jewish Colonial Correspondence: Letters of the Franks Family (1733–1748)*. Waltham, Mass.: Amer. Jewish Hist. Soc., 1968. 171p. Letters from New York to London, mostly from Abigail Franks to her son.

FREUDENTHAL, SAMUEL J.

BD252 Fierman, Floyd S. "Samuel J. Freudenthal: Southwestern Merchant and Civic Leader." *Amer. Jewish Hist. Quar.*, vol. 57 (March 1968), 353–435. F. (1863–1939) was a merchant of El Paso, Tex.

BD253 Freudenthal, Samuel J. *El Paso Merchant and Civic Leader from the 1880's through the Mexican Revolution*. Research and annotations by Floyd S. Fierman. El Paso: Texas Western College Pr., 1965. 44p. Southwestern Studies, vol. 3, no. 3. Monograph no. 11.

FRIEDENWALD, HARRY

BD254 Levin, Alexandra Lee. *Vision: A Biography of Harry Friedenwald*. Philadelphia: Jewish Publ. Soc. of America, 1964. 469p. F. (1864–1950) was an ophthalmologist.

GABELEIN, ARNO C.

BD255 Rausch, David A. "Arno C. Gabelein (1861–1945): Fundamentalist Protestant Zionist." *Amer. Jewish Hist.*, vol. 68 (1978), 43–56.

GOLDWATER, MICHAEL

BD256 Stern, Norton B., and William M. Kramer. "Some Further Notes on Michael Goldwater." *Western States Jewish Hist. Quar.*

GRAETZ, HEINRICH

BD257 Graetz, Heinrich. *Tagebuch und Briefe.* Ed. Reuven Michael. Tübingen: J. C. B. Mohr, 1977. Rev. by Harry Zohn, *Amer. Jewish Hist.*, vol. 68 (1979), 575–77.

GRATZ-SULZBERGER FAMILY

BD258 "Papers, 1747–1804." *Amer. Jewish Archives*, vol. 2, no. 2 (1950), 25–26. Comment on correspondence between members of this German-American Jewish family, a copy of which is in possession of the American Jewish Archives.

GRÜNEBAUM, ELIAS

BD259 Grünebaum, Elias. Papers. 2 boxes. In Bancroft Library, Univ. of California at Berkeley (MS 80-2263). Writings, notes, sermons, etc. G. (1807–1893) was a reform rabbi of Landau.

GUMBEL, EMIL JULIUS

BD260 Gumbel, Emil Julius. Papers, 1928–1960. 6 ft. In Leo Baeck Institute collections, New York (MS 72-231). Misc. scientific papers, reports, clippings, reprints of papers, MSS. and research materials. Mathematical statistician of Germany and New York.

GUSDORF, ALEXANDER

BD261 Gusdorf, Alexander. Papers, 1866–1926. 17 vols. In American Jewish Archives (MS 68-33). Records of a general store in Taos, N. Mex.

GUTHEIM, JAMES KOPPEL

BD262 Gutheim, James Koppel. Papers. In American Jewish Archives (MS 68-34). G. (1817–1866) was a rabbi of New Orleans.

HELLER, MAXIMILIAN

BD263 Heller, Maximilian. Papers, 1876–1930. 27 boxes. In American Jewish Archives (MS 67-1004). Rabbi's documents relating to the struggle of Bohemian emigrants to come to Chicago in the 1870's.

HIRSCH, EMIL G.

BD264 Bernard, Martin. "The Religious Philosophy of Emil G. Hirsch." *Amer. Jewish Archives*, vol. 4, no. 2 (1952), 61–82. The influence of Hirsch upon the reform movement within Judaism.

HIRSCH, HELMUT

BD265 Etzold, Thomas H. "An American Jew in Germany: The Death of Helmut Hirsch." *Jewish Social Studies*, vol. 35 (April 1973), 125–40. H., a young Jewish refugee who claimed American citizenship, was arrested for treason against Nazi Germany in 1937; the American government was unable to prevent his execution.

HUEBSCH, ADOLPH

BD266 Huebsch, Adolph. Papers. In American Jewish Archives (MS 68-37). Personal papers. H. (1830–1884) was a rabbi.

JACOBS, PHILLIP

BD267 Jacobs, Phillip. Papers, 1760–1832. 400 items. In collections of the Amer. Jewish Hist. Soc. (MS 68-139). A merchant (d. 1818) in New York City and upstate; accounts with Trinity Church, New York City and with the Protestant German Reform Church of Rhinebeck (Rhynbeck).

JACOBS, SAMUEL

BD268 Jacobs, Samuel. Papers, 1759–1786. 8 reels of microfilm. In the American Jewish Archives (MS 65-1727). J. (d. 1786) was a merchant of Montreal and St. Denis, Canada.

JASTROW, MARCUS

BD269 Jastrow, Marcus. Papers. In American Jewish Archives (MS 68-39). J. (1829–1903) was a rabbi.

KAHN, BERNHARD

BD270 Kahn, Bernhard. Papers. Ca. 200 items. In Leo Baeck Institute collections, New York (MS 75-715). Personal and agency papers. K. (1876–1955) was a social worker and Jewish communal leader, of Berlin, Germany, and New York City.

KALLEN, HORACE MEYER

BD271 Kallen, Horace Meyer. Papers. 22 ft. In the American Jewish Archives (MS 65-1728). Correspondence, articles, MSS., lectures, and clippings. Philosopher, educator, and writer.

KOHLER, KAUFMANN

BD272 Kohler, Kaufmann. Papers. In American Jewish Archives (MS 68-49). Rabbi (1843–1926).

KOHN, ABRAHAM

BD273 Goodman, Abram Vossen. "A Jewish Peddler's Diary 1842–43." *Amer. Jewish Archives*, vol. 3, no. 3 (1951), 81–111. Memoirs of struggles as German Jewish immigrant in rural areas before the Civil War.

KOHUT, GEORGE ALEX

BD274 Kohut, George Alex. Papers. 5 ft. In collections of the American Jewish Historical Society (MS 68-114). Incl. notes on Heinrich Heine and Jewish history Scholar (1874–1933).

KROHN, MOSES

BD275 Krohn, Moses. Papers. In American Jewish Archives (MS 68-51). Cigar manufacturer of Cincinnati.

KUHN, SETTIE S.

BD276 Kuhn, Settie S. "Papers, 1903–1948." *Amer. Jewish Archives*, vol. 2, no. 2 (1950), 26–27. The archives notes acquisition of letters addressed to S. S. Kuhn from celebrities of German origin.

LANDSBERG, MAX

BD277 Landsberg, Max. Papers. In American Jewish Archives (MS 68-52). L. (1845–1906) was rabbi of Rochester, N.Y.

LAUTERBACH, JACOB Z.

BD278 Lauterbach, Jacob Z. Papers. In American Jewish Archives (MS 68-53). Z. (1873–1942) was a Talmudic scholar.

LEESER, ISSAC

BD279 Korn, Bertram W. "Isaac Leeser: Centennial Reflections." *Amer. Jewish Archives*, vol. 19 (1967).

BD280 Leeser, Isaac. Papers, 1820–1866. 114 items. In collections of the American Jewish Historical Society (MS 68-147); also 29 items and 1 reel of microfilmed papers in the American Jewish Archives (MS 68-54).

BD281 Seller, Maxine S. "Isaac Leeser: A Jewish-Christian Dialogue in Antebellum Philadelphia." *Pa. Hist.*, vol. 35, no. 3 (July 1968), 231–42. German-Jewish immigrant from Westphalia.

BD282 Seller, Maxine S. "Isaac Leeser's Views on the Restoration of a Jewish Palestine." *Amer. Jewish Hist. Quar.*, vol. 58 (1968), 118–35. Early- and mid-19th century efforts to stimulate interest in the restoration of a Jewish Palestine.

BD283 Seller, Maxine Schwartz. "Isaac Leeser, Architect of the American Jewish Community." Diss., Univ. of Pa., 1965. 205p.

BD284 Sulzberger, Mayer. "No Better Jew, No Purer Man: Mayer Sulzberger on Isaac Lesser." *Amer. Jewish Archives*, vol. 21, no. 2 (November 1969), 140–48.

LEVIN, LEWIS CHARLES

BD285 Forman, John A. "Lewis Charles Levin. Portrait of an American Demagogue." *Amer. Jewish Archives*, vol. 12, no. 2 (October 1960), 150–94. On the career and personality of a notorious Know-Nothing agitator.

LEVY, AARON

BD286 Fish, Sidney M. *Aaron Levy, Founder of Aaronsburg, New York*. Publs., Amer. Jewish Hist. Soc., 1951. Rev. by A. Tarshish, *Amer. Jewish Archives*, vol. 4, no. 1 (1952), 1, 26–28.

LEWY, JULIUS

BD287 Lewy, Julius. Papers. 1,073 items. In American Jewish Archives (MS 68-59). Prof. of Semitics.

LYONS, SOLOMON

BD288 Lyons, Solomon. Papers. In the American Jewish Archives (MS 68-152). Incl. correspondence with his brother in Kremsier, Austria. L. was a broker of Philadelphia, 1788–1804.

MANN, JACOB

BD289 Mann, Jacob. Papers. In the American Jewish Archives (MS 68-61). M. (1888–1940) was prof., Hebrew Union College.

MARGOLIS, MAX LEOPOLD

BD290 *Max Leopold Margolis, Scholar and Teacher*. Philadelphia: Alumni Assoc., Dropsie College, 1952. 124p. Rev. by G. Kisch, *Historia Judaica*, vol. 14, no. 2, 169.

MARSHALL, LOUIS

BD291 Marshall, Louis. Papers. 96 ft. In the American Jewish Archives (MS 65-1729). Misc. correspondence, personal and business papers. M. (1856–1929) was a lawyer and philanthropist.

MERZBACHER, LEE

BD292 Cohn, Bernhard N. "Lee Merzbacher." *Amer. Jewish Archives*, vol. 6, no. 1 (1954), 21–24.

NAAR, DAVID

BD293 Kohn, S. Joshua. "David Naar of Trenton, New Jersey." *Amer. Jewish Hist. Quar.*, vol. 53 (June 1964).

PHILIPSON, DAVID

BD294 Marcus, Jacob Rader. "Dr. David Philipson's Place in American Jewish Historiography." *Amer. Jewish Archives*, vol. 3, no. 2 (1951), 28–31. Memoir of the historian (1862–1949) of Reform Judaism deeply influenced by German Jewish culture.

BD295 Philipson, David. Papers. 6 ft. In American Jewish Archives (MS 65-1734). Misc. correspondence, addresses, lectures, with documents and source materials pertaining to Jewish history, etc.

BD296 Philipson, David. "Strangers to a Strange Land." *Amer. Jewish Archives*, vol. 18 (1966), 133–38. Excerpts from diaries concerning the Jewish-Russian problem.

POSNER, ERNST

BD297 Franz, Eckhart G. "Ernst Posner und das Archivwesen Amerikas." *Jahrbuch für Amerikastudien*, vol. 15 (1970), 233–36. German-Jewish emigré archivist and teacher at American University, Washington.

PRITZ, CARL E.

BD298 Pritz, Carl E. "Collection, 1926–1947." *Amer. Jewish Archives*, vol. 2, no. 2 (1950), 29. The American Jewish Archives has acquired letters addressed to Carl E. Pritz.

PURVIN, JENNIE FRANKLIN

BD299 Purvin, Jennie Franklin. Papers. 7 ft. In American Jewish Archives (MS 65-1736). Correspondence and personal papers. P. (1873–1958) was a business executive of Mandel Bros. Store, Chicago.

ROHRHEIMER, RENA M.

BD300 Rohrheimer, Rena M. Papers, 1936–1950. 2 boxes. In the American Jewish Archives (MS 67-1023). R. was resident of Philadelphia, active in assistance to refugees from Nazi Germany.

ROSENAU, WILLIAM

BD301 Rosenau, William. Papers. 9 ft. In American Jewish Archives (MS 65-1737). Correspondence with religious leaders, government and education leaders. Misc. papers, clippings, articles. R. (1865–1943) was rabbi of Congreg. Oheb Shalom, Baltimore.

ROSENBAUM, BELLA W.

BD302 Rosenbaum, Bella W. "My Lifetime Memories of a Jewish Immigrant in Washington, D.C." *Amer. Jewish Archives*, vol. 19 (April 1967).

ROSEWATER FAMILY

BD303 Rosewater, Edward, and Victor Rosewater. Papers. 13 ft. In American Jewish Archives (MS 65-1738). Correspondence, political and historical materials, reports, etc., relating to the Rosewaters' interests in Nebraska; papers by V. R. (1854–1940); biography of E. R. (1841–1906), journalist and politician.

ROTH, BENJAMIN

BD304 Friedlander, Albert H. "An Ethical Letter, Benjamin M. Roth to His Son Solomon, 1854." *Amer. Jewish Archives*, vol. 6, no. 1 (1954), 6–12. Written on the eve of the son's departure for America. See also *Ibid.*, vol. 2, no. 2 (1950), 29, reporting the acquisition of a photostat letter from B. M. R. in Germany to his son in America.

SALOMON, HAYM

BD305 Salomon, Haym. Papers. 1 reel and 34 items. In the American Jewish Archives (MS 68-78). S. (1740–1785) was a merchant and banker of New York City and Philadelphia.

SANGER FAMILY

BD306 Rosenberg, Leon J. *Sanger's: Pioneer Texas Merchants*. Austin: Texas State Hist. Assoc., 1978. 135p. Rev. by Anna H. Morgan, *Ariz. and the West*, vol. 21 (1979), 201–02.

SARASOHN, KASRIEL HIRSCH

BD307 Sarasohn, Kasriel Hirsch. Papers. In the American Jewish Archives (MS 68-92). S. (1835–1905) was a journalist, editor, and communal leader, New York City.

SCHECHTER, SOLOMON

BD308 Mandelbaum, Bernard. *The Wisdom of Solomon Schechter*. New York: Burning Bush Pr., 1963. 137p. Religious leader, educated in Vienna and Berlin.

SCHLINGER, LEOPOLD

BD309 Schlinger, Leopold. Papers. 86 items. In the American Jewish Archives (MS 68-85). S. (1833–1894) was a naturalized citizen, resident of Texas.

SCHNEEBERGER, HENRY W.

BD310 Goldman, Israel M. "Henry W. Schneeberger: His Role in American Judaism." *Amer. Jewish Hist. Quar.*, vol. 56 (December 1967), 45–65. First American-born, university trained, ordained rabbi in the U.S.; at Baltimore 1876–1916.

SCHONBERG, MICHAEL

BD311 Schonberg, Michael. Papers, 1909–1922. In American Jewish Archives (MS 68-85). Resident of Newark, New Jersey.

SCHWARTZ, JACOB DAVID

BD312 Schwartz, Jacob David. Papers. In the American Jewish Archives (MS 68-88). S. (b. 1883), rabbi of Cincinnati.

SELIGMAN, JOSEPH

BD313 Hellman, George S. "Joseph Seligman, American Jew." *Publs., Amer. Jewish Hist. Soc.*, vol. 41, no. 1 (1951), 27–40. Prominent immigrant, Union patriot during the Civil War.

SHLESINGER, SIGMUND

BD314 Siegel, Burt A. "The Little Jew Was There—A Bibliographical Sketch of Sigmund Shlesinger." *Amer. Jewish Archives*, vol. 20, no. 1 (April 1968), 16–32. Heroism of a teenage immigrant from Germany as soldier in the Battle of Beecher Island.

SIMPSON, NATHAN

BD315 Simpson Nathan. Papers. 3 reels. In the American Jewish Archives (MS 65-1740). Correspondence, business papers; microfilm copies of originals in the British Public Records Office, London. S. (d. 1725) was a merchant of New York City.

SINGER, LOUIS E.

BD316 Singer, Louis E. "Now an American: The Autobiography of Louis E. Singer." *Amer. Jewish Archives*, vol. 22 (April 1970).

SONDERLING, JACOB

BD317 Sonderling, Jacob. "Five Gates: Casual Notes for an Autobiography." *Amer. Jewish Archives*, vol. 16, no. 2 (November 1964), 107–23. Native of Silesia; rabbi in Hamburg; emigré to the U.S. in 1923.

SONNE, ISAIAH

BD318 Sonne, Isaiah. Papers. 3329 items. In the American Jewish Archives (MS 68-98). S. (1877–1960) was a scholar of Cincinnati.

SONNESCHEIN, SOLOMON H.

BD319 Sonneschein, Solomon H. Papers. In the American Jewish Archives (MS 67-1024). 1 vol. Scholarly and literary subjects. S. (1839–1908) was a rabbi of Chattanooga.

SPIEGELBERG FAMILY

BD320 Fierman, Floyd S. *The Spiegelbergs of New Mexico, Merchants and Bankers 1844–1893*. Southwestern Studies, vol. 1, no. 4. El Paso: Texas Western Coll. Pr., ca. 1964. 48p.

STAAB, ABRAHAM

BD321 Fierman, Floyd S. "The Triangle and the Tetragrammaton." *N. Mex. Hist. Rev.*, vol. 37, no. 4 (1962), 310–21. S., born 1839 in Westphalia, subsequently a merchant in the Southwest. His influence on the design of the Cathedral at Santa Fe.

STEIN, PHILIP

BD322 Stein, Philip. Papers. In the American Jewish Archives (MS 68-100). S. (1844–1922) was a lawyer and judge of Chicago.

STEIN, SIGMUND

BD323 Dickinson, John K. *German and Jew. The Life and Death of Sigmund Stein*. Chicago: Quadrangle Books, 1967. 339p.

STOLZ, JOSEPH HENRY

BD324 Stolz, Joseph Henry. Papers. In American Jewish Archives (MS 68-102). Rabbi (b. 1877) and social worker of Los Angeles.

STRAUSS, BRUNO

BD325 Strauss, Bruno. Papers. 40 items. In Leo Baeck Institute collections, New York (MS 72-238). Writings relating to the Philosopher Hermann Cohen. S. (1889–1969) was German-Jewish scholar, professor of history and German language and literature at Centenary College of Louisiana (Shreveport).

German Jewish Biography *(cont.)*

STRAUSS, EDWARD

BD326 Strauss, Edward. Papers. Ca. 3 ft. In Leo Baeck Institute collections, New York (MS 72-239). Notes, diaries, MSS. pertaining to the history and philosophy of religion and related topics. S. (1876–1952) was a biochemist and Jewish religious philosopher, of Germany and New York City.

SZOLD, BENJAMIN

BD327 Szold, Benjamin. Papers. 86 items. In the American Jewish Archives (MS 67-1025). S. (1829–1902) was rabbi of Baltimore.

BD328 Wilhelm, Kurt. "Benjamin Szold." *Historia Judaica*, vol. 15 (1953), 49–58.

SZOLD, HENRIETTA

BD329 Dash, Joan. *Summoned to Jerusalem. The Life of Henrietta Szold*. New York: Harper & Row, ca. 1979. 348p. Rev. in *N.Y. Times Book Rev.*, 14 October 1979, 12. Life and work of S. (1860–1945), a prominent leader of Baltimore, founder of Hadassah.

BD330 Fineman, Irving. *Woman of Valor: The Story of Henrietta Szold*. New York: Simon & Schuster, 1961, 439p. Rev. by B. I. Schoolman, *Jewish Social Studies*, vol. 26, no. 1 (January 1964), 52–55.

BD331 Freund, Miriam. "Make My Eyes Look to the Future." *Publs. Amer. Jewish Hist. Soc.*, vol. 49 (March 1960), 159–72.

BD332 Levin, Jack L. *Henrietta Szold: Baltimorean*. Baltimore: Jewish Hist. Soc. of Maryland, 1976.

BD333 Lowenthal, Marvin. *Henrietta Szold, Life and Letters*. New York: n.p., 1942.

BD334 Szold, Henrietta. Papers, 1866–1945. In American Jewish Archives (MS 68-104). Materials concerning her community activities.

BD335 Zeitlin, Rosa. *Henrietta Szold, Record of a Life*. New York: Dial, 1952. 263p.

VOGELSTEIN, LUDWIG

BD336 Vogelstein, Ludwig. Papers. 6 ft. In Leo Baeck Institute collections, New York (MS 78-1245). Correspondence, personal papers, photos. Incl. correspondence with Julie Braun-Vogelstein, Heinemann and Rosa Vogelstein, Heinrich Braun, and the firm of Hirsch-Halberstadt. V. (1871–1934) was German-American industrialist and Jewish philanthropist.

WEIL, BRUNO

BD337 Weil, Bruno. Papers. Ca. 12 ft. In Leo Baeck Institute collections, New York (MS 72-240). Correspondence, early writings, diaries, notebooks, and memoirs, 1910–1948. MSS. and research materials on emigration and restitution problems, etc. W. (1883–1961) was a lawyer and politician of German and New York.

WEIL, GERTRUDE

BD338 Weil, Gertrude. Papers. 45 ft. In North Carolina State Office of Archives and History, Raleigh (MS 74-606). Records and family correspondence in German, English, and Yiddish. W. (1879–1971) was a suffragist and philanthropist of Goldsboro, N.C.

WEISSKOPF, GUSTAV

BD339 Weisskopf, Gustav. Papers. 277 items. In American Jewish Archives (MS 68-1153). Papers in German and Hebrew relating to W. (1820–1891) in Europe and the United States (San Francisco).

WISE, JONAH BONDI

BD340 Cauman, Sam. *Jonah Bondi Wise: A Biography*. New York: Crown Publ., 1967. 214p. Rev. by S. Chiel, *Amer. Jewish Hist. Quar.*, vol. 59, no. 2 (December 1969), 238–40. Ca. 1905 Wise spent a year in study in Germany and observed anti-Semitism.

WOLSEY, LOUIS

BD341 Wolsey, Louis. Papers. 4 ft. In the American Jewish Archives (MS 65-1745). Correspondence on church affairs. W. (1877–1953) was rabbi and communal leader of Philadelphia.

WOOG, EDWARD S.

BD342 Woog, Edward S. "Biography 1838–1909." *Amer. Jewish Archives*, vol. 2, no. 2 (1950), 30. Report of acquisition of typescript biography of a German Jewish immigrant.

WURMBRAND, MICHAEL

BD343 Grossmann, Kurt R., ed. *Michael Wurmbrand: The Man and His Work. New York: Philosophical Library, 1956. 127p. Correspondent of the Jewish Telegraphic Agency in Berlin, Prague and Paris; came to New York during World War II; wrote for *Aufbau* until his death in 1952.

ZAUSNER, PHILIP

BD344 Zausner, Philip. *Unvarnished; the Autobiography of a Union Leader.* New York: n.p., 1941. 381p. Jewish leader of the union of painters and decorators (b. 1884).

ZEISLER, SIGMUND

BD345 Zeisler, Sigmund. Papers. 176 items. In the American Jewish Archives (MS 68-113). Z. (1860–1931) was lawyer and publicist of Chicago.

ZIRNDORF, HEINRICH

BD346 Zirndorf, Heinrich. Papers. In the American Jewish Archives (MS 68-1156). 210 items and 1 vol. of misc. correspondence and personal papers. Z. (1829–1893) was rabbi and prof., Hebrew Union College.

BE

Hutterite Communities in the United States and Canada

BE1 Barclay, Harold B. "Plain and Peculiar People." *Alberta Anthropologist*, vol. 1, no. 3 (1967). Refers to the Hutterians.

BE2 Barclay, Harold B. "The Renewal of the Quest for Utopia." In: *Canadian Confrontations. Proceedings, Western Association of Sociology and Anthropology. December 28–30, 1969.* Banff, Alberta, 1969.

BE3 Bennett, John William. *Hutterian Brethren. The Agricultural Economy and Social Organization of a Communal People.* Stanford, Calif.: Stanford Univ. Pr., 1967. 298p. A study of six colonies in Saskatchewan.

BE4 Brednich, Rolf W. *The Bible and the Plough: The Lives of a Hutterite Minister and a Mennonite Farmer.* Ottawa: National Museums of Canada, 1981.

BE5 Brednich, Rolf W. "Die Hutterer: Ein Stück alter alpenländischer Kultur in der Neuen Welt." *Österreichische Zeitschrift für Volkskunde*, vol. 84 (1981), 141–53.

BE6 Brednich, Rolf W. "Die Hutterer und ihre Beziehungen zum südwestdeutschen Täufertum." *Allmende: Eine Alemannische Zeitschrift*, vol. 1, no. 3 (1981), 25–38.

BE7 Calgary Board of Education. *The People Called Hutterites.* Calgary, Alb.: n.p., 1974. Teaching unit: cassettes, filmstrips, photos, maps and printed materials.

BE8 David, Morris, and Joseph F. Krauter. *The Other Canadians.* Toronto: Methuen, 1971. Incl. discussion of the Hutterites.

BE9 Dempsey, Hugh A., and Edward Spiteri. *Hutterites-Spiteri: The Hutterite Diamond Jubilee.* Calgary, Alb.: Glenbow-Alberta Institute, 1978.

BE10 Holzach, Michael. *Das vergessene Volk: Ein Jahr bei den deutschen Hutterern in Kanada.* Hamburg: Hoffmann & Campe, 1980.

BE11 Horsch, John. *The Hutterite Brethren, 1528–1931: A Story of Martyrdom and Loyalty.* Cayley, Alb.: n.p., 1977.

BE12 Hostetler, John A. "Hutterites." In: *Encyclopedia of American Ethnic Groups.* Ed. Stephan Thernstrom. Cambridge: Harvard Univ. Pr., 1980, 471–73.

BE13 *The Hutterites.* Educational film produced by the National Film Board of Canada, Montreal. Black and white, 16 mm. 28 min. Available for purchase through Sterling Educational Films, 241 East 34th St., New York; for rental through Contemporary Films, Inc., New York; Evanston, Ill.; San Francisco.

BE14 Knill, William D. "The Hutterites: Cultural Transmission in a Closed Society." *Alberta Hist. Rev.*, vol. 16, no. 3 (Summer 1968), 1–10.

BE15 Ryan, John. "The Economic Significance of Hutterite Colonies in Manitoba." In: *Southern Prairies Field Excursion: Background Papers*. Montreal: Congress of the International Geographical Union, 1972.

BE16 Scheer, Herfried W. "Wo Meidung die härteste Strafe ist: Bericht über die altdeutsche Gemeinschaft der Hutterischen Brüder in Kanada." *Die geistige Welt*, vol. 49 (1971).

BE17 Steele, C. Frank. "Canada's Hutterite Settlement." *Canad. Geographical Jour.*, vol. 22 (June 1941), 314f.

BE18 Tschetter, Peter S. *Hutterian Brethren of Yesterday and Today*. Minburn, Alb.: n.p., 1966. 22p.

BF

Mennonite Communities in the United States

See also under Churches and Religious History *in* Section BB: Canadian Germans; Mennonites *under* Section IJ: Religion and Church History.

General

BF1 Alderfer, E. Gordon. "The Pioneer Culture of the Plain People." *Mennonite Life*, vol. 5, no. 4 (1950), 30–34.

BF2 Bargen, Bernhard. *Our Church Yearbook: A Guide*. Newton, Kans.: General Conference Mennonite Church, 1966. 15p.

BF3 Bartel, Lois Franz. "A Pioneer Home." *Mennonite Life*, vol. 17 (1962), 162–66.

BF4 Bender, Harold S. "Menno Simons and the North American Mennonites of Swiss-South German Background." *Mennonite Quar. Rev.*, vol. 35 (1961), 317–18.

BF5 Bender, Harold S. "Mennonite Colleges and Mennonite Research." *Mennonite Quar. Rev.*, vol. 16 (1942), 28–32. A call for historical and sociological research by Mennonites in their own culture.

BF6 Bender, Harold S. "The Mennonite Conception of the Church and Its Relation to Community Building." *Mennonite Quar. Rev.*, vol. 19, no. 1 (1945), 90–100.

BF7 Bender, Harold S. "Mennonite Inter-Group Relations." *Mennonite Quar. Rev.*, vol. 32 (1958), 48–58.

BF8 Bender, Harold S. "Mennonites in Art." *Mennonite Quar. Rev.*, vol. 27 (1954), 187–203.

BF9 Bender, Harold S., and C. Henry Smith. *Mennonites and Their Heritage: A Handbook of Mennonite History and Belief*. Scottdale, Pa.: Herald Pr., 1964. Based on the original edition of 1942: *Mennonites and Their Heritage: A Series of Six Studies Designed for Use in Civilian Public Service Camps*. Akron, Pa: Mennonite Central Committee, 1942. Rev. by M. Gingerich, *Mennonite Quar. Rev.*, vol. 19, no. 4 (1945), 299–300.

BF10 Bender, Paul. *Mennonite Secondary and Higher Education*. Goshen, Ind.: Mennonite Board of Education, 1964. 9 parts.

BF11 Bender, Titus W. "The Development of the Mennonite Mental Health Movement 1942–1971." Diss., Tulane Univ. School of Social Work, 1976.

BF12 Berg, P. H. "Mennonite Brethren Press." *Mennonite Life*, vol. 6, no. 1 (1951), 38–41.

BF13 Brackbill, Martin H. "A Communication on the Origins of the Early Eighteenth Century Pennsylvania Mennonite Immigrants." *Mennonite Quar. Rev.*, vol. 27, no. 1 (1953), 78–82.

BF14 Collins, Emilie. *The Plain People: High Ideals in Action.* Cleveland: Herbruck Mills, 1972.

BF15 Currie, Raymond, Leo Driedgar, and Rick Linden. "Abstinence and Moderation: Mixing Mennonite Drinking Norms." *Mennonite Quar. Rev.*, vol. 53 (October 1979).

BF16 Doerksen, John G. "Mennonite Brethren Bible College and College of Arts: Its History, Philosophy, and Development." Diss., Univ. of N. Dak., 1968. 250p.

BF17 Dyck, Cornelius J., ed. *An Introduction to Mennonite History.* Scottdale: Mennonite Publ. House, 1967. 324p. Rev. by H. J. Hillerbrand, *Historische Zeitschrift*, vol. 209, no. 1 (August 1969), 150. 3rd ed.: *An Introd. to Mennonite History: A Popular History of the Anabaptists and the Mennonites.* Scottdale, 1981. 460p.

BF18 Fast, Heinold. "Mennonite Students in Germany." *Mennonite Life*, vol. 20 (1965), 78–80.

BF19 Fast, Howard A. "Awakening to Human Needs." *Mennonite Life*, vol. 14 (1959), 163–67. Historical survey of Mennonite relief work.

BF20 Fretz, Clarence. "A History of the Winter Bible Schools in the Mennonite Church." *Mennonite Quar. Rev.*, vol. 16 (1942), 51–81, 178–95.

BF21 Fretz, J. Winfield. *Mennonite Colonization: Lessons from the Past for the Future.* Akron, Pa.: Mennonite Central Committee, 1944. 80p. Rev. by Melvin Gingerich, *Mennonite Quar. Rev.*, vol. 19, no. 3 (1945), 240.

BF22 Fretz, J. Winfield. "Should Mennonites Participate in Politics?" *Mennonite Life*, vol. 11 (1956), 139–40.

BF23 Gehman, Ernest G., trans. and ed. "The Mensch-Oberholtzer Papers." *Mennonite Quar. Rev.*, vol. 46 (October 1972).

BF24 Gingerich, Melvin. "Change and Uniformity in Mennonite Attire." *Mennonite Quar. Rev.*, vol. 40, no. 4 (1966), 243–59.

BF25 Gingerich, Melvin. "A Guide to Maps in Mennonite Books and Periodicals." *Mennonite Quar. Rev.*, vol. 27 (1953), 345–48. Maps for North America with references to German-speaking Mennonites in the hemisphere.

BF26 Gingerich, Melvin. "Mennonite Indentured Servants." *Mennonite Life*, vol. 16 (1961), 107–09, 128.

BF27 Gingerich, Melvin. "Rural Life Problems and the Mennonites." *Mennonite Quar. Rev.*, vol. 16 (1942), 167–73. On the means of preserving the heritage in a changing cultural setting.

BF28 Görtz, Hans-Jürgen. *Die Mennoniten.* Stuttgart: Evangelisches Verlagswerk, 1972. 286p. Depicts the Mennonite faith and church and a number of particular congregations in various regions of the earth.

BF29 Graeff, Arthur D. "Very Near the Truth," *Pa. Traveler*, vol. 1, no. 1 (1958), 38–39, 66–69. On the Mennonites; article prepared to commemorate Pastorius's arrival in Philadelphia, 1683. Rev. by P. A. Barba, "'S Pennsylfawnisch Deitsch Eck," Allentown *Morning Call*, 18 October 1958.

BF30 Habegger, Luann K. *Bonnets and Beards.* Berne, Ind.: Fred von Gunten, 1971. On the Mennonites.

BF31 Hershey, Mary J. "A Study of the Dress of the Old Mennonites of the Franconia Conference, 1700–1953." *Pa. Folklife*, vol. 9, no. 3 (1958), 24–47.

BF32 Hertzler, Silas. "Attendance at Mennonite Colleges and Affiliated Schools. 1941–1942." *Mennonite Quar. Rev.*, vol. 16 (1942), 260–68. "...1942–1943." *Ibid.*, vol. 17 (1943), 237–45. "...1943–1944." *Ibid.*, vol. 19, no. 1 (1945), 59–69. "...1949–1950." *Ibid.*, vol. 26 (1952), 48–62. "...1950–1951." *Ibid.*, 280–97. "...1959–1960." *Ibid.*, vol. 35 (1961), 238–41. "...1960–1961." *Ibid.*, vol. 36, no. 3 (1962), 276–79. "...1962–1963." *Ibid.*, vol. 38, no. 3 (1964), 300–03.

BF33 Horst, Irwin B. "The Menno Simons Historical Library and Archives." *Mennonite Life*, vol. 18, no. 1 (1963), 34. The library holds rare German imprints and broadsides.

BF34 Hostetler, John A. *God Uses Ink; the Heritage and Mission of the Mennonite Publishing House after Fifty Years.* Scottdale, Pa.: Mennonite Publ. House, 1958. 264p. History of the well known publishing house. Rev. by J. J. Stoudt, "'S Pennsylfawnisch Deitsch Eck," Allentown *Morning Call*, 8 November 1958.

BF35 Hostetler, John A. *Mennonite Life.* Scottdale, Pa.: Herald Pr., 1954. 32p. Rev. by P. A. Barba, "'S Pennsylfawnisch Deitsch Eck," Allentown *Morning Call*, 28 August 1954.

BF36 Juhnke, James C. "General Conference Mennonite Missions to the American Indians in the Late 19th Century." *Mennonite Quar. Rev.*, vol. 54, no. 2 (April 1980), 117–34.

BF37 Kaufmann, E. G. "Pioneers in Mennonite Education." *Mennonite Life*, vol. 17, no. 1 (1962), 16–19.

BF38 Kline, Collene. *Instructional Program for Elementary Amish and Mennonite Children.* New Holland, Pa.: BESL Center, n.d.

BF39 Klingelsmith, Sharon. "Women in the Mennonite Church, 1900–1930." *Mennonite Quar. Rev.*, vol. 54, no. 3 (July 1980), 163–207.

BF40 Klippenstein, Lawrence. *Mennoniten-Geschichte and Literatur: Eine Bücherliste.* Winnipeg, Man.: Mennonite Heritage Centre, 1981. 16p.

BF41 Krahn, Cornelius. *The Mennonites: A Brief Guide to Information.* Newton, Kans.: Faith & Life Pr., 1976. 2nd ed.

BF42 Krahn, Cornelius, Marianne Harms, and Sharon Klingelsmith. "Radical Reformation and Mennonite Bibliography 1975–76." *Mennonite Life*, vol. 32 (1977), 26–30.

BF43 Krahn, Cornelius, and Nelson P. Springer. "Radical Reformation Bibliography 1970–1972." *Mennonite Life*, vol. 28 (1973), 21–28.

BF44 Krahn, Cornelius, Nelson P. Springer, et al. "Radical Reformation and Mennonite Bibliography 1973–1974." *Mennonite Life*, vol. 30 (1975), 24–31.

BF45 Krahn, Cornelius, ed. *Smith's Story of the Mennonites.* Newton, Kans.: Mennonite Publ. Office, 1951. Rev. by H. W. Elkinton, *Amer.-German Rev.*, vol. 18, no. 1 (1951), 35–36.

BF46 Krahn, Cornelius, ed. "Some Letters of Bernhard Warkentin Pertaining to the Migration of 1873–75." *Mennonite Quar. Rev.*, vol. 24, no. 3 (1950), 248–62. Letters written in Illinois describe possibilities of settling in Minnesota and Dakota Territory.

BF47 Landis, Ira D. "Hans Herr—A Myth?" *Mennonite Research Jour.*, vol. 11, no. 3 (July 1970), 25, 32.

BF48 Liechty, Joseph C. "Humility: The Foundation of Mennonite Religious Life in the 1860's." *Mennonite Quar. Rev.*, vol. 54, no. 1 (January 1980), 5–31.

BF49 *The Mennonite Encyclopedia.* Ed. Cornelius Krahn and Melvin Gingerich. 4 vols. Hillsboro, Kans.: Mennonite Publ. Office, 1969–1973.

BF50 Mullen, Patricia F. *The Plain People.* Bethpage, N.Y.: C. J. Johnson, 1958. Rev. by E. L. Smith, "'S Pennsylfawnisch Deitsch Eck," Allentown *Morning Call*, 15 November 1958.

BF51 Mumaw, John R. "Current Forces Adversely Affecting the Life of the Mennonite Community." *Mennonite Quar. Rev.*, vol. 19, no. 2 (1945), 101–16.

BF52 Newcomb, Thomas L. *Buggies, Broadbrims, Bonnets and Beyond.* Garrettsville, Ohio: n.p., 1980. On the Amish-Mennonites and the Mennonites.

BF53 Newcomb, Thomas L. "Northeastern Ohio's Mennonite and Amish Folk." *Western Reserve Mag.*, July-August 1981, 70–74.

BF54 Pannabecker, Samuel Floyd. *Faith in Ferment: A History of the Central District Conference.* Newton, Kans., n.p., 1968. 385p. Mennonites in America.

BF55 Penner, Horst. "West Prussian Mennonites through Four Centuries." *Mennonite Quar. Rev.*, vol. 23, no. 4 (1949), 232–34. Trans. from the German. Migrations from Europe to southern Russia; to the United States and again recently to the British and American zones of occupation in Germany.

BF56 Prentis, Noble L. et al. "As Others Saw Them." *Mennonite Life*, vol. 25, no. 2 (April 1970), 59–62. German-American Mennonites.

BF57 Quiring, Horst. "Die Auswanderung der Mennoniten aus Preussen 1788–1870." *Mennonite Life*, vol. 6 (1951), 37f.

BF58 Raitz, Karl B. "Theology in the Landscape: A Comparison of Mormon and Amish-Mennonite Land Use." *Utah Hist. Quar.*, vol. 41 (Winter 1973), 23–34.

BF59 Redekop, Calvin. "A New Look at Sect Development." *Jour. for the Scientific Study of Religion*, vol. 13, no. 3 (September 1974), 345–52. Old Colony Mennonites and Mormons.

BF60 Redekop, Calvin. *The Old Colony Mennonites: Dilemmas of Ethnic Minority Life*. Baltimore: The Johns Hopkins Univ. Pr., 1969. 302p. Rev. by P. K. Conkin, *Jour. of Church and State*, vol. 12, no. 1 (Winter 1970), 156–57; J. Juhnke, *Jour. of Amer. Hist.*, vol. 57, no. 1 (June 1970), 217–18.

BF61 Redekop, Calvin. "The Sectarian Black and White: Old Colony Mennonites." Diss., Univ. of Chicago, 1959.

BF62 Redekop, Calvin, and John A. Hostetler. "The Plain People: An Interpretation." *Mennonite Quar. Rev.*, vol. 51 (October 1977), 266–77.

BF63 Schmidt, John F. "Bethel College and the Printed Word." *Mennonite Life*, vol. 18, no. 4 (October 1963), 181–83. The use of German in Bethel College publications.

BF64 Schmidt, John F. "I Was a Stranger." *Mennonite Quar. Rev.*, vol. 33 (1959), 245–49. Financial and other help given in aid of the Mennonite movement from Europe to the western states in the 1870's.

BF65 Smith, Charles Henry. *The Story of the Mennonites*. Berne, Ind.: Mennonite Book Concern, 1941, 823p. Rev. by H. S. Bender and Ernst Correll, *Mennonite Quar. Rev.*, vol. 16, no. 5 (1942), 270–75; W. K. Thomas, *Amer.-German Rev.*, vol. 8, no. 3 (1942), 34; Carl Wittke, *Amer. Hist. Rev.*, vol. 47, no. 3 (1942), 659–60. Rev. by H. S. Bender and E. Correll was answered by C. Henry Smith, in *Mennonite Quar. Rev.*, vol. 17 (1943), 246–52. 3rd ed., Newton, Kans.: Mennonite Publ. Office, 1950. 856p. Rev. by R. Friedmann, *Church History*, vol. 20, no. 2 (1951), 92–93. 4th ed. revised and enlarged by Cornelius Krahn. Newton, Kans.: Mennonite Publ. Office, 1957. 856p. Reissued as *Smith's Story of the Mennonites*. Ed. Cornelius Krahn. Newton, Kans.: Mennonite Publ. Office, 1981.

BF66 Sprunger, Keith L., and J. C. Juhnke. "Mennonite Oral History." *Mennonite Quar. Rev.*, vol. 54, no. 3 (1980), 244–47.

BF67 Suderman, Elmer F. "Two Mennonite Pioneers." *Mennonite Life*, vol. 18, no. 3 (July 1963), 127. Christian Krehbiel and C. H. Smith.

BF68 Umble, John Sylvanus. *Goshen College 1894–1954; A Venture in Christian Higher Education*. Goshen, Ind.: Goshen College, 1955. 284p. Rev. by N. E. Byers, *Mennonite Life*, vol. 11 (1956), 92–93; J. J. Detzler, *Ind. Mag. of Hist.*, vol. 52 (1956), 317.

BF69 Unruh, Wilfred J. *A Study of Mennonite Service Programs; a Historical and Empirical Study Prep. for the Inst. of Mennonite Studies, Associated Mennonite Biblical Seminaries, Elkhart, Ind., July 1965*. Elkhart: Inst. of Mennonite Studies, 1965.

BF70 Warkentin, A. *Who's Who among the Mennonites*. N.p.: n.p., 1943. Rev. by P. Erb., *Mennonite Quar. Rev.*, vol. 18, no. 4 (1944), 252–54.

BF71 Wenger, J. C. *Glimpses of Mennonite History*. Scottdale, Pa.: Mennonite Publ. House, 1940. 126p. Rev. by J. C. Meyer, *Amer. Hist. Rev.*, vol. 47, no. 1 (1941), 84–85. Reissued as *Glimpses of Mennonite History and Doctrine*. Scottdale, Pa.: Mennonite Publ. House, 1947. 258p. Rev. by H. Elkinton, *Amer.-German Rev.*, vol. 14, no. 4 (1948), 33; A. R. Suelflow, *Concordia Hist. Inst. Quar.*, vol. 23, no. 1 (1950), 44.

Mennonite Biography

BENDER, DANIEL H.

BF72 Bender, Daniel H. Papers. 2 ft. In the Mennonite Church Archives, Goshen, Ind. (MS 79-1820). Correspondence, diaries, lecture notes, etc. B. (1866–1945) was principal of Hesston Academy and Bible School and later president of Hesston College, Hesston, Kans.

BENDER, HAROLD S.

BF73 Bainton, Roland H. "Harold S. Bender." *Church Hist.*, vol. 31, no. 4 (December 1962), 476. A memorial tribute to B. (1897–1962).

BF74 Bainton, Roland H. et al. "The Meaning of the Life and Work of Harold S. Bender: A Symposium." *Mennonite Quar. Rev.*, vol. 38, no. 2 (1964), 175–211.

BF75 Dyck, Cornelius J. "Harold S. Bender: The Church Historian." *Mennonite Quar. Rev.*, vol. 38, no. 2 (1964), 130–37.

BF76 *Harold S. Bender; Educator, Historian, Churchman*. Scottdale, Pa.: Herald Pr., 1964. 141p. Offprint from the *Mennonite Quar. Rev.* for April 1964.

BF77 Hershberger, Guy F. "Harold S. Bender and His Time." *Mennonite Quar. Rev.*, vol. 38, no. 2 (1964), 83–112.

BF78 Hershberger, Guy F. *Recovery of the Anabaptist Vision; a Sixtieth Anniversary Tribute to Harold S. Bender*. Scottdale, Pa.: Mennonite Publ. House, 1957. 360p. Also issued in German translation: *Das Täufertum: Erbe und Verpflichtung*. Stuttgart: n.p., 1963. Rev. by R. Friedmann, *Mennonite Quar. Rev.*, vol. 38, no. 4 (1964), 376–77.

BF79 Kreider, Carl. "Harold S. Bender: The Educator." *Mennonite Quar. Rev.*, vol. 38, no. 2 (1964), 121–29. On B.'s teaching at Goshen College and Goshen College Biblical Seminary.

BF80 Waltner, Erland. "Harold S. Bender: The Ecumenical Mennonite." *Mennonite Quar. Rev.*, vol. 38, no. 2 (1964), 138–47.

BF81 Wenger, John C. "Harold S. Bender: A Brief Biography." *Mennonite Quar. Rev.*, vol. 38, no. 2 (1964), 113–20.

BERGTOLD, DANIEL F.

BF82 J. H. Lohrentz. "Daniel F. Bergtold 1876–1948." *Mennonite Life*, vol. 6, no. 3 (1951), 44. Prominent Mennonite preacher.

BURKHOLDER, CHRISTIAN

BF83 Landis, Ira D. "Bishop Christian Burkholder of Groffdale, 1746–1809." *Mennonite Quar. Rev.*, vol. 18, no. 3 (1944), 145–61.

CLAASSEN, CORNELIUS FRITZ

BF84 Claassen, Cornelius Fritz. Papers. In Mennonite Library and Archives, North Newton, Kans. (MS 80-2107). Correspondence and diaries. C. (1859–1941) was a Newton, Kans., banker.

COFFMAN, JOHN SAMUEL

BF85 Coffman, John Samuel. Papers. Ca. 3 ft. In Mennonite Church Archives, Goshen, Ind. (MS 79-1821). Correspondence, MSS., diaries, etc. C. (1848–1899) was Mennonite evangelist and editor at Mennonite Publ. Co., Elkhart, Ind.

BF86 Shank, Floyd A. "John S. Coffman, 1848–1899. Mennonite Evangelist." *Mennonite Hist. Bull.* vol. 4, no. 1 (March 1943), 1–2. Active in Pennsylvania, Indiana, and Michigan.

BF87 Umble, John S. "John Samuel Coffman: His Life and Work." *Mennonite Life*, vol. 14 (1959), 110–16.

DUERKSEN FAMILY

BF88 Duerksen, Jacob R. and Christena Duerksen. Papers. 4 ft. In Mennonite Library and Archives, North Newton, Kans. (MS 80-2110). Papers of Jacob D. (b. 1894), a missionary, and Christena D. (1919–1977).

FRIEDMANN, ROBERT

BF89 Bender, Harold S. "A Tribute to Robert Friedmann." *Mennonite Quar. Rev.*, vol. 35, no. 3 (1961), 242–47. Biographical sketch, bibliography, and list of his articles in the *Mennonite Encyclopedia*. An Austrian-American.

BF90 Friedmann, Robert. "My Way to the Mennonites." *Mennonite Life*, vol. 17, no. 3 (1962), 136–39. The author tells of his conversion and emigration to the United States.

FRIESEN, ABRAM A.

BF91 Friesen, Abram A. Papers, 1914–1948. 4 ft. In Mennonite Library and Archives, North Newton, Kans. (MS 80-2113). F. (1885–1948) was a member of the study commission sent to America by Mennonites of Russia in 1920–1921 to negotiate migration to America.

FRIESEN, HEINRICH B.

BF92 Friesen, Heinrich B. Papers. Ca. 1 ft. In Mennonite Library and Archives, North Newton,

Kans. (MS 80-2115). Memoirs and diaries. F. (1837–1926) was a Mennonite farmer who emigrated to America in 1879. Publ. in 1974 as *The Autobiography of H. B. Friesen 1837–1926*.

FRIESEN, J. JOHN

BF93 Friesen, J. John. Papers. 2 boxes. In Mennonite Library and Archives, North Newton, Kans. (MS 80-2116). MSS. on Mennonite history and doctrine. F. (1883–1972) was a lay historian and educator at Freeman, S. Dak., and Mountain Lake, Minn.

FUNK, JOHN F.

BF94 Schnell, Kempes. "John F. Funk, 1835–1930, and the Mennonite Migration 1873–1875." *Mennonite Quar. Rev.*, vol. 24, no. 3 (1950) 199–229; "John F. Funk's Land Inspection Trips as Recorded in His Diaries, 1872 and 1873." *Ibid.*, vol. 24, no. 4 (1950), 295–311. Reporting on Minnesota and Dakota Territory.

FUNK, JOSEPH

BF95 Horst, Irvin B. "Joseph Funk, Early Mennonite Printer and Publisher." *Mennonite Quar. Rev.*, vol. 31 (1957), 260–77.

GAEDDERT, GUSTAV RAYMOND

BF96 Gaeddert, Gustav Raymond. Papers, 1910–1971. 4 ft. In Mennonite Library and Archives, North Newton, Kans. (MS 80-2118). Correspondence, notes, and materials relating to the history of the Red Cross. G. (1895–1972) was an educator, historian, and relief worker in a Mennonite refuge settlement, of Topeka, Kans.

GALLE, WILLIAM

BF97 Galle, William. Papers, 1869–1920. 1 box. In Mennonite Library and Archives, North Newton, Kans. (MS 80-2119). Sermons and correspondence. G. (1849–1920) was a minister of Moundridge, Kans.

GOERING, JACOB

BF98 Hay, Charles A. *Memoirs of Rev. Jacob Goering, Rev. George Lochman, D.D., and Rev. Benjamin Kurtz, D.D., LL.D.* Philadelphia: n.p., 1887.

GOERING, SAMUEL JOSEPH

BF99 Goering, Samuel Joseph. Papers, ca. 1 ft. In Mennonite Library and Archives, North Newton, Kans. (MS 80-2120). G. (1892–1962) was a missionary.

GOERTZ, DAVID

BF100 Goertz, David. Papers. 1 box. In Mennonite Library and Archives, North Newton, Kans. (MS 80-2121). Misc. papers in German. G. (1862–1932) was evangelist in Brudertal Mennonite Church, Hillsboro, Kans.

GREBEL, CONRAD

BF101 Bender, Harold S. *Life and Letters of Conrad Grebel*. 2 vols. Vol. 1. *Conrad Grebel, the Founder of the Swiss Brethren*. Studies in Anabaptist and Mennonite History, no. 6. Goshen, Ind.: Mennonite Hist. Soc., Goshen College, 1950. 326p.

GUENGERICH, SAMUEL D.

BF102 Guengerich, Samuel D. Papers. Ca. 3 ft. In Mennonite Church Archives, Goshen, Ind. (MS 79-1823). Correspondence, diaries, records and documents. G. (1836–1929) was an Amish Mennonite educator, author, and publisher of Johnson County, Iowa.

HARDER, HENRY NOVALIS

BF103 Harder, Henry Novalis. Papers, 1942–1962. Ca. 7 ft. In Mennonite Library and Archives, North Newton, Kans. (MS 80–2122). Correspondence, papers and sermons. H. (1905–1963) was minister in Oklahoma, Idaho, and Illinois.

HARMS, HENRY H.

BF104 Harms, Henry H. Papers, 1874–1925. 1 box. In Mennonite Library and Archives, North Newton, Kans. (MS 80-2123). Documents relating to the 1874 migration from Russia and early years in Kansas.

HARMS, JOHN H.

BF105 Harms, E. M. "John H. Harms, Pioneer Mennonite Doctor." *Mennonite Life*, vol. 4, no. 4 (1949), 13–15.

HARTZLER, JONAS SMUCKER

BF106 Hartzler, Jonas Smucker. Papers, 1911–1946. In Mennonite Church Archives, Goshen, Ind. (MS 79-1824). Diaries, Bible course and sermon notes. H. (1857–1953) was clergyman, educator and editor, of Elkhart, Ind. Diaries also by his wife, Fannie (Stutzler) Hartzler.

HERMAN, ESTHER D.

BF107 Herman, Esther D. *As A Mennonite of Pioneer Ancestry.* Superior, Neb.: n.p., 1976.

HOHMAN, WALTER H.

BF108 Hohman, Walter H. Papers, 1940–1968. Ca. 2 ft. In Mennonite Library and Archives, North Newton, Kans. (MS 80-2125). Articles, compositions, research material on hymnody. H. (1892–1971) was director, Dept. of Music, Bethel Coll., North Newton Kans.

HORSCH, JOHN

BF109 Bender, Harold S. "John Horsch, 1867–1941: A Biography." *Mennonite Quar. Rev.*, vol. 21, no. 3 (1947), 131–44. H. (1867–1941) was a Mennonite historian, of Scottdale, Pa.

BF110 Correll, Ernst. "Notes on John Horsch as a Historian." *Mennonite Quar. Rev.*, vol. 21, no. 3 (1947), 145–50. On H.'s research and his American point of view toward Mennonite history.

BF111 Friedmann, Robert. "John Horsch und Ludwig Keller." *Mennonite Quar. Rev.*, vol. 21 (1947), 160–74.

BF112 Hershberger, Guy F. "John Horsch, a Proponent of Biblical Non-Resistance." *Mennonite Quar. Rev.*, vol. 21, no. 3 (1947), 156–59.

BF113 Horsch, John. Papers, 1873–1940. 8 ft. In Mennonite Church Archives, Goshen, Ind. (MS 79-1825). Correspondence, notes, and MSS. of writings chiefly relating to to modernist-fundamentalist controversy.

BF114 Wenger, John C. "The Theology of John Horsch." *Mennonite Quar. Rev.*, vol. 21, no. 3 (1947), 151–55.

HORSCH, MICHAEL M.

BF115 Horsch, Michael M. Papers. 1 box. In Mennonite Library and Archives, North Newton, Kans. (MS 80-2126). Sermons and correspondence from sisters in Germany. H. (1872–1941), minister from Germany, served in Oklahoma, California, and Nebraska.

JANZEN, JACOB HEINRICH

BF116 [Articles on Janzen.] *Mennonite Life*, vol. 6, no. 3 (1951), 33–43. Articles include a list of J.'s books.

BF117 Janzen, Jacob Heinrich. Papers. Ca. 15 ft. In Mennonite Library and Archives, North Newton, Kans. (MS 80-2127). Correspondence as immigrant leader and literary file. J. (1878–1950) was educator, literary figure, and minister in Russia and Ontario.

KAUFFMAN, DANIEL

BF118 Gingerich, Alice K. *Life and Times of Daniel Kauffman.* Scottdale, Pa.: Herlad Pr., 1954. 160p. Rev. by N. E. Byers, *Mennonite Life*, vol. 11 (1956), 93. K. (1865–1944) was clergyman, educator, and editor of the *Gospel Herald*, of Scottdale, Pa.

BF119 Kauffman, Daniel. Papers, 1907–1944. 1 ft. In Mennonite Church Archives, Goshen, Ind. (MS 79-1826). Correspondence; MSS. of books and articles.

KAUFMAN, EDMUND GEORGE

BF120 Kaufman, Edmund George. Papers. 15 ft. In Mennonite Library and Archives, North Newton, Kans. (MS 80-2128). K. (b. 1891), educator and historian, was president of Bethel Coll. (1932–1952).

KAUFMAN, FRIEDA

BF121 Kaufman, Frieda. Papers, 1910–1944. Ca. 1 ft. In Mennonite Library and Archives, North Newton, Kans. (MS 80-2129). Correspondence and MS. K. (1883–1944) was Mother of Bethel Deaconess Hospital, Newton, Kans.

KLIEWER, JOHN W.

BF122 Kliewer, John W. *Memoirs....* Newton, Kans.: Bethel College, 1943. 150p.

KREHBIEL, EDWARD BENJAMIN

BF123 Krehbiel, Edward, Benjamin Papers, 1903–1949. 1 box. In Mennonite Library and Archives, North Newton, Kans. (MS 80-2130). Correspondence, studies, articles. K. (1878–1950) was professor of history, Univ. of Chicago and Stanford Univ.

KREHBIEL, JOHN CARL

BF124 Melvin Gingerich. "John Carl Krehbiel (1811–1886), a Mennonite Pioneer in Iowa." *Mennonite Life*, vol. 15 (1960), 57–59.

KUHLMAN, ERNST

BF125 Kuhlman, Ernst. Papers, 1911–1974. 1 box. In Mennonite Library and Archives, North

Newton, Kans. (MS 80-2131). Correspondence to relatives in Kansas and newsletters from China in German and English. K. (1883–1975) was a German independent missionary to China, 1907–1948.

LINSCHEID, JOHN P.

BF126 Linscheid, John P. Papers, 1885–1975. Ca. 6 ft. In Mennonite Library and Archives, North Newton, Kans. (MS 80-2132). Includes family correspondence, genealogical material on L. and related Galician families. L. (1864–1937) was a minister; emigrated from Austrian Poland to Kansas.

MENSCH, JACOB B.

BF127 Mensch, Jacob B. MS. diary. In the Mennonite Archives of Eastern Pennsylvania at Kulpsville, Pa. Ed. and trans. by Raymond E. Hollenbach, 1966.

MILLER, ORIE O.

BF128 Erb, Paul. *Orie O. Miller: The Story of a Man and an Era*. Scottdale, Pa.: Mennonite Publ. House, 1969. 304p. The story of the Mennonite Central Committee.

MININGER, JACOB D.

BF129 Mininger, Jacob D. Papers, 1900–1941. Ca. 5 ft. In Mennonite Chuch Archives, Goshen, Ind. (MS 79-1827). Correspondence relating to mission work and counseling of conscientious objectors at Fort Leavenworth during World War I. M. (1879–1941) was a mission worker and evangelist.

MOYER, SAMUEL TYSON

BF130 Moyer, Samuel Tyson. Papers, 1920–1970. Ca. 3 ft. In Mennonite Library and Archives, North Newton, Kans. (MS 80-2133). Correspondence and reports from the field; MSS. of books and articles. M. (1893–1972) was minister to India and author.

NAVALL, DEDRICH

BF131 Navall, Lotte. "Dedrich Navall—Writer and Teacher." *Mennonite Life*, vol. 24, no. 4 (1969), 161–63. Emigrant from Russia who taught in the United States.

NEUFELD, HENRY T.

BF132 Neufeld, Henry T. Papers, 1913–1924. 1 box. In Mennonite Library and Archives, North Newton, Kans. (MS 80-2134). Correspondence; Cheyenne grammar materials. N. (1888–1968) was missionary to the Cheyenne in Oklahoma.

OBERHOLTZER, JOHN H.

BF133 Oberholtzer, John H. "A Letter of John H. Oberholtzer to Unnamed Friends in Germany, 1849." *Mennonite Quar. Rev.*, vol. 46 (October 1972). Trans. by Elizabeth Bender.

OYER, NOAH

BF134 Oyer, Noah. Papers, 1923–1930. Ca. 3 ft. In Mennonite Church Archives, Goshen, Ind. (MS 79-1828). Papers relating to church business. O. (1891–1931) was professor and dean, Goshen Coll., Goshen, Ind.

PENNER, HEINRICH D.

BF135 Penner, Heinrich D. Papers, 1913–1933. Ca. 1 ft. In Mennonite Library and Archives, North Newton, Kans. (MS 80-2135). P. (1862–1933) was minister and educator of Newton, Kans.

PENNER, PETER WILLIAM

BF136 Penner, Peter William. Papers, 1896–1950. 3 ft. In Mennonite Library and Archives, North Newton, Kans. (MS 80-2136). Correspondence, diaries, photo collection. P. (1876–1953) was a missionary.

PETERS, GERHARD A.

BF137 Peters, Gerhard A. Paper, 1911–1933. In Mennonite Library and Archives, North Newton, Kans. (MS 80-2137). Travel diaries and papers. P. (1880–1935) was teacher in Russia and Germany, and director of Girl's Home, Winnipeg.

PREHEIM, SAMUEL PETER

BF138 Preheim, Samuel Peter. Papers, 1925–1950. In Mennonite Library and Archives, North Newton, Kans. (MS 80-2138). Writings and MSS. on social and economic problems. P. (1881–1952) was pastor in Pennsylvania, Ohio, Nebraska, and South Dakota.

REGIER, AARON J.

BF139 Regier, Aaron J. Papers, 1910–1940. 1 box. In Mennonite Library and Archives, North Newton, Kans. (MS 80-2139). R. (1884–1947) was an educator.

REGIER, CORNELIUS C.

BF140 Regier, Cornelius C. Papers, 1919–1949. Ca. 3 ft. In Mennonite Library and Archives, North Newton, Kans. (MS 80-2140). Correspondence, genealogical material, historical notes. R. (1884–1950) was a college teacher.

BF141 Regier, Cornelius C. *Pioneer Experiences of Father, Mother, and Grandfather.* N.p.: n.p., 1963. 48p.

REGIER, EMIL

BF142 Regier, Emil. Papers, 1918–1939. In Mennonite Library and Archives, North Newton, Kans. (MS 80-2141). Correspondence as a noncombatant from Camp Funston, Kans., and service as a conscientious objector in World War I. R. (1895–1969).

REGIER, JOHN

BF143 Regier, John. Papers. Ca. 1 ft. In Mennonite Library and Archives, North Newton, Kans. (MS 80-2142). Diaries, account books and misc. papers. R. (1867–1945) was a farmer of Whitewater, Kans.

REGIER, JOHN M.

BF144 Regier, John M. Papers, 1912–1950. 1 ft. In Mennonite Library and Archives, North Newton, Kans. (MS 80-2143). Correspondence and notes for the Home Missions Board. R. (1885–1960) was minister of General Conference Mennonite churches.

REGIER, PETER K.

BF145 Regier, Peter K. Papers, 1922–1968. Ca. 7 ft. In Mennonite Library and Archives, North Newton, Kans. (MS 80-2144). Correspondence, sermons, Biblical studies, etc. R. (1891–1973) was a pastor.

REGIER, SAMUEL

BF146 Regier, Samuel. Papers, 1945–1964. 1 box. In Mennonite Library and Archives, North Newton, Kans. (MS 80-2145). Correspondence. R. (1892–1969) was a farmer in Kansas.

SAWATZKY, JACOB F.

BF147 Sawatzky, Jacob F. Papers, 1908–1964. Ca. 1 ft. In Mennonite Library and Archives, North Newton, Kans. (MS 80-2147). S. (1881–1966) was minister of General Conference Mennonite churches.

SCHELLENBERG, ABRAHAM

BF148 Schellenberg, T. R. "Editor Abraham L. Schellenberg." *Mennonite Life*, vol. 9 (1954), 19–28. On S. (1869–1941).

SCHROEDER, PETER R.

BF149 Dehnert, Celest S. "Peter R. Schroeder, Pastor and Conference Worker." *Mennonite Life*, vol. 4, no. 3 (1949), 38–41. S. (1888–1941) was pastor in the Midwest.

SCHWARZENDRUBER, JACOB

BF150 Umble, John. "Documents Relating to Bishop Jacob Schwarzendruber (1800–1868), Part II." *Mennonite Quar. Rev.*, vol. 20, no. 3 (1946), 230–39. A list of MSS. in the library of Bishop Schwarzendruber and his successors.

SHANK, CLARENCE

BF151 Shank, Clarence S. *A Mennonite Boy's World War I Experience.* Merion, Pa.: n.p., 1963. 48p.

SHOWALTER, JACOB A.

BF152 Schrag, Robert. "The Story of a Mennonite Millionaire Jacob A. Showalter 1879–1953." *Mennonite Life*, vol. 12 (1957), 64–69. Born in Friedelsheim, S. was a farmer of Harvey County, Kansas.

SMITH, C. HENRY

BF153 Smith, C. Henry. *Mennonite Country Boy; the Early Years of C. Henry Smith.* Newton, Kans.: Faith & Life Pr., 1962. 261p.

SPRUNGER, SAMUEL FERDINAND

BF154 Sprunger, Eva F. "Samuel Ferdinand Sprunger, Pastor, Conference Worker." *Mennonite Life*, vol. 8 (1953), 178–82. S. (1848–1923) was a prominent Mennonite preacher.

STEINER, MENNO SIMON

BF155 Steiner, Menno Simon. Papers, 1884–1911. Ca. 5 ft. In Mennonite Church Archives, Goshen, Ind. (MS 79-1829). Correspondence, diaries, notebooks, lectures and notes. S. (1866–1911) was a Mennonite leader and evangelist.

STOLL, JOSEPH

BF156 Stoll, Joseph. *The Lord is My Shepherd, The Life of Elizabeth Kemp Stutzman.* Aylmer, Ont.: Pathway Publ. Co., 1965. Rev. by C. R. Beam, "'S Pennsylfawnisch Deitsch Eck," Allentown *Morning Call*, 5 November 1966. Biography of a member of the Old Order Mennonite Church; set in Indiana and Ohio.

STUCKEY, JOSEPH

BF157 Yoder, Harry. "Joseph Stuckey and Central Conference." *Mennonite Life*, vol. 6, no. 2 (1951), 16–19.

STUCKY, JACOB

BF158 I. G. Neufeld. "Jacob Stucky, Pioneer of Two Continents." *Mennonite Life*, vol. 4, no. 1 (1949), 46–47. S. (1824–1893) was a Kansas Mennonite.

SUDERMAN, JOHN M.

BF159 Suderman, John M. Papers. Ca. 1 ft. In Mennonite Library and Archives, North Newton, Kans. (MS 80-2148). Correspondence, minutes and reports of the Mennonite Colonization Board and Board of Publications. S. (1876–1964) was a minister and hospital administrator, North Newton, Kans.

THIESSEN, ABRAHAM

BF160 Krahn, Cornelius. "Abraham Thiessen: A Mennonite Revolutionary?" *Mennonite Life*, vol. 24, no. 2 (April 1969), 73–77. Expelled from Russia; settled in Nebraska.

TSCHETTER, KATHARINA

BF161 Tschetter, Katharina. *My Life Story, 1880–1945*. Chicago: n.p., 1945. 46p. T. (b. 1880) was a Mennonite missionary in North Carolina, Tennessee, and Illinois.

UMBLE, JOHN SYLVANUS

BF162 Umble, John Sylvanus. Papers, 1881–1963. Ca. 8 ft. In Mennonite Church Archives, Goshen, Ind. (MS 79-1830). Correspondence, notebooks, addresses, research material on Mennonites. U. (1881–1966) was professor at Goshen Coll., Ind.

UNRAU, PETER

BF163 Unrau, Peter. Papers, 1845–1901. 1 box. In Mennonite Library and Archives, North Newton, Kans. (MS 80-2150). Correspondence, 1874–1879, from Mennonites in Russia to relatives in America; sermons. U. (1824–1915) was minister in Russia and Kansas.

UNRUH, RUDOLPH T.

BF164 Unruh, Rudolph T. Papers, 1932–1950. 1 box. In Mennonite Library and Archives, North Newton, Kans. (MS 80-2151). Documents relating to his experience in requesting recognition as a conscientious objector in the Army. U. (1899–1959) was a medical missionary and officer in the U.S. Army Medical Corps.

VOTH, HEINRICH

BF165 Froese, J. A. *Witness Extraordinary: A Biography of Elder Heinrich Voth, 1851–1918*. Hillsboro, Kans.: General Conference of the Mennonite Brethren Churches of North America, 1975.

VOTH, JOHN J.

BF166 Voth, John J. Papers, 1875–1885, 1903–1969. Ca. 5 ft. In Mennonite Library and Archives, North Newton, Kans. (MS 80-2152). Correspondence; file on pastoral work; genealogical materials of several families. V. (1891–1972) was an educator, minister, and relief worker in Germany.

WALLIS, MICHAEL

BF167 Wallis, Michael. "Mennonites: A Search for the Golden Time in the West." *Amer. West*, vol. 18, no. 6 (1981), 26–33.

WARKENTIN, BERNHARD

BF168 Haury, David A. "Bernhard Warkentin: A Mennonite Benefactor." *Mennonite Quar. Rev.*, vol. 49 (July 1975).

WEDEL, OSWALD HENRY

BF169 Wedel, Oswald Henry. Papers, 1930–1955. 1 box. In Mennonite Library and Archives, North Newton, Kans. (MS 80-2154). Correspondence; articles on European history. W. (1894–1957) was historian and professor of history.

WIEBE, JOHN E.

BF170 Wiebe, John E. Papers. 3 ft. In Mennonite Library and Archives, North Newton, Kans. (MS 80-2155). Correspondence with relatives in Europe. W. (1881–1973) was a Mennonite of Kansas.

BG
Amish-Mennonite People and Culture

See also Mennonites *under* Section IJ: Religion and Church History; *and* Indiana, Iowa, *and* Ohio *under* Part J: German-American Local History.

BG1 Beiler, Joseph F. "Eighteenth Century Amish in Lancaster County." *Mennonite Research Jour.*, vol. 17 (October 1976).

BG2 Beiler, Joseph F. *Old Order Shop and Service Directory of the Old Order Society*. Gordonville, Pa.: n.p., 1977.

BG3 Benjamin, Steven M. "The Old Order Amish: Their Culture, History, and Languages." In: *Papers from the Conference on German-Americana in the Eastern United States*. Morgantown: Dept. of For. Langs., West Virginia Univ., 1980, p.143–61.

BG4 Benjamin, Steven M. "The Old Order Amish and the University of Essen." *Newsletter of the Soc. for German-Amer. Studies*, vol. 2, no. 1 (1980–1981), 11–13.

BG5 Berns, Walter. "Ratiocinations: The Importance of Being Amish." *Harpers Mag.*, vol. 246 (1973), 36f.

BG6 Berry, Wendell. *The Unsettling of America. Culture and Agriculture*. New York: Avon Books, 1977. Touches on the culture of the Amish.

BG7 Buck, Roy C. "Bloodless Theatre: Images of the Old Order Amish in Tourism Literature." *Pa. Mennonite Heritage*, vol. 2 (July 1979), 2–11.

BG8 Buck, Roy C. "Boundary Maintenance Revisited: Tourist Experience in an Old Order Amish Community." *Rural Sociology*, vol. 43 (1978), 221–34.

BG9 Byler, Uria R. *Our Better Country; a History*. Gordonville, Pa.: Old Order Book Society ca. 1963. 271p.

BG10 Diaz-Plaja, Fernando. "Una Asombrosa Minoria: La de los Amish." In: *La vida norteamericana*. Madrid: Escelicer, S. L., 1955, p.123–27. A Spanish journalist describes the Amish settlements of Lancaster County, Pa.

BG11 Fisher, Gideon L. *Farm Life and Its Changes*. Gordonville, Pa.: Pequea Publs., 1978. Incl. information on the Amish.

BG12 Gehmann, Richard. "Plainest of Pennsylvania's Plain People: Amish Folk." With Photographs by William Albert Allard. *National Geographic Mag.*, vol. 128, no. 2 (1965), 226–53.

BG13 Gillin, J. P. "The Old Order Amish of Pennsylvania." In: *Anthropology*. Ed. S. B. Rapport and H. White. New York: N.Y. Univ. Pr., 1967, p.319–32. Excerpt from Gillin's The *Ways of Men*.

BG14 Hofer, Jesse W. *An Amish Boy Remembers from Behind Those Fences*. San Antonio, Tex.: Naylor Pr., 1973.

BG15 Horst, Mel, and Elmer L. Smith. *Among the Amish in Pennsylvania Dutchland*. Akron, Pa.: Applied Arts Associates, 1959. 42p. Rev. by P. A. Barba, "'S Pennsylfawnisch Deitsch Eck," Allentown *Morning Call*, 25 July 1959.

BG16 Hostetler, John A. "The Amish, Citizens of Heaven and America." *Pa. Folklife*, vol. 10, no. 1 (1959), 32–37.

BG17 Hostetler, John A. "The Amish in America." *Amer. Heritage*, vol. 3, no. 4 (1953), 4–8.

BG18 Hostetler, John A. *Amish Life*. Scottdale: Mennonite Publ. House, 1952. 32p. Rev. by P. A. Barba, "'S Pennsylfawnisch Deitsch Eck," Allentown *Morning Call*, 2 May 1953; *Pa. Mag. of Hist. and Biog.*, vol. 77 (1953), 378; M. A. Mook, *Mennonite Quar. Rev.*, vol. 49 (1975), 71.

BG19 Hostetler, John A. *Amish Society*. Baltimore: The Johns Hopkins Univ. Pr., 1963. 347p. Rev. by P. A. Barba, *Pa. Hist.*, vol. 31, no. 4 (1964), 489–90; P. A. Barba, "'S Pennsylfawnisch Deitsch Eck," Allentown *Morning Call*, 21 November 1964; C. J. Dyck, *Church Hist.* vol. 34, no. 1 (1965), 106–07; J. W. Fretz, *Mennonite Quar. Rev.*, vol. 39, no. 1 (January 1965), 82–84; P. E. Hammond, *Southern Folklore Quar.*, vol. 28, no.

3 (1964), 234–35; J. F. Schmidt, *Mennonite Life*, vol. 19, no. 3 (1964), 183; W. I. Schreiber, *Hist. Rev. of Berks Co.*, vol. 29, no. 1 (1964), 92–95; A. E. Schrock, *Western Pa. Hist. Mag.*, vol. 47, no. 2 (1965), 159–60; W. H. Smith, *Jour. of Amer. Hist.*, vol. 51, no. 1 (1965), 135–36; G. M. Stoltzfus, "'S Pennsylfawnisch Deitsch Eck," Allentown *Morning Call*, 4 April 1964; Arthur R. Schultz, *Amer.-German Rev.*, vol. 33, no. 3 (1967), 28–29; J. J. Stoudt, *Pa. Mag. of Hist. and Biog.*, vol. 88, no. 2 (1964), 238–39; and F. P. Weisenburger, *Ohio Hist.*, vol. 73, no. 3 (1964), 191. Rev. ed.: 1968. 369p. 3rd ed. Baltimore, 1980. 415p.

BG20 Hostetler, John A. *Educational Achievement and Life Styles in a Traditional Society, the Old Order Amish*. Washington D.C.: U.S. Dept. of Health, Education and Welfare, Office of Education, Bureau of Research, 1969. 523p.

BG21 Hostetler, John A. "Memoirs of Shem Zook (1798–1880): A Biography." *Mennonite Quar. Rev.*, vol. 38, no. 3 (1964), 303. Amish writer, publisher, and educator.

BG22 Kermes, Constantine. "Amish Album." *Pa. Folklife*, vol. 15, no. 4 (Summer 1966), 2–5.

BG23 Kollmorgen, Walter A. *Culture of a Contemporary Rural Community: The Old Order Amish of Lancaster County, Pa.* Rural Life Studies, No. 4. Washington, D.C.: Bureau of Agricultural Economics, 1942. Rev. in *Amer.-German Rev.*, vol. 9, no. 4 (1943), 40; M. Gingerich, *Mennonite Quar. Rev.*, vol. 17 (1943), 172–74 and *Mennonite Hist. Bull.*, vol. 4, no. 3 (1943), 4; Arthur D. Graeff, "'S Pennsylfawnisch Deitsch Eck," Allentown *Morning Call*, 20 March 1943; Joseph W. Yoder, *Hist. Rev. of Berks Co.*, vol. 8 (1942–1943), 89–90.

BG24 Luthy, David. "Amish Family Record Books." *Family Life*, March 1977, 17–18.

BG25 McKusick, Victor A., ed. *Medical Genetic Studies of the Amish: Selected Papers, Assembled with Commentary*. Baltimore: The Johns Hopkins Univ. Pr., 1978. 525p.

BG26 Madden, Robert W. "The Amish: A Simple, Ordered Life." In: *Life in Rural America*. Washington, D.C.: National Geographic Soc., 1977; p. 74–91. Photographic essay.

BG27 Mather, Boyd P. "That Amish Thing." *Christian Century*, vol. 83 (23 February 1966), 245–47.

BG28 Messerschmidt, H. Edgar. "Working with the Amish." *Amer.-German Rev.*, vol. 12, no. 6 (1946), 22–24.

BG29 Meyer, Carolyn. *Amish People: Plain Living in a Complex World*. Photos by Michael Ramsey, Gerald Dodds and C. Meyer. New York: Atheneum, 1976. 138p. Rev. by E. Hoagland, *New York Times Book Rev.*, 9 May 1976, 14–16; Christine Kreider, *Jour. of the Lancaster Co. Hist. Soc.*, vol. 80 (1976), 114–15. Juvenile reader.

BG30 Miller, Levi. "The Amish Word for Today." *Christian Century*, vol. 90 (1973), 70–73.

BG31 Mook, Maurice A. "The 'Big Valley' Amish of Central Pennsylvania: A Community of Cultural Contrasts." *Lycoming College Mag.*, vol. 24, no. 5 (1971), 1–5. Repr. *Pa. Folklife*, vol. 26, no. 2 (1976), 30–33.

BG32 Mook, Maurice A. "A Brief History of Former, Now Extinct, Amish Communities in Pennsylvania." *Western Pa. Hist. Mag.*, vol. 38, nos. 1–2 (1955), 33–46.

BG33 Mook, Maurice A. "'Crawford County Number Two': A Now Extinct Old Order Amish Community of the 1930's." *Western Pa. Hist. Mag.*, vol. 37 (1954), 33–46.

BG34 Mook, Maurice A. "Crawford County Number Three." *Mennonite Hist. Bull.*, vol. 14, no. 3 (1953), 6–8.

BG35 Mook, Maurice A. "A Defense of the Dutch—the Amish Dutch." "'S Pennsylfawnisch Deitsch Eck," Allentown *Morning Call*, 15 May 1954. Points out the "fantastic inaccuracies" in K. Bercovici's *On New Shores* (N.Y.: Century, 1925).

BG36 Mook, Maurice A. "An Early Amish Colony in Chester County." "'S Pennsylfawnisch Deitsch Eck," Allentown *Morning Call*, 26 February, 5 March 1955.

BG37 Mook, Maurice A. "Extinct Amish Mennonite Communities in Pennsylvania." *Mennonite Quar. Rev.*, vol. 30, no. 4 (1956), 267–76.

BG38 Mook, Maurice A. "The Nebraska Amish of Pennsylvania." *Mennonite Life*, vol. 17, no. 1 (1962), 27–30.

BG39 Mook, Maurice A. "The Number of Amish in Pennsylvania." "'S Pennsylfawnisch Deitsch Eck," Allentown *Morning Call*, 26 June 1954.

Statement of the location, number of congregations, and number of adult members of ten Old Order Amish communities in Pennsylvania.

BG40 Mook, Maurice A. "The Old Order Amish in Pennsylvania." In: *The Ethnic Experience in Pennsylvania*. Ed. John Bodnar. Lewisburg: Bucknell Univ. Pr., 1973, p.74–93.

BG41 Mook, Maurice A. "Our Neighbors and Brothers: The Amish." *Lycoming College Mag.*, vol. 24 (May 1971), 28–29.

BG42 Mook, Maurice A. "Pennsylvania Amish Communities that Failed." "'S Pennsylfawnisch Deitsch Eck," Allentown *Morning Call*, 21 August 1954.

BG43 Mook, Maurice A., and John A. Hostetler. "The Amish and Their Land." "'S Pennsylfawnisch Deitsch Eck," Allentown *Morning Call*, 8, 15, 22, 29 July 1961. See also *Landscape*, vol. 6, no. 3 (1957), 21–29. A study of the cultural landscape created by Amish settlement.

BG44 Naylor, Phyllis R. *An Amish Family*. Illus. by George Armstrong. Chicago: J. P. O'Hara, 1974. 181p. Juvenile.

BG45 Newcomb, Thomas L. *An Amish Language Development and Reading Program K–5*. Garrettsville, Ohio: n.p., 1980.

BG46 Newcomb, Thomas L. *A Brief Introduction to Amish Culture and Dialects*. Garrettsville, Ohio: n.p., 1980.

BG47 Newcomb, Thomas L. *Leseh, Schreivah und Rechlee: Reading, Writing and Arithmetic—Amish Style*. Garrettsville, Ohio: n.p., 1981.

BG48 Newswanger, K. and C. Newswanger. *Amishland*. New York: Hastings House, 1954. 128p. Rev. by J. A. Hostetler, *Pa. Mag. of Hist. and Biog.*, vol. 79 (1955) 393–94; M. A. Mook, "'S Pennsylfawnisch Deitsch Eck," Allentown *Morning Call*, 15 January 1955; in *Amer.-German Rev.*, vol. 21, no. 2 (1954), 39.

BG49 Nock, Albert J. "Utopia in Pennsylvania: The Amish." *Atlantic Monthly*, vol. 167, no. 4 (1941), 478–84. Customs and folk literature of the Amish.

BG50 Nordheimer, Jan. "Plain Sects 'Wintering' in Florida." Lancaster *Daily Intelligencer-Journal*, 20 March 1973. About the Amish.

BG51 Oestreich, Nelson. *The Amish: Two Perceptions*. Woodcuts by Nelson Oestreich; poems by James Ashbrook Perkins. New Wilmington, Pa.: Dawn Valley Pr., ca. 1976. 23p.

BG52 Olshan, Marc A. "Modernity, the Folk Society, and the Old Order Amish: An Alternative Interpretation." *Rural Sociology*, vol. 46 (1981), 297–309.

BG53 *Pennsylvania Amish Directory 1973: Lancaster and Chester Counties*. N.p.: n.p., 1973.

BG54 Rice, Charles S., and John B. Shenk. *Meet the Amish*. New Brunswick, N.J.: Rutgers Univ. Pr., 1947. 96p. Rev. by A. L. Shoemaker, *Western Folklore*, vol. 8, no. 1 (1949), 82–83. Pictorial study, with photos by C. S. Rice.

BG55 Rice, Charles S., and Rollin C. Steinmetz. *The Amish Year*. New Brunswick, N.J.: Rutgers Univ. Pr., 1956. 224p. Rev. by J. A. Hostetler, *Pa. Mag. of Hist. and Biog.*, vol. 81 (1957), 334–35; P. A. Barba, *Pa. Hist.*, vol. 24 (1957), 179–80; J. S. Weber, *Hist. Rev. of Berks Co.*, vol. 22 (1957), 53–54; R. S. Anderson, *N.Y. Hist.*, vol. 38 (1957), 210–11; E. Lang, *Ind. Mag. of Hist.*, vol. 53 (1957), 347–48; in *Md. Hist. Mag.*, vol. 52 (1957), 259; in *Amer.-German Rev.* vol. 24, no. 4 (1958), 38; T. G. James, *Western Folklore*, vol. 17 (1958), 224; N. L. Spelmann, *Ohio Hist. Quar.*, vol. 67 (1958), 74–75. Richly illustrated depiction of the everyday of life of the Amish in Lancaster County, Pennsylvania.

BG56 Ruth, John L. *A Quiet and Peaceable Life*. N.p.: Good Books, 1979. On the Amish.

BG57 Ruth, John L., with Burton Buller, cinematographer. *The Amish: A People of Preservation*. Film. Encyclopedia Britannica, dist. Rev. by S. J. Bronner, *Jour. of Amer. Folklore*, vol. 92 (1979), 121–23.

BG58 Schreiber, William I. "The Amish Way of Life." "'S Pennsylfawnisch Deitsch Eck," Allentown *Morning Call*, 1, 8, 15, 22 March 1958.

BG59 Schreiber, William I. "A Day with the Amish." *Amer.-German Rev.*, vol. 12, no. 3 (1945–46), 12–13.

BG60 Schreiber, William I. "Die 'Old Order Amish'—Mennoniten in Nordamerika: Ihre Sprache und Gebräuche." *Rheinisches Jahrbuch für Volkskunde*, vol. 13–14 (1964) 256–75.

BG61 Schreiber, William I. *Our Amish Neighbors*. Chicago: Univ. of Chicago Pr., 1962. 227p. Rev. by A. M. Milchunas, *Hist. Rev. of Berks Co.*, vol. 28, no. 3 (1963); H. G. Schmidt, *Agricultural Hist.*, vol. 37, no. 3 (1963), 174; F. P. Weisenburger, *Ohio Hist.*, vol. 72, no. 2 (1963), 158; J. C. Wenger, *Ind. Mag. of Hist.*, vol. 59, no. 1 (1963), 71–73; Z. Flacke, *Zeitschrift für Kulturaustausch*, vol. 14, no. 4 (1964), 276–77; J. J. Stoudt, *Pa. Mag. of Hist. and Biog.*, vol. 87, no. 2 (1965), 242–43. A study of the behavior of the Amish. 2nd ed., 1978.

BG62 Schrock, Alta. "Amish Americans: Frontiersmen." *Western Pa. Hist. Mag.*, vol. 26, nos. 1–2 (1943), 47–58.

BG63 Schwieder, Dorothy. "Utopia in the Midwest: The Old Order Amish and the Hutterites." *Palimpsest*, vol. 54 (May–June 1973), 9–23.

BG64 Shoemaker, Alfred L. "*Team* Mennonites," *The Pa. Dutchman*, vol. 8, no. 2 (1957), 38–42. Illustrated account of the types of buggies used by the Wengerites, a group of Lancaster County Mennonites who proscribe automobiles.

BG65 Smith, Elmer L. *The Amish People: Seventeenth-Century Tradition in Modern America: A Complete, Illustrated Story of the "Old Order" Sect of Southeastern Pennsylvania*. New York: Exposition Pr., 1958. 258p. Rev. by G. M. Stoltzfus, *Amer.-German Rev.*, vol. 24, no. 5 (1958), 38; J. J. Stoudt, *Hist. Rev. of Berks Co.*, vol. 23, no. 3 (1958), 88–89; and J. J. Stoudt, "'S Pennsylfawnisch Deitsch Eck," Allentown *Morning Call*, 5 April 1958.

BG66 Smith, Elmer L. "The Amish Population in Southeastern Pennsylvania." "'S Pennsylfawnisch Deitsch Eck," Allentown *Morning Call*, 22 August 1959.

BG67 Smith, Elmer L. *Studies in Amish Demography*. Harrisonburg, Va.: Research Council, Eastern Mennonite College, 1960. 106p. Rev. in *Amer.-German Rev.*, vol. 27, no. 6 (1961), 39.

BG68 Smith, Elmer Lewis. *The Amish Today, An Analysis of Their Beliefs, Behavior and Contemporary Problems*. Publs. of the Pa. German Folklore Soc., 1960, vol. 24, 1961. 346p. Rev. by M. Gingerich, *Amer.-German Rev.*, vol. 28, no. 4 (1962), 37.

BG69 Sprunger, Keith L., and J. C. Juhnke. "Mennonite Oral History." *Mennonite Quar. Rev.*, vol. 54, no. 3 (1980), 244–47.

BG70 Steinfeldt, Berenice. *The Amish of Lancaster County; A Brief but Truthful Account of the Actual Life and Customs of the Most Unique Class of People in the United States*. Lancaster, Pa.: I. Steinfeldt, 1943. 32p.

BG71 Stoltzfus, Grant M. "Tourism and the Amish Way of Life." *Pa. Folklife*, vol. 25, no. 1 (1975), 45f.

BG72 Tice, George A. *The Amish Portfolio*. Collection of 12 original photographic prints of the Pennsylvania Germans and their environment. Np.: n.p., 1968. Ed. limited to 50 copies.

BG73 Tortora, Vincent R. *The Amish Folk of the Pennsylvania Dutch Country*. Lancaster: Photo Arts Pr., 1958. Rev. by Elmer L. Smith, "'S Pennsylfawnisch Deitsch Eck," Allentown *Morning Call*, 10 January 1959.

BG74 Tortora, Vincent R. "The Amish in Their One-Room Schoolhouses." *Pa. Folklife*, vol. 11, no. 2 (1960), 42–46.

BG75 Tortora, Vincent R. *Old Order Amish*. Film. Rev. by Simon J. Bronner, *Jour. of Amer. Folklore*, vol. 92 (1979), 123–24.

BG76 Wagler, Jacob J. *The Life of Jake, an Amish Boy*. N.p.: n.p., 1971. Rev. by C. R. Beam, *Der Reggeboge*, vol. 5, nos. 3–4 (1971), 8–9.

BG77 Warner, James A. and Donald M. Denlinger. *The Gentle People: A Portrait of the Amish*. Soudersburg, Pa.: Mill Bridge Museum in coop. with Grossman, New York, 1969. 184p. Pictorial essays, mostly in color, based on the photographer's travel.

BG78 Yoder, Don. "The Horse and Buggy Dutch." *Pa. Folklife*, vol. 13, no. 3 (1963), 11–17.

BG79 Yoder, Don. "Plain Dutch and Gay Dutch." *The Pa. Dutchman*, vol. 8, no. 1 (1956), 34–55.

On the European origins and religious diversity of the Pennsylvania German "church" people and the sectarian groups.

BG80 Yoder, Don. "What to Read on the Amish." *Pa. Folklife*, vol. 18, no. 4 (Summer 1969), 14–19.

BG81 Zielinski, John M. *The Amish: A Pioneer Heritage.* Photos and Design by J. M. Zielinski. Des Moines: Wallace-Homestead Book Co., ca. 1975. 174p. A pictorial study.

BH

The Pennsylvania Germans

See also Section CI: German-American Literature; Section ED: Folklore; *and* Section EE: Folk Arts/Material Culture.

Bibliography/Sources/Historiography

BH1 Barba, P. A. "In Memoriam. Edwin Miller Fogel." *Publs., Pa. German Folklore Soc.*, vol. 14 (1949), 175–81.

BH2 Barba, Preston A. "A Tribute to Arthur D. Graeff." *Hist. Rev. of Berks Co.*, vol. 34, no. 3 (Summer 1969), 82–84. Pennsylvania-German historian.

BH3 Baumann, Roland M. "Dissertations on Pennsylvania History, 1866–1971: A Bibliography." *Pa. History: Quar. Jour. of the Pa. Hist. Assoc.*, vol. 39 (Jan. 1972), 72–114; Harrisburg: Pa. Hist. and Museum Commission, 1978. Rev. by C. D. Cashdollar, *Pa. Hist.*, vol. 47 (1980), 78–79; Helen M. Wilson, *West. Pa. Hist. Mag.*, vol. 63 (1980), 61–62.

BH4 Bechtel, Ernest. *Resources for Pennsylvania German Studies.* New Holland, Pa.: BESL Center, n.d.

BH5 Benjamin, Steven M. *An Annotated Bibliography of "'S Pennsylfawnisch Deitsch Eck."* Madison, Wis.: n.p., 1978. Column in the Allentown *Morning Call*; ed. P. A. Barba.

BH6 Benjamin, Steven M. *A Bibliography of Works Published in the Yearbooks of the Pennsylvania German Folklore Society.* Occasional Papers of the Society for German-Amer. Studies, no. 4. Morgantown: Dept. of For. Langs., West Va. Univ., 1979. 9p.

BH7 Bining, Arthur C., Robert L. Brunhouse, and Norman B. Wilkinson, comp. *Writings on Pennsylvania History: A Bibliography: A List of Secondary Materials Compiled under the Auspices of the Pennsylvania Historical Commission.* Harrisburg: The Pa. Hist. and Museum Commission, 1946. 565p. *See* esp. p.47–74.

BH8 Bodnar, John E. *Ethnic History in Pennsylvania: A Selected Bibliography.* Harrisburg: Pa. Hist. and Museum Commission, 1974. 47p.

BH9 [Buffington, Albert F.] "Publications of Albert F. Buffington." In: *Ebbes fer Alle—Ebber Ebbes fer Dich. Essays in Memoriam Albert Franklin Buffington.* Publs. of the Pa. German Soc., vol. 14. Ed. A. F. Buffington et al. Breinigsville, Pa.: The Pa. German Soc., 1980, p.xii–xv.

BH10 *Check List of Pennsylvania Newspapers.* Vol. 1. *Philadelphia.* Harrisburg: Pa. Hist. Commission, 1942.

BH11 Fegley, Nelson P., Kirke Bryan, and Franklin A. Stickler. "Emily Krause Preston." *Bull., Hist. Soc. of Montgomery Co.*, vol. 3, no. 4 (April 1943), 266. Obituary of former librarian and curator of the Society.

BH12 Gilbert, Russell W. "Progress and Problems in Pennsylvania German Research." *Susquehanna Univ. Studies*, vol. 5, no. 3 (1955), 137–62.

BH13 Hostetler, John A. "Maurice A. Mook (1904–1973): An Appreciation." *Pa. Folklife*, vol. 26, no. 2 (1976–77), 34–37. Incl. a bibliography of his writings.

BH14 Lamberton, John Porter. *A List of the Serials in the Principal Libraries of Philadelphia and Its Vicinity*. Bull. of the Free Library of Philadelphia, no. 8. Philadelphia: Pr. of Allen, Lane & Scott, 1908. 309p. *Supplement*: Philadelphia, 1910. 88p.

BH15 Milspaw, Yvonne A. "The Pennsylvania Germans: A Selected Bibliography." *Middle Atlantic Folklife Assoc. Newsletter*. Fall 1980.

BH16 Pennsylvania Historical and Museum Commission. *Book and Publication List, 1979–80*. Harrisburg: Pa. Hist. and Mus. Comm., 1979.

BH17 Reichard, Harry H. "John Baer Stoudt, D.D., An Appreciation." *Pa. German Folklore Soc. Publs.*, vol. 9 (1946), 221–229.

BH18 Rosenberger, Homer Tope. "Analysis of the Literature on the Pennsylvania Germans in These Seventy-Five Years." In: *The Pennsylvania Germans, 1891–1965 (Frequently Known as the "Pennsylvania Dutch")*, by H. T. Rosenberger. 75th Anniversary Vol. of the Pa. German Soc. Lancaster: Pa. German Soc., 1966, p.381–422.

BH19 Salisbury, Ruth, ed. *Pennsylvania Newspapers: A Bibliography and Union List*. Pittsburgh: Pa. Library Assoc., 1969. 2nd ed. 1978; ed. Glenora E. Rossell.

BH20 Trussell, John B. *Pennsylvania Historical Bibliography*. I. *Additions through 1970*. II. *Additions through 1973*. Harrisburg: Pa. Hist. and Mus. Comm., 1979. Rev. by H. M. Wilson, *Western Pa. Hist. Mag.*, vol. 63 (1979), 61–62.

BH21 Wall, Carol. *Bibliography of Pennsylvania History: A Supplement*. Harrisburg: Pa. Hist. and Mus. Comm., 1976. 252p.

BH22 Ward, Robert E. "Eine Bibliographie deutsch-amerikanischer Originalwerke im Besitz der Deutschen Gesellschaft von Pennsylvanien." *German-Amer. Studies*, vol. 1, no. 1 (1969), 33–48.

BH23 Washburn, David E., ed. *The Peoples of Pennsylvania: An Annotated Bibliography of Resource Materials*. Pittsburgh: Univ. of Pittsburgh Pr., 1981. 231p.

BH24 Wilkinson, Norman B. *Bibliography of Pennsylvania History*. Ed. S. K. Stevens and D. H. Kent. Harrisburg: Pa. Hist. and Mus. Comm., 1957. 826p. Rev. by D. L. Smith, *Ohio Hist. Quar.*, vol. 67 (1958), 292–93.

BH25 Yoder, Don. "The Pennsylvania Germans: A Preliminary Reading List." *Pa. Folklife*, vol. 21, no. 2 (1971–72), 2–17. Sources on Pennsylvania German culture.

BH26 Zecher, Peg. "His First Hundred Years: A Good Foundation." *Pa. Folklife*, vol. 29, no. 4 (1979–80), 32–34. On Prof. Phares H. Hertzog.

Historical Societies/Archives/Study Programs

GENERAL

BH27 Barba, Preston A. "[Pennsylvania-German] Historical Societies." "'S Pennsylfawnisch Deitsch Eck," Allentown *Morning Call*, 12 August 1967. Then flourishing in eastern Pa.: The Moravian Hist. Soc., Fereinicht Pennsylvaanisch Deitsch Folk (1960–), Historic Schaefferstown, Inc., Thomas Royce Brendle Memorial Library and Open Air Folklife Museum, Goschenhoppen Historians, Inc., and Lancaster-Mennonite Conference Hist. Soc.

BH28 Bressler, Leo A. "The Pennsylvania German." *Amer.-German Rev.*, vol. 18, no. 4 (1952), 11–14; no. 5, 13–15. A magazine published in Lebanon, Pa., 1900–1914.

BH29 Brow, Victoria D. and Deborah M. Miller. *Pennsylvania Directory of Historical Organizations 1976*. Harrisburg: Pa. Hist. and Museum Comm., 1976.

BH30 Buffington, Albert Franklin. Buffington Tape Recording Collection. The Pennsylvania German Society. Over 60 recordings made by Prof. Buffington in the course of his oral researches among Pennsylvania-Dutch-speaking informants.

BH31 Butterfield, L. H. "A Survey of the Benjamin Rush Papers." *Pa. Mag. of Hist. and Biog.*, vol. 70 (1946), 78–111. Incl. a number of letters by, to, or about Rush.

BH32 Carson, Hampton L. *A History of the Historical Society of Pennsylvania*. Philadelphia: n.p., 1940. 2 vols.

BH33 Carter, E. A. "A Symposium on Pennsylvania German Studies." *Amer.-German Rev.*, vol. 8, no. 3 (1942), 28–29. Conference held 10 January 1942, under the auspices of the Carl Schurz Memorial Foundation.

BH34 Clemens, Gurney W. "The Berks County Historical Society." *Publs., Pa. German Folklore Soc.*, vol. 7 (1942), 53–80.

BH35 Coley, Robert E. "The Pennsylvania German Materials in the Ganser Library, Millersville State College." In: *Papers from the Conference on German-Americana in the Eastern United States*. Ed. Steven M. Benjamin. Occasional Papers of the Soc. for German-Amer. Studies, No. 8. Morgantown: W. Va. Univ., Dept. of For. Langs., 1980, p. 61–67.

BH36 Daly, John. *Descriptive Inventory of the Archives of the City and County of Philadelphia*. Philadelphia: n.p., 1970.

BH37 Doll, Eugene E. "Research in Pennsylvania German Areas: Taking Stock." *Amer.-German Rev.*, vol. 25, no. 1 (1958), 31–32.

BH38 Dugan, Elaine K. and Marilyn M. Kramer. "Lancaster County Imprints from the German-American Imprint Collection in the Franklin and Marshall College Library." *Jour. of the Lanc. Co. Hist. Soc.*, vol. 79 (1975), 208–33.

BH39 Evans, Frank B., and Martha L. Simonetti. *Summary Guide to the Pennsylvania State Archives*. Ed. D. H. Kent. Harrisburg: Pa. Hist. and Museum Commission, Div. of Public Records, 1963. 41p.

BH40 Fine, John S., Harry W. Pfund, and Robert T. McCracken. [Addresses.] *Yearbook, German Soc. of Pa.*, vol. 3 (1952). For Pastorius celebration, Philadelphia, 1952.

BH41 Fleming, Elizabeth. "The Use of Audio-Visual Aids in the Teaching of Pennsylvania History." *Pa. Hist.*, vol. 12, no. 3 (1945), 234–40.

BH42 Friedrich, Gerhard. "The A. H. Cassel Collection at Juniata College." *Amer.-German Rev.*, vol. 7, no. 6 (August 1941), 18–21.

BH43 Funke, Anneliese Marckwald. "The Cassel Collection." *Pa. Mag. of Hist. and Biog.*, vol. 67 (1943), 152–60. Origin, history and description of one of the major collections of Pennsylvania-German literature.

BH44 German Society of Pennsylvania. "German Society of Pennsylvania. 200 Years." *Amer.-German Rev.*, vol. 31, no. 2 (1964), 19. Incl. the Joseph Horner Memorial Library.

BH45 Germantown. Official Town Records. In Historical Society of Pennsylvania, Manuscript Department.

(1) *Grund- und Lager Buch* for Germantown prior to 1707. Pastorius's original plan. Typescript also on file at the Philadelphia Archives.

(2) *Rathsbuch der Germantownischen Gemeinde*, or General Court Book of the Corporation. A book of rules, regulations, ordinances, and election returns. In German and Dutch languages.

(3) Records of the Court of Record of Germantown. The Historical Society of Pennsylvania holds a 19th-century copy. See *Collections of the Hist. Soc. of Pa.*, vol. 1, 243–58 for an abridgement of this material.

(4) *Gesetz Buch*. At the Hist. Soc. of Pa. among the Pastorius Papers, vol. 1. Trans. and publ. by S. W. Pennypacker in "Laws, Ordinances, and Statutes . . ." *Pa. Ger. Soc., Procs. and Addresses*, vol. 9 (1898).

BH46 *The Goschenhoppen Region. A Folklife Journal Devoted to the History and Folk Culture of America's Oldest Existing Pennsylvania Dutch Community*. Vol. 1–, 1968–. Quarterly. Discontinued with vol. 2, no. 2.

BH47 *Guide to the Manuscript Collections in the Historical Society of Pennsylvania*. Philadelphia: Hist. Soc. of Pa., 1940. Rev. by Roy F. Nichols, *Pa. Hist.*, vol. 9 (1942), 81–82.

BH48 Hellerich, Mahlon A. "A History of the Lehigh County Historical Society." *Procs., Lehigh Co. Hist. Soc.*, vol. 33 (1979), 1–44.

BH49 *Hostetter [Book] Sales Catalogues, nos. 1 and 2*. Lancaster, Pa., October, November 1946.

BH50 James, Alfred Proctor. *Index—The Western Pennsylvania Historical Magazine. Vols. 1–43, 1918–1960*. Richmond, Va.: Cavalier Pr., 1963. 557p. Rev. by J. W. Fawcett, *Western Pa. Hist. Mag.*, vol. 47, no. 2 (1963), 164–67.

BH51 James, Judie. "Come to Ursinus: Land of the Pennsylvania Dutch." *The Ursinus Weekly*, vol. 74, no. 15 (1975), 1–2. On the Pennsylvania Dutch Studies Program at Ursinus College.

BH52 Johnson, Elmer E. S. "The Schwenkfelder Historical Library." *Publs., Pa. German Folklore Soc.*, vol. 7 (1942), 31–40. Library and museum of household goods, photographs, etc., in Pennsburg, Pa.

BH53 Kulp, Clarence, Jr. "The Goschenhoppen Historians." *Pa. Folklife*, vol. 16, no. 4 (1967), 16–24.

BH54 von Kummer, Ruth L. "Dr. Parsons Authors Text." *Ursinus Weekly*, vol. 75 (13 May 1976), 1, 2. Author of *The Pennsylvania Dutch: A Persistent Minority* (Boston, 1976).

BH55 Mann, Horace M. "The Bucks County Historical Society." *Publs., Pa. German Folklore Soc.*, vol. 7 (1942), 9–28.

BH56 Marshall College, Mercersburg, Pa. Papers, 1837–1853. 2 ft. In Franklin and Marshall College Library, Lancaster (MS 60-1097). Minutes of the trustees and faculty; papers of the first president Friedrich August Rauch and early faculty.

BH57 Newcomb, Thomas. *Private Library and Archives: Summary List of Holdings on Amish, Mennonite and Pennsylvania Dutch Topics.* Garrettsville, Ohio: n.p., 1980. 6p.

BH58 Parsons, William T. "Pennsylvania Dutch Studies at Ursinus College, 1976." *Pa. Folklife*, vol. 25, no. 3 (1976), 47–48.

BH59 *Pennsylvania County and Regional Histories.* New Haven: Research Publications, 1973. Microform.

BH60 "Pennsylvania Dutch Studies Achievement Report, 1973–74." *Ursinus College Bull.*, September 1974, 3–6.

BH61 *Pennsylvania Ethnic Studies Newsletter.* Vol. 1–, ca. 1975–. Ed. Jos. Makarewicz. UCIS/Publications, G-6 Mervis Hall, Univ. of Pittsburgh.

BH62 *Pennsylvania German Heritage.* No. 1–, March 1964–. Bulletin published jointly by the Pennsylvania German Society and the Pennsylvania German Folklore Society, Allentown. News and information; list of publications.

BH63 "Pennsylvania German Institute." *Hist. Rev. of Berks Co.*, vol. 7 (1941–1942), 91. A meeting held at the Carl Schurz Memorial Foundation, 10 January 1942.

BH64 Pennypacker, Samuel W. and John S. Fisher. Papers, 1886–1940. In the Pennsylvania State Archives.

BH65 Pfund, Harry W. *A History of the German Society of Pennsylvania*. Philadelphia: The German Soc. of Pa., 1944. 38p. 2nd rev. ed.: *A History of the German Society of Pennsylvania: Bicentenary Edition, 1764–1964*. Philadelphia: The Society, 1964. 46p.

BH66 Reformed Church (Market Square, Germantown). Records, 1751–. In the Presbyterian Historical Society, Philadelphia. Trans. by William J. Hinke in the 1930's.

BH67 Reichel, William. Papers. 1 box. In the Historical Society of Pennsylvania. Misc. manuscripts, Northampton County, Pa.

BH68 Rice, Howard C., Jr. "Soundings in the Sinclair Hamilton Collection." *Princeton Univ. Library Chronicle*, vol. 20 (1958), 29–38. The collection in the Princeton University Library includes Pennsylvania German materials.

BH69 Richman, Irwin, comp. *Historical Manuscript Depositories in Pennsylvania*. Harrisburg: Pa. Hist. and Museum Commission, 1965. 73p.

BH70 Rosenberger, Homer Tope. "Outstanding Collections of Pennsylvania German Material." In: *The Pennsylvania Germans, 1891–1965*, by H. T. Rosenberger. Lancaster: The Pa. German Soc., 1966, 508–62.

BH71 Rupp, Israel Daniel. Papers, 1700–1848. 35 items. In the collections of the Evangelical and Reformed Historical Society, Lancaster (MS 70-182). Papers dealing with the histories of the Pennsylvania counties, 1700–1848; letters to R. (1803–1878) by contemporary historians and assemblages of materials made while preparing the country histories.

BH72 St. Michael-Zion Lutheran Church (Philadelphia). Archives, 1745–1927. In Lutheran The-

Historical Societies *(cont.)*

ological Seminary Library, Philadelphia. Church records, minutes of meetings in German and English; a history of the congregation by Carl F. Haussman.

BH73 St. Michael's Lutheran Church [Germantown, Pa.]. Register of vital events, 1746–. Treasurers' accounts, minutes of Elders' meetings, etc. from the 18th Century.

BH74 "'76 Pennsylvania Dutch Summer Study." *The Ursinus Weekly*, vol. 75, no. 16 (May 1976), 1, 3. On plans for a Pennsylvania German studies program of the Ursinus College summer school 1976.

BH75 Shryock, Richard H. "The Pennsylvania Germans as Seen by the Historian." In: *The Pennsylvania Germans, 1891–1965*. Ed. Homer T. Rosenberger. Lancaster: Pa. Ger. Soc., 1966, p. 239–58.

BH76 "'S Pennsylfawnisch Deitsch Eck." Allentown *Morning Call*. 23 March 1935–ca. March 1971. Ed. Preston A. Barba. Weekly column devoted to the literature, lore and history of the Pennsylvania Germans.

BH77 Thommen, Joggi. [Letter.] Ed. and trans. Walter L. Robbins, *Schaefferstown Bull.*, vol. 6, no. 1 (March 1972), 1–3. A Swiss MS. letter discovered in the Generallandesarchiv, Karlsruhe, dated 11 October 1736. Written by T. from America soon after he arrived in Conestoga, Pa., on the ship Princess Augusta.

BH78 Wainwright, Nicholas B. *One Hundred and Fifty Years of Collecting by the Historical Society of Pennsylvania, 1824–1974*. Philadelphia: Hist. Soc. of Pa., 1974. 105p.

BH79 Wood, Ralph C. "The Second Period of the German Society of Pennsylvania and the Mühlenberg Legend." In: *Yearbook, German Society of Pennsylvania*. Vol. 1. Philadelphia: The Society, 1950.

BH80 *Yearbook* (German Society of Pennsylvania). Vol. 1–, 1950–. Ed. Ernst Jockers. Philadelphia: German Society of Pa.

BH81 Yeich, Edwin B. "Using Local Resources for the Course in Pennsylvania History." *Pa. Hist.*, vol. 12, no. 2 (1945), 167–70.

PENNSYLVANIA GERMAN SOCIETY

BH82 Brendle, Thomas R. "The Pennsylvania German Society." *Pa. Hist.*, vol. 23 (1956), 340–345.

BH83 Graeff, Arthur D. "The First Half-Century of the Pennsylvania German Society: 1890–1940." *Hist. Rev. of Berks Co.*, vol. 31, no. 2 (Spring 1966), 59–60, 65–66. See also, "'S Pennsylfawnisch Deitsch Eck," Allentown *Morning Call*, 6 November 1965, for Graeff's address at the 75th anniversary meeting, Lancaster, 23 October 1965.

BH84 Johnson, Elmer E. S. "The Pennsylvania German Society Meeting [October 1943]." *Amer.-German Rev.*, vol. 10, no. 2 (December 1943), 28.

BH85 Minderhout, Mary Alice. "Pennsylvania German Society Plans Workshop." *Pa. Ethnic Studies Newsletter*, vol. 2, no. 5 (1976–77), 11.

BH86 Pennsylvania German Society. *Proceedings and Addresses* (Philadelphia). Vols. 1–50, 1891–1941. The Society, founded in 1891, is located in Breinigsville, Pa.

BH87 Pennsylvania German Society. *Proceedings and Addresses at Its Fiftieth Anniversary*. Vol. 1. Lancaster: The Society, 1941. Rev. by P. A. Barba, "'S Pennsylfawnisch Deitsch Eck," Allentown *Morning Call*, 28 October 1944.

BH88 Pennsylvania German Society. *Publications of the Pennsylvania German Society*. Vol. 1–, 1968–. A continuation of the *Proceedings* of the Pennsylvania German Society, vol. 1–63 (1891–1966) and the *Yearbook* of the Pennsylvania German Folklore Society, vols. 1–28 (1936–1966).

BH89 *Der Reggeboge*. Vol. 1–, 1967–. Ed. Frederick S. Weiser. Quarterly. Journal of the Pennsylvania German Society.

BH90 Rosenberger, Homer T. "Founding of the Pennsylvania German Society in 1891." In: *The Pennsylvania Germans, 1891–1965*. Lancaster: Pa. Ger. Soc., 1966, p. 73–90.

BH91 Zimmerman, Thomas C. "Puritan and Cavalier, Why Not the Pennsylvania Germans?" "'S Pennsylfawnisch Deitsch Eck," Allentown *Morning Call*, 23 November 1967. Repr. of an address given on the occasion of the formation of a Pennsylvania German Society, 15 April 1891.

Museums/Restorations/Festivals/Tour Guides

See also Section BI: Pennsylvania Local History and Exhibitions/Museums/Collections under Section EE: Folk Arts/Material Culture.

GENERAL

BH92 Aurand, Ammon Monroe. *Where to Dine in the Pennsylvania Dutch Region; a Guide to Travel Information, Historic Places, Points of Interest, Antique Dealers, Card and Gift Shops, Rare Book Dealers.* Rev. ed. N.p.: Aurand, 1946. 32p.

BH93 Best, Martha S. "The Folk Festival Seminars: Folk Art and Antique Collecting." *Pa. Folklife*, vol. 19, no. 4 (ca. 1970), 20–24.

BH94 Bitner, Mabel E. "The Pennsylvania State Museum." *Publs., Pa. Ger. Folklore Soc.*, vol. 7 (1942), 43–49.

BH95 Breininger, Lester P. "The Folk Festival's Bookstore." *Pa. Folklife*, vol. 23 (1974). See Folk Festival Supplement, p.14–15.

BH96 Burgwyn, Diane. *The 1776 Guide for Pennsylvania.* New York: Harper & Row, 1975. 248p.

BH97 Evans, E. Estyn. "The Pennsylvania Dutch Folk Festival: A European Report." *Pa. Folklife*, vol. 12, no. 1 (Spring 1961), 44–48.

BH98 Garvan, Beatrice B., and Charles F. Hummel. *The Pennsylvania Germans. A Celebration of Their Arts 1683–1850. An Exhibition Organized by the Philadelphia Museum of Art and the Henry Francis du Pont Winterthur Museum.* Philadelphia: Philadelphia Museum of Art, 1982. 197p. Catalogue of an exhibit which opened 17 October 1982 at the Philadelphia Museum of Art, displaying 350 examples of folk art, furniture, manuscripts, musical instruments, metal, glass, woven fabrics, pewter and ceramics.

BH99 Gleysteen, Jan. "The Springs Folk Festival." *Mennonite Life*, vol. 22, (1967), 102–04. An annual *Volksfest* held at Springs, Somerset Co., Pa.

BH100 *Hershey, Pennsylvania, Dutch Days.* Hershey: Pennsylvania Dutch Days Committee, 1949–. Annual program booklet.

BH101 Kulp, Clarence, Jr. "The Goschenhoppen Historians." *Pa. Folklife*, vol. 16, no. 4 (Summer 1967), 16–24. Efforts made at Woxall, Pa., in recent years to preserve Pennsylvania Dutch architecture and folkways.

BH102 Light, Richard. "The Hershey Museum." *Publs., Pa. German Folklore Soc.*, vol. 7 (1942), 85–90.

BH103 "Pennsylvania's County and Community Fairs." *Commonwealth* (Harrisburg), vol. 2, no. 7 (1948). Special number.

KUTZTOWN, PA. FESTIVAL

BH104 Bandler, Michael J. "Kutztown Girds for the Pennsylvania Dutch Fete." *New York Times*, 20 June 1965, Sec. XX p.13.

BH105 Britt, Ken. "Pennsylvania's Old-Time Dutch Treat." *National Geographic Mag.*, vol. 143 (1973), 564–78. On the Kutztown festival.

BH106 DeChant, Alliene Saeger. "Sixteen Years of the [Kutztown] Folk Festival." *Pa. Folklife*, vol. 14, no. 4 (1965), 10–13.

BH107 DeLong, Marsha. "Granges at the Kutztown Folk Festival." *Pa. Folklife*, vol. 23 (1974), Folk Festival Supplement, 38–41.

BH108 DeLong, Nancy A. "The Kutztown Folk Festival Is for Children Too." *Pa. Folklife*, vol. 24 (1975), Folk Festival Supplement, 10–12.

BH109 "Festival Highlights." *Pa. Folklife*, vol. 21 (1972), 19–30. Incl. photos of the 1972 festival.

BH110 Gensler, LeRoy. "A Look at the Folk Festival." *Pa. Folklife*, vol. 21 (1972), Folk Festival Supplement, 2–6.

BH111 Hartmann, Joseph E. "Folk Festival Music." *Pa. Folklife*, vol. 29 (1980), 6–7. At the Kutztown Folk Festival.

BH112 Jentsch, Theodore W. "Cooking for the Lord." *Pa. Folklife*, vol. 28 (1979), Folk Festival Supplement, 10–11. Pennsylvania German food served at the Kutztown festival.

BH113 Nazzaro, William J. "A German Dance Invasion." *Philadelphia Bull.*, 11 July 1979. A dance group from the Palatinate visits the Folk Festival.

BH114 "Program of the 14th Annual Pennsylvania Dutch Folk Festival June 29–30, July 1–6, Kutztown. Pageant of Pennsylvania Dutch Folklife (As Found among the Gay Dutch Sixty Years Ago)." *Pa. Folklife*, vol. 13, no. 3 (1963), 28–32. "Program, 15th Annual Pennsylvania Dutch Folk Festival, July 3–11, 1964, Kutztown." *Pa. Folklife*, vol. 13, no. 4 (July 1964), 32–39. "Program, 16th Annual Festival, July 3–10, 1965, Kutztown." 9p. Incl. "Men of One Master," dramatic piece with music—"an epic of the Pennsylvania Amish struggle to survive."

BH115 Sommer, Antje. "Gute Socha fer Hame tzu Nemma." *Pa. Folklife*, vol. 28, no. 1 (Autumn 1978), 25–28. Food specialties available at the Kutztown festival.

BH116 Stinsmen, John E. "Music on the Main Stage." *Pa. Folklife*, vol. 24 (1975), Folk Festival Supplement, 50–51.

BH117 Stinsmen, John E. "Sounds of the Folk Festival: A Visitor's Walking Tour." *Pa. Folklife*, vol. 22 (1973), Folk Festival Supplement, 2–7.

BH118 Stinsmen, John E. "'Swing Your Partner': Folk Dancing at the Festival." *Pa. Folklife*, vol. 20, no. 4 (1971), 22–24.

BH119 "30 Years of the Kutztown Folk Festival: A Photo Essay." *Pa. Folklife*, vol. 29, no. 3 (1979–1980), 120–23.

BH120 Williams, Maynard O. "Pennsylvania Dutch Folk Festival." *National Geographic Mag.*, vol. 102, no. 4 (October 1952), 503–16.

BH121 Yoder, Don. "Twenty-Five Years of the Folk Festival." *Pa. Folklife*, vol. 23 (1974), Folk Festival Supplement, 2–7. On the annual festival at Kutztown.

LANDIS VALLEY FARM MUSEUM

BH122 Breneman, Mae G. H. "Pennsylvania Farm Museum, Landis Valley," *Amer.-German Rev.*, vol. 20, no. 6 (1954), 10–13.

BH123 "Collectors in the Dell. Opening of the Landis Valley Museum." *Time*, vol. 37 (26 May 1941), 48.

BH124 Landis, Henry K. "A Folk Museum—Why?" "'S Pennsylfawnisch Deitsch Eck," Allentown *Morning Call*, 22 May 1943.

BH125 "Landis Valley Museum." *Amer.-German Rev.*, vol. 7, no. 4 (April 1941), 2–38. An issue devoted to the new museum. Fully illustrated.

BH126 MacPherson, Robert B. "A Farm and 250,000 Relics Become a Museum [The Landis Valley Farm Museum]." *New York Times*, 22 May 1966, Sec. XX, p.5.

BH127 "The Old Coppershop." *Amer. German Rev.*, vol. 12, no. 4 (1946), 10–11. On an old coppershop acquired by the brothers Landis for the Landis Valley Museum.

BH128 Reichmann, Felix. "The Landis Valley Museum." *Publs., Pa. German Folklore Soc.*, vol. 7 (1942), 93–102.

BH129 Reichmann, Felix. "Two Inscriptions from the Landis Valley Museum." *Amer.-German Rev.*, vol. 8, no. 5 (June 1942), 11–12, 38.

Pennsylvania German History and Culture

See also Section BI: Pennsylvania Local History; Section IJ: Religion and Church History; Section IK: Lutherans and the Lutheran Church; *and specific groups under* Section IL: Other Denominations.

GENERAL

BH130 Aurand, A. M. *Child Life of the Pennsylvania Germans*. N.p.: Aurand Pr., 1947. 32p. *Home Life of the Pennsylvania Germans*. N.p.: Aurand Pr., 1947. *Social Life of the Pennsylvania Germans*. N.p.: Aurand Pr., 1947. 31p.

BH131 Barba, P. A., comp. "The Autograph Album of Annie Trexler." "'S Pennsylfawnisch Deitsch Eck," Allentown *Morning Call*, 18, 25 February 1956. Autographs in prose and verse dedicated to Annie Trexler of Long Swamp, Pa.

BH132 Bechtel, Ernest. *Definition of a Pennsylvania German.* New Holland, Pa.: BESL Center, n.d.

BH133 Bechtel, Ernest. *Reflections on Pennsylvania German Culture.* New Holland, Pa.: BESL Center, n.d.

BH134 Beidelman, William. *The Story of the Pennsylvania Germans: Embracing an Account of Their Origin, Their History and Their Dialect.* Easton, Pa., 1898. Repr. Detroit: Gale Research Co., 1969. 254p.

BH135 Bergfeld, Annabelle W. "The Pennsylvania Dutch." *South Atlantic Quar.*, vol. 49, no. 3 (1950), 324–31.

BH136 Berky, Andrew S. "Yesteryear in Dutchland." *The Pa. Dutchman*, vol. 8, no. 1 (1956), 10–15. The portfolio of the H. Winslow Fegley photographs in the Schwenkfelder Library presents a revealing study of Pennsylvania German culture.

BH137 Biddle, Gertrude B., and Sarah D. Lowrie, eds. *Notable Women of Pennsylvania.* Philadelphia: Univ. of Pa., 1942. Rev. by Elsie Singmaster, *Mennonite Quar. Rev.*, vol. 16 (1942), 290. Incl. sketches of Anna Eva Weiser, Sally Wister, Rebecca Gratz, and Molly Pitcher.

BH138 Bittlingmayer, George, and Alexander Waldenrath. "The German in Early Pennsylvania Agriculture." *German-Amer. Studies*, vol. 10 (Fall 1975), 45–60.

BH139 Bockelman, Wayne, and Owen Ireland. "The Internal Revolution in Pennsylvania: An Ethnic-Religious Interpretation." *Pa. Hist.*, vol. 41 (April 1974), 125–59.

BH140 Bokum, Hermann. "The American Germans." "'S Pennsylfawnisch Deitsch Eck," Allentown *Morning Call*, 9, 16 February 1963. Excerpts from *The Stranger's Gift* (1836), presenting an early description of the Pennsylvania Germans. See also *The Pa. Dutchman* for 15 January 1951.

BH141 Brand, Millen. *Fields of Peace: A Pennsylvania German Album.* Photographs by George A. Tice. Garden City: Doubleday, 1970. 150p. Photographs and lyrical prose in celebration of the Pennsylvania way of life.

BH142 Brenner, Scott Francis. *Pennsylvania Dutch: The Plain and the Fancy.* Harrisburg: Stackpole Co., 1957. 244p. Rev. by J. J. Stoudt, *Pa. Mag. of Hist. and Biog.*, vol. 82 (1958), 242–43; A. Mulder, *Mich. Hist.*, vol. 42 (1958), 117–18; and W. E. Lass, *N. Dak. Hist.*, vol. 25 (1958), 84–86.

BH143 Cressman, Elmer W. *The History of Pennsylvania.* New York: Noble & Noble, 1944. 128p. Rev. by M. W. Hamilton, *Hist. Rev. of Berks Co.*, vol. 9, no. 4 (1944), 118–19.

BH144 Daniele, Joseph W. "Die Deutschen aus Pennsylvanien." *Early American Life*, vol. 4 (April–June 1973), 42–59.

BH145 DeChant, Alliene S. *Of the Dutch I Sing.* Kutztown: Kutztown Publ. Co., 1951. Rev. by G. Hanstein, *Amer.-German Rev.*, vol. 18, no. 3 (1953), 38; J. S. Weber, *Hist. Rev. of Berks Co.*, vol. 16, no. 3 (1951), 117.

BH146 Doll, Eugene E. "Meet Mrs. Royall." *Amer.-German Rev.*, vol. 10, no. 6 (1944), 8–10, 34. Enthusiastic reactions of a traveler among the Pennsylvania Germans.

BH147 Doll, Eugene E., ed. "With Mrs. Royall Among the Pennsylvania Germans." "'S Pennsylfawnisch Deitsch Eck," Allentown *Morning Call*, 2, 9, 16, 23, 30 June 1945; 7 July 1945. From a favorable travel account of the Pennsylvania Germans, written in 1829.

BH148 Dunkelberger, George F. "The Characteristics of the Pennsylvania German People." "'S Pennsylfawnisch Deitsch Eck," Allentown *Morning Call*, 19, 26 June 1943.

BH149 *Ebbes fer Alle—Ebber Ebbes fer Dich. Something for Everyone—Something for You. Essays in Memoriam Albert Franklin Buffington.* Publs. of the Pa. German Soc., vol. 14. Breinigsville: The Pa. German Soc., 1980. 534p.

BH150 Eberlein, Harold D., and Cortlandt Van Dyke Hubbard. *The Church of Saint Peter in the Great Valley, 1700–1940: The Story of a Colonial Country Parish in Pennsylvania.* Richmond, Pa.: n.p., 1944.

BH151 Egle, William H. "The First Historian of the Pennsylvania Germans." *Pa. Folklife*, vol. 18, no. 4 (Summer 1969), 46–49.

BH152 Gibbons, Phebe E. *"Pennsylvania Dutch" and Other Essays*. Philadelphia, 1874. Repr. New York: AMS Pr., 1971.

BH153 Gilbert, Russell W. *A Picture of the Pennsylvania Germans*. Gettysburg: Pa. Hist. Assoc., 1947. 65p. Rev. by E. E. Doll, *William and Mary Quar.*, vol. 5, no. 4 (1948), 601–02. Rev. ed.: Gettysburg, 1958. Rev. by J. J. Stoudt, "'S Pennsylfawnisch Deitsch Eck," Allentown *Morning Call*, 8 November 1958; P. A. Barba, *Pa. Hist.*, vol. 26, no. 3 (1959), 284–85. 3rd ed.; Gettysburg 1962. 71p. Rev. by A. G. Faust, *Western Pa. Hist. Mag.*, vol. 46, no. 2 (1963), 196–98.

BH154 Graeff, Arthur D. "The Big Switch." *Hist. Rev. of Berks Co.*, vol. 32 (1967), 40–41, 67, 71–72. On the roles of Pennsylvania Germans in partisan politics, 1754–1965.

BH155 Graeff, Arthur D. "Echoes From the Past." "'S Pennsylfawnisch Deitsch Eck," Allentown *Morning Call*, 20 February, 10 April, 7 August; 9 October 1943; 31 May, 21 June 1947; 8 May 1948.

BH156 Graeff, Arthur D. "Es Schneckeharn Verzaehlt." "'S Pennsylfawnisch Deitsch Eck," Allentown *Morning Call*, 10, 17, 24 April; 1 May 1948. A series on the canals of eastern Pennsylvania.

BH157 Graeff, Arthur D. *The History of Pennsylvania*. Philadelphia: Winston, 1944. 312p. Rev. by M. Hamilton, *Hist. Rev. of Berks Co.*, vol. 9, no. 4 (1944), 118; E. W. Thompson, *Pa. Mag. of Hist. and Biog.*, vol. 68, no. 4 (1944), 436–37; E. E. Wildman, *Amer.-German Rev.*, vol. 10, no. 6 (1944), 38–39; P. A. Barba, "'S Pennsylfawnisch Deitsch Eck," Allentown *Morning Call*, 24 June 1944.

BH158 Graeff, Arthur D. *It Happened in Pennsylvania*. Philadelphia: Winston, 1947. 183p. Rev. by D. R. Shenton, *Amer.-German Rev.*, vol. 14, no. 4 (1948), 34.

BH159 Graeff, Arthur D. "John Fritz and National Defense." "'S Pennsylfawnisch Deitsch Eck," Allentown *Morning Call*, 21 August 1943.

BH160 Graeff, Arthur D. *The Keystone State—Its Geography, History and Government*. Philadelphia: Winston, 1953. 412p. Rev. by P. A. Barba, "'S Pennsylfawnisch Deitsch Eck," Allentown *Morning Call*, 14 March 1953.

BH161 Graeff, Arthur D. "1942 in Pennsylvania German History." *Publs., Pa. Ger. Folklore Soc.*, vol. 7 (1942), 163–70; "1944 in Pennsylvania German History." *Ibid.*, vol. 9 (1946), 231–34; "1945 in Pennsylvania German History." *Ibid.*, vol. 10 (1947), 241–46; "1946 in Pennsylvania German History." *Ibid.*, vol. 11 (1948), 171–76; ; "1947 in Pennsylvania German History." *Ibid.*, vol. 12 (1949), 291–302; "1948 in Pennsylvania German History." *Ibid.*, vol. 13 (1949), 243–60; "1949 in Pennsylvania German History." *Ibid.*, vol. 14 (1950), 183–90.

BH162 Graeff, Arthur D. "Outstanding Events in 1945." "'S Pennsylfawnisch Deitsch Eck," Allentown *Morning Call*, 2 March 1946.

BH163 Graeff, Arthur D. "Pennsylvania Bound!" "'S Pennsylfawnisch Deitsch Eck," Allentown *Morning Call*, 31 July 1943.

BH164 Graeff, Arthur D. "Pennsylvania Dutchmen Contributed to Growth of Leading Steel State." "'S Pennsylfawnisch Deitsch Eck," Allentown *Morning Call*, 6 July 1946.

BH165 Graeff, Arthur D. *The Pennsylvania Germans. A Study in Stability*. Allentown, Pa.: n.p., 1945. 36p. Rev. by G. E. Pettingill, *Hist. Rev. of Berks Co.*, vol. 10, no. 4 (1945), 120; W. H. Oda, "'S Pennsylfawnisch Deitsch Eck," Allentown *Morning Call*, 17 February 1945. Also publ. at Plymouth Meeting, Pa.: Mrs. C. Naaman Keyser, 1945, as No. 20 in the Keyser "Home Craft Course" series.

BH166 Graeff, Arthur D. "The Pennsylvania Germans as Soldiers." In: *The Pennsylvania Germans*. Ed. Ralph Wood. Princeton: Princeton Univ. Pr., 1942, p.227–36.

BH167 Graeff, Arthur D. "Pennsylvania Governors—Joseph Ritner, John Wanamaker—Builders of Ships." "'S Pennsylfawnisch Deitsch Eck," Allentown *Morning Call*, 8 July 1944.

BH168 Graeff, Arthur D. "Renascence of History." *The Pa. Dutchman*, vol. 6, no. 5 (1955), 36–38. Discussion of the factors involved in the rebirth of Pennsylvania German history.

BH169 Hark, Ann. *Blue Hills and Shoofly Pie*. Philadelphia: Lippincott, 1952. 284p. Rev. by Arthur D. Graeff, *Amer.-German Rev.*, vol. 19, no. 2 (1952), 34. Stories about the Pennsylvania Dutch. Rev. by J. Hostetler, *Pa. Mag. of Hist. and Biog.*, vol. 77 (1953), 359–60; and P. A. Barba, "'S Pennsylfawnisch Deitsch Eck," Allentown *Morning Call*, 24 January 1953.

BH170 Hark, Ann. "Who are the Pennsylvania Dutch?" *House and Garden*, vol. 79, no. 6 (June 1941), 21, 64.

BH171 Harter, Thomas H. "The Pennsylvania Germans." "'S Pennsylfawnisch Deitsch Eck," Allentown *Morning Call*, 16 January 1960. From a paper originally read before the Bellefonte, Pa. Study Club, 27 January 1914.

BH172 Henninger, James F. "Your Neighbors." "'S Pennsylfawnisch Deitsch Eck," Allentown *Morning Call*, 27 February; 6, 13 March 1943.

BH173 Hoechst, Coit R. "The Pennsylvania Dutch." *Western Pa. Hist. Mag.*, vol. 35, no. 1 (1952), 1–16.

BH174 Hollenbach, Raymond E. "Account of a Hired Girl in a Pennsylvania German Family One Hundred Years Ago." "'S Pennsylfawnisch Deitsch Eck," Allentown *Morning Call*, 23 May 1964.

BH175 Hollenbach, Raymond E. "Rosenthal—Valley of Roses." "'S Pennsylfawnisch Deitsch Eck, Allentown *Morning Call*, 25 February; 4 March 1967. About a locality now known as Hawk Mountain.

BH176 Hopple, Lee C. "European and Spatial Origins of the Pennsylvania Dutch." *Pa. Folklife*, vol. 28, no. 4 (1979), 2–11.

BH177 Hopple, Lee C. "Plain Dutch Settlement in Southeastern Pennsylvania." *Pa. Geographer*, vol. 11, no. 3 (1971), 1–5.

BH178 Hopple, Lee C. "Spatial Development of the Southeastern Pennsylvania Plain Dutch Community to 1970." *Pa. Folklife*, vol. 21, no. 2 (1971), 18–40; no. 3 (1972), 36–45.

BH179 Hopple Lee C. "Spatial Organization of the Southeastern Pennsylvania Plain Dutch Group Cultural Region to 1975." *Pa. Folklife*, vol. 29, no. 1 (1979), 13–26. On locations of the Amish, Dunkard, Mennonite, and Schwenkfelder people in southeastern Pennsylvania; the degree of assimilation of these groups.

BH180 Hornberger, Mark A. "The Spatial Distribution of Ethnic Groups in Selected Counties in Pennsylvania, 1800–1880; A Geographic Interpretation." Diss., Pa. State, 1974.

BH181 Hosch, Heinz L. "Pennsylvania Dutch or Pennsylvania German? A Historical Assessment." In: *Papers from the Conference on German-Americana in the Eastern United States*. Occasional Papers of the Soc. for Ger.-Amer. Studies, no. 8. Ed. Steven M. Benjamin. Morgantown: W. Va. Univ., Dept. of For. Langs., 1980, p.117–23.

BH182 Hostetler, John A. "Revived Interest in Pennsylvania-German Culture." *Mennonite Life*, vol. 11 (1956), 65–72.

BH183 Hostetler, John A. "Why is Everybody Interested in the Pennsylvania Dutch?" "'S Pennsylfawnisch Deitsch Eck," Allentown *Morning Call*, 7, 14 January 1956.

BH184 Jentsch, Theodore W. "Old Order Mennonite Farm Life in the East Pennsylvania Valley." *Pa. Folklife*, vol. 24, no. 1 (1974), 18–28.

BH185 Jordan, Mildred. *The Distelfink Country of the Pennsylvania Dutch*. Illus. by Howard Berelson. New York: Crown Publs., Inc., 1978. 174p. Rev. by F. S. Weiser, *Pa. Mag. of Hist. and Biog.*, vol. 103 (January 1979), 137–38.

BH186 Kelly, Donald S. "Patterns of Pioneer Migration and Population in Mid-Western Pennsylvania." Diss., Ball State Univ., 1975.

BH187 Kermes, Constantine. "Folk Images of Rural Pennsylvania." *Pa. Folklife*, vol. 24, (1975), Supplement, 2–7.

BH188 Klees, Frederic. *The Pennsylvania Dutch*, New York: Macmillan, 1950. 451p. Rev. in *Amer.-German Rev.*, vol. 17, no. 4 (1951), 37; by R. W. Gilbert, *Pa. Hist.*, vol. 18, no. 2 (1951), 161–62; A. H. Finckh, *Amer.-German Rev.*, vol. 17, no. 6 (1951), 37–38; P. Wallace, *Amer. Hist. Rev.*, vol. 56 (1951), 676; C. Weygandt, *Annals of the Amer. Academy of Political and Social Sciences*, vol. 274 (1951), 250; J. S. Weber, *Hist. Rev. of Berks Co.*, vol. 16, no. 2 (1951), 45–46; P. A. Barba, "'S Pennsylfawnisch Deitsch Eck," Allentown *Morning Call*, 17 February 1951.

BH189 Klein, Philip S. *Pennsylvania Politics, 1817–1832. A Game Without Rules*. Philadelphia: Hist. Soc. of Pa., 1940. 430p. Rev. by A. E. Martin, *Miss. Valley Hist. Rev.*, vol. 28, no. 1 (1941), 97–98; W. E. Smith, *Pa. Hist.*, vol. 8, no. 3 (1941), 255–56. Incl. discussion of ethnic and religious factions.

BH190 Kriebel, Marth A. *Retracing Our Roots*. N.p.: n.p., 1976. Pa. Dutch Series, Ursinus Col-

Pennsylvania German History *(cont.)*
lege, no. 8. 61p. A brief history of the Pennsylvania Germans.

BH191 Lawton, Arthur J. "1967 Living History." *Pa. Folklife*, vol. 16, no. 4 (1967), 10–15.

BH192 Lemon, James. *The Best Poor Man's Country: A Geographical Study of Early Southeastern Pennsylvania*. Baltimore: The Johns Hopkins Univ. Pr., 1972. 295p. Repr. New York: Norton, 1976. Rev. by G. S. Dunbar, *Pacific Hist. Rev.*, vol. 42, no. 1 (1973); C. V. Earle, *Md. Hist. Mag.*, vol. 68, no. 1 (1973), 218–19; J. T. Main, *Jour. of Amer. Hist.*, vol. 59 no. 3 (December 1972), 689–90. Incl. discussion of the German Mennonites. Religious affiliation rather than national origin was a principal factor guiding the selection of land types and farming techniques.

BH193 Lentz, Oliver. "Stubborn Heads." "'S Pennsylfawnisch Deitsch Eck," Allentown *Morning Call*, 30 January; 6 February 1943.

BH194 Livingood, Louis J. "Autumn Days." "'S Pennsylfawnisch Deitsch Eck," Allentown *Morning Call*, 20, 27 November; 11 December 1943.

BH195 McKnight, W. J. *A Pioneer Outline History of Northwestern Pennsylvania*. Philadelphia: n.p., 1905.

BH196 MacLeish, Archibald. "Rediscovering the Simple Life." *McCall's*, vol. 99 (1972), 79–87. On the plain people of Pennsylvania.

BH197 Mast, Christian Z., and Robert E. Simpson. *Annals of the Conestoga Valley in Lancaster, Berks, and Chester Counties, Pennsylvania*. Scottdale, Pa.: n.p., 1942. 689p. Compendium of 200 years of local history.

BH198 Mendels, Judy. "Schweizer Reminiszenzen im Lande der Pennsylvania Dutch." *Echo* (Bern), vol. 36, no. 12 (1956), 15–17.

BH199 Miller, Lester M. *The Pennsylvania Dutch*. Reading, Pa.: n.p., 1958. 34p. Rev. by P. A. Barba, "'S Pennsylfawnisch Deitsch Eck," Allentown *Morning Call*, 19 April 1958.

BH200 Mook, Maurice A., ed. "The Changing Pattern of Pennsylvania German Culture, 1855–1955: A Panel Discussion." *Pa. Hist.*, vol. 23, no. 3 (1955), 311–339. Includes: R. W. Gilbert, "Family Life and Recreation"; A. F. Buffington, "Language"; W. J. Rupp, "Church Life and Work"; J. A. Hostetler, "The Mennonites and Amish"; W. E. Boyer, "Arts and Crafts."

BH201 Myers, Richmond E. *The Long Crooked River*. Boston: n.p., 1949. 380p. Rev. by H. J. Young, *Md. Hist. Mag.*, vol. 44, (1949), 217–18. On the Susquehanna River.

BH202 Nock, Albert J. "Utopia in Pennsylvania." In: *Atlantic Essays*. Ed. S. N. Bogorad and Cary B. Graham. Boston: Heath, 1958, p.280–91.

BH203 Nolan, J. Bennett. "An Introduction to Southeastern Pennsylvania History." *Americana Illustrated*, vol. 37, no. 3 (1943), 450–84.

BH204 Nolan, James Bennett, ed. *Southeastern Pennsylvania: A History of the Counties of Berks, Bucks, Chester, Delaware, Montgomery, Philadelphia and Schuylkill*. 3 vols. New York: Lewis Hist. Publ. Co., 1943. Rev. by G. E. Pettengill, *Hist. Rev. of Berks Co.*, vol. 9, no. 3 (1944), 87.

BH205 Parsons, William T. *Ethnic Heritage: The Legacy of the Pennsylvania Dutch*. Collegeville: Inst. on Pa. Dutch Studies, Ursinus College, 1975. 22p.

BH206 Parsons, William T. *The Pennsylvania Dutch: A Persistent Minority*. Boston: Twayne, 1976. 316p. Rev. C. H. Glatfelter, *Der Reggeboge*, vol. 12, no. 2 (April 1978), 22–24; W. Vander Hill, *Jour. of Amer. Hist.*, vol. 63, no. 4 (March 1977), 1019–21; Russell S. Nelson, Jr., *Pa. Hist.*, vol. 45 (1978), 184–85.

BH207 Parsons, William T., and William K. Munro. "Pennsylvania-Palatinate Informal Folk Cultural Exchanges." *Pa. Folklife*, vol. 30 (1980–1981), 120–22.

BH208 "The Passing of the Pennsylvania German." "'S Pennsylfawnisch Deitsch Eck," Allentown *Morning Call*, 16 September 1944. From the *Schwenksville Item*, 15 August 1912.

BH209 *Das Pennsylvanisch Deutsch Lese und Koloring Buch*. Aylmer, Ont.: Pathway Publ., 1976. Incl. glossary.

BH210 Pennsylvania Dutch Tourist Bureau, comp. and ed. *Pennsylvania Dutch Guide Book*. Lancaster: n.p., 1959. 96p. Revised ed., Lancaster: n.p., 1960. 100p.

BH211 Pfautz, John Eby. "The Pennsylvania Churches and Sects (1878)." *Pa. Folklife*, vol. 17, no. 2 (Winter 1967–1968), 44–46.

BH212 Post, Albert. "Early Efforts to Abolish Capital Punishment in Pennsylvania." *Pa. Mag. of Hist. and Biog.*, vol. 68, no. 1 (1944), 38–53.

BH213 Primiano, Leonard. "Student Life at a Pennsylvania Dutch College." *Pa. Folklife*, vol. 26, no. 1 (1976), 34–38.

BH214 Rice, William S. "Some Pennsylvania Landmarks Revisited." *Amer.-German Rev.*, vol. 13, nos. 5–6 (1947), 17–19. With drawings from the author's sketchbook.

BH215 Rippley, La Vern J. "A Note on the Pennsylvania Germans and the Russian Germans." *Work Papers of the Amer. Hist. Soc. of Germans from Russia*, vol. 19 (1975), 60–61.

BH216 Robacker, Earl F. *Touch of the Dutchland*. New York: Merriam, 1965. 240p.

BH217 Rosenberger, Homer T. "Migrations of the Pennsylvania Germans to Western Pennsylvania." *Western Pa. Hist. Mag.*, vol. 53, no. 4 (October 1970), 319–35; vol. 54 (January 1971), 58–76.

BH218 Rosenberger, Homer Tope. *The Pennsylvania-Germans, 1891–1965 (Frequently Known as the "Pennsylvania Dutch")*. 75th Anniversary Vol. of the Pa. German Society. Publs., Pa. German Soc.; vol. 63. Lancaster: Pa. German Soc., 1966. 619p. Rev. by P. S. Klein, *Amer. Hist. Rev.*, vol. 73, no. 3 (1968), 933–34; A.D.G., *Hist. Rev. of Berks Co.*, vol. 32, no. 3 (Summer 1967), 102–03; M. Rubincam, *National Genealogical Soc. Quar.*, vol. 56 (June 1968), 151–52; J. J. Stoudt, *Pa. Mag. of Hist. and Biog.*, vol. 91 (1967), 380–81; A. J. Wahl, *Pa. Hist.*, vol. 35, no. 1 (January 1968). Incl. "How the Pennsylvania Germans Fared During World War I," p.129–51; "Gradual Recovery," p.152–93; "Tidal Wave of Popular Interest in the Pennsylvania Germans," p.194–229; "Sustained Interest During World War II," p.230–53; "The Crest of the Wave 1945–1965," p.254–328; "Pennsylvania German Nobel and Pulitzer Prize Winners, Jane Addams, Pearl S. Buck, J. J. Pershing, Conrad Richter," p.423–47; "Other Pennsylvania Germans, 1891–1965, Who Attained Eminence—A Representative List," p.448–507. Also incl. bibliography and list of archives and museums.

BH219 Royall, A.N. "Eastern Pennsylvania: A Railroad and the Germans." In: *Mirror for Americans. Life and Manners in the United States 1790–1870 as Recorded by American Travelers*. 3 vols. Ed. W. S. Tryon. Chicago: Univ. of Chicago Pr., 1952, vol. 1, p.68–77.

BH220 Rupp, William J. "Mental Health Among the Pennsylvania Dutch." "'S Pennsylfawnisch Deitsch Eck," Allentown *Morning Call*, 11, 18 June 1955.

BH221 Schaefer, Richard H. "The Union Church in Pennsylvania." "'S Pennsylfawnisch Deitsch Eck," Allentown *Morning Call*, 7 April 1951.

BH222 Scherer, Karl. "The Fatherland of the Pennsylvania Dutch." *Mennonite Research Jour.*, vol. 15 (July 1974), 25–29.

BH223 Severs, Susan R., and Abraham R. Horne. "Anglicizing the Pennsylvania Dutch: 1966 and 1875." *Pa. Folklife*, vol. 16, no. 3 (Spring 1967), 46–48.

BH224 Smith, Edward C., and Virginia Van Horn Thompson. *Traditionally Pennsylvania Dutch*. New York: Hastings House, 1947. 81p. Large-format illus. work with full-page sketches by Edward C. Smith.

BH225 Smith, Norman S. "The Pennsylvania Germans and Some of Their Deeds." *Pa. Dutch News and Views*, vol. 3, no. 3 (1971), 5–6.

BH226 Stauffer, Elmer C. "In the Pennsylvania Dutch Country." *National Geographic Mag.*, vol. 80, no. 1 (July 1941), 37–74.

BH227 Stevens, Sylvester K. *Pennsylvania. Birthplace of a Nation*. New York: Random House, 1964.

BH228 Stevens, Sylvester K. *Pennsylvania History in Outline*. Harrisburg: Pa. Historical Commission, 1942. 32p.

BH229 Stevens, Sylvester K. "Pennsylvania's First Year in World War II." *Pa. Hist.*, vol. 10 (1943), 94–104. Some men of Pennsylvania-German background who were prominent in the armed forces.

BH230 Stevens, Sylvester K. *Some Pennsylvania Leaders*. Harrisburg: Pa. Hist. Commission, 1942. 16p.

BH231 Stoudt, John J. "The Cultural Contributions of the Pennsylvania Germans." *Hist. Rev. of Berks Co.*, vol. 25, no. 2 (1960), 40–45, 62–65.

BH232 Stoudt, John Joseph. *The Pennsylvania Dutch: An Introduction to Their Life and Culture*. Allentown: Schlechters, 1950. 32p. Rev. by P. A. Barba, "'S Pennsylfawnisch Deitsch Eck," Allentown *Morning Call*, 7 October 1950.

BH233 Stoudt, John Joseph. *Sunbonnets and Shoofly Pies: A Pennsylvania Dutch Cultural History*. South Brunswick, N. J.: A. S. Barnes, 1973. 272p. Rev. by F. Weiser, *Pa. Mag. of Hist. and Biog.*, vol. 98, no. 2 (April 1974), 280–82.

BH234 Struble, George G. "The French Element Among the Pennsylvania Germans." *Pa. Hist.*, vol. 22, no. 3 (1955), 267–76.

BH235 Sutter, Sem C. "Mennonites and the Pennsylvania German Revival." *Mennonite Quar. Rev.*, vol. 50 (January 1976).

BH236 "Ursinus College Professor Asked Question Which Led to Book on the Pennsylvania Dutch." *Norristown* (Pa.) *Times Herald*, July 1978. On William T. Parsons and his work *The Pennsylvania Dutch: A Persistent Minority* (Boston, 1976).

BH237 Waldenrath, Alexander. "Three Studies in German Culture in Pennsylvania: The Manuscripts of Charles C. More; German Churches of the Lehigh Valley; and Rural Pennsylvania German Newspress in the 18th Century." *German-Amer. Studies*, vol. 9 (1975), 16–42.

BH238 Wallower, Lucille. *The Pennsylvania Dutch*. Written with assistance of Patricia L. Gump. Bryn Mawr, Pa.: Better Govt. Associates, 1971. 74p. For juvenile readers.

BH239 Watson, J. "The Germans in Pennsylvania." "'S Pennsylfawnisch Deitsch Eck," Allentown *Morning Call*, 8 June 1967. Excerpts from Watson's *Annals of Philadelphia and Pennsylvania* (1850).

BH240 Weigel, Harold W. "Pennsylvania Dutch à la Viennoise." *Modern Lang. Jour.*, vol. 38 (1954), 148–49.

BH241 Weiser, Frederick S. "Art in Pennsylvania German Churches." *Der Reggeboge*, vol. 10, no. 2 (1976), 18–19.

BH242 Weygandt, Cornelius. "Pennsylvania Dutch Cultivation." *The Pa. Dutchman*, vol. 5, no. 1 (1953), 3.

BH243 Weygandt, Cornelius. *The Plenty of Pennsylvania*. New York: H. C. Kinsey & Co., 1942. 319p. Rev. in *Amer.-German Rev.*, vol. 9, no. 4 (April 1943), 43; by P. A. Barba, "'S Pennsylfawnisch Deitsch Eck," Allentown *Morning Call*, 5 December 1942; H. R. Warfel, *Pa. Hist.*, vol. 10 (1943), 154–55.

BH244 Wierman, Nancy K. "The Pennsylvania Dutchman." *Pa. Folklife*, vol. 28, no. 2 (1978), 2–11.

BH245 Wildes, Harry E. *The Delaware*. The Rivers of America Series. New York: Farrar and Rinehart, 1940. 398p. Rev. by B. Penrose, *Pa. Mag. of Hist. and Biog.*, vol. 65, no. 2 (1941), 234–35.

BH246 Wood, Ralph. "Lutheran and Reformed, Pennsylvania German Style." In: *The Pennsylvania Germans*. Ed. Ralph Wood. Princeton: Princeton Univ. Pr., 1942, p.87–102.

BH247 Wood, Ralph, ed. *The Pennsylvania Germans*. Contributions by Arthur D. Graeff, Walter M. Kollmorgen, Clyde S. Stine, Ralph Wood, Richard H. Shryock, Albert F. Buffington, Paul Musselman, and Harry Hess Reichard. Princeton: Princeton Univ. Pr., 1942. 299p. Rev. by G. W. Clemens, *Hist. Rev. of Berks Co.*, vol. 7 (1941–42), 119–20; P. A. Barba, *Mod. Lang. Notes*, vol. 58, no. 6 (1943), 489–92; D. Cunz, *Monatshefte für deutschen Unterricht*, vol. 35, no. 1 (1943), 48; E. Doll, *Pa. Mag. of Hist. and Biog.*, vol. 68, no. 3 (1944), 320–22; A. B. Faust, *Mod. Lang. Jour.*, vol. 26, no. 8 (1942), 630–31; L. Gannett, *N. Y. Herald-Tribune: Books*, 19 May 1942; R. Hommel, *Amer.-German Rev.*, vol. 8, no. 6 (1942), 31–32; O. Springer, *Amer. Speech*, vol. 19, no. 2 (1944), 130–34; C. Wittke, *Miss. Valley Hist. Rev.*, vol. 29, no. 2 (1942), 257; A. E. Zucker, *Amer. Hist. Rev.*, vol. 48, no. 2 (1943), 364–65. See *Amer.-German Rev.*, vol. 9, no. 4 (1943), 43 and vol. 10, no. 4 (1944), 40.

BH248 Wood, Ralph C. "The Pennsylvania Germans." *Western Pa. Hist. Mag.*, vol. 40, no. 2 (1957), 109–14.

BH249 Writers' Program. Pennsylvania. *Pennsylvania Cavalcade*. Works Projects Administration and Pa. Federation of Historical Societies. Philadelphia: Univ. of Pa. Pr., 1942. 462p. Rev. in *Amer.-German Rev.*, vol. 9, no. 4 (1943), 41; by S. L. Davis, *Pa. Mag. of Hist. and Biog.*, vol. 67 (1943), 94–95.

BH250 Yoder, Don. "The Bush-Meeting Dutch." *Pa. Folklife*, vol. 12, no. 2 (Summer 1961), 14–17.

BH251 Yoder, Don. "Let's Take our Blinders Off." *Pa. Folklife*, vol. 11 (1 May 1951). A warning against the narrowness of the "blood-conscious" cultural societies: "at no time in Pennsylvania's rich past was... [a] particular group the only one at work shaping Pennsylvania history."

BH252 Yoder, Don. "Pennsylvania Germans." In: *Encyclopedia of American Ethnic Groups*. Ed. Stephan Thernstrom. Cambridge: Harvard Univ. Pr., 1980, p. 770–72.

BH253 Yoder, Don. "Plain Dutch and Gay Dutch: Two Worlds in the Dutch Country." *The Pa. Dutchman*, vol. 8, no. 1 (Summer 1956), 34–55.

BH254 Yoder, Don, ed. "The Sausage Culture of the Pennsylvania Germans." In: *Food in Perspective. Proceedings of the Third International Conference on Ethnological Food Research, Cardiff, Wales, 1977*. Ed. Alexander Fenton and Trefor M. Owen. Edinburgh: John Donald, 1981, p. 409–425.

BH255 Yoder, Paul D. "The Story of a Changed Inscription." "'S Pennsylfawnisch Deitsch Eck," Allentown *Morning Call*, 15 May 1943.

BH256 Zimmerman, Thomas C. "Ancestral Virtues of the Pennsylvania Germans." "'S Pennsylfawnisch Deitsch Eck," Allentown *Morning Call*, 7 December 1967. Reprint of an address delivered before the Chautauqua at Mt. Gretna, 17 July 1893.

COLONIAL

BH257 Aldridge, Alfred Owen. "Franklin's Letter on Indians and Germans." *Procs., Amer. Philosophical Soc.*, vol. 94, no. 4 (1950), 391–95.

BH258 Barba, P. A. "Kidnapped by the Indians." "'S Pennsylfawnisch Deitsch Eck," Allentown *Morning Call*, 8, 15 December 1945.

BH259 Barba, Preston A. "Negro Slavery and the Pennsylvania Germans." "'S Pennsylfawnisch Deitsch Eck," Allentown *Morning Call*, 14 March 1959.

BH260 Barakat, Robert A. "The Herr and Zeller Houses." *Pa. Folklife*, vol. 21, no. 4 (1971–1972), 2–22. The Herr house was built in 1717.

BH261 Bender, Harold S. "The First Mennonite Minister in America." *Mennonite Life*, vol. 13 (1958), 174–77. Wilhelm Rittenhaus of Mühlheim, elected Mennonite Minister in 1690.

BH262 Biegener, E. M. "Heinrich Bernhard Koester (1662–1749)." *Concordia Hist. Inst. Quar.*, vol. 22, no. 4 (1949), 158–66. K. was one of 40 persons who settled with Johann Kelpius on the Wissahickon in 1694; active in spreading Lutheranism.

BH263 Bining, Arthur Cecil. *Pennsylvania Iron Manufacture in the Eighteenth Century*. Harrisburg: Pa. Hist. and Museum Commission, 1973. 215p. Repr. 1979. Rev. by R. E. Carlson, *Pa. History*, vol. 41 (1974), 357–59; F. A. Zahrosky, *Western Pa. Hist. Mag.*, vol. 57 (1974), 121–22; M. H. Hellerich, *Der Reggeboge*, vol. 9, no. 1 (1975), 23–24.

BH264 Brendle, Thomas R. "Moses Dissinger: Evangelist and Patriot." *Publs., Pa. German Soc.*, vol. 58 (1959), 91–192. Rev. by Arthur D. Graeff, "'S Pennsylfawnisch Deitsch Eck," Allentown *Morning Call*, 10 October 1959.

BH265 Buchwalter, Grace M. "Naturalization of German Settlers in Pennsylvania." *Amer.-German Rev.*, vol. 17, no. 6 (1951), 22–23. Describes the situation and conditions of naturalization before 1740.

BH266 Butterfield, L. H. ed. *A Letter by Dr. Benjamin Rush Describing the Consecration of the German College at Lancaster in June, 1787*. Lancaster: Franklin and Marshall College, 1945. 37p. Rev. by Th. Woody, *William and Mary Quar.*, 3rd Ser., vol. 3, no. 3 (1946), 450–52.

BH267 Casino, Joseph. "Anti-Popery in Colonial Pennsylvania." *Pa. Mag. of Hist. and Biog.*, vol. 105 (1981), 279–310.

BH268 Clark, Delber W. *The World of Justus Falckner.* Philadelphia: Muhlenberg Pr., 1946. 189p. Rev. by Don Yoder, "'S Pennsylfawnisch Deitsch Eck," Allentown *Morning Call,* 26 February 1949; M. V. Palsits, *Amer. Hist. Rev.,* vol. 52 (1947), 805.

BH269 Cohen, Norman S. "The Philadelphia Election Riot of 1742." *Pa. Mag. of Hist. and Biog.,* vol. 92, (July 1968), 306–19. Unruly sailors and newly arrived German immigrants were used in the political conflict between the proprietary party and the Quakers.

BH270 "A Communication on the Relation of Franconia and Lancaster Mennonites in Colonial Pennsylvania." *Mennonite Quar. Rev.,* vol. 26 (April 1952), 161–63. Communications between two settlements in 1773.

BH271 Doll, Eugene E. "Dr. Rush on the Integration of the Germans in Pennsylvania." *Amer.-German Rev.,* vol. 10, no. 2 (December 1943), 38.

BH272 Dorpalen, Andreas. "The German Element in Early Pennsylvania Politics, 1789–1800: A Study in Americanization." *Pa. Hist.,* vol. 9 (1942), 176–90. Finds active political participation only with Americanization. Rural conservative Germans support the Federalists.

BH273 Edwards, Jane Spencer. "Wills and Inventories of the First Purchasers of the Welsch Tract." *Pa. Folklife,* vol. 23 (Winter 1973–74).

BH274 [Ernst, Johann Friedrich.] "A Letter from Pastor Johann Friedrich (John Frederick) Ernst." Trans. and ed. by Edith von Zemenszky. *Pa. Folklife,* vol. 26 (Summer 1977), 34–45. Active in rural Pennsylvania and New York state 1782–1802.

BH275 Ernst, Johann Friedrich. Papers, 1776–1787. 1 vol. In collections of the Historical Society of Pennsylvania (MS 62-4720). Letter in German to correspondents in Pennsylvania.

BH276 Fretz, J. Herbert. "The Germantown Antislavery Petition of 1688." *Mennonite Quar. Rev.,* vol. 33, no. 1 (1959), 42–59. See also his "Germantown Anti-Slavery Protest." *Mennonite Life,* vol. 13 (1958), 183–86. The petition of 1688, signed by Francis Daniel Pastorius and other Mennonite leaders.

BH277 Friedrich, Gerhard. "The Earliest History of Germantown: An Unknown Pastorius Manuscript." *Bull., Friends' Hist. Assoc.,* vol. 33, no. 1 (1944), 17–19. Also in *Pa. Hist.,* vol. 8, no. 4 (1941), 314–16. See *Amer.-German Rev.,* vol. 8, no. 1 (1941), 7–8.

BH278 Friedrich, Gerhard. "Pastorius' Naturalization Paper." *Bull., Friends' Hist. Assoc.,* vol. 30, no. 1 (1941), 4–7. With a facsimile from the Cassel Collection at Juniata College.

BH279 "German Redemptioners Take Ship to Pennsylvania." In: *Heritage of America.* Ed. H.S. Commager and Allen Nevins. Boston: Little, Brown, 1949, p.76–79.

BH280 Gibson, James E. "John Augustus Otto." *Papers of the Berks Co. Hist. Soc.,* vol. 13, no. 1 (1947), 14–18. Son of Dr. Bodo Otto, physician in the Revolutionary War era.

BH281 Glatfelter, Charles H. "The Eighteenth Century German Lutheran and Reformed Clergymen in the Susquehanna Valley." *Pa. Hist.,* vol. 20, no. 1 (1953), 57–68.

BH282 Godschalk, Jacob et al. "A Pennsylvania Letter of 1745 to Mennonite Leaders in Holland." *Mennonite Hist. Bull.,* vol. 32 (October 1971), 3–4.

BH283 Graeff, Arthur D. "Daniel Rupp: The Number of Pennsylvania Germans, 1680–1776." "'S Pennsylfawnisch Deitsch Eck," Allentown *Morning Call,* 29 July 1944.

BH284 Graeff, Arthur D. "Echoes from the Past: First Protest Against Slavery." "'S Pennsylfawnisch Deitsch Eck," Allentown *Morning Call,* 20 January 1945.

BH285 Graeff, Arthur D. "Freiheits Bell." "'S Pennsylfawnisch Deitsch Eck," Allentown *Morning Call,* 3 July 1943.

BH286 Harper, John W., and Martha B. Harper. "The Palatine Migration—1723—from Schoharie to Tulpehocken." *Hist. Rev. of Berks Co.,* vol. 25, no. 3 (Summer 1960), 80–82.

BH287 Hawke, David. *The Colonial Experience.* Indianapolis: n.p., 1966. Incl. discussion of the German-Americans on the frontier in colonial Pennsylvania.

BH288 Heavner, Robert O. "Economic Aspects of Indentured Servitude in Colonial Pennsylvania." Diss., Stanford, 1976.

BH289 Heimer, Roger C. *A Pioneer Family in Colonial Pennsylvania*. Philadelphia: Dorrance, 1978. 139p.

BH290 Heisey, M. Luther. "The Indian Treaty of 1744." *Papers, Lancaster Co. Hist. Soc.*, vol. 48, no. 3 (1944), 57–70. On the conference between the Six Nations and the governments of Pennsylvania, Maryland and Virginia.

BH291 Helfferich, Johann H. "The Journal of Rev. Johann Heinrich Helfferich." Trans. by William U. Helfferich. *Pa. Folklife*, vol. 28, no. 4 (1979), 17–24. Diary of a transatlantic voyage.

BH292 Hershberger, Guy F. "A Newly Discovered Pennsylvania Mennonite Petition of 1755." *Mennonite Quar. Rev.*, vol. 33 (1959), 143–51.

BH293 Hess, Robert L. "Johann Philipp Streiter (ca. 1705–1756)." TS in possession of Charles H. Glatfelter (1980). Biogaphy of a Lutheran minister.

BH294 Hirsch, Helen. "Philadelphus Philadelphia, Scientist and Magician." *Amer.-German Rev.*, vol. 24, no. 6 (1958), 35–36. Jacob Meyer of Philadelphia, son of early settlers in Germantown; returned to Europe in 1750 to win fame as an astrologer, alchemist, and conjuror.

BH295 Huebener, Theodore. "Die ersten deutschen Siedler waren Krefelder." *New Yorker Staats-Zeitung und Herold*, vol. 146, no. 40 (1980), Sec. A, p.11.

BH296 Illick, Joseph E. *Colonial Pennsylvania*. New York: Scribner's, 1976. 359p. Biographical material on major and minor figures, with considerable attention to Conrad Weiser. Rev. by B. H. Newcomb, *Jour. of Amer. Hist.*, vol. 64, no. 1 (June 1977), 119–20.

BH297 Ireland, Owen S. "The Ethnic-Religious Dimension of Pennsylvania Politics, 1778–1779." *William and Mary Quar.*, vol. 30 (1979), 423–48.

BH298 Ireland, Owen S. "Germans against Abolition: A Minority's View of Slavery in Revolutionary Pennsylvania." *Jour. of Interdisciplinary Hist.*, vol. 3 (1973), 685–706.

BH299 Johannsen, Robert W. "The Conflict between the Three Lower Counties on the Delaware and the Province of Pennsylvania 1682–1704." *Del. Hist.*, vol. 5 (1952), 96–132. A few German settlers were involved.

BH300 Johnson, Hildegard Binder. "The Germantown Protest of 1688 Against Negro Slavery." *Pa. Mag. of Hist. and Biog.*, vol. 65, no. 2 (1941), 145–56.

BH301 Johnson, William Thomas. "Some Aspects of the Relations of the Government and German Settlers in Colonial Pennsylvania, 1683–1754." *Pa. Hist.*, vol. 11, no. 2 (1944), 81–102; no. 3 (1944), 200–07.

BH302 Jordan, John W. *Adm. Hubley, jr. Lt. Colo. Comdt. 11th Penna. Regt., His Journal, Commencing at Wyoming, July 30th 1779*. Philadelphia: n.p., 1909.

BH303 Kaufman, David B. "English and German." "'S Pennsylfawnisch Deitsch Eck," Allentown *Morning Call*, 4, 11 January 1964. Relations between Anglo-Saxon and German groups in 18th-century Pennsylvania.

BH304 Kehl, James A. "Albert Gallatin: Man of Moderation." *Western Pa. Hist. Mag.*, vol. 61 (January 1978), 31–45.

BH305 Keller, Kenneth W. "Diversity and Democracy: Ethnic Politics in Southeastern Pennsylvania, 1788–1799." Diss., Yale, 1971.

BH306 Kephart, Calvin I. "William Rittenhouse, First Mennonite Bishop in America." *Mennonite Quar. Rev.*, vol. 18, no. 1 (1944), 49–55. See also the reply by H. S. Bender.

BH307 Klein, H. M. J. "The Church People in Colonial Pennsylvania." *Pa. Hist.*, vol. 9 (1942), 37–47. On the conflicts between the German "church people" and the sectarians.

BH308 Kriebel, Martha B. "Women Servants and Family Life in Early America." *Pa. Folklife*, vol. 28 (Autumn 1978), 2–9. Discusses women in the Pennsylvania German communities; statistical data on some Schwenkfelder households.

BH309 Kreider, Harry Julius. "Justus Falckner" (1672–1723). *Concordia Hist. Inst. Quar.*, vol. 27, no. 2 (July 1954), 86–94. F. was the first Lutheran home missionary pastor, "the patriarch of the Lutheran Church in America."

BH310 Lichtenthaeler, Frank E. "Overland Barriers of the Susquehanna Corridor." *Hist. Rev. of Berks Co.*, vol. 10, no. 3 (April 1945), 67–73.

BH311 Lichtenthaeler, Frank E. "Storm Blown Seed of Schoharie." *Publs., Pa. Ger. Folklore Soc.*, vol. 9 (1944), 3–105.

BH312 Lineback, Donald J. "An Annotated Edition of the Diary of Johann Heinrich Müller (1702–1782), Pietist and Printer of the American Revolution." Diss., Univ. of N. Car., 1975–1976.

BH313 Lockyer, Timothy J. "Walking with the Lord: Rachel Bahn." *Pa. Mag. of Hist. and Biog.*, vol. 103 (1979), 484–96.

BH314 Loomis, C. Grant. "The Indians of Pennsylvania. An Early Letter of Pastorius." *American-Ger. Rev.*, vol. 9, no. 5 (June 1943), 21–23, 36.

BH315 Lord, Arthur C. "The Pre-Revolutionary Agriculture of Lancaster County, Pennsylvania." *Jour. of the Lancaster Co. Hist. Soc.*, vol. 79 (1975), 23–42.

BH316 Lourdes, Joan de, Sr. "Elections in Colonial Pennsylvania." *William and Mary Quar.*, vol. 11, no. 3 (1954), 385–401.

BH317 Massey, James E. "The Bertolet-Herbein Cabin." *Amer.-German Rev.*, vol. 26, no. 3 (1960), 12–14. One of the oldest pioneer houses in the Pennsylvania German area.

BH318 McCauley, Sr. Janet. "Pioneering German Jesuits in Colonial Pennsylvania, 1741–1781. Parts IV and V." *Social Justice Rev.*, vol. 58 (1965), 269–72, 304–08, 342–44; vol. 58 (January–February 1966), 379–82, 414–18, 451–56; 59 (March–June 1966), 25–27, 62–65, 99–101; vol. 60 (July–August 1966), 145–47.

BH319 Mattice, Paul B. "The Palatine Emigration from Schoharie to the Tulpehocken." *Hist. Rev. of Berks Co.*, vol. 10, no. 1 (October 1944), 16–21.

BH320 Miller, Peter. Register Book H. 1765–1777. In the Library of the American Philosophical Society, Philadelphia (MS 76-923). Copies of depositions sworn before Peter Miller as notary public. Documents in German and English.

BH321 Milspaw, Yvonne A. "Pioneer Churches of Central Pennsylvania: Plain Walls and Little Angels." *Pioneer America*, vol. 12 (1980), 76–96.

BH322 Nash, Gary B. "City Planning and Political Tension in the Seventeenth Century: The Case of Philadelphia." *Procs., Amer. Philosophical Soc.*, vol. 112 (1968), 54–73.

BH323 Neff, Larry M., trans. "The Stamp Act Repealed: Text of a 1766 Broadside." *Der Reggeboge*, vol. 11, no. 1 (1977), 1–2.

BH324 Nolan, J. Bennett. "A Clerical Visitor in 1787." *Hist. Rev. of Berks Co.*, vol. 7 (1941–1942), 114–15. Travel description, with references to German settlers.

BH325 Parsons, Phyllis Vibbard. "The Early Life of Daniel Claus." *Pa. Hist.*, vol. 29, no. 4 (1962), 357–72. Claus emigrated from the Palatinate in 1749.

BH326 Parsons, William R. "The 'Pennsylfawnisch Deitsch' Community for Independence, 1758–1783." In: *Germany and America: Essays on Problems of International Relations and Immigration.* Ed. Hans L. Trefousse. New York: Columbia Univ. Pr., 1980, p.73–88.

BH327 Prince, Carl E. "John Israel: Printer and Politician on the Pennsylvania Frontier, 1798–1805." *Pa. Mag. of Hist. and Biog.*, vol. 91 (January 1967), 46–55. The article points out the conflicts between Jeffersonians and Federalists in western Pennsylvania.

BH328 Pennsylvania Colony. Land Office. *Early Pennsylvania Land Records: Minutes of the Board of Property of the Province of Pennsylvania.* Ed. W. H. Egle. Forew. by George E. McCracken. Baltimore: Genealogical Publ. Co., 1976. 787p. Repr. of the 1893 ed. of Land Office Minute Books 1685–1739.

BH329 Rothermund, Dietmar. "The German Problem of Colonial Pennsylvania." *Pa. Mag. of Hist. and Biog.*, vol. 84, no. 1 (1960), 3–21. Discussion of the problem of "withdrawal" vs. assimilation.

BH330 Rothermund, Dietmar. *The Layman's Progress. Religious and Political Experience in Colonial Pennsylvania, 1740–1770.* Philadelphia: Univ. of Pennsylvania Pr., 1961. 202p. Rev. by J. M. Coleman, *Pa. Hist.*, vol. 29 (1962), 440–41; W. B. Miller, *Pa. Mag. of Hist. and Biog.*, vol. 86 (1962), 481–82. Cf. his "Denominations and Political Behavior in Colonial Pennsylvania, 1740–1770." Diss., Univ. of Pa., 1959.

BH331 Rubincam, Milton. "William Rittenhouse, America's Pioneer Paper Manufacturer and Mennonite Minister." *Publs., Pa. German Soc.*, vol. 58 (1959), 1–89. Publ. under the combined title *William Rittenhouse and Moses Dissinger—Two Eminent Pennsylvania Germans*. Publs., Pa. German Soc., vol. 58. Scottdale: Herald Pr., 1959. 192p.

BH332 Rush, Benjamin. *An Account of the Manners of the German Inhabitants of Pennsylvania*. Ed. William T. Parsons. Collegeville: Inst. on Pa. Dutch Studies, 1974. 25p. Repr. of the original article of 1789. See also "'S Pennsylfawnisch Deitsch Eck," Allentown *Morning Call*, 22, 29 September; 6, 13, 20, 27 October 1962 for a repr. of this pamphlet as it had been edited in 1875 by I. Daniel Rupp.

BH333 Schelbert, Leo. "From Reformed Preacher in the Palatinate to Pietist Monk in Pennsylvania: The Spiritual Path of Johann Peter Müller, 1709–1796." In: *Germany and America: Essays on Problems of International Relations and Immigration*. Ed. Hans L. Trefousse. New York: Columbia Univ. Pr., 1980, p.139–50.

BH334 Schultz, Selina G. "David Schultz, Surveyor (1717–1797)." *Schwenkfeldiana*, vol. 1, no. 5 (1945), 52–61.

BH335 Shryock, Richard H. "The Medical Reputation of Benjamin Rush: Contrasts over Two Centuries." *Bull. of the Hist. of Medicine*, vol. 45 (1971), 507–52.

BH336 Sifton, Paul G. "Pierre Eugène Du Simitiere (1737–1784): Collector in Revolutionary America." Diss., Univ. of Pennsylvania, ca. 1960. A Swiss-American collector and cultural historian.

BH337 Simon, Grant M. "Dissenters and Founders." *Amer.-German Rev.*, vol. 25, no. 1 (1958), 17–19. Mennonites and German Quakers in the early life of Pennsylvania.

BH338 Stern, Malcolm H. "Two Jewish Functionaries in Colonial Pennsylvania." *Amer. Jewish Hist. Quar.*, vol. 57 (September 1967), 24–51.

BH339 Stoudt, John J. "Early Pennsylvania Religious Movements." *Amer.-German Rev.*, vol. 8, no. 4 (1942), 9–10, 31.

BH340 Tappert, Theodore G. "Colonial Lutheran Churches." *Amer.-German Rev.*, vol. 9, no. 1 (1942), 18–22.

BH341 Tappert, Theodore G. "Helmuth and the Fries Rebellion in 1799." *Lutheran Quar.*, vol. 17 (1965), 265–69. On. J.H.C. Helmuth, Lutheran pastor in Lancaster and Philadelphia, 1769–1820.

BH342 Tappert, Theodore G. "John Caspar Stoever and the Ministerium of Pennsylvania." *Lutheran Church Quar.*, vol. 21, no. 2 (1948), 180–84.

BH343 Tees, Francis H. et al. *Pioneering in Penn's Woods*. Philadelphia: n.p., ca. 1937.

BH344 Tolles, Frederick B. "The Culture of Early Pennsylvania." *Pa. Mag. of Hist. and Biog.*, vol. 81 (1957), 119–37. Incl. comments on the early German immigrants.

BH345 Tully, Alan. "Englishmen and Germans: National-Group Contact in Colonial Pennsylvania, 1700–1755." *Pa. Hist.*, vol. 45 (July 1978), 237–56.

BH346 Waldenrath, Alexander. "Johann Heinrich Miller: German-American Patriot." *Der Reggeboge*, vol. 8, no. 1 (1974), 9–11.

BH347 Weaver, Glenn. "Benjamin Franklin and the Pennsylvania Germans." *William and Mary Quar.*, vol. 14 (1957), 536–59.

BH348 Weiser, Frederick S. "The Concept of Baptism among Colonial Pennsylvania German Lutheran and Reformed Church People." *Lutheran Hist. Conference Essays and Reports*, vol. 4 (1970), 1–45.

BH349 Weiser, Frederick S. "Human Idiosyncrasy in Estate Records: A Sample." *Der Reggeboge*, vol. 13, no. 2 (1979), 11–15. Examples of curious wills among early Pennsylvania documents, 1755–1801.

BH350 Wellenreuther, Herman. *Glaube und Politik in Pennsylvania 1681–1776. Die Wandlungen der Obrigkeitsdoktrin und des Peace Testimony der Quäker*. Köln: Böhlau, 1972. Rev. by Udo Sautter, *Pa. Mag. of Hist. and Biog.*, vol. 97, no. 2 (1973), 282; G. Hershberger, *Amer. Hist. Rev.*, vol. 80, part 2 (1975), 1381–82.

BH351 Winters, R. L. "John Caspar Stoever: Colonial Pastor and Founder of Churches." *Publs., Pa. German Soc.* (Norristown), vol. 53 (1948), 1–171. See also his article "John Caspar Stoever, Lutheran Pioneer." *Lutheran Church Quar.*, vol. 18, no. 3 (1945), 285–96.

BH352 Wood, Ralph. "Lutheran and Reformed, Pennsylvania-German Style." In: *The Pennsylvania Germans*. Princeton: Princeton Univ. Pr., 1942, p. 87–102.

BH353 Wood, Ralph. "Pennsylvania. The Colonial Melting Pot." In: *The Pennsylvania Germans*. Ed. Ralph Wood. Princeton: Princeton Univ. Pr., 1942, p. 1–26.

BH354 Yoder, Don, ed. "Notes and Documents: Eighteenth-Century Letters from Germany." *Pa. Folklife*, vol. 19, no. 3 (Spring 1970), 30–33. Contains (1) *Amerikabriefe* addressed to George Hechler of Lower Salford, Montgomery Co., by his brother Michael from Unterelsass, 1784, and (2) a letter of Jacob Rupp of Heppenheim (Pfalz), 1786, and a reply by Rudolph Landes, Bedminster Township, Bucks Co.

BH355 Yoder, Donald, ed. "Notes and Documents [on Jean Bertolet]." *Pa. Folklife*, vol. 16, no. 1 (Autumn 1966), 44–48. On Bertolet, an emigrant to Pennsylvania in 1726, and his descendants.

BH356 Zimmerman, John J. "Benjamin Franklin and the Pennsylvania Chronicle." *Pa. Mag. of Hist. and Biog.*, vol. 81 (1957), 351–64. On Pennsylvania politics in 1767.

REVOLUTIONARY ERA

BH357 Becker, Laura L. "The American Revolution as a Community Experience: A Case Study of Reading, Pennsylvania." Diss., Pennsylvania, 1978.

BH358 Cook, Ross K. "Five Adam Koch's [sic]—Berks County Revolutionary Soldiers." *Hist. Rev. of Berks Co.*, vol. 8 (1942–1943), 115–17.

BH359 Graeff, Arthur D. "The Hessians in Berks." "'S Pennsylfawnisch Deitsch Eck," Allentown *Morning Call*, 16 December 1944.

BH360 Graeff, Arthur D. "Washington's Bodyguard." "'S Pennsylfawnisch Deitsch Eck," Allentown *Morning Call*, 16 February 1963. Pennsylvania Germans under the command of Major von Heer.

BH361 Hellerich, Mahlon H. "Pennsylvania Germans in the American Revolution: The Emergence of Local Leadership in Lehigh County." *Der Reggeboge*, vol. 10, no. 2 (1976), 1–17.

BH362 Hellerich, Mahlon L. "The Revolutionary Generation: An Evaluation." *Procs., Lehigh Co. Hist. Soc.*, vol. 31 (1976), 33–42.

BH363 Ireland, Owen S. "The Ethnic-Religious Dimension of Pennsylvania Politics, 1778–1779." *William and Mary Quar.*, vol. 30 (July 1973), 423–48.

BH364 Jordan, John Woolf. "Bethlehem during the Revolution." *Pa. Hist. Mag.*, vol. 12 (1888), 385f.; vol. 13 (1889), 71f.

BH365 Kaufman, David B. "Allentown during the Revolution, According to 'Ben'." *Procs., Lehigh Co. Hist. Soc.*, vol. 31 (1976), 11–20. Based on Benjamin F. Trexler's *Skizzen aus dem Lecha-Thale* (Allentown, 1880–1886).

BH366 Keller, Kenneth W. "Diversity and Democracy: Ethnic Politics in Southeastern Pennsylvania, 1788–1799." Diss., Yale, 1971.

BH367 Kemp, Franklin W. "Baron Bose Comes to Berks." *Hist. Rev. of Berks Co.*, vol. 30, no. 1 (1964–1965), 19–20. Charles Augustus von Bose, German-born staff officer of the Pulaski Legion, was killed in an engagement at Little Egg Harbor Township.

BH368 Kraybill, Mary Jean. *A Guide to Select Revolutionary War Records Pertaining to the Mennonites and Other Pacifist Groups in Southeastern Pennsylvania and Maryland, 1775–1800, no. 2.* Harrisonburg, Pa.: Eastern Mennonite College, 1974.

BH369 Marshall, Christopher. "Revolutionary Prisoners in Reading." *Hist. Rev. of Berks Co.*, vol. 7 (1941–1942), 52–53. Extracts from a diary describing the Hessian prison camp at Reading.

BH370 Montgomery, Morton L. *History of Berks County ... in the Revolution, 1774–1783.* Reading, Pa.: Berks Co. Daughters of the American Revolution, 1975.

BH371 Parsons, William T. *The Preachers' Appeal of 1775.* Collegeville: Publs. of the Pa. Dutch Studies Program, Ursinus College, 1975. 58p. Lutheran and Reformed German Pastors plead for independence.

BH372 "Pennsylvania Mennonites and the Revolution." *Mirror* (Lancaster Co. Mennonite Conference Hist. Soc.), vol. 8, no. 3 (1976), 1f.

BH373 Reed, John F. "The Papers of Henry Juncken, Tory, and His Wife, of Springfield Township." *Bull., Hist. Soc. of Montgomery Co.*, vol. 14, no. 4 (Spring 1965), 315–30. A Tory sympathizer who fled to London in 1781.

BH374 Richards, Henry M. *The Pennsylvania German in the Revolutionary War, 1765–1783.* Lancaster: n.p., 1908. Repr. Baltimore: Genealogical Publ. Co., 1978. Rev. by M. Rubincam, *National Genealogical Soc. Quar.*, vol. 67 (1979), 68–69.

BH375 Sachse, Julius F. *The Braddock Expedition: Conditions of Pennsylvania during the Year 1775. Publs., Pa. German Soc.*, vol. 25 (1917). Trans. of a French pamphlet found in the Ducal Library at Gotha, Germany.

BH376 Scheidt, David L. "The Lutherans in Revolutionary Philadelphia." *Concordia Hist. Inst. Quar.*, vol. 49 (Winter 1976), 148–59.

BH377 Schmidt, Louis H. "The Liberty Bell 1753–1953." *Amer.-German Rev.*, vol. 19, no. 5 (1953), 19. Hidden in the German Reformed Church of Northampton, when Gen. Howe's troops approached Philadelphia in 1777.

BH378 Soderberg, Gertrude L. "Captain John Soder's Company, 1776." *National Genealogical Soc. Quar.*, vol. 53, no. 1 (1965), 35. A company of Germans led by Captain Soder of Berks County was called up to defend Philadelphia.

BH379 Sprout, Oliver S. "Tories at the 'Dutch' Mill." *Papers of the Lancaster Co. Hist. Soc.*, vol. 56, no. 2 (1952), 36–43. How certain colonists of German descent provided flour and horses for the British army.

BH380 Stemmons, John D. *Pennsylvania in 1780.* Salt Lake City: n.p., 1978. A collection of Colonial tax lists.

BH381 Von Reck, Philip Georg Friedrich. "Early Descriptions of Philadelphia and Germantown." "'S Pennsylfawnisch Deitsch Eck," Allentown *Morning Call*, 26 March 1966. His diary, excerpted from the Hallesche *Nachrichten*.

BH382 Waldenrath, Alexander. "The German Language Newspress of Pennsylvania during the American Revolution." *German-Amer. Studies*, vol. 6 (Fall 1973), 43–56.

BH383 Waldenrath, Alexander. "The Pennsylvania-Germans: Development of Their Printing and Their Newspress in the War for American Independence." In: *The German Contribution to the Building of the Americas: Studies in Honor of Karl J. R. Arndt.* Ed. G. K. Friesen and W. Schatzberg. Hanover: Univ. Pr. of New England, 1977, p.47–74.

BH384 Wentz, Richard E. "The American Character and the American Revolution: A Pennsylvania-German Sampler." *Jour. of the Amer. Academy of Religion*, vol. 44 (March 1976).

German Language in Pennsylvania/Bilingualism

See also Section CJ: Pennsylvania German Dialect Literature *and* Section DC: Dialects of German—United States and Canada.

BH385 Anderson, Keith O., and Willard M. Martin. "Language Loyalty among the Pennsylvania Germans: A Status Report on Old Order Mennonites in Pennsylvania and Ontario." In: *Germanica Americana 1976: Symposium on German-American Literature and Culture.* Ed. E. A. Albrecht and J. Anthony Burzle. Lawrence: Max Kade Doc. and Research Center, Univ. of Kans., 1977, p.73–80.

BH386 Buffington, Albert F. "A Pennsylvania German Goddesdienscht." *Der Reggeboge*, vol. 13, no. 2 (1979), 1–10. Worship service described and transcribed by B. on 4 September 1955 at the Grobbekarrich (Grubb's Church) in Snyder County.

BH387 Enninger, Werner, and Susan Good. *Pennsylvania German-English Interlanguages.* Newark: Univ. of Delaware, 1974. Interim Project No. 02–16 776–17.

BH388 Feer, Robert A. "Official Use of the German Language in Pennsylvania." *Pa. Mag. of Hist. and Biog.*, vol. 76 (1952), 394–405.

BH389 Gehman, Henry Snyder. "What the Pennsylvania Dutch Dialect has Meant in My Life." *Pa. Folklife*, vol. 17, no. 4 (1968), 8–11.

BH390 Gilbert, Russell W. "An All Pennsylvania-German Church Service." *Amer.-German Rev.*, vol. 22, no. 6 (1956), 15. At Botschaft Church, Snyder County.

BH391 Gilbert, Russell W. "The Oratory of the Pennsylvania Germans at the Versammlinge." *Susquehanna Univ. Studies*, vol. 4 (1951), 187–213.

BH392 Gilbert, Russell W. "Pennsylvania German Versammling Speeches." *Pa. Speech Annual*, vol. 13, (1956), 3–20.

BH393 Gilbert, Russell W. "Religious Services in Pennsylvania German." *Susquehanna Univ. Studies*, vol. 5, no. 4 (1956), 277–89. Rev. by P. A. Barba, "'S Pennsylfawnisch Deitsch Eck," Allentown *Morning Call*, 29 September 1956. Background and history of German and Pennsylvania-German worship services.

BH394 Gilbert, Russell W. "Worship in the Pennsylvania German Dialect Continues." *Susquehanna Univ. Studies*, vol. 6 (1959), 411–21.

BH395 Gladfelter, Millard E. "The Pennsylvania Dutch Dialect in a Teacher's Life." *Pa. Folklife*, vol. 18, no. 1 (1968), p.44–48. In this symposium on the Pennsylvania German dialect, there are also contributions by Homer L. Kreider, "The Pennsylvania Dialect and What It Has Meant to Me," and Charles D. Spotts, "What the Pennsylvania German Dialect Has Meant to a Non-Pennsylvania German."

BH396 Jackson, Gregory L. "Bi-Lingual German Churches in the Lutheran Church in America." *German-Amer. Studies*, vol. 9 (1975), 11–15. At the present time the bilingual churches continue gradually to lose their members and pastors.

BH397 Newcomb, Thomas L. *Bilingual-Bicultural Instruction with Pennsylvania German Speaking Children: A Source Book for the Classroom Teacher*. Garrettesville, Ohio: n.p., 1980.

BH398 "Pennsylvania German Dialect Expected to Survive." *Lebanon Daily News*, 19 July 1976. An interview with Dr. Willard Martin of the Pennsylvania State University.

BH399 Riley, Jobie E. "The Rhetoric of the German-Speaking Pulpit in Eighteenth-Century Pennsylvania." *Jour. of Lancaster Co. Hist. Soc.*, vol. 81, no. 3 (1977), 138–59.

BH400 Rosenberger, Homer Tope. "Awakening of Interest in the Pennsylvania Germans and Their Dialect, 1868–1890." In: *The Pennsylvania Germans, 1891–1965 (Frequently Known as the "Pennsylvania Dutch")*, by H. T. Rosenberger. 75th Anniversary Vol. of the Pa. German Society. Lancaster: Pa. German Soc., 1966, p.53–72.

BH401 Rosenberger, Homer Tope. "How Can the Pennsylvania German Culture and Dialect be Preserved in a Dignified Way?" In: *The Pennsylvania Germans, 1891–1965*. Lancaster: Pa. German Soc., 1966, p.563–93.

BH402 Rosenberger, Homer Tope. "Pennsylvania German Dictionaries and Grammars, 1891–1965." In: *The Pennsylvania Germans, 1891–1965*. Lancaster: Pa. German Soc., 1966, p.360–80.

BH403 Springer, Otto. "On Defining the Sources of Colonial Speech." In: *Arbeiten zur germanischen Philologie und zur Literatur des Mittelalters*. München: Fink, 1975, p.11–34.

BH404 Waldenrath, Alexander. "The Germans and Their Language in Early Pennsylvania." *Bull. of the Pa. State Modern Lang. Assoc.*, vol. 56, no. 1 (1978), 3–6.

Agriculture and Industry

BH405 Adams, Ruth C. "How to Love the Land and Live With Your Love." *Organic Gardening and Farming*, vol. 19 (May 1972), 68–72.

BH406 Allen, George. "The Rittenhouse Paper Mill and Its Founder." *Mennonite Quar. Rev.*, vol. 16 (1942), 108–28. First American paper mill, operated by William Rittenhouse.

BH407 *Baer's Agricultural Almanac for the Year 1977*. Ed. Gerald S. Lestz, of John Baer's Sons of Lancaster, Pa. New York: Grosset & Dunlap, 1976. The 152nd issue of this publication.

BH408 Barakat, Robert A. "Glossary of Pennsylvania German Terms Related to Construction and

Tobacco Agriculture." *Pa. Folklife*, vol. 26, no. 4 (1977), 21–35.

BH409 Barakat, Robert A. "Tobaccuary: A Study of Tobacco Curing Sheds in Southeastern Pennsylvania." Diss., Pennsylvania, 1972.

BH410 Bartholomew, Ann. "Agriculture in Lehigh County to 1920." *Procs., Lehigh Co. Hist. Soc.*, vol. 32 (1978), 74–99.

BH411 Bartholomew, Craig. "Anthracite and Industrial Growth in the Lehigh Valley." *Procs., Lehigh Co. Hist. Soc.*, vol. 32 (1978), 129–83.

BH412 Baver, Russell S. "Golden Fields in the Golden Years." *Pa. Folklife*, vol. 9, no. 4 (1958), 12–17. Early methods of sowing, harvesting, threshing and marketing on the Pennsylvania German farm.

BH413 Berky, Andrew S. *An Account of Some Hosensack Valley Mills*. Pennsburg, Pa.: Schwenkfelder Library, 1958. 70p.

BH414 Bining, Arthur C. "Early Ironmasters of Pennsylvania." *Pa. Hist.*, vol. 18, no. 2 (1951), 93–103. Besides the English ironmasters there were men like Heinrich Wilhelm Stiegel, John Probst, and Peter Schoenberger, of German descent.

BH415 Borie, Beaveau, IV. "Threshing Methods in the Pennsylvania German Area." Diss., Univ. of Pennsylvania, 1974. 284p.

BH416 Boyer, Melville J. "Fort Allen—Postwar Business." *Procs., Lehigh Co. Hist. Soc.*, vol. 31 (1976), 21–32. On the business enterprises of John Jacob Weiss and sons.

BH417 Bressler, Leo A. "Agriculture Among the Germans in Pennsylvania during the Eighteenth Century." *Pa. Hist.*, vol. 22, no. 2 (1955), 102–33.

BH418 Bucher, Robert C. "Grain in the Attic." *Pa. Folklife*, vol. 13, no. 2 (Winter 1962–1963), 7–15. Storage of grain in the days before barns; hoists and bins built into 18th-century farmhouses.

BH419 Burnett, Robert B. "A Portrait of the Iron Industry." *Hist. Rev. of Berks Co.*, vol. 45 (1980), 127–29, 131, 154–56. On Charming Forge, Pa.

BH420 Fletcher, Stevenson W. "The Expansion of the Agricultural Frontier." *Pa. Hist.*, vol. 18, no. 2 (1951), 119–29. Roles of the Germans and Scotch-Irish in the development of early Pennsylvania agriculture.

BH421 Fletcher, Stevenson W. *Pennsylvania Agriculture and Country Life, 1640–1840*. Harrisburg: Pa. Hist. and Museum Commission, 1950. 605p. Rev. by W. T. Utter, *Ohio State Archaeological and Hist. Quar.*, vol. 62, no. 1 (1953), 87–89; P. A. Barba, "'S Pennsylfawnisch Deitsch Eck," Allentown *Morning Call*, 19 January 1952.

BH422 Fletcher, Stevenson W. *Pennsylvania Agriculture and Country Life 1840–1940*. Harrisburg: Pa. Hist. and Museum Commission, 1955. 619p.

BH423 Gagliardo, John G. "Germans and Agriculture in Colonial Pennsylvania." *Pa. Mag. of Hist. and Biography*, vol. 83, no. 2 (1959), 192–218.

BH424 Gehret, Ellen J., and Alan G. Keyser. "Flax Processing in Pennsylvania: From Seed to Fiber." *Pa. Folklife*, vol. 22, no. 1 (1972), 10–34.

BH425 Geist, George W. "The Oldest Mine in Pennsylvania." *Amer.-German Rev.*, vol. 8, no. 2 (1941), 28, 29.

BH426 Gemmell, Alfred. "The Charcoal Iron Industry in the Perkiomen Valley." *Bull. of the Hist. Soc. of Montgomery Co.*, vol. 6, no. 3 (1948), 186–258.

BH427 Hollenbach, Raymond E. "Die Bittner's Corner Miehl." "'S Pennsylfawnisch Deitsch Eck," Allentown *Morning Call*, 30 August; 6 September 1947. Records kept by the owner of an historic mill.

BH428 Hollenbach, Raymond E. "Gibs un Glee." "'S Pennsylfawnisch Deitsch Eck," Allentown *Morning Call*, 25 June; 2 July 1949. Early Pennsylvania farming.

BH429 Hollenbach, Raymond E. "The Pennsylvania Germans and Grape Culture." "'S Pennsylfawnisch Deitsch Eck," Allentown *Morning Call*, 3, 10, 17 February 1951.

BH430 Hollenbach, Raymond E. "Sheep and Wool on Local Farms in Bygone Days." "'S Pennsylfawnisch Deitsch Eck," Allentown *Morning Call*, 29 February 1964.

BH431 Johnson, Warren A., Victor Stoltzfus, and Peter Craumer. "Energy Conservation in Amish Agriculture." *Science*, vol. 198 (1977), 373–78.

BH432 Kollmorgen, Walter M. *The Culture of a Contemporary Rural Community; the Old Order Amish of Lancaster County, Pennsylvania*. U.S. Bureau of Agricultural Economics, Rural Life Studies, No. 4. Washington, D.C., 1942. 105p.

BH433 Kollmorgen, Walter M. "The Pennsylvania German Farmer." In: *The Pennsylvania Germans*. Ed. Ralph Wood. Princeton, N.J.: Princeton Univ. Pr., 1942, p.29–55.

BH434 Lemon, James T. "The Agricultural Practices of National Groups in Eighteenth-Century Southeastern Pennsylvania." *Geographical Rev.*, vol. 56, no. 4 (October 1966), 467–96.

BH435 Long, Amos. *The Pennsylvania German Family Farm: A Regional Architectural and Folk Cultural Study of an American Agricultural Community*. Publs. of the Pennsylvania German Soc., No. 4. Breinigsville, Pa., 1972. 518p. Rev. by J. T. Lemon, *Agricultural Hist.*, vol. 48 (1974), 238; W. M. Kollmorgen, *Annals of the Assoc. of Amer. Geographers*, vol. 64 (1974), 578–79.

BH436 Lord, Arthur C. "Donegal Mills: A Case Study in Historical Geography." *Jour. of the Lancaster Co. Hist. Soc.*, vol. 81 (1977), 117–37. Pennsylvania-German owners.

BH437 Lord, Arthur C. "The Pre-Revolutionary Agriculture of Lancaster County, Pennsylvania." *Jour. of the Lancaster Co. Hist. Soc.*, vol. 79 (1975), 23–42.

BH438 Myers, Richmond E. "Eighteenth Century Industrial Bethlehem." "'S Pennsylfawnisch Deitsch Eck," Allentown *Morning Call*, 20 January, 1964, Repr. from the *Procs. of the Pa. Acad. of Science*, vol. 37 (1963).

BH439 Rice, William S. "Mount Hope Furnace." *Amer.-German Rev.*, vol. 17, no. 5 (1951), 28–29. The Grubb family were the first to build blast furnaces in Lancaster Co.

BH440 Rosenberger, Homer Tope. "The Agricultural Revolution, 1891–1965, and Its Effect Upon the Pennsylvania Germans." In: *The Pennsylvania Germans, 1891–1965 (Frequently Known as the "Pennsylvania Dutch")*, by H. T. Rosenberger. 75th Anniversary Vol. of the Pa. German Society. Lancaster: Pa. German Soc., 1966, p.329–59.

BH441 Schultz, George W. "Colebrookdale—Mother of Pennsylvania's Iron Industry." *Hist. Rev. of Berks Co.*, vol. 10, no. 1 (1944), 13–15. The first furnace in Pennsylvania erected by Thomas Rutter in 1720.

BH442 Summar, Donald J. "A History of the Kreider Machine Company." *Jour. of the Lancaster Co. Hist. Soc.*, vol. 76 (1972).

BH443 Talbot, Elizabeth P. "The Philadelphia Furniture Industry 1850–1880." Diss., Pennsylvania, 1980. 331p.

BH444 Vadasz, Thomas P. "The History of an Industrial Community: Bethlehem, Pennsylvania, 1741–1920." Diss., William and Mary College, 1975.

BH445 Weiser, Charles. "Lehigh County Agricultural Society, 1852–1976." *Procs., Lehigh Co. Hist. Soc.*, vol. 31 (1976), 117–38.

BH446 Wittlinger, Carlton O. "The Small Arms Industry of Lancaster County 1710–1840." *Pa. Hist.*, vol. 24 (1957), 121–36.

BH447 Yates, W. Ross. "Discovery of the Process for Making Anthracite Iron." *Pa. Mag. of Hist. and Biography*, vol. 98, no. 2 (April 1974), 206–23. The development of a hot blast furnace "upon a principle said to be in use in Germany" by Henry Jordan & Co. Based on experiments by Frederck W. Geissenhainer, emigrant to the U.S. in 1793, who smelted and refined iron in eastern Pennsylvania until 1833. G. served as pastor of the (Lutheran) Old Swamp Church in New York City.

The Press and the Schools

See also Christopher Saur *under* Section IB: Colonial Era.

BH448 Barba, Preston A. "The First Printer in the Lehigh Valley." "'S Pennsylfawnisch Deitsch Eck," Allentown *Morning Call*, 18 January 1958. On Johann Brandmiller, a Moravian preacher and printer.

BH449 Bell, Whitfield J., Jr. "Benjamin Franklin and the German Charity Schools." *Procs., Amer. Philosophical Soc.*, vol. 99 (1955), 381–87.

BH450 Bixler, Miriam E. "Ellen A. Brubaker, Pioneer Free Kindergartner." *Jour. of the Lancaster Co. Hist. Soc.*, vol. 71, no. 3 (1967), 165–75.

BH451 Boyer, Melville J. "Teaching in Lehigh County, 1817-1841." *Procs., Lehigh Co. Hist. Soc.*, vol. 29 (1972), 63–79.

BH452 Bridenbaugh, Carl. "The Press and the Book in Eighteenth Century Philadelphia." *Pa. Mag. of Hist. and Biography*, vol. 65, no. 1 (1941), 1–30.

BH453 Brown, H. Glenn. *A Directory of the Book-Arts and Book Trade in Philadelphia to 1820.* New York: N.Y. Public Library, 1950. 129p. Rev. by R. P. Bristol, *Md. Hist. Mag.*, vol. 46 (1951), 305.

BH454 Dwyer, John A. "Some Factors Influencing Public Opinion on Free Schools in Pennsylvania, 1800-1835." Diss., Temple Univ., 1956.

BH455 Finckh, Alice H. "Lankenau School Sixty Years." *Amer.-German Rev.*, vol. 16, no. 4 (1950), 9–11. A Philadelphia girls' school.

BH456 Ford, Thomas H. "The Reading Public Schools and the War Effort." *Hist. Rev. of Berks Co.*, vol. 9 (1944), 102–05.

BH457 Freidel, Frank B. "A Plan for Modern Education in Early Philadelphia." *Pa. Hist.*, vol. 14 (1947), 175–84. Plans drawn up by Francis Lieber for Girard College.

BH458 Goodell, Robert H. "John L. Boswell and 'The Columbia Spy'." *Procs., Lancaster Co. Hist. Soc.*, vol. 47 (1943), 35–43. Mentions some ventures of the Pennsylvania Germans in publishing in the English language.

BH459 Hamilton, Milton W. "The *Reading Adler*, 1796–1913." *Hist. Rev. of Berks Co.*, vol. 9 (1944), 46–50.

BH460 Hamilton, Milton W. "A Veteran Printing Press." *Hist. Rev. of Berks Co.*, vol. 7 (1941–1942), 85–86.

BH461 Hamilton, Milton W. "World War II and Higher Education in Berks County." *Hist. Rev. of Berks Co.*, vol. 9 (1944), 106–08.

BH462 Harbold, P. M. "Schools and Education in the Borough of Lancaster." *Procs., Lancaster Co. Hist. Soc.*, vol. 46 (1942), 1–44. German elementary schools, 1736–1755, and their teachers.

BH463 Helffrich, William A. "Catechetical Instruction in 1841." Trans. by David B. Kaufman. "'S Pennsylfawnisch Deitsch Eck," Allentown *Morning Call*, 12 August; 2 December, 1967. Excerpted from the *Lebensbild aus dem Pennsylvanisch-Deutschen Predigerstand*... (Allentown, 1906).

BH464 Hess, Ernest M. "A Study of the Influence of Mennonite Schools on Their Students in the Lancaster Conference of the Mennonite Church." Diss., Ohio State Univ., 1975.

BH465 Hocker, Edward W. *The Sower Printing House of Colonial Times*. Norristown: Pa. German Soc., 1948.

BH466 Hollenbach, Raymond E. "The Early Schools of Heidelberg Township." "'S Pennsylfawnisch Deitsch Eck," Allentown *Morning Call*, 14, 21, 28 May; 4, 11, 18 June, 1960. Church schools and free schools in a German community.

BH467 Hommel, Rudolf. "The First Printer in Allentown, Pa." "'S Pennsylfawnisch Deitsch Eck," Allentown *Morning Call*, 26 May 1945.

BH468 Jones, Alfred S. "Old Time School Teachers." *Hist. Rev. of Berks Co.*, vol. 45 (1980), 136–43, 157–60.

BH469 Kaufman, David B. "The Inception of the Public School System." "'S Pennsylfawnisch Deitsch Eck," Allentown *Morning Call*, 1 June 1968.

BH470 Kemp, A. F. "Berks County Schools in World War II." *Hist. Rev. of Berks Co.*, vol. 9 (1944), 99–101.

BH471 Kiefer, Monica. "Early American Childhood in the Middle Atlantic Area." *Pa. Mag. of*

The Press and the Schools (cont.)

Hist. and Biography, vol. 68, no. 1 (1944), 3–37. Some references to Pennsylvania-German children's books.

BH472 Klinefelter, Walter. "The ABC Books of the Pennsylvania Germans." *Publs., Pa. Ger. Folklore Soc.*, vol. 7 (1973), 1–104. Bibliography, p. 79–104.

BH473 Klinefelter, Walter. "Solomon Meyer, Printer and Publisher." *Der Reggeboge*, vol. 15, nos. 3–4 (July–October 1981), 1–19. In York, Pa., 1777-ca. 1800.

BH474 Kloss, Heinz. "James C. Lins, Political Columnist." "'S Pennsylfawnisch Deitsch Eck," Allentown *Morning Call*, 25 August 1951; 13 November 1965. Born in 1860, Lins conducted a dialect column in Reading.

BH475 Loth, Paul Edward. "A Study of Certain Christian Elementary Day Schools Situated in Metropolitan Philadelphia." Diss., Temple Univ., 1960.

BH476 McPherson, Donald S. "The Fight Against Free Schools in Pennsylvania: Popular Opposition to the Common School System, 1834–1874." Diss., Pittsburgh, 1977.

BH477 McMullen, Haynes. "The Founding of Social Libraries in Pennsylvania." *Pa. Hist.*, vol. 32 (April 1965), 130–152.

BH478 Martin, John D., ed. *Christopher Dock: Pioneer Christian Schoolmaster on the Skippack*. Harrisonburg, Va.: Christian Light Publs., 1971.

BH479 Miller, C. William. *Benjamin Franklin's Philadelphia Printing, 1728–1766: A Descriptive Bibliography*. Philadelphia: Amer. Philosophical Soc., 1974. Rev. by Horst Dippel, *Amerikastudien*, vol. 23 (1978), 347–49.

BH480 Minor, William Penn. "The Progress of Printing in Luzerne County." *Procs. and Collections of the Wyoming Hist. and Genealogical Soc.*, vol. 6 (1901), 106–12.

BH481 Myers, Charles Bennett. "Public Secondary Schools in Pennsylvania during the American Revolutionary Era, 1760–1800." Diss., Geo. Peabody Coll. for Teachers, 1968. 281p. Incl. the Philadelphia Academy, Germantown Academy, Friends public schools, Bethlehem Seminary for Young Ladies and Nazareth Hall.

BH482 Nolan, J. Bennett. *Newspapers of Berks County, Pennsylvania: 1789–1900*. Reading: Hist. Soc. of Berks Co., 1951.

BH483 "Pennsylvania Ethnic Newspapers: An Historical Bibliography." *Pa. Ethnic Studies Newsletter*, vol. 2, no. 2 (1976–1977), 2–3.

BH484 Reger, Willy L. "The Pilger Publishing House." *Hist. Rev. of Berks Co.*, vol. 7 (1941–1942), 78–80.

BH485 Reichmann, Felix. "Christopher Sower Exhibition." *Amer.-German Rev.*, vol. 10, no. 3 (February 1944), 8–10, 29.

BH486 Reichmann, Felix. *Christopher Sower, Sr., 1694–1758, Printer in Germantown: An Annotated Bibliography*. Philadelphia: Carl Schurz Memorial Foundation, 1943.

BH487 Robacker, Earl F. "Books Not for Burning." *Pa. Folklife*, vol. 9, no. 1 (Winter 1957/58), 44–52. Suggestions to the collector of Pennsylvania German printed materials.

BH488 Roy, Donald E. "Selected Pittsburgh Imprints, 1807–1860, in the Library of the Historical Society of Western Pennsylvania." *Western Pa. Hist. Mag.*, vol. 44 (1961), 175–97. Incl. some German imprints.

BH489 Schach, Paul. "Schuylkill Seminary in Reading, 1881–1886." *Hist. Rev. of Berks Co.*, vol. 10 (1945), 110–13.

BH490 Schnabel, Susan J. "Freeland Seminary." *Bull., Hist. Soc. of Montgomery Co.*, vol. 14 (1964), 81–120. A boys' preparatory school.

BH491 Shoemaker, Alfred L. "Adams County Printers." *The Pa. Dutchman*, vol. 4, no. 10 (1953), 11–13.

BH492 Shoemaker, Alfred L. "Biographical Sketches of Dauphin County Publishers." *The Pa. Dutchman*, vol. 3, no. 21 (April 1952), 7–8.

BH493 Shoemaker, Alfred L. "Biographical Sketches of Lebanon County Publishers." *The Pa. Dutchman*, vol. 3, no. 20 (15 March 1952), 7.

BH494 Shoemaker, Alfred L. "Biographies of Hanover Publishers." *The Pa. Dutchman*, vol. 4, no. 22 (15 February 1953), 15.

BH495 Shoemaker, Alfred L. "Central Pennsylvania Newspapers." *The Pa. Dutchman*, vol. 5 (1 March 1954), 14.

BH496 Shoemaker, Alfred L. "A Check List of Imprints of the German Press of Lehigh County, Pennsylvania, 1807–1900, with Biographies of the Printers." *Procs., Lehigh Co. Hist. Soc.*, vol. 16 (1947), 1–240.

BH497 Shoemaker, Alfred L. "A Check List of Imprints of the German Press of Northampton County, Pennsylvania, 1766–1905, with Biographies of the Printers." *Publs., Northampton Co. Hist. and Genealogical Soc.*, vol. 4. Easton, Pa., 1943. 162p. Rev. by P. A. Barba, "'S Pennsylfawnisch Deitsch Eck," Allentown *Morning Call*, 18 March 1944.

BH498 Shoemaker, Alfred L. "The Ephrata Printers." *The Pa. Dutchman*, vol. 4, no. 9 (January 1953), 11–13.

BH499 Shoemaker, Alfred L. "German Newspapers of Central Pennsylvania." *The Pa. Dutchman*, vol. 5 (1954), no. 12, 10f.; no. 13, 4. Checklist covering the period 1821–1875.

BH500 Shoemaker, Alfred L. "German Newspapers of the Coal Regions." *The Pa. Dutchman*, vol. 5, no. 14 (March 1954), 10–11. For the period 1826–1875.

BH501 Shoemaker, Alfred L. "Hanover Newspapers." *The Pa. Dutchman*, vol. 4, no. 12 (1953), p. 15; "Union County German Newspapers." *Ibid.*, vol. 4, no. 13 (1953), 12, 14; "Westmoreland County German Newspapers." *Ibid.*, vol. 4, no. 11 (1953), 15; "York County Checklist." *Ibid.*, vol. 5, no. 11 (1954), 10.

BH502 Stine, Clyde S. "The Pennsylvania Germans and the School." In: *The Pennsylvania Germans*. Ed. Ralph Wood. Princeton: Princeton Univ. Pr., 1942, p.105–27.

BH503 Studer, Gerald C. *Frederick Goeb, Master Printer*. Somerset, Pa.: Goeb Bible Sesquicentennial, 1963. 32p.

BH504 Studer, Gerald C. "Master Printer Goeb: The Goeb Bible." *Jour. of the Alleghenies*, vol. 1, no. 2 (Summer 1963), 6–10. Friedrich Goeb (1782–1829) arrived from Germany in 1804 and became a printer-publisher in Chambersburg and Somerset.

BH505 Swope, E. Pierce. "Der Libanoner Morgenstern." "'S Pennsylfawnisch Deitsch Eck," Allentown *Morning Call*, 13 June 1964. Samplings of materials printed 1818–1820.

BH506 Thompson, D. W. "Oldest American Printing Press." *The Pa. Dutchman*, vol. 6, no. 3 (1954), 28–33. Evidence to show that the Goodman press is the oldest of existing Ephrata presses.

BH507 Waldenrath, Alexander. "Rural Pennsylvania German Newspress in the 18th Century." *German-Amer. Studies*, vol. 9 (Spring 1975), 33–42.

BH508 Waldenrath, Alexander, and Julius M. Herz. "The 'Friedens-Bote': A Major German Language Newspaper of the Lehigh Valley." *Procs., Lehigh Co. Hist. Soc.*, vol. 30 (1974), 72–80. Published ca. 1812 to 1932.

BH509 Wood, Ralph. "Journalism among the Pennsylvania Germans." In: *The Pennsylvania Germans*. Princeton: Princeton Univ. Pr., 1942, p.131–64.

BI
Pennsylvania Local History

Berks County

BI1 Albright, Raymond W. "Daniel Bertolet of Oley." *Hist. Rev. of Berks Co.*, vol. 10, no. 3 (1945), 74–79.

BI2 Albright, Raymond W. *Two Centuries of Reading, Pennsylvania, 1748–1948*. Reading: n.p., 1948.

BI3 Arnold, Robert A. "The Krauss Organ and Church of the Most Blessed Sacrament." *Hist. Rev. of Berks Co.*, vol. 33 (Summer 1968), 98–101. On the organ of the German Roman Catholic Church in Bally, built in the 1790's.

BI4 Barba, Preston A. "Carl A. Bruckman—Printer and Publisher." *Hist. Rev. of Berks Co.*, vol. 9, no. 3 (1944), 81–83.

BI5 Barba, Preston A., trans. "Hard Times in Berks County, An Historical Narrative by L. A. Wolleneber; Conrad Weiser's Home." "'S Pennsylfawnisch Deitsch Eck," Allentown *Morning Call*, 27 January 1945.

BI6 Birch, Edith W. "The Benevolent Society—Reading's Oldest Charity." *Hist. Rev. of Berks Co.*, vol. 10, no. 1 (1944), 7–12.

BI7 Blatt, Milton K. and Luella E. Blatt. *Salem (Belleman's) Church, Centre Township, Berks Co., Pennsylvania.* ... N.p.: n.p., 1976.

BI8 Boyer, Geoffrey F. "The Berks Voters—1850–1966." *Hist. Rev. of Berks Co.*, vol. 32 (Autumn 1967), 120–23, 138–40. On the factors which keep Berks Co. generally in the Democratic column.

BI9 Braun, Fritz. "Tulpehocken in Pennsylvanien vor 250 Jahren von Deutschen besiedelt." *Mitteilungen zur Wanderungsgeschichte der Pfälzer*, Jahrgang 1973/1, Band 7, Heft 10, 357; 1973/2, Heft 11, 385; 1973/3, Heft 12, 425.

BI10 Burkholder, Albert N. "Bully Lyon—Detective and Factotum." *Hist. Rev. of Berks Co.*, vol. 9 (1943–1944), 6–10. Incl. material on Philip Huber, of the Knights of the Golden Circle, 1863.

BI11 Burnett, Robert B. "A Portrait of the Iron Industry." *Hist. Rev. of Berks Co.*, vol. 45 (1980), 127–29, 131, 154–56. On Charming Forge, Pa.

BI12 Butz, Charles Allaban. "The Longswamp Church." "'S Pennsylfawnisch Deitsch Eck," Allentown *Morning Call*, 17 April 1943.

BI13 *Church Book and Protocol of the Evangelical Lutheran Congregation Down at the Tulpehocken near Northkill*. Trans. by J. W. Early. N.p.: n.p., 1899; 1907.

BI14 Claussen, W. E. "The Revolutionary War—in Lower Berks." *Hist. Rev. of Berks Co.*, vol. 34, no. 2 (Spring 1969), 58–59, 70–73.

BI15 Clemens, Gurney W. "The Berks County Historical Society." *Publs., Pa. Ger. Folklore Soc.*, vol. 7 (1942), 55–80.

BI16 Clemens, Gurney W. "Frederick Fox—Chairmaker." *Hist. Rev. of Berks Co.*, vol. 9 (1943–1944), 14–15. On the MS. book of Frederick Fox, chairmaker in Reading, 1841–1847.

BI17 Clemens, Gurney W. "Nagle's Company First at Cambridge." *Hist. Rev. of Berks Co.*, vol. 7 (1941–1942), 107–110.

BI18 Cook, Ross K. "Five Adam Koch's (sic)—Berks County Revolutionary Soldiers." *Hist. Rev. of Berks Co.*, vol. 8 (1942–1943), 115–17.

BI19 Craigie, Carter W. "Folk Festival Geisinger." *Pa. Folklife*, vol. 18, no. 4 (Summer 1969). Howard Geisinger founded the Kempton Farm Museum in Berks County.

BI20 Dech, Elmer A. "The North Heidelberg Church [Berks Co.]." *Hist. Rev. of Berks Co.*, vol. 34, no. 3 (Summer 1969), 85–86, 101–104. History of a 225-year-old Moravian church; the present building dates from 1846.

BI21 DeChant, Alliene S. *Down Oley Way.* Kutztown: Kutztown Publ. Co., 1953. Rev. L. J. Livingood, *Hist. Rev. of Berks Co.*, vol. 19, no. 1 (1953), 29. Personalities, occupations and places in the Oley Valley of Berks County.

BI22 Dieffenbach, Ray J. *Altalaha Lutheran Church Baptisms, November 1757–November 1851.* Rehrersburg: n.p., 1978. Records from Rehrersburg, Tulpehocken Township, Berks County.

BI23 Dieffenbach, Victor C. "Peddlers I Remember." *Pa. Folklife*, vol. 14, no. 1 (1964), 38–48. Boyhood reminiscences of an octogenarian resident of Berks County.

BI24 Dundore, M. Walter. "A Population Study of the Pennsylvania Germans in Berks and Neighboring Counties." *Hist. Rev. of Berks Co.*, vol. 28, no. 4 (1963), 113–17.

BI25 Early, J. W. *Lutheran Ministers of Berks County . . . .* Reading: n.p., 1902.

BI26 Ford, Raymond West. "Germans and Other Foreign Stock: Their Part in the Evolution of Reading, Pennsylvania." Diss., Pennsylvania, 1963.

BI27 Frankhouser, Earle M. "The Big Spring Farm." *Hist. Rev. of Berks Co.*, vol. 31, no. 2 (Spring 1966), 48, 50, 62–63. On the settlement of Palatines from New York in 1723 at what is now Big Spring Farm.

BI28 Fryer, Benjamin A. "Battalion Days in Berks." *Hist. Rev. of Berks Co.*, vol. 7 (1941–1942), 103–06. Battalion days, 1780's to the 1870's. German surnames.

BI29 Fryer, Benjamin A. "Hotels on Penn Street." *Hist. Rev. of Berks Co.*, vol. 8 (1942–1943), 12–13. German-American hostelries.

BI30 Gehret, Bruce K. "Early Baseball in Reading." *Hist. Rev. of Berks Co.*, vol. 8 (1942–1943), 105–110. Pennsylvania Germans active in organization and participation in the sport.

BI31 Gilbert, Russell W. "Pennsylvania German Wills in Berks County." *Hist. Rev. of Berks Co.*, vol. 21, no. 1 (1955), 8–12.

BI32 Glase, Peter, and William A. Glase. Papers and business records, 1852–1885. In Eleutherian Mills Hist. Library, Geeenville, Del. (MS 73-535). Farmers and merchants of Oley township; incl. daybooks and ledgers.

BI33 Goldstein, Franklin. "The People, Yes—Berks County in World War I." *Hist. Rev. of Berks Co.*, vol. 22, no. 2 (1957), 42–47, 59–66. On the behavior and attitude of Pennsylvania Germans in Berks toward the Germans in World War I.

BI34 Graeff, Arthur D. "Building Canals in Berks." *Hist. Rev. of Berks Co.*, vol. 33 (1968), 78–81; 130–31; 140–44; vol. 34 (1968–1969), 20–23, 28–29. From the plans of David Rittenhouse in the 1790's to the sale of the properties to the Reading Railroad in the 1930's.

BI35 Graeff, Arthur D. "Merchandise in 1752." "'S Pennsylfawnisch Deitsch Eck," Allentown *Morning Call*, 23 November 1940. Prices paid for staples in Berks County.

BI36 Graeff, Arthur D. "Two Hundred Years of Worship, 1744–1944." "'S Pennsylfawnisch Deitsch Eck," Allentown *Morning Call*, 23 September 1944. History of Union Church of North Heidelberg, Berks County.

BI37 Graeff, Marie E. *Two Hundred Fifty Years: Tulpehocken 1723–1973 as Told in Articles Which Appeared in the Historical Review of Berks County.* Womelsdorf: Tulpehocken Settlement Hist. Soc., 1973.

BI38 Hamilton, Milton W. "Morton L. Montgomery—Historian of Berks." *Hist. Rev. of Berks Co.*, vol. 8 (1942–1943), 99–104. Incl. a bibliography of Montgomery's works.

BI39 Hellstrom, O. Henry. "The Brewing Industry in Reading, Until 1880." *Hist. Rev. of Berks Co.*, vol. 7 (1941–1942), 39–43. Frederick Lauer and other brewers.

BI40 *A Historical Booklet Published in Connection with the 200th Anniversary of Christ Lutheran Church at Stouchsburg, Berks Co., Pennsylvania.* N.p.: n.p., 1943.

BI41 *History of the Reading Hospital, 1867–1942.* Reading: Eagle Pr., 1942. 287p. Rev. M.D.I., *Hist. Rev. of Berks Co.*, vol. 8 (1942–43), 88.

BI42 Hoch, Daniel K. "Journey to Weiser Park." *Hist. Rev. of Berks Co.*, vol. 15, no. 4 (1949), 238–41. Description of the Conrad Weiser home and Memorial Park at Womelsdorf.

BI43 Hopkins, Phoebe Bertolet. "The DeTurk House of Oley." *Hist. Rev. of Berks Co.*, vol. 31, no. 2 (Spring, 1966), 56–58, 69–72. Isaac DeTurk,

Berks County *(cont.)*

desc. of a French Huguenot, came to Pennsylvania in 1708. His progeny joined Zinzendorf and the Moravians.

BI44 Hostetter, William D. "Horse-Car Railways in Reading." *Hist. Rev. of Berks Co.*, vol. 8 (1942–1943), 2–11.

BI45 Huston, Ralph D. "The Telephone Comes to Berks County." *Hist. Rev. of Berks Co.*, vol. 8 (1942–1943), 14–18. First line built by Henry W. Spang.

BI46 Impink, Mary Dives. "The Walking Tour of Downtown Reading." *Hist. Rev. of Berks Co.*, vol. 31, no. 4 (Autumn 1966), 123–25, 143. Reminiscences of Conrad Weiser and the Palatines; German churches.

BI47 "In Memoriam David Fulmer Hottenstein, M.D. 1906–1980. D. February 2, 1980." *Der Reggeboge*, vol. 14, no. 2 (April 1980), 19. Physician of Kutztown.

BI48 Jentsch, Theodore W. "Kutztown's Plain People." *Pa. Folklife*, vol. 27 (1978) Supplement, 8–11.

BI49 John Conrad Weiser Family Association. *Tulpehocken Settlement Family Festival, 1972–1973*. N.p.: n.p., ca. 1973. Program of events with an historical sketch of the Tulpehocken Creek area, Lebanon and Berks counties, Pa.

BI50 Jones, Alfred S. "Old-Time School Teachers." *Hist. Rev. of Berks Co.*, vol. 45 (1980), 136–43, 157–60. See also *Berks Co. Hist. Soc. Annals*, vol. 1, 1–12.

BI51 Jones, George M. "Memorials of Historic Interest in Charles Evans Cemetery." *Hist. Rev. of Berks Co.*, vol. 7 (1941–1942), 110–12. Military memorials, incl. German surnames.

BI52 Jones, George M. "Thirty-Sixth Pilgrimage (of the Historical Society of Berks County)." *Hist. Rev. of Berks Co.*, vol. 7 (1941–1942), 54–55. Mention of the Hershey Museum, Zion Lutheran Church at Manheim, Landis Valley Museum, and "Fort Zeller."

BI53 Kaufman, David B. "More About Allemaengel *Addenda*." "'S Pennsylfawnisch Deitsch Eck," Allentown *Morning Call*, 21, 28 January, 4 February 1967. History of a locality in Berks County.

BI54 Kaufman, David B. "Some Historical Facts of the Oley Valley in Berks County." "'S Pennsylfawnisch Deitsch Eck," Allentown *Morning Call*, 20, 27 April, 1963.

BI55 Kessler, Carol. "Ten Tulpehocken Inventories: What Do They Reveal about a Pennsylvania German Community?" *Pa. Folklife*, vol. 23, no. 2 (1973), 16–30.

BI56 Kiebach, Raymond E. "The Neversink Union Sunday School." *Hist. Rev. of Berks Co.*, vol. 45 (1979), 7, 36–38.

BI57 Kinsey, Ralph Wilhelm. "The Wilhelms: Reading Industrialists." *Hist. Rev. of Berks Co.*, vol. 31, no. 2 (1965), 42–47.

BI58 Kistler, John L. *Baptismal Records of Jerusalem Lutheran and Reformed Church, Berks County, Pennsylvania*. Washington: n.p., 1959.

BI59 Kistler, John L. *The History of Jerusalem "Allemaengel" Church . . . 1747–1947*. N.p.: n.p., 1947.

BI60 Kline, Pearl B., and Janice C. De Long. *Bernville, Pennsylvania, 1851–1976*. Bernville: Bicentennial Committee, 1976. 148p.

BI61 Klingaman, Arthur K. "History of Albany Township, Berks County." *Der Reggeboge*, vol. 8, nos. 3–4 (1974), 1–33.

BI62 Knudsen, Gunnar. *Two Living Centuries: The Story of Trinity Lutheran Church, Reading.* . . . N.p.: n.p., 1952. See also his "Trinity Lutheran Church—the First Two Hundred Years." *Hist. Rev. of Berks Co.*, vol. 16, no. 3 (1951), 66–72, 93. History of a German-English church in Reading.

BI63 Kuby, Alfred H. "A Pastor for the Reformed Church at Tulpehocken, 1742." Trans. by Frederick S. Weiser. *Der Reggeboge*, vol. 7, nos. 3–4 (1973), 2–4.

BI64 Logan, Helen Kille. "Annals of Strausstown." *Hist. Rev. of Berks Co.*, vol. 31, no. 1 (1966), 71–78, 88–90.

BI65 Marisseau, Merrill R. *A History of Zion's (Spies) Evangelical and Reformed Church, 1757–1960*. N.p.: n.p., 1960. In Alsace Township, Berks Co.

BI66 Mast, Harry C. "Bicycling in Berks." *Hist. Rev. of Berks Co.*, vol. 8 (1942–1943), 19–21.

BI67 Mast, Harry C. "Reading's First Stenographers." *Hist. Rev. of Berks Co.*, vol. 7 (1941–1942) 44–46.

BI68 Mast, Harry C. "The Tinkers of Berks County." *Hist. Rev. of Berks Co.*, vol. 9, no. 3 (1944), 78–80.

BI69 Mercer, Albert M., and Daniel G. Hartman. "1866—Boyertown—1966." *Hist. Rev. of Berks Co.* vol. 31, no. 3 (1966), 78–84, 99–107. A sketch of local history from the Palatinate to centennial; economic and social developments.

BI70 Miller, H. Robert. "Plumpton Manor." *Hist. Rev. of Berks Co.*, vol. 9, no. 3 (1944), 70–72. The first grant of land in Berks Co. given in 1722 to Letitia, daughter of William Penn.

BI71 Mohn, Viola Kohl. *Shadows of the Rhine Along the Tulpehocken. [Book One]*. Ed. Henry C. Westenberger. Lebanon, Pa.: Lebanon Co. Hist. Soc., 1970, ca. 1972. p. 133–91. Also as: *Hist. Papers and Addrs., Lebanon Co. Hist. Soc.*, vol. 14, no. 5.

BI72 Mohn, Viola Kohl. "Shadows of the Rhine along the Tulpehocken, Book 2." *Papers and Addrs., Lebanon Co. Hist. Soc.*, vol. 14 (1972), 237–336.

BI73 Nelson, Vernon H. "The Moravian Contribution to the Tulpehocken Region." *Der Reggeboge*, vol. 7, no. 2 (1973), 3–16.

BI74 "A New Mournful Song Containing the History of Susanna Cox, Who Was Hanged in Reading for Infanticide in the Year 1809, from the German." "'S Pennsylfawnisch Deitsch Eck," Allentown *Morning Call*, 22 July 1944. Printed here in English and in German.

BI75 Nolan, J. Bennett. "Daniel Boone's Pennsylvania Birthplace." *Amer.-German Rev.*, vol. 9, no. 6 (August 1943), 24–27. Boone was born 2 November 1734 (N.S.) on a farm in Berks Co.

BI76 Nolan, J. Bennett. "Reading's First Bookstore." *Hist. Rev. of Berks Co.*, vol. 7, no. 1 (1941), 22–24.

BI77 Nolan, J. Bennett. "Thomas Penn and the Town of Reading." *Hist. Rev. of Berks Co.*, vol. 10, no. 1 (1944), 6.

BI78 "Old Womelsdorf Organ." *Berks and Schuylkill Journal* (Reading), 7 September 1872.

BI79 Palmer-Poroner, Bruno J. "The Establishment of Libraries in Reading, Pennsylvania." *Hist. Rev. of Berks Co.*, vol. 6 (1941), 99–106.

BI80 Palmer-Poroner, Bruno J. "The Library Movement in Reading, 1820–1860." *Hist. Rev. of Berks Co.*, vol. 7 (1941–1942), 70–74.

BI81 Rahn, Kathryn. "Lasting Memories." *Pa. Dutch News and Views*, vol. 3, no. 1 (1971), 11. On farm life in the vicinity of Womelsdorf.

BI82 Regner, Sidney L. "The Earliest Jews in Berks County." *Hist. Rev. of Berks Co.*, vol. 7 (1941–1942), 47–48. Settlement in Schaefferstown.

BI83 Riegel, Lewis Edgar. "Reminiscences of a Boyhood in Reading, 1883–1890." *Pa. Folklife*, vol. 16, no. 3 (Spring 1967), 2–19.

BI84 Riegel, Lewis Edgar. "Reminiscences of Centerport [Berks Co.] 1876–1885." *Pa. Folklife*, vol. 14 no. 2 (1964), 34–47.

BI85 Robacker, Earl F. "Dream in Dutchland." *N.Y. Folklore Quar.*, vol. 12 (1956), 287–90. Chat about the Dutch Village in Bethel, Berks Co., Pa.

BI86 Rockland, [Berks Co.,] Pennsylvania. *Christ (Mertz) Lutheran Church: A Commemorative Booklet*. N.p.: n.p., 1947.

BI87 Schach, Paul. "Facts and Fallacies About Berks County Dutch." *Hist. Rev. of Berks Co.*, vol. 10, no. 3 (1945), 80–82.

BI88 Scholl, C. R. "The Miller Six-Lever Padlock." *Hist. Rev. of Berks Co.*, vol. 10, no. 4 (1945), 117.

BI89 Shaner, Richard H. "Kutztown's Mennonites." *Pa. Folklife*, vol. 14, no. 4 (1965), 21–30. Incl. an "Index of Penn Valley Mennonite families, 1965."

BI90 Smith, Patricia E. "Our Early Drugs and Druggists." *Hist. Rev. of Berks Co.*, vol. 9 (1943–1944), 3–5.

BI91 Smythe, Thomas B. "Early Berks County Alumni of the University of Pennsylvania." *Hist. Rev. of Berks Co.*, vol. 6 (1941–1942), 81–84. Incl. John Peter Gabriel Muhlenberg, George Ege, Bodo Otto, Jr., John Diemer, Benjamin and Samuel Weiser.

BI92 Snyder, Charles Fischer. "The Tulpehocken Path." *Hist. Rev. of Berks Co.*, vol. 32 (Winter 1966–1967). Historical associations of this westward road from Womelsdorf to Sunbury.

BI93 Springer, Edna F. "Dutch Pinafore—Gilbert and Sullivan in Reading." *Hist. Rev. of Berks Co.*, vol. 9, no. 4 (1944), 112–17.

BI94 Stailey, Harry N. "Brecknock Township, Berks County, Pennsylvania: An Index of Early Landholders in Southern Berks County Reflects a Mennonite Community in the Mid-1700's." *Pa. Mennonite Heritage*, vol. 4, no. 1 (1981), 20–24.

BI95 Steinmetz, Mary Owen. "Early Reading Muster Rolls." *Hist. Rev. of Berks Co.*, vol. 7 (1941–1942), 113–14.

BI96 Steinmetz, Mary Owen. "Gottlob Jungmann." *Hist. Rev. of Berks Co.*, vol. 13 (January 1948), 50–51.

BI97 Steinmetz, Mary Owen. "Horse Thieves and Organizations for Their Detection." *Hist. Rev. of Berks Co.*, vol. 8 (1942–1943), 77–79.

BI98 Stetler, Henry Gruber. *Socialist Movement in Reading, Pennsylvania, 1896–1936. A Study in Social Changes.* Storrs, Conn.: n.p., 1943. Diss., Columbia, 1943. Bibliography, p.190–94.

BI99 Stoltzfus, Grant M. "Amish Backgrounds in Berks County." *Hist. Rev. of Berks Co.*, vol. 16, no. 2 (1951), 38–42.

BI100 Stoudt, John Joseph. "Was America's First Autobiography Written in Oley?" *Hist. Rev. of Berks Co.*, vol. 26, no. 3 (1961), 87. On the autobiography of Johann Frantz Regnier, *Das Geheimnis der Zinzendorfischen Sekte*.

BI101 Strunck, Amos. *Beamten von Berks Caunty für jedes Jahr von 1752–1860, Gleichfalls die Stimme der Caunty bey den Präsident und Gouvernors Wahlen.* Reading: Carl Kessler, 1859. 124p.

BI102 Stupp, Irene M. "Stouchburg's Past." *Hist. Rev. of Berks Co.*, vol. 31, no. 1 (Winter 1965–1966), 19–22, 32–33. A German community.

BI103 Styer, Amy. "The Bernhard Adam Cemetery." *Hist. Rev. of Berks Co.*, vol. 45 (1980), 56–59, 64–66, 68. Concerns the John Schwartz family. See also the *Pa. Ethnic Studies Newsletter*, vol. 2, no. 3 (January 1977), 2–3.

BI104 *Tulpehocken Church Records 1730–1800. Christ (Little Tulpehocken) Church and Altalaha Church, Rehrersburg.* Sources and Documents, The Pennsylvania German Society, no. 7. Breinigsville, Pa.: The Society, 1982.

BI105 *Two Hundredth Anniversary Historical Booklet. Salem Reformed Church Congregation of Spangsville....* N.p.: n.p., 1936. On Oley, Pa.

BI106 Wallace, Tony. "William Parsons and the Widow Finney's Town." *Hist. Rev. of Berks Co.*, vol. 8 (1942–1943), 38–41. Family strife as a result of a Moravian conversion.

BI107 Weiser, Frederick S. "European Origins of Some Early Members of Saint Joseph's (Hill) Lutheran Church." *Hist. Rev. of Berks Co.*, vol. 32 (1967), 52–54.

BI108 Weiser, Frederick S., and Vernon Nelson. "The Registers of Reed's Church (Zion and Saint John's Lutheran Church, Tulpehocken)." *Hist. Rev. of Berks Co.*, vol. 31, no. 1 (Winter 1965–1966), 14–18, 27. Marion Township, Berks Co.

BI109 Wetzel, Daniel J. "First Reformed Church: 1753–1953." *Hist. Rev. of Berks Co.*, vol. 19, no. 2 (1953), 46–50, 57–61. History of the oldest German Reformed Church in Reading, Pa.

BI110 Wetzel, Daniel Jacob. *Two Hundredth Anniversary History of the First Reformed Church...Reading....* N.p.: n.p., 1953.

BI111 Yoder, Donald. "Kutztown and America." *Pa. Folklife*, vol. 14, no. 4 (1965), 2–9. A sesquicentennial salute.

BI112 Yost, Ivy Kemp. "The Landis Store Story." *Pa. Folklife*, vol. 29, no. 2 (Winter 1979–1980), 50–55. Reminiscences about a Pennsylvania locality in Berks Co.

Central Region

BI113 Aaronsburg, Pa. *The Citizens of Aaronsburg and of Centre County, Pennsylvania Present the Issue of an Ideal; A Dramatic Ceremony Commemorating the Founding of Aaronsburg, Pennsylvania [by]* W. R. Gordon; Narrated by Cornel Wilde, Presented at Aaronsburg, Sunday, October 23, 1949 at 2:00 p.m. N.p.: n.p., 1949. 16p.

BI114 Albright S. C. *The Story of the Moravian Congregation at York [Pennsylvania]*. York: Maple Pr., ca. 1927. 243p.

BI115 *Amish Farm and Home Directory of Lancaster and Lebanon Districts, Pennsylvania*. Gordonville: comp. and distrib. by the Old Order Map Committee, 1965. Introd. by Joseph F. Beiler. Rev. *Hist. Rev. of Berks Co.*, vol. 32, no. 2 (Spring 1967), 70. A list of heads of households, churches, etc.

BI116 Barrick, Mac E. "Rural Economics in Central Pennsylvania 1850–1867." *Pa. Folklife*, vol. 22, no. 1 (Autumn 1972), 42–45. An account given in the 19th century by a Lutheran minister.

BI117 Baver, Russell S. "Scenes Along the S. and L." *Pa. Dutch News and Views*, vol. 3, no. 1 (1971), 5–8. Along the Schuylkill and Lehigh Railroad between Reading and Slatington.

BI118 Beaver, Irwin M. *History of the Grindstone Hill Reformed Charge*. Chambersburg, Pa.: J. G. Schaff's Sons, 1892. 53p. In Franklin Co.

BI119 Beers, Paul B. *Profiles from the Susquehanna Valley: Past and Present Vignettes of Its People, Times and Towns*. Harrisburg: Stackpole, 1973.

BI120 Boyer, D. S., and J. F. Wampole. *History of the Freeburg Lutheran Charge...* Freeburg: n.p., 1891. Chapman Township, Snyder Co.

BI121 Brumbach, John C. *History of Christ Reformed Church...* N.p.: n.p., 1947. Incl. history of the Conewago settlement, Germany Township, Adams Co. and its Reformed church.

BI122 Buffington, Albert F. "Seller Nixnutz," "'S Pennsylfawnisch Deitsch Eck," Allentown *Morning Call*, 22, 29 May, 5 June, 31 July, 14 August 1948. Broadcasting in German from Station KOK, Sunbury.

BI123 Carter, John H. "The Himmel Church." *Procs. and Addrs., Northumberland Co. Hist. Soc.*, (1936) 67–97. Himmel's Congreg., Washington Township, Northumberland County.

BI124 *The Church Book Belonging to the Evangelical Lutherans. Parish Registers of the Union Church of Concordia, Adams Co., Pa. 1824–1833 and of the Mount Joy Evangelical Lutheran Church 1851–1943*. Ed. and in part trans. by Frederick S. Weiser. Gettysburg: n.p., 1969. 160p.

BI125 Crist, Robert Grant. *Peace Church [Cumberland County, Hampden Township]*. Camp Hill: n.p., 1966.

BI126 Dunkelberger, George F. *The Story of Snyder County From Its Earliest Times...* Selinsgrove: Snyder Co. Hist. Soc., 1948. 982p. Rev. M. Rubincam, *National Genealogical Soc. Quar.*, vol. 38, no. 3 (1950), 93; H. T. Rosenberger, *Pa. Hist.*, vol. 16, no. 3 (1949), 249–50. P.249–71 deal with the dialect and characteristics of the Pennsylvania Germans.

BI127 Earnest, Mrs. Franklin M. "The Dreisbach Church." *Procs. and Addrs., Northumberland Co. Hist. Soc.*, vol. 11 (1939), 95–112. A church in Buffalo Valley, Dreisbach. E. Buffalo Township, Union County.

BI128 *Emmanuel Evangelical Lutheran Church, Penns Creek, Snyder Co., Pa. Parish Records, 1844–1882*. Trans. by Frederick S. Weiser. Biglerville, Pa.: n.p., 1975. 38p.

BI129 *The Evangelical Lutheran Church, Waynesboro, Franklin County, Pennsylvania: Parish Registers, 1818–1919*. Ed. Frederick S. Weiser. Gettysburg: n.p., 1970. 286p.

BI130 *First Evangelical Lutheran Church, Carlisle, Cumberland Co., Pennsylvania: Parish Registers, 1768–1923*. Ed. Frederick S. Weiser. Gettysburg: n.p., 1970. 706p.

BI131 *The First Record Book of Salem Evangelical Lutheran Church at Killinger, Dauphin Co., Pennsylvania, in the Lykens Valley, 1770–1859*. Trans. by the Rev. A. S. Leiby in 1947; ed. Frederick S. Weiser. Gettysburg: n.p., 1968. 102p.

BI132 Flower, Milton E., and Lenore E. Flower. *This is Carlisle: A History of a Pennsylvania Town.* Carlisle: n.p., 1944. 72p. Rev. by A. S. Schach, *Pa. Hist.*, vol. 12, no. 4 (1945), 328.

BI133 Focht, D. H. *Discourse Portraying the History of the Grindstone Hill Evangelical Lutheran Church in Franklin County, Pennsylvania, Delivered...December 25, 1854...* Gettysburg: n.p. 1855. 46p.

BI134 Freidinger, Mildred L. *200th Anniversary, 1753–1953, Grace Evangelical and Reformed Church...Shippensburg, Pennsylvania.* N.p.: n.p., 1953.

BI135 *Friedrich Heinrich Gelwicks—Shoemaker and Distiller—Accounts, 1760–1783, Manheim Township, York County, Pennsylvania.* Pa. German Soc. Sources and Documents Series, no. 4. Breinigsville: The Society, ca. 1979.

BI136 Gilbert, D. M., ed. *Centennial of Zion Lutheran Church, Harrisburg.* Harrisburg: Herr Publ. Co., 1896.

BI137 Gilbert, Russell W. "An All Pennsylvania-German Church Service." *Amer.-German Rev.*, vol. 22, no. 5 (1956), 15. Church services in the dialect at Botschaft Church, Snyder County, Pa.

BI138 Gilbert, Russell W. "Blooming Grove, the Dunker Settlement of Central Pennsylvania." *Pa. Hist.*, vol. 20, no. 1 (1953), 22–39. Rev. by P. A. Barba, "'S Pennsylfawnisch Deitsch Eck," Allentown *Morning Call*, 2 May 1953.

BI139 Gilbert, Russell W. "The Pennsylvania German Wills of Northumberland County." *Northumberland Co. Hist. Soc., Procs. and Addresses*, vol. 17 (1949), 123–53.

BI140 Gipe, Florence M. *A 200th Anniversary History of St. Luke's Lutheran Church.* N.p.: n.p., 1973. In York Co., Chanceford Township.

BI141 Glatfelter, Armand, ed. *Das Siebental Revisited: The People of Seven Valleys.* York, Pa.: Mehl Ad-Associates, 1981.

BI142 Glatfelter, Charles H. *A History of St. Jacob's (Stone) Church, Brodbecks, Pennsylvania.* N.p.: n.p., 1956. In York County.

BI143 [Goering, Jacob.] *Personal Record of Pastor Jacob Goering (1755–1807) and Records of Baptisms he Performed 1780–1789, in the Vicinity of York, Pennsylvania, and of Baptisms and Marriages, 1791–1792, in the Vicinity of Hagerstown, Maryland.* Gettysburg: n.p., 1971. 22p.

BI144 Grace, Alonzo G. "The Aaronsburg Story." *Amer.-German Rev.*, vol. 19, no. 6 (1953), 3, 40. On the village in Centre Co., Pennsylvania founded in 1786 by Aaron Levy (1742–1815). Site of conferences for the promotion of world unity.

BI145 Halverson, Deborah. "The John Kreider Farm." *Early Amer. Life*, vol. 10, no. 1 (February 1979), 26–29. History of the brick farmhouse built in the early 19th century or before near the former Union Canal linking the Schuylkill and Susquehanna Rivers.

BI146 Hatch, Carl E. *York, Pennsylvania, in the Depression 1930's.* York: Strine Publ. Co., 1974.

BI147 Hatch, Carl E., and Richard E. Kohler, eds. *Reminiscences of an Old Man on Life in York County, Pennsylvania, during the Nineteenth Century: Diary of Henry Bott.* York: Strine Publ., 1973.

BI148 Hay, Ellis S. *One Hundred and Forty-Four Years: A Sketch of Emmanuel Reformed Church, Hanover, Pennsylvania, 1765–1909.* N.p.: n.p., n.d. In York Co.

BI149 Heister, Jesse W. *Mattawana Mennonite Church: 100th Anniversary, 1871–1971.* Mattawana, Pa.: Mattawana Mennonite Church, 1971. In Mifflin Co.

BI150 *The History of St. Thomas United Church of Christ. Formerly Wenrich's Evangelical and Reformed Church...* N.p.: n.p., 1957. Located in Lower Paxton Township, Dauphin Co.

BI151 Hoenstein, Floyd G. *A History of the Zion Evangelical Lutheran Church of Hollidaysburg, Pa.* Hollidaysburg: n.p., 1953. 64p. Blair Co.; a church founded in 1803.

BI152 Hosch, Heinz L. "Das Siebenthal—Siewedahl: The Formal and Informal German Expressions from Seven Valleys." In: *Das Siebental Revisited: The People of Seven Valleys.* Ed. Armand Glatfelter. York: n.p., 1981, p.236–40. Also: "Mei Siewedahl." *Ibid.*, p.243, and "York County, the Codorus, Seven Valleys." *Ibid.*, p.xi–xxi.

BI153 "Jubilees." *Social Justice Rev.*, vols. 35–36 (1942–1943), 322–59, 138–39, 176. Remembering John B. Vornholt, Pius Niermann, John A.

Schaffeld, Lawrence Mutter, Edwin Fussenegger, William Schaefers, Charles H. Krekenberg, Central Verein of Pennsylvania.

BI154 Keffer, Marion Christina. "The Early Days of Zion Evangelical Lutheran Church, Founded 1806 at Sherwood, York County." *York Pioneer and Hist. Soc., Report*, 1960, 13–22.

BI155 King, Trennis. A. *History of the Maple Grove Mennonite Church, Belleville, Pennsylvania, 1806–1974*. Belleville: n.p., 1974. In Mifflin Co.

BI156 Kohler, Daniel. "Biblical Fourth of July Sermon, Delivered Sunday, the 4th of July 1841... at Coxtown, Pa." Trans. by Luther A. Pflueger. "'S Pennsylfawnisch Deitsch Eck," Allentown *Morning Call*, 28 June, 5 July, 1941. Possibly Coxton at Duryea, Luzerne Co.

BI157 Lewis, Arthur H. *The Aaronsburg Story*. New York: Vanguard, ca. 1955. 253p. On Aaron Levy and the founding of Aaronsburg.

BI158 *Lischy's Reformed Church (Also Known as Saint Peter's Church), North Codorus Township, York County, Pennsylvania*. Gettysburg: n.p., 1971. 31p.

BI159 Lubold, D. G. "Jacob's Church: Its History and Records." *Publs., Hist. Soc. of Schuylkill Co.*, vol. 1 (1907), 247–76. In Pine Grove Township, Schuylkill Co.

BI160 McFall, Nancy J. "Preserving York's Architectural Heritage." *Pa. Folklife*, vol. 16, no. 3 (Spring 1967), 20–23.

BI161 Martin, David S. *History of St. Paul's (Sand Hill) Lutheran Church*.... N.p.: n.p., 1952. In Derry Township, Dauphin Co.

BI162 Metzger College, Carlisle, Pa. Records, 1798–1850, 1881–1912. Ca. 2 ft. In Dickinson College Library (MS 73–453). Student records, accounts, and miscellaneous papers; notebook of George Metzger (1782–1879), founder of Metzger College.

BI163 Mook, Maurice A. *Population Trends in Lycoming County Since 1960*. Williamsport: n.p., 1971.

BI164 Moyer, Nevin W. *With the Forefathers of Wenrich's Church*... N.p.: n.p., 1922. Lower Paxton Township, Dauphin Co.

BI165 Mulcahy, George. "Catholic Backgrounds in Lewisburg, Union County, Pa." *Records of the Amer. Catholic Hist. Soc.*, vol. 61, no. 2 (1950), 98–100. Beginnings of a community that was intended to be a haven for Dutch and German Catholic immigrants.

BI166 *Parish Register, Saint Matthew's Lutheran Church, Hanover, York Co., Pennsylvania, 1743–1893*. Ed. Frederick S. Weiser, Gettysburg: n.p., 1969. 3 parts: 364, 103, 253p.

BI167 *The Parish Registers of Benders Church, Butler Township, Adams Co., Pa., for the Evangelical Lutheran and Reformed Congregations, 1786–1860*. Trans. by Frederick S. Weiser. Hanover, Pa.: n.p., 1978. 216p.

BI168 "The Pastors of Conewago, 1750–1880." *Records of the Amer. Catholic Hist. Soc.*, vol. 60, no. 3 (1949), 144–46. Catholic German mission.

BI169 Prentice, J. Stuart. *The First United Church of Christ... in Carlisle, Pennsylvania, 1763–1963*. Carlisle: n.p., ca. 1963.

BI170 Rader, Herbert. "Early History of St. Paul's (Summer Hill) Church." *Publs., Hist. Soc. of Schuylkill Co.*, vol. 5 (1945), 1–15. South Manheim Township, Schuylkill Co.

BI171 *Register of Marriages and Baptisms Kept by the Rev. Traugott Frederick Illing*. Harrisburg: n.p., 1891. In Lower Swatara Township, at Middletown, Dauphin Co.

BI172 Renno, John R. *A Brief History of the Amish Church in Belleville*. Danville, Pa.: n.p., 1976. 26p.

BI173 Russ, William A. "Snyder County Germans as Viewed by an Outsider." "'S Pennsylfawnisch Deitsch Eck," Allentown *Morning Call*, 17, 24 July 1943.

BI174 *Saint Jacob's (Stone) Church, Lutheran and Reformed, near Brodbecks, Codorus Township, York Co., Pa.: Parish Registers, 1756–1884*. Ed. Frederick S. Weiser. Hanover: n.p., 1972. 266p.

BI175 *Saint Paul's Church, Lutheran and Reformed Union, Ringtown, Union Township, Schuylkill Co., Pennsylvania. Baptisms 1810–1884; Burials 1841–1944*. Ed. Frederick S. Weiser. Hanover: n.p., 1971. 210p.

BI176 *Saint Paul's Evangelical Lutheran Church...Parish Registers, 1757–1866.* N.p.: n.p., 1976 In Dauphin Co., Derry Township.

BI177 Sauers, Roy W. "Pennsylvania Dutch Life along Switzer Run and Penn's Creek." *Pa. Folklife*, vol. 31 (1981–1982), 38–42.

BI178 Schumacher, Daniel. "Daniel Schumacher's *Baptismal Register*." Trans. and introd. Frederick S. Weiser. *Publs. of the Pa. Ger. Soc.*, no. 1. Allentown: The Society, 1968. P.185–399. Rev., *Concordia Hist. Inst. Quar.*, vol. 42 (February 1969), 47–48.

BI179 Shank, Clarence. *A Brief History of the Marion Mennonite Congregation.* Marion, Pa.: Mennonite Historical Commission, 1968. 52p. Also in *Cumberland Valley Mennonite Hist. Bull.* for January 1968. In Franklin Co.

BI180 Shannon, Lester G. "The Lutheran Church in the Upper Susquehanna Valley." *Procs. and Addrs., Northumberland Co. Hist. Soc.*, vol. 22 (1958), 100–30.

BI181 Snyder, Charles F. "Post Offices of Northumberland County." *Procs., Northumberland Co. Hist. Soc.*, vol. 26 (1974), 109–28.

BI182 Stauffer, Elmer C. "Conewago Chapel." *The Pa. Dutchman*, vol. 7, no. 4 (1956), 28–33. German Jesuit fathers established the Conewago settlement near Gettysburg, Pa., in the first half of the 18th century.

BI183 Steinmetz, Andrew. "Regina Leininger. A Penn's Creek Massacre Episode." *Amer.-German Rev.*, vol. 8, no. 2 (1941), 4–7. In Snyder Co.

BI184 Stroup, John Martin, and Raymond Martin Bell. *The Pioneers of Mifflin County, Pa.* Lewiston: n.p., 1942. 41p.

BI185 Stroup, Martin J. *The Amish of the Kishacoquilias Valley.* Lewiston: Mifflin Co. Hist. Soc., ca. 1967. 19p.

BI186 Troutman, Carrie Haas. "Pioneer Days in Mahantongo Valley." "'S Pennsylfawnisch Deitsch Eck," Allentown *Morning Call*, 2, 9, 16 October 1948.

BI187 *200th Anniversary 1771–1971. St. Peter's United Church of Christ (Hoffman's Church)...* N.p: n.p., 1971. In Lykens Township, Dauphin Co.

BI188 Unger, C. W. "The Summer Hill Record Book." *Publs., Hist. Soc. of Schuylkill Co.*, vol. 5 (1945), 51–62.

BI189 Unger, C. W., and William H. Dietrich. "Early Tombstone Inscriptions at Summer Hill." *Publs., Hist. Soc. of Schuylkill Co.*, vol. 5 (1945), 16–50.

BI190 Walter, Charlotte D., ed. "Vital Statistics: Record of Deaths, 1852–53–54." *Procs., Northumberland Co. Hist. Soc.*, vol. 26 (1974), 133–43. Recorded at the Northumberland Co. Courthouse, Sunbury.

BI191 Weiser, Jacob. Letters. In possession of John Conrad Weiser Family Association (in 1967). Trans. and ed. Frederick S. Weiser. Correspondence from Jacob W. in the Mahantongo Valley, Northumberland Co., Pa., to Frederick W., his brother, in Delaware Co., Ohio.

BI192 Yoder, Don. "Notes and Documents: Articles on the Amish from the *Reformirte Kirchenzeitung* (1860)." *Pennsylvania Folklife*, vol. 16, no. 2 (Winter 1966–1967), 46–48. A church paper published at Chambersburg.

BI193 Youngman, Caroline Vandegrift. "Printer John Jungmann." *Northumberland Co. Hist. Soc. Procs.*, vol. 15 (1946), 215–45.

BI194 Zahn, C. T. "The Earliest Records of Saint David's Sherman's Church, West Mannheim Township, York County, Pennsylvania." Trans. and ed. by Frederick S. Weiser. *Der Reggeboge*, vol. 11, no. 2 (1977), 9–21.

Lancaster County

BI195 Bachman, Calvin George. *The Old Order Amish of Lancaster County.* Publs., Pa. German Soc., nos. 49, 60. Lancaster, 1942, 1961. Rev. by J. Umble, *Mennonite Quar. Rev.*, vol. 17 (1943), 207–36; F. Reichmann, *Pa. Mag. of Hist. and Biog.*, vol. 68, no. 2 (1944), 211–12; *Amer.-German Rev.*, vol. 9, no. 4 (1943) 36; vol. 10, no. 4 (1944), 32; G. M. Stoltzfus, *Amer.-German Rev.*, vol. 28, no. 3, 36.

BI196 Barnes, Horace R. "Industries of Lancaster County." *Papers, Lancaster Co. Hist. Soc.*, vol. 48, no. 2 (1944), 41–56. Mills, iron industry, mining, gun making, etc.

BI197 Beck, Herbert H. "Elizabeth Furnace Plantation (Warwick Township, Lancaster Co., Pa.)." *Jour. of the Lancaster Co. Hist. Soc.*, vol. 69, no. 1 (1965), 25–41. Blast furnace operations founded on a 400-acre plantation by Jacob Huber and Heinrich Wilhelm Stiegel in the eighteenth century.

BI198 Beck, Herbert H. "Graveyard of the Revolutionary Soldiers at Lititz." *Hist. Papers and Addrs. of the Lancaster Co. Hist. Soc.*, vol. 37 (1933), 1–5.

BI199 Beck, Herbert H. "Lititz." *The Pa. Dutchman*, vol. 8, no. 1 (Summer 1956), 24–27.

BI200 Beck, Herbert H. "Rock Springs and Their Historic Surroundings." *Papers, Lancaster Co. Hist. Soc.*, vol. 47 (1943), 45–58.

BI201 Bentley, Elizabeth P., comp. *Index to the 1850 Census of Pennsylvania: Lancaster County.* Baltimore: Genealogical Publ. Co., 1975. 156p. An index covering about 10,000 residents.

BI202 Bowman, John J. "Lancaster's Part in the World's Watch-Making Industry." *Papers of the Lancaster Co. Hist. Soc.*, vol. 49, no. 2 (1945), 29–50.

BI203 Braun, Fritz, and Frederick S. Weiser. "Marriages Performed at the Evangelical Lutheran Church of the Holy Trinity, 1748–1767." *Publs. of the Pa. German Soc.*, vol. 7. Breinigsville: Pa. German Soc., 1973. Also publ. in German as no. 34 of the *Schriften zur Wanderungsgeschichte der Pfälzer: Trauungen im Kirchenbuch der Trinity Lutheran Church in Lancaster, Pennsylvanien, 1748–1767 (mit deutschen Herkunftsangaben).*

BI204 Brener, David. "Lancaster's First Jewish Community, 1715 to 1804: The Era of Joseph Simon." *Jour. of the Lancaster Co. Hist. Soc.*, vol. 80 (Michaelmas, 1976), 211–321.

BI205 Denlinger, A. Martha. *Real People: Amish and Mennonites in Lancaster County, Pennsylvania.* Scottdale: Herald Pr., 1975. 96p.

BI206 Dunlap, Raymond L., ed. *Churches of Today and Yesterday in Southern Lancaster County.* Lancaster: Fellowship of Solanco Churches, 1968. 20p.

BI207 Dyke, Samuel E. "The Bachman Family of Cabinetmakers, 1766–1894." *Jour. of the Lancaster Hist. Soc.*, vol. 69, no. 3 (Trinity 1965), 168–80. John B. emigrated from Switzerland with his father in 1766.

BI208 Edye, Abner M. "A Lancaster City Boy in the Gay Nineties. Part III." *Jour. of the Lancaster Co. Hist. Soc.*, vol. 77 (1973), 143–61. Incl. a discussion of Amish burial customs.

BI209 Erb, Mrs. Martin S. *History of the Neffville Mennonite Church, Lancaster, Pa., 1952–56.* N.p.: n.p., n.d. 19p.

BI210 Fox, J. T. "History of the New Bloomfield Charge." 6p. TS. In archives of the Hist. Soc. of the Reformed Church, Lancaster, Pa.

BI211 Franklin College, Lancaster. Records, 1787–1853. 3 ft. In the Franklin and Marshall College Library (MS 60-1128). Incl. letters of G.H.E. Muhlenberg, Caspar Diedrich Weiberg, J.H.C. Helmuth, F. V. Melsheimer.

BI212 Gallagher, Tom. *Pennsylvania German Study Unit on Lancaster, Pennsylvania.* New Holland: BESL Center, n.d.

BI213 Gehman, Henry Snyder. *History of Bergstrasse Ev. Lutheran Church, 1752–1977.* Ephrata: n.p., 1978. Located near Ephrata, Lancaster Co.

BI214 Gerberich, Albert H., and Gaius Marcus Brumbaugh. *Lancaster County, Pennsylvania, Tax Lists, 1751, 1756, 1757, 1758.* National Genealogical Soc. Publ., no. 4. Washington, D.C.: ca. 1933. 35p. Repr. Washington, 1972.

BI215 Getz, Jane C. "The Economic Organization Practices of the Old Order Amish of Lancaster County, Pennsylvania." *Mennonite Quar. Rev.*, vol. 20 (1946), 53–80, 98–127.

BI216 Goodell, Robert H. "The First Columbia Bridge." *Papers of the Lancaster Co. Hist. Soc.*, vol. 46 (1942), 97–127. German-American stockholders and promoters.

BI217 Goodell, Robert H. "Matthias Zahm's Diary." *Papers of the Lancaster Co. Hist. Soc.*, vol. 47 (1943), 61–92. Excerpts 1821–1849 from the diary of a Lancaster resident touching on civic affairs and the history of the Zahm family.

BI218 *Guide to Lancaster and South-Central Pennsylvania.* Lititz, Pa.: n.p., 1973.

BI219 Hark, Ann. "A Freindschaft Revisited." *Amer.-German Rev.*, vol. 29, no. 6 (1963), 30–33. Account of a visit to an Amish family in Lancaster County.

BI220 Heiges, George L. "Apothecaries of Lancaster County 1760 to 1900." *Papers of the Lanc. Co. Hist. Soc.*, vol. 50, no. 2 (1946), 33–69.

BI221 Heiges, George L. "The Evangelical Lutheran Church of the Holy Trinity, Lancaster, Pa. Part One, 1730–1861. Part Two, 1862–1980." *Jour. of the Lancaster Co. Hist. Soc.*, vol. 83 (1979), 2–71, 74–156.

BI222 Heiges, George L. "Gen. S. P. Heintzelman Visits His Hometown of Manheim." *Jour. of the Lancaster Co. Hist. Soc.*, vol. 68 (Trinity, 1964), 85–109. Selections from the *Diary* of S. P. Heintzelman.

BI223 Heiges, George L., annotator. "Lancaster in 1876: Observing the Centennial Year." *Jour. of the Lancaster Co. Hist. Soc.*, vol. 80 (1976), 3–30, 77–108, 129–56, 193–210.

BI224 Heisey, M. Luther. "A Biography of Paul Zantzinger." *Papers of the Lancaster Co. Hist. Soc.*, vol. 47 (1943), 113–19. Businessman active in civic affairs, 1732–1817. Notes on the Z. family.

BI225 Heisey, M. Luther. "The Borough Fathers." *Papers of the Lancaster Co. Hist. Soc.*, vol. 46 (1942), 45–82. Biographies of numerous German-Americans.

BI226 Heisey, M. Luther. "A Brief Postal History of Lancaster County." *Papers of the Lancaster Co. Hist. Soc.*, vol. 48, no. 1 (1944), 1–37.

BI227 Heisey, M. Luther. "Obituaries of Former Members." *Papers of the Lancaster Co. Hist. Soc.*, vol. 46 (1942), vi–viii; vol. 47 (1943), v–viii.

BI228 Heisey, M. Luther. "Two-Hundredth Anniversary of Lancaster's Incorporation as a Borough." *Papers of the Lancaster Co. Hist. Soc.*, vol. 46 (1942), 83–92.

BI229 Heisey, M. Luther, and Henry W. Holcombe. "Local Penny Dispatch and Internal Revenue Stamps." *Papers of the Lancaster Co. Hist. Soc.*, vol. 47 (1943), 26–35.

BI230 Heller, Mary Belle S. "College Hill in the '80's and '90's: Memoirs of a Franklin and Marshall Daughter." *Jour. of the Lancaster Co. Hist. Soc.*, vol. 75 (1971), 19–37.

BI231 Herman, Stewart W. "Daniel Herman, Pioneer." *Jour. of the Lancaster Co. Hist. Soc.*, vol. 79 (1975), 131–41.

BI232 Hopf, Claudia, and Carrol Hopf. "Restoring an Eighteenth-Century Lancaster Farm House." *Der Reggeboge*, vol. 5, no. 1 (1971), 7–11.

BI233 Huebener, Mary Augusta. *A Brief History of Lititz, Pennsylvania.* Lititz: n.p., ca. 1947. 23p.

BI234 *Jerusalem Evangelical Lutheran Church, Rothsville, Lancaster Co., Pennsylvania. Parish Registers, 1846–1954.* Comp. Frederick S. Weiser. Biglerville: n.p., 1978. 144p.

BI235 Keller, David, R. "Nativism or Sectionalism: A History of the Know-Nothing Party in Lancaster County, Pennsylvania." *Jour. of the Lancaster Co. Hist. Soc.*, vol. 75 (1971), 41–100.

BI236 Kendig, John D. "'In This Place'—Manheim, 1866. Two Diaries and a Local Newspaper." *Pa. Folklife*, vol. 29, no. 2 (Winter 1979–1980), 56–71. Diaries of Benjamin Hostetter Hershey and Harriet A. Arndt, supplemented with data from the Manheim *Sentinel* for 1866.

BI237 Kieffer, Elizabeth C. "Libraries in Lancaster." *Papers of the Lancaster Co. Hist. Soc.*, vol. 48, no. 3 (1944), 71–80.

BI238 Klein, Frederick Shriver. *Old Lancaster, Historic Pennsylvania Community from Its Beginnings to 1865.* Illus. by Charles X. Carlson. Forew. by H. M. J. Klein. Lancaster: Early America Series, Inc., 1964. 159p. Rev. by M. J. Boyer, *Pa. Hist.*, vol. 32, no. 1 (1965), 98–99.

BI239 Lancaster, Pa. Evangelical Lutheran Church of the Holy Trinity. *Birth and Baptismal Register.* Reading: The Pa. German Society, 1893–1896. *Proceedings and Addrs., Pa. German Society*, vol. 3 (1893), Part 6, p.191–292; *Ibid.*, vol. 6 (1896), Part 2, p.251–283.

BI240 Landis, Berta C., and Eleanor J. Fulton. "Military Records of Lancaster Countians, 1784–1815." *Papers of the Lancaster Co. Hist. Soc.*, vol. 48, no. 4 (1944), 81–108.

BI241 Landis, Ira D. "Mennonite Background of the Present School System." *Mennonite Hist. Bull.*, vol. 4, no. 2 (June 1943), 1, 4. Esp. the Landis Schoolhouse, Roseville, Lancaster Co.

BI242 Landis, Ira D. "The Reply of the Lancaster Conference to the John H. Oberholtzer Constitution of 1847." *Mennonite Quar. Rev.*, vol. 29, no. 1 (1955), 74–76.

BI243 Lippold, John W. "Old Trinity Steeple." *Hist. Papers and Addrs. of the Lancaster Co. Hist. Soc.*, vol. 31, no. 9 (1927), 127–33.

BI244 Long, John D. "The Nickel Mines of Lancaster County." *Jour. of the Lancaster Co. Hist. Soc.*, vol. 80, (1976), 158–77.

BI245 Lynch, Charles O., John Ward, and Willson Loose. "A History of Brewing in Lancaster County, Legal and Otherwise." *Jour. of the Lancaster Co. Hist. Soc.*, vol. 70, no. 1 (Hilarymas, 1966), 1–100.

BI246 Madeira, Sheldon. "A Study of the Education of the Old Order Amish Mennonites of Lancaster County, Pennsylvania." Diss., Pennsylvania, 1955.

BI247 Martin, C. H. "Early Presidential Elections in Lancaster County." *Papers of the Lancaster Co. Hist. Soc.*, vol. 47 (1943), 93–105.

BI248 Mayhill, R. Thomas. *Lancaster County, Pennsylvania: Deed Abstracts and Revolutionary War Oaths of Allegiance.* Knightstown, Pa.: n.p., 1973.

BI249 *Memorial Volume of the Ev. Lutheran Church of the Holy Trinity, Lancaster, Pennsylvania....* Lancaster: n.p., 1861.

BI250 "Mennonite Agriculture in Colonial Lancaster County, Pennsylvania." "'S Pennsylfawnisch Deitsch Eck," Allentown *Morning Call*, 24, 31 August; 7, 14 September 1946. Also in *Mennonite Quar. Rev.*, vol. 19, no. 4 (1945), 254–72.

BI251 Musser, Edgar A. "John Musser's Plantation in Southeast Lancaster." *Jour. of the Lancaster Co. Hist. Soc.*, vol. 83 (1979), 158–85.

BI252 Musser, Edgar A. "Old St. Mary's of Lancaster, Pennsylvania: The Jesuit Period, 1741–1785;" "St. Mary's Church, Lancaster, Pa.: 1785–1877." *Jour. of the Lancaster Co. Hist. Soc.*, vol. 71, no. 2 (Easter 1967), 69–126; vol. 73, no. 3 (Trinity 1969), 97–184. With extensive notes on several German immigrant priests.

BI253 Reichmann, Felix. "Amusements in Lancaster 1750–1940." *Hist. Papers and Addrs., Lancaster Co. Hist. Soc.*, vol. 45 (1941), 25–55.

BI254 Reichmann, Felix. "History of Amusements in Lancaster, Pa." *Papers of the Lancaster Co. Hist. Soc.*, vol. 44, no. 2 (1941), 25–26.

BI255 Reichmann, Felix. *Subject-Index to the Proceedings of the Lancaster Co. Hist. Soc., 1895–1939.* Lancaster: Lancaster Co. Hist. Soc., 1940. 66p.

BI256 Reichmann, Felix. "Two Inscriptions from the Landis Valley Museum." *Amer.-German Rev.*, vol. 8, no. 5 (1942), 11–12, 38.

BI257 Rhodes, Irwin S. "Early Legal Records of Jews of Lancaster County, Pennsylvania." *Amer. Jewish Archives*, vol. 12 (1960), 96–108.

BI258 Richards, Luther. "Lancaster in 1830." *Jour. of the Lancaster Co. Hist. Soc.*, vol. 69, no. 1 (Hilarymas 1965), 1–9. With list of residents by trades and professions.

BI259 Rink, Franz, and Frederick S. Weiser, eds. "Records of the Muddy Creek Moravian Congregation." *Der Reggeboge*, vol. 10 (December 1976), 5–15.

BI260 Rodriguiz, Janice E. "The Lancaster of Leonard Eichholtz, 1750–1817." *Jour. of the Lancaster Co. Hist. Soc.*, vol. 79 (Michaelmas 1975), 175–207.

BI261 Rodriguiz, Janice E. "The Lost Cow." *Jour. of the Lancaster Co. Hist. Soc.*, vol. 75 (1971), 115–18. Appraisal of lost items columns in Christopher Saur's *Pennsylvanische Berichte*.

BI262 Rush, Benjamin. *A Letter Describing the Consecration of the German College at Lancaster in June 1787.* Lancaster: n.p., 1945. 4p. With portrait and facsimiles.

BI263 Russell, George E. "Migrations to and from Lancaster County, Pennsylvania." *National Genealogical Soc. Quar.*, vol. 55 (June 1967), 101–02.

BI264 Schwalm, Glenn P. and Frederick S. Weiser, trans. and eds. *Records of Pastoral Acts at Trinity Evangelical Lutheran Church, New Holland, Lancaster County, 1730–1799*. Sources and Documents Series of the Pennsylvania German Society, vol. 2. Breinigsville: The Society, 1977.

BI265 [Seltenreich Reformed Church, Earl Township (near New Holland), Lancaster Co., Pa.] *Church Records, 1746–1800*. Gettysburg: n.p., 1971. 35p.

BI266 Shindle, Richard E. "History of the Lancaster City Police Department, 1742–1977." *Jour. of the Lancaster Co. Hist. Soc.*, vol. 82 (1978), 126–59.

BI267 Spotts, Charles D. "Brickerville Old Zion Reformed Church." *Jour. of the Lancaster Co. Hist. Soc.*, vol. 77 (1973), 61–87.

BI268 Spotts, Charles D., ed. *Denominations Originating in Lancaster County, Pennsylvania*. Community Historians Annual, no. 2. Lancaster: Franklin and Marshall College Library, 1963. 41p.

BI269 Stevens, S. K. [State of Pennsylvania Acquires the Landis Valley Museum.] *Pa. Hist.*, vol. 8, no. 3 (1941), 243–44. See also *Amer.-German Rev.*, vol. 7, no. 4.

BI270 Summar, Donald J. "A History of the Kreider Machine Company." *Jour. of the Lancaster Co. Hist. Soc.*, vol. 76 (Hilarymas 1972), 41–44.

BI271 Watson, John. "Lancaster and Lancaster County." "'S Pennsylfawnisch Deitsch Eck," Allentown *Morning Call*, 4 May 1967. Excerpts from Watson's *Annals* (Philadelphia, 1843).

BI272 Weaver, Glenn. "A History of St. John's (Center) Reformed Church, East Earl Township, Lancaster County." *Procs., Lancaster Co. Hist. Soc.*, vol. 49, no. 3 (1945), 53–84.

BI273 Weiser, Frederick S. *A Congregation Named Saint John's...* Maytown, Pa.: n.p., 1967. In East Donegal Township, Lancaster Co.

BI274 Weiser, Frederick S. "The Earliest Records of Holy Trinity Evangelical Lutheran Church, Lancaster, Pennsylvania, 1730–1744." In: *Ebbes fer Alle—Ebber Ebbes fer Dich: Essays in Memoriam, Albert Franklin Buffington*. Publs., Pa. Ger. Soc., vol. 14. Breinigsville, The Society, 1980, p.397–434.

BI275 Weiser, Frederick S. *The Lutheran Church in New Holland, Pennsylvania, 1730–1980*. New Holland: n.p., ca. 1980.

BI276 Wenger, J. C. *Hans Herr*. Lancaster: Hans Herr House Restoration Committee, 1970. Rev. in *Mennonite Research Jour.*, vol. 11, no. 3 (July 1970), 35.

BI277 Wood, Jerome H. *Conestoga Crossroads: Lancaster, Pennsylvania, 1730–1790*. Harrisburg: Pa. Hist. and Museum Commission, 1979. Rev. by Stephanie G. Wolf, *Pa. Hist.*, vol. 47 (1980), 377–78. See also the diss., Brown Univ., ca. 1968: "Conestoga Crossroads: The Rise of Lancaster, Pennsylvania, 1730–1789."

BI278 Worner, William F. "Heller's Salem Reformed Churchyard, Lancaster County, Pennsylvania." *National Genealogical Soc. Quar.*, vol. 38, nos. 1 and 2 (1950), 9–12, 53–57. Inscriptions recorded from gravestones.

BI279 Yoder, Donald Herbert. "*Der Fröhliche Botschafter*. An Early American Universalist Magazine." *Amer.-German Rev.*, vol. 10, no. 5 (1944), 13–16. Issued in Lancaster, 1829–1838.

BI280 *Zion Evangelical Lutheran Church, Manheim, Lancaster Co., Pennsylvania. Parish Registers, 1771–1921*. Ed. Frederick S. Weiser. Hanover, Pa.: n.p., 1973. 285p.

Lebanon County

BI281 *Bi-Centennial, the Moravian Church, Lebanon, Pennsylvania*. N.p.: n.p., 1947.

BI282 Butz, C. A. *Bethel Herald*. Annville, Pa.: Journal Publ. Co., 1906. Church leaflet.

BI283 Graeff, Arthur D. *Lebanon County Through the Centuries*. Philadelphia: Edward Stern Co., 1945. 36p.

BI284 Heisey, John W., tr. and ed. "Extracts from the Diary of the Moravian Pastors of the Hebron Church, Lebanon, 1755–1814." *Pa. Hist.*, vol. 34, no. 1 (January 1967), 44–63.

BI285 *Historic Schaefferstown Record,* formerly *Schaefferstown Bull.* Quarterly. Vol. 1–, 1967–. Publ. by Historic Schaefferstown, Inc. Ed. C. Richard Beam, 406 Spring Dr., Millersville, Pa.

BI286 *The History of St. Jacob's (Kimmerling's) Church*... N.p.: n.p., 1970. A Reformed congregation in Lebanon Township, Lebanon Co.

BI287 *The History of St. Paul's United Church of Christ*...*Schaefferstown, Pa.* N.p.: n.p., 1965. In Heidelberg Township, Lebanon Co.

BI288 Leaman, Mary E., and Joan B. Leaman, eds. *The Story of Stumptown Mennonite Church: In Celebration of 200 Years as a Congregation, 1781–1981.* Bird-in-Hand, Pa.: Stumptown Mennonite Church, 1981.

BI289 Manbeck, Beverly. "Lebanon County Historical Sites: A Survey in Pictures." *Procs. and Addrs., Lebanon Co. Hist. Soc.,* vol. 40, no. 4 (1980). Entire issue.

BI290 Mohn, Viola Kohl. "Shadows of the Rhine along the Tulpehocken." Ed. Henry C. Westenberger. *Lebanon Co. Hist. Soc., Hist. Papers and Addrs.,* vol. 14, no. 5 (1970), 133–91. "Book 2." *Ibid.,* vol. 14 (1972), 237–336.

BI291 *Salem Evangelical Church, Lebanon, Lebanon County, Pennsylvania Baptismal Registers 1773–1876.* 533p. *Marriage Records 1794–1876.* 281p. *Burial Records, 1773–1876.* 214p. Gettysburg: Lutheran Theological Seminary, 1969.

BI292 *Two Hundred Twenty-Fifth Anniversary, Weisenberg Church, New Tripoli, Pennsylvania.* Prep. with the assistance of Raymond E. Hollenbach. N.p.: n.p., 1976. Weisenberg Township, Lebanon Co.

BI293 Wallace, Paul A. W. *Lebanon Valley College: A Centennial History.* Annville: Lebanon Valley College, 1966. 280p. Rev. by A. D. Sumberg, *Pa. Mag. of Hist. and Biography,* vol. 90 (1966), 554–55. A foundation of the United Brethren Church.

BI294 Weaver, Christine E. "Revolutionary War Soldiers Buried in Lebanon County." *Papers and Addrs., Lebanon Co. Hist. Soc.,* vol. 15, no. 1 (1976), 57–72.

BI295 Weiser, Frederick S. *A Church of Many Names: The Story of Trinity Lutheran Church, Colebrook, Pennsylvania*... Colebrook: n.p., 1971.

In South Londonderry Township, Lebanon Co.; Lutheran congregation.

Lehigh County and Region

BI296 Albright, Donald B. "The Band Plays On." *Procs., Lehigh Co. Hist. Soc.,* vol. 31 (1976), 139–47.

BI297 "[Allentown, Lehigh Co.] Ev. Reformirter Kirchenbau—1773." "'S Pennsylfawnisch Deitsch Eck," Allentown *Morning Call,* 13 August 1966. Second building of the Zion Reformed Church, Allentown.

BI298 Barba, Preston A., comp. *They Came to Emmaus.* Emmaus: Publ. by the Borough of Emmaus, 1959. Rev. by J. J. Stoudt, *Amer.-German Rev.,* vol. 27, no. 2 (1960), 35. History and description of life in a Pennsylvania town.

BI299 Berky, Andrew S. "The Schoolhouse Near the Old Spring: A History of the Union School and Church Association, Dillingersville, Pennsylvania, 1735–1955." *Publs., Pa. Ger. Soc.,* vol. 56 Norristown: The Society, 1955. 173p. Rev. by P. A. Barba, "'S Pennsylfawnisch Deitsch Eck," Allentown *Morning Call,* 19 November 1955.

BI300 "The Burgenland Migration to the Lehigh Valley: Naturalization Records of Lehigh Valley." *Pa. Ethnic Studies Newsletter,* vol. 1, no. 3 (1975–1976), 4–5.

BI301 Gray, Leslie R. "The George Zewitz (Savitz) Mill." *Procs., Lehigh Co. Hist. Soc.,* vol. 29 (1972), 46–49.

BI302 Haas, Arthur M. "The Allemaengel Road." "'S Pennsylfawnisch Deitsch Eck," Allentown *Morning Call,* 19, 26 November, 3 December 1966. The first road to Allemangel through Lehigh and Berks Counties.

BI303 Hammer, Carl, Jr. "Late German Documents from Organ Church." *Amer.-German Rev.,* vol. 7 (1951), 14–16. Organ congregation, Lynn Township, Lehigh Co.

BI304 Heindel, Ned D., and Natalie I. Foster. "The Allentown Academy: America's First German Medical School." *Pa. Folklife*, vol. 30 (1980–1981), 2–8.

BI305 Helffrich, William A. "Catechetical Instruction in 1841." Trans. by David B. Kaufman. "'S Pennsylfawnisch Deitsch Eck," Allentown *Morning Call*, 12 August, 2 December, 1967. Excerpted from his *Lebensbild aus dem Pennsylvanisch-Deutschen Predigerstand* ... (Allentown, 1906).

BI306 Hellerich, Mahlon H. "The Churches of Lehigh County, 1732–1784." *Procs., Lehigh Co. Hist. Soc.*, vol. 31 (1976), 60–88.

BI307 Hellerich, Mahlon H. "The Development of Allentown, 1811–1873." *Procs., Lehigh Co. Hist. Soc.*, vol. 32 (1978), 46–68.

BI308 Hellerich, Mahlon H., and Adrienne Snelling. "Lehigh Heritage." *Procs., Lehigh Co. Hist. Soc.*, vol. 33 (1979), 47–182. A pictorial history.

BI309 Heyl, John K. "The Peter Steckel House." "'S Pennsylfawnisch Deitsch Eck," Allentown *Morning Call*, 28 August 1943.

BI310 *History of Christ Lutheran and Reformed Church, Shoenersville, Pa.* N.p.: n.p., 1930. Hanover Township, Lehigh Co.

BI311 Hollenbach, Raymond E. "Ausschteier." "'S Pennsylfawnisch Deitsch Eck," Allentown *Morning Call*, 5 December 1964. A will, quoted from the account book of Benjamin Schmoyer, Lehigh County, 1842.

BI312 Hollenbach, Raymond E. "Public Sale of Personal Property of the Deceased Adam Scheurer, Whitehall Township, Lehigh County, May 17, 1805." "'S Pennsylfawnisch Deitsch Eck," Allentown *Morning Call*, 16 February 1946. Inventory of goods offered in a public sale.

BI313 Hollenbach, Raymond E. *Two Hundredth Anniversary of Heidelberg Union Church* ... N.p.: n.p., 1940. In Heidelberg Township, Lehigh Co.

BI314 Hollenbach, Raymond E. "Weisenberg Church." "'S Pennsylfawnisch Deitsch Eck," Allentown *Morning Call*, 15, 22, 29 April 1967. A Lehigh Co. church.

BI315 Howland, Garth A. "An Architectural History of the Moravian Church, Bethlehem, Pa." *Transactions, Moravian Hist. Soc.*, vol. 14, nos. 1–2 (1947), 51–132.

BI316 *Israel Trexler vs. William G. Mennig, St. Paul's Church Case, 1873–1876.* 3 vols. Philadelphia: Philadelphia Lutheran Seminary, Mount Airy, n.d. In Allentown, 1873–1876.

BI317 Kaufman, David B. "Helffrich on Fogelsville during the Civil War." *Procs., Lehigh Co. Hist. Soc.*, vol. 32 (1978), 208–24. Excerpts from W. A. Helffrich's *Lebensbild aus dem Pa.-Deut. Predigerstand* (Allentown, 1906).

BI318 [Klick, Richard C.] *One Hundred Ninetieth Anniversary St. Paul's Evangelical Lutheran Church, Allentown, Pennsylvania, 1762–1952.* Allentown: n.p., 1952.

BI319 Myers, Richmond E. *Lehigh Valley: The Unexpected.* Easton: Northampton Co. Hist. and Genealogical Soc., 1972.

BI320 *Regeln der Deutschen Lutherischen Jordan Kirche in Süd-Wheithall, Lecha County.* Allentown: n.p., 1871.

BI321 Schmoyer, Melville B. "Some of the Highlights and Shadows During Two Hundred Years' History of Lehigh (Zion's) Lutheran Congregation." N.p.: n.p., n.d. Copy on deposit in the Lutheran Archives Center, Lutheran Theological Seminary, Philadelphia.

BI322 Schuler, Henry Addison (1850–1908). "Ziegel Church." *The Pa. German*, vol. 12 (1911), 234. A parish near Fogelsville, Lehigh Co.

BI323 Trexler, Ben (pseud. "Ben"). *Skizzen aus dem Lecha-Thale.* Allentown: Trexler and Hartzell, 1880–1886. 260p. Retold in English by David B. Kaufman, "'S Pennsylfawnisch Deitsch Eck," Allentown *Morning Call*, 6, 13 March, 25 April, 9 May, 6, 20, 27 June, 11 July, 17 October 1964; 12, 19 June, 11, 18 September, 4 December 1965. Colonial life, frontier experiences, local customs, etc.

BI324 Waldenrath, Alexander. "German Churches of the Lehigh Valley." *German-Amer. Studies*, vol. 9 (Spring 1975), 26–32.

BI325 William, David G. "The Lower Jordan Valley Pennsylvania German Settlement." *Procs., Lehigh Co. Hist. Soc.*, vol. 18 (1950), 181p. Rev. by P. A. Barba, "'S Pennsylfawnisch Deitsch Eck,"

Allentown *Morning Call*, 18 August 1951; G. D. Harmon, *Pa. Hist.*, vol. 18, no. 2 (1951), 176–77.

Montgomery County

BI326 Alderfer, E. Gordon. *The Montgomery County Story*. Norristown: n.p., 1951. 302p. Rev. P. A. Barba, "'S Pennsylfawnisch Deitsch Eck," Allentown *Morning Call*, 18 August, 1951. Germans in the early history of the county.

BI327 Barker, Charles R. "The 'Old Dutch Church' in Lower Merion." *Bull., Hist. Soc. of Montgomery Co.*, vol. 9, no. 3 (1954), 185–230; no. 4 (1955), 281–346. Historical sketch and founders of a church organized in 1765; discussion of German immigration to Pennsylvania.

BI328 Beck, Clara A. "History of Whitpain Township." *Bull., Hist. Soc. of Montgomery Co.*, vol. 5, no. 2 (1946), 106–17; vol. 5, no. 3 (1946), 179–218. Incl. a sketch of John Philip Boehm's Reformed Church.

BI329 Beck, Clara A. "St. John's Lutheran Church, Centre Square [Montgomery Co.]" *Bull. Hist. Soc. of Montgomery Co.*, vol. 5 (ca. 1946), 52–72.

BI330 Berky, Andrew S. *An Account of Some Hosensack Valley Mills*. Pennsburg, Pa.: Schwenkfelder Library, 1958. 70p.

BI331 Brecht, George R. "Some Facts about Plymouth Township Public Schools." *Bull., Hist. Soc. of Montgomery Co.*, vol. 4 (1944), 137–51.

BI332 Cassel, Mary. Diary, 1858–1863. Copied by Herbert Harley, 1944. In the Hist. Soc. of Montgomery Co.

BI333 De Long, Calvin M. *Two Hundred Twenty-Five Years at New Goshenhoppen, 1727–1952*. Allentown: Schlechter's, 1952.

BI334 Doebler, Harold F., and George A. Ludwig. *St. Peter's Lutheran Church, Barren Hill, Pa., 1752–1952*. N.p.: n.p., 1952. In Whitemarsh Township, Montgomery Co.

BI335 Doll, Donald Goodyear, and David L. Wilson. *St. Paul's Lutheran Church, Ardmore, Pennsylvania, Through Two Hundred Years, 1765–1965*. N.p.: n.p., 1965. In Lower Merion Township, Montgomery Co.

BI336 Dougherty, D. J. "Goshenhoppen, the Third Oldest Parish in Pennsylvania." *Records, Amer. Catholic Hist. Soc.*, vol. 52, no. 3 (1941), 185–87. Catholic St. Paul, Goshenhoppen, founded in 1741; first minister the Rev. Theodor Schneider, S. J.

BI337 Dunne, John R. "The Goshenhoppen Registers: Fifth Series; Baptisms; 1807–18." *Records of the Amer. Catholic Hist. Soc.*, vol. 61, no. 1 (1950), 57–63; no. 2, 112–23; no. 3, 185–92; no. 4, 248–62. Church registers by Father Paul Erntzen of the old Pa. mission at Goshenhoppen, now Bally, from 1807–1818.

BI338 Faust, Alvin B. "History of the Faust Tannery and Sidelights on the Life of Alvin D. Faust." *Bull. of the Hist. Soc. of Montgomery Co.*, vol. 3 (1942), 172–81.

BI339 Fink, Leo Gregory. *From Bally to Valley Forge. Historical Monograph of the Catholic Church in the Perkiomen Valley from 1741 to 1952*. Philadelphia: n.p., 1953. 46p.

BI340 Fink, Leo Gregory. "Traditions of Bally." *Records, Amer. Catholic Hist. Soc.*, vol. 54, no. 2 (1943), 81–109. Church life in a congregation with German ministers and members in Bally, Pa.

BI341 "Free Inhabitants in Douglas Township in the County of Montgomery, State of Pennsylvania, According to the Census of 1850; . . . Norriton . . . ; Towamencin; Limerick; Lower Providence; Springfield; Cheltenham; Whitepain [Whitpain]; Upper Merion; Perkiomen; Montgomery; Frederick; Upper Salford Township . . ." *Bull., Hist. Soc. of Montgomery Co.*, vol. 14, no. 3 (Fall 1964), 211–303; no. 4 (Spring 1965), 331–84; vol. 15, nos. 1 and 2 (Spring 1966), 37–85; no. 3 (Fall 1966), 38–103; no. 4 (Spring 1967), 55–68, 69–88, 89–108. Immigrants from Germany are listed at the end.

BI342 Groshens, David E. "Legal Lotteries in Early Pennsylvania." *Bull., Hist. Soc. of Montgomery Co.*, vol. 4, no. 1 (October 1943), 15–32. Mention of lotteries held for German churches and for schools in German townships.

BI343 Groshens, David E. "Men of Montgomery County Who Aided Ratification of our Federal Constitution by the Commonwealth of Pennsylvania." *Bull., Hist. Soc. of Montgomery Co.*, vol. 5, no. 2 (1946), 125–34. English, Welsh and Germans "fused" into Americans.

BI344 Hagey, Henry D. In: *Some Local History of Franconia Township*. Ed. Joyce Clemmer Munro. Telford, Pa.: by the editor, 1979. Genealogical data about the Hagey family and a contribution to the study of Pennsylvania German folk culture.

BI345 Harding, George M. "Historical Murals in the Montgomery County Courthouse." *Pa. Hist.*, vol. 20, no. 3 (1953), 219–36. Murals represent historical scenes from the lives of Muhlenberg, Rittenhouse and others.

BI346 Heckler, James Y. *History of Franconia Township*. Harleysville: Carroll D. Henricks, 1960. 112p. Rev. by H. T. Rosenberger, *National Genealogical Soc. Quar.*, vol. 52, no. 3 (1964), 169; also in "'S Pennsylfawnisch Deitsch Eck," Allentown *Morning Call*, 5 January 1963. On an early and important settlement in America.

BI347 Heckler, James Y. *The History of Harleysville and Lower Salford Township*. Schwenksville: Robert C. Bucher, 1958. 225p. German settlement in Montgomery Co. Orig. published in 1886.

BI348 Heckler, James Y. *History of Lower Salford Township, in Sketches, Commencing with a History of Harleysville*. Harleysville, Pa.: Weekly News Office, 1888. 456p. Also publ. by B. L. Gehman, Harleysville, in 1886: *History of Harleysville and Historical Sketches of Lower Salford Township, Montgomery County, Pa.*

BI349 Hollenbach, Raymond E. "Salford Mennonite Meetinghouse." "'S Pennsylfawnisch Deitsch Eck," Allentown *Morning Call*, 30 April 1966. Mennonite church built in 1738, rebuilt 1770 and 1850; Lower Salford Township, Montgomery Co.

BI350 Hoover, Margaret Hocker. "The Trappe Neighbors of Henry Melchior Muhlenberg as Mentioned in His Journals, vol. 3, 1777–1787." *Bull., Hist. Soc. of Montgomery Co.*, vol. 16, no. 3 (1966), 139–60.

BI351 Hoover, Margaret Hocker. "Trappe [Pa.], 1834–1836." *Der Reggeboge*, vol. 7, no. 1 (1973), 1–16.

BI352 Jones, Mrs. A. Conrad. "Our Society: Some Milestones in Its Sixty Years," *Bull., Hist. Soc. of Montgomery Co.*, vol. 3 (1942), 75–83.

BI353 Kline, J. J. *Ist dieses nicht das gelobte Land? ...Falkner Swamp Reformed Church...* N.p.: n.p., 1975. On the Falkner Swamp United Church of Christ, near Gilbertsville, Montgomery Co.

BI354 Kline, Raymond A. *The Past and Present of St. Paul's Lutheran Church, Red Hill, Pennsylvania (1739–1970)*. N.p.: n.p., ca. 1970. At New Goshenhoppen, Upper Hanover Township, Montgomery Co.

BI355 Kulp, Clarence, Jr. "The Goschenhoppen Historians." *Pa. Folklife*, vol. 26, no. 4 (1967), 16–24. Measures taken at Woxall, Pa., to preserve Pennsylvania-Dutch architecture and folkways.

BI356 Moyer, Clayton C., and Charles F. Brobst. *Little Zion Lutheran Church, 1730–1970*. N.p.: n.p., ca. 1970. In Franconia Township, Montgomery Co.

BI357 Muhlenberg, Henry Melchior. [Account of the history of Barren Hill congregation, Whitemarsh Township, Montgomery County. Written in 1774.] See *Bull., Hist. Soc. of Montgomery Co.*, vol. 11 (1959), 282–97.

BI358 Munro, Joyce W. *Willing Inhabitants: A Short Account of Life in Franconia Township, Montgomery County, Pennsylvania*. Souderton: Provident Books, ca. 1980.

BI359 Parsons, William T. "The United States Census of 1850; Montgomery County." *Bull., Hist. Soc. of Montgomery Co.*, vol. 14, no. 2 (Spring 1964), 121–93. Names from Upper Providence, Pottsgrove and Hatfield Townships.

BI360 Pearce, Josiah S. "Early Recollections of Ardmore." *Bull., Hist. Soc. of Montgomery Co.*, vol. 4, no. 2 (1944), 65–136; vol. 4, no. 3 (1944), 169–247; vol. 5, no. 4 (1945), 297–344. Excellent history. Repr. from the Ardmore *Chronicle* of 1906–1907.

BI361 Price, Charles H., Jr. *A History of Christ Reformed Church at Indian Creek (Indianfield)....* Telford, Pa.: n.p., 1966. In Franconia Township, Montgomery Co.

BI362 Rosenberger, Homer T. "On a Montgomery County Heritage." *Der Reggeboge*, December 1969. 14p.

BI363 *St. Luke's Reformed Church (Evangelical and Reformed), Trappe, Pa....* N.p.: n.p., 1943.

BI364 Shellenberger, Paul M. "History of Public Education in Norristown." *Bull., Hist. Soc. of Montgomery Co.*, vol. 3 (1942), 98–143, 214–59.

BI365 Shoemaker, Alfred L. "Biographical Sketches of Montgomery County Publishers." *The Pa. Dutchman*, vol. 3, no. 17 (1 February 1952), 7.

BI366 Stickler, Franklin A. "The Pilgrimage to the Old Trappe Church, Saturday, September 19th, 1942." *Bull., Hist. Soc. of Montgomery Co.*, vol. 3, no. 4 (April 1943), 314–16. Celebration of the Muhlenberg bicentenary.

BI367 Unger, Claude W., trans. "The Old Goschenhoppen Lutheran Burial Register, 1752–1772." *Pa. Folklife*, vol. 17, no. 2 (Winter 1967–1968), 32–35.

Northeastern Region

BI368 Barba, Preston A. "Great Affliction and Frontier Life in Northampton County." "'S Pennsylfawnisch Deitsch Eck," Allentown *Morning Call*, 1, 8 June 1957. Excerpts from *The History of the Keller Family* by Eli Keller, 1905.

BI369 Bergey, Nelson H. "Some Accounts of the Early German Settlements of Bradford County." "'S Pennsylfawnisch Deitsch Eck," Allentown *Morning Call*, 12, 19, 26 January; 2 February 1946.

BI370 Dunkelberger, George F. "The Beginnings of Susquehanna University." *Northampton Co. Hist. Soc. Procs.*, vol. 16 (1948), 135–63.

BI371 *Eighteenth Century Vital Records from the Early Registers of the Moravian Congregation at Schoeneck, Northampton County, Pennsylvania.* Comp. by Charles H. Sandwick, Sr. Easton: Jacobsburg Hist. Soc., 1978. 71p.

BI372 Gallagher, John P. *A Century of History: The Diocese of Scranton 1868–1968.* Scranton: The Diocese of Scranton, 1968. 615p. Incl. some German congregations. Rev. by E. Halsey, *Amer. Catholic Hist. Soc. of Philadelphia, Records*, vol. 80, no. 4 (December 1969), 255–58.

BI373 Gollin, Gillian Lindt. "Bethlehem Transformed: The Secularization of a Moravian Settlement." *Pa. Hist.*, vol. 37, no. 1 (January 1970), 53–63.

BI374 Lehigh Coal Mine Co. "Jacob Weiss, of Northampton County... Having Discovered a Certain Coal Mine...." [Philadelphia: n.p., 1792.] Broadside. Dated 13 February 1792. In Historical Soc. of Pa.

BI375 Miner, Charles. *History of Wyoming (Pa.), In a Series of Letters, From Charles Miner to His Son, William Penn Miner, Esq.* Philadelphia: n.p., 1845.

BI376 Moravian Church, Bethlehem. *The Handbook of the Moravian Congregation of Bethlehem, Pa....* Bethlehem: n.p., 1890. 130p.

BI377 Schwarze, Edmund. *History of the Hopedale Moravian Church, Newfoundland, Pennsylvania.* Stroudsburg: n.p., 1912. 16p.

BI378 Trachtenberg, Joshua. *Consider the Years: The Story of the Jewish Community of Easton, 1752–1942.* Easton, Pa.: Centennial Committee of Temple Brith Sholom, 1944. 327p. Rev. by I. S. Meyer, *Pa. Hist.*, vol. 12, no. 3 (1945), 248–49.

BI379 Weiser, Frederick S., ed. "Parochial Register of the Indian Creek Reformed Church, 1753–1851." *Publs., Pa. German Soc.*, vol. 3 (1970), 117–19.

BI380 Yates, W. Ross, et al., eds. *Bethlehem of Pennsylvania: The First One Hundred Years, 1741–1841.* Bethlehem: Bethlehem Chamber of Commerce, 1968. 226p. Rev. by D. F. Durnbaugh, *Pa. Mag. of Hist. and Biography*, vol. 93, no. 3 (July 1969), 419–21.

BI381 Yates, W. Ross, ed. *Bethlehem of Pennsylvania: The Golden Years, 1841–1920.* Bethlehem: Bethlehem Book Committee, 1976. 362p. Rev. by M. H. Hellerich, *Der Reggeboge*, vol. 11, no. 1 (1977), 19–23; Robert F. Oaks, *Pa. Hist.*, vol. 45 (1978), 286–87.

Philadelphia—Germantown

BI382 *Eine Addresse an die freien Leute von Pennsylvanien, von der Correspondenz-Committee für die Stadt Philadelphia von den Freunden des James Ross* .... Philadelphia: Carl Cist, 1799. 24p.

BI383 *Annals of the First Troop Philadelphia City Cavalry, 1774–1914.* Philadelphia: n.p., 1915.

BI384 Bridenbaugh, Carl, and Jessica Bridenbaugh. *Rebels and Gentlemen. Philadelphia in the Age of Franklin.* New York: Reynal & Hitchcock, 1942. 393p. Rev. by L. Dodson, *Pa. Mag. of Hist. and Biography*, vol. 67, no. 2 (April 1943), 166–72.

BI385 Burstein, Alan N. "Residential Distribution and Mobility of Irish and German Immigrants in Philadelphia, 1850–1880." Diss., Univ. of Pa., 1975.

BI386 Burt, Nathaniel. *The Perennial Philadelphians: The Anatomy of an American Aristocracy.* Boston: Little Brown, 1963. 625p. Rev. by C. Angoff, *Jewish Social Studies*, vol. 28, no. 2 (April 1966), 118–19.

BI387 Crous, Ernst. "Krefelder Mennoniten und die Begrüdung von Germantown." *Archiv für Sippenforschung*, vol. 28 (1962), 469–70.

BI388 Demme, C. R. *Zum Andenken an die hundertjährige Jubelfeier in der deutschen Evangelischen Lutherischen St. Michaelis-Kirche in Philadelphia.* Philadelphia: Conrad Zentler, 1843.

BI389 Dolan, Jay. "Philadelphia and the German Catholic Community." In: *Immigrants and Religion in Urban America.* Ed. Randall M. Miller and Thomas D. Marzik. Philadelphia: Temple Univ. Pr., 1977. Rev. by A. M. Greeley, *Jour. of Amer. Hist.*, vol. 64, no. 4 (March 1978), 1133–34.

BI390 Dorr, Benjamin. *An Historical Account of Christ Church, Philadelphia.* Philadelphia: n.p., 1841.

BI391 Eller, Vernand. "A Tale of Two Printers—One City." *Brethren Life and Thought*, vol. 16 (1971), 49–57. Benjamin Franklin and Christopher Sauer.

BI392 Gapp, Samuel Vogt. "Philip Henry Gapp and the Philadelphia German Home Mission, 1850–1864." *Transactions of the Moravian Hist. Soc.* (Nazareth, Pa.), vol. 17, pt. 2 (1960), 231–68.

BI393 Gerhard, Elmer Schultz. "Frederick Graff and the Philadelphia Waterworks." *Amer.-German Rev.*, vol. 13, no. 3 (1947), 30–34. Historical account.

BI394 "A Germantown Chronology." *Amer.-German Rev.*, vol. 25, no. 1 (1958), 13–16.

BI395 Gillingham, Harold. "History of the Union School." Unpublished manuscript in the Germantown Historical Society. A history by a former headmaster of the school.

BI396 Graber, Ellis. "Germantown Commemorates 275th Anniversary." *Mennonite Life*, vol. 13 (1958) 167–68.

BI397 Graeff, Arthur D. "The Graeff House." "'S Pennsylfawnisch Deitsch Eck," Allentown *Morning Call*, 1 May 1965. Project for the rebuilding of the 18th-century structure at 7th and Market Sts., Philadelphia.

BI398 Hershberg, Theodore, Alan N. Burstein, P. Ericksen, Stephanie Greenberg and William L. Yancy. "A Tale of Three Cities: Blacks and Immigrants in Philadelphia, 1850–1880, 1930, and 1970." *Annals of the American Acadamy of Political and Social Sciences*, vol. 441 (1979), 55–81.

BI399 Kent, Homer A. "Beginnings at Germantown: Their Challenge for Today." *Brethren Life and Thought*, vol. 19 (1974), 225–28.

BI400 Linke, Marian. "A Hundred Years St. Thomas Lutheran Church, Germantown." *Amer.-German Rev.*, vol. 22, no. 5 (1956), 28–29.

BI401 London, Hannah R. "Portraits of Rebecca Gratz by Thomas Sully." *Antiques*, vol. 98 (July 1970), 115–17. Rebecca Gratz of Philadelphia was the daughter of Michael G. (1740–1811), a merchant of Philadelphia who emigrated from Silesia in 1759.

BI402 *Philadelphia Gazette Democrat.* 1838–. Ed. Erwin Single. German-language weekly publ. by the Staats-Herold Corp.

BI403 [Philadelphia Lutheran and Reformed Congregations and Churches.] In: *Pastors and People: German Lutheran and Reformed Churches in the Pennsylvania Field, 1717–1793*, by Charles H. Glatfelter. Vol. 1. Publs. of the Pa. German Soc., vol. 13. Breinigsville: The Soc., 1980, p.411–20.

BI404 Richards, J. W. "A Historical Sketch of the Evangelical-Lutheran Church of St. Michael's, Germantown, Pennsylvania." 2 vols. MS. 1845. In the Lutheran Seminary Library, Mt. Airy, Philadelphia.

BI405 Richards, John. *Quaint Old Germantown in Pennsylvania: 60 Former Landmarks Drawn on Zinc, 1863–88.* Comp. and annotated by Julius F. Sachse. Philadelphia: n.p., 1913.

BI406 Rosenbaum, Jeanette W. "Hebrew German Society Rodeph Shalom in the City and County of Philadelphia (1800–1950)." *Publs., Amer. Jewish Hist. Soc.*, vol. 41, no. 1 (1951), 83–93.

BI407 Rosenberger, Arthur S. "N. B. Grubb, Editor and Minister." *Mennonite Life*, vol. 6, no. 1 (1951), 42–45. Grubb (1850–1938) served for forty years as pastor of the Mennonite Church, Philadelphia.

BI408 Rosengarten and Denis (firm). Records, 1818–1853. 20,000 items. In Historical Soc. of Pennsylvania (MS 61-370). Business papers, some family and personal correspondence in English and German. Chemists of Philadelphia.

BI409 Schild, Karl. "75 Jahre der Tabor-Gemeinde in Philadelphia." *Kirchliches Monatsblatt*, vol. 30 (1973), 210–11.

BI410 Schoff, Kitt, and Ella W. Haines. "German Sectarian and British Friend." *Amer.-German Rev.*, vol. 26, no. 2 (1959), 17–19. The early years of Germantown Academy, founded as a bilingual school in 1761.

BI411 Shelly, Andrew R. "Germantown: Mennonite Gateway to North America." *Mennonite Life*, vol. 26 (December 1971), 160.

BI412 Shelly, Andrew R. "Germantown Looks to Bicentennial." *Mennonite Weekly Rev.*, vol. 53, no. 43 (1975), 2.

BI413 Shelly, William H. "Mennonite Landmarks in Germantown." *Mennonite Life*, vol. 13 (1958), 170–73.

BI414 Shover, John L. "The Emergence of a Two-Party System in Republican Philadelphia, 1924–1936." *Jour. of Amer. Hist.*, vol. 60, no. 4 (March 1974), 985–1002. On the German-Americans and their role in the development of the two-party system.

BI415 Shover, John L. "Ethnicity and Religion in Philadelphia Politics, 1924–40." *Amer. Quar.*, vol. 25 (December 1973), 499–515.

BI416 Shryock, Richard H. "Historical Traditions in Philadelphia and in the Middle Atlantic Area: An Editorial." *Pa. Mag. of Hist. and Biography*, vol. 67 (1943), 115–41. Incl. comments on the position of the local Germans.

BI417 Sibole, Edward Emory. *Historical Sketch of St. John's Evangelical Lutheran Church, Philadelphia. Centennial. A Brief Narrative of Events in the First 100 Years, 1806–1906.* Philadelphia: n.p., ca. 1906. 136p.

BI418 Springer, Ruth L., and Louise Wallman. "Two Swedish Pastors Describe Philadelphia, 1700 and 1702." *Pa. Mag. of Hist. and Biography*, vol. 84, no. 2 (1960), 194–218. Andreas Rudman and Andreas Sandel describe the sects and denominations in Philadelphia.

BI419 Talbot, Elizabeth P. "The Philadelphia Furniture Industry 1850 to 1880." Diss., Pennsylvania, 1980. 331p.

BI420 Tinkcom, Harry M., Margaret Tinkcom, and Grant Simon. *Historic Germantown, From the Founding to the Early Part of the Nineteenth Century; a Survey of the German Township...* Philadelphia: Amer. Philosophical Soc., 1955. 154p. Rev. by C. Bridenbaugh, *Pa. Mag. of Hist. and Biography*, vol. 79 (1955), 512–13; V. E. Lewis, *Pa. Hist.*, vol. 23 (1956), 309–10. An architectural study of Germantown houses.

BI421 Watson, John F. "In and About Germantown." "'S Pennsylfawnisch Deitsch Eck," Allen-

Philadelphia—Germantown *(cont.)*

town *Morning Call,* 13, 20, 27 July 1968. Repr. from Watson's *Annals of Philadelphia and Pennsylvania in the Olden Time* (Philadelphia, 1830.)

BI422 Wenger, J. C. "Germantown, a Mennonite Gateway." *Mennonite Life,* vol. 13 (1958), 175–77.

BI423 West Philadelphia Maennerchor. Records, 1896–1906. 13 vols. In Historical Soc. of Pennsylvania (MS 61-708). Minutes of meetings; 12 manuscript song books in German.

BI424 Whiteman, Maxwell. "Isaac Leeser and the Jews of Philadelphia: A Study in National Jewish Influence." *Publs., Amer. Jewish Hist. Soc.,* vol. 48 (1959), 207–44. Leeser (1806–1868) was a prominent leader among the German and Dutch Jews of Philadelphia.

BI425 Wolf, Edwin, and Maxwell Whiteman. *The History of the Jews of Philadelphia from Colonial Times to the Age of Jackson.* Philadelphia: Jewish Publ. Soc. of America, 1957.

BI426 Wolf, Stephanie G. *Urban Village: Population, Community and Family Structure in Germantown, Pennsylvania, 1683–1800.* Princeton: Princeton Univ. Pr., 1976. 361p. Rev. by Bruce Daniels, *Canad. Jour. of Hist.,* vol. 12 (1977), 280–81; R. V. Wells, *Jour. of Amer. Hist.,* vol. 64, no. 4 (March 1978), 1083–84.

BI427 Yoder, Don, ed. "Personalia from the 'Amerikanischer Correspondent' 1826–1828." *Pa. Folklife,* vol. 17, no. 2 (1967–1968), 36–41. Philadelphia newspaper.

Southeast—Bucks County, Chester County

BI428 *The Accounts of Two Pennsylvania German Furniture Makers—Abraham Overholt of Bucks County, 1790–1846, and Peter Ranck, of Lebanon County, 1794–1817.* Sources and Documents of the Pennsylvania Germans, Vol. 3. Trans. and ed. Alan G. Keyser, Larry M. Neff and Frederick S. Weiser. Breinigsville: Pa. German Soc., 1978.

BI429 Ball, Duane E. "The Process of Settlement in Eighteenth Century Chester County, Pennsylvania: A Social and Economic History." Diss., Pennsylvania, 1973.

BI430 Bieber, Edmund Ellis. *Springfield Church [Springfield Township, Bucks Co.]* .... N.p.: n.p., 1953.

BI431 Eby, Warren S. "A Lutheran Mission in Northampton Township in 1748." *Papers, Bucks Co. Hist. Soc.,* vol. 6 (1932), 44–52.

BI432 Fackenthal, B. F. *Saint John Reformed Church of Riegelsville, Pa., Showing the Development of the Congregation from Its Organization in 1849 to January 1, 1911.* ... Riegelsville: n.p., 1911. 221p. In Bucks Co.

BI433 Fretz, Herbert. *The History of the Deep Run Mennonite Congregation of Bucks County, Pa.* Bedminster: n.p., 1949. 52p.

BI434 Jentsch, Theodore. "Old Order Mennonite Family Life in the East Pennsylvania Valley." *Pa. Folklife,* vol. 24 (Autum 1974), 18–27.

BI435 Matthews, Sara. "German Settlement of Northern Chester County in the Eighteenth Century." *Pa. Folklife,* vol. 27, no. 4 (1977–1978), 25–32.

BI436 Petersmann, Sabra H. "Goschenhoppen Heritage. Wills of the 18th Century." *The Goschenhoppen Region* (Zionville, Pa.), vol. 3, no. 2 (1970), 9–16.

BI437 Schultz, George W. "Ironmaster Rutter and the Pietists of 1696." *Amer.-German Rev.,* vol. 10, no. 4 (1944), 26–28. In Bucks Co., Pa.

BI438 Schuyler, William B. "The Beginnings of the Perkiomen Valley Missions." *Records of the Amer. Catholic Hist. Soc.,* vol. 61, no. 2 (1950), 101–09.

BI439 Schuyler, William B. *The Pioneer Catholic Church of Chester County, Saint Agnes, West Chester, Pennsylvania, 1793–1943.* Philadelphia: Peter Reilly, 1944. 283p.

BI440 Siskind, Aaron, and William Morgan. *Bucks County: Photographs of Early Architecture.* New York: Horizon Pr., 1974. 112p.

BI441 Twiss, Beth Ann. "Peter Muhlenberg Slept Here. The Moore House at Valley Forge." *Pa. Folklife*, vol. 29, no. 2 (Winter 1979-1980), 85-94.

Western Counties

BI442 Auerheim, Solomon A. Papers, 1854-1888. 24 items. In American Jewish Hist. Soc. collections, Waltham, Mass. (MS 78-4). A. (b. 1838) was a dry goods merchant of Bradford, Pa.

BI443 Baynham, Edward E. "Henry Kleber, Early Pittsburgh Musician." *Western Pa. Hist. Mag.*, vol. 25, nos. 3-4 (1942), 113-20. Also in the *Amer.-German Rev.*, vol. 10, no. 1 (October 1943), 24-26, 35.

BI444 Beachy, Alvin J. *The Amish of Somerset County, Pennsylvania: A Study in the Rise and Development of the Beachy Amish Mennonite Churches.* Hartford: Hartford Seminary Foundation, 1952.

BI445 Beachy, Alvin J. "The Amish Settlement in Somerset County, Pennsylvania." *Mennonite Quar. Rev.*, vol. 28 (1954), 263-92.

BI446 Beachy, Alvin J. "The Rise and Development of the Beachy Mennonite Churches." *Mennonite Quar. Rev.*, vol. 29 (1955), 118-40.

BI447 Blackburn, E. Howard, and W. H. Welfley. *History of Bedford and Somerset Counties, Pennsylvania....* 3 vols. New York/Chicago: Lewis Publ. Co., 1906.

BI448 Burgess, Ellis B. "The Evangelical Lutheran Church of Western Pennsylvania." *Western Pa. Hist. Mag.*, vol. 26 (1943), 21-46.

BI449 *Catholic Pittsburgh's One Hundred Years.* Symposium Prepared by the Catholic Historical Society of Western Pennsylvania. Chicago: Loyola Univ. Press, 1943. 287p.

BI450 Emerich, Roy, and Al Krochka. "A Home Away from Home." *Pa. Ethnic Studies Newsletter*, vol. 2, no. 2 (1976-1977), 3-5. On Jacob Schmidt and the German Home, Farrell, Mercer Co., Pa.

BI451 Feldman, Jacob S. "Pioneers of a Community: Regional Diversity among the Jews of Pittsburgh, 1845-1861." *Amer. Jewish Archives*, vol. 32 (1980), 119-24.

BI452 Herr, Fred R. "Herr's Island." *Western Pa. Hist. Mag.*, vol. 53, no. 3 (July 1970), 211-26.

BI453 Hommel, Rudolf. "An Eventful Trip to Pittsburgh in 1790." "'S Pennsylfawnisch Deitsch Eck," Allentown *Morning Call*, 11 September 1943.

BI454 Lady, David B. *A History of St. Paul's Orphans' Home of the Reformed Church in the United States, Greenville, Mercer Co., Pa.* Philadelphia: The Reformed Church in the U.S., 1917. 335p.

BI455 Lambing, A. A. *A History of the Catholic Church in the Diocese of Pittsburg and Alleghany from its Establishment to the Present Time.* New York/Cincinnati/St. Louis: Benziger Bros., 1880. 531p.

BI456 Livengood, William S. "The First Bible West of the Alleghenies." "'S Pennsylfawnisch Deitsch Eck," Allentown *Morning Call*, 23 October 1954. Repr. from the *Monthly Bull.* for March 1946, of the Dept. of Internal Affairs, Commonwealth of Pennsylvania.

BI457 Mook, Maurice A. "The Amish Communities at Atlantic, Pennsylvania." *Mennonite Quar. Rev.*, vol. 28 (1954), 293-301.

BI458 Mook, Maurice A. "Joseph Johns: German Amish City Father." "'S Pennsylfawnisch Deitsch Eck," Allentown *Morning Call*, 16, 23 April 1955. The pioneer founder of Johnstown, Pa., was a lifelong member of the Amish church.

BI459 Reibel, Daniel B. "The Kunstfest at Old Economy [Ambridge, Pa.]" *Pa. Folklife*, vol. 20 (Autumn 1970), 23-27. Restoration and museum exhibits described; *Kunstfest* crafts festival was held in June 1969.

BI460 Reel, Caspar, and Conrad Reel. Papers, 1774-1832. 7 vols. In Hist. Soc. of Western Pennsylvania (MS 70-2150). Accounts, daybooks, etc. Father and son were tanners and leather workers.

BI461 Roy, Donald E. "Selected Pittsburgh Imprints, 1807–1860, in the Library of the Historical Society of Western Pennsylvania." *Western Pa. Hist. Mag.*, vol. 44 (1961), 175–97.

BI462 Ruff, Paul Miller. *The German Church Records of Westmoreland County, Pennsylvania, 1772–1791.* Aliquippa, Pa.: n.p., 1979. The ministry of John William Weber, of the Reformed Church. Also Vol. 2: Aliquippa, Pa.: n.p., n.d.

BI463 St. Peter's Evangelical Reformed Church, Pittsburgh. Records, 1839–1857. 50 vols. In Univ. of Pittsburgh Libraries: Archives of Industrial Society (MS 80-458). Incl. church records, minutes, reports, births, deaths, baptisms. Mainly in German.

BI464 Schermerhorn, John Freeman. Papers, 1809–1906. 255 items. Univ. of Missouri Library, Western Hist. MS. Collection (MS 61-54). S. (1786–1851) was a frontier preacher, working in Pittsburgh and Indiana. Papers consist of correspondence and family documents.

BI465 Studer, Gerald. "Mennonites in Southwestern Pennsylvania." *Mennonite Life*, vol. 20, no. 4 (1965), 177–82.

BI466 Turner, Charles W. "An Immigrant Butcher's Diary." *Western Pa. Hist. Mag.*, vol. 34, no. 2 (1951), 135–44. Letters by the immigrant August Ketterer of Freiburg, Germany from 1859 on.

BI467 Van Newkirk, Elizabeth H. "Frostburg after Hours Recreation, 1871–1877." *Jour. of the Alleghenies*, vol. 9 (1973), 21–31. References to a German singing society.

BI468 Wallace, Paul A. W. "Jacob Eyerly's Journal, 1794: The Survey of Moravian Lands in the Erie Triangle." *Western Pa. Hist. Mag.*, vol. 45, no. 1 (1962), 5–23. John Jacob Eyerly, Jr., 1757–1800, of Northampton Co., Pa. sought a grant of lands on French and Conneaut Creeks for his church's Indian mission.

BI469 Weslager, C. A. "Reminiscences of Beltzhoover and Allentown: Two Old-Time Western Pennsylvania Boroughs." *Western Pa. Hist. Mag.*, vol. 49, no. 3 (July 1966), 251–62. The Beltzhoover quarter of Pittsburgh had a marked German character.

BI470 Yoder, Edward. "The Mennonites of Westmoreland County, Pennsylvania." *Mennonite Quar.*

Rev., vol. 5, no. 3 (1941), 155–86. The Rev. Abraham Stauffer was among the earliest settlers to arrive from Lancaster County, in 1790.

Pennsylvania Germans in Other States and Canada

See also Virginia Local History *and* Maryland Local History *under* Part J: German-American Local History.

BI471 Boyer, George R. "Pennsylvania Germans Move to Kansas." *Pa: Hist.*, vol. 32, no. 1 (1964), 25–48.

BI472 Dundore, M. Walter. "Pennsylvania German Transplants in Illinois." "'S Pennsylfawnisch Deitsch Eck," Allentown *Morning Call*, 23, 30 April 1960.

BI473 Dundore, M. Walter. "The Saga of the Pennsylvania Germans in Wisconsin." *Publs., Pa. Ger. Folklore Soc.*, vol. 19 (1955), 33–166.

BI474 Graeff, Arthur D. "In Dixieland." "'S Pennsylfawnisch Deitsch Eck," Allentown *Morning Call*, 7, 14, 21 February 1953. On the "trail of the Pennsylvania Germans through Maryland, Virginia and the Carolinas."

BI475 Graeff, Arthur D. "On the Trail of the Pennsylvania Germans." "'S Pennsylfawnisch Deitsch Eck," Allentown *Morning Call*, 16, 23, 30 May; 6, 13 June 1953.

BI476 Graeff, Arthur D. "The Pennsylvania Germans in Ontario, Canada." *Publs., Pa. Ger. Folklore Soc.*, vol. 11 (1946), 1–80.

BI477 Hammer, Carl, Jr. *Rhinelanders on the Yadkin [N.C.]. The Story of the Pennsylvania Germans in Rowan and Cabarrus.* Salisbury, N.C.: Rowan Prtg. Co., 1943. 130p. Rev. by J. W. Frey, *Amer.-German Rev.* vol. 9, no. 6 (August 1943), 33–34; P. A. Barba, "'S Pennsylfawnisch Deitsch Eck," Allentown *Morning Call*, 1 May 1943; R. E. Leake, *N. Car. Hist. Rev.*, vol. 20, no. 4 (1943), 373–74; C. Wittke, *Jour. of Engl. and Germanic Philology*, vol. 42, no. 4 (1943), 616–17; D. Cunz, *William and Mary College Quar.*, vol. 23, no. 4

(1943), 534. A history of German settlements in Rowan and Cabarrus counties, N.C.

BI478 Heilbron, Bertha L. "Some Sources for Northwest History. Pennsylvania German Baptismal Certificates in Minnesota." *Minn. Hist.*, vol. 27, no. 1 (1946), 29–32.

BI479 Ludwig, G. M. "The Influence of the Pennsylvania Dutch in the Middle West." *Yearbook*, Pa. Ger. Folklore Soc., no. 10 (1945). Allentown: The Society, 1947. 101p.

BI480 "Pennsylvania Dutch Home Life." *Pa. German Folklore Soc. of Ontario*, vol. 7 (1979), 149–74.

BI481 Reaman, G. Elmore. "The Pennsylvania Germans in Ontario." "'S Pennsylfawnisch Deitsch Eck," Allentown *Morning Call*, 20 January 1951.

BI482 Schreiber, William I. "Pennsylvania German Pioneers in Ohio." "'S Pennsylfawnisch Deitsch Eck," Allentown *Morning Call*, 9, 16, 23 November 1957.

BI483 Shoemaker, Alfred L. "Pennsylvania Dutch Canada." *The Pa. Dutchman*, vol. 7, no. 4 (1956), 9–13.

BI484 Smith, Elmer L., and John G. Stewart. "A Dutch Get-Together." "'S Pennsylfawnisch Deitsch Eck," Allentown *Morning Call*, 24 October 1964. Third annual meeting of ethnic Pennsylvania Dutch residents in Shenandoah County, Virginia. At Jerome, Va., 4 October 1964.

BI485 Wust, Klaus G. "The Pennsylvania Germans in North Carolina: A Challenge to Future Historians." "'S Pennsylfawnisch Deitsch Eck," Allentown *Morning Call*, 18 July 1964.

Pennsylvania Biographies and Memoirs

BI486 Adams, Arthur. "Gaius Marcus Brumbaugh." *New England Hist. and Genealogical Register*, vol. 107, no. 2 (1953), 81–82. German-American physician, 1862–1952.

BI487 [Bachman, J.] "Diary of J. Bachman." *Pa. Dutch News and Views*, vol. 4, no. 1 (1972), 8, 11. Written in 1869.

BI488 Barba, Preston A. "Carl A. Bruckmann—Printer and Publisher." *Hist. Rev. of Berks Co.*, vol. 9 (April 1944.)

BI489 Barba, P. A. "The Pennsylvania German Who Conquered Paris." "'S Pennsylfawnisch Deitsch Eck," Allentown *Morning Call*, 8 February 1958. On Charles Rudy, pioneer of the direct method of teaching languages; expert in adult education.

BI490 Barba, P. A., ed. "Letters of a Rural Pennsylvania German Pastor." "'S Pennsylfawnisch Deitsch Eck," Allentown *Morning Call*, 3 March 1956. Letters sent to the Rev. William Helffrich in 1866 and 1886.

BI491 Barba, P. A., ed. "An Old Letter." "'S Pennsylfawnisch Deitsch Eck," Allentown *Morning Call*, 19 March 1955. Translation of a letter written by John Jacob Pflueger in 1819, describing the hardships of his journey to America and his experiences in the new land.

BI492 Bare, Daniel Mathias. *Looking Eighty Years Backward, and a History of Roaring Springs, Pa.* Findlay, Ohio: College Pr., 1920. 247p. Autobiography of B. (1834–1925) with a setting in Morrison's Cove, Pa., and Roaring Springs.

BI493 Bechtel, Louise S. *The Boy with the Star Lantern. Edwin DeTurck Bechtel 1880–1957.* New York: n.p. 1960.

BI494 Berger, Margaret E. "Reminiscing." *Pa. Dutch News and Views*, vol. 4, no. 1 (1972), 5. A teacher's recollections of a one-room school.

BI495 Bergey, Nelson H. "Johannes (Nasz) Naas." "'S Pennsylfawnisch Deitsch Eck," Allentown *Morning Call*, 6 January 1945.

BI496 [Bernhardt Arnt's emigration.] In: *Geschichte der Deutschen im Staate New York*, by Friedrich Kapp. New York: n.p., 1869, p.304–05. Describes the circumstances of A.'s emigration from Baumholder (Pfalz) to Philadelphia in 1731.

BI497 "Biographical Sketch of Dr. Constantin Hering, Compiled by His Daughter." *Mitteilungen des Deut. Pionier-Vereins von Philadelphia*, Heft 4 (1907), 1–15.

BI498 [Bott, Henry.] *Reminiscences of an Old Man on Life in York County, Pennsylvania, during the Nineteenth Century. Diary and Recollections of Henry Bott.* Ed. Carl E. Hatch and Richard E. Kohler. York, Pa.: Stine Publ. Co., 1973. 15p. Paper.

BI499 Boyer, Melville J. "Letters to a Homeopath." *Procs., Lehigh Co. Hist. Soc.*, vol. 30 (1974), 19–45. From letters addressed to Constantine Hering.

BI500 Breininger, Lester P. "The Biography of Jacob S. Yoder." *Tulpehocken Turtle*, vol. 2 (November 1971), 2–11.

BI501 Brumbaugh, Thomas B. "A Pennsylvania-German Diary (1847–1868)." *German-Amer. Studies*, vol. 10 (Fall 1975), 2–11. From an original by Charles Hartman preserved in the Lancaster Archives, Historical Commission of the United Church of Christ.

BI502 Burkholder, Wealthy A. *Some Things I Remember.* Rockton, Pa.: Keystone Pr., 1928. 24p. Life on a Pennsylvania farm described by a lay worker (b. 1819) for the Brethren (Dunkard) Church.

BI503 Clepper, Henry. "Rise of the Forest Conservation Movement in Pennsylvania." *Pa. Hist.*, vol. 12, no. 3 (1945), 200–16. Tribute to Joseph T. Rothrock, "father of Pennsylvania forestry."

BI504 Crist, Jacob Bishop. "Memoirs of a Lutheran Minister, 1850–1881." Ed. Don Yoder. *Pa. Folklife*, vol. 16, no. 3 (1967), 34–41. Crist held pastorates in various locations in Pennsylvania.

BI505 Davis, Henry Hunter. "Autobiography of Henry Hunter Davis." MS. in private hands, of a Methodist preacher, 1850's to 1870's. Partial copy avail. at the Pennsylvania Folklife Society.

BI506 Day, Richard E. "Hasenclever, Peter (1716–1793), Iron Manufacturer." *Dictionary of Amer. Biography*, vol. 8 (1932), 379f.

BI507 Derr, Emerson L. "Simon Snyder, Governor of Pennsylvania 1808–17." Ed. D. thesis, Pennsylvania State Univ., 1961.

BI508 "Dr. Gaius M. Brumbaugh, Dec'd." *National Genealogical Soc. Quar.*, vol. 40, no. 3 (1952), 108. A well-known member of a Pennsylvania and Maryland family.

BI509 Duhring, Herman Louis. Papers, 1860–1922. 100 items. In Dickinson College Library, Carlisle (MS 73-437). Correspondence and memorabilia. D. (1840–1917) was an Episcopal clergyman; papers incl. letters to his son, Herman Louis D., an architect in Philadelphia.

BI510 Dunbar, Gary S. "Henry Chapman Mercer, Pennsylvania Folklife Pioneer." *Pa. Folklife*, vol. 12, no. 2 (1961), 48–56.

BI511 Eisenberg, William Edward. *This Heritage.* Winchester: n.p., 1954. Ca. 365p. Biography of Christian Streit (b. 1749), Lutheran minister of Somerset Co., Pa.

BI512 Fetterhoff, John. *The Life of Rev. John Fetterhoff.* Chambersburg, Pa.: n.p., 1883.

BI513 [Fisher, Sidney George.] "The Diary of Sidney George Fisher 1861." *Pa. Mag. of Hist. and Biography*, vol. 88, no. 1 (January 1964), 70–93; no. 2, 199–226; no. 3, 328–67; no. 4, 456–84. Deals mainly with the life of the Philadelphia aristocracy in the 19th century, 1861–1863.

BI514 Freund, Elisabeth D. *Crusader for Light: Julius R. Friedlander, Founder of the Overbook School for the Blind, 1832.* Philadelphia: Dorrance, 1959. 153p. Rev. by H. C. Gordon, *Pa. Mag. of Hist. and Biography*, vol. 84, no. 3 (1960), 391–93. See also "Julius Friedlander, 1803–1939." *Amer.-German Rev.*, vol. 11, no. 4 (1945), 9–11, by the same author. J. R. Friedlander emigrated from Germany in 1832.

BI515 Frick, Willis G. "John R. Kooken: Minister, Educator, Diplomat and Soldier." *Bull., Hist. Soc. of Montgomery Co.*, vol. 14 (1966), nos. 1–2, p. 5–13. B. in Pennsylvania in 1815, K. founded the German Reformed Church of the Ascension, Norristown.

BI516 Gehman, Henry S. "Reminiscences of a Pennsylvania Octogenarian." *Historic Schaefferstown Record*, vol. 6, no. 3 (1972), 11–12; vol. 7, no. 1 (1973), 12.

BI517 Gerhard, Elmer Schultz. "The First Preacher of Univeralism in Pennsylvania." *Hist. Rev. of Berks Co.*, vol. 14, no. 1 (1948), 15–19. An account of Dr. George De Benneville.

BI518 Gerhard, Elmer Schultz. "Lorenz Ibach: The Stargazing Blacksmith." *Hist. Rev. of Berks Co.*, vol. 14 (January 1949), 46f.

BI519 Gibson, James E. "Bodo Otto, Jr." *Procs., N.J. Hist. Soc.*, vol. 66, no. 4 (1948), 171–83. On the son of Bodo Otto, senior physician of the Valley Forge encampment.

BI520 Girvin, J. Barry. "The Life of William Uhler Hensel." *Jour. of the Lancaster Co. Hist. Soc.*, vol. 70, no. 4 (Michaelmas 1966), 185–248. Pa. political figure (1851–1915).

BI521 Gratz Family, Philadelphia. Business and legal records, 1762–1921. In the Hist. Soc. of Pennsylvania collections (MS 60-2336).

BI522 Groff, Clyde L. "The Mylins, Hans and Martin." *Jour. of the Lancaster Co. Hist. Soc.*, vol. 75 (Trinity 1971), 107–14.

BI523 Hallman, Kenneth Hillegass and Harvey Earl Faulk. "George Welker: The Miller of New Goshenhoppen." *Hist. Soc. of Montgomery Co. Bull.*, vol. 10 (April 1957).

BI524 Harley, Herbert. "A Palatine Boor: A Short Comprehensive History of the Life of Christopher Laver." *Bull., Hist. Soc. of Montgomery Co.*, vol. 16, no. 4 (Spring 1969), 286–97.

BI525 Harper, Simon. "Diary of Simon Harper." 1861, Center County, Pa. In possession of John W. Harper, Schenectady, N.Y.

BI526 Hay, Charles A. *Memoirs of Rev. Jacob Goering, Rev. George Lochmann, D.D., and Rev. Benjamin Kurtz, D.D., LL.D.* Philadelphia: n.p., 1887.

BI527 Heckman, Marlin L. "Abraham Harley Cassel: Nineteenth Century Pennsylvania German Book Collector." *Publs. of the Pa. German Soc.*, vol. 7 (1973), 105–224.

BI528 Heisey, M. Luther. "The Diary of Harriet Amelia Arndt for 1865." *Papers of the Lancaster Co. Hist. Soc.*, vol. 50, no. 3 (1946), 73–76.

BI529 Helfferich, William U., trans. "The Journal of Rev. Johann Heinrich Helfferich." *Pa. Folklife*, vol. 28, no. 4 (1978–1979), 7–24. Diary of a transatlantic voyage in 1771.

BI530 Herman, Stewart W. "Daniel Herman, Pioneer." *Jour. of the Lancaster Co. Hist. Soc.*, vol. 79 (Trinity 1975), 131–41.

BI531 Herz, Julius M. "'O Zionsville, Built on a Hill': Two Cultural Worlds in the Life and Works of Eli Keller." *Procs., Lehigh Co. Hist. Soc.*, vol. 34 (1980), 189–205.

BI532 Hibshman, Jacob. Papers. 739 items, 1763–1880. In Pennsylvania State Univ. Library (MS 69-451). H. (1772–1852) was a U.S. representative and judge, Lancaster Co.

BI533 Hoffman, Johannes W. "The Diary of Johannes Wilhelm Hoffman." Trans. by Charles T. Zahn. *Der Reggeboge*, vol. 6, nos. 2–3 (1972), 6–17.

BI534 Hollenbach, Raymond E. "Henrich Christof Bleicherodt, Indentured Servant of Jacob and Johannes Clemens." "'S Pennsylfawnisch Deitsch Eck," Allentown *Morning Call*, 3 February 1967.

BI535 Hollenbach, Raymond E. "An Octogenarian Pennsylvania Dutchman." *Der Reggeboge*, vol. 9, no. 2 (1975), 18–22. Hollenbach's remarks upon receiving a citation from the Pennsylvania German Society.

BI536 Hollinshead, Benjamin M. "Mountain Mary, Die Baerrick Maria." "'S Pennsylfawnisch Deitsch Eck," Allentown *Morning Call*, 20, 27 November 1965. Repr. of an old account of a visit to the recluse "Mountain Mary," Maria Jung (Young).

BI537 Homan, Wayne E. [Article on Thomas Conrad Porter, President of the Pennsylvania German Society at the time of his death in 1901.] *Hist. Rev. of Berks Co.*, vol. 33 (Spring 1968).

BI538 Hummel, William W. "Abraham Reincke Beck: Portrait of a Schoolmaster." *Jour. of the Lancaster Co. Hist. Soc.*, vol. 60 (December 1964), 1–40. Biography and selected letters of a noted teacher.

BI539 "In Memoriam Daniel Miller." Transactions of the *Hist. Soc. of Berks Co.*, vol. 3 (1910–1916), 460–61.

BI540 *In memoriam of John Knecht.* Hellertown, Pa.: Laubach, Printer, 1891. 23p.

BI541 Johnson, M. F. "Henry Dolfinger, Business Leader." *Americana Illus.*, vol. 35, no. 2

(1941), 389–93. Philadelphia citizen; family's origins in Ergenzingen, Baden.

BI542 Jones, Henry Z. "Abraham Lauck of Wallau." *Der Reggeboge*, vol. 13, no. 1 (1979), 18–19.

BI543 Joyner, Peggy S. et al., eds. "George Erion, the Ragman." *Der Reggeboge*, vol. 11, no. 1 (1977), 3–17. From an 18th century account book. Farmer and rag dealer in Pennsylvania and Virginia.

BI544 Kiess, George. MS. Diary. Original in possession of Dr. Arthur D. Graeff. See "'S Pennsylfawnisch Deitsch Eck," Allentown *Morning Call*, 31 July 1943. Farmer of Pennsylvania, native of Möhringen.

BI545 Kistler, Richard C. "The Professor is Busy." "'S Pennsylfawnisch Deitsch Eck," Allentown *Morning Call*, 7 August 1948. Interview with Fred Jakob Holben, professor of agriculture, Pennsylvania State Univ.

BI546 Klein, Philip Shriver. "John Andrew Shulze—Dark Horse." *Hist. Rev. of Berks Co.*, vol. 7 (1941–1942), 34–38. Governor of Pennsylvania, 1823–1829.

BI547 Kulp, Isaac C., ed. "The Voyage of Bishop Naas, 1733." *Pa. Folklife*, vol. 30 (1980–81), 29–35. Dunkard preacher.

BI548 Labenberg, Judith K. "Clinton Lesher Aaron Schmoyer, alias Grandpa." *Procs., Lehigh Co. Hist. Soc.*, vol. 32 (1978), 100–11.

BI549 Landis, Charles I. *Jasper Yeates and His Times*. Lancaster: n.p., ca. 1922. 33p.

BI550 Lutz family. Papers, 1785–1874. 100 items. In the Hist. Soc. of Pennsylvania (MS 60-2807). Business papers.

BI551 [Memorial address for William Pepper, M.D., LL.D., held at the Univ. of Pa., 29 November 1898] In: *Procs., Philosophical Soc. Held at Philadelphia....* Memorial vol. 1. Philadelphia, The Soc., 1900. See also the biographical sketch by P. C. Croll in *The Pa. German*, vol. 7 (1906), 51–55. On P. (1843–1898).

BI552 Oda, Wilbur Harry. "John George Homan." *Hist. Rev. of Berks Co.*, vol. 13 (1948), 66–71. See also "John George Homan. Man of Many Parts." *The Pa. Dutchman*, vol. 1 (1949–1950), no. 16.

BI553 "Philip C. Croll—Antiquarian, Author, and Man of God." *Hist. Rev. of Berks Co.*, vol. 18, no. 1 (1952), 8–11. A native of Berks Co., Croll founded the *Pa. German Mag.*

BI554 Pomp, John Nicholas. "Autobiography." Trans. by Don Yoder. *The Pa. Dutchman*, vol. 1, no. 8 (23 June 1949), 5f. Pomp served as Reformed minister in Pa., 1765ff. Recalls his early life in Germany (1734–1765).

BI555 Ranck, Henry Haverstick. *The Life of the Reverend Benjamin Bausman*. Philadelphia: n.p., 1912.

BI556 Rapp, David H. "Philip Jacob Michael: Ecclesiastical Vagabond or 'Echt Reformirter' Pastor." *Pa. Folklife*, vol. 28, no. 3 (1978–1979), 14–26. An 18th-century Pennsylvania German.

BI557 "Raymond W. Albright in Memoriam." *Hist. Rev. of Berks Co.*, vol. 31 (1965), 101.

BI558 Redlich, Fritz. "Eric Bollmann, a Forgotten Citizen of Two Worlds." *Amer.-German Rev.*, vol. 16, no. 1 (1944), 23–25. Businessman, diplomat and soldier of fortune, 1769–1821.

BI559 Rosenberger, Homer T. *Adventures and Philosophy of a Pennsylvania Dutchman*. Bellefonte, Pa.: Pennsylvania Heritage, 1971. 665p. Rev. in *Der Reggeboge*, vol. 5, nos. 3–4 (1971), 9–10; Millard E. Glatfelter, *Pa. Hist.*, vol. 40 (1973), 110–12; Mac E. Barrick, *Newsletter of the Soc. for German-Amer. Studies*, vol. 2, no. 3 (1980–1981), 6–7.

BI560 Roth, George L. "Cyriacus Spangenberg." *Pa. Hist.*, vol. 11, no. 4 (1944), 284–89. Hessian Reformed Church pastor in Somerset Co., Pa.

BI561 Royer, B. Franklin. "William Stober, a Pioneer on Antitum." *Trans., Kittochtinny Hist. Soc.*, Chambersburg, vol. 12, 379–90.

BI562 Schaefer, John N. "Lebenslauf of John Nicholas Schaefer." Trans. by William T. Parsons. *Pa. Folklife*, vol. 28, no. 3 (1979), 2–13.

BI563 Schmidt, Edgar E. "To the Memory of Adolf Müller." *Bull., Hist. Soc. of Montgomery Co.*, vol. 4 (1943), 45–46. Horticulturist and popularizer of the dogwood.

BI564 Schneider, Robert I. "Country Butcher: An Interview with Newton Bachman." *Pa. Folklife*, vol. 20, no. 4 (1971), 17–21.

BI565 Sell, Harvey T. "Johann Conrad Yeager and His Son Joshua Yeager." "'S Pennsylfawnisch Deitsch Eck," Allentown *Morning Call*, 30 August 1941.

BI566 Shoemaker, Alfred L. "Henry Dulheuer, The Old Traveler." *The Pa. Dutchman*, vol. 3, no. 17 (1 February 1952), 1, 3.

BI567 Shoemaker, Alfred L. "Notes on Charles F. Egleman." *Hist. Rev. of Berks Co.*, vol. 13, no. 4 (July 1948), 99.

BI568 Shoemaker, Alfred L. "Peter Montelius—Printer and Teacher." *The Pa. Dutchman*, vol. 3, no. 9 (1 October 1951), 3.

BI569 Sinkler, Charles. "Rebecca Gratz of Philadelphia." *Genealogical Mag. and Hist. Chronicle*, vol. 54, (1951), 47–49. The supposed original of Scott's character of Rebecca in *Ivanhoe*.

BI570 Stange, Douglas C. "William A. Passavant [1821–1894, Lutheran Leader]: A Servant to All Men, Black or White." *Western Pa. Hist. Mag.*, vol. 50, no. 3 (July 1967), 187–98.

BI571 Stapleton, Ammon. "The Life and Character of Daniel Bertolet, Jr., of Oley, Pa." *The Evangelical* (Harrisburg), 6 October 1904. See also: *Hist. Rev. of Berks Co.*, April 1945, 74–79.

BI572 Stickler, Franklin A. "Adolf Müller." *Bull., Hist. Soc. of Montgomery Co.*, vol. 4 (1943), 39–44. Forester; active in public park and conservation programs.

BI573 "Swarr, Carl S." *Der Reggeboge*, vol. 5, nos. 3–4 (1971), 7–8. Resolution adopted by the Pennsylvania German Society upon his death.

BI574 Thorpe, Francis Newton. *William Pepper, M.D., LL. D. (1843–1898). Provost of the Univ. of Pennsylvania*. Philadelphia/London: Lippincott, 1904. 555p.

BI575 Weaver, Samuel P. *Autobiography of a Pennsylvania Dutchman*. New York: n.p., 1953. Rev. by George D. Harmon, *Pa. Hist.*, vol. 21, no. 2 (1954), 185–87; J. B. Nolan, *Pa. Mag. of Hist. and Biography*, vol. 78, no. 1 (1954), 133.

BI576 Wirt, George H. "Joseph Trimble Rothrock, Father of Forestry in Pennsylvania." *Amer. German Rev.*, vol. 8, no. 3 (1942), 5–8. Also in "'S Pennsylfawnisch Deitsch Eck," Allentown *Morning Call*, 24 September 1955.

BI577 Wust, Klaus. "Jacob Funk, Jr." "'S Pennsylfawnisch Deitsch Eck," Allentown *Morning Call*, 10 December 1966. A young Colonial Pennsylvania German who planned a seaport near the site of Washington, D.C.

BI578 Yoder, Donald H., ed. "He Rode with McKendree: Selections from the Autobiography of Jacob Bishop Crist." *Western Pa. Hist. Mag.*, vol. 27, nos. 1–2 (1944), 51–78.

BI579 Yrigoyen, Charles, Jr. "Emanuel V. Gerhart, Churchman, Theologian, and First President of Franklin and Marshall College." *Jour. of the Lancaster Co. Hist. Soc.*, vol. 78, no. 1 (1974), 1–28.

BI580 Zehner, Olive G. "Cornelius Weygandt." *The Pa. Dutchman*, vol. 5, no. 1 (1953), 2.

BI581 Zug, John. Papers, 1834–1842. 1 ft. In Dickinson College Library, Carlisle (MS 73-478). Z. was teacher and lecturer.

BJ
Refugees from National-Socialist Germany

General

See also Section CA: Philosophical and Theological Relations; Section CH: Emigré Authors/Refugees from Nazi Germany; *and* Part K: Biography. Prominent Americans of German Descent.

BJ1 American Federation of Jews from Central Europe. *Twenty Years, 1940–1960*. New York: n.p., 1961. 159p. Incl. studies on the economic and religious adjustment of those who immigrated since 1933.

BJ2 Berendsohn, Walter A. "Probleme der Emigration aus dem Dritten Reich." *Aus Politik und Zeitgeschichte* (Bonn), 8 August 1956, p.497–512 and 15 August, 1956, p.513–26.

BJ3 Bock, Sigrid. "Zur bürgerlichen Exilforschung." *Weimarer Beiträge*, vol. 21, no. 4 (1975), 99–129.

BJ4 Cirtautas, K. C. *The Refugee*. Forew. by Dominique Pire and Pitirim A. Sorokin. Postscript by Romano Guardini. New York: Citadel, 1963. 160p.

BJ5 Committee for Aid to German and Austrian Scholars. Records, 1946–1948. 425 items. In the Univ. of Chicago Library. (MS 64-71). The committee provided books, food, and supplies to emigré scholars.

BJ6 Council for a Democratic Germany. *A Declaration of the Council for a Democratic Germany*. N.p.: n.p., 1944. Mimeogr. pamphlet. The last futile attempt to form a broadly based Free German front in the United States.

BJ7 Council for a Democratic Germany. *Erklärungen an die Mitglieder und Freunde des Rates für ein demokratisches Deutschland*. N.p.: n.p., October 1945. Mimeogr. pamphlet.

BJ8 Council for a Democratic Germany. New York. *Rede des Chairman Paul Tillich. Zusammenkunft der New Yorker Unterzeichner der Deklaration des "Council for a Democratic Germany."* New York: n.p., 1944. Mimeogr. pamphlet of speech 17 June 1944.

BJ9 Davie, Maurice R. *Refugees in America*. New York: Harper, 1947. A committee study on immigration from Europe 1933–1944.

BJ10 Edinger, Lewis J. *German Exile Politics*. Berkeley: Univ. of Calif. Pr., 1956.

BJ11 Ernst, Robert. "The Asylum of the Oppressed." *South Atlantic Quar.*, vol. 40 (January 1941), 1–10. On the refugees from Nazi Germany.

BJ12 *Europe and the German Refugees*. Frankfurt: Institut zur Förderung öffentlicher Angelegenheiten, 1952. 94p.

BJ13 *Exil und Innere Emigration*. Ed. Reinhold Grimm and Jost Hermand. Wissenschaftl. Paperbacks: Literaturwiss., no. 17. Frankfurt: Athenäum Vlg., 1972. 210p. Rev. by Guy Stern, *Monatshefte*, vol. 66, no. 3 (Fall 1974), 325–27. Third Wisconsin Workshop. Treats exile in historico-political perspective. Contributions by Hans Mayer, David R. Bathrick, Theo. Ziolkowski, Karl Schröter, and Frank Trommler.

BJ14 Friedman, Saul S. "Official United States Policy toward Jewish Refugees, 1938–1945." Diss., Ohio State, 1969. 425p. "American anti-Semitism, combined with self-concern born of the Depression, and anti-alienism...in Congress prevented President Roosevelt from inaugurating changes" in U.S. immigration policies.

BJ15 Friedmann, Friedrich Georg. "Auswanderung und Rückkehr—Gedanken zur nationalsozialistischen Universität." In: *Die deutsche Universität im Dritten Reich. Eine Vortragsreihe der Universität München*. München: n.p., 1966. Also in: *Das Parlament* (Weekly), 21 September 1966.

BJ16 Friedrich-Ebert-Stiftung. Bad Godesberg. *Die deutsche politische Emigration 1933–1945*. Bad

Godesberg: Friedrich-Ebert-Stiftung, 1972. 135p. Exhibition catalogue.

BJ17 Frühwald, Wolfgang, and Wolfgang Schieder, eds. *Leben im Exil. Probleme der Integration deutscher Flüchtlinge im Ausland 1933–1945.* Hamburg: Hoffmann and Campe, 1981. 285p. Rev. by J. Strelka, *German Quar.*, vol. 55, no. 4 (November 1982), 610–11.

BJ18 Genezi, Haim. "American Interfaith Cooperation on Behalf of Refugees from Nazism, 1933–1945." *Amer. Jewish Hist.*, vol. 70 (March 1981), 347–61.

BJ19 Gittig, Hans, ed. *Bibliographie zur Geschichte des antifaschistischen Widerstandes.* Berlin: Deutsche Staatsbibliothek, 1959.

BJ20 Goldner, Franz. *Die österreichische Emigration 1938–45.* Wien: Herold Vlg., ca. 1972. No. 6 in a series of works on the Austrian resistance and emigration, 1938–1945.

BJ21 Heintz, Georg. *Index der "Neuen Weltbühne" 1933–1939.* Deutsches Exil 1933–1945, vol. 1. Worms: Heintz, 1972. 104p. Exile periodical.

BJ22 Hirsch, Julius, and Edith Hirsch. "Berufliche Eingliederung und wirtschaftliche Leistung der deutschjüdischen Einwanderung in die Vereinigten Staaten (1934–1960)." In: *American Federation of Jews from Central Europe, Twenty Years...1940–1960.* New York: n.p., 1961, p.41–70.

BJ23 Jackman, Jarrell C. "Exiles in Paradise: German Emigrés in Southern California, 1933–1950." *Southern Calif. Quar.*, vol. 61 (1979), 183–205.

BJ24 Jacobson, Claire. *The German Petty Bourgeoisie in Transition; Imperial Germany and Yorkville, U.S.A.* Ann Arbor: University Microfilms, 1958.

BJ25 Kettenacker, Lothar, ed. *Das "Andere Deutschland" im Zweiten Weltkrieg. Emigration und Widerstand in internationaler Perspektive.* Stuttgart: Klett, 1977. 320p.

BJ26 Klaus, Erwin H. "Die fortschrittliche deutschamerikanische Bewegung." *Aufbau Almanach* (New York) 1941, p.73–82.

BJ27 Kuehl, Michael. "Die exilierte demokratische Linke in U.S.A." *Zeitschrift für Politik*, N.F., vol. 4 (July 1957), 273–89.

BJ28 Laqueur, Walter Z. *Young Germany.* New York: Basic Books, 1962.

BJ29 Lazin, Frederick A. "The Response of the American Jewish Community to the Crisis of German Jewry, 1933–39." *Amer. Jewish Hist.*, vol. 68 (March 1979), 283–304.

BJ30 Link, Werner. "German Political Refugees in the United States during the Second World War." In: *German Democracy and the Triumph of Hitler. Essays in Recent German History.* Ed. A. J. Nicholls and E. Matthias. New York: St. Martin's Pr., ca. 1972, p.241–60.

BJ31 Lowenstein, Ludwig. "Die Entwicklung des 'New World Club'." *American Federation of Jews from Central Europe. Twenty Years...1940–1960.* New York: n.p., 1961, p.71–76.

BJ32 Maass, Ernest. "Integration and Name-Changing among Jewish Refugees from Central Europe in the U.S." *Names*, vol. 6 (September 1958).

BJ33 Matthias, Erich. *Sozial-Demokratie und Nation: Zur Ideengeschichte der sozialdemokratischen Emigration 1933–1938.* Stuttgart: Deutsche Verlags-Anstalt, 1952. 363p. Rev. by H. Kohn, *Amer. Hist. Rev.*, vol. 58 (1953), 914–16.

BJ34 Nawyn, William E. "American Protestant Churches Respond to the Plight of Germany's Jews and Refugees, 1933–1941." Diss., Iowa, 1980. 624p.

BJ35 Raddatz, Fritz J. "Exil contra Emigration." *Merkur*, vol. 32 (1978), 148–50.

BJ36 Ragg, Albrecht. "The German Socialist Emigration in the United States, 1933 to 1945." Diss., Loyola Univ. of Chicago, 1977.

BJ37 Reimer, Jürgen. "Quellen: Materialien zur politischen Emigration und zum innerdeutschen Widerstand gegen das Dritte Reich." *Internat. wissenschaftliche Korrespondence zur Geschichte der deutschen Arbeiterbewegung*, vol. 5 (December 1967), 1–38.

BJ38 Saenger, Gerhart. *Today's Refugees, Tomorrow's Citizens: A Story of Americanization.*

General *(cont.)*

New York: Harper, 1941. 286p. Rev. by Franz Hoellering, *Nation*, vol. 153, no. 5 (1941), 97–98.

BJ39 Sauer, Paul. "Die USA als Zufluchtsland für Verfolgte des nationalsozialistischen Regimes." In: *USA und Baden-Württemberg in ihren geschichtlichen Beziehungen*. Ed. Geo. Haselier. Stuttgart: n.p., 1976, p.66–70.

BJ40 Schaber, Will, ed. *Aufbau-Reconstruction: Dokumente einer Kultur im Exil*. Introd. by Hans Steinitz. New York: Overlook Pr., 1972. 416p.

BJ41 Schau, Friedrich. *Die Emigrationspresse der Sozialisten 1938 bis 1945*. Wien: Europa, 1968. 44p.

BJ42 Spalek, John M., in collab. with Adrienne Ash and Sandra H. Hawrylchak. *Guide to the Archival Materials of the German-Speaking Emigration to the United States after 1933/Verzeichnis der Quellen und Materialien der deutschsprachigen Emigration in den U.S.A. seit 1933*. Charlottesville: Univ. Pr. of Virginia, for the Bibliographic Soc. of the Univ. of Virginia, 1979. 1133p. Describes and furnishes locations of the papers, letters, literary works, memorabilia, etc. of near 700 distinguished emigré writers and scholars.

BJ43 Sternfelt, Wilhelm. "Die Emigrantenpresse." *Deutsche Rundschau*, vol. 76 (1950), 250–59.

BJ44 Stock, E. "Washington Heights' 'Fourth Reich': The German Emigrés' New Home." *Commentary*, vol. 11 (June 1951), 581–88.

BJ45 Strauss, Herbert A. "Zur sozialen und organisatorischen Akkulturation deutsch-jüdischer Einwanderer in den U.S.A." In: *Leben im Exil: Probleme der Integration deutscher Flüchtlinge im Ausland 1933 bis 1945*. Ed. Wolfgang Frühwald and Wolfgang Schieder. Hamburg: Hoffmann and Campe, 1981, p.235–60.

BJ46 Szajkowski, Zosa. "The Attitude of American Jews to Refugees from Germany in the 1930's." *Amer. Jewish Hist. Quar.*, vol. 61 (December 1971), 101f.

BJ47 Tartakower, Arieh, and Kurt Grossmann. *The Jewish Refugee*. New York: Institute of Jewish Affairs, 1944.

BJ48 Tutas, Herbert E. *N S—Propaganda und deutsches Exil 1933–1939*. Deutsches Exil 1933–1945, vol. 4. Worms: Georg Heintz, 1973. 194p. Incl. the full facsimile reprint of the "Leitheft" (guidelines) of the Reich Security Office (Reichssicherheitshauptamt) concerning treatment of the German exiles in the media, 1937.

BJ49 United States. Displaced Persons Commission. *The D P Story*. Washington, D.C.: n.p., 1952.

BJ50 United States. House of Representatives. *Walter Report. Expellees and Refugees of German Ethnic Origin*. Washington, D.C.: n.p., 1950. 87p.

BJ51 Walter, Hilde. "Die Flucht nach Amerika. Amerikanische Bürger helfen Nazi-Verfolgten bei der Rettung." *New Yorker Staats-Zeitung und Herold*, no. 44, 31 October 1971. A first-hand account of emergency assistance to refugees, 1940.

BJ52 Worms. Stadtbibliothek. *Verbrannt, verboten, verdrängt? Literatur und Dokumente der deutschen Emigration nach 1933 als Zeugnisse des antifaschistischen Widerstandes sowie N S—Schrifttum*. Worms: Stadtbibliothek, 1973. 79p. Exhibit to commemorate 40th anniversary of the book-burning, 10 May 1933.

BJ53 Wyman, David S. *Paper Walls: America and the Refugee Crisis, 1938–41*. Amherst: Univ. of Mass. Pr., 1968. 306p. Rev. by R. A. Divine, *Jour. of Amer. Hist.*, vol. 41, no. 2 (September 1969), 428–29; H. L. Feingold, *Amer. Jewish Hist. Quar.*, vol. 59 (1969), 129–31; L. Dinnerstein, *Jewish Social Studies*, vol. 31, no. 4 (October 1969), 338–39. Indictment of the United States for its failure to live up to its ideal of asylum. A maze of bureaucratic regulations hindered rather than helped those who were fleeing Hitler's terror.

Memoirs/Refugee Experiences

See also Section CI: German-American Literature *and* Part K: Biography. Prominent Americans of German Descent.

BJ54 Auernheimer, Raoul. "For Instance, Myself." *Amer.-German Rev.*, vol. 12, no. 5 (1946), 27, 29, 38. A brief account of the author's experiences as a recent immigrant.

BJ55 Barschak, Erna. *My American Adventure*. New York: n.p., 1945. 248p. Reactions of a German refugee to the American environment.

BJ56 Berl-Lee, Maria. *Schaumwein aus meinem Krug*. Wien: Bergland, 1974.

BJ57 Bermann Fischer, Gottfried. *Bedroht—Bewahrt. Weg eines Verlegers*. Vom Arzt zum Verleger, durch Nazijahre, Exil und Wiederaufbau hindurch; die Autobiographie spiegelt Geschichte und kulturelles Leben eines halben Jahrhunderts. Frankfurt a. Main: S. Fischer Vlg., 1967, 1970.

BJ58 Bettelheim, Bruno. *The Informed Heart. Autonomy in a Mass Age*. Glencoe, Ill.: Free Press, 1970. The social philosopher and psychologist reflects on experiences in surviving internment in Dachau and Buchenwald and establishing a career in America.

BJ59 Bonn, Moritz J. *Wandering Scholar*. New York; John Day, 1948. 403p. Rev. by H. Kohn, *Annals of the Amer. Academy of Political and Social Science*, vol. 261 (1949), 192–93. Autobiography of a liberal economist of Germany and professor in the United States.

BJ60 Brecht, Arnold. *The Political Education of Arnold Brecht: An Autobiography, 1884–1970*. Princeton: Princeton Univ. Pr., 1970. 544p. Government official in the Weimar Republic; professor of political science in the U.S.

BJ61 Cassirer, Toni. *Aus meinem Leben mit Ernst Cassirer*. New York: n.p., 1950.

BJ62 Deutsch, Julius. *Ein weiter Weg*. Zürich: Amalthea, 1960. Memoirs of a refugee.

BJ63 Drucker, Peter F. *The Adventures of a Bystander*. New York: Harper and Row, 1979. The early years 1908–1935 of a writer and economist who came to the U.S. from Vienna in 1933.

BJ64 Epstein, Fritz T. "Hamburg und Osteuropa: Zum Gedächtnis von Professor Richard Salomon (1884–1966)." *Jahrbücher für Geschichte Osteuropas*, vol. 15 (March 1967). See also the obituary of Professor Salomon, *New York Times*, 4 Feb. 1966, p.31. Distinguished emigré professor of history.

BJ65 Fraenkel, Heinrich. *Farewell to Germany*. London: B. Harrison, 1959.

BJ66 Freeman, Joseph. *Never Call Retreat*. New York: Farrar & Rinehart, 1943. 756p. Life of Paul Schuman, b. 1900 in Vienna, who in 1941 escaped a Nazi concentration camp and began a new life in America.

BJ67 Goetz, Curt, and Valérie von Martens. *Wir wandern, wir wandern: Der Memoiren dritter Teil*. Stuttgart: Deutsche Verlagsanstalt, 1963.

BJ68 Hallgarten, George W. F. *Als die Schatten fielen*. Berlin: Ullstein, ca. 1969. 368p. Memoirs of a political refugee who came to New York in 1938.

BJ69 Hammer, Walter. *Hohes Haus in Henkers Hand: Rückschau auf die Hitlerzeit, auf Leidensweg und Opfergang deutscher Parlamentarier*. 2nd rev. ed. Frankfurt: Europäische Verlangsanstalt, 1956.

BJ70 Hauser, Heinrich. *Time Was. Death of a Junker*. Trans. by Barrows Mussey. New York: Reynal and Hitchcock, 1942. 316p. Autobiography of man whose life spanned three Germanys—Empire, Republic, and Third Reich—before he emigrated to the United States.

BJ71 Hilsenrad, Helen. *Brown Was the Danube*. New York: Thomas Yoseloff, 1966. 492p. Autobiography of a refugee from Austria.

BJ72 Hirsch, Felix E. "Gerhart Seger: In the Tradition of Carl Schurz." *Amer.-German Rev.*, vol. 33, no. 3 (1967), 26–27. Member of the Reichstag in 1935; a militant socialist, editor of the *Neue Volkszeitung*; emigrated to the U.S. in 1935.

BJ73 Kohn, Hans. *Bürger vieler Welten. Ein Leben im Zeitalter der Weltrevolution*. Mit Geleitwort von Arnold J. Toynbee. Trans. from Engl. by Anna Katharina Ulrich-Debrunner. Frauenfeld: Huber, 1965. 276p. Rev. by R. Weltsch, *Neue Rundschau*, vol. 77 (1966), 519–25.

BJ74 Kohn, Hans. *Living in a World Revolution. My Encounters with History*. New York: Trident, 1964. 211p.

BJ75 Kraus, H. P. *A Rare Book Saga. An Autobiography*. London: Andre Deutsch, 1979. 386p. Refugee from Vienna; a rare book dealer who came to America via Sweden. See also his *In Retrospect, 100 Outstanding Manuscripts Sold in the Last Four Decades by H. P. Kraus*.

BJ76 Lazarsfeld, Paul F. "An Episode in the History of Social Research: A Memoir." In: *The Intellectual Migration. Europe and America, 1930–1960*. Ed. Donald Fleming and Bernard Bailyn. Cambridge: Harvard Univ. Pr., 1969, p.270–337.

BJ77 Lehmann-Haupt, Helmut. "Odyssee einer Bücherfreundes." *Philobiblon*, vol. 23, no. 2 (1979), 106–26. Memoirs and reminiscences of the American critic, bibliophile, and editor.

BJ78 Lips, Eva. *Rebirth in Liberty*. New York: n.p., 1942. 304p. Memoirs of a German refugee intellectual and writer. For her life in Germany, see her *Savage Symphony*.

BJ79 Lembeck, Fred, and Wolfgang Giere. *Otto Loewi: Ein Lebensbild in Dokumenten*. Berlin: Springer-Vlg., 1968. 241p. Rev. by Abram Kanof, *Amer. Jewish Histor. Quar.*, vol. 58, no. 4 (June 1969), 526. Medical scientist and Nobel Prize winner who fled Nazi Germany and came to the U.S.

BJ80 Lothar, Ernst. *Das Wunder des Überlebens*. Hamburg: Paul Szolnay, 1961.

BJ81 Lowe, Adolf. "In Memoriam: Eduard Heimann 1889–1967." *Social Research*, vol. 34 (1967), 609–12. Professor of economics and social science at the New School, New York and Hamburg University.

BJ82 Marcuse, Ludwig. *Mein Zwanzigstes Jahrhundert*. München: Paul List, 1960.

BJ83 Mayer, Carl. "In Memoriam: Albert Salomon 1891–1966." *Social Research*, vol. 34 (1967), 213–25.

BJ84 Niers, Gerd. "Abschied von Otto Fürth." *Aufbau*, 11 January 1980.

BJ85 Richter, Fritz. *Wenn du drüben bist...Geschichte eines Schlesiers in Amerika*. Stuttgart: Behrendt Vlg., 1949.

BJ86 Robitaillé, Adrien. "Walter Ruhman." *Arts et Pensée*, vol. 1, no. 3 (1951), 87–91. Mentioned in the *Canad. Hist. Rev.*, vol. 32, no. 3 (1951), 296. Biog. of a German-born doctor; interned in 1939 in England as political refugee; began his career as artist after 1940 in Canada.

BJ87 Schoenberner, Franz. *The Inside Story of an Outsider*. New York: Macmillan, 1949. 273p.

BJ88 Simons, Erna. *Snapshots of New York; Tagebuchblätter 1938*. Stuttgart: Rottacker, 1949. 119p.

BJ89 Stampfer, Friedrich. "Heimkehr aus der Emigration." *Neue Volks-Zeitung*, 16 August 1947, p.7.

BJ90 Stampfer, Friedrich. *Mit dem Gesicht nach Deutschland. Eine Dokumentation über die sozialdemokratische Emigration aus dem Nachlass von Friedrich Stampfer . . . .* Herausgegeben im Auftrag der Kommission für Geschichte des Parlamentarismus und der politischen Parteien von Erich Matthias. Ed. Werner Link. Düsseldorf: Droste, 1968. 785p. Rev. by S. Bahne, *Historische Zeitschrift*, vol. 211 (1971), 176–78. Stampfer, former editor of *Vorwaerts* (Germany); came to America in 1940.

BJ91 Steiner, Frank Charles. "Manfred George: His Life and Works." Diss., State Univ. of New York at Albany, 1977. 248p.

BJ92 Stolper, Toni. *Ein Leben in Brennpunkten unserer Zeit. Wien, Berlin, New York: Gustav Stolper, 1888–1947*. Tübingen: Wunderlich H. Leins, 1960. 502p. The Austrian Stolper was editor, commentator and investment counselor in New York; founder of *Der deutsche Volkswirt*. Rev. by C. Landauer, *Jour. of Mod. Hist.*, vol. 34 (1962), 105–06.

BJ93 Victor, Walther. *Kehre wieder über die Berge*. New York: Willard Publ. Co., 1945. Autobiographical.

BJ94 Victor, Walther. *Ein Paket aus Amerika*. Weimar: Thüringer Volksverlag, 1950.

BJ95 Wagner, Friedelind. *Heritage of Fire*. New York: Harper, 1945. 225p. Granddaughter (b. 1918) of Richard Wagner. Memoirs of youth in Germany, schooling in England, and later residence in the United States.

BJ96 Warburg, Max M. *Aus meinen Aufzeichnungen*. Ed. Hugo Bieber. New York: Eric M. Warburg, [1950]. 158p.

BJ97 Wehner, Alfred. *From Hitler Youth to U.S. Citizen*. New York: Carlton, 1972.

BJ98 Zassenhaus, Hiltgunt. *Walls: Resisting the Third Reich*. Boston: Beacon Pr., 1974. Reminiscences of the Resistance; author was later a physician practicing in Baltimore.

BJ99 Zoff, Otto. *Tagebücher aus der Emigration (1939–1944)*. Eds. Liselotte Zoff and Hans-Joachim Pavel. Epilogue by Hermann Kesten. Heidelberg: L. Schneider, 1968. 293p.

BJ100 Zweig, Friderike M. *Spiegelungen des Lebens*. Wien: Hans Deutsch Verlag, 1964.

BK
Switzerland-American Relations/Swiss-Americans

General

BK1 *Amerikanische Schweizer Zeitung. American Swiss Gazette*. 1868– . German and English language weekly. Ed. Franz X. Amrein. 1 Union Square West, New York 10003.

BK2 B., L. "Helvetica in American Libraries and Archives." *Newsletter of the Swiss-Amer. Hist. Soc.*, vol. 1, no. 3 (1965), 4–6.

BK3 Boeschenstein, Hermann. *Im Roten Ochsen. Geschichte einer Heimkehr*. Schaffhausen: Meier, 1977. 231p.

BK4 Boeschenstein, Hermann. *Unter Schweizern in Kanada*. Bern: n.p., 1974.

BK5 Bovay, Emile-Henri. "From Saanen in the Canton of Berne to Nipissing—A Little Known Episode of Swiss Emigration to Canada." *Newsletter of the Swiss-Amer. Hist. Soc.*, vol. 10 (March 1974), 17–18.

BK6 Brunner, Emil. "*Was hat Amerika uns, was haben wir Amerika zu geben?*" Series of the Swiss-Amer. Soc. for Cultural Relations, vol. 4. Basel.: n.p., 1945.

BK7 Burkhard, Marianne. "In Memoriam, Corine Honegger-Baumann." *Swiss-Amer. Hist. Soc. Newsletter*, vol. 17, no. 2 (1981), 3–4.

BK8 Escher, Henry. Papers. 1 box and 1 package. In New York Public Library (MS 69-830). Incl. the records of the Swiss Benevolent Soc. of N.Y.: lists of officers and index volumes; papers relating to Swiss immigrants, together with an unpublished history of the Swiss in America, written by E. (1832–1892).

BK9 Gruenewald, Rosa W. *The Story of a Dairy Barn: Being an Account of the Importance of the Swiss People to Green County and the State of Wisconsin*. Monroe, Wis.: n.p., 1980.

BK10 Liniger, Hans. *Schweizerische Auswanderung in Vergangenheit und Zukunft*. vol. 1. *Das Grundsätzliche*. Luzern: n.p., [1948].

BK11 M., H. K. "Some Resources in the New York Public Library for the Study of Swiss in the United States." *Newsletter of the Swiss-Amer. Hist. Soc.*, vol. 1, no. 3 (1965), 6.

BK12 Meier, Heinz K. *Friendship under Stress. U.S.-Swiss Relations 1900–1950*. Bern: Herbert Lang and Co., 1970. 423p. Rev. by W. M. Franklin, *Amer. Hist. Rev.*, vol. 77 (1972), 1092–93.

BK13 Meier, Heinz K. "Les relations de la Suisse avec la Grande Bretagne et les Etats-Unis." *Revue d'histoire de la deuxième guerre mondiale*, vol. 121 (January 1981), 41–47.

BK14 Meier, Heinz K. "The United States and Switzerland in the Nineteenth Century." Diss., Emory Univ., 1959. Publ. under the same title: The Hague: Mouton and Co., 1963. 208p. Study of emigration to America, commercial and diplomatic relations to 1900. Rev. by L. F. Burckhardt, *Amer.-German Rev.*, vol. 30, no. 4 (1964), 39; V. R. Greene, *Amer. Quar.*, vol. 16, no. 1 (1964), 119–

General *(cont.)*

20; L. Schelbert, *Amer. Hist. Rev.*, vol. 74, no. 1 (October 1968), 109.

BK15 Peyer, Hans Conrad. "Zürich und Übersee um die Wende vol 18. zum 19. Jahrhundert." In: *Beiträge zur Wirtschafts- und Stadtgeschichte. Festschrift für Hektor Ammann.* Wiesbaden: 1965, p.205–19.

BK16 Rappard, William E. "Pennsylvania and Switzerland: The American Origins of the Swiss Constitution...." In: *Univ. of Pennsylvania Bicentennial Conference. Studies in Political Science and Sociology.* Philadelphia: n.p., 1941, p.49–121.

BK17 Rippinger, Joel. "The Swiss-American Congregation: A Centennial Survey." *Amer. Benedictine Rev.*, vol. 32 (1981), 87–99.

BK18 Robbins, Walter L., ed. "Swiss and German Emigrants to America in Rotterdam, 1736. Excerpts from the Travel Diary of Hieronymus Annoni." *Newsletter of the Swiss-Amer. Hist. Soc.*, vol. 1, no. 3 (October 1965), 16–18.

BK19 Schelbert, Leo. "Eighteenth Century Migration of Swiss Mennonites to America." *Mennonite Quar. Rev.*, vol. 42 (July 1968), 163–83; (October 1968), 285–300. The movement of a small group of refugees from religious persecution to a "New Zion" in Pennsylvania or Carolina.

BK20 Schelbert, Leo. "Swiss." In: *Encyclopedia of American Ethnic Groups.* Ed. Stephan Thernstrom. Cambridge: Harvard Univ. Pr., 1980, p.981–87.

BK21 *Die Schweiz und die Vereinigten Staaten von Amerika. Beziehungen der Schweiz zu den Vereinigten Staaten. Die schweizerische Auswanderung. Bibliographie.* Bern: Bibliographische Auskunftsstelle der Landesbibliothek, 1964. 58p. A list of 550 books and articles.

BK22 *Schweizerische Amerikanistengesellschaft. Bulletin no. 31.* 1967. Genève: Musée et Institut d'Ethnographie. 58p. *Bulletin no. 32.* 1968. Genève: Musée et Institut d'Ethnographie. *Bulletin no. 35.* 1971. 43p. *Bulletin no. 36.* 1972. 85p.

BK23 Straumann, Heinrich. "Switzerland and the English-Speaking World." In: *Contexts of Literature: An Anglo-Swiss Approach. Twelve Essays.* Schweizer Anglistische Arbeiten, vol. 75. Bern: Francke, 1973.

BK24 *The Swiss American.* German-language Monthly. Ed. Anton Haemmerle. Sponsored by the North American Swiss Alliance. 603 Forest Ave., Paramus, N.J. 07652. Title varies: November 1941, *Der Schweizer*; December 1941–, *The Swiss American.* Articles in English and German.

BK25 *Swiss Canadian News.* Monthly. 1960–. Ed. A. Mettler. Publ. by the Swiss Club, Toronto.

BK26 *Swiss Journal/Schweizer Journal.* 1918–. Ed. S. Muschi and L. Muschi. Weekly newspaper in English, French, German and Italian languages. Swiss Publ. Co., San Fransisco.

BK27 Walbruck, Harry A., adapt. *Wilhelm Tell heute.* Skokie, Ill.: National Textbook Co., ca. 1974. A retelling of the drama with photographs of its staging in the New Glarus, Wis., William Tell festival.

BK28 Zollinger, James Peter. *The Swiss Benevolent Society of New York. A Brief History of Its First One Hundred Years, 1846–1946.* New York: The Society, 1947. 52p.

Swiss-American Historical Society

BK29 Meier, Heinz K. "History of the Swiss American Historical Society. Part II. A Crisis and A Radical Change." *Newsletter, Swiss-Amer. Hist. Soc.*, vol. 9 (May 1973), 4–15. The Soc. is located in Washington, D.C.

BK30 Meier, Heinz K. *The Swiss-American Historical Society, 1927–1977.* Norfolk: Donning, 1977. 82p.

BK31 Schelbert, Leo. "Swiss-American Historical Society." *International Migration Rev.*, vol. 3, no. 3 (Summer 1969), 64–66.

BK32 Senn, Alfred, ed. *The Swiss Record. Yearbook of the Swiss-Amer. Hist. Soc.*, vol. 2 (1950). Madison, Wis.: n.p., 1950. 112p. Incl. "Andreas Dietsch and Helvetia, Mo.," by G. Schulz-Behrend; "The Rev. Michael Schlatter," by John C. Schoop; "The Most Rev. Vincent Wehrle, First Bishop of Bismarck, N. D.," by B. Pfaller; "Herman Charles Honegger," by A. Bartholdi; and "The Swiss Benevolent Society of Philadelphia," by J. C. Schoop.

BK33 Swiss-American Historical Society. *The Swiss in the United States*. A Compilation Prepared for the Swiss-Amer. Hist. Soc. as the Second Volume of Its Publications. Ed. John Paul von Grueningen. Madison: The Society, 1940. 158p.

BK34 *The Swiss Record*. Vol. 1–, 1949–. Yearbook of the Swiss-American Hist. Soc.

C

Philosophical, Intellectual, and Literary Relations

CA
Philosophical and Theological Relations

General

CA1 Curti, Merle. *The Growth of American Thought*. New York: Harper and Bros., 1943. 848p. A general study on the relat ons between the German and American university systems.

CA2 Dowie, J. Iverne, and J. Thomas Tredway. *Immigration of Ideas: Studies in North Atlantic Community*. Rock Island, Ill.: Augustana Hist. Soc., 1968. Rev. by A. W. Anderson, *Jour. of Amer. Hist.*, vol. 55, no. 3 (December 1968), 642–44.

CA3 Flower, Elizabeth, and Murray G. Murphy. *A History of Philosophy in America*. New York: Capricorn Books, Putnam's Sons, 1977. 2 vols. 435, 497p. Incl. sections on New England logic and Transcendentalism, the St. Louis Hegelians, C. S. Peirce, William James.

CA4 Schneider, Herbert W. *A History of American Philosophy*. New York: Columbia Univ. Pr., 1946. 646p.

CA5 Van Tassel, David D., and Robert W. McAhren, eds. *European Origins of American Thought*. Chicago: Rand McNally, 1969. 146p.

Theological Interrelations/Biblical Criticism/Unitarianism

CA6 Bainton, Roland H. "Yale and German Theology in the Middle of the Nineteenth Century." *Zeitschrift für Kirchengeschichte*, vol. 66, no. 3 (1954–1955), 294–302.

CA7 Bowden, Henry Warner. "Philip Schaff and Sectarianism: The Americanization of a European Viewpoint." *Jour. of Church and State*, vol. 8, no. 1 (Winter 1966), 97–106.

CA8 Bowden, Henry Warner. "Robert Baird: Historical Narrative and the Image of a Protestant America—1855." *Jour. of Presbyterian Hist.*, vol. 47 (1969), 149–72.

CA9 Brown, Arthur W. *Always Young for Liberty*. Syracuse: Syracuse Univ. Pr., 1956. On the Biblical criticism of William Ellery Channing.

CA10 Brown, C. G. "Christocentric Liberalism in the Episcopal Church." *Hist. Mag. of the Protestant Episcopal Church*, vol. 37, no. 1 (March 1968), 5–38. Mention of Schleiermacher, Ritschl, Lotze, p.33–35.

CA11 Brown, Ira V. "The Higher Criticism Comes to America." *Jour. of the Presbyterian Hist. Soc.*, vol. 38, no. 4 (December 1960), 193–212. The influence of German Biblical critics.

CA12 Brown, Jerry Wayne. "Conflict and Criticism. Biblical Studies in New England: 1800–1860." Diss., Princeton, 1964. 254p.

CA13 Brown, Jerry Wayne. *The Rise of Biblical Criticism in America, 1800–1870. The New England Scholars*. Middletown, Conn.: Wesleyan Univ. Pr., 1969. 212p. Rev. by C. A. Holbrook, *New England Quar.*, vol. 43 (March 1970), 172–74. Comprehensive interpretation of the influence of German Biblical scholarship upon the Andover Seminary and Harvard University schools of thought.

CA14 Buckminster, Joseph S. "Notice of Griesbach's Edition of the New Testament, New Printing at Cambridge." *Monthly Anthology* (1808), 18–21; "Griesbach's *New Testament* [rev.]" *Ibid.*, vol. 10 (1811), 403–21.

CA15 Buckminster, Joseph S. "On the Accuracy and Fidelity of Griesbach." *General Repository and Rev.*, vol. 1 (1812), 89–101.

CA16 Burr, Nelson R. "'The American Church Historian and the Biblical View of History.' Addr. before the Anglican Assoc. of Historians, Wash-

Theological Interrelations *(cont.)*

ington, D.C., December 28, 1969." *Hist. Mag. of the Protestant Episcopal Church*, vol. 39 (1970), 347–59. Influences of Hegel, Marx, Spengler, among others, on the American Biblical view of history.

CA17 Burton, James. "The Influence of Religion upon Karl Follen." M.F.S. thesis, Maryland, 1950.

CA18 Caruthers, J. Wade. *Octavius Brooks Frothingham, Gentle Radical*. University, Ala.: Univ. of Alabama Pr., 1977. 279p. Rev. by Joseph H. Dorn, *New England Quar.*, vol. 51 (1978), 124–27. Biography of a liberal Unitarian churchman.

CA19 Cashdollar, Charles D. "Auguste Comte and the American Reformed Theologians." *Jour. of the Hist. of Ideas*, vol. 39 (January–March, 1978), 61–79. On the interaction between Comtean positivism and the positions of Reformed theologians and academicians such as Noah Porter, W. M. Gillespies and editors of literary and theological journals of the 1850's to 1870's.

CA20 Cashdollar, Charles D. "European Positivism and the American Unitarians." *Church Hist.*, vol. 45 (December 1976), 490–506. Comte aided in transforming denominational Unitarianism of the 1830's into the radicalism of the later decades.

CA21 Chable, Eugene R. "A Study of the Interpretation of the New Testament in New England Unitarianism." Diss., Columbia, 1955. Biblical criticism.

CA22 Clark, Allen S. "Andrews Norton: A Conservative Unitarian." Honors Thesis, Harvard Univ., 1942. A study in the controversy over Biblical criticism in the 1830's.

CA23 Clemmer, Robert. "Historical Transcendentalism in Pennsylvania." *Jour. of the Hist. of Ideas*, vol. 30 (September–December 1969), 579–92. Rev. by W.P.H., *Hist Mag. of the Protestant Episcopal Church*, vol. 39 (1970), 217. The Mercersburg movement in theology seen as a "valid American expression of Hegelian idealism paralleling New England transcendentalism."

CA24 Coppes, Leonard John. "Hermann Gunkel: A Presentation and Evaluation of His Contributions to Biblical Research—Chiefly in the Area of the Old Testament." Th.D. diss, Westminster Theological Seminary, 1968. 254p.

CA25 Cross, Barbara M. *Horace Bushnell: Minister to a Changing America*. Chicago: Univ. of Chicago Pr., 1958. Bushnell and the issue of Biblical criticism.

CA26 Davis, Lawrence B. *Immigrants, Baptists and the Protestant Mind in America*. Urbana-Champaign: Univ. of Illinois Press, 1973. 230p.

CA27 Glover, Willis B. *Evangelical Nonconformists and Higher Criticism in the Nineteenth Century*. London: Independent Pr., 1954. Biblical criticism.

CA28 Goliber, Thomas J. "Philip Schaff (1819–1893): A Study in Conservative Biblical Criticism." Diss., Kent State, 1976.

CA29 Gottschalk, Stephen. *The Emergence of Christian Science in American Religious Life*. Berkeley: Univ. of Calif. Pr., 1974. 334p.

CA30 Gower, Joseph Francis, Jr. "The 'New Apologetics' of Isaac Thomas Hecker (1819–1888): Catholicity and American Culture." Diss., Notre Dame, 1978. 281p.

CA31 Harvey, Van A. "D. F. Strauss' Life of Jesus Revisited." *Church Hist.*, vol. 30 (1961), 191–211.

CA32 Hatch, Carl E. "The First Heresy Trial of Charles August Briggs: American Higher Criticism in the 1890's." Diss., State Univ. of N.Y., Buffalo, 1964. Examines the impact of higher criticism on American theology.

CA33 Herbst, Jurgen. "Francis Greenwood Peabody: Harvard's Theologian of the Social Gospel." *Harvard Theol. Rev.*, vol. 54 (January 1961), 45–69.

CA34 Herbst, Jurgen. "German Theological Science and American Religion." In: *The German Historical School in American Scholarship. A Study in the Transfer of Culture*. Ed. Jurgen Herbst. Ithaca: Cornell Univ. Pr., 1965, p.73–97. Americans who went to German universities to acquire tools of scholarship brought home ideas as well.

CA35 Hodgson, Peter C. *The Formation of Historical Theology*. New York: Harper & Row, 1966.

CA36 Hodgson, Peter C., ed. *Ferdinand Christian Baur: On the Writing of Church History*. New York: Oxford Univ. Pr., 1968. 380p. Translations of B.'s *The Epochs of Church Historiog-*

raphy (1852) and the Introduction to *Lectures on the History of Christian Dogma* (1865–67).

CA37 Holifield, E. Brooks. "Mercersburg, Princeton, and the South: The Sacramental Controversy in the Nineteenth Century." *Jour. of Presbyterian Hist.*, vol. 54 (Summer 1976), 238–57.

CA38 Holmes, J. Derek. "Von Hugel's Letter to Ryder on Biblical Inspiration and Inerrancy." *Hist. Mag. of the Protestant Episcopal Church*, vol. 38 (June 1969).

CA39 Johnson, Kathryn L. "The Mustard Seed and the Leaven: Philip Schaff's Confident View of Christian History." *Hist. Mag. of the Protestant Episcopal Church*, vol. 50 (1981), 117–70.

CA40 Kitagawa, Joseph. "The Life and Thought of Joachim Wach." In: *Joachim Wach. Comparative Study of Religion*. New York: Columbia Univ. Pr., 1958. The eminent German-born theologian Joachim Wach (d. 1956) taught at the University of Chicago.

CA41 Krummel, Carl F. "Catholicism, Americanism, Democracy, and Orestes Brownson." *Amer. Quar.*, vol. 6 (Spring 1954) 19–31. Argues that his Catholicism was never liberal.

CA42 Lueking, F. Dean. "Roots of the Radical Right." *Lutheran Quar.*, vol. 18 (1966), 197–204. A brief survey of Protestantism's "Radical Right" in 19th-century America.

CA43 McLoughlin, William G. "Pietism and the American Character." *Amer. Quar.*, vol. 17 (Summer 1965), 163–86.

CA44 Maxwell, Jack Martin. "The Liturgical Lessons of Mercersburg: An Examination of the Issues Which Emerged during the Mercersburg Liturgical Controversy with a View toward Establishing Procedural and Theoretical Principles for the Liturgical Committee in the Reformed Tradition." Th.D. Diss., Princeton Theological Seminary, 1969. 447p.

CA45 Moore, William P. "American Identity and the Decline of Biblical Religion: A Theoretical and Empirical Examination of the Significance of 'Higher Criticism' in the American Experience." Diss., Starr King School for the Ministry, Berkeley, California, 1966. 49 l.

CA46 Nichols, James Hastings. *Romanticism in American Theology: Nevin and Schaff at Mercersburg*. Chicago: Univ. of Chicago Pr., 1961. 322p. Rev. by S. E. Ahlstrom, *Church Hist.*, vol. 30, no. 4 (1961), 496–97; B. M. Cross, *New England Quar.*, vol. 34, no. 4 (1961), 554–56. R. W. Albright, *Amer.-German Rev.*, vol. 28, no. 3 (1962), 36–37; W. R. Hutchison, *Amer. Quar.*, vol. 14, no. 1 (1962), 98–99. The development of theology, particularly within the Reformed Church, 1800–1850.

CA47 Nichols, James Hastings, ed. *The Mercersburg Theology*. New York: Oxford Univ. Pr., 1966. 384p. Under the leadership of Philip Schaff, the Mercersburg movement was a protest against many Puritan attitudes in mid-19th-century American religion. Rev. by K. M. Plummer, *Church Hist.*, vol. 37, no. 2 (June 1968), 222–23; G. H. Bricker, *Jour. of Presbyterian Hist.*, vol. 46, no. 2 (June 1968), 150–51.

CA48 Niebuhr, Richard R. *Schleiermacher on Christ and Religion*. New York: Scribner's, 1964. 267p. A new ed. and new introduction to this study of Schleiermacher's theological thought.

CA49 Niebuhr, Richard R. "Schleiermacher on Language and Feeling." *Theology Today*, vol. 17 (July 1960), 150–67. The importance of Schleiermacher's hermeneutics for German as well as for American theology.

CA50 Noone, Bernard J. "A Critical Analysis of the American Catholic Response to Higher Criticism as Reflected in Selected Catholic Periodicals—1870 to 1908." Diss., Drew Univ., 1976.

CA51 Pelikan, Jaroslav. "Luther Comes to the New World." In: *Luther and the Dawn of the Modern Era: Papers for the Fourth Internat. Congress for Luther Research*. Studies in the Hist. of Christian Thought. Ed. Heiko A. Oberman. Leiden: Brill, 1974, p.1–10.

CA52 Penzel, Klaus. "Church History and the Ecumenical Quest. A Study of the German Background and Thought of Philip Schaff." Diss., Union Theological Seminary in the City of New York, 1962. 377p.

CA53 Puknat, Siegfried B. "Auerbach and Channing." *PMLA*, vol. 72 (1957), 962–76. Channing's reception in Europe and Germany.

CA54 Puknat, Siegfried B. "Channing and German Thought." *Procs., Amer. Philosophical Soc.*, vol. 101 (1957), 195–203.

CA55 Puknat, Siegfried B. "DeWette in New England." *Procs., Amer. Philosophical Soc.*, vol. 102 (1960), 376–95.

CA56 Schaff, Philip. *America: A Sketch of Its Political, Social and Religious Character*. Ed. Perry Miller. Cambridge: Harvard Univ. Pr., 1961. 241p. Reissue of the famous set of lectures delivered in Germany by the young professor of theology in Mercersburg Seminary.

CA57 Schneider, Carl E. "Americanization of Karl August Rauschenbusch, 1816–1899." *Church Hist.*, vol. 24 (1955), 3–14.

CA58 Schober, Franz. "W. E. Channings Gedankengut: Eine Untersuchung seiner weltanschaulichen Grundideen." Diss., Erlangen, 1956. Publ.: Weltz: Scheinfeld, 1956. 127p.

CA59 Schroeder, Philip J. "August Hermann Francke, 1663–1963." *Concordia Theological Monthly*, vol. 34 (November 1963), 664–68. An evaluation and testimony.

CA60 Schulz-Behrend, G. "The Swedenborgians at Jasper, Iowa—The Disappointment of Hermann Diekhöner." *Amer.-German Rev.*, vol. 12, no. 4 (1946), 27–28. Based on C. A. Hawley's history of the Jasper colony in *The Iowa Jour. of Hist. and Politics*, vol. 33 (1935).

CA61 Shriver, George H. "Philip Schaff as a Teacher of Church History." *Jour. of Presbyterian Hist.*, vol. 47 (March 1969), 74–92. Schaff while a student at Berlin was strongly influenced by Neander.

CA62 Shriver, George Hite, Jr. "Philip Schaff's Concept of Organic Historiography Interpreted in Relation to the Realization of an 'Evangelical Catholicism' within the Christian Community." Diss., Duke Univ., 1960.

CA63 Smith, H. Shelton. *Horace Bushnell*. New York: Oxford Univ. Pr., 1965.

CA64 Smith, John A. "The Schmucker Myth and the Evangelical Alliance." *Jour. of the Lancaster Co. Hist. Soc.*, vol. 77 (1973), 107–23.

CA65 Stuart, Moses. Papers. In the Andover Newton Theological Library. Microform copies are located in the Yale Divinity School Library.

CA66 Sveino, Per. *Orestes A. Brownson's Road to Catholicism*. New York: Humanities Pr., 1971. 339p. Intellectual biography focusing on his religious-philosophical views before his conversion.

CA67 Tice, Terence N. *Schleiermacher Bibliography with Brief Introductions, Annotations and Index*. Princeton: Princeton Theolog. Seminary, 1966. 168p. Part 3 lists unpublished dissertations, journal articles and references to S. in more general studies.

CA68 Tredway, John Thomas. "Eucharistic Theology in American Protestantism: 1820–1860." Diss., Northwestern Univ., 1964. 331p. Includes an analysis of the "American Lutheran" position.

CA69 Wentz, Abdel Ross. "The Philosophic Roots of S. S. Schmucker's Thought." *Lutheran Quar.*, vol. 18 (August 1966), 245–59. Leader of the anticonfessional theology in the first half of the 19th century.

CA70 Williams, Daniel Day. *The Andover Liberals. A Study in American Theology*. New York: King's Crown Pr., 1941.

CA71 Williams, George Huntston, ed. *The Harvard Divinity School*. Boston: Beacon, 1954. The rise of Biblical criticism in America.

CA72 Wright, Conrad. *The Beginnings of Unitarianism in America*. Boston: Starr King Pr., 1955.

CA73 Yrigoyen, Charles. "Emanuel V. Gerhart: Apologist for the Mercersburg Theology." *Jour. of Presbyterian Hist.*, vol. 57 (Winter 1979), 485–500.

The Eighteenth Century and Before

GENERAL

CA74 Baeumer, Max L. "Simplicity and Grandeur: Winckelmann, French Classicism, and Jefferson." In: *Studies in Eighteenth-Century Culture*.

Ed. Roseann Runte. Madison: Univ. of Wisconsin Pr. for the Amer. Soc. for 18th Century Studies, 1978, p.63–78.

CA75 Benton, Robert M. "The John Winthrops and Developing Scientific Thought in New England." *Early Amer. Lit.*, vol. 7 (1973), 272–80.

CA76 Benz, Ernst. "Ecumenical Relations between Boston Puritanism and German Pietism: Cotton Mather and August Hermann Francke." *Harvard Theological Rev.*, vol. 54, no. 3 (1961), 159–93.

CA77 Brown, Madison. "Thomas Jefferson and Things German: Preliminary Findings." *The Report of the Soc. for the Hist. of the Germans in Md.*, vol. 37 (1978), 29–33.

CA78 Bultmann, William, and Phyllis W. Bultmann. "The Roots of Anglican Humanitarianism: A Study of the Membership of the S.P.C.K. and the S.P.G., 1699–1720." *Hist. Mag. of the Protestant Episcopal Church*, vol. 33, no. 1 (March 1964), 3–48. Incl. mention of the relations of the Anglicans with Continental figures such as William Mecke, August H. Francke, John Frederick Ostervald, and Anthony W. Boehme.

CA79 Cannon, Donald Quayle. "Christoph D. Ebeling: A German Geographer of America." Diss., Clark Univ., 1967. 285p. Ebeling (1741–1817) was an important link between the Old and New Worlds.

CA80 Carpenter, Kenneth E. *Dialogue in Political Economy: Translations from and into German in the 18th Century.* Boston: Kress Library of the Harvard Business School, 1977. 91p.

CA81 Chestnut, Paul I. "The Universalist Movement in America, 1770–1803." Diss., Duke, 1974. Reference to Benjamin Rush in Pennsylvania.

CA82 Commager, Henry Steele. *The Empire of Reason: How Europe Imagined and America Realized the Enlightenment.* Garden City: Doubleday, 1977. 172p.

CA83 Cope, Thomas D. "The Apprentice Years of Mason and Dixon." *Pa. Hist.*, vol. 11, no. 3 (1944), 155–70. Mention of Mason's revision of the astronomical tables of Tobias Mayer of Göttingen.

CA84 D'Elias, Donald J. *Benjamin Rush: Philosopher of the American Revolution.* Philadelphia: Amer. Philosophical Soc., 1974. Rev. by R. Lokken, *William and Mary Coll. Quar.*, vol. 32 (1975), 533–34; J. A. Schutz, *Amer. Hist. Rev.*, vol. 81 (1976), 963; J. M. Coleman, *Jour. of Amer. Hist.*, vol. 62 (1976), 974–75.

CA85 Dippel, Horst. "American and European Revolutionary Ideals in the Works of Thomas Paine. Amerikanische und europäische Revolutionsideale bei Thomas Paine." *Amerikastudien/Amer. Studies*, vol. 21, no. 2 (1976), 203–15.

CA86 Evans, Evan L. "Jacob Boehme's Contribution to the English Speaking World." Diss., Kiel, 1956.

CA87 Graham, John. *Lavater's Essays on Physiognomy: A Study in the History of Ideas.* Bern: Lang, 1979. 130p.

CA88 Greene, John C. "American Science Comes of Age, 1780–1820." *Jour. of Amer. Hist.*, vol. 55, no. 1 (June 1968), 22–41. The work of Pursh (a German resident in England), Henry Muhlenberg, and Count Rumford seen in the perspective of general European advances in natural history.

CA89 Greene, John C. "Early Scientific Interest in the American Indian: Comparative Linguistics." *Papers of the Amer. Philosophical Soc.*, vol. 104 (1960), 511–17. Benjamin S. Barton's studies of Indian languages and his influence on German Philologists.

CA90 Hindle, Brooke. *The Pursuit of Science in Revolutionary America, 1735–1789.* Chapel Hill: Univ. of N. Car. Pr., 1967. 410p.

CA91 Hirsch, Helmut. "Mesmerism and Revolutionary America." *Amer.-German Rev.*, vol. 10, no. 1 (October 1943), 11–14.

CA92 Hirsh, Helen. "Philadelphus Philadelphia, Scientist and Magician." *Amer.-German Rev.*, vol. 24, no. 6 (1958), 34–36. Jacob Meyer of Philadelphia, son of early settlers in Germantown, returned to Europe in 1750 to become famous as astrologer, alchemist and conjurer.

CA93 Jantz, Harold. "America's First Cosmopolitan." *Procs., Mass. Hist. Soc.*, vol. 84 (1973), 3–25. On the alchemical and related literature surrounding George Starkey and Eirenaeus Philalethes; the association of John Winthrop the Younger (1606–1676) with Continental scholars.

CA94 Jantz, Harold S. "Christian Lodowick of Newport and Leipzig." *R.I. Hist.*, vol. 3 (1944),

The Eighteenth Century and Before *(cont.)*

105–17; vol. 4 (1945), 13–26. Rev. D. Cunz, *Monatshefte*, vol. 38 (1946), 60. A German-born physician who came to America in 1684, played a part in New England intellectual history, and published a well-known English-German dictionary.

CA95 Jantz, Harold S. "German Thought and Literature in New England, 1620–1820." *Jour. of Engl. and Germanic Philology*, vol. 41, no. 1 (1942), 1–45. A marshalling of evidence to show that there were significant New England-German contacts from the early decades of British settlement.

CA96 Jantz, Harold S. "Henning Witte and Increase Mather." *New England Quar.*, vol. 18 (1945), 408.

CA97 Kraus, Michael. *The Atlantic Civilization: Eighteenth Century Origins*. Ithaca, N.Y.: Cornell Univ. Pr., 1949. 325p. New ed., New York: Russell & Russell, 1961. Rev. by R. R. Palmer, *Amer. Hist. Rev.*, vol. 55 (1950), 868–70; F. B. Tolles, *William and Mary Quar.*, vol. 7 (1950), 472–74; O. Zeichner, *N.Y. Hist.*, vol. 31 (1950), 430–31.

CA98 Kraus, Michael. "Scientific Relations Between Europe and America in the Eighteenth Century." *Scientific Monthly*, vol. 55 (September 1942), 259–72.

CA99 Loomis, C. Grant. "An Unnoted German Reference to Increase Mather." *New England Quar.*, vol. 14 (1941), 374–76. Mather's letter dealing with attempts to spread the gospel among the Indians was reprinted in *Unterredungen*, September 1964.

CA100 McDermott, John F. "Voltaire and the Freethinkers in Early St. Louis." *Revue de Littérature Comparée*, vol. 16 (1936), 720–31.

CA101 Mayo, Robert S. *Herder and the Beginnings of Comparative Literature*. Univ. of N. Car. Studies in Comparative Literature, no. 48. Chapel Hill: Univ. of N. Car. Pr., 1969.

CA102 Metcalf, George J. "A Linguistic Clash in the Seventeenth Century." *German Life and Letters*, vol. 23, no. 1 (October 1969), 31–38. Arguments centering about Grotius' hypothesis of the Germanic origins of the peoples of the Americas.

CA103 Noel, Patricia S., and Eric P. Carlson. "The Faculty of Psychology of Benjamin Rush." *Jour. of the Hist. of the Behavioral Sciences*, vol. 9 (1973), 369–77.

CA104 Schiller, Friedrich. "Universal History." *Clio—An Interdisciplinary Jour. of Intellectual Hist. and the Philosophy of Hist.* (Indiana and Purdue), vol. 7, no. 2 (1978). First English translation.

CA105 Stoudt, John Joseph. "Die Ausstrahlung der Marburger theologischen Fakultät auf das geistige Leben Amerikas im 18. Jahrhundert." *Zeitschrift für Religious- und Geistesgeschichte*, vol. 15, no. 1 (1963), 34–54.

CA106 Sweet, William Warren. *Religion in Colonial America*. New York: Scribner's, 1942. 367p. Rev. by H. C. Reed, *Pa. Mag. of Hist. and Biog.*, vol. 67 (1943), 412–14.

CA107 Toms, D. Victoria. "The Intellectual and Literary Background of Francis Daniel Pastorius." Diss., Northwestern, 1953.

CA108 Wilkinson, R. S. "The Alchemical Library of John Winthrop." *Ambix*, vol. 13 (1965), 139–86.

CA109 Wilkinson, R. S. "The Problem of the Identity of Eirenaeus Philalethes." *Ambix*, vol. 12 (1964), 24–43.

CA110 Wilkinson, Ronald Sterne. "'Hermes Christianus': John Winthrop, Jr., and Chemical Medicine in Seventeenth Century New England." In: *Science, Medicine and Society in the Renaissance. Essays to Honor Walter Pagel*. Ed. Allen G. Debus. New York: n.p., 1972, p.221–41. On the association of Winthrop with Johann von Rist of Wedel on the Elbe.

FRANKLIN, BENJAMIN

CA111 Aiken, John R. "Benjamin Franklin, Karl Marx, and the Labor Theory of Value." *Pa. Mag. of Hist. and Biog.*, vol. 90 (1966), 378–84. On Franklin's contribution to the development of Marx's law of value.

CA112 Aldridge, Alfred Owen. *Benjamin Franklin and Nature's God*. Durham, N. Car.: Duke Univ. Pr., 1967. 279p. Touches on Franklin's relations with the German sectarians. Rev. by Ira V. Brown, *Pa. Hist.*, vol. 35, no. 1 (January 1968), 93–94.

CA113 Baumgarten, Eduard. *Benjamin Franklin, der Lehrmeister der amerikanischen Revolution.* Frankfurt a. M.: V. Klostermann, 1936. 248p.

CA114 Benz, Ernst. "Franklin and the Mystic Rocket." *Amer.-German Rev.*, vol. 29, no. 5 (1963), 24–26. On the emblems and drawing in Franklin's 1751 ed. of the *Vier Bücher vom wahren Christenthum* by Johann Arndt.

CA115 Kahn, Robert L. "Franklin, Grimm and J. H. Landolt." *Procs., Amer. Philosophical Soc.*, vol. 99 (1955), 401–04.

CA116 Kahn, Robert L. "Georg Forster and Benjamin Franklin." *Procs., Amer. Philosophical Soc.*, vol. 102 (1958), 1–6.

CA117 Meinhardt, Günther. "Gottfried Achenwall und Benjamin Franklin: Beziehungen des Elbinger Gelehrten zu dem amerikanischen Staatsmann." *Westpreußen-Jahrbuch*, vol. 22 (1972), 83–86.

RITTENHOUSE, DAVID

CA118 Ford, Edward. *David Rittenhouse, Astronomer-Patriot, 1732–1796.* Philadelphia: Univ. of Pa. Pr., 1946. 228p.

CA119 Hindle, Brooke. *David Rittenhouse.* Princeton: Princeton Univ. Pr., 1964. 394p. Astronomer and instrument maker.

CA120 Montague, William E. *David Rittenhouse. His Life and Achievements...* Norristown, Pa.: n.p., 1924. 27p.

CA121 Rice, Howard C., Jr. *The Rittenhouse Orrery, Princeton's Eighteenth-Century Planetarium, 1767–1954.* Princeton: Princeton Univ. Pr., 1954.

CA122 "Rittenhouse, David." *Dictionary of Scientific Biography*, vol. 11, p.471–73.

CA123 Rittenhouse, David. Papers. In the Library of the American Philosophical Soc. (MS 61-782 and MS 76-937); and collections of the Hist. Soc. of Pennsylvania (MS 61-501). Photocopies of his correspondence and scientific writings.

THOMPSON, BENJAMIN (COUNT RUMFORD)

CA124 Brown, Sanborn C. *Benjamin Thompson, Court Rumford.* Cambridge: M.I.T. Pr., 1979. 376p. Biography of the expatriate (1753–1814), scientist, inventor, spy.

CA125 Brown, Sanborn C. *Count Rumford: Physicist Extraordinary.* London: Heinemann, 1964.

CA126 Brown, Sanborn C. *Men of Physics. Benjamin Thompson, Count Rumford.* Oxford: Pergamon Pr., 1967. 207p.

CA127 Brown, Sanborn C. and Kenneth Scott. "Count Rumford: International Informer." *New England Quar.*, vol. 21 (1948), 34–49.

CA128 Cummings, A. D. "Eighteenth Century's Fuel Efficiency Expert." *Discovery*, vol. 8 (1947), 120–33, 151–52.

CA129 Davis, Tenney L. [Thompson, Benjamin. Count Rumford.] *Dictionary of Amer. Biography*, vol. 18, 449.

CA130 Einstein, Lewis. [Count Rumford.] In: *Divided Loyalties: Americans in England during the War of Independence.* Boston/New York: Houghton Mifflin, 1933., p.114–50.

CA131 Jaffe, Bernard. [Count Rumford.] In: *Men of Science in America.* New York: Simon & Schuster, 1944. 1944, p.52–77.

CA132 Larsen, Egon. *Graf Rumford. Ein Amerikaner in München.* München: Prestel Vlg., 1961. This scientist was a native of Woburn, Mass. (1753), but lived in his later years in Europe.

CA133 Sokolow, Jayme A. "Count Rumford and Late Enlightenment Science, Technology, and Reform." *Eighteenth Century*, vol. 21 (1980), 67–86.

CA134 Sparrow, W. J. *Knight of the White Eagle. A Biography of Benjamin Thompson, Count Rumford.* London: Hutchinson, 1964.

CA135 Thompson, Benjamin. *The Collected Works of Count Rumford.* Ed. Sanborn C. Brown. Cambridge: Belknap Pr. of Harvard Univ. Pr., 1968. 3 vols. 507, 523, 504p. American-born early 19th-century scientist and social reformer who resided in München. Incl. papers on the nature of heat, economy of fuel, armament, light and color, and public institutions.

Early Nineteenth-Century Intellectual Relations

GENERAL

CA136 Baker, Jacob. *Human Magnetism: Its Origin, Progress, Philosophy and Curative Qualities, with Instruction for Its Application.* Worcester, Mass.: Jacob Baker & M. D. Phillips, ca. 1843. 31p.

CA137 Baker, William D., Jr. "The Influence of Mesmerism in 19th-Century American Literature." Diss., Northwestern Univ., 1950. 144p.

CA138 Betts, John R. "Mind and Body in Early American Thought." *Jour. of Amer. Hist.*, vol. 55, no. 4 (March 1968), 787–805. American interest in physical fitness stimulated by British and German forerunners.

CA139 Burwick, Fred L. "The Göttingen Influence on George Bancroft's Idea of Humanity." *Jahrbuch für Amerikastudien*, vol. 11 (1966), 196–212.

CA140 Duffy, John J. "From Hanover to Burlington: James Marsh's Search for Unity." *Vt. Hist.*, vol. 28 (1970), 27–48.

CA141 Ekirch, Arthur A., Jr. "Frederick Grimke: Advocate of Free Institutions." *Jour. of the Hist. of Ideas*, vol. 11 (1950), 75–92. On Grimke's comments on American democracy. G. was a South Carolinian of German and French ancestry.

CA142 Fabian, Bernhard. *Alexis de Tocquevilles Amerikabild. Genetische Untersuchungen über Zusammenhänge mit der zeitgenössischen, insbesondere der englischen Amerika-Interpretation.* Beiheft zum *Jahrbuch für Amerikastudien*, no. 1. Heidelberg: Winter, 1957. 158p.

CA143 Firda, Richard A. "The *North American Review*, 1815–1860: A Study in the Reception of German-American Cultural Influences." Diss., Harvard, 1966–1967.

CA144 Giltner, John Herbert. "Moses Stuart: 1780–1852." Diss., Yale, 1956. 600p.

CA145 Hart, Thomas R., Jr. "George Ticknor's *History of Spanish Literature*." *PMLA*, vol. 69 (1954), 76–88. T.'s debt to his teacher Bouterwek in Göttingen.

CA146 Horlick, Allan S. "Phrenology and the Social Education of Young Men." *Hist. of Education Quar.*, vol. 11 (Spring 1971), 28–38.

CA147 Howe, Mark A. *The Life and Letters of George Bancroft.* 2 vols. N.p.: n.p., n.d. Repr. Port Washington, N.Y.: Kennikat Pr., 1971.

CA148 Johnson-Cousin, Danielle. "The Reception of Madame de Stael's *De l'Allemagne* in North America." In: *Actes du VIIe congrés de l'Association Internationale de Littérature Comparee/Proceedings of the 7th Congress of the International Comparative Literature Assoc. I. Littératures américaines: Dépéndance, indépendance, interdépendance...* Ed. Milan V. Dimić and Juan Ferraté. Stuttgart: Bieber, 1979, p.151–57.

CA149 Kimball, Marie. "Europe Comes to Jefferson." *Amer.-German Rev.*, vol. 15, no. 3 (1949), 15–17, 30.

CA150 Lombard, C. M. "Mme. de Staël's Image in American Romanticism." *College Lang. Assoc. Jour.*, vol. 19 (September 1975) 57–64.

CA151 McCann, Gary Grayson. "Motley's Concept of Freedom as a Schillerian Ideal." Diss., Louisiana State, 1963–1964. John Lothrop Motley spent two years in study at Göttingen before launching his career as writer and historian.

CA152 McGiffert, A. C., Jr. "James Marsh (1794–1842): Philosophical Theologian, Evangelical Liberal." *Church Hist.*, vol. 38, no. 4 (December 1969), 437–58. Shows Marsh as "less a Transcendentalist after Coleridge than one who went beyond New England orthodoxy in another direction."

CA153 Nye, Russel. *George Bancroft: Brahmin Rebel.* New York: Knopf, 1944. 340p. Rev. by J. A. Krout, *Amer. Lit.*, vol. 17, no. 1 (1945), 87–89. Incl. a study of Bancroft's life in Germany.

CA154 Preyer, R. O. "The Dream of a Spiritualized Learning and Its Early Enthusiasts (German, British and American)." In: *Geschichte und Gesellschaft in der amerikanischen Literatur.* Ed. Karl Schubert and Ursula Müller-Richter. Heidelberg. Quelle & Meyer, 1975, p.62–85.

CA155 Richey, Homer G. *Memorandum of the German Edition of Jefferson's Notes on Virginia.* Charlottesville: Alderman Library, 1952. 4p.

CA156 Ryder, Frank G. "An American View of Germany—1817." *Amer.-German Rev.*, vol. 25, no. 3 (1959), 16–19. "George Ticknor on the German Scene." *Ibid.*, vol. 25, no. 4 (1959), 28–30. Ticknor's reaction to Germany and German life.

CA157 Schiller, Andrew. "A Letter from George Bancroft." *New England Quar.*, vol. 33, no. 2 (1960), 225–32. Notes on poetic juvenilia and translations from the German by the young Bancroft in Europe, 1818–1823.

CA158 Schnetzler, Barbara Verena. *Die Frühe amerikanische Frauenbewegung und ihre Kontakte mit Europa (1836–1869).* Europ. Hochschulschriften, Reihe III, vol. 11). Frankfurt/Bern: Lang, ca. 1973. 148p.

CA159 Stange, Douglas C. "The Making of an Abolitionist Martyr: Harvard Professor Charles Theodore Christian Follen (1796–1840)." *Harvard Library Bulletin*, vol. 24, no. 1 (1976), 17–24. Follen's early death put him in the pantheon of abolitionists.

CA160 Tyack, David B. *George Ticknor and the Boston Brahmins.* Cambridge: Harvard Univ. Pr., 1967. 289p. Rev. by I. H. Bartlett, *Jour. of Amer. Hist.*, vol. 54, no. 3 (December 1967), 651–52; N. Burt, *Pa. Mag. of Hist. and Biography*, vol. 92, no. 1 (1968), 131–33. Study of the man, his circle, and his time.

HUMBOLDT, ALEXANDER VON

CA161 de Terra, Helmut. "Alexander von Humboldt's Correspondence with Jefferson, Madison, and Gallatin." *Papers of the Amer. Philosophical Soc.*, vol. 103, no. 6 (15 December 1959), 783–806. On Baron von H. (1769–1859).

CA162 de Terra, Helmut. "Studies of the Documentation of Alexander von Humboldt: The Philadelphia Abstract of Humboldt's American Travels. Humboldt Portraits and Sculpture in the United States." *Procs. of the Amer. Philos. Soc.*, vol. 102, no. 6 (15 December 1958), 560–89.

CA163 Humboldt, Alexander von. Letters, 1793–1859. In the Library of the Amer. Philosophical Soc., Philadelphia. (MS 60-3216). Photocopies of originals owned by other U.S. institutions. Among the addressees are the naturalists Johann Gottfried Flügel, G. H. E. Muhlenberg, Karl Ludwig Wildenow.

CA164 Trevor-Roper, H. R. "The Last Universal Man: Alexander von Humboldt." *Horizon*, vol. 1, no. 6 (1959), 56–69, 128.

CA165 Wassemann, Felix M. "Six Unpublished Letters of Alexander von Humboldt to Thomas Jefferson." *Germanic Rev.*, vol. 29 (1954), 191–200. From the years 1804–1825.

Kant and Kantianism

CA166 Beck, Lewis W. "[Arthur O.] Lovejoy as a Critic of Kant." *Jour. of the Hist. of Ideas*, vol. 33 (1972), 471–84.

CA167 Blau, Joseph Leon. "Kant in America. 1. Brownson's Critique of the *Critique of Pure Reason*." *The Jour. of Philosophy*, vol. 51 (December 1954), 874–80. Brownson's criticism of the epistemology is marked by independence of judgment and analytical acuteness.

CA168 Handy, William J. *Kant and the Southern New Critics.* Austin: Univ. of Texas Pr., 1963. 112p. Rev. H. Baker, *Sewanee Rev.*, vol. 72, no. 4 (Autumn 1964), 681–90; H. J. Lang, *Jahrbuch für Amerikastudien*, vol. 11 (1964), 349. The Kantian generative idea and the theories of Ransom, Tate, Brooks, and others.

CA169 "Kant and Kantism." *Methodist Quar. Rev.*, Ser. III, vol. 5 (1845), 43–55. Dated Wesleyan Univ., 16 September 1844.

CA170 Laberge, Pierre, et al. eds. *Proceedings of the Ottawa Congress on Kant in the Anglo-American and Continental Traditions, Held October 10–14, 1974.* Ottawa: Univ. of Ottawa Pr., 1976.

CA171 Lovejoy, Arthur O. *The Reason, the Understanding, and Time.* Baltimore: The Johns Hopkins Univ. Pr., 1961. 210p. Ideas of reason, understanding and time in German philosophy from Kant to Hegel and in the American and British Transcendentalist movements.

CA172 Michael, Emily. "[Charles S.] Peirce's Adaptation of Kant's Definition of Logic: The Early Manuscripts." *Transactions of the Charles S. Peirce Soc.*, vol. 14 (1978), 176–83.

CA173 Murphey, Murray G. "Kant's Children: The Cambridge Pragmatists." *Trans. of the Charles S. Peirce Soc.*, vol. 4, no. 1 (Winter 1968), 3–33. Pragmatism arose in discussions of the Metaphysical Club in 1871–1872, with C. I. Lewis, Royce, and James present.

Samuel Taylor Coleridge

CA174 Appleyard, J. *Coleridge's Philosophy of Literature. The Development of a Concept of Poetry, 1791–1819.* Cambridge: Harvard Univ. Pr., 1966. 266p.

CA175 Beach, Joseph Warren. "Coleridge's Borrowings from the German." *Engl. Literary Hist.*, vol. 9, no. 1 (1942), 36–58. A good level-headed summary of this provoking problem.

CA176 Carafiol, Peter Coulter. "James Marsh: Transcendental Puritan." Diss., Claremont Graduate School, 1974. See *ESQ: Journal of the American Renaissance*, vol. 21 (1975), 127–36. On Marsh's edition of Coleridge's *Aids to Reflection* and its Kantian background.

CA177 Carafiol, Peter Coulter. "James Marsh's American *Aids to Reflection*: Influence through Ambiguity." *New England Quar.*, vol. 49 (1976), 27–45.

CA178 Dewey, John. "James Marsh and American Philosophy." *Jour. of the Hist. of Ideas*, vol. 2, no. 2 (1941), 131–50. Lecture del. at the Univ. of Vermont, 26 November 1929, at the centenary of Marsh's "Introduction" to Coleridge's *Aids to Reflection*. Excellent appraisal of the Germanic content of Marsh's philosophy.

CA179 Duffy, John J. *Coleridge's American Disciples. The Selected Correspondence of James Marsh.* Amherst: Univ. of Mass. Pr., 1973. 272p. Rev. by Stephen H. Wurster, *Church Hist.*, vol. 43, no. 2 (June 1974), 282.

CA180 Duffy, John J. "Problems in Publishing Coleridge: James Marsh's First American Edition of *Aids to Reflection*." *New England Quar.*, vol. 43 (June 1970), 193–208.

CA181 Loades, Anne. "Coleridge as Theologian: Some Comments on His Reading of Kant." *Jour. of Theological Studies*, vol. 29 (1978), 410–26.

CA182 Lovejoy, Arthur O. "Coleridge and Kant's Two Worlds." *Engl. Literary Hist.*, vol. 7 (1940), 341–62.

CA183 MacKinnon, D. M. "Coleridge and Kant." In: *Coleridge's Variety: Bicentennial Studies.* Ed. John Beer. Pittsburgh: Univ. of Pittsburgh, 1975, p.183–203, 253.

CA184 Marsh, James. Papers, 1821–1874. 80 items. In the University Archives, Univ. of Vermont (MS 64-795). Sermon, correspondence concerning S. T. Coleridge; letter to George Ripley. M. 1794–1842.

CA185 Marsh, James. *Selected Works.* Introd. by Peter C. Carafiol. Delmar, N.Y.: Scholars' Facsimiles Reprints, 1976. 3 vols. 576, 510, 757p. Incl. an edition of Coleridge's *The Friend* and of his *Aids to Reflection*; translation of Herder's *Spirit of Hebrew Poetry* and of Hegewisch's *Introduction to Historical Chronology.* Repr. of the original edition, 1822–.

CA186 Orsini, G.N.G. *Coleridge and German Idealism. A Study in the History of Philosophy.* With Unpublished Material from Coleridge's Manuscripts. Carbondale: Southern Illinois Univ. Pr., 1969. 320p.

CA187 Orsini, G.N.G. "Coleridge and Schlegel Reconsidered." *Compar. Lit.*, vol. 16 (1964), 97–118. A. W. Schlegel, an influence upon Coleridge.

CA188 Priestmann, Donald G. "Godwin, Schiller and the Polemic of Coleridge's *Osorio*." *Bull. of Research in the Humanities*, vol. 82, no. 2 (Summer 1979), 236–48. Wordsworth's *Borderers* and Schiller's *Robbers* read by Coleridge as expositions of Godwin's principles.

CA189 Swift, David E. "Yankee in Virginia: James Marsh at Hampden-Sydney, 1823–1926." *Va. Mag. of Hist. and Biography*, vol. 80 (July 1972), 312–32.

CA190 Wieden, Fritz. "S. T. Coleridge's Assimilation of Ideas from Schiller's Early Writings." In:

Analecta Helvetica et Germanica: Eine Festschrift zu Ehren von Hermann Boeschenstein. Ed. Achim Arnold, Hans Eichner et al. Bonn: Bouvier, 1979, p. 170–81.

CA191 Wieden, Fritz. "Samuel Taylor Coleridge as a Student of German Literature." Diss., Toronto, 1963.

CA192 Yoder, Richard. "The Influence of Coleridge in America 1817–1836." Diss., Pennsylvania, 1964.

Ralph Waldo Emerson

CA193 Baumgarten, Eduard. "Mitteilungen und Bemerkungen über den Einfluss Emersons auf Nietzsche." *Jahrbuch für Amerikastudien*, vol. 1 (1956), 93–152.

CA194 Bishop, Jonathan. *Emerson on the Soul.* Cambridge: Harvard Univ. Pr., 1964.

CA195 Braham, Lionel. "Emerson and Boehme: A Comparative Study in Mystical Ideas." *Mod. Lang. Quar.*, vol. 20 (1959), 31–35.

CA196 Brown, Stuart G. "Emerson's Platonism." *New England Quar.*, vol. 18, no. 3 (1945), 325–45.

CA197 Cameron, Kenneth W. "Emerson Transmits News from Germany." *Emerson Soc. Quar.*, no. 2 (1956), 2–7.

CA198 Cameron, Kenneth W. "Emerson's Anecdote from Goethe of St. Philip Neri and the Nun." *Emerson Soc. Quar.*, vol. 11 (1958), 62f.

CA199 Cameron, Kenneth W. "Emerson's 'Bacchus' and Beethoven." *Emerson Society Quar.*, no. 43 (1966), 34. With a reproduction of the source.

CA200 Cameron, Kenneth W. "History and Biography in Emerson's Unpublished Sermons." *Procs., Amer. Antiquarian Soc.*, vol. 66 (1957), 101–18. Mentions of German sources for the sermons.

CA201 Cameron, Kenneth W. "A New Source for Emerson's Lectures." *Emerson Soc. Quar.*, no. 20 (1960), 10–25. On Mme. De Staël's *Germany*, published in English, London, 1813.

CA202 Cameron, Kenneth W. *Ralph Waldo Emerson's Reading.* Raleigh, N. Car.: Thistle Pr., 1941. 144p. Unpublished letters, lists of withdrawals from libraries, etc.

CA203 Conroy, Stephen S. "Emerson and Phrenology." *Amer. Quar.*, vol. 16 (Summer 1964), 215–17.

CA204 Doderer, Hans. "Der junge Emerson und Deutschland." *Germanisch-Romanische Monatsschrift*, vol. 36 (1955), 147–61.

CA205 Els, Rüdiger. *Ralph Waldo Emerson und "Die Natur" in Goethes Werken: Parallelen von "Nature" (1836) und "Nature" (1844) mit dem Prosahymnus "Die Natur" und sein möglicher Einfluss.* Mainzer Studien zur Amerikanistik, no. 8. Frankfurt: Lang, 1977. 253p.

CA206 Emerson, Ralph Waldo. *The Journals and Miscellaneous Notebooks of Ralph Waldo Emerson.* Ed. William H. Gilman and others. Cambridge: Belknap Pr. of Harvard Univ. Pr., 1960–1978. 14 vols. Volume 6, *1824–1838*, issued in 1966. 422p. Rev. by R. M. Aderman, *Jour. of Amer. Hist.*, vol. 54, no. 1 (1967), 130–31.

CA207 Emerson, Ralph Waldo. [Unpublished Letter to Louis Prang.] *Amer. Lit.*, vol. 43, no. 2 (May 1971), 257–58. Dated Concord, September 1868. Acknowledges receipt of chromolithographs sent to Emerson by Prang.

CA208 Emerson, Ralph Waldo, and Thomas Carlyle. *The Correspondence of Emerson and Carlyle.* Ed. with an Introd. by Joseph Slater. New York: Columbia Univ. Pr., 1964. 662p. Rev. by C. A. Brown, *Amer. Quar.*, vol. 17 (1965) 595–97; V. C. Hopkins, *Amer. Lit.*, vol. 37 (1965), 329–31; H. J. Jones, *New England Quar.*, vol. 38, no. 2 (1965), 245–47. Inclusive new edition with ancillary correspondence.

CA209 Feuer, Lewis S. "Ralph Waldo Emerson's Reference to Karl Marx." *New England Quar.*, vol. 33, no. 3 (1960), 378–79.

CA210 Fletcher, Richard M. "Emerson's *Nature* and Goethe's *Faust*." *Amer. Notes and Queries*, vol. 12 (1974), 102.

CA211 Hammel, H. "Emerson and Nietzsche." *New England Quar.*, vol. 19 (1946), 63–84.

CA212 Harding, Walter, comp. *Emerson's Library.* Charlottesville: Univ. of Virginia Pr. for the Bibliographic Soc. of America, 1967. 338p. Rev. by W. A. Katz, *Publs., Bibliographic Soc. of Amer.*, vol. 62, no. 1 (1968), 150–52.

CA213 Harris, W. T. "Emerson's Relation to Goethe and Carlyle." In: *The Genius and Character of Emerson.* Lectures at the Concord School of Philosophy. Ed. F. B. Sanborn. Boston: Osgood & Co., 1885, p.386–419.

CA214 Hopkins, Vivian C. "The Influences of Goethe on Emerson's Aesthetic Theory." *Philological Quar.*, vol. 27, no. 4 (1948), 325–44.

CA215 Hubbard, Stanley. *Nietzsche and Emerson.* Basel: Verlag für Recht und Gesellschaft, 1958. 195p.

CA216 Luedtke, Luther S., and Winfried Schleiner. "New Letters from the Grimm-Emerson Correspondence." *Harvard Library Bull.*, vol. 25, no. 4 (1977), 399–465. Two letters from Gisela von Arnim Grimm to Ralph and Ellen Emerson.

CA217 McCormick, John O. "Emerson's Theory of Human Greatness." *New England Quar.*, vol. 26, no. 3 (1953), 291–314. References to E.'s interest in Goethe.

CA218 Marcuse, Ludwig. "Emerson in Modern Germany." *Emerson Soc. Quar.*, no. 12 (1958), 50–51.

CA219 Pochmann, Henry A. "The Emerson Canon." *Univ. of Toronto Quar.*, vol. 12, no. 4 (1943), 476–84. Examination of a misdated passage in E.'s *Journals* bearing upon his knowledge of German Transcendental philosophy.

CA220 Porte, Joel. "Emerson, Luther and American Character." *Forum* (Houston), vol. 13, no. 3 (1976), 8–13.

CA221 Randel, William Pierce. "A Late Emerson Letter." *Amer. Lit.*, vol. 12, no. 4 (1941), 496f. Concerning the Emerson-Grimm relationship.

CA222 Sowd, David. "Peter Kaufman's Correspondence with Emerson." *ESQ: A Jour. of the Amer. Renaissance*, vol. 20 (1974), 91–100.

CA223 Strauch, Carl F. "Emerson's Sacred Science." *PMLA*, vol. 73 (1958), 237–50. Incl. an evaluation of Goethe's and Schelling's influence on the formulation of the "sacred science."

CA224 Wahr, Fred B. "Emerson and the Germans." *Monatshefte*, vol. 33, no. 2 (1941), 49–63.

CA225 Wahr, Frederick B. "Emerson and Goethe, Emerson and the Germans." *Amer. Transcendentalist Quar.*, vol. 15, no. 1 (1972), 3–82.

CA226 Wellek, René. "Emerson and German Philosophy." *New England Quar.*, vol. 16, no. 1 (1943), 41–62.

The Transcendentalist Movement

CA227 Albanese, Catherine L. *Corresponding Motion: Transcendental Religion and the New America.* Philadelphia: Temple Univ. Pr., 1977. 210p. Rev. by W. A. Clebsch, *Jour. of Amer. Hist.*, vol. 65, no. 3 (December 1978), 774–75. An interpretation of Transcendentalist religious thought from *Nature* (1836) to the last issue of the *Dial* (1844).

CA228 Allen, Margaret Vanderhaar. *The Achievement of Margaret Fuller.* N.p.: Penn State Univ. Pr., 1979. 260p.

CA229 Barbour, Brian M., ed. *American Transcendentalism: An Anthology of Criticism.* Notre Dame, Ind.: Notre Dame Univ. Pr., 1973. 302p.

CA230 Barr, Eileen S. "Margaret Fuller D'Ossoli." *Western Humanities Rev.*, vol. 6 (1952), 37–52.

CA231 Berry, Edward G. "Margaret Fuller Ossoli, 1810–1850." *Dalhousie Rev.*, vol. 30 (1951), 369–77. A centenary note on her character and career.

CA232 Blausett, Barbara R. N. "Melville and Emersonian Transcendentalism." Diss., Texas, 1963.

CA233 Boller, Paul F., Jr. *American Transcendentalism, 1830–1860: An Intellectual Inquiry.* New York: Putnam's, 1974. 227p. Rev. by P. K. Conkin, *Jour. of Amer. Hist.*, vol. 62, no. 4 (March 1976), 988–89.

CA234 Brockway, Philip J. *Sylvester Judd (1813–1853): Novelist of Transcendentalism.* Orono: Univ. of Maine Pr., 121p. Rev. by R. Stewart, *Amer. Lit.*, vol. 13, no. 3 (1941), 272–74.

CA235 Buell, Lawrence. *Literary Transcendentalism: Style and Vision in the American Renaissance.* Ithaca: Cornell Univ. Pr., 1975. 347p.

CA236 Burton, Katherine (Kurz). *Celestial Homespun. The Life of Isaac Thomas Hecker.* New York: Longmans, 1943. 393p.

CA237 Cameron, Kenneth Walter. "Notes on Two Hellenic Romances [Lydia Maria Child's *Philothea* (1836) and Frances Wright's *A Few Days in Athens* (1822)]." *Amer. Transcendenta Quar.*, no. 6 (Second Quarter, 1970), part 3, 1f. Both works are indebted to the literature of Romantic Hellenicism transmitted from Wieland through Shelley and Emerson.

CA238 Caponigri, A. Robert. "European Influences on the Thought of Orestes Brownson: Pierre Leroux and Vincenzo Gioberti." In: *No Divided Allegiance. Essays in Brownson's Thought.* Ed. Leonard Gilhooley. New York: Fordham Univ. Pr., 1980. 193p.

CA239 Carafiol, Peter C. "James Marsh to John Dewey: The Fate of Transcendentalist Philosophy in American Education." *ESQ: Jour. of the Amer. Renaissance*, vol. 24 (1978), 1–11.

CA240 Carpenter, Frederic I. "Charles Sanders Peirce, Pragmatic Transcendentalist." *New England Quar.*, vol. 14 (1941), 34–48. Kantian and Emersonian elements in Peirce.

CA241 Carpenter, Hazen C. "Emerson and Christopher Pearse Cranch." *Amer. Quar.*, vol. 16, no. 1 (1964), 18–42.

CA242 *Catalogue of a Portion of the Libraries of the Late Rev. Convers Francis and his Sister Lydia Maria Child*... Boston: Charles F. Libbie & Co., 1887. 111p. Reproduced in offset in the *Amer. Transcendentalist Quar.*, no. 6 (Second Quarter, 1970), part 2.

CA243 Child, Lydia Maria. *The Collected Correspondence of Lydia Maria Child 1817–1880.* Millwood, N.Y.: Kraus Microform, 1978. Ca. 2500 letters in a microfiche ed. with introductory essay and a detailed index.

CA244 Collins, Robert E. *Theodore Parker: American Transcendentalist. A Critical Essay and a Collection of His Writings.* Metuchen, N.J.: Scarecrow Pr., 1973. 271p.

CA245 Crowe, Charles. *George Ripley: Transcendentalist and Utopian Socialist.* Athens: Univ. of Georgia Pr., 1967. 316p. Rev. by I. V. Brown, *Jour. of Amer. Hist.*, vol. 55 (1968), 131–32; L. Buell, *New England Quar.*, vol. 41, no. 3 (September 1968), 461–3; M. Cunliffe, *Amer. Hist. Rev.*, vol. 74, no. 3 (February 1969), 1087–88.

CA246 Cummins, Roger William. "The Second Eden: Charles Lane and American Transcendentalism." Diss., Minnesota, 1967. Founded Fruitlands in 1843.

CA247 Dirks, John E. *The Critical Theology of Theodore Parker.* New York: Columbia Univ. Pr., 1948. 152p.

CA248 Durning, Russell E. "Margaret Fuller and Germany." In: *Margaret Fuller, Citizen of the World.* Beiheft zum Jahrbuch für Amerikastudien, 26. Heft. Heidelberg: Winter, 1968, p.77–129. Based on his "Margaret Fuller, Citizen of the World: an Intermediary between European and American Literatures," diss. submitted at the Univ. of N. Car., 1965. 301p. Rev. by J. W. Thomas, *Jahrbuch für Amerikastudien*, vol. 15 (1970), 292–93.

CA249 Durning, Russell E. "Margaret Fuller's Translation of Goethe's 'Prometheus'." *Jahrbuch für Amerikastudien*, vol. 12 (1967), 240–45.

CA250 Dwight, John Sullivan. Papers, 1832–1892. 6 vols. In the Boston Public Library (MS 69-4). Correspondence, chiefly concerning Brook Farm and the *Harbinger*.

CA251 Elliott, Fannie Mae and Lucy Clark. *Charles Timothy Brooks: A Checklist of Works in the Library of the Univ. of Virginia.* Charlottesville: Univ. of Virginia Pr., 1960. 9p.

CA252 Fertig, Walter L. "John Sullivan Dwight, Transcendentalist and Literary Amateur of Music." Diss. Univ. of Maryland 1953. 137p.

CA253 Gilley, Leonard. "Transcendentalism in *Walden*." *Prairie Schooner*, vol. 42 (Fall 1968), 204–07. "Thoreau's spiritual quest in the light of Darwin, Goethe, Oriental mysticism and the legend of Icarus."

CA254 Gilmore, William James. "Orestes Brownson and New England Religious Culture, 1803–1827." Diss., Virginia, 1971. Abstract in *Church Hist.*, vol. 42, no. 1 (March 1973), 120. A cultural biography of the formative years of Orestes Brownson.

CA255 Gittleman, Edwin. *Jones Very: The Effective Years, 1833–1840*. New York: Columbia Univ. Pr., 1967. 436p.

CA256 Goddard, H. C. *Studies in New England Transcendentalism*. New York: Hillary House, 1960. 217p. Repr. of work originally issued in 1908.

CA257 Golemba, Henry L. *George Ripley*. Boston: Twayne, 1977. 172p. Rev. L. Rohler, *Jour. of Amer. Hist.*, vol. 65, no. 2 (September 1978), 469.

CA258 Harris, W. T. "The Philosophy of Bronson Alcott and the Transcendentalists." In: *A. Bronson Alcott. His Life and Philosophy*. By F. B. Sanborn and W. T. Harris. 2 vols. Boston: Roberts, 1893, p.544–664.

CA259 Harris, William T. "What is Most Valuable to Us in German Philosophy and Literature." In: *Poetry and Philosophy of Goethe*... Ed. Marion V. Dudley. Chicago: Griggs, 1887, p.219–51.

CA260 Holden, Vincent F. *The Yankee Paul: Isaac Thomas Hecker*. Milwaukee: Bruce, 1958. 508p.

CA261 Hudson, Herbert E. "Recent Interpretations of Parker: An Evaluation of the Literature since 1936." *Procs., Unitarian Hist. Soc.*, vol. 13 Part 1 (1966), 1–38. Incl. a bibliography of Theodore Parker, 1937–1967.

CA262 Hunter, Doreen. "'Frederick Henry Hedge, What Say You?'" *American Quar.*, vol. 32, no. 2 (Summer 1980), 186–201. Essay on Hedge's place in the Transcendentalist movement.

CA263 Hutchison, William R. *The Modernist Impulse in American Protestantism*. Cambridge: Harvard University Pr., 1976. 384p.

CA264 Hutchison, William R. "To Heaven in a Swing: the Transcendentalism of Cyrus Bartol." *Harvard Theological Rev.*, vol. 56 (1963), 275–95. Bartol had little access to German sources and influences.

CA265 Hutchison, William R. *The Transcendentalist Ministers; Church Reform in the New England Renaissance*. New Haven: Yale Univ. Pr., 1959, 240p. Rev. by D. B. Parke, *Jour. of Religion*, vol. 41, no. 1 (January 1961), 68–69. Kantianism and German idealist philosophy as informing the "gathering of forces." Stresses the adherence of the reformers to the N. Engl. church tradition.

CA266 Isely, Jeter A. and Elizabeth R. Isely. "A Note on George Ripley and the Beginnings of New England Transcendentalism." *Procs., Unitarian Hist. Soc.*, vol. 13, part 2 (1961), 75–81.

CA267 Ishikawa, Jesse. "Convers Francis to Theodore Parker: Boston in 1844." *ESQ Emerson Society Quar.*, vol. 24 (First quarter 1978), 20–29. Francis, moderator of the Transcendental Club, comments on his feelings about some of his more noted peers.

CA268 Joost, Nicholas. "The *Dial*: A Journalistic Emblem and Its Tradition." *Studies in Philology*, vol. 64 (January 1967), 167–81. A look at journals sharing the title *Dial*.

CA269 Lebow, Marcia Wilson. "A Systematic Examination of the *Journal of Music and Art* ed. by John Sullivan Dwight: 1852–1881, Boston, Mass." Diss., Univ. of Calif., Los Angeles, 1969, 424p. Analysis of content, style of criticism, and its educational influence.

CA270 Lerner, Saul. "The Concepts of History, Progress and Perfectibility in Nineteenth Century American Transcendentalist Thought." Diss., Kansas, 1966. A study in the history and migration of ideas.

CA271 Link, Franz H. "Goethe und die Renaissance des neuenglischen Geisteslebens im 19. Jahrhundert." *Amer. Transcendentalist Quar.*, vol. 14 (1972), 94–99.

CA272 Long, Orie W. *Frederic Henry Hedge: A Cosmopolitan Scholar*. Portland: n.p., 1940. Rev. by C. Von Klenze, *Germanic Rev.*, vol. 15 (1940), 304–06.

CA273 Long, Orie W. *Literary Pioneers.* New York: Russell & Russell, 1963. New edition of a standard study of the Transcendentalists.

CA274 Luker, Ralph E. "God, Man and the World of James Warley Miles, Charlestown's Transcendentalist." *Hist. Mag. of the Protestant Episcopal Church*, vol. 39 (1970), 101–36. A student of Kant.

CA275 Marquardt, Hertha. "Die erste Goethe-Biographin in Amerika. Margaret Fullers geplantes *Life of Goethe*." In: *Festschrift zum 75. Geburtstag von Theodor Spira*. Ed. H. Viebrock and W. Erzgräber. Heidelberg: Winter, 1960, p.309–17.

CA276 Mead, David. "Some Ohio Conversations of Amos Bronson Alcott." *New England Quar.*, vol. 22 (1949), 358–72.

CA277 Miller, Perry. "Theodore Parker: Apostasy Within Liberalism." *Harvard Theological Rev.*, vol. 54, no. 4 (1961), 275–95. Parker, the student of De Wette, seen in a new light.

CA278 Miller, Perry. "Thoreau in the Context of International Romanticism." *New England Quar.*, vol. 34 (1961), 147–59. T. interpreted as one of the Romantic "Sorgenkinder des Lebens."

CA279 Miller, Perry, ed. *The Transcendentalists: An Anthology.* Cambridge: Harvard Univ. Pr., 1950. 521p. Rev. by F. DeW. Miller, *Amer.-German Rev.*, vol. 17, no. 1 (1950), 38. Repr. under the title *The American Transcendentalists. Their Prose and Poetry.* Baltimore: Johns Hopkins Univ. Pr., 1981. 400p.

CA280 Myerson, Joel. "Frederic Henry Hedge and the Failure of Transcendentalism." *Harvard Library Bull.*, vol. 23 (October 1975), 396–410.

CA281 Myerson, Joel. "A History of the Transcendental Club." *ESQ: Jour. of the American Renaissance*, vol. 23 (1977), 27–35.

CA282 Myerson, Joel. "Introduction." In: *Critical Essays on Margaret Fuller.* Ed. Joel Myerson. Boston: G. K. Hall & Co., 1980, p.vii–xvi. Bibliography of the literature about Margaret Fuller.

CA283 Myerson, Joel. *Margaret Fuller. An Annotated Secondary Bibliography.* New York: Burt Franklin (1977). 272p.

CA284 Myerson, Joel. *Margaret Fuller: A Descriptive Bibliography.* Pittsburgh: Univ. of Pittsburgh Pr., 1978. Standard bibliography of writings by Margaret Fuller.

CA285 Newbrough, G. F. "Reason and Understanding in the Works of Theodore Parker." *South Atlantic Quar.*, vol. 47 (1949), 64–75.

CA286 Ossoli, Sarah Margaret (Fuller) Marchesa d'. Papers, 1836–1904. ca. 360 items. In the Boston Public Library. (MS 73-26–73-27). Incl. a journal for 1840–1842, papers, correspondence.

CA287 Parker, Theodore. Papers, ca. 1843–1860. 62 items. In the Boston Public Library (MS 73-27) By P. (1810–1860).

CA288 Pochmann, Henry. ["Margaret Fuller and Germany."] In: *Critical Essays on Margaret Fuller.* Ed. Joel Myerson. Boston: G. K. Hall, 1980, p.228–46. Excerpted from *German Culture in America 1600–1900. Philosophical and Literary Influences.* H. A. Pochmann, with the Assistance of Arthur R. Schultz. Madison: Univ. of Wisconsin Pr., 1957, p.440–47, 760–68.

CA289 Pochmann, Henry A. *New England Transcendentalism and St. Louis Hegelianism: Phases in the History of American Idealism.* Philadelphia: Carl Schurz Memorial Foundation, 1948. 146p. Rev. Perry Miller, *Amer. Lit.*, vol. 21 (1949), 368–70.

CA290 Porte, Joel. *Emerson and Thoreau: Transcendentalists in Conflict.* Middletown, Conn.: Wesleyan Univ. Pr., 1966.

CA291 Rider, Daniel E. "The Musical Thought and Activities of the New England Transcendentalists." Diss., Minnesota, 1964. 341p.

CA292 Rieger, Wolfgang. "The *Dial*: Geschichte und Wertung einer Zeitschrift (Boston, 1840–1844)." Diss., Bonn, 1955.

CA293 Robinson, David M. "Margaret Fuller and the Transcendental Ethos: Woman in the Nineteenth Century." *PMLA*, vol. 97, no. 1 (January 1982), 83–98. Develops the link between idealistic philosophy and the idea of Goethean self-culture and her move toward social reform.

CA294 Schultz, Arthur R. "Margaret Fuller—Transcendentalist Interpreter of German Literature." In: *Critical Essays on Margaret Fuller.* Ed. Joel Myerson. Boston: G. K. Hall & Co., 1980, p.195–208. Repr. from the *Monatshefte für deutschen Unterricht.* vol. 34 (1942).

CA295 Shivers, Frank R., Jr. "A Western Chapter in the History of American Transcendentalism." *Bull. of the Hist. and Philosophical Soc. of Ohio,* vol. 15 (1957), 117–30.

CA296 Simon, Myron, and Thornton H. Parsons, eds. *Transcendentalism and its Legacy.* Ann Arbor: Univ. of Michigan Pr., 1966. 228p. Collection of essays by Kenneth Burke, René Wellek, Joe Lee Davis and others.

CA297 Smith, H. S. "Was Theodore Parker a Transcendentalist?" *New England Quar.,* vol. 23 (1950), 351–64.

CA298 Stern, Guy. "Blücher, Brooks, and August Kopisch: A Report on an Unpublished Translation." *German-Amer. Studies,* vol. 5 (1972), 8–11.

CA299 Stern, Madeline B. "Elizabeth Peabody's Foreign Library (1840)." *Amer. Transcendentalist Quar.,* vol. 20, Supplement 1973, 5–12.

CA300 Thomas, J. Wesley. "A Hitherto Unpublished Critique of Goethe." *Jour. of Engl. and Germanic Philology,* vol. 48, no. 4 (1949), 588–94. In James Freeman Clarke's essay fragment on *Hermann und Dorothea.*

CA301 Thomas, J. Wesley. *James Freeman Clarke, Apostle of German Culture to America.* Boston: John W. Luce, 1949. 168p. Rev. by D. Cunz, *Miss. Valley Hist. Rev.,* vol. 37 (1950), 720–21; H. A. Pochmann, *Amer. Lit.,* vol. 23 (1950), 147–48; A. R. Schultz, *Jour. of Engl. and Germanic Philology,* vol. 53 (1951), 135–36; M. C. Turpie, *Amer. Hist. Rev.,* vol. 56 (1950), 676.

CA302 Thomas, J. Wesley. "John Sullivan Dwight: A Translator of American Romanticism." *Amer. Lit.* vol. 21 (1950), 427–41.

CA303 Thomas, J. Wesley. "New Light on Margaret Fuller's Projected 'Life of Goethe'." *Germanic Rev.,* vol. 24 (1949), 216–23.

CA304 Thomas, J. Wesley. "The *Western Messenger* and German Culture." *Amer.-German Rev.,* vol. 11, no. 1 (1944), 17–18.

CA305 Thomas, J. Wesley, ed. *The Letters of James Freeman Clarke to Margaret Fuller.* Hamburg: Cram, de Gruyter, 1957. 157p. Rev. by G. P. Clark, *Jour. of Engl. and Germanic Philology,* vol. 57 (1958), 564-66.

CA306 Vogel, Stanley. *German Literary Influences on the American Transcendentalists.* New Haven: Yale Univ. Pr., 1955. 196p. Rev. by R. W. Albright, *Amer.-German Rev.,* vol. 22, no. 1 (1955), 34–35; D. S. R. Coelland, *Mod. Lang. Rev.,* vol. 51 (1956), 460–61; E. H. Davidson, *Jour. of Engl. and Germanic Philology,* vol. 55 (1956), 338–39; B. Q. Morgan, *Compar. Lit.,* vol. 8 (1956), 252–53; H. A. Pochmann, *Mod. Lang. Notes,* vol. 71 (1956), 138–41; J. W. Thomas, *Books Abroad,* vol. 29 (1955), 471–72.

CA307 Wellek, René. "The Minor Transcendentalists and German Philosophy." *New England Quar.,* vol. 15, no. 4 (1942), 652–80.

CA308 Wells, Ronald Vale. *Three Christian Transcendentalists: James Marsh, Caleb Sprague Henry, and Frederic Henry Hedge.* Columbia Studies in American Culture, no. 12. New York: Columbia Univ. Pr., 1943. 238p. Rev. C. S. Ellsworth, *Miss. Valley Hist. Rev.,* vol. 30 (1944), 608. Repr. New York: Octagon Books, 1972. 290p.

CA309 Williams, Paul Osborne. "The Transcendental Movement in American Poetry." Diss., Pennsylvania, 1962. 504p.

CA310 Wilmes, D. R. "F. B. Sanborn and the Lost New England World of Transcendentalism." *Colby Library Quar.,* vol. 16 (1980), 237–47.

CA311 Wilson, John B. "Grimm's Law and the Brahmins." *New England Quar.,* vol. 16 (1943), 106–09; also vol. 38 (1965), 234–39. Prof. Kraitsir of Poland introduces new theories of historical linguistics to the Transcendentalists.

CA312 Wilson, John B. "Horace Mann's Aides: The New England Transcendentalists." *Educational Forum,* vol. 31 (May 1967), 487–95.

CA313 Wilson, John B. "A Transcendental Minority Report." *New England Quar.,* vol. 29 (1956), 147–58. The attitude of Elizabeth Peabody toward German idealism; her interest in Herder, Carl Schurz, Froebel, and the Kindergarten movement.

Hegel and Hegelianism

CA314 Anderson, Paul R. "Quincy (Ill.), an Outpost of Philosophy." *Jour. Ill. State Hist. Soc.*, vol. 34, no. 1 (1942), 50–83. Contacts of the Quincy Hegelians with the St. Louis group.

CA315 Baumgaertel, Gerhard. "Hegel in der Philosophie der Bewegung von St. Louis." *Zeitschrift für Philosophische Forschung*, vol. 14 (1960), 285–91.

CA316 Bayrhoffer, Karl Theodor. *Das Wesen des Universums und die Gesetze des Humanismus, dargestellt aus dem Standpunkt der Vernunft*. Ottawa, Ill., n.p., 1871. 100p. Native American student (b. 1812) of Hegel and materialist philosophy, author of philosphical tracts and articles in the *Jour. for Speculative Philosophy*. Resided for many years in Marburg and Leipzig.

CA317 Bowers, David F. "Hegel, Darwin, and the American Tradition." In: *Foreign Influences in American Life*. Ed. David F. Bowers. Princeton Univ. Pr., 1944, p.146–71.

CA318 Dahlstrand, Frederick Charles. "Amos Bronson Alcott: An Intellectual Biography." Diss., Kansas, 1977. 609p. Seen particularly in his relation to Hegelianism.

CA319 Dibble, Jerry A. "Strategies of the Mental War: Carlyle and Hegel and the Rhetoric of Idealism." *Bull., N.Y. Public Library*, vol. 80 (1976), 84–104.

CA320 Dykhuizen, George. "John Dewey and the University of Michigan." *Jour. of the Hist. of Ideas*, vol. 23 no. 4 (1962), 513–44. The neo-Hegelianism of the early Dewey and George Sylvester Morris.

CA321 Easton, Loyd D. "German Philosophy in Nineteenth Century Cincinnati—Stallo, Conway, Nast and Willich." *Bull., Hist. and Philosophical Soc. of Ohio*, vol. 20 (1962), 4–28.

CA322 Easton, Loyd D. "Hegel in the Light of his First American Followers." In: *Akten des XIV. Internat. Kongresses für Philosophie*. Vienna: n.p., 1970, vol. 5, p.617–23.

CA323 Easton, Loyd D. "Hegelianism in Nineteenth-Century Ohio." *Jour. of the Hist. of Ideas*, vol. 23, no. 3 (1962), 355–78. The group of J. B. Stallo, Peter Kaufmann, Moncure Conway, and August Willich.

CA324 Easton, Loyd D. *Hegel's First American Followers. The Ohio Hegelians: John B. Stallo, Peter Kaufmann, Moncure Conway, August Willich, with Key Writings*. Athens: Ohio Univ. Pr., 1966. 353p. Rev. by J. Barnett, *Bull. of the Cincinnati Hist. Soc.*, vol. 25 (1967), 154f.; R. J. Fechner, *Jour. of Amer. Hist.*, vol. 54 (1967), 679f.; R. L. Perkins, *Register of the Ky. Hist. Soc.*, vol. 65, no. 3 (July 1967), 254–56. Hegel in relation to phenomenalism; as process-philosopher; as precursor to modern linguistic philosophy.

CA325 Easton, Loyd D. "Moncure Conway and German Philosophy." In: *Spahr Lectures in Americana*. N.p.: 1970, vol. 4, p.203–22.

CA326 Goetzmann, William H., and Dixon Pratt, eds. *The American Hegelians: An Intellectual Episode in the History of Western America. Anthology of Essays Portraying a Different Kind of Western America . . . an Intellectual Movement, from Its Beginnings with the Transcendentalists in New England, to St. Louis, and Closing of the Circle in New England with the Concord School . . .* New York: Knopf, 1973. 397p. Rev. by J. V. Metzgar, *Historian*, vol. 36 (1974), 569–71.

CA327 Harmon, Francis B. "The Social Philosophy of the St. Louis Hegelians." Diss., Columbia, 1943. 112p.

CA328 Harris, William T. "George William Frederick Hegel (1770–1831)." In: *Library of the World's Best Literature*. Ed. Charles Dudley Warner. New York: R. S. Peale & J. A. Hill, ca. 1897, vol. 12, p.7161–73, with extracts from Hegel's writings, p.7174–83.

CA329 Harris, William T. "Outlines of Hegel's Logic." *Jour. of Speculative Philosophy*, vol. 3 (1869), 257–81. A compend of translations from Hegel's *Philosophical Propadeutics*, ed. by Karl Rosenkranz, 1840.

CA330 Harris, William T. Rev. of Hegel's *Philosophy of Right*. Trans. from the German by S. W.

Hegel and Hegelianism *(cont.)*

Dyde. London, 1895. In: *Philosophical Rev.*, vol. 6 (May 1897), 288-93.

CA331 Harris, William T. "Trendelenburg and Hegel." *Jour. of Speculative Philosophy*, vol. 9 (January 1875), 70-80.

CA332 Holt, W. Stull. "Hegel, the Turner Hypothesis, and the Safety-Valve Theory." *Agricultural Hist.*, vol. 22 (1948), 175-76. Hegel as possible source for Turner.

CA333 Koepsel, Werner. *Die Rezeption der Hegelschen Ästhetik im 20. Jahrhundert*. Bonn: Bouvier, 1975. 381p.

CA334 LeDuc, Thomas. *Piety and Intellect at Amherst College, 1865-1912*. New York: Columbia Univ. Pr., 1946. On the teaching of Hegelianism at Amherst.

CA335 *The Legacy of Hegel. Proceedings of the Marquette Hegel Symposium 1970*. Ed. J. J. O'Malley et al. The Hague: Nijhoff, 1973. 308p.

CA336 Marcuse, Herbert. *Reason and Revolution. Hegel and the Rise of Social Theory*. London / New York: Oxford Univ. Pr., ca. 1941. 431p.

CA337 Mueller, Gustav Emil. Papers, 1952-1959. In Univ. of Oklahoma Library. (MS 62-1840). Manuscripts of three books in German language on the subject of Hegel and the history of philosophy.

CA338 O'Brien, Michael. "W. J. Cash, Hegel, and the South." *Jour. of Southern Hist.*, vol. 44 (August 1978), 379-398. Wilbur Joseph Cash was author of the well-known work *The Mind of the South* (1941).

CA339 Pickens, Donald K. "A Note in Oklahoma History: Henry C. Brokmeyer Among the Creek Indians." *Chronicles of Okla.*, vol. 45 (1967), 73-76.

CA340 Pochmann, Henry A. "Emerson and the St. Louis Hegelians." *Amer.-German Rev.*, vol. 10, no. 3 (1944), 14-17.

CA341 Pochmann, Henry A. "Hegel and Plato Contend for the West." *Amer.-German Rev.*, vol. 9, no. 6 (August 1943), 8-13. Special reference to the encounters between Brokmeyer and Alcott.

CA342 Pochmann, Henry A. "The Hegelization of the West." *Amer.-German Review*, vol. 9, no. 5 (June 1943), 24-31, 37. Hegelian influence in a frontier society.

CA343 Rozwene, Edwin. "Edmundo O'Gorman and the Idea of America." *Amer. Quar.*, vol. 10 (1958), 99-115. The Mexican historian attacks Hegelian influence in American historiography, i.e., F. J. Turner and Herbert F. Bolton.

CA344 Setton, Kenneth M. "Hegel in America." *Library Chronicle of the Univ. of Pa.*, vol. 28 (Spring 1962), 81-87. Influences in New England and St. Louis.

CA345 Steinhauer, Kurt. ed. *Hegel: Bibliography*. New York: Bowker, 1981. 896p.

CA346 Townsend, Harvey Gates. "The Pragmatism of Peirce and Hegel." *Philosophical Rev.*, vol. 37, no. 4 (July 1938), 297-303.

CA347 Watson, David. "The Neo-Hegelian Tradition in America." *Jour. of Amer. Studies*, vol. 14, no. 2 (August 1980), 219-34.

Francis Lieber

CA348 Brown, Bernard E. *American Conservatives: The Political Thought of Francis Lieber and John W. Burgess*. New York: Columbia Univ. Pr., 1951. 191p. Rev. by T. L. Cook, *Amer. Quar.*, vol. 6 (1954), 86-90.

CA349 Lieber, Francis. Papers. In Henry S. Huntington Library, San Marino, Calif. Letters from persons in Europe and America, ed. by Mrs. Lieber. *Also*: 32 letters in the Rhees Collection. Misc. papers and article on Know-Nothingism (MS).

CA350 Robson, C. B. "Francis Lieber's Theories of Society, Government, and Liberty." *Jour. of Politics*, vol. 4, no. 2 (1942), 227-49.

CA351 Sallet, Richard. "On Francis Lieber and His Contribution to the Law of Nations of Today." In: *Recht im Dienste der Menschenwürde*.

Festschrift für Herbert Kraus. Ed. Göttinger Arbeitskreis. Würzburg: Holzner, 1964. 547p.

CA352 Smith, Wilson. "Francis Lieber's Moral Philosophy." *Huntington Library Quar.*, vol. 18, no. 4 (1955), 395–408.

Friedrich List

CA353 Bell, John F. "Frederick List, Champion of Industrial Capitalism." *Pa. Mag. of Hist. and Biography*, vol. 66 (1942), 56–83.

CA354 Brinkmann, Carl. *Friedrich List.* Berlin: Duncker Humblot, 1949. 359p. Rev. by Svend Laursen, *Amer. Hist. Rev.*, vol. 58, no. 2 (1952), 440–41.

CA355 Brown, R. W. *Friedrich List—The Father of German Railroads—His Residence in Dauphin and Schuylkill Counties, Pennsylvania.* Harrisburg: Dauphin Co. Hist. Soc., 1950. 11p.

CA356 Eckert, Robert. "Der Amerikaaufenthalt Friedrich Lists in seiner Bedeutung für das Listsche System." Diss., Erlangen-Nürnberg, 1964. 109p.

CA357 Garbe, Otfreid. "Friedrich List: His Impact on the Economic Independence of the United States." In: *Germany and America: Essays on Problems of International Relations and Immigration.* Ed. Hans L. Trefousse. New York: Columbia Univ. Pr., 1980, p.151–60.

CA358 Gehrig, Hans. *Friedrich List und Deutschlands politisch-ökonomische Einheit.* Leipzig: Koehler & Amelang, 1956. 450p. Comprehensive presentation of List's life and work.

CA359 Gehring, Paul. *Friedrich List, Jugend- und Reifejahre 1789–1825.* Introd. by Oskar Kalbfell. Tübingen: Mohr, 1964. 527p. Rev. by K. E. Born, *Historische Zeitschrift*, vol. 201, no. 2 (1965), 496–97.

CA360 Gendebien, Albert W. "Friedrich List and Lafayette College." *Pa. Hist.*, vol. 29 (1962), 123–39. List had been invited to accept the post of Principal of the projected college in 1828.

CA361 List, Friedrich. "The Dream of Friedrich List." *Amer.-German Rev.*, vol. 31, no. 2 (1964), 33–35. From a letter of 1836 on problems of trade and tariffs.

CA362 List, Friedrich. *Friedrich List. Wegbereiter einer neuen Wirtschaft. Hauptgedanken aus seinen Schriften.* Ed. Hans Gehrig. Berlin: Erich Schmidt, 1966. 179p. Selections from List's writings.

CA363 *Mitteilungen der List-Gesellschaft, Basel.* Basel: n.p., n.d. Publ. in 1964 in honor of the economist's 175th anniversary.

Marxism and Socialist Thought

CA364 Bathrick, David. "Brecht's Marxism and America." In: *Essays on Brecht. Theater and Politics.* Ed. Siegfried Mews and H. Knust. Chapel Hill: Univ. of North Carolina Pr., 1974, p.209–25. Examination of the successive phases of Brecht's reception in various contexts in America.

CA365 Baxandall, Lee, comp. *Marxism and Aesthetics: A Selective Annotated Bibliography.* New York: Humanities Pr., 1968.

CA366 Bell, Daniel. "The Background and Development of Marxian Socialism in the United States." In *Socialism and American Life.* Ed. Donald D. Egbert and Stow Persons. Princeton: Univ. of Princeton Pr., 1952. Vol. 1, p.215–405.

CA367 Bestor, Arthur E., Jr. "The Evolution of the Socialist Vocabulary." *Jour. of the Hist. of Ideas*, vol. 9, no. 3 (June 1948), 259–302.

CA368 Breines, Paul. "Germans, Journals and Jews—Madison, Men, Marxism and Mosse: A Tale of Jewish-Leftist Identity Confusion in America." *New German Critique*, vol. 20 (1980), 81–103. A circle of Germans, Jews, Leftists and Marxists who philosophize in Madison, Wis.

CA369 Broderick, Francis L. "German Influence on the Scholarship of W. E. B. Du Bois." *Phylon Quar.*, vol. 19 (1958), 367–71. Du Bois studied in Berlin under Adolph Wagner and G. von Schmoller, 1892–1894.

CA370 Brüning, Eberhard. "Probleme der Wechselbeziehungen zwischen der amerikanischen und der deutschen sozialistischen und proletarisch-revolutionären Literatur." In: *Zur Geschichte der sozialistischen Literatur 1918–1933. Elf Vorträge gehalten auf einer internat. Konferenz in Leipzig vom 23. bis 25. Januar 1962*. Hrsg. von der Deut. Akad. der Künste zu Berlin. Berlin: Aufbau-Verlag, 1963.

CA371 Dannenberg, Karl. *Karl Marx, the Man and His Work, and the Constructive Elements of Socialism*. 3 lectures and 2 essays. New York: Radical Review Publ. Assoc., 1918. 122p.

CA372 Diggins, John P. "Getting Hegel Out of History: Max Eastman's Quarrel with Marxism." *Amer. Hist. Rev.*, vol. 79 (February 1974), 38–71.

CA373 Du Bois, W.E.B. *The Autobiography of W.E.B. Du Bois. A Soliloquy on Viewing My Life from the Last Decade of Its First Century*. New York: International Publishers, 1968. 448p. (Available from Kraus International Publications, Millwood, N.Y.)

CA374 Easton, Loyd D. "August Willich, Marx, and Left-Hegelian Socialism." *Cahiers de L'icea*, August, 1965, 101–37.

CA375 Foner, Philip S. "Marx's *Capital* in the United States." *Science and Society*, vol. 31 (1967), 461–66.

CA376 Hale, William H. "When Karl Marx Worked for Horace Greeley." *Amer. Heritage*, vol. 8, no. 3 (1957), 20–25, 110–11. Marx's articles in the *N.Y. Tribune*, 1851–1860.

CA377 Herreshoff, David. *American Disciples of Marx: From the Age of Jackson to the Progressive Era*. Detroit: Wayne St. Univ. Pr., 1967. 215p. Rev. by R. M. Miller, *Procs., Amer. Antiquarian Soc.*, vol. 376 (March 1968); R. Drinnon, *Canad. Jour. of Hist.*, vol. 3 (September 1968), 105; M. Polner, *Jour. of Amer. Hist.*, vol. 55, no. 3 (December 1968), 647–48. On early Marxists in America; mutual influences between America and Marxist ideologues.

CA378 Herreshoff, David. *The Origins of American Marxism*. New York: Monad, 1973.

CA379 Hook, Sidney. *Marx and the Marxists; the Ambiguous Legacy*. New York: Van Nostrand, 1955. 254p.

CA380 Hughes, H. Stuart. "Franz Neumann between Marxian and Liberal Democracy." In: *The Intellectual Migration*. Ed. D. Fleming and B. Bailyn. Cambridge: Harvard Univ. Pr., 1969, p.446–62.

CA381 Johnson, Oakley C. *Marxism in United States History before the Russian Revolution (1876–1917)*. New York: Humanities Pr., 1974. 196p. Rev. by H. H. Quint, *Jour. of Amer. Hist.*, vol. 62, no. 1 (1975) 162–63.

CA382 Jones, Clifton. "The Socialist Party of the United States. A Bibliography of Secondary Sources, 1945–1974." *Labor Hist.*, vol. 19, no. 2 (Spring 1978), 253–79.

CA383 Koch, Rainer. *Demokratie und Staat bei Julius Fröbel 1805–1893. Liberales Denken zwischen Naturrecht und Social-Darwinismus*. Veröffentlichungen des Instituts für Europ. Geschichte, Mainz, vol. 84. Wiesbaden: Steiner, 1978. 298p. Rev. by Thomas Nipperdey, *Historische Zeitschrift*, vol. 229, no. 1 (October and August 1979), 183–87. A refugee from the Revolution of 1848, active in America between 1850 and 1857.

CA384 Kreuter, Kent, and Gretchen Kreuter. "The Vernacular History of A. M. Simons." *Jour. of Amer. Studies*, vol. 2 (1968), 65–81. Simons' was the first Marxist interpretation of the American past; a part of the vernacular attack on the genteel tradition.

CA385 Lachs, John. *Marxist Philosophy. A Bibliographical Guide*. Chapel Hill: Univ. of N. Car. Pr., 1967. A checklist of 1,500 entries.

CA386 Lens, Sidney. *Radicalism in America*. New York: Thomas Y. Crowell, 1966. 371p. Incl. a chapter "Enter Karl Marx," p.149–70.

CA387 Marx, Karl, and Friedrich Engels. *The American Journalism of Marx and Engels. A Selection from the New York Daily Tribune*. Ed. Henry M. Christman. Introd. by Charles Blitzer. New York: New American Library, 1966. 267p.

CA388 Marx, Karl, and Friedrich Engels. *Letters to America.* New York: International Publishers, ca. 1961. Selections from the correspondence of Marx and Engels with American socialists and labor leaders, Jos. Weydemeyer, Friedrich Sorge, Hermann Schlueter, Florence Kelley, and John Swinton.

CA389 "Marxism and the American Christian Church: 1876–1917." *Political Affairs*, vol. 45 (July 1966), 53–63.

CA390 Matthias, Erich. *Sozial-Demokratie und Nation: Zur Ideengeschichte der sozialdemokratischen Emigration 1933–1938.* Stuttgart: Deutsche Verlags-Anstalt, 1952. 363p. Rev. by Hans Kohn, *Amer. Hist. Rev.*, vol. 58, no. 4 (1953), 914–16.

CA391 Obermann, Karl. "Die Beziehungen von Marx und Engels zur amerikanischen Arbeiterbewegung in der Zeit zwischen der ersten und der zweiten Internationale." *Zeitschrift für Geschichtswissenschaft*, vol. 12, no. 1 (1964), 62–71.

Later Nineteenth Century Figures

CA392 Apel, K. O. "From Kant to Peirce: The Semiotical Transformation of Transcendental Logic." In: *Procs., Third Internat. Kant Congress.* Ed. Lewis White Beck. Dordrecht: D. Reidel, 1972, p.90–104.

CA393 Barzun, Jacques. *Darwin, Marx, Wagner. Critique of of a Heritage.* 2nd ed., rev. Garden City: Doubleday, 1958. 378p.

CA394 Bense, Max. *Semiotik. Allgemeine Theorie der Zeichen.* Internat. Reihe Kybernetik und Information, vol. 4. Baden-Baden: Agis, 1967. 79p. Exposition of C. S. Pierce's studies in semiotics.

CA395 Bishop, Donald H. "The Carus-James Controversy." *Jour. of the Hist. of Ideas*, vol. 35, no. 1 (1974), 509–20.

CA396 Blackmore, John T. *Ernst Mach: His Work, Life, and Influence.* Berkeley/Los Angeles: Univ. of California Pr., 1972. 414p. Austrian physicist; father of many of the current schools of philosophical empiricism.

CA397 Brostowin, Patrick R. "John Adolphis Etzler: Scientific-Utopian During the 1830's and 1840's." Diss., New York Univ., 1969. 394p. German-born immigrant of 1831; revolutionary prophet associated with John A. Roebling.

CA398 "Carus, Paul (b. Ilsenburg, Germany, 18 July 1952; d. LaSalle, Ill., 1 February 1919.)" *Dictionary of Scientific Biography*, vol. 15, p.79–80.

CA399 "Carus, Paul." *Dictionary of Amer. Biography*, vol. 3, p.548–49.

CA400 "C. S. Peirce and the Scientific Philosophy of Ernst Mach." *Actes du XIIe Congrès international d'histoire des sciences.* Paris: n.p., 1968, p.33–40.

CA401 Esposito, Joseph L. "Peirce and *Naturphilosophie*." *Trans., Charles S. Peirce Soc.*, vol. 13, no. 2 (Spring, 1977), 122–41. On Peirce and German idealist philosophers, esp. Schelling and Hegel.

CA402 Haggerty, William J. "Realism in the Philosophy of Orestes A. Brownson." Diss., Boston Univ., 1961.

CA403 Hartmann, Wilfried, ed. *Max Scheler Bibliographie.* Stuttgart-Bad Canstatt: Fromm, 1963. 128p. An early phenomenologist whose reputation has prospered in America.

CA404 Hay, William H. "Paul Carus: A Case Study of Philosophy on the Frontier." *Jour. of the Hist. of Ideas*, vol. 17 (1956), 498–510.

CA405 Jackson, Carl T. "The Meeting: East and West: The Case of Paul Carus." *Jour. of the Hist. of Ideas*, vol. 29, no. 1 (January–March 1968), 73–92. Carus, b. in the Harz in 1852, came to the U.S. in the 1880's. He developed his views on Monistic philosophy in his journal *The Open Court* from 1887 on.

CA406 Kegley, Jacquelyn Ann. "Royce and Husserl: Some Parallels and Food for Thought." *Transactions of the Charles S. Peirce Soc.*, vol. 14 (1978), 184–99.

CA407 Kuklick, Bruce. *Josiah Royce: An Intellectual Biography.* Indianapolis: Bobbs-Merrill, 1972. 270p. Rev. by E. Pomeroy, *Jour. of Amer. Hist.*, vol. 59, no. 4 (March 1973), 1028–29. Examination of Royce's idealist metaphysics and epistemology.

CA408 Kuklick, Bruce. *The Rise of American Philosophy: Cambridge, Massachusetts, 1860–1930.* New Haven: Yale University Press, 1977. 652p. Rev. by E. H. Madden and P. H. Hare, *Transactions of the Charles S. Peirce Soc.*, vol. 14 (1978), 53–71. A study of the line of New England thinkers from Bower through Peirce, Royce, and Münsterberg to Whitehead and Lewis seen against the background of world developments in philosophy.

CA409 Leonard, William Ellery. "Paul Carus." *Dial*, vol. 66 (1919), 452–55.

CA410 Marcuse, Ludwig. "Amerikanischer und deutscher Pragmatismus." *Der Monat*, vol. 8, no. 88 (1955–1956), 33–45.

CA411 Meyer, Donald Harvey. "Paul Carus and the Religion of Science." *Amer. Quar.*, vol. 14, no. 4 (1962), 597–607.

CA412 Müller, Gustav E. "John Dewey's Aesthetik." *Neue Schweizer Rundschau*, vol. 9 (1952), 542–49. An analysis of *Art and Experience* which points out Dewey's similarity to Schiller in his approach to the educational value of art.

CA413 Sheridan, James Francis. "Paul Carus: A Study of the Thought and Work of the Editor of the Open Court Publishing Co." Diss., Univ. of Illinois, Urbana, ca. 1957.

CA414 Steinkraus, Warren E. "Writings By and About Borden Parker Bowne (1847–1910)." *Bull., N.Y. Public Library*, vol. 73, no. 6 (1969), 398–414. Prof. Bowne's philosophical views spring primarily from the philosophy of Lotze, to whom he dedicated his *Metaphysics* of 1882.

CA415 Vigener, Gerhard. *Die zeichentheoretischen Entwürfe von F. de Saussure und Charles S. Peirce als Grundlage einer linguistischen Pragmatik.* Tübingen: Narr, 1979. 180p.

CA416 Wilkinson, G.D. "John B. Stallo's Criticism of Physical Science." Diss., Columbia, 1941.

Friedrich Nietzsche

CA417 Anghinetti, Paul W. "Alienation, Rebellion, and Myth: A Study of the Works of Nietzsche, Jung, Yeats, Camus, and Joyce." Diss., Florida State, 1969.

CA418 Bridgewater, Patrick. *Nietzsche in Anglosaxony: A Study of Nietzsche's Impact on English and American Literature.* Leicester: Leicester Univ. Pr.; New York: Humanities Pr., 1972. 236p. The Nietzschean impact on Jack London, Theodore Dreiser, Eugene O'Neill, John Gould Fletcher, Wallace Stevens, Mencken and others.

CA419 Carus, Paul. *Nietzsche and Other Exponents of Individualism.* New York: Haskell House, 1972. 150p. Repr.

CA420 Coffin, Arthur B. *Robinson Jeffers. Poet of Inhumanism.* Madison: Univ. of Wisconsin Press, 1971. 324p.

CA421 Donadio, Stephen L. "The Dream of Art Triumphant: An Essay on Nietzsche and Henry James." Diss., Columbia, 1974.

CA422 Donadio, Stephen L. *Nietzsche, Henry James, and the Artistic Will.* New York: Oxford Univ. Pr., 1978. 347p.

CA423 Drimmer, Melvin. "Nietzsche in American Thought, 1895–1925." Diss., Rochester, 1965. 738p.

CA424 Fleckenstein, Joan P. "Eugene O'Neill's Theatre of Dionysius: The Nietzschean Influence upon Selected Plays." Diss., Wisconsin, 1973.

CA425 Frisby, Elisabeth Stein. "Nietzsche's Influence on the Superman in Science Fiction Literature." Diss., Florida State, 1979. 185p.

CA426 Gilman, S. L. "Nietzsches Emerson-Lektüre: Eine unbekannte Quelle." *Nietzsche Studien: Internationales Jahrbuch für die Nietzsche-Forschung*, vol. 9 (1980), 406–31.

CA427 Green, Gregory. "The Old Superman and the Sea: Nietzsche, the Lions, and the 'Will to Power'." *Hemingway Notes*, vol. 5, no. 1 (1979), 14–17.

CA428 Humma, John B. "From Transcendental to Descendental: The Romantic Thought of Blake, Nietzsche, Lawrence." Diss., Univ. of Southern Illinois, 1970. 312p. An examination of the Nietzschean "way of the senses," "blood-knowledge," sensual "going under."

CA429 Kauffmann, LeRoy Culbertson. "The Influence of Friedrich Nietzsche on American Literature." Diss., Pennsylvania, 1963.

CA430 Kunne-Ibsch, Elrud. *Die Stellung Nietzsches in der Entwicklung der modernen Literaturwissenschaft*. Tübingen: Niemeyer, 1972. 277p.

CA431 Mann, Thomas. "Nietzsche's Philosophie im Lichte unserer Erfahrung." *Die neue Rundschau*, Autumn 1947, 359–89. Also Stockholm: Bermann-Fischer Vlg., 1947.

CA432 Marcuse, Ludwig. "Nietzsche in Amerika zu seinem fünfzigsten Todestag." *Neue Schweizer Rundschau*, vol. 4, no. 2 (August 1950), 222–31. See also his "Nietzsche in Amerika." *South Atlantic Quar.*, vol. 50 (1951), 330–39.

CA433 Poulard, Regina. "O'Neill and Nietzsche: The Making of a Playwright and Thinker." Diss., Loyola Univ., 1974.

CA434 Reichert, Herbert, and Karl Schlechta. *International Nietzsche Bibliography*. N. Car. Studies in Comparative Literature, no. 29. Chapel Hill: Univ. of N. Car. Pr., 1960.

CA435 Shaw, George Bernard. "Nietzsche in English." In: *Nietzsche: A Collection of Critical Essays*. Modern Studies in Philosophy. Ed. Robert C. Solomon. Garden City: Doubleday, 1973, p.386–89. Reprinted essay.

CA436 Snider, Nancy V. "An Annotated Bibliography of English Works on Friedrich Nietzsche." Diss., Michigan, 1962. 138p. 700 titles of the years 1894 to 1960.

CA437 Solomon, Robert C., ed. *Nietzsche: A Collection of Critical Essays*. Modern Studies in Philosophy. Garden City: Doubleday, 1973. 391p. New and reprinted essays; bibliography.

CA438 Stavrou, C. N. *Whitman and Nietzsche. A Comparative Study of Their Thought*. Chapel Hill: Univ. of N. Car. Pr., 1964. 231p. Rev. by W. D. Williams, *German Life and Letters*, vol. 19 (1966), 117.

CA439 Strong, Bryan. "Images of Nietzsche in America, 1900–1970." *South Atlantic Quarterly*, vol. 70 (Autumn 1971), 575–94.

CA440 Suelflow, August R. "Nietzsche and Schaff on American Lutheranism." *Concordia Hist. Inst. Quar.*, vol. 23, no. 4 (1950), 145–58. Summarizes a talk given by Nietzsche in 1865 which was based on Schaff's *Amerika*.

CA441 Takizawa, Juzo. "Schopenhauer and Nietzsche in Bellows's Work." In: *American Literature in the 1950's. Annual Report 1976*. Tokyo: Tokyo Chap., Amer. Lit. Soc. of Japan, 1977, p.50–59.

H. L. Mencken

CA442 Douglas, George H. *H. L. Mencken: Critic of American Life*. Hamden: Archon, 1978. 248p. Rev. by D. C. Stenerson, *Jour. of Amer. Hist.*, vol. 66, no. 1 (June 1979), 189–90. Concentrates on M.'s social commentary in the decade of the 'twenties. Less a thinker than one who dramatizes ideas.

CA443 Fecher, Charles A. *Mencken: A Study of His Thought*. New York: Random House, 1978. 391p.

CA444 Hollingdale, R. J. "The True Disciple." *Menckeniana*, no. 19 (Fall 1966), 5–7. On M. as a disciple of Nietzsche.

CA445 La Belle, M. Maurice. "H. L. Mencken's Comprehension of Friedrich Nietzsche." *Compar. Lit. Studies*, vol. 7 (1970), 43–49.

CA446 Stenerson, Douglas C. *H. L. Mencken: Iconoclast from Baltimore*. Chicago: Univ. of Chicago Pr., 1971. 287p. Shows how the Nietzschean element in M.'s philosophy has been exaggerated. The work is a guide to the enduring portions of the Mencken literary legacy. Rev. by Ann Massa, *Jour. of Amer. Studies*, vol. 8 (1974), 403–04.

CA447 Turaj, Frank. "H. L. Mencken's Philosophical Skepticism." *Menckeniana*, vol. 48 (1973), 12–16.

Die Freie Gemeinde / Free Thought Movement

CA448 *Amerikanischer Turner-Kalender für das Jahr 1887*. Milwaukee: Freidenker Publ. Co., 1887. 120p.

CA449 Cooper, Berenice. "Die Freie Gemeinde: Freethinkers on the Frontier." *Minn. Hist.*, vol. 41, no. 2 (Summer 1968), 53–60.

CA450 Demerath, N.J., 3rd., and Victor Thiessen. "On Spitting Against the Wind: Organizational Precariousness and American Irreligion." *Amer. Jour. of Sociology*, vol. 81 (May 1966), 674–87. Dissolution and destruction of the Sauk City, Wis. free thought movement.

CA451 Dodel, F. W., ed. and comp. *Requiescat. Eine Mustersammlung von Grabreden für Freidenker. Nebst einem Anhang von Citaten und Gedichten zum Einflechten bei Begräbnisreden*. Milwaukee: n.p., 1900.

CA452 *Freidenker-Almanach für das Jahr 1887*. Milwaukee: Freidenker Publ. Co., 1887. 124p.

CA453 *Das Freie Wort. / Voice of Freedom*. German-language periodical sponsored by the Freie Gemeinde. 2617 West Fond du Lac Ave., Milwaukee, Wis. 53206.

CA454 Post, Albert. *Popular Freethought in America, 1825–1950*. Studies in History, Economics and Public Law, no. 497. New York: Columbia Univ. Pr., 1943. 258p.

CA455 Prahl, Augustus J. "The Ideological Background of the American Turner." *Compar. Lit. News-Letter*, vol. 3, no. 2 (1944), 11–13.

CA456 Schlicher, J. J. "Edward Schroeter the Humanist: I. The Early Years of Storm and Stress. II. Work and Honor at Sauk City." *Wis. Mag. of Hist.*, vol. 28 (1944), 169–83, 307–24. Associated with the Freie Gemeinde, Sauk City, from 1854 to 1888.

CA457 Vonnegut, Clemens. ["Dillettant."] *Versuch eines Leitfadens zum Unterricht in der Sittenlehre im freidenkerischen Sinne*. Milwaukee: n.p., 1890. 32p.

CA458 Warren, Sidney. *American Freethought, 1860–1914*. Columbia Univ. Studies in History, Economics and Public Law, no. 504. New York: Columbia Univ. Pr., 1943.

Twentieth Century Figures

CA459 Adler, Felix. *An Ethical Philosophy of Life...* New York: Appleton, 1913. 380p. A spiritual autobiography by A. (1851–1933), German-born leader of the ethical culture movement.

CA460 Ambacher, Michel. *[Herbert] Marcuse et la civilisation américaine*. Paris: Anbier-Montaigne, 1969. 134p. A critique and analysis; his roots in exile, persecution, Hegelianism, Marxism, Freud.

CA461 Barnouw, Dagmar. "'Beute der Pragmatisierung': Adorno und Amerika. In: *Die USA und Deutschland: Wechselseitige Spiegelungen in der Literatur der Gegenwart*. Ed. Wolfgang Paulsen. Bern: Francke, 1976, p.61–83.

CA462 Bové, Paul A. *Destructive Poetics: Heidegger and Modern American Poetry*. New York: Columbia Univ. Pr., 1980. 304p. Concerning Whitman, Stevens, and Olson.

CA463 Boydston, Jo Ann. *John Dewey's Personal and Professional Library. A Checklist*. Carbondale: Southern Illinois Univ. Pr., 1982. 128p.

CA464 Dewey, John. *German Philosophy and Politics.* New York: Holt, 1915. 134p. New York: Putnam's, 1942. Repr. New York: Arno Press. Facsimiles ed. Select Bibliographies Reprint Series.

CA465 Dewey, John. *Leibniz's New Essays Concerning the Human Understanding. A Critical Exposition.* Chicago: S. C. Griggs & Co., 1888. 272p. Repr. in: *The Early Works of John Dewey, 1882–1898.* 5 vols. MLA-CEAA Textual Ed. 1969–1972. Vol. 1 (1882–1888): *Collected Essays.* Ed. Jo Ann Boydston. 1969. 493p.

CA466 "Dietrich Bonhoeffer." *Union Seminary Quar. Rev.,* vol. 23 (Fall 1967), 3–90. Essays by leading interpreters on one of the most important European influences on American theology.

CA467 Feigl, Herbert. "The Wiener Kreis in America." In: *The Intellectual Migration.* Ed. Donald Fleming and Bernard Bailyn. Cambridge: Harvard Univ. Pr., 1969, p.630–73. Espec. the schools of logical positivism and scientific empiricism.

CA468 Gottstein, W. K. "Albert Schweitzer and America." *Amer.-German Rev.,* vol. 16, no. 4 (1950), 6–8, 31.

CA469 Guise, Alice M. "What Are Poets For? Coleridge and Heidegger." Diss., American Univ., 1976. 44p. Applying Heideggerian theory in approaching the later poems of Coleridge.

CA470 Jay, Martin. "The Frankfurt School in Exile." *Perspectives in Amer. Hist.,* vol. 6 (1972), 339–85.

CA471 *Karl Jaspers in Übersetzungen.* Weltliteratur in Übersetzungen, Reihe I, Bd. 1. Frankfurt a. Main: Hans W. Bentz Verlag, 1961. 31p. Bibliography of translations.

CA472 Krüger, Marlis. "Wissenssoziologie zwischen Ideologie und Wissenschaft. Zur Rezeption der Wissenssoziologie Karl Mannheims in Amerika. Eine Kritik amerikanischer wissenssoziologischer Theorien." Diss., Berlin, 1967. 211p.

CA473 Link, Arthur S. "Woodrow Wilson and the Study of Administration." *Procs., Amer. Philosophical Soc.,* vol. 112 (1968), 431–33. Cites German influences on Wilson's thought.

CA474 McDonnell, Joseph W. "John Dewey and Martin Buber on Communication and Community." Diss., Univ. of Southern California, 1978.

CA475 Marshall, M. E. "William James, Gustav Fechner, and the Question of Dogs and Cats in the Library." *Jour. of the Hist. of the Behavioral Sciences,* vol. 10 (July 1974), 304–12. On James's perception of the (changing) relationship between his own thought and that of Gustav Fechner (1890–1909).

CA476 May, Henry F. *The End of American Innocence. A Study of the First Years of Our Own Time 1912–1917.* New York: Knopf, 1959. 413p. Incursions of new attitudes and ideas: Freud, Nietzsche, Marx, philosophical naturalism, Menckenism, monism.

CA477 Moonan, Willard. "Writings about Martin Buber in English: A Selective Bibliography." *Bull. of Bibliography,* vol. 32 (1978), 28–32. Buber's thought has had a broad influence on contemporary philosophy, psychiatry, education, theology, and social theory.

CA478 Rhoades, Yolande Jacqueline Muris. "Faith and Responsibility in H. Richard Niebuhr and Dietrich Bonhoeffer: A Comparison of Their Concepts of God and Their Understandings of Christian Ethics." Diss., Emory Univ., 1969. 368p.

CA479 Roth, Guenther. "Max Weber's Empirical Sociology in Germany and the United States. Tensions between Partisanship and Scholarship." *Central European Hist.,* vol. 2, no. 3 (September 1969), 196–215.

CA480 Schoolman, Morton. "Marcuse's Aesthetics and the Displacement of Critical Theory." *New German Critique,* vol. 8 (1976), 54–79.

CA481 Segal, Sol. "Science and Values: A Comparative Study of the Relations between Science and Values, Particularly Ethical Values, in the Writings of John Dewey and Frederick Engels." Diss., N.Y. Univ., 1961. 454p.

CA482 Trigg, Hugh Larimore. "The Impact of a Pessimist: The Reception of Oswald Spengler in America, 1919–1939." Diss., George Peabody Collection for Teachers, 1968. 189p.

CA483 Twitchell, Kenaston. "Frank Buchman: Twentieth Century Catalyst." *Procs., Lehigh Co. Hist. Soc.*, vol. 30 (1974), 7–18.

CA484 Verene, Donald Phillip. "Ernst Cassirer. A Bibliography." *Bull. of Bibliography*, vol. 24, no. 5 (September–December 1964), 104–05. German philosopher resident in the United States from 1941; a list of the principal books, articles and reviews by and about Cassirer.

CA485 Vivas, Eliseo. "Herbert Marcuse: 'Philosopher' *en titre* of the New Nihilists." *Intercollegiate Rev.*, vol. 6 (Winter 1969–1970).

CA486 Von Hofe, Harold. *Briefe von und an Ludwig Marcuse*. Zürich: Diogenes, 1975. 357p.

CA487 Von Hofe, Harold. "Ludwig Marcuse." In: *Deutsche Exilliteratur seit 1933*. Ed. John M. Spalek and Joseph Strelka. vol. 1. *Kalifornien*. 2 Teile. Bern: Francke, 1976, p.527–41.

CA488 Wegner, Robert A. "Dewey's Ideas in Germany: The Intellectual Response, 1901–1933." Diss., Univ. of Wisconsin, 1978.

CA489 Yoder, John Howard. *Reinhold Niebuhr and Christian Pacifism*. Zeist: Heerewegen, 1954. 23p.

Freud and Psychoanalysis

CA490 Abraham, Karl. Papers. 500 items. In MS. Div., U.S. Library of Congress (MS 79-1764). Psychologist (1877–1925). Correspondence with Freud, Rank, Jung, Ernest Jones, and others.

CA491 Bach, William G. "The Influence of Psychoanalytic Thought on Benjamin Spock's *Baby and Child Care*." *Jour. of the Hist. of Behavioral Sciences*, vol. 10, no. 1 (January 1974), 91–94.

CA492 Bentz, Hans W. *Sigmund Freud in Übersetzungen. Sigmund Freud Translated*... Introd. by M. Bayer-Meissen. Frankfurt a.M.: Bentz, 1961. 60p. *Weltliteratur in Übersetzungen*, Reihe I, Bd. 2.

CA493 Bernfeld, Siegfried. Papers, 1854–1970. 6,000 items. In MS Division, Library of Congress (MS 77-1492.) In German and English; research materials and writings on Freud and his correspondents and other psychoanalytic subjects.

CA494 Burnham, John C. "From Avant-Garde to Specialism: Psychoanalysis in America." *Jour. of the Hist. of the Behavioral Sciences*, vol. 15 (April 1979), 128–34.

CA495 Burnham, John C. "Psychoanalysis in American Civilization before 1918." Diss., Stanford Univ., 1958.

CA496 Burnham, John Chynoweth. *Psychoanalysis and American Medicine: 1894–1918. Medicine, Science, and Culture*. New York: Internat. Universities Pr., 1967. 249p. Rev. J. A. Carrigan, *Jour. of Amer. Hist.*, vol. 41 (1969), 406–07.

CA497 Clark, Ronald W. "Sigmund Freud's Sortie to America." *Amer. Heritage*, vol. 31, no. 3 (1980), 34–43.

CA498 Covert, Catherine L. "Freud on the Front Page: Transmission of Freudian Ideas in the American Newspaper of the 1920's." Diss., Syracuse Univ., 1975.

CA499 Cromer, Ward, and Paula Anderson. "Freud's Visit to America: Newspaper Coverage." *Jour. of the Hist. of the Behavioral Sciences*, vol. 6 (October 1970), 349–53.

CA500 Crunden, Robert M. "Freud, Erikson, and the Historian: A Bibliographical Survey." *Canad. Rev. of Amer. Studies*, vol. 4 (Spring 1973), 48–64.

CA501 Farau, Alfred. *Einfluß der österreichischen Tiefenpsychologie auf die amerikanische Psychotherapie der Gegenwart*. Wien: n.p., 1953.

CA502 Freud, Sigmund. *Sigmund Freud in Übersetzungen*. Weltliteratur in Übersetzungen, Reihe I, Band 2. Frankfurt a. M.: Hans W. Bentz Verlag, 1961. 60p. Bibliography of translations.

CA503 "Freudian Influences in the American Social Sciences." *Amer. Jour. of Sociology*, November 1939. The entire issue is devoted to this topic.

CA504 Fromm, Erich. *Beyond the Chains of Illusion: My Encounter with Marx and Freud*. New York: Simon & Schuster, 1962. 182p.

CA505 Grinstein, A. "Freud's First Publications in America." *Jour. of the Amer. Psychological Assoc.*, vol. 19 (1971), 241–64.

CA506 Hale, Nathan. "The Americanization of Sigmund Freud: The Popularization of Freud in America, 1909–1933." Diss., Univ. of Calif., Berkeley, 1966.

CA507 Hale, Nathan G., Jr. *Freud and the Americans: The Beginnings of Psychoanalysis in the United States, 1876–1917.* New York, Oxford Univ. Pr., 1971. 574p. Rev. by G. N. Grob, *Jour. of Amer. Hist.*, vol. 59, no. 2 (September 1972), 450–51; D. J. Kevles, *Amer. Hist. Rev.*, vol. 79 (1974), 881; P. A. Robinson, *N.Y. Times Book Rev.*, 26 December 1971, 4, 16. A richly detailed history of the American movement in the decade following Freud's lectures at Clark University.

CA508 Jahoda, Marie. "The Migration of Psychoanalysis: Its Impact on American Psychology." In: *The Intellectual Migration. Europe and America, 1930–1960.* Ed. Don Fleming and Bernard Bailyn. Cambridge: Belknap Pr. of Harvard Univ. Pr., 1969, p.420–45.

CA509 Jahoda, Marie. "Some Notes on the Influence of Psychoanalytic Ideas on American Psychology." *Human Relations*, vol. 16, no. 2 (1963), 111–29.

CA510 Jones, Robert A. "Freud and American Sociology, 1909–1949." *Jour. of the Hist. of the Behavioral Sciences*, vol. 10, no. 1 (January 1974), 21–39.

CA511 Koelsch, W. "Freud Discovers America." *Va. Quar. Rev.*, vol. 46, no. 1 (Winter 1970), 114–32.

CA512 Matthews, F. H. "The Americanization of Sigmund Freud: Adoptions of Psychoanalysis before 1917." *Jour. of Amer. Studies*, vol. 1, no. 1 (April 1967), 39–62.

CA513 Oberndorf, Clarence Paul. *A History of Psychoanalysis in America.* New York: Harper & Row, 1964. 280p.

CA514 Putnam, James Jackson. *James Jackson Putnam and Psychoanalysis: Letters between Putnam and Sigmund Freud, Ernest Jones, William James, Sandor Ferenczi, and Morton Prince, 1877–1917.* Ed. Nathan G. Hale, Jr. Trans. Judith Bernays Heller. Cambridge: Harvard Univ. Pr., 1971. 384p. Rev. by J. C. Burnham, *Jour. of Amer. Hist.*, vol. 59, no. 1 (June 1972), 180–81. Putnam was a partisan of Freud from 1909.

CA515 Quen, Jacques M. and Eric T. Carlson, eds. *American Psychoanalysis: Origins and Development.* The Adolph Meyer Seminars. New York: Brunner/Mazel, 1978. 216p.

CA516 Rieff, Philip. *Freud, the Mind of the Moralist.* New York: Viking, 1959. 397p. Repr. Garden City: Doubleday, 1961. 441p. On Freud's place in intellectual history.

CA517 Rieff, Philip. "Freud's Contribution to Political Philosophy." Diss., Univ. of Chicago, 1954. 424 l.

CA518 Robinson, Paul A. *The Freudian Left: Wilhelm Reich, Geza Roheim, Herbert Marcuse.* New York: Harper & Row, 1969. 253p.

CA519 Ruitenbeek, Hendrik M. *Freud and America.* New York: Macmillan; London: Collier-Macmillan, 1966. Influence of Freudian thought on the American character.

CA520 Schneider, Louis. *The Freudian Psychology and Veblen's Social Theory.* New York: King's Crown Pr., 1948. 270p. Repr. Westport, Conn.: Greenwood Pr., 1974.

CA521 Steere, Geoffrey H. "Freudianism and Child-Rearing in the Twenties." *Amer. Quar.*, vol. 20, no. 4 (Winter 1968), 759–67. On the impact of Freud on life in 20th-century America.

CA522 Weiss, Edoardo. Papers, 1919–1970. 3,000 items. In the Ms. Div., U.S. Library of Congress (MS 80-2090). W. was a psychoanalyst, associated with Freud.

Paul Tillich

CA523 Adams, James Luther. *Paul Tillich's Philosophy of Culture, Science and Religion.* New York: Harper & Row, 1965. 313p. Rev. by J. A. Lacy, *Amer. German Rev.* vol. 33, no. 2 (1966),

Paul Tillich *(cont.)*

39. Limited to his writings prior to 1945; shows T.'s orientation toward German classical philosophy.

CA524 Comstock, W. Richard. "Two Ontologies of Power: A Comparison of Santayana and Tillich." *Harvard Theological Rev.*, vol. 60 (January 1967), 39–67. Congruent methods along with similarities and differences in their thought.

CA525 Corvin, William R. "The Rhetorical Practice of Paul Tillich." Diss., Oklahoma, 1968.

CA526 Craighead, Houston Archer, Jr. "Process and Being: The Concept of God in the Philosophies of Charles Hartshorne and Paul Tillich." Diss., Texas, 1970. 190p.

CA527 Ferre, Nels F. S. et al. "Paul Tillich: Retrospect and Future." *Religion in Life*, vol. 35 (Winter 1966), 662–718. A series of articles on the legacy of Paul Tillich.

CA528 Kiesling, Christopher. "A Translation of Tillich's Idea of God." *Jour. of Ecumenical Studies*, vol. 4, no. 4 (Fall 1967), 700–15.

CA529 Lyons, James R., ed. *The Intellectual Legacy of Paul Tillich*. Detroit: Wayne State Univ. Pr., 1968. 115p.

CA530 Midgley, Louis C. "Ultimate Concern and Politics: A Critical Examination of Paul Tillich's Political Theology." *Western Political Quar.*, vol. 20 (March 1967), 31–50. Tillich held that political ideas and decisions have inherently religious foundations.

CA531 Stumme, John Richard. "Socialism in Theological Perspective: A Study of Paul Tillich, 1918–1933." Diss., Union Theological Seminary of New York, 1976. 365p.

CA532 Tillich, Paul. *An meine deutschen Freunde: die politischen Reden Paul Tillichs während des Zweiten Weltkriegs über die "Stimme Amerikas."* Introd. and notes by Karin Schäfer-Kretzler. In: *Gesammelte Werke*. Vol. 3. Stuttgart: Evangelisches Verlagswerk, 1973. 367p. Texts of 84 radio messages broadcast in 1942, 1943 and 1944.

CA533 Tillich, Paul. *The Future of Religions*. Ed. Jerald C. Brauer. Westport: Greenwood Pr., 1976. Repr. of ed. of 1966.

CA534 Tillich, Paul. *My Search for Absolutes*. Ed. Ruth Nanda Anshen. Credo Perspectives Series. New York: Simon & Schuster. ca. 1967. An autobiography dealing with both the German and the American phases of his life. Illustrated by Saul Steinberg.

CA535 Tillich, Paul. *My Travel Diary: 1936*. Trans. by Maria Pelikan. Ed. Jerald C. Brauer. New York: Harper & Row, 1970. 192p. Reminiscences of his activities in 1936, espec. his European visit from April to September.

CA536 Tillich, Paul. *On the Boundary; An Autobiographical Sketch*. New York: Scribner's, 1966. 104p. Newly translated from Part I of *The Interpretation of History*.

CA537 Weigel, Gustave. "Contemporaneous Protestantism and Paul Tillich." *Theological Studies*, vol. 11 (1950), 177–202. See also the *Rev. of Religion*, vol. 15, nos. 1–2, 109.

CA538 Wheat, Leonard F. *Paul Tillich's Dialectical Humanism: Unmasking the God above God*. Baltimore: The Johns Hopkins Univ. Pr., 1970. 287p. Rev. by Robert Kysar, *Christian Century*, vol. 88 (1971), 1062–64.

CA539 White, Frank Torbit. "Systematic Theological Principles of Friedrich Schleiermacher and Paul Tillich." Diss., Columbia, 1966. 266p. Comparison and contrast of the two systems.

CA540 Wright, Elliot. "Paul Tillich as Hero." *Christian Century*, vol. 91 (1974), 530–33.

CB

Elementary and Secondary Schools—Educational Theory

General

CB1 Barlow, Thomas A. *Pestalozzi and American Education*. Boulder: Univ. of Colo. Libraries, 1977. 180p.

CB2 Beck, Earl R. "The German Discovery of American Education." *Hist. of Education Quar.*, vol. 5, no. 1 (1965), 3–13. German observers were impressed by the emphasis on the development of individual abilities in the American elementary and adult systems.

CB3 Bennett, Fordyce R. "Bronson Alcott: The Transcendentalist Reformer as Educator." Diss., Illinois, Urbana-Champaign, 1976.

CB4 Carter, John P. "German Influences on the American Community School Movement." Diss., Virginia, 1979. 364p.

CB5 Collins, Charles R. J. "The Herbartian Teachers College, University of Buffalo School of Pedagogy, 1895–1898." Diss., State Univ. of New York at Buffalo, 1969. 101p.

CB6 Deschamp, Daniel R. "Adolph Unruh, Ph. D.: An Examination of His Career in Education and Major Ideas as Revealed through His Writing for Professional Journals, 1932–1977." Diss., St. Louis Univ., 1979.

CB7 Dunkel, Harold B. *Herbart and Education*. New York: Random House, 1969. 146p.

CB8 Dunkel, Harold B. *Herbart and Herbartianism. An Intellectual Ghost Story*. Chicago: Univ. of Chicago Pr., 1970. 301p. On the American influence of Johann Friedrich Herbart.

CB9 Dunkel, Harold B. "Herbartianism Comes to America." *Hist. of Education Quar.*, vol. 9 (Summer 1969), 202–33; vol. 9 (Fall 1969), 376–90.

CB10 Dunson, Alvis A. "Notes on the German Influence on Education in Early Missouri." *Amer.-German Rev.*, vol. 25, no. 5 (1959), 17–19.

CB11 Gutek, Gerald Lee. "An Examination of Joseph Neef's Theory of Ethical Education." *Hist. of Education Quar.*, vol. 9 (Summer (1969), 187–201.

CB12 Gutek, Gerald Lee. *Joseph Neef: The Americanization of Pestalozzianism*. University: Univ. of Alabama Pr., 1978. 159p. Rev. Jean Baker, *Jour. of Amer. Hist.*, vol. 65, no. 4 (March 1979), 1115–16.

CB13 Hackensmith, Charles W. *Biography of Joseph Neef: Educator in the Ohio Valley, 1809–1854*. New York: Carlton, 1973. Rev. W. B. Hendrickson, *Ind. Mag. of Hist.*, vol. 70 (1974), 182–84.

CB14 Harris, William Torrey. "Herbart and Pestalozzi Compared." *Educational Rev.*, vol. 5 (May 1893), 417–23.

CB15 Herbst, Jürgen, comp. *The History of American Education*. Goldentree Bibliographies in American History. Northbrook, Ill.: Alton Publ. Corp., 1974. 153p.

CB16 Little, Lawrence C. *Bibliography of American Doctoral Dissertations in Religious Education 1885 to 1959*. Pittsburgh: Univ. of Pittsburgh Pr., 1962. 215p.

CB17 Meyer, Adolphe E. *Educational History of the American People*. New York: McGraw-Hill, 1957. 444p. Rev. by L. A. Cremin, *Amer. Quar.*, vol. 10 (1958). 496–97. Incl. the influences of Pestalozzi, Herbart, and Froebel.

CB18 Morris, Monica C. "Teacher Training in Missouri before 1871." *Mo. Hist. Rev.*, vol. 43 (1948), 18–37. Swiss and German influences 1815–1834.

CB19 Osgood, John C. "Johann Heinrich Pestalozzi. *My Fate and Experiences as Director of my Educational Institutes in Burgdorf and Iferten*. An

General *(cont.)*

Annotated Translation with an Introd. and Appendixes." Diss., Harvard Univ., 1959.

CB20 Park, Roberta J. "Joseph Neef and William Maclure: Early Pioneers in American Physical Education." *Physical Educator*, vol. 31 (31 March 1974), 23–26.

CB21 Rossi, Peter H., and Alice S. Rossi. "Some Effects of Parochial School Education in America." *Daedalus* vol. 90, no.2 (Spring 1961), 300–28.

CB22 Ryon, Roderick N. "Public Sponsorship of Special Education in Pennsylvania from 1818 to 1834." *Pa. Hist.*, vol. 34, no. 3 (July 1967), 240–49. Infl. of Pestalozzi and Fellenberg.

CB23 Schreiber, Theodore. "First Pestalozzian in the New World." *Amer.-German Rev.*, vol. 9, no. 1 (1942), 25–27. On Josef Neef.

CB24 Silber, Käte, ed. *Pestalozzis Beziehungen zu England und Amerika*. Zürich: Morgarten Vlg., Conzett & Huber, 1963. 135p.

CB25 Smith, Timothy L. "Protestant Schooling and American Nationality, 1800–1850." *Jour. of Amer. Hist.*, vol. 53 (March 1967), 679–95.

CB26 Steiger, Ernst. *Heinrich Pestalozzi, Held des Geistes und der Aufopferung, Szenario zu einem Grossfilm nach historischen Motiven*...New York: Aehren Vlg., 1944. 161p.

The Kindergarten

CB27 B., H. D. "The 'First' Kindergarten Controversy," *Mo. Hist. Rev.*, vol. 44 (1949), 101–02. The tax-supported kindergarten established in St. Louis by Susan Blow in 1873.

CB28 Baylor, Ruth Markendorff. *Elizabeth Palmer Peabody: Kindergarten Pioneer*. Philadelphia: Univ. of Pennsylvania Pr., 1965. 228p. Based on an Ed. D. Diss., New York Univ. 1960.

CB29 Blow, Susan E. *Letters to a Mother on the Philosophy of Froebel*. New York: Appleton, 1899.

CB30 Blow, Susan E. *Songs and Music of Friedrich Froebel's Mother Play*. Prepared and arranged by Susan Blow. New York: Appleton, 1895.

CB31 Cavallo, Dom. "From Perfection to Habit: Moral Training in the American Kindergarten, 1860–1920." *Hist. of Education Quar.*, vol. 16 (Summer 1976), 147–61.

CB32 Downs, Robert. *Friedrich Froebel*. Boston: Twayne, 1978.

CB33 Froebel, Friedrich. *Autobiography*... Trans. and annotated by Emilie Michaelis... and H. Keatley Moore... Syracuse, N.Y.: C. W. Bardeen, 1889. 167p. A work made up of two long autobiographical letters by Froebel, to the Duke of Meiningen and the philosopher K. C. F. Krause. Bibliography of books by and about Froebel, p.145–52.

CB34 Froebel, Friedrich. *Mother-Play, and Nursery Songs*. Illus. with Fifty Engravings. With Notes to Mothers. Trans. by Elizabeth Palmer Peabody. Boston/New York: n.p., 1879. 192p.

CB35 Gillan, Dennis Patrick. "Some American Uses of Froebel." Diss., Rutgers, 1969. Publ. New Brunswick: Rutgers Univ. Pr., 1969. 219p. On Froebel's impact on the thought of Elizabeth Peabody, Francis Parker, Susan Blow and John Dewey.

CB36 Harris, William Torrey. "Kindergarten—Educational Results." In: *St. Louis. Board of Education. 23rd Annual Report for the Year Ending August 1, 1877*, p.212–23.

CB37 Harris, William Torrey. "The Kindergarten—Its Philosophy." In: *St. Louis. Board of Education. 22nd Annual Report for the Year Ending August 1, 1876*, p.79–119.

CB38 Harris, William Torrey. "Kindergarten in St. Louis—The History and Philosophy of Its Methods." In: *St. Louis. Board of Education. 25th Annual Report for the Year Ending August 1, 1879*, p.127–37. Also in: *United States. Bureau of Education. Report of the Commissioner for the Year 1896–97*. Vol. 1, p.899–922.

CB39 Harris, William Torrey. "The Kindergarten Methods Contrasted with the Methods of the

American Primary School." *National Education Assoc. Jour. of Procs. and Addresses*, 1889, 448–53.

CB40 Hocker, Edward W. "The First American Kindergarten Teacher." *Amer.-German Rev.*, vol. 8, no. 3 (1942), 9–10, 36. Caroline Louisa Frankenberg, at Columbus, Ohio, in 1838.

CB41 Kraus-Boelte, Maria, and John Kraus. *The Kindergarten Guide. An Illustrated Hand-Book, Designed for the Self-Instruction of Kindergartners, Mothers and Nurses.* Vol. 1: *The Gifts.* New York: E. Steiger, ca. 1893; 1900. 552p. Incl. an extensive catalogue of educational realia for the kindergarten. Originally issued in 1877.

CB42 Langzettel, Marian B. Papers. Ca. 215 items. In the New York Hist. Soc. collections. (MS 69-788). Papers on educational matters from L. (1861–1929), founder of the Froebel League School for Children.

CB43 Leidecker, Kurt. "The 101st Year of the Kindergarten." *Amer.-German Rev.*, vol. 7, no. 5 (1941), 6–8.

CB44 Nunis, Doyce B., Jr. "Kate Douglas Wiggin, Pioneer in California Kindergarten Education." *Calif. Hist. Soc. Quar.*, vol. 41 (1962), 291–307.

CB45 Peabody, Elizabeth Palmer, and Mary Tyler Mann. *Guide to the Kindergarten and Intermediate Class* [by E. P. Peabody] *and Moral Culture of Infancy* [by M. Mann]. Rev. ed. New York: E. Steiger, 1877. 216p. Copyrighted 1869. With 10 pages of songs and a catalog of kindergarten materials available from Steiger.

CB46 Phifer, Betty T. "The Origin and Development of the Kindergarten Idea in Newark, New Jersey, 1870–1915." Diss., Rutgers, 1977.

CB47 Pösche, Hermann, ed. *Friedrich Fröbels Kindergarten-Briefe.* Wien/Leipzig: Pichler, 1887.

CB48 Snider, Denton J. *Life of Friedrich Froebel, Founder of the Kindergarten.* Chicago: Sigma Publ. Co., ca. 1900. 470p.

CB49 Weber, Evelyn. *The Kindergarten: Its Encounter with Educational Thought in America.* New York: Teachers College Pr., 1969. 282p. Rev. by S. Cohen, *Jour. of Amer. Hist.*, vol. 56, no. 4 (March 1970), 939–40.

CB50 Weber, Evelyn Irene. "The Kindergarten: Its Encounter with Educational Thought in America." Diss., Wisconsin, 1966. 341p. A history of the kindergarten since 1837.

Secondary Schooling/Teacher Training

CB51 Beauchamp, Edward R. "An American *Gymnasium*, the Round Hill School, 1823–34." *Educational Forum*, vol. 37 (January 1973), 159–67.

CB52 Cater, Harold D. "Henry Adams Reports on a German Gymnasium." *Amer. Hist. Rev.*, vol. 53, no. 1 (1948), 59–74. The Friedrich Wilhelm Werder Gymnasium in Berlin, 1858–1859.

CB53 Johnson, Henry. *The Other Side of Main Street. A History Teacher from Sauk Centre . . .* New York: Columbia Univ. Pr., 1943. 263p. Autobiography by a proponent (b. 1867) of the teaching of history and the social sciences in the schools.

CB54 Klaeger, Max L. "A Comparison Study of the Preparation of Art Teachers for American and German Secondary Schools." Diss., Minnesota, 1956.

CB55 Marr, Harriet Webster. "The Round Hill School for Boys, 1823–1833." *Old-Time New England*, vol. 49 (1959), 48–55.

CB56 Rippley, LaVern J. "The German-American Normal Schools." In: *Germanica-Americana 1976: Symposium on Ger.-Amer. Literature and Culture.* Ed. E. A. Albrecht and J. A. Burzle. Lawrence: Max Kade Document and Research Center, Univ. of Kansas, 1977, p.63–71.

CB57 Voigt, Frieda. "The National Teacher's Seminary (1878–1919)." *Hist. Messenger of the Milwaukee Co. Hist. Soc.*, vol. 25, no. 4 (December 1969), 137–39.

CC
Germanic Influences in American Higher Learning

Educational Theory/Reform/ Philosophy of Education

CC1 Burgess, Charles Orville. "The Educational State in America: Selected Views on Learning as the Key to Utopia, 1800–1924." Diss., Wisconsin, 1962. 268p. Focuses on the Utopian theorists William Maclure, Joseph Neef, Robert Owen, Robert Dale Owen, and G. Stanley Hall.

CC2 Burnside, Houston Marvin. "John Dewey and Martin Buber: A Comparative Study." Diss., Claremont Grad. School and Univ. Center, 1970. 296p. A thesis in the theory and practice of education.

CC3 Conant, James B. *Probleme der Universitäten in Deutschland und in den USA*. Tübinger Universitätsreden, no. 22. Tübingen: J.C.B. Mohr, 1965. 22p. Rev. by R. Vierhaus, *Jahrbuch für Amerikastudien*, vol. 12 (1967), 281–83.

CC4 Cook, Francis E. "William Torrey Harris in the Public Schools." *United States. Bureau of Education. Annual Report of the Superintendent of Instruction*, 1909–1910.

CC5 Cordasco, Francesco. *Daniel Coit Gilman and the Protean Ph.D*. Leiden: n.p., 1960.

CC6 Evans, Henry Ridgely. "William Torrey Harris, United States Commissioner of Education, 1889 to 1906." *School Life*, vol. 15, no. 8 (April 1930), 144–47.

CC7 Feuer, Lewis S. "H. A. P. Torrey and John Dewey: Teacher and Pupil." *Amer. Quar.*, vol. 10 (1958), 34–54. Impact of German thought, mainly of Kant and Leibniz, on Dewey via his teacher Torrey.

CC8 Fraenkel, Ernst. "Akademisches Prüfungswesen in Deutschland und in den USA (Ein Vergleich." *Jahrbuch für Amerikastudien*, vol. 12 (1967), 61–73.

CC9 Friedmann, Friedrich Georg. "Amerikanisches und deutsches Universitätssystem. Ein Vergleich." *Zeitschrift für Politik*, vol. 12 (1966), 309–23.

CC10 Gerhard, Dietrich. "Development and Structure of Continental European and American Universities—a Comparison." *Jahrbuch für Amerikastudien*, vol. 12 (1967), 19–35.

CC11 Gougher, Ronald L. "Comparison of English and American Views of the German University, 1840–1865: A Bibliography." *Hist. of Education Quar.*, (Winter 1969), 477–91.

CC12 Harris, William Torrey. [Bibliography of his writings.] In: *The St. Louis Movement in Philosophy*. Ed. Charles M. Perry. Norman, Okla.: n.p., 1930, p.97–140.

CC13 Harris, William Torrey. "German Reform in American Education." *Western* (St. Louis), vol. 3 (September 1872), 326–34.

CC14 Herbst, Jurgen. "Francis Greenwood Peabody: A Bibliography." *Unitarian Hist. Soc. Procs.* vol. 13, part 2 (1961), 86–97. Articles, lectures, sermons and books by Peabody, some in the German language.

CC15 Herbst, Jurgen. "German Wissenschaft and American Philosophy." Chap. 3 in: *The German Historical School and American Scholarship*... Ithaca: Cornell, 1965, p.53–71.

CC16 Herbst, Jurgen. "Herbert Spencer and the Genteel Tradition in American Education." *Educational Theory*, vol. 11 (1961), 99–111. Argues that Spencer's emphasis on science contributed to the decline of German influence in American higher education.

CC17 Herbst, Jurgen. "Liberal Education and the Graduate Schools: An Historical View of College Reform." *Hist. of Education Quar.*, vol. 2 (December 1962), 244–58.

CC18 Hofstadter, Richard, and C. DeWitt Hardy. *The Development and Scope of Higher Education in the United States.* New York: n.p., 1952.

CC19 Hofstadter, Richard, and Walter P. Metzger. *The Development of Academic Freedom in the United States.* New York: Columbia Univ. Pr., 1955. 527p. Rev. by G. H. Klubertanz, *Hist. Bull.*, vol. 34 (1956), 248–50.

CC20 Holzner, Burkart. *Amerikanische und deutsche Psychologie. Eine vergleichende Darstellung.* Würzburg: Holzner, 1961. 408p. Rev. by K.-A. Jochheim, *Jahrbuch für Amerikastudien*, vol. 9 (1964), 356–57. A comparison of the disciplines as developed in the U.S. and Germany. Based on a dissertation of the same title submitted at Bonn, 1958.

CC21 Leidecker, Kurt. *Yankee Teacher: The Life of William Torrey Harris.* New York: Philosophical Library, 1946. 648p.

CC22 Metzger, Walter P. *Academic Freedom in the Age of the University.* New York: n.p., 1955. Incl. treatment of the German influence on American universities.

CC23 Metzger, Walter P. "The German Contribution to the American Theory of Academic Freedom." *Bull. of the Amer. Assoc. of Univ. Professors*, vol. 41 (1955), 214–30.

CC24 Phelps, Reginald H., and Ruth Jaeger. "The German Example and American Higher Education. Karl Follen in Cambridge. Werner Jaeger." In: *Germans in Boston.* Boston: Goethe Society of New England, 1981, p.15–22.

CC25 Reagan, Gaylord B. L. "The Emergence of the Graduate Fellow, 1865–1910: Changing Conceptions and Changing Roles." Diss., Oregon, 1978.

CC26 Rockwell, Leo L. "Academic Freedom, German Origin and American Development." *Bull. of the Amer. Assoc. of Univ. Professors*, vol. 36, no. 2 (1950), 225–36.

CC27 Shryock, Richard H. "The Academic Profession in the United States." *Bull., Amer. Assoc. of Univ. Professors*, vol. 38 (Spring 1952), 32–70.

CC28 Shuster, George N. *In Amerika und Deutschland. Erinnerungen eines amerikanischen College Presidenten.* Trans. by Leni Gruber. Frankfurt: Knecht, 1965. 280p.

CC29 Smith, Shirley W. *James Burrill Angell, an American Influence.* Ann Arbor: Univ. of Michigan Pr., 1954. On Angell's study at München and his appraisal of the academic atmosphere of the German university.

CC30 Smith, Wilson, ed. *Theories of Education in Early America, 1655–1819.* Indianapolis: Bobbs-Merrill, 1973. 442p.

CC31 Travers, Paul Donald. "Interest in European Education and the Development of Comparative Education as a Subject of Study in American Universities and Colleges in the Nineteenth Century." Diss., George Peabody College for Teachers, 1967.

CC32 Ulich, Robert. *Philosophy of Education.* New York, American Book Co., 1961. 286p.

CC33 Ulich, Robert. *Professional Education as a Humane Study.* New York: Macmillan, 1956. 145p.

CC34 Ulich, Robert. *Religious Perspectives of College Teaching in the Preparation of Teachers.* New Haven: Edward W. Hazen Found., ca. 1951. 32p.

CC35 Weinberg, Julius. "E. A. Ross: The Progressive as Nativist." *Wis. Mag. of Hist.*, vol. 50 (Spring 1967), 242–53.

CC36 Wilson, John G. "Horace Mann's Aides: The New England Transcendentalists." *Educational Forum*, vol. 31 (May 1967), 487–95.

History of American Higher Education

CC37 Ahern, Patrick A. *The Catholic University of America, 1887–1896; the Rectorship of John J. Keane.* Washington, D.C.: n.p., 1948.

CC38 Arnold, Matthew. *Schools and Universities on the Continent.* Ed. R. H. Super. Ann Arbor:

History of American Higher Education (cont.)

Univ. of Michigan Pr., 1964. Incl. the essay "Superior or University Instruction in Prussia." Calls for university reform along the lines of the Prussian program.

CC39 Becker, Carl L. *Cornell University: Founders and the Founding*. Ithaca: Cornell Univ. Pr., 1967. 256p.

CC40 Bestor, Arthur E., Jr. "The Transformation of American Scholarship, 1875–1917." *Library Quar.*, vol. 23 (1953), 164–79. Stressing the rise of professional librarianship and the Dewey classification system.

CC41 Bingham, Wanda D. "The Germanic Impact on the American Professor in the Late Nineteenth Century." Diss., Univ. of Kentucky, 1978. 127p.

CC42 Bishop, Morris. *A History of Cornell*. Drawings by Alison M. Kingsbury. Ithaca: Cornell Univ. Pr., 1962. 651p.

CC43 Cunz, Dieter. "Contributions of the German Element to the Growth of the University of Maryland." *Report, Soc. for the Hist. of Germans in Md.*, vol. 26 (1945), 7–15. Enumerates teachers of German descent at the University throughout its 140-year history.

CC44 Damm, Helmut Henry. "The University of Michigan from 1850 to 1917 As a Leading Center of German Influences during the Nation's Economic Take-Off Period." Diss., Michigan, 1970. 259p.

CC45 Diehl, Carl. *Americans and German Scholarship, 1770–1870*. New Haven: Yale Univ. Pr., 1978. 208p. Rev. by R. W. Ewton, *German Studies Rev.*, vol. 1 (1978), 354; Jurgen Herbst, *Amer. Hist. Rev.*, vol. 83 (1978), 1324; L. Veysey, *Jour. of Amer. Hist.*, vol. 66 (1979), 141. American scholarship in the humanities owes its largest debt to 19th-century German scholarship. This work details the Americans' difficult and protracted effort to assimilate German learning.

CC46 Dohrmann, George, III. "Medical Education in the United States as Seen by a German Immigrant: The Letters of George Dohrmann, 1897–1901." *Jour. of the Hist. of Medicine and Allied Sciences*, vol. 33, no. 4 (October 1978), 477–506. An immigrant of 1892, D. was trained in medicine in Illinois and corresponded with his parents in Germany.

CC47 Duberman, Martin. *Black Mountain: An Exploration in Community*. New York: Dutton, 1972. 527p. Rev. by P. K. Conkin, *Jour. of Amer. Hist.*, vol. 60 (1973), 510–12; H. C. Ferrell, *Jour. of Southern Hist.*, vol. 39 (1973), 469–70; G. B. Tindall, *N. Car. Hist. Rev.*, vol. 50 (1973), 197–99; F. G. Davenport, *Amer. Hist. Rev.*, vol. 80 (1975), 524–25; D. E. Whisnant, *South Atlantic Quar.*, vol. 73 (1974), 277–78. An experimental college established in 1933 with a staff incl. several distinguished emigré teachers.

CC48 French, John C. *A History of the University Founded by Johns Hopkins*. Baltimore: The Johns Hopkins Pr., 1946. 492p.

CC49 Hawkins, Hugh. "Charles W. Eliot, Daniel Coit Gilman, and the Nurture of American Scholarship." *New England Quar.*, vol. 39 (1966), 291–308. They looked to the example of the German universities.

CC50 Hawkins, Hugh. *Pioneer: A History of the Johns Hopkins University, 1874–1889*. Ithaca: Cornell Univ. Pr., 1960. 368p.

CC51 Heindel, Ned D., and Natalie I. Foster. "The Allentown Academy: America's First German Medical School." *Pa. Folklife*, vol. 30 (1980–1981), 2–8.

CC52 Herbst, Jurgen. "The American College and the Problem of Professional Education." Chap. 2 in: *The German Historical School in American Scholarship. A Study in the Transfer of Culture*. Ed. Jurgen Herbst. Ithaca: Cornell, 1965, p. 23–51.

CC53 Herbst, Jurgen. "The First Three American Colleges: Schools of the Reformation." *Perspectives in Amer. Hist.*, vol. 8 (1974), 7–52.

CC54 Herbst, Jurgen. *The German Historical School in American Scholarship: A Study in the Transfer of Culture*. Ithaca: Cornell Univ. Pr., 1965. 262p. Rev. by J. Braeman, *Jour. of Higher Education*, vol. 37 (February 1966), 101–103; M. Cunliffe, *History*, vol. 51 (Feb. 1966), 127–28; O. A. Dieter, *Quar. Jour. of Speech*, vol. 52 (April 1966), 194–95; S. Fraser, *Peabody Jour. of Education*, vol. 43 (January 1966), 243–44; R. H. Gabriel, *Jour. of Amer. Hist.*, vol. 52, no. 3 (1965), 607–09; F. Gilbert, *History and Theory*, vol. 5 (1966), 217–19; H. Hawkins, *Hist. of Education*

Quar., vol. 5 (September 1965), 191–92; D. W. Hoover, *Amer. Quar.*, vol. 18 (Spring 1966), 104–08; G. G. Iggers, *Amer. Hist. Rev.*, vol. 71 (January 1966), 708–09; M. R. P. McGuire, *Manuscripta*, vol. 10, no. 1 (March 1966) 57–58; W. J. Mommsen, *Jahrbuch für Amerikastudien*, vol. 12 (1967), 288–90; B. C. Shafer, *Jour. of Mod. Hist.*, vol. 38, no. 3 (September 1966) 314–15; *Wis. Mag. of Hist.* vol. 50 (1967), 178–79.

CC55 Hogan, Patrick E. *The Catholic University of America, 1896–1903; the Rectorship of Thomas J. Conaty.* Washington, D.C.: n.p., 1949.

CC56 Klein, H.M.J. *History of Franklin and Marshall College 1787–1948.* Lancaster: Franklin and Marshall College Alumni Assoc., 1952. 357p.

CC57 Peckham, Howard H. *The Making of the University of Michigan.* Ann Arbor: Univ. of Michigan Pr., 1967. 276p.

CC58 Ringer, Fritz K. "The German Academic Community." In: *The Organization of Knowledge in Modern America, 1860–1920.* Ed. Alexandra Oleson and John Voss. Baltimore: John Hopkins Univ. Pr., 1979, p.409–29.

CC59 Sack, Saul. *History of Higher Education in Pennsylvania.* Harrisburg: Hist. and Museum Commission, 1963. 2 vols. 817p. Rev. J. Walton, *Md. Hist. Mag.*, vol. 59 (1964), 308–09.

CC60 Schmidt, George P. *The Liberal Arts College: A Chapter in American Cultural History.* New Brunswick: Rutgers Univ. Pr., 1957. 310p. Rev. by R. J. Storr, *Amer. Hist. Rev.*, vol. 63 (1958), 744.

CC61 Storr, Richard J. *The Beginnings of Graduate Education in America.* Chicago: n.p., 1953. Rev. by H. L. Swint, *Pa. Hist.*, vol. 21, no. 2 (1954), 189–90; J. G. Dwyer, *Catholic Hist. Rev.*, vol. 40, no. 1 (1954), 88–89; E. Ellis, *Pa. Mag. of Hist. and Biography*, vol. 78, no. 1 (1954), 129–30.

CC62 Storr, Richard J. *Harper's University: The Beginnings. A History of the University of Chicago.* Chicago: n.p., 1966. 411p.

CC63 Tappan, Henry Philip. Papers, 1840–1936. 24 vols. In the University of Michigan, Michigan Hist. Collections (MS 65–585). Correspondence by T. (1805–1881) relating to his scholarly interest.

CC64 Ulich, Heinrich Gottlob Robert. *The Education of Nations: A Comparison in Historical Perspective.* Rev. ed. Cambridge: Harvard Univ. Pr., 1961. 325p. A general study of the educational heritage of the West.

CC65 Ulich, Heinrich Gottlob Robert. *History of Educational Thought.* New York: Amer. Book Co., 1945. 412p. Incl. bibliog., p.351–403.

CC66 Veysey, Laurence. *The Emergence of the American University.* Chicago/London: n.p., 1965.

CC67 Veysey, Laurence. "From Germany to America." A Review Essay. *Hist. of Education Quar.*, vol. 13 (Winter 1973), 401–07.

Development of the Graduate Disciplines in America

ART HISTORY/THE HUMANITIES

CC68 Braun-Vogelstein, Julie. Papers. Ca. 52 ft. In Julie Braun-Vogelstein collection. Bequest to the Leo Baeck Institute collections, New York (MS 78-1222–1223). Incl. personal correspondence, business correspondence of German-American art historian and archaeologist (1883–1971); MSS. about art history.

CC69 Calder, William M., III. "Die Geschichte der klassischen Philologie in den Vereinigten Staaten." *Jahrbuch für Amerikastudien*, vol. 11 (1966), 213–40.

CC70 Diehl, Carl C. "Vision and Vocation; The Assimilation of Modern Scholarship in the Humanities in Germany and America, 1770–1870." Diss., Yale Univ., 1975. 298p.

CC71 Eisler, Colin. "Kunstgeschichte American Style." In: *The Intellectual Migration. Europe and America, 1930–1960.* Ed. Donald Fleming and Bernard Bailyn. Cambridge: Harvard Univ. Pr., 1969, 544–629. On the democratization and Americanization of European art historians and scholars.

CC72 Goetze, Albrecht Ernst Rudolf. Papers, 1923–1971. In Yale University Library (MS 80-

Development of the Graduate Disciplines *(cont.)*

756). Assyriologist who emigrated to the U.S. from Germany in 1934; professor and director of the American School of Oriental Research, Baghdad.

CC73 Grodecki, Louis. "Berenson, Woelfflin et la critique de l'art moderne." *Critique*, vol. 10 (1955), 657–75.

CC74 Koehler, Wilhelm Reinhold Walter. Papers, 1912–1941. 2 ft. In Harvard University Archives (MS 76-1979.) Notes and documents by K. (1884–1959), a teacher of fine arts and German art and culture, Harvard.

CC75 Levin, Harry. "Two *Romanisten* in America: Spitzer and Auerbach." In: *The Intellectual Migration. Europe and America, 1930–1960*. Ed. Donald Fleming and Bernard Bailyn. Cambridge: Harvard Univ. Pr., 1969, p.463–84.

CC76 Mueller-Vollmer, Kurt. "Rezeption und Neuansatz: Phänomenologische Literaturwissenschaft in den Vereinigten Staaten." *Zeitschrift für Literaturwissenschaft und Linguistik*, vol. 5, no. 17 (1975), 10–24.

GEOGRAPHY

CC77 Fuchs, Gerhard. "Der Wandel zum anthropogeographischen Denken in der amerikanischen Geographie." Diss., Marburg, 1967. Publ. in *Marburger geographische Schriften*, heft 32. Marburg: n.p., 1967.

CC78 Hartshorne, Richard. "The Concept of Geography as a Science of Space, from Kant and Humboldt, to Hettner." *Annals of American Geography*, vol. 48 (1958), 97–108. A learned and discerning treatment of the influence of German geography.

CC79 Herbst, Jurgen. "Social Darwinism and the History of American Geography." *Papers of the Amer. Philosophical Soc.*, vol. 105, no. 6 (1961), 538–44. The college teaching of geography as influenced by Swiss and German tradition.

CC80 Johnson, Hildegard Binder. "A Note on Thünen's Circles." *Annals of the Assoc. of Amer. Geographers*, vol. 52 (June 1962), 213–20. On the origin of the modern central place theory in American geography.

CC81 Leighly, John. "Carl Ortwin Sauer, 1889–1975." *Annals of the Assoc. of Amer. Geographers*, vol. 66 (1976), 337–48. German-American scholar and geographer.

CC82 Sauer, C. O. "The Formative Years of [Friedrich] Ratzel in the United States." *Annals of the Assoc. of American Geographers*, vol. 61 (June 1971), 245–54.

CC83 Warntz, William. *Geography Now and Then: Some Notes on the History of Academic Geography in the United States.* New York: Amer. Geographic Soc., 1964. 162p.

LINGUISTIC SCIENCE AND FOLKLORE

CC84 Crosby, Donald A. *Horace Bushnell's Theory of Language in the Context of Other Nineteenth-Century Philosophies of Language.* Studies in Philosophy, no. 221. The Hague: Mouton, 1976. 300p.

CC85 Hymes, Dell. "Alfred Louis Kroeber 1876–1960." In: *Portraits of Linguists*... Ed. Thomas A. Sebeok. Bloomington: Indiana Univ. Pr., 1966. Vol. 1, p.400–36.

CC86 Hymes, Dell. "Pre-War Prague School and Post-War American Anthropological Linguistics." In: *The Transformational-Generative Paradigm and Modern Linguistic Theory.* Ed. E.F.K. Koerner, with J. Odmark and J. H. Shaw. Amsterdam: Benjamins, 1975, p.359–80.

CC87 Koerner, Ernst F. K. "The Humboldtian Trend in Linguistics." In: *Studies in Descriptive and Historical Linguistics: Festschrift for Winfred P. Lehmann.* Ed. Paul J. Hopper. Amsterdam: Benjamins, 1977, p.145–58. See also *Cahiers Linguistiques d'Ottawa*, vol. 5 (1977), 27–40.

CC88 Mattoso-Camara, J., Jr. "Wilhelm von Humboldt et Edward Sapir." In: *Actes du Xe Congrès International des Linguistes, Bucarest, 28 août—2 septembre 1967.* Eds. Alexander Graur et al. 4 vols. Bucarest: Ed Acad. R.S.R., 1969–1970, p.327–32.

CC89 Müller-Vollmer, Kurt. "Wilhelm von Humboldt und der Anfang der amerikanischen Sprachwissenschaft: Die Briefe an John Pickering." In: *Humboldt-Tagung, 1st, Gras-Ellenbach, Germany, 1972; 2nd, Aachen, 1974. Universalismus und Wissenschaft im Werk und Wirken der Brüder Humboldt [Beiträge zu 2 Tagungen 1972 (Gras-Ellenbach) und 1974 (Aachen)] im Auftrag der Humboldt-Gesellschaft hrsg. von Klaus Hammacher, mit einem Anhang, Wilhelm von Hum-*

boldts Briefe an John Pickering, hrsg. von Kurt Müller-Vollmer. Frankfurt am M.: Klostermann, 1976, p.259–334.

CC90 Pätsch, Gertrud. "[Wilhelm von] Humboldts Beitrag zur modernen Sprachwissenschaft." *Wissenschaftl. Zeitschrift der Humboldt-Universität zu Berlin.* Gesellschafts- und Sprachwissenschaftl. Reihe, vol. 17, no. 3 (1968), 353–56.

CC91 Penn, Julia M. *Linguistic Relativity Versus Innate Ideas: The Origins of the Sapir-Whorf Hypothesis in German Thought.* Janua Linguarum, Ser. Minor, no. 120. The Hague: Mouton, 1972. 62p. Cf. the diss. of the same title submitted to the Univ. of Texas, 1966, 86p.

CC92 Pribić, Nikola R. "TALVJ—Pioneer in Comparative Studies of Slavic Folklore in America." In *Miedzynarodowy Kongres Slawistów w Warszawie 1973. Steszenzenia Referatów i komunikatów.* Warsaw: PAN, 1973, p.957–58.

CC93 Pribić, Nikola R. "TALVJ in America." In: *Serta Slavica in Memoriam Aloisii Schmaus.* Ed. Wolfgang Gesemann et al. München: Trofenik, 1971, p.589–606.

CC94 Read, Allen Walker. "The Spread of German Linguistic Learning in New England During the Lifetime of Noah Webster." *American Speech*, vol. 41 (October 1966), 163–81.

CC95 Sebeok, Thomas A., ed. *Portraits of Linguists: A Biographical Source Book for the History of Western Linguistics, 1746–1963.* Bloomington: Indiana Univ. Pr., 1967. 2 vols. 1280p.

CC96 Seidel, Eugen. "Wilhelm von Humboldt und die vergleichende Sprachwissenschaft." *Wissenschaftl. Zeitschrift der Humboldt-Univ. zu Berlin. Gesellschafts- und sprachwissenschaftl. Reihe*, vol. 17, no. 3 (1968), 357–58.

PSYCHOLOGY

CC97 Alpert, Barry. "Fielding Dawson: Not as Jung as He Used to Be." *Open Letter* (Toronto), 2nd Ser., no. 7 (1974), 72–83.

CC98 Ansbacher, Heinz L. "Alfred Adler and G. Stanley Hall: Correspondence and General Relationships." *Jour. of the Hist. of the Behavioral Sciences*, vol. 7 (October 1971), 337–52.

CC99 Benjamin, Ludy T., Jr. "Psychology at the University of Nebraska, 1889–1930." *Nebr. Hist.*, vol. 56 (Fall 1975), 375–87.

CC100 Benoit, Ray. "The Mind's Return: Whitman, Teilhard, and Jung." *Walt Whitman Rev.*, vol. 13 (March 1967), 21–28. Argues Whitman's anticipation of ideas of Teilhard and Jung.

CC101 Bickman, Martin. *The Unsounded Centre: Jungian Studies in American Romanticism.* Chapel Hill: Univ. of North Carolina Pr., 1980. 182p.

CC102 Drake, Carlos G. "Jung and His Critics." *Jour. of Amer. Folklore*, vol. 80 (October–December 1967), 321–33. Defends his concepts of the archetype and collective unconscious against recent criticisms by anthropologists.

CC103 Freeman, Frank S. "The Beginnings of Gestalt Psychology in the United States." *Jour. of the Hist. of Behavioral Sciences*, vol. 13 (October 1977), 352–53. On the work of Robert Morris Ogden of Cornell University; translator of Koffka.

CC104 Hale, Matthew. "Psychology and Social Order: An Intellectual Biography of Hugo Münsterberg." Diss., Maryland, 1977. 451p.

CC105 Heider, Fritz. "Gestalt Theory: Early History and Reminiscences." *Jour. of the Hist. of the Behavioral Sciences*, vol. 6 (April 1970), 131–39.

CC106 Keogh, Andrew. "Authenticity and Self-Actualization: A Rapprochement between the Philosophy of Heidegger and the Psychology of Maslow." Diss., Toronto, 1978.

CC107 Kohs, Samuel Calmin. Papers. 4 ft. In the American Jewish Hist. Soc. (MS 72-7). K. (1916–1960) was a psychologist and social worker. Correspondence and misc. papers dealing with the National Coordinating Committee for Aid to Refugees and Emigrants from Germany.

CC108 Mackaness, William Howard. *A Biographical Study of the Life of Rudolf Dreikurs, M. D., With Special Emphasis Placed upon His Work in Relating the Theoretical Principles of Individual Psychology to the Modern Classroom Setting.* Ed. D. Diss., Univ. of Oregon, 1963. 314p. D., a student of Adler, was director of the Alfred Adler Institute, Chicago.

CC109 Meier, Carl Alfred. *Jung's Analytical Psychology and Religion.* Carbondale: Southern Illi-

Development of the Graduate Disciplines (cont.)

nois Univ. Pr., ca. 1977. From lectures delivered at Andover Newton Theological School, in 1959. By a student of Jung.

CC110 Rank, Otto. Papers. 25 boxes. In Columbia University Libraries (MS 62-1). Incl. many MSS. of R. (1884–1939), a psychiatrist.

CC111 Roper, Gordon. "Robertson Davies' *Fifth Business* and That Old Fantastical Duke of Dark Corners, C. G. Jung." *Jour. of Canad. Fiction*, vol. 1, no. 1 (1972), 33–39.

CC112 Wertheimer, Max. Papers, 1885–1943. 9 cartons. In New York Public Library (MS 74-575). W. (1880–1943) was a psychologist; pioneer of Gestalt psychology. Incl. letters to W. from European colleagues, many in German; also papers of Wilhelm Wertheimer and E. M. von Hornbostel on subjects of music and ethnology. Correspondents of M. Wertheimer incl. Max Born, Einstein, Jung, W. Köhler, Karl Mann.

SOCIAL SCIENCES AND HISTORY

CC113 Adorno, Theodor W. "Scientific Experiences of a European Scholar in America." In: *The Intellectual Migration*. Ed. Donald Fleming and Bernard Bailyn. Cambridge: Harvard Univ. Pr., 1969, p.338–70. Published in German as "Wissenschaftliche Erfahrungen in Amerika." *Neue Deutsche Hefte*, no. 122, vol. 16, no. 2 (1969), 3–42. Autobiographical memoir centering on Adorno's stay in the United States from 1937 to 1953.

CC114 Alliband, Terry T. "Plains History and Cultural Anthropology." *Plains Anthropologist*, vol. 17, no. 56 (1972), 85–90.

CC115 Arendt, Hannah. Papers, 1935–1963. 3 ft. In MS. Div., Library of Congress (MS 65-891). A. (1906–1975), author, historian and social scientist. Correspondence, manuscripts, drafts of writings and lectures, etc. This collection has been increased to 28,000 items consisting of papers, correspondence, files, 1898–1976 (MS 80-2028). *Also*: Papers, 1958–1965 131 items. In Leo Baeck Institute, New York (MS 70-1559). Incl. the MS. of her book on Rachel Varnhagen.

CC116 Bandelier, Adolph F. *The Southwestern Journals of Adolph F. Bandelier, 1885–1888*. Ed. Charles H. Lange, Carroll L. Riley and Elizabeth M. Lange. Albuquerque/Santa Fe: Univ. of N. Mex. Pr./School of American Research, 1975. 702p.

CC117 Becker, Howard. "Deutsches Gedankengut in der amerikanischen Sozialpsychologie und Soziologie der Gegenwart." *Jahrbuch für Amerikastudien*, vol. 3 (1958), 15–21.

CC118 Bernard, L. L., and Jessie Bernard. *Origins of American Sociology. The Social Science Movement in the United States*. New York: Crowell, 1943. 866p.

CC119 "Boas, Franz." *Dictionary of Scientific Biography*, vol. 2, p.207–13; vol. 11, p.219a. American anthropologist, b. in Minden, Germany.

CC120 Boas, Franz. *The Ethnography of Franz Boas: Letters and Diaries of Franz Boas Written on the Northwest Coast from 1886 to 1931*. Comp. and ed. Ronald Rohner. Trans. by Hedy Parker. Chicago: Univ. of Chicago Pr., 1969. 331p.

CC121 Boas, Franz. "Unter den Eskimos. Ethnologische Studie." *Deutsch-Amerikanisches Magazin*, vol. 1 (1887), 613–23.

CC122 Brew, J. O., ed. *One Hundred Years of Anthropology*. Harvard Univ. Pr., 1968. 276p.

CC123 Buck, Paul, ed. *Social Science at Harvard, 1860–1900: From Inculcation to the Open Mind*. Cambridge: Harvard Univ. Pr., 1965. 320p.

CC124 Cunningham, Raymond J. "The German Historical World of Herbert Baxter Adams, 1874–1876." *Jour. of Amer. Hist.*, vol. 68 (1981), 261–75.

CC125 Dorfman, Joseph. "The Role of the German Historical School in American Economic Growth." *Papers & Procs. of the 76th Annual Meeting of the Amer. Economic Association, Detroit, December 28–30, 1954*, vol. 45 (May, 1955), 17–39.

CC126 Elbogen, Ismar. Papers, 1897–1943. 3 ft. In Leo Baeck Institute collections, New York (MS 70-1582, MS 78-1228). Misc. correspondence about Judaic studies. E. (1874–1943), historian of Judaism and professor in Germany and New York City.

CC127 Glazer, Nathan. "Hannah Arendt's America." *Commentary* vol. 60 (September 1975), 61–67.

CC128 Goldschmidt, Walter Rochs, ed. *The Anthropology of Franz Boas: Essays on the Centennial of His Birth*. American Anthropological

Association, Memoir no. 89. Menasha, Wis.: American Anthropological Association, 1959. 165p. See also Memoir no. 61, with contributions by A. L. Kroeber, Ruth Benedict, and others.

CC129 Goode, William J. "Die Beziehungen zwischen der amerikanischen und der deutschen Soziologie." *Kölner Zeitschrift für Soziologie und Sozialpsychologie*, vol. 11 (1959), 165–80.

CC130 Hays, H. R. *From Ape to Angel. An Informal History of Social Anthropology.* New York: Knopf, 1958. 440p. The diffusion into American university study of various schools: the American influence of Ratzel, Schurtz, Bastian, Freud, Frobenius, Graebner, and Franz Boas.

CC131 Helm, June, ed. *Pioneers of American Anthropology: The Uses of Biography.* American Ethnological Society Monographs, no. 43. Washington, D.C.: n.p., 1966. 247p. Essays on the achievements of such anthropologists as Franz Boas, Zelia Nuttall, Erminnie Smith, and Alice Fletcher.

CC132 Herbst, Jurgen. "From Moral Philosophy to Sociology. Albion Woodbury Small." *Harvard Educational Rev.*, vol. 29 (1959), 227–44. On the development of graduate study in America, 1875–1925, as influenced by European example.

CC133 Herbst, Jurgen. "The German Influence and American Social Science." In: *The German Historical School in American Scholarship...* Ed. Jurgen Herbst. Ithaca: Cornell, 1965, p.203–30.

CC134 Herbst, Jurgen. "Nineteenth Century German Scholarship in America: A Study of Five German-Trained Social Scientists." Diss., Harvard Univ., 1958.

CC135 Herbst, Jurgen. "Scholarship and Social Action." In: *The German Historical School in American Scholarship. A Study in the Transfer of Culture.* Ed. Jurgen Herbst. Ithaca: Cornell Univ. Pr., 1965, p.161–202.

CC136 Herbst, Jurgen. "The Science of History and Politics." In: *The German Historical School in American Scholarship. A Study in the Transfer of Culture.* Ed. Jurgen Herbst. Ithaca: Cornell Univ. Pr., 1965, p.99–128.

CC137 Herbst, Jurgen. "The Sciences of Society: Political Economy and Sociology." In: *The German Historical School in American Scholarship...* Ed. Jurgen Herbst. Ithaca: Cornell, 1965, Chap. 6, p.129–59.

CC138 Hughes, H. Stuart. "Franz Neumann between Marxism and Liberal Democracy." In: *The Intellectual Migration. Europe and America, 1930–1960.* Ed. Donald Fleming and Bernard Bailyn. Cambridge: Harvard Univ. Pr., 1969, p.446–62. Prominent political scientist (1900–1954); b. in Kattowitz, Poland and emigrated to U. S. in 1936.

CC139 Hinsley, Curtis M., Jr. "The Development of a Profession: Anthropology in Washington, D.C., 1846–1903." Diss., Wisconsin, 1976.

CC140 Hyatt, Marshall. "The Emergence of a Discipline: Franz Boas and the Study of Man." Diss., Univ. of Delaware, 1979. 363p.

CC141 Jogland, Herta H. "Die Anfänge der amerikanischen Soziologie." *Schmollers Jahrbuch für Gesetzgebung, Verwaltung und Volkswirtschaft*, vol. 82 (1962, part 2), 407–44.

CC142 Kahn, Ludwig W. "Some Sociological Aspects of Literature." *Mod. Lang. Jour.*, vol. 25, no. 6 (1941), 460–66. Discusses Max Weber's theory.

CC143 Krippendorf, Ekkehart. "Profil einer Disziplin: Versuch über Herkunft und Stand der Politischen Wissenschaft in den Vereinigten Staaten." *Politische Vierteljahrschrift*, vol. 6 (1965), 184–204.

CC144 Kroeber, Theodora. *Alfred Kroeber. A Personal Configuration.* Berkeley: Univ. of California Pr., 1979, 304p. On the life and scholarly development of the distinguished anthropologist.

CC145 MacNeish, June Helm. *Pioneers of American Anthropology; the Uses of Biography...Contributions by Jacob Gruber and others.* Seattle: Univ. of Washington Pr., ca. 1966. 247p. Incl. papers on Franz Boas by R. P. Rohner and Mrs. Tom Johnson.

CC146 Roth, Günther, and Reinhard Bendix. "Max Webers Einfluss auf die amerikanische Soziologie." *Kölner Zeitschrift für Soziologie und Sozialpsychologie*, vol. 11 (1959), 38–53.

CC147 Stammer, Otto, ed. Trans. Kathleen Morris. *Max Weber and Sociology Today.* New York: Harper & Row, 1971. 256p. Contributions by Talcott Parsons, Raymond Aron, Karl Deutsch, Carl Friedrich et al. From a German original: *15. Deutscher Soziologentag 1964.* Publ. for the Deutsche Gesellschaft für Soziologie. Tübingen: Mohr, 1965.

CC148 Steward, Julian H. *Alfred Kroeber*. Leaders of Modern Anthropology Series. New York: Columbia Univ. Pr., 1973. 137p.

CC149 Stocking, George, Jr. "Franz Boas and the Culture Concept in Historic Perspective." *Amer. Anthropologist*, vol. 68, no. 4 (1966), 867–82.

CC150 Wehler, Hans-Ulrich. "Nachwort zu 'Uncle Sam' von John W. Burgess." *Jahrbuch für Amerikastudien*, vol. 8 (1963), 261–66. The political scientist Burgess in his relations with German thought in the 19th century.

CC151 Wells, G. A. *Herder and After. A Study in the Development of Sociology*. Anglica Germanica, no. 1. The Hague: Mouton, 1959. 283p.

CC152 Zunz, Leopold. Papers. 4 ft. In Leo Baeck Institute collections, New York (MS 72-241). German Jewish scholar, religious historian, and teacher (1794–1886). Correspondence, diaries, MSS., and misc. papers, in part photocopies from originals in the Zunz Archives, National and University Library, Jerusalem. Correspondents incl. prominent figures of the early 19th century.

SCIENCES

CC153 American Philosophical Society, Philadelphia. Manuscript writings on science, 1720–1958. In the Soc. Library (MS 61–950). Incl. papers by Johann Beckmann, Fred. Henry Cramer, Fred. Augustus Genth, Jacob Stauffer.

CC154 Bates, Ralph S. *Scientific Societies in the United States*. New York: n.p., 1945. After the Civil War scientific societies took on a guild or professional nature—no longer the club for amateurs of philosophy.

CC155 Berger, David. "The Brain Drain. A Documentation." *Amer.-German Rev.*, vol. 35, no. 2 (1969), 30–33. Espec. the emigration of medical specialists to the United States.

CC156 Bernstein, Jeremy. "Profiles. [I. L. Rabi.]" *New Yorker*, 13 October 1975, 47–110; 20 October 1975, 47–102.

CC157 Coben, Stanley. "The Scientific Establishment and the Transmission of Quantum Mechanics to the United States, 1919–1932." *Amer. Hist. Rev.*, vol. 76, part 2 (April 1971), 442–46. The new physics was transmitted by young physicists who studied in European universities in the twenties. At the same time some young European physicists joined departments in leading universities in the U.S.

CC158 Dresden, Arnold. "The Migration of Mathematicians." *Amer. Mathematical Monthly*, vol. 49 (1942), 415.

CC159 Haines, George, and Frederick H. Jackson. "A Neglected Landmark in the History of Ideals." *Miss. Valley Hist. Rev.*, vol. 34 no. 2 (1947), 201–20. On the Congress of Science held in September 1904, St. Louis. Hugo Münsterberg was first vice president of a panel where German and German-American scholars were brought together.

CC160 Hendrickson, Walter B. "The St. Louis Academy of Science: The Early Years." *Mo. Hist. Rev.*, vol. 61 (1966), 83–94. The leading spirit in the founding of the academy was George Engelmann, scientist and physician educated at Würzburg and Paris, who came to St. Louis in 1836.

CC161 Jackson, Charles O., and Charles W. Johnson. "The Summer of '44: Observations on Life in the Oak Ridge Community." *Tenn. Hist. Quar.*, vol. 32, no. 3 (Fall 1973), 233–248. Incl. the presence of a number of German scientists.

CC162 Jackson, Charles O., and Charles W. Johnson. "The Urbane Frontier: The Army and the Community of Oak Ridge, Tennessee, 1942–1947." *Military Affairs*, vol. 41, no. 1 (1977), 8–14.

CC163 Kaufman, Martin. *Homeopathy in America: The Rise and Fall of a Medical Heresy*. Baltimore: The Johns Hopkins Univ. Pr., 1971. 205p.

CC164 Lasby, Clarence. *Project Paperclip. German Scientists and the Cold War*. New York: Atheneum, 1972. A group of post-World War II programs designed to "exploit" the German scientists and technicians by bringing them to the United States.

CC165 Lawrence, George H. W. "Linnaeus Comes to Pittsburgh." *Carnegie Mag.*, June 1969, 185–89. The microscope of the Harmony Society.

CC166 Plaut, Alfred. "Rudolf Virchow and Today's Physicians and Scientists." *Bull. of the Hist. of Medicine*, vol. 72, no. 3 (1953), 236–51.

CC167 Rahn, Hartmut. "Das Physikstudium in der Bundesrepublik im Vergleich mit Frankreich, England, den USA und der Schweiz." *Deutsche Uni-*

versitätszeitung, vol. 20 (1965), Teil I, Heft 1, 16–23; Teil II, Heft 2, 10–16.

CC168 Rezneck, Samuel. "The European Education of an American Chemist and Its Influence in 19th-Century America: Eben Norton Horsford." *Technology and Culture*, vol. 11 (July 1970), 366–88.

CC169 Rossiter, Margaret W. *The Emergence of Agricultural Science. Justus Liebig and the Americans, 1840–1880*. Studies in the Hist. of Science and Medicine, no. 9. New Haven: Yale Univ. Pr., 1975. 275p. Rev. by Eric E. Lampard, *Amer. Hist. Rev.*, vol. 81, no. 5 (December 1976), 1244–45; W. D. Rasmussen, *Jour. of Amer. Hist.*, vol. 63, no. 3 (December 1976), 713–14. Growth of Liebig's influence after the publication of his first book in 1841.

CC170 "Science, Education, and the Brain Drain. [Symposium]" (1) Gerhard Stoltenberg. "What the Government is Doing." (2) David Schendler. "What the Reform Movement Wants." *Amer. German Rev.*, vol. 33, no. 2 (1966–1967), 6–10.

CC171 Shryock, Richard H. "An Indifference to Basic Science during the Nineteenth Century." *Archives Internationales d'Histoire des Sciences*, October 1948, 50–65.

CC172 "Stallo, Johann B." *Dictionary of Scientific Biography*, vol. 12, p.606–10. B. Sierhausen, Oldenburg; active in Cincinnati as scientist, author, philosopher, judge.

CC173 Stallo, Johann Bernhardt. *The Concepts and Theories of Modern Physics*. Ed. Percy W. Bridgman. Cambridge: Harvard Univ. Pr., 1960. 325p. Reprint of Judge Stallo's classic work of 1882.

CC174 Sturtevant, Alfred H. "The Early Mendelians." *Papers of the Amer. Philosophic Soc.*, vol. 109, no. 4 (1965), 199–204. On C. B. Davenport of Harvard University and others who supported the Mendelian theories.

CC175 Szilard, Leo. "Reminiscences." Ed. Gertrud Weiss Szilard and Kathleen R. Winsor. In: *The Intellectual Migration. Europe and America, 1930–1960*. Ed. D. Fleming and B. Bailyn. Cambridge: Harvard Univ. Pr., 1969, p.94–151.

CC176 Ulam, S., H. W. Kuhn, A. W. Tucker, and Claude E. Shannon. "John Von Neumann, 1903–1957." In: *The Intellectual Migration. Europe and America, 1930–1960*. Ed. Donald Fleming and Bernard Bailyn. Cambridge: Harvard Univ. Pr., 1969, p.235–69. A sketch based on articles in the *Bull. of the Amer. Mathematical Soc.*, vol. 64, no. 3, part 2 (May 1958). Von Neumann was a native of Hungary.

CC177 Walsh, Anthony A. "The American Tour of Dr. Spurzheim." *Jour. of the Hist. of Medicine and Allied Sciences*, vol. 27 (April 1972), 187–205. Noted phrenologist.

CC178 Weiner, Charles. "A New Site for the Seminar: The Refugees and American Physics in the Thirties." In: *The Intellectual Migration. Europe and America, 1930–1960*. Ed. Donald Fleming and Bernard Bailyn. Cambridge: Harvard Univ. Pr., 1969, p.190–234.

CC179 Whyte, Lancelot. "Stallo versus Matter." *Anglo-German Rev.*, vol. 1 (1961). On the scientific philosophy of Johann Bernhard Stallo.

Refugee Scholars in America

CC180 Bentwich, Norman D. *Rescue and Achievement of Refugee Scholars. The Story of Displaced Scholars and Scientists, 1933–1952*. New York: Dover, 1951. 107p.

CC181 Boyers, Robert, ed. *The Legacy of the German Refugee Intellectuals*. New York: Schocken, 1972. 307p. Rev. by M. Jay, *Jour. of Mod. Hist.*, vol. 45 (1973), 45; P. Gleason, *Internat. Mig. Rev.*, vol. 8 (1974), 96–97; L. Kain, *German Quar.*, vol. 47 (1974), 91–92; J. J. Weingartner, *Historian*, vol. 35 (1973), 291–92. Essays by W. Kaufmann, George McKenna (Hannah Arendt), Henry Hatfield (Thomas Mann), Irving Fetscher (B. Brecht), E. Kahler, and others. A repr. of *Salmagundi*, issue for Fall 1969-Winter 1970.

CC182 Bühler, Charlotte. "Die Wiener Psychologische Schule in der Emigration." *Psychologische Rundschau*, vol. 16 (1965), 187–96. Supplements the study by A. Wellek.

CC183 Crawford, Rex, ed. *The Cultural Migration*. Philadelphia, Univ. of Pennsylvania Pr., 1953.

CC184 "Die deutsche Emigration nach 1933: Ihr Einfluss auf das amerikanische Geistesleben." *Frankfurter Allgemeine Zeitung*, 27 May 1964.

CC185 Donnelly, J. B. "The Vision of Scholarship. Johns Hopkins after the War." *Md. Hist. Mag.*, vol. 73 (1978), 137–62. Sketches of emigré scholars—Spitzer, Feise, Schirokauer—who taught at Johns Hopkins.

CC186 Duggan, Stephen, and Betty Drury. *The Rescue of Science and Learning: The Story of the Emergency Committee in Aid of Displaced Foreign Scholars*. New York: Macmillan, 1948. 214p. Rev. by K. Birnbaum, *Annals of the Amer. Academy of Social and Political Science*, vol. 261 (1949), 196–97.

CC187 Falk, Gerhard. "The Immigration of the European Professors and Intellectuals to the United States and Particularly the Niagara Frontier during the Nazi Era, 1933–1941." Diss., St. Univ. of New York at Buffalo, 1970. 301p. An analysis of the impact of the assimilative process upon the emigrés.

CC188 Fermi, Laura. *Illustrious Immigrants. The Intellectual Migration from Europe, 1930–41*. Chicago: Chicago Univ. Pr., 1968. 440p. Rev. by p. Gay, *N.Y. Times Book Rev.*, 7 April 1968, 8; G. L. Mosse, *Amer. Hist. Rev.*, vol. 74 (1968), 763–64; J. Gilbert, *Wis. Mag. of Hist.*, vol. 52 (1968), 191. Extended compilation of lists of intellectual exiles, writers, scientists, artists. Many of the accounts are based on personal acquaintance.

CC189 Fleming, Donald. "Emigré Physicists and the Biological Revolution." In: *The Intellectual Migration*. Ed. D. Fleming and B. Bailyn. Cambridge: Harvard Univ. Pr., 1969, p.152–89.

CC190 Fleming, Donald, and Bernard Bailyn, eds. *The Intellectual Migration. Europe and America, 1930–1960*. Cambridge: Belknap Pr. of Harvard Univ. Pr., 1969. 748p. Fourteen essays and memoirs covering many fields of intellectual endeavor. Accounts by American-born scholars of the impact of the refugees on American culture, together with reports by the emigrés themselves of their involvement with America. Incl. a list of 300 notable figures with biographical data. Rev. by G. L. Mosse, *Wis. Mag. of Hist.*, vol. 53, no. 2 (Winter 1969–1970), 147–48; Nathan Glazer, *N.Y. Times Book Rev.*, 7 September 1969, 1, 54–55.

CC191 Gay, Peter. "Weimar Culture: The Outsider as Insider." In: *The Intellectual Migration. Europe and Amerika*. Ed. Donald Fleming and Bernard Bailyn. Cambridge: Harvard Univ. Pr., 1969, p.11–93. The Weimar intellectual scene as background for the later intellectual emigrés.

CC192 Holborn, Louise M. "Deutsche Wissenschaftler in den Vereinigten Staaten in den Jahren nach 1933." *Jahrbuch für Amerikastudien*, vol. 10 (1965), 15–26. From an address before the Deutsche Gesellschaft für Amerikastudien, meeting in Frankfurt, 21 May 1964.

CC193 Huebsch, B. W. "Culture in Exile." *Saturday Rev. of Lit.*, 2 July 1938, 17.

CC194 Johnson, Alvin. "The Refugee Scholar in America." *Survey Graphic*, vol. 21 (1941), 228f.

CC195 Kent, Donald P. *The Refugee Intellectual: The Americanization of the Immigrants of 1933–1941*. New York: Columbia Univ. Pr., 1953. 317p. Rev. by O. Handlin, *N.Y. Times Book Rev.*, 26 April 1953; E. L. Fackt, *Amer.-German Rev.*, vol. 19, no. 6 (1953), 37f.; O. Seidlin, *Books Abroad*, vol. 28 (1954), 228.

CC196 Von Klimpt, Werner E. Papers, 1939–1960. 1 carton. In the New York Public Library (MS 69-893). Incl. diaries and notebooks (in German) of German scholar (b. 1900) kept in U.S. 1939–46; writings and watercolor sketchbook.

CC197 Mandler, Jean Matter, and George Mandler. "The Diaspora of Experimental Psychology: The Gestaltists and Others." In: *The Intellectual Migration. Europe and America, 1930–1960*. Ed. Donald Fleming and Bernard Bailyn. Cambridge: Harvard Univ. Pr., 1969, p.371–419.

CC198 Marcuse, Herbert. "Der Einfluss der deutschen Emigration auf das amerikanische Geistesleben: Philosophie und Soziologie." *Jahrbuch für Amerikastudien*, vol. 10 (1965), 27–33.

CC199 Mayer, Carl. In Memoriam: Albert Salomon, 1891–1966. *Social Research*, vol. 34, no. 2 (1967), 213–225. Sociologist and student of the sociology of culture on the Graduate Faculty of the New School for Social Research.

CC200 Von Mises, Richard. Papers, 1903–1953. In American Institute of Physics, Center for History and Philosophy of Physics, New York (MS 65-1720). Physicist, native of Germany (1883–1953). MSS. and correspondence, in German language.

CC201 Neumann, Franz L., et al. *The Cultural Migration: The European Scholar in America.* Introd. by Rex Crawford. Philadelphia: Univ. of Pa. Pr., 1953. New York, 1961. 156p. Incl. essays by Erich Von Neumann, Henri Peyre, Erwin Panofsky, Wolfgang Köhler, and Paul Tillich. Essay on "The Social Sciences," p.4–26.

CC202 Plessner, Monika. "Die deutsche University im Exile in New York und ihre amerikanische Gründer." *Frankfurter Hefte*, vol. 19 (1964), 181–86.

CC203 Priebe, Paul M., and Michael W. Rubinoff. "Hitler's Gift to the University of Denver." *Western States Jewish Hist. Quar.*, vol. 9 (October 1976). Emigré scholars.

CC204 Pross, Helge. *Die deutsche akademische Emigration nach den Vereinigten Staaten 1933–1941.* Berlin: Duncker and Humblot, 1955. 69p.

CC205 Radio Bremen. *Auszug des Geistes: Bericht über eine Sendereihe.* Bremer Beiträge, no. 4. Bremen: Verlag B. C. Heye, 1962. Series of interviews with Hannah Arendt, W. Gropius, Fr. Dessauer, Paul Tillich, H. Rothfels, M. Delbrück and others.

CC206 Riemer, Svend. "Die Emigration der deutschen Soziologen nach den Vereinigten Staaten." *Kölner Zeitschrift für Soziologie*, vol. 11 (1959), 100–12.

CC207 Scheyer, Ernst. "Geistiges Leben in der Emigration." *Jahrbuch der schlesischen Friedrich-Wilhelms Universität zu Breslau* (Würzburg), vol. 5 (1960), 271–95.

CC208 Speier, Hans. "The Social Conditions of the Intellectual Exile." In: *Social Order and the Risk of War*, by H. Speier. New York: n.p., 1952, p.87f.

CC209 Steinitz, Hans. "Vierzig Jahre Universität im Exil: Ein Jubiläum der New Yorker School for Social Research." *Aufbau*, 14 September 1973.

CC210 Stokes, Lawrence D. "Canada and an Academic Refugee from Nazi Germany: The Case of Gerhard Herzberg." In: *Immigrants: A Portrait of the Urban Experience.* Robert Harney and Harold Troper. Toronto: Van Nostrand Reinhold, 1975, p.150–70.

CC211 Stourzh, Gerald. "Bibliographie der deutschsprachigen Emigration in den Vereinigten Staaten, 1933–1963. Geschichte und Politische Wissenschaft." 2 Parts. *Jahrbuch für Amerikastudien*, vol. 10 (1965), 59–77, 232–66; vol. 11 (1966), 260–317. Well organized marshalling of the scholarly writings of refugee historians and social scientists.

CC212 Tillich, Paul. *Die politische und geistige Aufgabe der deutschen Emigration.* N.p.: n.p., 1938. Hectographed.

CC213 Wellek, Albert. "Der Einfluss der deutschen Emigration auf die Entwicklung der nordamerikanischen Psychologie." *Jahrbuch für Amerikastudien*, vol. 10 (1965), 34–58. An excellent survey of emigration during the Nazi era.

CC214 Wellek, Albert. "The Impact of the German Immigration on the Development of American Psychology." *Jour. of the Hist. of Behavioral Sciences*, vol. 4 (July 1968), 207–29.

CC215 Wetzel, Charles John. "The American Rescue of Refugee Scholars and Scientists from Europe 1933–1945." Diss., Wisconsin, 1964. 446p.

CC216 Wunderlich, George. Papers, 1897–1951. Ca. 2700 items; in the MS Div., Library of Congress (MS 59-221). International lawyer and judge who emigrated to the U.S. in 1936. Became Professor at the Univ. of Pennsylvania.

CD
Germanistic Study in the United States and Canada

General

CD1 Bathrick, David. "On Leaving Exile: American *Germanistik* in Its Social Content." In: *German Studies in the United States: Assessment and Outlook*. Eds. Walter F. W. Lohnes and Valters Nollendorfs. *Monatshefte* Occasional vol. 1. Madison: Univ. of Wisconsin Pr., 1976, p.252–57.

CD2 Bayerschmidt, Carl F. [History of the Department of Germanic Languages at Columbia University.] In: *A History of the Faculty of Philosophy, Columbia University*. New York: Columbia Univ. Pr., 1957. Rev. by W. Neuse, *German Quar.*, vol. 33 (1960), 84.

CD3 Benjamin, Steven M. "The SGAS Directory of German-Americanists: A Progress Report." *Newsletter, Soc. for German Amer. Studies*, vol. 2, no. 4 (1980–1981), 3–4.

CD4 Bernd, Clifford. "Die Leistungen der amerikanischen neueren Germanistik während des letzten Jahrzehnts (1951–1961)." *Wirkendes Wort*, vol. 15, no. 5, (October 1965), 343–50.

CD5 Brown University. Department of German. *Newsletter*. November 1980. 8p.

CD6 Daemmrich, Horst. "Die Germanistik in den Vereinigten Staaten: Studium und Forschung." *Colloquia Germanica*, vol. 3 (1969), 316–32.

CD7 Demetz, Peter. "Americanische Studien zur deutschen Dichtung." *Merkur*, vol. 14, no. 1 (1960), 94–97.

CD8 "Doctoral Degrees in the Field of German Languages and Literature Granted in 1949." *Monatshefte für deut. Unterricht*, vol. 42 (1950), 49–51. Also listed in subsequent years.

CD9 Freund, Folk. "Germanistik in den U S A: Quousque tandem... aut Quo Vadis?" *Moderna Språk*, vol. 72 (1978), 271–76.

CD10 Frey, John R. "German Literature." In: *Modern Literature*, vol. 2: *Italian, Spanish, German, Russian, and Oriental Literature*. Ed. Victor Lange. Englewood Cliffs: Prentice-Hall, 1968. Rev. by R. Grimm, *German Quar.*, vol. 42 (May 1969), 418–20. On Germanists and Germanistic study in the United States.

CD11 "German at Thiel College [Greenville, Pa.]." *Amer.-German Rev.*, vol. 24 (1958), no. 5, 25–26.

CD12 *German Studies in America*. Series edited by Heinrich Meyer. Bern: Herbert Lang & Cie. Vol. 1–, 1968–.

CD13 Gillespie, Gerald. "German and Comparative Literature." In: *German Studies in the United States: Assessment and Outlook*. Eds. Walter F. W. Lohnes and Valters Nollendorfs. *Monatshefte* Occasional vol. 1. Madison: Univ. of Wis. Pr., 1976, p.155–67.

CD14 Habicht, Werner, ed. *English and American Studies in German. Summaries of Theses and Monographs. A Supplement to Anglia, 1968*. Tübingen: Max Niemeyer, 1969. 101p. The initial contribution of a projected annual supplement.

CD15 Haile, H. G. "Outline for Graduate Study in German Literature." *Monatshefte*, vol. 62 (1970), 135–40.

CD16 Hatfield, Henry C., and Joan Merrick. "Studies of German Literature in the United States, 1939–1946." *Mod. Lang. Rev.*, vol. 43 (1948), 353–92.

CD17 Helbig, Louis F. "Der amerikanische Germanistenverband zwischen Tradition und Wandel." *Deutsche Studien*, vol. 12 (1974), 265–73.

CD18 Helbig, Louis F., and Heinz D. Osterle. *German Studies in America*. Bloomington, Ind.: Institute of German Studies, 1978. 74p.

CD19 Helbig, Louis F., and Eberhard Reichmann. *Teaching Postwar Germany in America: Papers and Discussions.* German Studies at Indiana University, no. 2. Bloomington: Indiana Univ. Pr., Fall, 1972. 250p. Thirteen contributions by West German, East German, American and Canadian scholars on interdisciplinary German studies. Rev. by E. Helms, *Amerikastudien*, vol. 19, no. 2 (1974), 370–71.

CD20 Hildebrand, Janet Elizabeth. "Methods for Teaching College German in the United States, 1753–1903: An Historical Study." Diss., Univ. of Texas at Austin, 1977. 230p.

CD21 Hoff, Richard. "German Language Club of Carleton College." *Mitteilungen des Instituts für Auslandsbeziehungen*, vol. 7 (1957), 186–87.

CD22 Hohlfeld, Alexander Rudolf. "The Early History of the Central Division of the Modern Language Association." *PMLA*, vol. 50 (1945), 1387–91.

CD23 Hohlfeld, Alexander Rudolf. "The Wisconsin Project on Anglo-German Literary Relations." In: *German Literature in British Magazines 1750–1860*, by W. Roloff, M. Mix, and M. Nicolai. Ed. B. Q. Morgan and A. R. Hohlfeld. Madison: Univ. Wisconsin Pr., 1950, p.3–32.

CD24 Koenig, Karl F. "German at Colgate." *Amer.-German Rev.*, vol. 8, no. 2 (1941), 30–31.

CD25 Lange, Victor. "Thoughts in Season." In: *German Studies in the United States: Assessment and Outlook.* Ed. Walter F. W. Lohnes and Valters Nollendorfs. *Monatshefte* Occasion vol. 1. Madison: Univ. of Wisconsin Pr., 1976, p.5–16.

CD26 Learned, Marion D. "Germanistik und schöne Literatur in Amerika." *Pädagogische Monatshefte*, vol. 2, no. 3 (1900–1901), 97–101.

CD27 Liedloff, Helmut. "German Climate in Illinois." *Amer.-German Rev.*, vol. 31, no. 1 (1964), 33–36. The NDEA Summer Institute in German at Southern Illinois Univ., Carbondale.

CD28 Liedtke, Kurt E. H. "A Case for German." *Amer.-German Rev.*, vol. 32, no. 4 (1966), 35. Why college students ought to consider learning German.

CD29 Liedtke, Kurt E. H. "Der Deutschunterricht am San Francisco State College." *Zeitschrift für Kulturaustausch*, vol. 12 (1962), 325–26.

CD30 Lohnes, Walter, F. W., and Valters Nollendorfs. *German Studies in the United States: Assessment and Outlook.* Madison: Univ. of Wisconsin Pr., 1976. 263p. Rev. by H. Slessarev, *German Quar.*, vol. 51, no. 1 (January 1978), 110–13; Gerhard H. Weiss, *Unterrichtspraxis*, vol. 10, no. 1 (Spring 1977), 117–18. A collection of essays on problems of the profession, its *raison d'être* in the present academic, social, and cultural situation.

CD31 Maier, Wolfgang M. L., comp. *Who is Who in German Studies in the U S A.* Beltsville, Md.: n.p., 1978. A directory with bio-bibliographical references and data on Germanists.

CD32 Markey, T. L. "Malice in Wonderland: The Linguist's Future in the German Department." *German Quar.*, vol. 50, no. 1 (1977), 10–20.

CD33 Martin, Horst. "Die Hochschulgermanistik in Kanada." In: *Deutsch als Muttersprache in Kanada: Berichte zur Gegenwartslage.* Ed. L. Auburger et al. Wiesbaden: Steiner, 1977, p.107–13.

CD34 Mieder, Wolfgang. "Deutsche Volkskunde und amerikanische Germanistik." *Unterrichtspraxis*, vol. 6, no. 2 (1973), 34–40.

CD35 Miller, W. Marion. "American Doctoral Degrees Granted in the Field of Modern Languages in 1948 and 1949." *Mod. Lang. Jour.*, vol. 33 (1950) 392–96, 624–90.

CD36 Mollenhauer, Peter. "Dissertations in Progress [in Germanic Language and Literature]." *Monatshefte*, vol. 59, no. 3 (1967), 255.

CD37 Neumann, Gerda. "Germanistik in Amerika. Nachlassendes Interesse am Deutschunterricht." *Deutscher Forschungsdienst*, vol. 18 (1971). Supplement, p.1–2.

CD38 Reichmann, Eberhard. "Germanistik oder Deutsche Studien: Zur Situation des Faches im Ausland." In: *Rezeption der deutschen Gegenwartsliteratur im Ausland: Internationale Forschungen zur neueren deutschen Literatur. Tagungsbeiträge eines Symposiums der Alexander von Humboldt Stiftung, Bonn . . . 21. bis 26. Okt. 1975 in Ludwigsburg.* Ed. Dietrich Papenfuss and

General *(cont.)*

Jürgen Söring. Stuttgart: Kohlhammer, 1976, p.57–67.

CD39 Rippley, La Vern J. "The German-Americans: A Course Proposal." *Unterrichtspraxis*, vol. 9, no. 2 (1976), 24–30.

CD40 Rose, Ernst. "Die Leistungen der amerikanischen Germanistik während des letzten Jahrzehnts (1939–1951)." *Wirkendes Wort*, vol. 3 (1952), 34–46.

CD41 Rudnytsky, Leo D. "The Changing Aspects of Teaching German." In: *The Study of Foreign Languages*. Ed. Joseph S. Roucek. New York: Philosophical Library, 1968.

CD42 Sammons, Jeffrey L. "Die amerikanische Germanistik: Historische Betrachtungen zur gegenwärtigen Situation." In: *Germanistik International: Vorträge und Diskussionen auf dem . . . Symposium "Germanistik im Ausland" vom 23. bis 25. Mai 1977 in Tübingen*. Ed. Richard Brinkmann, E. Kennosuke and Fritz Hackert. Tübingen: Niemeyer, 1978., p.105–20.

CD43 Schaum, K. "Die Grillparzer-Forschung in Amerika im 20. Jahrhundert." In: *Das Grillparzer-Bild des 20. Jahrhunderts: Festschrift . . . zum 100. Todestag von Franz Grillparzer*. Ed. Heinz Kindermann. Wien/Köln/Graz: Böhlau, 1972.

CD44 Shaw, Leroy R. "German on Television at the University of Texas." *German Quar.*, vol. 34 (1961), 146–53.

CD45 Spuler, R. "A Study of 'Germanistik' in America: The Reception of German Classicism, 1870–1905." Diss., Ohio State University, 1980.

CD46 Spuler, Richard C. "Mediating German Culture: American Germanistik." *Yearbook for German-Amer. Studies*, vol. 16 (1981), 9–26. Finds reflections of Wilhelminian Germany in American *Germanistik*: remnants of racist-chauvinistic attitudes.

CD47 Stambaugh, Ria, and Petrus Tax. "Die Altgermanistik in Chapel Hill: Bericht der Lage und der allgemeinen Problematik." *Jahrbuch für Internationale Germanistik*, vol. 5, no. 1 (1973), 146–55.

CD48 Stern, Guy. "The Future of German Studies: A Graduate Dean's Perspective." *Unterrichtspraxis*, vol. 7, no. 2 (1974), 7–14.

CD49 Theurer, Louise H. "The German Language House, New Jersey College for Women, 1929–1954." *Amer.-German Rev.*, vol. 21, no. 1 (1955), 13–15.

CD50 *Versuch. Literarische Beiträge amerikanischer College-Studenten.* Ed. B. Mitchell and G. Barisas. Lawrence: German Dept., Univ. of Kansas, n.d.

CD51 Waldenrath, Alexander. "German-America: Another Approach to Language Instruction." *Bull., Pa. State Mod. Lang. Assoc.*, vol. 55, no. 2 (1977), 8–12.

CD52 Waldenrath, Alexander. "The Role of German-American Culture in Teaching German." *Die Schatzkammer*, vol. 2 (Spring 1976), 26–32.

CD53 Weber, Berta. "Folklore for Teachers. Deutsche Volkskunde im Sprachunterricht." *Bull., Pa. State Mod. Lang. Assoc.*, vol. 50, no. 1 (Fall 1971), 12–15. On the use of folklife, dress, music and the like in German classes.

CD54 Willson, Leslie A. "Alte und Neue Fenster oder wie man deutsche Literatur in den U S A vermittelt." *Akzente*, vol. 22, no. 2 (April 1975), 113–20. A survey of American publishing in the field of textbook editions of German authors.

Germanistic Scholars and Teachers in America

GENERAL LISTINGS

CD55 Monatshefte. Fall issue. Annual listing of current "Personalia" for the entire field of United States and Canadian Germanists. Besides the faculties of German departments, it includes promotions and new appointments, visitors, and doctoral degrees awarded in the previous year. Cf. "Personalia 1976–77." *Monatshefte*, vol. 68, no. 3 (Fall 1976), 270–333.

ACKERMANN, ELFRIEDE

CD56 Planitz, Karl-Heinz. "Elfriede Ackermann. In memoriam." *German Quar.*, vol. 31 (1958), 309–10. Active in the Chicago high schools, 1890–1958.

ALEWYN, RICHARD

CD57 Kahn, Ludwig W. "In memoriam Richard Alewyn (1902–1979)." *German Quar.*, vol. 53, no. 1 (January 1980), 128–29.

ALMSTEDT, HERMANN N.

CD58 Almstedt, Hermann N. Papers, 1895–1954. 1 box. In the Western Hist. MS. Collection, Univ. of Missouri Library (MS 61-241). A. (1873–1954) was professor of German, Univ. of Missouri.

CD59 B., H. "Hermann N. Almstedt. In memoriam...." *Monatshefte*, vol. 46 (1954), 348–49.

AMANN, PAUL

CD60 Amann, Paul. Papers. In Leo Baeck Institute collections, New York (MS 75-712). Philologist and author, professor of German. Letters, misc. MSS., research materials for stories, essays, plays, lectures. Transcripts and translations of prominent Continental literary figures: Romain Rolland, Hermann Broch, Georges Duhamel, C. Isherwood, Hans Kohn, and others.

APPELT, EWALD PAUL

CD61 Hanhardt, Arthur M. "Ewald Paul Appelt." *Monatshefte*, vol. 46 (1954), 347–48.

CD62 Neuse, Werner. "Ewald Paul Appelt In Memoriam...." *German Quar.*, vol. 27 (1954), 219–20.

ARNDT, KARL J. R.

CD63 Friesen, Gerhard K., and Walter Schatzberg, eds. *The German Contribution to the Building of the Americas: Studies in Honor of Karl J. R. Arndt.* Hanover, N. H.: Clark Univ. Pr. and Univ. Pr. of New England, 1977. 410p. With "Bibliography of Publications of Karl J. R. Arndt," p.xi–xvi.

ARON, ALBERT WILLIAM

CD64 Morgan, Bayard Q. "Albert William Aron, 1885–1945." *Zeitschrift für deutsche Philologie*, vol. 70 (1948), 212. See also: John J. Parry. "Albert William Aron—In memoriam." *Jour. of Engl. and Germanic Philology*, vol. 45 (1946), 123–24.

AUERBACH, ERICH

CD65 Wellek, René. "Erich Auerbach in Memoriam." *Compar. Lit.*, vol. 10 (1958), 93–94. Famous authority in Romance literature at Yale University.

BARBA, PRESTON ALBERT

CD66 Heyl, John K. "In Memoriam: Preston Albert Barba." *Der Reggeboge*, vol. 5, nos. 3–4 (1971), 3.

CD67 "Klo." "Prof. Preston A. Barba †." *Zeitschrift für Kulturaustausch*, Jahrgang 22, no. 1 (1972), 63. Professor of German Languages and Literature, Muhlenberg College; editor of "'S Pennsylfawnisch Deitsch Eck."

CD68 Ward, Robert E. "Preston A. Barba In Memoriam." *German-Amer. Studies*, vol. 5 (1972), 200–02. With a list of his principal writings.

BELL, CLAIR HAYDEN

CD69 Bell, Clair Hayden. Papers, 1905–1965. In the Bancroft Library, Univ. of California, Berkeley (MS 75-257). Professor of German, Univ. of California.

BERGSTRAESSER, ARNOLD

CD70 "Arnold Bergstraesser." *Amer.-German Rev.*, vol. 30, no. 4 (1964), 37.

CD71 "Arnold Bergstraesser." *Zeitschrift für Kulturaustausch*, vol. 14 (1964), 128.

CD72 Fraenkel, Ernst. "Arnold Bergstraesser, 14. Juli 1896–24. Februar 1964." *Jahrbuch für Amerikastudien*, vol. 9 (1964), 10; *ibid.*, vol. 10 (1965), 8–14. (Memorial service at the Univ. of Freiburg, 14 July 1964.)

CD73 Hodeige, Fritz, ed. *Atlantische Begegnungen: eine Freundesgabe für Arnold Bergstraesser*, von Carl J. Friedrich et al. Ed. F. Hodeige and Carl Rothe. Freiburg/Br.: Rombach, 1964.

BIERWIRTH, HEINRICH C.

CD74 Bierwirth, Heinrich C. *Aus dem Leben eines Deutsch-Amerikaners.* Yarmouth Port, Mass.: n.p., 1947. Cf. *Amer.-German Rev.*, vol. 15 (1949), no. 4, 39. Rev. by C. E. Pauck, *Mod. Lang. Jour.*, vol. 33 (1949), 79; C. D. Vail, *Mod. Lang. Quar.*, vol. 10 (1949), 103. Reminiscences of a German scholar and teacher.

CD75 Bierwirth, Heinrich C. Papers. In Harvard Univ. Archives (MS 65–1891). Misc. correspondence and autobiographical MSS.; instructor and professor of German at Harvard.

CD76 Howard, William G. "Heinrich Conrad Bierwirth." *Amer.-German Rev.*, vol. 11, no. 3 (1945), 33–36.

BLOOMFIELD, LEONARD

CD77 Bloch, Bernard. "Leonard Bloomfield 1887–1949." In: *Portraits of Linguists*... Ed. Thomas A. Sebeok. Bloomington: Indiana Univ. Pr., 1966. Vol. 1, p.508–17.

CD78 Hosford, Helga. "Bloomfield as a Teacher of Elementary German." *Proceedings of the Pacific Northwest Conference on Foreign Languages*, vol. 25, no. 2 (1974), 194–99.

CD79 Moulton, William G. "Leonard Bloomfield as Germanist." (1967). In: *A Leonard Bloomfield Anthology*. Ed. Charles F. Hockett. Bloomington: Indiana Univ. Pr., 1970, p.512–23.

CD80 Sturtevant, Edgar H. "Leonard Bloomfield." In: *Portraits of Linguists* .... Ed. Thomas A. Sebeok. Bloomington: Indiana Univ. Pr., 1966. Vol. 1, p.518–21.

BLUME, BERNHARD

CD81 Blume, Bernhard. "Einwanderungen. Antwort auf eine Rundfrage: Was verdanke ich meiner Heimat?" *Dimension*, vol. 9, no. 1 (1976), 152–63. See also *Schwaben unter sich—über sich*. Frankfurt: W. Weidlich Vlg., 1976.

CD82 Heller, Peter. "Aesthetic Analysis and the Disinherited Mind: The *Festschrift* für Bernhard Blume." *German Life and Letters*, vol. 23 (1970), 169–77.

CD83 Seidlin, Oskar. "In Memoriam Bernhard Blume (1901–1978)." *German Quar.*, vol. 51 (November 1978), 441–42. Professor of German at Mills College.

BOESCHENSTEIN, HERMANN

CD84 "Großes Bundesverdienstkreuz für Professor Boeschenstein." *Der Courier*, 29 October 1970, p.17, 22.

CD85 "Herman Boeschenstein ausgezeichnet." *Zeitschrift für Kulturaustausch*, vol. 21, no. 1 (1971), 106. The scholar-teacher of the Univ. of Toronto honored by the German government.

CD86 Milnes, Humphrey. "Hermann Boeschenstein." *German Life and Letters*, vol. 23 (October 1969), 1–6. With list of writings.

BORN, HEINZ GEORGE FRANK

CD87 Maurer, Karl W. *Heinz George Frank Born. June 23, 1911, Died June 24, 1967. A Profile. A Memorial Address October 10, 1967*. Publ. for the Hölderlin Soc. and University College. Manitoba: Univ. of Manitoba, n.d. 24p. Graduate student at the Univ. of Manitoba, a native of Germany.

BOYESEN, HJALMAR HJORTH

CD88 Glasrud, Clarence A. *Hjalmar Hjorth Boyesen*. Northfield, Minn.: Norwegian-Amer. Hist. Assoc., 1963. 245p.

VON BRADISH, JOSEPH A.

CD89 "Joseph A. von Bradish ausgezeichnet." *Zeitschrift für Kulturaustausch*, vol. 14 (1964), 278. Recipient of Österreichisches Ehrenkreuz für Wissenschaft und Kunst 1. Klasse.

BUFFINGTON, ALBERT F.

CD90 "Publications of Albert F. Buffington." In *Ebbes fer alle—ebber ebbes fer dich: Essays in Memoriam, Albert Franklin Buffington*. Publs., Pa. German Soc., vol. 14. Breinigsville, Pa. 1980. p.xiii–xv. See also: Weiser, Frederick S. "Preface." *Ibid.*, p.xi–xii.

CANAAN, GERSHON

CD91 "Die ersten Träger der Verdienstmedaille des Instituts für Auslandsbeziehungen. Gershon Canaan." *Zeitschrift für Kulturaustausch*, vol. 18, no. 1 (1968), 69. Remembering the promoter of the "Deutscher Tag" in Texas in 1963.

CARLSON, HAROLD GOTTFRIED

CD92 Viehmeyer, L. Allen. "Harold Gottfried Carlson In Memoriam." *German-Amer. Studies*, vol. 5 (1972), 193–94. Teacher and scholar in German and American literature and language.

CLARK, ROBERT T.

CD93 Seidlin, Oskar. "Robert T. Clark. In memoriam." *Report, Soc. for the Hist. of the Germans in Md.*, vol. 30 (1959), 119–20. Germanist, author of studies on J. G. Herder and the Germans in Louisiana.

COENEN, FREDERIC EDWARD

CD94 Friederich, Werner P. "Frederic Edward Coenen 1903–1973." *German Quar.*, vol. 47 (1974), 167. Professor of German at the Univ. of North Carolina.

CD95 Mews, Siegfried, ed. *Studies in German Literature of the Nineteenth and Twentieth Centuries. Festschrift for Frederick E. Coenen.* Univ. of N. Car. Studies in German Lang. and Literature, no. 67. Chapel Hill: Univ. of N. Car. Pr., 1970.

COMPTON, OTELIA AUGSPURGER

CD96 Schreiber, Clare A. "Otelia Augspurger Compton." *Amer.-German Rev.*, vol. 11, no. 3 (1945), 14–16. Wife of Professor Compton of Wooster College.

CUNZ, DIETER

CD97 "Auszeichnung für Professor Dieter Cunz." *Zeitschrift für Kulturaustausch*, vol. 12 (1962), 371. Recipient of the Bundesverdienstkreuz Erster Klasse.

CD98 Knoche, Walter. "Dieter Cunz: A List of Published Writings 1934–1969." *The Report of the Soc. for the Hist. of the Germans in Md.*, vol. 34 (1970), 19–22.

CD99 Prahl, Augustus J., et al. "Dieter Cunz (1910–1969): Tributes and Memories." *Report of the Soc. for the Hist. of the Germans in Md.*, vol. 34 (1970), 9–18.

DEILER, J. HANNO

CD100 Moehlenbrock, Arthur H. "J. Hanno Deiler, Cultural Pioneer of the South." *Amer.-German Rev.*, vol. 8, no. 3 (1942), 25–27.

FABER DU FAUR, CURT

CD101 Henel, Heinrich. "Curt von Faber du Faur: In Memoriam." *Germanic Rev.*, vol. 41, no. 3 (May 1966), 155–56.

CD102 Weigand, Hermann J. "In memoriam Curt von Faber du Faur." *Monatshefte*, vol. 58 (1966), 157–59.

FAUST, ALBERT BERNHARDT

CD103 Cunz, Dieter. "Albert Bernhardt Faust." *Report of the Soc. for the Hist. of the Germans in Md.*, vol. 28 (1953), 86–88. Historian in the field of German-American studies, 1870–1951.

CD104 Faust, Albert B. Papers. 10 ft. In Cornell University Library. collection of Regional History and University Archives, Ithaca, N.Y. (MS 62-3887). See also MS 77-173; Additions 1938–1940. On F. (1891–1945); correspondence, articles, speeches, clippings and materials for the study of the German element in the United States.

CD105 Lange, Victor. "In Memory of Albert Bernhardt Faust, 1870–1951." *Amer.-German Rev.*, vol. 17 (1951), no. 4, 28.

FEISE, ERNST

CD106 Neuse, Werner. "In memoriam Ernst Feise (1884–1966)." *German Quar.*, vol. 39 (1966), 547–48.

CD107 Steinhauer, Harry. "Ernst Feise (1884–1966)." *Monatshefte*, vol. 58 (1966), 353–54.

FIFE, ROBERT HERNDON

CD108 Bayerschmidt, Carl F. "In memoriam: Robert Herndon Fife." *Germanic Rev.*, vol. 34 (1959), 3.

CD109 [Obituary.] *Amer.-German Rev.*, vol. 25, no. 1 (1958), 36. Professor of German at Columbia University.

FLEISCHHAUER, WOLFGANG

CD110 Riechel, Donald C., ed. *Wege der Worte: Festschrift für Wolfgang Fleischhauer; anlässlich seines 65. Geburtstags und des 40. Jahres seines Wirkens als Professor der deutschen Philologie an der Ohio State University mit Beiträgen von Freunden, Kollegen und Schülern.* Köln: Böhlau, 1978. 401p. "Dedication," by Charles W. Hoffmann, p.xv–xvii; "Bibliographie W.F.," p.400–01.

FORCHHEIMER, FREDERICK

CD111 Bohlmann, Theodor. In memoriam Dr. Frederick Forchheimer. N.p.: n.p., 1913. 12p.

FRANCKE, KUNO

CD112 Francke, Kuno. Papers, 1890–1930. 3 boxes. In Harvard Univ. Archives (MS 65-1241). Incl. correspondence, 1915–1917; F. (1855–1930) was professor of German at Harvard University.

FREUND, MAX

CD113 "Max Freund 85 Jahre." *Zeitschrift für Kulturaustausch*, vol. 14 (1964), 127. Professor at Rice Univ., retired.

FUERST, NORBERT

CD114 Durzak, Manfred, Eberhard Reichmann and Ulrich Weisstein, eds. *Texte und Kontexte: Studien zur deutschen und vergleichenden Literaturwissenschaft. Festschrift für Norbert Fuerst zum 65. Geburtstag.* Bern: Francke, 1973. 336p. See also "Bibliographie Norbert Fuerst 1940–1972." *Ibid.*, 327–29.

GALINSKY, HANS

CD115 "Hans Galinsky zum 65. Geburtstag." *Amerikastudien*, vol. 19, no. 2 (1974), 199–200.

GAUSEWITZ, WALTER

CD116 "In Memoriam: Walter Gausewitz, 1898–1971." *Monatshefte*, vol. 64, no. 3 (Fall 1972), 217.

GERHARD, MELITTA

CD117 Spaethling, Robert. "Melitta Gerhard zum Gedächtnis (1891–1981)." *German Quar.*, vol. 55, no. 4 (November 1982), 630–31.

GILDERSLEEVE, BASIL LANEAU

CD118 Krumpelmann, John T. "Basil Laneau Gildersleeve, Classicist and Germanist." *Amer.-German Rev.*, vol. 27, no. 3 (1961), 25–27.

GLEIS, PAUL G.

CD119 Prahl, Augustus J. "Paul G. Gleis." *Report of the Soc. for the Hist. of the Germans in Md.*, vol. 29 (1956), 82–83. Professor of German philology at the Catholic University, 1887–1955.

GUDDE, ERWIN G.

CD120 "Erwin G. Gudde 75 Jahre." *Zeitschrift für Kulturaustausch*, vol. 14 (1964), 127. G. (1889–1969) was founder of the American Name Society.

CD121 "Erwin G. Gudde †." *Zeitschrift für Kulturaustausch*, vol. 19, no. 3 (1969), 284.

CD122 Gudde, Erwin G. "Vita nostra brevis est." *Names*, vol. 7 (1959), 1–16. Autobiography.

HAMMERSCHLAG, LUDWIG

CD123 Zucker, Adolf E., and A. J. Prahl. "Ludwig Hammerschlag In memoriam." *Report, Soc. for the Hist. of the Germans in Md.*, vol. 32 (1966), 70–71. A political exile of the Nazi era, who taught German from 1946–1957 at the University of Maryland.

HEFFNER, R.-MERRILL S.

CD124 Ingraham, Mark H. "Merrill Heffner." *Monatshefte*, vol. 55 (1963), 147–48.

CD125 "R.-M. S. Heffner: Publications." *Monatshefte*, vol. 55 (1963), 236f.

HELLER, OTTO

CD126 Hohfeld, A. R. "Otto Heller." *Monatshefte für deutschen Unterricht*, vol. 33 (1941), 331.

CD127 "Otto Heller 1863–1941. In memoriam." By Adolf Busse, *German Quar.*, vol. 14 (1941), 232–33.

CD128 Zucker, A. E. "Otto Heller." *Jour. of English and Germanic Philology*, vol. 41 (1942), 398–99.

HENEL, HEINRICH E. K.

CD129 Sammons, Jeffrey L. "Heinrich E. K. Henel 1905–1981 in memoriam." *German Quar.*, vol. 54, no. 3 (May 1981), 401–03.

CD130 Sammons, Jeffrey L., and Ernst Schürer, eds. *Lebendige Form: Interpretationen zur deutschen Literatur. Festschrift für Heinrich E. K. Henel.* München: Fink, 1970. "Bibliographie 1928–1968," p.291–96.

HEUSER, FREDERICK WILLIAM JUSTUS

CD131 Bayerschmidt, Carl F. "Frederick W. J. Heuser." *Germanic Rev.*, vol. 33 (1958), 164–67.

CD132 Heuser, Frederick William Justus. Papers, 1894–1957. 2500 items. In the Columbia University Libraries (MS 67-796). Professor of German, Columbia University.

CD133 Keil, Günther. "Frederick W. J. Heuser. Nachruf und Würdigung." *German Quar.*, vol. 34 (1961), 282–83.

HILL, CLAUDE

CD134 Ley, Ralph, Maria Wagner, Joanna M. Ratych and Kenneth Hughes, eds. *Perspectives and Personalities. Studies in Modern German Literature Honoring Claude Hill.* Beiträge zur neueren Literaturgeschichte. 3rd Ser. no. 37. Heidelberg: Winter, 1978. 326p.

HOFACKER, ERICH PAUL

CD135 "In Memoriam. Erich Paul Hofacker" (1898–1976). *German Quar.*, vol. 49, no. 4 (November 1976), 602.

HOHLFELD, ALEXANDER RUDOLF

CD136 "In Memoriam Alexander Rudolf Hohlfeld." *Monatshefte*, 48 (1956), 243–44. B. in Dresden, d. Madison, Wis.; scholar in Germanic literature.

CD137 "To Professor Hohlfeld on His Ninetieth Birthday." *Monatshefte*, vol. 47 (1955), 369–70.

JANTZ, HAROLD

CD138 Kurth, Lieselotte, William McClain and Holger Homann, eds. *Traditions and Transitions: Studies in Honor of Harold Jantz.* München: Delp, 1972. 262p. See also: "Harold Jantz: An Appreciation," *ibid.*, p.5–8; and Morgan H. Pritchett, "Bibliography of Publications of Harold Jantz." *Ibid.*, p.9–11.

JENTE, RICHARD

CD139 Coenen, F. E. "In memoriam Richard Jente 1888–1952." *Monatshefte*, vol. 44 (1952), 420–21.

CD140 Holmes, Urban T. "Richard Jente (1888–1952)." *Studies in Philology*, vol. 49 (1952), 551–52.

CD141 Taylor, Archer. "Richard Jente, 1888–1952." *Jour. of Amer. Folklore*, vol. 66, no. 261 (1953), 200. Tribute and biography.

KEIL, GUENTHER

CD142 Rose, Ernst. "In Memoriam Guenther Keil (1890–1967)." *German Quar.*, vol. 40 (1967), 506–08.

VON KLENZE, CAMILLO

CD143 Busse, A. "Camillo von Klenze." *Amer.-German Rev.*, vol. 9, no. 5 (1943), 38.

CD144 Hohlfeld, A. R. "Camillo von Klenze, 1863–1943." *Monatshefte für deutschen Unterricht*, vol. 35 (1943), 296.

KLOSS, HEINZ

CD145 "Statt einer Festschrift: Bibliographie der Veröffentlichungen von Heinz Kloss." *Vierteljahresschrift für Nationalitätenfragen*, vol. 28, no. 2 (1971), 51–69.

KRUMPELMANN, JOHN T.

CD146 Hammer, Carl, Jr. "John T. Krumpelmann." In: *Studies in German Literature.* Baton Rouge: Louisiana State Univ. Pr., 1963, p.xiii–xviii; Hammer, Carl, Jr. "Publications of John T. Krumpelmann." *Ibid.*, p.165–69.

KURATH, HANS

CD147 Scholler, Harald, and John Reidy, eds. *Lexicography and Dialect Geography. Festgabe for Hans Kurath.* (ZDL Beihefte, N. F., Heft 9). Wiesbaden: Steiner, 1973. Incl. Harald Scholler. "A Eulogy for Hans Kurath," p.1–4; "Publications of Hans Kurath," p.268–71.

KURRELMEYER, WILLIAM

CD148 Albrecht, Erich. "Bibliography of William Kurrelmeyer." *Mod. Lang. Notes*, vol. 68 (1953), 291–98. K. (1874–1957) was professor of German at Johns Hopkins University.

CD149 Kurrelmeyer, William. Papers. 1610 items. In the Johns Hopkins University Library (MS 60-1647). Correspondence and misc. papers.

CD150 McClain, William H. "William Kurrelmeyer: German-American 1874–1957." *Report of the Soc. for the Hist. of the Germans in Md.*, vol. 37 (1978), 8–18.

CD151 McClain, William H. "William Kurrelmeyer, In memoriam." *German Quar.*, vol. 31 (1958), 66.

CD152 Sehrt, Edward H. "William Kurrelmeyer, In Memoriam." *Report of the Soc. for the Hist. of the Germans in Md.*, vol. 30 (1959), 115–16. See also: Taylor Starck. "William Kurrelmeyer 1874–1957. A Tribute." *Ibid.*, vol. 32 (1966), 9–12.

LANGE, VICTOR

CD153 "Victor Lange Receives Golden Medal." *Amer.-German Rev.*, vol. 32, no. 4 (1966), 37.

LEARNED, MARION DEXTER

CD154 Eddy, Beverley D. "Marion Dexter Learned: Spokesman for the German American Heritage." *John and Mary's Journal. Publ. by the Dickinson College Friends of the Library.* Spring 1976, no. 2, 14–24.

CD155 Learned, Marion Dexter. Papers. 3215 items in Dickinson College Library, Carlisle, Pa. (MS 66-471). Additionally, 500 items, incl. photographs of documents in German archives relating to German settlement in the U.S. In Historical Society of Pennsylvania (MS 61 599). Professor of German.

LEDERER, MAX

CD156 "In Memory of Max Lederer." *Books Abroad*, vol. 24 (1950), 316–17. Consultant on German literature at the Library of Congress.

LEHMANN, WINFRED P.

CD157 Hopper, Paul J., ed. *Studies in Descriptive and Historical Linguistics: Festschrift for Winfred P. Lehmann*. Amsterdam: Benjamins, 1977. 502p. "List of Publications 1938–1976," p.1–18.

LOOMIS, C. GRANT

CD158 Beeler, M. S. "C. Grant Loomis (1901–1963)." *Western Folklore*, vol. 22 (1963), 229–30. Memorial tribute to Professor Loomis as folklorist and former editor of *Western Folklore*.

LOUIS, ANDREW

CD159 Kahn, Robert L., ed. *Studies in German: In Memory of Andrew Louis*. Rice Univ. Studies, vol. 55, no. 3. Houston, Texas: Rice Univ. Pr., 1969.

LUDWIG, HERMANN ERNST

CD160 Ladenson, Alexander. "Hermann Ernst Ludwig, 1809–1856." *Library Quar.*, vol. 14 (1944), 126–31. Bibliographer.

MANKIEWICZ, FRANK

CD161 Schueler, Herbert. "Frank Mankiewicz. In memoriam." *German Quar.*, vol. 15 (1942), 2–4.

MANSCHINGER, GRETA HARTWIG

CD162 "Greta Hartwig Manschinger in Memoriam." *German-Amer. Studies*, vol. 5 (1972), 196–97.

MARCKWARDT, ALBERT H.

CD163 Moulton, William G. "A Biography and Bibliography of Albert H. Marckwardt." In: *Studies in Honor of Albert H. Marckwardt*. Ed. James E. Alatis. Washington, D.C.: Teachers of English to Speakers of Other Languages, 1972, p.1–14.

MAURER, KARL-WERNER

CD164 "K. W. Maurer, 1870—Manitoba—1970." *Canad. Ethnic Studies*, vol. 1, no. 2 (December 1969), 77f.

CD165 Schludermann, Brigitte, Victor G. Doerksen, Robert J. Glendinning and Evelyn S. Firchow, eds. *Deutung und Bedeutung: Studies in German and Comparative Literature Presented to Karl-Werner Maurer*. The Hague: Mouton, 1973. Includes: L. A. Willoughby, "Karl-Werner Maurer: An English Tribute," p.11–13; Haraldur Bessason, "From Troy to Uppsala: A Manitoba Tribute," p.14–15; Zenta Maurina, "Übersetzung als Umdichtung: Karl-Werner Maurer gewidmet," p.366–73; "Karl-Werner Maurer: A Selected Bibliography," p.379–85.

MAUTNER, FRANZ H.

CD166 "Österreichische Gelehrte im Ausland: Franz H. Mautner, U S A." *Österreichische Hochschulzeitung*, 1 October 1962.

MEISNEST, FREDERICK W.

CD167 "Frederick W. Meisnest. In memoriam." *German Quar.*, vol. 30 (1957), 58. Professor of German in Seattle.

MEMMING, GERRIT

CD168 Planitz, Karl-Heinz. "Gerrit Memming, 1904–1965." *German Quar.*, vol. 38 (1965), 402–03. Professor of German, Albright College.

MEYER, HEINRICH

CD169 Mommsen, Katharina. "Novarum rerum cupidus. Nachruf auf den Herausgeber der German Studies in America: Heinrich Meyer (1904–1977)." *German Studies Rev.*, vol. 1, no. 3 (October 1978), 336–41. See also *Sonderprospect Verlag Peter Lang*. Bern: Peter Lang, 1978. p.30–31. B. Nürnberg, d. Nashville.

MORGAN, BAYARD QUINCY

CD170 Bluhm, Heinz. "Review Essay: Bayard Quincy Morgan." *Mod. Lang. Jour.*, vol. 50 (1966), 426–28. Morgan's contributions to the study of German literature.

CD171 Boeninger, Helmut R., et al. "Memorial Resolution Bayard Quincy Morgan 1883–1967." *Monatshefte*, vol. 59 (1967), 148–49.

CD172 F., N. "B. Q. Morgan at Eighty." *Monatshefte*, vol. 55 (1963), 102–06.

CD173 Strothmann, F. W. "Bayard Quincy Morgan (1883–1967)." *German Quar.*, vol. 40 (1967), 317.

NEUSE, WERNER

CD174 Lederer, H., and J. Seyppel, eds. *Festschrift für Werner Neuse.* Berlin: Die Diagonale, 1967–1968. Incl.: Stephen A. Freeman. "A Tribute to Werner Neuse,"; W. Neuse. "Vierzig Sommer Deutsche Schule des Middlebury College,"; "Veröffentlichungen von Werner Neuse," Wolfgang Panzer, "Vermont und seine Landschaft—vom Philoberg gesehen."

NORDMEYER, HENRY W.

CD175 Frank, Luanne T., and Emery E. George, eds. *Husbanding the Golden Grain: Studies in Honor of Henry W. Nordmeyer.* Ann Arbor: Dept. of Germanic Languages and Literatures, Univ. of Michigan, 1973. 337p.; see also; Mary C. Crichton, ed. "Henry W. Nordmeyer: Bibliography of Publications." p.1–4.

OTT, JOHN HENRY

CD176 Owen, Ralph Dornfeld. "John Henry Ott of Northwestern College—In Memoriam." *Amer.-German Rev.*, vol. 12, no. 4 (1946), 36.

PEARSON, ALFRED JOHN

CD177 Herriott, F. I. "Alfred John Pearson, An Appreciation—Professor of German Language and Literature, Drake University 1907–1939." *American Imago*, 3rd Ser., vol. 22 (1941), 515–42. Native of Sweden, b. 1869; granted Yale Ph.D. degree in 1896.

PEISEL, GERTRUDE

CD178 Planitz, Karl-Heinz. "In Memoriam: Gertrude Peisel." *German Quar.*, vol. 40 (1967), 508.

PEKARY, CHARLOTTE H.

CD179 Berger, Dorothea. "Charlotte H. Pekary (1894–1967)." *German, Quar.*, vol. 40 (1967), 318–19.

PENZL, HERBERT

CD180 Rauch, Irmengard, and Gerald F. Carr, eds. *Linguistic Method: Essays in Honor of Herbert Penzl.* The Hague: Mouton, 1979. 630p. Incl. "Selected Bibliography of Herbert Penzl," p.11–18.

PFEFFER, J. ALAN

CD181 Jonas, Klaus W. *Deutsche Weltliteratur: Von Goethe bis Ingeborg Bachmann: Festgabe für J. Alan Pfeffer.* Tübingen: Niemeyer, 1972. 304p.; incl. "Veröffentlichungen von J. Alan Pfeffer."

POCHMANN, HENRY A.

CD182 Ward, Robert E. "Henry A. Pochmann in memoriam." *German-Amer. Studies*, vol. 7 (1974), 1–2. Professor of American Literature, Univ. of Wisconsin (1901–1973).

POLITZER, HEINZ

CD183 Angress, Ruth K. "Heinz Politzer (1910–1978)." *German Quar.*, vol. 51 (1978), 442–43. Writer and scholar, a native of Austria. Was granted the Ph.D. degree by Bryn Mawr in 1950.

CD184 Hagedorn, Karen. "Bibliographie [of Heinz Politzer.]" In: "Heinz Politzer e il centenario di Grillparzer." Claudio Magris. *Studi Germanici*, vol. 10 (1972), p.697–703.

POSNER, ERNST

CD185 Mommsen, Wolfgang A. "Ernst Posner, Mittler zwischen deutschem und amerikanischem Archivwesen." *Der Archivar*, Jahrg. 20, Heft 3 (July 1967), 217–30.

PRAHL, AUGUSTUS J.

CD186 Murphy, Charles D. "Augustus J. Prahl: 1901–1970." *The Report of the Soc. for the Hist. of the Germans in Md.*, vol. 35 (1972), 9–15.

PREITZ, MAX

CD187 Schröder, Walter Johannes. "Eine 'Deutsche Sommerschule' in den Vereinigten Staaten. Max Preitz zum 80. Geburtstag." *Muttersprache*, vol. 75, no. 12 (1965), 360–65.

PRICE, LAWRENCE MARSDEN

CD188 *In Honorem Lawrence Marsden Price.* Berkeley: Univ. of California Pr., 1952. Calif. Univ. Publs. in Modern Philology. 454p. Rev. by E. Feise, *Mod. Lang. Notes*, vol. 69 (1954), 616–18; F. Reichmann, *William and Mary Quar.*, vol. 11 (1954), 152–54.

PROKOSCH, EDUARD

CD189 Penzl, Herbert. "Eduard Prokosch und die amerikanische Sprachwissenschaft." In: *Österreich und die angelsächsische Welt. Kulturbegeg-*

Germanistic Scholars and Teachers in America (cont.)

nungen und Vergleiche. Ed. Otto Hietsch. Wien: Braumüller, 1961, p.217–22.

PURIN, CHARLES M.

CD190 "Charles M. Purin, In memoriam." *Monatshefte*, vol. 49 (1957), 279–50. Professor of German, Milwaukee.

REHDER, HELMUT

CD191 Jennings, Lee B., and G. Schulz-Behrend, eds. *Vistas and Vectors. A Volume Honoring the Memory of Helmut Rehder*. Austin: Dept. of Germanic Languages, Univ. of Texas, 1977. Helmut Rehder, b. Bergedorf-Hamburg, d. Austin, Texas. Incl. "Bibliography of Helmut Rehder."

CD192 Lehmann, W. P., J. Christopher Middleton, and W. Gordon Whaley. *In Memoriam Helmut Rehder*. Austin: Univ. of Texas Pr., 1977. 17p. Incl. Bibliography of the writings.

REICHERT, HERBERT W.

CD193 Mews, Siegfried. "In Memoriam. Herbert W. Reichert (1917–1978)." *German Quar.*, vol. 51 (1978), 278.

CD194 Reichmann, Felix. Papers, 1951–1965. 2 ft. In Cornell Univ. Libraries, Collection of Regional History and University Archives (MS 71-1628). Asst. Director of Cornell Univ. Libraries; correspondence, reports on library matters, research notes, misc. papers.

ROEDDER, ERWIN CARL

CD195 Herwig, John. "Erwin Carl Roedder (1873–1945)." In: *U S A und Baden-Württemberg in ihren geschichtlichen Beziehungen*. Ed. G. Haselier. Stuttgart: n.p., 1976, p.95–97.

CD196 Liptzin, Sol. "Edwin Carl Roedder at Seventy." *Monatshefte für deut. Unterricht*, vol. 35 (1943), 97–100.

CD197 Whyte, John. "Edwin C. Roedder—In memoriam." *Amer.-German Rev.*, vol. 12, no. 2 (1945), 35, 37.

ROELKER, BERNARD

CD198 Roelker, Bernard. Papers. Ca. 50 items. In Harvard University Archives. (MS 76 2002). R. (1816–1888) was teacher of German at Harvard.

ROESELER, ROBERT OSWALD

CD199 "In Memoriam: Robert Oswald Roeseler, 1882–1971." *Monatshefte*, vol. 64 (Spring 1972), no. 1, 1.

RUEBNER, MAURICE

CD200 Ward, Robert E. "Maurice Ruebner in Memoriam." *German-Amer. Studies*, vol. 5 (1972), 202.

SALINGER, HERMAN

CD201 Phelps, Leland R., and A. Tilo Alt, eds. *Creative Encounter—Festschrift for Herman Salinger*. Chapel Hill: University of N. Car. Pr., 1978. Incl. "The Publications of Herman Salinger."

SAPIR, EDWARD

CD202 C. E. Voegelin. "Edward Sapir (1884–1939)." In: *Portraits of Linguists...* Ed. Thomas A. Sebeok. 2 vols. Bloomington: Indiana Univ. Press, 1966. Vol. 1, p.489–92.

SCHERER, GEORGE A. C.

CD203 "George A. C. Scherer 1912–1966." and "In Memory of George A. C. Scherer." *German Quar.*, vol. 39 (1966), 287–88.

SCHINNERER, OTTO PAUL

CD204 Robert H. Fife, "Otto Paul Schinnerer (1890–1942). In memoriam." *Germanic Rev.*, vol. 17 (1942), 312–14. *See also* obit. in *Monatshefte für deutschen Unterricht*, vol. 34 (1942), 436.

SCHIROKAUER, ARNO

CD205 McClain, William. "Arno Schirokauer, In memoriam..." *Monatshefte*, vol. 46 (1954), 346–47.

CD206 Stammler, Wolfgang. "Arno C. Schirokauer." *Mod. Lang. Notes*, vol. 71 (1956) 1–4.

CD207 Strich, Fritz, ed. *Arno Schirokauer*. Germanistische Studien. Hamburg: Hauswedell, 1957. 451p. Rev. by H. S. Schultz, *Mod. Philology*, vol. 58 (1960), 119.

CD208 Werbow, Stanley N. "Arno C. Schirokauer." *Report of the Soc. for the Hist. of the Germans in Md.*, vol. 29 (1956), 73–75. Professor of Germanic philology at the Johns Hopkins Univ., 1899–1954.

SCHREIBER, KARL FREDERICK

CD209 Bluhm, Heinz. "In memoriam Karl Frederick Schreiber, March 21, 1886–March 2, 1960." *Monatshefte*, vol. 52 (1960), 194–95.

SCHUMANN, DETLEV W.

CD210 Schmitt, Albert R., ed. *Festschrift für Detlev W. Schumann zum 70. Geburtstag.* München: Delp, 1970. Incl. "Bibliographie der Veröffentlichungen und Rezensionen von Detlev W. Schumann."

SEHRT, HENRY EDWARD

CD211 Raven, Frithjof A., and James C. King, eds. *Germanic Studies in Honor of Henry Edward Sehrt, Presented by His Colleagues, Students, and Friends on the Occasion of His Eightieth Birthday, March 3, 1968.* N.p.: Miami Univ. Pr., 1968. 264p.

SEIDLIN, OSKAR

CD212 Gillespie, Gerald, and Linda Gillespie DeMichiel. "Die Schriften Oskar Seidlins." In: *Herkommen und Erneuerung: Essays für Oskar Seidlin.* Ed. Gerald Gillespie and Edgar Lohnes. Tübingen: Niemeyer, 1976, p.415–26.

SENN, ALFRED

CD213 Benson, Morton. "In memoriam Alfred Senn (1899–1967)." *German Quar.*, vol. 51, no. 3 (May 1978), 425.

CD214 Benson, Morton. "In Memoriam. Alfred Senn." *Names*, vol. 26, no. 3 (September 1978), 285–86.

CD215 Senn, Alfred. *Aus meinem Leben.* Bala-Cynwyd, Pa.: n.p., 1952. 50p.

SINGER, SAMUEL

CD216 Schirokauer, Arno, and Wolfgang Paulsen, eds. *Corona. Studies in Celebration of the Eightieth Birthday of Samuel Singer.* Durham: Duke Univ. Pr., 1941. 282p. Rev. by N. E. Eliason, *Southern Folklore Quar.*, vol. 6 (1942), 69–70; H. W. Pfund, *Amer.-German Rev.*, vol. 7, no. 6 (1941), 35.

SPERBER, HANS

CD217 Fleischhauer, Wolfgang. "Hans Sperber 1885–1963." *Monatshefte*, vol. 56 (1964), no. 3, 107–10. Professor of German and Linguistics at Ohio State Univ.; came to America from Austria in 1934. See also the appreciation by Fleischhauer in the *Zeitschrift für deutsche Philologie*, 1965.

SPITZER, LEO

CD218 M[alkiel], Y[akov.] "Leo Spitzer (1887–1960)." In: *Portraits of Linguists. A Biographical Source Book for the History of Western Linguists 1746–1963.* Ed. Thomas A. Sebeok. 2 vols. Bloomington: Indiana Univ. Pr., 1966. Vol. 1, p.522–25.

CD219 Wellek, René. "Leo Spitzer (1887–1960)." *Compar. Lit.* vol. 12 (1960), 310–34. Memoir and bibliography of the German-born scholar and critic.

SPOHR, CARL W.

CD220 Ward, Robert E. "Carl W. Spohr In Memoriam." *German-Amer. Studies*, vol. 5 (1972), 197.

STARCK, TAYLOR

CD221 Betz, Werner, Evelyn S. Coleman, and Kenneth Northcott, eds. *Taylor Starck Festschrift.* London/The Hague: Mouton, 1964. 276p.

STEIN, JACK MADISON

CD222 Hatfield, Henry. "[Jack Madison Stein.] In Memoriam." *German Quar.*, vol. 53 (May 1977), 393–94; incl. Guy Stern. "Memories of Jack Stein," 394–95.

STRODTMANN, ADOLF

CD223 Timpe, Eugene F. "Adolf Strodtmann: Eine verspätete Anerkennung." *Zeitschrift für Kulturaustausch*, vol. 21, no. 3 (1971), 26–27.

TAYLOR, ARCHER

CD224 Arlt, Gustave O. "Archer Taylor." *Humaniora*, no. 11 (1960), 1–7.

CD225 Hand, Wayland D. "Archer Taylor (1890–1973)." *Jour. of Amer. Folklore*, vol. 87, no. 343 (January–March 1974), 3–9. Archer Taylor Memorial Issue.

CD226 Lee, Hector H. "Archer Taylor 1890–1973." *Western Folklore*, vol. 32 (1973), 262–64.

CD227 Loomis, C. Grant. "Bibliography of the Writings of Archer Taylor." *Humaniora*, no. 11 (1960), 356–74.

CD228 Pargellis, Stanley. "A(rcher) T(aylor): Friend of Libraries." *Humaniora*, no. 11 (1960), 97–101.

CD229 Taylor, Archer. *Selected Writings on Proverbs*. Ed. Wolfgang Mieder. Helsinki: Suomalainen Tiedeakatemia, 1975. 203p. Incl. "Bibliography of Archer Taylor's Proverb Studies," p. 195–203.

CD230 Ward, D[onald]. "Archer Taylor 1890–1973." *Fabula*, vol. 15 (1974), 124–27. Obituary.

THAU, KARL

CD231 "Karl Thau In Memoriam." *Report of the Soc. for the Hist. of the Germans in Md.*, vol. 32 (1966), 73. Co-founder of German-American societies in Baltimore.

URZIDIL, GERTRUDE

CD232 Niers, Gerd. "In Memoriam Gertrude Urzidil." *Jour. for German-Amer. Studies*, vol. 12, no. 4 (Winter 1977), 107.

VAIL, CURTIS C. D.

CD233 "Curtis C. D. Vail, In memoriam." *Mod. Lang. Quar.*, vol. 18 (1957), 177–82; *PMLA*, vol. 72 (1957), no. 5, 1; *Amer.-German Rev.*, vol. 24, no. 2 (1957), 32. Chairman, Dept. of German, Univ. of Washington, 1903–1957.

CD234 Rey, W. H. "Curtis C. D. Vail in Erinnerung." *German Quar.*, vol. 31 (1958), 1–3.

VIËTOR, KARL

CD235 Atkins, Stuart P. "Karl Viëtor, November 29, 1892–June 7, 1951." *Germanic Rev.*, vol. 26 (1951), 171–72.

CD236 "Karl Viëtor." *Amer.-German Rev.*, vol. 17, no. 6 (1951), 34.

CD237 Schneider, Heinrich. "Karl Viëtor: In Memoriam." *Monatshefte*, vol. 43 (1951), 341–44.

VOIGT, FRIEDA

CD238 Ward, Robert E. "Frieda Voigt in Memoriam." *German-Amer. Studies*, vol. 7 (1974), 3–4.

WALTHER, HUGO J.

CD239 Rosenberg, Ralph P. "The First American Doctorate in German Literature." *Amer.-German Rev.*, vol. 21 (1955), no. 3, 34. Hugo J. Walther's degree at Columbia University, 1886.

CD240 Rosenberg, Ralph P. "Hugo Julius Walther." *Germanic Rev.*, vol. 29 (1954), 224–29.

WALZ, JOHN ALBERT

CD241 B., H. "John Albrecht Walz, In Memoriam." *Monatshefte*, vol. 46 (1954), 390.

CD242 Nolte, Fred O., H. W. Pfund, and George J. Metcalf, eds. *Studies in Honor of John Albrecht Walz*. Lancaster: Lanc. Pr., 1941. 335p. Rev. by A. E. Zucker, *Amer.-German Rev.*, vol. 8, no. 4 (1942), 35–36; E. H. Sehrt, *Mod. Lang. Notes*, vol. 58 (1943), 308–10.

WARD (WARD-LEYERLE), ROBERT

CD243 Tolzmann, Don H. "Dr. Robert Ward-Leyerle und das Deutsch-Amerikanertum." *Der Milwaukee Herold*, 1 November 1973.

WARFEL, HARRY R.

CD244 Deakin, Motley, and Peter Lisca, eds. *From Irving to Steinbeck: Studies of American Literature in Honor of Harry R. Warfel*. Gainesville: Univ. of Florida Pr., 1972. 140p. See "An Appreciation," p. 3–10, by M. Deakin and Alfred Reid.

WEBER, BETTE NANCE

CD245 Wetzels, Walter D. "In memoriam Betty Nance Weber (1943–1979)." *German Quar.*, vol. 52, no. 4 (November 1979), 526. A member of the Dept. of Germanic Languages at the Univ. of Texas, Austin, 1972–1979.

WEIGAND, HERMANN

CD246 Faber du Four, Curt v. "Rede zu Hermann Weigands 65. Geburtstag." *Monatshefte*, vol. 50 (1958), 86–90.

CD247 "Hermann Weigand Honored." *Monatshefte*, vol. 60 (1968), 44. Recipient of the Knight Commander's Cross of the German Order of Merit.

WERNAER, ROBERT MAXIMILIAN

CD248 Wernaer, Robert Maximilian. Papers, 1912–1949. 2 ft. In Harvard University Archives (MS 76-2029). Teacher of German at Harvard: correspondence, mss., notes.

WHYTE, JOHN

CD249 Coogan, Daniel F. "In memoriam John Whyte 1887–1952." *Monatshefte*, vol. 44 (1952), 303–04.

CD250 Gaede, William R., and Daniel Coogan. *John Whyte—His Life and Thought*. Brooklyn: Brooklyn College Pr., 1954. 183p. Rev. in *Amer.-German Rev.*, vol. 21, no. 1 (1954), 37.

CD251 Taub, L. Leo. "John Whyte in memoriam." *German Quar.*, vol. 25 (1952), 255–57.

WOLFF, HANS M.

CD252 Guthke, Karl S. "Hans M. Wolff. Statt eines Nachrufs." *Monatshefte*, vol. 51 (1959), 193–96. Germanist at the Univ. of California; with a list of publications.

WOODS, BARBARA ALLEN

CD253 Dornberg, Otto. "In memoriam Barbara Allen Woods (1928–1978)." *German Quar.*, vol. 52, no. 1 (January 1979), 155. Professor of German at the Univ. of Rhode Island, 1957 to 1978.

WOOLEY, E. O.

CD254 Wooley, E. O. "Five Decades of German Instruction in America." *Monatshefte für deut. Unterricht*, vol. 36, no. 7 (1944), 359–70. Reminiscences of a teacher.

ZEYDEL, EDWIN H.

CD255 Slessarev, Helga. "In Memoriam—Edwin H. Zeydel." *Monatshefte*, vol. 66 (1975), 152.

ZIEGLSCHMID, A. J. F.

CD256 Friedmann, Robert. "A. J. F. Zieglschmid, an Obituary." *Mennonite Quar. Rev.*, vol. 24 (1950), 364–65.

ZUCKER, A. E.

CD257 Knoche, Walter, and Klaus Wust. "A. E. Zucker (1890–1971)." *The Report (Soc. for the Hist. of the Germans in Md.*, vol. 35 (1972), 16–18.

CE
German-American Literary Relations—General

Library Holdings and Special Collections

See also Appendix.

CE1 Bircher, Martin. "Deutsche Barock-Literatur: Die Sammlung Harold Jantz in Baltimore." *Philobiblon*, vol. 19 (1975), 101–26. Collection of Baroque literature in the Library of The Johns Hopkins University, Baltimore.

CE2 Bluhm, Heinz. "Scope and Significance of the *Newberry Goetheana*." *German Quar.*, vol. 37, no. 3 (1964) 230–38. In Chicago.

CE3 Broch, Hermann. Materials. In Yale Univ. Library. Incl. a carbon copy of TS. of *Der Tod des Vergil* (1945). Letters addresses to Gertrude Geiringer by Broch; TS. of poem by Broch. Correspondence exchanged between Hermann Broch de Rottermann and Franziska Broch, Manfred Durzak and Bertold Hack.

CE4 "Collection of German-Americana Established." *Candid Campus* (Univ. of Cincinnati), 29 May 1974; "The University of Cincinnati is Celebrating." *LJ/SLJ Hotline*, 17 June 1974. The Heinrich H. Fick Collection of German-Americana, University of Cincinnati Main Library.

CE5 Committee on Manuscript Holdings, American Literature Group, Modern Language Association of America, comp. and ed. *American Literary Manuscripts: A Checklist of Holdings in Academic, Historical and Public Libraries in the United States*. Austin: Univ. of Texas Pr., 1961. 421p.

CE6 Conard, Robert C, "Report on the Böll Archive at the Boston University Library." *Univ. of Dayton Rev.*, vol. 10 (1973), no. 2, 11–14. A collection of 165 large MS. boxes containing published and unpublished MSS. of Böll became available to the public at Boston Univ. Library.

CE7 Faber du Faur, Curt von. *German Baroque Literature. A Catalogue of the Collection in the Yale University Library.* New Haven: Yale Univ. Pr., 1958. 496p. Rev. by A. G. de Capua, *Monatshefte*, vol. 51 (1959), 211–13; Stuart Atkins, *German Quar.*, vol. 32 (1959), 174–75; G. Schulz-Behrend, *Mod. Lang. Quar.*, vol. 20 (1959), 202–04; Archer Taylor, *Library Quar.*, vol. 29 (1959), 57–59; C.K. Pott, *Publs., Bibliographic Soc. of America*, vol. 54 (1960), no. 1, 71–74.

CE8 Faber du Four, Curt von. *German Baroque Literature: A Catalogue of the Collection in the Yale University Library.* Vol. 2. New Haven: Yale Univ. Pr., 1969, 185p. The 2nd vol. adds some 550 titles acquired since 1958.

CE9 Faber du Faur, Curt von. "Modern German Literature in Letters to Kurt Wolff." *Yale Univ. Library Gazette*, vol. 23 (1948), 25–29.

CE10 Gehman, Sander L. "The Wilhelm Scherer Library: A Bibliography of the Works Printed Prior to 1700." *Archiv*, vol. 206 (1970), 433–46. In the holdings of Case Western Reserve University, Cleveland.

CE11 *German Baroque Literature: A Descriptive Catalogue of the Collection of Harold Jantz and a Guide to the Collection on Microfilm.* 2 vols. New Haven: Research Publications, 1974. 550p.

CE12 Grossman, Kurt Richard. Papers, 1938–1966. Ca. 10 ft. In Leo Baeck Institute, New York City (MS 75-713). Correspondence, MSS., source and research material, memos and printed matter of the political journalist and author. Correspondents include Einstein, Th. Mann, Ernst Toller, Veit Valentin, and Stephen Wise.

CE13 Grossman, Walter. "The Gillman-Harvard Manuscript of Schiller's *Wallensteins Tod*." *Harvard Library Bull.*, vol. 11, no. 3 (Autumn 1957), 319–45. Provenience and description of the MS; list of variants from the standard text.

CE14 ["Gutzkow Papers."] *Ex Libris* (Johns Hopkins Univ.), vol. 18, no. 1 (September 1963). Received by the univ. from William Kurrelmeyer, a collection of books and MSS., incl. 1600 letters by notable German writes. Of these, 224 were written by Karl Gutzkow to his publisher.

CE15 Heuser, F. W. J. *First Editions of the German Romantic Period.* New York: Modern Language Association, 1942. Rev. by W. Kurrelmeyer, *Mod. Lang. Notes*, vol. 58, no. 4 (1943), 328.

CE16 Hirschfeld, Kurt. Papers. Ca. 6 ft. In Leo Baeck Institute Collections, New York City (MS 75-714). Dramaturge and theater director of Germany and Switzerland; correspondence, notes, misc. papers and research material, chiefly relating to the theater. MSS. of Max Frisch, E. E. Kisch, Ernst Wiechert and Carl Zuckmayer; correspondents incl. Albert Bassermann, Max Brod, E. Piscator, Carl Zuckmayer.

CE17 *The Hofmannsthal Collection in the Houghton Library: A Descriptive Catalogue of Printed Books.* Prep. by James E. Walsh. Heidelberg: L. Stiehm, 1974. 250p. The catalogue lists 774 items of Hofmannsthal materials which had been removed from Austria to America in 1938 and later acquired by the Houghton Library. Catalogue includes 10 facsimiles. Rev. by Ilsedore B. Jonas, *Mod. Lang. Notes*, vol. 93, no. 3 (April 1978), 534–37.

CE18 Huebsch, Benjamin W. Papers, 1893–1964. 10,515 items. In the MS. Division, Library of Congress (MS 66-1421). New York publisher, 1876–1964; correspondence, literary MSS., Incl. materials of Werfel, Dorothea Angermann, Peter Brauer, G. Hauptmann, Stefan Zweig.

CE19 Jonas, Klaus W. "Mein Weg zu Thomas Mann: Aus den Erinnerungen eines Sammlers und Bibliographen." *Börsenblatt für den Deutschen Buchhandel*, vol. 31 (26 September 1975), p. 285–95.

CE20 Jonas, Klaus W. "Thomas Mann-Archive und -Sammlungen in Amerika." In: *Thomas Mann, 1875–1975: Vorträge in München—Zürich—Lübeck.* Ed. B. Bludau, H. Eckhard, and H. Koopmann. Frankfurt: Fischer Vlg., 1977, p. 534–43.

CE21 Kahler, Erich. Papers, 1910–1970. In the Leo Baeck Institute, New York City (MS 72-232). Cultural historian, sociologist and educator. MSS. of writings on the Jews in Germany; correspondence, 1910–1931 between K. and Friedrich Gundolf; letters from Richard Beer-Hofman, Hermann Broch, Martin Buber, Albert Einstein and others. Gift of Mr. and Mrs. Kahler.

CE22 Kersten, Kurt. Papers, 1940–1958. Ca. 2 ft. In Leo Baeck Institute collections, New York City (MS 75-716). Journalist and political publicist of Germany and New York. Misc. papers, research materials and notes. Correspondents incl. Julius Bab, Lion Feuchtwanger, O. M. Graf, Kurt Hiller, Theodor Heuss, Erika Mann, Anna Seghers, and many others.

CE23 Klarmann, Adolf, and Rudolf Hirsch. "A Note on the Alma Mahler Werfel Collection." *Library Chronicle* (Univ. of Pennsylvania), vol. 35 (1969), 33–35. A collection of 5,000 items acquired by the Univ. of Pa. library.

CE24 Kobler, Franz. Papers, 1933–1971. Ca. 7 ft. In Leo Baeck Institute, New York (MS 75-718). Lawyer and historian of Vienna, London, and Berkeley. Misc. notes, MSS., research materials and correspondence. Correspondents incl. Else Lasker-Schüler, Ernst Lissauer. Some writings on the Stefan George Kreis, as well as on Jewish history.

CE25 Kopp, W. La Marr. "The Allison-Shelley Collection of Anglica-Americana Germanica." In: *Germanica Americana 1976: Symposium on German-American Literature*. Ed. Erich A. Albrecht and J. Anthony Burzle. Lawrence: Max Kade Document and Research Center, Univ. of Kansas, 1977, p.1–5.

CE26 Lazarus, Emma. Correspondence 1868–1887. 86 items. In Columbia University Library (MS 62–237).

CE27 Lindau, Paul. Papers, 1867–1930. In Leo Baeck Institute collections, New York City (MS 75-721). Misc. papers and correspondence of German theater critic, playwright and stage director. Incl. letters of Julius Bauer, Udo Brachvogel, Stefan Grossman, Rudolf Mosse, Leopold Sonnemann, and Theodor Wolf.

CE28 Loewenberg, Jakob. Papers, 1876–1964. In Leo Baeck Institute, New York City (MS 75-723). In part microfilmed letters of the poet Detlev Liliencron in the Library of the State University, Hamburg. Correspondence of Loewenberg, German author and teacher, with R. Dehmel, Gustav Falke, Gustav Karpeles, Liliencron and Meier Spanier. Also misc. diaries, papers, and memorabilia.

CE29 Müller, F. Max. Papers. 67 items. In Univ. of Oregon Library (MS 60-416). Student of linguistics and oriental antiquities (1823–1900). Incl. letters to Moncure Conway 1872–1901.

CE30 Phelps, Leland R., ed. *The Harold Jantz Collection: Proceedings of a Sponsored Conference to Introduce the Collection to Specialists in German-American Literary Relations*. Durham: Duke Univ. Center for International Studies, 1981. 145p.

CE31 Polzer, Victor. Papers, 1899–1965. Ca. 300 items. In: Leo Baeck Institute New York City (MS 75-725). Journalist, editor and translator of Vienna and New York City. Misc. papers and correspondence in German and English. Correspondents incl. Hermann Broch and Thomas Mann.

CE32 Roth, Joseph. Papers. Ca. 2 ft. In Leo Baeck Institute, New York City (MS 72-236). Austrian journalist and author; extensive correspondence 1906–1939; personal papers; documents; misc. memorabilia; film about Roth.

CE33 Sahlin, Nils G. "The *Faust* Puppet Play Manuscripts in the William A. Speck Collection of Goetheana, Yale University." Diss., Yale, 1972.

CE34 Salm, Peter. "Die Scherer-Bibliothek. In Cleveland wiedergefunden." *Frankfurter Allegemeine Zeitung* 18 September 1965. Wilhelm Scherer Collection, Case Western Reserve Univ.

CE35 Sammons, Christa. "Faust at Yale." *Yale Univ. Library Gazette*, vol. 53 (1978), 150–58.

CE36 Sammons, Christa, and Richard E. Schade. "Yale University's Faber du Faur Collection: 20 Years After." *Wolfenbütteler Barock-Nachrichten*, vol. 5 (1978), 175–76. See also Faber du Faur's *German Baroque Literature*.

CE37 "Scherer Collection Displayed in Showcase at Freiberger [Library]." [Western] *Reserve Tribune* (Cleveland), 4 November 1965. Library of famous 19th-century literary historian Wilhelm Scherer had been acquired by Western Reserve University in 1887.

CE38 Schoenberner, Franz. Papers, 1899–1968. In Hoover Institution, Stanford California (MS 75-672). German author and editor. Misc. writings pertinent to intellectual history and political history of the 20th century.

CE39 Schwarzschild, Leopold. Papers, 1933–1962. Ca. 7 ft. In Leo Baeck Institute, New York City (MS 72-237). Political publicist, economist,

Library Holdings and Special Collections (cont.)

and journalist of Germany and New York, Leopold Schwarzschild. Incl. MSS., research materials, personal papers, etc., and correspondence with such figures as Bruno Frank, Hermann Kesten, Alfred Polgar, Franz Werfel and Carl Zuckmayer.

CE40 Schweitzer, Christoph E. "Deutsche Dichterhandschriften in der Historical Society of Pennsylvania." *Jahrbuch der deutschen Schillergesellschaft*, vol. 8 (1964), 344–81.

CE41 *A Select Assembly of Notable Books and Manuscripts from the Allison-Shelley Collection of Anglica Americana Germanica*. Forew. Philip A. Shelley. University Park: Penn. State Univ. 1972. 107p. Catalog of an exhibition of a distinguished collection of English translations of German writings, presented by Philip Allison Shelley to the Pattee Library of The Pennsylvania State Univ. Libraries.

CE42 Ward, Robert E. "Eine Bibliographie deutschamerikanischer Originalwerke im Besitz der Deutschen Gesellschaft von Pennsylvanien." *German-Amer. Studies*, vol. 1, no. 1 (1969), 33–48.

CE43 Ward, Robert E. "The German-American Library of H. H. Fick: A Rediscovery." *German-Amer. Studies*, vol. 1, no. 1 (1969), 49–68; vol. 2, no. 1, 2–29.

CE44 Yale University Library. *Junges Deutschland*. Journal published between 1843 and 1849. First, original ed. by J. H. Detmold, F. Dingelstedt, F. Freiligrath, George Herwegh and W. Weitling. Purchased for library from Associates' and Harper Funds.

Bibliographies and Sources

CE45 Albrecht, Erich A., comp., with the assistance of Hildegard Pross. *Grundriss zur Geschichte der deutschen Dichtung aus den Quellen von Karl Goedeke*. Band 15. 4. Teil: *Nordamerika (USA)*, Berlin: Akademie-Vlg, 1964. p.518–661. Thorough presentation of writings in German by American and German-American authors in the first third of the 19th century.

CE46 "American Bibliography." Annually in the April supplement of *PMLA*. Since 1966—for the year 1965—continued as the *MLA International Bibliography* (see entry **CE75**).

CE47 "Anglo-German Literary Bibliography." Annually in July issue of the *Jour. of Engl. and Germanic Philology*. Ed. John R. Frey. Lists publications dealing with the literary relations between England, the U.S. and Canada, and Germany. Includes reviews.

CE48 "Articles on American Literature Appearing in Current Periodicals." *Research in Progress*. Published issue by issue (and later in a single annual list) in *Amer. Lit.*, vol. 1., 1920–.

CE49 *Auslanddeutschtum und Dichtung*. Sonderheft der Halbmonatsschrift des Deutschen Ausland-Instituts in Stuttgart *Der Auslandsdeutsche* (Stuttgart), vol. 12, no. 2 (1929).

CE50 *Autobiographien*. Hrsg. vom International P.E.N.–Zentrum deutschsprachiger Autoren im Ausland. London: n.p., 1970.

CE51 Baldensperger, F., and W. P. Friedrich. *Bibliography of Comparative Literature*. Chapel Hill: Univ. of N. Car. Pr., 1950. 701p. With a apter on "German Influence upon America," p.621–22.

CE52 Bateson, F. W., ed. *The Cambridge Bibliography of English Literature*. New York: Macmillan, 1941–1957. 3 vols. "Literary Relations with Germany." Vol. 1, p.54f.; vol. 2, p.50f.; vol. 3, p.26f.

CE53 Bergstraesser, Arnold, ed. *Deutsche Beiträge zur geistigen Überlieferung*. Chicago: Henry Regnery. Vol. 1–, 1947–.

CE54 "Bibliography of Comparative Literature (YCGL)." Annually. Vol. 1–, 1952–. Vols. 1–9 issued as the *Univ. of N. Car. Studies in Compar. Lit.* Vols. for 1952–1960 publ. by the Univ. of N. Car. Pr. Since 1960 publ. at Bloomington by Indiana Univ.

CE55 Cardinal, Clive H. von. "A Preliminary Check List of Studies on German-Canadian Creative Literature. Part 1. General Studies. Part 2. Specific Studies." *Canad. Ethnic Studies* vol. 1, no. 1 (April 1969); vol. 2, no. 1 (June 1970).

CE56 "Contemporary American Literature: A Checklist of Recent German Publications in American Studies." *Amer. Studies Internat.*, vol. 16, no. 2 (1977), 36–46.

CE57 Dobert, Eitel Wolf. *Deutsche Demokraten, die Achtundvierziger und ihre Schriften.* Göttingen: n.p., 1958. Based on a diss., Maryland, 1955.

CE58 Fittbogen, Gottfried. "Die Dichtung der Auslandsdeutschen." *Deutsches Volkstum*, vol. 2 (1929), 826–31.

CE59 Fittbogen, Gottfried. "Volkstum und Dichtung, insbesondere bei den Auslandsdeutschen." *Monatschrift für höhere Schulen*, vol. 36 (1937), 321–33.

CE60 "Franco-German Studies: A Current Bibliography." Annually in *Bull. of Bibliography and Dramatic Index* (Boston: F. W. Faxon Co.). First and second installments in *Romanic Rev.*, vol. 36, no 3 (1945), 191–199 and vol. 37, no. 4 (1946), 346–348.

CE61 Gieselberg, Margarita. "Beiträge zum Thema 'Deutsche im Ausland,' in der *Zeitung für Kulturaustausch* 1951–1967... Bibliographie." *Zeitschrift für Kulturaustausch*, vol. 18 (1968), 41–46.

CE62 Gilby, William K. "Imprints of German-Canadian Creative Literature: First Supplement." *Canad. Ethnic Studies*, vol. 5, nos. 1–2 (1973), 85–90.

CE63 Grossberg, Mimi, ed. *Österreichische Autoren in Amerika. Geschick und Leistung der österreichischen literarischen Emigration in den Vereinigten Staaten.* Ausstellungs-Katalog mit bio-bibliografischen Notizen. Wien: n.p., c. 1970. Exhibition catalogue.

CE64 Hendrick, George. "American Literary Manuscripts in Continental Libraries." *Bull. of Bibliography*, vol. 25 (May–August 1967), 49–58. On the principal MS. collections in European libraries.

CE65 Hill, Ruth A., and Elsa de Bondell. *Children's Books from Foreign Languages: English Translations from Published and Unpublished Sources.* New York: H. W. Wilson for the Amer. Library Assoc., 1937.

CE66 House, Roy Temple. "*Books Abroad* at Twenty-Five." *Amer.-German Rev.*, vol. 19, no. 1 (1952), 14–15.

CE67 Jakobsh, Frank K. "German and German-Canadian Literature as Contained in the *Berliner Journal*." *German-Canad. Yearbook*, vol. 5 (1979), 108–20.

CE68 Kindermann, Heinz. "Auslandsdeutsche Dichtung. Eine neue Sammelaufgabe des Deutschen Ausland-Instituts in Stuttgart." *Der Auslanddeutsche*, vol. 18 (1935), 562–67.

CE69 Kirkham, E. Bruce, and John W. Fink, comps. *Indices to American Literary Annuals and Gift Books 1825–1865.* New Haven: Research Publications, 1975. 628p. Bibliographical information about and contents of 469 works; with indexes.

CE70 Klein, Karl K. "Auslanddeutsches Schrifttum." In: *Reallexikon der deutschen Literaturgeschichte.* Ed. Paul Merker and W. Stammler. Berlin: n.p., 1931, vol. 4, p.1–11.

CE71 Klein, Karl K. *Literaturgeschichte des Deutschtums im Ausland: Schrifttum und Geistesleben der deutschen Volksgruppen im Ausland vom Mittelalter bis zur Gegenwart.* Rev. ed. incl. bibliography by Alexander Ritter. Hildesheim: Olms, 1979. 494p. Rev. *New Yorker Staats-Zeitung und Herold*, vol. 146, no. 4 (1980), Sec. B, 7. The section on "Bibliographie 1945–1978. Vereinigte Staaten von Amerika" was contributed by Don Heinrich Tolzmann. The work as a whole includes extensive discussions of the Pennsylvania sectarians and pietists, Pennsylvania German writings in general and German writings in the U.S. and Canada.

CE72 Klippenstein, Lawrence. "Canadian Mennonite Writings: A Bibliographical Survey, 1970–1980.". *German-Canad. Yearbook*, vol. 6 (1981), 284-93.

CE73 *Lyrica Germanica: A Journal for German Lyric Poetry.* Ed. John Fitzell. Twice a Year. Vol. 1–, ca. 1974–1977. The editor: 46 Ridgeview Road, Jamesburg, N.J. 08831. For original German lyric poetry and translations into English of German poetry written before 1880.

CE74 *Mitteilungsblatt* of the Association of German Language Authors in America (AGLAA). 3 issues yearly. Don Heinrich Tolzmann, Pres. 2545 Harrison Ave., Cincinnati. Founded 1974.

CE75 Modern Language Association of America. *MLA International Bibliography*, 1921–. (Publ. as supplements to *PMLA*, v. 39–.) Annual. Since 1966 (covering 1965) has listed books, articles, and monographs on English, American, Germanic, Romance, Scandinavian, Dutch, Celtic, and East European languages and literatures, linguistics, and folklore.

CE76 Mummendey, Richard. *Language and Literature of the Anglo-Saxon Nations as Presented in German Doctoral Dissertations, 1885–1950. A Bibliography*. Charlottesville, Univ. of Virginia Pr. for the Bibliographical Soc. of America, 1954. 200p. Rev. by C.D.C. Vail, *Mod. Lang. Quar.*, vol. 16 (1955), 281.

CE77 Reding, Josef. "Deutsche Literatur in amerikanischen Dissertationen." *Welt und Wort* (Tübingen), vol. 9, no. 3 (1954), 81–82.

CE78 Ritter, Alexander. "Deutschsprachige Literatur der Gegenwart im Ausland." In: *Deutsche Gegenwartsliteratur*. Ed. Manfred Durzak. Stuttgart: Reclam, 1981, p.632–61.

CE79 Ritter, Alexander. "Literaturwissenschaft und deutschsprachige Literatur des Auslands: Eine Tour d'Horizon zum Forschungsstand." *Deutschkanadisches Jahrbuch*, vol. 4 (1978), 214–24.

CE80 Ritter, Alexander. "Zwischen literarkritischem Vorbehalt und kulturpolitischer Empfindlichkeit: Die deutschsprachige Literatur des Auslands." *Literatur und Kritik* (Wien), vols. 146–147 (ca. 1980), 416–30. Article of the same title in *Germanistische Mitteilungen: Zeitschrift des belgischen Germanisten- und Deutschlehrerverbandes*, vol. 11 (1980), 71–88.

CE81 Roloff, Walter, Morton E. Mix, and Martha Nicolai. *German Literature in British Magazines, 1750–1860*. Ed. B. Q. Morgan and A. R. Hohlfeld. Madison: Univ. of Wisconsin Pr., 1949. 364p. 5500 items in the bibliography, p.128–364.

CE82 Spiller, Robert E., Willard Thorp, Thomas H. Johnson, Henry S. Canby, and Richard M. Ludwig, eds. *Literary History of the United States: Bibliography Supplement II*. New York: Macmillan, 1972. 366p. Pages p.286–91 repr. as "Literary History of the United States. German and Pennsylvania German." *German-Amer. Studies*, vol. 3, no. 1 (1971), 24–28.

CE83 Steiger, Ernst. *Steigers literarischer Monatsbericht*. 2 vols. May 1869–April 1871.

CE84 Suderman, Elmer F. "American Mennonite Fiction: A Contribution toward a Bibliography." *Mennonite Life*, vol. 22 (1967), 131–33.

CE85 Ward, Robert E. "A Bibliography of Works on German-American Literature." Youngstown State Univ., 1970. 28p. Multilithed.

CE86 Ward, Robert E. *Dictionary of German-American Creative Writers from the 17th Century to the Present. Vol. 1. Bibliographical Handbook*. Cleveland: German-Amer. Publ., 1978. 76p.

CE87 Willibrand, W. A. "On the 25th Anniversary of *Books Abroad*." *German Quar.*, vol. 25, no. 4 (1952), 239–42.

CE88 Wirth, Albrecht: "Deutsche überseeische Literatur." *Internationale Literaturberichte*, vol. 4 (1897), 97, 117.

CE89 Zenker, E., comp. *Veröffentlichungen deutscher sozialistischer Schriftsteller der revolutionären und demokratischen Presse 1918–1945. Bibliographie*. Berlin: n.p., 1966.

Translation: Issues and Problems

CE90 Adler, Jeremy. "Rilke auf Englisch: Zu einigen Übersetzungen der *Duineser Elegien*." *Literatur und Kritik*, no. 128 (1978), 494–500.

CE91 Ball, David. "On Translating Goethe's *Faust*." *Germanic Rev.*, vol. 55 (1980), 27–30.

CE92 Barnstorff, Hermann. "German Literature in Translation Published by *Poet Lore*, 1891–1939." *Mod. Lang. Jour.* vol. 25, no. 9 (1941), 711–15. Lists about 60 titles and authors.

CE93 Barnstorff, Hermann. "Translations and Interpretations of *Faust I*, [lines] 682–683." *Mod. Lang. Notes*, vol. 58, no. 4 (1943), 288–91.

CE94 Bell, Gerda. "Henry von Heiseler as a Translator of English Poetry [into German]." *Monatshefte*, vol. 60, no. 4 (1968), 379–93.

CE95 Briffault, Herman. "The Plight of the Literary Translator, Especially in the U.S.A." *Babel*, vol. 10 (1964), 12–14.

CE96 Brower, Reuben A. *On Translation*. New York: Oxford Univ. Pr., 1966. Repr. of 1959 edition.

CE97 Buehne, S. Z. "Translating Middle High German into Modern English." *Babel*, vol. 10 (1964), 110–13. Hartmann's "Gregorius."

CE98 Burkhard, Arthur. [Rev. of E. H. Zeydel's *Goethe the Lyrist*.] *Yearbook of Compar. and General Literature*, 1956. Translating Goethean lyrics is "a self-defeating task."

CE99 *Chartoteca translationum alphabetica: Internationale Bibliographie der Übersetzungen auf Karteikarten... Zusammengestellt und hrsg. von Hans W. Bentz*. Frankfurt: Bentz, 1957–. Serie I. 1. Übersetzungen deutschsprachiger Autoren ins Englische. Serie VIII. 1. Übersetzungen amerikanischer Autoren ins deutsche.

CE100 Cordasco, Francesco. *The Bohn Libraries. History and Checklist*. New York: Franklin, 1951. 110p. Famous series of the world's classics in English translation.

CE101 Exner, Richard. "On Translating Late Rilke: Remarks on Some Recent Examples." *Chicago Rev.*, vol. 29, no. 3 (1978), 153–61.

CE102 Fairley, Barker. "On Translating *Faust*." *German Life and Letters*, vol. 23 (1969), 54–62.

CE103 Fleischmann, Wolfgang B. "Translation Problems Related to Rendering the Work of Certain Contemporary American Poets into German." *Jahrbuch für Amerikastudien*, vol. 7 (1962), 176–82.

CE104 Frantz, Adolf Ingram. *Half a Hundred Thralls to Faust. British and American Translators 1823–1940*. Chapel Hill: Univ. of N. Car. Pr., 1949. 315p.

CE105 Gittleman, Sol. "American Germans and Edward Fitzgerald's Rubaiyat of Omar Khayyam." *Amer. German Rev.*, vol. 29, no. 1 (1962), 23–24. Among many translations of Omar, that of H. W. Nordmeyer is most successful.

CE106 Gugelberger, Georg M. "Endlessly Describing Novel Experiences: Peter Handke Translations In/and America." *Dimension*, vol. 8, nos. 1–2 (1975), 180–90. How Handke fares at the hands of his translators.

CE107 Hamburger, Michael. "Brief Afterthoughts on Versions of a Poem by Hölderlin ["Hälfte des Lebens."]" *Mod. Poetry in Translation*, nos. 41–42 (March 1981), 33–36.

CE108 Hammer, Carl. "Nineteenth Century German Drama in English." *German Quar.*, vol. 30 (1957), 32–36. A survey of translations published in the United States.

CE109 Handler, Gary. "A Textual Omission in the English Translation of *Der Prozess*." *Mod. Lang. Notes*, vol. 83, no. 3 (1968), 454–56.

CE110 *Index translationum 1932–1938*. Paris: International Institute of Intellectual Cooperation, 1933–1939. *Index translationum*. New Series. Vol. 1–, 1949–. Paris: UNESCO.

CE111 Johnson, E. D. "On Translating Thomas Wolfe." *Amer. Speech*, vol. 32 (1957), 95–101. Compares German, French, Spanish, Norwegian translations of Wolfe's works.

CE112 Ita, J. M. "Note on Willa and Edwin Muir's Translation of Kafka's Novel *Das Schloss—The Castle*." *Ibadan*, vol. 29 (1971), 102–05.

CE113 Jonas, Klaus W. "In Memoriam: Helen T. Lowe-Porter 1876–1963." *Monatshefte*, vol. 55, no. 6 (1963), 322–24. Translator of Thomas Mann.

CE114 Kahl, Günter. "Would + Infinitive Perfekt Aktiv und seine Übersetzung ins Deutsche." *Die neueren Sprachen*, N.F., vol. 14, no. 4 (1965), 426–30.

CE115 Kallos, Alexander. "Twentieth Century German Literature in English." In: *Views and Reviews of Modern German Literature: Festschrift für Adolf D. Klarmann*. Ed. Karl S. Weimar. München: Delp, 1974, p. 277–84.

CE116 Kann, Hans Joachim. *Übersetzungsprobleme in den deutschen Übersetzungen dreier angloamerikanischer Kurzgeschichten: Aldous Huxley: "Green Tunnels"; Ernest Hemingway: "The Killers" und "A Clean, Well-lighted Place."* Mainzer amerikanistische Beiträge, vol. 10. München: Hueber, 1968. 144p. Based on a München Diss., 1968 of same title. Rev. by T. Klimek, *Jahrbuch für Amerikastudien*, vol. 15 (1970), 281–83.

CE117 Knight, Max. "Adventures in Translation." *Amer.-German Rev.*, vol. 34, no. 1 (1967–1968), 24–29. By the translator of Morgenstern and Nestroy.

CE118 Krumpelmann, John T. "Classical German Drama in Recent English Translation." *German Quar.*, vol. 39, no. 1 (January 1966), 77–91.

CE119 Latimer, Renate. "On Translating Stifter's *Nachsommer*." *Mod. Austrian Lit.*, vol. 12, no. 2 (1979), 67–79.

CE120 Lautermilch, Steven. "On Translating Rilke." *Studia Mystica*, vol. 1, no. 4 (1978), 52–55.

CE121 Lewisohn, Ludwig. "Foreword." In: *Thirty-One Poems by Rainer Maria Rilke*. Trans. by L. Lewisohn. New York: n.p., 1946.

CE122 Link, Franz H. "Solange das Sunlicht meiner Raison anhellt: Bemerkungen zu einer neuen deutschen Übersetzung der Werke Edgar Allan Poes." *Neusprachliche Mitteilungen*, vol. 70 (1966), 233–38.

CE123 Longyear, Christopher Rudston. "Linguistically Determined Categories of Meaning: A Comparative Analysis of Meaning in 'The Snows of Kilimanjaro' in English and German." Diss., Michigan, 1961.

CE124 Lowe-Porter, H. T. "Translating Thomas Mann." *Symposium*, vol. 9 (1955), 260–77. Personal experiences in translating Mann.

CE125 McEachran, Frank. "On Translating Nietzsche into English." *Nietzsche Studien: Internationales Jahrbuch für die Nietzsche-Forschung*, 1977, vol. 6, p. 295–99.

CE126 Merkel, Gottfried F., ed. *On Romanticism and the Art of Translation. Studies in Honor of Edwin Hermann Zeydel*. Princeton Univ. Pr. for the Univ. of Cincinnati, 1956. 267p. Rev. in *Amer.-German Rev.*, vol. 22, no. 6 (1956), 38.

CE127 Mönnig, Richard, ed. *Translations from the German; English 1948–1964*. 2nd rev. ed. Bad Godesberg: Inter Nationes; Göttingen: Vandenhoeck and Ruprecht, 1968. 509p. Rev. by M. L. Baeumer, *Monatshefte*, vol. 61 (1969), 210–12. Lists 8300 translations into English and 3500 books on Germany written by English-using authors.

CE128 Morgan, Bayard Quincy. Copies of translations by M. reproduced from TS. on microfilm. In Columbia University Library. Hebbel's *Agnes Bernauer*, *Die Nibelungen*, etc.

CE129 Morgan, Bayard Quincy. *A Critical Bibliography of German Literature in English Translation 1481–1927. Supplement Embracing the Years 1928–1955*. New York/London: Scarecrow Pr., 1965. 2 vols. 690, 901p. Rev. by L. Newman, *Mod. Lang. Rev.*, vol. 61 (1966), 722–24; G. N. Davis, *Mod. Lang. Notes*, vol. 82 (1967), 503–06.

CE130 Morgan, Bayard Quincy. "On Translating Feminine Rhymes." In: *On Romanticism and the Art of Translation. Studies in Honor of Edwin Hermann Zeydel*. Ed. Gottfried F. Merkel. Princeton: Princeton Univ. Pr., 1956, p. 163–69.

CE131 Morgan, Bayard Quincy. "What is Translation For?" *Symposium*, vol. 10 (1956), 322–28. Answer: For the enrichment of our literature and life.

CE132 Muir, Edwin, and Willa Muir. "Translating from the German." In: *On Translation*. Ed. Reuben A. Brower. Cambridge: Harvard Univ. Pr., 1959, p. 93–96.

CE133 Mulholland, Gabrielle. "Some Problems in Translating Grillparzer." *German Life and Letters*, vol. 19 (1966), 178–89. Review of translations by Arthur Burkhard.

CE134 O'Neill, Patrick. *German Literature in English Translation*. Toronto: Univ. of Toronto Pr., 1981. 242p. A select bibliography of German authors available in book form in English, according to the primary criterion of literary excellence.

CE135 Pettegrove, James P. "Einiges über O'Neill—Übersetzungen ins Deutsche." *Maske und Kothurn*, vol. 17 (1971), 40–47.

CE136 Probst, Gerhard F. "Bemerkungen zu H. T. Lowe-Porters englischer Übersetzung von Thomas Manns *Tonio Kröger*." *Germanic Notes*, vol. 7 (1976), 51–53.

CE137 Reichert, Klaus. "Zur Technik des Übersetzens amerikanischer Gedichte." *Sprache im technischen Zeitalter*, no. 21 (1967), 1–16.

CE138 Riedel, Walter E. "A Checklist of Literature Translated from the German and Published in Canada." *German-Canad. Yearbook*, vol. 5 (1979), 283-99.

CE139 Riedel, Walter E. "Some German Ripples of Holden Caulfield's 'Goddam Autobiography': On Translating and Adapting J. D. Salinger's *The Catcher in the Rye*." *Canad. Rev. of Compar. Literature/Revue Canadienne de Littérature Comparée*, vol. 7 (1980), 196-205.

CE140 Sadleir, Michael. *Nineteenth Century Fiction...* London/Constable; Univ. of California, 1951. 2 vols. A bibliography of fiction in translation.

CE141 Salinger, Herman. "On Translating Lyric Poetry." In: *Reality and Creative Vision in German Lyrical Poetry*. Ed. August Closs. London: Butterworths, 1963, p.14-29.

CE142 Sandri-White, Alex. "How to Translate German Slang into American English." *Die lebenden Sprachen*, vol. 9 (September 1964), 66-68.

CE143 Shaw, Frank. "Kommentar zur englischen Übersetzung [von Grass' *Katz und Maus* und *Die Blechtrommel*, by R. Manheim]." *Die lebenden Sprachen*, vol. 12, no. 4-5 (1967), 147-48.

CE144 Sherry, Charles. "Translating Peter Bichsel. Some Remarks." *Dimension*, vol. 10 (1977), 66-73.

CE145 Smith, Murray F. *A Selected Bibliography of German Literature in English Translation, 1956-60: A Second Supplement to Bayard Quincy Morgan's A Critical Bibliography of German Literature in English Translation*. Metuchen: Scarecrow, 1972. 398p.

CE146 Thirlwall, John C. *In Another Language: A Record of the Thirty-Year Relationship Between Thomas Mann and His English Translator, Helen Tracy Lowe-Porter*. New York: Knopf, 1966. 209p. Rev. by R. W. Leonhardt, *N.Y. Times Book Rev.*, 10 July 1966, 1, 52.

CE147 Thomas, J. Wesley. "James Freeman Clarke as a Translator." *Amer.-German Rev.*, vol. 10, no. 2 (1943), 31-33.

CE148 Thomas, J. Wesley. "James Freeman Clarke's Criticism of Margaret Fuller's Translation of *Tasso*." *Monatshefte*, vol. 41, no. 2 (1949), 89-92.

CE149 Upward, C. [Rev. of Uwe Johnson's *Mutmassungen über Jakob*. Trans. into English by Ursula Molinaro. London: Jonathan Cape, 1963.] *Die lebenden Sprachen*, vol. 10, no. 3 (May-June 1965), 84-86. Criticism and close analysis of the translation technique.

CE150 Van Hoof, Henry. *Internationale Bibliographie der Übersetzung. International Bibliography of Translation*. München-Pullach: Vlg. Dokumentation, 1972. 591p.

CE151 Weaver, Warren. *Alice in Many Tongues: The Translations of "Alice in Wonderland."* Madison: Univ. of Wisconsin Pr., 1964. 147p. Rev. by E. L. Bassett, *Mod. Philology*, vol. 63 (1965), 171-75. Incl. examples from and discussion of German translations.

CE152 Weisstein, Ulrich. "Dialect as a Barrier to Translation: The Case of German Literature." *Monatshefte*, vol. 54, no. 5 (1962), 233-43.

CE153 Weisstein, Ulrich. "Recent Translations of Twentieth-Century German Poetry and Drama: A Collective Review." *German Quar.*, vol. 37, no. 4 (1964), 516-26.

CE154 Wirl, Julius. "Englische Übertragungen von Rilkes Erster Duineser Elegie." In: *Österreich und die angelsächsische Welt. Kulturbegegnungen und Vergleiche*. Ed. Otto Hietsch. Wien/Stuttgart: Braumüller, 1961, vol. 1, p.432-53.

CE155 Zeydel, Edwin H. "Can We Rely on Translations?" *Mod. Lang. Jour.*, vol. 25, no. 5 (1941), 402-04. On gross errors found in a translation of Schnitzler's *Literatur*.

CE156 Zeydel, Edwin H. "The English Versions of Walther's 'Under der Linden': A Study in Translation." *Mod. Lang. Jour.*, vol. 37 (1953), 10-18. On versions by Dole and Morgan.

CE157 Zimmermann, U. "Translating *Jenny Treibel*." In: *Formen realistischer Erzählkunst: Festschrift für Charlotte Jolles*. Ed. Jörg Thunecke. Nottingham: Sherwood, 1979, p.602-09.

CE158 Zurbrigg, Lloyd Alvin. "A Theory of Translation for Musical Texts from German into English with Appended Translations." Diss., Indiana, 1963. 197p.

CE159 Zuther, Gerhard H. W. "Problems in Translation: Modern American Dramas in German." Diss., Indiana, 1959.

Comparative Literature/Mutual Interactions Between German and American Literatures

CE160 Arndt, Karl J. R. "'Dauer im Wechsel': Grimmelshausen's ungarische Wiedertäufer and Rapp's Harmoniegesellschaft." In: *Traditions and Transitions: Studies in Honor of Harold Jantz*. Ed. Lieselotte E. Kurth et al. München: Delp, 1972.

CE161 Baker, Marilyn Joyce. "Against Humanism; Alienation in the Works of Elie Wiesel, Günter Grass, and Kurt Vonnegut." Diss., Univ. of South. California, 1977.

CE162 Barsch, Karl-Heinrich. "Origin and Development of the Nineteenth-Century Short Story in Germany, France, Russia, and the U.S.A." Diss., Colorado, 1977.

CE163 Bell, Robert F. "Perspectives on Witch Hunts: Lion Feuchtwanger and Arthur Miller." In: *Deutsches Exildrama und Exiltheater. Akten des Exilliteratur-Symposiums der University of South Carolinia 1976*. Ed. Wolfgang Elfe. Frankfurt: Lang, 1977, p.113–18.

CE164 Benoit, Ray. "The Mind's Return: Whitman, Teilhard, and Jung." *Walt Whitman Rev.*, vol. 13 (March 1967), 21–28. Argues Whitman's anticipation of the ideas of Teilhard and Jung.

CE165 Brumm, Anne-Marie L. "The Poet Visits the City: A Study of Carl Sandburg, R. M. Rilke, and Federico Garcia Lorca." Diss., Michigan, 1976.

CE166 Brumm, Ursula. "Amerikanische Dichter und europäische Geschichte: Nathaniel Hawthorne und Mark Twain." In: *Geschichte und Fiktion: Amerikanische Prosa im 19. Jahrhundert/ History and Fiction: American Prose in the 19th Century*. Eds. Alfred Weber and Hartmut Grandel, Göttingen: Vandenhoeck & Ruprecht, 1972, p.85–108.

CE167 Butcher, Philip, ed. *The Minority Presence in American Literature, 1600–1900: A Reader and Course Guide*. Washington: Howard Univ. Pr., 1977. 2 vols. 452, 421p.

CE168 Clements, Robert J. "Dürer's Knight, Death and the Devil: Five Literary Readings." *Canad. Rev. of Compar. Lit.*, vol. 6 (1979), 1–8. In Hugo, Sienkiewicz, Gatsos, Jarrell, and Borges.

CE169 Dean, O. C., Jr. "German-American Language and Literary Influences." *Amer. Speech*, vol. 47 (1972), no. 3–4, 292–98.

CE170 Dorsey, John Thomas. "The Courtroom Drama in Postwar Germany and America." Diss., Univ. of Illinois at Urbana–Champaign, 1979. 218p. In the writings of Levitt, Weiss, Arthur Miller, H. Kipphardt, Berrigan, and Enzensberger.

CE171 Edgington, K. Ann. "Abstraction as a Concept in the Criticism of Gertrude Stein and Wassily Kandinsky." Diss., American Univ., 1976. 72p.

CE172 Faulhaber, Uwe K. "German-American and German-English Literary Relations." In: *German Literature: An Annotated Reference Guide*. New York: Garland, 1979, p.266–69.

CE173 Feuerlicht, Ignace. "*Erlkönig* and *The Turn of The Screw*." *Jour. of Engl. and Germanic Philology*, vol. 58 (1959), 68–74. Parallels between Goethe's poem and James's ghost story, in the light of psychoanalytic interpretation.

CE174 Fleischmann, W. B. "Amerikanische Dichtkunst und deutsche, 1945–1965." In: *Nordamerikanische Literatur im deutschen Sprachraum seit 1945: Beiträge zur Rezeption*. Eds. Horst Frenz and H.-J. Lang. München: Winkler, 1973, p.65–78.

CE175 Frenzel, Ivo. "Ernst Jünger—Norman Mailer." *Deutsche Universitätszeitung*, vol. 5 (1950), no. 22, 12–14.

CE176 Friedmann, Melvin F. "American and European Fiction: The Contemporary Interaction." *Compar. Lit.*, vol. 17, no. 4 (1965), 342–45.

CE177 Galinsky, Hans. *Amerikanisch-deutsche Sprach- und Literaturbeziehungen: Systematische Übersicht und Forschungsbericht 1945–1970*. Frankfurt a.M.: Athenäum, 1972. 253p. Rev. in *Jour. of European Studies*, vol. 4 (1972), 92–94.

CE178 Galinsky, Hans. "Amerikanische Literaturgeschichtsschreibung und die Möglichkeit eines deutschen Beitrags." *Jahrbuch für Amerikastudien*, vol. 9 (1964), 55–90.

CE179 Galinsky, Hans K. "Zwei Jahrhunderte amerikanisch-deutscher Literaturbeziehungen (1776–1976)." *Nassauische Annalen*, vol. 89 (1979), 49–77.

CE180 Garland, Gary. "Mann and Jeffers: Myth Definition and Subsequent Technique." *Robinson Jeffers Newsletter*, vol. 37 (1973), 7–11.

CE181 George, N. F. "The *Chymische Hochzeit* of Thomas Pynchon." *Pynchon Notes*, vol. 4 (1980), 5–22.

CE182 Görres, Ida. "Zwei Bücher: Ein Vergleich (Ernst Wiechert und Ernest Hemingway)." *Frankfurter Hefte*, vol. 2 (1947), 856–63.

CE183 Gordon, Caroline. "Notes on Hemingway and Kafka." In: *Kafka. A Collection of Critical Essays*. Ed. Ronald Grey. Englewood Cliffs, N.J.: Prentice-Hall, 1962, p.75–83.

CE184 Gowa, Ferdinand. "Present Trends in American and German Literary Criticism." *Germanic Rev.*, vol. 28 (1953), 99–112. An examination of parallels and differences.

CE185 Grimm, Reinhold, and Henry J. Schmidt. "Foreign Influences in German Expressionist Poetry." In: *Expressionism Reconsidered: Relationships and Affinities*. Ed. Gertrud Bauer Pickar and Karl Eugene Webb. Houston German Studies 1. München: Fink, 1979, p.9–18.

CE186 Hainebach, Hans. "German Publications on the United States, 1933–1945." *Bull., N.Y. Public Library*, vol. 52, no. 9 (1948), 435–49; no. 10, 501–23. Books dealing with the U.S. which were publ. for the first time in Germany or German-occupied countries.

CE187 Hanak, Miroslav J. "Nietzsche, Dostoevsky, and Faulkner: Rebellion against Society in the Light of the New Left." In: *Actes du VIe Congrés de l'Association International de Littérature comparée*. Ed. Michel Cadot et al. Stuttgart: Bieber, 1975, p.739–43.

CE188 Heinz, Heide. "Herman Melvilles Erzählung *Bartleby* im Vergleich zu Franz Kafkas Roman *Der Prozess*." *Saarbrücker Beiträge zur Ästhetik*, 1966, 59–66.

CE189 Hittmair, Hans. "E.T.A. Hoffmann und E. A. Poe, ein Vergleich." Diss., Innsbruck, 1952.

CE190 Hoffmeister, Werner. "Critical Realism in Germany and America: Fontane and Howells." *Yearbook of German-American Studies*, vol. 16 (1981), 27–38.

CE191 Hoffmeister, Werner. "Der realistische Gesellschaftsroman bei Theodor Fontane und William Dean Howells: Eine deutsch-amerikanische Parallele." *Fontane Blätter*, vol. 3, no. 8 (1976), 600–07.

CE192 Hofrichter, Laura. "From Poe to Kafka." *Univ. of Toronto Quar.*, vol. 29 (1960), 405–19.

CE193 Howard, Ursula Elisabeth. "The Mystical Trends in the Poetry of Emily Dickinson and Annette von Droste-Hülshoff." Diss., Univ. of Illinois at Urbana–Champaign, 1974.

CE194 Hübner, Paul. "Prekäre Gleichgewichte—Albee, Hofmannsthal und Camus." *Wirkendes Wort*, vol. 19 (1969), 28–34.

CE195 Hunt, Joel A. "Mann and Whitman: Humaniores Litterae." *Compar. Lit.*, vol. 14 (1962), 266–71.

CE196 Hunt, Joel A. "Thomas Mann and Faulkner: Portrait of a Magician." *Wis. Studies in Contemporary Lit.*, vol. 8 (Summer 1967), 431–36.

CE197 Jäger, Dietrich. "Das Verhältnis zwischen Wirklichkeit und menschlicher Ordnung als Thema der Lyrik. Robert Frost und Wallace Stevens im Vergleich mit europäischen Dichtern." *Die neueren Sprachen*, N.F., vol. 17 (1968), 65–83.

CE198 Jäger, Dietrich. "Der verheimlichte Raum in Faulkners 'A Rose for Emily' und Brittings 'Der Schneckenweg'." *Literatur in Wissenschaft und Unterricht*, vol. 1 (1968), 108–16.

CE199 Jolivet, Philippe. "Le personnage de Thomas Becket dans 'Der Heilige' de C. F. Meyer, 'Murder in the Cathedral' de T. S. Eliot et 'Becket ou l'honneur de Dieu' de Jean Anouilh." *Etudes Germaniques*, vol. 16 (July–September 1961), 235–41.

CE200 Kaes, Anton. "Dokumentarismus—Fiktionalität—Politik: Anmerkungen zum deutschen und amerikanischen Dokumentartheater der 20er und 30er Jahre." In: *Theater und Drama in Amerika: Aspekte und Interpretationen.* Ed. E. Lohner and R. Haas. Berlin: Schmidt, 1978, p.91–107.

CE201 Kearney, E. I., and L. S. Fitzgerald. *The Continental Novel: A Checklist of Criticism in English 1900–1966.* Metuchen, N.J.: Scarecrow Pr., 1968. 460p. Concentrates on criticism published in America.

CE202 Keyser, Samuel Jay, and Alan Prince. "Folk Etymology in Sigmund Freud, Christian Morgenstern, and Wallace Stevens." *Critical Inquiry,* vol. 6 (1979), 65–78.

CE203 Kilchenmann, Ruth J. "Die amerikanische und die deutsche Kurzgeschichte: Beziehungen und Einflüsse." In: *Procs., IVth Congress of the International Comparative Literature Assoc.* Ed. Francois Jost. 2 vols. The Hague/Paris: n.p., 1966, vol. 2, p.1105–1112.

CE204 Kraus, Michael. "Literary Relations between Europe and America in the Eighteenth Century." *William and Mary College Quar.,* 3rd Ser., vol. 1, no. 3 (1944), 210–34.

CE205 Krumpelmann, John T. "Ethnic Endeavors by Quasi-Residents of our Nineteenth-Century Southwest." In: *Ethnic Literature Since 1776: The Many Voices of America.* Ed. W. T. Zyla and W. M. Aycock. Vol. 1. *Proceedings, Compar. Literature Symposium.* Lubbock, Tex.: Texas Tech Pr., 1978, p.233–41.

CE206 Kühnelt, Harro H. "E. A. Poe und Alfred Kubin: Zwei künstlerische Gestalten des Grauens." *Wiener Beiträge zur englischen Philologie,* vol. 65 (1957), 121–41.

CE207 Lawson, Richard H. "Thematic Similarities in Edith Wharton and Thomas Mann." *Twentieth Century Lit.,* vol. 23 (1977), 289–98.

CE208 Lease, Benjamin. "The Chemistry of Genius: Herman Melville and Anton Bruckner." *Personalist,* vol. 48 (Spring 1967), 224–41.

CE209 Lennox, Sara. "'We Could Have Had Such a Damned Good Time Together': Individual and Society in *The Sun Also Rises* and *Mutmassungen über Jakob.*" *Mod. Lang. Studies,* vol. 7, no. 1 (1977), 82–90. On the probable reasons for Uwe Johnson's use of Hemingway's line.

CE210 Lennox, Sara Jane K. "The Fiction of William Faulkner and Uwe Johnson: A Comparative Study." Diss., Wisconsin, 1973.

CE211 Lewis, Paul. "The Intellectual Functions of Gothic Fiction: Poe's 'Ligeia' and Tieck's 'Wake Not the Dead'." *Compar. Lit. Studies,* vol. 16 (1979), 207–21.

CE212 Liedloff, Helmut. "Two War Novels. A Critical Comparison. [Hemingway's *A Farewell to Arms* and Remarque's *Im Westen nichts Neues*]." *Revue de Littérature Comparée,* vol. 42 (1968), 390–406.

CE213 Liptzin, Sol. "Lafcadio Hearn, Hugo von Hofmannsthal, and Stefan Zweig." In: *The Old Century and the New: Essays in Honor of Charles Angoff.* Ed. Alfred Rosa. Rutherford: Fairleigh Dickinson Univ. Pr., 1978, p.186–91.

CE214 LoCicero, Donald. "Arthur Schnitzler and Eugene O'Neill: Masks, Pipe-Dreams, and Reality." *Jour. of the Internat. Arther Schnitzler Research Assoc.,* vol. 4, no. 3 (1965), 27–42. See also: "Schnitzler, O'Neill, and Reality." *Ibid.,* no. 3, 4–26.

CE215 Lyons, Charles R. "Some Variations of *Kindermord* as Dramatic Archetype." *Compar. Drama,* vol. 1, no. 1 (1967), 56–70. In Shakespeare, Albee, Brecht, and Beckett.

CE216 Lyons, Charles R. "Two Projections of the Isolation of the Human Soul: Brecht and Albee." *Drama Survey,* vol. 4 (Summer 1965), 121–38. Brecht's *Im Dickicht der Städte* and Albee's *The Zoo Story.*

CE217 Lyons, Nathan. "Kafka and Poe—and Hope." *Minn. Rev.,* vol. 5 (May–July 1964), 158–68.

CE218 McCormick, John O. "Thomas Wolfe, André Malraux, Hermann Hesse: A Study in Creative Vitality." Diss., Harvard, 1951.

CE219 McNeir, Waldo F. *Studies in Comparative Literature.* Baton Rouge: Louisiana State Univ. Pr., 1962. 311p.

CE220 Malsch, Wilfried. "Vom Vorbild zum Schreckbild: Politische U S A-Vorstellungen deutscher Schriftsteller von Thomas Mann zu Reinhard Lettau." In: *Die U S A und Deutschland: Wechselseitige Spiegelungen in der Literatur der Gegenwart*. Ed. Wolfgang Paulsen. Bern: Francke, 1976, p.29–51.

CE221 Mandel, Josef Lorenz. "Gerhart Hauptmann and Eugene O'Neill: A Parallel Study of Their Dramatic Technique in Selected Naturalistic Plays." Diss., Univ. of North Carolina, 1976.

CE222 Maucher, Gisela M. "Das Problem der dichterischen Wirklichkeit im Prosawerk von E.T.A. Hoffmann und E. A. Poe." Diss., Washington Univ., 1964. 205p. See also *Mitteilungen der E.T.A. Hoffmann Gesellschaft* (Bamberg), vol. 12 (1966), 31–32.

CE223 Musgrave, Marian E. "Sexual Excess and Deviation as Structural Devices in Günter Grass's *Blechtrommel* and Ishmael Reed's *Free-Lance Pallbearers*." *College Lang. Assoc. Jour.*, vol. 22 (1979), 229–39.

CE224 Nettesheim, Josefine. "Kriminelles, Kriminalistisches und Okkultes in der Dichtung der Droste und Edgar Allan Poes." *Jahrbuch des Wiener Goethe Vereins*, vol. 74 (1970), 136–46.

CE225 Osterle, Heinz D. "Uwe Johnson, Jahrestage: Das Bild der U S A." *German Quar.*, vol. 48 (1975), 505–18.

CE226 Ozana, Anna. "Varianten des 'Einfachen Lebens' von Henry D. Thoreau bis Ernst Wiechert." *Welt und Wort*, vol. 8 (1953), 145–49.

CE227 Padgett, Jacqueline O. "The Poet in War: Walt Whitman and Wolfgang Borchert." *Monatshefte*, vol. 72 (1980), 149–61. Their images, stylistic preferences, and concept of the poet's role were alike. Notes the influence of *Leaves of Grass* in Borchert's prose and dramas.

CE228 Paulsen, Wolfgang, ed. *Die USA und Deutschland. Wechselseitige Spiegelungen in der Literatur der Gegenwart. Zum 200jährigen Bestehen der Vereinigten Staaten am 4. Juli 1976*. Bern and München: Francke, 1976. 194p. 8. Amherster Kolloquium zur Modernen Deutschen Literatur. Rev. by J. K. Fugate, *Monatshefte*, vol. 70 (1978), 344–46.

CE229 Pinsker, Sanford. *The Schlemiel as Metaphor: Studies in the Yiddish and American Jewish Novel*. South Carbondale: Southern Illinois Univ. Pr., 1971. Submitted as diss., Univ. of Washington, 1967. 278p.

CE230 Raddatz, Fritz J. "Zur Bilanz von Princeton [Die Gruppe 47 in Princeton]." *Frankfurter Hefte*, vol. 21 (1966), 495–97.

CE231 Rajec, Elizabeth M. "Kafka and Philip Roth: Their Use of Literary Onomastics (Based on *The Professor of Desire*)." *Literary Onomastics Studies*, vol. 7 (1980), 69–86.

CE232 Ratner, Marc. "Georg Brandes and Hjalmar Hjorth Boyesen: An Exchange of Critical Views." *Scandinavian Studies*, vol. 33 (November 1961) 218–30.

CE233 Riese, Teut Andreas. "The Idea of Evil in American and European Literature." In: *Diverging Parallels: A Comparison of American and European Thought and Action*. Ed. A.J.N. den Hollander. Leiden: Brill, 1971, p.185–201.

CE234 Ryan, Judith. "Ezra Pound und Gottfried Benn: Avant-Garde, Faschismus und ästhetische Autonomie." In: *Faschismus und Avant-Garde*. Ed. Reinhold Grimm and Jost Hermand. Königstein: Athenäum, 1980, p.20–34.

CE235 Rysten, Felix S. A. "False Prophets in Fiction: Camus, Dostoevsky, Melville, and Others." Diss., Univ. of Southern California, 1968. 272p. Incl. discussion of Kafka and A. Malraux.

CE236 Sandrock, James P., and John A. A. ter Haar. "Die Lutherbibel als literarischer und kultureller Brückenschlag." *Zeitschrift für Kulturaustausch*, vol. 22, no. 1 (1972), 18–21. How Luther's Bible bridges between general German culture and the understanding of mythic and other allusions in many works of modern literature.

CE237 Sattin, Jerry Paul. "Allegory in Modern Fiction: A Study of *Moby-Dick*, the *Brothers Karamazov*, and 'Die Verwandlung'." Diss., Univ. of Illinois at Urbana–Champaign, 1978. 265p.

CE238 Shelley, Philip A., Arthur O. Lewis, and William W. Betts, eds. *Anglo-German and American-German Crosscurrents*. Vol. 1. Chapel Hill: Univ. of N. Car. Pr., 1957. 303p. Rev. by A. H. Marks, *Amer. Quar.*, vol. 10 (1958), 495; by Henry A. Pochmann, *Monatshefte*, vol. 51 (1959), 132–34; Karl J. R. Arndt, *Jour. of Engl. and Germanic Philology*, vol. 59, no. 2 (1960), 378–79; H. Bergholz, *Books Abroad*, vol. 34, no. 1 (1960), 77. Vol.

Comparative Literature/Mutual Interactions *(cont.)*

2. Chapel Hill: Univ. of N. Car. Pr., 1962. 322p. Rev. by Karl J. R. Arndt, *Jour. of Eng. and Germanic Philol.*, vol. 62, no. 4 (1963), 821–22; H. A. Pochmann, *Monatshefte*, vol. 56 (1964), no. 6, 310–11. A collection of eight studies.

CE239 Shelley, Philip Allison. "Annuals and Gift Books as American Intermediates of Foreign Literature." *Compar. Lit. News-Letter*, vol. 3 (1945), 59–62.

CE240 Shunami, Gideon. "Between the Epic and the Absurd: Brecht, Wilder, Dürrenmatt, and Ionesco. (A Comparison of Two Major Genres in Modern Drama)." *Genre*, vol. 8 (1975), 42–59.

CE241 Soudek, Ingrid H. W. "Man and the Machine: A Contrastive Study of Ernst Toller's *Die Maschinenstürmer* and Elmer Rice's *The Adding Machine.*" Diss., Michigan, 1974.

CE242 Spender, Stephen. "Rilke and the Angels, Eliot and the Shrines." *Sewanee Rev.*, vol. 61 (1953), 557–58. Contrasting attitude toward life in the *Duino Elegies* and the *Four Quartets*.

CE243 Stebner, Gerhard. "Whitman—Liliencron—W. H. Auden: Betrachtung und Vergleich motivähnlicher Gedichte." *Die neueren Sprachen*, N.F., vol. 9 (1960), 101–18.

CE244 Swann, C. S. B. "The Practice and Theory of Story-Telling: Nathaniel Hawthorne and Walter Benjamin." *Jour. of Amer. Studies*, vol. 12 (1978), 185–202.

CE245 Swigger, Ronald Thomas. "The Life of the World: A Comparison of Stevens and Rilke." Diss., Indiana, 1967. 198p.

CE246 Urzidil, Johannes. "Adalbert Stifter und Henry Thoreau." *Welt und Wort*, vol. 5 (1950), 225.

CE247 Vitt-Maucher, Gisela. "E.T.A. Hoffmanns *Ritter Gluck* und E. A. Poes *The Man of the Crowd*: Eine Gegenüberstellung." *German Quar.*, vol. 43 (1970), 35–46.

CE248 Weisstein, Ulrich. "Expressionism as an International Phenomenon: An Annotated Bibliography." In: *Expressionism as an International Literary Phenomenon: 21 Essays and a Bibliography*. Comp. by U. Weisstein. Paris: Didier, 1973, p.329–49.

CE249 Wehner, James V. "The Nature of Evil in Melville's *Billy Budd* and Mann's *Mario und der Zauberer.*" *Comparatist*, vol. 4 (1980), 31–46.

CE250 Wellek, René. *Confrontations. Studies in the Intellectual and Literary Relations between Germany, England, and the United States during the Nineteenth Century*. Princeton: Princeton Univ. Pr., 1965. 221p. Rev. by H. M. Jones, *Mod. Lang. Quar.*, vol. 26 (1965), no. 2, 353–54; W. B. Fleischmann, *Mod. Lang. Jour.*, vol. 49 (1966), 398–400; L. R. Furst, *Mod. Lang. Rev.*, vol. 61 (1966), 655–56; J. P. Pritchard, *Books Abroad*, vol. 40 (Autumn 1966), 462–63; C. S. Brown, *Compar. Lit.*, vol. 18 (1966), 182–83; H. A. Pochmann, *Mod. Lang. Notes*, vol. 83, no. 3 (1968), 496–97.

CE251 Wellek, René. "German and English Romanticism: A Confrontation." *Studies in Romanticism* (1964), no. 4, 35–36.

CE252 Wellek, René. *A History of Modern Criticism: Seventeen Fifty to Nineteen Fifty*. 4 vols. I. *The Late Eighteenth Century*. 358p. 1955. II. *The Romantic Age*. 459p. 1955. III. *The Age of Transition*. 389p. 1965. IV. *The Late Nineteenth Century*. 671p. 1965. New Haven: Yale Univ. Pr. Rev. by R. Macauley, *N.Y. Times Book Rev.*, 2 January 1966.

CE253 Wellek, René. *Konfrontationen. Vergleichende Studien zur Romantik*. Frankfurt: Suhrkamp, 1964.

CE254 Wellek, René. "Die Krise der vergleichenden Literaturwissenschaft." In: *Neuere deutsche Literatur. Wirkendes Wort*, Sammelband no. 3. Düsseldorf: Schwann, 1963, p.85–92.

CE255 Werge, Thomas. "Luther and Melville on the Masks of God." *Melville Soc. Extracts*, vol. 22 (May 1975), 6–7.

CE256 Willard, Nancy Margaret. "An Experiment in Objectivity: the Poetic Theory and Practice of William Carlos Williams and Rainer Maria Rilke." Diss., Michigan, 1963.

CE257 Wood, Frank. "German Parallels to the New Criticism." *Mod. Lang. Forum*, vol. 36 (1951), 8–20.

CE258 Zipes, Jack D. *The Great Refusal: Studies of the Romantic Hero in German and American Literature.* Bad Homburg: Athenäum, 1970. 158p. Cf. diss., Columbia, 1965: "Studies of the Romantic Hero in German and American Literature." 183p.

CF

Vogue and Reception of German Literature in America

General

CF1 Auerbach, Doris N. "The Reception of German Literature in America as Exemplified by the *New York Times*, 1945–1970." Diss., New York Univ., 1974.

CF2 Binder, Wolfgang. *Europäisches Drama und amerikanische Kritik: skandinavische, deutschsprachige und russische Dramatiker in der nordamerikanischen Kritik 1890–1914.* Nürnberg: Carl, 1974. 490p. See also his Diss., Erlangen, 1973 on the same subject. American critical approaches to European drama.

CF3 Blume, Bernhard. "Amerika und die deutsche Literatur." *Jahrbuch der Deutschen Akademie für Sprache und Dichtung 1959* (Darmstadt), 137–48.

CF4 Boerner, Peter. "Die deutsche Klassik im Urteil des Auslands." In: *Die Klassik-Legende: Second Wisconsin Workshop.* Ed. Reinhold Grimm and Jost Hermand. Frankfurt: Athenäum, 1971, p.79–107.

CF5 Cady, Frank C. "The Unitary Phenomenon: The Phenomenology of Martin Heidegger and the Poetry of Ezra Pound, William Carlos Williams, and Charles Olson." Diss., Stanford, 1973.

CF6 Carse, Alice F. "The Reception of German Literature in America as Exemplified by the *New York Times*: 1919–1944." Diss., New York Univ., 1974.

CF7 Charles, Robert Alan. "French Mediation and Intermediaries, 1750–1815." In: *Anglo-German and American-German Crosscurrents.* P. A. Shelley, A. O. Lewis, and W. W. Betts. Chapel Hill: Univ. of N. Car. Pr., 1957–1962, vol. I (1957), p.1–38.

CF8 Crispyn, Robert L. "The Currency and Reception of German Short Prose Fiction in England and America as Reflected in the Periodicals, 1790–1840." Diss., Pennsylvania State Univ., 1955.

CF9 David, Reinhard. "Das Bild des literarischen Deutschland in den amerikanischen Zeitschriften vor 1817." Diss., Göttingen, 1966.

CF10 Davis, Edward Z. *Translations of German Poetry in American Magazines, 1741–1810.* Philadelphia: n.p., 1905. Repr. Detroit: Gale Research Co., 1966.

CF11 Demetz, Peter. "Die Literatur der Bundesrepublik in den Vereinigten Staaten: Kritische Notizen." In: *Perspectives and Personalities. Studies in Modern German Literature Honoring Claude Hill.* Ed. R. Ley, M. Wagner, J. M. Ratych and K. Hughes. Heidelberg: Winter, 1978, p.110–17.

CF12 Dietel, Günther. "Studien zur Aufnahme der deutschen Literatur in Amerika 1919–1939." Diss., Jena, 1952. Rev. by H. Zohn, *Amer.-German Rev.*, vol. 19, no. 3 (1953), 38–39.

CF13 Dunbar, John R. "The Reception of European Literary Naturalism in the United States, 1870–1900." Diss., Harvard Univ., 1948. 128p.

CF14 Durzak, Manfred. "Die Rezeption der deutschen Literatur nach 1945 in den U S A." In: *Die deutsche Literatur der Gegenwart. Aspekte und Tendenzen.* Stuttgart: Reclam, 1971, p.437–47.

CF15 Earnest, Ernest. *Expatriates and Patriots: American Artists, Scholars, and Writers in Eu-*

General *(cont.)*

rope. Durham: Duke Univ. Pr., 1968. Survey of motives and attitudes of Americans in Europe from 1783 to 1929.

CF16 Fourier, Ruth G. "The Literary Criticism of the *Dial*, 1920–1929." Diss., Vanderbilt, 1959.

CF17 Galinsky, Hans K. "America's Image of German Literature: A Neglected Field of American-German Literary Relations." *Compar. Lit. Studies*, vol. 13 (1976), 165–92.

CF18 Gordon, John. "The Reception of German Literature in America as Exemplified by the *New York Herald Tribune*: 1935–1966." Diss., New York Univ., 1975.

CF19 Granville, Robert Mannix. "The Reception of German Literature in America as Exemplified by the *Saturday Rev. of Lit.*: 1945–1970." Diss., New York Univ., 1975.

CF20 Haberland, Paul M. "The Reception of German Literature in Baltimore's Literary Magazines, 1800–1875." *German-Amer. Studies*, vol. 7 (1974), 69–92. A survey of some 45 separate runs of belletristic and popular journals; finds a favorable attitude toward German literature in Baltimore, especially in the earlier portion of the period.

CF21 Heinsohn, Wolfgang E. "The Reception of German Literature in America as Exemplified by the *New York Times*. Part 1. 1870 to 1918." Diss., New York Univ., 1974.

CF22 Heller, Peter. "Die deutsche Literatur aus amerikanischer Sicht." *Welt und Wort*, vol. 11 (1956), 105–07.

CF23 Hofacker, Erich P. *German Literature as Reflected in the German-Language Press of St. Louis prior to 1898*. St. Louis: n.p., 1946.

CF24 Jantz, Harold S. "Samuel Miller's Survey of German Literature, 1803." *Germanic Rev.*, vol. 16 (1941), 267–68.

CF25 Kaes, Anton. *Expressionismus in Amerika: Rezeption und Innovation*. Tübingen: Niemeyer, 1975. 162p. Rev. by Elizabeth Chadwick, *Monatshefte*, vol. 70 (1978), 90–92; B. Zimmermann, *German Quar.*, vol. 51 (1978), 555–56. Cf. "Rezeption und Innovation: Zur Wirkungsgeschichte des deutschen Expressionismus in Amerika." Diss., Stanford, 1973.

CF26 Kopp, W. LaMarr. "The Currency of German Literature in the United States, 1945–1960." Diss., Pennsylvania State, 1964–1965.

CF27 Kopp, William LaMarr. *German Literature in the United States, 1945–1965*. Chapel Hill: Univ. of N. Car. Pr., 1967. 230p. Rev. by D. Milburn, *Monatshefte*, vol. 62, no. 2 (Summer 1970), 174–75; U. Weisstein, *Jour. of Eng. and Germanic Philology*, vol. 68 (1969), 148–51; J. D. Zipes, *Germanic Rev.*, vol. 44, no. 3 (May 1969), 239–41; in *Zeitschrift für Kulturaustausch*, vol. 19, no. 1 (1969), 64–65. A critical evaluation of the influx of German-language literature into the United States; incl. a title list of German works in translation and selective bibliography, p. 154–220.

CF28 Kremer, Sabine. "Die deutsche Literatur in der kritischen Würdigung der Auslandspresse. Unter besonderer Berücksichtigung der grossen amerikanischen Tagespresse in den Jahren 1945–1960." Diss., Wien, 1965.

CF29 Morgan, Bayard Quincy. "Sources of German Influences on American Letters." *Amer.-German Rev.*, vol. 10, no. 3 (1944), 4–7, 35.

CF30 Morgan, Bayard Quincy. "Traces of German Influence in American Letters." *Amer.-German Rev.*, vol. 10, no. 4 (1944), 15–18.

CF31 Paolucci, Anne. "Benn, Pound, and Eliot: The Monologue Art of German Expressionism and Anglo-German Modernism." *Rev. of National Lit.*, vol. 9 (1978), 10–24.

CF32 Papenfuss, Dietrich, and Jürgen Söring, eds. *Rezeption der deutschen Gegenwartsliteratur im Ausland: Internationale Forschungen zur neueren deutschen Literatur. Tagungsbeiträge eines Symposiums der Alex. von Humboldt-Stiftung, Bonn-Bad Godesberg, veranstaltet vom 21. bis 26. Oktober 1975 in Ludwigsburg*. Stuttgart: Kohlhammer, 1976. 448p.

CF33 Pinsker, Sanford. "The Schlemiel's Family Tree." In: *The Schlemiel as Metaphor. Studies in the Yiddish and American Jewish Novel*. Pref. by Harry T. Moore. Carbondale: Southern Ill. Univ. Pr., 1971, p. 50–54.

CF34 Pochmann, Henry A., Arthur R. Schultz et al. *German Culture in America, 1600–1900: Philosophical and Literary Influences*. Madison: Univ. of Wisconsin Pr., 1957. 866p. Rev. by H. Frenz, *Amer.-German Rev.*, vol. 23, no. 3 (1957), 38; in *Yearbook of Compar. and General Lit.*, vol. 6

(1957), 76–80; C. Wittke, *Amer. Hist. Rev.*, vol. 62 (1957), 927–29; by H. F. Peters, *Miss. Valley Hist. Rev.*, vol. 44 (1957), 109–12; J. W. Thomas, *Amer. Lit.*, vol. 29 (1957), 327–28; C. Gohdes, *Mod. Philology*, vol. 55 (1957), 136–38; C. G. Cleaver, *Minn. Hist.*, vol. 35 (1957), 327–28; J. Dunner, *Wis. Mag. of Hist.*, vol. 41 (1957), 140–41; A.J. App, *Social Justice Rev.*, vol. 50 (July–August 1957); M. Gaither, *Ind. Mag. of Hist.*, vol. 53 (1957), 447–49; G. N. Shuster, *Key Reporter*, vol. 22, no. 4 (1957), 6; A. Werner, *Congress Weekly*, 28 October 1957; in *Book Exchange* (July 1957); in *Regesten* (July–August 1957); in *Mennonite Life*, vol. 12 (1957), 92; in *Bücher aus Amerika*, no. 82 (May 1957); S. Taubert, *Börsenblatt für den deut. Buchhandel*, no. 97 (1957), 1479–80; A. E. Zucker, *Mod. Lang. Notes*, vol. 73 (1958), 555–57; D. Cunz, *German Quar.*, vol. 31 (1958), 324–28; P. A. Shelley, *Monatshefte*, vol. 50 (1958), 280–84; E. E. Doll, *Pa. Mag. of Hist. and Biography*, vol. 82 (1958), 131–32; G. Cardwell, *Ohio Hist. Quar.*, vol. 67 (1958), 87–89; C. Bode, *Mod. Lang. Rev.*, vol. 52 (1958), 117; S. E. Ahlstrom, *Church Hist.*, vol. 27 (1958), 285–87; H. Kloss, *Mitteilungen des Instituts für Auslandsbeziehungen*, vol. 7 (1958), 313–14; P. A. Barba, "'S Pennsylfawnisch Deitsch Eck," Allentown *Morning Call*, 11 January, 1958; A. H. Marks, *Amer. Quar.*, vol. 10 (1958), 494–94; L. Lewis, *Jahrbuch für Amerikastudien*, vol. 3 (1958), 218; W. Fischer, *ibid.*, 268–71; F. Ernst, *Das historisch-politische Buch*, vol. 6, no. 1 (1958), 30–31; C. David, *Etudes Germaniques*, vol. 12 (1958), 183–84; R. T. Voigt, *Thought*, vol. 32 (1958), 614–15; *Mo. Hist. Rev.*, vol. 52 (1958), 288; H. W. Pfund, *Pa. Hist.*, vol. 26 (1959), 191–93; K. G. Wust, *Books Abroad*, vol. 33 (1959), 472; *Report, Soc. for the Hist. of the Germans in Md.*, vol. 30 (1959), 23–25; A. C. Kern, *Philological Quar.*, vol. 38 (1959), 127–28; F. Reichmann, *Jour. of Eng. and Germanic Philology*, vol. 59 (1960), 745–49. Repr. Westport, Conn.: Greenwood Press, 1978.

CF35 Rie, Robert. "Amerika und die österreichische Literatur." *Wort in der Zeit*, vol. 7 (1961), no. 4, 42–45.

CF36 Sander, Volkmar. "Der deutsche Bildungsroman in Amerika." *Deutsche Rundschau*, vol. 87 (1961), 1032–38.

CF37 Sander, Volkmar. "Die *New York Times Book Review*: Zur Rezeption deutscher Literatur in den U S A." *Basis. Jahrbuch für deutsche Gegenwartsliteratur*, vol. 4 (1973), 86–97.

CF38 Sander, Volkmar. "Zur Rezeption der deutschen Literatur in Amerika." In: *Theorie und Kritik. Zur vergleichende u. neueren deutschen Literatur: Festschrift für Gerhard Loose*... Ed. Stefan Grunwald and Bruce A. Beatie. Bern/München: Francke, 1974, p.57–65.

CF39 Sander, Volkmar. "Zur Rezeption der deutschen Literatur in der New York Times." In: *Die U S A und Deutschland: Wechseitige Spiegelungen in der Literatur der Gegenwart*... Ed. Wolfgang Paulsen. 8. Amherster Kolloquium zur modernen deutschen Literatur. Bern: Francke, 1976, p.160–73.

CF40 Saul, C. T. "Deutschsprachige Literatur in den U S A." *Die Schule* (Hannover), vol. 3 (1948), 114f.

CF41 Schlesinger, Eva. "The Reception of German Literature in America as Exemplified by the *Atlantic Monthly*, 1919–1944." Diss., New York Univ., 1975–1976.

CF42 Thomas, J. Wesley. *Amerikanische Dichter und die deutsche Literatur*. Goslar, 1950. Cf. *Amer.-German Rev.*, vol. 19, no. 4 (1953), 39. Rev. by H. A. Pochmann, *Monatshefte*, vol. 45 (1953), 60; Henry Pochmann, *Amer. Lit.*, vol. 26 (1954), 452–53; Arthur R. Schultz, *Jour. of Eng. and Germanic Philology*, vol. 53 (1954) 135–36; C. Lazenby, *Amer.-German Rev.*, vol. 18 (1951), no. 2, 38; J. G. Frank, *Monatshefte*, vol. 44 (1952), 120–21; W. P. Friedrich, *Compar. Lit.*, vol. 4 (1952), 89–90; D. Cunz, *Books Abroad*, vol. 26 (1952), 174–75; H. Frenz, *Ind. Mag. of Hist.*, vol. 48 (1952), 97–98.

CF43 Thomas, J. Wesley. "German Literature in the Old South." *Amer.-German Rev.*, vol. 19, no. 2 (1952), 8–10, 33. On George Calvert, Elizabeth Ellet, Mary Lee, translators; William G. Simms.

CF44 Totten, Christine M. "Das dichtende Deutschland—aus amerikanischer Sicht." *Welt und Wort*, vol. 20, no. 2 (1965), 39–40.

CF45 Townsend, Stanley R. "Die moderne deutsche Literatur in Amerika." *Die Sammlung. Zeitschrift für Kultur und Erziehung*, vol. 9 (1945), 247–53.

CF46 Trout, Thomas J. "The *Knickerbocker* and German Influence." Diss., Bowling Green Univ., 1973.

CF47 Vogel, Stanley M. "The Flowering of German Literature in New England." In: *John Quincy Adams: Pioneer of German-American Literary Studies*. Ed. Anneliese Harding. Cambridge, Mass.: Harvard Univ. Pr., 1979, p.52–63.

CF48 Vogel, Stanley M. "The Reception of 20th Century German Literature in the United States." *Proceedings, Second International Comparative Literature Congress*. Univ. of N. Car. Studies in Compar. Lit., no. 24. Chapel Hill: Univ. of N. Car. Pr., 1959, p.548–57.

CF49 Waidson, H. M. "Zeitgenössische deutsche Literatur in Englischer Übersetzung." *Deutschunterricht für Ausländer*, vol. 8 (1958), 65–71.

German and German-American Themes and Motifs in American Literature

CF50 Barba, Preston A. "The Pennsylvania German in Fiction, 1935–1955." *The Pa. Dutchman*, vol. 7, no. 4 (1956), 22–27.

CF51 Bender, Elizabeth Horsch. "Three Amish novels." *Mennonite Quar. Rev.*, vol. 19 (October 1945), 273–84. On the literary merit and authenticity of Helen R. Martin's *Sabina, A Story of the Amish* (1950), Ruth Lininger Dobson's *Straw in the Wind* (1937), and Joseph W. Yoder's *Rosanna of the Amish* (1940).

CF52 Berman, Marshall. "Sympathy for the Devil: Faust, the '60s and the Tragedy of Development." *Amer. Rev.*, vol. 19 (1974), 23–75.

CF53 Betts, William W., Jr. "The Fortunes of Faust in American Literature." Diss., Pennsylvania State, 1954. 150p. On the use of the Faust legend in American literature.

CF54 Breitenbach, Edgar. "Des Kaysers Abschied and the First Dance of Death in America." *Der Reggeboge*, vol. 12, no. 1 (1978), 4–9. *See also* his article "Des Kaysers Abschied: Das Totentanzmotiv unter den Deutschen Pennsylvaniens," *Philobiblon*, vol. 22 (1978), 42–49.

CF55 Cameron, Alex J. "The Image of the Physician in the American Novel 1859 to 1925." Diss., Notre Dame, 1973.

CF56 Carter, Everett. "The Haymarket (Chicago) Affair in Literature." *Amer. Quar.*, vol. 2 (1950), 270–78.

CF57 Cary, Meredith. "Faustus Now." *Hartford Studies in Lit.*, vol. 4 (1972), 167–73. Science fiction.

CF58 *Children's Catalogue, 7th ed*. New York: H. W. Wilson Co., 1947–1948. With Supplement. See list of English-language children's books about Germany and Switzerland, p.302–03.

CF59 Danis, Edward J. "The Popularity of the German 'Professorenroman' or the Archaeological Novel in Late Nineteenth Century America." Diss., Pennsylvania State, 1980. 237p.

CF60 Davenport, Basil, ed. *Deals with the Devil*. New York: Dodd, Mead & Co., 1958. 332p. Twenty-five stories, American and British, on the motif of the pact with the Devil.

CF61 Dell, Robert M. "The Representation of the Immigrant on the New York Stage—1881 to 1910." Diss., New York Univ., 1961.

CF62 Dryud, David L. "Varieties of Marginality: The Treatment of the European Immigrant in the Middlewestern Frontier Novel." Diss., Purdue, 1979. 258p.

CF63 Eisele, Susanne. "Das Deutschlandbild in der amerikanischen Literatur des zweiten Weltkrieges." Diss., Erlangen, 1961.

CF64 Ezrahi, Sidra DeKoven. "The Holocaust in Literature: A Comparative Study of Modes of Literary Response to the Holocaust." Diss., Brandeis, 1976. 483p.

CF65 Fine, David M. *The Immigrant and American Fiction, 1880–1920*. Metuchen: Scarecrow Pr., 1977. 182p. Rev. by Elinor Grumet, *Amer. Jewish Archives*, vol. 30 (1978), 80–82.

CF66 Flanagan, John T. "A Bibliography of Middle Western Farm Novels." *Minn. Hist.*, vol. 23 (1942), 156–58.

CF67 Flanagan, John T. "The German in American Fiction." In: *In the Trek of the Immigrants: Essays Presented to Carl Wittke*. Ed. O. Fritiof Ander. Rock Island, Ill.: Augustana Publ. House, 1964, p.95–115.

CF68 Fritchie, Barbara. Papers. 1 vol. In Maryland Historical Society Library (MS 67-1450). Correspondence, clippings bearing on the factual and fictional aspects of Whittier's story; dedication in 1927 of the restored Fritchie home, Frederick, Md.

CF69 Gallagher, Kent Grey. "The Foreigner in American Drama to 1830: A Study in Attitudes." Diss., Indiana, 1962. 302p.

CF70 Gallagher, Kent Grey. *The Foreigner in Early American Drama: A Study in Attitudes*. The Hague: Mouton, 1966. 206p.

CF71 Halley, Anne. "Der 'väterliche Deutsche': Ein Stereotyp des Ausländers im Werk amerikanischer Schriftstellerinnen." In: *Die U S A und Deutschland: Wechselseitige Spiegelungen in der Literatur der Gegenwart*... Ed. Wolfgang Paulsen. 8. Amherster Kolloquium zur modernen deutschen Literatur. Bern/München: Francke, 1976, 138–51. Cites the instances of works by Jean Stafford, Hortense Calisher, Mary McCarthy, Katherine A. Porter, Sylvia Plath, Lillian Hellman, et al.

CF72 Harap, Louis. *The Image of the Jew in American Literature: From Early Republic to Mass Immigration*. Philadelphia: Jewish Publ. Soc. of America, 1975. 586p.

CF73 Jost, Francois. "German and French Themes in Early American Drama." *Jour. of General Education*, vol. 28 (1976), 190–222.

CF74 Keuhr, Wanda L. "The Ethnic Character as a Device in American Drama, 1930–1950." Diss., Florida, ca. 1969.

CF75 Kloberdanz, Timothy J. "Homesteaders, Housemaids and Other Heroes: The Black Sea Germans in American Literature and Local History." *Heritage Rev.*, no. 20 (1978), 13–19.

CF76 Kraus, Joe W. "Missouri in Fiction: A Review and a Bibliography." *Mo. Hist. Rev.*, vol. 42 (1948), 209–25, 310–24.

CF77 Krumpelmann, John T. "Midsummer Night's Dreams." *Monatshefte*, vol. 46 (1954), 281–82. Longfellow dreaming of Goethe, Bayard Taylor of Uhland.

CF78 Lawrence, Elwood. "The Immigrant in American Fiction." Diss., Western Reserve Case, 1944.

CF79 Liptzin, Sol. *The Jew in American Literature*. New York: Bloch, 1966. 251p. Rev. by C. I. Glicksberg, *Jewish Social Studies*, vol. 30, no. 4 (October 1968), 278–79. The image of the Jew in literature; his contribution to American literature.

CF80 Lutz, Hartmut. "Indians through German vs. U.S. Eyes." *Bull. of Interracial Books for Children*, vol. 12, no. 1 (1981), 3–8.

CF81 MacDonald, J. Frederick. "The Foreigner in Juvenile Series Fiction, 1900–1945." *Jour. of Popular Culture*, vol. 8 (Winter 1974).

CF82 McGranahan, Donald V. and Ivor Wayne. "German and American Traits Reflected in Popular Drama." *Human Relations*, vol. 1 (August 1948), 429–55. Repr. as "A Comparative Study of National Characteristics." In: *Experiments in Social Process: A Symposium on Social Psychology*. Ed. James G. Miller. New York: McGraw Hill, 1950, Chap. 7. An experimental comparison of national traits exemplified in the 62 "most popular" plays in each country, 1909–1910 and 1927.

CF83 McKenzie, Ruth. "Life in a New Land. Notes on the Immigrant Theme in Canadian Fiction." *Canad. Lit.*, no. 7 (Winter 1961), 24–33.

CF84 McManus, Jo A. "*Rosemary's Baby*: A Unique Combination of Faust, Leda, and 'The Second Coming'." *McNeese Rev.* (McNeese State College, Iowa), vol. 20 (1971–1972), 33–36.

CF85 "Mennonites in American and Canadian Literature." Art. in the *Mennonite Encyclopedia*, vol. 3, p.353–74.

CF86 Mersand, Joseph. "The European and Ethnic Presence in American Literature." *Eng. Jour.*, vol. 66, no. 3 (1977), 42–55.

CF87 Meyer, Roy W. *The Middle Western Farm Novel in the Twentieth Century*. Lincoln: Univ. of Neb. Pr., 1965. 265p.

CF88 Musgrave, Marian E. "Deutsche und Deutschland in der schwarzen und weissen amerikanischen Literatur des zwanzigsten Jahrhunderts." In: *Die U S A und Deutschland: Wechselseitige Spiegelungen in der Literatur der Gegenwart*... Ed. Wolfgang Paulsen. 8. Amherster Kolloquium zur modernen deutschen Literatur. Bern/München: Francke, 1976, p.119–37. Incl. a bibliography of American novels dealing with the subject matter of Germany.

CF89 Nichols, Charles H. "The Image of the European Father in American Writing." *Jahrbuch für Amerikastudien*, vol. 5 (1960), 26–33. The underlying identification is that of Europe with the "Father."

CF90 Pfeil, Sigmar. "Bemerkungen zu einigen bedeutenden amerikanischen Kriegsromanen über den zweiten Weltkrieg." *Zeitschrift für Anglistik und Amerikanistik*, vol. 13 (1965), 61–74.

CF91 Royer, Mary. "The Amish and Mennonite Theme in American Literature for Children." *Mennonite Quar. Rev.*, vol. 19 (October 1945), 285–91.

CF92 Sapiro, Leland. "The Faustus Tradition in the Early Science Fiction Story." *Riverside Quar.* (Univ. of Saskatchewan), vol. 1 (1964–1965), 3–18, 43–57, 118–25.

CF93 Schirmer, Gustav. *Die Schweiz im Spiegel der englischen und amerikanischen Literature*. Zürich and Leipzig: n.p., 1929.

CF94 Shenk, Stanley Coffman. "American Mennonite Fiction." *Mennonite Life*, vol. 23 (July 1968), 119–20. A list of 30 novels during the years 1900–1970.

CF95 Shenk, Stanley Coffman. "The Image of the Mennonites in American Novels, 1900–1970." *Mennonite Quar. Rev.*, vol. 46 (July 1972). *See also his* "The Image of the Mennonites in American Novels, 1900–1970." Diss., New York Univ., 1971. 498p.

CF96 Shenton, Donald Radcliffe. "Contemporary Fiction on the Pennsylvania-Germans." "'S Pennsylfawnisch Deitsch Eck," Allentown *Morning Call*, 3, 10 July 1943.

CF97 Suderman, Elmer F. "American Mennonite Fiction: A Contribution toward a Bibliography." *Mennonite Life*, vol. 22 (July 1967), 131–33.

CF98 Suderman, Elmer F. "Fiction and Mennonite Life." *Midcontinent Amer. Studies Jour.*, vol. 10 (Spring 1969), 16–24. Culture and character in six novels treating the Mennonite Germans from Russia.

CF99 Suderman, Elmer F. "The Mennonite Character in American Fiction." *Mennonite Life*, vol. 22 (July 1967), 123–30. As discerned in the writings of Caroline Chesebro, Gordon Friesen, Rudy Wiebe, and Warren Kliewer.

CF100 Ward, Robert E. "Englischsprachige Literatur über Deutsche in Amerika." *German-Amer. Studies*, vol. 3, no. 2 (1971), 46–48.

CF101 Weinberg, Daniel E. "Viewing the Immigrant Experience in America Through Fiction and Autobiography—With a Select Bibliography." *Hist. Teacher*, vol. 9 (May 1976).

CF102 Werner, William L. "The First Novel about the Pennsylvania Germans." "'S Pennsylfawnisch Deitsch Eck," Allentown *Morning Call*, 2 November 1957.

CF103 Wilkinson, N. B. "Current Writings on Pennsylvania." *Pa. Hist.*, vol. 16 (1949), 326–30. Incl. novels with Pennsylvania German background.

CF104 Winther, Sophus Keith. "The Emigrant Theme." *Amer. Quar.*, vol. 34 (1978), 31–43. On "emigrant novels" by Moberg, Rölvaag, Winther and Boyer.

CF105 Wisse, Ruth Roskies. "The Schlemihl as Hero in Yiddish and American Fiction." Diss., McGill, 1969.

CF106 Wittke, Carl. "The Immigrant Theme on the American Stage." *Miss. Valley Hist. Rev.*, vol. 39 (1952), 211–32.

CF107 Wittke, Carl. "Melting-Pot Literature." *College Eng.*, vol. 7 (1946), 189–97.

American Writings on German and German-American Themes and Subjects

CF108 Alexander, Lloyd. *Border Hawk: August Bondi*. New York: n.p., 1958. Children's book based on the life of August Bondi, a Kansas Forty-Eighter and supporter of John Brown.

CF109 Bach, Marcus. *The Dream Gate*. Indianapolis: Bobbs-Merrill, 1949. 318p. Rev. by E. Suderman, *Mennonite Life*, vol. 5, no. 4 (1950), 47. Fictionalized account of life among the Hutterites in South Dakota.

CF110 Bennett, Gertrude Ryder. *The Hessian Lieutenant Left His Name*. Francestown, N. H.: Golden Quill Pr., ca. 1976. 272p. Bibliography. Poems about Michael Bach, "Hessian Lieutenant." Based on primary sources—diaries, reports, and letters.

CF111 Bohning, Elizabeth E. "The Nibelungenlied in 19th Century American Periodicals." *German Quar.*, vol. 28 (1955), 14–18.

CF112 Carroll, Curt. *The Golden Herd*. New York: Morrow, 1950. 249p. Novel dealing with the German colonists in New Braunfels, Texas.

CF113 Derleth, August. *Seven Who Waited*. New York: Scribner's, 1943. 230p.

CF114 Derleth, August. *Shadow of Night*. New York: Scribner's, 1943. 354p. The central character of the novel is a German intellectual in Sac Prairie.

CF115 Derleth, August. *Wisconsin Earth: A Sac Prairie Sampler; Shadow of Night; Place of Hawks; Village Year; A Sac Prairie Journal*. Sauk City: Arkham House, 1948.

CF116 Dunham, B. Mabel. *Kristli's Trees*. Toronto: McClelland & Steward Ltd. 1949. 197p. Rev. by P. A. Barba, "'S Pennsylfawnisch Deitsch Eck," Allentown *Morning Call*, 17 December 1949. The story of the boy Kristli Eby who is brought up among the "plain people" living in Waterloo County, Ontario.

CF117 Eby, Kermit. *The God in You*. Chicago: Univ. of Chicago Pr., 1954. 161p. Excellent fictional portrayal of "plain" life in the rural Midwest. Deals with the church and social problems from the point of view of the Church of the Brethren.

CF118 Edrington, William C. *Ticket from Turner's Station*. Deerfield Beach, Fla.: n.p., 1967. 361p. Fiction about early small town life and a German farmer.

CF119 Fast, Howard. *The Hessian*. New York: Morrow, 1972. 192p. A novel.

CF120 Fisher, Frances Hope. *Written in the Stars*. New York: Harper, 1951. 304p. A novel about Albrecht Dürer.

CF121 Freitag, George H. *The Lost Land*. New York: Coward-McCann, 1947. 314p. On the Kreitzers, immigrant farmers in an Ohio mill town, early 20th century.

CF122 Good, Merle, comp. *People Pieces, a Collection of Mennonite and Amish Stories*. Ed. M. Good. Illus. by Allan Eitzen. Scottdale, Pa.: Herald Pr., 1974. 172p.

CF123 Green, Paul. *Trumpet in the Land*. Schoenbrunn Amphitheater, New Philadelphia, Ohio, 1 July–31, August 1975. Historical play about the Moravian missionary David Zeisberger.

CF124 Greene, Patterson. *Papa Is All*. New York: Samuel French, 1942. 134p. Rev. by Clyde F. Lytle: "'Papa is all'." *Hist. Rev. of Berks Co.*, vol. 8 (1942–1943), 55. Adverse review of the play and the production. Three-act comedy dealing with Pennsylvania-German life.

CF125 Harnack, Curtis. *The Work of an Ancient Hand*. London: Weidenfeld & Nicolson, 1961. 318p. Stories about scattered, but related, elements in an Iowan German-immigrant farm community.

CF126 Hearon, Shelby. *A Prince of a Fellow*. Garden City Doubleday, 1978. Portrait of a woman named Avery Krause. Rev. in *New Yorker*, 5 June 1978, 116–17. Fiction set in a small central-Texas town.

CF127 Heyen, William. *The Swastika Poems*. New York: Vanguard, 1976/77. A "remarkable book of poems" on a young German-American's encounter with people in post-Hitlerian Germany.

CF128 Jordan, Mildred. *Proud to Be Amish*. New York: Crown Publs., 1968. Rev. by E. M. Dudley, *Hist. Rev. of Berks Co.*, vol. 34, no. 3 (Summer 1969). Juvenile fiction, grades 3 to 7.

CF129 Krause, Herbert. *The Thresher*. Indianapolis: Bobbs-Merrill, 1946. An impressive farm novel.

CF130 Leland, Charles G. *Mother Pitcher's Poems for Little People*. Philadelphia: n.p., 1864. 54p.

CF131 Leland, Charles G. "Rudolstein, or the Romance of the Nightingale, by Carlos." *Nassau Monthly* (Princeton), vol. 3, no. 7 (June 1844), 211–12.

CF132 Leland, Charles Godfrey. *Hans Breitmann's Ballads*. Philadelphia, ca. 1870. Repr. New York: Dover Publications, 1965. 260p.

CF133 Leland, Charles Godfrey. "Ursachen zum lieben, [by] Carlos." *Nassau Monthly* (Princeton), vol. 2, no. 7 (June 1843), 219.

CF134 Long, Lucile. *Anna Elizabeth, A Dunker Maid of 1748*. Illus. by Iney Goughnour. Elgin, Ill.: Brethren Publ. House, 1942. 125p.

CF135 Manfred, Frederick. *Green Earth*. New York: Crown Publ., ca. 1978. 721p. Novel of an American-Frisian family set in the Midwest of the early 20th century. The author, born in "Siouxland," Iowa, descended from Frisian-Saxon forebears, is the author of 23 books. Rev. by Helga Sandburg, *N.Y. Times Book Rev.*, 22 January 1978.

CF136 Mannin, Ethel Edith (Mrs. Reginald Reynolds). *Bavarian Story*. New York: Appleton, 1950. 314p. Set in post-war Germany.

CF137 Michener, James. *Centennial*. New York: Random House, 1974. 909p. Illus. Massive novel of the conquest of the West. A principal character, a Pennsylvania German Mennonite, moved to Colorado and established Zendt's farm. Hans Brumbaugh is the entrepreneur from St. Louis. Story is told against the background of farming, cattle and sheep raising, mining, etc.

CF138 Miller, Clara Bernice. *The Crying Heart*. Scottdale, Pa.: Herald Pr., 1962. Rev. by C. R. Beam, "'S Pennsylfawnisch Deitsch Eck," Allentown *Morning Call*, 7 January 1967. Novel with Iowa Amish background.

CF139 Miller, Clara Bernice. *Katie*. Scottdale, Pa.: Herald Pr., ca. 1967. 288p. Rev. by C. R. Beam, "'S Pennsylfawnisch Deitsch Eck," Allentown *Morning Call*, 7 January 1967. Novel of life among the Amish.

CF140 Mook, Maurice A. "Not So Plain and Much Too Fancy." "'S Pennsylfawnisch Deitsch Eck," Allentown *Morning Call*, 25 June 1955. Review of the Broadway musical *Plain and Fancy*.

CF141 Morrah, Dave. *Cinderella Hassenpfeffer, and Other Tales Mein Grossfader Told*. New York: Rinehart, 1948. 60p.

CF142 Morrah, Dave. *Fräulein Bo-Peepen and More Tales mein Grossfader Told*. New York: Holt Rinehart & Winston, ca. 1953. 79p.

CF143 Morrah, Dave. *Heinrich Schnibble, and Even More Tales mein Grossfader Told*. New York: Rinehart, 1955. 111p.

CF144 Morrah, Dave. *Who ben Kaputen der Robin? Mein Grossfader's Rhymers and Fable Tellen*. Garden City: Doubleday, 1960. 96p.

CF145 Morrah, Dave. *Der Wizard in Ozzenland. Mein Grossfader's Rhymers and Fable Tellen, mit also Heinrich Schnibble's Deutscher Wordenboke*. Garden City: Doubleday, 1962. 96p.

CF146 Mundis, Jerrold J. (pseud.) *Gerhardt's Children*. New York: Atheneum, 1976. 305p. Novel about four generations of a large German-American family established by Gerhardt Sproul.

CF147 Neusbaum, Frank and Kathryn M. Popp. *Ephrata. Play in Two Parts*. New York: Dramatists Play Service, 1943. Cf. "'S Pennsylvawnisch Deitsch Eck," Allentown *Morning Call*, 12 June 1943.

CF148 Nitzsche, Elsa K. *Marriage by Lot: A Novel Based on Moravian History*. Allentown, Pa.: Pa. German Folklore Soc. Publ., vol. 22 (1958). 149p.

CF149 Parker, Olivia (i.e., Frances Faviell). *Dancing Bear. Berlin de profundis*. New York: Norton, 1954. 246p. Postwar Berlin.

CF150 Pieper, Charlotte. *Wooden Shoe Hollow*. New York: Exposition Pr., 1951. 243p. Novel.

CF151 Pine, Hester. *The Waltz is Over*. New York: Farrar & Rinehart, 1943. 371p. Careful delineation of "Germanic" traits in the story of Marta Nordlander and her family—their Americanization in three generations from 1845 to 1942.

CF152 Porter, Katherine Ann. *Ship of Fools*. Boston: Little, Brown, 1962. 297p. A sharply drawn exhibit of late Nazi-era Germans observed on a voyage from Vera Cruz to Europe.

CF153 Richter, Conrad. *The Free Man*. New York: Knopf, 1943. 155p. Rev. by P. A. Barba, "'S Pennsylfawnisch Deitsch Eck," Allentown *Morning Call*, 2 October 1943, and *Hist. Rev. of Berks Co.*, vol. 9 (1943–1944), 22–24. Colonial Pennsylvania is the setting of the story of Henner Dellicker, native of the German Rhineland, indentured servant who escaped to the frontier and fought for freedom under the name of Henry Free. Rev. by J. J. Stoudt, *Pa. Mag. of Hist. and Biography*, vol. 69, no. 2 (1945), 185–86.

CF154 Richter, Conrad. *Over the Blue Mountain*. New York: Knopf, 1967. Juvenile novel based on an old Pennsylvania Dutch rain legend.

CF155 Richter, Conrad. *A Simple Honorable Man*. New York: Knopf, 1962. 310p. Novel of the life of a Lutheran minister in rural Pennsylvania at the turn of the century.

CF156 Richter, William Benson (pseud. Benson Williams.) *Life and Loves of Von Steuben*. Boston: Christopher, 1952. 224p.

CF157 Rimland, Ingrid. *The Wanderers. The Saga of Three Women Who Survived*. St. Louis: Concordia Publ. House, 1977. 352p. Novel. Tells of the thousand-mile winter trek of Mennonites attempting to escape Russian persecution in the 1940's. The survivors found a haven in Paraguay and moved thence to Canada and the United States. Written by an eyewitness who took up English at the age of 30.

CF158 Seyfert, Ella Mae. *Amish Moving Day*. New York: Crowell, 1942. 126p. Rev. by Grace Wenger, *Amer.-German Rev.*, vol. 9, no. 1 (1942), 34; P. A. Barba, "'S Pennsylfawnisch Deitsch Eck," Allentown *Morning Call*, 21 November 1942. Story of a Pennsylvania Amish family who moved to a new farm in Maryland. Juvenile fiction, ages 8–12.

CF159 Singmaster, Elsie. "Dinner Was Late." "'S Pennsylfawnisch Deitsch Eck," Allentown *Morning Call*, 12 June 1943. Author lived 1879–1958.

CF160 Singmaster, Elsie. "The Great Book." Excerpted from *Stories of Pennsylvania*. "'S Pennsylfawnisch Deitsch Eck," Allentown *Morning Call*, 9 March 1963. The story of Peter Mueller, Reformed pastor who succeeded Conrad Beissel as head of the Ephrata Cloister.

CF161 Singmaster, Elsie. *A High Wind Rising*. Boston: Houghton Mifflin, 1942. Rev. by P. A. Barba, "'S Pennsylfawnisch Deitsch Eck," Allentown *Morning Call*, 12 December 1942. A story of the heroic Pennsylvania Germans during the French and Indian wars.

CF162 Singmaster, Elsie. *I Heard of a River: The Story of the Germans in Pennsylvania*. Philadelphia: Winston, 1948. 209p. Rev. by P. A. Barba, "'S Pennsylfawnisch Deitsch Eck," Allentown *Morning Call*, 29 October 1949, Juvenile story of the first Mennonites in Lancaster County.

CF163 Singmaster, Elsie. *The Magic Mirror*. Boston: Houghton Mifflin, 1934. 284p.

CF164 Singmaster, Elsie. *Martin Luther. The Story of His Life*. Philadelphia: Muhlenberg Pr., ca. 1939.

CF165 Singmaster, Elsie. *Pennsylvania's Susquehanna*. Harrisburg: n.p., 1950. Rev. by J. G. D'Arcy Paul, *Md. Hist. Mag.*, vol. 46 (1951), 148–49.

CF166 Singmaster, Elsie. "Regina." "'S Pennsylfawnisch Deitsch Eck," Allentown *Morning Call*, 8 April 1944. Repr. from *Stories of Pennsylvania*.

CF167 Singmaster, Elsie. *Rifles for Washington*. Illus. by Frank E. Schoonover. Boston: Houghton, Mifflin Co., 1938. 321p.

CF168 Singmaster, Elsie. "Sorrel Dan, 1775." "'S Pennsylfawnisch Deitsch Eck," Allentown *Morning Call*, 27 March, 1943.

CF169 Singmaster, Elsie. *Stories of Pennsylvania*. Illus. by Alden Turner. Harrisburg: Pennsylvania Book Service, ca. 1937.

CF170 Singmaster, Elsie. *The Story of Lutheran Missions*. Columbus, S. Car.: Woman's Missionary Societies of the Lutheran Church, ca. 1917. 221p.

CF171 Smith, DeCost. *Martyrs of the Oblong and Little Nine*. Caldwell, Idaho: Caxton Pr., 1948. 311p. Account of the relations between the Mo-

American Writings (cont.)

hawks, Delawares and Moravian missionaries in the 18th century. Sufferings and persecution of Mohican Indians converted to Christianity, 1700–1813.

CF172 Steuber, William F. *The Landlooker.* Indianapolis: Bobbs-Merrill, 1957. 367p. Novel set in German Wisconsin of 1871.

CF173 Stone, Nancy. *Whistle up the Bay.* Grand Rapids: Eerdmans, 1966. 219p. Rev. by F. S. Ceasar, *Mich. Hist.*, vol. 50, no. 3 (1966), 263–64. Historical novel dealing with a Swiss immigrant family.

CF174 Sykes, Hope. *The Joppa Door.* New York: Putnam, 1937. 274p. Story of a German girl in her migrations to Palestine and subsequently to the United States, establishing a large family with her Russian-born German husband.

CF175 Toepfer, Amy Brungardt, and Agnes Dreiling. *Conquering the Wind.* Garwood, N.J.: Victor C. Leiker, 1967. 208p.

CF176 Vrooman, John J. *The Promised Land. The Story of the Palatine Emigration from Their Rhineland Homes to the Hudson and Schoharie Valleys.* Johnstown and New York: The Baronet Lith. Co., 1958. Centering on the fortunes of the Weisers, father and son.

CF177 Wendt, Lloyd. *Bright Tomorrow.* Indianapolis: Bobbs-Merrill, 1945. Farm novel; anti-German feeling in a South Dakota community during World War II.

CF178 Wilbur, Marguerite E. *John Sutter, Rascal and Adventurer.* New York: Liveright, 1949. 371p. Rev. by R. K. Wyllys, *Pacific Hist. Rev.*, vol. 17 (1949), 400–01. Fictionalized biography.

CF179 Woiwode, Larry. *Beyond the Bedroom Wall (A Family Album).* New York: Farrar, Straus, Giroux, 1975. 619p. Chronicle of life in the Neumiller family of North Dakota. A powerfully felt study of acculturation in the Midwestern setting.

CF180 Wonsetler, Adelaide Hill. *Liberty for Johanny.* Illus. by John C. Wonsetler. N.p.: Longmans Publs., 1943. 287p. Tale of adventures that befall a Mennonite farmer boy of Pennsylvania during the American Revolution.

CF181 Yoder, Joseph Warren. *Rosanna of the Amish.* Huntingdon, Pa.: Yoder Publ. Co., 1940. 319p. Rev. by A. E. Zucker, *Amer.-German Rev.*, vol. 8, no. 3 (1942), 34.

CF182 Yoder, Joseph Warren. *Rosanna's Boys. A Sequel to Rosanna of the Amish.* Huntingdon, Pa.: n.p., 1948. 345p.

CF183 Zietlow, E. R. *Zietlow.* New York: Knopf, 1960. A study of the old and the new ways on a ranch in South Dakota.

American Authors: Their Germanic Interests and Influences

ADAMS, JOHN QUINCY

CF184 Adams, Thomas B. "John Quincy Adams: Patriot in Literature." In: *John Quincy Adams: Pioneer of German-American Literary Studies.* Ed. Anneliese Harding. Boston: Harvard Univ. Printing Office, 1979, p.19–25.

CF185 Allen, David G. "John Quincy Adams' Mission to Prussia." In: *John Quincy Adams: Pioneer of German-American Literary Studies.* Ed. Anneliese Harding. Boston: Harvard Univ. Printing Office, 1979, p.26–39.

CF186 Finckenstein, Hans-Werner (Graf von). "A Man of Letters on a Diplomatic Mission." In: *John Quincy Adams: Pioneer of German-American Literary Studies.* Ed. Anneliese Harding. Boston: Harvard Univ. Printing Office, 1979, p.40–51.

CF187 Harding, Anneliese, ed. *John Quincy Adams: Pioneer of German-American Literary Studies.* Cambridge, Mass.: Harvard Univ. Printing Office, 1979. 100p.

CF188 Morris, Walter J. "The Father of German Studies in America: John Quincy Adams." In: *John Quincy Adams: Pioneer of German-American Literary Studies.* Ed. Anneliese Harding. Cambridge, Mass.: Harvard Univ., 1979, p.68–86.

CF189 Morris, Walter John. "John Quincy Adams: Germanophile." Diss., Pennsylvania State, 1963.

CF190 Morris, Walter John. "John Quincy Adams's German Library, With a Catalogue of His German Books." *Procs. Amer. Philosophical Soc.*, vol. 118 (September 1974), 321–33.

CF191 Morris, Walter John. "J. Q. Adams' Verse Translations of C. F. Gellert's Fables." In: *Helen Adolf Festschrift*. Ed. S. Z. Buehne et al. New York: Ungar, 1968, p.138–65.

AIKEN, CONRAD

CF192 Carlile, Robert E. "Great Circle: Conrad Aiken's Musico-Literary Technique." *Ga. Rev.*, vol. 22 (1968), 27–36. Aiken's mode of composition seen as paralleling Mozart.

ALLSTON, WASHINGTON

CF193 Allston, Washington. "The Paint King." *Monthly Anthology and Boston Rev.*, vol. 7 (1809), 391–95. A poem; parody of German and Danish ballads as translated by M. G. Lewis and Walter Scott.

BELLOW, SAUL

CF194 Chavkin, Allan. "Baron Humboldt and Bellow's Von Humboldt Fleischer: Success and Failure in *Humboldt's Gift*." *Notes on Contemporary Lit.*, vol. 10, no. 2 (1980), 11–12.

CF195 Kathe, Barbara Ann. "Self Realization: The Jungian Process of Individuation in the Novels of Saul Bellow." Diss., Drew Univ., 1979. 269p.

CF196 Rodrigues, Eusebio L. "Herzog and Hegel." *Notes on Mod. Amer. Lit.*, vol. 2 (1978), item 16.

BOYLE, KAY

CF197 Boyle, Kay. *Smoking Mountain: Stories of Postwar Germany*. New York: McGraw, 1951. 273p.

BRAND, MILLEN

CF198 Brand, Millen. *Local Lives. Poems About the Pennsylvania Dutch*. New York: Clarkson N. Potter/Crown Publ., 1975. 544p. Rev. by W. Stafford, *N.Y. Times Book Review*, 18 May 1975, 22. Rev. by D. H. Tolzmann, *German-Amer. Studies*, vol. 10 (Fall 1975), 74–75. On the life of Mennonite, Amish, Quaker, and Brethren groups in Pennsylvania.

BRANDES, GEORGE

CF199 Liptzin, Sol. "Georg Brandes and Richard Beer-Hoffmann." *Mod. Austrian Lit. Jour. of the Internat. Arthur Schnitzler Research Assoc.*, vol. 12, no. 1 (1979), 19–29.

BROOKS, CHARLES TIMOTHY

CF200 Schoenfeldt, Arthur. "Charles Timothy Brooks, Translator of German Literature." *Amer.-German Rev.*, vol. 18 (1952), 22–23.

CF201 Shelley, Philip A. "Anastasius Grün and Charles T. Brooks." *PMLA*, vol. 57 (1942), 586–87.

CF202 Stern, Guy. "Blücher, Brooks, and August Kopisch: A Report on an Unpublished Translation." *German-Amer. Studies*, vol. 5 (1972), 8–11. Unpubl. translations by C. T. Brooks among the papers of the late Edward Carey Gardiner, now in the library of the Pa. Hist. Soc. Stern prints one example, "Blücher am Rhein" by Kopisch, from among the poetic translations there discovered.

BROWN, CHARLES BROCKDEN

CF203 Brown, Charles B. *The Rhapsodist and Other Uncollected Writings*. Ed. Harry R. Warfel. New York: Scholars Facsimiles and Reprints, 1943. 156p.

CF204 Frank, John G. "The Wieland Family in Charles Brockden Brown's *Wieland*." *Monatshefte*, vol. 42, no. 7 (1950), 347–53. A long-range illumination of German ideas in this major work (1798) of "the father of the American novel."

CF205 Hemenway, Robert E., and Dean H. Keller. "Charles Brockden Brown, America's First Important Novelist: A Check List of Biography and Criticism." *Publs., Bibliographic Soc. of America*, vol. 60, no. 3 (1966), 349–62. Incl. the German sources of Brown's novels.

CF206 Preu, James A. "The Tale of Terror." *Eng. Jour.*, vol. 47 (1958), 243–47.

CF207 Soldati, Joseph A. "The Americanization of Faust: A Study of Charles Brockden Brown's *Wieland*." *Emerson Soc. Quar.*, vol. 74 (1974), 1–14.

CF208 Wiley, Lulu R. *The Sources and Influence of the Novels of Charles Brockden Brown.* New York: Vantage Pr., 1950. 381p.

BROWNE, JOHN ROSS

CF209 Weisert, John J. "John Ross Browne, Proto-Innocent in Germany." *Amer.-German Rev.*, vol. 25 (1959), no. 3, 131–35. About Browne's *An American Family in Germany* (1867).

CALVERT, GEORGE HENRY

CF210 Everson, Ida. *George Henry Calvert, American Literary Pioneer.* New York: Columbia Univ. Pr., 1944. 330p. Rev. by D. J. Gordon, *Rev. of Eng. Studies*, vol. 21 (1945), 251; B. J. Loewenberg, *Miss. Valley Hist. Rev.*, vol. 32, no. 1 (1945), 135–36.

CF211 Hagge, C. W. "G. H. Calvert's Translations from the German." *Mod. Lang. Notes*, vol. 57 (1942), 283–84.

CF212 Hoyt, William D., Jr. "The Calvert-Stier Correspondence. Letters from America to the Low Countries, 1797–1828." *Md. Hist. Mag.*, vol. 38 (1943), 123–40, 261–72, 337–44. Rosalier Stier Calvert reads Gesner in trans. with approbation; George, Jr., attends Göttingen.

CF213 Pfund, Harry W. "George Henry Calvert, Admirer of Goethe." In: *Studies in Honor of John Albrecht Walz.* Lancaster: Lancaster Pr., 1941, p. 117–61.

CATHER, WILLA

CF214 Andes, Cynthia J. "The Bohemian Folk Practice in 'Neighbour Rosicky'." *Western Amer. Lit.*, vol. 7, no. 1 (1972) 63–64. On a story by Willa Cather.

CF215 Bennett, Mildred R. *The World of Willa Cather. Fragments of Inheritance, Place, Childhood Friends, Scholarship, Methods of Writing and Literary Experience.* New York: Dodd, Mead, 1951. 226p. Cather in her prairie town home in the latter 1880's.

CF216 Budz, Judith Kaufman. "The Immigrant Experience on the Great Plains." *Ill. School Jour.*, vol. 55 (1975), 21–27. On Willa Cather.

CF217 Pfund, Harry W. "Willa Cather's German Characters." *Amer.-German Rev.*, vol. 21, no. 5 (1955), 9–11, 31.

CHESEBROUGH, CAROLINE

CF218 Werner, William L. "The First Novel about the Pennsylvania Germans." "'S Pennsylfawnisch Deitsch Eck, Allentown *Morning Call*, 2 November 1957. A novel by Caroline Chesebrough ran serially in the *Atlantic Monthly* from March through December 1869 and was published in book form by Estes, Lauriat and James R. Osgood Co., Boston, 1871.

CLEMENS, SAMUEL L. (PSEUD. MARK TWAIN)

CF219 Fairley, Barker. "Raabe and Mark Twain: A Point of Contact." *Jahrbuch der Raabe-Gesellschaft*, vol. 4 (1963), 76–77.

CF220 Fiedler, Leslie. "An American Abroad." *Partisan Rev.*, vol. 33 (Winter 1966), 77–91. On Twain's image of Europe; he saw it as an instrument for defining America.

CF221 Hemminghaus, Edgar H. "Mark Twain's German Provenience." *Mod. Lang. Quar.*, vol. 6, no. 4 (1945), 459–78.

CF222 Hibler, Leo von. "Mark Twain und die deutsche Sprache." *Anglia*, vol. 65, nos. 1–3 (1941), 200–13.

CF223 Hietsch, Otto. "Mark Twain und Johann Strauss." *Jahrbuch für Amerikastudien*, vol. 8 (1963), 210–11. A letter of Twain's dated June 1899 testifies to his meeting Strauss.

CF224 Klotz, Herbert E. "Goethe and Mark Twain." *Notes and Queries*, vol. 7 (1960), 150–51.

CF225 Krumpelmann, John T. *Mark Twain and the German Language.* Baton Rouge, La.: Louisiana St. Univ. Pr., 1953. 21p. Rev. by W. A. Willibrand, *Books Abroad*, vol. 28 (1954), 350; in *Monatshefte*, vol. 46 (1954), 155; by H. Hever, *Archiv für das Studium der neueren Sprachen*, vol. 192 (1956), 71–72.

CF226 MacGowan, Gault. "Mark Twain in Heidelberg." *Mark Twain Quar.*, vol. 9 (1951), 30.

CF227 McKeithan, D. M. "Mark Twain's Letters of Thomas J. Snodgrass." *Philological Quar.*, vol. 32 (1953), 353–65. Twain reports on a performance of *Lohengrin* in Mannheim.

CF228 Parsons, Coleman O. "The Background of *The Mysterious Stranger*." *Amer. Lit.*, vol. 32, no.

1 (1960), 55–74. Incl. discussion of possible German influences.

CF229 Scott, Arthur L. "Mark Twain Looks at Europe." *South Atlantic Quar.*, vol. 52 (1953), 399–413.

CF230 Smith, Henry N. "Mark Twain's Image of Hannibal: From St. Petersburg to Eseldorf." *Univ. of Texas Studies in English*, vol. 37 (1958), 3–23.

CF231 Vagts, Alfred. "Mark Twain at the Courts of the Emperor." *Jahrbuch für Amerikastudien*, vol. 9 (1964), 149–51. Twain meets European royalty.

CF232 Wecter, Dixon. "Mark Twain as Translator from the German." *Amer. Lit.*, vol. 13, no. 3 (1941), 257–63.

CF233 Weisert, John J. "Once Again: Mark Twain and German." *Mark Twain Jour.*, vol. 12, no. 4 (1965), 16.

CF234 Wilson, James D. "*The Mysterious Stranger* and Goethe's *Faust*." In: *Actes du VIIe congrès de l'Assoc. Internationale de Littérature Comparée... Literature of America: Dependence, Independence, Interdependence*. Ed. Milan V. Dimić and Juan Ferraté. Stuttgart: Bieber, 1979, p. 159–64.

CONNELLY, MARC

CF235 Krumpelmann, John T. "Marc Connelly's *The Green Pastures* and Goethe's *Faust*." In: *Studies in Comparative Literature*. Ed. Waldo F. McNeir. Baton Rouge: La. State Univ. Pr., 1962, p. 199–218.

COOPER, JAMES FENIMORE

CF236 Baym, Max I. and Percy Matenko. "The Odyssey of *The Water-Witch* and a Susan Fenimore Cooper Letter." *N.Y. Hist.*, vol. 51, no. 1 (January 1970). Deal in part with Cooper's visit to Dresden in 1830.

CF237 McCarthy, H. T. "James Fenimore Cooper: The European Novels." In: *The Expatriate Perspective. American Novelists and the Idea of America*. Fairleigh Dickinson Univ. Pr., 1974, p. 125–46.

CF238 Riese, Teut Andreas. "Fenimore Cooper als Gestalter deutscher Geschichte: Betrachtungen zu seinem Roman *Die Heidenmauer*." *Ruperto-Carola*, vol. 41 (1967).

CF239 Stockton, Edwin L. "The Influence of the Moravians upon the Leather-Stocking Tales." *Transactions, Moravian Hist. Soc.*, vol. 20 (1964), part 1. Cf. his diss. of the same title, Florida State Univ., 1961.

CF240 Wehmeyer, William Anthony. "The European Novels of James Fenimore Cooper: A Critical Study." Diss., Notre Dame, 1962. 291p.

CF241 Williams, J. Gary. "Cooper and European Catholicism: A Reading of *The Heidenmauer*." *Emerson Soc. Quar.*, vol. 22 (1976), 149–58. The novel becomes C.'s "vehicle for a public admonition against undervaluing the spiritual worth of Catholicism."

CRANE, HART

CF242 Bassoff, Bruce. "[Hart] Crane's 'For the Marriage of Faustus and Helen,' III, 1–23." *Explicator*, vol. 31 (1973), item 53.

CF243 "Decorum and Terror: Homage to Goethe and Hart Crane." *Pacific Spectator*, vol. 10 (1956), 292–94. Poem.

CF244 Dickinson-Brown, Roger. "Crane's 'For the Marriage of Faustus and Helen,' II 7–8 and 11–12." *Explicator*, vol. 31 (1973), item 66.

CF245 Hendrick, George. "Hart Crane Aboard the Ship of Fools." *Twentieth Century Lit.*, vol. 9 (April 1963), 1–9.

CRANE, STEPHEN

CF246 Helm, Johannes. "In Memory of Stephen Crane." *Amer.-German Rev.*, vol. 26, no. 1 (1959), 16–17, 36. On Crane's last days at Badenweiler and recent efforts to erect a memorial to him there.

CF247 Hough, Robert L. "Crane and Goethe: A Forgotten Relationship." *Nineteenth-Century Fiction*, vol. 17, no. 2 (1962), 135–48. Goethean psychology of color and the structure of the *Red Badge of Courage*. "Whether Crane knew Goethe or the Impressionists first, he put color to the same uses."

DOCTOROW, E. L.

CF248 Ditsky, John. "The German Source of *Ragtime*: A Note" *Ontario Rev.*, vol. 4 (1976), 84–86. Heinrich v. Kleist.

CF249 Faber, Marion. "Michael Kohlhaas in New York: Kleist and E. L. Doctorow's *Ragtime*." In: *Heinrich von Kleist Studies*. Ed. A. Ugrinsky et al. Hofstra Univ. Cultural and Intercultural Studies, no. 3. New York: AMS Pr., ca. 1979, p.147–56.

CF250 Gelus, Marjorie and Ruth Crowley. "Kleist in *Ragtime*: Doctorow's Novel, Its German Source and Its Reviewers." *Jour. of Popular Culture*, vol. 14 (1980), 20–26.

CF251 Helbling, Robert E. "E. L. Doctorow's *Ragtime*: Kleist Revisited." In: *Heinrich von Kleist Studies*. Ed. A. Ugrinsky et al. Hofstra Univ. Cultural and Intercultural Studies, no. 3. New York: AMS Pr., ca. 1979, p.157–67.

CF252 Knorr, Walter L. "Doctorow and Kleist: 'Kohlhaas' in *Ragtime*." *Mod. Fiction Studies*, vol. 22 (Summer 1976), 224–27.

CF253 Kurth-Voigt, Lieselotte E. "Kleistian Overtones in E. L. Doctorow's *Ragtime*." *Monatshefte*, vol. 69 (1977), 404–14.

CF254 Neumeyer, Peter F. "E. L. Doctorow, Kleist, and the Ascendancy of Things." *C E A Critic: An Official Jour. of the College Eng. Assoc.*, vol. 39, no. 4 (1977), 17–21.

DREISER, THEODORE

CF255 Leisy, Ernest E. "Dreiser's Mennonite Origin." *Mennonite Life*, vol. 9 (1954), 179–80.

CF256 Staab, Wolfgang. "Das Deutschlandbild Theodore Dreisers." Diss., Mainz, 1961.

DUNLAP, WILLIAM

CF257 Grinchuk, Robert. "The Plays of William Dunlap: A Study of Popular Culture." Diss., Minnesota, 1966.

DUPONCEAU, PETER STEPHEN

CF258 Krumpelmann, John T. *Duponceau and German Letters*. Britannica et Americana, vol. 4. Hamburg: Cram de Gruyter & Co., 1959. 235p. On D. (1760–1844).

CF259 Krumpelmann, John T. "Duponceau and Weimar." *Die Neueren Sprachen*, N. F. vol. 8 (1959), 57–61.

ELIOT, THOMAS STEARNS

CF260 Barry, John. "*The Waste Land*: a Possible German Source." *Compar. Lit. Studies*, vol. 9 (1972), 429–42. On the influence of Spengler.

CF261 Beare, R. L. "T. S. Eliot and Goethe." *Germanic Rev.*, vol. 28 (1953), 243–53. A summary of Eliot's views on Goethe.

CF262 Curtius, Ernest Robert. "T. S. Eliot und Deutschland." *Der Monat*, vol. 1, no. 3 (1948), 75.

CF263 Hochwald, Ilse E. "Eliot's *Cocktail Party* and Goethe's *Wahlverwandtschaften*." *Germanic Rev.*, vol. 29 (1954), 254–59. Eliot used the Goethean novel as a source.

CF264 Howarth, Herbert. "Eliot and Hofmannsthal." *South Atlantic Quar.*, vol. 59 (1960), 500–09.

CF265 Howarth, Herbert. "Eliot, Beethoven, and J.W.N. Sullivan." *Compar. Lit.*, vol. 9 (1957), 322–32. Quarter op. 132 and the form of Eliot's *Four Quartets*.

CF266 Lees, F. N. "T. S. Eliot and Nietzsche." *Notes and Queries*, vol. 11 (October 1964), 386–87.

CF267 Peacock, Ronald. "T. S. Eliot on Goethe." In: *The Discontinuous Tradition: Studies in German Literature in Honor of Ernest Ludwig Stahl*. Ed. Peter F. Ganz. New York: Oxford Univ. Pr., 1971, p.67–78.

CF268 Steinmann, Martin. "Coleridge, T. S. Eliot and Organism." *Mod. Lang. Notes*, vol. 71 (1956), 339–40. Points to the line A. W. Schlegel–Coleridge–Eliot.

CF269 Takayanagi, Shunichi. "Virgil, Theodore Haecker and T. S. Eliot." *Eng. Lit. and Lang.* (Tokyo), vol. 8 (1971), 37–63.

CF270 Weigand, Elsie. "Rilke and Eliot." *Germanic Rev.*, vol. 30 (1955), 198–210. Centering around the Ninth Duino Elegy and "Burnt Norton."

CF271 Wood, Frank. "T. S. Eliot and Rilke." *Germanic Rev.*, vol. 27 (1952), 246–59.

ENGLE, PAUL

CF272 Engle, Paul. *Always the Land.* New York: Random House, 1941. A farming family in Iowa through the generations.

FITZGERALD, F. SCOTT

CF273 Qualls, Barry V. "Physician in the Counting House: The Religious Motif in *Tender Is the Night*." *Essays in Literature* (Western Ill. Univ.), vol. 2 (1975), 192–208. F.'s interest in Spengler's *Decline of the West* may be a key to a reading of the novel as an essentially religious drama.

CF274 Schmid, Hans. "The Switzerland of Fitzgerald and Hemingway." *Fitzgerald-Hemingway Annual* (1978), 261–71.

FRANKLIN, BENJAMIN

CF275 Blair, Walter. "Franklin's Massacre of the Hessians." In: *Toward a New American Literary History and Essays in Honor of Arlin Turner.* Ed. Louis J. Budd, Edwin H. Cady, and Carl L. Anderson. Durham, N. Car.: Duke Univ. Pr., 1980, p. 84–90.

CF276 Gallacher, Stuart A. "Franklin's *Way to Wealth*." *Jour. of Eng. and Germanic Philology*, vol. 48, no. 2 (1949), 229–51. Franklin's knowledge of German proverbs.

CF277 Kahn, Robert L. "Addendum Concerning a Lost Franklin-Raspe Letter (1770)." *Procs., Amer. Philosophical Soc.*, vol. 100 (1956), 279.

CF278 Kahn, Robert L. "A Meeting between Lichtenberg and Franklin." *German Life and Letters*, vol. 9 (1956), 64–67.

CF279 Kahn, Robert L. "Some Unpublished Raspe–Franklin Letters." *Procs., Amer. Philosophical Soc.*, vol. 99, no. 3 (1955), 127–32. Correspondence with Rudolf Erich Raspe, author of the Münchhausen tales, between 1766 and 1780.

CF280 Kahn, Robert L. "Three Franklin–Raspe Letters." *Procs., Amer. Philosophical Soc.*, vol. 99 (1955), 397–400. Further correspondence with R. E. Raspe.

CF281 Walz, Hans. "Benjamin Franklin in Hannover 1766." *Hannoversche Geschichtsblätter*, nos. 1–2, 1967. In German.

HARTE, BRET

CF282 Lewis, Ward B. "Bret Harte and Germany." *Revue de Littérature Comparée*, vol. 54 (1980), 213–24.

HAWTHORNE, NATHANIEL

CF283 Alsen, Eberhard. "Hawthorne: A Puritan Tieck. A Comparative Analysis of the Tales of Hawthorne and the *Märchen* of Tieck." Diss., Indiana, 1967. 228p. Finds similarities in motifs, characters, form, and artistic intent.

CF284 Alsen, Eberhard. "Poe's Theory of Hawthorne's Indebtedness to Tieck." *Anglia*, vol. 91 (1973), 342–56.

CF285 Brumm, Ursula. "Amerikanische Dichter und europäische Geschichte: Nathaniel Hawthorne—Mark Twain." In: *Geschichte und Fiktion: Amerikanische Prosa im 19. Jahrhundert/ History and Fiction...* Ed. Alfred Weber and Hartmut Grandel. Göttingen: Vandenhoeck & Ruprecht, 1972, p. 85–108.

CF286 Dameron, J. L. "Hawthorne and *Blackwood's* Review of Goethe's *Faust*." *Emerson Soc. Quar.*, no. 19 (1960), 25.

CF287 Devlin, James E. "A German Analogue for 'The Ambitious Guest'." *Amer. Transcendental Quar.*, vol. 17 (1973), 71–74.

CF288 Herndon, Jerry A., and Sidney P. Moss. "The Identity and Significance of the German Jewish Showman in Hawthorne's 'Ethan Brand'." *College Eng.*, vol. 23 (February 1962), 362–63.

CF289 Krumpelmann, John T. "Hawthorne's 'Young Goodman Brown' and Goethe's 'Faust'." *Die Neueren Sprachen*, vol. 11 (1956), 516–21.

CF290 Male, Roy R., Jr. "Hawthorne and the Concept of Sympathy." *PMLA*, vol. 68 (1953), 138–48. Touches on affinities with Goethe and German Romanticism.

CF291 Marks, Alfred H. "German Romantic Irony in Hawthorne's Tales." *Symposium*, vol. 7 (1954), 274–305. Like F. Schlegel, Tieck and others, Hawthorne used self-mockery, self-conscious narration and contradictory tones to heighten artistic effect.

CF292 Napier, Elizabeth R. "Aylmer as 'Scheidekünstler': The Pattern of Union and Separation in Hawthorne's 'The Birthmark'." *South Atlantic Bull.*, vol. 41 (November 1976), 32–35.

CF293 Rowe, John C. "The Internal Conflict of Romantic Narrative: Hegel's *Phenomenology* and Hawthorne's *The Scarlet Letter.*" *Mod. Lang. Notes*, vol. 95 (1980), 1203–31.

CF294 Schwarz, Peter. "Zwei mögliche 'Faust'- Quellen für Hawthorne's Roman *The Scarlet Letter.*" *Jahrbuch für Amerikastudien*, vol. 10 (1965), 198–205.

CF295 Sokoloff, B. A. "Ethan Brand's Twin." *Mod. Lang. Notes*, vol. 73 (1958), 413–14. The role of the German in Hawthorne's work.

CF296 Stein, William B. "The Faust Myth and Hawthorne." Diss., Florida, 1951.

CF297 Stein, William B. *Hawthorne's Faust*. Gainesville: Univ. of Florida Pr., 1953. 172p. Rev. by S. T. Williams, *Books Abroad*, vol. 28 (1954), 352; R. H. Pearce, *Mod. Lang. Notes*, vol. 71 (1955), 61–63. A study of the Devil-archetype.

CF298 Stoehr, Taylor. "Physiognomy in Hawthorne." *Huntington Library Quar.*, vol. 37 (1973–1974), 355–400. H.'s interest in phrenological science, physiognomical speculation and related occultisms.

CF299 Van Leer, David M. "Aylmer's Library: Transcendental Alchemy in Hawthorne's 'The Birthmark'." *ESQ, Jour. of the Amer. Renaissance*, vol. 22 (1976), 211–20.

"H. D."

CF300 Eder, Doris. "Freud and H. D." *Book Forum. An Internat. Transdisciplinary Quar.*, vol. 1 (1975), 365–69. A review article on H. D.'s *Tribute to Freud* (Boston: Godine, 1974).

HEMINGWAY, ERNEST

CF301 Bataille, Georges. "Hemingway à la lumière de Hegel." *Critique*, vol. 9 (1953) 195–210.

CF302 Kann, Hans-Joachim. "Ernest Hemingway's Knowledge of German." *Jahrbuch für Amerikastudien*, vol. 15 (1970), 221–32.

CF303 Ruhm, Herbert. "Hemingway in Schruns." *Commonweal*, vol. 99 (1973), 344–45. H. spent the winters and 1925 and 1926 in Schruns, Austria.

HERGESHEIMER, JOSEPH

CF304 Justus, James H. "Joseph Hergesheimer's Germany: A Radical Art of Surfaces." *Jour. of Amer. Studies*, vol. 7 (1973), 47–66.

HORGAN, PAUL

CF305 Horgan, Paul. "How Dr. Faustus Came to Rochester." *Harper's*, vol. 172 (1936), 506–15.

HOWELLS, WILLIAM DEAN

CF306 Altenbernd, A. Lynn. "The Influence of European Travel on the Political and Social Outlook of Henry Adams, William Dean Howells, and Mark Twain." Diss., Ohio State, 1955.

CF307 Betts, William W., Jr. "The Relations of William D. Howells to German Life and Letters." In: *Anglo-German and American-German Crosscurrents*. Ed. P. A. Shelley, A. O. Lewis, and Wm. W. Betts. 2 vols. Chapel Hill: Univ. of N. Car. Pr., 1957–1962. Vol. 1, p. 189–240.

CF308 Graeff, Arthur D. "William Dean Howells." "'S Pennsylfawnisch Deitsch Eck," Allentown *Morning Call*, 13 May, 1944.

CF309 Howells, William D. *A Hazard of New Fortunes*. New York: n.p., 1890. German characters appear p. 64–66, 109, 118.

CF310 Howells, William Dean. "A Little German Capital." Essay. *The Nation*, vol. 2, 4 January 1866, 11–13.

IRVING, WASHINGTON

CF311 Brooks, E. L. "A Note on Irving's Sources." *Amer. Lit.*, vol. 25 (1953), 229–30. Musäus's legends of Rübezahl.

CF312 Brooks, Elmer L. "A Note on the Source of *Rip Van Winkle*." *Amer. Lit.*, vol. 25, no. 4 (1953), 495–96. The *London Magazine* in March 1822 carried what was probably the first English version of Irving's most likely source, a translation from Büsching's *Volkssagen, Märchen und Legenden*.

CF313 Buell, Thomas C. "The Professional Idler: Washington Irving's European Years: *The Sketch Book* and Its Sequels." Diss., Univ. of Washington, 1966.

CF314 Hoffman, Daniel G. "Irving's Use of American Folklore in 'The Legend of Sleepy Hollow'." *PMLA*, vol. 68 (1953), 425–35. Irving's knowledge of Othmar's *Volkssagen* and Musäus's *Volksmärchen*.

CF315 Irving, Washington. *Astoria: or, Anecdotes of an Enterprise beyond the Rocky Mountains*. Ed. and introd. by Edgeley W. Todd. Oklahoma Univ. Pr., 1964. 556p. Annotated ed. of a classic of American business history, on Astor's venture to the mouth of the Columbia.

CF316 Kleinfeld, H. L. "A Census of Washington Irving Manuscripts." *Bull., N.Y. Public Library*, vol. 68 (1964), 13–32.

CF317 Krumpelmann, John T. "Revealing the Source of Irving's *Rip Van Winkle*." *Monatshefte*, vol. 47 (1955), 361–62. Also in *Archiv für das Studium der neueren Sprachen*, vol. 193 (1957), 39–40. On Bayard Taylor's discovery in the *Atlantic Monthly* 1868.

CF318 McClary, Ben H. "Irving's Literary Borrowing." *Notes and Queries*, vol. 16 (February 1969), 57–58.

CF319 Myers, Andrew B., ed. *A Century of Commentary (1860–1974) on the Works of Washington Irving*. Tarrytown, N.Y.: Sleepy Hollow Restorations, 1976. 504p. Reprintings of 45 selections, often excerpts from books.

CF320 Myers, Andrew Breen. "Washington Irving, Fur Trade Chronicler: An Analysis of Astoria with Notes for a Corrected Edition." Diss., Columbia Univ., 1964. 303p.

CF321 Reichart, Walter A. "Baron von Gumppenberg, Emily Foster and Washington Irving." *Mod. Lang. Notes*, vol. 60, no. 5 (1945), 333–35.

CF322 Reichart, Walter A. "Concerning the Source of Irving's 'Rip van Winkle'." *Monatshefte*, vol. 48 (1956), 94–95. On Büsching's *Volks-Sagen, Märchen und Legenden* (1812), as the likeliest.

CF323 Reichart, Walter A. "Washington Irving and Friedrich Schiller." *Jahrbuch der deutschen Schillergesellschaft*, vol. 3 (1959), 210–17. Points out Irving's enthusiasm for Schiller's dramatic and historical writings.

CF324 Reichart, Walter A. *Washington Irving and Germany*. Ann Arbor: Univ. of Mich. Pr., 1957. 212p. Rev. by A. L. Altenbernd, *Jour. of Eng. and Germanic Philology*, vol. 57 (1958), 562–63; H. Oppel, *Die neueren Sprachen*, N.F., vol. 6 (1957), 493–94; H. Papajewski, *Germanisch-Romanische Monatsschrift*, N.F., vol. 8 (1958), 315–16; Henry A. Pochmann, *Amer. Lit.*, vol. 30 (1958), 247–49; W. W. Pusey, *Germanic Rev.*, vol. 33 (1958), 237–39; H. W. Rudman, *Books Abroad*, vol. 32 (1958), 83–84; F. G. Ryder, *German Quar.*, vol. 31 (1958), 250; Arthur R. Schultz, *Monatshefte*, vol. 51 (1959), 205; C. Wegelin, *Compar. Lit.*, vol. 10 (1958), 268–69; E. Teichmann, *Revue de Litt. Comparee*, vol. 34 (1960), 745–49; K. Wirzberger, *Zeitschrift für Anglistik und Amerikanistik*, vol. 7 (1959), 327–28. On Irving's travels in Germany and their effects on his writings.

CF325 Reichart, Walter A. "Washington Irving and the Theatre." *Maske und Kothurn*, vol. 14 (1968), 341–50.

CF326 Reichart, Walter A. "Washington Irving in der Dresdner und Pariser Gesellschaft 1822–1825." *Jahrbuch des Wiener Goethe-Vereins*, vol. 77 (1973), 134–46.

CF327 Reichart, Walter A. "Washington Irving's Friend and Collaborator: Barham John Livius, Esq." *PMLA*, vol. 56 (June 1941), 513–31.

CF328 Reichart, Walter A. "Washington Irving's Interest in German Folklore." *N.Y. Folklore Quar.*, vol. 13 (1957), 181–92.

CF329 Reichart, Walter A. "Washington Irvings Quelle für seinen Rip van Winkle." *Archiv*, vol. 193 (1957), 291.

CF330 Reichart, Walter A. "Washington Irvings Reise durch Österreich." *Jahrbuch des Wiener Goethe-Vereins*, vol. 66 (1963), 120–26.

CF331 Zug, Charles. "The Construction of 'The Devil and Tom Walker': A Study of Irving's Later Use of Folklore." *N.Y. Folklore Quar.*, vol. 24 (December 1968), 243–60.

JAMES, HENRY

CF332 Blanke, Gustav H. "Henry James als Schriftsteller zwischen Amerika und Europa." *Die Neueren Sprachen*, N.F., vol. 5, no. 2 (1956), 59–71. Also in: *America, Vision und Wirklichkeit. Beiträge deutscher Forschung zur amerikanischen Literaturgeschichte*. Ed. Franz H. Link. Frankfurt: Athenäum, 1968, p.212–28.

CF333 Büschges, Gisela. "Die Kultureinwirkung Europas auf den Amerikaner bei Henry James." Diss., Freiburg, 1952.

CF334 Enkvist, Nils E. "Henry James and Julio Reuter: Two Notes." *Neuphilologische Mitteilungen*, vol. 57 (1956), 318–24.

CF335 Feuerlicht, Ignace. "'Erlkönig' and *The Turn of the Screw*." *Jour. of Eng. and Germanic Philology*, vol. 58 (1959), 68–74. Finds parallels between Goethe's poem and James's ghost story when viewed in the light of psychoanalytic interpretation.

CF336 Gale, Robert L. "Freudian Imagery in James's Fiction." *Amer. Imago*, vol. 11 (1954), 181–90.

CF337 Hasler, Jörg. *Switzerland in the Life and Work of Henry James: The Clare Benedict Collection of Letters from Henry James*. Cooper Monographs on English and Amer. Langs. and Lit. no. 10. Bern: Francke, 1966. 164p. Rev. by M. Le Breton, *Études Anglaises*, vol. 19 (1966), 310; O. Cargill, *Mod. Philology*, vol. 65, no. 2 (1967), 179–80.

CF338 Hovanec, Evelyn A. "Henry James and Germany." Diss., Pittsburgh, 1973.

CF339 Lemco, Gary. "Henry James and Richard Wagner: The American." *Hartford Studies in Lit.*, vol. 6 (1974), 147–58.

CF340 Reinke, Charlotte. "Die Frau von der hinteren Veranda." *Weltstimmen*, vol. 22 (1953), no. 2, p.57–62. European society in James's novels.

CF341 Steinkamp, Egon. "Das Fremdheitserlebnis bei Henry James." Diss., Münster, 1956. Europe and America in James's life and art.

JARRELL, RANDALL

CF342 Beck, Charlotte H. "The Rilkean Spirit in the Poetry of Randall Jarrell." *Southern Literary Jour.*, vol. 12, no. 1 (1979), 3–17.

JEFFERS, ROBINSON

CF343 Coffin, Arthur B. *Robinson Jeffers. Poet of Inhumanism*. Madison: Univ. of Wisconsin Pr., 1971. 300p. Shows that the "ideas of Nietzsche were the dominant influence on Jeffers' thinking..."

JOYNE, EDWARD SOUTHEY

CF344 Pusey, William W. "Edward Southey Joyne's 'Old Letters from Germany'." In: *Studies in Nineteenth Century and Early Twentieth Century Literature: Essays in Honor of Paul K. Whitaker*. Ed. Norman H. Binger and A. Wayne Wonderley. Lexington, Ky.: Apra Pr., 1974, p.135–58.

KEY, FRANCIS SCOTT

CF345 Marks, Lillian Bayly. "Count de Benjowsky and 'The Star-Spangled Banner'." *Md. Hist. Mag.*, vol. 70 (Spring 1975), 90–91.

KRAUSE, HERBERT

CF346 Flanagan, John T. "Thirty Years of Minnesota Fiction." *Minnesota History*, vol. 24 (1950), 129–47. On Krause's novels, *Wind Without Rain* and *The Thresher*, "farm" fiction with strong German background.

KRIEGER, MURRAY

CF347 Free, William J. "Murray Krieger and the Place of Poetry." *The Ga. Rev.*, vol. 22 (1968), 236–46. Incl. Krieger's response to Kant, Coleridge and Lessing.

LANIER, SIDNEY

CF348 De Bellis, Jack. "Sidney Lanier and German Romance: An Important Qualification." *Compar. Lit. Studies*, vol. 5, no. 2 (1968), 145f. Lanier derived ideas through Carlyle, was not interested in Richter or Novalis, however, and did not read any German writers in the original.

CF349 Lewis, Arthur O., Jr. "Sidney Lanier's Knowledge of German Literature." In: *Anglo-German and American German Crosscurrents*. Ed. P. A. Shelley, A. O. Lewis, and W. W. Betts. 2 vols. Chapel Hill: Univ. of N. Car. Pr., 2 vols. Chael Hill: Univ. of N. Car. Pr., 1957–1962. Vol. I, p.155–88.

CF350 Lewis, Arthur O., Jr. "Sidney Lanier's Study of German." *Amer.-German Rev.*, vol. 22, no. 3 (1956), 30–32.

LAZARUS, EMMA

CF351 Kramer, Aaron. "The Link between Heinrich Heine and Emma Lazarus." *Amer. Jewish Hist. Soc.*, vol. 45 (1956), 248–57.

CF352 Schappes, M. U., ed. "The Letters of Emma Lazarus, 1868–1885." *Bull., N.Y. Public Library*, vol. 53, no. 7 (1949), 315–34; no. 8, 367–86; no. 9, 419–46. Letters addressed to Emerson, Higginson et al., touching on German literature.

LELAND, CHARLES GODFREY

CF353 Lang, Anton. "Charles Godfrey Leland und sein Hans Breitmann." Diss., 1932, Göttingen. 807p.

CF354 Leland, Charles Godfrey. Papers, 1835–1906. 5,000 items. In the Hist. Soc. of Pa. (MS 60-2089). Multifarious writings and some manuscripts.

CF355 Smith, Ralph Carlisle. "Charles Godfrey Leland. The American Years, 1804–1869." Diss., Univ. of New Mexico, 1962. 498p.

CF356 Varesano, Angela-Marie Joanna. "Charles Godfrey Leland: The Eclectic Folklorist." Diss., Univ. of Pa., 1980. 454p. An intellectual biography, with emphasis on his interest in folklore studies.

LONDON, JACK

CF357 Bukoski, Anthony. "Jack London's Wolf Larsen: Nietzschean Super Man at All?" *Jack London Newsletter*, vol. 7 (1974), 109–10.

CF358 Littell, Katherine. "The 'Nietzschean' and the Individualist in Jack London's Socialist Writings." *Amer. Studies/Amerikastudien*, vol. 22 (1977), 309–23.

CF359 Parkay, Forrest W. "The Influence of Nietzsche's *Thus Spake Zarathustra* on London's *The Sea-Wolf*." *Jack London Newsletter*, vol. 4 (1971), 16–24.

CF360 Watson, Charles N., Jr. "Nietzsche and *The Sea-Wolf*: A Rebuttal." *Jack London Newsletter*, vol. 9 (1976), 33–35.

LONGFELLOW, HENRY WADSWORTH

CF361 Burwick, Frederick. "Longfellow and German Romanticism." *Compar. Lit. Studies*, vol. 7 (1970), 12–42.

CF362 Davis, Rose M. "'The Tents of Grace' in Longfellow's *Evangeline*: Their History and Fate." *Pa. Hist.*, vol. 18 (1951), 269–92. References to the missionary activities of the Moravians Zinzendorf, Zeisberger, Heckewelder and others.

CF363 Galinsky, Hans. "Echowirkungen von Coleridges *Kubla Khan* und *Dejection: An Ode* in Longfellow's erstem Heine-Essay (1942)." *Jahrbuch für Amerikastudien*, vol. 3 (1958), 112–35.

CF364 Griffith, John W. "Longfellow and Herder and the Sense of History." *Texas Studies in Lit. and Lang.*, vol. 13 (1971), 249–65.

CF365 Hammer, Carl, Jr. *Longfellow's "Golden Legend" and Goethe's "Faust."* Baton Rouge: La. State Univ. Pr., 1952. 35p. Rev. by L. Polak, *Eng. Studies*, vol. 34 (1953), 221–22; Horst Frenz, *Amer.-German Rev.*, vol. 19, no. 5 (1953), 34–35; W. A. Willibrand, *Books Abroad*, vol. 28 (1954), 480; in *Monatshefte*, vol. 46 (1954), 155. In this examination of parallels, the author concludes that L. derived "afflatus" from "Faust."

CF366 Hammer, Carl, Jr. "Longfellow's Lyrics 'From the German'." In: *Studies in Compar. Lit..* Ed. Waldo F. McNeir. Baton Rouge: La. State Univ. Pr., 1962, p.155–72.

CF367 Hart, Loring E. "The Beginnings of Longfellow's Fame." *New England Quar.*, vol. 36 (1963), 63–76. Incl. discussion of the reception of *Hyperion*.

CF368 Hilen, Andrew, ed. *The Diary of Clara Crowninshield: A European Tour with Longfellow, 1835–36*. Seattle: Univ. of Washington Pr., 1956. 304p. Rev. by N. H. Pearson, *Mod. Lang. Quar.*, vol. 19 (1958), 184–85; C. L. Johnson, *Compar. Lit.*, vol. 10 (1958), 279–81; Wilbert Snow, *Mod. Lang. Notes*, vol. 73 (1958), 367–68.

CF369 Huebener, Theodore. "Longfellow's Estimate of Heine." *German Quar.*, vol. 21, no. 2 (1948), 117–19.

CF370 "Hymn of the Moravian Nuns of Bethlehem (At the Consecration of Pulaski's Banner)." "'S Pennsylfawnisch Deitsch Eck," *Allentown Morning Call*, 19 March 1966. On the writing of the poem by H. W. Longfellow.

CF371 Johnson, Carl L. "Longfellow's Beginnings in Foreign Languages." *New England Quar.*, vol. 20 (1947), 317–28.

CF372 Johnson, Carl L. *Professor Longfellow of Harvard*. Eugene, Ore.: Oregon Univ. Pr., 1944. 122p. Rev. in *Amer. Lit.*, vol. 16, no. 3 (1944), 260–61.

CF373 Kornbluth, Martin L. "Longfellow's *Hyperion* and Goethe's *Wilhelm Meisters Lehrjahre*." *Emerson Soc. Quar.*, no. 31 (1963), 55–59.

CF374 Krumpelmann, John T. "Longfellow's Shakespeare Studies in Heidelberg." *Die neueren Sprachen*, vol. 13 (1964), no. 9, 405–13.

CF375 Lefcourt, Charles R. "Longfellow's First Goethe Lectures." *Eng. Rec.*, vol. 18 (December 1967), 15–18.

CF376 Longfellow, Henry W. *Hyperion*. New York: n.p., 1839. 2 vols. On microfilm in Wright's American Fiction series. Reel L-8 1707.

CF377 Longfellow, Henry W. *The Letters of Henry Wadsworth Longfellow*. Ed. Andrew Hilen. Vol. I. *1814–1836*. 576p. Vol. II. *1837–1843*. 654p. Cambridge: Belknap Pr. of Harvard Univ. Pr., 1967. Rev. by H. M. Jones, *New England Quar.*, vol. 40, no. 3 (1967), 445–47; Edward Wagenknecht, *N.Y. Times Book Rev.*, 28 May 1967, 6. Incl. L.'s extensive European travel letters; afford a view of L. as student, teacher of languages, and traveler.

CF378 Moyne, Ernest J., and F. Mustanoja Tauno. "Longfellow's *Song of Hiawatha* and *Kalevala*." *Amer. Lit.*, vol. 25, no. 1 (1953), 87–89. "The meter in Hiawatha is the meter of Kalevala as it appears in A. Schiefner's German translation, used by Longfellow."

CF379 Schacht, Frank E. "Die weissen und die blauen Blätter. Henry Wadsworth Longfellows Aufzeichnungen und Vorlesungen über Jean Pauls Leben und Werke." *Hesperus* (Bayreuth), vol. 20 (1960), 32–36.

CF380 Shelley, Philip A. "An Exchange of Letters (of Niclas Müller) with Longfellow." *PMLA*, vol. 60, no. 2 (1945), 611–16. N. Müller, a Forty-Eighter, corresponded with Longfellow about Müller's poetry and translations (1864).

CF381 Silz, Walter. "Longfellow's Translation of Goethe's 'Über allen Gipfeln'." *Mod. Lang. Notes*, vol. 71 (1956), 344–45.

CF382 Voss, Krafft Helmut. "The Longfellow Tradition at Geisenheim." *Amer.-German Rev.*, vol. 21, no. 2 (1954), 33–34. The Longfellow Memorial plaque was bestowed upon Theo. Heuss and John J. McCloy at Geisenheim, Longfellow's favorite sojourn in the Rheingau.

LOWELL, JAMES RUSSELL

CF383 Bayley, John. "Lowell and Hölderlin: A Note and Suggestion." *Agenda*, vol. 18 (1980), no. 3, 30–33.

MACLEISH, ARCHIBALD

CF384 Maier, Kurt S. "A Fellowship in German Literature: Thomas Mann, Agnes Meyer, and Archibald MacLeish." *Quar. Jour. of the Library of Congress*, vol. 36 (1979), 385–400.

MARTIN, HELEN RIEMENSNYDER

CF385 Seaton, Beverly. "Helen Riemensnyder Martin's 'Caricature' of the Pennsylvania Germans." *Pa. Mag. of Hist. and Biography*, vol. 104 (January 1980).

MELVILLE, HERMAN

CF386 Bagley, Carol Lenore. "Melville's Trilogy: Symbolic Precursor of Freudian Personality Structure in the History of Ideas." Diss., Washington State, 1966.

CF387 Betts, William W., Jr. "*Moby Dick*, Melville's Faust." *Lock Haven Bull.*, vol. 1, no. 1 (1959), 31–44.

CF388 Bezanson, Walter E. "Melville's Reading of Arnold's Poetry." *PMLA*, vol. 69 (1954), 365–91. Melville's preoccupation with Goethe, Schiller and Heine stimulated by Arnold.

CF389 D'Avanzo, Mario. "Melville's 'Bartleby' and John Jacob Astor." *New England Quar.*, vol. 41 (June 1968), 259–64.

CF390 Dettlaf, Shirley M. "Hebraism and Hellenism in Melville's *Clarel*: The Influence of Arnold, Goethe, and Schiller." Diss., Univ. of Southern Calif., 1978. "Arnold's ideas may have helped M. see a theme running through his extensive reading which already included Goethe and Schiller, two German Hellenes who had greatly influenced Arnold."

CF391 Fite, Olive L. "Billy Budd, Claggart, and Schopenhauer." *Nineteenth-Century Fiction*, vol. 23, no. 3 (1968–1969), 336–43.

CF392 Hillway, Tyrus. "Melville's Use of Two Pseudo-Sciences." *Mod. Lang. Notes*, vol. 64, no. 3 (1949), 145–50. M.'s interest in Lavater's *Physiognomy*.

CF393 Kosok, Heinz. *Die Bedeutung der Gothic Novel für das Erzählwerk Herman Melvilles.* Hamburg: Cram, de Gruyter, 1963. 157p. Britannica et Americana, vol. 12. Rev. by H. J. Lang, *Jahrbuch für Amerikastudien*, vol. 9 (1964), 319–24. Cf. diss. of same title, Marburg, 1961.

CF394 Mabbott, Thomas O. "A Source for the Conclusion of Melville's *Moby Dick*." *Notes and Queries*, vol. 181, 26 July 1941, 47–48. From Southey's *Commonplace Book*, 1st Ser., or from Southey's source, the Eastern voyages of Johann Albrecht Mandelslo in 1638–1640.

CF395 McIntosh, James. "Melville's Use and Abuse of Goethe: The Weaver-Gods in *Faust* and *Moby-Dick*." *Amerikastudien*, vol. 25 (1980), 158–73.

CF396 Poenicke, Klaus. "A View from the Piazza: Herman Melville and the Legacy of the 'European Sublime'." *Compar. Lit. Studies*, vol. 4 (1967), 267–81.

CF397 Rogers, Jane E. "The Transcendental Quest in Emerson and Melville." Diss., Pittsburgh, 1974.

CF398 Slochower, Harry. "Freudian Motifs in *Moby-Dick*." *Complex*, vol. 3 (1955), 16–25.

CF399 Wais, Kurt. "Die Errettung aus dem Schiffbruch: Melville, Mallarme und einige deutsche Voraussetzungen." *Deut. Vierteljahrschrift für Literaturwissenschaft und Geistesgeschichte*, vol. 34 (1960), 21–45. Reliance on the 18th-century topos "Schiffbruch."

MENCKEN, HENRY L.

CF400 Adler, Betty, and John Wilhelm. *H.L.M.: The Mencken Bibliography*. Baltimore: The Johns Hopkins Univ. Pr., 1961. 367p.

CF401 Angoff, Charles. *H. L. Mencken: A Portrait from Memory*. New York: Th. Yoseloff, 1956. 240p.

CF402 Angoff, Charles. "Mencken as a 'German' American." *Chicago Jewish Forum*, vol. 25 (1967), 143–46.

CF403 Banks, Dean. "H. L. Mencken and 'Hitlerism,' 1933–1941: A Patrician Libertarian Besieged." *Md. Hist. Mag.*, vol. 71 (Winter 1976), 498–515. Examination of M.'s reaction against Nazism and his public stand.

CF404 Bode, Carl. "Henry Louis Mencken." *Report, Soc. for the Hist. of the Germans in Md.*, vol. 29 (1956), 70–73.

CF405 Bode, Carl. *Mencken*. Carbondale: Southern Ill. Univ. Pr., 1969. 452p.

CF406 Brooks, Van Wyck. "Mencken in Baltimore." *Amer. Scholar*, vol. 20, no. 4 (1951), 409–21. M.'s German-American background.

CF407 Cheslock, Louis. "HLM Talks about Max Brodel." *Menckeniana*, vol. 55 (1975), 6–8.

CF408 Cunz, Dieter. "H. L. Mencken." *New Yorker Staatszeitung*, 12 February 1956. M.'s German ancestry.

CF409 Dolmetsch, Carl R. "H. L. Mencken as a Critic of Poetry." *Jahrbuch für Amerikastudien*, vol. 11 (1966), 83–95.

CF410 Fecher, Charles A. "Mencken and Goethe." *Menckeniana*, no. 75 (Fall 1980), 43–49.

CF411 Forgue, Guy Dean. *H. L. Mencken. L'Homme, l'oeuvre, l'influence*. Paris: M. J. Minard, Lettres modernes, 1967. 496p. Rev. by Anne M. Witmer, *Jahrbuch für Amerikastudien*, vol. 15 (1970), 305–07.

CF412 Gordon, Douglas. "A Last Glimpse of Mencken." *Md. Hist. Mag.*, vol. 51 (1956), 337–40. The visit of André Siegfried to Mencken in January 1956.

CF413 Kemler, Edgar. *The Irreverent Mr. Mencken*. Boston: Little, Brown, 1950. 317p.

CF414 Manchester, William. *Disturber of the Peace. The Life of H. L. Mencken*. New York: Harper, 1951. 336p. Reissued as *H. L. Mencken. Disturber of the Peace*. New York: Collier, 1967. Mentions the unpublished "Battle of the Wilhelmstrasse" depicting Mencken's experiences in Germany as war correspondent in 1916.

CF415 Mayfield, S. *The Constant Circle. H. L. Mencken and His Friends*. New York: Delacorte Pr., 1968. 307p.

CF416 Mencken, Henry L. *H. L. Mencken on Music: A Selection of His Writings on Music, Together with an Account of H. L. Mencken's Musical Life and a History of the Saturday Night Club.* Ed. Louis Cheslock. New York: Knopf, 1961. 222p.

CF417 Mencken, H. L. *Letters of H. L. Mencken.* Selected and annotated by Guy J. Forgue. New York: Knopf, 1961. 506p.

CF418 Mencken, H. L. Mencken-Weisberger collection, 1925–1956. 13 boxes. In Univ. of Pennsylvania Libraries (MS 68-455). Letters to Siegfried Weisberger (Peabody Bookstore) and misc. papers relating to *The American Language.*

CF419 Mencken, H. L. Papers, 1890–1956. 30 ft. In Enoch Pratt Free Library, Baltimore (MS 61-911).

CF420 Mencken, H. L. Papers, 1901–1919. In Duke Univ. Library (MS 72-879). Magazine articles, clippings on world drama. Collected by M. while drama critic for the Baltimore *Herald* and Baltimore *Sun.*

CF421 Mencken, H. L. Papers. 139 letters, 1916–1948. In Henry L. Huntington Library, San Marino, Calif. (MS 62-369).

CF422 Mencken, H. L. Papers. 7 boxes. In Baker Library, Dartmouth College (MS 65-1852). Carbons of correspondence, 1921–1951; MSS., etc.

CF423 Mencken, H. L. Papers, 1935–1956. Ca. 150 items. In Univ. of Virginia Library (MS 69-1295).

CF424 Mencken, H. L. Papers. 110 letters. In Temple Univ. Library (MS 70-1909). Letters from M. to Leary's Book Store, Philadelphia.

CF425 Mencken, H. L. Papers. In: Bode, Carl. Papers, 1941–1974. 3 ft. of Menckeniana. In Univ. of Maryland Library, College Park (MS 76-1670).

CF426 "Minority Report: Second Series." *Menckeniana: A Quar. Rev.*, no. 33 (Spring 1970), 1–4. M.'s autobiographical notes of his life around the time of World War I.

CF427 Moseley, Merritt W., Jr. "H. L. Mencken and the First World War." *Menckeniana*, no. 58 (Summer 1976), 8–15.

CF428 Motsch, Markus F. "A Dose of Kultur." *Menckeniana*, no. 19 (Fall 1966), 8–11. On M.'s reception of German literature.

CF429 Motsch, Markus F. "H. L. Mencken and German Kultur." *German-Amer. Studies*, vol. 6 (1973), 21–42. Summary statement of M.'s proclivities: Nietzsche, the literary naturalists, classical music, bourgeois *Gemütlichkeit.*

CF430 Peters, Otto. "H. L. Mencken's Attitude towards Germany." Diss., Berlin, 1956.

CF431 Puknat, Siegfried B. "Mencken and the Sudermann Case." *Monatshefte*, vol. 51 (1959), 183–89.

CF432 Ruland, Richard. "The Disappearance of H. L. Mencken." *Menckeniana*, no. 20 (Winter 1966), 7–8. How M.'s espousal of German culture lost him his reading public in the 1930's.

CF433 Turaj, Frank. "Mencken and the Nazis: A Note." *Md. Hist. Mag.*, vol. 67, no. 2 (Summer 1972), 176–78. In answer to Stuart P. Sherman's unfair attack, shows that M. had only repugnance for Hitler and the Nazis.

CF434 Wagner, Philip. *H. L. Mencken.* Minneapolis: Univ. of Minn. Pr., 1966. 48p.

CF435 Williams, W. H. A. *H. L. Mencken.* Boston: Twayne, 1977. 179p. Rev. by Ronald Lora, *Jour. of Amer. Hist.*, vol. 65, no. 3 (December 1978), 813–14.

CF436 Wycherly, H. Alan. "Mencken and Knopf: The Editor and His Publisher." *Amer. Quar.*, vol. 16, no. 3 (1964), 460–72. Friendly association of M. and Alfred A. Knopf from 1913 on.

CF437 Zucker, A. E. "A Mencken Reminiscence." *Report, Soc. for the Hist. of the Germans in Md.*, vol. 29 (1956), 68–69.

MICHENER, JAMES A.

CF438 Kings, John. *In Search of Centennial: A Journey with James A. Michener.* Photographs by T. Dalton, James A. Michener, and the author. New York: Random House, 1978. 143p.

MOTLEY, JOHN LOTHROP

CF439 Porterfield, Allan W., "When Boston Took Up German." *German Quar.*, vol. 22, no. 2 (1949), 84–94. Motley's novel *Morton's Hope*, first American novel set against a German background, 1839.

OLSON, CHARLES

CF440 Stein, Charles Frederick. "The Secret of the Black Chrysanthemum: Charles Olson's Use of the Writings of C. G. Jung." Diss., Univ. of Connecticut, 1979. 285p.

O'NEILL, EUGENE

CF441 Alexander, Doris M. "Psychological Fate in *Mourning Becomes Electra.*" *PMLA*, vol. 68 (1953), 923–34. Freudian touches in the O'Neill play.

CF442 Alexander, Doris M. "*Strange Interlude* and Schopenhauer." *Amer. Lit.*, vol. 25, no. 2 (1953), 213–28.

CF443 Brashear, William R. "O'Neill's Schopenhauer Interlude." *Criticism*, vol. 6 (Summer 1964), 256–65.

CF444 Burns, Sr. M. Vincentia. "The Functions of Wagner's Theory of the Union of the Arts in the Dramaturgy of Eugene O'Neill." Diss., Univ. of Pa., 1943.

CF445 Hambright, Jeanne K. "The Journey Out: Contributions of German Dramatic Expressionism in the Social Protest Plays of Eugene O'Neill." Diss., Tufts, 1973.

CF446 Hinden, Michael. "*The Emperor Jones*: O'Neill, Nietzsche, and the American Past." *Eugene O'Neill Newsletter*, vol. 3, no. 3 (1980), 2–4.

CF447 Hinden, Michael C. "Tragedy: The Communal Vision: A Critique and Extension of Nietzsche's Theory of Tragedy with Attention Devoted to the Early Plays of Eugene O'Neill." Diss., Brown, 1972.

CF448 Jordan, John Wingate. "An Examination of Eugene O'Neill's Plays in the light of C. G. Jung's Collected Works and Recorded Conversations." Diss., Univ. of Houston, 1979. 602p.

CF449 LaBelle, Maurice M. "Dionysius and Despair: The Influence of Nietzsche upon O'Neill's Drama." *Educational Theater Jour.*, vol. 25 (1973), 436–42.

CF450 Lichtman, Myla Ruth. "Mythic Plot and Character Development in Euripides *Hippolytus* and Eugene O'Neill's *Desire under the Elms*: A Jungian Analysis." Diss., Univ. of Southern Calif., 1979.

CF451 Nolan, Patrick J. "*The Emperor Jones*: A Jungian View of the Origin of Fear in the Black Race." *Eugene O'Neill Newsletter*, vol. 4, nos. 1–2 (1980), 6–9.

CF452 Olson, Esther J. "An Analysis of the Nietzschean Elements in the Plays of Eugene O'Neill." Diss., Minnesota, 1956.

CF453 Pickering, Christine P. "The Works of Eugene O'Neill: A Greek Idea of the Theatre Derived from the Philosophy of Friedrich Nietzsche." Diss., East Texas State Univ., 1972.

CF454 Spiller, Robert E. "Nobelpreisträger Eugene O'Neill und die Weltliteratur unserer Zeit." *Universitas* (Stuttgart), vol. 12 (1957), 1277–80.

CF455 Stein, Daniel A. "O'Neill and the Philosohers: A Study of Nietzschean and Other Philosophical Influences on Eugene O'Neill." Diss., Yale, 1967.

CF456 Steinhauer, Harry. "Eros and Psyche, a Nietzschean Motif in Anglo-American Literature." *Mod. Lang. Notes*, vol. 64, no. 4 (1949), 217–28. Nietzsche and O'Neill.

CF457 Törnqvist, Egil. "Nietzsche and O'Neill: A Study in Affinity." *Orbis Litterarum*, vol. 23 (1968), 97–126.

PERCIVAL, JAMES GATES

CF458 Rutledge, Joyce S. "New Findings in the German Studies of James Gates Percival (1795–1856)." *Mod. Lang. Notes*, vol. 89 (1974), 404–21.

POE, EDGAR ALLAN

CF459 Benson, Adolph B. "Scandinavian References in the Works of Poe." *Jour. of Eng. and Germanic Philology*, vol. 40, no. 1 (1941), 73–90.

CF460 Cohen, Hubert I. "Hoffmann's 'The Sandman': A Possible Source for 'Rappaccini's Daughter'." *Emerson Soc. Quar.*, vol. 68 (1972), 148–53.

CF461 Dieckmann, Lieselotte. "E.T.A. Hoffmann und E. A. Poe: Verwandte Sensibilität bei

American Authors: German Influence *(cont.)*

verschiedenen Sprach- und Gesellschaftsraum." In: *Dichtung, Sprache, Gesellschaft: Akten des IV. Internat. Germanisten-Kongresses 1970 in Princeton.* Ed. V. Lange and H.-G. Roloff. Frankfurt: Athenaeum, 1971, p.273–80.

CF462 Lloyd, Rosemary. "Sur Hoffmann, Poe et Baudelaire." *Bull. Baudelairien*, vol. 11, no. 3 (1976), 11–12.

CF463 Lubell, Albert J. "Poe and A. W. Schlegel." *Jour. of Eng. and Germ. Philology*, vol. 52 (1953), 1–12. "Schlegel's *Lectures on Dramatic Art and Literature* profoundly influenced Poe's philosphy of literary art."

CF464 McNeal, Thomas H. "Poe's 'Zenobia'," *Mod. Lang. Quar.*, vol. 11, no. 2 (1950), 205–16. Satire on Margaret Fuller and her German-influenced Transdendentalism.

CF465 Mohr, Franz Karl. "Der Einfluss von Eichendorff's *Ahnung und Gegenwart* auf Poes *Die Maske des roten Todes*." *Der Wächter*, vol. 32 (1951), 45–52. In English: "The Influence of Eichendorff's *Ahnung und Gegenwart* on Poe's *Masque of the Red Death*." *Mod. Lang. Quar.*, vol. 10, no. 1 (1949), 3–15.

CF466 Panek, Leroy L. "'Maelzel's Chess-Player,' Poe's First Detective Mistake." *Amer. Lit.*, vol. 48, no. 2 (November 1976), 370–72. Poe did not conjecture that an amputee operated the "automaton."

CF467 Pitcher, Edward W. "From Hoffmann's 'Das Majorat' to Poe's 'Usher' via 'The Robber's Tower': Poe's Borrowings Reconsidered." *Amer. Transcendentalist Quar.*, no. 39 (Summer 1978), 231–36. "The Robber's Tower" is a story by John Hardman.

CF468 Thompson, Gary R. "Poe and Romantic Irony." In: *Papers on Poe: Essays in Honor of John Ward Ostrom.* Ed. Richard P. Veler. Springfield, Ohio: Chantry Music Pr. at Wittenberg Univ., 1972, p.28–41.

CF469 Thompson, Gary R. "Poe's Romantic Irony: A Study of the Gothic Tales in a Romantic Context." Diss., Southern Calif., 1967. 342p.

CF470 Von der Lippe, George B. "Beyond the House of Usher: The Figure of E.T.A. Hoffmann in the Works of Poe." *Mod. Lang. Studies*, vol. 9, no. 1 (1978–1979), 33–41.

CF471 Von der Lippe, George B. "The Figure of E.T.A. Hoffmann as *Doppelgänger* to Poe's Roderick Usher." *Mod. Lang. Notes*, vol. 92 (1977), 525–34.

CF472 Zeydel, Edwin H. "Edgar Allan Poe's Contacts with German as Seen in his Relations with Ludwig Tieck." In: *Studies in German Literature of the Nineteenth and Twentieth Centuries. Festschrift for Prof. Frederic E. Coenen.* Ed. Siegfried Mews. Chapel Hill: Univ. of N. Car. Pr., 1970, p.47–54.

PORTER, KATHERINE ANN

CF473 Givner, Joan. "The Genesis of *Ship of Fools*." *Southern Lit. Jour.*, vol. 10, no. 1 (1977), 14–30.

CF474 Hertz, Robert N. "Sebastian Brant and Porter's *Ship of Fools*." *Midwest Quar.*, vol. 6 (July 1965), 389–401.

CF475 Townsend, Stanley R. "*The Ship of Fools* and *The Magic Mountain*." *Program*, Mod. Lang. Assoc., December 1964.

POUND, EZRA

CF476 Baumann, Walter. "Ezra Pound and Hermann Broch: A Comparison." *Seminar*, vol. 4, no. 2 (1970), 100–12.

CF477 Bush, Ronald. "Pound and Spengler: Another Look." *Paideuma*, vol. 5 (Spring 1976), 63–66.

CF478 Davenport, Guy. "Pound and Frobenius." *Eng. Institute Essays*, 1953, 33–59. Pound objects to the world's neglect of Leo Frobenius, the German student of cultures. Considers the effect of Frobenius on Pound's writings. See essay of same title in *Motive and Method in the "Cantos of Ezra Pound."* Ed. Lewis Leary. New York: Columbia Univ. Pr., 1954. Rev. by R. Mayo, *Mod. Lang. Notes*, vol. 71 (1954), 313.

CF479 Demetz, Peter. "Ezra Pound's German Studies." *Germanic Rev.*, vol. 31 (1956), 279–92. Particularly the Heine "translations" by Pound.

CF480 Klink, R. M. "Pound and Spengler." *Paideuma*, vol. 5 (Spring 1976), 67–68.

CF481 Schneeman, Peter. "Pound's 'Englischer Brief': A Look Toward Germany." *Paideuma*, vol. 7 (1978), 309–16.

RICHTER, CONRAD

CF482 Flanagan, John T. "Conrad Richter, Romancer of the Southwest." *Southwest Rev.*, vol. 48 (1958), 189–96.

CF483 Graham, Alice D. "Pennsylvania-German Elements in the Work of Conrad Richter." M. A. Thesis, Pa. State Univ., 1960.

CF484 Kohler, Dayton. "Conrad Richter: Early American." *College Eng.*, vol. 8 (February 1947), 221–27. An evaluation and review of Richter's accomplishment in the imaginative recreation of the American past.

CF485 La Hood, Marvin J. *Conrad Richter's America*. The Hague: Mouton, 1975. 145p. Rev. by John T. Flanagan, *Amer. Lit.*, vol. 48, no. 1 (March 1976), 93.

CF486 La Hood, Marvin J. "Major Themes in the Fiction of Conrad Richter, and His Place in the Tradition of the American Frontier Novel." Diss., Notre Dame, 1962. 244p.

CF487 La Hood, Marvin J. "Richter's Pennsylvania Trilogy." *Susquehanna Univ. Studies*, vol. 8 (June 1968).

CF488 Young, David Lee. "The Art of Conrad Richter." Diss., Ohio State Univ., 1964. 169p.

ROBINSON, THÉRÈSE A. L. (TALVJ)

CF489 Pribić, Nikola. "Goethe, Talvj und das südslawische Volkslied." In: *Vergleichen und Verändern. Festschrift für Helmut Motekat*. Ed. Albrecht Goetze and Günther Pflaum. München: Hueber, 1970, p.17–27. Also in: *Balkan Studies*, vol. 10 (1970), 135–44.

CF490 Pribić, Nikola R. "TALVJ—Pioneer in Comparative Studies of Folklore in America." In: *American Contributions to the VII. International Congress* of Slavists. The Hague: Mouton, 1973, p.495–504.

CF491 Pribić, Nikola R. "TALVJ in America." In: *Serta Slavica in Memoriam Aloisii Schmaus*. Ed. W. Gesemann et al. München: R. Trofenik, 1971, p.589–606.

ROETHKE, THEODORE

CF492 Kunitz, Stanley. "Roethke: Poet of Transformations." *New Republic*, vol. 152 (January 1965), 23–29. The poet's relation to the system of C. G. Jung and Maud Bodkin.

ROTH, PHILIP

CF493 Davidson, Arnold E. "Kafka, Rilke, and Philip Roth's *The Breast*." *Notes on Contemporary Lit.*, vol. 5, no. 1 (1975), 9–11.

CF494 Roth, Philip. "In Search of Kafka and Other Answers." *N.Y. Times Book Rev.*, 15 February 1976, 6–7.

SHECUT, J.L.E.W.

CF495 Doyle, James. "Mennonites and Mohawks: The Universalist Fiction of J.L.E.W. Shecut." *Mennonite Quar. Rev.*, vol. 51 (January 1977).

SIMMS, WILLIAM GILMORE

CF496 Thomas, J. Wesley. "The German Sources of William Gilmore Simms." In: *Anglo-German and American-German Crosscurrents*. Ed. P. A. Shelley, A. O. Lewis, and W. W. Betts. 2 vols. Chapel Hill: Univ. of N. Car. Pr., 1957–1962. Vol. I, p.127–54.

STEGNER, WALLACE

CF497 Ellis, James. "Wallace Stegner's Art of Literary Allusion: The Marriage of Heaven and Hell and Faust in 'Maiden in a Tower'." *Studies in Short Fiction*, vol. 17 (1980), 105–11.

STEVENS, WALLACE

CF498 Adams, Richard P. "Wallace Stevens and Schopenhauer's *The World as Will and Idea*." *Tulane Studies in Eng.*, vol. 20 (1972), 135–68.

CF499 Bates, Milton. "Major Man and Overman: Wallace Stevens' Use of Nietzsche." *Southern Rev.*, vol. 15 (1979), 811–39.

CF500 Crasnow, Ellman. "Poems and Fictions: Stevens, Rilke, Valéry." In: *Modernism, 1890–1930*. Ed. Malcolm Bradbury and James W. McFarlane. Hassocks, Eng. / Atlantic Highlands, N.J.: Humanities Pr., 1978, p.369–82.

CF501 Hines, Thomas J. *The Later Poetry of Wallace Stevens: Phenomenological Parallels with Husserl and Heidegger*. Lewisburg, Pa.: Bucknell Univ. Pr., 1976. 298p.

CF502 Kermode, Frank. "Dwelling Poetically in Connecticut." In: *Wallace Stevens: A Celebration*. Ed. Frank A. Doggett and Robert Buttell. Princeton: Princeton Univ. Pr., 1980, p.256–73. On Stevens and Heidegger.

SUCKOW, RUTH

CF503 Kissane, Leedice McAnelly. "Ruth Suckow: Interpreter of the Mind of Mid-America (1900–1933)." Diss., Minnesota, 1967. 379p. Examines the treatment of immigrants in the work of Suckow.

TAYLOR, BAYARD

CF504 Frenz, Horst. "Bayard Taylor and the Reception of Goethe in America." *Jour. of Eng. and Germanic Philology*, vol. 41, no. 2 (1942), 125–39. Taylor's service as translator and critic is reviewed; he is shown to have been ahead of his time in estimating the importance of Goethe.

CF505 Frenz, Horst, and Philip A. Shelley, eds. "Bayard Taylor's German Lecture on American Literature." *Jahrbuch für Amerikastudien*, vol. 2 (1957), 89–133.

CF506 Krumpelmann, John T. *Bayard Taylor and German Letters*. Hamburg: de Gruyter & Co., 1959. 235p. Rev. by C. Duffy, *Amer. Lit.*, vol. 22, no. 3 (1960), 334–35; G. Friedrich, *Books Abroad*, vol. 34, no. 3 (1960), 294; S. B. Puknat *German Quar.*, vol. 34, no. 2 (1961), 207–08; H. Bock, *Jahrbuch für Amerikastudien*, vol. 6 (1960), 338; P. A. Shelley, *Mod. Philology*, vol. 60, no. 1 (1962), 71–75; R. Asselineau, *Revue de Littérature Comparée*, vol. 36 (1962), 463–65.

CF507 Krumpelmann, John T. "Bayard Taylor and Schiller." In: *Contributions to the Humanities 1954*. La. State Univ. Studies, Humanistic Ser., no. 5. Baton Rouge: La. State Univ. Pr., 1955, p.11–24.

CF508 Krumpelmann, John T. "Bayard Taylor as a Literary Mediator between Germany and the South Atlantic States." *Die neueren Sprachen*, N.F., vol. 4, no. 9 (1955), 415–18.

CF509 Krumpelmann, John T. "The Genesis of Bayard Taylor's Translation of Goethe's *Faust*." *Jour. of Eng. and Germanic Philology*, vol. 42, no. 4 (1943), 551–62.

CF510 Prahl, Augustus J. "Bayard Taylor and Goethe." *Mod. Lang. Quar.*, vol. 7, no. 2 (1946), 205–17. Accounting for T.'s admiration of Goethe.

CF511 Prahl, Augustus J. "Bayard Taylor in Germany." *German Quar.*, vol. 18, no. 1 (1945), 16–25. Resumé of T.'s visits to Germany—1844 to 1878.

CF512 Shelley, Philip Allison. "Bayard Taylor and Schiller's *Don Carlos*." In: *Anglo-German and American-German Crosscurrents*. Ed. P. A. Shelley, A. O. Lewis, and W. W. Betts. 2 vols. Chapel Hill: Univ. of N. Car. Pr., 1957–1962. Vol. II (1962), p.33–96.

CF513 Smyth, Albert Henry. *Bayard Taylor*. Detroit: Gale Research Corp., 1970. 320p. Repr. of the 1896 original.

TICKNOR, GEORGE

CF514 Ryder, Frank G. "First American Commentary on *Faust*." *Amer.-German Rev.*, vol. 19, no. 3 (1953), 9–11. T.'s notes and explications written in 1815–1816 during his stay in Göttingen.

CF515 Ryder, Frank G. "George Ticknor and Goethe—Boston and Göttingen." *PMLA*, vol. 67, no. 7 (1952), 960–72.

CF516 Ryder, Frank G. "George Ticknor and Goethe: Europe and Harvard." *Mod. Lang. Quar.*, vol. 14 (1953), 413–24.

CF517 Ryder, Frank G., ed. *George Ticknor's The Sorrows of Young Werther*. Chapel Hill: Univ. of N. Car. Pr., 1952. 108p. Rev. by Stuart Atkins, *Amer.-German Rev.*, vol. 19, no. 3 (1953), 38; H. H. Remak, *German Quar.*, vol. 26 (1953), 196–97; C. Hammer, *Monatshefte*, vol. 46 (1954), 60–61. Ticknor's trans. here published for the first time. See also "George Ticknor's *Sorrows of Young Werther*." *Compar. Lit.*, vol. 1 (1949), 360–72. Incl. introd. and critical analysis.

VONNEGUT, KURT

CF518 Metzger, Michael M. "Deutschland und die Deutschen in den Werken Kurt Vonneguts." In: *Die U S A und Deutschland: Wechselseitige Spiegelungen in der Literatur der Gegenwart. 8. Amherster Kolloquium*. Ed. Wolfgang Paulsen. Bern/München: Francke, 1976, p.152–59.

CF519 Seltzer, Leon F. "Dresden and Vonnegut's Creative Testament of Guilt." *Jour. of Amer. Culture*, vol. 4, no. 4 (1981), 55–69.

WALEY, ARTHUR

CF520 Bridgewater, Patrick. "Arthur Waley and Brecht." *German Life and Letters*, vol. 17, no. 3 (1965), 216–32.

WELLES, ORSON

CF521 Mesnil, Michel. "Orson Welles et *le Jugement*." *Esprit*, no. 423 (1973), 973–85.

WHARTON, EDITH

CF522 Lawson, Richard H. *Edith Wharton and German Literature*. Bonn: Bouvier Vlg. Herbert Grundmann, 1975. 150p. The author's interest in Goethe, Fouqué, Keller, Nietzsche, Sudermann, Schnitzler. Based on an analysis of texts of novels and letters.

CF523 Lawson, Richard H. "Hermann Sudermann and Edith Wharton." *Revue de la Littérature Comparée*, vol. 41 (1967), 125–31.

CF524 Lawson, Richard H. "The Influence of Gottfried Keller on Edith Wharton." *Revue de la Littérature Comparée*, vol. 42 (July–September 1968), 366–79.

CF525 Lawson, Richard H. "Nietzsche, Edith Wharton, and 'The Blond Beast'." In: *Actes du VII⁰ congrès de l'Assoc. Internationale de Littérature Comparée ... Literature of America: Dependence, Independence, Interdependence*. Ed. Milan V. Dimić and Juan Ferraté. Stuttgart: Bieber, 1979, p. 169–72.

CF526 McHaney, Thomas L. "Fouqué's *Undine* and Edith Wharton's *Custom of the Country*." *Revue de Littérature Comparée*, vol. 45 (1971), 180–86.

CF527 Puknat, S. B., and E. M. Puknat. "Edith Wharton and Gottfried Keller." *Compar. Lit.*, vol. 21, no. 3 (1969), 245–54. Comparative study of *Ethan Frome* and *Romeo und Julia auf dem Dorfe*.

WHITMAN, WALT

CF528 Allen, Gay W. "A Note on Comparing Whitman and Nietzsche." *Walt Whitman Rev.*, vol. 11 (September 1965), 74–76.

CF529 Aspiz, Harold. "Educating the Kosmos: 'There Was a Child Went Forth'." *Amer. Quar.*, vol. 18, no. 4 (Winter 1966), 654–66. A phrenological system as the basis for this poem of Whitman's.

CF530 Bergman, Herbert. "Whitman on Beethoven and Music." *Mod. Lang. Notes*, vol. 66, no. 8 (1951), 556–58.

CF531 Black, Stephen A. "Whitman and Psychoanalytic Criticism. A Response to Arthur Golden." *Lit. and Psychology*, vol. 20, no. 2 (1970), 79–81. See also Arthur Golden. "A Reply." *Ibid.*, 83–92.

CF532 Bluestein, Gene. "The Advantages of Barbarism: Herder and Whitman's Nationalism." *Jour. of the Hist. of Ideas*, vol. 24, no. 1 (1963), 115–26.

CF533 Falk, Robert P. "Walt Whitman and German Thought." *Jour. of Eng. and Germanic Philology*, vol. 40, no. 3 (1941), 315–30. A clear-headed synthesis.

CF534 Frenz, Horst. "Walt Whitman's Letters to Karl Knortz." *Amer. Lit.*, vol. 20, no. 2 (1948), 155–63.

CF535 Frenz, Horst. *Whitman and Rolleston. A Correspondence*. Ind. Univ. Publs., Humanities Ser. no. 26. Bloomington: Ind. Univ. Pr., 1951. Rev. by Henry A. Pochmann, *Monatshefte*, vol. 45 (1953), 108; Frank Wood, *Compar. Lit.*, vol. 5 (1953), 373–75; R. G. Silver, *Mod. Lang. Notes*, vol. 68 (1953), 139.

CF536 Fulghum, W. B., Jr. "Whitman's Debt to Joseph Gostwick." *Amer. Lit.*, vol. 12, no. 4 (1941), 491–96.

CF537 Kemnitz, Charles. "A Construction of Hegelian Spirit in Whitman's 'As I Ebb'd with the Ocean of Life'." *Walt Whitman Rev.*, vol. 26 (1980), 59–63.

CF538 Kisler, Karl M. "Walt Whitman, seine persönlichen und künstlerischen Beziehungen zu Oesterreich und Deutschland." Diss., Wien, 1953.

CF539 Little, William A. "Walt Whitman and the *Nibelungenlied*." *PMLA*, vol. 80, no. 5 (1965), 562–70. Sources of Whitman's knowledge of the poem.

CF540 Livingston, James L. "With Whitman and Hegel around the Campfire." *Walt Whitman Rev.*, vol. 15 (June 1969), 122–24.

CF541 McAleer, John S. "Whitman and Goethe: More on the 'Van Rensellaer Letter'." *Walt Whitman Rev.*, vol. 8 (December 1962), 83–85.

CF542 Parsons, Olive W. "Whitman the Non-Hegelian." *PMLA*, vol. 58, no. 4 (December 1943), 1073–93. To correct the tendency to overemphasize Hegelian influence.

CF543 Shephard, Esther. "Possible Sources of Some of Whitman's Ideas and Symbols in Hermes Mecurin's Trismegistus and Other Works." *Mod. Lang. Quar.*, vol. 14 (1953), 60–81. W. "may have used the writings of Hermes and of Jacob Boehme as a source for some of his symbols."

CF544 Springer, Otto. "Walt Whitman and Ferdinand Freiligrath." *Amer.-German Rev.*, vol. 11, no. 2 (1944), 22–26, 38.

CF545 Stavrou, C. N. *Whitman and Nietzsche. A Comparative Study of Their Thought*. Chapel Hill: Univ. of N. Car. Pr., 1964. 231p.

CF546 Tisiker, Monica R. "Jacob Boehme's Influence on Some Poems in Leaves of Grass." *Walt Whitman Rev.*, vol. 20 (1974), 15–27.

CF547 "Walt Whitman und Goethe." *Neuphilologische Zeitung*, vol. 1 (1949), no. 5, 68.

WILDER, THORNTON

CF548 Frenz, Horst. "Thornton Wilder's Visits to Postwar Germany." *Amer.-German Rev.*, vol. 24, no. 1 (1957), 8–10. Most honored and beloved American writer in Germany.

CF549 Germer, Rudolf. "Thornton Wilders Bühnenstück *The Matchmaker* und seine literarischen Vorbilder." *Jahrbuch für Amerikastudien*, vol. 12 (1967), 137–46.

CF550 Kosok, Heinz. "Thornton Wilder: ein Literaturbericht." *Jahrbuch für Amerikastudien*, vol. 9 (1964), 196–227.

CF551 Riegl, Kurt. "Max Reinhardt als Vorbild für Thornton Wilders Caesar." *Die neueren Sprachen*, vol. 17 (1968), 356–58.

CF552 Riegl, Kurt. "Max Reinhardt, Thornton Wilder und *The Merchant of Yonkers*." In: *Österreich und die angelsächsische Welt. Kulturbegegnungen und Vergleiche*. Ed. Otto Hietsch. Vol. 2. Wien and Stuttgart: Braumüller, 1968, p.564–85.

CF553 Riegl, Kurt. "Zu den Unterschieden zwischen den gedruckten Fassungen von Thornton Wilders *The Matchmaker* und *The Merchant of Yonkers*." *Jahrbuch für Amerikastudien*, vol. 12 (1967), 147–58.

CF554 Williams, Michael Vincent. "Thornton Wilder's Anglo-American and German Critics: A Bibliography." Diss., Univ. of South Carolina, 1979. 374p.

WILLIAMS, WILLIAM CARLOS

CF555 Davis, Robert Gorham. "A Note on 'The Use of Force' and Freud's 'The Dream of Irma's Injection'." *William Carlos Williams Newsletter*, vol. 2, no. 1 (Spring 1976), 9–10. The story seen in relation to an early passage in *The Interpretation of Dreams*.

CF556 Galinsky, Hans. "An American Doctor-Poet's Image of Germany: An Approach to the Work of William Carlos Williams." *Studium Generale*, vol. 21 (1968), 74–93.

CF557 Hurry, David. "William Carlos Williams' *Paterson* and Freud's Interpretation of Dreams." *Lit. and Psychology*, vol. 28 (1978), 170–77.

WILLIAMSON, THAMES

CF558 Shoemaker, Alfred L. "D is for Dutch." *The Pa. Dutchman*, vol. 5, no. 2 (1953), 5, 15. Points out the strong influence of Fogel's *Beliefs and Superstitions of the Pennsylvania Germans* on Thames Williamson's novel, *D is for Dutch*.

WOLFE, THOMAS

CF559 Frenz, Horst. "Bemerkungen über Thomas Wolfe." *Die Neueren Sprachen* (1953), no. 9, 371–77. On W.'s European and German popularity; his admiration for Goethe.

CF560 Halperin, Irving. "Hunger for Life. Thomas Wolfe, a Young Faust." *Amer.-German Rev.*, vol. 30, no. 6 (1964), 12–14, 31. W.'s sojourn in Germany.

CF561 Ledig-Rowohlt, H. M. "Thomas Wolfe in Berlin." *Amer. Scholar*, vol. 22 (1953), 185–201. W.'s visits in 1935 and 1936; the use he made of these visits in *You Can't Go Home Again*. See also *Der Monat*, vol. 1 (1948), 69–77.

CF562 Oertel, Ferdinand. "Die Europa-Erfahrung Thomas Wolfes." Diss., Köln, 1954.

CF563 Reeves, Paschal. "The Second Homeland of His Spirit: Germany in the Fiction of Thomas

Wolfe." In: *Americana-Austriaca: Beiträge zur Amerikakunde.* vol. 2. Ed. Klaus Lanzinger. Wien: W. Braumüller, 1970, p. 53–60.

CF564 Schmid, Hans. "A Note on Thomas Wolfe's Oktoberfest-Letter." *Harvard Library Bull.*, vol. 18 (1970), 367–70.

CF565 Stanton, Edgar Emmett, Jr. "Hegel and Thomas Wolfe." Diss., Florida State, 1961.

CF566 Unger, Gerda. "Amerika und Europa im Urteil von Thomas Wolfes Romanen." Diss., Wien, 1953.

Reception and Influence of German Authors in America

ARNIM, BETTINA VON

CF567 Collins, Hildegard Platzer, and Philip Allison Shelley. "The Reception in England and America of Bettina von Arnim's *Goethe's Correspondence with a Child.*" In: *Anglo-German and American-German Crosscurrents.* Ed. P. A. Shelley, A. O. Lewis, and W. W. Betts. Chapel Hill: Univ. of N. Car. Pr., 1957–1962. 2 vols. Vol. II (1962), p. 97–174.

BENN, GOTTFRIED

CF568 Hohendahl, Peter Uwe. "Die Rezeption Gottfried Benns in den Vereinigten Staaten und Frankreich: Ein kritischer Vergleich." *Deutsche Vierteljahrschrift für Literaturwiss. u. Geistesgeschichte*, vol. 41 (1967), 233–57.

CF569 Lohner, Edgar. *Gottfried Benn Bibliographie, 1912–1956.* Wiesbaden: n.p., 1958. Incl. list of translations.

BÖLL, HEINRICH

CF570 Stewart, Keith. "The American Reviews of Heinrich Böll: A Note on the Problems of the Compassionate Novelist." *Univ. of Dayton Rev.*, vol. 11, no. 2 (1974), 5–10.

CF571 White, Ray Lewis. *Heinrich Böll in America, 1954–1970.* New York, Hildesheim: Olms, 1979. 170p.

BRECHT, BERTOLT

CF572 Bentley, Eric R. "How Brecht's "Circle" Came Full Circle." *N.Y. Times*, 20 March 1966. B. had to be played first in France before he would be accepted on Broadway.

CF573 Campbell, Johnstone. "American Culture and the Art of Bertolt Brecht: A Succession of Dawns." Diss., Stanford Univ., 1976. 203p. A study of the interaction of American culture with Brecht's dramatic practice and political thought.

CF574 Davis, R. G. "[Walter] Benjamin, Storytelling, and Brecht in the USA." *New German Critique*, vol. 17 (1979), 143–56.

CF575 Dial, Joseph. "Brecht in den U S A: Zur Stellung der New Yorker Aufführung der *Mutter Courage* (1935) und des *Galilei* (1947) in der Geschichte des epischen Theaters." *Weimarer Beiträge*, vol. 24, no. 2 (1978), 160–72.

CF576 Esslin, Martin. "A Descriptive List of Brecht's Works." In: *Brecht. The Man and His Work.* Martin Esslin. New York: n.p., 1961, p. 273–326. List of translations, time of composition, first performances, and publication data.

CF577 Gassner, John. "Varieties of Epic Theatre in the Modern Drama." *Compar. Lit. Studies.* Special Advance Issue, 1963.

CF578 Grimm, Reinhold. "FBI 'Subjekt' Bertolt Brecht. Zum V. Internationalen Brecht-Kongress." *German Quar.*, vol. 53, no. 3 (May 1980), 348–51. See also "Als Helene Weigel dem FBI Kochrezepte vorlas." *Frankfurter Allgemeine Zeitung*, 8 May 1979. Criticism of the congress held in West Germany in Autumn 1978.

CF579 Himelstein, Morgan Y. "The Pioneers of Brecht in America." *Mod. Drama*, vol. 9 (1966), 178–89.

CF580 Huettich, Gunner. "Zwischen Klassik und Kommerz: Brecht in Los Angeles." *Brecht Heute*, 1974, 125–37.

CF581 Jorns, David L. "Brechtian Epic Elements in the American Federal Theatre." M.A. thesis, Oklahoma State, 1967.

CF582 Lyon, James K. *Bertolt Brecht in America.* Princeton Univ. Pr., 1980. 408p. Rev. by John

German Authors: Influence *(cont.)*

Simon, *N.Y. Times Book Rev.*, 11 January 1981, 3, 26–27. Incl. Bibliography, p.385–96.

CF583 Lyon, James K. "Bertolt Brecht's Hollywood Years: The Dramatist as a Film Writer." *Oxford German Studies*, vol. 6 (1971), 145–74.

CF584 Lyon, James K. "Zur New Yorker Aufführung von Brechts Furcht und Elend des Dritten Reiches." In: *Deutsches Exildrama und Exilliteratur. Akten des Exilliteratur-Symposiums der University of South Carolina 1976*. Jahrbuch für Internat. Germanistik A 3. Frankfurt: Lang, 1977, p.67–76.

CF585 Lyon, James K., ed. "Der Briefwechsel zwischen Bertolt Brecht und der New Yorker Theatre Union von 1935." *Brecht-Jahrbuch* 1975, 136–55.

CF586 Nubel, Walter, comp. "Brecht in America. Productions of Brecht's Plays in America up to the Time of His Death." In: *Brecht. The Man and His Works*. Ed. Martin Esslin. New York, 1961, p.340–51.

CF587 Roswell, May MacGinnis. "Bertolt Brecht's Plays in America." Diss., Maryland, 1961. 134p.

CF588 Schevill, James. "Bertolt Brecht in New York." *The Tulane Drama Rev.*, vol. 6 (1961), 98–107.

CF589 Thomson, Philip. "'*Exegi momentum*': The Fame of Bertolt Brecht." *German Quar.*, vol. 53, no. 3 (May 1980), 337–47.

CF590 Torbruegge, Marylin K. "Turandot in Columbus." *Brecht-Jahrbuch* 1977, 169–73.

CF591 Weisstein, Ulrich. "Brecht in America: a Preliminary Survey." *Mod. Lang. Notes*, vol. 78, no. 4 (1963), 373–96.

CF592 Willett, John. *The Theatre of Bertolt Brecht. A Study from Eight Aspects*. New York: n.p., 1960. Incl. lists of English and French translations, p.21–61.

BROCH, HERMANN

CF593 Jonas, Klaus W. "Hermann Broch. Eine Bibliographische Studie." *Philobiblon*, vol. 9 (1965), 291–323.

BÜCHNER, GEORG

CF594 Emigh, John S. "An Analysis, Adaptation, and Production Book of Georg Büchner's *Woyzeck*." M.F.A. Thesis, Tulane, 1967.

CF595 Houseman, John. "Orson Welles and *Danton's Death*." *Yale/Theatre*, vol. 3, no. 3 (1970), 91–93.

CF596 Mackay, Barbara. "Leonce and Lena." *Yale/Theatre*, vol. 3 (1970), 68–82.

CF597 Marks, Jonathan. "Jonathan Miller's *Danton's Death*." *Yale/Theater*, vol. 3, no. 3 (1970), 99–105.

CF598 Rosenberg, Ralph. "Georg Büchner's Early Reception in America." *Jour. of Eng. and Germanic Philology*, vol. 44 (1945), 270–73. Support of Büchner by the Socialists may have impeded the recognition of his literary importance.

CF599 Simon, John. "On Danton's Death." *Yale/Theatre*, vol. 3, no. 3 (1970), 35–44.

CHAMISSO, ADELBERT VON

CF600 [Biographical sketch.] *Dictionary of Scientific Biography*, vol. 15, 81–83. German scientist and author.

CF601 De Brugger, Ilse I. M. "Adelbert von Chamisso en el Mundo Nuovo (1816)." In: *Algunos Aspectos de la Cultura Literaria de Mayo*. La Plata: n.p., 1961, 249–76.

CF602 Gudde, Erwin G. "Chamisso and California's State Flower." *Amer.-German Rev.*, vol. 8, no. 4 (1942), 33–34.

DROSTE-HÜLSHOFF, ANNETTE

CF603 Dees, Helmut. "Annette von Droste-Hülshoffs Dichtung in England und Amerika." Diss., Tübingen, 1966. 217p. Close study and evaluation of the work of her translators. Rev. by L. W. Tusken, *Monatshefte*, vol. 59 (1967), 282–83.

DÜRRENMATT, FRIEDRICH

CF604 Brock, D. Heyward. "Dürrenmatt's *Der Besuch der alten Dame*: The Stage and Screen Adaptations." *Lit./Film Quar.*, vol. 4 (1976), 60–67.

CF605 Knapp, Mona. "Die Verjüngung der alten Dame: Zur Initialrezeption Dürrenmatts in den Vereinigten Staaten." *Text und Kritik: Zeitschrift für Literatur*, vol. 56 (1977), 58–66.

CF606 Loram, Ian C. "'Der Besuch der alten Dame' and 'The Visit'." *Monatshefte*, vol. 53, no. 1 (January 1961), 15–21.

EICHENDORFF, JOSEPH KARL BENEDICT, FREIHERR VON

CF607 Seidlin, Oskar. "1957: The Eichendorff Year." *German Quar.*, vol. 31 (1958), 183–87. On E. (1788–1857).

FREUD, SIGMUND

CF608 Bettelheim, Bruno. *Freud and Man's Soul.* New York: Alfred A. Knopf., 1982. 112p. Rev. by Frank Kermode, *N.Y. Times Book Rev.*, 6 February 1983, 9, 25. Adverse critique of the accuracy and success of the Standard Edition of Freud's writings, as translated by James Strachey and his collaborators.

CF609 Foster, Ruel E. "Freudian Influences on the American Autobiographical Novel." Diss., Vanderbilt Univ., 1942. 165p.

CF610 Hoffman, Frederick J. *Freudianism and the Literary Mind.* 1st ed., 1945. 2nd ed. Baton Rouge: Louisiana Univ. Pr., 1957. 350p. Examination of 20th-century writers exhibiting interest in Freudian thought.

CF611 Morrison, Claudia C. *Freud and the Critic: The Early Use of Depth Psychology in Literary Criticism.* Chapel Hill: Univ. of N. Car. Pr., 1968. 248p. Rev. by L. Fraiberg, *Amer. Lit.*, vol. 41, no. 2 (May 1969), 314–15; P. K. Tompkins, *Quar. Jour. of Speech*, vol. 55 (1969), 196. Emphasis on the figures of Brooks, Krutch, Aiken, and D. H. Lawrence.

CF612 Noland, Richard W. "Psychoanalysis and Literature." *Bucknell Rev.*, vol. 14 (December 1966), 110–23.

CF613 Siever, W. David. *Freud on Broadway.* New York: n.p., 1955. Influence on the stage and theater.

CF614 Slochower, Harry. "Freud and Marx in Contemporary Literature." *Sewanee Rev.*, vol. 49, no. 3 (1941), 316–24.

CF615 Smith, Joseph H. *The Literary Freud: Mechanisms of Defense and the Will.* New Haven: Yale Univ. Pr., 1980. Rev. by Ned Lukacher, *Mod. Lang. Notes*, vol. 95 (1980), 1367–74.

GEORGE, STEFAN

CF616 Landmann, Georg P., comp. *Stefan George in fremden Sprachen; Übersetzungen seiner Gedichte in die europäischen Sprachen ausser den slawischen.* Düsseldorf: H. Küpper, 1973. 768p. Bibliography. Incl. all translations in anthologies and periodicals to 1960.

GERSTÄCKER, FRIEDRICH

CF617 Gerstäcker, Friedrich. *California Gold Mines.* Forew. by Joseph A. Sullivan. California Centennial Series, vol. 6. Oakland, Calif.: Biobooks, 1946. Selections from an undated edition by Harper's of Gerstäcker's *Travels Round the World*, based on his *Reisen*. G. (1816–1872).

CF618 Gerstäcker, Friedrich. *Die Flusspiraten des Mississippi.* Neubearb. von Marianne Simons. Heidelberg-Waibstadt: Kemper, 1948. 229p.

CF619 Gerstäcker, Friedrich. "Friedrich Gerstäcker in Arkansas. Selections from his *Streif- und Jagdzüge durch die Vereinigten Staaten Nordamerikas.*" Trans. by Clarence Evans and Liselotte Albrecht. *Ark. Hist. Quar.*, vol. 5 (1946), 39–57. A depiction of frontier life.

CF620 Gerstäcker, Friedrich. "Gerstäcker and the Konwells of White River Valley." Trans. by Clarence Evans. *Ark. Hist. Quar.*, vol. 10 (1951), 1–36. Three excerpts from the *Streif- und Jagdzüge*.

CF621 Gerstäcker, Friedrich. *Die Rache des weissen Mannes. Mississippi-Bilder. Auszüge.* Wien: Breitschopf, 1947. 93p.

CF622 Gerstäcker, Friedrich. *Scenes of Life in California.* Trans. from the French version by Revilliod by George Cosgrave. Forew. by R. E. Cowan. San Francisco: Grabhorn Pr., 1942. 188p. Rev. by J. W. Caughey, *Pacific Hist. Rev.*, vol. 13 (1943), 350. Based on Gerstäcker's *Kalifornische Skizzen* (1856).

CF623 Krumpelmann, John T. "Gerstäcker's *Germelshausen* and Lerner's *Brigadoon.*" *Monatshefte für deutschen Unterricht*, vol. 40 (1948), 396–400. See also *N.Y. Times*, 30 March 1947: "Reader Questions Origin of 'Brigadoon' And Asks Author Lerner's Reply."

GOETHE, JOHANN WOLFGANG VON

CF624 Atkins, Stuart P. *The Testament of Werther in Poetry and Drama.* Cambridge: Harvard Univ. Pr., 1949. 322p.

CF625 Biermann, Berthold. "Goethe im Urteil der Amerikaner." *Neue Schweizer Rundschau*, vol. 17 (1949), 317-23.

CF626 Broadbent, Thomas L. "A Goethe Note from the San Francisco *Sonntagsgast*: Implications and Deductions." *German Quar.*, vol. 44, no. 2 (March 1971), 168-71. Touches on the satire in "Das Neueste von Plundersweilen."

CF627 Browne, W. H. Rev. of *Poems and Ballads of Goethe*. Aytoun and Martin. *Southern Mag.*, vol. 9 (1871), 755-57.

CF628 Friesen, Gerhard. "Mignon in America." *Jour. of German-Amer. Studies*, vol. 14 (1979), 1-26. On the parodies and adaptations of Goethe's "Kennst du das Land."

CF629 Goethe, J. W. von. *Faust I*. Trans. by Carlyle F. MacIntyre. Norfolk, Conn.: New Directions, 1941. Rev. by W. A. Braun, *Germanic Rev.*, vol. 18, no. 3 (1943), 229-31.

CF630 Goethe, J. W. von. *Goethe's Faust, Parts One and Two*. Trans. and ed with introd. and notes by George Madison Priest. 2nd rev. ed. New York: Knopf, 1941. 454p. Rev. by Heinrich Meyer, *Amer.-German Rev.*, vol. 8 (1941), no. 2, 32; Mary Colum, *N.Y. Times Book Rev.*, 30 November 1941; W. A. Braun, *Germanic Rev.*, vol. 18, no. 3 (1943), 229-31; in *Amer.-German Rev.*, vol. 8, no. 4 (1941), 42.

CF631 Goldschmit-Jentner, R. K. *Eine Welt schreibt an Goethe*. Heidelberg: n.p., 1947. Rev. by Carl J. Hammer, *Germanic Rev.*, vol. 24, no. 4 (1949), 311-12.

CF632 Gudde, Erwin G. "Aaron Burr in Weimar." *South Atlantic Quar.*, vol. 40, no. 4 (1941), 360-67.

CF633 Hammer, Carl, ed. *Goethe after Two Centuries*. Baton Rouge: Louisiana State Univ. Pr., 1952. 118p.

CF634 Harris, W. T. "Goethe's Faust." In: *The Life and Genius of Goethe. Lectures at the Concord School of Philosophy*. Ed. F. B. Sanborn. Boston: Ticknor & Co., 1886, p.368-445.

CF635 Harris, William T. "Goethe's Wilhelm Meister." In: *Poetry and Philosophy of Ed. N. V. Dudley*. Chicago: Griggs, 1887, p.12-37.

CF636 Goethe Harris, William Torrey. "The Lesson of Goethe's Faust." [Cincinnati]: n.p., 1897. 18p. Repr. from the *Independent*, vol. 49, nos. 5 and 12 (August 1897), 998-99, 1035-36. Also in *Educational Foundations*, vol. 17 (April 1906), 614-24.

CF637 Hatfield, James T. "Götz von Berlichingen in America." *Germanic Rev.*, vol. 24 (1949), 177-83.

CF638 Hohlfeld, Alexander R. *Fifty Years with Goethe, 1901-1951*. Madison: Univ. of Wisconsin Pr., 1953. 400p. Collected studies and monographs on Goethe's life and works.

CF639 Igo, John. "A Calendar of Fausts." *Bull., N.Y. Public Library*, vol. 71 (1967), no. 1, 5-25. Faust characters created in the literature of the last 400 years.

CF640 Jarrell, Randall, trans. *Goethe's Faust, Part I: An English Translation*. New York: Farrar, Straus & Giroux, 1976.

CF641 Klein, Manfred. "Goethe and the Genteel Tradition in America." Diss., Boston Univ., 1961. 429p. On Goethe's vogue and reputation, 1865-1912.

CF642 Kornbluth, Martin L. "The Reception of *Wilhelm Meister* in America." *Symposium*, vol. 13 (1959), 128-34.

CF643 Krumpelmann, John T. *Southern Scholars in Goethe's Germany*. Chapel Hill: Univ. of N. Car. Pr., 1965. 200p. Rev. by C. Hammer, *La. Hist.*, vol. 8, no. 1 (Winter 1967), 110-111; A. E. Zucker, *German Quar.*, vol. 40 (1967), 279f.

CF644 Lewisohn, Ludwig. "Goethe's Poetry in the Lands of English Speech." In: *Goethe and the Modern Age: The Internat. Convocation at Aspen, Colorado*. Ed. Arnold Bergstraesser. Chicago: n.p., 1950, p.192-212.

CF645 Link, Franz H. "Goethe und die Renaissance des neu-englischen Geisteslebens im 19. Jahrhundert." *Die neueren Sprachen*, vol. II (1954), 63-73. Also in: *Amerika, Vision und Wirlichkeit*. Ed. F. H. Link. Frankfurt/Bonn: Athenäum, 1968, p.85-95.

CF646 Long, Orie W. "Goethe's American Visitors." *Amer. German Rev.*, vol. 15, no. 6 (1949), 24–28. Account of the early Göttingen group who "contributed... to Goethe's understanding of America" and gave "a significant impulse to the promotion of American interest in the poet."

CF647 Long, Orie W. "Werther in America." *Studies in Honor of John Albrecht Walz.* Lancaster, Pa.: Lancaster Pr., 1941, 86–116.

CF648 Melz, Charles F. "Goethe and America." *College Eng.*, vol. 10 (1949), 425–31. Deals chiefly with Emerson as an interpreter of Goethe.

CF649 Menchen, Georg. "Goethe's *Faust I* in New York: Gespräch mit Fritz Bennewitz." *Goethe*, vol. 97 (1980), 126–31.

CF650 Morgan, Bayard Q. "Goethe's *Faust* in Recent Translation." *Stanford Studies in Lang. and Lit.*, 1941, 275–86. The versions of Andrews, Buchanan, Cookson, Coxwile, Priest (1st ed.), Raphael, Shawcross, Todhunter, and Van der Smissen.

CF651 Olschner, Leonard M. "Zur frühen amerikanischen Rezeption von Goethes *Wahlverwandtschaften*." *Archiv für das Studium d. neueren Sprachen u. Literaturen*, vol. 212 (1975), 30–48.

CF652 Puknat, E. M. and S. B. Puknat. "Goethe and Modern American Poets." *German Quar.*, vol. 42 (January 1969), 21–36. Responses range from awe to ambivalence and rebellion.

CF653 Reichart, Walter A. "Goethe und Goethe-Literatur in Amerika." *Germanisch-Romanische Monatsschrift*, vol. 33 (1951), 47–54. On the Bicentennial of Goethe's birth (1949) and resultant publications.

CF654 Schwartz, Steven Gary. "Victorian Translations of Goethe's *Faust*, 1833–1885." Diss., Michigan, 1974.

CF655 Shelley, Philip Allison. "A German Art of Life in America: The American Reception of the Goethean Doctrine of Self-Culture." In: *Anglo-German and American-German Crosscurrents.* Eds. Philip A. Shelley, Arthur O. Lewis, Jr. and William W. Betts. Chapel Hill: Univ. of N. Car. Pr., 1957–1962. 2 vols. Vol. I, p.241–90.

CF656 Stern, Madeleine B. "The First German *Faust* Published in America." *American Notes and Queries*, vol. 10 (1972), 115–16.

CF657 Sundermeyer, William K. "Gettysburg College Goethe Album." *Amer.-German Rev.*, vol. 19, no. 5 (1953), 3–6. A souvenir album presented by Goethe to Countess Egloffstein; had been lost since 1891, but found in the archives of Gettysburg College.

CF658 Wallach, Martha K. "Goethe's American Utopia in *Wanderjahre* and Two Nineteenth Century German Experiments in the United States: The Harmony Society and the Oschwald Association." *Procs. of the Pacific Northwest Conference on Foreign Languages*, vol. 26, no. 1 (1975), 125–28. The ideals of Goethe's *Auswandererstaat* were realized by the followers of Oschwald who "might have known Goethe's *Wanderjahre*, but not by the harmonists."

CF659 Willoughby, Leonard A. "Die Goethe-Forschung in Amerika seit 1949." *Euphorion*, vol. 48 (1954), 220–36.

CF660 Zeydel, Edwin H. "Goethe's Reputation in America." In: *Essays on Goethe.* Ed. William Rose. London: Cassel & Co., 1949, p.207–32.

CF661 Zeydel, Edwin H., ed. and trans. *Goethe, the Lyrist, 100 poems in New Translations facing the Originals, with a Biographical Introduction, and an Appendix on Musical Settings to the Poems.* Chapel Hill: Univ. of N. Car. Pr., 1955. 182p. Rev. by Fred K. Scheibe, *Amer.-German Rev.*, vol. 22, no. 3 (1956), 38–39.

GOTTHELF, JEREMIAS (BITZIUS)

CF662 Andrews, John S. "The Reception of Gotthelf in British and American Periodicals." *Mod. Lang. Rev.*, vol. 51 (1956), 543–54.

CF663 Waidson, H. M. "Jeremias Gotthelf's Reception in Britain and America." *Mod. Lang. Rev.*, vol. 43, no. 2 (1948), 223–38.

GRASS, GÜNTER

CF664 Kellen, Konrad. "Grass and Johnson in New York." *Amer.-German Rev.*, vol. 31, no. 5 (1965), 35–37. Program of readings held on May 10 at the Poetry Center, YMHA.

CF665 White, Ray L. *Günter Grass in America: The Early Years.* Hildesheim: Georg Olms Verlag, 1981.

GRILLPARZER, FRANZ

CF666 Burkhard, Arthur. "England und Amerika, Kanada, Irland." In: *Grillparzer im Ausland.*

German Authors: Influence *(cont.)*

Cambridge: n.p., 1969, p.11–16. Rev. by W. E. Yates, *Mod. Lang. Rev.*, vol. 66, no. 1 (January 1971), 225–26.

CF667 Burkhard, Arthur. *Franz Grillparzer in England und America*. Wien: Bergland, 1961. 82p. Rev. by J. M. Herz, *Amer.-German Rev.*, vol. 28, no. 1 (1961), 37–37; T. C. Dunham, *Monatshefte*, vol. 55, no. 3 (1963), 136–37; D. Lasher-Schlitt, *Mod. Lang. Notes*, vol. 79, no. 4 (1964), 479–80; W.A. Little, *German Quar.*, vol. 39 (1966), 104–06.

CF668 Hecken, Dorothea. "Das Grillparzerbild im angloamerikanischen Ausland. Mit einer Studie über den deutschen literarischen Einfluss in Amerika." Diss., Berlin—Humboldt Univ., 1944.

CF669 McCormick, John. "Falling Asleep over Grillparzer: An Interview with Robert Lowell." *Poetry*, vol. 81 (1953), 269–79.

CF670 Schaum, Konrad. "Die Grillparzer-Forschung in Amerika im 20. Jahrhundert." In: *Das Grillparzer-Bild des 20. Jahrhunderts: Festschrift der Österreichischen Akad. der Wissenschaften zum 100. Todestag von Franz Grillparzer.* Ed. Heinz Kindermann. Wien: Bohlau, 1972, p.263–84.

CF671 Straubinger, O. Paul. "Grillparzer-Bibliographie 1937–1953." *Jahrbuch der Grillparzer-Gesellschaft*, 3rd Ser., vol. 1 (1953), 34–80.

CF672 Strelka, Joseph. "Die amerikanische Grillparzer-Literatur 1970–75: Ein Forschungsbericht." *Jahrbuch der Grillparzer-Gesellschaft*, vol. 13 (1978), 101–12.

CF673 Whiton, John. "Grillparzer-Forschung in Kanada." In: *Das Grillparzer-Bild des 20. Jahrhunderts. Festschrift...zum 100. Todestag von Franz Grillparzer.* Ed. Heinz Kindermann. Wien: Bohlau, 1972, p.193–202.

GRIMM, JACOB AND WILHELM

CF674 Dilkey, M. C., and H. Schneider. "John Mitchell Kemble and the Brothers Grimm." *Jour. of Eng. and Germanic Philology*, vol. 40, no. 4 (1941), 461–73.

CF675 *Grimm's Fairy Tales*. Trans. by Margaret Hunt, revised by James Stern. New York: Pantheon, 1944. 864p. Rev. by L. J. Davidson, *Western Folklore*, vol. 8, no. 2 (1949), 190–91.

CF676 Hand, Wayland. "Die Märchen der Brüder Grimm in den Vereinigten Staaten." In: *Brüder Grimm Gedenken 1963. Gedenkschrift zur hundertsten Wiederkehr des Todestages von Jacob Grimm.* Ed. Ludwig Denecke and Ina-Maria Greverus. Marburg: Elwert, 1963, p.525–44.

HAUPTMANN, GERHART

CF677 Blankenagel, John C. "Early Reception of Hauptmann's *Die Weber* in the United States." *Mod. Lang. Notes*, vol. 68 (1953), 334–40. The play was forbidden by the Newark authorities but was performed in New York and Chicago without protest, 1894–1895.

CF678 Cappel, Edith. "The Reception of Gerhart Hauptmann in the United States." Diss., Columbia, 1952.

CF679 Emerson, Helen. "A Criticism of Charles Henry Meltzer's Translation of *Hanneles Himmelfahrt* and *Die Versunkene Glocke*." *German Quar.*, vol. 21, no. 3 (1948), 163–74.

CF680 Jonas, Klaus W. "Gerhart Hauptmann in Amerika und England." *Börsenblatt für den deutschen Buchhandel*, vol. 25, no. 52 (1969), 1601–09.

CF681 Reichart, Walter A. "Bibliographie der gedruckten und ungedruckten Dissertationen über Gerhart Hauptmann und sein Werk. Unter Mitarbeit von Manfred Kremkus und Harold Culbertson." *Philobiblon*, vol. 11, no. 2 (June 1967), 121–34.

CF682 Reichart, Walter A. "Fifty Years of Hauptmann Study in America (1894–1944): A Bibliography." *Monatshefte für deutschen Unterricht*, vol. 37, no. 1 (1945), 1–31.

CF683 Reichart, Walter A. "Die früheste Hauptmann-Kritik in Amerika." In: *Marginalien zur poetischen Welt: Festschrift für Robert Mühlher zum 60. Geburtstag.* Ed. Alois Eder et al. Berlin: Duncker & Humblot, 1971, p. 271–81.

CF684 Reichart, Walter A. "Gerhart Hauptmann: His Work in America." *Amer. German Rev.*, vol. 29 (1962–63), no. 2, 4–6, 31.

CF685 Reichart, Walter A. "Gerhart Hauptmann's Dramas on the American Stage." *Maske und Kothurn*, vol. 8 (1962), 223–32.

CF686 Reichart, Walter A. "Hauptmann Study in America: A Continuation Bibliography." *Monatshefte*, vol. 54, no. 6 (1962), 296–310.

CF687 Weisert, John J. "Critical Reception of Hauptmann's *Sunken Bell* on the American Stage." *Monatshefte*, vol. 43, no. 4–5 (1951), 221–34.

HEBBEL, FRIEDRICH

CF688 Alt, Arthur Tilo. Die kritische Rezeption Friedrich Hebbels in den U S A. *Hebbel-Jahrbuch* 1978, 163–80.

CF689 Reichart, Walter A. "Hebbel in Amerika und England: Eine Bibliographie." *Hebbel-Jahrbuch* 1961, 118–35.

HEINE, HEINRICH

CF690 Arnold, Armin. *Heine in England and America. A Bibliographical Checklist.* Introd. by W. Rose. London: Linden Pr., 1959. 80p. Rev. by S. Liptzin, *German Quar.*, vol. 33, no. 4 (1960), 395–96.

CF691 Gohdes, Clarence. "Heine In America: A Cursory Survey." *Ga. Rev.*, vol. 11 (1959), 44–49.

CF692 Liptzin, Sol. *The English Legend of Heinrich Heine.* New York: n.p., 1954. On the reception of Heine in the English-speaking world.

CF693 Weiss, Gerhard. "Die Aufnahme Heinrich Heines in Grossbritannien und den Vereinigten Staaten von Nordamerika (1828 bis 1856); eine Studie zur Rezeption des Menschen und Prosakünstlers." Diss., Mainz, 1955.

CF694 Werner, Alfred. "Heine in America." *Amer.-German Rev.*, vol. 22, no. 6 (1956), 4–6. Also in: *The Sword and the Flame: Selections from Heinrich Heine's Prose.* New York: n.p., 1960, p.91–97.

CF695 Wilhelm, Gottfried and Eberhard Galley. *Heine Bibliographie.* Weimar: Arion, 1960. 2 vols. 191, 294p.

HERDER, JOHANN GOTTFRIED

CF696 Bluestein, Gene. "Herder's Folksong Ideology." *Southern Folklore Quar.*, vol. 26, no. 2 (June 1962), 137–144. Herder's influence on Whitman, Emerson, Rourke, and Lomax.

HESSE, HERMANN

CF697 Bareis, Otto. *Hermann Hesse: Eine Bibliographie der Werke über Hermann Hesse.* Part 1. Basel: n.p., 1962. Part 2. *Zeitschriften und Zeitungsaufsätze.* Basel: n.p., 1964.

CF698 Bentz, Hans W., comp. *Hermann Hesse in Übersetzungen. 289 Übersetzungsnachweise in 27 Sprachen, erschienen zwischen 1945 und 1965.* Weltliteratur in Übersetzungen, Reihe I, Band 3. Frankfurt: Bentz, 1964. 38p.

CF699 Bredsdorff, Morten. "Hermann-Hesse—en Romantiker i U S A." *Dansk Udsyn*, vol. 51 (1971), 97–102.

CF700 Butler, C. "The Defective Art of Hermann Hesse." *Jour. of European Studies*, vol. 5, no. 1 (March 1975), 41–54.

CF701 Cook, Bruce. "Hermann Hesse's Curious Appeal. Today's Young Embrace a German Writer from the Past." *National Observer*, 14 September 1970.

CF702 "Cultivating Hesse." *Times Literary Supplement*. 31 August 1973.

CF703 Ford, Richard J. "Herman Hesse: Prophet of the Pot Generation." *Catholic World*, vol. 212 (1970), 15–19.

CF704 Freedman, Ralph. *Hermann Hesse. Pilgrim of Crisis.* New York: Pantheon Books, ca. 1978. 432p. Rev. by Peter Gay, *N.Y. Times Book Rev.*, 21 January 1979, 3, 24–25.

CF705 Gajek, Bernhard. "Hesses Wirkung in den U S A: Überlegungen zu seinem 100. Geburtstag." *Schweizer Monatshefte: Zeitschrift für Politik, Wirtschaft, Kultur*, vol. 57 (1977), 295–309.

CF706 *The Herman Hesse 1975 Calendar.* Illus. by Milton Glaser, with an Astrologer's Note by Helen Weaver, and Text from the Writings of Hermann Hesse. New York: Farrar Straus & Giroux, 1974.

CF707 Hertz, Peter D. "*Steppenwolf* as a Bible." *Ga. Rev.*, vol. 25 (1971), 439–49.

CF708 Jonas, Klaus W. "Additions to the Bibliography of Hermann Hesse." *Publs., Bibliographical Soc. of America*, vol. 49 (1955), 358–60.

CF709 Jonas, Klaus W. "Hermann Hesse in Amerika. Bibliographie." *Monatshefte*, vol. 44, no. 2 (1952), 95–99.

CF710 Jonas, Klaus W. "Hermann Hesse in Germany, Switzerland, and America." *Annali Instituto Universitario Orientale, Napoli, Sezione Germanica*, vol. 12 (1969), 267–80.

CF711 Jonas, Klaus W. "Hermann Hesse in Switzerland and America." *Stechert-Hafner Book News*, vol. 24 (1968), 37–40.

CF712 Maierhöfer, Fränzi. "Auf der Suche nach Entpersönlichung. Zur Entdeckung Hermann Hesses in Amerika." *Hochland*, vol. 63 (1971), 483–91.

CF713 Michels, Volker. "Hesse in den U S A—Hesse bei uns." *Westermanns Monatshefte*, vol. 5 (May 1971), 52–59.

CF714 Michels, Volker, ed. *Materialien zu Hermann Hesses "Der Steppenwolf."* Frankfurt: Suhrkamp, 1972. 417p. Reviews the details of his reception in America.

CF715 Mileck, Joseph. *Hermann Hesse and His Critics: The Criticism and Bibliography of Half a Century.* Chapel Hill: Univ. of N. Car. Pr., 1958.

CF716 Mileck, Joseph. "Hesse Bibliographies." *Monatshefte*, vol. 49 (1957), 201–05.

CF717 Mileck, Joseph. "The Horst Kliemann Hermann-Hesse Archiv at the University of California in Berkeley." *German Quar.*, vol. 34, no. 3 (1961), 248–56.

CF718 Mileck, Joseph. "Trends in Literary Reception: The Hesse Boom." *German Quar.*, vol. 51 (1978), 346–54.

CF719 Otten, Anna, ed. *Hesse Companion.* Albuquerque: Univ. of New Mexico Pr., 1977. 324p. Rev. by P. H. Stanley, *German Studies Rev.*, vol. 1 (1978), 216. A collection of essays on Hesse by American Germanists.

CF720 Pfeifer, Martin. *Hermann-Hesse-Bibliographie: Primär- und Sekundärschrifttum in Auswahl.* Berlin: Erich Schmidt Verlag, 1973. 104p. Incl. sections on the literature in the U.S., Japan, the U.S.S.R., and France.

CF721 Pfeifer, Martin, ed. *Herman Hesses weltweite Wirkung: Internationale Rezeptionsgeschichte.* Frankfurt: Suhrkamp, 1977. 364p. Section on "U S A," p.155–71. Bibliography of translations, p.275–348.

CF722 Schwarz, Egon. "Hermann Hesse, the American Youth Movement and Problems of Literary Evaluation." *PMLA*, vol. 85 (1970), 977–87. Also published in the German language in 1970: *BASIS, Jahrbuch für deutsche Gegenwartsliteratur*, Band 1. Ed. Reinh. Grimm and Jost Hermand. Frankfurt: Athenäum, 1970, 116–33.

CF723 Steiner, George. "Hermann Hesse." *New Yorker*, vol. 44, 18 January 1969, 87–90.

CF724 Timpe, Eugene F. "Hermann Hesse in the United States." *Symposium*, vol. 23, no. 1 (1969), 73–79.

CF725 Unseld, Siegfried. "Hermann Hesse's Watchword, 'Be Yourself': Hesse's Impact Today." *Dimension*, vol. 9, no. 3 (1976), 446–61. With personal reminiscences.

CF726 Weyr, Thomas. "Hermann Hesse and the American-German Review." *Amer.-German Rev.*, vol. 35 (1969), no. 2, 1.

CF727 Winston, Krishna. "The Hermann Hesse Phenomenon." *American P.E.N.*, vol. 6, no. 1 (Winter 1974), 37–46. A review of four recent translations.

CF728 Ziolkowski, Theodor. "Hermann Hesse in den U S A." In: *Hermann Hesse heute.* Ed. Adrian Hsia. Bonn: Bouvier, 1980, p.1–24.

CF729 Ziolkowsky, Theodore. "Saint Hesse among the Hippies." *Amer.-German Review*, vol. 35, no. 2 (1969), 19–23.

HOCHHUTH, ROLF

CF730 Bentley, Eric, ed. *The Storm Over 'The Deputy': Essays and Articles about Hochhuth's Explosive Drama.* New York: n.p., 1964. 254p. Rev. by N. Lamm, *Jewish Social Studies*, vol. 28, no. 2 (April 1966), 124–26. On the Broadway production and the reaction to the play.

HOFFMANN, E.T.A.

CF731 Dose, Claus Dieter. "The Reception of E.T.A. Hoffmann in the United States, 1940–1976." Diss., New York Univ., 1980. 281p.

HOFMANNSTHAL, HUGO VON

CF732 Pick, Robert, and Ann C. Weaver. "Hugo von Hofmannsthal in England and America. A Bibliography." In: *Hofmannsthal. Studies in Commemoration.* Ed. F. Norman. London: Univ. of London, Inst. of Germanic Langs. and Literatures, 1963, p.119-47.

KAFKA, FRANZ

CF733 Benson, Ann T. "The American Criticism of Franz Kafka, 1930-1948." Diss., Tennessee, 1958. 161p.

CF734 Benson, Ann T. "Franz Kafka: An American Bibliography." *Bull. of Bibliography*, vol. 22 (1958), 112-14.

CF735 Boegeman, Margaret Byrd. "Paradox Gained: Kafka's Reception in English from 1930 to 1949 and His Influence on the Early Fiction of Borges, Beckett, and Nabokov." Diss., Univ. of California, Los Angeles, 1977.

CF736 Born, Jürgen. "Die Aufnahme und der Einfluss Franz Kafkas in Amerika." Diss., Freie Universität, Berlin, 1958.

CF737 Caputo-Mayr, Maria Luise. "Franz Kafka. Bibliography: Editions and Translations. Part 4. Addenda." *Newsletter, Kafka Soc. of America*, no. 1 (1980), 40-53.

CF738 Caputo-Mayr, Maria Luise, and Julius M. Herz. "Editions and Translations, Part 3: Einzelveröffentlichungen und andere Prosa." *Newsletter, Kafka Soc. of America*, no. 2 (1979), 17-59.

CF739 Caputo-Mayr, Maria Luise, and Julius M. Herz. "Franz Kafka Bibliography: A Selection of Secondary Titles 1975-1980." *Newsletter, Kafka Soc. of America*, no. 1 (1980), 18-39.

CF740 Flores, Angel. "Bibliographical Index of the Works Available in English." In: *Franz Kafka Today.* Ed. A. Flores and Homer Swander. Madison: Univ. of Wis. Pr., 1958, p.251-85.

CF741 Flores, Angel. "Franz Kafka: Bibliography and Criticism—A New, Up-to-Date Bibliography." In: *The Kafka Problem.* Ed. A. Flores. New York: n.p., 1963, 455-77.

CF742 Flores, Angel. *Franz Kafka: A Chronology and Bibliography.* Houlton, Me.: n.p., 1944.

CF743 Heidinger, Maurice. "'Intrinsic' Kafka Criticism in America (1949-1963)." Diss., Indiana Univ., 1965. 149p.

CF744 Hemmerle, Rudolf. *Franz Kafka: Eine Bibliographie.* München: n.p., 1958.

CF745 Järv, Harry. *Die Kafka-Literatur.* Malmö/Lund: n.p., 1961.

CF746 Jaffe, Adrian. "Franz Kafka et le héros solitaire dans le roman américain contemporain." *Roman*, vol. 1 (March 1951), 142-49.

CF747 Jonas, Klaus W. "Franz Kafka: An American Bibliography." *Bull. of Bibliography*, vol. 20 (1953), 212-16, 231-33. Primary and secondary literature in America through 1948. Repr. Folcroft, Pa.: Folcroft Library Editions, 1972. 10p.

CF748 Kolman, Maria A. "The Literary Fortune of Franz Kafka: A Critical Survey of the German, English and Slavic Secondary Literature." Diss., Colorado, 1973.

CF749 Kowal, Michael. "Kafka and the Emigrés: A Chapter in the History of Kafka Criticism." *Germanic Rev.*, vol. 41, no. 4 (November 1966), 291-301.

CF750 Weinberg, Helen. *The New Novel in America: The Kafkan Mode in Contemporary Fiction.* Ithaca: Cornell Univ. Pr., ca. 1970. 248p. Rev. by B. H. Gelfant, *Amer. Lit.*, vol. 43 (1971), 147-49. The spiritual "activist" mode distinguished from the "absurdist" exemplified by Kafka's *Castle.*

CF751 Weinberg, Helen Arnstein. "The Kafkan Hero and the Contemporary American Activist Novel." Diss., Western Reserve, 1966. 297p.

KOTZEBUE, AUGUST F. F.

CF752 Behrmann, Alfred. "Kotzebue on the American Stage." *Arcadia*, vol. 4 (1969), 274-84.

CF753 Matlaw, Myron. "English Versions of *Die Spanier in Peru.*" *Mod. Lang. Quar.*, vol. 16 (1955), 63-67.

CF754 Matlaw, Myron. "Some Kotzebue Plays in England and America: *The Stranger* and *Pizarro.*" Diss., Chicago, 1954.

KRAUS, KARL

CF755 Daviau, Donald G. "Karl Kraus in English Translation." *Psychoanalytic Rev.*, vol. 65 (1978), 95–108. A review article.

KÜRNBERGER, FERDINAND

CF756 Lang, Hans-Joachim. "Ferdinand Kürnberger One Hundred Years Later." In: *The Harold Jantz Collection: Proceedings of a Sponsored Conference to Introduce the Collection to Specialists in German-American Literary Relations*. Ed. Leland R. Phelps. Durham: Duke Univ. Center for Internat. Studies, 1981, p.51–70.

LENAU, NIKOLAUS

CF757 Arndt, Karl J. R. "Lenau's Last Poem, *An die Ultraliberalen in Deutschland*." *Germanic Rev.*, vol. 19 (1944), 180–89.

CF758 Berges, Ruth. "Lenau's Quest in America." *Amer.-German Rev.*, vol. 28, no. 4 (1962), 14–17.

LILIENCRON, DETLEV VON

CF759 Loewenberg, Ernst L. "Liliencron und Amerika." *Monatshefte für deutschen Unterricht*, vol. 37 (1945), 428–36.

LUTHER, MARTIN

CF760 Green, Lowell C. "Luther Research in English-Speaking Countries since 1971." *Luther Jahrbuch*, vol. 44 (1977), 105–26.

MANN, HEINRICH

CF761 Weisstein, Ulrich. "Heinrich Mann in America: A Critical Survey." *Books Abroad*, vol. 33 (1960), 281–84.

CF762 Weisstein, Ulrich. "Professor Unrat, Small Town Tyrant, and The Blue Angel: Translations, Versions and Adaptations of Heinrich Mann's Novel in Two Media." In: *Actes du VIe Congrés de l'Association Internat. de Littérature Comparée*... Ed. Michel Cadot, M. V. Dimić, D. Malone and Miklós Szabolcsi. Stuttgart: Bieber, 1975, p.251–57.

MANN, KLAUS

CF763 Dirschauer, Wilfried. *Klaus Mann und das Exil*. Deutsches Exil 1933–1945, Eine Schriftenreihe. Band 2. Worms: Heintz, 1973. 151p.

MANN, THOMAS

CF764 Ahn, S.-H. "Exilliterarische Aspekte in Thomas Manns Roman Doktor Faustus." Diss. (DAI, vol. 37 (1977), 3226C).

CF765 Berger, Willy Richard. *Die mythologischen Motive in Thomas Manns Roman Joseph und seine Brüder*. Literatur und Leben, N.F., Bd. 14. Köln / Wien: Böhlau, 1971. 312p.

CF766 Binger, Norman H. "Thomas Mann's Analysis of Democracy." *Germanic Notes*, vol. 1, no. 2 (1970), 10–12.

CF767 Brennan, Joseph Gerard. *Thomas Mann's World*. New York, 1942; 1962.

CF768 Bürgin, Hans. *Das Werk Thomas Manns*. Frankfurt a. M.: S. Fischer Vlg., 1959. Lists editions of works in translation in 31 countries.

CF769 Bürgin, Hans, and Hans-Otto Mayer, comps. *Thomas Mann: Eine Chronologie seines Lebens*. Frankfurt a. M.: S. Fischer Vlg., 1965. 284p. For his years in America, see p.134–53, 153–234.

CF770 Frey, Erich. "Thomas Mann's Exile Years in America." *Mod. Lang. Studies*, vol. 6, no. 1 (1976), 83–92.

CF771 Guerard, Albert. "What We Hope from Thomas Mann." *Amer. Scholar*, vol. 15, no. 1 (1946), 35–43.

CF772 Hatfield, Henry. "Thomas Mann and America." *Salmagundi*, vols. 10–11 (1969–1970), 174–85.

CF773 Jonas, Klaus W. *Fifty Years of Thomas Mann Studies; A Bibliography of Criticism*. Minneapolis: Univ. of Minn. Pr., 1955. 217p. Repr. New York: Kraus Reprint, 1969. 217p.

CF774 Jonas, Klaus W. "Die Hochschulschriften des In- und Auslandes über Thomas Mann." In: *Betrachtungen und Überblicke: Zum Werk Thomas Manns*. Ed. Georg Wenzel. Berlin: Aufbau, 1966, p.511–31.

CF775 Jonas, Klaus W. "Thomas Mann, Caroline Newton and Princeton." *Börsenblatt für den deutschen Buchhandel*, vol. 27 (30 July, 1971), A277–85.

CF776 Jonas, Klaus W. "Thomas Mann Collections." *Monatshefte*, vol. 50 (1958), 145–56. Collections of Harvard, Yale, and private owners Caroline Newton and Alfred A. Knopf.

CF777 Jonas, Klaus W. *Die Thomas Mann Literatur*. Ed. K. W. Jonas. Berlin: E. Schmidt, ca. 1972. Prepared in cooperation with the Thomas-Mann Archiv, Zürich.

CF778 Jonas, Klaus W. "Thomas Mann. Manuscripte in europäischen Sammlungen." *Jahrbuch für Amerikastudien*, vol. 4 (1959), 236–48.

CF779 Jonas, Klaus W. "Thomas Mann und Agnes E. Meyer." *Neue Deutsche Hefte*, no. 148 (1975), 706–18.

CF780 Jonas, Klaus W. "Thomas Mann und Agnes E. Meyer: Zwei unveröffentlichte Briefe." *Börsenblatt für den deutschen Buchhandel*, vol. 27 (21 May, 1971), A 213–20.

CF781 Jonas, Klaus W. "Thomas Manns Manuscripte." *Philobiblon*, vol. 9 (September 1965), 153–74.

CF782 Jonas, Klaus W. "Two Previously Unpublished Thomas Mann Letters to Agnes E. Meyer." *Books Abroad*, vol. 45 (1971), 627–36. In translations by D. L. Ashliman.

CF783 Jonas, Klaus W., and Ilsedore B. Jonas, eds. *Thomas Mann Studies*. Vol. II. Philadelphia: Univ. of Pa. Press, 1967. 440p. A list of 4,000 items of criticism for the period 1954 to 1965.

CF784 "Kein Deutschland Komitee in U S A: Ein Dementi Thomas Manns." *Aufbau* (N.Y.), 3 December 1943.

CF785 Köpke, Wulf. "Thomas Mann und Ludwig Lewisohn: Ein Beitrag zum Thema 'Thomas Mann und Amerika' aufgrund unveröffentlichten Briefe Thomas Manns." *Colloquia Germanica*, vol. 11 (1978), 123–48.

CF786 Lange, Victor. "Thomas Mann: Die Princetoner Jahre." In: *Thomas Mann, 1875–1975: Vorträge in München—Zürich—Lübeck*. Ed. Beatrix Bludeau, Eckhard Heftrich, and Helmut Koopman. Frankfurt: S. Fischer Vlg., 1976, p.566–85.

CF787 Lehnert, Herbert. "The Burgher in Exile." *Soundings*, vol. 8, no. 1 (1976), 48–61. On Thomas Mann.

CF788 Mann, Golo. *Thomas Mann: Erinnerungen an meinen Vater...Thomas Mann in Übersetzungen: Bibliographie*. Bonn: Inter Nationes, 1965.

CF789 Mann, Michael. "Thomas Mann and the United States of America: A Twenty-Year Relationship." In: *Perspectives and Personalities: Studies in Modern German Literature Honoring Claude Hill*. Ed. R. Ley, M. Wagner, et al. Heidelberg: Winter, 1978, p.274–81.

CF790 Mann, Thomas. *Briefe 1937–1947*. Ed. Erika Mann. Frankfurt a. M.: S. Fischer Vlg., 1963.

CF791 Mann, Thomas. *Ein Briefwechsel*. New York: Rotograph Co., 1937. 4p.

CF792 Mann, Thomas. *Deutsche Hörer! 25 Radiosendungen nach Deutschland*. Stockholm: Bermann-Fischer Vlg., 1942. 151p. Reissued in Stockholm in 1945 as: *Deutsche Hörer! 55 Radiosendungen nach Deutschland*. 2. erweiterte Ausgabe. See also: *Deutsche Hörer! Eine Auswahl aus den Rundfunkbotschaften an das deutsche Volk*. London: Freier deutscher Kulturbund in Grossbritannien, 1944. 23p.

CF793 Mann, Thomas. *Dieser Friede*. Stockholm: n.p. n.d. 28p. 1st ed.

CF794 Mann, Thomas. *Leiden an Deutschland. Tagebuchblätter aus den Jahren 1933 und 1934*. Los Angeles: Pazific Pr., 1946. 90p.

CF795 Mann, Thomas. "A Letter from Thomas Mann to Hermann J. Weigand." *PMLA*, vol. 87 (1972), 306–08.

CF796 Mann, Thomas. *The Letters of Thomas Mann to Caroline Newton*. Princeton: Princeton Univ. Pr., 1971. 112p.

CF797 Mann, Thomas. *Letters to Paul Amman, 1915–1952*. Middletown, Conn: Wesleyan Univ. Pr., 1960.

CF798 Mann, Thomas. *Vom kommenden Sieg der Demokratie*. Berlin: Suhrkamp Vlg., 1946. 40p.

CF799 Mann, Thomas. *Vom zukünftigen Sieg der Demokratie.* 2nd ed. Zürich: Vlg. Oprecht, 1938. A slightly expanded version of an address given in fifteen cities of the United States in the spring of 1938.

CF800 Neumann, Erich, Hans Bürgin, and Walter A. Reichart. Fortsetzung und Nachtrag zu Hans Bürgins Bibliographie *Das Werk Thomas Manns.* In: *Betrachtungen und Überblicke: Zum Werk Thomas Manns.* Ed. Georg Wenzel. Berlin: Aufbau, 1966, p.491–510.

CF801 Ordon, Edmund. "Thomas Mann's 'Joseph'-Cycle and the American Critic." *Monatshefte für deutschen Unterricht,* vol. 35 (1943), 286–96, 318–30.

CF802 Perl, Walter H. *Thomas Mann 1933–1945: Vom deutschen Humanisten zum amerikanischer Weltbürger.* New York: Friedr. Krause, 1945. 64p.

CF803 Prausnitz, Walther G. "Thomas Mann: Artist in Exile." *Discourse,* vol. 8 (1965), 105–18.

CF804 Pringsheim, Klaus H. "Thomas Mann in America." *Amer.-German Rev.,* vol. 30, no. 3 (1964), 24–34. Political aspects of Mann's presence in the United States, 1938 to 1952. Article of same title, but presumably in German, in *Neue deutsche Hefte,* vol. 13 (1966), no. 109, p.20–46.

CF805 Pringsheim, Klaus H. "Thomas Mann in Exile: Roosevelt, McCarthy, Goethe, and Democracy." In: *Thomas Mann: Ein Kolloquium.* Ed. Hans H. Schulte and Gerald Chapple. Modern German Studies, no. 1. Bonn: Bouvier, 1978, p.20–34.

CF806 Pross, Harry. "On Thomas Mann's Political Career." *Jour. of Contemporary Hist.,* vol. 2, no. 2 (April 1967), 65–80.

CF807 Ramras, Herman. "Main Currents in American Criticism of Thomas Mann." Diss., Wisconsin, 1950.

CF808 Reichart, Walter A. "Thomas Mann: An American Bibliography." *Monatshefte für deutschen Unterricht,* vol. 37, no. 6 (1945), 389–408.

CF809 Riesenman, Catherine Patricia. "The Early Reception of Thomas Mann's *Doktor Faustus*: History and Main Problems." Diss., Indiana, 1966. 305p. Reception in Europe and America.

CF810 Seinfelt, Frederick W. "Thomas Mann and Some American and British Writers." In: *George Moore: Ireland's Unconventional Realist.* Philadelphia: Dorrance, 1975. 309p.

CF811 *Thomas Manns Bekenntnis für ein freies Deutschland: Rede die am 21. April 1937 in New York gehalten wurde.* New York: n.p., 1937. 4p.

CF812 White, John F. "Thomas Mann in America: The Rhetorical and Political Experience of an Exiled Artist." Diss. Minnesota, 1971.

CF813 Wysling, Hans, ed. "Thomas Mann—Erich von Kahler Briefwechsel im Exil: Aus den Beständen des Thomas-Mann-Archives der Eidgenössischen Technischen Hochschule." *Blätter der Thomas Mann Gesellschaft,* vol. 10 (1970), 5–62.

CF814 Wysling, Hans, Dieter Schwarz, and Herbert Wiesner, eds. "Die ersten Jahre des Exils: Briefe von Schriftstellern an Thomas Mann. Erster Teil: 1933. Zweiter Teil: 1934–1935. Dritter Teil: 1936–1939." *Blätter der Thomas Mann Gesellschaft,* vol. 13 (1973), 5–34; *ibid.,* vol. 14 (1974), 5–37; *ibid.,* vol. 15 (1975), 4–42.

CF815 Zerner, Marianne. "Thomas Mann in Standard English Anthologies." *German Quar.,* vol. 18, no. 4 (1945), 178–88. Critical study of extant translations of *Tonio Kröger, Der Tod in Venedig,* and *Der Bajazzo.*

MARX, KARL/MARXISM

CF816 Clecak, Peter. "Marxism, Literary Criticism, and the American Academic Scene." *Science and Society,* vol. 31, no. 3 (Summer 1967), 275–301.

CF817 Dayananda, James Y. "Marxist Contribution to Edmund Wilson's Literary Criticism." Diss., Temple Univ., 1969. 200p. Finds a para-Marxist rather than a doctrinaire Marxist ideology; touches on W.'s debt to Freud for insights in his psychological criticism.

CF818 Eagleton, Terry. *Marxism and Literary Criticism.* Berkeley: Univ. of Calif. Pr., ca. 1968. 96p.

CF819 Peck, David. *American Marxist Literary Criticism: 1926–1941: A Bibliography.* American Institute for Marxist Studies, Bibliographical Series, no. 10. New York: Institute for Marxist Studies, 1975. 42p.

CF820 Peck, David. "Marxist Literary Criticism in the United States, 1941–1966: A Bibliography." *Bull. of Bibliography*, vol. 35, no. 4 (ca. 1975), 172–79.

CF821 Peck, David. "The New Marxist Criticism: A Bibliography." *The Minn. Rev.*, vol. 2–3 (Spring/Fall 1974), 127–32; vol. 7 (Fall 1976), 100–05.

CF822 Peck, David R. "Salvaging the Marxist Criticism of the 30's." *Minn. Rev.*, vol. 4 (1975), 59–84.

CF823 Raina, M. L. "Marxism and Literature—A Select Bibliography." *College Eng.*, vol. 34 (1972), 308–14.

CF824 Rudich, Norman, ed. *Amerikanische Literaturkritik in Engagement: Beiträge zur marxistischen Literaturtheorie und Literaturgeschichte.* Berlin: Akademie-Vlg., 1978. 220p.

CF825 Sühnel, Rudolf. "The Marxist Trend in Literary Criticism in the USA in the Thirties." *Jahrbuch für Amerikastudien*, vol. 7 (1962), 52–66.

MEINHOLD, WILLIAM

CF826 Krause, Carolyn L. "Wilhelm Meinhold: His Life and Works, and Reception in England and America." Diss., Northwestern Univ., 1971.

NORDAU, MAX

CF827 Foster, Milton P. "The Reception of Max Nordau's *Degeneration* in England and America." Diss., Univ. of Michigan, 1954. 138p.

NOVALIS (FRIEDRICH VON HARDENBERG)

CF828 Black, Greta A. "Novalis, Friedrich von Hardenberg in English Translation. Being an Account of Novalis in England and America." Diss., London Univ., 1936. 634p.

CF829 Hiebel, Frederick. *Novalis: German Poet, European Thinker, Christian Mystic.* Chapel Hill: Univ. of N. Car. Pr., 1954. Incl. a bibliography of editions in the English language.

NESTROY, JOHANN NEPOMUK

CF830 Straubinger, O. Paul. "The Reception of Raimund and Nestroy in England and America." In: *Österreich und die angelsächsische Welt. Kulturbegegnungen und Vergleiche.* Ed. Otto Hietsch. Vol. 1. Wien: Braumüller, 1961, p.481–94.

REMARQUE, ERICH MARIA

CF831 [Remarque, E. M.] *Three Comrades.* Adapted by F. Scott Fitzgerald. Ed., with an afterword by Matthew Bruccoli. Carbondale/Edwardsville: South. Ill. Univ. Pr., 1978. 290p. Fitzgerald's screenplay adaptation of Remarque's novel, done in 1937.

CF832 Wegner, Irene. "Zur Rezeption der Romane Erich Maria Remarques." In: *Erzählte Welt: Studien zur Epik des 20. Jahrhunderts.* Ed. Helmut Brandt and Nodar Kakabadse. Friedrich-Schiller Universität Jena, Sektion Literatur-und Kunstwissenschaft. Berlin: Aufbau, 1978, p.384–99, 457f.

RICHTER, JEAN PAUL ("JEAN PAUL")

CF833 Brewer, Edward V. *The New England Interest in Jean Paul Friedrich Richter.* Univ. of Calif. Pubs. in Modern Philology, vol. 27, no. 1. Berkeley: Univ. of California Pr., 1943. 25p. Rev. by W. F. Mainland, *Mod. Lang. Rev.*, vol. 40, no. 1 (1945), 78–79; E. Rose, *German Quar.*, vol. 20 (1945) 157–58. See *Amer.-German Rev.*, vol. 11, no. 4 (1945), 27.

RILKE, RAINER MARIA

CF834 Auden, W. H. "Rilke in English." *New Republic*, 6 September 1959, 135–36.

CF835 Becker, Carol C. "A Rilke Tradition in American Poetry: Theodore Roethke, Delmore Schwartz, Randall Jarrell, John Berryman, Anne Sexton, and Sylvia Plath." Diss., Rutgers, 1979. 263p.

CF836 Comerford, Mollie J. "Rilke in English: 1946 to 1966." *Germanic Rev.*, vol. 42, no. 4 (November 1967), 301–09. A bibliography.

CF837 Huettich, Gunner. "Rilke in Amerika: Gestern heute morgen." In: *Rilke: Kleine Hommage zum 100. Geburtstag.* Ed. Heinz L. Arnold. München: Text und Kritik, 1975, p.121–28.

CF838 Jonas, Ilsedore B. and Klaus W. Jonas. "From Muzot to Harvard: The Odyssey of Rainer Maria Rilke's Manuscripts." *Jahrbuch für Amerikastudien*, vol. 9 (1964), 129–44.

CF839 Jonas, Klaus W. "Rainer Maria Rilke in America and England." *Stechert-Hafner Book News*, vol. 21 (1967), 81–84.

CF840 Jonas, Klaus W. "Rainer Maria Rilke in Amerika." *Börsenblatt für den deutschen Buchhandel*, no. 82, vol. 19 (11 October 1963), 1864f.

CF841 Mason, Eudo C. *Rilke, Europe and the English-Speaking World*. Cambridge: Cambridge Univ. Pr., 1961. 257p. Rev. by H. F. Peters, *German Quar.*, vol. 36 (1962), 299–301.

CF842 Obermüller, Paul and Herbert Steiner, comps. and eds. *Katalog der Rilke-Sammlung Richard von Mises, unter Mitarbeit von Ernst Zinn*. Frankfurt a. M.: Insel, 1966. 431p. Rev. by K. W. Jonas, *Monatshefte*, vol. 59 (1967), 365–67.

CF843 Puknat, E. M. and S. B. Puknat. "American Literary Encounters with Rilke." *Monatshefte*, vol. 60 (1967), no. 3, 245–56. The involvement of poets from Eliot to MacLeish, Hemingway, J. D. Salinger, Tennessee Williams, and others, with Rilke and his writings.

CF844 Ritzer, Walter. *Rainer Maria Rilke. Bibliographie*. Wien: n.p., 1951.

CF845 Schroeder, Adolf E. "Rainer Maria Rilke in America—A Bibliography, 1926–1951." *Monatshefte*, vol. 44, no. 1 (1952), 27–38. See also K. W. Jonas's rev. of Walter Ritzer's bibliography in *Papers of the Bibliographic Soc. of America*, vol. 45 (1951), 371–74.

CF846 Von Mises, Richard. *Rilke in English: A Tentative Bibliography*. Comp. by Richard Von Mises in collaboration with B. J. Morse and M. D. Herter Norton. Cambridge, Mass.: n.p., 1947.

CF847 Wirl, Julius. "Englische Uebertragungen von Rilkes Erster Duineser Elegie." In: *Österreich und die angelsächsische Welt. Kulturbegegnungen und Vergleiche*. Ed. Otto Hietsch. Vol. 1. Wien: Braumüller, 1961, p. 432–53.

SCHILLER, FRIEDRICH VON

CF848 Arndt, Karl J. R. "Mozart and Schiller on the Wabash." *Monatshefte*, vol. 38, no. 4 (1946), 244–48.

CF849 Beck, Carl. "Schiller und die alten deutschen Studenten." *German-Amer. Annals*, N.S., vol. 3 (ca. 1905), 290–91.

CF850 Burkhard, Arthur. "Charles T. Brooks's *Mary Stuart*." In: *Studies in German Literature*. Ed. Carl J. Hammer. Baton Rouge: Louisiana Univ. Pr., 1963, p. 3–17, 149–151. Rev. by Erich Hofacker, *German Quar.*, vol. 37, no. 4 (1964), 550. An unpubl. trans. of Schiller's play discovered at Brown University.

CF851 Dummer, E. Heyse. "Schiller in English." *Monatshefte*, vol. 35, no. 6 (October 1943), 334–37.

CF852 Frey, John R. "American Schiller Literature: A Bibliography." *Jour. of Eng. and Germanic Philology*, vol. 57 (1958), 633–43. From 1905 to 1957.

CF853 Frey, John R. "Maria Stuart 'Off Broadway,' 1957." *Amer.-German Rev.*, vol. 24, no. 6 (1958), 6–8, 27. Production by Tyrone Guthrie of *Mary Stuart* at the Phoenix Theater, New York, in 1957.

CF854 Frey, John R. "Schiller in Amerika, insbesondere in der amerikanischen Forschung." *Jahrbuch der Deutschen Schillergesellschaft*, vol. 3 (1959), 338–67.

CF855 Guthke, Karl S. "Schiller auf der Bühne der Vereinigten Staaten." *Maske und Kothurn*, vol. 5 (1960), 227–42.

CF856 Jessen, Karl Detlev. "Schillerrede." *German-Amer. Annals*, N.S., vol. 3 (1905), 185.

CF857 Jetter, Marianne R. "Wilhelm Tell and Modern Students." *German Quar.*, vol. 30 (1957), 45–48. On the reaction of Canadian students.

CF858 Jost, Francois. "John Wilkes Booth and Abraham Lincoln: The Reenactment of a Murder." *Mod. Lang. Notes*, vol. 93 (1978), 503–55. Suggests the relevance of Schiller's play *Die Räuber* to the pattern of murder chosen by Booth. Booth had played Karl Moor in New York three years earlier.

CF859 Knepler, Henry W. "Schiller's *Maria Stuart* on the Stage in England and America." In: *Anglo-German and American-German Crosscurrents*. Ed. Philip A. Shelley, Arthur O. Lewis, and William W. Betts. Chapel Hill: Univ. of N. Car. Pr., 1957–1962. 2 vols. Vol. II, p. 5–32. Also in *Theatre Annual*, vol. 16 (1959), 30–50.

CF860 Robinson, Heidi. "Der gesellschaftsfeindliche 'innere' bzw. 'ganze Mensch': Missdeutungen in der Englischen Rezeption und Überlieferung von Schillers Kulturtheorie." *Arcadia*, vol. 15 (1980), 129–48.

CF861 Trainer, James. "The First English Translation of 'Kabale und Liebe'." *Mod. Lang. Rev.*, vol. 59, no. 1 (1964), 65–72. Fresh review of the question as to who translated the play in 1795.

CF862 Willson, A. Leslie, ed. *A Schiller Symposium.* Austin, Texas: n.p., 1960. 132p. Rev. by G. Baumgaertel, *Amer.-German Rev.*, vol. 27, no. 6 (1961), 37–38. From addresses by Harold Jantz, Helmut Rehder, Oscar Seidlin, Stephen Spender, and Herman Weigand.

SCHLEGEL, FRIEDRICH AND WILHELM

CF863 Schilling, Hanna-Beate. "The Role of the Brothers Schlegel in American Literary Criticism as Found in Selected Periodicals, 1812–1833: A Critical Bibliography." *Amer. Lit.*, vol. 43 (1972), 563–79.

SCHNITZLER, ARTHUR

CF864 Allen, Richard H. *An Annotated Arthur Schnitzler Bibliography: Editions and Criticism in German, French, and English, 1879–1965.* Foreword by Robert O. Weiss. Univ. of N. Car. Studies in Germanic Langs. and Literatures, no. 56. Chapel Hill: Univ. of N. Car. Pr., 1966. 166p.

CF865 Allen, Richard H. "Arthur Schnitzler's Works and Their Reception: An Annotated Bibliography." Diss., Michigan, 1964. 226p.

CF866 Foltinek, Herbert. "Arthur Schnitzler in Amerika." In: *Österreich und die angelsächsische Welt. Kulturbegegnungen und Vergleiche.* Ed. Otto Hietsch. Vol. 1. Wien: Braumüller, 1961, p.207–16.

CF867 Kann, Robert A. *Arthur Schnitzler: Reflections on the Evolution of His Image.* Wisconsin Studies in Contemporary Literature, no. 4. Madison: Univ. of Wisconsin Pr., 1967.

CF868 Schrumpf, Beatrice M. "The Reception of Arthur Schnitzler in the United States." M.A. thesis, Columbia, 1931.

CF869 Walton, Sarah L. "Arthur Schnitzler on the New York Stage." Diss., Indiana, 1966–1967.

SCHOPPE, AMALIE

CF870 Ashliman, D. L. "Amalie Schoppe in America." *Hebbel-Jahrbuch*, 1973, 127–36.

SEUME, JOHANN GOTTFRIED

CF871 Kahn, Robert L. "Seume's Reception in England and America." *Mod. Lang. Rev.*, vol. 52 (1957), 65–71.

STIFTER, ADALBERT

CF872 Eisenmeier, Edward. "Erster Nachtrag zu 'Stifters Werk in Amerika und England,' eine Bibliographie." *Adalbert Stifter-Institut des Landes Oberösterreich*, vol. 9 (1960), nos. 3–4, 129–32.

CF873 Reichert, Walter A., and Werner H. Grilk. "Stifters Werk in Amerika und England: Eine Bibliographie." *Vierteljahrschrift des Adalbert-Stifter-Instituts Oberösterreich*, vol. 9 (1960), 39–42.

CF874 Schneider, Franz. "Stifter im Western der Vereinigten Staaten." *Adalbert Stifter-Institut des Landes Oberösterreich*, vol. 9, nos. 1–2 (1961), 43–45.

STORM, THEODOR

CF875 Silz, Walter. "Storm-Forschung in den Vereinigten Staaten." *Schriften der Theodor Storm-Gesellschaft*, vol. 17 (1968), 41–46.

TIECK, LUDWIG

CF876 Matenko, Percy. *Ludwig Tieck and America.* Chapel Hill: Univ. of N. Car. Pr., 1954. Rev. by H. W. Hewett-Thayer, *Germanic Rev.*, vol. 30 (1955), 159–60; B. Q. Morgan, *Compar. Lit.*, vol. 7 (1955), 179; C. Wegelin, *Mod. Lang. Notes*, vol. 70 (1955), 535–37; E. H. Zeydel, *Mod. Lang. Quar.*, vol. 16 (1955), 279–81; F. G. Ryder, *German Quar.*, vol. 28 (1955), 286–87; H. A. Pochmann, *Amer. Lit.*, vol. 27 (1955–1956), 444–45. A study of the nature and extent of Tieck's reception in America to 1900.

WALTER VON DER VOGELWEIDE

CF877 Scheibe, Fred K. "The Life and Works of Walther von der Vogelweide and Their Reception in the English Speaking Countries." Diss., Cincinnati, 1954.

WEDEKIND, FRANK

CF878 Funke, Lewis. "Theatre: Wedekind's 'The Awakening of Spring'." *N.Y. Times*, 13 May 1964. A review of the production.

CF879 Weisgall, Hugo. *The Tenor. One-Act Opera.* Libretto by Karl Shapiro and Ernst Lert. Bryn Mawr: n.p., 1956. Based on Wedekind's *Der Kam-*

Reception and Influence *(cont.)*

mersänger—*The Court Singer*, trans. by A. W. Boesche.

WIELAND, CHRISTIAN MARTIN

CF880 Kurth-Voigt, Lieselotte E. "The Reception of C. M. Wieland in America." In: *The German Contribution to the Building of the Americas. Studies in Honor of Karl J. R. Arndt.* Ed. G. K. Friesen and W. Schatzberg. Hanover, N.H.: Univ. Pr. of New England, 1977, p.97–133.

CF881 Reiman, Donald H., introd. *Oberon: A Poem from the German of Wieland.* Romantic Context, no. 106. New York: Garland, 1978. Repr. of Sotheby's trans., 1798.

CF882 Wieland, Christian Martin. *Oberon*... Ed. A. B. Faust., 1940. See *Jour. of Eng. and Germanic Philology*, vol. 40, no. 2 (1941), 272. Rev. by Henry A. Pochmann, *Mod. Lang. Notes*, vol. 56, no. 3 (1941), 225–27; Carl Wittke, *Miss. Valley Hist. Rev.*, vol. 27, no. 4 (1941), 682–3.

CF883 Wright, Wyllis, E. "A Newly Discovered Edition of Wieland's *Trial of Abraham*." *Mod. Lang. Notes*, vol. 65, no. 4 (1950), 246–47. Earliest printing of Wieland in America by Perkins in Boston.

ZWEIG, STEFAN

CF884 Klawiter, Randolph. *Stefan Zweig: A Bibliography.* Chapel Hill: Univ. of N. Car. Pr., 1965. 191p. Rev. by D. A. Prater, *Jour. of Eng. and Germanic Philology*, vol. 65, no. 4 (October 1966), 784–85.

CG

Reception of American Literature in Germany

American Studies in Europe

CG1 "American Studies Enjoys High Rate of Growth Abroad." *Amer. Studies News*, vol. 5 (August 1966), 1–5. On the growth of programs and courses; teachers of American subjects at European universities in 1966–1967.

CG2 Beck, Earl R. "Friedrich Schönemann, German Americanist Historian." *The Historian*, vol. 26, no. 3 (1964), 381–404. On the career of a "father of Amerikakunde."

CG3 Fabian, Bernhard. "Jahrestagung der deutschen Gesellschaft für Amerikastudien." *Die Neueren Sprachen*, N.F., vol. 5 (1956), 490–94.

CG4 Fischer, Walter. "Die Amerikanistik im gegenwärtigen Universitätslehrplan und in den Prüfungsordnungen der deutschen Länder." *Neuphilologische Zeitung*, vol. 3 (1951), 412–17.

CG5 Galinsky, Hans. "American Studies in Germany." In: *American Studies in Transition.* Ed. Marshall W. Fishwick. Philadelphia: n.p., 1964, p.232–52.

CG6 Galinsky, Hans. "Developments in American Studies in the German Universities, 1963–64." "Current Bibliography, 1962–63, 1963–64." *EAAS News Letter* (London), vols. 8–9 (1962–1964, 1965), 29–30, 51–62, passim. See also *ibid.*, vol. 10 (1965–1966).

CG7 Gavin, J. "Salzburg Seminar in American Studies." *Amer.-German Rev.*, vol. 16, no. 4 (1950), 23–25.

CG8 Gusinde, Martin. "Bibliographic Contributions to Americanistic Studies." *Anthropos* (Fribourg), vol. 53 (1958), 1014–17.

CG9 Hartig, Paul. "American Studies Seminar, Berlin, 1958." *Die Neueren Sprachen*, N.F., vol. 7 (1958), 176–77. See also his "Amerikakunde als Aufgabe." *Neuphilologische Zeitung*, vol. 3 (1951), 219–20.

CG10 Helmcke, Hans. "Jahrestagung der Deutschen Gesellschaft für Amerikastudien... 1958, etc." In: *Die Neueren Sprachen*, vol. 59 (1959) through vol. 10, N.F. (1961). Annual reports.

CG11 Hofmann, Christa. "Die Anglistik-Amerikanistik in der Deutschen Demokratischen Republik." *Zeitschrift für Anglistik und Amerikanistik*, vol. 8 (February 1960), 171-85.

CG12 Holthusen, Hans Egon. "America Mediatrix." *Merkur*, vol. 11 (1957), 698-702. On the periodical *Perspektiven*, German ed. of *Perspectives*.

CG13 Jacob, Ernst G. "38. Amerikanisten-Congress (IAC)." *Zeitschrift für Kulturaustausch*, vol. 18 (1968), no. 4, 328-29. Report on a congress held in Stuttgart.

CG14 *Jahrbuch für Amerikastudien*. Im Auftrag der Deutschen Gessellschaft für Amerikastudien. Ed. Ernst Fraenkel, Hans Galinsky, Dietrich Gerhard and H.-J. Lang. Heidelberg: Winter, Vol. 1-, 1955-.

CG15 Lanzinger, Klaus. "Tätigkeit des Amerika-Instituts der Universität Innsbruck 1956-1966." In: *Americana-Austriaca: Festschrift des Amerika-Instituts...anlässlich seines zehnjährigen Bestehens*. Wien, Stuttgart: Braumüller, 1966, p.17-31.

CG16 Laurien, Hanna-Renate. "Amerikanistentagung in Altenberg, 1957." *Die Neueren Sprachen*, N.F., vol. 7 (1958), 69-72.

CG17 Link, Franz H. "American Studies at Frankfurt University." *Amer.-German Rev.*, vol. 21, no. 5 (1955), 6-8.

CG18 Link, Franz H. "Das Studium der amerikanischen Literatur an den Pädagogischen Hochschulen." In: *Mölichkeiten der Amerikastudien an den deutschen Pädagogischen Hochschulen*. N.p.: U.S. Information Service, Germany, 1964, p.49-60.

CG19 Ludwig, Heinz. "Amerikakundliche Tagung in Wesel." *Die Neueren Sprachen*, N.F., vol. 8 (1960), 192-96.

CG20 Mannes, Marya. "America in Salzburg." *Harper's*, vol. 232 (February 1966), 91-95. Problems in communication amongst the fellows and faculty of the Salzburg Seminar in American Studies.

CG21 Münch, Rudolf. "Erfahrungen einer amerikanischen Studienwoche." *Neuphilologische Zeitung*, vol. 3 (1951), 130-38.

CG22 Oehme, Ruthardt. *Verzeichnis amerikanischer Zeitschriften an den deutschen wissenschaftlichen Bibliotheken Westdeutschlands, einschl. der öffentlichen wissenschaftlichen Bibliothek Berlin*. Freiburg: Universitätsbiliothek, 1949. 94p.

CG23 Oppel, Horst. "Forschungsbericht zur deutschen Amerikanistik." *Die Neueren Sprachen*, vol. 51, N.F. vol. 1 (1952), 292-302.

CG24 "Overseas Seminars in American Studies." *Amer. Studies News*, vol. 4 (April 1966), 20-23, 24-25; vol. 6 (Autumn 1967), 20-22. Places and dates of seminars and conferences in various countries.

CG25 Pivec, Karl. "Das Amerika-Institut der Universität Innsbruck." In: *Americana-Austriaca: Festschrift des Amerika-Institutes...anlässlich seines zehnjährigen Bestehens*. Wien: Braumüller, 1966, p.1-16.

CG26 Röske, Elfriede. "Amerikalehrgänge in Salzburg." *Die Neueren Sprachen*, N.F., vol. 7 (1958), 125-27.

CG27 Salewsky, Rudolf. "Amerikatagung in Rhöndorf." *Die Neueren Sprachen*, N.F., vol. 6 (1957), 355-57.

CG28 Seyppel, Joachim. "Forderungen zur Amerikanistik." *Neuphilologische Zeitung*, vol. 3 (1951), 288-91.

CG29 Skard, Sigmund. *American Studies in Europe: Their History and Present Organization*. 2 vols. Philadelphia: Univ. of Pa. Pr., 1958. 735p. Rev. by J. Loiseau, *Amer. Quar.*, vol. 10 (1958), 488-91; D. H. Dougherty, *Annals of the Amer. Academy of Political and Social Science*, vol. 123 (1959), 195-96; W. Thorp, *Amer. Lit.*, vol. 31 (1959), 342-45; W. Fischer, *Jahrbuch für Amerikastudien*, vol. 4 (1959), 285-87; F. Krog, *Histor. Zeitschrift*, vol. 191 (1960), 411; E. H. Rovit, *Books Abroad*, vol. 34 (1960), 306. Vol. 1 incl. a discussion of American Studies in Germany.

CG30 Smith, Henry Nash. "The Salzburg Seminar." *Amer. Quar.*, vol. 1 (1949), 30–37. Description of the program for 1947–1948.

CG31 Spiller, Robert E. "American Studies Abroad: Culture and Foreign Policy." *Annals of the Amer. Academy of Political and Social Science*, vol. 366 (July 1966), 1–16. Notes the establishment of chairs, courses, degrees and societies devoted to American studies in foreign countries.

CG32 United States Information Service. *Möglichkeiten der Amerikastudien*. Bad Godesberg: United States Information Service, 1966. Publ. of the American Embassy.

CG33 Wächtler, Kurt. "Amerikastudien als Aufgabe und Problem des Englischunterrichts." *Der fremdsprachliche Unterricht*, vol. 1, no. 1 (1967), 46–55.

American Literature in German Translation—General

CG34 *Amerikanisches Theater, Eine Einführung in Themen und Inhalt amerikanischer Bühnenwerke, die in deutschen Übersetzungen erschienen sind*. Nauheim: Theater-Abteilung der amerikanischen Hohn Kommission, 1949. 96p.

CG35 Brown, Soi-Daniel Webster, II. "German Translations of Works by Black American Authors, 1945–1975." Diss., Brown, 1967–1977.

CG36 Mummendey, Richard. *Belles Lettres of the United States of America in German Translations: A Bibliography*. Charlottesville: Univ. of Virginia Pr., 1961. 199p. *Die schöne Literatur der Vereinigten Staaten von Amerika in deutschen Übersetzungen, eine Bibliographie*. Bonner Beiträge zur Bibliotheks- und Bücherkunde, No. 6. Bonn, 1961. 199p. Rev. by A. M. Cohn, *Library Quar.*, vol. 32 (1962), 254–55. Lists 1887 translations from American originals.

CG37 Riedel, Walter A. "Kanadische Kurzprosa in deutscher Übersetzung." *German-Canad. Yearbook*, vol. 4 (1978), 205–13.

American Drama and Film in Germany

CG38 Brüning, Eberhard. "Amerikanische Dramen an den Bühnen der Deutschen Demokratischen Republik und Berlins von 1945 bis 1955." *Zeitschrift für Anglistik und Amerikanistik*, vol. 7 (1959), 246–69.

CG39 Brüning, Eberhard. "Haupttendenzen des amerikanischen Dramas der dreissiger Jahre. Ein Beitrag zur Literaturgeschichte der Vereinigten Staaten unter Berücksichtigung des Einflusses amerikanischer Dramatik auf die Spielplangestaltung deutscher Bühnen nach dem zweiten Weltkrieg." Diss. Univ. Leipzig, 1961.

CG40 Frenz, Horst. "American Playwrights and the German Psyche." *Die Neueren Sprachen*, N.F., vol. 10, no. 4 (April 1961), 170–78.

CG41 Frenz, Horst. "Amerikanische Dramatiker auf den Bühnen und vor der Theaterkritik der Bundesrepublik." In: *Nordamerikanische Literatur im deutschen Sprachraum seit 1945: Beiträge zur Rezeption*. Ed. H. Frenz and H.-J. Lang. München: Winkler, 1973, p.79–102.

CG42 Frenz, Horst. "A German Home for Mannerhouse." *Theatre Arts*, vol. 40, no. 8 (1956), 62–63, 95. Report on a year's study of American plays on German stages.

CG43 Karsch, Walther. "American Drama and the German Stage." In: *The German Theater Today. A Symposium*. Ed. Leroy R. Shaw. Austin: Univ. of Texas Pr., 1963, p.33–46.

CG44 Kracht, Fritz A. "Rise and Decline of U.S. Theater on German Stages." *Amer.-German Rev.*, vol. 32 (1966), no. 5, 13–15. Covers the years from 1945 to 1965.

CG45 Schreyvogel, Friedrich. "Das moderne England und Amerika im Wiener Burgtheater." In: *Österreich und die angelsächsische Welt: Kulturbegegnungen und Vergleiche*. Ed. Otto Hietsch. Vol. II. Wien: Braumüller, 1968, p.537–46.

CG46 Sollors, Werner. "*Wurzeln: Roots* in West Germany." *Amer. Studies Internat.*, vol. 17, no. 3 (1979), 40–45.

American Themes and Settings in German Literature

CG47 Akselrod, Rose-Marie. "Deutsche Literatur an der Indianergrenze." *Ky. For. Long. Quar.*, vol. 4 (1957), 113–18. Writers like Strubberg, Pater Hörmann, Schenck, etc., active in Texas in the second part of the the 19th century.

CG48 Ashliman, D. L. "The Image of Utah and the Mormons in Nineteenth-Century Germany." *Utah Hist. Quar.*, vol. 35 (1967), 209–27. Cf. his diss., "The American West in Nineteenth Century German Literature." Rutgers, 1970.

CG49 Ashliman, D. L. "Mormonism and the Germans: An Annotated Bibliography, 1848–1966." *Brigham Young Univ. Studies*, vol. 8 (Autumn 1967), no. 1, 73–94.

CG50 Ashliman, D. L. "The Novel of Western Adventure in Nineteenth-Century Germany." *Western American Lit.*, vol. 3, no. 2 (Summer 1968), 133–45.

CG51 Beissel, Rudolf. "Der Indianerroman und seine wichtigsten Vertreter." *Karl May Jahrbuch* (Radebeul bei Dresden: Karl May Verlag), vol. 1 (1918).

CG52 Bender, Elizabeth H. "The Anabaptist Novelettes of Adolf Stern and Wilhelm Heinrich Riehl." *Mennonite Quar. Rev.*, vol. 18, no. 3 (1944), 174–85.

CG53 Bender, Elizabeth H. "Ernst von Wildenbruch's Drama *Der Mennonit*. An Historical and Literary Critique." *Mennonite Quar. Rev.*, vol. 18, no. 1 (1944), 22–35.

CG54 Bender, Elizabeth H. "The Mennonites in German Literature." M.A. thesis, Minnesota, 1944.

CG55 Bender, Elizabeth H. "The Portrayal of the Swiss Anabaptists in Gottfried Keller's *Ursula*." *Mennonite Quar. Rev.*, vol. 17 (1943), 136–50. On the authenticity of the historical framework and portrayals in Keller's novel.

CG56 Billington, Ray A. "The Plains and Deserts through European Eyes." *Western Historical Quar.*, vol. 10 (1979), 467–89. In writings by Karl May, Wilhelm Frey and others.

CG57 Bock, Hellmut. "Von Cooper's 'Lederstrumpf' bis Carl Mays 'Old Shatterhand': 150 Jahre Wildwest-Literatur." *Blätter für Erwachsenenbildung in Schleswig-Holstein. Sonderheft Anglistik und Amerikanistik*. Kiel: n.p., 1961, 4–26.

CG58 Brooks, George R. "The American Frontier in German Fiction." In: *The Frontier Re-Examined*. Ed. John F. McDermott. Urbana: Univ. of Ill. Pr., 1967, p.155–67.

CG59 Cobbs, Alfred L. "The Image of the Black in German Literature." In: *The Harold Jantz Collection...* Ed. Leland R. Phelps. Durham: Duke Univ. Center for International Studies, 1981. 145p.

CG60 Cronholm, Anna-Christie. "Die nordamerikanische Sklavenfrage im deutschen Schrifttum des 19. Jahrhunderts." Diss., Freie Universität Berlin, 1958. 107p.

CG61 Davids, Jean-Ulrich. *Das Wildwest-Romanheft in der Bundesrepublik: Ursprünge und Strukturen*. Tübingen: Tübinger Vereinigung für Volkskunde, 1975. 317p.

CG62 Dippel, Horst. *Americana Germanica: Bibliographie deutscher Amerikaliteratur 1770–1800*. Amerikastudien; eine Schriftenreihe, Bd. 31. Stuttgart: Metzler, 1976. 214p. Rev. by M. Nirenberg, *German Quar.*, vol. 50, no. 3 (May 1977), 376–77.

CG63 Eickhorst, William. "The Treatment of the South in Modern German Literature." *Ariz. Quar.*, vol. 15 (1959), 217–28.

CG64 Ethe, Hermann. "Der transatlantisch-exotische Roman und seine Hauptvertreter in der modernen deutschen Literatur." In: *Essays und Studien*. Berlin: n.p., 1972, p.47–101.

CG65 Frey, John R. "George Washington in German Fiction." *Amer.-German Rev.*, vol. 12, no. 5 (1946), 25–26, 37.

CG66 Gilman, Sander. "The Image of Slavery in Two Eighteenth Century German Dramas." *Germanic Rev.* vol. 45 (1970), 26–40. *Die Mohrin zu Hamburg*, by Ernst L. M. Rathelf, 1775, and *Die Negersklaven, Ein Lustspiel in einem Aufzug*, 1779.

CG67 Gleis, P. G. "Columbus in Forgotten German Literature." *Amer.-German Rev.*, vol. 9, no. 1 (1942), 7–9.

CG68 Grossberg, Mimi. *Amerika im austroamerikanischen Gedicht, 1938–1978*. Wien: Bergland Vlg., 1978. 64p. Anthology of poems largely on the themes of exile and adjustment to the New World: Ferd. Bruckner, Ernst Lothar, Josef Luitpold, Johannes Urzidil, and others. Rev. by Gerd Niers, *Jour. of German Amer. Studies*, vol. 13 (1978), 128.

CG69 Hollyday, Guy T. "Albert von Halfern's *Der Squire*, a Novel about Life in Early Arkansas." *Ark. Hist. Quar.*, vol. 27 (1968), 226–45.

CG70 Klemm, Frederick A. "Four German-American Novelists of New World Adventure." *Amer.-German Rev.*, vol. 7, no. 6 (1941), 26–29. On Gerstäcker, Sealsfield, Strubberg, and Möllhausen.

CG71 Lutz, Hartmut. "'North American Indians' in Kinder- und Jugendliteratur und Unterricht: Ein Bericht über *American Studies* in der Schule." *Amerikastudien*, vol. 24 (1979), 120–51.

CG72 Mann, Klaus. "Dream America." *Accent*, vol. 8 (1947–1948), 173–84. On Romantic, infantile, and irresponsible qualities in the writings of Karl May, a likely influence on Hitler.

CG73 Plischke, H. *Von Cooper bis Karl May, Geschichte des völkerkundlichen Reise- und Abenteuerromans*. Düsseldorf: Droste, 1951. 208p. Rev. by D. Cunz, *Books Abroad*, vol. 26 (1952), 371; J. T. Krumpelmann, *Jour. of Eng. and Germanic Philology*, vol. 52 (1953), 432–33. Treats Cooper, Ruppius, Sealsfield, Gerstäcker, Möllhausen, Strubberg, May and others.

CG74 Riemann, Robert. *Die Entwicklung des politischen und exotischen Romans in Deutschland*. Leipzig: n.p., 1911. 33p.

CG75 Rohrer, Max. *Amerika im deutschen Gedicht*. Anthology. Stuttgart: Böhm, 1948. 175p. Rev. by J. G. Frank, *Monatshefte*, vol. 44 (1948), 120–21; Z. Kukierelli, *Amer.-German Rev.*, vol. 16 (1950), no. 6, 38–39.

CG76 Stammel, Heinz Josef. *Der Cowboy: Legende und Wirklichkeit von A–Z: Ein Lexikon der amerikanischen Pioniergeschichte*. Gütersloh / Berlin: Bertelsmann Lexikon-Verlag, 1972, 416p.

CG77 Van de Luyster, Nelson. "Emigration to America as Reflected in the German Novel of the 19th Century: Especially in the Fiction of Bitzius, Laube, Gutzkow, Auerbach, Freytag, Storm, Keller, Spielhagen, Heyse, and Raabe." Diss., North Carolina, 1943.

CG78 Von Hofe, Harold. "The Halberstadt Poets and the New World." *Germanic Rev.*, vol. 32 (1957), 243–54. American themes in the works of Gleim, Jacobi, Tiedge, Göckingk, and others.

CG79 Woodson, Leroy H. *American Negro Slavery in the Works of Strubberg, Gerstäcker, and Ruppius*. Washington: Catholic Univ. Pr., 1949. 340p. Rev. by A. J. Prahl, *Mod. Lang. Notes*, vol. 65 (1950), 214–15; J. T. Krumpelmann, *Monatshefte*, vol. 43 (1951), 243. Based on a diss. submitted at Catholic University, 1948.

The Image of America in German Literature

CG80 Bauschinger, Sigrid, H. Denkler, and W. Malsch, eds. *Amerika in der deutschen Literatur: Neue Welt—Nordamerika—USA. Wolfgang Paulsen zum 65. Geburtstag*. Stuttgart: Ph. Reclam Jun., 1975. 416p. Rev. by G. A. Fetz, *German Studies Rev.*, vol. 1 (1978), 102–03.

CG81 Billington, Ray A. *Land of Savagery, Land of Promise: The European Image of the American Frontier in the Nineteenth Century*. New York: Norton, 1981. 364p.

CG82 Boerner, Peter. "Amerikabilder der europäischen Literatur: Wunschprojektion und Kritik." *Amerikastudien*, vol. 23 (1978), 40–50. Esp. in Goethe, Carl Spindler, Lenau, Herder and Duden.

CG83 Böschenstein, Hermann. "Is There a Canadian Image in German Literature?" *Seminar*, vol. 3 (1967), 1–20.

CG84 Cobbs, Alfred L. "Selected Studies on the Image of America in Post-War German Literature." Diss., Univ. of Cincinnati, 1974.

CG85 Deutsche Demokratische Republik. Zentralinstitut für Bibliothekswesen. *U.S.A. im Spiegel der Literatur*. Leipzig: Verlag für Buch- und Bibliothekswesen, 1957. 132p. Bibliography of translations from the English.

CG86 Doerry, Karl W. "Three Versions of America: Sealsfield, Gerstäcker, and May." *Yearbook of German-Amer. Studies*, vol. 16 (1981), 39–50.

CG87 Durzak, Manfred. "Abrechnung mit einer Utopie: Zum Amerika-Bild im jüngsten deutschen Roman." *Basis*, vol. 4 (1973), 98–121.

CG88 Durzak, Manfred. *Das Amerika-Bild in der deutschen Gegenwartsliteratur. Historische Voraussetzungen und aktuelle Beispiele*. Stuttgart: Kohlhammer, 1979. 236p. Rev. by Jürgen Koppensteiner, *German Quar.*, vol. 53, no. 3 (May 1980), 371–73. Reprints a group of his articles.

CG89 Galinsky, Hans K. "America's Image in German Literature: A Neglected Field of American-German Literary Relations." *Compar. Lit. Studies*, vol. 13 (1976), 165–92.

CG90 Galinsky, Hans K. "Deutschlands literarisches Amerikabild: Ein kritischer Bericht zu Geschichte, Stand und Aufgaben der Forschung." In: *Deutschlands literarisches Amerikabild: Forschungen zur Amerikarezeption der deutschen Literatur*. Ed. Alexander Ritter. Hildesheim: Olms, 1977, p.4–27.

CG91 Helinski, Maureen M. "The Image of America in German Drama, 1890–1930." Diss., Johns Hopkins Univ., 1971.

CG92 Heuer, Helmut. "Zur Problematik des Amerikabildes in den Englisch-Lehrbüchern der Volksschule." *Jahrbuch für Amerikastudien*, vol. 12 (1967), 227–39.

CG93 Hollyday, Guy T. *Anti-Americanism in the German Novel 1841–1862*. German Studies in America, no. 27. Bern / Frankfurt a. M. / Las Vegas: Peter Lang, 1977. 212p. Rev. by Jeffrey L. Sammons, *German Quar.*, vol. 51 (1978), 541–42; W. Thorp, *Pa. Mag. of Hist. and Biography*, vol. 102 (1978), 535–36; Ruth-Ellen Boetcher Joeres, *Monatshefte*, vol. 72, no. 2 (Summer 1980), 194–95. Analysis of novels of R. F. Eylert, Franz von Elling, Ferd. Kürnberger, Albert von Halfern, Adelbert von Baudissin, Friedrich Gerstäcker, Otto Ruppius, and Armand Strubberg.

CG94 Jantz, Harold. "America im deutschen Dichten und Denken." In: *Deutsche Philologie im Aufriss*. Ed. W. Stammler. Berlin: Schmidt, 1955, p.145–204. 2nd ed. 1960. Cols. 309–72.

CG95 Laemmle, Peter. "'Geheimnis und Amerika liegen dicht nebeneinander': Zur Amerika-Sehnsucht in der jüngsten deutschen Literatur." *Akzente*, vol. 23 (1976), 418–27.

CG96 Laws, Page R. "Mythic Images of America: Four Recent European Novels." Diss., Yale, 1979. 252p. Novels by Handke, Robbe-Grillet, Uwe Johnson, and M. Butor.

CG97 Malsch, Wilfried. "Neue Welt, Nordamerika und USA als Projektion und Problem." In: *Amerika in der deutschen Literatur: Neue Welt, Nordamerika, USA. Wolfgang Paulsen zum 65. Geburtstag*. Ed. S. Bauschinger et al. Stuttgart: Reclam, 1975, p.9–16.

CG98 Malsch, Wilfried. "Vom Vorbild zum Schreckbild: Politische USA-Vorstellungen deutscher Schriftsteller von Thomas Mann bis zu Reinhard Lettau." In: *Die USA und Deutschland: Wechselseitige Spiegelungen in der Literatur der Gegenwart. Zum zweihundertjährigen Bestehen der Vereinigten Staaten am 4. Juli 1976*. Ed. Wolfgang Paulsen. 8. Amherster Kolloquium zur modernen deutschen Literatur. Bern: Francke, 1976, p.29–51.

CG99 Martini, Fritz. "Auswanderer, Rückkehrer, Heimkehrer: Amerikaspiegelungen im Erzählwerk von Keller, Raabe und Fontane." In: *Amerika in der deutschen Literatur: Neue Welt, Nordamerika, USA. Wolfgang Paulsen zum 65. Geburtstag*. Ed. S. Bauschinger et al. Stuttgart; Reclam, 1975, p.178–204.

CG100 Michelsen, Peter. "Americanism and Anti-Americanism in German Novels of the XIXth Century." *Arcadia*, vol. 11 (1976), 272–87. In Goethe, Fr. Schlegel, Zschokke, Sealsfield, Gerstäcker, von Bülow, and Kürnberger.

CG101 Osterle, Heinz D. "The Lost Utopia: New Images of America in German Literature." *German Quar.*, vol. 54 (1981), 427–46.

CG102 Pick, Robert. "Mit europäischen Augen. Amerika im Spiegel der europäischen Literaturkritik." *Der Monat*, vol. 2, no. 18 (1950), 658–64.

CG103 Ritter, Alexander. "Amerika-Literatur 1945–1976: Eine Bibliographie zum literarischen Amerikabild Deutschlands und zu verwandten Themen." In his *Deutschlands Amerikabild: Neuere Forschungen zur Amerikarezeption der deutschen Literatur*. Hildesheim: Olms, 1977, p.562–606. With a bibliography by A. Ritter. Incl. articles by Albert R. Schmitt, Karl J. R. Arndt, and Harold Jantz.

CG104 Ritter, Alexander, ed. *Deutschlands literarisches Amerikabild. Neuere Forschungen zur Amerikarezeption der deutschen Literatur*. (Germanistische Texte und Studien, vol. 3. Hildesheim/N.Y.: Olms Vlg, 1977. 672p. Rev. by Jürgen Koppensteiner, *German Quar.*, vol. 53, no. 3 (May 1980), 371–73. A collection of 30 articles, mostly in reprint; incl. "Bibliographie zum literarischen Amerikabild... 1945–1976."

CG105 Ruland, Richard. *America in Modern European Literature: From Image to Metaphor*. New York: N.Y. Univ. Pr., 1976. 197p.

CG106 Sammons, Jeffrey L. "Land of Limited Possibilities: America in the Nineteenth-Century German Novel." *Yale Review*, vol. 68 (1978–1979), 35–52.

CG107 Schlunk, Jurgen E. "The Image of America in German Literature and in the New German Cinema: Wim Wenders' The American Friend." *Lit./Film Quar.*, vol. 7 (1979), 215–22.

CG108 Schroeder, Samuel. "Amerika in der deutschen Dichtung von 1850 bis 1890." Diss., Heidelberg, 1934.

CG109 Theobaldy, Jürgen. "Begrenzte Weiten: Amerika-Bilder in der westdeutschen Lyrik." *Akzente*, vol. 23 (1976), 402–07.

CG110 Wagner, Lydia E. "The Reserved Attitude of the Early German Romanticists toward America." *German Quar.*, vol. 16 (1943), 8–12.

CG111 Wehe, Walter. "Das Amerikaerlebnis in der deutschen Literatur." *Geist der Zeit*, vol. 17 (1939).

CG112 Williams, Cecil B. "The German Picture of American Literature." *Descant*, vol. 5 (1960), 33–37.

CG113 Willson, A. Leslie. "Another Planet: Texas in German Literature." In: *Texas and Germany: Crosscurrents*. Ed. Joseph B. Wilson. Rice Univ. Studies, vol. 63, no. 3. Houston: Rice Univ., 1977, p.101–09.

CG114 Wittke, Carl. "The American Theme in Continental European Literatures." *Miss. Valley Hist. Rev.*, vol. 28 (1941), 3–26.

CG115 Zipes, Jack. "Die Freiheit trägt Handschellen im Land der Freiheit: Das Bild der Vereinigten Staaten in der Literatur der DDR." In: *Amerika in der deutschen Literatur: Neue Welt, Nordamerika, USA. Wolfgang Paulsen zum 65. Geburtstag*. Ed. S. Bauschinger et al. Stuttgart: Reclam, 1975, p.329–52.

Vogue and Influence of American Literature in Germany—General

CG116 Arnold, Armin. "Foreign Influences in German Expressionist Prose." In: *Expressionism as an International Literary Phenomenon: 21 Essays and a Bibliography*. Ed. Ulrich Weisstein. Paris: Didier, 1973, p.79–96.

CG117 Ballinger, Sara Elizabeth. "The Reception of the American Novel in German Periodicals, 1945–1957." Diss., Indiana, 1959.

CG118 Bungert, Hans. "Zur Rezeption zeitgenössischer amerikanischer Erzählliteratur in der Bundes-Republik." In: *Die Amerikanische Literatur der Gegenwart: Aspekte und Tendenzen*. Ed. Hans Bungert. Stuttgart: Reclam, 1977, p.252–62.

CG119 Christadler, Martin. "Autobiographien—Essayisten—Lyriker." In: *Nordamerikanische Literatur im deutschen Sprachraum seit 1945: Beiträge zur Rezeption*. Ed. H. Frenz and H.-J. Lang. München: Winkler, 1973, p.111–36.

CG120 Combecher, Hans. "Amerikanische Lyrik in der Oberstufe." *Praxis des neusprachlichen Unterrichts*, vol. 3 (1956), 81–84. American poets in the German classroom.

CG121 Doderer, Klaus. "Die angelsächsische Short Story und die deutsche Kurzgeschichte." *Die Neueren Sprachen*, N.F., vol. 2 (1953), 417–24.

CG122 Engelmann, Helmut. "Englische und amerikanische Gedichte in der Realschule." *Die Neueren Sprachen*, N.F., vol. 9 (1960), 329–41.

CG123 Feller, Max Carl. "Die Aufnahme amerikanischer Literatur in der deutschsprachigen Schweiz." Diss., Humboldt Univ., Berlin, 1949. 108p.

CG124 Frenz, Horst, and Hans-Joachim Lang, eds. *Nordamerikanische Literatur im deutschen Sprachraum seit 1945: Beiträge zur Rezeption*. München: Winkler, 1973. 271p. Incl.: "Die Rezeption der nordamerikanischen Gegenwartsliteratur," "Die neue Welt der amerikanischen Klassik," and "Regional- und Einflußstudien: DDR, Österreich, Schweiz," and bibliography.

CG125 Frenz, Horst, and John Hess. "Die nordamerikanische Literatur in der Deutschen Demokratischen Republik." In: *Nordamerikanische Literatur im deutschen Sprachraum seit 1945: Beiträge zur Rezeption*. Ed. H. Frenz and H.-J. Lang. 1973, p.171–99.

CG126 Frey, John R. "America and Her Literature Reviewed by Postwar Germany." *Amer. German Rev.*, vol. 20, no. 4 (1954), 4–6, 31. Reaction in an extremely America-conscious Germany.

CG127 Frey, John R. "Post-War German Reactions to American Literature." *Jour. of Eng. and Germanic Philology*, vol. 54 (1955), 173–94.

CG128 Frey, John R. "Postwar Germany: Enter American Literature." *Amer.-German Rev.*, vol. 21, no. 1 (April 1954), 9–12.

CG129 Gaither, Mary, and Horst Frenz. "German Criticism of American Drama." *Amer. Quar.*, vol. 7 (1955), 111–22.

CG130 Galinsky, Hans. "Gedanken zu einer neuen Geschichte der amerikanischen Literatur." *Die Neueren Sprachen*, N.F., vol. 3 (1954), no. 7/8, 318–37.

CG131 [Galinsky, Hans.] *Literatur und Sprache der Vereinigten Staaten. Aufsätze zu Ehren von H. G.* Ed. Hans Helmcke, Klaus Lubbers, and R. Schmidt-von Bardeleben. Heidelberg: Winter, 1969. 247p.

CG132 Galinsky, Hans. "Understanding Twentieth-Century America through Its Literature: A German View." *Midcontinent. Amer. Studies Jour.*, vol. 8 (Fall 1967), 58–68. Holds that the sociocritical function is especially well served by American writers.

CG133 Galinsky, Hans K. "The Uses of American English in Modern German Drama and Poetry: Brecht, Benn, Bachmann." In: *Teilnahme und Spiegelung: Festschrift für Horst Rüdiger*. Ed. B. Allemann, E. Koppen, and Dieter Gutzen. Berlin: De Gruyter, 1975, p.499–530.

CG134 Garten, H. F. "Foreign Influence in German Expressionist Drama." In: *Expressionism as an International Literary Phenomenon: 21 Essays and a Bibliography*. Ed. Ulrich Weisstein. Paris: Didier, 1973, p.59–68.

CG135 *Germans in America: Aspects of German-American Relations in the Nineteenth Century*. Symposium. 30 April–1 May 1981. The Graduate School and University Center, City University of New York. Cosponsored by the Goethe House, New York. Papers by James M. Bergquist, Steven M. Benjamin, John R. Costello, Franzi Ascher-Nash, Richard Spuler, Jeffrey Sammons, Maria M. Wagner, Volkmar Sander and others.

CG136 Graf, Emil. "Die Aufnahme der englischen und amerikanischen Literatur in der deutschen Schweiz, 1800–1830." Diss., Zürich, 1951.

CG137 Grimm, Reinhold and Henry J. Schmidt. "Foreign Influences on German Expressionist Poetry." In: *Expressionism as an International Literary Phenomenon: 21 Essays and a Bibliography*. Ed. Ulrich Weisstein. Paris: Didier, 1973, p.69–78.

CG138 Haas, Rudolf. "Einige Bemerkungen zu Schulausgaben amerikanischer Dramen und Gedichte." *Jahrbuch für Amerikastudien*, vol. 8 (1963), 84–91.

CG139 Haas, Rudolf. "Über die Rezeption amerikanischer Romane in der Bundesrepublik 1945–1965." In: *Nordamerikanische Literatur im deutschen Sprachraum seit 1945: Beiträge zur Rezeption*. Ed. H. Frenz and H.-J. Lang. München: Winkler, 1973, p.20–46.

CG140 Heuermann, Hartmut. "Angloamerikanische Literatur und der deutsche Leser." *Neusprachliche Mitteilungen aus Wissenschaft und Praxis*, vol. 29 (1976), 193–99.

CG141 Hewett-Thayer, Harvey W. *American Literature as Viewed in Germany, 1818–1861*. Chapel

Vogue and Influence (cont.)

Hill: Univ. of N. Car. Pr., 1958. 83p. Rev. by W. W. Pusey, *Amer.-German Rev.*, vol. 25, no. 6 (1959), 38; W. L. Miner, *Amer. Quar.*, vol. 11 (1959), 200; F. G. Ryder, *German Quar.*, vol. 33 (1960), 393f.; J. W. Thomas, *Monatshefte*, vol. 52 (1960), 200–01; C. Wegelin, *Compar. Lit.*, vol. 12 (1960), 61–62; A. E. Zucker, *Mod. Lang. Notes*, vol. 76 (1961), 93–95.

CG142 Hewett-Thayer, Harvey W. "German Criticism of American Literature in the First Part of the Nineteenth Century." Diss., Princeton, 1950.

CG143 Keiser, Robert. *Die Aufnahme englischen Schrifttums in der deutschen Schweiz von 1830 bis 1860.* Züricher Beiträge zur vergleichenden Literatur. Zürich: Juris Verlag, 1962. 111p. Rev. by C. Janslin, *Germanistik*, vol. 4 (1963), 615–16; L. M. Price, *Jour. of Eng. and Germanic Philology*, vol. 63, no. 2 (1964), 311–12; M. B. Benn, *Compar. Lit.*, vol. 17 (1964), 285; J. Voisin, *Études anglaises*, vol. 19 (1966), 195. Also takes cognizance of American writings.

CG144 Kosok, Heinz. "Englische und amerikanische Kurzdramen im Englischunterricht der Oberstufe." *Die Neueren Sprachen*, N.F., vol. 14 (1965), 520–31.

CG145 Krebs, Karl. "Die amerikanische Kurzgeschichte in der Schule." *Die Neueren Sprachen*, N.F., vol. 5 (1956), 306–08.

CG146 Kühnelt, Harro H. "Die Aufnahme der nordamerikanischen Literatur in Österreich." In: *Nordamerikanische Literatur im deutschen Sprachraum seit 1945: Beiträge zur Rezeption.* Ed. H. Frenz and H.-J. Lang. München: Winkler, 1973, p. 200–24.

CG147 Kwiat, Joseph J. and Gerhard Weiss. "Responses of German Men of Letters to American Literature, 1945–1955." In: *Americana-Austriaca. Beiträge zur Amerikakunde.* Ed. Klaus Lanzinger. Bd. 2. Wien: W. Braumüller, 1970, p. 30–44.

CG148 Lang, Hans-Joachim. "Amerikanische Kurzgeschichten in deutschen Schulausgaben." *Jahrbuch für Amerikastudien*, vol. 8 (1963), 92–97.

CG149 Lang, Hans-Joachim. "Erzähler." In: *Nordamerikanische Literatur im deutschen Sprachraum seit 1945: Beiträge zur Rezeption.* Ed. H. Frenz and H.-J. Lang. München: Winkler, 1973, p. 137–62.

CG150 Leitel, Erich. "Die Aufnahme der amerikanischen Literatur in Deutschland: Übersetzungen der Jahre 1914–1944. Mit einer Bibliographie." Diss., Jena, 1958. 276p.

CG151 Locher, Kaspar T. *German Histories of American Literature: A Chronological and Critical Description of All German Historical Accounts of American Literature which Appeared between 1800 and 1950.* Chicago: Univ. of Chicago Pr., 1955. 268p. Rev. by E. E. Doll, *Amer.-German Rev.*, vol. 25, no. 3 (1958), 37–38.

CG152 Locher, Kaspar T. "The Reception of American Literature in German Literary Histories in the Nineteenth Century." Diss., Chicago, 1948. 459p.

CG153 Lubbers, Klaus. "Amerikanische Kurzgeschichten, Romane, Gedichte und Drama in deutschen Schulausgaben: Kritische Übersicht und Vorschläge." *Die Neueren Sprachen*, N.F., vol. 14, no. 4 (1965), 180–90.

CG154 Lubbers, Klaus. "Zur Rezeption der amerikanischen Kurzgeschichte in Deutschland nach 1945." In: *Nordamerikanische Literatur im deutschen Sprachraum seit 1945: Beiträge zur Rezeption.* Ed. H. Frenz and H.-J. Lang. München: Winkler, 1973, p. 47–64.

CG155 Mews, Siegfried. "The Reception of Weltliteratur in Germany, 1871–1890. A Study in Literary Taste." Diss., Illinois, 1966–1967.

CG156 Möhl, Gertrud. *Die Aufnahme amerikanischer Literatur in der deutschsprachigen Schweiz während der Jahre 1945–1950.* Züricher Beiträge zur vergleichenden Literaturgeschichte, vol. 9. Zürich: n.p., 1961. Cf. diss. submitted at Zürich, 1961, of same title.

CG157 Motekat, Helmut. "The Modern Short Story in Germany. An Aspect of American Influence on Contemporary German Literature." In: *Essays in Comparative Literature.* St. Louis, Mo.: Washington Univ. Studies, 1961, p. 21–40.

CG158 Nichols, Charles H. "Amerikanische Literatur an Gymnasien." *Praxis des neusprachlichen Unterrichts*, vol. 12, no. 4 (1965), 305–10.

CG159 Nirenberg, Morton. *The Reception of American Literature in German Periodicals, 1820–1850.* Heidelberg: Carl Winter, 1970. 130p. Rev. by G. T. Hollyday, *German Quar.*, vol. 46, no. 3 (May 1973), 472–74; I. L. Carlson, *Germanistik*, vol. 12, no. 3 (1971), 513. Cf. the diss. of the same title submitted at Johns Hopkins, 1970. 267p.

CG160 Oppel, Horst. "American Literature in Postwar Germany: Impact or Alienation?" In: *Studies in Comparative Literature*, Ed. Waldo F. McNeir. Louisiana St. Univ. Pr., 1962. Vol. 7, p.259–72. Also in: *Die Neueren Sprachen*, N.F., vol. 11, no. 1 (1962), 1–10.

CG161 Oppel, Horst. "Amerikanische Literatur (Einfluss auf die deutsche)." In: *Reallexikon der deutschen Literaturgeschichte.* 2nd ed. Berlin: Merker-Stammler, 1955, cols. 47–60.

CG162 Oppel, Horst. "Die amerikanische Literatur in Deutschland und das Problem der literarischen Wertung." In: *Festschrift für Walther Fischer.* Ed. Horst Oppel. Heidelberg: Winter, 1959, p.127–44.

CG163 Pocher, Wilhelm. "Die Rezeption der englischen und der amerikanischen Literatur in Deutschland in den Jahren 1918 bis 1933. Untersucht an Hand der Zeitschrift 'Das literarische Echo / Die Literatur' unter besonderer Berücksichtigung der Epik." Diss., Jena, 1972. 238 leaves. TS.

CG164 Price, Lawrence Marsden. *The Reception of United States Literature in Germany.* Univ. of N. Car. Studies in Compar. Lit., no. 39. Chapel Hill: Univ. of N. Car. Pr., 1967. 246p. Rev. by J. D. Zipes, *Germanic Rev.*, vol. 43, no. 1 (1968), 75–76. Survey of criticism, translations, literary influences, theatrical performances, etc. in German-speaking Europe. 40 pages of bibliographies covering the full range of American literature from Colonial times to the present.

CG165 Riley, Thomas A. "New England Anarchism in Germany." *New England Quar.*, vol. 18 (March 1945), 25–38.

CG166 Schönfelder, Karl-Heinz. "Amerikanische Literatur in Europa: Methodologisches zu geschmacksgeschichtlichen Überlegungen." *Zeitschrift für Anglistik und Amerikanistik*, vol. 7 (1959), 35–37. Reply to H. Straumann.

CG167 Sinde, Wolfgang. "Englische und amerikanische Literatur in Reclams Universal-Bibliothek." *Zeitschrift für Anglistik und Amerikanistik*, vol. 10 (1962), 279–88. English and American authors published in trans. by Reclam (Ost) since 1945. 15 items were "aus dem Amerikanischen."

CG168 Skard, Sigmund. *The American Myth and the European Mind: American Studies in Europe, 1776–1960.* Philadelphia: Univ. of Pa. Pr., 1961. 112p. Rev. in *Amer. Quar.*, vol. 14, no. 2 (1962), 214–15; P. d'A. Jones, *Miss. Valley Hist. Rev.*, vol. 49, no. 2 (1962), 366–67.

CG169 Springer, Anne M. *The American Novel in Germany. A Study of the Critical Reception of Eight American Novelists between the Two World Wars.* Hamburg: DeGruyter, 1960. 116p. Rev. by G. Konx, *Amer. Quar.*, vol. 13 (1961), 202–03; F. W. Lorch, *Amer. Lit.*, vol. 34 (1962), 440–41; H. Bock, *Jahrbuch für Amerikastudien*, vol. 6 (1961), 337–38; K.-H. Wirzberger, *Zeitschrift für Anglistik und Amerikanistik*, vol. 14 (1966), 217–18.

CG170 Straumann, Heinrich. "Amerikanische Literatur in Europa: Eine geschmacksgeschichtliche Überlegung." *Anglia*, vol. 76 (1958), 208–16.

CG171 Timpe, Eugene F. *American Literature in Germany 1861–1872.* Chapel Hill: Univ. of N. Car. Pr., 1964. 95p. Rev. by G. Hendrick, *Amer. Lit.*, vol. 37 (1966), 339; H.-J. Lang, *Jahrbuch für Amerikastudien*, vol. 11 (1966), 364–66; U. Weisstein, *Jour. of Eng. and Germanic Philology*, vol. 65 (1966), 571–74. Cf. diss. "The Reception of American Literature in Germany, 1861–1871." Univ. of Southern California, 1960.

CG172 Wager, Willis: *American Literature: A World View.* New York: N.Y. Univ. Pr., 1968. 292p. The American writer in relation to broad Europen and Oriental influences.

CG173 Wehdeking, Volker Christian. *Der Nullpunkt: Über die Konstituierung der deutschen Nachkriegsliteratur (1945–1948) in den amerikanischen Kriegsgefangenenlagern.* Stuttgart: Metzler, 1971. 208p. Rev. by H. F., *Jahrbuch für Amerikastudien*, vol. 18 (1973), 288–90.

CG174 Wildi, Max. "Der angelsächsische Roman und der Schweizer Leser." Diss., Zürich, 1944. 81p.

CG175 Wolpers, Theodore. "Die amerikanische *Short Story* in der Schule: Gesichtspunkte und Vorschläge für eine representative Auswahl." *Die Neueren Sprachen*, N.F., vol. 5 (1956), 286–304.

CG176 Zuther, Gerhard H. W., comp. *Eine Bibliographie der Aufnahme amerikanischer Literatur in deutschen Zeitschriften 1945–1960*. München: Franz Frank, 1965. 142p. Lists reviews, articles, and dissertations under headings of the American author. Bibliography of sources. 2400 items analyzing the contents of 70 German periodicals. Rev. by H.-J. Lang, *Jahrbuch für Amerikastudien*, vol. 11 (1966), 364–66; K.-H. Wirzberger, *Zeitschrift für Anglistik und Amerikanistik*, vol. 15, no. 3 (1966), 324–25; by K. J. R. Arndt, *Mod. Lang. Jour.*, vol. 50 (1966), 442.

Influence and Reception of American Authors in Germany

ALBEE, EDWARD

CG177 Rule, Margaret W. "The Reception of the Plays of Edward Albee in Germany." Arkansas, 1971.

BELLAMY, EDWARD

CG178 Bowman, Sylvia et al. *Edward Bellamy Abroad: An American Prophet's Influence*. New York: Twayne, 1963.

BRYANT, WILLIAM CULLEN

CG179 Bryant, William Cullen. *Amerikanische Gedichte in deutscher Nachbildung nebst Einleitung von Adolf Laun*. Bremen: Heyse, 1863. 175p.

CLEMENS, SAMUEL (PSEUD. MARK TWAIN)

CG180 Asselineau, Roger. *The Literary Reputation of Mark Twain from 1920 to 1950*. Paris: n.p., 1954. 241p. The Bibliography, p.68–226, lists many entries of German criticism.

CG181 Lederer, Max. "Mark Twain in Vienna." *Mark Twain Quar.*, vol. 7, no. 1 (1944), 1–12.

CG182 Michel, Robert. "The Popularity of Mark Twain in Austria." *Mark Twain Quar.*, vol. 8 (1950), 5–6, 19.

CG183 Schönfelder, Karl Heinz. *Mark Twain: Leben, Persönlichkeit und Werk*. Halle: n.p., 1961. 118p. Lists reprints and translations that have appeared in East Germany.

CG184 Stiehl, Karl. "Mark Twain und die Wiener Presse zur Zeit seines Aufenthaltes in Wien, 1897–1899." Diss., Wien, 1953.

COOPER, JAMES FENIMORE

CG185 Arndt, Karl J. R. "The Cooper-Sealsfield Exchange of Criticism." *Amer. Lit.*, vol. 15 (1943), 16–24.

CG186 Bodensohn, Annaliese. *Im Zeichen des Manitu. Coopers "Lederstrumpf" als Dichtung und Jugendlektüre*. Frankfurt: Dipa, 1963. 192p. (Untersuchungen zur Jugendlektüre, vol. 4).

CG187 Kozeluk, Alfons. "Charles Sealsfield und J. F. Cooper." Diss., Wien, 1949.

CG188 Liljegren, S. B. "Die Menschenauffassung der Romantik und Fenimore Cooper." *Wissenschaftliche Zeitschrift der Ernst Moritz Arndt-Univ. Greifswald*, vol. 5 (1955–1956), 157–60.

CG189 Lüdeke, H. "James Fenimore Cooper and the Democracy of Switzerland." *Eng. Studies*, vol. 27 (1946), 33–44

CG190 Rossbacher, Karlheinz. *Lederstrumpf in Deutschland: Zur Rezeption James Fenimore Coopers beim Leser der Restaurationszeit*. München: Wilh. Fink Verlag, 1972. 114p. Rev. by Klaus Lanzinger, *Amerikastudien*, vol. 19, no. 1 (1974), 180–81.

CG191 Thorp, Willard. "Cooper beyond America." *N.Y. Hist.*, vol. 35 (1955), 522–39.

CG192 Zaeckel, Eugene. "Der Einfluss J. F. Coopers und W. Irvings auf die deutsche Literatur." Diss., Wien, 1944.

CRANE, STEPHEN

CG193 Bastein, Friedel H. *Die Rezeption Stephen Cranes in Deutschland*. Anglo-Amer. Forum, vol. 3. Frankfurt: Lang, 1977. 361p.

DOS PASSOS, JOHN

CG194 Porter, John. *Bibliography of John Dos Passos*. Chicago: Normandie House, 1950.

DREISER, THEODORE

CG195 Schmidt-von Bardeleben, Renate. "Dreiser on the European Continent: Part One: Theodore Dreiser, the German Dreisers, and German." *Dreiser Newsletter*, vol. 2, no. 2 (1971), 1–2. See also: "Dreiser on the European Continent," *ibid.*, vol. 3, no. 1 (1972), 1–8.

CG196 Wentz, John C. "*An American Tragedy* as Epic-Theater: The Piscator-Dramatization." *Mod. Drama*, vol. 4 (1962), 365–76.

ELIOT, THOMAS STEARNS

CG197 "Eliot: Gedichte auf deutsch." *Gegenwart*, vol. 7, no. 6 (1952), 182f.

CG198 Fink, E. O. "Die übersetzerische Rezeption des lyrischen Werkes von T. S. Eliot im deutschsprachigen Raum." Diss., Hamburg, 1978–1979. 221p. See DAI, vol. 39 (1978–1979), 612C.

CG199 Galinsky, Hans. *T. S. Eliots "Murder in the Cathedral" im Unterricht der Oberstufe*. Braunschweig: n.p., 1964.

CG200 Germer, Rudolf. "T. S. Eliots 'Waste Land': Die Geschichte seiner Wirkung und Beurteilung in den Jahren 1922–1956 unter besonderer Berücksichtigung der Rezeption in England, Amerika, Deutschland und Frankreich." Diss., Freiburg i. Br., 1957. 229p.

CG201 Lohner, Edgar. "Gottfried Benn und T. S. Eliot." *Neue deutsche Hefte*, vol. 3 (1956–1957), 100–07.

EMERSON, RALPH WALDO

CG202 Christadler, Martin. "Ralph Waldo Emerson in Modern Germany." *Emerson Soc. Quar.*, no. 38 (1965), 112–30.

CG203 Duffy, Charles. "Material Relating to R. W. Emerson in the Grimm *Nachlass*." *Amer. Lit.*, vol. 30 (1959), 523–28. The critic Hermann Grimm.

CG204 Luedtke, Luther S. "Adolph Holtermann: Translator of Emerson." *Amer. Transcend. Quar.*, vol. 29 (1976), 46–52.

CG205 Luedtke, Luther S. "Emerson in Western Europe (1955–1975)." *Amer. Transcend. Quar.*, vol. 31 (1978). Supplement, 24–42. Incl. bibliography.

CG206 Luedtke, Luther S. "First Notices of Emerson in England and Germany, 1835–1842." *Notes and Queries*, vol. 22 (1975), 106–08.

CG207 Luedtke, Luther S. "German Criticism and Reception of Ralph W. Emerson." Diss., Brown Univ., 1972.

CG208 Urzidil, Johannes. "Weltreise in Concord." *Neue Literarische Welt*, 10 May 1953.

FAST, HOWARD

CG209 Kopka, Hans W. K. "Eine erste ausführliche Fast-Bibliographie." *Zeitschrift für Anglistik und Amerikanistik*, vol. 1 (1953), 97–107.

FAULKNER, WILLIAM

CG210 Ait Daraou, Ahmet. "The German Reception of William Faulkner: Books and Dissertations, 1950–1979." Diss., Univ. of S. Car., 1980. 323p.

CG211 Pusey, William W., III. "William Faulkner's Works in Germany to 1940: Translations and Criticism." *Germanic Rev.*, vol. 30 (1955), 211–26.

CG212 Zindel, Edith. *William Faulkner in den deutschsprachigen Ländern Europas: Untersuchungen zur Aufnahme seiner Werke nach 1945*. Hamburg: Lüdke Verlag, 1972. 552p. Rev. by A. Bleikasten, *Miss. Quar.*, vol. 27 (1974), 353–56.

FITZGERALD, F. SCOTT

CG213 Bryer, Jackson R., comp. *The Critical Reputation of F. Scott Fitzgerald*. Hamden, Conn.: Archon Books, 1967. 434p. Checklist incl. foreign books and articles.

FRANKLIN, BENJAMIN

CG214 Hausel, Helmut. "Benjamin Franklin, 1706–1790, im literarischen Deutschland seiner Zeit." Diss., Erlangen, 1952.

CG215 Hegemann, Daniel V. "Franklin and Germany: Further Evidence of His Reputation in the 18th Century." *German Quar.*, vol. 26 (1953), 187–94.

CG216 Kahn, Robert L. "An Account of a Meeting with Benjamin Franklin at Passy on October 9,

Influence and Reception (cont.)

1777, from Georg Forster's English Journal." *William and Mary Quar.*, vol. 12 (1955), 472–74.

CG217 Kahn, Robert L. "Franklin, Grimm and J. H. Landolt." *Papers of the Amer. Philosophical Soc.*, vol. 99 (1955), 401–04. Baron Friedr. Melchior von Grimm supplies Landolt with a letter of introduction to Franklin.

CG218 Kahn, Robert L. "Georg Forster and Benjamin Franklin." *Papers of the Amer. Philosophical Soc.*, vol. 102 (1958), 1–6.

CG219 Kahn, Robert L. "A Meeting between Lichtenberg and Franklin." *German Life and Letters*, vol. 9 (1956), 64–67.

CG220 Slessarev, Helga. "Susanne von Bandener and Benjamin Franklin." *Amer. Notes and Queries*, vol. 4 (June 1966), 149–50. This German poet claimed that Franklin was her uncle.

CG221 Vagts, Alfred. "Benjamin Franklin—Influence and Symbol." *Amer.-German Rev.*, vol. 23, no. 2 (1956), 7–9. F.'s influence in Germany; the German editions of his works.

CG222 Wild, Reiner. "Prometheus-Franklin: Die Gestalt Benjamin Franklins in der deutschen Literatur des 18. Jahrhunderts." *Amerikastudien*, vol. 23, no. 1 (1978), 30–39.

FROST, ROBERT

CG223 Lichtenstein, Erich, reviewer. "Lyrik von Robert Frost, deutsch." *Neue literarische Welt*, 30 October 1953.

HARTE, BRET

CG224 Timpe, Eugene F. "Bret Harte's German Public." *Jahrbuch für Amerikastudien*, vol. 10 (1965), 215–20.

HAWTHORNE, NATHANIEL

CG225 Schmitt-von Mühlenfels, Astrid. "Hawthorne's *The Scarlet Letter* als Fernsehfilm: Darstellung, Deutung und Umdeutung." *Literatur in Wissenschaft und Unterricht* (Kiel), vol. 7 (1974), 39–46.

CG226 Timpe, Eugene F. "Hawthorne in Germany." *Symposium*, vol. 19 (1956), 171–79. Assessment of his popular and critical reception.

HEMINGWAY, ERNEST

CG227 Asselineau, Rogert, ed. *The Literary Reputation of Hemingway in Europe*. Introd. by H. Straumann. New York: N.Y. Univ. Pr., 1965. 210p. Rev. by W. L. Miner, *Amer. Lit.*, vol. 37 (1966), 501–02; D. N. Curley, *Books Abroad*, vol. 40 (1966), 82; L. Fietz, *Jahrbuch für Amerikastudien*, vol. 11 (1966), 357–59; C. Baker, *Compar. Lit. Studies*, vol. 3 (1966), 67–69. Eight essays on the critical and popular response. Helmut Papajewski writes on Hemingway in Germany.

CG228 Bentz, Hans W. *Ernest Hemingway in Übersetzungen*. Frankfurt: Bentz, 1963. 34p. Rev. by W. White, *Bull. of Bibliography*, vol. 24 (1966), 241–42.

CG229 Gurtler, Lea. "Der Bestseller Hemingway." Diss., Innsbruck, 1950.

CG230 Kirshner, Sumner. "From the Gulf Stream into the Main Stream: Siegfried Lenz and Hemingway." *Research Studies of Washington State Univ.*, vol. 35 (June 1967), 141–47.

CG231 Kruse, Horst. "Hinrich Kruses *Weg un Uemweg* und die Tradition der Short Story Hemingways." *Germanisch-Romanische Monatsschrift*, vol. 43 (N.F., vol. 12), 1962, 286–301.

CG232 Kvam, Wayne E. "The Critical Reaction to Hemingway in Germany, 1945–1965." Diss., Wisconsin, 1969.

CG233 Mucharowski, Hans-Günter. *Die Werke von Ernest Hemingway. Eine Bibliographie der deutschsprachigen Hemingway-Literatur und der Originalwerke von 1923–1954*. Hamburg: n.p., 1955. 48p.

CG234 White, William. "'The Old Man and the Sea' as a German Textbook." *Publs., Bibliographical Soc. of America*, vol. 60 (1966), 89–90.

HOWELLS, WILLIAM DEAN

CG235 Timpe, Eugene F. "Howells and His German Critics." *Jahrbuch für Amerikastudien*, vol. 11 (1966), 256–59.

IRVING, WASHINGTON

CG236 Gontrum, Peter. "The Legend of Rip van Winkle in Max Frisch's *Stiller*." In: *Studies in Swiss Literature*. Ed. Manfred Jurgensen. Brisbane: Univ. of Queensland, 1971. p.97–102.

CG237 Reichart, Walter A. "The Earliest German Translations of Washington Irving's Writings: A Bibliography." *Bull., N.Y. Pub. Lib.*, vol. 61 (1957), 491–98.

CG238 Reichart, Walter A. "The Early Reception of Washington Irving's Works in Germany." *Anglia*, vol. 74 (1956), 345–63.

CG239 Reichart, Walter A. "Washington Irving's Influence on German Literature." *Mod. Lang. Rev.*, vol. 52 (1957), 536–53.

JAMES, HENRY

CG240 Baumgaertel, Gerhard. "The Reception of Henry James in Germany." *Symposium*, vol. 12 (1959), 19–31. A survey of criticism.

CG241 Hennecke, Hans. "Henry James in Deutschland." *Der Monat*, vol. 5 (1952), no. 53, 554–56. On James's *The Siege of London*.

CG242 Uhlig, H. "Henry James, deutsch." *Texte und Zeichen*, vol. 1 (1955), 262–66.

LONDON, JACK

CG243 Chomet, Otto. "Jack London: Works, Reviews and Criticism Published in German—A Bibliography." *Bull. of Bibliography*, vol. 19 (1949), 211–15, 239f.

McCULLERS, CARSON

CG244 Bondy, Barbara. "Eine Dichterin Amerikas: Zu den deutschsprachigen Ausgaben der Werke Carson McCullers." *Deutsche Rundschau*, vol. 89, no. 7 (1963), 76–79.

MELVILLE, HERMAN

CG245 Kühnelt, Harro H. "The Reception of Herman Melville's Works in Germany and Austria." *Innsbrucker Beiträge zur Kulturwissenschaft*, vol. 4 (1956), 111–21.

CG246 Mangold, Charlotte W. "Herman Melville in German Criticism from 1900 to 1955." Diss., Maryland, 1959.

CG247 Phelps, Leland R. "*Moby-Dick* in Germany." *Compar. Lit.*, vol. 10 (1958), 349–55.

CG248 Phelps, Leland R. "The Reaction to *Benito Cereno* and *Billy Budd* in Germany." *Symposium*, vol. 13 (1959), 294–99. With *Moby-Dick*, these two works form the foundation of Melville's reputation in Germany.

CG249 Walter, Josef. "Herman Melville's Influence upon Gerstäcker's South Sea Novels." Diss., Freiburg, 1952.

MILLER, ARTHUR

CG250 Dotzenrath, Theo. "Arthur Miller's *All My Sons* als Schullektüre." *Die Neueren Sprachen*, N.F., vol. 8 (1959), 33–40.

CG251 Reitemeier, Rüdiger. "Arthur Millers *All My Sons* auf der Oberstufe." *Die Neueren Sprachen*, N.F., vol. 13 (1964), 166–72.

CG252 Rischbieter, Henning. "Arthur Millers Fall: Sein neues Stück am Burgtheater." *Theater heute*, vol. 5 (1964), no. 12, 28f.

CG253 Van Allen, Harold. "An Examination of the Reception and Critical Evaluation of the Plays of Arthur Miller in West Germany from 1950–1961." Diss., Arkansas, 1964. 226p.

MITCHELL, MARGARET

CG254 Pusey, William W., III. "Gone With the Wind in Germany." *Ky. For. Lang. Quar.*, vol. 5 (1955), 180–88.

O'HARA, JOHN

CG255 Zachrau, Thekla. "The Reception of John O'Hara in Germany." *John O'Hara Jour.*, vol. 2, no. 1 (1979–1980), 1–12.

O'NEILL, EUGENE

CG256 Bryer, Jackson H. "Forty Years of O'Neill Criticism, a Selected Bibliography." *Mod. Drama*, vol. 4 (1961), 196–216.

CG257 Frenz, Horst. "Eugene O'Neill in Deutschland." *Euphorion*, vol. 50 (1956), 307–27.

CG258 Frenz, Horst. "Eugene O'Neill on the German Stage." *Theatre Annual*, vol. 11 (1953), 24–34.

CG259 Frenz, Horst. "Eugene O'Neill's Plays Printed Abroad." *Eng. Jour.*, vol. 5 (1944), 340–41.

CG260 Frenz, Horst. "List of Foreign Editions and Translations of Eugene O'Neill's Dramas." *Bull. of Bibliography*, vol. 18 (September–December 1943), 33–34.

CG261 Frenz, Horst. "Three European Productions of *The Hairy Ape*." *The Eugene O'Neill Newsletter*, vol. 1, no. 3 (1978), 10–12. English, German, and French productions.

CG262 Kahl, Kurt. "O'Neill Entdeckungen: Frühe Stücke in Wien und Wupperthal." *Theater heute*, vol. 4, no. 2 (1963), 40.

CG263 Luft, Friedrich. "Berliner Theater: Zwei wesentliche Ereignisse der Spielzeit." *Westermanns Monatshefte*, vol. 98, no. 1 (1957), 78–79. On *A Long Day's Journey into Night*.

CG264 Sturm, Clarence. "Scholarly Criticism of Eugene O'Neill in Periodicals, 1960–1975, With a Bibliographical Overview of the American and German Studies." Diss., Oklahoma State Univ., 1977. 419p.

PAINE, THOMAS

CG265 Aldridge, A. O. "The Influence of Thomas Paine in the United States, England, France, Germany, and South America." *Procs., Second Internat. Compar. Lit. Congress*. Univ. of North Carolina Studies in Compar. Lit., vol. 24. Chapel Hill: Univ. of N. Car. Pr., 1959, p.369–82.

CG266 Arnold, Hans. "Die Aufnahme von Thomas Paine's Schriften in Deutschland." *PMLA*, vol. 74 (1959), 354–86.

CG267 Gabrielli, Vittorio. "Thomas Paine fra l'America e l'Europa." *Studi Americani*, vol. 1 (1955), 9–53.

POE, EDGAR ALLAN

CG268 Bandy, William T. *The Influence and Reputation of Edgar Allan Poe in Europe*. Baltimore: Edgar Allan Poe Soc., 1962. 15p.

CG269 Kühnelt, Harro H. "Die Aufnahme und Verbreitung von E. A. Poes Werken im Deutschen." In: *Festschrift für Walther Fischer*. Heidelberg: n.p., 1959, p.195–224. Incl. Bibliography.

CG270 Kühnelt, Harro H. "Deutsche Erzähler im Gefolge von E. A. Poe." *Rivista di Letterature Moderne e Comparate* (Firenze), vol. 2 (1951), 457–65.

CG271 Kühnelt, Harro H. "E. A. Poe und die phantastische Erzählung im österreichischen Schrifttum von 1900–1920." *Schlern Schriften* (Innsbruck), vol. 104 (1953), 131–43.

SALINGER, JEROME D.

CG272 Kraul, Fritz. "Jerome D. Salingers Roman 'Der Fänger im Roggen' als Pflichtlektüre im Deutschunterricht der Oberstufe." *Der Deutschunterricht*, vol. 20, no. 1 (March 1968), 79–86.

SINCLAIR, UPTON

CG273 Bantz, Elizabeth. "Upton Sinclair: Book Reviews and Criticism Published in German and French Periodicals." *Bull. of Bibliography*, vol. 18 (1946), 204–06.

CG274 Uhlig, Helga. "Zum Abdruck des Romans *König Kohle* von Upton Sinclair in der *Roten Fahne* 1921." *Wissenschaftliche Zeitschrift der Humboldt-Universität zu Berlin. Gesellschafts- und sprachwissenschaftl. Reihe*, vol. 25 (1976), 249–52.

STEINBECK, JOHN

CG275 Liedloff, Helmut. *Steinbeck in German Translation: A Study of Translational Practices*. Carbondale: South. Illinois Univ. Pr., 1965. 104p. Rev. by W. Francke, *Anglia*, vol. 85 (1966), 251; W. French, *Compar. Lit. Studies*, vol. 3 (1966), 351–52; F. Genschmer, *Mod. Lang. Jour.*, vol. 50 (1966), 239. Four translated texts are compared with the original; bibliography of Steinbeck translations into German, 1940–1941.

THOREAU, HENRY DAVID

CG276 Lacey, James Francis. "Henry David Thoreau in German Criticism: 1881–1965." Diss., New York Univ., 1968. 182p.

CG277 Timpe, Eugene F. "Thoreau in Germany." *Thoreau Soc. Bull.*, no. 93 (1965), 1–3.

WARREN, ROBERT PENN

CG278 Poenicke, Klaus. "Robert Penn Warren: Kunstwerk und kritische Theorie." Diss., Freie Univ., Berlin. Repr. *Jahrbuch für Amerikastudien*, 1959. Supplement no. 4. 160p. See also *Jahrbuch für Amerikastudien* vol. 5 (1960), 349–51.

WHITMAN, WALT

CG279 Allen, Gay Wilson. *Twenty-Five Years of Walt Whitman Bibliography, 1918–1942*. Boston: Faxon, 1943. 57p.

CG280 Allen, Gay Wilson, ed. *Walt Whitman Abroad: Critical Essays from Germany, France, Scandinavia* . . . Syracuse: Syracuse Univ. Pr., 1955. 290p.

CG281 Cosentino, Vincent. "Walt Whitman's Influence on Thomas Mann, the 'Non-Political' Writer." In: *Vergleichen und Verändern. Festschrift für Helmut Motekat*. Ed. Albrecht Goetze and Günther Pflaum. München: Hueber, 1970, p. 224–42.

CG282 Hatfield, Henry. "Drei Randglossen zu Thomas Manns *Zauberberg*, Hans Castorp und Walt Whitman." *Euphorion*, vol. 56 (1962), 365–68.

CG283 Hess, John. "Reception of Whitman in the German Democratic Republic." *Walt Whitman Rev.*, vol. 22 (1976), 30–35.

CG284 Hunt, Joel A. "Mann and Whitman, Humaniores Litterae." *Compar. Lit.*, vol. 14 (1962), 266–71.

CG285 Lang, Hans-Joachim. "Walt Whitman in Germany." In: *Walt Whitman in Europe Today*. Ed. Roger Asselineau and William White. Detroit: n.p., 1972, p. 12–15.

CG286 McCormick, E. A. *Die sprachliche Eigenart von Walt Whitmans 'Leaves of Grass' in deutscher Übertragung*. Sprache und Dichtung, no. 79. Bern / Stuttgart: n.p., 1953. 118p. Rev. by J. W. Thomas, *Monatshefte*, vol. 46 (1954), 287–88; I. Meidinger-Geise, *Welt und Wort*, vol. 9 (1954), 134.

CG287 Pongs, Hermann. "Walt Whitman und Stefan George." *Compar. Lit.*, vol. 4 (1952), 289–322.

CG288 Roecklinger, Gertrude. "Walt Whitmans Einfluss auf die deutsche Lyrik." Diss., Wien, 1951–1952.

CG289 Scherrinsky, Harald. "Walt Whitman in modernen deutschen Übersetzungen." *Neuphilologische Zeitschrift*, vol. 3 (1950), 189–91.

CG290 Schumann, Detlev W. "Enumerative Style and Its Significance in Whitman, Rilke, Werfel." *Mod. Lang. Quar.*, vol. 3 (1942), 171–204.

CG291 Schumann, Detlev W. "Observations on Enumerative Style in Modern German Poetry." *PMLA*, vol. 59 (1944), 1111–55.

CG292 Warfel, Harry R., ed. *Studies in Walt Whitman's "Leaves of Grass" Written by Scholars at Philipps Univ., Marburg / Lahn*. Marburg: n.p., 1954. 116p.

CG293 Wirzberger, Karl-Heinz. "Ein Hundert Jahre *Leaves of Grass*." *Zeitschrift für Anglistik und Amerikanistik*, vol. 4 (1956), 77–87. Rev. by J. W. Thomas, *Jahrbuch für Amerikastudien*, vol. 8 (1963), 351–53.

CG294 Wood, Frank. "Three Poems on Whitman." *Compar. Lit.*, vol. 4 (1952), 44–53. Mention of W.'s impact on Arno Holz, Herbert Eulenberg, and Johannes R. Becher.

WILDER, THORNTON

CG295 Bischoff, Dietrich. "Columbus in Göttingen." *Deutsche Universitätszeitung*, vol. 3, no. 20 (1947), 8.

CG296 Fehse, Klaus-Dieter. "Thornton Wilders *The Skin of Our Teeth* als Oberstufenlektüre." *Die Neueren Sprachen*, vol. 22 (1973), 27–38.

CG297 Frenz, Horst. "The Reception of Thornton Wilder's Plays in Germany." *Mod. Drama*, vol. 3 (1960), 123–37.

CG298 Fussell, Paul, Jr. "Thornton Wilder and the German Psyche." *Nation*, vol. 186 (1958), 394–95.

CG299 Gontrum, Peter. "The Influence of Thornton Wilder on Max Frisch." *Procs. of the Pacific Northwest Conference on For. Languages*, vol. 29, no. 1 (1978), 14–17.

CG300 Goldstone, Richard. "Interview mit Thornton Wilder. Friedenspreis des deutschen Buchhandels 1957." *Der Monat*, vol. 9 (1957), no. 108, 46–53.

CG301 Kosok, Heinz. "Thornton Wilder: A Bibliography of Criticism." *Twentieth Century Lit.*, vol. 9 (1963), 93–100.

CG302 Mauranges, Jean-Paul. "Der Einfluss Thornton Wilders auf das literarische Schaffen von Friedrich Dürrenmatt und Max Frisch." In: *Nordamerikanische Literatur im deutschen Sprachraum seit 1945: Beiträge zur Rezeption*. Ed. H. Frenz and H.-J. Lang. München: Winkler, 1973, p. 225–50.

CG303 Schimpf, Sigurd. "Thornton Wilders Theaterstücke und ihre Inszenierungen auf den deutschen Bühnen." Diss., Kiel, 1966.

CG304 Voss, Renate. "Die Umsetzung von Thornton Wilders 'The Skin of our Teeth' im

Influence and Reception (cont.)

deutschsprachigen Raum: Übersetzungen und Aufführungen." Diss., Kiel, 1963.

CG305 "Das Wilder-Gespräch. Schillerndes Spiegelbild unserer Zeit." *Deutsche Universitätszeitung*, vol. 2 (1947), no. 16, 10–14.

CG306 Williams, Michael V. "Thornton Wilder's Anglo-American and German Critics: A Bibliography." Diss., Univ. of S. Car., 1979. 374p.

WILLIAMS, TENNESSEE

CG307 Dobson, Eugene, Jr. "The Reception of the Plays of Tennessee Williams in Germany." Diss., Arkansas, 1967. 322p.

CG308 Frenz, Horst, and Ulrich Weisstein. "Tennessee Williams and His German Critics." *Symposium*, vol. 14, no. 4 (1960), 258–75.

CG309 Wendt, Ernst. "Zeit der Anpassung: Tennessee Williams' neues Stück in den Hamburger Kammerspielen." *Theater heute*, vol. 2, no. 2 (1962), 18–20.

WILLIAMS, WILLIAM CARLOS

CG310 Bonheim, Helmut and Reingard Nischik. "William Carlos Williams in Germany." *William Carlos Williams Newsletter*, vol. 4, no. 1 (1978), 14–18.

CG311 Galinsky, Hans. "William Carlos Williams. Eine Vergleichende Studie zur Aufnahme seines Werkes in Deutschland, England und Italien (1912–1965). Teil I: Deutschland." *Jahrbuch für Amerikastudien*, vol. 11 (1966), 96–175.

WINTHROP, THEODORE

CG312 Bergmann, Frank. "A Note on Two Nineteenth-Century German Editions of Theodore Winthrop's *John Brent*." *Bull., N.Y. Pub. Lib.*, vol. 72, no. 10 (December 1968), 656–58. On W.'s reputation in Germany from 1864 on. *John Brent* (1862) is an early novel of Western life.

WOLFE, THOMAS

CG313 Kracht, Fritz Andreas. "Die Thomas Wolfe-Kritik in den Vereinigten Staaten und Deutschland." Diss., München, 1953. 161p.

CG314 Pusey, William W., III. "The German Vogue of Thomas Wolfe." *Germanic Rev.*, vol. 23, no. 2 (1948), 131–48. W. received an enthusiastic reception in Germany.

WRIGHT, RICHARD

CG315 Brown, Soi-Daniel. "Invisible Man's Appearance in Germany: An Analysis of Potential Critical Response to the German Translation." *Amerikastudien*, vol. 26 (1981), 213–18.

American Influences on German Authors

BLEI, FRANZ

CG316 Kühnelt, Harro H. "Franz Blei und die Literatur der Vereinigten Staaten." In: *Romantic Reassessment. Essays in Honor of Professor Tyrus Hillway*. Ed. E. A. Stürzl. Salzburg: Inst. für Englische Sprache und Literatur, 1977, p. 129–55.

BRANT, SEBASTIAN

CG317 Zeydel, Edwin H. "Sebastian Brant and the Discovery of America." *Jour. of Eng. and Germanic Philology*, vol. 42 (1943), 410–11. Evidence of Brant's interest in the first voyage of Columbus.

BRECHT, BERTHOLT

See Canadian- and American-German Authors, Including Writers in Exile, *under* Section CI: German-American Literature.

BRENTANO, SOPHIE

CG318 Von Hofe, Harold. "Sophie Mereau Brentano and America." *Mod. Lang. Notes*, vol. 75 (1960), 427–31.

BROCH, HERMANN

CG319 Jonas, Klaus W. "Hermann Broch. Eine bibliographische Studie." *Philobiblon*, vol. 9 (1965), 291–323.

COURTHS-MAHLER, HEDWIG

CG320 Schmidt, Josef. "Hedwig Courths-Mahlers Die Pelzkönigin: Deutsch-Kanadische Märchen und sanfte Protest." In: *Analecta Helvetica et Germanica: Eine Festschrift zu Ehren von Hermann Boeschenstein*. Ed. A. Arnold, Hans Eichner, Edmund Heier and S. Hoefert. Bonn: Bouvier, 1979, p.310–22.

DÜRRENMATT, FRIEDRICH

CG321 Mauranges, Jean-Paul. "L'image de l'Amérique dans l'oeuvre de Dürrenmatt: Une perspektive théologique?" *Seminar. A Jour. of Germanic Studies*, vol. 12 (1976), 156–73.

EBELING, CHRISTOPH DANIEL

CG322 Stewart, Gordon M. *The Literary Contributions of Christoph Daniel Ebeling*. Amsterdam: Rodopi, 225p. Cf. his diss., Johns Hopkins, 1978. 18th-century geographer and historian. On Ebeling's literary activities and his relations with America.

EDSCHMID, KASIMIR

CG323 Lewis, Ward B. "Kasimir Edschmid's Image of America and Her Relation to Germany." *Mod. Lang. Studies*, vol. 10, no. 2 (1980), 69–79.

EICHENDORFF, JOSEPH VON

CG324 Maler, Anselm. "Die Entdeckung Amerikas as romantisches Thema: Zu Eichendorffs 'Meerfahrt' und ihren Quellen." *Germanisch-Romanische Monatsschrift*, N.F. vol. 25 (1975), 47–74. Echoes of biographies of Columbus, the *Kolumbus* of Campe, Washington Irving, and Humboldt.

ENZENSBERGER, HANS MAGNUS

CG325 Peter, Klaus. "Supermacht USA: Hans Magnus Enzensberger über Amerika, Politik und Verbrechen." In: *Amerika in der deutschen Literatur: Neue Welt, Nordamerika, USA. Wolfgang Paulsen zum 65. Geburtstag*. Ed. S. Bauschinger et al. Stuttgart: Reclam, 1975, p.368–81.

FONTANE, THEODOR

CG326 Correll, Ernst. "Theodor Fontane's *Quitt*." *Mennonite Quar. Rev.*, vol. 16, no. 4 (1942), 221–22. F.'s novel dealing with Mennonites of Oklahoma.

CG327 Davis, Arthur L. "Theodor Fontane's Interest in America as Revealed by His Novel *Quitt*." *Amer.-German Rev.*, vol. 19 (1953), no. 3, 28–29.

CG328 Enns, Erwin. "'Quitt' oder: Wie man auch Mennonit werden kann. Anmerkungen zu einem Fontane-Roman." *Mennonitisches Jahrbuch 1979*. Konferenz der Süddeutschen Mennonitengemeinde. Karlsruhe: H. Schneider, 1979.

CG329 Keune, Manfred E. "Das Amerikabild in Theodore Fontanes Romanwerk." *Amsterdamer Beiträge zur neueren Germanistik*, vol. 2 (1973), 1–25.

CG330 Loewen, Harry. "From Prussianism to Mennonitism: Reality and Ideals in Theodor Fontane's Novel 'Quitt'." *Jour. of German-Amer. Studies*, vol. 15 (1980), 25–38.

CG331 Salamon, George. "'Wer is(t) John Maynard?': Fontanes tapferer Steuermann und sein amerikanisches Vorbild." *Fontane Blätter 1965*, no. 2, 25–40.

CG332 Zieglschmid, A. J. F. "Truth and Fiction and Mennonites in the Second Part of Theodor Fontane's Novel *Quitt*: The Indian Territory." *Mennonite Quar. Rev.*, vol. 16, no. 4 (1942), 223–46. Sources and backgrounds of the novel.

FRISCH, MAX

CG333 Durzak, Manfred. "Max Frisch und Thornton Wilder: Der vierte Akt von *The Skin of Our Teeth*." In: *Frisch: Kritik—Thesen—Analysen. Beiträge zum 65. Geburtstag*. Ed. Manfred Jurgensen. Bern: Francke, 1977, p.97–120.

CG334 Mayer, Siegfried. "Zur Funktion der Amerikakomponente im Erzählwerk Max Frischs." In: *Max Frisch: Aspekte des Prosawerks*. Ed. Gerhard P. Knapp. Bern: Lang, 1978, p.205–35.

CG335 Stine, Linda J. "Chinesische Träumerei—amerikanisches Märchen: Märchenelemente in Bin und Still." In: *Max Frisch: Askpekte des Prosawerks*. Ed. Gerhard P. Knapp. Bern: Lang, 1978, p.37–51.

GERSTÄCKER, FRIEDRICH

CG336 Bukey, Anita, and Evan Burr Bukey. "Frederick Gerstaecker and Arkansas." *Ark. Hist. Quar.*, vol. 31, no. 1 (Spring 1972), 3–14.

CG337 Bukey, Anita, and Evan Burr Bukey, trans. and eds. "Arkansas After the War: From the Journal of Frederick Gerstäcker." *Ark. Hist. Quar.*, vol. 32 (Autumn 1973), 255–73.

CG338 Evans, Clarence. "A Cultural Link between Nineteenth-Century Germany and the Ar-

American Influences on German Authors *(cont.)*
kansas Ozarks." *Mod. Lang. Jour.*, vol. 35 (1951), 523–30. Symbolism of the motif of the sinking village of Germelshausen. G.'s experiences in Arkansas as a source for *Germelshausen*.

CG339 Evans, Clarence. "Friedrich Gerstäcker, Social Chronicler of the Arkansas Frontier." *Ark. Hist. Quar.*, vol. 6 (1948), 440–49. Pointing out the value of G.'s reports about the frontier.

CG340 Gudde, Erwin G. "Friedrich Gerstaecker: World Traveller and Author, 1816–1872." *Jour. of the West*, vol. 7, no. 3 (July 1968), 345–50.

CG341 Kolb, Alfred. "Friedrich Gerstäcker and the American Dream." *Mod. Lang. Studies*, vol. 5, no. 1 (1975), 103–08. G.'s frontier America, where man gives noble battle to the forces of nature, becomes his personal perception of the American dream.

CG342 Kolb, Alfred. "Friedrich Gerstäcker and the American Frontier." Diss., Syracuse Univ., 1966. 161p. G. as myth-maker.

CG343 Kolb, Alfred. "Gerstäcker's America." *Thoth* (Dept. of Eng., Syracuse Univ.), vol. 7 (1966), 12–21.

CG344 Landa, Bjarne E. "The American Scene in Friedrich Gerstäcker's Works of Fiction." Diss., Minnesota, 1953.

CG345 Matthews, Earl L. "The Search for the Erkswine Grave." *Ark. Hist. Quar.*, vol. 11, no. 2 (1952), 113–23. E. was killed by a bear while hunting with Gerstäcker in Arkansas. His grave was found by following Gerstäcker's account. Cf. Evans, Clarence. "Gerstäcker and the Konwells of White River Valley." *Ark. Hist. Quar.*, vol. 10 (1951), no. 1, 1–36.

CG346 Moltmann, Günter. "Überseeische Siedlungen und weltpolitische Spekulationen: Friedrich Gerstäcker und die Frankfurter Zentralgewalt." In: *Russland-Deutschland-Amerika: Festschrift für Fritz Epstein*. Wiesbaden, 1978, p.56–72.

CG347 Morris, Robert L. "Three Arkansas Travelers." *Ark. Hist. Quar.*, vol. 4, no. 3 (1945), 226–31. Three trips of Fr. Gerstäcker through Arkansas between 1838 and 1841 as recorded in his writings.

CG348 Prahl, Augustus J. "America in the Works of Gerstäcker." *Mod. Lang. Quar.*, vol. 4 (1943), 213–24.

CG349 Prahl, Augustus J. "Friedrich Gerstäcker, the Frontier Novelist." *Ark. Hist. Quar.*, vol. 14 (1955), 43–50.

CG350 Schutz, H. "Friedrich Gerstäcker's Image of the German Immigrant in America." *German-Amer. Studies*, vol. 5 (1972), 98–116.

CG351 Thomas, J. Wesley. "William Gilmore Simms' *Helen Halsey* as the Source for Gerstäcker's Germelshausen." *Monatshefte*, vol. 45 (1953), 141–44.

CG352 Van de Luyster, Nelson. "Gerstäcker's Novels about Emigrants to America." *Amer.-German Rev.*, vol. 20, no. 5 (1954), 22–23, 36.

GOETHE, JOHANN WOLFGANG VON

CG353 Arndt, Karl J. R. "The Harmony Society and Wilhelm Meisters Wanderjahre." *Compar. Lit.*, vol. 10 (1958), 193–202. Goethe's interest in the Harmonists between 1821 and 1829.

CG354 Baumann, Walter. "Goethe und Amerika." *Jahrbuch für internationale Germanistik*, vol. 2, no. 3 (1976), 187–92.

CG355 Edinger, Dora. "Children of Goethe's Friends in America." *Amer.-German Rev.*, vol. 16, no. 2 (1949), 24–26, 36.

CG356 Feuerle, Lois M. "Goethe's *Wilhelm Meisters Wanderjahre*: A Document in the History of Utopian Thought." Diss., Kansas, 1970.

CG357 Franck, Wolf. "Goethe for America." *Amer. Scholar*, vol. 20, no. 2 (1951), 206–14. G.'s interest in America and his American visitors.

CG358 Hammer, Carl, Jr. "Goethe, Prevost and Louisiana." *Mod. Lang. Quar.*, vol. 16 (1955), 332–38. G.'s interest in Louisiana aroused by Prevost's *Manon Lescaut*.

CG359 Lange, Victor. "Goethes Amerikabild: Wirklichkeit und Vision." In: *Amerika in der deutschen Literatur; Neue Welt, Nordamerika, USA. Wolfgang Paulsen zum 65. Geburtstag*. Ed. S. Bauschinger et al. Stuttgart: Reclam, 1975, p.63–74.

CG360 Long, Orie W. "Goethe's American Visitors." *Amer.-German Rev.*, vol. 15 (1949), 24–28.

CG361 Müller-Seidel, Walter. "Auswanderungen in Goethes dichterische Welt: Zur Geschichte einer sozialen Frage." *Jahrbuch des Wiener Goethe-Vereins*, vols. 81–83 (1977–1979), 159–83.

CG362 Niers, Gerd. "Einige Bemerkungen zu Goethes Amerika-Bild in den beiden Wilhelm-Meister-Romanen." *Jour. of German-Amer. Studies*, vol. 14 (1979), 46–58.

CG363 Pfund, Harry W. "'Amerika, du hast es besser:' The Main Aspects of Goethe's Interest in America." *German Soc. of Pennsylvania. Yearbook*, vol. 1 (1950), 33–43.

CG364 Remak, Henry H. H. "Amerikanischer Geist in Goethes 'Wilhelm Meister'." In: *Festschrift für Werner Neuse*. Berlin: Verlag die Diagonale, 1967–1968, p.34–43.

CG365 Riley, Thomas A. "Goethe and Parker Cleaveland." *PMLA*, vol. 67, no. 4 (1952), 350–74. Cleaveland, 1780–1858, mineralogist, geologist, and professor at Bowdoin College, highly esteemed by Goethe.

CG366 Schultz, Arthur R. "Goethe and the Literature of Travel." *Jour. of Eng. and Germanic Philology*, vol. 48, no. 4 (1949), 445–68. Incl. Goethe's knowledge of books dealing with America.

CG367 Sell, Friedrich C. "American Influences upon Goethe." *Amer.-German Rev.*, vol. 9, no. 4 (1943), 15–17.

CG368 Sühnel, Rudolf. "Amerika aus Goethes Sicht—heute." In: *Geschichte und Gesellschaft in der amerikanischen Literatur*. Ed. Karl Schubert and Ursula Müller-Richter. Heidelberg: Quelle & Meyer, 1975, p.175–87.

CG369 Urzidil, Johannes. *Das Glück der Gegenwart: Goethes Amerikabild*. Zürich: Artemis, 1958. 58p. Rev. by D. Cunz, *Books Abroad*, vol. 33 (1959), 58; H. W. Pfund, *Amer.-German Rev.*, vol. 26 (1960), no. 4, 39.

CG370 Wadepuhl, Walter. "Goethe's Interest in America." *Amer.-German Rev.*, vol. 15, no. 6 (1949), 29–32. G. "had an understanding knowledge of America" and a prophetic eye for its future greatness.

GRASS, GÜNTER

CG371 Stone, Edward. "The *Tin Drum* and *Moby-Dick*." *Melville Soc. Extracts*, vol. 33 (1978), 22–23.

GRIMM, HERMAN

CG372 Kreuzer, Helmut. "Ralph Waldo Emerson und Herman Grimm: Zur Rezeption des Amerikaners in Deutschland und zum Amerikabild in der deutschen Literatur." In: *Formen realistischer Erzählkunst: Festschrift für Charlotte Jolles*. Ed. Jörg Thunecke. Nottingham: Sherwood, 1979, p.448–56.

CG373 Kreuzer, Helmut. "Ralph Waldo Emerson, Herman Grimm and the Image of the American in German Literature." *Forum* (Houston), vol. 14, no. 1 (1976), 15–23.

GRIMMELSHAUSEN, HANS JAKOB CHRISTOFFEL VON

CG374 Bender, Elizabeth. "Grimmelshausen and the Hutterites." *Mennonite Life*, vol. 18, no. 4 (October 1963), 187–89.

CG375 Schulz-Behrend, George. "Der englisch-redende Simplicissimus." *Argenis*, vol. 1 (1977), 41–61.

CG376 Zieglschmid, A. J. F. "Die ungarischen Wiedertäufer bei Grimmelshausen." *Zeitschrift für Kirchengeschichte*, vol. 59, nos. 3–4 (1948), 352–87.

HANDKE, PETER

CG377 Mauranges, Jean-Paul. "Peter Handke, *Der kurze Brief zum langen Abschied*: Amérique et classicisme, deux images compatibles." *Austriaca*, vol. 5, no. 9 (1979), 29–49.

CG378 Nägele, Rainer. "Amerika als Fiktion und Wirklichkeit in Peter Handke's Roman *Der kurze Brief zum langen Abschied*." In: *Die USA und Deutschland: Wechselseitige Spiegelungen in der Literatur der Gegenwart...8. Amherster Kolloquium zur modernen deutschen Literatur*. Ed. Wolfgang Paulsen. Bern: Francke, 1976, p.110–15.

HAUPTMANN, GERHART

CG379 Muller, Siegfried H. "Gerhart Hauptmann's Relation to American Literature and His Concept of America." *Monatshefte*, vol. 44 (1952), no. 7, 333–39.

HEINE, HEINRICH

CG380 Hermand, Jost. "'Auf andere Art so grosse Hoffnung': Heine und die USA." In: *Amerika in der deutschen Literatur: Neue Welt, Nordamerika, USA. Wolfgang Paulsen zum 65. Geburtstag.* Ed. S. Bauschinger et al. Stuttgart: Reclam, 1975, p.81–92.

CG381 Jaffe, Adrian. "Uncle Tom in the Penal Colony: Heine's View of Uncle Tom's Cabin." *Amer.-German Rev.*, vol. 19, no. 3 (1953), 5–6. H. reacts rather to the religious than to the social implication of Mrs. Stowe's novel.

HEINSE, JOHANN JAKOB WILHELM

CG382 Von Hofe, Harold. "Heinse, America, and Utopianism." *PMLA*, vol. 72 (1957), 390–402.

HERDER, JOHANN GOTTFRIED

CG383 "Herder über Franklin." *Amer.-German Rev.*, vol. 33 (1967), no. 6, 21. Quotation from Herder in appreciation of Franklin's autobiography.

CG384 Schmitt, Albert R. *Herder und Amerika.* Studies in German Literature, vol. 10. The Hague: Mouton, 1967. 186p. Rev. by H. J. Vaemrich, *Germanic Rev.*, vol. 43, no. 4 (1968), 286–87. Cf. "Herder und Amerika." Diss., Univ. of Pennsylvania, 1962.

HERMLIN, STEPHAN

CG385 Durzak, Manfred. "Ambrose Bierce und Stephan Hermlin: Zur Rezeption der amerikanischen Short Story in Deutschland." *Arcadia*, vol. 11 (1976), 38–66.

HESSE, HERMANN

CG386 Field, G. Wallis. "Hermann Hesse as Critic of English and American Literature." *Monatshefte* vol. 53 (1961), 147–58. Hesse as reviewer of English and American authors.

HOFMANNSTHAL, HUGO VON

CG387 Fiedler, L. M. "Hugo von Hofmannsthal und die Weltliteratur." *Acta Litteraria Academiae Scientiarum Hungaricae (Budapest)*, vol. 18 (1976), 85–99.

CG388 Lewis, Hanna Ballin. "English and American Influence on Hugo von Hofmannsthal." Diss., Rice Univ., 1964. 232p.

CG389 Lewis, Hanna Ballin. "Hofmannsthal and America." In: *Studies in German: In Memory of Andrew Louis.* Ed. Robert L. Kahn. Rice Univ. Studies, vol. 55, no. 3. Houston: Rice Univ., 1969, p.131–41.

HUMBOLDT, ALEXANDER VON

CG390 de Terra, Helmut. "Motives and Consequences of Alexander von Humboldt's Visit to the United States, 1804." *Procs. of the Amer. Philos. Soc.*, vol. 104, no. 3 (15 June 1960), 314–16.

CG391 Meyer-Abich, Adolph. "Humboldt's Exploration in the American Tropics." *Texas Quar.*, vol. 1 (1958), 125–35. Expeditions in North and South America; his visit with Jefferson.

CG392 Meyer-Abich, Adolph. "Die Neue Welt in der Perspektive Alexander von Humboldts." *Erdkunde*, vol. 13 (1959), 395–411.

CG393 Pfeiffer, Gottfried. "Alexander von Humboldts Entwicklungsjahre und amerikanische Reise." *Ruperto Carolo Mitteilungen der Vereinigung der Freunde der Studentenschaft der Universität Heidelberg*, 1945, 128–50.

JACOBI, FRIEDRICH HEINRICH

CG394 Von Hofe, Harold. "Jacobi, Wieland and the New World." *Monatshefte*, vol. 49 (1957), 187–92. Knowledge and use of Robertson's *History of America*.

JOHST, HANS

CG395 Hermann, Helmut G. "Ausgebeutete Amerika-Romantik: Hans Johst und der 'Parteigenosse' Thomas Paine." In: *Amerika in der deutschen Literatur: Neue Welt, Nordamerika, USA. Wolfgang Paulsen zum 65. Geburtstag.* Ed. S. Bauschinger et al. Stuttgart: Reclam, 1975, p.315–22.

JOHNSON, UWE

CG396 Kurz, Paul K. "Deutschstunde in New York: Uwe Johnsons Roman *Jahrestage.*" *Stimmen der Zeit*, vol. 187 (1971), 191–99.

CG397 Lennox, Sara. "Die *New York Times* in Johnsons *Jahrestagen.*" In: *Die USA und Deutschland: Wechselseitige Spiegelungen in der Literatur der Gegenwart. Zum zweihundertjährigen Beste-*

hen der Vereinigten Staaten am 4. Juli 1976. 8. Amherster Kolloquium zur modernen deutschen Literatur. Ed. Wolfgang Paulsen. Bern: Francke, 1976, p.103–09.

CG398 Lennox, Sara. "Yoknapatawpha to Jerichow, Uwe Johnson's Appropriation of William Faulkner." *Arcadia*, vol. 14 (1979), 160–76.

CG399 Post-Adams, Rae. "Von Mecklenburg bis Manhatten: Amerikabilder in den *Jahrestagen*." *Text und Kritik*, vol. 65–66 (1980), 120–26.

JUNG, JOHANN HEINRICH ("JUNG-STILLING")

CG400 Wust, Klaus. "Jung-Stilling and the American Backwoods." *The Report (Soc. for the Hist. of the Germans in Maryland)*, vol. 34 (1970), 35–39.

JÜNGER, ERNST

CG401 Peters, H. F. "Ernst Jünger's Concern with E. A. Poe." *Compar. Lit.*, vol. 10 (1958), 144–49.

KAFKA, FRANZ

CG402 David, Claude. "L'Amérique de Franz Kafka." In: *Dialog: Literatur und Literaturwissenschaft im Zeichen deutsch–französischer Begegnung. Festgabe für Josef Kunz*. Ed. Rainer Schönhaar. Berlin: E. Schmidt, 1973, p.194–204.

CG403 Greenberg, Martin. "Kafka's Amerika." *Salmagundi*, vol. 1, no. 3 (1966), 74–84.

CG404 Heuer, Helmut. "Die Amerikavision bei William Blake und Franz Kafka." Diss., München, 1960.

CG405 Jahn, Wolfgang. "Kafka's Handschrift zum Verschollenen (Amerika)." *Jahrbuch der deut. Schillergesellschaft*, vol. 9 (1965), 541–42.

CG406 Jahn, Wolfgang. *Kafka's Roman "Der Verschollene" ("Amerika")*. Stuttgart: Metzler, 1965. 158p. Rev. by E. E. Reed, *German Quar.*, vol. 40 (1967), 139–40; C. B. Bedwell, *Monatshefte*, vol. 59 (1967), 276–77. Includes suggestions as to Kafka's source in a travel account.

CG407 Loos, Gerhard. *Franz Kafka und Amerika*. Frankfurt a. M.: Vittorio Klostermann, 1968. 90p.

CG408 Lyons, Nathan. "Kafka and Poe—and Hope." *Minn. Rev.*, vol. 5 (May–July 1965), 158–68.

CG409 Moseley, Edwin M. "The American Dream Become Nightmare: Franz Kafka and Others." In: *Czechoslovakia Past and Present*. Vol. II. *Essays on the Arts and Sciences*. Ed. Miloslav Rechcigl, Jr. The Hague: Mouton, 1968 (i.e., 1970), p.1012–21.

CG410 Northey, Anthony D. "Franz Kafkas Verbindung zu Amerika." In: *Franz Kafka: Eine Aufsatzsammlung nach einem Symposium in Philadelphia*. Ed. Maria Luise Caputo-Mayr. Berlin: Agora, 1978, p.5–16.

CG411 Ruland, Richard E. "A View from Back Home: Kafka's *Amerika*." *Amer. Quar.*, vol. 13 (1961), 33–42. The immigrant theme in K.'s novel.

CG412 Thalman, Jörg. *Wege zu Kafka. Eine Interpretation des Amerikaromans*. Frauenfeld: Huber, 1966. 298p.

CG413 Uyttersprot, H. "Franz Kafka's *Der Verschollene (Amerika)*." *Merlyn*, vol. 3 (1965), 409–24.

CG414 Wirkner, Alfred. *Kafka und die Aussenwelt: Quellenstudien zum Amerika-Fragment. Mit einem Anhang: Der Reisbericht des Dr. Soukup*. Stuttgart: Klett, 1976. 113p.

KAISER, GEORG

CG415 Kauf, Robert. "Georg Kaiser, der Amerikanismus, and America." In: *Georg Kaiser: Eine Aufsatzsammlung nach einem Symposium in Edmonton, Kanada*. Berlin: Agora, 1980, p.251–62.

KERR, ALFRED

CG416 Loram, Ian C. "Alfred Kerr's America." *German Quar.*, vol. 38 (1965), 164–71.

KIPPHARDT, HEINAR

CG417 Gong, Alfred. "The Case of J. Robert Oppenheimer." *Amer.-German Rev.*, vol. 31, no. 5 (1965), 27–28, 39.

KÜRNBERGER, FERDINAND

CG418 Kürnberger, Ferdinand. *Der Amerikamüde: Amerikanisches Kulturbild*. Ed. Friedemann Beyer. Weimar: Kiepenheuer, 1973. Repr.

CG419 Sammons, Jeffrey L. "The Lorenzo Da Ponte Episode in Ferdinand Kürnberger's *Der Amerika-Müde*." *Jour. of German-Amer. Studies*, vol. 15 (1980), 48–56.

CG420 Steinlein, Rüdiger. "Ferdinand Kürnbergers *Der Amerikamüde*: Ein 'amerikanisches Kulturbild' als Entwurf einer negativen Utopie." In: *Amerika in der deutschen Literatur: Neue Welt, Nordamerika, USA. Wolfgang Paulsen zum 65. Geburtstag.* Ed. S. Bauschinger et al. Stuttgart: Reclam, 1975, p.154–77.

KUNERT, GÜNTER

CG421 Osterle, Heinz D. "Denkbilder über die USA: Günter Kunert's Der andere Planet." *Basis. Jahrbuch für deutsche Gegenwartsliteratur*, vol. 7 (1977), 137–55.

LA ROCHE, SOPHIE

CG422 Lange, Victor. "Visitors to Lake Oneida: An Account of the Background of Sophie von La Roche's Novel, *Erscheinungen am See Oneida.*" *Symposium*, vol. 2 (1948), 48–78. Fritz von La Roche, Sophie's eldest son, spent some time in the U.S. as a soldier and provided material for the novel.

LENAU, NIKOLAUS

CG423 Arndt, Karl J. R. "The Effect of America on Lenau's Life and Work." *Germanic Rev.*, vol. 33 (1958), 125–42. With particular reference to his contacts with the Harmonists at Economy, Pa.

CG424 Berges, Ruth. "Lenau's Quest in America." *Amer.-German Rev.*, vol. 28, no. 4 (1961–1962), 14–17.

CG425 Blanchard, Homer. "Lenau's Ohio Venture." *Ohio Hist.*, vol. 78 (1969), 237–51.

CG426 Durzak, Manfred. "Nach Amerika. Gerstäckers Widerlegung der Lenau-Legende." In: *Amerika in der deutschen Literatur: Neue Welt—Nordamerika—USA.* Ed. S. Bauschinger. Stuttgart: Reclam, 1975, p.135–53.

CG427 Theiner, Paul. "Lenau, Sealsfield and the American Experience." In: *Actes du VIIe congrés de l'Association Internat. de Littérature Comparee/Procs., 7th Congress of the Internat. Comp. Lit. Assoc., I. Littératures amêricaines...* Ed. Milan V. Dimić and J. Ferraté. Stuttgart: Bieber, 1979, p.437–41.

LICHTENBERG, GEORG CHRISTOPH

CG428 Von Hofe, Harold. "Lichtenberg and America." In: *Vistas and Vectors*. Ed. Lee B. Jennings and G. Schulz-Behrend. Austin: Dept. of Germanic Languages, Univ. of Texas, 1977, p.114–19.

MACKAY, JOHN HENRY

CG429 Riley, Thomas A. "New England Anarchism in Germany." *New England Quar.*, vol. 18 (1945), 25–38. Benjamin Tucker's influence on John Henry Mackay.

MANN, THOMAS

CG430 Briner, Andres. "Conrad Beissel and Thomas Mann." *Amer.-German Rev.*, vol. 26, no. 2 (1959), 24–25, 38. Mann's character in *Dr. Faustus* was a Pennsylvania-German religious leader of the 18th century.

CG431 Briner, Andres. "Wahrheit und Dichtung um J. C. Beissel: Studie um eine Gestalt in Thomas Manns 'Dr. Faustus'." *Schweizerische Musikzeitung*, no. 10 (October 1958), 365–69.

CG432 Frey, Erich A. "An American Prototype in Thomas Mann's Königliche Hoheit." *Ky. For. Lang. Quar.*, vol. 13 (1966), 125–29.

CG433 Haile, H. G. "Thomas Mann und der Anglizismus." *Monatshefte*, vol. 51 (1959), 263–69. A vindication of Mann's Anglicisms; not slips but consciously used for effect.

CG434 Leppmann, Wolfgang. "Der Amerikaner im Werke Thomas Manns." *German Quar.*, vol. 38 (1965), 619–29.

CG435 Politzer, Heinz. "America in the Later Writings of Thomas Mann." *Mod. Lang. Forum*, vol. 37 (1952), 91–100. The linguistic and cultural influence of America, espec. with respect to *Dr. Faustus.*

CG436 Riley, Anthony W. "Notes on Thomas Mann and English and American Literature." *Compar. Lit.*, vol. 17 (1965), 57–72.

CG437 Singer, Irving. "Death in Venice: Visconti and Mann." *Mod. Lang. Notes*, vol. 91 (1976), 1348–59.

CG438 Suhl, Abraham. "Anglicismen in Thomas Manns Doktor Faustus." *Monatshefte für deutschen Unterricht*, vol. 40 (1948), 391–97.

MAY, KARL

CG439 Cracroft, Richard H. "The American West of Karl May." *Amer. Quar.*, vol. 19 (Summer 1967), 249–58.

CG440 Hohendahl, Peter U. "Von der Rothaut zum Edelmenschen: Karl Mays Amerikaromane." In: *Amerika in der deutschen Literatur: Neue Welt, Nordamerika, U.S.A. Wolfgang Paulsen zum 65. Geburtstag.* Ed. S. Bauschinger et al. Stuttgart: Reclam, 1975, p.229–45.

CG441 Lohr, Otto. "Stimmt Karl Mays Amerikabild?" *Mitteilungen des Instituts für Auslandsbeziehungen*, vol. 7 (1958), 274–75.

CG442 Mann, Klaus. "Cowboy Mentor of the Führer." *Living Age*, vol. 352 (November 1940), 221. Concerning Karl May.

CG443 Poppe, Werner. "'Winnetou': Ein Name und seine Quellen." *Jahrbuch der Karl May Gesellschaft 1972/73* (1972), 248–53.

CG444 Raddatz, Werner. *Das abenteuerliche Leben Karl Mays.* Gütersloh: Mohn, 1965.

CG445 Schmidt, Arno. *Sitara und der Weg dorthin, eine Studie über Wesen, Werk und Wirkung Karl Mays.* Frankfurt: S. Fischer, 1969.

CG446 Schmiedt, Helmut. *Karl May. Studien zu Leben, Werk und Wirkung eines Erfolgsschriftstellers.* Königstein/Ts: Hain, 1979. 267p. Rev. by J. L. Sammons, *German Quar.*, vol. 53, no. 4 (November 1980), 486–88.

CG447 Stadler, Ernst A. "Karl May: The Wild West under the German Umlaut." *Bull., Mo. Hist. Soc.*, vol. 21, no. 4, part 1 (1965), 295–307.

CG448 Stolte, Heinz. "Die Reise ins Innere: Dichtung und Wahrheit in den Reiseerzählungen Karl Mays." *Jahrbuch der Karl May Gesellschaft 1975*, 11–33.

MÖLLHAUSEN, BALDUIN

CG449 Miller, David H. "A Prussian on the Plains: Balduin Möllhausen's Impressions." *Great Plains Journal*, vol. 12 (Spring 1973), 175–93.

CG450 Möllhausen, Heinrich Balduin. "Over the Santa Fe Trail through Kansas in 1858." Trans. by J. Anthony Burzle. Ed. and Annotated by Robert Taft. *Kans. Hist. Quar.*, vol. 16 (1948), 337–80.

NIETZSCHE, FRIEDRICH

CG451 Seidler, Ingo. "'Den Blick fernhin auf Nordamerika richten': Zur Amerikaperspektive Nietzsches." In: *Amerika in der deutschen Literatur: Neue Welt, Nordamerika, USA. Wolfgang Paulsen zum 65. Geburtstag.* Ed. S. Bauschinger et al. Stuttgart: Reclam, 1975, p.218–28.

NOSSACK, HANS ERICH

CG452 Mueller, G. H. S. "Hans Erich Nossack and Sherwood Anderson's Winesburg, Ohio." *The Winesburg Eagle: The Official Publ. of the Sherwood Anderson Soc.*, vol. 3, no. 1 (1977), 7.

PAQUET, ALFONS

CG453 Weisstein, Ulrich. "Keine amerikanische Tragödie: Alfons Paquets dramatischer Roman Fahnen, Text, Inszenierung und Kritik." In: *Amerika in der deutschen Literatur: Neue Welt, Nordamerika, U.S.A. Wolfgang Paulsen zum 65 Geburtstag.* Ed. S. Bauschinger. Stuttgart: Reclam, 1975, p.272–93.

PLENZDORF, ULRICH

CG454 Langenbruch, Theodor. "Goethe and Salinger as Models for Ulrich Plenzdorf's Novel *Die neuen Leiden des jungen W.*" *Perspectives on Contemporary Literature*, vol. 2, no. 2 (1976), 60–70.

CG455 Tabah, Mireille. "Die neuen Leiden des jungen W. Ulrich Plenzdorf entre Goethe et Salinger." *Études Germaniques*, vol. 30 (1975), 335–44.

REMARQUE, ERICH MARIA

CG456 Gross, Ingrid E. "Remarque's *Weltanschauung.* A Study in Fictional Dualism." Diss., Louisiana State Univ., 1980–1981.

RILKE, RAINER MARIA

CG457 Jonas, Klaus W. "Rilke and America." *Etudes Germaniques*, vol. 9 (1954), 55–59. See also *German Life and Letters*, vol. 8 (1954), 45–49.

CG458 Wojcik, Jan. "Emerson and Rilke: A Significant Influence?" *Mod. Lang. Notes*, vol. 91 (1976), 565–74.

ROTH, JOSEPH

CG459 Rollka, Bodo. "Joseph Roths Amerikabild." *Literatur und Kritik*, vol. 70 (1972), 590–98.

RUPPIUS, OTTO

CG460 Graewert, Theodor. "Otto Ruppius und der Amerikaroman im 19. Jahrhundert." Diss., Jena, 1935.

CG461 Schrader, Frederick Franklin, trans. "A Career in America." *Amer.-German Rev.*, vol. 9, no. 3 (February 1943), 28–33. Chapters of autobiography.

SCHILLER, JOHANN FRIEDRICH VON

CG462 Blegen, Theodore C. "A Note on Schiller's Indian Threnody." *Minn. Hist.*, vol. 39 (1965), 198–200.

CG463 Jantz, Harold. "Schiller's 'Indian Threnody.'" In: *Schiller 1759/1959*. Urbana: Univ. of Illinois Pr., 1959, p.58–75.

CG464 Jantz, Harold. "William Tell and the American Revolution." In: *A Schiller Symposium, In Observance of the Bicentenary of Schiller's Birth. Essays by Harold Jantz and others.* Ed. A. Leslie Willson. Austin: Dept. of Germanic Languages, Univ. of Texas, 1960, p.65–81.

CG465 Stadler, Gabrielle. *Dichterverehrung und national Repräsentanz im literarischen Leben des 19. Jahrhunderts: Studien zur Geschichte der Schillervereine im 19. Jahrhundert.* München: n.p., 1977. 298p.

SCHLAF, JOHANNES

CG466 Lewis, Ward B. "The New World and the Yankee: Emigration as a Theme in the Works of Johannes Schlaf." *German-Amer. Studies*, vol. 6 (1973), 3–20. S. employs the stereotypes common to his time; no reflection of first-hand experience.

CG467 Lewis, Ward B. "Walt Whitman: Johannes Schlaf's 'Neuer Mensch'." *Revue de Littérature Comparée*, vol. 47 (1973), 596–611.

SCHLEGEL, AUGUST WILHELM VON

CG468 Von Hofe, Harold. "August Wilhelm Schlegel and the New World." *Germanic Rev.*, vol. 35 (1960), 279–87.

CG469 Von Hofe, Harold. "August Wilhelm Schlegel's American Emigration Plans. Biographical-Literary Notes." In: *Wert und Wort. Festschrift für Else M. Fleissner.* Aurora, N.Y.: Wells College, ca. 1965, p.22–31.

SCHLEGEL, FRIEDRICH VON

CG470 Von Hofe, Harold. "Friedrich Schlegel and the New World." *PMLA*, vol. 76 (1961) 63–67.

STIFTER, ADALBERT

CG471 Browning, Barton W. "Cooper's Influence on Stifter: Fact or Scholarly Myth?" *Mod. Lang. Notes*, vol. 89 (1974), 821–28.

WASSERMANN, JAKOB

CG472 Blankenagel, John C. "Jakob Wassermann's Views of America." *German Quar.*, vol. 27 (1954), 51–57. Identifies certain biases and distortions in W.'s view of American culture.

WEDEKIND, FRANK

CG473 Gittleman, Sol. "Frank Wedekind's Image of America." *German Quar.*, vol. 39 (1966), 570–80.

CG474 Seidlin, Oskar. "Frank Wedekind's German-American Parents." *Amer.-German Rev.*, vol. 12, no. 6 (1946), 24–26.

ZSCHOKKE, HEINRICH

CG475 Albrecht, Erich. "Heinrich Zschokke's Version of the Founding of Maryland." *Amer.-German Rev.*, vol. 8 (1942), 15–16, 34.

CG476 Kochert, Sr. Laurene Marie. "The Concept of America in the Works of Heinrich Zschokke." M. A. thesis, Catholic Univ. of America, 1947.

CG477 Oppel, Horst. "Die deutsche Siedlung in Louisiana im Spiegel des Amerika-Romanes der Goethezeit: Heinrich Zschokkes 'Prinzessin von Wolfenbüttel'." In: *Studies in German Literature.* Ed. Carl J. Hammer, Jr. Baton Rouge: Louisiana St. Univ. Pr., 1963, p.18–38. See also *Die Wissenschaft von deutscher Sprache...Festschrift für Friedr. Maurer.* Stuttgart, 1963, p.347–60.

ZUCKMAYER, CARL

CG478 Kvam, Wayne. "Zuckmayer, Hilpert and Hemingway." *PMLA*, vol. 91 (1976), 194–205.

CG479 Mews, Siegfried. "From Karl May to Horace A. W. Tabor: Carl Zuckmayer's View of America." *Mosaic*, vol. 6, no. 2 (1973), 125–42.

CG480 Steiner, Pauline, and Horst Frenz. "Anderson and Stalling's *What Price Glory?* and Carl Zuckmayer's *Rivalen.*" *German Quar.*, vol. 20 (1947), 239–52.

CH
Emigré Authors/Refugees from Nazi Germany

CH1 Apsler, Alfred. "Writers from Across the Sea." *Eng. Jour.*, vol. 9 (1947), 19–24.

CH2 Arnold, Heinz L., ed. *Deutsche Literatur im Exil 1933–1945. I. Dokumente. II. Materialien.* Frankfurt: Athenäum Fischer Taschenbuch Vlg. 1974. 312, 385p.

CH3 Arnold, Heinz L., and Hans-Albrecht Walter. "Die Exil-Literatur und ihre Erforschung: Ein Gespräch." *Akzente*, vol. 20 (1973), 481–508.

CH4 Ash, Adrienne. "German Poetry in Exile: 1933–1945." Diss., Texas, 1972.

CH5 Bahr, Erhard. "Der Schriftstellerkongress 1943 an der Universität von Kalifornien." In: *Deutsche Exilliteratur seit 1933. Bd. 1: Kalifornien.* Ed. J. M. Spalek and J. Strelka. Bern: Francke, 1976, p.40–61.

CH6 Bander, Carol. J. "Exilliteratur und Exil im Spiegel der deutschsprachigen Presse der Westküste: 1933–1949." In: *Deutsch Exilliteratur seit 1933. Bd. 1: Kalifornien.* Ed. J. M. Spalek and J. Strelka. Bern: Francke, 1976, p.195–213.

CH7 Bander, Carol J. "The Reception of Exiled German Writers in the Nazi and Conservative German Press of California, 1933–1950." Diss., Univ. of Southern California, 1973.

CH8 Benecke, Hans. *Deutsche Literatur im Exil 1933–1945.* Frankfurt: n.p., 1962.

CH9 Bentley, Eric Russell. "German Writers in Exile, 1933–1943." *Books Abroad*, vol. 17 (1943), 313–17.

CH10 Berendsohn, Walter A. "Die deutsche Literatur der Flüchtlinge aus dem Dritten Reich und ihre Hintergründe." *Colloquia Germanica*, vol. 5 (1971), 1–156.

CH11 Berendsohn, Walter A. "Emigrantenliteratur 1933–1947." In: *Reallexikon der deutschen Lieraturgeschichte.* Ed. W. Kohlschmidt and W. Mohr. Berlin: W. de Gruyter, 1958. Vol. 1, p.336–43. With useful bibliographical notes: lists of works, journals, secondary studies.

CH12 Berendsohn, Walter A. *Die humanistische Front. Teil I. Von 1933 bis zum Kriegsausbruch 1939.* Zürich: Europa Vlg., 1946.

CH13 Berendsohn, Walter A. *Die humanistische Front. Einführung in die deutsche Emigranten-Literatur. Teil II. Vom Kriegsausbruch 1939 bis Ende 1946.* First publ. of a MS. completed in 1949 and held in possession of the Deutsche Bibliothek, Frankfurt a. M., Worms: G. Heintz, 1976. 236p. Rev. by W. D. Elfe, *German Quar.*, vol. 51 (1978), 248–51.

CH14 Berglund, Gisela. *Deutsche Opposition gegen Hitler in Presse und Roman des Exils. Eine Darstellung und ein Vergleich mit der historischen Wirklichkeit.* Stockholm: Almquist & Wiksell, 1972. 410p.

CH15 *Bericht I*. Ed. Helmut Müssener. Stockholmer Koordinationsstelle zur Erforschung der deutschsprachigen Exil-Literatur. Stockholm: Deutsches Institut der Universität Stockholm, 1970.

CH16 *Bericht II*. Stockholmer Koordinationsstelle zur Erforschung der deutschsprachigen Exil-Literatur. Stockholm: hrsg. Deutsches Institut der Universität Stockholm, 1971.

CH17 Berthold, Werner. "Exilliteratur der Jahre 1933–1945 in der Deutschen Bibliothek." *Jahrbuch für Internat. Germanistik*, vol. 6, no. 2 (1974), 108–24.

CH18 Berthold, Werner. *Exil-Literatur 1933–1945.* Frankfurt: Weisbecker, 1966. 324p. Ausstellung der Deutschen Bibliothek, Frankfurt a. M., Mai bis August 1965. Exhibit and Catalogue.

CH19 Berthold, Werner. "Die Sondersammlung Exil-Literatur 1933–1945." In: *Die Deutsche Bibliothek. Festgabe für Hanns W. Eppelsheimer zum 75. Geburtstag.* Ed. Kurt Köster. Frankfurt: Klostermann, 1966, p.136–48.

CH20 Berthold, Werner, and Christa Wilhelmi, eds. *Exil-Literatur 1933–1945.* Frankfurt a. M.: n.p., 1965.

CH21 Bilke, Jörg Bernhard. "Exilliteratur und DDR—Germanistik: Zur Ideologiekritik 'parteilicher' Wissenschaft." *Deutsche Studien*, vol. 13 (1975), 277–92.

CH22 "Books the Nazis Banned." *N.Y. Public Library Bull.*, vol. 46 (1942), 945–48.

CH23 Brenner, Hildegard. "Deutsche Literatur im Exil 1933–1947." In: *Handbuch der deutschen Gegenwartsliteratur.* Ed. Hermann Kunisch. München: n.p., 1965, p.677–94.

CH24 Breycha-Vauthier, A. C. *Die Zeitschriften der österreichischen Emigration, 1934–1946.* Wien: Österreichische Nationalbibliothek, 1960. 28p. Incl. several Austro-American publications.

CH25 Broerman, Bruce Martin. "The German Historical Novel in Exile after 1933." Diss., SUNY-Albany, 1975–1976.

CH26 Bruhns, Maike. "Das Amerika-Bild deutscher Emigranten." Diss., Hamburg, 1971.

CH27 Carpenter, Charles Whitney. "Exiled German Writers in America 1932–50." M. A. Thesis, Univ. of Southern California, 1952.

CH28 Cazden, Robert E. *German Exile Literature in America, 1933–1950: A History of the Free German Press and Book Trade.* Chicago: Amer. Library Assoc., 1970. 250p. Rev. by F. Reichmann, *Library Quar.*, vol. 41, no. 1 (January 1971), 69–70; E. F. Ritter, *German-Amer. Studies* vol. 5 (1972), 179–80; Jos. P. Strelka, *Mod. Lang. Jour.*, vol. 57 (1973), 149. Bibliographical reference work on German-language publishing, importing and distribution of German writing in the U.S.

CH29 Cazden, Robert E. "Plight of the Emigré Author in America." In: *German Exile Literature in America, 1933–1950.* Chicago: Amer. Library Assoc., 1970, p.137–62.

CH30 Cazden, Robert E. "Retail Distributors of Free German Publications in the United States, 1933–1950." In: *German Exile Literature in America, 1933–1950.* Chicago: Amer. Library Assoc., 1970, Appendix, p.175–177.

CH31 Dahlke, Hans. *Geschichtsroman und Literaturkritik im Exil.* Berlin, Weimar: Aufbau-Vlg., 1976. 452p. Rev. by Ehrhard Bahr, *German Quar.*, vol. 51 no. 4 (November 1978), 559–62.

CH32 Deutsche Bibliothek, Frankfurt a. M. *Exil-Literatur 1933–1945.* Ed. Kurt Köster. Frankfurt: Deutsche Bibliothek, 1965. 364p. 2nd enlarged and revised ed., Frankfurt: Buchhändler Vereinigung, 1966. 324p. 3rd ed. Frankfurt, 1967. 352p. Exhibition of works in the Deutsche Bibliothek, May–August 1965.

CH33 "Die deutsche Emigration nach 1933: Ihr Einfluss auf das amerikanische Geistesleben." *Frankfurter Allgemeine Zeitung*, 27 May 1964.

CH34 Dickson, Paul. "Das Amerikabild in der deutschen Emigranten-Literatur seit 1933." Diss., München, 1951.

CH35 Durzak, Manfred. "Deutschsprachige Exilliteratur: Vom moralischen Zeugnis zum literarischen Dokument." In: *Die deutsche Exilliteratur 1933–1945.* Stuttgart: Reclam, 1973, p.9–26.

CH36 Durzak, Manfred. "Das Elend der Exilliteratur-Forschung." *Akzente*, vol. 21 (1974), 186–88.

CH37 Durzak, Manfred. "Die Exilsituation und USA." In: *Die deutsche Exilliteratur 1933–1945.* Stuttgart: Reclam, 1973, p.145–58.

CH38 Durzak, Manfred. "Laokoons Söhne: Zur Sprachproblematik im Exil." *Akzente*, vol. 21 (1974), 54–63.

CH39 Durzak, Manfred. "Literarische Diaspora: Stationen des Exils." In: *Die deutsche Exilliteratur 1933–1945.* Stuttgart: Reclam, 1973, p.40–55.

CH40 Durzak, Manfred, ed. *Die deutsche Exilliteratur 1933–1945.* Stuttgart: Reclam, 1973. 624p. Rev. by E. A. Frey, *German Quar.*, vol. 49, no. 4 (November 1976), 510. Consists of (1) essays on the history of exile in various countries; (2) presentation of *Exiloeuvres* from Heinrich Mann, Thomas Mann through Zuckmayer—25 prominent authors in all; and (3) bio-bibliographic data on ca. 400 authors.

CH41 Elfe, Wolfgang D. "Das Emergency Rescue Committee." In: *Deutsche Exilliterature seit 1933*. Bd. 1: *Kalifornien*. Ed. J. M. Spalek and J. Strelka. Bern: Francke, 1976.

CH42 "Emigrantenliteratur." In: *Deutsche Literatur seit 1945 in Einzeldarstellungen*. Ed. D. Weber. 2nd ed. Stuttgart: n.p., 1971.

CH43 *Exil. Literarische und Politische Texte aus dem deutschen Exil 1933-1945*. 3 Vols. Vol. 2. *Erbärmlichkeit und Grösse des Exils*. Ed. Ernst Loewy et al. Frankfurt a. M.: Fischer Taschenbuch Vlg., 1982. 467p.

CH44 *Exile Literature 1933-45*. Bad Godesberg: Inter Nationes; Köln: Verlagsgesellschaft Rudolf Müller, 1968. 73p. Report on a conference held in Luxemburg, January 1968.

CH45 Feilchenfeldt, Konrad. "Zur Erforschung der Exilliteratur: Nach Erscheinen des ersten Bandes der von John B. Spalek und Joseph Strelka herausgegebenen *Studien*." *Euphorion*, vol. 71 (1977), 406-20.

CH46 Fraser, James H. "German Exile Publishing: The Malik-Aurora Verlag of Wieland Herzfelde." *German Life and Letters*, vol. 27 (January 1974), 115-24. History of the press from founding in 1916. Moved to New York in 1939.

CH47 Frühwald, Wolfgang, and Wolfgang Schieder, eds. *Leben im Exil: Probleme der Integration deutscher Flüchtlinge im Ausland 1933 bis 1945*. Hamburg: Hoffman & Campe, 1981. 285p.

CH48 Fry, Varian. "What has Happened to Them Since: Writers I Helped Escape from France." *Publishers Weekly*, 23 June 1945, 2434-37. See also the "Reply," *ibid.*, 28 July 1945, 307.

CH49 George, Manfred. "Deutsche Schriftsteller in den U.S.A." *Neue Schweizerische Rundschau*, N.F., vol. 17 (1949-1950), 312-16.

CH50 Görlich, Ernst J. "Österreichische Dichter in angelsächsischer Emigration: mit unveröffentlichten Briefen Theodor Kramers an den Verfasser." In: *Österreich und die angelsächsische Welt. Kulturbegegnungen und Vergleiche*. Vol. 1. Ed. Otto Hietsch. Wien: Braumüller, 1961, p.197-206.

CH51 Goldschmidt Kunzer, Ruth. "Die deutsche Literatur und Kultur im Exil und die Universitäten in Kalifornien." In: *Deutsche Exilliteratur seit 1933*. Bd. 1. *Kalifornien*. Ed. J. M. Spalek and J. Strelka. Bern: Francke, 1976, p.147-67.

CH52 Green, Geoffrey Dennis. "Writers in Exile: Chapters in the Critical Examination of Literature and Society." Diss., SUNY Buffalo, 1977. 306p. One of the exiles here discussed is Erich Auerbach.

CH53 Gregor-Dellin, Martin. "Klaus Manns Exilromane." In: *Die deutsche Exilliterature 1933-1945*. Ed. M. Durzak. Stuttgart: Reclam, 1973, p.457-63.

CH54 Grossberg, Mimi. *Austrian Writers in the United States 1938-1968*. Austrian Institute and the Austrian Forum, Inc., New York, 5-26 April 1968. 27p. Catalogue of exhibit. Bio-bibliographical notes on 62 authors, poets, and writers of Austrian origin who were exiled from Hitler's Europe in the thirties and forties.

CH55 Grossberg, Mimi. *Geschick und Leistung der österreichischen literarischen Emigration von 1938 in den Vereinigten Staaten*. New York, 1967. Mimeographed.

CH56 Grossberg, Mimi. *Österreichs literarische Emigration in den Vereinigten Staaten 1938*. Wien/Frankfurt/Zürich: Europa Vlg., 1970. 65p.

CH57 Grossberg, Mimi, and Viktor Suche, eds. *Österreichische Autoren in Amerika. Geschick und Leistung der österreichischen literarischen Emigration ab 1938 in den Vereinigten Staaten*. Wien: Dokumentationsstelle für neuere Österreichischen Literatur, 1970. Rev. by J. Erhardt, *German-Amer. Studies*, vol. 5 (1972), 184-85.

CH58 Halfmann, Horst, ed. *Zeitschriften und Zeitungen des Exils 1933-1945: Bestandsverzeichnis der Deutschen Bücherei*. Leipzig: Deutsche Bücherei, 1969.

CH59 Hamburger, Michael. "Einige Bemerkungen zur Kategorie Exil-Literatur." *Literatur und Kritik*, no. 128 (1978), 481-84.

CH60 Hansen, Thomas S. "The *Deutschlandroman* in Exile: Anti-Fascist Criticism in the Political Prose of Klaus Mann, Walter Mehring, Bernard von Brentano and Gustav Regler." Diss., Harvard, 1976-1977.

CH61 Heeg, Günther. *Die Wendung zur Geschichte: Konstitutionsprobleme antifaschistischer Literatur im Exil*. Stuttgart: Metzler, 1977. 222p.

CH62 Heintz, Georg. "Deutsche Exilliteratur. Bericht über eine Tagung." *Muttersprache*, vol. 80 (1970), 171–79.

CH63 Heintz, George, ed. *Deutsches Exil 1933–1945. Eine Schriftenreihe*. Worms: Vlg. George Heintz, ca. 1972. No. 1 of the series is an *Index der "Neuen Weltbühne" 1933–1939*. 104p.

CH64 Hermand, Jost. "Schreiben in der Fremde: Gedanken zur deutschen Exilliteratur seit 1789." In: *Exil und Innere Emigration: Third Wisconsin Workshop*. Ed. Reinhold Grimm and Jost Hermand. Frankfurt a. M.: Athenäum, 1973, p.7–30.

CH65 Hoffer, Peter T. *Klaus Mann*. Boston: Twayne Publ., 1978. Rev. by Herbert Lehnert, *German Quar.*, vol. 52 (1979), 134–35.

CH66 Hohendahl, Peter U., and Egon Schwarz, eds. *Exil und Innere Emigration. II. Internationale Tagung in St. Louis*. Frankfurt: Athenäum, 1973. 170p.

CH67 Hohendahl, Peter Uwe. "Das Symposium in Stockholm über deutsche Exilliteratur." *German Quar.*, vol. 42, no. 1 (January 1970), 151–54.

CH68 Jarmatz, Klaus. *Literatur im Exil*. Berlin: Dietz, 1966. 302p. Rev. by H. Osterle, *Germanic Rev.*, vol. 43, no. 3 (1968), 224f.

CH69 Johnson, E. Bond. "Der European Film Bund und die Exilschriftsteller in Hollywood." In: *Deutsche Exilliteratur seit 1933. Bd. 1: Kalifornien*. Ed. J. M. Spalek and J. Strelka. Bern: Francke, 1976, p.135–46.

CH70 Jonas, Klaus W. "Amerikanische Germanistik und deutsche Exilliteratur." *Alma mater philippina* (Marburg) 1974, 8–11.

CH71 Jonas, Klaus W. "Amerika's Beitrag zur Erforschung der deutschsprachigen Exilliteratur." *Börsenblatt für den Deutschen Buchhandel*, vol. 30, no. 77 (27 September 1974), A. 281–86.

CH72 Kamla, Thomas A. *Confrontation with Exile: Studies in the German Novel*. Europäische Hochschulschriften, No. 137. Bern: Lang, 1975. 182p. Rev. by W. D. Elfe, *Monatshefte*, vol. 70 (1978), 202–23. A study of 16 German novels in which the theme of exile is central.

CH73 Kamla, Thomas A. "The German Exile Novel during the Third Reich: The Problem of Art and Politics." *German Studies Rev.*, vol. 3 (1980), 395–413.

CH74 Kamla, Thomas A. "The Theme of Exile in the Novel of the German Emigration." Diss., Wisconsin, 1973.

CH75 Kantorowicz, Alfred. *Politik und Literatur im Exil: Deutschsprachige Schriftsteller im Kampf gegen den Nationalsozialismus*. Hamburg: Christians, 1978. 346p.

CH76 Kesten, Hermann. *Der Geist der Unruhe*. Köln: Kiepenheuer & Witsch, 1959.

CH77 Kesten, Hermann. *Meine Freunde die Poeten*. München: Kindler, 1959. 248p. Heinr. Mann, H. von Hofmannsthal, Thomas Mann, A. Kolb, C. Sternheim, G. Kaiser, A. Döblin, W. Hegemann, and others.

CH78 Kesten, Hermann, ed. *Deutsche Literatur im Exil: Briefe europäischer Autoren 1933–1949*. München: Kurt Desch, 1964. 380p. Repr. Frankfurt: Fischer Taschenbuch Verlag, 1973. 315p.

CH79 Koepke, Wulf. "Die Exilschriftsteller und der amerikanische Buchmarkt." In: *Die deutsche Exilliteratur seit 1933. Bd. 1: Kalifornien*. Ed. J. M. Spalek and J. Strelka. Bern: Francke, 1976., p.89–116.

CH80 Krispyn, Egbert. *Anti-Nazi Writers in Exile*. Athens: Univ. of Georgia Pr., 1978. 200p. Rev. by T. S. Hansen, *German Quar.*, vol. 52 (January 1979), 135–37; D. Pike, *Monatshefte*, vol. 72, no. 2 (Summer 1980), 206–08; Alexander Stephan, *Zeitschrift für Kulturaustausch*, 1979, 338; B. S. Chamberlain, *Amer. Hist. Rev.*, vol. 84 (1979), 793.

CH81 Krispyn, Egbert. "Exil als Lebensform." In *Exil und Innere Emigration. II. Internationale Tagung in St. Louis*. Ed. P. U. Hohendahl and E. Schwarz. Frankfurt: Athenäum, 1973, p.101–18.

CH82 League of American Writers, Exiled Writers Committee. *We Must Save Them All: A Report*. New York: n.p., ca. December 1940.

CH83 Leopold, Werner. "Der Dichter in der Fremde." *Der Auslandsdeutsche*, vol. 15 (1932), 9.

CH84 Lewis, Ward B. "Message from America: The Verse of Walt Whitman as Interpreted by

German Authors in Exile." *German Life and Letters*, vol. 29 (1976), 215–27.

CH85 Lindt, Peter. *Schriftsteller im Exil: Zwei Jahre deutsche literarische Sendung am Rundfunk in New York.* New York: Willard Publ. Co., 1944. Repr. 1974 in Nendeln: Kraus Reprint. Interviews with leading literary figures.

CH86 Maas, Lieselotte, and Eberhard Lämmert, eds. *Handbuch der deutschen Exilpresse 1933–45.* I. *Bibliographie A–K.* II. *Bibliographie L–Z.* Sonderveröffentlichung der Deutschen Bibliothek. München: Hanser, 1977. 352, 480p. Rev. by T. S. Hansen, *German Quar.*, vol. 51 (1978), 112–14. Guide to approx. 400 periodicals, journals and newspapers established and operated by emigrés from Germany and the Sudetenland. Author indexes.

CH87 Malone, Dagmar Emilie. "Die literarischen Kontroversen innerhalb der Exil-Literatur der dreissiger Jahre." Diss., Univ. of Southern Calif., 1970.

CH88 Mann, Erika. *Music in War Time.* New York?: n.p., 1942. 7 leaves. Statement in a public polemic with Deems Taylor over the question of employing musicians who are Nazis.

CH89 Mann, Golo. "Deutsche Literatur im Exil." *Neue Rundschau*, vol. 79 (1968), 38–49.

CH90 Mann, Klaus. *Der Wendepunkt.* Berlin: G. B. Fischer, 1960.

CH91 Mayer, Hans. "Und Saßen an den Ufern des Hudson: Anmerkungen zur deutschen literarischen Emigration." *Akzente* 23 (1976), 439–446.

CH92 Mews, Siegfried. "Quo Vadis? Zur Situation der amerikanischen Exilforschung anlässlich des Exilsymposiums in Riverside, Kalifornien im April 1980." *Arbeitskreis Heinrich Mann Mitteilungsblatt.* Special Issue, 1981, 192–203.

CH93 Middell, Eike, Alfred Dreifuss, Volker Frank, Wolfgang Gersch, Thea Kirfel, Lenk und Jürgen Schebera. *Exil in den U S A mit einem Bericht "Shanghai—Eine Emigration am Rande."* Kunst und Literatur im antifaschistischen Exil 1933–1945, vol. 3. Leipzig: Reclam, 1979. 590p.

CH94 Mierendorff, Marta. "Exilliteraturforschung an der University of Southern California in Los Angeles (USC). *Jahrbuch für Internationale Germanistik*, vol. 6, no. 2 (1974), 129–33.

CH95 Mitchell, Janis. "Exile and Historical Existence in the Writings of Franz Werfel, Alfred Döblin and Hermann Broch." Diss., Pennsylvania State, 1976–1977.

CH96 Moeller, Hans-Bernhard. "Exilautoren als Drehbuchautoren." In: *Deutsche Exilliteratur seit 1933.* Bd. 1: *Kalifornien.* Ed. J. M. Spalek and J. Strelka. Bern: Francke, 1976, p. 676–714.

CH97 Moeller, Hans-Bernhard. "Die internationale Situation der Germanistik: Opposition und Resignation. Deutsche Schriftsteller im Exil. Ein Symposium der Modern Language Association of America. (St. Louis, April 1972)." *Colloquia Germanica. Internat. Zeitschrift für germanistische Sprach- und Literaturwissenschaft*, vol. 7 (1973), 59–67.

CH98 Moore, Erna M. "Exil in Hollywood: Leben und Haltung deutscher Exilautoren nach ihren autobiographischen Berichten." In: *Deutsche Exilliteratur seit 1933.* Bd. 1: *Kalifornien.* Ed. J. M. Spalek and J. Strelka. Bern: Francke, 1976, p. 21–39.

CH99 Niers, Gerd. "Ein Panorama deutscher Exilliteratur: Dokumentausstellung in der Heilbronner Stadtbücherei." *Aufbau*, vol. 46, 13 April 1979.

CH100 Nyssen, Elke. *Geschichtsbewußtsein und Emigration: Der historische Roman der deutschen Antifaschisten 1933–1945.* München: Wilh. Fink Vlg., 1974. 192p. Rev. by W. K. Faulhaber, *German Quar.* vol. 49, no. 4 (November 1976), 510–11.

CH101 Osterle, Heinz D. "Die Deutschen im Spiegel des sozialkritischen Romans der Emigranten, 1933–1950." 2 vols. Diss., Brown Univ., 1964. 617p.

CH102 Osterle, Heinz D. "The Other Germany: Resistance to the Third Reich in German Literature." *German Quar.*, vol. 41, no. 1 (January 1968), 1–22.

CH103 Paul, Carol L. "The Relationship between the American Liberal Press and the German Writers in Exile, 1933–1945." Diss., Univ. of Southern Calif., 1974.

CH104 Pfanner, Helmut F. "Die Rolle der Frau im Exil: Im Spiegel der deutschsprachigen Literatur in New York." In: *Analecta Helvetica et Germanica: Eine Festschrfit zu Ehren von Hermann Boeschenstein.* Ed. Achim Arnold, Hans Eichner et al. Bonn: Bouvier, 1979, p.342–59.

CH105 Pfanner, Helmut F. "Schreiben als Selbstbestätigung: Erzählen im Exil." In: *Erzählung und Erzählforschung im 20. Jahrhundert.* Ed. Rolf Kloepfner und Gisela Janetzke-Dillner. Berlin: Kohlhammer, 1981, p.83–94.

CH106 Pfanner, Helmut F. "Der Tod im Exil: Zu Gebrauch und Verbreitung eines literarischen Motivs." *Arbeitskreis Heinrich Mann Mitteilungsblatt.* Special Issue, 1981, 238–47.

CH107 Pfeiler, William K. *German Literature in Exile: The Concern of the Poets.* Lincoln: Univ. of Nebraska Pr., 1957. 142p. Rev. by T. O. Brandt, *Amer.-German Rev.*, vol. 24, no. 3 (1958), 37; H. Cohn, *Books Abroad*, vol. 32 (1958), 448; R. Exner, *German Quar.*, vol. 32 (1959), 281f.; H. Von Hofe, *Mod. Lang Quar.*, vol. 19 (1958), 83–84.

CH108 "Press in Exile. German Anti-Nazi Periodicals 1933–1945." *Wiener Library Bull.* (London), vol. 3 (1949), no. 31 and vol. 4 (1950), no. 1.

CH109 Reinhold, Ernest. "German Exile Literature: Problems and Proposals." *Western Canad. Studies in Mod. Lang. and Lit.*, vol. 2 (1970), 75–87.

CH110 Reszler, André. *Le national-socialisme dans le roman allemand contemporain (1933–1958).* Genève: n.p., 1966.

CH111 Röder, W. "Zur Situation der Exilforschung in der Bundesrepublik Deutschlands." In: *Exil und Innere Emigration. II. Internationale Tagung in St. Louis.* Ed. P. U. Hohendahl and E. Schwarz. Frankfurt: Athenäum, 1973, p.141–53.

CH112 Roloff, Gerhard. *Exil und Exilliteratur in der deutschen Presse 1945–1949. Ein Beitrag zur Rezeptionsgeschichte.* Deutsches Exil 1933–1945, Bd. 10. Worms: Heintz, 1976. 313p. Rev. by E. Bahr, *German Quar.*, vol. 51 (1978), 559–62.

CH113 Sándor, András. "Ein amerikanischer Verleger und die Exilautoren." In: *Deutsche Exilliteratur seit 1933.* Bd. 1. *Kalifornien.* Eds. J. M. Spalek, Joseph Strelka, and Sandra H. Hawrylchak. Bern: Francke, 1976, p.117–34.

CH114 Schaber, Will, ed. *Aufbau, Reconstruction: Dokumente einer Kultur im Exil, mit einem Geleitwort von Hans Steinitz.* Woodstock, N.Y.: Overlook Pr., 1972/Köln: Kiepenheuer und Witsch. 416p. Materials for a cultural history of an important publication.

CH115 Schau, Friedrich. *Die Emigrationspresse der Sozialisten 1938 bis 1945.* Wien: Europa, 1968. 44p.

CH116 Schneider, Sigrid. *Das Ende Weimars im Exilroman: Literarische Strategien zur Vermittlung von Faschismustheorien.* Münich: Saur, 1980. 575p.

CH117 Schwarz, Egon. "Was ist und zu welchem Ende studieren wir Exilliteratur?" In: *Exil und Innere Emigration. II. Internationale Tagung in St. Louis.* Ed. P. U. Hohendahl and E. Schwarz. Frankfurt: Athenäum, 1973, p.155–64.

CH118 Schwarz, Egon and Matthias Wegner, eds. *Verbannung: Aufzeichnungen deutscher Schriftsteller im Exil.* Hamburg: Christian Wegner Vlg., 1964. 340p.

CH119 Söffke, Günther. *Deutsches Schrifttum im Exil (1933–1950). Ein Bestandsverzeichnis.* Bonner Beiträge zur Bibliotheks- und Bücherkunde, Bd. 11. Bonn: Bouvier, 1965. 64p. A collection of 600 items acquired from the library of Hein Kohn.

CH120 Sorell, Walter. "English Language is No Sanctuary." *Saturday Rev. of Lit.*, 25 August 1945. An article on writers in exile.

CH121 Spalek, John M. *Guide to the Papers of Twentieth Century German and Austrian Exiles in the United States.* Charlottesville: Univ. Pr. of Virginia, 1978.

CH122 Spalek, John M. "Exilliteratur und Exilliteraturforschung in den U S A." *Colloquia Germanica*, Special Exile Literature Issue, vol. 5, no. 1–2 (1971), 157–66.

CH123 Spalek, John M. "Literature in Exile: the Comparative Approach." In: *Deutsches Exildrama und Exiltheater. Akten des Exilliteratur-Symposiums der Univ. of South Carolina 1976.* Jahrbuch für Internat. Germanistik A 3. Frankfurt: Lang, 1977, p.14–26.

CH124 Spalek, John M., Joseph Strelka, and Sandra H. Hawrylchak, eds. *Deutsche Exilliteratur seit 1933.* Bd. 1. Teil 1. *Kalifornien.* Teil 2. *Bib-*

liographie und Quellenkunde. Bern: Francke, 1976. 868, 216p. Band 2. *Die deutsche Literatur seit 1933 im Osten der Vereinigten Staaten.* Bern: Francke / Albany: SUNY, 1977. Rev. by Manfred Durzak, *German Quar.*, vol. 50, no. 3 (May 1977), 346–49; B. M. Broerman, *Colloquia Germanica*, vol. 2 (1978), 189–92; Siegfried Mews, *Jour. of Eng. and Germanic Philology*, vol. 76, no. 4 (1977), 612–15; Helmut Pfanner, *Monatshefte*, vol. 68, no. 4 (Winter 1976), 437–40; Alexander Stephan, *Zeitschrift für Kulturaustausch*, vol. 27 no. 2 (1977), 84.

CH125 Steiner, Carl. "Untersuchungen zum historischen Roman der deutschen Emigrantenliteratur nach 1933." Diss., George Washington Univ., 1966.

CH126 Stephan, Alexander. *Die deutsche Exilliteratur 1933–1945. Eine Einführung.* München: Beck, 1979. 376p. Rev. by Thomas S. Hansen, *German Quar.*, vol. 54, no. 1 (January 1981), 101–02. Incl. extensive bibliography.

CH127 Stern, Guy. "Das Amerikabild der Exilliteratur: Zu einem unveröffentlichten Filmexposé von Alfred Neumann." In: *Amerika in der deutschen Literatur: Neue Welt, Nordamerika, U S A. Wolfgang Paulsen zum 65. Geburtstag.* Ed. S. Bauschinger et al. Stuttgart: Reclam, 1975, p.323–28.

CH128 Stern, Guy. "Exile Literature: Sub-Division or Misnomer?" *Colloquia Germanica*, vol. 5, Exile Literature Issue, no. 1–2 (1971), 167–78.

CH129 Stern, Guy. "Hinweise und Anregungen zur Erforschung der Exilliteratur." In: *Exil und Innere Emigration. II. Internationale Tagung in St. Louis.* Ed. P. U. Hohendahl and E. Schwarz. Frankfurt: Athenäum, 1973, p.9–17.

CH130 Stern, Guy. "Ob und wie sie sich anpaßten: Deutsche Schriftsteller im Exilland USA." In: *Leben im Exil: Probleme der Integration deutscher Flüchtlinge im Ausland 1933 bis 1945.* Ed. Wolfgang Frühwald and Wolfgang Schieder. Hamburg: Hoffmann & Campe, 1981, p.68–76.

CH131 Stern, Guy. "Die Thematik 'Flucht und Exil' innerhalb und ausserhalb des Dritten Reiches: Eine Konfrontation." In: *Deutsche Exilliteratur: Literatur im Dritten Reich.* Ed. W. Elfe, J. Hardin and G. Holst. Akten des 2. Exilliteratur-Symposiums der Univ. of South Carolina. Bern: Lang. 1979, p.60–78.

CH132 Stern, Guy. "Über das Fortleben des Exilromans in den sechziger Jahren." In: *Revolte und Experiment. Die Literatur und Sprache im europäischen Mittelalter: Festschrift für Karl Langosch zum 70. Geburtstag.* Ed. Wolfgang Paulsen. Darmstadt: Wissenschaftliche Buchgesellschaft, 1973, p.165–85.

CH133 Stern, Guy and Dorothy Wartenberg. "Flucht und Exil: Werkthematik und Autorenkommentare." In: *Gegenwartswartsliteratur und Drittes Reich: Deutsche Autoren in der Auseinandersetzung mit der Vergangenheit.* Ed. Hans Wagener. Stuttgart: Reclam, 1977, p.111–32.

CH134 Sternfeld, Wilhelm. "Die Emigrantenpresse." *Deutsche Rundschau*, vol. 76 (1950), 250–59.

CH135 Sternfeld, Wilhelm, and Eva Tiedemann. *Deutsche Exil-Literatur 1933–1945. Eine Bio-Bibliographie.* Veröffentlichungen der Deutschen Akademie für Sprache und Dichtung, no. 29. Darmstadt: Lambert Schneider, 1962. 405p. Rev. by R. E. Cazden, *Library Quar.*, vol. 33 (1963), 283f. 2nd revised ed. Forew. by Hanns W. Eppelsheimer. Heidelberg: Lambert Schneider, 1970. 612p. Rev. by Helmut F. Pfanner, *German Quar.*, vol. 45 (November 1972), 775–76.

CH136 Strauss, Herbert A., and Leonard P. Liggio. "Einwanderung und Radikalismus in der politischen Kultur der Vereinigten Staaten von Amerika." In: *Deutsche Exilliteratur seit 1933.* Ed. J. M. Spalek, Joseph Strelka, and Sandra H. Hawrylchak. Bd. 1. Teil. 1. *Kalifornien.* Bern: Francke, 1976, p.168–94.

CH137 Strelka, Joseph P. "Material Collectors, Political Rhetoricians, and Amateurs: Current Methodological Problems in German Exile Literature Studies." In: *Protest—Form—Tradition: Essays on German Exile Literature.* Ed. Joseph P. Strelka, Robert F. Bell and Eugene Dobson. University, Ala.: Univ. of Alabama Pr., 1979, p.1–14

CH138 Strelka, Joseph P. "Probleme der Erforschung der deutschsprachigen Exilliteratur seit 1933." *Colloquia Germanica*, vol. 10 (1976–1977), 140–53.

CH139 Strelka, Joseph P., Robert F. Bell and Eugene Dobson, eds. *Protest—Form—Tradition; Essays on German Exile Literature.* University, Ala.: Univ. of Alabama Pr., 1979. 144p. Rev. by David Pike, *Compar. Lit. Studies*, vol. 16 (1979), 365–66; Jacob Erhardt, *Newsletter, Soc. for Ger-*

man-Amer. Studies, vol. 2, no. 3 (1980–1981), 5–6.

CH140 Sudhof, Siegfried. "Literatur des Exils 1933–1945." *Jahrbuch für Internationale Germanistik*, vol. 2, no. 4 (1976), 242–50.

CH141 "Symposium on Transplanted Writers." *Books Abroad*, Autumn 1942.

CH142 Tabori, Paul, ed. *The Pen in Exile: An Anthology of Writers in Exile*. New York: Living Books, 1966. 252p.

CH143 Trommler, Frank. "Emigration und Nachkriegsliteratur: Zum Problem der geschichtlichen Kontinuität." In: *Exil und innere Emigration: Third Wisconsin Workshop*. Ed. Reinhold Grimm and Jost Hermand. Frankfurt: Atheneum, 1972, p.73–97.

CH144 Vielig, J. "Die Bibliothek der Emigrationsliteratur in Frankfurt a. M." *Panorama* (Speyer), vol. 4, no. 12 (1960), 6.

CH145 Von Hofe, Harold. "German Literature in Exile." *German Quar.*, vol. 17 (1944), 28–31, 88–92, 145–54, 263–72. On Alfred Döblin, Heinrich and Thomas Mann, and Franz Werfel.

CH146 Walter, Hans-Albert. "Das Bild Deutschlands im Exilroman." *Neue Rundschau*, vol. 77 (1966), 437–58.

CH147 Walter, Hans-Albert. *Deutsche Exilliteratur 1933–1945* [retitled ... *1933–1950*]. 9 vols. projected, 1972–. Vol. 1. *Bedrohung und Verfolgung bis 1933*. Darmstadt, Neuwied: Luchterhand, 1972. ca. 240p. Vol. 2. *Asylpraxis und Lebensbedingung in Europa*. Darmstadt: Luchterhand, 1972. ca. 240p. Vol. 4. *Exilpresse*. Stuttgart: Metzler, 1978. ca. 850p. Vol. 7. *Exilpresse I*. Darmstadt: Luchterhand, 1974. 424p. Rev. by J. Strelka, *German Quar.*, vol. 50, no. 3 (May 1977), 340–42. Vol. 8. *Exilpresse II*. Sammlung Luchterhand, vol. 191. Neuwied: Luchterhand 1974. ca. 350p.

CH148 Walter, Hans-Albert. "Deutsche Literatur im Exil: Ein Modellfall für die Zusammenhänge von Literatur und Politik." *Merkur*, vol. 25 (1971), 77–84.

CH149 Walter, Hans-Albert. "Emigrantenliteratur und deutsche Germanistik." *Colloquia Germanica*, vol. 5 (1971), 313–20.

CH150 Walter, Hans-Albert. "Die Helfer im Hintergrund: Zur Situation der deutschen Exilverlage 1933–1945." *Frankfurter Hefte*, vol. 20 (February 1965), 121–32.

CH151 Wegner, Matthias. *Exil und Literatur. Deutsche Schriftsteller im Ausland 1933–1945*. Athenäum Bücher zur Dichtkunst. Frankfurt/Bonn: Athenäum, 1967. 247p. Groups and ideologies among emigré writers. Bibliography. Rev. by H. Osterle, *Germanic Rev.*, vol. 43, no. 3 (1968), 225–28.

CH152 Weiskopf, Franz Carl and Kurt Pinthus. *Geschichte der deutschen Literatur im Exil. (Unter fremden Himmeln: Ein Abriss deutscher Literatur im Exil 1933–1945*. Berlin: Dietz, 1948.

CH153 Weisstein, Ulrich. "Literaturkritik in deutschen Exilzeitschriften: Der Fall *Das Wort*." In: *Exil und Innere Emigration. II. Internationale Tagung in St. Louis*. Ed. P. U. Hohendahl and E. Schwarz. Frankfurt: Athenäum, 1973, p.19–46.

CH154 Werner, Renate. "Transparente Kommentare: Überlegungen zu historischen Romanen deutscher Exilautoren." *Poetica*, vol. 9 (1977), 324–51.

CH155 Winkler, A. "Hermann Kesten im Exil (1933–1940)." Diss., 1980. [*DAI*, vol. 41 (1980), 49C.]

CH156 [Yale University Library.] *List of manuscripts, correspondence, and works by exiled German authors in the Yale University Library*. New Haven: Yale Univ. Library, unpublished.

CH157 Ziolkowski, Theodore. "Form und Protest: Das Sonett in der Literatur des Exils und der inneren Emigration." In: *Exil und Innere Emigration: Third Wisconsin Workshop*. Ed. Reinhold Grimm and Jost Hermand. Frankfurt: Athenäum, 1973, p.153–72.

CI
German-American Literature

Source: Goedeke, Karl, ed. *Grundriss*..., see entry CI4.

German American (U.S.A.) Writers, Including Writers in Exile

SOURCES, COLLECTIONS AND ANTHOLOGIES

CI1 Adolf, Helen, comp. *Dem neuen Reich entgegen.* N.p.: n.p., 1930. Collection of German-American writings.

CI2 Adolf, Helen, comp. *Im neuen Reich.* N.p.: n.p., 1932. Collection of German-American writings.

CI3 Felsmeyer, R., ed. *Dein Herz ist deine Heimat.* Wien: n.p., 1955. Anthology of Austrian-American poems.

CI4 Goedeke, Karl, ed. *Grundriss zur Geschichte der deutschen Dichtung aus den Quellen.* Berlin: Akademie-Vlg., 19–. Esp. vol. 15. Part IV. [*Ausland.*] *Nordamerika (USA).* Ed. Erich A. Albrecht and Hildegard Pross. Berlin: Akademie-Vlg., 1964, p. 518-661.

CI5 Gong, Alfred, ed. *Interview mit Amerika—50 deutschprachige Autoren in der neuen Welt.* München: Nymphenburger Vlgshandlung, 1962. Anthology.

CI6 Grossberg, Mimi, ed. *Amerika im austroamerikanischen Gedicht, 1938-1978.* Wien: Bergland Vlg., ca. 1979. Anthology. Contributions by Ferd. Bruckner, Ernst Lothar, Josef Luitpold, Johannes Urzidil.

CI7 Grossberg, Mimi, ed. *Kleinkunst aus Amerika. Gedichte, Chansons, Prose von in Amerika lebenden Autoren.* Wien: Europäischer Vlg., 1964. 64p. Rev. by J. Erhardt, *German-Amer. Studies*, vol. 1, no. 1 (1969), 76-77.

CI8 Grossberg, Mimi, ed. *Österreichisches aus Amerika. Vers und Prosa. Ein Geschenkbuch.* Wien: Bergland Vlg., ca. 1975. 64p. Anthology of contemporary Austrian and Austrian-American writers.

CI9 *Junge Lyrik.* Stuttgart: Carl Schurz Memorial Foundation, 1956.

CI10 Kahn, Lisa, ed. *Reisegepäck Sprache: deutschschreibende Schriftstellerinnen in den U S A 1938-1978.* München: Fink, 1979. 145p. Rev. by B. Eichmann-Leutenegger, *Neue Zürcher Zeitung*, 18 November 1980; J. Glenn, *Jour. of German-Amer. Studies*, vol. 15, no. 2 (June 1980), 57. Anthology of writings.

CI11 Kaiser, Bruno. *Das Wort der Verfolgten. Gedichte und Prosa, Briefe und Ausrufe deutscher Flüchtlinge von H. Heine und G. Herwegh bis B. Brecht und T. Mann.* Ed. Oswald Mohr (pseud.) Basel: n.p., 1945; Berlin: n.p., 1948.

CI12 Longsdorf, Kenneth D. "A Patchwork of Novels about the Plain People." *The Pa. Dutchman*, vol. 2 (15 May 1951).

CI13 *Morgenröte: Ein Lesebuch.* New York: Aurora, 1947.

CI14 Pratschke, Gottfried, ed. *Aber den Feind sollten wir nicht lieben.* Wien: Europäischer Vlg., 1969. Anthology of Austrian-American writers and others.

CI15 Pratschke, Gottfried, ed. *Alle Wunder dieser Welt.* Wien: Europäischer Vlg., 1968. Anthology containing poems by Austrian-American poets and others.

CI16 Pratschke, Gottfried, ed. *Das ist mein Land.* Wien: Europäischer Vlg., 1966. Anthology.

CI17 Pratschke, Gottfried, ed. *Du, unsere Zeit*. Wien: Europäischer Vlg., 1965. Anthology of poems by Austrian-American poets and others.

CI18 Pratschke, Gottfried, ed. *Licht vor dem Dunkel der Angst*. Wien: Europäischer Vlg., 1963. Anthology of Austrian-American writers and others.

CI19 Pratschke, Gottfried, ed. *Liebe, Menschgewordenes Licht*. Wien: Europäischer Vlg., 1964. Anthology of Austrian-American poets and others.

CI20 Pratschke, Gottfried, ed. *Ein Wort ins Herz der Welt*. Wien: Europäischer Vlg., 1967. Anthology of poems.

CI21 Schlösser, Manfred, and H. R. Ropertz. *An den Wind geschrieben, Lyrik der Freiheit: Gedichte der Jahre 1933–45*. Darmstadt: Agora Vlg., 1960.

CI22 Tabori, Paul, ed. *The Pen in Exile: An Anthology of Writers in Exile*. New York: Living Books, 1966. 252p.

CI23 Ward, Robert E. "Contemporary German-American Poetry." *German-Amer. Studies*, vol. 4 (1972), 2–22. Examples of the poetry of émigré and native-born writers in the German language.

CI24 Ward, Robert E. *Deutsche Lyrik aus Amerika. Eine Auswahl*. New York: The Literary Society Foundation, Inc., 1969. 109p. Anthology of lyric poetical selections from Pastorius to the present day. With biobibliographies of 65 authors. Rev. by G. Gerbaux, *New Yorker Staats-Zeitung und Herold*, 5 April 1970; E. Ritter, *Monatshefte* vol. 62, no. 4 (Winter 1970), 418–19.

CI25 *Zwischen gestern und morgen. Neue österreichische Gedichte*. London: n.p., 1942. Anthology.

EARLY STUDIES (TO 1940)

CI26 Bittinger, Lucy Forney. "German-American Literature." *Lutheran Quar.* (Gettysburg), vol. 43 (1913), 375–88.

CI27 *Ein Blüthenstrauss von Liedern und Gedichten dem Herrn Heinrich Mühlsiepen gewidmet....* St. Louis: n.p., 1893.

CI28 Börnstein, Heinrich. *Hausbibliothek des Anzeigers des Westens*. St. Louis: n.p., 1855–1856. 4 vols. in 2.

CI29 Bosse, Georg von. [German-American Literature]. In: *Das deutsche Element in den Vereinigten Staaten under besonderer Berücksichtigung seines politischen, ethischen, sozialen und erzieherischen Einflusses*. Stuttgart: n.p., 1908, p.427–47.

CI30 Busse, Karl. "Deutsch-Amerikanische Dichtung." *Bulletin literarischen Unterrichts*, vol. 14, no. 3 (January 1897), 33–36; 21 January, no. 4, 49–51; 28 January, no. 5, 65–67.

CI31 Butz, Caspar. "Deutsch-amerikanische Literatur." *Deutsch-Amerikanische Monatshefte*, vol. 2 (1864), 572f.

CI32 *California-Album. Eine Erinnerung, vom Strande des Stillen Meeres für Deutsch-Amerikaner*. Ed. and publ. by Charles J. Brick. San Francisco: n.p., 1883.

CI33 Cronau, Rudolf. "Noteworthy Authors and Poets." In: *German Achievements in America*. New York: n.p., 1916, p.155–71.

CI34 "Deutsch-amerikanische Literatur." In: *Der grosse Brockhaus*, 15th ed. Vol. 4 (Leipzig, 1929), 546–48.

CI35 "Deutsch-amerikanische Turnerei und Poesie." *Jahrbuch der deutsch-amerikanischen Turnerei*, vol. 3 (1894), 173–74.

CI36 *Deutsche Arbeiter-Dichtung. Eine Auswahl Lieder und Gedichte deutscher Proletarier*. Stuttgart: n.p., 1893. 5 vols.

CI37 Faust, Albert B. "Die Dialektdichtung in der deutsch-amerikanischen Literatur." *Freidenker Almanach für das Jahr 1896* (Milwaukee), 1896, p.69–94.

CI38 Fick, Heinrich H. "Der Baum in der Poesie." *Freidenker-Almanach* (Milwaukee), 1893, p.68–78.

CI39 Fick, Heinrich H. "Die deutsche Muse in Amerika." *Amerikanischer Turner-Kalender für das Jahr 1894* (Milwaukee), 1894, p.50–64.

CI40 Fick, Heinrich H. *Humor in der deutsch-amerikanischen Poesie*. N.p.: n.p., n.d.

CI41 Goebel, Julius. "Die deutsche Erhebung von 1870 im Spiegel der deutsch-amerikanischen Dichtung." In: *Jahrbuch der Deutschamerikaner* *für das Jahr 1918*. Ed. Michael Singer. Chicago: n.p., 1918.

CI42 Heide, Heinrich R. "Poesie im Lande der Prosa." *New Yorker Staats-Zeitung*, 15 April 1927, p.7.

CI43 "Iowa's deutsche Dichter und Schriftsteller." In: *Die Deutschen von Iowa und deren Errungenschaften*, by Joseph Eiboeck. Des Moines: n.p., 1900, p.198–219.

CI44 Klauprecht, Emil. "Deutsch-Amerikanische Literatur." *Fliegende Blätter* (Cincinnati), no. 35, 14 August 1847.

CI45 Kleeberg, Minna. "Die deutsche Dichtkunst in Amerika." *Der deutsche Pionier*, vol. 6 (1874), 217.

CI46 Knortz, Karl. "Deutsch-Amerikanische Literatur." In: *Das Deutschtum in den Vereinigten Staaten*, by K. Knortz. Hamburg: n.p., 1898, p.39–55.

CI47 Kreyssig, Friedrich. "Der deutsch-amerikanische Abenteuer-Roman." In: *Vorlesungen über den deutschen Roman der Gegenwart*, by F. Kreyssig. Berlin: n.p., 1871, p.159–62.

CI48 Leffel, Heinrich von. "Zur deutschen Literatur in Nordamerika." *Die Glocke*, vol. 2, no. 1 (1907), 227–29; no. 2, 370–73. Reviews of recently published works. Author resided in Santa Monica, California.

CI49 Leser, L. L. "Deutsch-Amerikanische Dichtung." In: *Das Buch der Deutschen in Amerika*. Ed. Max Heinrici. Philadelphia: n.p., 1909, p.399–420.

CI50 Metzenthin-Raunick, Selma Marie. "Deutsche Literatur in Texas." In: *Handwörterbuch des Grenz- und Auslanddeutschtums*. Ed. Carl Petersen and Otto Scheel. Breslau: F. Hirt, 1933.

CI51 Metzenthin-Raunick, Selma Marie. "Deutsch-texanische Schriftsteller." *Die Literatur* (Stuttgart), vol. 32 (1927), 11. Trans. by Temple House as "Two Texas Writers." *Bunker's Monthly*, May 1928.

CI52 Metzner, Henry. "Die Hebung der deutschamerikanischen Literatur." *Amerikanischer Turner-Kalender für das Jahr 1886* (Milwaukee) 1886, p.73–74.

CI53 Michel, Friedrich, ed. *Jahrbuch des Verbandes deutscher Schriftsteller in Amerika*. New York: n.p., 1911.

CI54 *Musenklänge aus dem Süden. Eine Sammlung von Original-Gedichten von Hugo Weidmann, Christian Friedrich Vogler, Georg Hoffmann and Franz Melchers*. Charleston, S. Car.: n.p., 1858. 176p.

CI55 [Nordau, Max.] "Ein Brief von Max Nordau." *Deutsch-Amerikanische Dichtung*, vol. 1 (1888–1889), 35. Expresses his hope for the development of German-American poetry.

CI56 *Prairie Blume*. La Grange, Tex.: Texas German Literary Society, 1857–1861. Anthology.

CI57 [Pseudonyms of German-American writers]. *Milwaukee Sunday Free Press*, 27 September 1903.

CI58 Rattermann, Heinrich A. "Deutschamerikanische Dichter und Dichtung des 17. und 18. Jahrhunderts." *Deutsch-Amerikanische Geschichtsblätter*, vol. 14 (1914), 103–13.

CI59 Scherr, Johannes, comp. *Bildersaal der Weltliteratur*. N.p.: n.p., 1888. Incl. some German-American poems.

CI60 Stapel, Wilhelm. "Deutsche Dichtung in Amerika." *Deutsches Volkstum: Monatsschrift für das deut. Geistesleben*, vol. 17 (1914), 504f.

CI61 Uhlendorf, Bernhard A. "Politische Lyrik der Deutschen in Amerika." *Der deutsche Gedanke*, vol. 3 (1926), 115–24.

CI62 Voigt, Rudolf. "Deutsche Literatur in Amerika." In: *Der deutsche Führer durch die Weltausstellung*. Chicago: Gutenberg Publ., 1934.

CI63 Wayland, John W. "Literary Activities and Associations." In: *A History of Shenandoah County, Va*. Strasburg: n.p., n.d., p.481–97. A supplement to the lists of German imprints in Seidensticker.

CI64 Wayland, John W. "List of publications by Lutherans in the United States." *Evangelical Rev.*, vol. 12 (1860–1861), 542–74.

CI65 Wayland, John W. "Publications by Lutherans in the United States." *Evangelical Rev.*, vol. 8 (1856–1857), 64–84.

GENERAL STUDIES AND MONOGRAPHS

CI66 App, Austin. "Deutsch-amerikanische Sehnsucht: Studien über deutsche Dichtung in U S A." *Klüter Blätter*, vol. 26 (1975), 5.

CI67 Bartscht, Waltraud. "A Texas-German Civil War Romance." *Schatzkammer*, vol. 3, no. 1 (1977), 38–40.

CI68 Bockstahler, Oscar L. "Contributions to American Literature by Hoosiers of German Ancestry." *Ind. Mag. of Hist.*, vol. 38, no. 3 (1942), 231–50. W. V. Moody, Theodore Dreiser, and many others.

CI69 Brause, Herman F. "Betrachtungen zur deutschamerikanischen Dichtung." *Mitteilungsblatt des Verbands deutschsprachiger Autoren in Amerika*, vol. 1, no. 1 (1974).

CI70 Condoyannis, George E. "German American Prose Fiction before 1914." In: *Papers from the Conference on German-Americana in the Eastern United States*. Ed. S. M. Benjamin. Occas. Papers of the Soc. for German-Amer. Studies, no. 8. Morgantown, W. Va.: Dept. of Foreign Langs., W.Va. Univ., 1980, p.38–54.

CI71 Condoyannis, George E. "German-American Prose Fiction from 1850 to 1918." Diss., Columbia, 1953. 641p.

CI72 Condoyannis, George E. "German-American Prose Fiction: Synopses of 38 Works." *German-Amer. Studies*, vol. 4 (1972), 1–126. Extracts from the dissertation submitted at Columbia Univ., 1953.

CI73 Davis, Richard Beale. "Three Poems from Colonial North Carolina." *The N. Car. Hist. Rev.*, vol. 46 (1969), 33–41. One poem is in German—probably of Moravian origin.

CI74 Dolmetsch, Christopher L. "The German Literature of Virginia's Shenandoah Valley, 1789–1854: A Historical, Linguistic and Literary Study." Diss., Wisconsin, 1979. 303p.

CI75 Fahnenbruck, Heinz T. "Die Frühzeit der deutsch-amerikanischen Literatur Ohios." *Cincinnati Kurier*, in installments from 17 February 1967.

CI76 Fisher, Dexter, ed. *Minority Language and Literature: Retrospective and Perspective*. New York: Mod. Lang. Assoc., 1977. 160p. A collection of 16 essays on the relationship of minority literature to the mainstream literary tradition.

CI77 "German-American Literature." *South Central Bull.*, vol. 41 (1981), 50.

CI78 Glanz, Rudolf. "Jews in Early German American Literature." *Jewish Social Studies*, vol. 4, no. 2 (1942), 99–120.

CI79 Glanz, Rudolf. *Jews in Relation to the Cultural Milieu of the Germans in America Up to the 1880's*. New York: n.p., 1947. Trans. from the *YIVO bleter*—Jour. of the Yiddish Scientific Institute. 55p.

CI80 Görlich, Ernst. "Österreichische Dichter in angelsächsischer Emigration: mit unveröffentlichten Briefen Theodor Kramers an den Verfasser." In: *Österreich und die angelsächsische Welt. Kulturbegegnungen und Vergleiche*, Ed. Otto Hietsch. Wien: Braumüller, vol. 1 (1961), p.197–206.

CI81 Govier, Robert Allen. "German Poetry in New Braunfels, Texas." M.A. thesis, Univ. of Texas, 1962.

CI82 Hammer, Carl, Jr. "A Glance at Three Centuries of German-American Writing." In: *Proceedings, Comparative Literature Symposium, Ethnic Literatures Since 1776: The Many Voices of America*. Vol. 1. Ed. W. T. Zyla and W. M. Aycock. Lubbock: Texas Tech Pr., 1978, p.217–32.

CI83 Heaney, Howell J. "A Century of Early American Children's Books in German, 1738–1837." *Phaedrus*, vol. 6, no. 1 (1979), 22–26. Repr. in *Pa. Folklife*, vol. 29 (1979–1980), 75–79.

CI84 Herzog, Marvin I., Barbara Kirshenblatt-Gimblett, Dan Miron, and Ruth Wisse, eds. *The Field of Yiddish: Studies in Language, Folklore, and Literature*. Philadelphia: Institute for the Study of Human Issues, 1980. 499p.

CI85 Jantz, Harold. "German Men of Letters in the Early United States." In: *The German Contribution to the Building of the Americas: Studies in Honor of Karl J. R. Arndt*. Ed. G. K. Friesen and W. Schatzberg. Hanover, N.H.: Clark Univ. Pr. and Univ. Pr. of New England, 1977, p.75–95.

CI86 Kahn, Lisa. "American Women Writers who Write in German." *MELUS*, vol. 5, no. 4 (1978), 63–70.

CI87 Kahn, Lisa. "Contemporary Texas-German Authors." In: *Retrospect and Retrieval, the German Element in Review: Essays on Cultural Preservation*. Ed. Dona B. Reeves and Glen E. Lich. Ann Arbor: University Microfilms, 1978, p.61–81.

CI88 Kahn, Lisa. "Die deutsche Sprache ist unsere Heimat: Deutsch-amerikanische Schriftstellerinnen." *Der Literat*, vol. 21 (1979), 49–50, 52.

CI89 Kahn, Lisa. "'...I desire that you remember the ladies...': Contemporary German-American Women Authors: A Survey." *Schatzkammer der deutschen Sprachlehre, Dichtung und Geschichte*, vol. 4 (1978), 53–65.

CI90 Krahn, Cornelius. "Literary Efforts among the Mennonites of Russian Background." *Mennonite Life*, vol. 24, no. 4 (October 1969), 166–68.

CI91 Merrill, Peter C. "Eugène Sue's German-American Imitators." *South Central Bull.*, vol. 39, no. 3 (1979), 109. Summary of paper of South Central Mod. Lang. Assoc., 12 October 1979.

CI92 Merrill, Peter C. "The Serial Novel in the German-American Press of the Nineteenth Century." *German-Amer. Studies*, vol. 13 (1978), 16–22.

CI93 Metzger, Erika A. "Deutsche Lyrik in Amerika." *German-Amer. Studies*, vol. 9 (1974), 2–10. Surveys the range and treatment of topics in the lyric poetry of German-American writers from 1700 to the present.

CI94 Miller, Edmund E. "Das *New Yorker Belletristische Journal*, 1851–1911." *Amer.-German Rev.*, vol. 8, no. 2 (December 1941), 24–27.

CI95 Mitchum, Nelson. "The Isolation of the Immigrant and Expatriate." *Lakehead Univ. Rev.*, vol. 2 (Fall 1972), 87–103. Discussion of Canadian immigrant fiction.

CI96 Niers, Gerd. "Deutschamerikanische Literatur oder deutschsprachige Literatur in Amerika." *New Yorker Staats-Zeitung und Herold*, 24–25 January 1976.

CI97 Niers, Gerd. "Deutschamerikanische-Studien: Aspekte einer neuen Forschungsdisziplin—Was ist 'deutschamerikanische Literatur'?" *Aufbau*, vol. 45, no. 7 (1979), 5.

CI98 Peters, Victor. "Russlanddeutsches Schrifttum in Nordamerika." *German-Canad. Yearbook*, vol. 3 (1976), 282–83.

CI99 Pochmann, Henry A., et al. "The Mingling of Tongues." In: *Literary History of the United States*. Ed. Robert E. Spiller et al. 3 vols. New York: Macmillan, 1948, Vol. 2, p.676–93 and vol. 3, p.284–94. 3rd ed., rev., 1963, p.58–62. Treats the Pennsylvania German dialect writings, Yiddish, and High German writings.

CI100 Poore, Carol Jean. "German-American Socialist Literature in the Late Nineteenth Century." Diss., Univ. of Wiconsin—Madison, 1979. Analysis of available primary material in poetry, drama, and fiction by German socialist immigrants; their newspapers, theaters and cultural organizations.

CI101 Riese, Teut Andreas. "Man's Rebirth in the Wilderness. The Immigrant Writer's View." In: *Vistas of a Continent: Concepts of Nature in America*. Ed. Teut Andreas Riese. Heidelberg: Winter, 1979, p.51–60.

CI102 Rose, Ernst. "Amerikas neuere Lyrik." *New Yorker Staats-Zeitung und Herold*, 27 January 1954.

CI103 R[ose], E[rnst]. "German-American Literature." In: *Cassell's Encyclopedia of Literature*. Ed. S. H. Steinberg. London: Cassell's, 1953. 2 vols. "German-American Literature," by E. R. in vol. 1, p. 247–48. Parts 2 and 3 of this work, in vol. 2, carry brief biographies of 90 German-American authors.

CI104 Shenk, Stanley C. "American Mennonite Fiction." *Mennonite Life*, vol. 23 (July 1968), 119–20. Supplements the bibliography on Mennonites in novels, July 1967.

CI105 Scherer, Anton. "Die Literatur der Donauschwaben als Mittlerin zwischen Völkern und Kulturen." *Lenau Forum*, vol. 3, nos. 3–4 (1971), 111–27.

CI106 Scholtes, Waldemar. "Ethnic Groups as Portrayed in Modern Transylvanian Saxon Novels." Diss., Univ. of Waterloo, 1976–77.

CI107 Schweitzer, Christoph E., ed. *Deliciae Hortenses or Garden Recreations (1711)*. Columbia, S. Car.: Camden House, 1981. 150p.

CI108 Spuler, Linus. *Deutsches Schrifttum in den Vereinigten Staaten von Amerika: Beiträge von Amerika-Schweizern*. Beilage zum Jahresbericht der kantonalen höheren Lehranstalten Luzern, 1959–1960. N.p.: n.p., 1960. 75p.

CI109 Spuler, Linus. "Von deutschamerikanischer Dichtung." *German-Amer. Studies*, vol. 1, no. 1 (1969), 8–16.

CI110 Stern, Desider. *Werke von Autoren Jüdischer Herkunft in deutscher Sprache. Eine Bio-Bibliographie*. 2nd ed. München: B'Nai B'rith, 1969. 407p. The original ed. of 1967 was entitled: *Bücher von Autoren jüdischer Herkunft in deutscher Sprache*. Also publ. Wien: Stern, 1970. Rev. by M. Grossberg, *German-Amer. Studies*, vol. 5 (1972), 189–92. To accompany an exhibit at Universitäts-Bibliothek Frankfurt a.M. 27 April–14 May 1969.

CI111 Stuecher, Dorothea D. "Double Jeopardy: German-American Women Writers in the Nineteenth Century." Diss., Minnesota, 1980–1981. 279p.

CI112 Suderman, Elmer F. "Fiction and Mennonite Life." *Mid-Continent. Amer. Studies Jour.*, vol. 10 (1969), 16–24.

CI113 Tolzmann, Don H. "Contemporary German-American Literature: 1970–1976." In: *German-American Literature*. Ed. D. H. Tolzmann. Metuchen: Scarecrow, 1977, p.308–11.

CI114 Tolzmann, Don Heinrich. "Deutschamerikanische Dichtung 1675–1973." *Der Milwaukee Herold*, 2 August 1973.

CI115 Tolzmann, Don Heinrich. "Musenklänge aus Cincinnati." *Cincinnati Hist. Soc. Bull.*, vol. 35, no. 2 (Summer 1977), 115–29.

CI116 Tolzmann, Don Heinrich, ed. *German-American Literature*. Metuchen, N.J.: Scarecrow Pr., 1977. 341p. Rev. by Charlotte Anderson, *Unterrichtspraxis*, vol. 11, no. 2 (Fall 1978), 130–32. Thirty-four articles collected from recent publications in the field, on German-American literature, the press and theater, and regional writings of Pennsylvania, Wisconsin and Texas.

CI117 Trommler, Frank. "Vom Vormärz zum Bürgerkrieg. Die Achtundvierziger und ihre Lyrik." In: *Amerika in der deutschen Literatur*. Ed. Sigrid Bauschinger et al. Stuttgart: Reclam, 1975, p.93.

CI118 Trout, Thomas J. "The *Knickerbocker* and German Influence." Diss., Bowling Green Univ., 1973. A popular literary journal publ. in New York in the mid-19th century.

CI119 Ward, Robert E. "Amerikas deutschsprachige Dichter aus Baden-Württemberg." *Badische Heimat*, no. 4 (November 1974), 105–10.

CI120 Ward, Robert E. "The Case for German-American Literature." In: *The German Contribution to the Building of the Americas: Studies in Honor of Karl J. R. Arndt*. Ed. G. K. Friesen and W. Schatzberg. Hanover, N.H.: Clark Univ. Pr. and Univ. Pr. of New England, 1977, 373–91.

CI121 Ward, Robert E. "Clevelands deutschamerikanische Dichter." *Wächter und Anzeiger*, 21 June 1968, p.4.

CI122 Ward, Robert E. "Lutherische Pastoren, die zur deutschamerikanischen Literatur beigetragen haben." *German-Amer. Studies*, vol. 6 (1973), 68–71.

CI123 Ward, Robert E. "Reflections on Some German Poems by Lutheran Pastors in America." *Concordia Hist. Inst. Quar.*, vol. 44, no. 3 (August 1971), 114–21.

CI124 Ward, Robert E., Jacob Erhard, and Irene Heydle. "Deutschamerikanische Dichter: Ihr Leben und Schaffen." Continued series in the *Wächter und Anzeiger* (Cleveland), 7 February–28 April 1969.

CI125 Weber, Brom. "Ethnic Literatures in Pre-Revolutionary America." *Procs. of the Compar. Lit. Symposium* (Lubbock, Tex.), vol. 9 (1978), 35–47.

CI126 Willibrand, W. A. "Occasional German Verse at Westphalia, Missouri, in the 1880's." *Studies in German Literature*. Ed. Carl Hammer, Jr. Baton Rouge, Univ. of Louisiana Pr., 1963, p.39–47, 155–56.

CI127 Witte, Karsten. "'Das verlangte / nicht erlangte Canaan / bey den Lust-Gräbern': Zur Kolonialliteratur in North Carolina." *Arcadia*, vol. 8 (1973), 300–06.

CI128 Wood, Ralph C. "German American Poetry." *Amer.-German Review*, vol. 23, no. 4 (1957), 3. Notes on Kurt Baum and others.

Canadian-German Literature

See also The Arts/Music/Literary Life *under* Section BB: Canadian Germans/German Life and Culture in Canada.

ANTHOLOGIES

CI129 Bartsch, Ernst. *Die weite Reise. Kanadische Erzählungen und Kurzgeschichten*. Berlin: Vlg. Volk und Welt, 1974. 400p. A collection of 29 stories.

CI130 Boeschenstein, Hermann, ed. *Heiteres und Satirisches aus der deutschkanadischen Literatur*. Toronto: German-Canadian Hist. Assoc., 1980. 117p. Writings by John Adam Rittinger, Walter Roome, Ernst Loeb, and Rolf Max Kully.

CI131 De Fehr, William, et al., eds. *Harvest Anthology of Mennonite Writing in Canada, 1874–1974*. Winnipeg: Centennial Committee of the Mennonite Hist. Soc. of Canada, 1974. 182p.

CI132 Epp, Georg K., ed. *Unter dem Nordlicht: Anthology of German Mennonite Writing in Canada*. Altona, Man.: D. W. Friesen / Mennonite German Soc. of Canada, 1977. 292p.

CI133 Epp, Reuben. *Biem Aunsiedle*. R.E.C. Recordings (Winnipeg, Man.), 1974. LP record of Low-German stories.

CI134 Epp, Reuben. *Plattdietsche Schreftsteckja*. Steinbach, Man.: Derksen Printers, 1972.

CI135 Friesen, Gerhard K. "German-Canadian Poetry under the Star-Spangled Banner." *German-Canad. Yearbook*, vol. 6 (1981), 103–14.

CI136 Friesen, John W. "Mennonites and Hutterites in Twentieth-Century Alberta Literature with Special Reference to Educational Implications." *Alberta Jour. of Educational Research*, vol. 22 (1976), 102–28.

CI137 Froeschle, Hartmut. "Eine Anthologie deutschkanadischer Dichtung in den Jahrbüchern." *German-Canad. Yearbook*, vol. 5 (1979), 101–07.

CI138 Froeschle, Hartmut, ed. *Nachrichten aus Ontario. Deutschsprachige Literatur in Kanada*. Auslandsdeutsche Literatur der Gegenwart, no. 6. Hildesheim: Georg Olms, 1980. 262p. Anthology of lyric poetry, stories and essays.

CI139 Goerzen, Jakob W. *Germanic Heritage. Canadian Lyrics in Three Languages, English, Low German, German*. Edmonton: n.p., 1963. 169p.

CI140 Goerzen, Jakob W. *Ute Griksche Hellje Schrefte. Proowe Plautditscha Ewasating*. Edmonton: n.p., 1968. 168p.

CI141 Kloss, Heinz, and Arnold B. Dyck, eds. *Ahornblätter. Deutsche Dichtung aus Kanada*. Würzburg: Holzner, 1961. 115p. Incl. some Mennonite writers.

CI142 Thiessen, J. "Canadian Mennonite Literature." *Canad. Lit.*, vol. 51 (Winter 1972), 65–72.

CANADA: GENERAL STUDIES

CI143 Cardinal, Clive H. von. "Some Polish- and German-Canadian Poetry." *Canad. Ethnic Studies*, vol. 1, no. 2 (December 1969), 67f.

CI144 Debor, H. W. "Gibt es deutsch-kanadische Literatur?" *Der Nordwesten*, 22 November 1966, 11, 18.

CI145 Epp, Georg K. "Der mennonitische Beitrag zur deutschkanadischen Literatur." *Mennonitisches Jahrbuch*, 1978, 40–47; also: *German-Canad. Yearbook*, vol. 6 (1981), 140–48.

CI146 Friesen, Gerhard K. "Yankee 'sche Eigenheiten': Anti-Americanism in a 19th-century German-Canadian Poem." *German-Canad. Yearbook*, vol. 6 (1981), 15–29.

CI147 Fröschle, Hartmut. "Die deutschkanadische Literatur: Umfang und Problemstellungen." In: *Annalen 1, Symposium 1976, Deutschkanadische Studien*. Ed. Karin Gürttler and Friedhelm Lach, p. 18–30.

CI148 Froeschle, Hartmut. "Gibt es eine deutschkanadische Literatur?" *Deutschkanadisches Jahubuch*, vol. 3 (1976), 174–87.

CI149 Froeschle, Hartmut, ed. *Drei frühe deutschkanadische Dichter*. Toronto: German-Canad. Hist. Assoc., 1978. 112p. Incl. work of Eugen Funken, Heinrich Rembe, and Emil Querner.

CI150 Gross, Konrad. "Literary Criticism in German on English-Canadian Literature." *German-Canad. Yearbook*, vol. 6 (1981), 305–10.

CI151 Jeffrey, David L. "Biblical Hermeneutic and Family History in Contemporary Canadian Fiction: Wiebe and Laurence." *Mosaic*, vol. 11 (1978), 87–106. Allusions to Heine's "Loreley" in Laurence's *Stone Angel*; role of the Mennonite family in Wiebe's *Blue Mountain of China*.

CI152 Jelen, Walter. "Ein Land [Kanada] sucht seine Dichter." *Bunte Illustrierte Weltspiegel*, no. 44 (26 October 1972), 7.

CI153 Kloss, Heinz. "Bemerkungen zur deutsch-kanadischen Literatur." *German-Canad. Yearbook*, vol. 3 (1976), 188–92.

CI154 Kloss, Heinz. "Randbemerkungen zur deutsch-kanadischen Literatur." *Mitteilungen des Instituts für Auslandsbeziehungen*, vol. 7 (1957), 191–92. A critical-bibliographical article.

CI155 Krahn, Cornelius. "Russo-Mennonite Literatur in Canada and U.S.A." In: *Germanica Americana 1976: Symposium on German-Amcrican Literature and Culture*. Ed. E. A. Albrecht and J. Anthony Burzle. Lawrence: Max Kade Document and Research Center, Univ. of Kansas, 1977, p.95–100.

CI156 Oberholz, Vera. "Dichten dies unschuldigste aller Geschäfte." *Der Nordwesten*, 14 June 1966, 6. The Hölderlin-Gesellschaft at the Univ. of Manitoba.

CI157 Pearlman, R. "Jewish-Canadian Creative Literature: A Preliminary Check List of Authors and Pseudonyms." *Canad. Ethnic Studies*, vol. 1, no. 1 (1969).

CI158 Riedel, Walter, ed. *Kanada*. Forew. by Walter Riedel. Stuttgart: Erdmann, 1976. 416p. In the series "Moderne Erzähler der Welt," sponsored by the Institut für Auslandsbeziehungen, Stuttgart.

CI159 Thiessen, J. "Canadian Mennonite Literature." *Canad. Lit.*, no. 51 (Winter 1972), 65–72.

CI160 "Was bleibet aber stiften die Dichter."—Zur Gründung der Hölderlin-Gesellschaft in der Universität von Manitoba unter Litung von Professor Dr. K. W. Maurer." *Manitoba-Courier*, June 23, 1966, p.10.

CI161 Wieden, Fritz. "Deutschkanadische Literatur: Ein Überblick." In: *Deutsch als Muttersprache in Kanada: Berichte zur Gegenwartslage*. Ed. L. Auburger et al. Wiesbaden: Steiner, 1977, p.69–76.

Specific Canadian- and American-German Authors, Including Writers in Exile

AMANN, PAUL

CI162 Amann, Paul. Papers, 1911–1958. In the collections of the Leo Baeck Institute, New York (MS 75-712). A. (1884–1958) was an emigré scholar and author, Professor at Champlain College, Plattsburgh, New York.

ANNEKE, MATHILDE FRANZISKA (GEISLER)

CI163 Anneke, Fritz, and Mathilde F. Anneke. Papers, 1791–1884. 2 vols. and 8 boxes. In State Hist. Soc. of Wisconsin (MS 62-2085). See Alice E. Schmidt. *Guide to the Manuscripts of the Wisconsin Historical Society*. Madison: n.p., 1944, p.8–9. Incl. correspondence with persons prominent in early Milwaukee history.

CI164 Brümmer, Franz. *Lexikon der deutschen Dichter und Prosaisten des 19. Jahrhunderts bis zur Gegenwart*. Leipzig: n.p., 1913, vol. 1, p.65–66. Bibliography of A.'s writings.

CI165 Dobert, Eitel W. *Deutsche Demokraten in Amerika: Die Achtundvierziger und ihre Schriften*. Göttingen: Vandenhoek & Ruprecht, 1958, p.24–26. Biography and bibliography of A.'s writings.

CI166 Edinger, Dora. "A Feminist Forty-Eighter (Mathilde Franziska Anneke)." *Amer.-German Rev.*, vol. 8, no. 5 (1942), 18–19, 38.

CI167 *Ein ehrengerichtlicher Prozess.* Leipzig: Wigand, 1846. 79p. A lost imprint.

CI168 Friesen, Gerhard K. "A Letter from M. F. Anneke: A Forgotten German-American Pioneer in Women's Rights." *Jour. of German-Amer. Studies*, vol. 12, no. 2 (Spring 1977), 34–46. The letter dated Milwaukee 26 April 1877 is addressed to Alexander Jonas; it is a hitherto unpublished self-appraisal.

CI169 Genzmer, George Harvey. ["Mathilde F. Geisler-Annike."] *Dictionary of Amer. Biography*, vol. 7, (1932), 262–63.

CI170 Goedeke, Karl, ed. *Grundriss.* . . . New series, vol. 1 (1962), p.249–50.

CI171 Hense-Jensen, Wilhelm. *Wisconsins Deutsch-Amerikaner bis zum Schluss des neunzehnten Jahrhunderts*, 2 vols. Milwaukee: n.p., 1902, p.14–18. On Mathilde F. Anneke.

CI172 Krueger, Lillian. "Mathilde Franziska Anneke, an Early Wisconsin Journalist." *Wis. Mag. of Hist.*, vol. 21 (1938), 160–67.

CI173 Ruben, Regina. *Mathilde Franziska Anneke.* Hamburg: n.p., n.d. 32p.

CI174 Schulte, Wilhelm. *Fritz Anneke: Ein Leben für die Freiheit in Deutschland und in den USA.* Dortmund: Verlag des Historischen Vereins Dortmund, 1961. 100p. Rev. in *Amer.-German Rev.*, vol. 27, no. 6 (1961), 38–39.

CI175 Wagner, Maria. "Feminismus, Literatur und Revolution: Ein unveröffentlichtes Manuskript aus dem Jahre 1850." *German Quar.*, vol. 50 (1977), 121–29. Centers on M. F. Anneke.

CI176 Wagner, Maria. "Mathilde Anneke's Stories of Slavery in the German-American Press." *MELUS*, vol. 6, no. 4 (1979), 9–16.

CI177 Wagner, Maria. *Mathilde Franziska Anneke. Ein deutsche Dichterin des Vormärz und amerikanische Feministin.* Frankfurt: Fischer Taschenbuch-Vlg., 1980.

CI178 Wagner, Maria. *Mathilde Franziska Anneke in Selbstzeugnissen und Dokumenten.* Frankfurt: Fischer Taschenbuch-Vlg., ca. 1980. 442p.

CI179 Wagner, Maria. "Representation of Slavery in German-American Prose Fiction." In: *Papers for a Symposium on German-Americana, April 27–28, 1979.* Ed. LaVern J. Rippley and Steven M. Benjamin. Occasional Papers of the Soc. for German-Amer. Studies, no. 10. Morgantown, W. Va.: Dept. of Foreign Langs. W. Va. Univ., 1980, p.130–43.

CI180 Wagner, Maria. "Zerbrochene Ketten: Ein Beitrag zum literarischen Feminismus." In: *Perspectives and Personalities: Studies in Modern German Literature Honoring Claude Hill.* Ed. R. Ley, M. Wagner, J. M. Ratych and K. Hughes. Heidelberg: Winter, 1978, p.340–48. Deals with M. F. Anneke.

CI181 Zündt, E. A. "Mathilde Franziska Anneke (1885)." *Ebbe und Fluth* (Milwaukee), 1894, 327.

ASCHER-NASH, FRANZI

CI182 Ascher-Nash, Franzi. *Essays aus jüngster Zeit.* Beckingen: Literarische Union, 1976. Incl. essays on German-American literature.

CI183 Ascher-Nash, Franzi. *Gedichte eines Lebens.* Darmstadt: Bläschke, 1976.

CI184 Ascher-Nash, Franzi. *Die wahre Perspektive meines Lebens.* Cincinnati: Vlg. des Verbandes deutschsprachiger Autoren in Amerika, 1978.

ASMUS, GEORGE

CI185 Asmus, George. *Gedichtbüchelchen.* Leipzig: Mayer, ca. 1897.

AUSLÄNDER, ROSE

CI186 Ausländer, Rose. *Aschensommer: Ausgewählte Gedichte.* Ed. B. Mosblech. München: Deut. Taschenbuch Vlg., 1978. Rev. by Jerry Glenn, *Jour. of German-Amer. Studies*, vol. 13 (1978), 127–28.

CI187 Ausländer, Rose. *Doppelspiel.* Rev. by Jerry Glenn, *World Lit. Today*, vol. 58 (1978), 618.

CI188 Ausländer, Rose. *Es bleibt noch viel zu sagen.* Ed. B. Mosblech. Köln: Literar. Vlg. Helmut Braun, 1978. 47p. Rev. by Jerry Glenn, *Jour. of German-Amer. Studies*, vol. 13 (1978), 127–28.

CI189 Ausländer, Rose. *Gesammelte Gedichte.* Ed. H. E. Kaufer and B. Mosblech. Leverkusen: Literar. Vlg. Helmut Braun, 1976. 423p. Repr. 1977, 1978. Rev. by Jacob Erhardt, *German-Amer.*

Canadian- and American-German Authors *(cont.)*

Studies, vol. 11, nos. 3–4 (Winter 1976), 91–92; Jerry Glenn, *World Lit. Today*, vol. 51 (1977), 277.

CI190 Ausländer, Rose. *Mutterland. Gedichte.* Köln: Literarischer Vlg. Braun, 1978. 70p. Rev. by Jerry Glenn, *Mod. Austrian Lit.*, vol. 12 (1979), 443–44.

CI191 Ausländer, Rose. *Noch ist Raum.* Duisburg: Gilles Francke, 1976. 128p. Poems: Rev. by Jerry Glenn, *Jour. of German-Amer. Studies*, vol. 12, no. 4 (Winter 1977), 98–99.

CI192 Ausländer, Rose. *Ohne Visum. Poesie und kleine Prosa.* Düsseldorf: Sassafras, 1974. 44p. Rev. by Jerry Glenn, *Books Abroad*, vol. 50 (1976), 154.

CI193 Ausländer, Rose. *Sechsunddreissig Gerechte. Gedichte.* Hamburg: Hoffmann & Campe, 1967. 64p.

CI194 Ausländer, Rose. *Selected Poems.* Trans. by Ewald Osers. Tisbury, Wilts.: London Magazine Editions, 1977. 72p. Rev. by Jacob Erhardt, *Jour. of German-Amer. Studies*, vol. 12, no. 4 (Winter 1977), 97–98.

CI195 Erhardt, Jacob. "Einführung in das lyrische Werk von Rose Ausländer." *German-Amer. Studies*, vol. 2, no. 2 (1970), 55–62.

CI196 Glenn, Jerry H. "Blumenworte / Kriegsgestammel: The Poetry of Rose Ausländer." *Mod. Austrian Lit.*, vol. 12, nos. 3–4 (1979), 127–46.

BACHMAN, J. FRED

CI197 Stahl, Albert G. "Novelist J. Fred Bachman." *The Pa. Dutchman*, vol. 4, no. 10 (1953), 9, 15.

BAUER, WALTER

CI198 Bauer, Walter. *Lebenslauf. Gedichte 1929 bis 1974.* München: Desch, 1975. 144p.

CI199 Froeschle, Hartmut. "Walter Bauer: Sein dichterisches Werk mit besonderer Berücksichtigung seines Kanada-Erlebnisses." *German-Canad. Yearbook*, vol. 5 (1979), 77–100.

CI200 Watt, F. W. "A Different Son: Walter Bauer's Canadian Poetry." *Canad. Forum*, vol. 59 (September 1979), 20–24.

BAUM, KURT

CI201 Baum, Kurt. *Am Leben entlang. Amerika-Ausgabe. Gedichte und Balladen.* Drawings by Willy Knapp. Chicago: Gutenberg Publ., 1933. 52p.

CI202 Baum, Kurt. *Pokale und Kelche. Gedichte.* New York: Deutscher Akademischer Bund, ca. 1910.

CI203 Baum, Kurt. *Zeitgedichte.* Chicago: A. Kroch, ca. 1915. 64p.

CI204 "Curt Baum." *Amer.-German Rev.*, vol. 28, no. 4 (1962), 36. Obituary tribute.

CI205 Voigt, Frieda. "Kurt Baum: German Poet in Milwaukee." *Hist. Messenger* (Milwaukee Public Library), vol. 24, no. 3 (1968), 73–78.

BAYRHOFFER, KARL THEODOR

CI206 [Biographical sketch] *Mitteilungen des deutschen Pionier-Vereins zu Philadelphia*, vol. 11, (ca. 1908), 21.

BECHER, ULRICH

CI207 Becher, Ulrich. *New Yorker Novellen. Ein Zyklus in drei Nächten.* Berlin: Aufbau, 1969. 324p.

BECK, CARL (KARL; CHARLES)

CI208 Beck, Carl. Papers. In: Harvard University Archives. See *Harvard University Faculty...Deceased before 1940. Papers Consisting Mainly of Items Others than Correspondence, c. 1770–1940* (MS 76-1964). On B. (1798–1866).

CI209 Goedeke, Karl, ed. *Grundriss...*, vol. 15 (1964), Ausland part 4, p.544–47. Bio-bibliography.

CI210 Rattermann, Heinrich A. "Karl Beck." *Deutsch-Amerikanisches Mag.*, vol. 1 (1887), 483–88.

BECKER, JOHANN P.

CI211 Becker, Johann P. *Psalmen in Reimform.* Geneva: n.p., 1875.

BEHR, HANS HERMANN

CI212 Legge, Robert J. "Hans Hermann Behr." *Calif. Hist. Soc. Quar.*, vol. 32 (1953), 243–62. On B. (1818–1904), a German Forty-Eighter, botanist in California.

BEIDENKAPP, GEORG

CI213 Beidenkapp, Georg. *Brennende Lieder und Strophen*. New York: n.p., 1900.

CI214 Beidenkapp, Georg. *Sankta Libertas*. New York: n.p., 1893.

BEISSEL, JOHANN CONRAD

CI215 McCort, Dennis. "Johann Conrad Beissel: Colonial Mystic Poet." *German-Amer. Studies*, vol. 8 (1974), 1–26; repr. in *German-Amer. Lit.* Ed. Don H. Tolzmann. Metuchen, N.J.: Scarecrow Pr., 1977, p.108–27.

BENIGNUS, WILHELM

CI216 Benignus, Wilhelm. *Lieder eines Pilgers*. New York: Max Schmetterling, 1912. Copy in Deutsche Gesell. von Pa.

BERGHOLD, ALEXANDER

CI217 Rippley, LaVern J. "Alexander Berghold, Pioneer Priest and Prairie Poet." *The Report. A Jour. of German-Amer. Hist.*, no. 37 (1978), 43–56.

BERL-LEE, MARIA

CI218 "Maria Berl-Lee im Literarischen Verein." *New Yorker Staats-Zeitung und Herold*, vol. 146, no. 10 (1980), Sec. A, p.8.

BERLEMANN, F. W.

CI219 Berlemann, F. W. *Daheim ist's gut. Gedichte*. N.p.: n.p., n.d. Copy in Deut. Gesell. von Pa.

BESENSTIEL, HANS

CI220 Broadbent, T. L., "Hans Besenstiel: Immigrant Satirist." *Western Humanities Rev.*, vol. 12 (1958), 151–57. On the author of letters-to-the-editor in the Salt Lake City *Beobachter* in the 1890's.

BEYSCHLAG, CARL

CI221 Beyschlag, Carl. *Eisele und Beisele im westvirginischen Feldzuge*. A lost imprint. See E. W. Dobert. *Deutsche Demokraten in Amerika*... Göttingen: Vandenhoeckt & Ruprecht, 1958.

CI222 [Bio-bibliography.] In: *Deutsche Demokraten in Amerika*...., by Eitel W. Dobert. Göttingen: Vandenhoeck & Ruprecht, 1958, p.33–34.

BINDER, HEINRICH

CI223 Binder, Heinrich. *Gedichte*. Introd. by G. Thomann. N.p.: n.p., n.d.

CI224 Binder, Heinrich. *Liederklänge aus vier Jahrzehnten*. New York: Stechert, 1895. 142p.

BOKUM, HERMANN

CI225 Hermann Bokum. *Discourse on the State of the German Population in the United States*. New York: J. P. Callender, 1836. Delivered July 31 1836 in Central Presbyterian Church on Broome Street, New York.

BORKHOLDER (BURK(G)HALTER), CHRISTIAN

CI226 Goedeke, Karl, ed. *Grundriss*..., vol. 7, p.579; vol. 15 (1964), Ausland part 4, p.547–48. Bio-bibliography of B. (1784–ca. 1859), a Quaker; author of *Geist der Sprachen* (Cincinnati, 1845). Lived in Warren Co., Ohio.

BÖRNSTEIN, HEINRICH

CI227 Vagts, Alfred. "Heinrich Börnstein, Ex- and Repatriate." *Mo. Hist. Soc. Bull.*, vol. 12, no. 2 (1956), 105–27. A Forty-Eighter active in St. Louis public life; spent his last years as theater director in Vienna.

BOSECKER, LUDWIG

CI228 Goedeke, Karl, ed. *Grundriss*..., vol. 15 (1964), Ausland part 4, p.548. B. was a resident of Pennsylvania, ca. 1830–1836. Bio-bibliography.

BRACHVOGEL, UDO

CI229 Brachvogel, Udo. Papers, 1873–1925. 6 boxes and 1 vol. In New York Public Library (MS 68-1073). Misc. writings, MSS. of poems, letters received, copybooks. Incl. MS. translation of Hawthorne's *Scarlet Letter*.

BRACKLOW, THEODOR

CI230 Theodor Bracklow. *Die Erscheinung. Epische Zeitgedichte*. 4th ed. New York: n.p., 1854.

BRAUSE, HERMAN F.

CI231 Herman F. Brause. *Auf fernen Wegen. Gedichte*. Vienna: Europäischer Vlg., ca. 1975.

CI232 Tolzmann, Don H. "Herman Brause: Auf fernen Wegen." *Der Milwaukee Herold*, 23 August 1973. German-American poet.

BRECHT, BERTOLT

CI233 Bathrick, David. "Brecht's Marxism and America." In: *Essays on Brecht: Theater and Politics*. Ed. Siegfried Mews and Herbert Knust. Chapel Hill: Univ. of N. Car. Pr., 1974, p.209–25.

CI234 Baxandall, Lee. "The Americanization of Bert Brecht." *Brecht Heute*, vol. 1 (1971), 150–67.

CI235 Baxandall, Lee. "Brecht in America, 1935." *Tulane Drama Rev.*, vol. 12 (1967), 69–87.

CI236 Bentley, Eric R. "An Un-American Chalk Circle." *Tulane Drama Rev.*, vol. 10, no. 4 (1966), 64–77.

CI237 Brandt, Thomas O. "Bertolt Brecht und sein Amerikabild." *Universitas* (Stuttgart), vol. 21 (1966), 719–34.

CI238 Brecht, Bertolt. *Gedichte 1941–1947: Gedichte im Exil, in Sammlungen nicht enthaltene Gedichte, Gedichte und Lieder aus Stücken.* Frankfurt a.M.: Suhrkamp Vlg., 1964.

CI239 "Brecht in Exile." *Times Literary Supplement*, 23 November 1973, p.1413–15; 30 November 1973, p.1477. Review article.

CI240 Esslin, Martin. *Brecht. The Man and His Work*. Garden City: Doubleday, 1960.

CI241 Fetscher, Irving. "Bertolt Brecht and America." *Salmagundi*, vol. 10–11 (1969–1970), 246–72.

CI242 Grimm, Reinhold. *Bertolt Brecht und die Weltliteratur*. Nürnberg: Hans Carl, 1961. 96p. Rev. by T. O. Brandt, *German Quar.*, vol. 39 (1966), 117–18.

CI243 Helmetag, Charles H. "Mother Courage and Her American Cousins in *The Skin of Our Teeth*." In: *Theater und Drama in Amerika: Aspekte und Interpretationen*. Ed. Edgar Lohner and Rud. Haas. Berlin: Schmidt, 1978, p.263–77. See also *Mod. Lang. Studies*, vol. 8, no. 3 (1978), 65–69.

CI244 Hermsdorf, Klaus. "Brecht's Prosa im Exil." *Weimarer Beiträge*, vol. 24, no. 2 (1978), 30–42.

CI245 Hook, Sidney. "Bert Brecht, Sidney Hook and Stalin." *Encounter*, vol. 93 (March 1978), 93. Constitutes a reply to Martin Esslin's: "Icon and Self-Portrait: Images of Brecht." *Ibid.*, December 1977, 30–39; rejoinder by M. Esslin, *ibid.*, April, 1978, 90.

CI246 Hoover, Marjorie L. "'Ihr geht gemeinsam den Weg nach unten': Aufstieg und Fall Amerikas im Werk Bertolt Brechts?" In: *Amerika in der deutschen Literatur: Neue Welt, Nordamerika, USA. Wolfgang Paulsen zum 65. Geburtstag.* Ed. S. Bauschinger, H. Denkler, and A. Malsch. Stuttgart: Reclam, 1975, p.294–314.

CI247 Kaes, Anton. "Brecht und der Amerikanismus: Zum Verhältnis von Theater und Massenkultur in den zwanziger Jahren." *Jahrbuch für Internationale Germanistik*, vol. 2, no. 3 (1976), 439–49.

CI248 Lyon, James K. *Bertolt Brecht's American Cicerone. With an Appendix Containing the Complete Correspondence between Bertolt Brecht and Ferdinand Reyher.* Bonn: Bouvier Vlg., 1978. 256p. Article of same title in *Brecht Heute—Brecht Today: Jahrbuch der Internationalen Brecht-Gesellschaft*, vol. 2 (1972), 187–208. Study of a literary friendship extending from 1928 to 1956.

CI249 Michaels, Jennifer E. "Chaplin and Brecht: *The Gold Rush* and *The Rise and Fall of the City of Mahagonny*." *Lit./Film Quar.*, vol. 8 (1980), 170–81.

CI250 Oehme, Walter. "Brecht in der Emigration." *Neue deutsche Literatur*, vol. 11, no. 6 (1963), 180–85.

CI251 Parmalee, Patty Lee. *Brecht's America*. Forew. by John Willett. Columbus, Ohio: Ohio St. Univ. Pr., for Miami Univ., 1980. 306p. Based on a diss. submitted at the Univ. of California, Irvine, 1970. Mostly a discussion of American sources in Brecht's work; and his image of America. Rev. S. Mews, *German Quar.*, vol. 55, no. 3 (May 1982), 455–56.

CI252 Ruland, Richard. "The American Plays of Bertolt Brecht." *Amer. Quar.*, vol. 15, no. 3 (1963), 371–89.

CI253 Schürer, Ernst. "Revolution from the Right: Bertolt Brecht's American Gangster Play *The Resistible Rise of Arturo Ui*." *Perspectives in Contemporary Lit.*, vol. 2, no. 2 (1976), 24–46.

CI254 Seliger, Helfried. *Das Amerikabild Bertolt Brechts*. Bonn: Bouvier Vlg., 1974. 296p.

CI255 Seliger, Helfried. "Bertolt Brecht und Amerika." Diss., McGill Univ., 1973.

CI256 Weisstein, Ulrich. "Bertolt Brecht. Die Lehren des Exils." In: *Die deutsche Exilliteratur 1933–1945.* Ed. Manfred Durzak. Stuttgart: Reclam, 1973, p.373–97.

CI257 Wirth, Andrezej. "Der Amerika-Gestus in Brechts Arbeitsjournal." In: *Die USA und Deutschland: Wechselseitige Spiegelungen in der Literatur der Gegenwart.* Ed. W. Paulsen. Bern: Francke, 1976, p.52–60.

CI258 Woods, Barbara Allen. "English Sayings in Brecht's Plays: A Preliminary Survey." *Proverbium* (Helsinki), (1966), no. 6, 121–29. Their provenience from his varied reading; few direct borrowings are found.

BRENDEL, FRIEDRICH

CI259 [Bio-bibliography.] In *Deutsche Demokraten in Amerika ...*, by E. W. Dobert. Göttingen: Vandenhoeck & Ruprecht, 1958, p.40. On B. (1820–1876).

BRETHAUER, OTTO

CI260 [Bio-bibliography.] In: *Deutsche Demokraten in Amerika ...*, by E. W. Dobert. Göttingen: Vandenhoeck & Ruprecht, 1958, p.40. On B. (1830–1882).

CI261 *Schnedderedengg—An Illustrated Journal of Humor, Satire, Belletristik, Theater and Music.* (New York) 1873–.

BROCH, HERMANN

CI262 Breuer, Robert. "Hermann Broch—Poet and Philosopher." *Amer.-German Rev.*, vol. 23, no. 3 (1957), 12–14. On B. (1886–1951); his life in the United States; his papers at Yale.

CI263 Broch, Hermann. *Briefe.* Zürich: Rhein Vlg., 1957.

CI264 Broch, Hermann. Papers. 9 ft. and 1450 items. In Yale Univ. Library, the Yale Collection of German Literature (MS 68-1446). Correspondence and literary, philosophical and misc. writings. B. (1886–1951) was an author, philosopher, and literary scholar of Germany and U.S., 1914–1951.

CI265 Broch, Hermann. *Die unbekannte Grösse.* Zürich: Rhein Vlg., 1961.

CI266 Brude-Firnau, Gisela. "Hermann Broch-Dr. Daniel Brody, Korrespondenz 1930–1933: Nach den in der Broch-Sammlung befindlichen Materialien, mit Einleitung, Annotationen und dokumentarischem Anhang." 2 vols. Diss., Yale Univ., 1969.

CI267 Nettl, Paul. "Hermann Broch." *Amer.-German Rev.*, vol. 17, no. 6 (1951), 35. Obituary.

CI268 Sammons, Christa. "Hermann Broch Archive: Yale University Library." *Mod. Austrian Lit.* vol. 5, nos. 3–4 (1972), 18–69.

CI269 Sammons, Christa. "Recent Additions to the Hermann Broch Archive." *Yale Univ. Library Gazette*, vol. 53 (1979), 217–20.

CI270 Strelka, Joseph. "Hermann Broch als Exil-Autor." *Mod. Austrian Lit.*, vol. 8, nos. 3–4 (1975), 100–12.

CI271 Strelka, Joseph, ed. *Broch heute.* Bern: Francke, 1978. 154p.

CI272 Watt, Roderick. "America in the Works of Hermann Broch: The Symbol and the Reality." *New German Studies* (Hull, Engl.), vol. 3 (1975), 16–30.

BRONNER, LUISE

CI273 Luise Bronner. *Mosaik. Gedichte.* Darmstadt: Blaschke, 1978. German-Amer. writer in Brookline, Mass.

BRUNNER, CONSTANTIN

CI274 Aron, Willy. *Constantin Brunner: A Contribution to a Bibliography of Writings by and about Him.* New York: n.p., 1942. 7p.

BUFE, FRANZ GUSTAV

CI275 Bufe, Franz Gustav. *Licht und Schatten. Diverse Gedichte.* Moline, Ill.: n.p., 1906.

BUTZ, CASTAR

CI276 Johnson, Hildegard Binder. "Caspar Butz of Chicago—Politician and Poet. Part 1 & 2." *Amer.-German Rev.*, vol. 12, no. 6 (1946), 4–7; vol. 13 (October 1946), no. 1, 9–11.

CANISIUS, THEODORE

CI277 Zucker, A. E. "Dr. Theodore Canisius, Friend of Lincoln." *Amer.-German Rev.*, vol. 16, no. 3 (1950), 13–15. Editor, diplomat, author; a native of Illinois.

CLAUSEN, EMMA

CI278 Clausen, Emma. *Im Vorübergehen—Gedichte*. Los Angeles: n.p., 1956. 158p. B. 1867 in Husum, Schleswig.

CI279 Clausen, Emma. *Kleinigkeiten, Gedanken in Vers und Spruch*. Los Angeles: Commonwealth Pr., 1958. 73p. Poems.

COHEN, LEONARD

CI280 Cohen, Leonard. *Flowers for Hitler. Poems*. 1st ed. Canada, 1964. Reissued London: Jonathan Cape, 1973.

COHN, RUTH C.

CI281 Cohn, Ruth C. *Inmitten aller Sterne*. New York: P. T. Fisher. 2nd ed., 1952. 24p. Poems.

CONZE, ALEXANDER

CI282 Knoche, Carl H. "Alexander Conze: An Early Milwaukee German-American Poet." *German-Amer. Studies*, vol. 5 (1972), 148–62. Author of the "Oregon Lied" and other popular poems. Joined the U.S. forces in the war against Mexico and was killed at the battle of Buena Vista in 1847.

CUNZ, DIETER

CI283 Brown, John D. M. "National Hymn." German translation by Dieter Cunz. *Report of the Soc. for the Hist. of the Germans in Md.*, vol. 28 (1953), 6; also: *Amer.-German Rev.*, vol. 19, no. 5 (1953), 29.

CZOKOR, FRANZ THEODOR

CI284 Czokor, Franz Theodor, ed. *Zeuge einer Zeit. Briefe aus dem Exil 1933–1950*. München: n.p., 1964.

DEMBITZ, LEWIS N.

CI285 Weisert, John J. "Lewis N. Dembitz and *Onkel Toms Hütte*." *Amer.-German Rev.*, vol. 19, no. 3 (1953), 7–8. D. (1833–1907), lawyer and legal advisor to the Kentucky legislature, translated the novel for *Der Beobachter am Ohio* (Louisville, 1853).

DEUTSCH, GOTTHARD

CI286 Deutsch, Gotthard. *Selected List of the Writings of G. D.* Cincinnati: n.p., 1916. 11p.

CI287 Deutsch, Gotthard. *Unlösbare Fesseln. Erzählungen*. Frankfurt a. M.: n.p., 1903. 198p.

DIETZGEN, JOSEPH

CI288 Dietzgen, Joseph. *Gesammelte Schriften*. Ed. Eugen Dietzgen. 4th ed. Berlin: n.p., 1930. Essays on topics such as Monistic philosophy and social reform. Published in Europe and America.

DÖBLIN, ALFRED

CI289 Erhardt, Jacob. *Alfred Döblins "Amazonas"-Trilogy*. Deutsches Exil 1933–1945, Bd. 3. Worms: Georg Heintz, 1974. 123p.

DOERNENBURG, EMIL

CI290 Doernenburg, Emil. *De Profundis. Gedichte*. Braunschweig: B. Goeritz, 1922.

CI291 Doernenburg, Emil. *Deutsch-amerikanische Balladen und Gedichte*. Philadelphia: n.p., 1933. 245p.

CI292 Doernenburg, Emil. *Lieder eines Einsamen*. Leipzig: Xenien-Vlg., 1928.

CI293 Doernenburg, Emil. *Sturm und Stille. Gedichte*. New York: International News Co., 1916.

DOMIN, HILDE

CI294 Stern, Dagmar C. "Hilde Domin: From Exile to Ideal." Diss., Indiana, 1977.

DORSCH, EDUARD

CI295 Dorsch, Eduard. Papers, 1886–1914. 3 vols. and 137 items. In the Michigan Historical Collections, Univ. of Michigan Library (MS 65-234). Correspondence of D., physician and German-American author, mainly in German.

CI296 "Eduard Dorsch and Otto Roser: German-American Poets in Michigan." *Mich. Hist.*, vol. 11, no. 2 (1969), 61–69.

DRESCHER, MARTIN

CI297 D.M., [i.e., Martin Drescher.] [Rev. of George Sylvester Viereck. *A Game at Love and Other Plays*. New York: Brentano, ca. 1906.] *Die Glocke*, vol. 1 (1906), 310–11.

CI298 Voigt, Frieda. "Martin Drescher, A German-American Poet." *Canad. Mod. Lang. Rev.* (Toronto) vol. 24 (Winter 1966). 3p.

CI299 Ward, Robert E. "An Unpublished Poem by Martin Drescher in His Own Handwriting." *German-Amer. Studies*, vol. 3, no. 2 (1971), 1.

DRESCHER, SAMUEL

CI300 Goedeke, Karl, ed. *Grundriss*..., vol. 15 (1964), Ausland part 4, p.548–49. Schwenkfelder poet.

DUBBS, JOSEPH HENRY

CI301 Dubbs, Joseph Henry. "Conrad Bucher." "'S Pennsylfawnisch Deitsch Eck," Allentown *Morning Call*, 15 July 1944. Poem repr. from *Home Ballads and Metrical Versions* by J. H. Dubbs. Philadelphia: Fischer, 1888.

CI302 Dubbs, Joseph Henry. "The Emigrants," and "The Grave of Henry Antes." "'S Pennsylfawnisch Deitsch Eck," Allentown *Morning Call*, 17 February 1945 and 13 October 1945. Selections from Dubbs' *Home Ballads and Metrical Versions*. Philadelphia: n.p., 1888.

CI303 Dubbs, Joseph Henry. "The Tory Preacher." "'S Pennsylfawnisch Deitsch Eck," Allentown *Morning Call*, 19 August 1944. Repr. from *Home Ballads and Metrical Versions*.

DULON, RUDOLF

CI304 [Bio-bibliography.] In: *Deutsche Demokraten in America*..., by E. W. Dobert. Göttingen: Vandenhoeck & Ruprecht, 1958, p.67–71. On D. (1807–1869).

DYCK, ARNOLD

CI305 "Arnold Dyck." *Zeitschrift für Kulturaustausch*, vol. 20, no. 4 (October–December 1970), 407.

CI306 Dyck, Arnold. "Dave Niedorp and the Spook." Trans. by Elmer F. Sudermann. *Mennonite Life*, vol. 26 (April 1971), 59–60. From: *Onse Lied*, p.37–39. Dyck writes about the Mennonites of German-Russian background.

CI307 Dyck, Arnold. "Old Man Stobbe Goes to the Doctor." *Mennonite Life*, vol. 24, no. 4 (October 1969), 170.

CI308 Hadley, Michael L. "Arnold Dyck's 'Verloren in der Steppe', a Mennonite *Bildungsroman*." *Canad. Ethnic Studies*, vol. 1, no. 2 (December 1969).

CI309 Hadley, Michael L. "Education and Alienation in Dyck's *Verloren in der Steppe*: A Novel of Cultural Crisis." *German-Canad. Yearbook*, vol. 3 (1976), 199–206.

CI310 Klassen, N. J. "Arnold Dyck—An Appreciation." *Mennonite Life*, vol. 26 (April 1971), 59.

CI311 Knoop, Aedwig. "Arnold Dyck—At the End of the Road." *Mennonite Life*, vol. 26 (April 1971), 56–58. Trans. by Elmer F. Suderman.

CI312 Peters, Elisabeth. "Arnold Dyck—Our Last Visit." *Mennonite Life*, vol. 26 (April 1971), 54–55.

CI313 Peters, Elisabeth. "Der Mennonitendichter Arnold Dyck in seinen Werken." M.A. Thesis, Univ. of Manitoba, 1968.

CI314 Peters, Elisabeth. "A Tribute to Arnold Dyck." *Mennonite Life*, vol. 24, no. 1 (January 1969), 3–5.

CI315 Suderman, Elmer F. "Arnold Dyck Explains the Origin of Low German." *Mennonite Life*, vol. 24, no. 1 (January 1969), 5–7.

CI316 Suderman, Elmer F. "The Comic Spirit of Arnold Dyck." *Mennonite Life*, vol. 24, no. 4 (October 1969), 169–70.

CI317 Thiessen, Jack. "Arnold Dyck—The Mennonite Artist." *Mennonite Life*, vol. 24, no. 2 (April 1969), 77–83.

EGELMANN, J. CARL FRIEDRICH

CI318 Goedeke, Karl, ed. *Grundriss*..., vol. 15 (1964), Ausland part 4, p.549–50. Bio-bibliography of E. (1762–1860), publisher of almanacs and newspapers, Reading, Pa.

EHRMANN, MAX

CI319 Ehrmann, Bertha. *Max Ehrmann, A Poet's Life*. Boston: Bruce Humphries, 1951. 119p. Rev. by W. H. Jansen, *Ind. Mag. of Hist.*, vol. 47, no. 4 (1951), 389–91. Poet of German parentage, of Terre Haute, Ind.

EMERSON, EDWIN

CI320 Fischer, Hanns. "Colonel Edwin Emerson. Versuch einer Würdigung." *Jahrbuch der Albertus Univ. zu Königsberg*, vol. 11 (1961). 22p. American publicist and war correspondent, born in Germany.

ESSELEN, CHRISTIAN

CI321 [Bio-bibliography.] In: *Deutsche Demokraten in Amerika...*, by E. W. Dobert. Göttingen: Vandenhoeck & Ruprecht, 1958, p.74–77. E. (1823–1859) was an editor and writer.

CI322 Edinger, Dora. "Christian Esselen: Citizen of Atlantis." *Mich. Hist.*, vol. 34, no. 2 (1950), 133–43.

ETZLER, JOHN ADOLPHUS

CI323 Thoreau, Henry David. [Rev. and comment on Etzler's *The Paradise Within the Reach of All Men, Without Labor, by Power of Nature and Machinery*.] See: "Paradise (to be) Regained." In: *Reform Papers*, by H. D. Thoreau. Ed. Wendell Glick. Princeton: Princeton Univ. Pr., 1973, p.19–47.

FAUST, ALBERT B.

CI324 Faust, Albert B. *The Bank War, An American Historical Drama in Six Scenes*. New York: n.p., 1944. 86p.

FELMAYER, RUDOLF

CI325 Felmayer, Rudolf. *Dein Herz ist deine Heimat*. Wien: n.p., 1955. By an Austrian émigré writer.

FEUCHTWANGER, LION

CI326 Fanning, Rita M. "Das Amerikabild in den Werken Lion Feuchtwangers, 1921–1952." Diss., Univ. of Southern California, 1971.

CI327 Kahn, Lothar. *Insight and Action: The Life and Work of Lion Feuchtwanger*. Rutherford / Madison / Teaneck, N.J.: Fairleigh Dickinson Univ. Pr., 1975. 392p. Rev. by John M. Spalek, *German Quar.*, vol. 51 (1978), 393–95.

CI328 Keilbach, Herta M. "A Bibliography of Lion Feuchtwanger's Works in English Translation." Diss., Univ. of Southern California, 1973.

CI329 Pischel, Joseph. *Lion Feuchtwanger: Versuch über Leben und Work*. Leipzig: Ph. Reclam jun., 1976. 279p. Rev. by J. M. Spalek, *German Quar.*, vol. 51 (1978), 393–95.

CI330 Reich-Ranicke, Marcel. "Lion Feuchtwanger: oder der Weltruhm des Emigranten." In: *Die deutsche Exilliteratur 1933–1945*. Ed. Manfred Durzak. Stuttgart: Reclam, 1973, p.443–56. Also in: *Frankfurter Hefte*, vol. 28 (1973), 357–66.

CI331 Wertheim, Ursula. "Das Amerikabild in Lion Feuchtwangers Roman *Die Füchse im Weinberg*: Zum Problem des historischen Romans bei Feuchtwanger." In: *Erzählte Welt: Studien zur Epik des 20. Jahrhunderts*. Ed. H. Brandt and N. Kakabadse. Berlin: Aufbau, 1978, p.123–40, 430–35.

FICK, HEINRICH H.

CI332 Fick, Henry H. *Der deutschamerikanische Pestalozzi*. N.p.: n.p., n.d.

CI333 Fick, Henry H. *Erfolgreicher Deutschunterricht in öffentlichen Schulen*. N.p.: n.p., n.d.

CI334 Fick, Henry H. *Meine deutschamerikanischen Poetenbekanntschaften*. N.p.: n.p., n.d.

CI335 Fick, Henry H. *Wir in Amerika*. N.p.: n.p., n.d.

CI336 Fick, Henry H. "Der 22. Februar." *Freidenker-Almanach für das Jahr 1892* (Milwaukee), 25–37.

CI337 Tolzmann, Don H. "The Last Cincinnati German Poet: Heinrich H. Fick." *German-Amer. Studies*, vol. 11 (1976), 1–16; repr. in his *German-American Literature*. Metuchen, N.J.: Scarecrow Pr., 1977, p.273–84. Incl. a list of the writings of Fick: fiction, essays, occasional pieces, and German-American literary history.

CI338 Ward Robert E. "The German-American Library of H. H. Fick: A Rediscovery." Part 1. *German-Amer. Studies*, vol. 1, no. 1 (1969), 49–68. Part 2. *Ibid.*, vol. 2, no. 1 (1970), 2–29.

FLEISSER, MARIE LUISE

CI339 Schmitz, Walter. "Hier ist Amerika oder nirgends: Die negative Erlösung in Marie Luise Fleissers Roman *Eine Zierde für den Verein*." *Text + Kritik*, vol. 64 (1979), 61–73.

FOLLEN, KARL (CHARLES)

CI340 Follen, Karl. Papers. In Harvard Univ. Archives, *Harvard Univ. Faculty...Deceased Before 1940* (MS 76–1965). Chiefly correspondence, 1725–ca. 1940.

CI341 Goedeke, Karl, ed. *Grundriss...*, vol. 8, p.139; vol. 15 (1964), Ausland part 4, p.550–65. Bio-bibliography of F. (1796–1840).

CI342 Holinger, Cora L. "Charles Follen. A Sketch of His Life in New England." *Amer.-German Rev.*, vol. 14, no. 5 (1948), 20–22.

CI343 Huebener, Theodore. "The First German Grammar and Reader for American Schools." *German Quar.*, vol. 22 (1949), 95–101. On: Charles Follen's grammar.

CI344 "Karl Follen in Amerika." *Telegraph für Deutschland*, February 1845, 137–40, 141–44; March 1845, 157–59, 163–64, 166–68, 170–72, 174–45, 178–80, 182–84, 186–7, 190–91. Incl. poems, excerpts from journals, and letters from Follen and to Follen.

CI345 Legge, James Grancille. *Rhyme and Revolution in Germany. A Study in German History, Life, Literature and Character 1813–1850*. London: n.p., 1918. See p.32 and 217 for comments on Karl Follen.

CI346 Prutz, Robert Eduard. *Gedichte. Neue Sammlung*. Zürich: Winterthur, 1843. "An L[udwig] F[ollen], October 1842." A poem about the Follen brothers.

CI347 Schneider, Heinrich. "Karl Follen: A Re-Appraisal and Some New Biographical Materials." *Report of the Soc. for the Hist. of the Germans in Md.*, vol. 30 (1959), 73–86. Unpublished letters from Follen to Franz Lieber and to John Quincy Adams.

CI348 Szépe, Helena. "Zur Problematik von Karl Follens *Grossem Lied*." *Monatshefte*, vol. 63 (1971), 335–40.

CI349 Whittier, John Greenleaf. "Follen." [Broadside] Haverhill: n.p., 1842. Also in *The Writings*, by John Greenleaf Whittier. Vol. 4. London: n.p., 1889, p.29–34; also vol. 3, p.24–28.

FOLLENIUS, PAUL

CI350 Muench, Friedrich. "Paul Follenius." Trans. 2nd ed. by Ralph Gregory. *Bull. of the Mo. Hist. Soc.*, vol. 23 (July 1967), 325–47. Excerpts from Muench's *Erinnerungen aus Deutschlands trübster Zeit* (St. Louis, 1873).

FRANK, BRUNO

CI351 Hoyt, Walter Carl-Alexander. "Conflict in Change: A Study of the Prose–Fiction of Bruno Frank." Diss., Rutgers Univ., 1979. 302p. Writer in exile who lived in California until his death in 1945.

FREY, EGON

CI352 Frey, Egon. *Werktagslied*. Wien: Europäisches Vlg., 1968. On F. (1892–1972).

CI353 Ward, Robert E. "Dr. Egon Frey in Memoriam." *German-Amer. Studies*, vol. 6 (1973), 1–2. Obituary of Viennese-born physician of New York, author of German-language poems, novellas and novels.

FREYTAG-LORINGHOVEN, ELSA (PLÖTZ) VON

CI354 von Freytag-Loringhoven, Elsa. Papers. 3 ft. In: Univ. of Maryland Library, College Park (MS 80-2327). Papers in English and German of F.-L. (1847–1927), author and poet.

FRIEBERT, STUART

CI355 Friebert, Stuart. *Der Gast, und sei er noch so schlecht*. Duisburg: Gilles & Francke, 1973. 52p. Excerpts from his work.

CI356 Friebert, Stuart. *Kein Trinkwasser. Gedichte von Stuart Friebert*. Note by Karl Krolow. Andernach: Atelier Vlg., 1969. 60p.

CI357 Friebert, Stuart. *Nicht hinauslehnen: Gedichte*. München: Delp, 1975. 64p.

CI358 Friebert, Stuart. *Die Prokuristen kommen. Gedichte*. Halten: Ueli Kaufmann & Co, Lenos-Presse (Basel), 1972. 58p.

FRIEDMANN, ROBERT

CI359 Gross, Leonard, ed. "Conversations with Robert Friedmann." *Mennonite Quar. Rev.*, vol. 48, no. 2 (April 1974), 141–73.

CI360 Klaassen, Walter. "Robert Friedmann as Historian." *Mennonite Quar. Rev.*, vol. 48, no. 2 (April 1974), 125–40.

CI361 Klingelsmith, Sharon L., comp. "Bibliographical and Research Notes: A Bibliography of the Anabaptist-Mennonite Writings of Robert Friedmann." *Mennonite Quar. Rev.*, vol. 48, no. 2 (April 1974), 246–55.

FRIEDRICH, GERHARD

CI362 Friedrich, Gerhard. *When Quakers Meet, and Other Poems*. Guilford College: n.p., 1943. 50p. Incl. a collection of poems in German originally intended for the cycle *Du tiefes Leben*.

FROMM, ERICH

CI363 Hausdorff, Don. *Erich Fromm*. New York: Twayne, 1972. 180p. Critical study in Twayne's United States Authors series.

FUNCKEN, EUGEN

CI364 Erb, Peter C. "The Canadian Poems of Eugen Funcken, C.R." *German-Canad. Yearbook*, vol. 4 (1978), 225–33.

GEHRING, ALBERT

CI365 Gehring, Albert. *Maskenfest. Gedichte*. Cleveland: n.p., n.d. 35p.

CI366 Gehring, Albert. *Phantasien und Betrachtungen*. Cleveland: n.p., 1916. 94p.

GEILFUSS, GEORG EDWARD ("GEORGE EDWARD")

CI367 Edward, George. *Komödie des Lebens. Roman aus Amerika*. Freiburg im Breisgar: n.p., n.d. 608p. G. (1869–1969) was a poet of Chicago, who returned to Europe in 1931.

CI368 Stoll, Karl-Heinz. "The Literary Activity of Georg Edward." *German-Amer. Studies* vol. 1, no. 1 (1969), 17–32.

GOETZ, GUSTAV FRIEDRICH

CI369 Goedeke, Karl, ed. *Grundriss* . . . , vol. 15 (1964), Ausland part 4, p.564–65. Bio-bibliography of G. (b. ca. 1765), author of Pennsylvania.

GOLDBECK, FRIEDRICH W. F.

CI370 Robinson-Zwahr, Robert R. "Friedrich Wilhelm Ferdinand Goldbeck." *German-Amer. Studies*, vol. 10 (Fall 1975), 12–19. German-Texas poet, b. 1831 in Hannover. Study incl. some genealogical data on the Bremer family.

GONG, ALFRED

CI371 Gong, Alfred. *Happening in der Park Avenue. New Yorker Geschichten*. München: Piper, 1969. 222p. Seven stories by a German author who came to New York in 1952.

GOOD, MERLE

CI372 Pinsker, Sanford. "The Mennonite as Ethnic Writer: A Conversation with Merle Good." *Jour. of Ethnic Studies*, vol. 3, no. 2 (Summer 1975), 57–64.

GRAF, OSKAR MARIA

CI373 Eckert, Brita, and Werner Berthold, eds. *Oskar Maria Graf: Briefe aus dem Exil: Aus unveröffentlichten Beständen der Deutschen Bibliothek*. Frankfurt: Buchhändler-Vereinigung, 1978. 72p.

CI374 Graf, Oskar Maria. *Das bayrische Dekameron*. New York: n.p., 1939.

CI375 Graf, Oskar Maria. *Die Flucht ins Mittelmässige: Ein New-Yorker Roman*. Frankfurt: Nest Verlag, 1959. 504p. Novel on the life of refugees in New York in the 1950's—twenty years after their emigration; partly autobiographical.

CI376 Graf, Oskar Maria. "My Family and America." *Amer.-German Rev.*, vol. 9, no. 5 (1943), 141–6.

CI377 Graf, Oskar Maria. Papers. 55 boxes. In Univ. of New Hampshire Library, Durham (MS 73-194). Correspondence, MSS. clippings, memorabilia, personal library. Letters from prominent German men of letters of his time, 1933–1967. See *Literaturwissenschaftliches Jahrbuch* (Berlin), vol. 11 (1971), 369–86, for a description of the collection.

CI378 Graf, Oskar Maria. *Prisoners All*. New York: n.p., 1943.

CI379 Graf, Oska Maria. *Ua—Pua*! Mit 30 Kreidezeichnungen von Georg Schrimpf . . . . Regensburg: F. L. Habbel: n.p., 1921. 59p. "Indianer-Dichtungen."

CI380 Heydt, Alfred von der. "Oskar Maria Graf." *German Quar.*, vol. 41 (1968), no. 3, 401–12.

CI381 Pfanner, Helmut F. *Oskar Maria Graf: Eine kritische Bibliographie*. Bern München: Francke, 1976. 767p. Rev. by Ilsedore B. Jonas, *German Quar.*, vol. 51, no. 1 (January 1978), 120–22.

CI382 Recknagel, Rolf. *Ein Bayer in America: Oskar Maria Graf—Leben und Werk*. Berlin: Nation, 1975; Guhl: Klaus Vlg. 460p.

GROSS, WILLIAM

CI383 Gross, Elizabeth L. "Poet William Gross." *The Pa. Dutchman*, vol. 4, no. 10 (1953), 12. Brief account of the Mennonite poet; checklist of his broadsides.

GROSSBERG, MIMI

CI384 Grossberg, Mimi. *Gedichte und kleine Prosa*. Wien: Bergland Vlg., 1972. Rev. by J. Erhardt, *German-Amer. Studies*, vol. 7 (Spring 1974), 93.

CI385 Grossberg, Mimi. "Der New Yorker literarische Kreis von 1938." *Literatur und Kritik*, vol. 119 (1977), 547–57.

CI386 Grossberg, Mimi. *Versäume, verträume. Alte und neue Gedichte*. Wien: Europäischer Vlg., 1957.

CI387 Johns, Jorun. "Mimi Grossberg: Eine Bibliographie bis Ende 1978." *Mod. Austrian Lit. Jour. of the Arthur Schnitzler Research Assoc.*, vol. 12, nos. 3–4 (1979), 317–24.

GROSSBERG, NORBERT

CI388 Grossberg, Norbert. *Die Schaukel*. Wien: Europäischer Vlg., 1966.

GROSCH (GROSH), GEORGE

CI389 Goedeke, Karl, ed. *Grundriss...*, vol. 15 (1964), Ausland part 4, p.564–66. Bio-bibliography of G., author of Marietta, Ohio; editor of Universalist journal.

GROVE, FREDERICK PHILIP (FELIX PAUL GREVE)

CI390 Giltrow, Janet. "Grove in Search of a New Audience." *Canad. Lit.*, vol. 90 (1981), 92–107. On Frederick Grove, Canadian novelist.

CI391 Grove, Frederick P. *Fruits of the Earth*. New Canadian Library, no. 49, N.p.: n.p., n.d. Novel.

CI392 Healy, J. J. "Grove and the Matter of Germany: The Warkentin Letters and the Art of Liminal Disengagement." *Studies in Canad. Lit.*, vol. 6 (1981), 170–87.

CI393 Kaye, Frances W. "Hamlin Garland and Frederick Philip Grove: Self-Conscious Chroniclers of the Pioneers." *Canad. Rev. of Amer. Studies*, vol. 10 (Spring 1979), 31–39.

CI394 Keith, W. J. "F. P. Grove's 'Difficult' Novel: *The Master of the Mill*." *Ariel: A Rev. of Internat. Engl. Lit.*, vol. 4, no. 2 (1973), 34–48.

CI395 Keith, W. J. "Grove's Search for America." *Canad. Lit.*, vol. 59 (Winter 1974), 57f.

CI396 McMullin, Stanley E. "Grove and the Promised Land." In: *Writers of the Prairies*. Ed. Donald G. Stephens. Vancouver: Univ. of British Columbia Pr., 1973, p.67–76.

CI397 Pacey, Desmond, and J. C. Mahanti. "Frederick Philip Grove: An International Novelist." *Internat. Fiction Rev.*, vol. 1, no. 1 (1974), 17–26.

CI398 Pache, Walter. "Der Fall Greve: Vorleben und Nachleben des Schriftstellers Felix Paul Greve." *German-Canad. Yearbook*, vol. 5 (1979), 121–36.

CI399 Riley, Anthony W. "The German Novels of Frederick Philip Grove." *Inscape* (Univ. of Ottawa), vol. 9, no. 1 (1974), 55–66.

CI400 Spettigue, Douglas O. "Frederick Philip Grove." *Queen's Quar.*, Winter 1971, 614–15.

CI401 Spettigue, Douglas O. "The Grove Enigma Resolved." *Queen's Quar.*, Spring 1972, 1–2.

CI402 Spettigue, Douglas O., and Anthony W. Riley. "Felix Paul Greve Redivivus: Zum früheren Leben des kanadischen Schriftstellers Frederick Philip Grove." *Seminar*, vol. 9 no. 2 (1973), 148–55.

CI403 Stick, K. P. "Grove's New World Bluff." *Canad. Lit.*, vol. 90 (1981), 111–23. On Frederick Philip Grove.

CI404 Stobie, Margaret R. *Frederick Philip Grove*. TWAS no. 246. New York: Twayne, 1973. 206p.

CI405 Stobie, Margaret R. "'Frederick Philip Grove' and the Canadianism Movement." *Studies in the Novel* (North Texas St. Univ.), vol. 4 (1972), 173–85.

CI406 Stobie, Margaret. "Grove's Letters from the Mennonite Reserve." *Canad. Lit.*, vol. 59 (Winter 1974), 67–80.

CI407 Webber, Bernard. "Grove in Politics." *Canad. Lit.*, vol. 63 (Winter 1975), 126–27.

GRUBER, JOHN

CI408 Cunz, Dieter. "John Gruber and His Almanac." *Md. Hist. Mag.*, vol. 47 (June 1952), 89–102.

GRUNEWALD, DORA

CI409 Grunewald, Dora. "Kunst und Leben." *Der Milwaukee Herold*, 18 October 1973. German-

Canadian- and American-German Authors *(cont.)*

American poet, b. 1895 in Hanau; high school teacher of languages. A volume of her verse, entitled *Gedichte*, has been published.

CI410 Grunewald, Dora. "Was ist Poesie? Vortrag." Milwaukee: n.p., 1974.

CI411 Ritter, Erwin F. "Dora Grunewald: Reminiscences." *German-Amer. Studies*, vol. 7 (1974), 5–12. The essay by Ritter has been repr. in *German-American Literature*, ed. D. H. Tolzmann. Metuchen: Scarecrow Pr., 1977, p. 291–97.

GUETERMANN, ERIKA

CI412 Guetermann, Erika. *Maschine und Magnolia*. Stuttgart: Deutsche Verlagsanstalt, 1966. 87p. Rev. by H. Adolf, *Books Abroad*, Autumn 1967, 440–41. E. Guetermann, who emigrated in 1938, writes about the United States.

HÄRTING, CARL

CI413 Härting, Carl. "Chicago. Zweiter Preisgekrönter Aufsatz." *Die Glocke*, vol. 3 (1908), 57–60.

HARRO-HARRING, PAUL (HARRO PAUL HARRING)

CI414 Harro-Harring, Paul. *Dolores: A Novel of South America*. New York: Publ. by the Author; Montevideo: Libreria Hernandez, 1846. 356p. The story of Rio de la Plata and the Revolution in Brazil, led by Garibaldi (1834–1836). Harring (1798–1870) lived in Rio de Janeiro in 1842–1843. After an adventurous career in political reform, he took refuge in the United States. The second ed. of *Dolores* was issued by Harring in 1847. The title is expanded to include: . . . *Episodes on Politics, Religion, Socialism, Psychology, Magnetism, and Sphereology*.

HARTMANN, SADAKICHI

CI415 Knox, George. "A Complex Fate: Sadakichi Hartmann, Japanese-German Immigrant Writer and Artist." *German-Amer. Studies*, vol. 7 (Spring 1974), 38–49. Sketch of the engrossing life and frustrated work of Hartmann. Journalist and writer in New York; art historian 1898–1916.

CI416 Knox, George, and Harry W. Lawton. *The Whitman-Hartmann Controversy. Including Conversations with Walt Whitman and other Essays*. Bern / Frankfurt a.M. / München: Lang, 1976. 137p. An attempt to clarify the relationship between Hartmann and Whitman and the circumstances surrounding the founding of a Whitman Society. The present work includes: "Notes of a Conversation with the Good Gray Poet by a German Poet and Traveller," "An Early Estimate of Walt Whitman by Ferdinand Freiligrath (Hartmann's translation)."

HARTZLER, HENRY BURNS

CI417 Hartzler, Henry Burns. *Poems*. Harrisburg, Pa.: n.p., ca. 1920.

HASSAUREK, FRIEDRICH

CI418 Hassaurek, Friedrich. *Four Years Among the Ecuadorians*. Ed. C. Harvey Gardiner. Carbondale/Edwardsville: Southern Ill. Univ. Pr., 1967. 196p. With an introduction by C. Harvey Gardiner on H.'s life and work. Reissue of: *Four Years Among Spanish-Americans*. New York: Hurd & Houghton, 1967.

CI419 Hassaurek, Friedrich. Papers. In Library of the Ohio Hist. Soc. (MS 60-2620). Misc. personal, political, professional papers; MSS. of writings.

CI420 Merrill, Peter C. "Friedrich Hassaurek's *The Secret of the Andes*: An Exotic Romance by a Forty-Eighter." In: *Papers from the St. Olaf Symposium on German-Americana*. Ed. La Vern J. Rippley and Steven M. Benjamin. Occasional Papers of the Soc. for German-Amer. Studies, no. 10. Morgantown, W.Va.: Dept. of Foreign Languages, W.Va. Univ., 1980, p. 87–95.

CI421 Wittke, Carl F. "Friedrich Hassaurek: Cincinnati's Leading Forty-Eighter." *Ohio Hist. Quar.*, vol. 68 (1959), 1–17.

HEHL, MATTHAEUS GOTTFRIED

CI422 Hehl, Matthaeus Gottfried. "Carminum and Poematum Mattaei, è pluribus selectorum fasciculus secundus." Handwritten volume in possession of the Moravian Archives, Southern Province, Winston-Salem, N.C. 336p. The book contains 185 poems to mark various occasions in the author's experience. All but three are in German.

CI423 Schweitzer, Christoph E. "The Significance of a Newly Discovered Volume of Verse by Matthaeus Gottfried Hehl." *Yearbook of German-Amer. Studies*, vol. 16 (1981), 67–72.

HEILBUT, IVAN

CI424 Heilbut, Ivan. *Meine Wanderungen. Gedichte*. New York: n.p., 1942. 71p.

HEINZEN, KARL

CI425 Friesen, Gerhard. "A Pseudo-Heinzen Poem." *Jour. of German-Amer. Studies*, vol. 13

(1978), 41–51. The "Neues Wintermärchen," published anonymously in 1872, was generally attributed to Heinzen (1809–1880). It is here ascribed to Otto Hörth, an editor of the *Frankfurter Zeitung*.

CI426 Friesen, Katherine, and Gerhard K. Friesen. "Karl Heinzen's German-American Writings: Some Literary Aspects." *German-Amer. Studies*, vol. 7 (1974), 107–29; repr. in: Don H. Tolzmann, ed. *German-American Literature*. Metuchen, N.J.: Scarecrow Pr., 1977, p.179–95. Account of Heinzen's literary career, with emphasis on his dramas.

CI427 Heinzen, Karl. "Louisville Platform." In the Labadie Collection of the Univ. of Michigan Library. Copy also in the Univ. of Kentucky Library. The original English text of the Louisville Platform of a proposed new reform party, drawn up by Karl Heinzen.

CI428 Heinzen, Karl. MSS. In Niedersächsische Staats- und Universitätsbibliothek, Göttingen (Nachlass Seidensticker, no. 25.6835, no. 90). MS. describing Heinzen's expulsion from Bern, winter 1847.

CI429 Wittke, Carl. *Against the Current. The Life of Karl Heinzen, 1809–1880*. Chicago: Univ. of Chicago Pr., 1945. 342p. Rev. by A. E. Zucker, *Monatshefte für deutschen Unterricht*, vol. 37, no. 6 (1945), 448–49; Dieter Cunz, *Amer. Hist. Rev.*, vol. 50, no. 4 (1945), 815–17; Elmer Ellis, *Miss. Valley Hist. Rev.*, vol. 32, no. 1 (1945), 110–11; J. T. Flynn, *Annals of the Amer. Academy of Political and Social Science*, (September 1945), 197; P. L. Johnson, *Catholic Hist. Rev.*, vol. 31, no. 2 (1945), 212–13; H. Larsen, *Jour. of Mod. Hist.*, vol. 17, no. 2 (1945), 174–75.

CI430 Wittke, Carl. "Freiligrath and Heinzen." *Monatshefte für deutschen Unterricht*, vol. 34, no. 7 (1942), 425–35.

CI431 Wittke, Carl. "Karl Heinzen's Literary Ambitions." *Monatshefte für deutschen Unterricht*, vol. 37, no. 2 (1945), 88–98.

HELFFENSTEIN, SAMUEL

CI432 Goedeke, Karl, ed. *Grundriss...*, vol. 15 (1964), Ausland part 4, p.567–69. Bio-bibliography of H. (1775–1866), minister of Montgomery Co., Pa.; author of poems, sermons, songs and hymns.

HELLER, PETER

CI433 Heller, Peter. *Menschentiere*. Buffalo, N.Y.: n.p., 1975. Special issue of his *Lyrik und Prosa*.

CI434 Heller, Peter. *Prosa in Versen*. Darmstadt: Bläschke, 1975.

HELMUTH, JUST(US) HEINRICH (HENRY) CHRISTIAN

CI435 Goedeke, Karl, ed. *Grundriss...*, vol. 15 (1964), Ausland part 4, p.569–73. Bio-bibliography of H. (1745–1825), Pennsylvania-German Lutheran minister, author of hymns, juvenile books, sermons.

HEMPEL, MAX

CI436 Hempel, Max. *Gedichte*. St. Louis; Co-operative Printing House, 1909.

HENKEL, AMBROSE

CI437 Goedeke, Karl, ed. *Grundriss...*, vol. 15 (1964), Ausland part 4, p.573–75. Bio-bibliography of H. (1786–1870), an author and printer of Virginia.

CI438 Henkel, Ambrose. *Kurzer Zeitvertreib. Lieder*. Dayton: n.p., 1851.

CI439 Stewart, John, and Elmer L. Smith. "The Henkel ABC Books." *Shenandoah Valley Studies*, nos. 49 and 50. "'S Pennsylfawnisch Deitsch Eck," Allentown *Morning Call*, 11, 18 February, 1967. On works produced at the Henkel Press.

HENSCHEL, GEORGE

CI440 Henschel, George. *Bridge over Yesterday, Including Kinderschpiel and Other Poems*. New York: Vantage Pr., 1976. 163p. Writer of North Carolina.

HERING, CONSTANTIN

CI441 Hering, Constantin. *Drei Novelletten*. Sondershausen: n.p., 1863.

HERMANN-NEISSE, MAX

CI442 Hermann-Neisse, Max. *Letzte Gedichte*. New York: Barthold Fles, 1942. 252p.

CI443 Hermann-Neisse, Max. *Mir bleibt mein Lied: Auswahl aus unveröffentlichten Gedichten*. New York: Fles, 1942. 184p.

CI444 Lorenz, Rosemarie. *Max Herrmann-Neisse*. Germanistische Abhandlungen, vol. 14. Stuttgart:

Canadian- and American-German Authors *(cont.)*

Metzler, 1966. 192p. Rev. H. Pappe, *Germanic Rev.*, vol. 42, no. 1 (January 1967), 74–75.

HERMLIN, STEPHAN

CI445 Durzak, Manfred. "Der 'Zwang zur Politik.' Georg Kaiser und Stephan Hermlin im Exil." *Monatshefte*, vol. 68, no. 4 (Winter 1976), 373–86.

HESSE, ALICE

CI446 Hesse, Alice. *Rippled Memories.* New York: Harbinger House, 1943. 69p.

HEYM, STEFAN

CI447 Zachau, Reinhard Konrad. "Stefan Heym in Amerika: Eine Untersuchung zu Stefan Heyms Entwicklung im amerikanischen Exil 1935–1952." Diss., Pittsburgh, 1978. 273p.

HINTERLEITNER, G. A.

CI448 Hinterleitner, G. A. *Eine ernsthafte Kriegsgeschichte in Versen.* Pottsville, Pa.: H. J. Hendler & Co., 1871. Copy in Deut. Gesell. von Pa.

HIRSH, HELMUT

CI449 Hirsh, Helmut. *Amerika, du Morgenröte. Verse eines Flüchtlings (1939–1942).* New York: Willard Publ. Co., 1947.

HOCHBAUM, ELFRIEDA

CI450 Hochbaum, Elfrieda. *Burning Arrows.* Boston: Humphries, 1963. On H. (1877–1962); a study in novelistic form of the author's German-American girlhood in Chicago. Introd. and notes by Elfrieda Pope Bestelmeyer.

CI451 Hochbaum, Elfrieda. Papers, 1906–1963. 4 ft. and 26 ft. microfilm. In Cornell Univ. Libraries, Collection of Regional History and University Archives (MS 70-1096). Author, in Ithaca, N.Y.

IDELER, L.

CI452 Ideler, L. *Weisse und rote Rosen.* St. Louis: L. Lange, 1929.

ILGEN, PEDRO

CI453 Ilgen, Pedro. *Stechaepfel. Ein Frühlingsgedicht von Pedro Ilgen . . .* Highland, Ill.: n.p., ca. 1890. 48p. I. (b. 1869).

CI454 Ilgen, Pedro. *Sulamith. Königsnocturnen, Meer- und Wanderlieder.* St. Louis: J. Meyer, ca. 1907. 50p; Leipzig: Volger, 1908.

CI455 Ilgen, Pedro. *Tiefgluth. Dichtungen.* St. Louis: J. Meyer, 1906. 37p.

ILLING, OSCAR

CI456 Illing, Oscar. *Rosen und Dornen. Gedichte.* Ellenville, N.Y.: German-American Author's Agency, ca. 1908. Copy in Deut. Gesell. von Pa.

JOCKERS, ERNST

CI457 Jockers, Ernst. *Wandlungen. Gedichte.* New York: Westermann, n.d. Copy in Deut. Gesell. von Pa.

JORDAN, MILDRED A.

CI458 Jordan, Mildred A. *Apple in the Attic.* New York: Knopf, 1942. 200p. Rev. by Elizabeth Drew, *Atlantic Monthly*, October 1942; B. Sherman, *N.Y. Times*, 13 September 1942.

CI459 Jordan, Mildred A. *One Red Rose Forever.* New York: Knopf, 1941. 550p. Rev. by A. E. Zucker, *Amer.-German Rev.*, vol. 8, no. 2 (1941), 33. Fictionalized life of Baron Stiegel of Lancaster County.

CI460 Jordan, Mildred. *The Shoe-Fly Pie.* New York: Knopf, 1944. 118p. Rev. by D. B. Johnston, *Hist. Rev. of Berks Co.*, vol. 9, no. 4 (1944), 118. A present-day story of a Pennsylvania German farm family.

JÜRGENSEN, MATHILDE

CI461 Jürgensen, Mathilde. *Heimatliebe. Gedichte.* 3rd ed. New York: n.p., 1921. Copy in Deut. Gesell. von Pa.

KAHN, LISA

CI462 Kahn, Lisa. *Feuersteine.* Zürich: Strom-Vlg., 1978. Rev. Jerry Glenn, *World Lit. Today*, vol. 54 (1980), 105.

CI463 Kahn, Lisa. *Klopfet an so wird euch nichts aufgetan.* Darmstadt: Bläschke, 1975.

CI464 Kahn, Lisa. "Onkel Konrads Hütte." *Jour. of the German-Texan Heritage Soc.*, vol. 3, no. 1 (1980), 26–28.

CI465 Kahn, Lisa. *Utahs Geheimnisse.* Berlin: Stoedtner, 1982.

KAHN, ROBERT L.

CI466 Kahn, Robert L. *Denver im Frühling.* Ed. Lisa Kahn. Berlin: Stoedtner, 1980.

KAUFMANN, EDWARD

CI467 Kaufmann, Edward. *O höre. Gedanken, die immer wieder auferstehn*. New York: Mary S. Rosenberg, 1953. 59p. Poetry and prose by a refugee writer.

KEMP, ELLWOOD L.

CI468 Kemp, Ellwood L. "The German Exiles." "'S Pennsylfawnisch Deitsch Eck," Allentown *Morning Call*, 15, 22, 29 April, 1944. Repr. from *An Idyl of the War—The German Exiles and Other Poems*, by Ellwood L. Kemp (Philadelphia, 1883.) The title poem is based upon the incidents attendant on the expulsion of the Germans from the Palatinate and their subsequent settlement in Pennsylvania.

KERR, ALFRED

CI469 Unger, Alfred H. "Emigrantentragödie— Alfred Kerr." *Literatur und Kritik*, no. 128 (1978), 456–58. Biography.

KESTEN, HERMANN

CI470 Kesten, Hermann. "Preface." In: Heine, Heinrich. *Germany. A Winter's Tale 1844*. English Version by Herman Salinger. Introd. by Hermann Kesten. New York: L. B. Fischer Publ. Corp., 1944, p.i–xix.

CI471 Seifert, Walter. "Exil als politischer Akt: Der Romancier Hermann Kesten." In: *Die deutsche Exilliteratur 1933–1945*. Ed. M. Durzak. Stuttgart: Reclam, 1973, p.464–72.

KIRCHHOFF, THEODORE

CI472 Giegold, Georg. "Theodor Kirchhoff (1828–1899)." *Die Glocke*, vol. 1 (1906) 220–222. Poet, writer, essayist for German and American journals. Native of Kiel, Germany; traveled extensively in the West.

KLATT, MARGARETE

CI473 Klatt, Margarete. *Brücke zur Heimat*. Illus. by Fritz Sonntag. Arolsen: Weizacker Vlg., 1950. 93p. Poems by the German-American poet.

CI474 Klatt, Margarete. *Meine Welt. Gedichte*. New York: Arrowhead Publishers, 1943. 59p.

KNORTZ, KARL

CI475 Frenz, Horst. "Karl Knortz, Interpreter of American Literature and Culture." *Amer.-German Rev.*, vol. 13, no. 2 (1946), 27–30. On K. (1841–1918).

CI476 Knortz, Karl. Papers, 1870–1912. 750 items. In New York Public Library (MS 72-1045). Educator and journalist; selections from K.'s literary correspondence with German and German-American authors.

KOLLBRUNNER, (OTTO) OSKAR

CI477 "Drei Gedichte aus dem Nachlass Oskar Kollbrunners." *German-Amer. Studies*, vol. 10 (Fall 1975), 76–77. On K. (1895–1932).

CI478 Spuler, Linus. "New Yorker Gedichte. Zur Grosstadtdichtung des Schweizer-Amerikaners Oskar Kollbrunner." *Euphorion*, vol. 47 (1953), 341–50. Kollbrunner resided in the U.S. from 1913 to 1928.

CI479 Spuler, Linus. *Oskar Kollbrunner. Leben, Werk und literarhistorische Stellung eines Schweizer Dichters in der Neuen Welt*. Frauenfeld: Huber, 1955. 121p. Rev. by J. Mendels, *Amer.-German Rev.*, vol. 21, no. 6 (1955), 36–37; D. Cunz, *Monatshefte*, vol. 47, 407–08; G. Schulz-Behrend, *Germanic Rev.*, vol. 30 (1955), 316; P. A. Ackermann, *Mod. Lang. Notes*, vol. 71 (1956), 235–36; E. Feise, *Jour. of Engl. and Germanic Philology*, vol. 55 (1956), 674–75; M. E. Valk, *German Quar.*, vol. 29 (1956), 290; G. Mueller, *Books Abroad*, vol. 30 (1956), 59. See *Amer.-German Rev.* vol. 22, no. 4 (1956), 38.

CI480 Spuler, Linus. "Otto Oskar Kollbrunner, Swiss-American Poet, 1895–1932." *Amer.-German Rev.*, vol. 21, no. 4 (1955), 9–11.

KOLLISCH, MARGARETE

CI481 Kollisch, Margarete. *Unverlorene Zeit. Ausgewählte Gedichte und Betrachtungen*. Wien: Österreichische Verlagsanstalt, 1971.

CI482 Kollisch, Margarete. *Wege und Einkehr. Ausgewählte Gedichte*. Wien: Berland Vlg., 1960. Rev. by Wilhelm Bartsch, *German-Amer. Studies*, vol. 7 (Spring 1974), 94–99.

KRAPF, NORBERT

CI483 Krapf, Norbert. *Finding the Grain: Pioneer Journals, Franconian Folktales, Ancestral Poems*. Jasper, Ind.: Dubois Co. Hist. Soc. and Herald Printing, Inc., 1977. 120p. Rev. by K. P. McCutchan, *Ind. Mag. of Hist.*, vol. 74 (1978), 161–62; D. T. Tolzmann, *Jour. of German-Amer. Studies*, vol. 13 (1978), 25.

KREISEL, HENRY

CI484 Gürttler, Karin R. "Alte Welt und Neue Welt in den Romanen Henry Kreisels: *The Rich Man* und *The Betrayal*." In: *Annalen III: Kontakte—Konflikte—Konzepte, Deutsch-kanadische Beziehungen, Symposium 1980.* Ed. K. R. Gürttler and Herfried Scheer. Montreal: Univ. of Montreal, 1981, p.106–19.

KREZ, KONRAD

CI485 [Biographical sketch.] In: *Soldiers' and Citizens' Album of Biographical Record.* Ed. H. O. Brown and M. A. W. Brown. Chicago: Grand Army Publ. Co., 1890, p.597–99.

CI486 "Ein deutscher Dichter in Wisconsin." *Der Milwaukee Herold*, 23 August 1973.

CI487 Roemer, Hans E. "Konrad Krez, Poet between Continents." *German-Amer. Studies*, vol. 3, no. 1 (1971), 12–17; repr. in *German-Amer. Literature.* Ed. Don H. Tolzmann. Metuchen: Scarecrow Pr., 1977, p.196–202.

KROMMER, ANNE

CI488 Krommer, Anne. *Spiegelungen.* Wien: Europäischer Vlg., 1971. German-language poems written in the U.S.; some were previously published in *Aufbau* and the *New Yorker Staatszeitung und Herold*.

KUNZE, JOHANN CHRISTOPH (JOHN CHRISTOPHER)

CI489 Goedeke, Karl, ed. *Grundriss...*, vol. 15 (1964), Ausland part 4, p.578–81. Bio-bibliography of K. (1744–1807), professor of Oriental languages, Columbia College; publisher of first Lutheran hymnal in English.

LAHMEYER, FRANZ

CI490 Wiley, Raymond A. "The German-American Verse of Dr. Franz Lahmeyer." *German-Amer. Studies*, vol. 7 (1974), 14–29. A hitherto unrecognised German-American poet who arrived in Baltimore from Hanover in 1833. Wrote a long poem urging emigration of oppressed Germans.

LANGE, AUGUST GOTTFRIED HEINRICH

CI491 Lange, August G. H. Aus stillen Stunden: Jugend-Gedichte. Scranton, Pa.: n.p., n.d. 131p. Copy in Deut. Gesell. von Pa. By L. (b. 1865).

CI492 Lange, August G. H. *Walpurgisnacht. Eine nordische Fantasie.* Philadelphia: n.p., 1913. Copy in Deut. Gesell. von Pa.

LANGE, HEINRICH

CI493 Lange, Heinrich. *Gedichte.* Vol. 1. New Albany, Ind.: n.p., 1867. 324p. Also publ. in 2 vols: New Albany, 1871. Philadelphia, 1871–1873. On L. (1836–1874).

LEHMUS, CHRISTIAN DANIEL

CI494 Goedeke, Karl, ed. *Grundriss...*, vol. 15 (1964), Ausland part 4, p.581–83. Bio-bibliography of L. (1785–1845), editor and translator, author of poems and newspaper pieces, of Indiana Co., Pa.

LEINEWEBER, CLEMENS HEINRICH

CI495 Leineweber, Clemens H. *Liebe und Tod, ein Trauerspiel des Herzens. Gedicht.* Milwaukee: Gutenberg, ca. 1936. 100p. Possibly a native of Fribourg, Switzerland, b. 1876.

CI496 Leineweber, Clemens H. *Wünsche und Weisen.* Washington, D.C.: n.p., 1946. 63p. Rev. by G. Hanstein, *Amer.-German Rev.*, vol. 13, nos. 5–6 (1946), 44.

LIEBER, FRANCIS (FRANZ)

CI497 *Encyclopedia Americana.* Rev. in *Amer. Monthly Rev.*, vol. 1 (1832), 322; vol. 2 (1833), 132. L. (1798–1872) was editor.

CI498 Freidel, Frank. "Francis Lieber, Charles Sumner, and Slavery." *Jour. of Southern Hist.*, vol. 9 (1943), 75–93.

CI499 Freidel, Frank. *Francis Lieber, Nineteenth Century Liberal.* Baton Rouge: Louisiana St. Univ. Pr., 1947. 445p. Rev. by A. E. Zucker, *Amer.-German Rev.*, vol. 15, no. 1 (1948), 23; D. Cunz, *Md. Hist. Mag.*, vol. 53, no. 4 (1948), 320; R. C. Madden, *Catholic Hist. Rev.*, vol. 34, no. 3 (1948), 346; H. H. Simms, *Jour. of Southern Hist.*, vol. 14, no. 3 (1948), 418; R. R. MacIver, *Annals of the Amer. Academy of Social and Political Science*, vol. 259 (1948), p.196; F. P. Weisenburger, *Miss. Valley Hist. Rev.*, vol. 35, no. 2 (1948), 313; *Amer. Lit.*, vol. 20, no. 3 (1948), 363; M. Curti, *Political Science Quar.*, vol. 63, no. 3 (1948), 442; C. E. Merriam, *Amer. Political Science Rev.*, vol. 42, no. 4 (1948), 781; L. L. Bernard, *Social Forces*, vol. 27, no. 2 (1948), 163; F. W. Johnston, *N. Car. Hist. Rev.*, vol. 26 (1949), 354–56; C. M. Destler,

N.Y. Hist., vol. 30 (1949), 83–85; E. E. Doll, *Pa. Mag. of Hist. and Biography*, vol. 73, no. 1 (1949), 108–09; *Ga. Hist. Quar.*, vol. 33 (1949), 275–77; W. E. Binkley, *Amer. Hist. Rev.*, vol. 55 (1950), 160–61.

CI500 Freidel, Frank. "Francis Lieber: Transmitter of European Ideas to America." *Bull. of the John Rylands Library*, vol. 38 (1956), 342–59.

CI501 Freidel, Frank. "Lieber's Contribution to the International Copyright Movement." *Huntington Library Quar.*, vol. 8, no. 2 (1945), 200–06. Lieber's essay of 1840 revived American agitation on this subject.

CI502 Freidel, Frank. "The Life of Francis Lieber (1800–1872), Editor of the *Encyclopedia Americana*." Diss., Wisconsin, 1942.

CI503 Hawgood, J. A., and J. S. Stephens, eds. "Document: A Letter from Baron Christian von Bunsen to Francis Lieber." Repr. from the *Univ. of Birmingham Hist. Jour.*, vol. 2, no. 1 (1949), 97–103.

CI504 Kennedy, Thomas J. "Francis Lieber (1798–1872): German-American Poet and Transmitter of German Culture to America." *German-Amer. Studies*, vol. 5 (1972), 28–50. Repr. in *German-American Literature*. Ed. D. H. Tolzmann. Metuchen: Scarecrow, 1977, p.28–50. L.'s literary connections on both sides of the Atlantic. Examination of his writings in German and English and his work as organizer of the *Encyclopedia Americana*.

CI505 Kirsch, August. "Franz Lieber: Turner, Freiheitskämpfer und Emigrant, 1798–1830." Diss., Köln, 1953.

CI506 Lieber, Francis. Papers, 1800–1879. 176 items and 3 vols. In South Caroliniana Library, Univ. of South Carolina (MS 66-570). Letters and reports to the trustees of South Carolina College. *Also*: Addition, 1810–1879. 106 items. (MS 74-993). Correspondence of L., collected by L.; many in German.

CI507 Lieber, Francis. Papers, 1815–1888. Ca. 6,000 items. In the Henry E. Huntington Library, San Marino, Calif. (MS 61-663). Correspondence, MSS. of L.'s writings before and during the Civil War.

CI508 Lieber, Francis. Papers, 1820–1951. 1242 items. In South Caroliniana Library, Univ. of South Carolina (MS 70-1883). Family letters, many in German; journals; scrapbook.

CI509 Lieber, Francis. Papers, 1841–1872. Ca. 250 letters. In Ms. Div., Library of Congress (MS 63-370). Relating to his writings on political ethics.

CI510 Lieber, Franz. *Tagebuch meines Aufenthaltes in Griechenland*. Leipzig: Brockhaus, 1823.

CI511 Sengfelder, Bernhard. *Franz Lieber. Ein deutsches Schicksal in Amerika*. Nürnberg: Olympia, 1949. 198p.

LEONHARDT, RUDOLPH

CI512 Leonhardt, Rudolph. *Nord und Süd im Krieg und Frieden*... See summary of action of this novel in *German-Amer. Studies*, vol. 4 (1972), 67–75. The author (1832–1901) was a native of Bodenfeld, Hannover.

LEXOW, FRIEDRICH

CI513 Lexow, Friedrich. *Vornehm und gering*. N.p.: n.p. 1872.

LINDT, PETER M.

CI514 Niers, Gerd. "In Memoriam Peter M. Lindt." *Jour. of German-Amer. Studies*, vol. 12, no. 1 (Spring 1977), 23–24. Austrian-born author and political-literary commentator; Pres., Social Scientific Soc. for Intercultural Relations, Inc.

LIPPARD, GEORGE

CI515 Lippard, George. *The Quaker City; or, The Monks of Monk-Hall. A Romance of Philadelphia Life, Mystery, and Crime*. Philadelphia: n.p., 1845. 494p. Issued in German as: *Die Quäkerstadt und ihre Geheimnisse. Amerikanische Nachtseiten. Nach dem hinterlassenen Manuscripte des Herrn K., Advokaten in Philadelphia*... 2nd ed. Leipzig: Wigand, 1846. 4 vols. The original German ed. was publ. in Philadelphia, 1844.

LIST, FRIEDRICH

CI516 List, Friedrich. *Reports on the Improvement of the Little Schuylkill*. Reading, Pa.: n.p., 1829. 16p. See: *Papers of James Madison*, vol. 78, p.27. On L. (1789–1846).

CI517 List, Friedrich. *Schriften, Reden, Briefe*. Berlin: n.p., 1928–1935. 10 vols.

CI518 Schilling, Karl F. "Die Stellung Friedrich Lists in der amerikanischen und deutschen Literatur." Diss., Hamburg, 1952.

LOEBEL, PAUL

CI519 Loebel, Paul. *Gedichte*. Chicago: W. H. Neebe, 1879. 32p.

LOEWEN, GERHARD

CI520 Dyck, Arnold. "The Poet Gerhard Loewen." *Mennonite Life*, vol. 3, no. 1 (1948), 22–23. Mennonite poet in Manitoba.

LOHRENZ, GERHARD

CI521 Lohrenz, Gerhard. *Lose Blätter 3. Teil*. Winnipeg: n.p., 1976. 168p. Parts 1 and 2, vols. 1 and 2 appeared in 1974.

LONGENECKER, STEPHEN L.

CI522 Longenecker, Stephen L. "Buffenmeyer's Bullets." *Jour. of the Lancaster Co. Hist. Soc.*, vol. 81 (1977), 164–65. Humorous tale of two Pennsylvania Germans speculating about the effect of a Confederate invasion of Lancaster County.

MAASS, JOACHIM

CI523 Sevin, Dieter. "Joachim Maass: Exil ohne Ende." *Colloquia Germanica*, vol. 14, no. 1 (1981), 1–25.

CI524 Sevin, Dieter. "Theodor Plievier und Joachim Maass: Der erfolgreiche und weniger erfolgreiche Exilautor in der Nachkriegszeit." *Jahrbuch für Internationale Germanistik* (Reihe A), vol. 10 (1981), 38–44.

MACLEA, SAMUEL

CI525 Cunz, Dieter, ed. "Samuel Maclea: Totentanz. Ein Jedermann Spiel aus dem 19. Jahrhundert." *Monatshefte*, vol. 39, no. 1 (1947), 25–53. First reprinting of a "Dance of Death" written in 1848 by a Baltimore German.

MAREK, KURT W.

CI526 Marek, Kurt W. Papers, 1929–1966. 50 items. In the Boston Univ. Library (MS 67-785). Correspondence, diaries and manuscripts by M. (b. 1915).

MANHEIM, WERNER

CI527 Manheim, Werner. "Die Sonette von der Vergänglichkeit." *German-Amer. Studies*, vol. 9 (Spring 1975), 47–58.

MANN, HEINRICH

CI528 Durzak, Manfred. "Exil-Motive im Spätwerk Heinrich Manns: Bemerkungen zu dem Roman *Der Atem*." In: *Heinrich Mann 1871–1971: Bestandsaufnahme und Untersuchung: Ergebnisse der Heinrich-Mann Tagung in Lübeck*. Ed. Klaus Matthias. München: Fink, 1973, p.203–19.

MANSCHINGER, GRETE

CI529 Manschinger, Grete. *Rendezvous in Manhattan. Amerikanischer Roman*. Wien: Cerny, 1948. 250p.

MARCHWITZA, HANS

CI530 Marchwitza, Hans. *Untergrund: Gedichte. A Collection of Anti-Fascist Poems*. New York: n.p., 1942. 40p.

MARWEDEL, FRIEDRICH AUGUST

CI531 Goedeke, Karl, ed. *Grundriss . . .*, vol. 15 (1964), Ausland part 4, p.597. New York bookdealer and author; came to America in 1828.

MARX, KARL T.

CI532 Marx, Karl T. *Deutschamerikanische Aphorismen*. München: Gabeva Vlg., 1957. 59p. Rev. in *Amer.-German Rev.*, vol. 23, no. 6 (1957), 38–39.

CI533 Marx, Karl T. *Der Feigling und andere Geschichten*. New York: n.p., 1942. 125p. Short stories and children's stories in German.

CI534 Marx, Karl T. "Rendezvous im 'König von Preussen'." *Amer.-German Rev.*, vol. 12, no. 3 (1946), 28–31, 38. An episode of the Revolutionary War, 1777 in a short story.

MAYER, BRANTZ

CI535 Patterson, Jerry E. "Brantz Mayer, Man of Letters." *Md. Hist. Mag.*, vol. 52 (1957), 275–89. M. (1809–1879) was a Baltimore littérateur and lawyer, descendant of prominent German-American forebears.

MAYER, ORLANDO BENEDICT

CI536 Chapman, John A. John A. Chapman's additions to John Belton O'Neall. *The Annals of Newberry*. Newberry, S. C.: Aull & Houseal, 1892, p.567–68.

CI537 Crosson, J. M. "The Newberry of Days that Are Past." *Newberry Herald and News*, 22 August 1905.

CI538 Mayer, Orlando B. *John Punterick; or The Apple Dumplings. A Chronicle of Dutch Fork.* Introd. by James E. Kibler, Jr. Spartanburg, S. Car.: The Reprint Co., 1979.

CI539 Mayer, Orlando B. *Malladoce, the Briton. His Wanderings from Druidism to Christianity.* Richmond, Va.: Everett Waddey, 1891.

CI540 "Orlando Benedict Mayer." *Cyclopedia of Eminent and Representative Men of the Carolinas of the Nineteenth Century.* Madison, Wis.: Brant & Fuller, 1892. Vol. 1, p.323–24.

CI541 Summer, Leland. *Newberry County, South Carolina: Historical and Genealogical.* Newberry: n.p., 1954, p.259–61.

MEYER, JOHANN JAKOB

CI542 Knief, Frederick C. "Johann Jakob Meyer." *Amer.-German Rev.*, vol. 17, no. 4 (1951), 8–9. M. (1870–1939) was an American-German writer and translator.

MICHEL, FRIEDRICH

CI543 Michel, Friedrich. *Deutsche und englische Gedichte.* New York: Verlag des Deutschen gesellig-wissenschaftlichen Vereins, 1924. Copy in Deut. Gesell. von Pa.

MIRBACH, HENRY

CI544 Koenig, Karl F. "Henry (Vater) Mirbach, Volksdichter." *Amer.-German Rev.*, vol. 16, no. 5 (1950), 25–27.

CI545 Mirbach, Henry. *Gedichte.* Syracuse, N.Y.: Syracuse Union Deutsche Zeitung für Central N.Y., 1939. Copy in Deut. Gesell. von Pa.

MÖLLING, KARL EDWIN

CI546 Mölling, Karl E. *Johanna von Aragon. Ein Trauerspiel in fünf Aufzügen.* Philadelphia: n.p., 1867. Copy in Deut. Gesell. von Pa.

MORTON, FREDERIC

CI547 Morton, Frederic. "I Love 83rd Street"; "Vhere iss Charlotte Street?" *Amer.-German Rev.*, vol. 35, no. 2 (1969), 25–29. Autobiographical reminiscences of an emigré writer from Hitler's Wien.

MUELLER, A. O.

CI548 Mueller, A. O. *Müllerlieder; Lieder und Gedichte von Müller von Davenport.* Davenport, Iowa: n.p., 1905. Copy in Deut. Gesell. von Pa.

MUELLER, GUSTAV

CI549 House, Roy Temple. "Gustav Mueller and the Schüttelreim; a Swiss-American's Contribution to a Unique German Verse Form." *Amer.-German Rev.*, vol. 14, no. 3 (1948), 21–23.

MÜLLER, NICLAS

CI550 Müller, Niclas. *Zehn gepanzerte Sonnete* [sic]. New York: n.p., 1862.

CI551 Shelley, Philip A. "Niclas Müller, German-American Poet and Patriot." *Studies in Honor of John Albrecht Walz.* Lancaster: Lancaster Press, Inc., 1941, p.1–20.

MUELLER, WILLIAM

CI552 Guyot, Wilma. "A Biographical Note on William Mueller (1845–1931)." *Bull., Hist. and Philosophical Soc. of Ohio*, vol. 20, no. 1 (1962), 88–91. German-born educator and author of Cincinnati.

CI553 Guyot, Wilma. "William Mueller, Writer." *Amer.-German Rev.*, vol. 28, no. 3 (1962), 14–15.

MUENCH, ADOLF

CI554 Muench, Adolf. "A Wedding with Obstacles." From the *Erzählungen* by Ad. Muench. Trans. by Ralph Gregory. *Bull., Mo. Hist. Soc.*, vol. 24, no. 4 (July 1968), 326–28. The *Erzählungen* of 1886 consist of three tales based on actual incidents of life in early Missouri.

MUENCH, FRIEDRICH

CI555 "The Life of Frederick Muench, an Autobiography." Trans. by Ralph Gregory. *Washington* [Missouri] *Citizen*, 13 September–15 November 1964.

MÜNSTERBERG, MARGARETE A.

CI556 Münsterberg, Margarete. *Singende Seele; Gedichte.* Berlin: Frigga Vlg., 1935. 96p. On M. (b. 1889).

NAAS, JOHANNES

CI557 Naas, Johannes. "Hymn of Trust (Verse)." Trans. by Ora W. Graber. *Brethren Life and Thought*, vol. 16 (1971), 59–61.

NEUBURGER, HANS

CI558 Neuburger, Hans. "Lyrik eines Deutschamerikaners." *Amer.-German Rev.*, vol. 26, no. 4 (1960), 30. Six poems.

NEUMANN, ALFRED

CI559 Brett, Doris Maria. "Alfred Neumanns Romane: Exil als Wendepunkt." Diss., Univ. of Cincinnati, 1975.

CI560 Neumann, Alfred. *Gitterwerk des Lebens*. Los Angeles: Pazifische Presse (1943). 65p. Poems.

CI561 Stern, Guy. "Alfred Neumann." In: *Deutsche Exilliteratur seit 1933*. Vol. 1. *Kalifornien*. Ed. J. M. Spalek and J. Strelka. Bern: Francke, 1976, p.542-70.

NIES, KONRAD

CI562 Harris, Edward P., and Don H. Tolzmann. "An Unpublished Letter of Konrad Nies to H. H. Fick." *German-Amer. Studies*, vol. 8 (1974), 86-88.

CI563 Nies, Conrad. *Gedichte und Lieder aus vier Erdteilen*. Leipzig: n.p., 1921.

CI564 Ward, Robert E. "Konrad Nies: German-American Literary Knight." *German-Amer. Studies*, vol. 3, no. 1 (1971), 7-11. Repr. in *German-American Literature*. Ed. D. H. Tolzmann. Metuchen: Scarecrow, 1977, p.245-51.

PARKINSON, FRANZISKA RAABE

CI565 Parkinson, Franziska Raabe. *When A Poet Speaks*. Mill Valley, Calif.: Wings Pr., 1955. 59p. Rev. in *Amer.-German Rev.*, vol. 23, no. 2 (1956), 37. Epigrammatic poems by the Emden-born musician and teacher.

PASTORIUS, FRANCIS DANIEL

CI566 "Francis Daniel Pastorius." In: *Literary History of the United States*. Ed. Robert E. Spiller et al. New York, 1948. Vol. 3, p.683-84. On P. (1651-ca. 1720).

PAULUS, HELMUT

CI567 Paulus, Helmut. *Amerika-Ballade*. Stuttgart: Silberburg Vlg., 1957.

PHILLIPP, ADOLF

CI568 Marx, Henry. "Adolf Phillipp: German-American Playwright, Singer, Composer." In: *Germanica Americana 1976: Symposium on German-American Literature and Culture*. Ed. E. A. Albrecht and J. Anthony Burzle. Lawrence: Max Kade Document and Research Center, Univ. of Kansas, 1977, p.43-47.

PINKUS, MAX

CI569 Reichart, Walter A., and C. F. Behl, eds. *Max Pinkus*. München: Bergstadt Vlg., 1958.

PINTHUS, KURT

CI570 Lewis, Ward B. "Starting Anew: the Exile Years of Kurt Pinthus." *German Life and Letters*, vol. 33 (1980), 234-44.

PLÜMACHER, MARIA P. O. (HÜNERWADEL)

CI571 Osborne, John C., and Chauncey J. Mellor. [Sketch of career and writings of Maria P. O. Hünerwadel Plümacher.] In: Maria Slonina. *German-Speaking Peoples in Tennessee*. Ed. David Lee. Knoxville: n.p., 1976, p.98-102. On P. (ca. 1840-1895), student of psychology and philosophy under Eduard v. Hartmann; native of Stein am Rhein, Switzerland; resided in Beersheba Springs, Tenn. to 1877.

PONTE, LORENZO DA (LORENZ DA PONTE VON CENEDA)

CI572 Ponte von Ceneda, Lorenz da. *Memoiren von L. da Ponte. Von ihm selbst in New-York herausgegeben*. Stuttgart: Franck'sche Buchhandlung, 1847. Copy in Newberry Library, Chicago.

CI573 Struble, George G. "Lorenzo da Ponte, Our Neglected Genius." *Procs., Northumberland Co. Hist. Soc.*, vol. 16 (1948), 67-68. Da Ponte, librettist of Mozart's "Don Giovanni," a grocer in Sunbury, Pa.

PREUSS, WOLFGANG

CI574 Preuss, Wolfgang. *American Rhapsody*. Harrisburg, Pa.: Evangelical Pr., 1941. 43p. Poems by a former German immigrant, in tribute to his new country.

RACINE, EVA SELMA

CI575 Racine, Eva S. *Ausgewählte Gedichte*. Philadelphia: Charles J. Racine, 1935. 28p. Poems.

RASTER, HERMANN

CI576 Raster, Hermann. Papers. Ca. 3,900 items. In the Newberry Library, Chicago (MS 61-724). Correspondence and misc. papers bearing on German influence on U.S. civilization. By R. (1827–1891).

RATH, GEORG

CI577 Rath, Georg. *Fabeln.* Peru, Nebr.: n.p., 1974.

CI578 Rath, Georg. *Klänge der Seele.* Peru, Nebr.: n.p., 1974.

RATTERMANN, HEINRICH A.

CI579 Scheibe, Fred Karl. "Heinrich Armin Rattermann: German-American Poet." *German-Amer. Studies,* vol. 1, no. 1 (1969), 3–7.

REITZEL, ROBERT

CI580 Donaldson, Randall Paul. "Robert Reitzel (1849–1898) and His German-American Periodical *Der Arme Teufel.*" Diss., Johns Hopkins, 1967–1977. Publ. as "Robert Reitzel and His German-American Journal *Der arme Teufel.*" In: *Papers from the Conference on German-Americana in the Eastern United States.* Ed. S. M. Benjamin. Occas. Papers of the Soc. for German-Amer. Studies, no. 8. Morgantown, W.Va.: Dept. of Foreign Langs., W.Va. Univ., 1980, p.1–11.

CI581 Ritter, Erwin F. "Robert Reitzel, A. T. (1849–1898)." *German-Amer. Studies,* vol. 5 (1972), 12–26. Repr. in: *German-American Literature.* Ed. D. H. Tolzmann. Metuchen: Scarecrow, 1977, p.228–36.

CI582 Zucker, Adolf E. "A Monument to Robert Reitzel: 'Der Arme Teufel', Berlin." *Germanic Rev.,* vol. 20 (April 1945), 141–52.

RENNERT, HANS

CI583 Rennert, Hans. *Gedichte und Uebersetzungen.* Philadelphia: n.p., 1917. 101p.

RICHTER, FRITZ

CI584 Richter, Fritz. *Wenn du drüben bist...Geschichten eines Schlesiers in Amerika.* Stuttgart: Behrend Vlg., 1949. 128p. Short stories by a German-born author, professor in Chicago.

RITTER, JACOB

CI585 Ritter, Jacob. *Sixty Odd Skeletons in the Form of a Sketch Book.* Harrisburg: n.p., 1845.

ROEMER, LOUIS

CI586 Roemer, Louis. *Zeit Gedichte.* New York: L. Roemer, 1938.

ROMBERG, JOHANNES C. N.

CI587 Metzenthin-Raunick, Selma. "Johannes Christlieb Nathanael Romberg, German Poet of Texas." *Amer.-German Rev.,* vol. 12, no. 3 (1946), 32–35. On R. (1808–1891).

RONDTHALER, EMANUEL

CI588 Goedeke, Karl, ed. *Grundriss...,* vol. 15 (1964), Ausland part 4, p.649–50. Bio-bibliography of R. (1764–1848), minister and teacher of the Church of the Brethren, Nazareth Hall; born in Pommern; died in Philadelphia.

ROSENBERG, W. L.

CI589 Rosenberg, W. L. *Irrfahrten, Eine Soziale Lebensgeschichte.* N.p.: n.p., 1880. B. 1850 in Hamm, Westf., lived in Boston, New York, Chicago after 1880.

CI590 Rosenberg, W. L. *Krieg dem Kriege. Gedichte.* N.p.: n.p., 1915.

CI591 Rosenberg, W. L. *Lieder und Gedichte.* N.p.: n.p., 1881.

ROTHENSTEINER, JOHN

CI592 Rothensteiner, John. *Heliotrope. A Book of Verse.* St. Louis: B. Herder, 1908.

RUDEBUSCH, EMIL F.

CI593 Rudebusch, Emil F. *Freie Menschen in der Liebe und Ehe...* Mayville, Wis.: n.p., 1895. 148p. A plea for sexual liberation for both men and women; call for the abolition of the hypocrisy and shame surrounding sexuality.

RUECKHEIM, MATHILDE

CI594 Rueckheim, Mathilde. *Vor seiner Fülle.* Chicago: n.p., 1900.

RÜTLINGER, JOHANN JAKOB

CI595 Rütlinger, Johann Jakob.. *Ländliche Gedichte.* N.p.: n.p., n.d. On R. (1790–1856).

RUPPIUS, OTTO

CI596 Hering, Christoph. "Otto Ruppius, der Amerikafahrer: Flüchtling, Exilschriftsteller, Rückwanderer." In: *Amerika in der deutschen Literatur: Neue Welt, Nordamerika, U S A. Wolfgang Paulsen zum 65. Geburtstag.* Ed. S. Bauschinger, H. Denkler, and Wilfried Malsch. Stuttgart: Reclam, 1975, p.124–34.

RUYTER, CLAUS

CI597 Ruyter, Claus. *Meine Lieder*. St. Louis: Julius Meyer, 1908. 247p. Includes music.

SAENGER, EDUARD

CI598 Saenger, Eduard. *Die fremden Jahre: Gedichte aus der Emigration*. Heidelberg/Darmstadt: n.p., 1959. 75p.

SAHL, HANS

CI599 Sahl, Hans. *Die hellen Nächte. Gedichte aus Frankreich*. New York: B. Fles, 1942. 70p. Rev. by E. Jockers, *Amer.-German Rev.*, vol. 8, no. 6 (1942), 33.

SAINT JOHN, STEPHEN

CI600 Shoemaker, Alfred L. "Stephen St. John." *The Pa. Dutchman*, vol. 4, no. 13 (1953), 3. On the author of *The American Harmonist*.

SARTORIUS, (CARL) CHRISTIAN WILHELM

CI601 Goedeke, Karl, ed. *Grundriss...*, vol. 15 (1964), Ausland part 4, p.650–56. Bio-bibliography of S. (1796–1872), who arrived in America in the 1830's. Author of "burschenschaftliche Dichtung."

SATTLER, OTTO

CI602 Sattler, Otto. *New York und die Welt. Gedichte*. New York: n.p., 1913.

CI603 Sattler, Otto. *Stille und Sturm. Gedichte*. New York: n.p., 1910.

SAUR, RUDOLPH

CI604 Saur, Rudolph. *Gedichte*. Washington, D.C.: n.p., 1898.

SAWATZKY, VALENTIN

CI605 Sawatzky, Valentin. *Heimatglocken, Lyrik und Balladen*. Virgil, Ont.: Niagara Pr., 1962. 97p.

CI606 Sawatzky, Valentin. *Lindenblätter. Ausgewählte Gedichte*. Virgil, Ont.: Niagara Pr., 1962. 90p.

SCHEFFAUER, HERMAN GEORGE

CI607 Scheffauer, Herman. Papers, 1893–1926. 1 box and 2 cartons. In Univ. of California Library, Berkeley, Bancroft Library (MS 80-2305). Literary correspondence and MSS. of writings by S. (1878–1927).

SCHEIBE, ANNA K.

CI608 Scheibe, Anna K. *Geschichten, Märchen und Gedichte*. Cincinnati: Verband deutschsprachiger Autoren in Amerika, 1980. 110p. Rev. *New Yorker Staats-Zeitung und Herold*, vol. 147, no. 1 (1981), Sec. A, 11. Incl. documents, articles and letters about the author as well as her paintings.

CI609 Scheibe, Anna K. *Die verborgene Welt. Geschichten, Gedanken und Gedichte einer deutschamerikanischen Hausfrau*. Wien: Europäischer Vlg., 1968.

CI610 Tolzmann, D. H. "In Memoriam Anna Katarina Scheibe." *Jour. of German-Amer. Studies*, vol. 14, no. 3 (1979), 145. German-American poet and artist.

SCHMIDT-BARRIEN, HEINRICH

CI611 Kruse, Horst. "Plattdeutsch in New York: Sprache als Schicksal in Heinrich Schmidt-Barriens 'De Spaaßmaker'." *Plattdeutsche Erzähler und plattdeutsche Erzählungen der Gegenwart: Portraits, Skizzen, Interpretationen*. Neumünster: n.p., 1968, p.116–31.

CI612 Schmidt-Barrien, Heinrich. *De Spaassmaker*. Hamburg-Wellingsbüttel: Fehrs-Gilde, 1960. 59p. Humorous story in Low-German dialect about the election of a president of a *plattdeutscher Verein* in New York City.

SCHNAUFFERS, CARL HEINRICH

CI613 Cunz, Dieter. "Carl Heinrich Schnauffers literarische Versuche." *PMLA*, vol. 59, no. 2 (1944), 524–39. Evaluates his poetry and play, his Turner lyrics; the influence of America on his writings.

SCHOLZ, HERMANN

CI614 Scholz, Hermann. *Ein Sommer in Manitoba*. München: Kurt Desch, ca. 1962. 288p. Novel.

SCHOPPE, AMALIE

CI615 Ashliman, D. L. "Amalie Schoppe in Amerika." *Hebbel-Jahrbuch 1973* (1972), p.127–36.

SCHURZ, CARL

CI616 Schurz, Carl. *Die Befreiung aus dem Kerker, ein Tatsachenbericht aus der deutschen Revolution 1848*. Bern: n.p., 1953. 52p.

CI617 Schurz, Carl. *Charles Summer, an Essay*. Ed. Arthur R. Hogue. Urbana: Univ. of Ill. Pr., 1951. 152p.

CI618 Schurz, Carl. *Flucht aus dem Spandaurer Zuchthaus. Mit einer Einleitung von Gerhart Eisler.* Berlin: n.p., ca. 1955. 96p.

SEALSFIELD, CHARLES

CI619 Arndt, Karl J. R. "Charles Sealsfield and the *Courrier des Etats-Unis*." *PMLA*, vol. 68 (1953), 170–88. New evidence that S. (1793–1864) was editor (1829–1830) of the French weekly published in New York.

CI620 Arndt, Karl J. R. "Charles Sealsfield in Amerika." *Zeitschrift für deutsche Philologie*, vol. 72 (1953), 169–82.

CI621 Arndt, Karl J. R. "Charles Sealsfield, 'The Greatest American Author'." *Procs., Amer. Antiquarian Soc.*, vol. 74, no. 2, (1964), 249–59.

CI622 Arndt, Karl J. R. "The Litigious Mr. Sealsfield." *Mod. Lang. Notes*, vol. 78, no. 5 (1963), 527–32. First publication of a draft for a claim by Sealsfield which he was about to file in the courts in Solothurn, Switzerland, against a neighbor.

CI623 Arndt, Karl J. R. "New Light on Sealsfield's *Cajütenbuch* and *Gesammelte Werke*." *Jour. of Engl. and Germanic Philology*, vol. 41, no. 2 (April 1942), 210–22.

CI624 Arndt, Karl J. R. "Newly Discovered Sealsfield Relationships Documented." *Mod. Lang. Notes*, vol. 87 (1972), 450–64.

CI625 Arndt, Karl J. R. "Plagiarism: Sealsfield or Simms?" *Mod. Lang. Notes*, vol. 69 (1954), 577–81. What of the claim that Sealsfield plagiarized Simms' *Guy Rivers*?

CI626 Arndt, Karl J. R. "Recent Sealsfield Discoveries." *Jour. of Engl. and Germanic Philology*, vol. 53 (1954), 160–71. Letters of Sealsfield to various addressees from 1823 to 1864.

CI627 Arndt, Karl J. R. "Sealsfield and Strubberg at Vera Cruz." *Monatshefte*, vol. 44, nos. 4–5 (1952), 225–28. Armand Strubberg claimed to have met Sealsfield as an American major at Vera Cruz.

CI628 Arndt, Karl J. R. "Sealsfield's Claim to Realism." *Monatshefte für deutschen Unterricht*, vol. 35, no. 5 (May 1943), 271–85. Reply to Norman L. Willey's essay, *ibid.*, vol. 24, no. 6 (October 1942), 295–306.

CI629 Arndt, Karl J. R. "Sealsfield's Command of the English Language." *Mod. Lang. Notes*, vol. 67, no. 5 (1952), 310–13.

CI630 Arndt, Karl J. R. "Sealsfield's Early Reception in England and America." *Germanic Rev.*, vol. 18, no. 3 (1943), 176–95.

CI631 Arndt, Karl J. R., and Henry Groen. "Sealsfield, the 'Greatest American Author'," *Amer.-German Rev.*, vol. 7, no. 5 (1941), 12–15.

CI632 Arns, E. (Lüty). "Charles Sealsfield, Besonderheit und Grenzen eines Schriftstellers." Diss., Bonn, 1955.

CI633 Ashby, Nanette. "The Sealsfield Controversy, a Study of Publication Conditions Affecting the Reception in America of the Works of Charles Sealsfield." Diss., Stanford, 1939. 158p.

CI634 Aufderheide, Elfriede. "Das Amerika-Erlebnis in den Romanen von Charles Sealsfield." Diss., Göttingen, 1946. 140p.

CI635 Baerent, Robert H. "Die Erzähltechnik in Charles Sealsfields *Cajütenbuch*: Die epische Integration des Romans." Diss., Connecticut, 1978. 218p.

CI636 Bauernfeind, Lieselotte. "Karl Postl—Charles Sealsfield. Die Demokratie im Lichte seines literarischen Schaffens und seiner Persönlichkeit." Diss., Wien, 1948. 177p. Copy on microfilm, Univ. of California Library.

CI637 Berger, Gottfried. "Das Bild der Vereinigten Staaten von Nordamerika in der deutschen Reiseliteratur des 19. Jahrhunderts, unter besonderer Berücksichtigung von Werk und Persönlichkeit des Österreichers Karl Postl." Diss., Wien, 1945.

CI638 Bornemann, Felix. *Sealsfield-Bibliographie 1945–1965: In Zusammenarbeit mit Hans Freising, hrsg. von Felix Bornemann.* Stuttgart: Vlg. der Charles Sealsfield-Gesellschaft, 1966. 24p. Jahresgabe der Charles Sealsfield Gesellschaft, 1966.

CI639 Carrington, Ulrich S. *The Making of an American: An Adaptation of Memorable Tales by Charles Sealsfield.* Forew. by Ray Allen Billington. Bicentennial Ser. in Amer. Studies, no. 2. Dallas: Southern Methodist Univ. Pr., 1974. 211p. Rev. by L. Kaufman, *Jour. of the West*, vol. 14 (1975), 156–57. Excerpts from the novels.

CI640 Castle, Eduard. "Charles Sealsfield in Amerika zur Berichtigung." *Zeitschrift für deutsche Philologie*, vol. 67 (November 1942), 57–66.

CI641 Castle, Eduard. *Das Geheimnis des Grossen Unbekannten: Die Quellenschriften mit Einleitung, Bildnis, Handschriftenproben und ausführlichem Personen- und Sachreigster.* Wien: n.p., 1943.

CI642 Castle, Eduard. *Der grosse Unbekannte. Das Leben von Charles Sealsfield.* Wien: Wulf Stratowa Vlg., 1952. 720p. Rev. by J. T. Krumpelmann, *Germanic Rev.*, vol. 28 (1953), 303–05.

CI643 Castle, Eduard. *Der grosse Unbekannte: Das Leben von Charles Sealsfield.* Wien: Karl Werner Vlg., 1955. 435p. Rev. by Karl J. R. Arndt, *Jour. of Engl. and Germanic Philol.*, vol. 56 (1957), 455–56; in *Monatshefte*, vol. 49 (1957), 374–75; by Ch. Schuster, *Amer.-German Rev.*, vol. 24, no. 2 (1957), 34–35; J. T. Krumpelmann, *German Quar.*, vol. 31 (1958), 247–48.

CI644 Castle, Eduard. "Der literarische Kolumbus der 'Neuen Welt.' Ein Gedenkblatt zu Charles Sealsfields 75. Todestag." *Solothurner Zeitung*, no. 199, 23 May 1939.

CI645 Emmel, Hildegard. "Recht oder Unrecht in der neuen Welt. Zu Charles Sealsfields Roman *Der Legitime und die Republikaner*." In: *Amerika in der deutschen Literatur: Neue Welt, Nordamerika, USA. Wolfgang Paulsen zum 65. Geburtstag.* Ed. S. Bauschinger et al. Stuttgart: Reclam, 1975, p.75–80.

CI646 Emmel, Hildegard. "Vision und Reise bei Charles Sealsfield." *Jour. of German-Amer. Studies*, vol. 15 (1980), 39–47.

CI647 Friesen, Gerhard. "Charles Sealsfield and the German Panoramic Novel of the 19th Century." *Mod. Lang. Notes*, vol. 84, no. 5 (1969), 734–75. A study of affinities in *Der Virey und die Aristokraten oder Mexiko im Jahre 1812*.

CI648 Fritz, Hubert. *Die Erzählweise in den Romanen Charles Sealsfields und Jeremias Gotthelfs: Zur Rhetoriktraditon im Biedermeier.* Europäische Hochschulschriften, no. 151. Bern: Lang, 1976. 225p.

CI649 Goedeke, Karl, ed. *Grundriss ...*, vol. 15 (1964), Ausland part 4, p.605–49. Bio-bibliography.

CI650 Grünzweig, Walter. "Charles Sealsfield and Timothy Flint." *Yearbook of German-Amer. Studies*, vol. 17 (1982), 1–20.

CI651 Grünzweig, Walter. "The Italian Sky in the Republic of Letters: Charles Sealsfield and Timothy Flint as Early Writers of the American West." *Yearbook of German-Amer. Studies*, vol. 17 (1982), 1–20. On the search for an "American" meaning of Sealsfields works.

CI652 Heller, Otto, and Theodore H. Leon. *The Language of Charles Sealsfield. A Study in Atypical Usage.* St. Louis: Washington Univ. Studies, 1941. 154p. Rev. by K. J. R. Arndt, *Germanic Rev.*, vol. 16 (1941), 151–52; *Monatshefte für deutschen Unterricht*, vol. 33 (1941), 335; *Amer.-German Rev.*, vol. 8, no. 4 (1942), 43; A. B. Faust, *Mod. Lang. Quar.*, vol. 3 (1942), 315–19; *Amer.-German Rev.*, vol. 9, no. 4 (1943), 39; by N. L. Willey, *Mod. Lang. Jour.*, vol. 27 (1943), 223; by A. J. Prahl, *Mod. Lang. Notes*, vol. 18 (1943), 155–56.

CI653 Hübner, Gertrud. "Charles Sealsfield und Sir Walter Scott." Diss., Wien, 1948. 146p.

CI654 Jantz, Harold. "Charles Sealsfield's Letter to Joel R. Poinsett." *Germanic Rev.*, vol. 27, no. 3 (1952), 155–64. His relation with the United States Secretary of War.

CI655 Jordan, E. L., trans. *America: Glorious and Chaotic Land: Charles Sealsfield Discovers the Young United States.* Englewood Cliffs, N.J.: Prentice Hall, Inc., 1969. 307p. Rev. by Marvin L. Brown, Jr., *William and Mary Quar.*, vol. 27, no. 1 (January 1970), 178–79; P. Showers, *N.Y. Times Book Rev.*, 26 October 1969, 70. Selections from the corpus of S.'s writings to give a comprehensive view of the America he saw.

CI656 Krumpelmann, John T. "Charles Sealsfield and Weimar." In: *The German Contribution to the Building of the Americas: Studies in Honor of Karl J. R. Arndt.* Ed. G. K. Friesen and W. Schatzberg. Hanover: Clark Univ. Pr. and the Univ. Pr. of New England, 1977, p.173–86.

CI657 Krumpelmann, John T. "Charles Sealsfield's Americanisms." *Amer. Speech*, vol. 16, no. 1 (1941), 26–31; no. 2, 104–11; vol. 19, no. 3 (1944), 196–99.

CI658 Krumpelmann, John T. "Sealsfield and Sources." *Monatshefte für deutschen Unterricht*, vol. 43, no. 7 (1951), 324–26. Sealsfield's use of river descriptions in the magazine *The Navigator*, for his story "Ralph Doughbys Brautfahrt."

CI659 Krumpelmann, John T. "Sealsfield Redivivus." *Amer. Speech*, vol. 43 (1968), 297–301. Americanisms in the language of Sealsfield.

CI660 Krumpelmann, John T. "Sealsfield Vindicated." *Monatshefte für deut. Unterricht*, vol. 50 (1958), 257–59.

CI661 Krumpelmann, John T. "Sealsfield's 'China Trees'." *Monatshefte*, vol. 43, no. 1 (1951), 44–45.

CI662 Krumpelmann, John T. "Sealsfield's Inebriated Robins." *Monatshefte*, vol. 46 (1954), 225–26.

CI663 Krumpelmann, John T. "Sealsfield's Observations Concerning the Blooming of Magnolias in Louisiana." *Mod. Lang. Notes*, vol. 84, no. 5 (1969), 769–98.

CI664 Krumpelmann, John T. "A Source for Local Color in Sealsfield's *Cajütenbuch*." *Jour. of Engl. and Germanic Philology*, vol. 43, no. 4 (1944), 429–33. Resemblances in diction with Jos. H. Ingraham's *The South-West by a Yankee* (New York, 1835).

CI665 McMillan, James B. "Lexical Evidence from Charles Sealsfield." *Amer. Speech*, vol. 18 (April 1943), 117–27. Additional words from Sealsfield to supplement the study by John T. Krumpelmann. See *Amer.-German Rev.*, vol. 8, no. 4 (April 1942), 44.

CI666 Magris, Claudio. "Der Abenteurer und der Eigentümer: Charles Sealsfields *Prärie am Jacinto*." In: *Austriaca. Beiträge zur österreichischen Literatur. Festschrift für Heinz Politzer zum 65. Geburtstag*. With Richard Brinkmann. Ed. Winfried Kudszus and Hinrich C. Seeba. Tübingen: Niemeyer, 1975, p. 151–70.

CI667 Ritter, Alexander. "Bemerkungen zur Exilsituation Charles Sealsfields anlässlich wiedergefundener Brieftexte." *Literaturwissenschaftliches Jahrbuch der Görres-Gesellschaft*, vol. 14 (1973), 395–420.

CI668 Ritter, Alexander. "Charles Sealsfield." In: *Deutsche Dichter des 19. Jahrhunderts: Ihr Leben und Werk*. Ed. Benno von Wiese. Berlin: Schmidt, 1979, p. 98–127.

CI669 Ritter, Alexander. "Charles Sealsfield." In: *Deutsche Schriftsteller im Porträt*. Vol. 4. *Das 19. Jahrhundert*. Ed. Hiltrud Häntzschel. München: n.p., 1981, p. 162–63.

CI670 Ritter, Alexander. "Charles Sealsfield (Karl Postl)—Die Deutung seines Werkes zwischen Positivismus and Funktionalität, europäischer Geistesgeschichte und amerikanischer Literaturgeschichte." *Literatur in Wissenschaft und Unterricht*, vol. 4 (1971), 270–88.

CI671 Ritter, Alexander. *Darstellung und Funktion der Landschaft in den Amerika-Romanen von Charles Sealsfield (Karl Postl): Eine Studie zum Prosa-Roman der deutschen und amerikanischen Literatur in der ersten Hälfte des 19. Jahrhunderts*. Kiel: n.p., 1969. 346p.

CI672 Ritter, Alexander. *Sealsfield-Bibliographie 1966–1975*. Stuttgart: Sealsfield Gesellschaft, 1976. 20p.

CI673 Ritter, Alexander. "Sealsfields Erzählformel seiner Amerika-Romane: Raum und Zeit als Welt und Geschichte—Anmerkungen zur Erzähltheorie am Beispiel des Romans *Kajütenbuch*." In: *The German Contribution to the Building of the Americas: Studies in Honor of Karl J. R. Arndt*. Ed. G. K. Friesen and W. Schatzberg. Hanover, N. H.: Clark Univ. Pr. and Univ. Pr. of New England, 1977, p. 187–216.

CI674 Robbins, Walter L. "A. Hoffmann's Influence on Sealsfield's 'Die Prärie am Jacinto'." *Germanic Notes*, vol. 6, no. 1 (1975), 5.

CI675 Schmidt, Albert J. "A European Commentary on Kentucky and Kentuckians, circa 1825." *Ky. Hist. Soc. Register*, vol. 57 (1959), 243–56. Excerpts from Sealsfield's *Americans as They Are*.

CI676 Schroeder, Adolf E. "A Century of Sealsfield Scholarship." *Report of the Soc. for the Hist. of the Germans in Md.*, vol. 32 (1966), 13–23.

CI677 Schroeder, Adolf E. "Charles Sealsfield in the Red River Valley." M.A. thesis, Louisiana State Univ., 1947.

CI678 Schroeder, Adolf E. "New Sources of Charles Sealsfield." *Jour. of Engl. and Germanic Philology*, vol. 46 (1947), 70–74. Adduces early works by C. C. Robin, Jedidiah Morse, and Thomas L. McKenny as sources.

CI679 Schulz, Paul. "Die Schilderung exotischer Natur im deutschen Roman mit besonderer Berücksichtigung von Charles Sealsfield." Diss., München, 1913.

CI680 Schuppen, Franz. *Charles Sealsfield: Karl Postl; ein österreichischer Erzähler der Biedermeierzeit im Spannungsfeld von Alter und Neuer Welt.* Frankfurt: Lang, 1981.

CI681 Sealsfield, Charles. *Sämtliche Werke.* Ed. Karl J. R. Arndt. Revised and enlarged ed. Hildesheim and New York: Olms, 1972–1977. 14 vols. Rev. by Morton Nirenberg, *German Quar.*, vol. 52, no. 1 (January 1979), 81–87. Review includes a frank discussion of the moral deficiencies found in Sealsfield's attitude toward his subject matter. Rev. by Alexander Waldenrath, *Monatshefte*, vol. 66, no. 4 (Winter 1974), 430–31.

CI682 Sehm, Gunter G. *Charles Sealsfields "Kajütenbuch" im Kontext der literarischen Tradition und der revolutionär-restaurativen Epoche des 19. Jahrhunderts.* Stuttgart: Charles Sealsfield-Gesellschaft, 1981.

CI683 Sehm, Gunter G. *Charles Sealsfields Sprache im "Kajütenbuch": Eine linguistische Studie.* Stuttgart: Sealsfield Gesellschaft, 1975. 28p.

CI684 Starnes, Thomas C., Jr. "Charles Sealsfield and Louisiana French." M.A. thesis, Louisiana State, 1957. 87p.

CI685 Theiner, Paul. "Lenau, Sealsfield and the American Experience." In: *Actes du VIIe congrès de l'Assoc. Internat. de Littérature Comparée. I. Littératures américaines: Dépendance, indépendance, interdépendance.* Ed. Milan V. Dimić and Juan Ferraté. Stuttgart: Bieber, 1979, p.437–41.

CI686 Willey, Norman L. "Charles Sealsfield as a Realist." *Monatshefte für deut. Unterr.*, vol. 34, no. 6 (1942), 295–306.

CI687 Willey, Norman L. "Sealsfield—a Replication." *Monatshefte für deut. Unterr.*, vol. 35, no. 7 (November 1943), 365–77. Reply to essay by Karl J. R. Arndt, *ibid.*, vol. 35, no. 5 (May 1943), 271–85.

CI688 Willey, Norman L. "Sealsfield's Unrealistic Mexico." *Monatshefte für deut. Unterr.*, vol. 48 (1956), 127–36. S.'s many mistakes indicate that he never visited Mexico.

CI689 Willey, Norman L. "Sealsfield's Working Methods." *Papers of the Mich. Academy of Science, Arts and Letters*, vol. 34 (1948), 299–315.

CI690 Urzidil, Johannes. "Sealsfield, Amerikaner aus Mähren." *Stimmen aus Böhmen.* London: Verlag der Einheit, 1944.

CI691 Zimpel, Helmut. *Karl Postls [Charles Sealsfields] Romane im Rahmen ihrer Zeit.* Frankfurter Quellen und Forschungen zur germanistischen und romanischen Philologie. Ed. E. Lommatsch, H. Naumann, and F. Schultz, no. 29. Frankfurt: M. Diesterweg, 1941. 127p.

SECKENDORF(F), GUSTAV ANTON VON (PSEUD. PATRIK PEALE)

CI692 Goedeke, Karl, ed. *Grundriss...*, vol. 6, p.461; vol 11, part 1, p.329; vol. 15 (1964), Ausland part 4, p.657. Bio-bibliography of von S. (1773–1823).

SEEL, ELSE

CI693 Böschenstein, H. "Else Seel, eine deutschkanadische Dichterin." *German Canad. Rev.*, vol. 10, no. 1 (1957), 17–19.

CI694 Boeschenstein, Hermann. "Else Seel, a German-Canadian Poetess." *Canad. Ethnic Studies*, vol. 1, no. 3 (December 1969), 51f.

CI695 Seel, Else. *Ausgewählte Werke: Lyrik und Prosa.* Ed. Rodney K. Symington. Toronto: German-Canad. Hist. Assoc., 1979. 211p.

CI696 Seel, Else. *Haus im Urwald.* Regina, Sask.: Western Printers, 1956. 25p. Rev. by E. Jockers, *Amer.-German Rev.*, vol. 23, no. 4 (1957), 31. Collection of poetry.

CI697 Seel, Else. "Die Witwe." *German-Canad. Yearbook*, vol. 3 (1976), 244–53.

CI698 Symington, Rodney T. K. "Else Seel: Eine Biographie im Nachlass." *Deutschkanadisches Jahrbuch*, vol. 3 (1976), 193–98.

SEELE, HERMANN

CI699 Seele, Hermann. *The Cypress and Other Writings of a German Pioneer in Texas.* Trans. by Edward C. Breitenkamp. Austin: Univ. of Texas Pr., 1979. 217p. Rev. by Terry G. Jordan, *Southwestern Hist. Quar.*, vol. 84 (1980), 260–61; Glen E. Lich, *Jour. of German-Amer. Studies*, 14 (1979), back cover. From the varied writings of a German-Texan from New Braunfels.

SEGER, GERHART

CI700 Hirsch, Felix F. "Gerhart Seger: In the Tradition of Carl Schurz." *Amer. German Rev.*, vol. 33 (April–May 1967), 26–27.

SEIB, CARRIE

CI701 Seib, Carrie. *Gedichte der höheren Kraft.* St. Louis: Geo. A. Seib, 1974. 692p.; St. Louis: Eden Publ. Co., 1974, 1975.

SEILER, CHRISTINE

CI702 Seiler, Christine. *Der knallrote Hahn.* Cincinnati: Vlg. des Verbands deutschsprachige Autoren, 1976.

SENN, FRITZ

CI703 Senn, Fritz. *"Das Dorf im Abendgrauen."* Gedichte. Ed. by Elisabeth Peters. Winnipeg: Verein zur Pflege der deutschen Sprache, 1974. 97p.

SHULTZE, DAVID

CI704 Shultze, David. *The Journals and Papers of David Shultze.* Trans. and ed. by Andrew Berky. Pennsburg, Pa.: n.p., 1953.

SIFF, HEINRICH (HENRY)

CI705 Siff, Heinrich. *Aus der Wüste. Gedichte.* 2nd ed. New York: Stuyvesant Pr., 1922. 143p.

CI706 Siff, Heinrich. *Gedichte.* . . . New York: n.p., ca. 1913.

CI707 Siff, Heinrich. *Tales from Beyond; or, a Glimpse behind the Veil.* New York: n.p., 1932. 196p.

SOLGER, REINHOLD

CI708 Denkler, Horst. "Die Schule des Kapitalismus: Reinhold Solgers deutsch-amerikanisches 'Seitenstück' zu Gustav Freytags *Soll und Haben*." In: *Amerika in der deutschen Literatur: Neue Welt, Nordamerika, U S A. Wolfgang Paulsen zum 65. Geburtstag.* Ed. Sigrid Bauschinger, Horst Denkler and Wilfried Malsch. Stuttgart: Reclam, 1975, p. 108–23. On S. (1817–1866).

CI709 Solger, Reinhold. *Hans von Katenfingen und seine Tante, geb. K.* Zürich: n.p., 1845. A satirical mock-epic in Byronese.

CI710 Solger, Reinhold. Papers. 250 items. In the MS. Div., Library of Congress (MS 66-1457). S. (1817–1866), a Forty-Eighter, worked as U.S. government official.

STADLER, ERNEST

CI711 Forster, Leonard. "Ernst Stadler and the University of Toronto." *Univ. of Toronto Quar.*, vol. 29, no. 1 (1959), 11–20. An appreciation of the promising young German poet and scholar who was killed in World War I before he could take up his appointment as Assoc. Professor of German.

STALLO, JOHANN BERNHARD

CI712 Stallo, Johann Bernhard. "Rede des Herrn Johann B. Stallo Gehalten beim Sängerfeste zu Indianapolis, 1867." *Deutsch-Amerikanisches Magazin*, vol. 1 (1887), 113–18.

STEIN, ELEANORE KATHARINA

CI713 Stein, Eleanore K. "Gedichte von Eleanore Katharina Stein." In the Max Kade Document and Research Center, Lawrence, Kans. Presented by Robert E. Ward. 1970.

STEIN, KURT M.

CI714 Stein, Kurt M. *Die allerschönste Lengevitch.* New York: Crown, 1953. 214p. Rev. ed. with additions of *Die schönste Lengevitch* (1925).

STEPLER, JOHANN HEINRICH

CI715 Stepler, Johann Heinrich. Papers. 445p. In Society for German-American Studies, Youngstown, Ohio. Literary remains collected by Robert E. Ward.

CI716 Ward, Robert E. "Dr. J. H. Stepler: Cleveland's German-American Pastor-Poet." *German-Amer. Studies*, vol. 5 (1972), 69–96.

STERNE, EMMA G.

CI717 Sterne, Emma G. *Incident in Yorkville.* New York: Farrar and Rinehart, 1943.

STICH, AUGUSTUS

CI718 Stich, Augustus. *Der moderne St. Crispin, eine Micheliade.* Philadelphia: n.p., 1861.

STOETZNER, FRIDEL

CI719 Stoetzner, Fridel. *The Transplanted.* Trans. by Lili Krakowski from *Die Pfeile treffen nicht mehr.* New York: McGraw-Hill, 1966. 275p. Rev. by R. B. Dooley, *N.Y. Times Book Rev.*, 11 December 1966, 66–67. Novel on the life of emigrés in America during the Hitler period.

STRODTMANN, ADOLF

CI720 Timpe, Eugene F. "Adolf Strodtmann: Eine verspätete Anerkennung." *Zeitschrift für Kulturaustausch*, vol. 21, no. 3 (1971), 26–27.

STRUBBERG, FRIEDRICH ARMAND

CI721 Armand (i.e., F. A. Strubberg). *An der Indianer-Grenze oder Treuer Liebe Lohn*. Weimar, 1894. 792p. 2 vols. Novel.

STRUVE, GUSTAV VON

CI722 Struve, Gustav von. *Briefwechsel zwischen einem ehemaligen und einem jetzigen Diplomaten*. Mannheim: n.p., 1845. 350p. By v. S. (1805–1870).

THORMÄHLEN, ANTON

CI723 Merrill, Peter C. "Anton Thormaehlen: German-American Poet in Milwaukee." *Milwaukee Hist.*, vol. 4 (nos. 3–4 (1981), 79–86.

CI724 Merrill, Peter C. "Anton Thormählen, Milwaukee Poet." In: *Germanica Americana 1976: Symposium on German-American Literature and Culture*. Ed. E. A. Albrecht and J. A. Burzle. Lawrence: Max Kade Document and Research Center, Univ. of Kansas, 1977, p.49–55.

TIPPMANN, HUGO KARL

CI725 Posselt, Erich. "The Story of an American Poet." *Amer.-German Rev.*, vol. 17, no. 1 (1950), 25–26. Hugo Karl Tippmann, b. 1875 in the Sudetenland, d. 1942 in New York.

CI726 Tippmann, Hugo Karl. *Amerikanische Balladen und andere Gedichte*. Forew. by Erich Posselt. New York: Arrowhead Pr., 1942. 159p.

TOLLER, ERNST

CI727 Spalek, John M. and Wolfgang Frühwald. "Ernst Tollers amerikanische Vortragsreise 1936/37. Mit bisher unveröffentlichten Texten und einem Anhang." *Literaturwissenschaftliches Jahrbuch der Görres-Gesellschaft* (Berlin), vol. 6 (1965), 267–312.

TOLZMANN, DON H.

CI728 "Herr Don Heinrich Tolzmann." *Der Milwaukee Herold*, 19 July 1973.

CI729 Tolzmann, Don H. *Abschied*. Cincinnati: Vlg. des Verbands deutschsprachiger Autoren, 1975. Poems.

CI730 Tolzmann, Don Heinrich. *Drei Gedichte: Neues Leben, Emigrant, Pennsylvanisch*. N.p.: n.p., n.d.

CI731 Tolzmann, Don Heinrich. *Handbuch eines Deutsch-Amerikaners: Gedichte*. Gordonville, Pa.: n.p. 1973. 58p.

TORBERG, FRIEDRICH (FR. KANTORBERG)

CI732 Torberg, Friedrich. *Mein ist die Rache, von Friedrich Torberg*. Los Angeles: Pazifische Presse (1943). 62p.

TRAVEN, B.

CI733 Baumann, Michael. "B. Traven." In: *Dictionary of Literary Biography: American Novelists*. Vol. 9, part 3. Detroit: Gale Research Co., 1981, p.99–105. On T. (b. 1890?).

CI734 Baumann, Michael. *B. Traven: An Introduction*. Albuquerque: Univ. of New Mex. Pr., 1976. 184p. Rev. by D. H. Tolzmann, *Jour. of German-Amer. Studies*, vol. 11, no. 2 (Fall 1976), 44–45. Contends that T. was a self-taught American-born German-American intellectual. Rev. James Atlas, *N.Y. Times Book Rev.*, 19 September 1976, 8, 12. Rev. by L. Schutte, *German Studies Rev.*, vol. 1 (1978), 381–82. Called the best and most comprehensive study of T. so far available in English.

CI735 Baumann, Michael. "A Discussion of Four B. Traven Questions, with Particular Attention to the *Death Ship*." Diss., Univ. of Pa., 1971.

CI736 Baumann, Michael. "Reflections on B. Traven's Language." *Mod. Lang. Quar.*, vol. 36 (1975), 403–17. Traven's prolonged stay in Germany from roughly 1900 to 1922 explains the peculiarities of his Germanic locutions in English.

CI737 Berman, Paul. "B. Traven, I Presume." *Mich. Quar. Rev.*, vol. 17 (1978), 82–96. A review article.

CI738 Hagemann, E. R. "A Checklist of the Work of B. Traven and the Critical Estimates and Biographical Essays on Him, Together with a Brief Biography." *Publs., Bibliographical Soc. of America*, vol. 53, no. 1 (1959), 37–67.

CI739 Humphrey, Charles Robert. "B. Traven: An Examination of the Controversy over His Identity, with an Analysis of his Major Work and His

Place in Literature." Diss., Texas, 1965. 288p. Claims that T. is an American Middle Westerner.

CI740 Jannach, Hubert. "B. Traven—An American or German Author?" *German Quar.*, vol. 36, no. 4 (1963), 459–68. Concludes that the German versions of the writings are the originals and the Amer. editions inferior translations from the German.

CI741 Jannach, Hubert. "The B. Traven Mystery." *Books Abroad*, vol. 35, no. 1 (1961), 28–29.

CI742 Jannach, Hubert. "A Literary Curiosity." *German Quar.*, vol. 38, no. 3 (1965), 404–06. Discovery of an article on Indian art by "B. Traven."

CI743 Kutt, Inge. "Facts and Guesses: the Differences between the First German and American Editions of B. Traven's *The Treasure of the Sierra Madre*." *Publs., Bibliographic Soc. of Amer.*, vol. 73 (1979), 315–32. "To read the real Traven is to read his German novels."

CI744 Lübbe, Peter. "Das Revolutionserlebnis im Werke von B. Traven." Diss., Rostock, 1965. 318p.

CI745 Lujan, Rosa E., and Miguel D. Pareja. "Marut y Traven: De la praxis al servicio de la ideología a la ideologia como praxis." *Texte Critico*, vol. 3 (1976), 14–20.

CI746 Mezo, Richard Eugene. "The Journey to Solipaz: A Study of B. Traven's Fiction." Diss., N. Dakota, 1978. 268p.

CI747 Miller, Charles. "B. Traven, American Author." *Texas Quar.*, vol. 6 (Winter 1963), 162–68. Traven insists: "I am not...of German race or blood...I am an American born in the U.S.A."

CI748 Miller, Charles. "B. Traven in the Americas." *Texas Quar.*, vol. 6 (Winter 1963), 208–11.

CI749 Miller, Charles H. "B. Traven, Continued." *N.Y. Times Book Rev.*, 20 November 1966, 84.

CI750 Ponick, Terrence Lee. "The Novels of B. Traven: Literature and Politics in the American Editions." Diss., Univ. of S. Carolina, 1976. 231p.

CI751 Raskin, Jonah. "In Search of Traven." In: *The Radical Reader*. Ed. S. Knight and M. Wilding. Sydney: Wild & Wolley, 1977, p.73–89.

CI752 Raskin, Jonah. *My Search for B. Traven*. New York: Methuen, 1980. 249p. A probe into his origins.

CI753 Recknagel, Rolf. *B. Traven—Beiträge zur Biografie*. Leipzig: Reclam, 1965. Other eds. 1970, 1971. 408p. Enlarged ed., with new documents and illustrations. Guhl: Klaus, 1977.

CI754 Richter, Armin. "B. Traven als Feuilletonist: Frühe unbekannte Arbeiten unter dem Pseudonym Ret Marut aufgefunden." *Zeitschrift für deutsche Philologie*, vol. 91 (1972), 585–606.

CI755 Richter, Armin. *Der Ziegelbrenner (1917–1921). Das individual-anarchistische Kampforgan des frühen B. Traven*. Bonn: Bouvier Vlg. Herbert Grundmann, 1977. 442p. Analysis and critique of the short-lived journal edited by "Traven." Rev. by M. L. Baumann, *German Quar.*, vol. 52, no. 4 (November 1979), 557–58.

CI756 Ruffinelli, Jorge. "Bibliografia de B. Traven." *Texte Critico*, vol. 3 (1976), 65–67.

CI757 Shabecoff, Philipp. "B. Traven Called Son of the Kaiser." *N.Y. Times*, 7 May 1967.

CI758 Smith, Bernard. "Speaking of Books: B(ashful). Traven." *N.Y. Times Book Rev.*, 22 November 1970, 2, 56. Citation of correspondence with T. by a former editor-in-chief at Alfred A. Knopf.

CI759 Traven, B. *The Night Visitor and Other Stories*. Introd. Charles Miller. New York: Hill & Wang, 1966. 235p. Rev. by William W. Johnson, *N.Y. Times Book Rev.*, 17 April 1966, 1, 41–43. Rev. is devoted to Traven's identity; states he is an American 76 years of age in 1966, b. in Chicago 5 March 1890, now living in Mexico.

CI760 West, Anthony. "The Great Traven Mystery." *New Yorker*, vol. 43, 22 July 1967, 82–87.

CI761 Woodcock, George. "On the Track of B. Traven." *Times Literary Supplement*, 27 August 1976, 1053. See also Michael L. Baumann, *ibid.*, 1 October 1976, 1255; and Nicolas Walter, *ibid.*, 8 October 1976, 1280.

CI762 Wyatt, Will. *The Man Who Was B. Traven*. London: Jonathan Cape, 1980. 338p. With genealogical table and illus.

TREHER, CHARLES W.

CI763 Treher, Charles W. *Snow Hill Cloister.* Publs., The Pa. German Soc., vol. 2. Allentown: The Soc., 1969. Rev. by R. W. Gilbert, "'S Pennsylfawnisch Deitsch Eck," Allentown *Morning Call*, 22 March 1969; *Amer.-German Rev.*, vol. 35, no. 5 (June–July 1969), 25; Arthur D. Graeff, *Hist. Rev. of Berks Co.*, vol. 34, no. 4 (Autumn 1969); M. J. Boyer, *Pa. Hist.*, vol. 37, no. 2 (April 1970), 206–07.

UNRUH, FRITZ VON

CI764 Unruh, Fritz von. Papers, 1922–1964. 103 items. In Syracuse Univ. Library (MS 79-1981). Correspondence and MSS. of German-American writer (1885–1970).

UNRUH, NIKOLAUS

CI765 Unruh, Nikolaus. *Gedichte und plattdeutsche Gespräche.* Steinbach, Man.: Derksen Printers, 1973.

URZIDIL, JOHANNES

CI766 "'Auszug des Geistes': Wiedergabe eines Gesprächs mit Johannes Urzidil in New York (mit Irmgard Bach) aus dem Jahr 1959. Zum Todestag des Schriftstellers am 2. November 1980." *Adalbert Stifter Inst. des Landes Oberösterreich: Vierteljahrschrift*, vol. 29 (1980), 166–75.

CI767 Berger, David. "A Conversation with Johannes Urzidil." *Amer.-German Rev.*, vol. 32, no. 1 (1965), 23–24.

CI768 Urzidil, Johannes. *Bist du es, Ronald? Erzählungen.* Zürich, Stuttgart: Artemis-Vlg., 1968. 327p. Seven stories from the New World and the Old.

CI769 Urzidil, Johannes. *Väterliches aus Prag und Handwerkliches aus New York.* Zwei Erzählungen. Zürich: Artemis, 1969.

CI770 Ward, Robert E. "Johannes Urzidil in Memoriam." *German-Amer. Studies*, vol. 5 (1972), 195.

VAN DER BERG, ROSE

CI771 Van der Berg, Rose. *Gedichte—Aus dem Leben—für das Leben.* Baltimore: n.p., 1956. 280p. Poems of German life in Baltimore and Washington.

VANDERSLOOT (VAN DER SLOOT), FRIEDRICH WILHELM

CI772 Goedeke, Karl, ed. *Grundriss...*, vol. 15 (1964), Ausland part 4, p.658. Bio-bibliography of V. (1773–1831), native of Dessau; minister and occasional contributor to magazines; died in York Co., Pa.

VIERECK, GEORGE SYLVESTER

CI773 Johnson, Niel M. *George Sylvester Viereck. German-American Propagandist.* Urbana: Univ. of Ill. Pr., 1972. 276p. Rev. by D. H. Tolzmann, *Internat. Migration Rev.*, vol. 7 (1973), 347. Biography of V. (1884–1962) not a critique of his literary career.

CI774 Viereck, George S. Papers, 1896–1959. 1287 items. In Univ. of Iowa Libraries, Iowa City (MS 71-228). Incl. correspondence, drafts of writings, poems in German and English, notebooks. Correspondents: E. Haldeman-Julius, William L. Langer, E. Ludwig.

CI775 Viereck, George S. Papers, 1929–1937. 3 boxes. In Yale Univ. Library (MS 61-3479). Correspondence.

VIERTEL, BERTHOLD

CI776 Pfäfflin, Friedrich, ed. "Berthold Viertel im amerikanischen Exil." *Marbacher Magazin*, vol. 9, (1978), 1–36.

CI777 Viertel, Berthold. *Fürchte dich nicht! Neue Gedichte.* New York: Berthold Fles, 1941. 183p. Anti-Fascist poems.

VOIGT, RUDOLF

CI778 Voigt, Frieda. "Letters and Postcards to My Husband from Oskar Maria Graf and Julius Bab." *German-Amer. Studies*, vol. 3, no. 2 (1971), 24–45.

CI779 Voigt, Rudolf. *Das sehnsüchtige Herz. Gedichte eines Deutschen in Amerika.* Osterode, Harz: Giebel & Ohlenschläger, 1953. Rev. by R. O. Roeseler, *Monatshefte*, vol. 46 (1954), 107.

VON GONTARD, PAUL CURT

CI780 Von Gontard, Paul Curt. *Off the Beaten Path. Stories of Crooks, Horse Thieves, Pintos, Desert Rats and Other Lively Characters of the Great West.* Illus. by Max Barsis. Culver City, Calif.: n.p., 1948. A book of verse.

WAGNER, ABRAHAM

CI781 Berky, Andrew S. *Practitioner in Physick; a Biography of Abraham Wagner 1717 [i.e., 1715]–1763.* Pennsburg: Schwenkfelder Library, 1954. 175p.

CI782 Wagner, Abraham. Papers. Ca. 40 items. In Schwenkfelder Library, Pennsburg, Pa. Letters, medical notes, poems and hymns. W. (1715–1763) was a physician and poet of Worcester, Pa.

WALDINGER, ERNST

CI783 Erhardt, Jacob. "Ernst Waldinger in Memoriam." *German-Amer. Studies*, vol. 2, no. 1 (1970), 1.

CI784 Kauf, Robert. "Ernst Waldinger: An Austro-American Poet." *Amer.-German Rev.*, vol. 27, no. 6 (1961), 11–13.

CI785 Kauf, Robert. "Ernst Waldinger im Exil." *Literatur und Kritik*, vol. 108 (1976), 474–89.

CI786 Kauf, Robert. "Stiller Dichter in lärmender Zeit: Zum 70. Geburtstag Ernst Waldingers." *Wiener Bücherbriefe*, vol. 6 (1966), 181–85.

CI787 Picard, Jacob. "Ernst Waldinger at Sixty." *Books Abroad*, vol. 31 (1957), 28–29. Austrian émigré poet, in the U.S. since 1938.

CI788 Waldinger, Ernst. *Glück und Geduld.* New York: Frederick Ungar, 1952. 144p. Rev. by Herman Salinger, *German Quar.*, vol. 27 (1954), 130. Austrian-born author; teacher at Skidmore College.

CI789 Waldinger, Ernst. *Ich kann mit meinem Menschenbruder sprechen.* Gedichte. Wien: Bergland, 1965.

CI790 Waldinger, Ernst. *Zwischen Hudson und Donau: Gedichte.* Wien: Bergland Vlg., 1958. 60p. Rev. by Ulrich Weisstein, *German Quar.*, vol. 31 (1958), 330.

WALZ, ERNST LUDWIG

CI791 Goedeke, Karl, ed. *Grundriss...*, vol. 15 (1964), Ausland part 4, p.658–59. Bio-bibliography of W., minister of Pa.; editor and author.

WEBER, JOHANN WILHELM

CI792 Goedeke, Karl, ed. *Grundriss...*, vol. 15 (1964), Ausland part 4, p.659. Bio-bibliography of W. (d. 1816), Reformed minister of Pa.

WEISELBERGER, CARL

CI793 Liddell, Peter, and Walter E. Riedel. "Der Erzähler und Journalist Carl Weiselberger." *German-Canad. Yearbook*, vol. 6 (1981), 167–71.

CI794 Weiselberger, Carl. *Carl Weiselberger: Eine Auswahl seiner Schriften.* Ed. Peter Liddell and Walter E. Riedel. Toronto: German-Canadian Historical Assoc., 1981. 240p.

WEISS, GEORG MICHAEL

CI795 Knowlton, James. "Georg Michael Weiss und sein 'Prediger': Ein frühes Beispiel der deutsch-amerikanischen Literatur." *German-Amer. Studies*, vol. 14 (1979), 27–35. Minister of the Reformed Church active in Pennsylvania and New York from 1727 on.

WEISS, PAUL

CI796 Goedeke, Karl, ed. *Grundriss...*, vol. 15 (1964), Ausland part 4, p.659–60. Bio-bibliography of W. (1763–1840), teacher and pastor at Nazareth Hall School, Bethlehem, Pa.

WEISSELBERG, MARIE ANNA

CI797 Vines, Mary Jo. "A Pioneer Poet of Texas." *Amer.-German Rev.*, vol. 14, no. 5 (1948), 28–30. Marie Anna Weisselberg (1835–1911), with selections from her poetry.

WEITLING, WILHELM

CI798 Wittke, Carl. "Wilhelm Weitling's Literary Efforts." *Monatshefte*, vol. 40, no. 2 (1948), 63–68. Biographical sketch and literary appreciation of a forgotten Forty-Eighter.

WERFEL, FRANZ

CI799 Arlt, Gustave O. "Franz Werfel and America." *Mod. Lang. Forum*, vol. 36 (1951), 1–7. The symbolism of the last novel by Werfel (1890–1945) shows how quickly and thoroughly the Americanization of Werfel took place.

CI800 Foltin, Lore B. *Franz Werfel.* Stuttgart: Metzler, 1972. 127p. Rev. by Vincent LoCicero, *German-Amer. Studies*, vol. 7 (Spring 1974), 99–101.

CI801 Foltin, Lore B. "The Franz Werfel Archives in Los Angeles." *German Quar.*, vol. 39, no. 1 (January 1966), 55–61.

CI802 Foltin, Lore B. *Franz Werfel, 1890–1945.* Pittsburgh: Univ. of Pittsburgh Pr., 1961. 102p.

CI803 Foltin, Lore B., and John M. Spalek. "Franz Werfels literarischer Nachlass." *Zeitschrift für Kulturaustausch*, vol. 19, no. 1 (1969), 39–44. Lists and describes the papers held at the Univ. of California, Los Angeles, Univ. of Pennsylvania, Yale, and elsewhere.

CI804 Frey, John R. "America and Franz Werfel." *German Quar.*, vol. 19, no. 2 (1946), 121–28.

CI805 Moeller, Hans-Bernhard. "America As a Counter-Image in the Works of Franz Werfel." In: *Vistas and Vectors. A Volume Honoring the Memory of Helmut Rehder*. Eds. Lee B. Jennings and G. Schulz-Behrend. Austin: Univ. of Texas, 1977, p.164–69.

CI806 Moeller, Hans-Bernhard. "Amerika als Gegenbild bei Franz Werfel." *Literatur und Kritik* (Wien), no. 81 (1974), 42–48.

CI807 Rolleston, James L. "The Usable Future: Franz Werfel's *Star of the Unborn* as Exile Literature." In: *Protest—Form—Tradition: Essays on German Exile Literature*. Eds. Joseph P. Strelka, Robert F. Bell, and Eugene Dobson. University: Univ. of Alabama Pr., 1979, p.57–80.

WIEBE, RUDY

CI808 Dueck, Allen K. *Rudy Wiebe as Storyteller: Vision and Art in Wiebe's Fiction*. Edmonton, Alb.: n.p., 1974.

CI809 Tefs, Wayne A. "Rudy Wiebe: Mystery and Reality." *Mosaic*, vol. 11 (1978), 155–58. On the Mennonite heritage in Wiebe's works.

WINTER-LOEWEN, MARIA

CI810 Winter-Loewen, Maria. *Gelegenheitsgedichte: Weihnachts- Neujahrs- Geburtstags- Hochzeits- Silber- und Goldene Jubiläums-Gedichte*. Steinbach, Man.: n.p., 1981. 174p.

WOLFF, ALBERT

CI811 Wolff, Albert. *Gedichte*. St. Paul: n.p., 1867.

WOLFF, HANS

CI812 Wolff, Hans. *Auch der Herbst kommt wieder*. New York: Theo. Gaus, 1958. 39p. Poems.

CI813 Wolff, Hans. *In den silbernen Nächten*. New York: Theo Gaus, 1950. 40p. Poems.

CI814 Wolff, Hans. *Lied des Lebens*. Gedichte. New York: Willard Publ. Co., 1945. Copy in Deut. Gesell. von Pa.

WOLLENWEBER, LUDWIG A.

CI815 Barba, Preston A. "Ludwig A. Wollenweber." *Hist. Rev. of Berks Co.*, vol. 7 (April 1942), 74–77.

WOOD, RALPH C.

CI816 Wood, Ralph C. "Das bucklige Männlein." *Amer.-German Rev.*, vol. 8, no. 6 (1941–1942), 27–30.

CI817 Wood, Ralph C. *Klumpendal, Ernstes und Heiteres aus dem Leben einer deutschen Gemeinde in den U S A*. Wolfshagen-Scharbeutz: Franz Westphal Vlg., 1955. 199p. Rev. by Heinrich Meyer, *Amer.-German Rev.*, vol. 22, no. 3 (1956), 37; Heinz Kloss, *Mitteilungen des Instituts für Auslandsbeziehungen*, vol. 6 (1956), 192; M. C. Lazenby, *Monatshefte*, vol. 49 (1957), 156. Excerpts printed in *Europa und die Niederdeutsche Welt*, vol. 19 (1956), 66–74.

ZECH, PAUL

CI818 Lewis, Ward B. "Literature in Exile: Paul Zech." *German Quar.*, vol. 43, no. 3 (May 1970), 535–38. Edited *Deutsche Blätter*, an exile journal.

ZELLER-EID, EMMY

CI819 *Gedichte von Emmy Zeller-eid*. In the Max Kade Document and Research Center, Univ. of Kansas. Presented by Robert E. Ward. 1970.

ZUCKMAYER, ALICE

CI820 Zuckmayer, Alice Herdan. *Die Farm in den grünen Bergen*. Frankfurt: Fischer, 1956. Adjustment to a new life in northern Vermont.

ZUCKMAYER, KARL (CARL)

CI821 Mews, Siegfried. "Carl Zuckmayer (27 December 1896–18 January 1977)." *German Quar.*, vol. 50, no. 3 (May 1977), 298–308.

CI822 Zuckmayer, Carl. *Als wär's ein Stück von mir. Horen der Freundschaft. Erinnerungen*. Frankfurt: Fischer, 1966. 600p.

CI823 Zuckmayer, Carl. "Aufruf zum Leben." *Aufbau*, vol. 8 (1942), no. 12, 3.

ZUENDT, ERNST ANTON

CI824 Ward, Robert E. "Ernst Anton Zuendt: Profile of a German Writer in the Midwest." *Grand Prairie Hist. Bull.*, vol. 14, no. 1 (1971), 1–6. Repr. in *German-American Literature*. Ed. D. H. Tolzmann. Metuchen: Scarecrow, 1977, p.212–15.

CJ
Pennsylvania German Dialect Literature

Collections and Monographs

CJ1 Aurand, A. Monroe. *Aurand's Collection of Pennsylvania-German Poetry and Prose*. Beaver Springs, Pa.: n.p., 1916.

CJ2 Aurand, A. Monroe. *Pennsylvania-German Dialect Stories and Poems*. Harrisburg: n.p., ca. 1940.

CJ3 Benjamin, Steven M. "Secondary Sources on Pennsylvania German Literature." In: *Papers from the Conference on German-Americana in the Eastern United States*. Ed. S. M. Benjamin. Morgantown, W. Va.: Dept. of Foreign Langs., W. Va. Univ., 1980, p.21–37.

CJ4 Boyer, Melville J. "Specimens of Sacred Pictorial Poetry." *Lehigh Co. Hist. Soc., Procs.* 1944, 44–53.

CJ5 Boyer, Walter E. "The German Broadside Songs of Pennsylvania." *Pa. Folklife*, vol. 10, no. 1 (1959), 14–19.

CJ6 Buehrle, R. K. "A Pennsylvania-German Anthology." *The Pa., German*, vol. 7 (1906), 422–23.

CJ7 Buffington, Albert F. "Literary Ownership Among the Pennsylvania Germans." *Der Reggeboge*, vol. 10, no. 1 (1976), 1–3.

CJ8 Buffington, Albert F. "The Pennsylvania German Prose and Poetry of Thomas H. Harter and Harvey M. Miller." In: *Ebbes fer Alle—Ebber Ebbs fer Dich: Essays in Memoriam, Albert Franklin Buffington*. Publs., Pa. German Soc., vol. 14. Breinigsville: The Soc., 1980, p.63–104.

CJ9 Burrison, John. "Bibliography of Pennsylvania Dutch Folktales." Diss., Univ. of Pa., 1966.

CJ10 Coley, Robert E., Marjorie Markoff and Scott Miller. "A Select Bibliography of Pennsylvania German Dialect Materials in the Ganser Library, Millersville State College." In: *Papers from the Conference on German-Americana in the Eastern United States*. Ed. Steven M. Benjamin. Morgantown, W. Va.: Dept. of Foreign Langs., W. Va. Univ., 1980, p.78–81.

CJ11 Dieffenbach, Victor C. *Der Oldt Bauer*. A collection of newspaper columns in the dialect, 1912–1950.

CJ12 *Ebbes fer Alle—Ebber Ebbes fer Dich: Essays in Memoriam Albert Franklin Buffington*. Publs., Pa. German Soc., vol. 14. Breinigsville: The Soc., 1980. 534p.

CJ13 Fischer, Joshua Francis. "Some Accounts of the Early Poets and Poetry of Pennsylvania." *Pa. Hist. Soc. Memoirs*, Part II (1830), p.53–102.

CJ14 "For Remembrance." "'S Pennsylfawnisch Deitsch Eck," Allentown *Morning Call*, 14 January 1967. Obituaries of Thomas R. Brendle, George Knecht, and William J. Rupp.

CJ15 Frey, J. William. "Dialect Writers: Then and Now." *The Pa. Dutchman*, vol. 1, no. 1 (1949–1950), 7 (on Henry Harbaugh). Vol. 1, no. 3 (1949–1950), 7 (on Tilghman K. Laufer).

CJ16 Frey, J. William. "Index for Pennsylvania Dutch Poetry." *The Pa. Dutchman*, vol. 2, no. 15 (1950–1951), 7. On Ralph S. Funk's *Index of First*

Collections and Monographs *(cont.)*

Lines presented to the Pennsylvania Dutch Folklore Center.

CJ17 Frey, J. William. "Where are the Dialect Columnists?" *The Pa. Dutchman*, vol. 2, no. 18 (1950–1951), 7.

CJ18 Frick, W. K. "Pennsylvania German Literature." *Muhlenberg Monthly*, vol. 5 (1888), 77–79, 104–08, 139–40.

CJ19 Funk, Ralph S. "Collecting and Editing Dialect Poetry." *Pa. Folklife*, vol. 10, no. 2 (1959–1960), 24–27.

CJ20 Funk, Ralph S. "On Collecting Dialect Poetry." *The Pa. Dutchman*, vol. 4, no. 1 (1952–53), 4. The author's collection of 2,700 Pennsylvania German selections by 209 authors.

CJ21 Funk, Ralph S. "Pen Names." *The Pa. Dutchman*, vol. 5, no. 8 (1953–1954), 7. Pseudonyms employed by dialect writers.

CJ22 Gehman, Ernest G. "Gedichde un Gschichde." Tape recording of readings of Pennsylvania-German poems and stories. Address: Gehman Products, 1531 Hillcrest Dr., Harrisonburg, Va., 22801.

CJ23 Gilbert, Russell W. "The Oratory of the Pennsylvania Germans at the Versammlinge." *Susquehanna Univ. Studies*, vol. 4, no. 3 (1951), 187–213. Rev. by P. A. Barba, "'S Pennsylfawnisch Deitsch Eck," Allentown *Morning Call*, 24 November 1851. On the content, purpose and style of speeches by Pennsylvania German speakers at church gatherings, folk festivals, reunions, etc.

CJ24 Gilbert, Russell W., Larry M. Neff and Arthur D. Graeff. "Little Church Book: A Collection of Worship Materials, Prayers, Psalms, and Hymns in the Dialect." *Der Reggeboge*, vol. 8, no. 2 (1974), 1–16.

CJ25 Gross, William H., ed. *Da Aussauga*. Freemansburg, Pa.: Fereinicht Pennsylfawnisch Deitsch Folk, Inc., December 1968. Incl. poetry and prose in the dialect.

CJ26 Harbaugh, Linn. "Some of Our Native Poets." *Papers of the Kittochtinny Hist. Soc.*, vol. 4 (1906), 204–29.

CJ27 Heckman, Oliver. "Pennsylvania Bibliography." *Pa. Hist.*, vol. 11, no. 1 (1944), 63–65. Fiction and nonfiction dealing with the Pa. Germans; publications of the past year.

CJ28 Heckman, Oliver. "What to Read about Pennsylvania. A Supplementary Bibliography of Pennsylvania Fiction." *Pa. Hist.*, vol. 10 (1943), 135–40. Incl. works dealing with the Pennsylvania Germans.

CJ29 Hinsey, E. O. "The Pennsylvania Dutchman and His Writings." Diss., Harvard, 1948.

CJ30 Hollenbach, Raymond E. "Pennsylvania-German Diaries." "'S Pennsylfawnisch Deitsch Eck," Allentown *Morning Call*, 8 April 1967.

CJ31 Kemp, Alwin F. "More Dialect Stories." *Pa. Folklife*, vol. 28, no. 3 (1978–1979), 43–45.

CJ32 Kemp, Alwin F. "Pennsylvania Dutch Dialect Stories." *Pa. Folklife*, vol. 18, no. 2 (1978), 27–33.

CJ33 Kloss, Heinz. [Critical notices, Reviews, Biographical Sketches of Pennsylvania German Dialect Authors.] "'S Pennsylfawnisch Deitsch Eck," Allentown *Morning Call*, between November 1948 and October 1957. "Tobias Witmer." 6 November 1948; "James C. Lins: Political Columnist." 25 August 1951; "Stages and Standards of Literary Development." 10 November 1951; "Tilghman Laufer: Writer of Rimes and Analyzer of Budgets." 24 November 1951; "Columnist—Advertiser—Early Radio Author—Being the Dialect Record of George W. Kunsman." 19 April 1952; "The Volksfreund Poet." 7 June 1952; "Edward Montgomery Eberman or Danny Kratzer: Popular German Columnist." 12, 19 December 1953; "Hiram Hollerbeck: Teller of Tales Once Widely Read." 28 March, 4 April 1953; "William H. Erb, Columnist." 7 November 1953; "Edmund Daniel Leisenring: Pennsylvania German Dialect Writer." 24 April, 1 May 1954; "A Plea for an Anthology of Pennsylvania German Prose." 30 October, 6 November 1954; "Snyder County's Edwin Charles." 19 February 1955; "En Bissel Pennsylvanisch vun Canada: New Writings by Andrew Schumacher." 26 May 1956. (A dialect columnist); "George K. Hoffmann: Columnist, Antiquarian, Chronicler of Olden Days." 28 January 1956; "Sim Schmalzgsicht: Once Locally Famous Allentown Humorist." (On Charles W. Weiser). 20 October 1956; "Uncle Mike: Unknown Sage from the Saucony." (Dialect columnist.) 22 September 1956; "En Bissel Wollenweberisch." (On Ludwig A. Wollenweber) 19 October 1957.

CJ34 Kloss, Heinz. "Pennsylvania German Dialect Writings: North and West." "'S Pennsylfawnisch Deitsch Eck," Allentown *Morning Call*, 28 January, 4, 11 February 1950. Writings in Ohio and Ontario, Canada.

CJ35 Kloss, Heinz. "Three Pennsylvania German Versions of the Parable of the Prodigal Son." "'S Pennsylfawnisch Deitsch Eck," Allentown *Morning Call*, 27 August 1949.

CJ36 Kloss, Heinz. "Zwei pennsylvaniadeutsche Lyriker." *Muttersprache*, 1955, no. 1, 28–29. On the dialect poems of Charles Calvin Ziegler and John Birmelin.

CJ37 Kloss, Heinz, ed. *Ich schwetz in der Muttersproch: Pfälzer Stimmen in Poesie und Prosa*. Bad Dürkheim: Vlg. Deutsche Volkbücher, 1936. Rev. by P. A. Barba, "'S Pennsylfawnisch Deitsch Eck," Allentown *Morning Call*, 27 March 1936; Erwin Roedder, *German Quar.*, vol. 10 (1937), 206–08.

CJ38 Kloss, Heinz, ed. *Lewendiche Schtimme aus Pennsilvani*. New York: n.p., 1929. Contains a few dialect poems and several long prose works.

CJ39 Knortz, Karl. "Sitten, Aberglaube, Sprache und Literatur der Deutsch-Pennsylvanier." In: *Streifzüge auf dem Gebiet amerikanischer Volkskunde: Altes und Neues*. Leipzig: Wortigs, 1902, p. 74–80.

CJ40 Kuhns, Levi O. "Language, Literature and Education." In: *The German and Swiss Settlements of Colonial Pennsylvania: A Study of the So-Called Pennsylvania Dutch*. New York: n.p., 1900, p. 115–52.

CJ41 Luckenbaugh, Hamilton. "Pen Names." *The Pa. Dutchman*, vol. 4, no. 7 (1952–1953), 4. Pseudonyms of dialect columnists.

CJ42 Martin, Willard M. "The Literature of the Pennsylvania Germans." In: *Pennsylvania 1776*. Ed. Robert Secor. University Park: Pennsylvania State Univ. Pr., 1975, p. 278–81.

CJ43 Messerschmidt, H. Edgar. "Ein anderer Ananias." *Amer.-German Rev.*, vol. 13, no. 5–6 (1947), 24–25. Anecdote reflecting the political attitude of the Pennsylvania Germans.

CJ44 Miller, Harvey M. *Collections of Pennsylvania Dutch Poems*. Elizabethville, Pa.: n.p., n.d.

CJ45 Monroe, Will S. *Poets and Poetry of the Wyoming Valley*. Scranton, Pa.: n.p., 1887.

CJ46 Neff, Larry M. "Preface." In: *Selections from Arthur Graeff's Scholla*; by Arthur D. Graeff. Publs. of the Pa. Ger. Soc., vol. 5. Breinigsville: The Soc., 1971, p. vii–xii.

CJ47 Pettengill, George E. "Reading and Berks County Authors: A Bibliography." *Hist. Rev. of Berks Co.*, vol. 8 (1943), 46–53, 80–83.

CJ48 Reichard, Harry H. "The Christmas Poetry of the 'Pennsylvania Dutch'." *Yearbook, Pa. German Folklore Soc.*, vol. 6 (1941), part IV, 17–87.

CJ49 Reichard, Harry Hess. [Introduction.] To "Drauss un Deheem," by Charles C. Ziegler. *Yearbook of the Pa. German Folklore Soc.*, vol. 1 (1936), 15–24.

CJ50 Reichard, Harry Hess. [Introduction.] To "En Quart Millich un en halb Beint Raahm," by Clarence F. Jobst. *Yearbook, Pa. German Folklore Soc.*, vol. 4 (1939), part IV, 7–28.

CJ51 Reichard, Harry Hess. "Pennsylvania German Literature." In: *The Pennsylvania Germans*. Ed. Ralph C. Wood. Princeton: Princeton Univ. Pr., 1942, p. 167–224.

CJ52 Reichard, Harry Hess. *The Reichard Collection of Early Pennsylvania German Dialogues and Plays*. Ed. and retranscribed by Albert F. Buffington. Publs., Pa. German Soc., vol. 61. Lancaster: The Soc., 1962. 439p. Rev. by P. A. Barba, "'S Pennsylfawnisch Deitsch Eck," Allentown *Morning Call*, 7 September 1962.

CJ53 Reichmann, Felix. "A Pennsylvania-German Satirical Poem." *Amer.-German Rev.*, vol. 10, no. 2 (1943–1944), 25, 33.

CJ54 Renn, Donald. "Pennsylvania Dutch Literature and Music." *The Pa. Dutchman*, vol. 1, no. 9 (1949–50), 8. Repr. from the *Lancaster New Era*, June 1950.

Collections and Monographs (cont.)

CJ55 Robacker, Earl F. *Pennsylvania German Literature: Changing Trends from 1683 to 1942.* Philadelphia: Univ. of Pennsylvania Pr., 1943. 217p. Rev. by P. A. Barba, "'S Pennsylfawnisch Deitsch Eck," Allentown *Morning Call*, 13 November 1943; Dieter Cunz, *German Quar.*, vol. 18 (1945), 106–07; Arthur D. Graeff, *Pa. Mag. of Hist. and Biography*, vol. 68 (1944), 117–20; Henry A. Pochmann, *Papers of the Bibliographical Soc. of America*, vol. 39 (1945), 78–83; in *Amer.-German Rev.*, vol. 10, no. 4 (1944), 38 and vol. 11, no. 4 (1945), 30; by William L. Werner, *Amer. Lit.*, vol. 6, no. 1 (1944), 45–47; Ralph C. Wood, *Amer. Hist. Rev.*, vol. 49 (1944), 492–94; F. Reichmann, *Library Quar.*, vol. 14, no. 1 (1944), 66–67; W. F. Mainland, *Mod. Lang. Rev.*, vol. 39, no. 4 (1944), 421–22; D. R. Shenton, *Amer.-German Rev.*, vol. 10, no. 3 (1944), 34; F. Frauchiger, *Books Abroad* (Spring 1944). See also the comment by P. A. Barba on Robacker's diss. of the same title submitted at New York University in 1941: "'S Pennsylfawnisch Deitsch Eck," Allentown *Morning Call*, 3 January 1942.

CJ56 Rosenberger, Francis C. "A Treasury of Pennsylvania German Literature." In: *Intimate Glimpses of the Pennsylvania Germans.* Waynesboro: n.p., 1966, p.55–95.

CJ57 Seifert, Lester W. J. "Pennsylvania-German Dialect Literature." *Amer.-German Rev.*, vol. 8, no. 4 (1942), 26–27; no. 5, 30–33.

CJ58 Shoemaker, Alfred L. [Notes on Pennsylvania German Dialect Writers and Columnists and the History of the Writing Tradition.] In: *The Pa. Dutchman*, vol. 1 (1949–1950) through vol. 5 (1953–1954): "Pumpernickle Bill: Dialect Writer" (On William S. Troxell). Vol. 1, no. 4, 1; "Pit Schweffelbrenner fum Shliffelstown" [On Edward H. Rauch]. Vol. 1, no. 10, 1; "Daniel C. Keller: Dialect Writer." Vol. 2, no. 12, (1950–1951) 4; "Der Foulks-Freund Pennsylvania Deitsch" [On writer Frank Bilger and his publication]. Vol. 3, no. 12, 3; "'John Schumacher' of the Reading Adler" [Dialect columnist]. Vol. 3, no. 13, 3; "J. Fred Wetter: Author of the Hansjoerg Dialect Column." Vol. 3, no. 15, 3; "George Keller DeLong: The Blind Dutch Poet." Vol. 3, no. 16, 1–2; "Deitsher Brief foom P. J. B. Bullfrog Shteddle" [On writer Phillip J. Barnhart]. Vol. 3, no. 16, 3; "Jacob S. Nace: Dutch Poet of Glabbord-Shettel." Vol. 3, no. 17, 7; "John W. Senft: Dutch Writer of Spring Grove, York County." Vol. 3, no. 17, 7; "The Pennsylvania German Poem in 'Der Deutsche in Amerika'" [The first published work in the dialect]. Vol. 3, no. 19, 3; "Der Olt Coxey: Noah B. Geiman" [Dialect columnist]. Vol. 3, no. 19, 7; "Some Notes on Der Alt Schulmeshter" [Questioning Frank G. Light's authorship of Der Alt Schulmeshter letters]. Vol. 3, no. 19, 7; "Solwell Files: Pen Name of Elwood D. Fisher" [Columnist]. Vol. 3, no. 20, 3; "Harry E. Blair: Author of Deitsher Brief foom H.E.B." [Columnist]. Vol. 3, no. 20, 7; "Edward Newman" [Columnist]. Vol. 3, no. 21, 2; "A Checklist of Dialect Literature." Vol. 4, no. 1 (1952–53), 6–7, 10; "Joseph H. Warner: Author of the 'Americanish Historie'" [A history book in Pennsylvania German]. Vol. 4, no. 1 (1952–1953), 10; "Henry Landis' Dialect Column." Vol. 4, no. 2, 9; "J. Lorenzo Rohrbaugh: "Adam and Eve Broadsides." Vol. 4, no. 6, 4–5; Dialect Writer." Vol. 4, no. 4, 9; "Unkel Yarrick" [Dialect columnist W. Edwin Charles]. Vol. 4, no. 7, 15; "Pen Names: Their Identification" [Pseudonyms of columnists]. Vol. 4, no. 7, 4; "Clinton County Dialect Poet" [On John Wise]. Vol. 4, no. 10, 2; "Yukel Dryfuse" [Dialect writer George K. Hoffman]. Vol. 4, no. 15, 13; "Canadian Dutch Writer" [Benjamin Sauder]. Vol. 5, no. 6 (1953–54), 8; "Dialect Columns." Vol. 5, no. 12, 6; "Tramp Poet" [On Louis Storck]. Vol. 5, no. 13, 6, 16.

CJ59 Stoudt, John Joseph. "Pennsylvania German Poetry Until 1816. A Survey." *German Life and Letters*, vol. 13, no. 2 (1960), 145–53.

CJ60 Stoudt, John Joseph, ed. "Pennsylvania German Poetry, 1685–1830." *Pa. Ger. Folklore Soc., Yearbook*, vol. 20 (1955). Allentown: The Soc., 1956. 287p. Rev. by E. E. Doll, *Amer.-German Rev.*, vol. 22, no. 5 (1955), 37; A. E. Zucker, *Hist. Rev. of Berks Co.*, vol. 22, no. 1 (1955), 24–25; R. W. Gilbert, *Pa. Hist.*, vol. 23, no. 4 (1955), 532–34; G. Friedrich, *Pa. Mag. of Hist. and Biography*, vol. 80 (1955), 373–75; A. Closs, *Die neueren Sprachen*, N.F., vol. 5 (1956), 261–2; and Don Yoder, "'S Pennsylfawnisch Deitsch Eck," Allentown *Morning Call*, 25 October 1958.

CJ61 "Vom Pennselfona Deutsches Eck Haasabaerrick, Pennselfona." *Pa. Mennonite Heritage*, vol. 1, no. 1 (1978), 17.

CJ62 Weisel, Blanche V. *An Index of 'S Pennsylfawnisch Deitsch Eck of the Allentown* Morning Call, *1935–1945.* State College, Pa.: n.p., 1949.

CJ63 Weiser, Frederick S. ["Introduction."] In: *Bilder un Gedanke: A Book of Pennsylvania German Verse*, by Russell W. Gilbert. Publs. of the Pa. German Soc., vol. 9. Breinigsville: The Soc., 1971, p.ix-x.

CJ64 "Wer sind die Autoren?" In: *Pennsilfaanischdeitsch: Erzählungen und Gedichte der Pennsylvaniadeutschen*. Comp. by Ralph C. Wood and Fritz Braun. Kaiserslautern: Heimatstelle Pfalz, 1966, p.96. Notes on John Birmelin, Lee Grumbine, Henry Harbaugh, Lloyd A. Moll, Charles C. More, Emanuel Rondthaler, Pierce E. Swope, Astor C. Wuchter and Charles C. Ziegler.

CJ65 Wood, Ralph C. "Journalism among the Pennsylvania Germans." In: *The Pennsylvania Germans*. Ed. R. C. Wood. Princeton: Princeton Univ. Pr., 1942, p.131-64.

CJ66 Wood, Ralph C. "Life, Death, and Poetry as Seen by the Pennsylvania Dutch." *Monatshefte für deutschen Unterricht*, vol. 37, no. 7 (1945), 453-65.

CJ67 Wood, Ralph C., and Fritz Braun, comps. *Pennsilfaanischdeitsch. Erzählungen und Gedichte der Pennsylvaniadeutschen*. Pfälzer in der weiten Welt, vol. 6. Kaiserslautern: n.p., 1966. 99p. Rev. by C. R. Beam, "'S Pennsylfawnisch Deitsch Eck," Allentown *Morning Call*, 10 December 1966.

CJ68 Yoder, Don. "Alamanac Album." *Pa. Folklife*, vol. 17, no. 2 (Winter 1967-1968) 12-19. Photoreproductions of Pennsylvania almanacs, English and German.

CJ69 Yoder, Don. "Dutch Writers from Morrison's Cove." *The Pa. Dutchman*, vol. 4, no. 3 (1952-1953), 3.

CJ70 Yoder, Don. "Hegins Valley in Song and Story." "'S Pennsylfawnisch Deitsch Eck," Allentown *Morning Call*, 11, 18, 15 January, 1, 8 February, 1947. Focus on Pennsylvania German writers in the area.

CJ71 Yoder, Don. "Pennsylvania Broadsides: II." *Pa. Folklife*, vol. 16, no. 3 (1967), 28-33. Hymns. Excellent illustrations.

Pennsylvania German Wit and Humor

CJ72 Aurand, A. Monroe. *Wit and Humor of the Pennsylvania Germans: A Collection of Anecdotes, Stories and Witticisms*. Harrisburg: n.p., 1946. 24p.

CJ73 Barrick, Mac E. "Pulpit Humor in Central Pennsylvania." *Pa. Folklife*, vol. 19, no. 1 (Autumn 1969), 28-36.

CJ74 Bressler, Leo A. "Pennsylvania German Wit and Humor." "'S Pennsylfawnisch Deitsch Eck," Allentown *Morning Call*, 23, 30 March, 6, 13, 20, 27 April, 4, 11, 18, 25 May, 1957. From a Pennsylvania State Univ. Master's thesis.

CJ75 Buffington, Albert F. "Glingerschteddel Schtories." *Der Reggeboge*, vol. 12, no. 1 (1978), 1-3. Earthy stories in Pennsylvania German dialect.

CJ76 Buffington, Albert F. "Lach hazhafdich: A Collection of 'Earthy' Pennsylvania German 'Schtories'," In: *Ebbes fer alle—ebber ebbes fer dich: Essays in Memoriam, Albert Franklin Buffington*. Publs., Pa. German Soc., vol. 14. Breinigsville: The Soc., 1980, p.37-59.

CJ77 Buffington, Albert F. "Pennsylvaanischdeitscher Gschpass, a Collection of Pennsylvania German Anecdotes, Jokes, and Stories." "'S Pennsylfawnisch Deitsch Eck," Allentown *Morning Call*, 5 August through 23 September, 1961; 14 July through September 8, 1862.

CJ78 Buffington, Albert F. "Pennsylvania German Humor; Some Representative Samples." *Keystone Folklore Quar.*, vol. 8, no. 2 (1963), 75-80.

CJ79 Frey, J. William. *Jake un Johnny 'n Buweg'schicht in siwwe Schtreech, vum J. William Frey. In der Pennsylvaanisch Schprooch frei iwwersetzt aus'm Wilhelm Busch seim "Max und Moritz."* Clinton, S. Car.: J. W. Frey, 1943. 53 leaves. Rev. by P. A. Barba, "'S Pennsylfawnisch Deitsch Eck," Allentown *Morning Call*, 7 August 1943. See *Amer.-German Rev.*, vol. 10, no. 4

Pennsylvania German Wit and Humor *(cont.)*

(1944), 34. Rev. by H. Gramm, *Hist. Rev. of Berks Co.*, vol. 9, no. 3 (1944), 87.

CJ80 Graeff, Arthur D. "Pennsylvania German Humor." "'S Pennsylfawnisch Deitsch Eck," Allentown *Morning Call*, 12, 19, 26 November, 3 December, 1949.

CJ81 "Humorous Tales Told by Contemporary Pennsylvania Germans." *Yearbook, Pa. German Folklore Soc.*, no. 15 (1950), 109–28.

CJ82 *Kurzweil un Zeitfortreib, ruhrende un' launige Gedichte in Pennsylvanisch-Deutscher Mundart*. York, Pa.: n.p., 1896.

CJ83 *Der Pennsylvaanisch Deitsch Eileschpiggel. En Zeiding, Schwetzbrief un Blanderschtick far die Deitsche*. [For Scholars and Laymen.] 1943–. Newspaper in dialect. Ed. William J. Frey, with Ralph C. Wood and Alfred L. Shoemaker.

CJ84 Shoemaker, Alfred L. *My Off is All; A Treasury of Pennsylvania Dutch Humor....* Lancaster: The Pennsylvania Dutch Folklore Center, Inc., ca. 1953.

CJ85 Stevens, S. K. "Of Men and Many Things." *Pa. Hist.*, vol. 12, no. 4 (1945), 312. Report on a humorous speech of J. William Frey on the subject of the Pennsylvania German language.

CJ86 Strong, Leah A. "Humor in the Lehigh Valley." *N.Y. Folklore Quar.*, vol. 15 (1959), 126–30.

CJ87 Yoder, Don. "The Snake-Bitten Dutchman." *Pa. Folklife*, vol. 16, no. 1 (Autumn 1966), 42–32. An example of the 'Dutchman' joke of the 19th century.

Pennsylvania German Dialect Writers

BAHN, RACHEL

CJ88 Barba, Preston A., ed. "Rachel Bahn: Pennsylvania German Poetess." *Publs., Pa. German Soc.*, vol. 3 (1970), 55–90.

CJ89 Betz, I. H. "Rachel Bahn: The York County Poetess." *The Pa. German*, vol. 7 (1906), 99–102.

CJ90 Lockyer, Timothy J. "Walking with the Lord: Rachel Bahn." *Pa. Mag. of Hist. and Biography*, vol. 103 (1979), 484–96. Pennsylvania German poet.

BAKER, LYMAN

CJ91 Buffington, Albert F. "Lyman Baker—the Bard of Bannerville." "'S Pennsylfawnisch Deitsch Eck," Allentown *Morning Call*, 10, 17 July 1954. On the life and works of Pennsylvania's most prolific bilingual poet.

BARBA, PRESTON A.

CJ92 Barba, Preston A. "'S Pennsylfawnisch Deitsch Eck." Dialect column, including some English, in Allentown *Morning Call*, 23 March 1935–5 April 1969. See also "The Last Eck." *Ibid.*, 5 April 1969.

CJ93 Barba, Preston A. [Reviews, Comments, Reprintings, Reminiscences, and Historical Notes on Pennsylvania German Authors and Pennsylvania German Literature]. In "'S Pennsylfawnisch Deitsch Eck," Allentown *Morning Call*. 10 August 1935. "Ludwig August Wollenweber." 8 January 1938. "Edward Hermany's Poem" ("Wie die Alde nooch der 'Heio' sin"). 25 November 1939. "Altzeit Fuhrmans Lied,", by Lewis Miller. 30 October 1943. "In Memoriam: Michael A. Gruber, 1855–1943." 6 May 1944. "In Memoriam, Lloyd A. Moll." 15 February 1947. "A Literary Discovery." (On Henry Harbaugh). 19 July 1947. "Pitt Schwefelbrenner" (On Edward H. Rauch). 3 July 1948. "Who was Tobias Witmer?" 14 October 1950. "In Memoriam, John Birmelin." 27 October 1956. "Sim Schmalzgsicht's Own Magazine." (On Charles W. Weiser and his publication). 2 November 1956. "Der Sim Schmalzgsicht vum Leder Eck Poshta." (On Charles W. Weiser). 10 December 1960. Rev. of *E Bissel vun dem un e Bissel vun Sellem: Mundartverse aus Pennsylvanien* (Kaiserslautern, 1960). 28 October 1961. "A Gift." (On Charles C. More). 20 July–31 August 1963. "Edward Hermany: A Pennsylvania German Poet, 1832–1896." 15 August–10 October 1964; 7–21 November 1964; 12 December 1964; 20 May 1967; 3 June–22 July 1967. "The Life and Works of Eli Keller, Pennsylvania German Poet."

CJ94 Barba, Preston A. "Wer aahalt, gewinnt." "'S Pennsylfawnisch Deitsch Eck," Allentown *Morning Call*, 28 August 1943.

BENDER, BEULAH HUMMEL

CJ95 Bender, Beulah Hummel. "Ghost Stories," told to LeRoy Person. *Der Reggeboge*, vol. 15, nos. 3-4 (July-October 1981), 20-24. In the Pennsylvania German dialect.

BIRMELIN, JOHN E.

CJ96 Barba, Preston A. "In Memoriam, John Birmelin." *Yearbook, Pa. German Folklore Soc.*, vol. 16 (1951), 1-5.

CJ97 Barba, Preston A. [Introduction] to *Gezwitscher: A Book of Pennsylvania German Verse*. Ed. John Birmelin. *Yearbook of the Pa. German Folklore Soc.*, vol. 3 (1938), part I, 5-17.

CJ98 Barba, Preston A. "John Birmelin—Distinguished Pennsylvania German Dialect Poet." *Hist. Rev. of Berks Co.*, vol. 16, no. 3 (1951), 79-80, 95-96.

CJ99 Barba, Preston A., ed. "The Later Poems of John Birmelin." *Yearbook, Pa. German Folklore Soc.*, vol. 16 (1951), 7-149. Rev. by Melville J. Boyer, "'S Pennsylfawnisch Deitsch Eck," Allentown *Morning Call*, 6 June 1953; by J. S. Weber, *Hist. Rev. of Berks Co.*, vol. 18, no. 4 (1953), 115-16.

CJ100 Birmelin, John. *Mami Gans: The Dialect Nursery Rhymes of John Birmelin*. Allentown: Schlechter's, 1953. Rev. by P. A. Barba, "'S Pennsylfawnisch Deitsch Eck," Allentown *Morning Call*, 11 December 1954.

CJ101 [Birmelin, John.] *The Poems of John Birmelin*. Ed. Preston A. Barba. *Yearbook, Pa. German Folklore Soc.*, vol. 16. Allentown: Schlechter's, 1953. 210p. Rev. by J. S. Weber, *Amer.-German Rev.*, vol. 20, no. 1 (1953), 36-37.

CJ102 Birmelin, John. "Die Schtowwerkepp." "'S Pennsylfawnisch Deitsch Eck," Allentown *Morning Call*, 22, 29 May 1943.

BIRMELIN, JOHN E.

CJ103 Birmelin, John E. *E bissel vun dem un e bissel vun sellem: Mundartverse aus Pennsylvanien*. Introd. by Fritz Braun. Kaiserslautern: Heimatstelle Pfalz, 1960. 63p. Rev. by P. A. Barba, "'S Pennsylfawnisch Deitsch Eck," Allentown *Morning Call*, 10 December 1960.

CJ104 Braun, Fritz. "Ein Wort über John Birmelin." In: *E Bissel vun dem un e Bissel vun Sellem: Mundartverse aus Pennsylvanien*. Ed. John Birmelin. Kaiserslautern: Heimatstelle Pfalz, 1960, p.5-8.

CJ105 Frey, J. William. "John Birmelin: Poet of the People." *The Pa. Dutchman*, vol. 2, no. 10 (1950-1951), 1.

CJ106 Rosenberger, Homer T. "John Birmelin, Poet of the People." In: *The Pennsylvania Germans, 1891-1965*. Ed. H. T. Rosenberger. *Publs., Pa. German Soc.*, vol. 63. Lancaster: The Pa. German Society, 1966, 215-17.

CJ107 "Tears for John Birmelin." *The Pa. Dutchman*, vol. 2, no. 10 (1950-1951), 1. Repr. from Allentown *Morning Call*, 5 September 1950.

CJ108 "A Tribute to John Birmelin." *The Pa. Dutchman*, Vol. 2, no. 10 (1950-51), 1, 8; repr. from the *Allentown Sunday Call-Chronicle*, September 1950.

CJ109 Waldenrath, Alexander. "John Birmelin's Poetry Mirrors His Native Berks." *Hist. Rev. of Berks Co.*, vol. 39 (Winter, 1973-1974), 8-11.

BLATT, MILTON

CJ110 Blatt, Milton. *Die Schlief-Schtey locher Minstrels*. N.p.: n.p., ca. 1946. Dialect play.

BOYER, WALTER E.

CJ111 Yoder, Don. "Work through the Schools: Walter E. Boyer." *The Pa. Dutchman*, vol. 1, no. 8 (1949-1950), 1. Dialect writer.

BROBST, SAMUEL K.

CJ112 Diehl, T. H. *Reminiscences of Rev. S. K. Brobst and His Times*. Allentown: n.p., n.d. 58p. Repr. from the *Lutheran Church Rev*.

CJ113 "Rev. Samuel K. Brobst." *Der deutsche Pionier*, vol. 8 (1876-1877), 424-27. Obituary.

CJ114 "Reverend Samuel K. Brobst: Sunday School Founder, Minister and Editor." *The Pa. German*, vol. 8 (1907), 360-64.

CJ115 Wood, Ralph C. "S. K. Brobst: Our Pennsylvania Dutch Language Leader." *The Pa. Dutchman*, vol. 1, no. 14 (1949-1950), 7.

BUFFINGTON, ALBERT F.

CJ116 Buffington, Albert F. "Maidel wilscht du heirathen: A Hybrid Poem." *Amer. German Rev.*, vol. 12, no. 5 (1945-1946), 30-33.

CASSEL, ABRAHAM H.

CJ117 Friedrich, Gerhard. "Abraham H. Cassel Invents an Anecdote." *Amer.-German Rev.*, vol. 9, no. 2 (1942), 19–20, 39.

CHARLES, EDWIN

CJ118 Kloss, Heinz. "Snyder County's Edwin Charles." "'S Pennsylfawnisch Deitsch Eck," Allentown *Morning Call*, 19 February 1955. On the life and dialect writings of Edwin Charles.

DELONG, GEORGE KELLER

CJ119 Shoemaker, Alfred L. "George Keller DeLong—the Blind Dutch Poet." *The Pa. Dutchman*, vol. 3, no. 16 (1952), 1–2.

DELONG, SOLOMON

CJ120 Handwerk, Walter T. "Obadiah Grouthomel." *The Pa. Dutchman*, vol. 5, no. 12 (1953–1954), 7. On the dialect columnist Solomon DeLong.

DIEFFENBACH, VICTOR C.

CJ121 Hartman, Joel. "The Pennsylvania Dutch Dialect Can Never Die Out: Der Alt Bauer." *The Pa. Dutchman*, vol. 1, no. 11 (1949–50), 1. On Victor C. Dieffenbach.

CJ122 *Der oldt Bauer Hut Eppes Tsu Sawge*. N.p.: n.p., n.d. Collection of newspaper columns in the dialect, 1912–1950.

DRUCKENBROD, RICHARD

CJ123 Druckenbrod, Richard. "Es Deitsch Schtick." Weekly column, Mondays, Allentown *Morning Call*, 1978–.

EBERMAN, EDWARD M.

CJ124 Kloss, Heinz. "Edward Montgomery Eberman or Danny Kratzer—Popular Pennsylvania German Columnist." "'S Pennsylfawnisch Deitsch Eck," Allentown *Morning Call*, 12, 19 December 1953.

ERB, WILLIAM H.

CJ125 Erb, Russel C. "My Father: Dr. William H. Erb." *The Pa. Dutchman*, vol. 1, no. 18 (1949–1950), 7.

CJ126 Kloss, Heinz. "William H. Erb, Columnist." "'S Pennsylfawnisch Deitsch Erk," Allentown *Morning Call*, 7 November, 1953. Account of the author of the column, "Der Gust un die Suf," with specimens of his writing.

EVELAN, RAY

CJ127 "Ray Evelan." *The Pa. Dutchman*, vol. 4, no. 7 (1952–1953), 1, 12. Autobiographical note by a dialect columnist.

FISHER, ELWOOD ("SOLWELL FILES")

CJ128 Beam, C. Richard. "Pennsylvania German Columnist, Solwell Files." *Hist. Schaefferstown Record*, vol. 6, no. 3 (1972), 8–9.

CJ129 Boyer, Melville J. "Pennsylvania German Columnist Solwell Files: Dialect Selections and Translations." *Procs., Lehigh Co. Hist. Soc.*, vol. 28 (1970), 5–207.

CJ130 Fisher, Elwood. "Briefe vum Solwell Files." Comp., ed., and trans. by Melville J. Boyer. "'S Pennsylfawnisch Deitsch Eck," Allentown *Morning Call*, 27 January–17 February, 1967.

FISHER, HENRY LEE

CJ131 Allen, George. "Two Pennsylvania-Dutch Poets. Part II. Henry Lee Fisher." *Amer.-German Rev.*, vol. 9, no. 1 (1942), 10–12, 37. Repr. in D. H. Tolzmann, ed. *German-American Literature*. Metuchen: Scarecrow Pr., 1977, p.141–50.

CJ132 Fisher, Henry Lee. "From York to Egypt (A Hiking Tour in the 1880's.)" From clippings taken from the *Reading Times*, October 1886. "'S Pennsylfawnisch Deitsch Eck," Allentown *Morning Call*, 16 November 1968. Written in the Pennsylvania German dialect.

FOGEL, EDWIN M.

CJ133 Fogel, Edwin M. "Twelvetide." *Publs., Pa. German Folklore Soc.*, vol. 6 (1941).

FRANKLIN, SARA

CJ134 Franklin, Sara. "The Immigrant Family." *Pa. Ethnic Studies Newsletter*, vol. 2, no. 4 (1976–1977), 2. Excerpts from stories written by fourth- and fifth-graders about the Klabumski family of Frankfurt.

FUNK, RALPH

CJ135 Barba, Preston A., ed. "The Poems of Ralph Funk." *Publs., Pa. German Soc.*, vol. 3 (1970), 115–238.

CJ136 Funk, Ralph. *The Dialect Poems of Ralph Funk*. Publs., Pa. German Soc., vol. 2. Allentown: The Soc., 1968. 328p. Rev. by R. W. Gilbert, "'S Pennsylfawnisch Deitsch Eck," Allentown *Morning Call*, 22 March 1969; Arthur D. Graeff, *Hist. Rev. of Berks Co.*, vol. 34, no. 4 (Autumn 1969); M. J. Boyer, *Pa. Hist.*, vol. 37, no. 2 (April 1970), 206–07.

CJ137 Funk, Ralph S. "The Pennsylvania German." In: *The Pennsylvania Germans, 1891–1965, Frequently Known as the "Pennsylvania Dutch."* Ed. Homer T. Rosenberger. Publs., Pa. German Soc., vol. 63. Lancaster: The Society, 1966, p.22–23. Dialect poem.

GILBERT, RUSSELL WIEDER

CJ138 Gilbert, Russell W. *Bilder un Gedanke. A Book of Pennsylvania German Verse*. Publs., Pa. German Soc., vol. 9. Breinigsville: The Soc., 1975. Rev. by Alexander Waldenrath, *German-Amer. Studies*, vol. 10 (1975), 71–74.

CJ139 Gilbert, Russell Wieder. *Jacob Appet. Der ritter underm zuber...* Philadelphia: n.p., 1943. A "medieval" poem by Appet, a supposed 13th-century author.

CJ140 Gilbert, Russell Wieder. [Pennsylvania German Dialect Poems.] *Der Reggeboge*, 1971–1980: "Ken Baam! Ken Katzegrautte!" Vol. 5, no. 1 (1971), 11; "Die Uhrzeeche." Vol. 6, no. 1 (1972), 10; "Die Windelschpell." Vol. 6, nos. 2–3 (1972), 23; "Mer kann's erreeche." Vol. 6, nos. 2–3 (1972), 22; "Glaab Yuscht!" Vol. 7, no. 2 (1973), 16; "Waahre Schpichte." Vol. 7, nos. 3–4 (1973), 5–6; "Die Yaahreszeide." Vol. 9, nos. 3–4 (1975), 26; "Der Oschderhaas." Vol. 10, no. 1 (1976), 15; "1776 un heit." Vol. 10, no. 2 (1976), 25; "Zwee Rebbebilder." Vol. 11, no. 2 (1977), 25; "Der alt Blechschmitt aus 'm Bloobarrig." Vol. 12, no. 3 (1978), 7–8; "Ken Abrillekalb." Vol. 14, no. 2 (1980), 19; "Sei Naama." Vol. 14, no. 2 (1980), inside cover.

GRAEFF, ARTHUR DUNDORE

CJ141 Barba, Preston A. "A Tribute to Arthur D. Graeff." *Hist. Rev. of Berks Co.*, vol. 24 (1969), 82–84.

CJ142 Graeff, Arthur D. *Selections from Arthur Graeff's "Scholla."* Introd. Larry M. Neff. Publs., Pa. German Soc., vol. 5. Breinigsville: The Soc., 1971. 202p. Collected from the newspaper columns in the *Reading Times*, starting in 1939.

GRUBER, JOHN

CJ143 Cunz, Dieter. "John Gruber and His Almanac." *Md. Hist. Mag.*, vol. 47, no. 2 (1952), 89–102. Founded in 1797 as a German almanac for the rural population of Maryland, Pennsylvania, and Virginia. English edition after 1822; German ed. 1797–1917. See also "'S Pennsylfawnisch Deitsch Eck," Allentown *Morning Call*, 10, 17 December 1955.

CJ144 Durnbaugh, Donald F. "Johann Adam Gruber. Pennsylvania German Prophet and Poet." *Pa. Mag. of Hist. and Biography*, vol. 83, no. 4 (1959), 382–408.

CJ145 "The Farmers' Bible: John Gruber's Hagerstown Almanac." *Valleys of History* (Hagerstown, Md.), vol. 2, no. 4 (1966), 6–9.

CJ146 Prahl, A. J. "The Hagerstown Almanack, a Venerable Institution." *Amer.-German Rev.*, vol. 8, no. 5 (1942), 7–10.

CJ147 Smith, Elmer L., and J. G. Stewart. "Gruber's Hagerstown Almanac." "'S Pennsylfawnisch Deitsch Eck," Allentown *Morning Call*, 9 January 1965.

GRUBER, MICHAEL A.

CJ148 Klopp, Donald S. *The Life and Work of Michael A. Gruber*. State College, Pa.: n.p., 1937. Incl. dialect poems and prose.

GRUMBINE, EZRA

CJ149 Grumbine, Ezra. *Der Prahl-Hans*. Lebanon, Pa.: n.p., 1917. Poetry in English and in the dialect.

GRUMBINE, LEE L.

CJ150 Croll, Philip C. "Lee L. Grumbine." *The Pa. German*, vol. 5 (1904), 145–48. Obituary.

CJ151 Richards, Henry M. "In Memoriam Lee L. Grumbine." *Procs. and Addrs., Pa. German Soc.*, vol. 14 (1905), 55–58.

"HANSYARRICK"

CJ152 Wood, Ralph C. "Who Was Hansyarrick?" "'S Pennsylfawnisch Deitsch Eck," Allentown *Morning Call*, 24 November 1945. Dialect columnist.

HARBAUGH, HENRY

CJ153 Allen, George. "Two Pennsylvania-Dutch Poets. Part I. Henry Harbaugh." *Amer.-German Rev.*, vol. 8, no. 6 (1942), 10–12, 34. Repr. In: *German-American Literature*. Ed. D. H. Tolzmann. Metuchen: Scarecrow, 1977, p.141–50. Poet and pastor (1817–1867).

CJ154 Barba, Preston A. "A Literary Discovery." "'S Pennsylfawnisch Deitsch Eck," Allentown *Morning Call*, 15 February, 1947. Discovery of four stanzas omitted in the printed version of Harbaugh's *Schulhaus an der Krick* solves the problem as to why the English translation had four extra stanzas.

CJ155 Bomberger, C. M. "Harbaugh's Harp." *The Pa. Dutchman*, vol. 3, no. 11 (1951–1952), 8. Excerpts from *Pennsylvania Dutch Sketches*.

CJ156 Croll, Philip C. "Rev. Henry Harbaugh, D. D." *The Pa. German*, vol. 5 (1904), 51–60.

CJ157 Dubbs, Joseph H. "The Blessed Memory of Henry Harbaugh." *The Pa. German*, vol. 10 (1909), 12–14.

CJ158 Harbaugh, Henry. *Harbaugh's Harfe*. Philadelphia: n.p., ca. 1902. Dialect poetry.

CJ159 Kieffer, Elizabeth C. "Henry Harbaugh in Lancaster." *Publs., Lancaster Co. Hist. Soc.*, vol. 46 (1942), 57–83. Pennsylvania-German pastor and poet and his contest with the First German Reformed congregation.

CJ160 Kieffer, Elizabeth C. *Henry Harbaugh: Pennsylvania Dutchman, 1817–1867*. Procs. and Addrs. of the Pa. German Soc., no. 51 (1945). 365p. Rev. by P. A. Barba, "'S Pennsylfawnisch Deitsch Eck," Allentown *Morning Call*, 9 March 1946. Incl. Harbaugh's dialect writings.

CJ161 Klein, H. M. "Diaries and Private Papers of Dr. Henry Harbaugh." *Procs., Northumberland Co. Hist. Soc.*, vol. 12 (1942), 179–203.

CJ162 Laubach, Samuel E. "The Life and Works of Henry Harbaugh." "'S Pennsylfawnisch Deitsch Eck," Allentown *Morning Call*, 15 May 1937.

HARTER, THOMAS HESS

CJ163 Harter, Thomas H. *Boonastiel: Being the Fun and Filosophy in the Pennsylvania "Dutch" Letters...of the Late Thomas Hess Harter*. 4th ed., revised and enlarged. Harrisburg: Aurand Pr., 1942. Rev. by P. A. Barba, "'S Pennsylfawnisch Deitsch Eck," Allentown *Morning Call*, 28 November 1942.

CJ164 Wood, Ralph C. "More Boonastiel Letters." "'S Pennsylfawnisch Deitsch Eck," Allentown *Morning Call*, 28 April 1945. On the writings of Thomas H. Harter.

HEILMAN, SAMUEL P.

CJ165 Heilman, Samuel P. *The Old Cider Mill*. Lebanon, Pa.: n.p., 1899. Dialect poetry dealing with rural life. Poems in English translation.

HERMANY, EDWARD

CJ166 Barba, Preston A. "Edward Hermany—A Pennsylvania German Poet (1832–1896)." "'S Pennsylfawnisch Deitsch Eck," Allentown Morning Call, 20, 27 July, 3, 10, 17, 24, 31 August 1963. Repr. from the *Lehigh Co. Hist. Soc., Procs.*, vol. 12 (1959), 37–76.

HILBURN, VALENTINE

CJ167 Weiser, Frederick S., ed. "The Friend of Children." *Der Reggeboge*, vol. 14, no. 4 (1980), 1–2. Repr. of the preface to Valentine Hilburn. *A Book of Aid for Learning the English Language*. Hellertown: Thomas N. Weber, 1857.

HOFFMAN, GEORGE K. ("YUKEL DRYFUSS")

CJ168 Kloss, Heinz. "George K. Hoffman—Columnist, Antiquarian, Chronicler of Olden Days." "'S Pennsylfawnisch Deitsch Eck," Allentown *Morning Call*, 28 January, 1956. Under the penname of "Yukel Dryfuss," Hoffman wrote letters in the Pennsylvania German dialect to the *Morning Call*, at the beginning of this century.

HOMAN, JOHN GEORGE

CJ169 Oda, Wilbur Harry. "John George Homan." *Hist. Rev. of Berks Co.*, vol. 13 (1948), 61–71. On H.'s writings in the Pennsylvania German dialect, 1802–1846.

CJ170 Oda, Wilbur Harry. "John George Homan. Man of Many Parts." The Pa. Dutchman, vol. 1 (1949–1950), 1.

HOWER, HARRY

CJ171 Yoder, Don. "Bad Luck Farm—the Story of Harry Hower." *The Pa. Dutchman*, vol. 2 (1 December 1951). H. (1870–1939) was a Pennsylvania German poet, entertainer, and columnist.

KELLER, ELI

CJ172 Herz, Julius M. "Eli Keller: Pennsylvania-German Poet, in Commemoration of the 150th Anniversary of His Birth." *German-Amer. Studies*, vol. 10 (1975), 35–44.

CJ173 "The Life and Works of Eli Keller, Pennsylvania German Poet, 1825–1919." "'S Pennsylvawnisch Deitsch Eck," Allentown *Morning Call*, 15 August through 12 December 1964; 20 May, 3–24 June, and 1–22 July 1967. Repr. from the *Pa. German Magazine* for June 1908. Extracts from Keller's *History of the Keller Family* (1905).

KLEES, FREDERIC

CJ174 Klees, Frederic. "Swan Song." In: *The Pennsylvania Dutch*. Ed. F. Klees. New York: Macmillan, 1950, p. 406–12.

KLINGER, IRWIN

CJ175 Klinger, Irwin. "Der Greemer (The Peddler)." *Der Reggeboge*, vol. 12, no. 1 (1978), 10–13; "Der viert Tschuler." *Der Reggeboge*, vol. 10, nos. 3–4 (1976), 1–4. Dramatic skits.

KNAUSS, OSCAR P.

CJ176 Kloss, Heinz. "Hiram Hollerheck—Teller of Tales Once Widley Read." "'S Pennsylfawnisch Deitsch Eck," Allentown *Morning Call*, 28 March, 4 April 1953. With some samples of the writing of an early dialect author.

KNECHT, GEORGE

CJ177 "Dr. George Knecht, Dentist, Astronomer, Poet." "'S Pennsylfawnisch Deitsch Eck," Allentown *Morning Call*, 2, 9, 16 April, 1966.

LAUFER, TILGHMAN K.

CJ178 "'Greitzweg' Philosophy." *The Pa. Dutchman*, vol. 1, no. 3 (1949–1950), 3. On Tilghman K. Laufer.

CJ179 Kloss, Heinz. "Tilghman Laufer—Writer of Rimes and Analyzer of Budgets." "'S Pennsylfawnisch Deitsch Eck," Allentown *Morning Call*, 24 November 1951.

LEISENRING, EDMUND

CJ180 Kloss, Heinz. "Edmund Daniel Leisenring—Pennsylvania German Dialect Writer." "'S Pennsylfawnisch Deitsch Eck," Allentown *Morning Call*, 24 April, 1 May 1954.

CJ181 Rattermann, Heinrich A. "Edmund Daniel Leisenring." *Der deutsche Pionier*, vol. 14 (1882–1883), 68–70.

LIGHT, JOSEPH H.

CJ182 Light, Joseph H. *Der Alt Schulmeshter*. Lebanon, Pa., 1928. Collection of dialect columns from the *Lebanon Semi-Weekly News*, in the late 1890's.

MAURER, MAE F.

CJ183 Maurer, Mae F. [Mrs. Mae F.] "Nau hock ich ewwe do." Poem. "'S Pennsylfawnisch Deitsch Eck," Allentown *Morning Call*, 11 January 1969.

MEYER, HENRY

CJ184 Buffington, Albert F. "Henry Meyer—An Early Pennsylvania German Poet." Yearbook, *Pa. German Folklore Soc.*, no. 19 (1955), p. 1–32. Recently discovered sources show Henry Meyer to have been one of the earliest dialect poets.

"MIKE"

CJ185 Kloss, Heinz. "Unkle Mike, Unknown Sage from the Saucony." "'S Pennsylfawnisch Deitsch Eck," Allentown *Morning Call*, 22 September 1956. A dialect writer whose identity has not been established; wrote a dialect column for the *Kutztown Patriot* in 1889.

MILLER, HARVEY M.

CJ186 Boyer, Walter E. "Solly Hulsbuck, the People's Poet." *The Pa. Dutchman*, vol. 4, no. 5 (1952), 1–2, 14–15. On the life and work of Harvey M. Miller.

CJ187 Miller, Harvey M. "Alle Daag." "'S Pennsylfawnisch Deitsch Eck," Allentown *Morning Call*, 28 August 1943.

CJ188 Miller, Harvey M. "Der bescht Thanksgiving." "'S Pennsylfawnisch Deitsch Eck," Allentown *Morning Call*, 27 November 1943.

CJ189 Miller, Harvey M. "'S iss alles iwwerduh." "'S Pennsylfawnisch Deitsch Eck," Allentown *Morning Call*, 18 September 1943.

MOLL, LLOYD A.

CJ190 Barba, Preston A. "In Memoriam, Lloyd A. Moll." Yearbook, *Pa. German Folklore Soc.*, vol. 12 (1947), 1–7.

CJ191 Moll, Lloyd A. "Am schwarze Baer." *Publs., Pa. German Folklore Soc.*, vol. 12 (1947), 9–146. Rev. by R. W. Gilbert, "'S Pennsylfawnisch Deitsch Eck," Allentown *Morning Call*, 5 March 1949; *Pa. Hist.*, vol. 16, no. 2 (1949), 155–56. Collects 25 of the 49 dialect sketches which had appeared at intervals between 1935 and 1939 in the "Pennsylfawnisch Deitsches Eck."

CJ192 Moll, Lloyd A. "Schtimme aus'm Kaerrichhof." "'S Pennsylfawnisch Deitsch Eck," Allentown *Morning Call*, 13 February, 3, 24 April, 5 June, 21 August, 25 September, 27 November 1943.

MORE, CHARLES C.

CJ193 Kloss, Heinz. "Zur Erinnerung an den pennsylvaniadeutschen Mundarterzähler Charles C. More." *Deutsche Kultur im Leben der Völker* (1941), 433–40.

CJ194 [More, Charles C.] "'S Wash Hellers ihra Chrischtdagzug." *Hist. Rev. of Berks Co.*, vol. 6, no. 2 (1941), 51–53. A Christmas story.

CJ195 Waldenrath, Alexander. "The Manuscripts of Charles C. More." *German-Amer. Studies*, vol. 9 (Spring 1975), 16–25. On More's intent and ambition to capture the spirit of his fellow Pennsylvanians in the medium of their dialect.

NEAGLEY, SAMUEL M.

CJ196 Yoder, Don. "A New Dutch Poet." *The Pa. Dutchman*, vol. 2, no. 2 (1950–1951), 5.

PETER, OSVILLE C.

CJ197 "Fliggle Payder (Der Fliggel Peder.)" "'S Pennsylfawnisch Deitsch Eck," Allentown *Morning Call*, 15 January 1966; 28 January 1967.

CJ198 Handwerk, Walter T., comp. *Fliggle Payder, The Humorous World of the Pennsylvania Dutch Country*. New York: Carlton Pr., 1966. O. C. Peter, "Der Fliggel Peder," perpetrated the pranks here recorded.

RAHN, CLARENCE

CJ199 [Dialect Humor.] 5 tape recordings made by Parre Rahn. In the Pennsylvania German Society.

RAUCH, EDWARD H.

CJ200 Barba, Preston A. "Pitt Schweffelbrenner." "'S Pennsylfawnisch Deitsch Eck," Allentown *Morning Call*, 19 July, 1947. Sketch of the life of R., Pennsylvania editor and writer.

CJ201 [Rauch, Edward H.] *Pennsylvanish Deitsh; de Campain Breefa fum Pit Schweffelbrenner [pseud.] un de Bevoy, si Alty. Gepublished olly woch, im "Father Abraham."* Lancaster: Rauch & Cochran, 1868. 46p. Campaign letters of U.S. Grant in the dialect.

CJ202 Rauch, Edward H. *Pennsylvania Dutch Rip Van Winkle. A Romantic Drama in Two Acts*. Trans. from the Original with Variations by E. H. Rauch ("Pit Schweffelbrenner"). Mauch Chunk, Pa.: Mauch Chunk Democrat Steam Print, 1883. Reissued Mauch Chunk, 1951. 32p.

REITNAUER, CLARENCE

CJ203 Reitnauer, Clarence. "Der Shdivvel Knecht." Pennsylvania German dialect column in the Pennsburg *Town and Country*. Also featured on radio station WBYO. Collected (1966–1975) by Mark Trumbore and publ. as *Der Shdivvel Knecht*. N.p.: n.p., n.d.

CJ204 Reitnauer, Clarence G. *Em Shdivvel Knecht Sei Pennsylfawnisch Deitsch Werdta Buch*. Pennsylvania Dutch Series, Ursinus College, no. 7. N.p.: n.p., 1976. 35p. Dialect-to-English dictionary. With "Introduction" by William T. Parsons, p.ii–iv.

CJ205 Reitnauer, Clarence G. *So schreibt der Shdivvel Knecht*. Collegeville, Pa.: Institute on Pennsylvania Dutch Studies, 1975. Reprints from the author's Pennsylvania German dialect column. With "Introduction" by William T. Parsons, p.i–ii.

RHOADS, THOMAS J. B.

CJ206 Leidy, Rosanne D. "Thomas J. B. Rhoads, Poet and Physician of Boyertown." *Hist. Rev. of Berks Co.*, vol. 26, no. 2 (1961), 50–51.

RUPP, WILLIAM J.

CJ207 Rupp, William J. "Der Huns John—A Unique Character." *The Pa. Dutchman*, vol. 2 (1 August 1951). Stories and legends about John Heinrich Heimbach, an old German dog peddler who was known throughout Berks and Lehigh counties.

SAUDER, BEN

CJ208 Sauder, Ben. *Der Nachbar an de Schtroas*. Norristown, Pa.: Pa. German Soc., 1955. 35p. Collection of the poems of Canada's Pennsylvania German Folk Poet. Rev. by P. A. Barba, "'S Pennsylfawnisch Deitsch Eck," Allentown *Morning Call*, 19 November 1955.

CJ209 Sauder, Benjamin. "Der Nachbar an de Schtroas vun Ben Sauder." *Publs. of the Pa. German Folklore Soc. of Ontario*, vol. 1 (1960). Rev. by P. A. Barba, "'S Pennsylfawnisch Deitsch Eck," Allentown *Morning Call*, 2 September 1961.

SCHANDEIN, LUDWIG

CJ210 Schandein, Ludwig. "Die Auswannerer, the Emigrants by Ludwig Schandein." Trans. by William T. Parsons. *Pa. Folklife*, vol. 28, no. 4 (1979), 25–31. A Palatine German poem printed in 1854.

"SCHNITZ UND GNEPP"

CJ211 "Schnitz und Gnepp." *Der Reggeboge*, vol. 11, no. 1 (1977), 24. Dialect poem.

SCHUMACHER, ANDREW

CJ212 Kloss, Heinz. "En Bissel Pennsylvanisch vun Canada—New Writings by Andrew Schumacher." "'S Pennsylfawnisch Deitsch Eck," Allentown *Morning Call*, 26 May 1956.

SHENTON, DONALD RADCLIFFE

CJ213 Shenton, Donald Radcliffe. "Everything Makes." "'S Pennsylfawnisch Deitsch Eck," Allentown *Morning Call*, 20 November 1943.

SHOWALTER, HENRY

CJ214 Harman, Joel. "Henry Showalter: Dialect Writer." *The Pa. Dutchman*, vol. 3, no. 2 (1951–1952), 7.

SIEGEL, CHARLES

CJ215 Yoder, Don. "Charles Siegel: Dialect Poet." "'S Pennsylfawnisch Deitsch Eck," Allentown *Morning Call*, 12 June 1948.

SNYDER, G. GILBERT

CJ216 "The Reading Wunnernaws." *The Pa. Dutchman*, vol. 1, no. 1 (1949–1950), 1. On dialect columnist G. Gilbert Snyder.

SOMMER, LINA

CJ217 Sommer, Lina. *So Sache: G'schichtelcher und Gedichtelcher von Lina Sommer*. Heidelberg: n.p., 1922. Dialect poetry and prose.

STORK, LUDWIG

CJ218 Shoemaker, Alfred L. "Tramp Poet." *The Pa. Dutchman*, vol. 5, no. 13 (1954), 6, 16. A collection of magazine and newspaper accounts of Ludwig Stork, 19th-century German "tramp poet."

SWOPE, PIERCE E.

CJ219 Buffington, Albert F. "Der Kasper Hufnagel (i.e., Pierce E. Swope, dialect columnist) verzeehlt." *Der Reggeboge*, vol. 13, no. 4 (October 1979), 5–8. An interview with the writer, incl. his article on flies: "Micke."

CJ220 "Dr. Pierce E. Swope Alias Kaspar Hufnagel." "'S Pennsylfawnisch Deitsch Eck," Allentown *Morning Call*, 29 August 1959. Dialect columnist.

TREXLER, BENJAMIN T.

CJ221 Kaufman, David B. "The Walking Purchase of 1737.; "'S Pennsylfawnisch Deitsch Eck," Allentown *Moring Call*, 29 January, 5 February 1966. Repr. from Trexler's *Skizzen aus dem Lecha Thale*. The original was written in the Pennsylvania-German dialect.

TROXELL, WILLIAM S.

CJ222 "[Allentown *Morning*] *Call* Columnist Pumpernickle Bill Dies." *Allentown Evening Chronicle*, 10 August 1957. On William S. Troxell.

CJ223 Frey, J. William. "Supplement to a Morphological and Syntactical Study of the Pennsylvania German Dialect of Pumpernickle Bill." TS. Univ. of Illinois, 1939.

CJ224 "Hail and Farewell." Allentown *Morning Call*, 12 August 1957. On William S. Troxell.

CJ225 Rosenberger, Homer Tope. "The Passing of William S. Troxell, Widely Known Columnist." In: *The Pennsylvania Germans, 1891–1965, Frequently Known as the "Pennsylvania Dutch."* Publs. of the Pa. German Soc., vol. 63. Lancaster: The Soc., 1966, p. 308–14.

CJ226 Shoemaker, Alfred L. "Pumpernickle Bill, Dialect Writer." *The Pa. Dutchman*, vol. 1, no. 4 (1949), 1.

CJ227 [Tribute to Troxell, William S.] *Procs., Lehigh Co. Hist. Soc.*, vol. 22 (1958), 289f.

VON NIEDA, JOHN WESLEY

CJ228 Kloss, Heinz. "John Wesley von Nieda: A Pennsylvania German Novelist." "'S Pennsylfawnisch Deitsch Eck," Allentown *Morning Call*, 23 July 1949.

WARNER, JOSEPH H. ("JOHANN KLOTZ")

CJ229 Klotz, Johann. "Americanisch Historie." "'S Pennsylfawnisch Deitsch Eck," 17 May–28 June 1958. Repr. of a humorous dialect version of American history.

WEISER, ANNE E.

CJ230 DeChant, Alliene. "Anne E. Weiser." *The Pa. Dutchman*, vol. 5, no. 1 (1953–1954), 8. On the dialect columnist.

WEISER, CHARLES W.

CJ231 Barba, Preston A. "Der Sim Schmalzgsicht vum Leder Eck Poshta." "'S Pennsylfawnisch Deitsch Eck," Allentown *Morning Call*, 3 November 1956. On the work of Charles W. Weiser, newspaperman and dialect columnist.

CJ232 Barba, Preston A. "Sim Schmalzgsicht's Own Magazine." "'S Pennsylfawnisch Deitsch Eck," Allentown *Morning Call*, 27 October 1956. On the magazine started by Weiser in 1913.

CJ233 Kloss, Heinz. "Sim Schmalzgsicht, Once Locally Famous Allentown Humorist." "'S Pennsylfawnisch Deitsch Eck," 20 October 1956.

CJ234 Kloss, Heinz. "Tobias Witmer." "'S Pennsylfawnisch Deitsch Eck," Allentown *Morning Call*, 6 November 1948.

WIEAND, PAUL

CJ235 "Paul Wieand: Pennsylvania Dutch Playwright." *The Pa. Dutchman*, vol. 1, no. 5 (1949–1950), 7.

WITMER, TOBIAS

CJ236 Barba, Preston A. "Who Was Tobias Witmer?" "'S Pennsylfawnisch Deitsch Eck," Allentown *Morning Call*, 3 July 1948. Pennsylvania German poet of the nineteenth century.

WOLF, JOHN M.

CJ237 Eisenhart, W. W. "Squire John M. Wolf: Dutch Dialect Writer." *The Pa. Dutchman*, vol. 2, no. 8 (1950–1951), 8.

WOLLENWEBER, LUDWIG A.

CJ238 Barba, Preston A. "Ludwig A. Wollenweber." *Hist. Rev. of Berks Co.*, vol. 7 (1941–1942), 74–77. Early writer on the Pennsylvania Germans in High German and the dialect; journalist (1807–1888) on German papers in Philadelphia and Reading.

CJ239 Kloss, Heinz. "En Bissel Wollenweberisch." "'S Pennsylfawnisch Deitsch Eck," Allentown *Morning Call*, 19 October 1957.

CJ240 Wollenweber, Ludwig A. *Aus den Aufzeichnungen von L. A. Woolenweber über seine Erlebnisse in Amerika, namentlich in Philadelphia*. Collegeville: Inst. on Pa. Dutch Studies, 1977. 94p. New ed. by William T. Parsons of a work originally publ. in the *Mitteilungen des Deutschen Pionier Vereins von Philadelphia* (1909).

CJ241 Wollenweber, Ludwig A. "Aus meinem Leben." *Mitteilungen des Deutschen Pionier Vereins von Philadelphia*, vol. 14 (1910), 1–28; vol. 15 (1910), 1–27.

WOOD, RALPH C.

CJ242 Wood, Ralph C. "Das bucklige Männlein." *Amer.-German Rev.*, vol. 8, no. 6 (1942), 27–30.

CJ243 Wood, Ralph Charles. "The Four Gospels. Translated into the Pennsylvania German Dialect." *Publs., Pa. German Soc.*, vol. 1 (1968), 7–184. Rev. in *Pa. Genealogical Mag.*, vol. 25, no. 4 (1968), 281–82; Excerpted in "'S Pennsylfawnisch Deitsch Eck," Allentown *Morning Call*, 13 April and 21 December, 1968. Rev. by R. W. Gilbert, *ibid.*, 17 August 1968.

CJ244 Wood, Ralph C., trans. *Es Evangelium vum Mattheus. Aus der griechische Schprooch ins Pennsilvenideitsch iwwersetzt vum Ralph Charles Wood*. Stuttgart: J. F. Steinkopf, 1955; Allentown, Pa., 1955. 56p. Rev. by Heinz Kloss, *Mitteilungen des Instituts für Auslandsbeziehungen*, vol. 6 (1956), 126; P. A. Barba, "'S Pennsylfawnisch Deitsch Eck," Allentown *Morning Call*, 24 March 1956.

WUCHTER, ASTOR C.

CJ245 Baver, Mrs. Russel S. "Northampton County Bobbelmaul." *The Pa. Dutchman*, vol. 4, no. 3 (1952–1953), 14. Notes on Astor C. Wuchter.

CJ246 Dieruff, Louis E. "Astor Wuchter: Dialect Poet." *The Pa. Dutchman*, vol. 1, no. 23 (1949–1950), 1.

ZARTMAN, ISAAC

CJ247 Buffington, Albert F. "Isaac Zartman: The Prolific Bilingual Poet." *Der Reggeboge*, vol. 5, no. 2 (1971), 3–18.

ZIEGLER, CHARLES C.

CJ248 Frey, J. William. "The Dutch in Word and Song." *The Pa. Dutchman*, vol. 1, no. 2 (1949–1950), 8. On Charles C. Ziegler.

D
Linguistics, Dialectology, and Sociology of Language

DA
General Studies

Demographics/Geography of Language

DA1 Eichhoff, Jürgen. *Wortatlas der deutschen Umgangssprachen.* Vol. I. München: Francke, 1977. Ca. 64p. 54 maps.

DA2 Fishman, Joshua A., Esther G. Lowy, Michael H. Gertner, and William G. Milan. *Language Resources in the United States.* Vol. I. *Guide to Non-English-Language Print Media.* Rosslyn, Va.: National Clearinghouse for Bilingual Education, 1981. 51p.

DA3 Galinsky, Hans. *Amerika und Europa. Sprachliche und sprachkünstlerische Wechselbeziehungen in amerikanistischer Sicht.* Berlin/München/Zürich: Langenscheidt, 1968. 316p. Survey of mutual interchanges in the area of language during the last 500 years. A collection of essays, incl. some that had appeared between 1960 and 1964.

DA4 Gilbert, Glenn G. *Linguistic Atlas of Texas German.* Austin: Univ. of Texas Pr., 1972; Marburg: Elwert. 25p., with 148 leaves of maps. Indicates the geographic distribution of features of syntax, vocabulary, semantics, and phonology of a dialect which is rapidly disappearing.

DA5 Gilbert, Glenn G. "The Linguistic Geography of Non-Official Languages in the United States." In: *Tenth International Congress of Linguistics. / Actes du Xe Congrès des Linguistes.* Vol. 2. *Résumés des communications. Abstracts of Papers...* Ed. Alexander Graur. Bucharest: n.p., 1967, p.203–08.

DA6 Gilbert, Glenn G. "Origin and Present-Day Location of German Speakers in Texas: A Statistical Interpretation." In: *Texas and Germany: Crosscurrents.* Ed. Joseph Wilson. Houston: Rice Univ., 1977, p.21–34. Repr. in: *Problems in Applied Educational Sociolinguistics: Readings on Language and Culture Problems of U.S. Ethnic Groups.* Ed. G. G. Gilbert and J. Ornstein. The Hague: Mouton, 1978, p.119–29.

DA7 Grabowitz, W. "Regionale und soziale Varianten des Amerikanisch-Englischen Lexikons in Kent County, Delaware, U.S.A." State examination thesis, Düsseldorf, 1978.

DA8 Kloss, Heinz. *Atlas of 19th and Early 20th Century German Settlements* [in America]. Marburg: Elwert, 1974. Rev. by J. Eichhoff, *Muttersprache,* vol. 86 (1976), 161–64. Also publ. in German: Marburg: Elwert, 1974.

DA9 Kloss, Heinz. "Demographische Grundtatsachen." In: *Deutsche Muttersprache in Kanada: Berichte zur Gegenwartslage.* Ed. L. Auburger, H. Kloss and H. Rupp. Wiesbaden: Steiner, 1977, p.3–6.

DA10 Kloss, Heinz. "Die Muttersprachenzählung von 1940 und die Zukunft der nichtenglischen Sprachen in den USA." *Erdkunde,* vol. 7, no. 3 (1953), 220–25.

DA11 Kloss, Heinz. "Sprachstatistischer Rahmen." In: *Deutsch als Muttersprache in den Vereinigten Staaten. Teil 1. Der Mittelwestern.* Ed. L. Auburger et al. Wiesbaden: Steiner, 1979, p.223–27.

DA12 Kloss, Heinz, and Grant D. McConnell, eds. *Linguistic Composition of the Nations of the World.* Vol. 2: *North America.* Québec: Presse Universitaire de Laval, 1978. 893p.

DA13 Kloss, Heinz, and Grant D. McConnell, eds. *The Written Languages of the World: A Survey of the Degree and Modes of Use.* Vol. 1: *The Americas.* Québec: Presse Universitaire de Laval, 1978. 633p.

DA14 Reed, Carroll. "Die Sprachgeographie des Pennsylvaniendeutschen." *Zeitschrift für Mundartforschung,* vol. 25 (1957), 29–39.

DA15 Ross, Werner. "Die Stellung der deutschen Sprache in der Welt." In: *Nationalismus in Germanistik und Dichtung: Dokumente des Germanistentages in München vom 17.–22. Oktober 1966.*

Demographics/Geography *(cont.)*

Ed. Benno von Wiese and Rudolf Henss. Berlin: Schmidt, 1967.

Theoretical and General Studies

DA16 Auburger, Leopold. "Vorbemerkung der Herausgeber." In: *Deutsch als Muttersprache in Kanada....* Ed. L. Auburger, Heinz Kloss, and Heinz Rupp. Wiesbaden: Steiner, 1977, p.vii–ix.

DA17 Barry, W. J., and C. Gutknecht. *A University Course in English Phonetics and a Comparative Study in English and German Phonology.* Vol. 2. *Theory.* In: *Linguistische Berichte*, Heft 14, 1971.

DA18 Bausinger, Hermann. *Volkskultur in der technischen Welt.* Stuttgart: W. Kohlhammer, 1961.

DA19 Blanke, Gustav. *Der Amerikaner, eine sozio-linguistische Studie.* Meisenheim am Glan: Hain, 1957. 336p.

DA20 Blanke, Gustav. *Amerikanischer Geist. Begriffs- und wortgeschichtliche Untersuchungen.* Meisenheim: Hain, 1956. 267p. Rev. by H. Galinsky, *Die neueren Sprachen*, NF, vol. 8, no. 1 (1959), 40–45.

DA21 Brewster, Paul G. "A Note on the Epithet 'Hessian'." *Amer. Speech*, vol. 18, no. 1 (1943), 72–73.

DA22 Clyne, Michael. "Some [German-English] Language Contact Phenomena at the Discourse Level." In: *Studies for Einar Haugen Presented by Friends and Colleagues.* Ed. Evelyn S. Firchow et al. The Hague: Mouton, 1972, p.132–45.

DA23 Clyne, Michael. "Zur Beschreibung des Gebrauchs von sprachlichem Lehngut unter Berücksichtigung der kontaktbedingten Sprachforschung." *Zeitschrift für Mundartforschung*, vol. 34 (1967), 217–25.

DA24 Curme, George O. *Grammar of the German Language.* 2nd rev. ed. New York: Ungar, 1952. 623p.

DA25 Darnell, Regna, ed. *Canadian Languages in Their Social Context.* Edmonton: Linguistic Research, 1973.

DA26 Darnell, Regna, ed. *Linguistic Diversity in Canadian Society.* Edmonton: Linguistic Research, 1971. Rev. by Bernard Saint-Jacques, *Canad. Jour. of Linguistics*, vol. 18 (1973), 183–89.

DA27 Davis, Lawrence M., ed. *Studies in Linguistics in Honor of Raven I. McDavid, Jr.* Univ. of Alabama Pr., 1972. 496p. Writings on dialectology, language structure, and language history.

DA28 D[obbie], E[lliot] V. K. "A Further Note on 'Hessian'." *Amer. Speech*, vol. 18, no. 4 (1943), 310.

DA29 Enninger, Werner, and Karl-Heinz Wandt. "Zur Notation von Repertoire-(dis)-kontinuität: Ein Komplement zur Terminologie im Bereich von 'Language Maintenance' und 'Language Shift'." In: *Angewandte Soziolinguistik.* Ed. Matthias Hartig. Tübingen: Gunter Narr, 1981, p.65–77.

DA30 Galinsky, Hans. *Amerikanische-deutsche Sprach- und Literaturbeziehungen: Systematische Übersicht und Forschungsbericht 1945–1970.* Frankfurt: Athenäum, 1972. 253p. Rev. in *Engl. and Amer. Studies in German.* A Supplement to *Anglia* 1972. Ed. Werner Habicht. Tübingen: Niemeyer, 1973, p.122–24. The first section offers a survey of Anglo-American influences on the development of German since 1945; the second is a general essay on mutual interchanges between languages.

DA31 Galinsky, Hans K. "Amerikanischenglische und gesamtenglische Interferenzen mit dem Deutschen und anderen Sprachen der Gegenwart." In: *Sprachliche Interferenz. Festschrift für Werner Betz.* Ed. Herbert Kolb et al. Tübingen: Niemeyer, 1977, p.463–517.

DA32 Galinsky, Hans K. *Regionalismus und Einheitsstreben in den Vereinigten Staaten. Ein sprachwissenschaftlicher Forschungsbericht.* Heidelberg: C. Winter, 1972. Rev. in *Engl. and Amer. Studies in German.* A Supplement to *Anglia* 1972.

Ed. W. Habicht. Tübingen: Niemeyer, 1973, p. 122–24.

DA33 Galinsky, Hans K. *Die Sprache des Amerikaners; Eine Einführung in die Hauptunterschiede zwischen amerikanischem und britischem Englisch der Gegenwart*. Heidelberg: Kerle, 1951–1952. 2 vols. Incl. a study of Americanisms in German.

DA34 Gilbert, Glenn G. "Linguistic Change in the Colonial and Immigrant Languages in the United States." In *Saga og Språk: Studies in Language and Literature Presented to Lee M. Hollander*. Ed. John M. Weinstock. Austin: Pemberton Pr., 1972, p. 223–31.

DA35 Gilbert, Glenn G. Rev. of W. Labov: *The Social Stratification of English in New York City*. In: *Language*, vol. 45 (1969), 469–76.

DA36 Gilbert, Glenn G., and Jacob Ornstein, eds. *Problems in Applied Educational Sociolinguistics: Readings on Language and Culture Problems of U.S. Ethnic Groups*. The Hague: Mouton, 1978; Berlin: DeGruyter, 1978. 144p.

DA37 Haugen, Einar. "The Analysis of Linguistic Borrowing." *Language*, vol. 26 (1950), 210–31.

DA38 Heller, Otto, and Theodore H. Leon. *The Language of Charles Sealsfield. A Study in Atypical Usage*. St. Louis: Washington Univ. Studies, 1941. 154p. Rev. by K. Arndt, *Germanic Rev.*, vol. 16 (1941), 151–52; A. B. Faust, *Mod. Lang. Quar.*, vol. 3 (1942), 315–19; N. Willey, *Mod. Lang. Jour.*, vol. 27 (1943), 223; A. Prahl, *Mod. Lang. Notes*, vol. 58 (1943), 155–56; *Monatshefte*, vol. 33 (1941), 335.

DA39 Kaufman, David D. "Language Relationships—Particularly English and German." "'S Pennsylfawnisch Deitsch Eck," Allentown *Morning Call*, 16, 23, 30 April 1966.

DA40 Keul, Norman C. "A Selected, Annotated Bibliography of English-German Contrastive Linguistics." *Die Unterrichtspraxis*, vol. 14, no. 1 (Spring 1981), 105–16.

DA41 Kloss, Heinz. ["Autobibliography."] *Europa Ethnica, Vierteljahresschrift für Nationalitätenfragen*, vol. 28, nos. 132 and 134 (1971), 60.

DA42 Kloss, Heinz. *Deutsch in der Begegnung mit anderen Sprachen: Im Fremdsprachen-Wettbewerb, als Mutter-Sprache im Übersee, als Bildungsbarriere für Gastarbeiter*. Eds. U. Engel and Irmgard Vogel. Institut für deutsche Sprache, Forschungsberichte no. 20. Tübinger Beiträge zur Linguistik. Tubingen: Narr, 1974. 204p. Rev. in: *German-Canad. Yearbook*, vol. 4 (1978), 356–58.

DA43 Kloss, Heinz. "Forschung im Dienst der Sprachen und Schulen. Bibliographie aus Anlass des 65. Geburtstag von Heinz Kloss." *Europa-Ethnica*, vol. 28, no. 2 (1971). 69p.

DA44 Kloss, Heinz. "Notes Concerning a Language-Nation Typology." In: *Language Problems of Developing Nations*. Ed. Joshua Fishman et al. New York: Wiley, 1968, p. 69–86.

DA45 [Kloss, Heinz.] "Statt einer Festschrift: Bibliographie der Veröffentlichungen von Heinz Kloss." *Vierteljahresschrift für Nationalitätenfragen*, vol. 28, no. 2 (1971), 51–69.

DA46 Kloss, Heinz. "Vom Lohr-Archiv und anderen Dokumenten zur Geschichte der deutschen Sprache in Übersee." *German-Amer. Studies*, vol. 9 (1975), 75–79.

DA47 Kloss, Heinz. "Who are the Shapers of New Cultural Tongues." "'S Pennsylfawnisch Deitsch Eck," Allentown *Morning Call*, 10 January 1953. The role of the intellectual in the formation of new literary languages.

DA48 Koerner, Ernst F. K. "The Humboldtian Trend in Linguistics." In: *Studies in Descriptive and Historical Linguistics: Festschrift for Winfred P. Lehmann*. Ed. Paul J. Hopper. Amsterdam: Benjamins, 1977, p. 145–58.

DA49 Kufner, Herbert L. *The Grammatical Structures of English and German*. Chicago: Univ. of Chicago Pr., 1963. Rev. by G. L. Baurley, *Zeitschrift für Anglistik und Amerikanistik*, vol. 13 (1965), 417–20.

DA50 Lehmann, Winfred P. *Historical Linguistics. An Introduction*. New York: Holt, Rinehart & Winston, 1962.

DA51 Moulton, William G. *The Sound of English and German*. Chicago: Univ. of Chicago Pr., 1963. Rev. by G. L. Baurley, *Zeitschrift für Anglistik und Amerikanistik*, vol. 13 (1965), 417–20.

DA52 Müller-Schotte, Hans. "Zur Stärke des Ausdrucks im Englischen und Deutschen." *Die*

Theoretical and General Studies (cont.)

Lebenden Sprachen, vol. 12, no. 4–5 (1967), 97–107. Superlatives, emphatic particles, intensification of verbs.

DA53 Nickel, Gerhard. "Sprachliche Missverständnisse. Strukturunterschiede zwischen dem Deutschen und dem Englischen." *Praxis des neusprachlichen Unterrichts* (1966), 1–12.

DA54 Penn, Julia M. "Linguistic Relativity versus Innate Ideas: The Origins of the Sapir-Whorf Hypothesis in German Thought in the Eighteenth and Nineteenth Centuries." Diss., Univ. of Texas, 1966.

DA55 Pyles, Thomas. *The Origins and Development of the English Language*. 2nd ed. New York: Harcourt Brace Jovanovich, 1971. For German loan words, *see* p. 283–84, 332–34.

DA56 Reed, Carroll E. *Dialects of American English*. Rev. ed. Amherst, Mass.: Univ. of Massachusetts Pr., 1977. 135p. Bibliography, p. 87–96.

DA57 Sapir, Edward. *Language*. New York: Harcourt, Brace, 1921.

DA58 Saporta, Sol. "Ordered Rules, Dialect Differences, and Historical Processes." *Language*, vol. 41 (1965), 218–24.

DA59 Wächtler, Kurt. *Das amerikanische Englisch in der Schule*. Berlin: Langenscheidt, 1963. Rev. by B. Carstensen, *Jahrbuch für Amerikastudien*, vol. 11 (1966), 366–68. On the relative merits of American and British English in German secondary school curricula.

DA60 Wächtler, Kurt. "Zur Stellung und Behandlung des amerikanischen English im Englischunterricht." *Praxis des neusprachlichen Unterrichts*, vol. 3 (1966), 244–50.

DA61 Whyte, John. "A Personal Adventure into the German and English Future Tenses." *Monatshefte für deutschen Unterricht*, vol. 35, nos. 3–4 (March–April 1943), 226–32.

DA62 Wilson, Joseph B. "Texas German and Afrikaans." *Jour. for Regional Cultures*, vol. 1, no. 1 (1981), 79–87.

DA63 Wise, C. M., and Morris Cohen. "The Language Problems of German-Speaking Invaders." *Quar. Jour. of Speech*, vol. 30 (1944), 402–16.

Multilingualism and Bilingualism

DA64 Adams, Marylin. "Linguistic Change in German Immigrants and Their Progeny: A Question of Contemporary Significance." M.A. Thesis, Univ. of Cincinnati, 1976.

DA65 Auburger, Leopold, and Heinz Kloss. *Deutsche Sprachkontakte in Übersee*. Tübingen: Gunter Narr Verlag, 1978.

DA66 Brunt, Richard. "An Investigation into German/English Language Contact in an Old Order Amish Isolate in Kent County, Delaware, U.S.A." M.A. thesis, Dept. of English, Univ. of Essen, 1979.

DA67 Buchheit, Robert H. "Language Maintenance and Shift among Mennonites in South-Central Kansas." *Yearbook of German-Amer. Studies*, vol. 17 (1982), 111–21.

DA68 Costello, John R. "Syntactic Change and Second Language Acquisition: The Case for Pennsylvania German." *Linguistics*, vol. 213 (1978), 29–50.

DA69 Dietz, Paul T. "The Transition from German to English in the Missouri Synod from 1910 to 1947." *Concordia Hist. Inst. Quar.*, vol. 22, no. 3 (1949), 97–127. Dispassionate treatment of the problem that has caused such great strife.

DA70 Enninger, Werner. "Aspekte des soziolinguistischen Systems einer dreisprachigen Interaktionsgemeinschaft in Kent County, Delaware, U.S.A.: Eine Fallstudie." Manuscript, Univ. of Essen, 1978. A study of the Old Order Amish in Kent County, Del.

DA71 Enninger, Werner. "Language Convergence in a Stable Triglossia Plus Trilingualism Situation." In: *Anglistik: Beiträge zur Fachwissenschaft und Fachdidaktik*. Ed. Peter Freese et al. Münster: n.p., 1979, p. 43–63. A study of the Delaware Old Order Amish.

DA72 Enninger, Werner. "Nonverbal Performatives: The Function of a Grooming and Garment

Grammar in the Organization of Nonverbal Role-Taking and Role-Making in One Specific Trilingual Social Isolate." In: *Understanding Bilingualism.* Ed. Werner Hüllen. Frankfurt: Peter Lang, 1980, p.25–65. A study of the Old Order Amish in Delaware.

DA73 Enninger, Werner. "Syntactic Convergence in a Stable Triglossia Plus Trilingualism Situation in Kent County, Delaware, U.S.A." In: *Sprachkontakt und Sprachkonflict. Zeitschrift für Dialektologie und Linguistik,* Beiheft no. 30. Ed. P. H. Nelde. Wiesbaden: Steiner, 1980, p.343–50.

DA74 Enninger, Werner, and Joachim Raith. "Linguistic Modalities of Liturgical Registers: The Case of the Old Order Amish Church Service." *Yearbook of German-Amer. Studies,* vol. 16 (1981), 115–30.

DA75 Enninger, Werner, and K. H. Wandt. "Social Roles and Language Choice in an Old Order Amish Community." *Sociologia Internationalis,* vol. 17, no. 1–2 (1979), 47–70.

DA76 Fishman, Joshua. *Advances in the Study of Societal Multilingualism. Contributions to the Sociology of Language,* vol. 9. The Hague: Mouton, 1978. 842p.

DA77 Fishman, Joshua. "Ethnic Community Mother Tongue Schools in the U.S.A.: Dynamics and Distribution." *Internat. Migration Rev.,* vol. 14 (1980), 235–47. Statistics on mother tongue schools, including those in the German language.

DA78 Fishman, Joshua. *Language and Nationalism.* Rowley, Mass.: Newbury House, 1973.

DA79 Fishman, Joshua A. *The Sociology of Language.* Rowley, Mass.: Newbury House, 1972. 105p.

DA80 Fishman, Joshua A. et al. *Language Loyalty in the United States: The Maintenance and Perpetuation of Non-English Mother Tongues by American Ethnic and Religious Groups.* New York: Yeshiva Univ. Prepubl. Duplicated ed., 1964; The Hague: Mouton, 1966; repr. New York: Arno Pr., 1978. 478p. Rev. by A. R. Schultz, *Amer.-German Rev.,* vol. 33, no. 1 (1967), 28–29; C. Wittke, *Catholic Hist. Rev.,* vol. 55, no. 4 (1970). The first comprehensive study of the factor of ethnicity in American culture. A massive statistical-sociological study by a panel of experts.

DA81 Frey, J. William. "Amish Triple Talk." *Amer. Speech,* vol. 20 (April 1945), 84–98.

DA82 Frey, J. William. "Some Observations on Bilingualism in Eastern York County." "'S Pennsylfawnisch Deitsch Eck," Allentown *Morning Call,* 15 February 1941, p.7.

DA83 Gaarder, A. Bruce. "Teaching the Bilingual Child: Research, Development, and Policy." *Mod. Lang. Jour.,* vol. 49 (1965), 165–75.

DA84 Galinsky, Hans. "Stylistic Aspects of Linguistic Borrowing: A Stylistic and Comparative View of American Elements in Modern German and British English." In: *Preprints of Papers for the Ninth International Congress of Linguistics.* Ed. Moritz Halle. Cambridge, Mass.: n.p., 1962, p.221–63. Also in: *Procs. of the Ninth International Congress of Linguistics, Cambridge, August 27–31, 1962.* Ed. Horace G. Lunt. The Hague, 1964, p.374–81. See also *Jahrbuch für Amerikastudien,* vol. 8 (1963), 98–135.

DA85 Gilbert, Glenn G. "Needs in Bilingual Research in Languages Other than Spanish and Amerindian in the Southwest." Symposium on Bilingual / Bicultural Education: Effects on Languages, Individuals, and Society. Univ. of Texas at El Paso, 12–14 June 1975. Mimeogr.

DA86 Gilbert, Glenn G., ed. *Texas Studies in Bilingualism. Spanish, French, German, Czech, Polish, Sorbian, and Norwegian in the Southwest....* Studia Linguistica Germanica, no. 3. Berlin: de Gruyter, 1970. 223p. 4 tables. Rev. by J. Eichhoff, *Monatshefte,* vol. 64 (1972), 400–01. Eleven studies, incl. articles by Gilbert, William Pulte, and J. B. Wilson.

DA87 Graham, Robert S. "The Transition from German to English in the German Settlements of Saskatchewan." *Jour. of the Canad. Linguistic Assoc.,* vol. 3 (1957), 9–13. Changes in phonological systems of second-generation German speakers at Luseland, Sask.

DA88 Haugen, Einar. *Bilingualism in the Americas: A Bibliography and Research Guide.* Publs. of the Amer. Dialect Soc., no. 26 (1956). 159p. Rev. by C. E. Reed, *Monatshefte,* vol. 50 (1958), 93–94.

DA89 Haugen, Einar. "Bilingualism, Language Contact, and Immigrant Languages in the United States: A Research Report, 1956–1970." In: *Cur-*

Multilingualism and Bilingualism *(cont.)*

rent Trends in Linguistics. Vol. 10. *Linguistics in North America*. Ed. Thomas A. Sebeok et al. The Hague: Mouton, 1973, p.505–91.

DA90 Haugen, Einar. "Problems of Bilingualism." *Lingua*, vol. 2 (1950), 271–90.

DA91 Kloss, Heinz. "Assimilationsfragen des Pennsylvaniadeutschtums." *Pfälzer Heimat*, vol. 3 (1952), 83–87. On the linguistic assimilation of the Pennsylvania Germans in recent times.

DA92 Kyeck-Janssen, C., and A. Hahn. "The Role of High German in the Trilingual Repertoire of an Old Order Amish Speech Community." In: *Project Trilingual Speech Community: Interim Report.* N.p.: English Dept., Univ. of Essen, 1978. Mimeogr. A community in Kent Co., Delaware.

DA93 Landis, Ira D., "The German-English Transition in Lancaster County [Pennsylvania]." *Amer.-German Rev.*, vol. 11, no. 5 (1945), 8–9, 27.

DA94 Leopold, Werner F. "Bilingualism of Occupation Children in Germany." In: *Brittanica. Festschrift für Hermann M. Flasdieck.... Ed. W. Iser and H. Schabram.* Heidelberg: Winter, 1960, p.106–79.

DA95 Leopold, Werner F. *Speech Development of a Bilingual Child*. 4 vols. Northwestern Univ. Studies in Humanities, nos. 6, 11, 18, and 19. Evanston: Northwestern Univ. Pr., 1939–1949. Rev. by R. A. Fowkes, *Germanic Rev.*, vol. 25 (1950), 131–33; E. Haugen, *Jour. of Engl. and Germanic Philol.*, vol. 52 (1953), 392–97; M. Joos, *Monatshefte*, vol. 46 (1954), 232–34; K. Malone, *Mod. Lang. Notes*, vol. 68 (1953), 508–09; O. Springer, *German Quar.*, vol. 28 (1955), 293–95.

DA96 Lourie, Margaret A., and Nancy F. Conklin, eds. *A Pluralistic Nation: The Language Issue in the United States*. Rowley, Mass.: Newbury House, 1978.

DA97 Missebach, Sabine. "Der Nativismus-Aspekt." In: *Project Trilingual Speech Community: Interim Report.* N.p.: Dept. of English, Univ. of Essen, 1978. Mimeogr. An Old Order Amish community in Kent Co., Delaware.

DA98 Pape, Martin. "Interactional Fencing." In: *Project Trilingual Speech Community: Interim Report.* N.p.: Dept. of English, Univ. of Essen, 1978. Mimeogr. An Old Order Amish community, Kent Co., Delaware.

DA99 Raith, Joachim. "Pennsylvania German—American English Bilingualism: A Case Study." In: *Deutsch in Kontakt mit anderen Sprachen / German in Contact with Other Languages*. Ed. C. Molony, H. Zobl and W. Stölting. Kronberg: n.p., 1977, p.104–28.

DA100 Raith, Joachim. "Phonologische Interferenzen im amerikanischen Englisch der anabaptistischen Gruppen deutscher Herkunft in Lancaster County, Pennsylvania: Unter Berücksichtigung von Sprachgemeinschaftstyp und Erwebskontext." *Zeitschrift für Dialektologie und Linguistik*, vol. 48 (1981), 35–52.

DA101 Raith, Joachim. *Sprachgemeinschaftstyp, Sprachkontakt, Sprachgebrauch: Eine Untersuchung des Bilingualismus der anabaptistischen Gruppen deutscher Abstammung in Lancaster County, Pennsylvania*. Diss., Univ. of Essen, 1978. Publ. in Wiesbaden: Steiner, 1981.

DA102 Raith, Joachim. "Sprachkonvergenz und Sprachgemeinschaftstyp: Eine soziolinguistische Analyse eines Sprachkontaktphänomens in Lancaster County (Pennsylvanien, U.S.A.)." Univ. of Essen, 1980. MS., 21p.

DA103 Raith, Joachim. "Types of Speech Community and Language Use." In: *Understanding Bilingualism: Life, Learning and Language in Bilingual Situations*. Ed. Werner Hüllen. Frankfurt: Peter Lang, 1980, p.131–46.

DA104 Röwer, Corinne. "Interim Report: Quantitative and Qualitative Aspects of English Interpenetration into the Pennsylvania German of the Delaware 'Botschaft' Scribe." MS., Dept. of English, Univ. of Essen, 1979. Study of an Old Order Amish community, Kent Co., Delaware.

DA105 Seifert, Lester W. J. "One Hundred Thirty Years of Divergent Development in One Dialect." Univ. of Kentucky Foreign Language Conference, 27–29 April 1967. Compares the speech of Oderbruck with that of informants whose ancestors emigrated to Wisconsin.

DA106 Seifert, Lester W. J. "The Problem of Speech-Mixture in the German Spoken in Northwestern Dane County, Wisconsin." *Transactions, Wis. Acad. of Sciences, Arts, and Letters*, vol. 39 (1949), 127–39.

DA107 Stanforth, Antony W. "Deutsch-englischer Lehnwortaustausch." In: *Wortgeographie und Gesellschaft. Festgabe für Ludwig Erich Schmitt...10. Feb. 1968.* Ed. W. Mitzka. Berlin: de Gruyter, 1968, p.526–60.

DA108 Urion, Carl. "A German-English Interlingual Key." In: *Linguistic Diversity in Canadian Society.* Ed. Regna Darnell. Edmonton: Linguistic Research, 1971, p.223–30.

DA109 Veith, Werner H. "Amerika-Emigranten am Niederrhein: Transferenzen im Wortschatz ihrer Nachfahren." In: *Lexicography and Dialect Geography. Festschrift for Hans Kurath.* Ed. Harald Scholler and John Reidy. Wiesbaden: Steiner, 1973, p.243–59.

DA110 Viereck, Wolfgang. "Wortmischung im Englischen und Deutschen." *Die Lebenden Sprachen*, vol. 10, no. 6 (November–December 1965), 162f.

DA111 Wandt, Karl-Heinz. "Methodische Probleme bei der Anwendung des Konstrukts der Domäne hinsichtlich der Sprachenauswahl einer multilingualen Sprachgemeinschaft." In: *Project Trilingual Speech Community: Interim Report.* Dept. of English, Univ. of Essen, 1978. Mimeogr. Based on a study of the Old Order Amish community, Kent County, Delaware.

DA112 Weinreich, Uriel. *Languages in Contact. Findings and Problems.* Publs. of the Linguistic Circle of New York, no. 1. Pref. by Andre Martinet. New York: n.p., 1953. 2nd printing: The Hague: Mouton, 1963; 6th printing: The Hague: Mouton, 1968. On the mixing of languages and the languages of immigrants to the U.S.A. Also publ. in German: München: Beck, 1976. 190p.

Law of Language Rights

DA113 Kloss, Heinz. *The Bilingual Tradition in the United States.* Rowley, Mass.: Newbury House, 1977. 347p. The author's study *Das Nationalitätenrecht...* of 1963 translated into English.

DA114 Kloss, Heinz. "Deutsche Sprachpolitik im Ausland." *Sprachforum*, vol. 2 (1957), 8–9.

DA115 Kloss, Heinz. *Les droits linguistiques des Franco-Américains aux États-Unis.* Québec: International Center for Research in Bilingualism, 1972. 80p.

DA116 Kloss, Heinz. *Grundfragen der Ethnopolitik im 20. Jahrhundert. Die Sprachgemeinschaften zwischen Recht und Gewalt.* Ethnos. Schriftenreihe der Forschungs-Stelle Marburg/Lahn, no. 7. Wien: Braumüller, 1969. 624p.

DA117 Kloss, Heinz. *Das Nationalitätenrecht der Vereinigten Staaten von Amerika.* Wien: Braumüller, 1963.

DA118 Kloss, Heinz. "Der sprachenrechtliche Rahmen." In: *Deutsch als Muttersprache in Kanada: Berichte zur Gegenwartslage.* Ed. L. Auburger et al. Wiesbaden: Steiner, 1977, p.53–57.

DA119 Luebke, Frederick C. "Laws Against Language: Legal Restrictions on Foreign Languages in the Great Plains States, 1917–1923." In: *Languages in Conflict. Linguistic Acculturation on the Great Plains.* Ed. Paul Schach. Lincoln: Univ. of Nebraska Pr., 1981, p.1–19.

DB
English and German Languages—Interactions

The German Language in America—Impact of English

See also Section AL: The German Language in American Life.

DB1 Albrecht, Erich A. "Deutsche Sprache, deutsche Literatur und deutscher Unterricht in New Orleans, Louisiana." *German-Amer. Studies*, vol. 3, no. 1 (1971), 18–21.

DB2 Albrecht, Erich A. "Deutsche Sprache in Kansas." In: *Deutsch als Muttersprache in den Vereinigten Staaten*. Teil 1: *Der Mittelwesten*. Ed. L. Auburger et al. Wiesbaden: Steiner, 1979, p.161–69.

DB3 Auburger, Leopold. "Zur Sprache Kanadadeutscher Zeitungstexte (Zusammenfassung der Forschungsergebnisse von Helga Wacker)." In: *Deutsch als Muttersprache in Kanada*... Ed. L. Auburger et al. Wiesbaden: Steiner, 1977, p.149–56.

DB4 Auburger, Leopold, Heinz Kloss and Heinz Rupp, eds. *Deutsch als Muttersprache in den Vereinigten Staaten*. Teil 1: *Der Mittelwesten*. Wiesbaden: Steiner, 1979. 343p. Rev. by H. Froeschle, *Germanistische Mitteilungen*, no. 12 (1980), 73–75; C. E. Reed, *Monatshefte*, vol. 72 (1980), 340–41. Reports on the German language in the several states and regions and within such communities as the Amish, the Germans from Russia, and the Mennonites. General bibliography on dialects and German language use in North America.

DB5 Baroni, Werner. "Deutsche Sprache in Chicago." In: *Deutsch als Muttersprach in den Vereinigten Staaten*. Teil 1: *Der Mittelwesten*. Ed. L. Auburger et al. Wiesbaden: Steiner, 1978, p.35–40.

DB6 Bartel, Klaus J. "German and the Germans at the Time of the American Revolution." *Mod. Lang. Jour.*, vol. 60 (1976), 96–100. The language situation in Pennsylvania in the eighteenth century.

DB7 "Bibliographie zu den Beiträgen." In: *Deutsch als Muttersprache in Kanada: Berichte zur Gegenwartslage*. Ed. L. Auburger et al. Wiesbaden: Steiner, 1977, p.169–75.

DB8 Carman, J. Neale. *Foreign Language Units of Kansas*. Vol. 1. *Historical Atlas and Statistics*. Lawrence: Univ. of Kans. Pr., 1962. 330p. Rev. by *Amer.-German Rev.*, vol. 29, no. 1 (1962), 36; S. J. Sackett, *Western Folklore*, vol. 22, no. 2 (1963), 139–40; E. Haugen, *Amer. Speech*, vol. 39, no. 1 (February 1964), 54–56. Vols. 2 and 3 in microfiche. Approx. 3,115 manuscript pages. Lawrence, Univ. of Kans. Pr., 1973. A monumental chronicle of the linguistic assimilation of early settlers in Kansas; a study of linguistic anglicization based on a wealth of materials from local history.

DB9 Carstensen, Broder. "Information zum geplanten Anglizismen-Wörterbuch." *Der fremdsprachliche Unterricht*, vol. 15 (1981), 218–20.

DB10 Dolmetsch, Christopher L. "Studies in Shenandoah Valley [Virginia] German: A Critical Survey." *Jour. of German-Amer. Studies*, vol. 12 (1977), 25–33.

DB11 Dow, James R. "Deutsch als Muttersprache in Iowa." In: *Deutsch als Muttersprache in den Vereinigten Staaten*. Teil 1: *Der Mittelwesten*. Ed. L. Auburger et al. Wiesbaden: Steiner, 1978, p.91–118.

DB12 Eichhoff, Jürgen. "Deutsch als Siedlersprache in den Vereinigten Staaten von Amerika." In: *Festchrift für Gerhard Cordes*. Eds. Friedhelm Debus and Joachim Hartwig. Neumünster: Wachholtz, 1976. Vol. 2, p.68–91.

DB13 Eichhoff, Jürgen. "Deutsche Sprache in Wisconsin." In: *Deutsch als Muttersprache in den Vereinigten Staaten*. Teil 1: *Der Mittelwesten*. Ed. L. Auburger et al. Wiesbaden: Steiner, 1979, p.65–75.

DB14 Eichhoff, Jürgen. "German in Wisconsin." In: *The German Language in America: A Symposium.* Ed. Glenn G. Gilbert. Austin: Univ. of Texas Pr., 1971, p.43–57.

DB15 Entz, W. "Die deutschsprachige Presse Westkanadas: Ihr Inhalt und ihre Sprache." *Seminar: A Jour. of Germanic Studies*, vol. 3 (1967), 37–52.

DB16 Gilbert, Glenn G. "Dative versus Accusative in the German Dialects of Central Texas." *Zeitschrift für Mundartforschung*, vol. 32 (1965), 288–96.

DB17 Gilbert, Glenn G. "English Loan Words in the German of Fredericksburg, Texas." *Amer. Speech*, vol. 40 (1965), 102–12.

DB18 Gilbert, Glenn G. "The German Language in Ellis County, Kansas." *Heritage of Kans.*, vol. 9, nos. 2/3 (1976), 8–16.

DB19 Gilbert, Glenn G. "The German Language in Texas: Some Needed Research." From a paper presented at San Marcos, Texas, 1978. 8p.

DB20 Gilbert, Glenn G. "Linguistic Change in the Colonial and Immigrant Languages in the United States." In: *Saga og Språk: Studies in Language and Literature Presented to Lee M. Hollander.* Ed. John M. Weinstock. Austin, Tex.: Pemberton Pr., 1972, p.223–31.

DB21 Gilbert, Glenn G. "The Phonology, Morphology, and Lexicon of a German Text from Fredericksburg, Texas." In: *Texas Studies in Bilingualism. Spanish, French, German, Czech, Polish...in the Southwest...* Ed. Glenn G. Gilbert. Studia Linguistica Germanica, no. 3. Berlin: de Gruyter, 1970, p.63–104.

DB22 Gilbert, Glenn G., Carroll E. Reed et al. "A Unified Proposal for the Study of the German Language in the United States: Discussion." In: *The German Language in America: A Symposium.* Ed. Glenn G. Gilbert. Austin: Univ. of Texas Pr., 1971, p.128–47.

DB23 Gilbert, Glenn G., ed. and introd. *The German Language in America: A Symposium.* Austin: Univ. of Texas Pr., 1971. 217p. Rev. by E. Haugen, *Amer. Anthropologist*, vol. 75 (1973), 1090–91; Werner H. Veith, *Zeitschrift für Dialektologie und Linguistik*, vol. 39 (1972), 339–41. With contributions by Eichhoff, Gilbert, Kloss, Pulte, Reed and Seifert. Bibliography, p.179–97.

DB24 Heard, Betty R. "A Phonological Analysis of the Speech of Hays County, Texas." Diss., Louisiana State Univ. and Mechanical College, 1969. Cites lexical forms used principally or exclusively by informants of German descent.

DB25 Heffner, Roe-Merrill S. "German Settlements in Wisconsin." *Conference on Non-English Speech in the United States, Bull., Amer. Council of Learned Soc.*, vol. 34 (1942), 19–26.

DB26 Howell, Richard W., and Jack Klassen. "Contrasting du/Sie Patterns in a Mennonite Community." *Anthropological Linguistics*, vol. 13 (1971), 68–74.

DB27 Johansen, Kjell. "The English of Kendall and Gillespie Counties, Texas." M.A. Thesis, Texas, 1961. Some information on the impact of Texas German on English.

DB28 Jordan, Gilbert J. "The Texas German Language of the Western Hill Country." In: *Texas and Germany: Crosscurrents.* Ed. Joseph Wilson. Rice Univ. Studies, vol. 63, no. 3. Houston: Rice Univ., 1977, p.59–71.

DB29 Kaufman, David D. "Language Relationships—Particularly English and German." "'S Pennsylfawnisch Deitsch Eck," Allentown *Morning Call*, 16, 23, 30 April 1966.

DB30 Kloss, Heinz. "Die deutsche Schriftsprache bei den Amischen." In: *Deutsch als Muttersprache in Kanada: Berichte zur Gegenwartslage.* Ed. L. Auburger et al. Wiesbaden: Steiner, 1977, p.97–98.

DB31 Kloss, Heinz. "Deutsche Sprache im Ausland." In: *Lexikon der germanistischen Linguistik.* Ed. Hans P. Althaus, Helmut Henne, and Herbert E. Wiegand. Tübingen: Niemeyer, 1973, vol. 2, p.377–87.

DB32 Kloss, Heinz. "German as an Immigrant, Indigenous, Foreign, and Second Language in the United States." In: *The German Language in America: A Symposium.* Ed. Glenn G. Gilbert. Austin: Univ. of Texas Pr., 1971, p.106–27.

DB33 Korda, G. "Aspekte der syntaktischen Variation eines Old Order Amish Isolats in Kent

The German Language in America *(cont.)*

County, Delaware." MS. of a state examination thesis, Univ. of Essen, 1979.

DB34 Krumpelmann, John T. "Americanisms Recorded by Duke Bernhard of Saxe-Weimar." In: *Festschrift für Walther Fischer*. Ed. Horst Oppel. Heidelberg: Winter, 1959, p.187–94.

DB35 Krumpelmann, John T. "Charles Sealsfield's Americanisms." *Amer. Speech*, vol. 16 (1941), 26–31, 104–11; vol. 19 (1944), 196–99. See also the comments of J. B. Macmillan, *Amer. Speech*, vol. 18 (1943), 117–27.

DB36 Lehmann, Winfred. "Lone Star German." In: *Texas and Germany: Crosscurrents*. Rice Univ. Studies, vol. 63. Ed. Joseph Wilson. Houston: Rice Univ., 1977, p.73–81.

DB37 Lewis, Brian A. "German in Colorado: Background for a Linguistic Survey." *German-Amer. Studies*, vol. 8 (1974), 106–13.

DB38 Lewis, Brian A. "Swiss German in Wisconsin: The Impact of English." *Amer. Speech*, vol. 48 (Fall-Winter 1973), 211–28.

DB39 Lewis, Brian A. "The Volga Germans in Colorado and Their Languages." *Work Papers of the Amer. Hist. Soc. of Germans from Russia*, vol. 17 (1975), 10–12.

DB40 M., L. B. "Von den Amischen im Mittelwesten." In: *Deutsch als Muttersprache in den Vereinigten Staaten*. Teil 1: *Der Mittelwesten*. Ed. L. Auburger et al. Wiesbaden: Steiner, 1979, p.199–208.

DB41 McCord, Stanley Joe. "A Historical and Linguistic Study of the German Settlement at Roberts Cove, Louisiana." Diss., Louisiana St. Univ. and Agricultural and Mechanical Coll., 1969. 301p. On a low-German dialect of a colony established in 1881 in Acadia Parish.

DB42 Martens, Hedda. "Language Attitudes of German Immigrants and Their Families Observed in Rochester, N.Y." Diss., Rochester, 1972.

DB43 Martin, Horst. "Zum Geschlecht englischer Wörter im Auslanddeutschen im Hinweis auf eine kanadische Spielart." *Muttersprache*, vol. 87 (1977), 321–25.

DB44 Mayer, Elizabeth M. *Deutschsprachige und die deutsche Sprache in Michigan*. Kalamazoo: n.p., 1974.

DB45 Mayer, Elizabeth M. "Deutsche Sprache in Michigan." In: *Deutsch als Muttersprache in den Vereinigten Staaten*. Teil 1: *Der Mittelwesten*. Ed. L. Auburger et al. Wiesbaden: Steiner, 1979, p.41–63.

DB46 Mieder, Wolfgang. "Angloamerikanische und deutsche Uberlieferung des Ausdrucks 'last (but) not least.'" *Sprachspiegel*, vol. 37 (1981), 131–34, 162–66.

DB47 Mieder, Wolfgang. "Bibliographische Skizze zur Überlieferung des Ausdrucks 'Iron Curtain'/'Eiserner Vorhang.'" *Muttersprache*, vol. 91 (1981), 1–14.

DB48 Milnes, Humphrey N. "Gesprochenes Deutsch in Kanada." *German-Canad. Rev.*, vol. 9 (1956), 7–11; *Mitteilungen des Instituts für Auslandsbeziehungen* (Stuttgart), vol. 7 (1957), 184–86. In Waterloo Co., Ontario.

DB49 Moore, Barbara J. "A Sociolinguistic Longitudinal Study (1969–1979) of a Texas German Community, Including Curricular Recommendations." Diss., Texas, 1980. 269p.

DB50 Neufeld, N. J. "Sprechen die Mennoniten in Kanada noch deutsch?" *Muttersprache*, vol. 65 (1955), 229–31.

DB51 Proechel, Glen. "Minnesota Liturgical German." Diss., Mankato St. Coll., 1973.

DB52 Pulte, William J. "German in Virginia and West Virginia." In: *The German Language in America: A Symposium*. Ed. Glenn G. Gilbert. Austin: Univ. of Texas Pr., 1971, p.58–69.

DB53 Reed, Carroll E., and Herbert F. Wiese. "Amana German," *Amer. Speech*, vol. 32 (1957), 243–56. An analysis of speech of the Iowa community, with a brief history.

DB54 Reimer, Gerhard. "Deutsch als Muttersprache unter den Mennoniten in Indiana." In: *Deutsch als Muttersprache in den Vereinigten Staaten*. Teil 1: *Der Mittelwesten*. Ed. L. Auburger et al. Wiesbaden: Steiner, 1979, p.17–22.

DB55 Reimer, Gerhard. "Deutsche Sprache unter den Amischen des Mittelwesten." In: *Deutsch* *als Muttersprache in den Vereinigten Staaten.* Teil 1: *Der Mittelwesten.* Ed. L. Auburger et al. Wiesbaden: Steiner, 1979, p.191–97.

DB56 Rein, Kurt. "Deutsche Minderheiten täuferischen Ursprungs im Mittelwesten der USA." In: *Deutsch als Muttersprache in den Vereinigten Staaten.* Teil 1: *Der Mittelwesten.* Ed. L. Auburger et al. Wiesbaden: Steiner, 1979, p.173–89.

DB57 Rein, Kurt. "Religiöse Minderheiten als Sprachgemeinschaftsmodelle. Deutsche Sprachinseln täuferischen Ursprungs in den Vereinigten Staaten von Amerika." Habilitations-Schrift, Univ. Marburg, 1973. Also in: *Zeitschrift für Dialektologie und Linguistik*, Beiheft 15. 197p.

DB58 Rettig, Lawrence. "Grammatical Structures in Amana German." Diss., Iowa, 1970. 136p. An analysis based on the reports of eight informants.

DB59 Rippley, LaVern J. "Deutsche Sprache in Minnesota." In: *Deutsch als Muttersprache in den Vereinigten Staaten.* Teil 1: *Der Mittelwesten.* Ed. L. Auburger et al. Wiesbaden: Steiner, 1979, p.77–90.

DB60 Rippley, LaVern J. "Zur sprachlichen Situation der Russlanddeutschen in den USA." In: *Deutsch als Muttersprache in den Vereinigten Staaten.* Teil 1: *Der Mittelwesten.* Ed. L. Auburger et al. Wiesbaden: Steiner, 1979, p.211–22.

DB61 Rittenhouse, Jack D. *Wendish Language Printing In Texas.* Los Angeles: Dawson's Bookshop, 1962.

DB62 Sachs, Emmy. "The Gender of English Loan Words in the German of Recent Immigrants." *Amer. Speech*, vol. 28, no. 4 (1953), 256–70.

DB63 Sacket, S. J. "Folk Speech in Schoenchen, Kansas." *Western Folklore*, vol. 19, no. 4 (1960), 277. In a Russian-German community.

DB64 Schach, Paul. "Comments on Some Pennsylvania-German Words in the Dictionary of Americanisms." *Amer. Speech*, vol. 29, no. 1 (1954), 45–54.

DB65 Scheer, Herfried. "Studien zur Sprache der Hutterer Brüder." Diss., McGill, 1972.

DB66 Schreiber, William I. "Die 'Old Order Amish'—Mennoniten in Nordamerika: ihre Sprache und Gebräuche." *Rheinisches Jahrbuch für Volkskunde*, vol. 13–14 (1964), 256–75.

DB67 Schroeder, Adolf E. "Deutsche Sprache in Missouri." In: *Deutsch als Muttersprache in den Vereinigten Staaten.* Teil 1: *Der Mittelwesten.* Ed. L. Auburger et al. Wiesbaden: Steiner, 1979, p.125–60.

DB68 Schurz, Carl. "Die deutsche Sprache in Amerika." *Zeitschrift für Amerikakunde*, vol. 12, no. 4 (1962), 331–32. Text of an address delivered at the 50th anniversary program of the Deutscher Liederkranz in New York, 1897.

DB69 Sebeok, Thomas A. "German Travelers and Language in America." *Amer. Speech*, vol. 18, no. 4 (1943), 279–82.

DB70 Seeger, Mary Anderson. "English Influence on the Language of the *Dodge County Pionier*, Mayville, Wisconsin." Diss., Wisconsin, 1970.

DB71 Seifert, Lester W. J. "Methods and Aims of a Survey of the German Language Spoken in Wisconsin." *Transactions, Wis. Academy of Sciences, Arts and Letters*, vol. 40, part 2 (1951), 201–10.

DB72 Seifert, Lester W. J. Wisconsin German Questionnaire, 1946. Univ. of Wisconsin. TS.

DB73 Sell, Rainer. "The German Language: Mirror of the German-American Struggle for Identity as Reflected in *Der deutsche Pionier* (1869–1887) and the Archives of *Der deutsche Pionier-Verein von Cincinnati*." *German-Amer. Studies*, vol. 11 (1976), 71–81.

DB74 "Sprechen Sie Deutsch." *New Yorker Staats-Zeitung und Herold*, vol. 146, no. 18 (1980): B–8. On the influence of English on the language of German-Americans and Continental Germans.

DB75 Spuler, Linus. "Deutsch in den Vereinigten Staaten." *Sprachspiegel: Mitteilungen des deutschschweizerischen Sprachvereins*, vol. 12, no. 4 (July–August 1956), 67–71.

DB76 Thierfelder, Franz. *Die deutsche Sprache im Ausland. Deutsche Philologie im Aufriss.* Ed. Wolfgang Stammler. 2 vols. Berlin: E. Schmidt, 1951; Hamburg: Decker Vlg. G. Schenck, 1956–57. 196, 402p. Rev. T. O. Brandt, *Amer.-German Rev.*, vol. 24, no. 3 (1958), 37; A. Closs, *Mod. Lang. Quar.*, vol. 20 (1959), 107–09; W. Neuse,

The German Language in America *(cont.)*

German Quar., vol. 31 (1958), 250–51. For the use and occurrence of German in the United States and Canada, see vol. 2, p. 345–502.

DB77 Thiessen, John. "The Language of the Canadian Mennonites." *Procs. of the Linguistic Circle of Manitoba and N. Dak.*, vol. 4 (1963), 34–37.

DB78 Thiessen, John. *Studien zum Wortschatz der kanadischen Mennoniten*. Deutsche Dialektgeographie, vol. 64. Marburg: Elwert, 1963. 207p. Rev. by K. W. Maurer, *Zeitschrift für Kulturaustausch*, vol. 14, no. 1 (1964), 55–56.

DB79 Travis, D. C. "Texas Symposium [Austin, 18–20 November 1968]: The German Language in America." *Die Unterrichtspraxis*, vol. 2, no. 1 (1969), 104–12.

DB80 Wacker, Helga. *Die Besonderheiten der deutschen Schriftsprache in den USA*. Duden-Beiträge: Die Besonderheiten der deutschen Schriftsprache im Ausland, no. 14. Mannheim: Bibliographisches Inst., 1964. 191p. Rev. by G. G. Gilbert, *Zeitschrift für Mundartforschung*, vol. 34 (1967), 83–86; S. Jäger, *Muttersprache*, vol. 78 (1968), 51–55; M. Clyne, *Muttersprache*, vol. 76 (1966), 287f.

DB81 Wacker, Helga. *Die Besonderheiten der deutschen Schriftsprache in Kanada und Australien*. Duden-Beiträge, no. 17. Mannheim: Bibliographisches Inst., 1964. 191p. Study based on the language of German-language newspapers. Rev. by Glenn G. Gilbert, *Zeitschrift für Mundartforschung*, vol. 34 (1967), 83–86.

DB82 Wacker, Helga. "Untersuchungen zur Gestalt der deutschen Schriftsprache beim Deutschtum der Vereinigten Staaten, Kanadas und Australiens... Auf Grund der Sprache der überseeischen deutschen Zeitungen." Diss., Tübingen, 1956. 507p.

DB83 Ward, Robert E. "Brigandedeutsch in Amerika." *Vierteljahrsschr. für das kulturelle Leben in Stadt und Land*, (Karlsruhe), vol. 3 (1968), 24–27.

DB84 Ward, Robert E. "Deutsche Sprache in Ohio." In: *Deutsch als Muttersprache in den Vereinigten Staaten. Teil 1: Der Mittelwesten*. Ed. L. Auburger et al. Wiesbaden: Steiner, 1979, p. 3–16.

DB85 Wilde, Henry. "Die deutsche Sprache in den U S A." *Condor* (Santiago de Chile), vol. 16, no. 274 (1954), 5.

DB86 Willibrand, W. A. "German in Okarche 1892–1902." Repr. from the *Chronicles of Okla.*, vol. 28 (Autumn 1950), 284–91.

DB87 Wilson, Joseph. "The Earliest Anglicisms in Texas German." *Yearbook of the Soc. for German-Amer. Studies*, vol. 16 (1981), 103–14.

DB88 Wilson, Joseph. "The German Language in Central Texas Today." In: *Texas and Germany: Crosscurrents*. Rice Univ. Studies, vol. 63, no. 3. Ed. Joseph Wilson. Houston: Rice Univ., 1977, p. 47–58.

DB89 Wilson, Joseph. "The German Language in Texas." *Die Schatzkammer*, vol. 2, no. 1 (1976), 43–49. Rev. by Glen E. Lich, *Jour. of German-Amer. Studies*, vol. 12, no. 4 (Winter 1977), 99–100.

DB90 Wilson, Joseph. "Lebendiges Deutsch: Anglicisms in Texas German." *Newsletter of the German-Texan Heritage Soc.*, vol. 3, no. 1 (1981), 19–23.

DB91 Wilson, Joseph, ed. *Texas and Germany: Crosscurrents*. Ed. Joseph Wilson. Rice Univ. Studies, no. 63. Houston: Rice Univ. 1977.

DB92 Wilson, Joseph B. "The Texas German of Lee and Fayette Counties." *Rice Institute Pamphlet*, vol. 47, no. 1 (1960), 83–98.

DB93 Wilson, Joseph B. "Unusual German Lexical Items from the Lee-Fayette County Area of Texas." In: *Texas Studies in Bilingualism.... * Ed. Glenn G. Gilbert. Berlin: de Gruyter, 1970, p. 142–50.

DB94 Wood, Ralph Charles. "Die deutsche Volkssprache in Nordamerika." *Wirkendes Wort*, vol. 11, no. 5 (July–August 1961), 202–09.

DB95 Wood, Ralph Charles. "Pennsylvania High German." *Germanic Rev.*, vol. 20, no. 4 (1945), 299–314.

DB96 Wood, Ralph Charles. "Zur Problematik der deutschen Volkssprache in Nordamerika." In: *Weltweite Wissenschaft vom Volke; Festgabe für J. W. Mannhardt*. Wien: R. M. Rohrer, 1958, p. 185–89.

The German Language in America—German Influence on English

See also Section AL: The German Language in American Life.

DB97 Albrecht, Erich A. "New German Words in Popular English Dictionaries." *German Quar.*, vol. 22 (1949), 10–16.

DB98 Aldrich, Ruth I. "A Festfest." *Amer. Speech*, vol. 49 (1974), 155–56.

DB99 Appuhn, Hans-Günter. "Das Apollo-Mondprogramm in sprachlicher Sicht." *Die Neueren Sprachen*, vol. 69 (n.s. 19) (1970): 209–22.

DB100 Ashcom, B. B. "Notes on the Language of the Bedford, Pennsylvania, Subarea." *Amer. Speech*, vol. 28 (1953), 241–55. Indications of Pennsylvania-German influence on the English of the Bedford area.

DB101 Atwood, E. Bagby. *The Regional Vocabulary of Texas*. Austin: Univ. of Texas Pr., 1962.

DB102 Benjamin, Renate L., and Steven M. Benjamin. "Origin of American English *fink*." *Comments on Etymology*, vol. 9, no. 15 (1980), 10–11.

DB103 Benjamin, Renate L., and Steven M. Benjamin. "The Origin of *Patzer*." *Comments on Etymology*, vol. 7, no. 14 (1978), 4–6.

DB104 Benjamin, Steven M., and Luanne von Schneidemesser. "German Loanwords in American English: A Bibliography of Studies, 1872–1978." *Amer. Speech*, vol. 54 (1979), 210–15.

DB105 Binger, Norman H. "German Elements in the American Vocabulary." *Semasia. Beiträge zur germanisch-romanischen Sprachforschung* (Amsterdam), vol. 2 (1975), 31–41.

DB106 Buffington, Albert F. "The Influence of the Pennsylvania German Dialect on the English Spoken in the Pennsylvania German Area." In: *Helen Adolf Festschrift*. Ed. S. Z. Büehne, J. L. Hodge, and L. B. Pinto. New York: Ungar, 1968, p.30–41.

DB107 Dorpalen, Andreas. "German Influences on the American Language." *Amer.-German Rev.*, vol. 7, no. 6 (1941), 13–14, 36.

DB108 Dunbar, Ronald W. "The Presence of German in the Jargon of the American Skier: A Sociological Look at the Past, Present, and Future." In: *Papers from the Conference on German-Americana in the Eastern United States*. Ed. Steven M. Benjamin. Morgantown, W. Va.: Dept. of Foreign Langs., W. Va. Univ., 1980, p.182–96.

DB109 Eichhoff, Jürgen. *Deutsch als Siedlersprache in Nordamerika und Probleme des wechselseitigen Einflusses zwischen dem Englischen und Deutschen: Bibliographie 1968–1974*. Madison: Dept. of German, Univ. of Wisconsin, 1974. Mimeogr. 4p. Supplement to the Bibliography by W. Viereck in *Orbis*, vol. 16-17 (1967–1968).

DB110 Eichhoff, Jürgen. "Deutsches Lehngut in der amerikanischen Pressesprache 1930–1971." *Jahrbuch für Amerikastudien*, vol. 17 (1972), 156–212. See also *Der Sprachdienst*, vol. 15 (1971), 173–74.

DB111 Eichhoff, Jürgen. "Zur Aussprache und Schreibung von Wörtern deutscher Herkunft im amerikanischen English." *Muttersprache*, vol. 81 (1971), 385–406.

DB112 Eichhoff, Jürgen. "Zur Systematik und Terminologie Deutsch-Englischer Lehnbeziehungen." *Festschrift für Hans Marchand*. The Hague: Mouton, 1968, p.32–45.

DB113 Feinsilver, Lilian M. "Like Influences from Yiddish and Pennsylvania German." *Amer. Speech*, vol. 33 (1958), 231–32.

DB114 Fischer, Heinz. "Kulturelle Sprachverwandtschaft zwischen dem Englischen und dem Deutschen. Deutsches Wortgut in einem Halbjahr des amerikanischen Nachrichtenmagazins TIME, 1964–1965." *Deutschunterricht für Ausländer* (München), vol. 15 (1965), 103–11.

DB115 Foster, Brian. "Foreign Influences." In: *The Changing English Language*, by Brian Foster. London: Macmillan, 1968, p.81–106. Traces lexical forms introduced into English from the German of the immigrants.

DB116 Frey, J. William. "The English of the Pennsylvania Germans in York Co., Pa." "'S Pennsylfawnisch Deitsch Eck," Allentown *Morning Call*, 18 May 1940.

DB117 Green, Archie. "'Dutchman': An On-the-Job Etymology." *Amer. Speech*, vol. 35 (1960), 270–74. Use of the word traced to the skill of German immigrant workers.

DB118 Haislund, Niels. "German Loanwords in American English." In: *Kopenhagener Germanistische Studien*. Vol. 1. *Festschrift für Peter Jørgensen*. Ed. K. Hyldgaard-Jensen and S. Steffensen. Kopenhagen: n.p., 1969, p.126–37.

DB119 Hamm, Joan. "The Effect of the Pennsylvania German Dialect upon the Intonation of English as Spoken in Dauphin and York Counties, Pennsylvania." M.A. thesis, Northeastern Illinois State College, 1970.

DB120 Harris, Jesse W. "German Language Influences in St. Clair County, Illinois." *Amer. Speech*, vol. 23 (1948), 106–10. Despite the large German element in the population, one finds relatively few traces in present-day English.

DB121 Heard, Betty R. "A Phonological Analysis of the Speech of Hays County, Texas." Diss., Louisiana State Univ. and Agricultural and Mechanical College, 1969. 308p. Some discussion of lexical items used by German informants.

DB122 Hosford, Helga. "Amerikanische Lehrbücher des Deutschen. Eine linguistische Analyse." In: *Proceedings, Pacific Northwest Conference on Foreign Languages. Twenty-Fourth Annual Meeting, May 4–5 1973 at Western Washington State College*. Walter C. Kraft. Corvallis: Oregon State Univ. Pr., vol. 24, p.77–82.

DB123 Huffines, Marion Lois. "English in Contact with Pennsylvania German." *German Quar.*, vol. 53, no. 3 (1980), 352–66.

DB124 Jarka, Horst. "The Language of Skiers." *Amer. Speech*, vol. 38, no. 3 (1963), 202–08. Words of German origin.

DB125 Jarka, Horst. "Skisportausdrücke im amerikanischen Englisch." *Die Lebenden Sprachen*, vol. 9 (1964), 161–64.

DB126 Kann, Hans-Joachim. "The 'Burger' Family." *Jahrbuch für Amerikastudien*, vol. 17 (1972), 213–15. From "hamburg steak" to "hamburger-steak."

DB127 Kann, Hans-Joachim. "DDR-Deutsch in TIME Magazine (1968–1973)." *Zeitschrift f. Dialektologie und Linguistik*, vol. 42 (1975), 63–65.

DB128 Kann, Hans-Joachim. "Entlehnungen aus dem Deutschen in *Time* 1972." *Muttersprache*, vol. 84 (1974), 430–44.

DB129 Kann, Hans-Joachim. "Neue Germanismen in *Time* 1975." *Der Sprachdienst*, vol. 21 (1977), 6–8; "...in *Time* 1976." *Ibid.*, vol. 22 (1977), 53–54; "...in *Time* 1977." *Ibid.*, vol. 22 (1978), 20–22; "...in *Time* 1978." *Ibid.*, vol. 23 (1979), 40–42.

DB130 Kloss, Heinz. "Found in Carman's Kansas Atlas: The Englings." *Amer. Speech*, vol. 50 (1975), 335–36.

DB131 Koenig, Karl. "Borrowings from the German (1930–1941)." *Mod. Lang. Jour.*, vol. 27, no. 7 (1943), 486–93.

DB132 Koenig, Karl. "German Loan Words in American, 1930–1940." *German Quar.*, vol. 15 (1942), 163–68.

DB133 Koziol, Herbert. "Der deutsche Einfluss auf den englischen Wortschatz." *Archiv*, vol. 178, nos. 3–4 (1941), 122–23. Rev. in: *Amer. Speech*, vol. 16, no. 3 (1941), 225.

DB134 Koziol, Herbert. "Zu Neubildungen und Lehnwörtern im amerikanischen Englisch." *Orbis*, vol. 10, no. 1 (1961), 169–74.

DB135 Kraemer, Heinz. "Der deutsche Einfluss auf den englischen Wortschatz." Diss., Tübingen Univ., 1952.

DB136 Kreider, Mary C. "'Dutchified English'—Some Lebanon Valley Examples." *Pa. Folklife*, vol. 12, no. 1 (1961), 40–43.

DB137 Kurath, Hans. "German Relics in Pennsylvania English." *Monatshefte*, vol. 37 (1945), 92–102.

DB138 Kurath, Hans. *Studies in Area Linguistics*. Bloomington, Ind.: Indiana Univ. Pr., 1972. Incl. discussion of loan words in English and Pennsylvania German, p.60–62, 107–13.

DB139 Kurath, Hans. *A Word Geography of the Eastern United States*. Ann Arbor: Univ. of Mich. Pr., 1949. 251p. Rev. by R. J. Menner, *Amer. Speech*, vol. 25 (1950), 122–26; C. C. Reed, *Mod. Lang. Quar.*, vol. 12 (1951), 245–47; N. E. Eliason, *Mod. Lang. Notes*, vol. 66 (1951), 487–89. For the distribution of words of Pennsylvania-German origin, see esp. p.32–36, maps nos. 23 and 24.

DB140 Kurath, Hans, and Raven I. McDavid, Jr. *The Pronunciation of English in the Atlantic States*. Ann Arbor: Univ. of Michigan Pr., 1959, 1961. Rev. by Samuel J. Keyser, *Language*, vol. 39 (1963), 303–13. With some discussion of Pennsylvania-German phonetic features.

DB141 Larson, Robert C. "The English Language of Carl Schurz, A Study of Its Germanic Background." Diss., Bonn, 1956. 805p.

DB142 Liedke, Herbert R. "The Evolution of the Ski-Lingo in America." *Monatschefte*, vol. 35 (1943), 116–24.

DB143 Livingood, Louis J. "Dutchisms in English." "'S Pennsylfawnisch Deitsch Eck," Allentown *Morning Call*, 19 August 1944.

DB144 Martens, Hedda. "Language Attitudes of German Immigrants and Their Families Observed in Rochester, N.Y." Diss., Univ. of Rochester, 1972.

DB145 Mencken, Henry L. *The American Language: An Inquiry Into the Development of English in the United States*. 4th ed., with 2 supplements, abridged, with annotations and new material by Raven I. McDavid, Jr. New York: Knopf, 1963. For comments on German dialects and their influence on English see p.192–95, 254–59, 472.

DB146 Mieder, Wolfgang. "Der Apfel fällt nicht weit von Deutschland: Zur amerikanischen Entlehnung eines deutschen Sprichwortes." *Sprachdienst*, vol. 15 (1981), 89–93.

DB147 Neubauer, Philip, and Arthur M. Z. Norman. "German and the G.I." *Amer. Speech*, vol. 31 (1956), 142–43. German expressions that have entered the lingo of American soldiers stationed in Germany.

DB148 Osterhues, Iris. "Die Sprache der Deutschstämmigen in den USA: Ein Verwandtschaftsnetz im nördlichen Mittelwesten." State examination thesis, Univ. of Oldenburg, 1979. 105p. Study of communities in Minnesota.

DB149 Palmer, Francis W. "Several Mennonite Americanisms." *Amer. Speech*, vol. 22, no. 1, part 1 (1947), 72–73.

DB150 Pfeffer, J. Alan. "Deutsches Lehngut im Wortschatz der Amerikaner von 1976." In: *Sprachliche Interferenz: Festschrift für Werner Betz zum 65. Geburtstag*. Ed. Herbert Kolb, H. Lauffer, K. O. Brogsitter et al. Tübingen: Niemeyer, 1977, p.518–25.

DB151 Rockwell, Leo L. "German Loan Words in American English." In: *Studies in Languages and Linguistics in Honor of Charles C. Fries*. Ed. A. H. Marckwardt. Ann Arbor: n.p., 1964, p.229–40.

DB152 Rockwell, Leo L. "Older German Loan Words in American English." *Amer. Speech*, vol. 20, no. 4 (1945), 247–57.

DB153 Rohrer, David. "The Influence of the Pennsylvania German Dialect on Amish English in Lancaster County." *Mennonite Research Jour.*, vol. 15 (1974), 34–35, 38–39, 47.

DB154 Rositzke, Harry H. "Some Dynamic Elements in the American Pronunciation of High German." *Monatshefte f. den Deut. Unterricht* 35, no. 1 (January 1943), 34–40.

DB155 Rothenberg, Julius G. "The English of 'Aufbau'." *Amer. Speech*, vol. 19, no. 2 (1944), 97–102. Interlingual influences in the English-German newspaper for refugees.

DB156 Sachs, Emmy. "The Gender of English Loan Words in the German of Recent Immigrants." *Amer. Speech*, vol. 28, no. 4 (1953), 256–70. The most important determinant is association with a German word or suffix of similar sound or meaning or with a group of German nouns liked by a common characteristic and having the same gender.

DB157 Schach, Paul. "The Pennsylvania German Contribution to the American Vocabulary." "'S Pennsylfawnisch Deitsch Eck," Allentown *Morning Call*, 12, 19 June 1954. Repr. from the *Hist. Rev. of Berks Co.*, vol. 19 (1953), 2–7.

DB158 Schach, Paul. "Pfälzische Entlehnungen in der amerikanischen Umgangssprache." *Rheinische Vierteljahrsblätter*, vol. 20 (1955), 223–36.

DB159 Schönfelder, Karl-Heinz. "Ausdrücke aus dem deutschen Bildungswesen im amerikanischen Englisch." *Zeitschrift für Anglistik and Amerikanistik*, vol. 3 (1955), 419–31.

DB160 Schönfelder, Karl-Heinz. "Deutsche Wortbildungselemente im amerikanischen Englisch." *Wissenschaftl. Zeitschrift der Universität Leipzig. Gesellschafts- und Sprachwissenschaftliche Reihe*, vol. 1, no. 5 (1951–1952), 8–18.

DB161 Schönfelder, Karl-Heinz. *Deutsches Lehngut im amerikanischen Englisch. Ein Beitrag zum Problem der Völker- und Sprachmischung*. Halle (Saale): VEB Max Niemeyer-Vlg., 1957. Reissued in the series *Wissen und Können, Reihe Gesellschaftswissenschaften*, no. 13, 1966. 200p.

DB162 Sergeantson, Mary S. *A History of Foreign Words in English*. London: Routledge & Kegan Paul, 2nd ed., 1961. 354p.

DB163 Soudek, Leo. "The Development and Use of the Morpheme *Burger* in American English." *Linguistics*, vol. 68 (1971), 61–89.

DB164 Soudek, Leo. "Further Members of the *Burger* Family." *Amer. Speech*, vol. 43 (1968), 74–76.

DB165 Spitzer, Leo. "Confusion Schmooshun." *Jour. of Engl. and Germanic Philology*, vol. 51, no. 2 (1952), 226–33. On the Yiddish basis of Brooklynese slang.

DB166 Springer, Otto. "On Defining the Sources of Colonial Speech." In: *Arbeiten zur germanischen Philologie und zur Literatur des Mittelalters*. München: Wilh. Fink Vlg., 1975, p.11–34.

DB167 Springer, Otto. "The Study of the English of the Pennsylvania Germans." In: *Perspectives on American English*. Ed. J. L. Dillard. The Hague: Mouton, 1980, p.195–204. Mutual influences between American English and Pennsylvania German.

DB168 Stanler, E. G. "The Use in English of the Word 'Schadenfreude'." *Notes and Queries*, vol. 9 (February 1962), 68–69.

DB169 Wächtler, Kurt. "Zur substantivischen Wortbildung mittels Lehnsuffix im amerikanischen Englisch." In: *Wortbildung, Syntax und Morphologie. Festschr. zum 60. Geburtstag von Hans Marchand am 1. Okt., 1967*. Ed. H. E. Brekle and L. Lipka. The Hague/Paris: n.p., 1968, p.230–42.

DB170 Weil, Dorothy. "Unnerstanning Cincinnada Dutch." Cincinnati *Enquirer Magazine*, 10 August 1980, 7–10.

DB171 Wild, S. "Deutsche Lehnübersetzungen im Amerikanisch-Englischen." *Neuphilologische Zeitschrift*, vol. 4 (1952), 196–98.

DB172 Wilson, Arthur Herman. "The English Spoken by Pennsylvania Germans in Snyder County, Pennsylvania." *Amer. Speech*, vol. 23 (1948), 236–38. Pennsylvania-German influences on the English of this relatively isolated region.

DB173 Wilson, H. Rex. "The Dialect of Lunenburg County, Nova Scotia: A Study of the English of the County, With Reference to Its Sources, Preservation of Relics, and Vestiges of Bilingualism." Diss., Univ. of Michigan, 1958.

DB174 Wilson, Joseph B. "The English Spoken by German-Americans in Central Texas." In: *Languages in Conflict: Linguistic Acculturation on the Great Plains*. Ed. Paul Schach. Lincoln: Univ. of Nebraska Pr., 1981, p.157–73.

DB175 Wrausmann, Ingrid. "Deutsches Wortgut im heutigen Amerikanischen." State Examination thesis, Univ. of München, 1971.

Anglo-American Influences on Standard German

DB176 "Anglicisms Irk German Purists." *N.Y. Times*, 3 December 1967.

DB177 Bald, Wolf-Dietrich. "Neologismen mit -in im Englischen und Deutschen." *Die lebenden Sprachen*, vol. 13, no. 4 (1968), 65–68.

DB178 Buchloh, Paul G. "Zur Sprache der Luft und Raumfahrt." *Deutscher Aerokurier*, vol. 12 (1973), 880–81.

DB179 Buchloh, Paul Gerhard, and Hans Finger. "Astronaut und Kosmonaut: Die Bezeichnungen für den Raumfahrer im Spiegel der Presse." *Die Neueren Sprachen*, N.F., vol. 17 (1968), 358–64.

DB180 Bungert, Hans. "Zum Einfluss des Englischen auf die deutsche Sprache seit dem Ende des zweiten Weltkrieges." *Jour. of Engl. and Germanic Philology*, vol. 62, no. 4 (1963), 703–17.

DB181 Burger, Antje. "Die Konkurrenz englischer und französischer Fremdwörter in der modernen deutschen Pressesprache." *Muttersprache*, vol. 76, no. 2 (February 1966), 33–48. On the tendency to borrow from American and British English more frequently than from the French.

DB182 Butter, G. P. "Anybody Here for *Blendwerkmädchen?*" *Mod. Lang.*, vol. 60 (1979), 46–49. On anglicisms in German.

DB183 Carstensen, Broder. "Amerikanische Einflüsse auf die deutsche Sprache." *Jahrbuch für Amerikastudien*, vol. 8 (1963), 34–55.

DB184 Carstensen, Broder. "Amerikanisches Englisch." In: *Amerikakunde*. Handbücher der Auslandskunde. Ed. P. Hartig. Frankfurt a. M.: Diesterweg, 1966.

DB185 Carstensen, Broder. *Englische Einflüsse auf die deutsche Sprache nach 1945*. Beiheft zum *Jahrbuch für Amerikastudien*, no. 13. Heidelberg: Winter 1965. 296p. Rev. by W. E. Collinson, *Mod. Lang. Rev.*, vol. 62, no. 1 (1967), 151–53; J. Eichhoff, *Monatshefte*, vol. 60, no. 4 (1968), 403–406; H. Eggers, *Jahrbuch für Amerikastudien*, vol. 12 (1967), 291–96; C. F. Bayerschmidt, *Amer. Speech*, vol. 41 (1966), 59–61; in *Lebende Sprachen*, vol. 11, no. 1 (1966), 7–8; and by A. Urbanová, *Muttersprache*, vol. 76 (1966), 177–81.

DB186 Carstensen, Broder. "'Wechselwähler' nach englisch 'floating voter'." *Die lebenden Sprachen*, vol. 24 (1979), 10–12.

DB187 Carstensen, Broder, and Hans Galinsky. *Amerikanismen der deutschen Gegenwartssprache: Entlehnungsvorgänge und ihre stilistischen Aspekte: mit umfassenden bibliographischen Nachträgen*. Heidelberg: Winter 1964. 80p. 2nd revised ed. Heidelberg, 1967. Rev. by K.-H. Schönfelder, *Zeitschrift für Anglistik und Amerikanistik*, vol. 13 (1965), no. 1, 7; 3rd ed., 1975.

DB188 Carstensen, Broder, Hannelore Griesel, and Hans-Günter Meyer. "Zur Intensität des englischen Einflusses auf die deutsche Pressesprache." *Muttersprache*, vol. 82 (1972), 238–43.

DB189 Charleston, Britta M. "The English Linguistic Invasion of Switzerland." *Engl. Studies*, vol. 40 (1959), 271–82. English syntax and idiom imposed on Swiss German.

DB190 Cohen, Gerald. "More on šmok." *Comments on Etymology*, vol. 14, no. 14 (1980), 11–16.

DB191 Crean, John E., Jr. "The Extended Modifier—English or German?" *Amer. Speech*, vol. 44 (1969), 272–78.

DB192 Daiber, Hans. "Amerikanismen der deutschen Sprache." *Neue deutsche Hefte*, no. 56 (1960), 1115–20.

DB193 Engels, Barbara. *Gebrauchsanstieg der lexikalischen und semantischen Amerikanismen in zwei Jahrgängen der "Welt" (1954 und 1964)*. Frankfurt a. M.: Lang, 1976. 257p. Comparative-quantitative study of American influences on the language of the newspaper *Die Welt*. Rev. in *Amer. Speech*, vol. 53 (1978), 78.

DB194 Engels, Barbara. "Der steigende Einfluss des amerikanischen Englisch auf die deutsche Zeitungssprache in 'Die Welt' (1954/1964)." In: *Grammatik und interdisziplinäre Bereiche der Linguistik: Akten des 11. Linguistischen Kolloquiums Aachen 1976*. Ed. Heinz Werner Viethen, Wolf-Dietrich Bald, and Konrad Sprengel. Tübingen: Niemeyer, 1977, p.165–74.

DB195 Erämätsä, Erik. "Adam Smith als Mittler englisch-deutscher Spracheinflüsse." *Zeitschrift für deutsche Wortforschung*, vol. 16, nos. 1–2 (1960), 25–31. Also publ. Helsinki, 1961. Rev. by W. Fleischhauer, *Jour. of Engl. and Germanic Philol.*, vol. 63, no. 3 (1964), 547–49.

DB196 Erämätsä, Erik. "Zum angloamerikanischen Einfluß auf die deutsche Gegenwartssprache." In: *Festschrift für Hugo Moser zum 60. Geburtstag am 19. Juni 1969*. Ed. Ulrich Engel, Paul Grebe and Heinz Rupp. Düsseldorf: Schwann, 1969, p.39–45.

DB197 F., A. "Amerikanismen." *Sprachspiegel*, vol. 20, no. 3 (1966), 74–75.

DB198 Fink, Hermann. *Amerikanismen im Wortschatz der deutschen Tagespresse, dargestellt am Beispiel dreier überregionaler Zeitungen* (Süddeutsche Zeitung, Frankfurter Allgemeine Zeitung, Die Welt). Mainzeramerikanistische Beiträge, no. 11. München: Hueber, 1970. 534p. Diss., Mainz 1968.

DB199 Fink, Hermann. "Der angloamerikanische 'Look' im Deutschen. Zur Verwendung eines Modewortes." *Muttersprache*, vol. 88 (1978), 51–69.

DB200 Fink, Hermann. "'Know-how' und 'Hifi-Pionier.' Zum Verständnis englischer Ausdrücke in der deutschen Werbesprache." *Muttersprache*, vol. 85 (1975), 186–203.

DB201 Fink, Hermann. "Ein 'Starangebot.' Englisches im Versandhauskatalog." *Muttersprache*, vol. 86 (1976), 368–82.

DB202 Friman, Kristi. *Zum angloamerikanischen Einfluß auf die heutige deutsche Werbesprache*. Studia Philologica Jyväskyläensie no. 9. Jyväskylä: Universität Jyväskylä, 1977. 353p.

DB203 Galinsky, Hans. "American Neologisms in German." *Amer. Speech*, vol. 55 (1980), 243–63.

DB204 Galinsky, Hans. "Der anglo-amerikanische Einfluß auf die deutsche Sprachentwicklung der beiden letzten Jahrzehnte: Versuch einer systematischen Übersicht." In: *Wortbildung, Syntax und Morphologie: Festschrift zum 60. Geburtstag von Hans Marchand am 1. Oktober 1967*. Ed. Herbert E. Brekle and Leonhard Lipka. The Hague: Mouton, 1968, p.67–81.

DB205 Ganz, Peter F. *Der Einfluss des Englischen auf den deutschen Wortschatz 1640–1815*. Berlin: Erich Schmidt, 1957. 257p.

DB206 Grosse, Siegfried. "Reklamedeutsch." *Wirkendes Wort*, vol. 16 (1966), 89–104.

DB207 Heald, David. "Anglicisms in German: An Unrepented Heretic Replies." *Mod. Lang.*, vol. 60 (1979), 218–20.

DB208 Hensel, Susan Z. "American English and General English Interferences with German in the Field of Technical Terminologies: A Study of German Reception and Integration of 'Transactional Analysis' Terminology." M.A. thesis, Mainz, 1977.

DB209 Kann, Hans-Joachim. "Hamburger, Cheeseburger usw. im Deutschen." *Die Lebenden Sprachen*, vol. 18 (1973), 167–69.

DB210 Kann, Hans-Joachim. "Spielfreude in der Sprache: Super- und Mini-." *Muttersprache*, vol. 83 (1973), 198–200.

DB211 Koekkoek, J. B. "The English Loanword *Manager* in Present Day German." *German Quar.*, vol. 30 (1957), 162–66.

DB212 Koekkoek, J. B. "A Note on the German Borrowing of American Brand Names." *Amer. Speech*, vol. 33 (1958), 236–37.

DB213 Koller, Werner. "Angloamerikanismen in der DDR-Zeitungssprache: Zur Untersuchung von G. Kristensson." *Deutsche Sprache*, 1978, 306–22. On Kristensson's *Angloamerikanische Einflüsse in DDR-Zeitungstexten*.

DB214 Koziol, Herbert. "Englische Wörter in deutschen Wörterbuchern aus der Zeit bis 1830." *Anzeiger der Österreichischen Akademie der Wissenschaften. Philos.-histor. Klasse 1973*, vol. 110 (1974), 219–23.

DB215 Krauss, Paul G. "The Anglo-American Influence on German." *Amer. Speech*, vol. 38, no. 4 (1963), 257–69; "The Continuing Anglo-American Influence on German." *Ibid.*, vol. 41 (February 1966), 28–38.

DB216 Krauss, Paul G. "Anglo-American Influence on German Sport Terms." *Amer. Speech*, vol. 36 (1961), 41–47; "English Sport Terms in German." *Ibid.*, vol. 37, no. 2 (1962), 123–29.

DB217 Kurrelmeyer, William. "American and Other Loan Words in German." *Jour. of Engl. and Germanic Philology*, vol. 63, no. 3 (1944), 286–301.

DB218 Leighton, Linda. "Die Sprache der Wochenschrift 'Der Spiegel'." M.A. thesis, Middlebury College, 1961.

DB219 Leisi, Ernst. "Recent English Influences on German Meanings." *Engl. Studies*, vol. 40 (1959), 314–18.

DB220 Leopold, Werner F. *English Influence on Postwar German*. Univ. of Nebraska Studies, N.S., no. 36. Lincoln: Univ. of Nebraska Pr., 1967. 84p. Rev. by J. Eichhoff, *Monatshefte*, vol. 60, no. 4 (1968), 406–409.

DB221 Lipka, Leonhard. "Wasserdicht und grasgrün. Zwei Wortbildungstypen der deutschen Gegenwartssprache." *Muttersprache*, vol. 77 (1967), 33f.

DB222 Martin, Bernhard. "Über die Namengebung einiger aus Amerika eingeführter Kulturpflanzen in den deutschen Mundarten (Kartoffel... Maiz, Tomate)." *Muttersprache*, vol. 16 (Ausgabe B), no. 1 (January 1966), 51–158.

DB223 Meyer, Hans-Günter. "Untersuchungen zum Einfluss des Englischen auf die deutsche Pressesprache, dargestellt an zwei deutschen Tageszeitungen." *Muttersprache*, vol. 84 (1974), 97–134.

DB224 Morgan, Estelle. "Some New German Words." *Notes and Queries*, vol. 6 (1959), 375–76. Borrowings from British and American English.

DB225 Palmer, P. M. "The Influence of English on the German Vocabulary to 1880: A Supplement." *Univ. of Calif. Publs. in Linguistics*, vol. 7, no. 2 (1960), 39–72. Supplement to the study by Peter F. Ganz.

DB226 Pfeffer, J. Alan. "Grunddeutsch und die deutschen Entlehnungen aus fremden Sprachen." *Wirkendes Wort*, vol. 23 (1973), 420–26.

DB227 Pfitzner, Jürgen. *Der Anglizismus im Deutschen: Zur Bestimmung seiner stilistischen Funktion in der heutigen Presse.* Stuttgart: Metzler, 1978. 254p. Cf. diss., Washington Univ., 1971–1972: "Der Anglizismus im deutschen: Ein Beitrag zur Bestimmung seiner stilistischen Funktion in der heutigen Presse."

DB228 Römer, Ruth. *Die Sprache der Anzeigenwerbung.* Sprache der Gegenwart, no. 4. Düsseldorf: n.p., 1968.

DB229 Schneider, Peter. *Die Sprache des Sports: Terminologie und Präsentation in Massenmedien; eine statistische vergleichende Analyse.* Düsseldorf: Pädagogischer Verlag Schwann, 1974. 517p. Analyses of news stories, reports, and commentary in the mass media.

DB230 Upward, Christopher. "Anglicisms in German: The Matter in Perspective." *Mod. Lang.*, vol. 60 (1979), 161–67.

DB231 Urbanová, Anna. "Zum Einfluss des amerikanischen Englisch auf die deutsche Gegenwartssprache (ein Beitrag zur Frage sprachlicher Kontakte)." *Muttersprache*, vol. 76, no. 4 (April 1966), 97–114.

DB232 Viereck, Wolfgang, ed. *Studien zum Einfluss der englischen Sprache auf das Deutsche.* Tübinger Beiträge zur Linguistik, no. 132. Tübingen: Narr, 1980. 210p.

DB233 Walz, John A. "English Influence on the German Vocabulary of the Eighteenth Century." *Monatshefte für deutschen Unterricht*, vol. 35, nos. 3–4 (March–April 1943), 156–64.

DB234 Wendelken, Peter. "Der Einfluß des Englischen auf das heutige Werbedeutsch." *Muttersprache*, vol. 77 (1967), 289–308.

DB235 Wilss, Wolfram. "Das Eindringen angloamerikanischer Fremdwörter in die deutsche Sprache seit Ende des zweiten Weltkrieges." *Muttersprache*, vol. 68 (1958), 180–88.

DB236 Zindler, Horst. "Anglizismen in der deutschen Pressesprache nach 1945." Diss., Kiel, 1960.

DC
Dialects of German—United States and Canada

General

See also German Language in Pennsylvania/Bilingualism *under* Section BH: The Pennsylvania Germans.

DC1 Arbuckle, John. "Phonology of the Volhynian German Dialect of the Edmonton [Alb.] Area." M.A. Thesis, Alberta Univ., 1961. TS.

DC2 Bausenhart, Werner A. "Mundart und Schriftsprache und ihr Verhältnis zur Sprachpflege und Spracherhaltung." *German-Canad. Yearbook*, vol. 1 (1973), 81–85.

DC3 Bausenhart, Werner A. "The Waterloo Pennsylvania German Dialect Community." In: *The Waterloo County Area: Selected Essays*. Ed. A. G. McLellan. Waterloo: Univ. of Waterloo, 1971, p.31–40.

DC4 Beardsley, Theodore S., Jr. "Belleville [Ill.] Dutch." In: *Studies in Honor of Lloyd A. Kasten*. Madison, Wis.: Hispanic Seminary of Medieval Studies, 1975, p.19–32.

DC5 Becker, Donald Allen. "Generative Phonology and Dialect Study; an Investigation of Three Modern German Dialects." Diss., Univ. of Texas at Austin, 1967.

DC6 Benjamin, Steven M., Jürgen Eichhoff, and Wolfgang Viereck. "Nachträge zur 'Bibliographie zur Erforschung der deutschen Mundarten und Sprachvarianten in den Vereinigten Staaten'." In: *Deutsch als Muttersprache in den Vereinigten Staaten. Teil 1: Der Mittelwesten*. Ed. L. Auburger et al. Wiesbaden: Steiner, 1979, p.307–35.

DC7 Clausing, Stephen D. "English Influence on the American German Dialects with a Comparison to American Icelandic." Diss., Wisconsin, 1981. 231p.

DC8 Conner, Cora, and Maurice Conner. "A German Dialect Spoken in South Dakota: Swiss-Volhynian." *Jour. of German-Amer. Studies*, vol. 7 (1974), 31–37. The dialect of Mennonites who migrated from Switzerland to the Pfalz ca. 1664 and thence to the Ukraine (Volhynia) via Galicia approximately a century later. Their dialect is basically a form of Pfälzisch.

DC9 D'Alquen, Richard. "Phonology of the Galician German Dialect of Stony Plain, Alberta [Can.]." M.A. thesis, Alberta Univ., 1962. TS.

DC10 Eberhardt, Elvire. "The Area of Origin of the Bessarabian German Dialect in Medicine Hat, Alberta." *Deutschkanadisches Jahrbuch*, vol. 3 (1976), 207–10. Based on the Ph.D. Diss., "The Bessarabian Dialect of Medicine Hat, Alberta," Univ. of Alberta, 1973.

DC11 Eichhoff, Jürgen. "Bibliography of German Dialects Spoken in the United States and Canada and Problems of German-English Language Contact Especially in North America, 1968–1976, with Pre-1968 Supplements." *Monatshefte*, vol. 68 (1976), 196–208.

DC12 Eikel, Fred. "New Braunfels German." *Amer. Speech*, vol. 41 (1966), 5–16, 254–60; vol. 42 (1967), 83–104. Some 85 per cent of the 14,000 residents of this community were bilingual in the 1940's.

DC13 Eikel, Fred. *The New Braunfels German Dialect*. Baltimore: n.p., 1954. Multilithed.

DC14 Eikel, Fred. "The New Braunfels German Dialect: Phonology and Morphology." Diss., Johns Hopkins, 1952.

DC15 Eikel, Fred. "The Use of Cases in New Braunfels German." *Amer. Speech*, vol. 24 (1949), 278–81.

DC16 Elliott, Nancy A. "The Dialect of Metzenseifen as Spoken in Cleveland, Ohio." Diss., Michigan State, 1971–1972. Metzenseifen is a rural community in Hungary which had been colonized by Germans.

DC17 Frazer, Timothy C. "The Speech Island of the American Bottoms: A Problem in Social History." *Amer. Speech*, 54 (1979), 185–93.

DC18 Frey, J. William. "A Comparison of Pennsylvania German with the Amana Dialect of Iowa." "'S Pennsylfawnisch Deitsch Eck," Allentown *Morning Call*, 29 August, 5 September 1942.

DC19 Gilbert, Glenn G. "Dative vs. Accusative in the German Dialects of Central Texas." *Zeitschrift für Mundartforschung*, vol. 32 (1965), 288–96.

DC20 Gilbert, Glenn G. "The German Dialect of Kendall and Gillespie Counties, Texas." *Zeitschrift für Mundartforschung*, vol. 31 (1964), 138–72. Based on his Ph.D. Diss., Harvard Univ., 1963. 318p.

DC21 Gilbert, Glenn G. "A Unified Proposal for the Study of the German Language in America: A Discussion." In: *The German Language in America; A Symposium*. Ed. with an Introd. by Glenn G. Gilbert. Austin: Univ. of Texas Pr., 1971, p.164–78.

DC22 Gommermann, Andreas. "Ein Fuldaer Siedlungsmundart aus der schwäbischen Türkei." In: *Das Jahrbuch der Ungarndeutschen: Unser Hauskalender 1978*. Stuttgart: n.p., 1978, p.125–28.

DC23 Gommermann, Andreas. "Hungarian and American Borrowings in a Twice Transplanted Fulda Dialect." In: *Languages in Conflict: Linguistic Acculturation on the Great Plains*. Ed. Paul Schach. Lincoln: Univ. of Nebraska Pr., ca. 1981, p.86–93.

DC24 Gommermann, Andreas. "Oberhessische Siedlungsmundart in Milwaukee, Wisconsin USA: Tochtermundart einer in Mucsi (Ungarn) gesprochenen Fuldischen Siedlungsmundart." Diss., Nebraska, 1975. On a dialect spoken in Milwaukee by ca. 200 persons.

DC25 Gumperz, John J. "The Swabian Dialect of Washtenaw County, Michigan." Diss., Univ. of Michigan, 1954.

DC26 Holtzmann, Jerome. "An Inquiry into the Hutterian German Dialect." M.A. thesis, Univ. of South Dakota, 1961.

DC27 Keel, William D. "On the *Heimatbestimmung* of the Ellis County (Kansas) Volga-German Dialects." *Yearbook of German-Amer. Studies*, vol. 17 (1982), 99–109.

DC28 McDavid, Raven J., Jr. "Two Decades of the Linguistic Atlas." *Jour. of Engl. Germanic Philology*, vol. 50 (1951), 101–10. On German dialects in the United States, see p.108.

DC29 McGraw, Peter A. "Amerikanische Hochschulschriften über deutsche Mundarten im Mittelwesten." In: *Deutsch als Muttersprache in den Vereinigten Staaten*. Teil 1: *Der Mittelwesten*. Ed. L. Auburger et al. Wiesbaden: Steiner, 1979, p.229–66.

DC30 McGraw, Peter A. "*Dane County Kölsch, Wisconsin, U S A*." Phonai 21, no. 12. Tübingen: Lautbibliothek der europäischen Sprachen und Mundarten, 1978. With 9.5 cm/sec tapes.

DC31 McGraw, Peter A. "The *Kölsch* Dialect of Dane County, Wisconsin: Phonology, Morphology, and English Influence." Diss., Wisconsin, 1973.

DC32 Mang, Lawrence H. "A German Dialect Spoken in the Edenwold-Zehner-Balgonie Area of Saskatchewan, Canada." M.A. thesis, Univ. of Washington, 1954. TS.

DC33 Miller, Cora A. "A Phonological and Morphological Study of a German Dialect Spoken near Freeman, South Dakota." M.A. thesis, Univ. of Nebraska, 1966. TS. On the speech of Mennonites in S. Dak.

DC34 Moser, Hugo. "Schwäbische Sprachinseln in Europa und Übersee." *Zeitschrift für württembergische Landesgeschichte*, vol. 12 (1953), 91–121.

DC35 Nabert, Kurt. "Deutsch in Ontario. III. Über einige deutsche Dialekte." In: *Deutsch als Muttersprache in Kanada: Berichte zur Gegenwartslage*. Ed. L. Auburger et al. Wiesbaden: Steiner, 1977, p.33–37.

DC36 Obernberger, Alfred. "The Dialect of the Hutterites in Canada." In: *Papers from the Conference on German-Americana in the Eastern United States*. Occasional Papers of the Soc. for German-Amer. Studies, no. 8. Ed. Steven M.

General *(cont.)*

Benjamin. Morgantown, W. Va.: Dept. of Foreign Langs., W. Va. Univ., 1980, p.124–30.

DC37 Olesch, Reinhold. "West Slavic Languages in Texas with Specific Reference to Sorbian in Lee County." In: *Texas Studies in Bilingualism. Spanish, French, German, Czech, Polish, Sorbian...in the Southwest.* Studia Linguistica Germanica, no. 3. Ed. Glenn G. Gilbert. Berlin: de Gruyter, 1970. A Texan community of trilingual Sorbs from near Bautzen, Obersachsen.

DC38 Pulte, William J., Jr. "An Analysis of Selected German Dialects of North Texas and Oklahoma." In: *Texas Studies in Bilingualism...* Studia Linguistica Germanica, no. 3. Ed. Glenn G. Gilbert. Berlin: de Gruyter, 1970, p.105–41.

DC39 Reed, Carroll E. "The Dialectology of American Colonial German." In: *The German Language in America: A Symposium.* Ed. Glenn G. Gilbert. Austin: Univ. of Texas Pr., 1971, p.3–13.

DC40 Reed, Carroll E., and Herbert F. Wiese. "Amana German." *Amer. Speech*, vol. 32 (1957), 243–56.

DC41 Rein, Kurt. "German Dialects in Anabaptist Colonies on the Great Plains." In: *Languages in Conflict: Linguistic Acculturation on the Great Plains.* Ed. Paul Schach. Lincoln: Univ. of Nebraska Pr., 1981, p.94–110.

DC42 Richter, Manfred. "Die deutschen Mundarten in Kanada: Ein Forschungsbericht." *Seminar*, vol. 3 (1967), 53–64.

DC43 Schach, Paul. "Some Approaches to the Study of German Dialects in America." In: *Papers from the St. Olaf Symposium on German-Americana.* Ed. L. J. Rippley and S. M. Benjamin. Morgantown, W. Va.: Dept. of Foreign Langs., W. Va. Univ., 1980, p.96–112.

DC44 Scheer, Herfried. "A Lexicological Analysis of the Hutterian German Dialect." Diss., McGill Univ., 1972.

DC45 Scheer, Herfried. "The Linguistic Heritage of the Hutterian Brethren." *German-Canad. Yearbook*, vol. 1 (1973), 91–94.

DC46 Scheer, Herfried. "Die Mundart der hutterischen Brüder. Ein sprachgeschichtliches Denkmal aus dem 16. und 18. Jahrhundert." In: *Deutsch als Muttersprache in Kanada. Berichte zur Gegenwartslage.* Ed. L. Auburger et al. Wiesbaden: Steiner, 1977, p.133–37.

DC47 Scheer, Herfried. "Research on the Hutterian German Dialect." *Canad. Ethnic Studies*, vol. 1, no. 2 (December 1969).

DC48 Scheer, Herfried W. "Studien zum Wortschatz der Mundart der Hutterischen Brüder." Diss., McGill Univ., 1971–1972.

DC49 Schirmunski, Viktor M. *Deutsche Mundartkunde.* Berlin: Akademie Vlg., 1962.

DC50 Seifert, Lester W. J. "Stress Accent in Dane County (Wisconsin) *Kölsch.*" *Monatshefte*, vol. 55, no. 4 (1963), 195–202.

DC51 Selzer, Barbara. "A Description of the Amana Dialect of Homestead, Iowa." M.A. thesis, Univ. of Illinois, 1941.

DC52 Sirks, Aina. "A Study of a Nebraska German Dialect." M.A. thesis, Nebraska, 1956. On the Volga German dialect.

DC53 Strauch, Gabriele L. "German American Dialects; State of Research in the Midwest: Ohio, Indiana, Illinois, Missouri and Kansas." *Zeitschrift für Dialektologie und Linguistik*, vol. 48 (1981), 313–28.

DC54 Viereck, Wolfgang. "German Dialects Spoken in the United States and Canada and Problems of German-English Language Contact especially in North America; a Bibliography." *Orbis*, vol. 16 (1967), 549–68; "Supplement," vol. 17 (1968), 532–35.

DC55 Viereck, Wolfgang. "Wandel deutscher Dialekte in den U S A." *Eintracht* (Chicago), 4 April 1967.

DC56 Viereck, Wolfgang, and Jürgen Eichhoff. "Bibliographie zur Erforschung der deutschen Mundarten in Kanada." In: *Deutsch als Muttersprache in Kanada: Berichte zur Gegenwartslage.* Ed. L. Auburger et al. Wiesbaden: Steiner, 1977, p.165–68.

DC57 Viereck, Wolfgang, and Jürgen Eichhoff. "Bibliographie zur Erforschung der deutschen Mundarten und Sprachvarianten in den Vereinigten Staaten." In: *Deutsch als Muttersprache in den Vereinigten Staaten. Teil 1: Der Mittelwesten.* Ed.

L. Auburger et al. Wiesbaden: Steiner, 1979, p. 267–305.

DC58 Vogel-Shire, Ilse. "Dialektstudie des Katharinenstädter Deutsch." M.A. thesis, Kansas, 1981.

The Pennsylvania German Dialect

DC59 Atwood, E. Bagby. *A Survey of Verb Forms in the Eastern United States.* Studies in American English, no. 2. Ann Arbor, Mich.: n.p., 1953. Treats also some morphological features of Pennsylvania German.

DC60 Aurand, Monroe. *Quaint Idioms and Expressions of the Pennsylvania-Germans.* Harrisburg: n.p., 1939.

DC61 Autenrieth, Georg C. *Pfälzisches Idiotikon (Palatine Idioms).* Zweibrücken: n.p., ca. 1899. Many of the usages cited in this dictionary are current in the Pennsylvania German dialect.

DC62 Barba, Preston A., and C. Richard Beam. "Alle Sadde Wadde (Alle Sarde Warde; Alle Sorde Worte)." "'S Pennsylfawnisch Deitsch Eck," Allentown *Morning Call*, 13 March 1947–12 July 1948, at irregular intervals; again 22 February 1964 through 24 August 1968. Pennsylvania German dialect word studies.

DC63 Bausenhart, Werner A. "The Terminology of Agronomy of the Pennsylvania German Dialect of Waterloo County, Ontario." M.A. thesis, Univ. of Waterloo, 1966. TS.

DC64 Bausman, E. [Introduction to the Word List.] *Harbaugh's Harfe: Gedichte in Pennsylvanisch-Deutscher Mundart.* Philadelphia: n.p., 1870, p. 111–13.

DC65 Beam, C. Richard. "A Guide for the Co-Workers of the Pennsylvania German Dictionary." "'S Pennsylfawnisch Deitsch Eck," Allentown *Morning Call*, 2, 9 July 1966.

DC66 Beam, C. Richard. *Kleines pennsylvaniadeutsches Wörterbuch. Abridged Pennsylvania German Dictionary.* Pfälzer in der Weiten Welt, Folge 8. Kaiserslautern: Heimatstelle Pfalz, 1970. 114p. With phonetic aids to pronunciation. Rev. by R. W. Gilbert, *Der Reggeboge*, vol. 5, no. 2 (1971), 18–23.

DC67 Beam, C. Richard. "Pennsylvania Dutch Language. An Introduction." Tape Cassette, 1981. Available through Spectrum Fidelity Magnetics, 49 Glenwood Ave., Lancaster, Pa. 17602.

DC68 Beam, C. Richard. *Pennsylvania German Dictionary: English to Pennsylvania Dutch.* Millersville, Pa.: n.p., 1981. Address the author at 406 Spring Dr., 17551.

DC69 Bechtel, Ernest W. *Instruction Sheet for Pennsylvania Dutch.* New Holland, Pa.: BESL Center, n.d.

DC70 Bechtel, Ernest W. "Original Expressions in Pennsylvania German." *Hist. Schaefferstown Record*, vol. 8 (1974), 36.

DC71 Bechtel, Ernest W. *Pennsylvania German Expressions.* New Holland, Pa.: BESL Center, n.d.

DC72 Bechtel, Ernest W. *Proper Words for Specific Situations.* New Holland, Pa.: BESL Center, n.d. On the Pennsylvania German dialect.

DC73 Bechtel, Ernest W. *Study of the Use of Positional or Directional Words in the Pennsylvania Dutch Dialect.* New Holland, Pa.: BESL Center, n.d.

DC74 Bender, Ruth. *A Study of the Pennsylvania-German Dialect as Spoken in Johnson County, Iowa.* Iowa City: n.p., ca. 1929. With a list of dialect words and their English translations.

DC75 Benjamin, Steven M. *An Annotated Bibliography of the Pennsylvania German Dialect as Spoken in Pennsylvania.* Madison, Wis.: n.p., 1978.

DC76 Benjamin, Steven M. "The Phonology of the Pennsylvania German Dialect as Spoken in the Counties of Berks, Lehigh, and Lancaster and in the Upper Susquehanna Region." Diss., Madison: Univ. of Wisconsin, 1978.

DC77 Benjamin, Steven M. "The Segmental Vocalic Phonemes of the Pennsylvania German Dialect as Spoken in Northumberland and Schuylkill Counties, Pennsylvania." Diss., Wisconsin, 1981. 282p.

DC78 Benjamin, Steven M. *A Select Bibliography on the Pennsylvania German Dialect. Occasional Papers of the Soc. for German-Amer. Studies*, no. 2. Morgantown, W.Va.: Dept. of Foreign Langs., W. Va. Univ., 1979. 17p.

DC79 Buehler, Allan M. *The Pennsylvania German Dialect and the Life of an Old Order Mennonite*. Cambridge, Ont.: n.p., 1977. 227p.

DC80 Buffington, Albert F. "The Changing Pattern of Pennsylvania German Culture, 1855–1955: Language." *Pa. Hist.*, vol. 23 (1956), 317–22.

DC81 Buffington, Albert F. "Dunnerwedder Compounds." "'S Pennsylfawnisch Deitsch Eck," Allentown *Morning Call*, 17 March 1945.

DC82 Buffington, Albert F. "'Dutchified' German." "'S Pennsylfawnisch Deitsch Eck," Allentown *Morning Call*, 1 June 1946.

DC83 Buffington, Albert F. "English Loan Words in Pennsylvania German." In: *Studies in Honor of John Albrecht Walz*. Lancaster: Lancaster Pr., 1941, p.66–85.

DC84 Buffington, Albert F. "Linguistic Variants in the Pennsylvania German Dialect." *Pa. German Folklore Soc.*, vol. 13 (1949), 217–52. Also in *The Pa. Dutchman*, vol. 1, no. 5 (1949). Rev. by A. D. Graeff, "'S Pennsylfawnisch Deitsch Eck," Allentown *Morning Call*, 15 October 1949.

DC85 Buffington, Albert F. "Ninety-One Ways to Spell a Word." "'S Pennsylfawnisch Deitsch Eck," Allentown *Morning Call*, 12 April 1952. A survey of the "Nixnutz's" fan mail has revealed ninety-one different spellings of the word "Nixnutz."

DC86 Buffington, Albert F. "The Origins, Peculiar Phonological Features, and Curious Connotations of Certain Pennsylvania German Words." "'S Pennsylfawnisch Deitsch Eck," Allentown *Morning Call*, 18 April, 11 July, 24 October, 28 November 1953; 10 March and 7 April 1956.

DC87 Buffington, Albert F. "Pennsylvania German as a Foundation for the Study of Standard German." *German Quar.*, vol. 24 (1951), 76–83. Rev. by P. A. Barba, "'S Pennsylfawnisch Deitsch Eck," Allentown *Morning Call*, 9 February 1952.

DC88 Buffington, Albert F. "The Pennsylvania German Dialect and Folklore of Somerset County." In: *Ebbes fer Alle—Ebber Ebbes fer Dich. Essays in Memoriam Albert Franklin Buffington*. Publs. of the Pa. German Soc., vol. 14. Breinigsville, Pa.: The Soc., 1980, p.3–33.

DC89 Buffington, Albert F. "The Pennsylvania German Dialect Today." *Commonwealth*, vol. 1 (1946), 10f.

DC90 Buffington, Albert F. "Pennsylvania German Sounds and Their Representation." *Pa. German Folklore Soc., Publs.*, vol. 16 (1953), 150–55.

DC91 Buffington, Albert F. "The Perennial Problems of Our Pennsylvania German Orthography." "'S Pennsylfawnisch Deitsch Eck," Allentown *Morning Call*, 4, 11 September 1948.

DC92 Buffington, Albert F. "Similarities and Dissimilarities between Pennsylvania German and the Rhenish Palatinate Dialects." *Pa. German Folklore Soc. Publs.*, vol. 3 (1970), 91–116.

DC93 Buffington, Albert F., and Preston A. Barba. *A Pennsylvania German Grammar*. Allentown: Schlechter's, 1954. 167p. See *Amer.-German Rev.*, vol. 21, no. 1 (1954), 37. Rev. by R. W. Gilbert, *Hist. Rev. of Berks Co.*, vol. 20, no. 1 (1954), 23–25; H. Kloss, *Deutschunterricht für Ausländer*, vol. 5 (1955), 135; H. Kloss, *Mitteilungen des Instituts für Auslandsbeziehungen*, vol. 5, nos. 1–2 (1955), 69–70; R. C. Wood, "'S Pennsylfawnisch Deitsch Eck," Allentown *Morning Call*, 24 July 1954. New edition: *Yearbook, Pa. German Folklore Soc. for 1963*, vol. 27 (1965).

DC94 Christmann, Ernst. "Das Pennsylvaniadeutsch als pfälzische Mundart." *Rheinisches Jahrbuch für Volkskunde*, vol. 1 (1950), 47–82.

DC95 Coleman, Clarence. "Pennsylvania Dutch Spoken Here Abouts." "As I Was Saying ..." "Schussel along with Schnitzel." "Imagine That." Recording. Herman F. Schnitzel, 1962.

DC96 Coley, Robert E., Marjorie Markoff and Scott Miller. "A Select Bibliography of Pennsylvania German Dialect Materials in the Ganser Library, Millersville State College." In: *Papers from the Conference on German-Americana in the Eastern United States*. Ed. Steven M. Benjamin. Morgantown, W. Va.: Dept. of Foreign Langs., W. Va. University, 1980, p.76–81.

DC97 Costello, John R. "Choosing an Orthography for a Patois Language, or, How Should One Spell Pennsylvania German?" *Hist. Schaefferstown Record*, vol. 8 (1973), 42–48.

DC98 Costello, John R. "A Glottochronological Study of Pennsylvania German." *Hist. Schaefferstown Record*, vol. 8, no. 1 (1974), 2–13.

DC99 Costello, John R. "A Lexical Comparison of Two Sister Languages: Pennsylvania German and Yiddish." *Pa. Folklife*, vol. 29, no. 3 (1979–1980), 138–42.

DC100 Costello, John R. "Pennsylvania German, Standard German, and the Reconstruction of Meaning." In: *Papers from the Conference on German-Americana in the Eastern United States*. Occasional Papers of the Soc. for German-Amer. Studies, no. 8. Ed. S. M. Benjamin. Morgantown, W. Va.: Dept. of Foreign Langs., W. Va. Univ., 1980, p. 131–42.

DC101 Costello, John R. "Phonemics as a Basis for Orthography: The Case for Pennsylvania German." *Hist. Schaefferstown Record*, vol. 10 (1976), 40–63.

DC102 Danner, E. R. *Pennsylvania Dutch Dictionary and Hand-Book*. Spring Grove, Pa.: n.p., 1951. 178p. English to Pennsylvania German dictionary with emphasis on the dialect of York County.

DC103 Deischer, Claude K. "My Experience with the Dialect." *Pa. Folklife*, vol. 23, no. 4 (1974), 47f.

DC104 Dorian, Nancy C. "The Dying Dialect and the Role of the Schools: East Sutherland Gaelic and Pennsylvania Dutch." In: *Georgetown Univ. Roundtable on Langs. and Linguistics 1978: Internat. Dimensions of Bilingual Education*. Ed. J. E. Alatis. Washington, D.C.: Georgetown Univ. Pr., 1979, p. 646–56.

DC105 Dürr, Gertrude A. "Sprachliche Bemerkungen zum Pennsylvania-Deutsch." In: *Textlinguistik und Semantik*. Ed. Wolfgang Meid and Karin Heller. Innsbruck: Inst. für Sprachwissenschaft der Universität Innsbruck, 1976, p. 237–49.

DC106 Enninger, Werner, and Karl-Heinz Wandt. "Pennsylvania German in the Context of an Old Order Amish Settlement: The Structural Instability of a Functionally Stable Variety." *Yearbook of German-Amer. Studies*, vol. 17 (1982), 123–43.

DC107 Frey, J. William. "Amish Triple-Talk." *Amer. Speech*, vol. 20, no. 2 (1945), 85–98.

DC108 Frey, J. William. "Early Grammatical Notes on Pennsylvania German." "'S Pennsylfawnisch Deitsch Eck," Allentown *Morning Call*, 14 August 1943.

DC109 Frey, J. William. *Frey's Pennsylvania Dutch Grammar*. Serialized in *The Pa. Dutchman*, 1949–1950. Repr. Collegeville: Institute on Pa. Dutch Studies, 1978. 32p.

DC110 Frey, J. William. "The German Dialect of Eastern York County, Pennsylvania." Diss., Univ. of Illinois, 1941.

DC111 Frey, J. William. "A Morphological and Syntactical Study of the Pennsylvania German Dialect of Pumpernickle Bill." M. A. thesis, Univ. of Illinois, 1939. TS. Rev. in "'S Pennsylfawnisch Deitsch Eck," Allentown *Morning Call*, 19 August 1939.

DC112 Frey, J. William. "Notes on the Diphthong 'oi' in Pennsylvania Dutch." *Amer. Speech*, vol. 18, no. 2 (1943), 112–16.

DC113 Frey, J. William. "Pennsylvania Dutch." *Pa. Folklife*, vol. 12, no. 3 (Fall 1961), 12–13. On dialect terms and hybrid English.

DC114 Frey, J. William. *Pennsylvania Dutch Grammar*. Lancaster, Pa.: n.p., 1961.

DC115 Frey, J. William. *The Pennsylvania-German Dialect of Pumpernickle Bill*. Urbana, Ill.: n.p., 1939. On the dialect as used by columnist William S. Troxell.

DC116 Frey, J. William. "The Phonemics of English Loan Words in Eastern York County Pennsylvania Dutch." *Amer. Speech*, vol. 17, no. 1 (1942), 94–101.

DC117 Frey, J. William. "The Present Status of Research in the Pennsylvania Dutch Dialect." *South Atlantic Bull.*, vol. 8 (1942), 7.

DC118 Frey, J. William. *A Simple Grammar of Pennsylvania Dutch*. Clinton, S. Car.: Jacobs Pr., 1942. 140p. Rev. by P. A. Barba, "'S Pennsylfawnisch Deitsch Eck," Allentown *Morning Call*, 7 November 1942; G. W. Clemens, *Hist. Rev. of Berks Co.*, vol. 8 (1942–1943), 54; H. L. Mencken, *Books*, N.Y. Herald-Tribune, 6 December 1942; F. Reichmann, *Amer.-German Rev.*, vol. 10, no. 4 (1944), 29. Repr. ca. 1981. Address: 406 Spring Dr., Millersville, Pa. 17551.

DC119 Frey, J. William. "Some Interesting and Unusual Pennsylvania German Words in Eastern York County." "'S Pennsylfawnisch Deitsch Eck," Allentown *Morning Call*, 4, 11, 18 September 1943.

DC120 Frey, J. William. *A Supplement to a Study of the Pennsylvania-German Dialect of Pumpernickle Bill*. Urbana, Ill.: n.p., 1939.

DC121 Frey, J. William. "This Question of Pennsylvania German Orthography." "'S Pennsylfawnisch Deitsch Eck," Allentown *Morning Call*, 14 November 1942.

DC122 Frey, J. William, ed. "Familiar Letters to Those Who Speak Pennsylvania Dutch." *The Pa. Dutchman*, vol. 3, no. 22 (1952), 1–7. Repr. of a series of letters signed "Zinzendorff," which appeared in the Easton *Free Press*, tending to discourage the use of the "degrading" Pa. Dutch tongue.

DC123 Gehman, Ernest G. "En Iwwerbligg auff die Pennsylveenje Deitsch Schbrooch." *Amer.-German Rev.*, vol. 34, no. 3 (1968), 30–32. Also in "'S Pennsylfawnisch Deitsch Eck," Allentown *Morning Call*, 19, 26 January 1963.

DC124 Gehman, Ernest G. "Lautlehre der Pennsylvania-Deutschen Mundart von Bally, Pennsylvania." Diss., Heidelberg Univ., 1949. 133p. A dialect phonology.

DC125 Gehman, Ernest G. "Pennsylvania German in the Shenandoah Valley." "'S Pennsylfawnisch Deitsch Eck," Allentown *Morning Call*, 16, 23, 30 March 1963. A course in Pennsylvania German taught at Eastern Mennonite College, Harrisburg.

DC126 Gehman, Sara. "Isaac Hunsicker's Copy-Books." *Amer. Speech*, vol. 9 (1934), 46–48.

DC127 Gerhard, Elmer S. "Pennsylvania German: The Picturesqueness and Directness of the Dialect." *Hist. Rev. of Berks Co.*, vol. 21 (1956), 98–106, 123–28.

DC128 Gladfelter, Millard E., H. L. Kreider, and C. D. Spotts. Symposium on the Pennsylvania Dutch Dialect. *Pa. Folklife*, vol. 18, no. 1 (1968), 44–48.

DC129 Graeff, Arthur D. "Our Dialect is not Dutch, It is not German, It is Pennsylvanish." "'S Pennsylfawnisch Deitsch Eck," Allentown *Morning Call*, 9 September 1944.

DC130 Graeff, Arthur D. "Vaterland and Mutterschproch." "'S Pennsylfawnisch Deitsch Eck," Allentown *Morning Call*, 9 September 1944.

DC131 Grumbine, Lee L. *The Pennsylvania-German Dialect*... Lancaster, Pa.: n.p., 1902. Includes examples of dialect literature.

DC132 Hershberger, Henry D. "Sounds and Spelling System." A booklet of nine pages attached to the cover of *Mark sei Efangeylium in Pa. Deitsch*. Sugarcreek, Ohio: Amish Committee for Translation, 1975.

DC133 Hollenbach, Raymond E. "Wibberwill Gnebb." "'S Pennsylfawnisch Deitsch Eck," Allentown *Morning Call*, 14 May 1966. Local names and lore of edible galls on the wild azalea.

DC134 Hosch, Heinz L. "Pennsylvania Dutch or Pennsylvania German? A Historical Assessment." In: *Papers from the Conference on German-Americana in the Eastern United States*. Occasional Papers of the Soc. for German-Amer. Studies, no. 8. Ed. Steven M. Benjamin. Morgantown, W. Va.: Dept. of Foreign Langs., W. Va. Univ., 1980, p. 117–23.

DC135 Huffines, Marion L. "Pennsylvania German: Maintenance and Shift." *Internat. Jour. of the Sociology of Lang.*, vol. 25 (1980), 43–57.

DC136 Kaess, Constance C. "Some Elements of Generative-Transformational Syntax in Pennsylvania German." M.A. thesis, Univ. of Illinois, 1971.

DC137 Kalbfleisch, Herbert Karl. "Pennsylvania German in Ontario German Newspapers 1835–1918." *Amer.-German Rev.*, vol. 23, no. 1 (1956), 31–33.

DC138 Kelz, Heinrich. "Der Einfluss des Englischen auf das Pennsylvaniadeutsche." *Miszellen* (Bonn) 1970, 1978, p. 127–64.

DC139 Kelz, Heinrich P. "Pennsylvaniadeutsch und Pfälzisch: ein Sprachlicher Vergleich." *Stimme der Pfalz* (Kaiserslautern), vol. 27 (1977), 23–24.

DC140 Kelz, Heinrich P. *Phonologische Analyse des Pennsylvaniadeutschen*. Hamburg: Buske, 1971. 152p. Based on a dissertation of the same title (Bonn, 1969). Publ. in: *Forschungsberichte des Instituts für Kommunikationsforschung und Phonetik der Univ. Bonn*, vol. 32 (1970). Rev. by D. Karch, *Phonetica*, vol. 26 (1972) 52–60; W. H. Veith, *Zeits. für Dialektologie und Linguistik*, vol.

37 (1970), 225-30, with reply and rebuttal by Kelz and Veith, *ibid.*, vol. 38 (1971), 218-26; Albert Buffington, *Der Reggeboge*, vol. 4, no. 2 (1970), 17-18.

DC141 Kelz, Heinrich P. "The 'R-Sound' in Pennsylvania German. A Phonological Problem." "'S Pennsylfawnisch Deitsch Eck," Allentown *Morning Call*, 1, 8 March 1969.

DC142 Kelz, Heinrich P. "Zur Phonotaktik des Pennsylvania-deutschen." *Orbis*, vol. 21 (1972), 337-66.

DC143 Klinger, Erwin. "Unbennich." *Der Reggeboge*, vol. 15, no. 1/2 (1981), 10-14. A Pennsylvania German dialect play.

DC144 Kloss, Heinz. *Die Entwicklung neuer germanischer Kultursprachen von 1800-1950*. München: Pohl, 1952. 254p. Rev. by P. A. Barba, "'S Pennsylfawnisch Deitsch Eck," Allentown *Morning Call*, 11 April 1953. Incl. a chapter on the development of the Pennsylvania German dialect.

DC145 Kloss, Heinz. "Pensilfaanisch-Deutsch in Ostkanada." *Pälzer Feierowend*, vol. 8, no. 48, 1 December 1956. Beilage zu "Die Rheinpfalz" (Ludwigshafen).

DC146 Kloss, Heinz. "Die Sprache der Pennsylvaniendeutschen und die Gegenwart." *Muttersprache* (Lüneburg), vol. 62 (1952), 337-41.

DC147 Kloss, Heinz. "What's In a Name." "'S Pennsylfawnisch Deitsch Eck," Allentown *Morning Call*, 2 October 1954. On the names given to the Pennsylvania German dialect.

DC148 Kloss, Heinz. "Who Are the Shapers of New Cultural Tongues?" "'S Pennsylfawnisch Deitsch Eck," Allentown *Morning Call*, 10 January 1953. Pennsylvania German can rise to the dignity of a literary language if it is shaped and shared by intellectuals who identify themselves with the body of speakers as a whole.

DC149 Kloss, Heinz. "Wo in Ostpennsylvanien spricht man deutsche Mundart?" *Deutschtum im Ausland*, vol. 26 (1943), 2-9.

DC150 Krämer, Julius. "Proben aus dem Pfälzischen Wörterbuch." *Pfälzer Heimat*, vol. 15 (1964), 146-51.

DC151 Kratz, Henry, and Humphrey Milnes. "Kitchener German: A Pennsylvania German Dialect." *Mod. Lang. Quar.*, vol. 14 (1953), 184-98, 274-83.

DC152 Kulp, Clarence, Jr. "A Study of the Dialect Terminology of the Plain Sects of Montgomery County, Pa." *Pa. Folklife*, vol. 12, no. 3 (1961), 41-47.

DC153 Kurath, Hans. "German Relics in Pennsylvania German." *Monatshefte f. deutschen Unterricht*, vol. 37 (1945), 96-102.

DC154 Kurath, Hans. "Pennsylvania German." *Conference on Non-English Speech in the United States.* Published in: *Amer. Council of Learned Societies Bull.*, no. 34 (1942), 12-18.

DC155 Kyger, M. Ellsworth. "The Pennsylvania-German Dialect in the Shenandoah Valley." "'S Pennsylfawnisch Deitsch Eck," Allentown *Morning Call*, 7 December 1963.

DC156 Lambert, Marcus B. *Pennsylvania-German Dictionary*. Introd. by Willard M. Martin. Repr. Exton, Pa.: Schiffer Ltd., 1977. From the *Pa. German Soc., Procs. and Addrs.*, vol. 30 (October 1919).

DC157 Lieber, Francis. "Pennsylvania German Dialect," ed. by Felix Reichmann from a manuscript in the Henry E. Huntington Library. See *Amer.-German Rev.*, vol. 11, no. 3 (1945), 24-27. Surviving portions of an essay written in 1835.

DC158 Master, Jane E. "It Wonders Me." *Hist. Rev. of Berks Co.*, vol. 32, no. 3 (Summer 1967), 92-94. On the Pennsylvania German dialect.

DC159 Moelleken, Wolfgang W., and Dieter Karch. *Siedlungspfälzisch im Kreis Waterloo, Ontario, Kanada*. Phonai, no. 18. Tübingen: Lautbibliothek der europäischen Sprachen und Mundarten, 1977. Ca. 260p.

DC160 Newcomb, Thomas L. *Abridged Pennsylvania German Glossary and Dictionary*. Garrettsville, Ohio: n.p., ca. 1980.

DC161 Newcomb, Thomas L. *A Brief Introduction to Amish Culture and Dialects*. Garrettsville, Ohio: n.p., 1980.

DC162 Oswald, Victor. "The Phones of a Lehigh County Dialect of Pennsylvania." Diss., Columbia Univ., New York, 1949. 91p.

DC163 "Pennsylvania German and High German: Folk-Cultural Questionnaire no. 19." *Pa. Folklife*, vol. 20, no. 3 (Winter 1971), 47–48.

DC164 *Pfäzisches Wörterbuch*. Estab. by Ernst Christmann. Ed. Julius Krämer. Vol. 1, parts 1–8. Wiesbaden: Steiner, 1965–1968. 1438 cols. Rev. by C. R. Beam, "'S Pennsylfawnisch Deitsch Eck," Allentown *Morning Call*, 25 September 1965; H. Stopp, *Pfälzer Heimat*, vol. 17 (1966), 158–60. Embraces forms used in Germany as well as in Palatine settlements abroad. 40,000 entries. See also "Proben aus dem Pfälzischen Wörterbuch." Ed. J. Krämer. *Pfälzer Heimat*, vol. 15 (1964), 146–51. Projected as a work in five volumes.

DC165 Rahn, C. R. *A Pennsylvania-Dutch Dictionary*. 2nd ed. Quakertown, Pa.: Meredith Publ., 1948. 104p. Pennsylvania-Dutch into English.

DC166 Reed, Carroll. "The Adaptation of English to Pennsylvania German Morphology." *Amer. Speech*, vol. 23, no. 3 (1949), 239–44. English has had relatively little influence on Pennsylvania German; the dialect has fitted its borrowings from English into its native categories.

DC167 Reed, Carroll. "Double Dialect Geography." *Orbis*, vol. 10 (1961), 308–19. The dialect of southeastern Pennsylvania: reports in the *Linguistic Atlas of the United States* compared with those in the *Linguistic Atlas of Pennsylvania German*.

DC168 Reed, Carroll. "English Archaisms in Pennsylvania German." *Publs., Amer. Dialect Soc.*, vol. 19 (1953), 3–7.

DC169 Reed, Carroll. "The Gender of English Loan Words in Pennsylvania German." *Amer. Speech*, vol. 17, no. 1 (1942), 25–29.

DC170 Reed, Carroll. "The German Dialect of Southeastern Pennsylvania." *Bull. of the New England Mod. Lang. Assoc.*, vol. 5 (1943), 26–31.

DC171 Reed, Carroll. "Loan-Word Stratification in Pennsylvania German." *German Quar.*, vol. 40 (1967), 83–86.

DC172 Reed, Carroll. "The Morphological History of Pennsylvania German." In: *Sprache und Literatur: Festschrift für Arval L. Streadbeck zum 65. Geburstag*. Ed. Gerhard P. Knapp et al. Bern: Peter Lang, 1981, p.39–45.

DC173 Reed, Carroll. "Pennsylvania German." *Le Maître Phonétique*, no. 106 (1957), 37–38.

DC174 Reed, Carroll. *The Pennsylvania German Dialect Spoken in the Counties of Lehigh and Berks: Phonology and Morphology*. Introd. in Collaboration with Lester W. Seifert. Seattle: Univ. of Washington Pr., 1949. 66p. Rev. in *Amer.-German Rev.*, vol. 16, no. 4 (1950), 38; P. A. Barba, "'S Pennsylfawnisch Deitsch Eck," Allentown *Morning Call*, 4 March 1950; P. Schach, *Zeitschrift für Mundartforschung*, vol. 23 (1956), 126–28. See diss. of same title: Brown Univ., 1941.

DC175 Reed, Carroll. "A Phonological History of Pennsylvania German." In: *Studies for Einar Haugen*. Ed. Evelyn Firchow et al. The Hague: Mouton, 1972, p.469–81.

DC176 Reed, Carroll. "The Question of Aspect in Pennsylvania German." *Germanic Rev.*, vol. 22 (1947), 5–12.

DC177 Reed, Carroll. "A Survey of Pennsylvania German Morphology." *Mod. Lang. Quar.*, vol. 9, no. 3 (1948), 322–42.

DC178 Reed, Carroll. "A Survey of Pennsylvania German Phonology." *Mod. Lang. Quar.*, vol. 8 (1947), 267–89.

DC179 Reed, Carroll E., and Lester W. F. Seifert. *A Linguistic Atlas of Pennsylvania German*. Marburg: n.p., 1954. 99p.; Marburg: Becker, 1954. 2p. and 90 maps. Rev. by A. Buffington, *Monatshefte*, vol. 51 (1959), 93–95; H. Kloss, *Mitteilungen des Instituts für Auslandsbeziehungen*, vol. 5 (1955), 69f.; P. Schach, *Zeitschrift für Mundartforschung*, vol. 23 (1955), 126–28; T. H. Wilbur, *German Quar.*, vol. 29 (1956), 54–55; P. Schach, *Mod. Lang. Quar.*, vol. 17 (1956), 182–83.

DC180 Reed, Carroll E., and Lester W. F. Seifert. "A Study of the Pennsylvania German Dialect Spoken in the Counties of Lehigh and Berks." *Mod. Lang. Quar.*, vol. 9, no. 4 (1948), 448–66. The introduction to the authors' dissertations, Brown Univ.

DC181 Reitnauer, Clarence G. *Em Shdivvel Knecht sei Werdta Buch*. Pennsylvania Dutch Studies, no. 7. Collegeville: Institute on Pennsylvania Dutch Studies, Ursinus College, 1976. 36p.

DC182 "Responses to Peculiar Dialect Words." *Pa. Dutch News and Views*, vol. 3, no. 1 (1971), 12. Native informants give definitions of three dialect words.

DC183 Richter, Manfred M. "The Phonemic System of the Pennsylvania German Dialect in Waterloo County, Ontario." Diss., Toronto, 1969. Publ. in Marburg: Elwert, 1975. Ca. 144p. Deutsche Dialektgeographie, vol. 78.

DC184 Rohrer, David M. "A Critical Examination of the 529 Words Appended to Alfred F. Shoemaker's Dissertation on the Pennsylvania German Dialect of the Arthur, Illinois Amish." Honors Paper, Millersville State College, 1975.

DC185 Rohrer, David M. "The Influence of the Pennsylvania German Dialect on Amish English in Lancaster County." *Mennonite Research Jour.*, vol. 15 (1974), 34–35, 38–39, 47.

DC186 Schach, Paul. "The Formation of Hybrid Derivatives in Pennsylvania German." *Symposium*, vol. 3 (1949), 114–29. Pennsylvania-German affixes plus English stem or English affixes plus Pennsylvania-German words are discussed.

DC187 Schach, Paul. "Hybrid Compounds in Pennsylvania German." *Amer. Speech*, vol. 23 (1948), 121–34. Study of forms which are partly German and partly English.

DC188 Schach, Paul. "Die Lehnprägungen der pennsylvaniadeutschen Mundart." *Zeitschrift f. Mundart-forschung*, vol. 22 (1954), 215–22.

DC189 Schach, Paul. "Pfälzische Entlehnungen in der amerikanischen Umgangssprache." *Rheinische Vierteljahrsblätter*, vol. 20 (1955), 223–36.

DC190 Schach, Paul. "Semantic Borrowing in Pennsylvania German." *Amer. Speech*, vol. 26, no. 4 (1951), 257–67. On the changes in meaning of native German words under pressure of the English language or alien cultural patterns.

DC191 Schach, Paul. "Types of Loan Translations in Pennsylvania German." *Mod. Lang. Quar.*, vol. 13, no. 3 (1952), 268–76.

DC192 Schach, Paul. "Zum Lautwandel im Rheinpfälzischen: Die Senkung von kurzem Vokal zu a vor r-Verbindung." *Zeitschrift für Mundartforschung*, vol. 26 (1958), 200–22.

DC193 Schmidt-von Bardeleben, Renate. "Die Einwirkung des amerikanischen Englisch auf das Pennsylvaniadeutsche: Mobilität und Stabilität eines Einwandererdialekts." *Amerikastudien / American Studies*, vol. 23, no. 2 (1978), 320–29.

DC194 Seifert, Lester W. J. "Causes of the Dialect Differences between and within Western Berks and Western Lehigh Counties, Pa." "'S Pennsylfawnisch Deitsch Eck," Allentown *Morning Call*, 15, 22, 29 March 1941; 26 July, 2 August 1941; 2 August 1942.

DC195 Seifert, Lester W. J. "A Contrastive Description of Pennsylvania German and Standard German Stops and Fricatives." In: *Approaches in Linguistic Methodology*. Ed. Irmengard Rauch and C. T. Scott. Madison, Wis.: Univ. of Wis. Pr., 1969, p.81–88.

DC196 Seifert, Lester W. J. "The Diminutives of Pennsylvania German." *Monatshefte*, vol. 39, no. 5 (1947), 285–93.

DC197 Seifert, Lester W. J. "Lexical Differences between Four Pennsylvania German Regions." *Pa. German Folklore Soc., Publs.*, vol. 11 (1946), 155–69.

DC198 Seifert, Lester W. J. "The Pennsylvania German Dialect Spoken in the Counties of Lehigh and Berks: Vocabulary." Diss., Brown Univ., 1941.

DC199 Seifert, Lester W. J. "The Word Geography of Pennsylvania German: Extent and Causes." Abstr. of Paper Presented at the Germanic Language Symposium, Austin, Texas, November 1968, Publ. in *The German Language in America: A Symposium*. Ed. Glenn G. Gilbert. Austin: Univ. of Texas Pr., 1971, p.14–42.

DC200 Shoemaker, Alfred L. "Moshey and Bellyguts." *The Pa. Dutchman*, vol. 8, no. 1 (1956), 16–17, 59. Etymology and usages in the Pennsylvania-German area.

DC201 Smith, Elmer L., J. E. Stewart, and M. E. Kyger. "The Pennsylvania Germans of the Shenandoah Valley." *Yearbook, Pa. Ger. Folklore Soc.*, vol. 26 (1962). Part IV: "Language."

DC202 Snader, Howard. *Glossary of 6167 English Words and Expressions and Their Berks County Pennsylvania Dutch Equivalents*. Temple, Pa.: the Author, 1948. 64p.

DC203 Snader, Howard. *The English Pennsylvania Dutch Dictionary. A Glossary of Words and Expressions with Their Pennsylvania Dutch Equivalents. Together with an Illus. Compilation of Many Unique and Fascinating Facets of Wonderful Pennsylvania Dutch People and Their Historical Background* ... Reading: Culinary Arts Pr., 1965. 96p. Rev. by C. R. Beam, "'S Pennsylfawnisch Deitsch Eck," Allentown *Morning Call*, 2 October 1965.

DC204 Springer, Otto. "Die Erforschung des Pennsylvania-Deutschen." In: *Arbeiten zur germanischen Philologie und zur Literatur des Mittelalters*. München: n.p., 1975, p.35–74. A bibliographic essay.

DC205 Springer, Otto. "Pennsylvania German *Ochdem* 'Atem' and the Problem of Hypercorrect Forms." *Monatshefte f. deutschen Unterricht*, vol. 35, nos. 3–4 (March–April 1943), 138–50.

DC206 Springer, Otto. "The Study of the Pennsylvania German Dialect." *Jour. of Engl. and Germanic Philol.*, vol. 42 (1943), 1–39. Rev. by P. A. Barba, "'S Pennsylfawnisch Deitsch Eck," Allentown *Morning Call*, 8 May 1943.

DC207 Springer, Otto. "A Working Bibliography for the Study of the Pennsylvania German Language and Its Sources." 2nd rev. ed. Philadelphia: Univ. of Pa., 1941. 17p. Mimeogr.

DC208 Stahr, John Summers. "Pennsylvania German." "'S Pennsylfawnisch Deitsch Eck," Allentown *Morning Call*, 23, 30 October, 6 November 1943.

DC209 Stewart, John, and Elmer L. Smith. "The Survival of German Dialects and Customs in the Shenandoah Valley (A Preliminary Survey)." *Report of the Soc. for the Hist. of Germans in Md.*, vol. 31 (1963), 66–70.

DC210 Tway, Patricia V. "A Dialect Study of the Pennsylvania German Area." M.A. thesis, Univ. of Pittsburgh, 1970.

DC211 Veith, Werner. "Noch einmal: Zur phonologischen Analyse des Pennsylvaniadeutschen." *Zeitschrift für Dialektologie und Linguistik*, vol. 38 (1971), 222–26.

DC212 Veith, Werner. "Pennsylvaniadeutsch: Ein Beitrag zur Entstehung von Siedlungsmundarten." *Zeitschr. f. Mundartforschung*, vol. 35 (1968), 254–83.

DC213 Waldenrath, Alexander. "The Emergence of Pennsylvania-German in the Eighteenth Century: A Mixture of English and German?" *Jour. for German-Amer. Studies*, vol. 13 (1978), 1–15.

DC214 Wood, Ralph C. "Pennsilfaanisch (Pennsylvaniadeutsch): Eine neudeutsche Sprache Nordamerikas." In: *Deutsche Philologie im Aufriss*, Ed. W. Stammler. Berlin: n.p., 1952, vol. 1, cols. 786–807. 2nd ed., Berlin, 1957, cols. 1931f.

DC215 Wood, Ralph C. "Die Pennsylvanische Schärfung." *Zeitschrift für Deutsche Philologie*, vol. 78 (1959), 225–38. In accentuation, the Pennsylvania-German dialect is closer to the dialect of the Trier-Cologne area than to the present language of the Palatinate.

DC216 Wood, Ralph C. "Schärfungspunkte im Pfälzischen." *Zeitschrift für Mundartforschung*, vol. 31 (1964), 180–86.

DC217 Wood, Ralph C. "Two Hundred Years of Pennsylvania German." *Yearbook of the German Soc. of Pa.*, vol. 2 (1951), 29–35.

DC218 Yoder, Donald H. "The Dialect Church Service in the Pennsylvania German Culture." *Pa. Folklife*, vol. 27, no. 4 (1977–1978), 21–23.

DC219 Yoder, Donald H. "Outsiders Discover our Dialect." "'S Pennsylfawnisch Deitsch Eck," Allentown *Morning Call*, 5, 12, 19 May 1945.

Swiss Dialect—Schwyzerdütsch

DC220 Lewis, Brian Arthur. "The Phonology of the Glarus Dialect in Green County, Wisconsin." Diss., Univ. of Wisconsin, 1968. 115p.

DC221 Lewis, Brian Arthur. "Swiss German in Wisconsin: The Impact of English." *Amer. Speech*, vol. 48 (Fall-Winter 1973), 211–28.

DC222 Lewis, Brian Arthur. "Über die Glarner Mundart in New Glarus, einer schweizerdeutschen Sprachinsel im amerikanischen Mittelwesten." In: *Bericht über das Jahr 1969*. Schweizerdeutsches Wörterbuch. Zürich: n.p.

[1970], p.9–17. See also: *Jahrbuch des Histor. Vereins des Kantons Glarus 1970.*

DC223 Wenger, Marion R. "Swiss Dialect Islands in Ohio and Indiana." M.A. Thesis, Ohio State, 1961.

DC224 Wenger, Marion R. "A Swiss-German Dialect Study: Three Linguistic Islands in Midwestern U.S.A." Ph.D. Diss., Ohio State, 1969. Abstract in *Mennonite Quar. Rev.*, vol. 46 (1972), 85f.

Low German Dialects—"Platt"

DC225 Auburger, Leopold. "Die monophthongalen Vokale des kanadischen Plaudietsch." In: *Deutsch als Muttersprache in Kanada: Berichte zur Gegenwartslage.* Ed. L. Auburger et al. Wiesbaden: Steiner, 1977, p.139–48.

DC226 Baerg, Marjorie. "Phonology and Inflections of Gnadenau Low German, a Dialect of Marion County, Kansas." Diss., Univ. of Chicago, 1960. TS.

DC227 Bender, Jan E. "Die getrennte Entwicklung gleichen niederdeutschen Sprachgutes in Deutschland und Nebraska." Diss., Univ. of Nebraska, 1971.

DC228 Bender, Jan E. "The Impact of English on a Low German Dialect in Nebraska." In: *Languages in Conflict: Linguistic Acculturation on the Great Plains.* Ed. Paul Schach. Lincoln: Univ. of Nebraska Pr., 1981, p.77–85.

DC229 Buchheit, Robert H. "Mennonite 'Plautdeutsch': A Phonological and Morphological Description of a Settlement in York and Hamilton Counties, Nebraska." Unpubl. Diss., Univ. of Nebraska, 1978. 267p.

DC230 Dehning, Gustav. "Plattdeutsch in Neu-York." *Muttersprache*, vol. 76 (1966), 261–63.

DC231 Donnelly, Dale J. "The Low German Dialect of Sauk County, Wisconsin: Phonology and Morphology." Diss., Wisconsin, 1969. 158p. Incl. a brief history of the settlement of northern Sauk Co. by Germans from Hanover, 1850–1900.

DC232 Dyck, Henry D. "Language Differentiation among the Low German Mennonites of Manitoba." *Mennonite Life*, vol. 22 (1967), 117–20.

DC233 Dyck, Henry D. "Language Differentiation in Two Low German Groups in Canada." Diss., Univ. of Pennsylvania, 1964. 107p.

DC234 Eichhoff, Jürgen. "Niederdeutsche Mundarten in Nordamerika: Geschichte und Bibliographie." *Niederdeutsches Jahrbuch*, vol. 104 (1981), 134–59.

DC235 Fleischhauer, Wolfgang. "Westphalian in Ohio." *Amer.-German Rev.*, vol. 30, no. 1 (1963), 26–30. Westphalian *Plattdeutsch* preserved in a small Ohio community.

DC236 Friesen, J. John. "Romance of Low German." *Mennonite Life*, vol. 2 (April 1947), 2–3.

DC237 Goerzen, Jakob W. "Low German in Canada. A Study of 'Plautdietsch' ('Ploudîtš') as Spoken by Mennonite Immigrants from Russia." Diss., Toronto, 1952. Reissued, Edmonton: n.p., 1970. 255p.

DC238 Goerzen, Jakob W. "The Phonology of Plautdietsch." Diss., Univ. of Alberta, 1950.

DC239 Goerzen, Jakob W. "Plautdietsch and English." *Mennonite Life*, vol. 7 (January 1952), 18.

DC240 Hameyer, Klaus. "Variation in Dialect Proficiency and Restructuring: Pomeranian Low-German Twenty-Five Years after Emigration." *Phonetica*, vol. 32 (1975), 24–37.

DC241 Harder, Bertha F. "Low German for Children: Rhymes and Poems." *Mennonite Life*, vol. 36, no. 3 (1981), 12–16.

DC242 Kehlenbeck, Alfred P. *An Iowa Low German Dialect.* Publs. of the Amer. Dialect Soc., no. 10. University, Ala.: American Dialect Soc., 1948. 82p.

DC243 Kliewer, Warren. "Low German Children's Rimes." *Mennonite Life*, vol. 14 (1959), 141f. Notes on a dialect preserved at Mountain Lake, Minn.

DC244 Krahn, Cornelius. "Mennonite Plattdeutsch." *Mennonite Quar. Rev.*, vol. 33 (1959), 256–59.

DC245 Krahn, Cornelius. "Plattdeutsch." *Mennonite Encyclopedia*, vol. 4, p.186–89.

DC246 Lehn, Walter I. "Rosental Low German, Synchronic and Diachronic Phonology." Ph.D. Diss., Cornell Univ., 1957.

DC247 Mierau, Eric. "A Descriptive Grammar of Ukrainian Low German." Diss., Indiana Univ., 1965. 123p. The Ukrainian Germans embrace 100,000 speakers in Canada, Russia, South and Central America.

DC248 Moelleken, Wolfgang W. "Diaphonic Correspondences in the Low German of Mennonites from the Fraser Valley, British Columbia." *Zeitschrift für Mundartforschung*, vol. 34 (1967), 240–53.

DC249 Moelleken, Wolfgang W. *Niederdeutsch der Molotschna- und Chortitza-Mennoniten in British Columbia, Kanada*. Tübingen: Phonai, 1972. 213p. With tape recording.

DC250 Nyman, Lennart. "Die niederdeutschen Mundarten der Russland-Mennoniten." In: *Beiträge zur historischen Grammatik und zur Dialektologie*. KBGL, no. 10. Copenhagen: Akademisk, 1978, p.43–56.

DC251 "Plattdeutsch Makes Comeback: North Germans Celebrate Their Private Language." *Internat. Herald Tribune*, 13 October 1978.

DC252 Schütte, Friedel. "Zwischen Mississippi und Ohio: Plattdeutsch durch die Prärie." *Neue Westfälische Rundschau* (Bielefeld), 4, 5, 8, 9, 10, 11 and 12 August 1967. Report on Midwestern settlers from eastern Westphalia.

DC253 Thiessen, John. "The Low German of the Canadian Mennonites." *Mennonite Life*, vol. 22 (1967), 110–15. *See also* his: "Das Niederdeutsche der Mennoniten." *Zeitschrift für Kulturaustausch*, vol. 15, no. 3 (1965), 165–67.

DC254 Thiessen, John. "Plattdeutsch in Kanada." *German-Canad. Yearbook*, vol. 3 (1976), 211–19.

DC255 Thiessen, John. *Studien zum Wortschatz der kanadischen Mennoniten*. Marburg: Elwert, 1963. 207p. Rev. by K. W. Maurer, *Zeitschrift für Kulturaustausch*, vol. 14 (1964), 55.

DC256 Thiessen, John. *Das Wörterbuch der kanadischen Mennoniten mit englischen und hochdeutschen Übersetzungen*. Marburg: Elwert, 1977.

DC257 Voss, Carl. "Auch in Nebraska spricht man Plattdütsch." *Der Milwaukee Herold*, 6 December 1973.

DC258 Wiens, Gerhard. "Russian in Low German." *Mennonite Life*, vol. 13 (1958), 75.

DC259 Willibrand, W. A. "English Loan Words in the Low German Dialect of Westphalia, Missouri." *Publs. of the Amer. Dialect Soc.*, vol. 27 (1957), 16–21.

DC260 Wust, Harald. "High German oder Low German." *Europa und die Niederdeutsche Welt*, vol. 19 (1955), 75–76. Report on a visit to Emden, Logan Co., Ill.

Yiddish Language in America

DC261 Davis, Lawrence P. "The Phonology of Yiddish-American Speech." Diss., Chicago, 1967.

DC262 Doroshkin, Milton. *Yiddish in America. Social and Cultural Foundations*. Carlisle: Fairleigh Dickinson Univ. Pr., ca. 1969.

DC263 Feinsilver, Lillian M. "Like Influences from Yiddish and Pennsylvania German." *Amer. Speech*, vol. 33 (1958), 231–32. Noting the similar effects produced by Yiddish and Pennsylvania German on American English.

DC264 Feinsilver, Lillian M. "Who Needs It?" *Amer. Speech*, vol. 41, no. 4 (1966), 270–73. A locution from Yiddish "Ver darf es?"

DC265 Feinsilver, Lillian M. "Yiddish Idioms in American English." *Amer. Speech*, vol. 37 (1962), 200–06.

DC266 Feinsilver, Lillian M. "The Yiddish is Showing." In: *Perspectives on American English*. Ed. J. L. Dillard. The Hague: Mouton, 1980, p.205–56. Yiddish expressions entering general American speech and writing.

DC267 Fisch, Harold. *The Dual Image: The Figure of the Jew in English and American Literature.* London: World Jewish Library; New York: Ktav Publ. Co., 1971. 149p. Revised, enlarged ed.

DC268 Gilman, Sander L. "Über das Jiddische heute und künftig: Interview mit dem Nobelpreisträger Isaac Bashevis Singer." *Neue deutsche Hefte*, vol. 161 (1979), 200–03.

DC269 Haslam, Gerald W. "Odets' Use of Yiddish-English in Awake and Sing." *Research Studies* (Washington State Univ.), vol. 34 (1966), 161–64.

DC270 Herzog, Marvin I., Barbara Kirshenblatt-Gimblet, Dan Miron and Ruth Wisse, eds. *The Field of Yiddish: Studies in Language, Folklore, and Literature.* Philadelphia: Institute for the Study of Human Issues, 1980. 499p.

DC271 Howard, John A. "Hebrew-German and Early Yiddish Literatures: A Survey of Problems." Diss., Univ. of Illinois, Urbana, 1973.

DC272 Kloss, Heinz. "Ein Paar Worte über das Jiddische in Kanada." In: *Deutsch als Muttersprache in Kanada: Berichte zur Gegenwartslage.* Ed. L. Auburger et al. Wiesbaden: Steiner, 1977, p. 129–30.

DC273 Landmann, Salcia. *Jiddisch, das Abenteuer einer Sprache.* Olten, Switz.: Walter, 1962. 469p.

DC274 Lermer, A. "Jidish in Kanade." *Di Tsukunft* (New York), 1972, p. 177–81.

DC275 Madison, Charles A. *Yiddish Literature: Its Scope and the Major Writers.* New York: Ungar, 1968. 540p. Rev. by B. Murdoch, *Mod. Lang. Rev.*, vol. 66 (1971), 236–37. Incl. chapters on the development of the Yiddish language, the United States, the Soviet Union, and Israel.

DC276 Markfield, Wallace. "The Yiddishization of American Humor." *Esquire*, vol. 64 (October 1965), 114–15, 136. The world is discovering an almost universal speech.

DC277 Rosten, Leo. *The Joys of Yiddish. A Relaxed Lexicon of Yiddish, Hebrew and Yinglish Words Often Encountered in English ...with Serendipitous Excursions into Jewish Humor, Habits ...Religion ...Folklore ...* New York: McGraw-Hill, 1968; London, 1970. 547p.

DC278 Rosten, Leo. "Yiddish and English. Towards a New Lexikon." *Encounter*, vol. 31, no. 3 (September 1968), 21–32. Yiddish words and phrasings entering English in the past 30–40 years.

DC279 Shenker, Israel. "From Nudnik to Peacenik, It's All Yiddish." *N.Y. Times*, 25 January 1969.

DC280 Spitzer, Leo. "Confusion Schmooshun." *Jour. of Engl. and Germanic Philology*, vol. 51, no. 2 (1952), 226–33. Yiddish as the basis of Brooklynese.

DC281 Shtarkman, Moyshe. "Highlights in the History of the Yiddish Word in America." *Zukunft*, vol. 75 (1970), 233–37. Celebrating the 100th anniversary of the Yiddish press in the U.S.; in Yiddish.

DC282 Weinberg, Werner. *Die Reste des Jüdischdeutschen.* Studia Delitzchiana, no. 12. Stuttgart: Kohlhammer, 1969. 116p. Rev. by J. Eichhoff, *Monatshefte*, vol. 64, no. 1 (Spring 1972), 58. Jüdischdeutsch, as used in Germany, America, and Israel, is not Yiddish, but German spoken by Jews (with admixture of Hebrew words). A grammatical analysis with extensive glossary.

DC283 Weinreich, Max. *History of the Yiddish Language: Concepts, Facts, Methods.* New York: YIVO Inst. for Jewish Research, 1973. 4 vols. 353, 397, 381, 393p. In Yiddish.

DC284 Weinreich, Max. "Old Yiddish Poetry in Linguistic-Literary Research." *Word*, vol. 1, no. 1 (1960).

DC285 Weinreich, Max. "Yidishkayt and Yiddish: On the Impact of Religion on Language in Ashkenazic Jewry." In: *Readings in the Sociology of Language.* Ed. Joshua A. Fishman. The Hague: Mouton, 1968, p. 382–413. Repr. from *Mordecai M. Kaplan Jubilee Volume.* New York: Jewish Theological Seminary of America, 1953, p. 481–514.

DC286 Weinreich, Uriel. *College Yiddish.* Yiddish Scientific Institute, New York, 1949. Rev. by A. F. Hubbell, *Amer. Speech*, vol. 25, no. 3 (1950), 209–10.

DC287 Weinreich, Uriel. *Modern English-Yiddish, Yiddish-English Dictionary.* New York: McGraw-Hill, 1968. 789p.

DC288 Weinreich, Uriel. *Yiddish Language and Folklore—A Selective Bibliography for Research*

Yiddish Language in America *(cont.)*

by Uriel Weinreich and Beatrice Weinreich. The Hague: Mouton, 1959. 66p.

DC289 Weinreich, Uriel, ed. *The Field of Yiddish: Studies in Language, Folklore, and Literature. Second Collection.* The Hague: Mouton, 1965. 289p.

DC290 Weisbert, Josef. "Sprachentfaltung: Zu M. Weinreichs Geschichte der jiddischen Sprache." *Zeitschrift für deutsche Philologie*, vol. 99 (1980), 100–10.

DC291 Yudel, Mark. "The Yiddish Language: Its Cultural Impact." *Amer. Jewish Hist. Quar.*, vol. 59 (December 1969), 210f.

DD

Dictionaries of "American" for German Speakers

DD1 Baader, Werner. *Modernes Wörterbuch, Amerikanisch-Deutsch, Deutsch-Amerikanisch.* 4th ed. Stuttgart: Gentner, 1947. 2 vols. 160p.

DD2 Bense, J. F. *A Dictionary of the Low-Dutch Element in the English Vocabulary.* The Hague: Nijhoff, 1939. Rev. by Henning Larsen, *Philol. Quar.*, vol. 20, no. 1 (1941), 95–96.

DD3 Bindewald, Rüdiger. *Deutsch-englisch, amerikanisches Wörterbuch.* Braunschweig: Westermann, 1949. 114p.

DD4 Friederici, Georg. *Amerikanisches Wörterbuch mit Hilfswörterbuch für den Amerikanisten. Deutsch-Spanisch-Englisch.* 2nd ed. Hamburg: Cram, de Gruyter, 1960. 831p. Orig. ed.: Hamburg, 1947. 722p.

DD5 Hietsch, Otto. "An Austro-American Glossary of Slang and Colloquial Speech. Erste Teilveröffentlichung des Forschungsvorhabens *An English-German German-English Dictionary of Slang and Colloquial Speech.*" Prep. for inclusion in: *Americana-Austriaca.* Ed. Klaus Lanzinger. Vol. 2. Amerika-Institut der Universität Innsbruck, 1967.

DD6 Hildebrandt, Lieselotte M. *Deutsche Phonetik für Amerikaner.* (Monograph Publishing on Demand, Sponsor Ser.) Ann Arbor: Univ. Microfilms International, 1976. 247p. Rev. by S. B. Barlau, *Monatshefte*, vol. 70, no. 2 (Summer 1978), 81–82. Textbook of German phonetics for American users.

DD7 Jacobs, Noah Jonathan. *Amerika im Spiegel der Sprache. Slang-Ausdrücke erklärt.* Bern / München: Francke, 1968. 110p. Prepared as a guide through difficult words and expressions in American slang.

DD8 Mayer, Arthur. *Amerikanisches Wörterbuch. Mit internationaler Aussprachebezeichnung.* 2 vols. in 1. *Amerikanisch-Deutsch; Deutsch-Amerikanisch.* Berlin: Axel Juncker, 1953. 487p. 4th ed. 1965. Rev. by J. R. Frey, *Jour. of Engl. and Germanic Philology*, vol. 53 (1954), 683; R.M.S. Heffner, *Monatshefte*, vol. 47 (1953), 52.

DD9 Neske, Fritz, and Ingeborg Neske. *dtv—Wörterbuch englischer und amerikanischer Ausdrücke in der deutschen Sprache.* München: Deut. Taschenbuch Verlag. 314p. Rev. by A. W. Stanforth, *Monatshefte*, vol. 63 (1971), 166–67.

DD10 Neuse, Werner. "German Words in Two Dictionaries of American English." *Monatshefte*, vol. 45 (1953), 246–48.

DD11 *Preussisches Wörterbuch.* Ed. Erhard Riemann. Comp. by E. Riemann, A. Schönfeldt, and U. Tolksdorf. Neumünster: Wachholtz, 1974–1976. Rev. by J. Eichhoff, *Monatshefte*, vol. 70 (1978), 315–17. The area here studied is significant in that it was the homeland of low-German speaking Mennonites who subsequently settled in Canada and the United States.

DD12 Rudolph, Horst Eduard. *Amerika-England: Worüber sie lachen. Ein humoristischer Lehrbehelf für Englisch-Lernende mit 110 Original-Karikaturen und einem Anhang mit Amerikanismen.* Wien: n.p., 1946. 161p.

DD13 Rudolph, Horst Eduard. *Amerikanisch in Abkürzungen. Eine Anlage zu jedem englisch-deutsch Wörterbuch*. Wien: Hollinek, 1946. 109p. Acronyms and abbreviations.

DD14 Spitzbardt, Harry, and Gerhard Gräf. *Amerikanisches Englisch*. Leipzig: VEB-Verlag Enzyclopädie, 1964. 125p.

DD15 Steiner, Arthur. *Amerikanisch wie es nicht im Wörterbuch steht*. Frankfurt: Scheffler, 1966. 157p.

DE
Names and Nicknames

Family Names

DE1 Droege, Geart B. "Frisian Family and Place Names." *Names*, vol. 3, no. 2 (1955), 89–97.

DE2 *Ethnic Names*. Ed. Fred Tarpley. Dept. of Literature and Language, East Texas State Univ., in Cooperation with the American Name Society. Commerce, Texas: Names Institute Pr., 1978. 14p. Incl. bibliographic references.

DE3 Gingerich, Melvin. "Mennonite Family Names in Iowa." *Annals of Iowa*, vol. 42 (Summer 1974), 397–403.

DE4 Glanz, Rudolf. "German-Jewish Names in America." *Jewish Social Studies*, vol. 23 (July 1961), 143–69.

DE5 Goertz, Adalbert. "Familiennamen in mennonitischen Lexika." *Archiv für Sippenforschung*, vol. 28 (1962), 457–59.

DE6 Gold, David L. "Jewish Surnames as a Key to Jewish Settlement History." *Yugntruf*, vol. 23 (1971), 10–11. In Yiddish.

DE7 Gold, David L. "R.M.R. and Beatrice L. Hall's 'Some Apparent Inconsistencies in American Family Names of Yiddish Origin'." *Names*, vol. 19 (1971), 223–28.

DE8 Graham, Robert S. "The Anglicization of German Family Names in Western Canada." *Amer. Speech*, vol. 30 (1955), 260–64.

DE9 Hilbig, Frederick Walter. "Anglicized German Surnames in America." M.A. Thesis, Univ. of Utah, 1955. "Americanization of German Surnames." Diss., Utah, 1958.

DE10 Kaganoff, Benzion C. *A Dictionary of Jewish Names and Their History*. New York: Schocken Publ., 1977. 250p.

DE11 Kaufman, David B. "German and Pennsylvania German Surnames." "'S Pennsylfawnisch Deitsch Eck," Allentown *Morning Call*, 21, 28 May, 4 June 1966.

DE12 Krahn, Cornelius. "Mennonite Names of Persons and Places." *Mennonite Life*, vol. 15, no. 1 (1960), 36–38.

DE13 Luthy, David. "New Names Among the Amish." *Family Life*, August/September 1972, 31–35; October 1972, 20–23; November 1972, 21–23; also February 1973, 13–15, and June 1973, 13–15.

DE14 Maass, Ernest. "Integration and Name Changing among Jewish Refugees from Central Europe in the United States." *Names*, vol. 6, no. 3 (1958), 129–71.

DE15 Markreich, Max. "Notes on Transformation of Place Names by European Jews." *Jewish Social Studies*, vol. 23 (October 1961), 265–84. Surnames derived from European place names.

DE16 Mockler, W. E. "Surnames of Trans-Allegheny Virginia, 1750–1800." *Names*, vol. 4 (1956), 1–17, 96–118. Examples of German names changed by order of the Monongalia Court.

DE17 Priblude, A. "Contemporary Family Names—Vanished Names: Toward the History of

Family Names *(cont.)*

Jewish Family Names." *Yiddishe Kultur*, vol. 34, no. 2 (1972), 55–56. Article in Yiddish.

DE18 Priblude, A. "Yiddish Names Borrowed from Other Peoples." *Sovetish Heymland*, vol. 12 (1971), 173–76. Article in Yiddish.

DE19 Rennick, Robert. "Hitlers and Others Who Changed Their Names and a Few Who Did Not." *Names*, vol. 17 (September 1969), 199–207. On families named "Hitler" during World War II. Ironically, they were almost all Jewish.

DE20 Schelbert, Leo, and Sandra Luebking. "Swiss Mennonite Family Names: An Annotated Checklist." *Pa. Folklife*, vol. 26, no. 4 (1977), 2–24.

DE21 Smith, Elmer L. "Amish Names." *Names*, vol. 16 (June 1968), 105–10.

DE22 Smith, Elmer L. "The Amish System of Nomenclature." "'S Pennsylfawnisch Deitsch Eck," Allentown *Morning Call*, 8 August 1959; also *Hist. Rev. of Berks Co.*, vol. 27 (1961), 21–25. Surnames, given names, and nicknames in southeastern Pennsylvania.

DE23 Stiens, Robert E. "Surname Inconsistencies in Northern Germany." *German-Amer. Studies*, vol. 9 (Spring 1975), 43–46.

DE24 United States Department of Justice. Immigration and Naturalization Service. *Foreign Versions of English Names, M-131*. Revised ed. Washington, D.C.: U.S. Govt. Printing Office, 1962. 22p.

DE25 Yoder, Donald Herbert. "Dutchified Surnames." "'S Pennsylfawnisch Deitsch Eck," Allentown *Morning Call*, 21 September 1946.

Nicknames

DE26 Kulp, Isaac Clarence, Jr. [Dialect nicknames among the Pennsylvania Germans.] *The Goschenhoppen Region*, vol. 1, no. 1 (1968), 6–7.

DE27 Mook, Maurice A. "Nicknames among the Amish." *Pa. Folklife*, vol. 17, no. 4 (1968), 20–23. See also *Names*, vol. 15 (1967), 111–18.

DE28 Schmidt, Mrs. H. R. "Nicknames Among the Mennonites from Russia." *Mennonite Life*, vol. 16, no. 3 (July 1961), 132.

DE29 Troyer, Lester O. "Amish Nicknames from Holmes County, Ohio." *Pa. Folklife*, vol. 17, no. 4 (1968), 24.

DE30 Yoder, Don H. "Notes and Documents: Nicknames from a Mennonite Family." *Pa. Folklife*, vol. 16, no. 3 (Spring 1967), 42–43.

DE31 Yoder, Eleanor. "Nicknaming in an Amish-Mennonite Community." *Pa. Folklife*, vol. 23, no. 3 (1974), 30–37.

Place Names

DE32 Alder, Douglas D. "The Ghost of Mercur." *Utah Hist. Quar.*, vol. 29 (1961), 33–42. The name "Merkur" had been given to a mine discovered in 1879 by a Bavarian prospector.

DE33 Beam, C. Richard. "Pennsylvania German Place Name Maps." *Hist. Schaefferstown Record*, vol. 11, no. 3 (1977), 29–39.

DE34 Beeler, Madison S. "America, the Story of a Name." *Names*, vol. 1 (1953), 1–14. Tracing the name to its Germanic roots.

DE35 Cheney, Roberta Carkeek. "Montana Place Names." *Montana. The Mag. of Western Hist.*, vol. 20, no. 2 (1970), 48–61. A few Swiss and German place names.

DE36 "Contributions to the Study of Missouri Place Names." Part II. "Kinderpost." *Comments on Etymology*, vol. 9, nos. 8–9 (1980), 3–11. Kinderpost, Missouri, and its names discussed by Priscilla Bradford and Anna O'Brien.

DE37 Cunz, Dieter. "German Street Names in Egg Harbor [New Jersey]." *Amer.-German Rev.*, vol. 22, no. 3 (1956), 27–29.

DE38 Davis, Harry. *A Short History of German Place Names.* Hamburg: Atlantic-Brücke, 1978. 36p.

DE39 Farkas, Zoltan J. "The Challenge of the Name 'America'." *Names*, vol. 13 (1965), 11–18. Origin, development, and use of the name.

DE40 Fennel, C. W. "Heidelberg und seine Töchter." *Deutsche in der Welt*, vol. 1, no. 3 (1960), 36–37. On Heidelberg as place name on the American continent.

DE41 Ferguson, Charles A. "Saints' Names in American Lutheran Church Dedications." *Names*, vol. 14 (June 1966), 76–82. Cultural and denominational implications of name choices.

DE42 Ganett, Henry. *American Names. A Guide to the Origin of Place Names in the United States.* Washington, D.C.: Public Affairs Pr., 1947. 334p. Cites, e.g., the occurrence of 37 post offices named "Berlin."

DE43 Gudde, Erwin G. *California Place Names: A Geographical Dictionary.* Berkeley: Univ. of California Pr., 1949. 431p. See also his *1,000 California Place Names... Based on California Place Names: A Geographical Dictionary.* Berkeley: n.p., 1947. 96p.

DE44 Heier, Edmund. "Russo-German Place-Names in Russia and in North America." *Names*, vol. 9 (1961), 260–68.

DE45 Hollenbach, Raymond E. "Geographic Names Known in Northern Lehigh Co., Pa." "'S Pennsylfawnisch Deitsch Eck," Allentown *Morning Call*, 22 February 1964.

DE46 Hummel, Ray O., Jr. *A List of Places Included in 19th Century Virginia Directories.* Richmond: Virginia State Library, 1960. 154p. Names are here listed according to patterns of national origin, incl. German.

DE47 Johnson, Gilbert. "Place Names in Langenburg Municipality." *Saskatchewan Hist.*, vol. 5 (1952), 33f.

DE48 Kane, Joseph Nathan. *The American Counties: A Record of the Origin of the Names of the 3,067 Counties, Dates of Creation, and Organization, Area, Population, Historical Data, etc.* New York: Scarecrow Pr., 1960. 500p.

DE49 Kenny, Hamill. *West Virginia Place Names, Their Origin and Meaning, Including the Nomenclature of the Streams and Mountains.* Piedmont, W. Va.: The Place Name Pr., 1945. 768p. Finds numerous West Virginia settlements of German origin.

DE50 Klinefelter, Walter. "German Place Names in York County." *Der Reggeboge*, vol. 14, no. 2 (1980), 3–8.

DE51 "Local Place Names." *Pa. Folklife*, vol. 19, no. 2 (1969), 47–48.

DE52 McGraw, Peter A. "A German Footnote on Cassidy's *Place-Names of Dane County, Wisconsin.*" *Amer. Speech*, vol. 48 (1973), 150–53.

DE53 MacReynolds, George, comp. *Place Names in Bucks County, Pennsylvania, Alphabetically Arranged in an Historical Narrative.* Doylestown: Bucks Co. Hist. Soc., 1942. 482p. Compiled from the archives of the Bucks Co. Hist. Soc.

DE54 Miegel, Charles H. "What's in a Street Name?" *Report of the Soc. for the Hist. of the Germans in Md.*, vol. 25 (1942), 27–30. Traces German sources of Baltimore street names.

DE55 Neuffer, Claude H. "Folk Etymology in South Carolina Place Names." *Amer. Speech*, vol. 41 (1966), 274–77. Some names of German origin.

DE56 Overman, William. *Ohio Town Names.* Akron: Atlantic Pr., 1958. 155p. Rev. by W. Coyle, *Ohio Hist. Quar.*, vol. 68 (1959), 427. Incl. references to German names.

DE57 Ramsay, Robert L. *The Place Names of Franklin County, Missouri.* Columbia: Univ. of Missouri Pr., 1954.

DE58 Ramsay, Robert L. "The Secrets of Franklin County Place Names: The German Heritage." *The Washington Missourian*, 30 August 1951, 1 B.

DE59 Resnick, Abraham. "A United States Place Name Glossary." *Jour. of Geography*, vol. 66 (1967), 435f. Analyzes the use of prefixes and suffixes in -berg, -burg, -feld, gross-, land-, stadt- and -wald.

DE60 Sealock, R. B., and P. A. Seely. *Bibliography of Place Name Literature: United States, Canada, Alaska, and Newfoundland.* 2nd ed. Chicago: Amer. Library Assoc., 1967. 331p. References on place names of German origin are listed on p.18, 113, 152, 175–79.

DE61 Shain, Samson A. "Old Testament Place Names in Pennsylvania." *Keystone Folklore Quar.*, vol. 6, no. 3 (Autumn 1961), 3–11.

DE62 Spieler, Gerhard G. "Pennsylvania Dutch Place Names." *The Pa. Dutchman*, vol. 5, no. 7 (1953), 5–6.

DE63 Stein, Herbert. "'Deutschland' in Amerika—Vom Germany Valley, Germany Creek, Germanya und anderen deutschen Namen." In: *Deutsch-Amerika Almanach 1958.* New York: Verlag Plattdütsche Post, 1957, p.80–82.

DE64 Stewart, George R. *American Place-Names: A Concise and Selective Dictionary for the Continental United States of America.* New York: Oxford Univ. Pr., ca. 1971. 12,000 entries, citing meaning, derivations, occasion for use, etc.

DE65 Stewart, George R. *Names on the Land. A Historical Account of Place-Naming in the United States.* New York: Random House, ca. 1945. 418p.

DE66 Ver Nooy, Amy. "Place-Names and Folklore in Dutchess County." *N.Y. Folklore Quar.*, vol. 20 (1964), 42–46. Reflecting Dutch, German, and Indian languages of the area.

DE67 Weidhaas, Walther E. "German Religious Influences on American Place Names." *Amer.-German Rev.*, vol. 23, no. 6 (1957), 33–34.

DE68 Wolle, Muriel S. "From 'Sailors Digging' to 'Miners Delight.'" *Western Folklore*, vol. 13, no. 1 (1954), 40–46. About the naming of mining towns.

Other

DE70 Cray, Edward. "More Ethnic and Place Names as Derisive Adjectives." *Western Folklore*, vol. 24 (1965), 197–98.

DE71 Freund, Max. "English Names and Misnomers for the Germans: Dutch, German, Teuton." In: *Studies in German in Memory of Andrew Louis.* Ed. Robert L. Kahn. Rice Univ. Studies, vol. 55, no. 3 (Summer 1969), 33–38.

DE72 Guthke, Karl S. "Names in German Speech." *Names*, vol. 5, no. 2 (1957), 80–88. The use and extension of personal names in general German vocabulary.

DE73 Hollenbach, Raymond E. "Ungeziffer." "'S Pennsylfawnisch Deitsch Eck," Allentown *Morning Call*, 25 July 1953. Pa. Dutch dialect names for insects and vermin and lore associated with them.

DE74 Krueger, John R. "Beer Brand Names in the United States." *Names*, vol. 12, no. 1 (1964), 6–9.

DE75 Kulp, Isaac Clarence, Jr. [Enumeration of local names for crafts and craftsmen among the Pennsylvania Germans.] *The Goschenhoppen Region*, vol. 1, no. 3 (1968), 8–17.

DE76 Majut, Rudolf. "Die Libelle im deutschen und englischen Sprachgebrauch." *Germanisch-Romanische Monatsschrift*, N.S., vol. 14 (October 1964), 403–20. German and English names for the dragonfly.

DE77 Petrea, H. S. "Names of Early Lutheran Churches." *Names*, vol. 17 (1970), 33–35. Also in *Names in South Carolina*, vol. 17 (Winter 1970), 33–35. Names and origins of churches in South Carolina.

DE78 Rupp, William J. *Bird Names and Bird Lore among the Pennsylvania Germans.* Publs., Pa. German Soc., no. 52 (1946). Norristown: The Soc., 1948.

DE79 Rupp, William J. "Pennsylvania German Bird Names." "'S Pennsylfawnisch Deitsch Eck," Allentown *Morning Call*, 9 April 1949.

DE80 Seits, Laurence E., ed. *Papers of the North Central Names Institute 1980*. Sugar Grove, Ill.: Waubonsee Community College Pr., 1980.

E

Folklore and Material Culture of the German-Americans

EA
General Works—Backgrounds

Bibliography / Sources / Background Studies

EA1 Ansari, Muhammad S. "Towards a Methodology [in Folklore Study]." *Folklore* (Calcutta), vol. 196 (1975), 138–49; vol. 197, 177–92, 199–200, 261–68. Parts 2 and 3 are titled "A Look at the Amish Country."

EA2 Ayres, Tom. "Anthropology, Folklore, and Secondary Education: An Annotated Bibliography." *Jour. of the Ohio Folklore Soc.*, vol. 4 (1977), 3–36.

EA3 Bayard, Samuel P. "Unrecorded Folk Traditions in Pennsylvania." *Pa. Hist.*, vol. 12, no. 1 (1945), 1–14. A call for the study of folk culture and of folk music in particular.

EA4 Benjamin, Steven M. *An Annotated Bibliography of "The Pennsylvania Dutchman," "The Dutchman," "Pennsylvania Dutchman," and "Pennsylvania Folklore."* Madison, Wis.: n.p., 1978.

EA5 Benjamin, Steven M. "A Bibliography of Works Published in the Yearbooks of the Pennsylvania German Folklore Society." *Occasional Papers of the Soc. for German-Amer. Studies*, vol. 4. Morgantown, W. Va.: Dept. of Foreign Languages, W. Va. Univ., 1979. 9p.

EA6 Boggs, Ralph S. "Folklore. Bibliography for 1951." *Southern Folklore Quar.*, vol. 16, no. 1 (1952), 1–78.

EA7 Bracher, James T. *Analytical Index to the Publications of the Texas Folklore Society, Vols. 1–36.* Dallas: Southern Methodist Univ. Pr., 1973.

EA8 Buffington, Albert F. "The Pennsylvania German Dialect and Folklore of Somerset County." In: *Ebbes fer Alle—Ebber Ebbes fer Dich: Essays in Memoriam, Albert Franklin Buffington.* Publs., Pa. German Soc., vol. 14. Breinigsville, Pa.: The Soc., 1980, p.3–33.

EA9 *Canadian-German Folklore.* Annual. Publ. by the Pa. German Folklore Soc. of Ontario. Vol. 5, Kitchener, 1975. Vol. 6, Kitchener, 1977.

EA10 Clarke, Mary W., and Charles S. Guthrie, eds. *Twenty-Year Index to the Kentucky Folklore Record, 1955–1974.* Bowling Green: Kentucky Folklore Society, 1975. 32p.

EA11 Comfort [Texas] Middle School. "Those Comforting Hills." Ethnic Folklore and Oral History Project. Director: Mrs. Betty Johannes. 1975.

EA12 Dorson, Richard M. *American Folklore.* Chicago: Univ. of Chicago Pr., 1959. 350p. Rev. by J. T. Flanagan, *Miss. Valley Hist. Rev.*, vol. 46 (1960), 749–51.

EA13 Dorson, Richard M. "American Folklore Bibliography." *Amer. Studies Internat.*, vol. 16 (Autumn 1977), 23–37. A survey of the state of bibliographic studies in the field of American folklore.

EA14 Drake, Milton, comp. *Almanacs of the United States.* New York: Scarecrow Pr., 1962. 2 vols. For chronological listings of Pennsylvania almanacs in German and in English from 1686 to 1850, see vol. 2, p. 911–1211. The earliest German entry there is *Der Teutsche Pilgrim: Mitbringende Einen Sitten-Calender auf 1731.* Philadelphia: Andreas Bradford. 14 1. Library locations are indicated.

EA15 Dundes, Alan. *Folklore Theses and Dissertations in the United States.* Austin: Univ. of Texas Pr., 1976. 610p.

EA16 Flanagan, Cathleen C., and John T. Flanagan. *American Folklore: A Bibliography, 1950–1974.* Metuchen, N. J.: Scarecrow Pr., 1977. 406p.

EA17 Fryer, Judith E. *Twenty-Five Year Index to "Pennsylvania Folklife" (Including the "Pennsylvania Dutchman" and "The Dutchman")*. Collegeville, Pa.: Pennsylvania Folklife Soc., 1980. 94p.

EA18 Glassie, Henry H. *Pattern in the Material Folk Culture of the Eastern United States.* Philadelphia: Univ. of Pennsylvania Pr., 1968.

EA19 Goldstein, Kenneth S. *A Guide for Field Workers in Folklore.* Hatboro, Pa.: American Folklore Soc., 1964.

EA20 Graeff, Arthur D. [Annual Report and Comment on Pennsylvania German Folklore: "1950 in Pennsylvania German Folklore," etc.] See *Publs., Pa. German Folklore Soc.* Vol. 15 (1951), 129–34; Vol. 16 (1953), 203–10; Vol. 17 (1954), 207–211; Vol. 19 (1955), 167–76; Vol. 20 (1956), 275–84; and Vol. 21 (1958), 301–09.

EA21 Hand, Wayland D. "Folklore Societies and the Research Effort." *Keystone Folklore Quar.*, vol. 14, no. 3 (Fall 1969), 97–104.

EA22 Hand, Wayland D. "German-American Folklore." *Jour. of Amer. Folklore*, vol. 60 (1947), 366–72.

EA23 Hand, Wayland D., ed. *Popular Beliefs and Superstitions from North Carolina* (1961). Vol. 6 in: Duke Univ., Durham, N. C., Library. Frank C. Brown Collection of North Carolina Folklore. *The Frank C. Brown Collection of North Carolina Folklore; The Folklore of North Carolina, Collected by Dr. Frank C. Brown during the Years 1912 to 1943, in Collaboration with the North Carolina Folklore Society... General editor: Newman Ivey White. Wood Engravings by Clare Leighton.* Durham: Duke Univ. Pr., 1952–64. 7 vols.

EA24 Haywood, Charles. *A Bibliography of North American Folklore and Folksong.* New York: Greenberg, 1951. 1292p. Rev. by L. J. Davidson, *Western Folklore*, vol. 10, no. 4 (1951), 338–39; 2nd rev. ed. New York: Dover, 1961. 1301p.

EA25 Hufford, David J. "History and Work of the Ethnic Culture Survey and State Folklorist Program of the Pennsylvania Historical and Museum Commission." *Keystone Folklore Quar.*, vol. 14 (1969), 166–75.

EA26 Jagendorf, Moritz. "Charles Godfrey Leland—Neglected Folklorist." *N.Y. Folklore Quar.*, vol. 19, no. 3 (1963), 211–19.

EA27 Kieffer, Elizabeth C. "Joseph Henry Dubbs as a Folklorist." *Pa. Folklife*, vol. 9, no. 1 (1958), 32–35. Professor of history and archaeology at Franklin and Marshall College until his death in 1910.

EA28 Kliewer, Warren. "Collecting Folklore among Mennonites." *Mennonite Life*, vol. 16 (1961), 109–12.

EA29 Leach, MacEdward, and Henry Glassie. *A Guide for Collectors of Oral Traditions and Folk Cultural Material in Pennsylvania.* Harrisburg: Pennsylvania Historical and Museum Commission, 1968. 70p. Suggestions on what to collect; examples of Pennsylvania lore.

EA30 Leach, Maria, and Jerome Fried. *The Standard Dictionary of Folklore, Mythology, and Legend.* Vol. 2: J–Z. New York: Funk & Wagnalls, 1950, p.533–1196. Rev. by C. Grant Loomis, *Western Folklore*, vol. 10, no. 3 (1951), 265–66; B. P. Miller, *Southern Folklore Quar.*, vol. 20, no. 2 (1951), 171–72. Incl. the folklore of the Pennsylvania Germans.

EA31 Lomax, Alan, and Sidney Robertson. *American Folksong and Folklore: A Regional Bibliography.* New York: Progressive Educ. Assoc., 1942.

EA32 Pieske, Christa. "Volkskundliche Aktivitäten in Pennsylvanien." *Zeitschrift für Volkskunde*, vol. 76 (1980), 89–92.

EA33 Reichmann, Felix. "The Landis Valley Museum. Objectives of a Pennsylvania Dutch Folklore Museum." *Publs., Pa. German Folklore Soc.*, vol. 7 (1942), 95–102.

EA34 Roth, Juliana. "Travel Journals as a Folklife Research Tool: Impressions of the Pennsylvania Dutch." *Pa. Folklife*, vol. 21, no. 4 (1971–1972), 28–38. Discussion and bibliography of journals and diaries describing life and customs of early Pennsylvania.

EA35 Shoemaker, Alfred L. "The Last Five Years." *The Pa. Dutchman*, vol. 5, no. 15 (1954), 3, 6. Work of the Pennsylvania Dutch Folklore Center at Franklin and Marshall College.

EA36 Shupp, Leonard E. "The Reverend Thomas Royce Brendle." "'S Pennsylfawnisch Deitsch Eck," Allentown *Morning Call*, 11 June 1966. Pennsylvania German folklorist.

EA37 Taft, Michael, comp. "A Bibliography for Folklore Studies in Nova Scotia." In: *Three Atlantic Bibliographies*. Comp. H. F. McGee, Jr., S. A. Davis, and M. Taft. Halifax: St. Mary's Univ. Dept. of Anthropology, 1975, p.102–205.

EA38 Thill, Richard S. "History and Purpose of the Omaha Folklore Project: A Synopsis Prepared for the Membership of the Nebraska Assoc. of Teachers of German." *Tenn. Folklore Soc., Bull.*, vol. 41 (1975), 175–77.

EA39 Viereck, Wolfgang. "Volkstums-Forscher in Chicago gesucht." *Abendpost* (Chicago), 8 January 1967, p.8.

EA40 Yoder, Don. "Folklife Studies Bibliography 1964. Periodicals, Part 1." *Pa. Folklife*, vol. 14, no. 4 (1965), 60–64.

EA41 Yoder, Don. "The Folklife Studies Movement." *Pa. Folklife*, vol. 13, no. 3 (1963), 43–57. A brief for the study of cultures of non-primitive areas in both their material and their oral phases.

EA42 Yoder, Don. "German Folklore in America: Discussion." In: *The German Language in America: A Symposium*. Ed. Glenn G. Gilbert. Austin: Univ. of Texas Pr., 1971, p.148–63.

EA43 Yoder, Don. "The Newspaper and Folklife Studies." *Pa. Folklife*, vol. 15, no. 3 (Spring 1966), 16–23. Excerpts and summaries of articles which appeared in the *Nordwestliche Post*, of Sunbury, Pa., in 1822.

EA44 Yoder, Don. "Pennsylvania German Folklore Research: A Historical Analysis." In: *The German Language in America: A Symposium*. Ed. G. G. Gilbert. Austin: Univ. of Texas Pr., 1971, p.70–105.

EA45 Yoder, Don. "Pennsylvania German and High German: Folk Cultural Questionnaire No. 19." *Pa. Folklife*, vol. 20, no. 3 (1971), 47.

General

See also Section AK: German-American Commemorations / Festivals / Celebrations *and* Museums / Resorations / Festivals / Tour Guides *under* Section BH: The Pennsylvania Germans.

EA46 Abernethy, Francis E. "Texas Folklore and German Culture." In: *Texas and Germany: Crosscurrents*. Ed. Joseph Wilson. Rice Univ. Studies, vol. 63, no. 3. Houston: Rice Univ., 1977, p.83–99.

EA47 Abernethy, Francis E., ed. *The Folklore of Texas Cultures*. Publs., Texas Folklore Soc., no. 38. Austin: Encino Pr., 1974.

EA48 Abernethy, Francis E., ed. *Some Still Do: Essays on Texas Customs*. Publs., Texas Folklore Soc., no. 39. Austin: Encino Pr., 1975.

EA49 Abernethy, Francis E. *What's Going On? (In Modern Texas Folklore)*. Publs., Texas Folklore Soc., no. 40. Austin: Encino Pr., 1976. 309p.

EA50 Beam, C. Richard. "Die Rumleefer (Tramps)." *Hist. Schaefferstown Record*, vol. 8 (1974), 59–60.

EA51 Best, Martha S. "The Folk Festival Seminars: Crafts and Customs of the Year." *Pa. Folklife*, vol. 18, no. 4 (Summer 1969).

EA52 Botkin, B. A., ed. *A Treasury of American Folklore*. New York: Crown Publs., 1944.

EA53 Brednich, Rolf W. *Mennonite Folklife and Folklore: A Preliminary Report*. Canadian Centre for Folk Culture Study. Papers. Ottawa: National Museum of Canada, 1977. 116p. Rev. by L. Klippenstein, *Canad. Ethnic Studies*, vol. 11 (1979), 184–85.

EA54 Byington, Robert H., and Kenneth S. Goldstein, eds. *Two Penny Ballads and Four Dollar Whiskey: a Pennsylvania Folklore Miscellany*. Hatboro: Folklore Associates for the Pa. Folklore Soc., 1966.

EA55 Camp, Charles, and Lucyann Kerry. *Voices of Tradition: Scenes and Stories of Maryland Folk Culture.* Film. Rev. by D. E. Whisnant, *Jour. of Amer. Folklore*, vol. 92 (ca. 1979), 516–17.

EA56 Connor, William L. "The Folk Culture of the Pennsylvania German: Its Value in Modern Education." *Publs., Pa. German Folklore Soc.*, no. 5 (1940), 1–46.

EA57 Costello, John R. "Cultural Vestiges and Cultural Blends among the Pennsylvania Germans." *N.Y. Folklore*, vol. 3 (1977), 101–13.

EA58 Creighton, Helen. *The Folklore of Lunenburg County, Nova Scotia.* Ottawa: E. Cloutier, 1950. 163p. Repr. Toronto: McGraw-Hill-Ryerson, 1976. Rev. by R. W. Boggs, *Southern Folklore Quar.*, vol. 15, no. 1 (1951), 17; *Canad. Hist. Rev.*, vol. 32, no. 2 (1951), 184. The people of the county are largely descended from German stock.

EA59 Dorson, Richard M. *Buying the Wind.* Chicago: Univ. of Chicago Pr., 1964. 600p. Rev. by P. H. Kennedy, *Southern Folklore Quar.*, vol. 21, no. 3 (September 1967), 287–90. Folklore of the U.S. by regions. Chap. 2 is devoted to the Pennsylvania Germans.

EA60 Dyck, Ruth, comp. "Ethnic Folklore in Canada: A Preliminary Survey." *Canad. Ethnic Studies*, vol. 7, no. 2 (1975), 90–101.

EA61 Evans, E. Estyn. "A Pennsylvania Folk Festival." *Ulster Folklife*, vol. 5 (1959), 14–19. Repr. in *Pa. Folklife*, vol. 12, no. 1 (1961), 44–48.

EA62 "Folklore of the Germans from Russia." Unpublished. Paper from Millard Lefler Junior High School, Lincoln, Nebraska. In the library of the Colorado State Univ.

EA63 Frey, J. William. "Remnants of Folklore in Eastern York County [Pa.]." "'S Pennsylfawnisch Deitsch Eck," Allentown *Morning Call*, 26 June 1943.

EA64 Geissler, Friedmar. "German Parallels to California Folk Beliefs." *Western Folklore*, vol. 19, no. 3 (July 1960), 199–200.

EA65 Gillespie, Angus K. "Pennsylvania Folk Festivals in the 1930's." *Pa. Folklife*, vol. 26, no. 1 (1976), 2–11.

EA66 Glanz, Rudolf. *The Jew in the old American Folklore.* New York: n.p., 1961. 294p. With bibliography.

EA67 Green, Archie. "John Neuhaus: Wobbly Folklorist." *Jour. of Amer. Folklore*, vol. 73, no. 289 (1960), 189–217. Mainly on ethnic industrial slang as recited by Neuhaus.

EA68 Hand, Wayland D., ed. *North Carolina Folklore: Popular Beliefs and Superstitions.* Durham: Duke Univ. Pr., 1961. 664p.

EA69 Hand, Wayland D., ed. *Popular Beliefs and Superstitions from North Carolina.* II. 4874–8569. Frank C. Brown Collection of North Carolina Folklore, no. 7. Durham: Duke Univ. Pr., 1964. 677p. Rev. by E. W. Wilborn, *N. Car. Hist. Rev.*, vol. 41, no. 4 (1964), 485–86.

EA70 Hess, Albert. "Deutsche Bräuche und Volkslieder in Maryhill (Waterloo County, Ontario)." *German-Canad. Yearbook*, vol. 3 (1976), 220–24.

EA71 Heilbron, Bertha L. "North Star Folklore in Minnesota History: A Bibliography." *Western Folklore*, vol. 9, no. 4 (1951), 366–71. Incl. the Germans and their influence in Minnesota.

EA72 High, N. H., W. G. Schweitzer, and J. W. Dyck, eds. *Canad.-German Folklore*, vol. 1. N.p.: Pa. German Folklore Soc. of Ontario, 1961. 144p. Rev. by P. A. Barba, "'S Pennsylfawnisch Deitsch Eck," Allentown *Morning Call*, 27 January 1962; *Amer.-German Rev.*, vol. 29, no. 2 (1962), 37. Twenty-four articles on the life and lore of Germans in Ontario.

EA73 Hoffman, W. J. "Folklore of the Pennsylvania Germans." "'S Pennsylfawnisch Deitsch Eck," Allentown *Morning Call*, 28 March, 4, 11, 18, 25 April 1959. Repr. of an article publ. in the *Jour. of Amer. Folklore* for July–September 1888.

EA74 Horst, Mary A. *Pennsylvania Dutch Fun, Folklore and Cooking.* Kitchener, Ont.: n.p., ca. 1977. 63p.

EA75 Hydinger, Gary D. "The Pennsylvania Germans: Folklore Studies from Autobiographical Sources." *Pa. Folklife*, vol. 26, no. 1 (1976), 25–33.

EA76 Johnson, Gilbert. "Swabian Folkways." *Saskatchewan Hist.*, vol. 13, no. 2 (1960), 73–75.

General Works—Backgrounds

EA77 Klymasz, Robert, ed. "Ethnic Folklore in Canada." *Canad. Ethnic Studies*, vol. 7, no. 2 (1975), 3–127.

EA78 Koch, William E., ed. *Folklore from Kansas: Customs, Beliefs, and Superstititons.* Lawrence: Regents Pr. of Kans., 1980. 467p.

EA79 Korson, George. *Black Rock; Mining Folklore of the Pennsylvania Dutch.* Publ. of the Pa. German Soc., no. 59. Baltimore: Johns Hopkins Univ. Pr., 1960. 453p. Rev. by J. F. Schmidt, *Mennonite Life*, vol. 17, no. 4 (1962), 191.

EA80 Korson, George, ed. *Pennsylvania Songs and Legends.* Philadelphia: Univ. of Pennsylvania Pr., 1949. 474p. Songs, legends, medical lore, proverbs, and tales. Rev. by A. E. Fife, *Western Folklore*, vol. 9, no. 2 (1950), 178–79; R. E. Gard, *Wis. Mag. of Hist.*, vol. 34, no. 2 (1951), 114–15. Incl. songs and tales of the Amish.

EA81 Kramer, Frank R. *Voices in the Valley: Mythmaking and Folk Belief in the Shaping of the Middle West.* Madison: Univ. of Wisconsin Pr., 1964. 300p.

EA82 Krapf, Norman. *Finding the Grain: Pioneer Journals, Franconian Folktales, Ancestral Poems.* Jasper, Ind.: Dubois County Hist. Soc. and Herald Printing, 1977. 120p. Rev. by J. J. Detzler, *The Old Northwest*, vol. 3 (1977), 465–67; K. P. McCutchan, *Ind. Mag. of Hist.*, vol. 74 (1978), 161–62; D. H. Tolzmann, *Jour. of German-Amer. Studies*, vol. 13 (1978), 25.

EA83 Kreider, Mary Catherine. "Languages and Folklore of the 'Hoffmansleit' (United Christians)." M.A. thesis, Pennsylvania State Univ., 1956.

EA84 Kring, Hilda Adam. "The Harmonists—A Folk-Cultural Approach." Diss., Univ. of Pennsylvania, 1969. 308p.

EA85 Lacey, Laurie, ed. *Lunenburg County* [Nova Scotia] *Folklore and Oral History Project '77.* Ottawa: National Museums of Canada, 1979.

EA86 Long, Amos. "The Rural Village." *Pa. Folklife*, vol. 29 (1979–1980), 124–32.

EA87 Milnes, Humphrey. "German Folklore in Ontario." *Jour. of Amer. Folklore*, vol. 67 (1954), 35–43.

EA88 Mumaw, John R. "Folklore among the Pennsylvania Germans in Wayne County, Ohio." M. A. Thesis, Univ. of Virginia, 1931.

EA89 Nielsen, George R. "Folklore of the German-Wends in Texas." In: *Singers and Storytellers.* Texas Folklore Soc. Publs., no. 30. Dallas: Southern Methodist Univ. Pr., 1961, p.244–59. Folk cures, wedding and funeral customs, beliefs and practices.

EA90 Pennsylvania Folklore Society of Ontario. *Canad.-German Folklore.* Vol. 2. Waterloo: Pennsylvania German Folklore Soc. of Ontario, 1967. 96p.

EA91 Reaman, G. Elmore. "Folklore, Folk Art and Characteristic Foods of the Province of Ontario." *German-Canad. Rev.*, vol. 10, no. 1 (1957), 8–10.

EA92 Sackett, S. J., and William E. Koch. *Kansas Folklore.* Lincoln: Univ. of Nebraska Pr., 1961. 225p. Rev. by W. Kliewer, *Mennonite Life*, vol. 17, no. 4 (1962), 191. On cooking and customs.

EA93 Schroeder, Adolf E. "The Contexts of Continuity: German Folklore in Missouri." *Kans. Quar.*, vol. 13 (1981), 89–102.

EA94 Schroeder, Adolf E. "The Survival of German Traditions in Missouri." In: *The German Contribution to the Building of the Americas: Studies in Honor of Karl J. R. Arndt.* Ed. G. K. Friesen and W. Schatzberg. Hanover: Univ. Press of New England, 1977, p.289–313.

EA95 Shaner, Richard H. *The America That Didn't Die; A Twentieth Century Folk Cultural Study of the Oley Valley of Pennsylvania.* Photographs by Robert Walch. Laureldale: Hunsberger Printers, 1971. 40p.

EA96 Shaner, Richard H. "Taverns and Tavern Lore of Dutchland." *Pa. Folklife*, vol. 22 (1973), Folk Festival Supplement, p.31–35.

EA97 Smith, Elmer L. "Shenandoah Valley Folklore." "The Almanac and Snow in July." "The Dog Days." "Decorated Brick Barns." "Summer Snow Scenes." "Whooping in the Hopper." "New Market Gunmaker." "All But the Squeal!" "'S Pennsylfawnisch Deitsch Eck," Allentown *Morning Call*, 13 July, 3, 10, 17 August, 2, 9 November, 14 December 1967.

EA98 Smith, Elmer L., and John G. Stewart. "Pennsylvania German Folklore in the Shenandoah Valley." "'S Pennsylfawnisch Deitsch Eck," Allentown *Morning Call*, 7, 13 April, 8–29 June, 6, 13 July, 7–28 September, 23, 30 November, 7–28 December 1963; 1, 8, 15 February, 14, 21 March 1964.

EA99 Starr, Frederick. "Some Pennsylvania German Lore." "'S Pennsylfawnisch Deitsch Eck," Allentown *Morning Call*, 15 August 1959. Repr. of an article publ. in the *Jour. of Amer. Folklore*, October and December 1891.

EA100 Stoudt, John Baer. *The Folklore of the Pennsylvania German*. Publs., Pa. German Soc., vol. 23. Part III. The Soc., 1972. p.3–155. Incl. 2 chapters on the Pennsylvania German ballad.

EA101 Stoudt, John Joseph. "Pennsylvania German Folklore. An Interpretation." *Publs., Pa. German Folklore Soc.*, vol. 16 (ca. 1952), 157–70.

EA102 Thonger, Richard. *A Calendar of German Customs*. Chester Springs: Dufour Editions, 1968. Food and drink, courting, rhymes and games through the seasons. Illus. with woodcuts, drawings and old engravings.

EA103 Troyer, Les. *Pennsylvania Dutch Lore*. Katmandu: Nepal: Summer Institute of Linguistics, Tribhuvan Univ., 1974. On the Amish of Holmes County.

EA104 Trumbore, Mark S. *A Superficial Collection of Pennsylvania German Erotic Folklore*. Pennsburg, Pa.: n.p., 1978. 90p.

EA105 Wintemberg, W. J. *Folklore of Waterloo County, Ontario*. Ottawa: King's Printer, 1950. 68p.

EA106 Wust, Klaus. "Folklore, Customs and Crafts of the [Shenandoah] Valley Settlers." *Hist. Preservation*, vol. 20, nos. 3–4 (1968), 28–39. An illustrated survey of German folklife.

EA107 Yoder, Don, ed. *American Folklife*. Austin: Univ. of Texas Pr., 1976. 304p. Incl. some references to German-American New Year's customs in the South.

EA108 Yoder, Don, ed. "Collectanea: Ore Mining and Basket Weaving in Maxatawny, the Sharadin Tannery at Kutztown, Occult Lore Recorded in Cumberland County." *Pa. Folklife*, vol. 26, no. 2 (1976–1977), 38.

EA109 Yoder, Don H. "Folklore from the Hegins and Mahantongo Valleys." "'S Pennsylfawnisch Deitsch Eck," Allentown *Morning Call*, 4–25 October, 2–22 November 1947.

EB

Sayings and Stories

Tale and Story

EB1 Barba, Preston A. "Der Tambour Yockel." "'S Pennsylfawnisch Deitsch Eck," Allentown *Morning Call*, 16 July 1949. Tambour Yockel was said to have challenged the Devil in the graveyard of the East Salisbury Church.

EB2 Beam, C. Richard. "Eulenspiegel in Pennsylvania." *Der Reggeboge*, vol. 5, no. 1 (1971), 3–6.

EB3 Bonner, Willard H. "The Flying Dutchman of the Western World." *Jour. of Amer. Folklore*, vol. 59, no. 223 (1946), 282–88. Captain Kidd in the 19th century legend "owes much to German folk lore."

EB4 Boyer, Walter E. "Adam and Eva im Paradies." *The Pa. Dutchman*, vol. 8, no. 2 (1957), 14–18. Popular broadsides published by German printers before 1850.

EB5 Brednich, Rolf W. "Hutterische Volkserzählungen." *Canad.-German Yearbook*, vol. 6 (1981), 199–224.

EB6 Brendle, Thomas Royce, and William S. Troxell, eds. and trans. *Pennsylvania German Folk Tales, Legends, Once-Upon-A-Time Stories, Maxims, and Sayings Spoken in the Dialect Popularly Known as the Pennsylvania Dutch.* Norristown: Pa. German Soc., 1944. 238p. Rev. by P. Schach, *Hist. Rev. of Berks Co.*, vol. 11, no. 1 (1945), 22.

EB7 Brown, Frank. "New Light on 'Mountain Mary'." *Pa. Folklife*, vol. 15, no. 3 (Spring 1966), 10–15. Widow of a German immigrant killed in the American Revolution. Her generosity became legendary.

EB8 Clarke, Kenneth, and Mary Clarke. "Another Note on Münchhausen Motifs." *Jour. of Amer. Folklore*, vol. 74, no. 292 (1961), 149–52. Münchhausen lore, types 1881 and 1900, in a telling by Charles Hanes of Colusa, California.

EB9 Dorson, Richard M. "More about Paul Bunyan and Holländer Michel." *Jour. of Amer. Folklore*, vol. 65, no. 257 (1952), 306–07. Expresses his doubts concerning Hauff's influence.

EB10 Gorelick, J. "Two Anecdotes of Immigrant Life." Trans. from the Yiddish by B. A. Botkin. *N.Y. Folklore Quar.*, vol. 18, no. 1 (Spring 1962), 65–67.

EB11 Gudde, Erwin G. "An American Version of Munchhausen." *Amer. Lit.*, vol. 13, no. 4 (1942), 372–90.

EB12 Hand, Wayland D. "Die Märchen der Brüder Grimm in den Vereinigten Staaten." In: *Brüder Grimm Gedenken 1963.* Ed. Ludwig Denecke and Ina-Maria Greverus. Hessische Blätter für Volkskunde, no. 54. Marburg: Elwert, 1963, p.525–44.

EB13 Heisey, M. Luther. "Stories Radiating from Conestoga Centre." *Papers of the Lancaster Co. Hist. Soc.*, vol. 56, no. 1 (1952), 1–19. Pennsylvania German folklore.

EB14 Helpert, Herbert, and Emma Robinson. "'Oregon' Smith, an Indian Folk Hero." *Southern Folklore Quar.*, vol. 6, no. 3 (1942), 163–68. At least one of this collection of stories is taken from Münchhausen.

EB15 Hudson, Wilson M. "Another Mexican Version of the Story of the Bear's Son." *Southern Folklore Quar.*, vol. 15, no. 2 (1951), 152–58. Notes the Germanic influences in this tale.

EB16 Jones, George Fenwick. "Reineke Fuchs and Brer Rabbit—Oral or Written Tradition." In: *Vistas and Vectors. A Volume Honoring The Memory of Helmut Rehder.* Ed. Lee B. Jennings and G. Schulz-Behrend. Austin: Dept. of Germanic Langs., Univ. of Texas, 1977.

EB17 Mankin, Carolyn. "Tales the German Texans Tell." In: *Singers and Storytellers.* Publs. of the Texas Folklore Soc., no. 30. Dallas: Southern Methodist Univ. Pr., 1961, p.260–65. Gives texts of seven tales.

EB18 Merritt, Arthur H. "Did Parson Weems Really Invent the Cherry Tree Story?" *N.Y. Hist. Soc. Quar.*, vol. 40 (1956), 252–63. A German-made tankard of 1776 depicts a scene similar to the cherry tree episode; it may indicate a European source for the story.

EB19 Minderhout, Mary Alice. *Pennsylvania German Mini-Units, 4th Grade: Holidays and Folk Art. The Folktale of Regina Leininger of the Pennsylvania Germans.* New Holland, Pa.: BESL Center, n.d.

EB20 Randolph, Mary Claire. "Red Satires and the Pied Piper of Hamelin." *Southern Folklore Quar.*, vol. 5, no. 2 (1941), 81–100. Parallels between the Germanic folk legend and Celtic folk satires.

EB21 Shoemaker, Alfred L. "Adam and Eve Broadsides." *The Pa. Dutchman*, vol. 4, no. 6 (October 1952), 4–5.

EB22 Smith, Grace P. "The European Origin of an Illinois Tale." *Southern Folklore Quar.*, vol. 6, no. 2 (1942), 89–94. Old World sources, mostly German, reached the New World in the form of a local legend.

EB23 "Spook Stories." *The Pa. Dutchman*, vol. 5, no. 9 (1954), 8–9. Ghost stories collected in Berks Co.

EB24 Thomas, J. Wesley. "Paul Bunyan and Holländer Michel." *Jour. of Amer. Folklore*, vol. 65, no. 257 (1952), 305–06. Comparison of Hauff's lumberjack with that of the American legend.

EB25 Weigel, Lawrence. "Laughter, A Good Medicine: Humorous Stories Told by Our People." *Jour. of the Amer. Hist. Soc. of Germans from Russia*, vol. 4, no. 2 (1981), 23–35.

EB26 Whittier, John Greenleaf. "Magicians and Witch Folk. Margaret Smith's Journal; Tales and Sketches." In: *The Writings of John Greenleaf Whittier*, Riverside Edition. Vol. 5. Boston: Houghton Mifflin & Co., 1866, 1904, p.399–411.

EB27 Yoder, Don. "The Saint's Legend in the Pennsylvania German Folk Culture." In: *UCLA Conference on American Folk Legend*. Pref. by W. D. Hand. Los Angeles: Univ. of California Pr., 1971, p.157–83.

Riddles / Proverbs / Inscriptions

EB28 Barrick, Mac E. "Early Proverbs from Carlisle, Pennsylvania (1788–1821)." *Keystone Folklore Quar.*, vol. 13 (1968), 193–218.

EB29 Becker, A., comp. "Pennsylvania German Riddles." "'S Pennsylfawnisch Deitsch Eck," Allentown *Morning Call*, 20, 27 August 1966.

EB30 Burress, Lee A., Jr. "Folklore Collecting in Wisconsin." *Jour. of the Ohio Folklore Soc.*, vol. 2, no. 3 (Autumn 1967), 125–33. Incl. collected sayings, many showing a syntactical relationship with German.

EB31 "Early Epitaphs of Goschenhoppen." *The Goschenhoppen Region*, vol. 1, no. 2 (Aller Heil 1968); vol. 1, no. 3 (Lichtmess 1969), 20.

EB32 Gabel, Marie. "Proverbs of Volga German Settlers in Ellis County [Kans.]." *Heritage of Kans.*, vol. 9, nos. 2–3 (1976), 55–58.

EB33 Gerhard, Elmer S. "Some Pennsylvania German Proverbs." *Hist. Rev. of Berks Co.*, vol. 20, no. 3 (1955), 71–75, 93–95.

EB34 Hommel, Rudolf. "Tavern Inscriptions." *Amer.-German Rev.*, vol. 9, no. 1 (1942), 31–32. In Bucks County.

EB35 Kaiser, Leo M. "German Verse in American Cemeteries." *Amer.-German Rev.*, vol. 26, no. 4 (1960), 25–28.

EB36 Kaiser, Leo M. "German Verse in Missouri Churchyards." *Zeitschrift für Kulturaustausch*, vol. 12, no. 4 (1962), 319–22. Gravestone verse inscribed in the period 1866 to 1917.

EB37 Kliewer, Warren. "Low German Children's Rimes." *Mennonite Life*, vol. 14 (1959), 141–42. Notes on the dialect verses preserved at Mountain Lake, Minnesota.

EB38 Kliewer, Warren. "Low German Proverbs." "More Low German Children's Rhymes." "Low German Sayings." *Mennonite Life*, vol. 13 (April 1958), 66; vol. 15 (October 1960), 173; vol. 15 (April 1960), 77.

EB39 Kloberdanz, Timothy J. "Proverbs and Proverbial Expressions among the Germans from Russia." *Jour. of the Amer. Hist. Soc. of Germans from Russia*, vol. 2, no. 1 (1979), 29–31.

EB40 Koch, Mary. "Volga German Proverbs and Proverbial Expressions from the Colony of Dreispitz." *Jour. of the Amer. Hist. Soc. of Germans from Russia*, vol. 2, no. 1 (1979), 32–37.

EB41 Kraemer, Julius. *Sprichwort Wahrwort*. Kaiserslautern: n.p., 1962. 62p. Rev. by P. A. Barba, "'S Pennsylfawnisch Deitsch Eck," Allentown *Morning Call*, 10 February 1962. On proverbs.

EB42 Kramer, Edmund P. *German Proverbs with Their English Counterparts*. Stanford: Stanford Univ. Pr., 1955. 116p. Rev. by J. B. MacLean, *Mod. Lang. Quar.*, vol. 18 (1957), 74–77.

EB43 Rubin, Ruth. "Yiddish Sayings and English Equivalents." *N.Y. Folklore Quar.*, vol. 15 (1959), 91–92.

EB44 Smith, Elmer L., and J. G. Stewart. "Shenandoah Valley Sayings." "'S Pennsylfawnisch Deitsch Eck," Allentown *Morning Call*, 5 June 1965.

EB45 Shoemaker, Alfred L. *Traditional Rhymes and Jingles of the Pennsylvania Dutch*. Lancaster: n.p., 1951.

EB46 Stoudt, John B. "Pennsylvania German Riddles and Nursery Rhymes." *Jour. of Amer. Folk-*

lore, vol. 19 (1906), 113-31. Incl. "Pennsylvania German Cradle Songs."

EB47 Weigel, Lawrence A. "German Proverbs from around Fort Hays, Kansas." *Western Folklore*, vol. 18 (1959), 98.

EC
Folk Music

Folk Song

See also Section GB: Secular Song.

EC1 Albrecht, Erich A. "Ein deutschamerikanisches Regenlied." *German-Amer. Studies*, vol. I, no. 1 (1969), 1-2.

EC2 Barba, Preston A. "In Polen steht ein Haus." "'S Pennsylfawnisch Deitsch Eck," Allentown *Morning Call*, 3 April 1948. Pennsylvania German version of a familiar folksong.

EC3 Begemann, Renate. "Die Lieder der Pennsylvania-deutschen in ihrem sozialen Kontext: Eine Analyse der Brendleschen Sammlung 1935-1950." Diss., Univ. Marburg, 1973. 335p.

EC4 Benjamin, Steven M. "The German-American Folksong. A Bibliographic Report." *Jour. of German-Amer. Studies*, vol. 14, no. 3 (1979), 140-44.

EC5 Bluestein, Eugene. "The Background and Sources of an American Folksong Tradition." Diss., Univ. of Minnesota, 1961. On Herder's theory of the folksong as the basis of national literatures.

EC6 Boyer, Walter E. "The Folksong Tradition in the Mahantongo Valley." *Northumberland Co. Hist. Soc., Procs. and Addrs.*, vol. 21 (1957), 148-62.

EC7 Boyer, Walter E. "The German Broadside Songs of Pennsylvania." *Pa. Folklife*, vol. 10, no. 1 (Spring 1959), 14-19.

EC8 Boyer, Walter E., Albert F. Buffington, and Don H. Yoder. *Songs Along the Mahantongo: Pennsylvania Dutch Folksongs*. Lancaster, Pa.: Pa. Dutch Folklore Center, 1951. Repr. Hatboro: Folklore Associates, 1964. 232p. Repr. Detroit: Gale Research Co. Rev. by J. Evanston, *Pa. Hist.*, vol. 19, no. 1 (1952), 111-12; J. G. Frank, *Monatshefte*, vol. 44, no. 2 (1952), 120-21; *Amer.-German Rev.*, vol. 18, no. 4 (1952), 34; A. D. Graeff, *Amer.-German Rev.*, vol. 17, no. 5 (1951), 37; A. Taylor, *Western Folklore*, vol. 25, no. 3 (July 1966), 207-08; R. C. Wood, "'S Pennsylfawnisch Deitsch Eck," Allentown *Morning Call*, 30 June 1951.

EC9 Brendle, Thomas. "Collecting Dialect Folk Songs." *Pa. Folklife*, vol. 11, no. 1 (1960), 50-52.

EC10 Brendle, Thomas, and William S. Troxell. "Pennsylvania German Songs." In: *Pennsylvania Songs and Legends*. Ed. George Korson. Philadelphia: Univ. of Pa. Pr., 1949, p.62-128. Contains 28 of the 200 songs in the Brendle-Troxell collection of folksong recordings at the Fackenthal Library, Franklin and Marshall College.

EC11 Britton, George. *Pennsylvania Dutch Folksongs*. Folkways Records, FA 2215; FP 615. Rev. in *Keystone Folklore Quar.*, vol. 1 (1956-1957), 29-30. Fourteen secular folksongs in Pennsylvania German dialect. With book of texts, translations and note. Roundup Records, Box 474, Somerville, Mass.

EC12 Bucher, Robert C., Clarence Kulp, Jr., and Alan G. Keyser, the "Goschenhoppen historians." Recorded folksongs of the Plain people of the Goschenhoppen area north of Philadelphia.

EC13 Buffington, Albert F. *Pennsylvania German Secular Folksongs*. Publs., Pa. German Soc., no. 8. Breinigsville: Pa. German Soc. 1974. 182p.

EC14 *Datt Drunne Deheem*. Lewis, Delaware: Arcadia Pr., 1974. Recorded Pennsylvania German songs and sayings.

EC15 Dinges, Herman, producer. *Schoencheneers German Folk Songs*. LP record. Copy at Greeley, Colorado, Public Library.

EC16 Frey, J. William. "The Folksong Tradition." In: *In the Dutch Country*. Lancaster: Pa. Dutch Folklore Center, 1953, p.40.

EC17 Frey, J. William. *Folksongs of the Pennsylvania Dutch. Interpreted by J. William Frey*. 3 sound discs. 78 rpm. Rutherford, N. J.: Nelson Cornell, n.d.

EC18 Frey, J. William, ed. "The Dutch in Word and Song." *The Pa. Dutchman*, vol. 1–5 (1941–1945). Regular feature.

EC19 Graeff, Marie K. "Folk Songs." *Pa. Folklife*, vol. 31 (1981–1982), 20–25.

EC20 Hark, Ann. "Trauer-Lieder." *Amer.-German Rev.*, vol. 27, no. 1 (1960–1961), 27–30. The ballad of Susanna Cox and other songs and stories of the Pennsylvania German area.

EC21 [Henkel, Paul.] *Kurzer Zeitvertreib, Bestehend in einigen Liedern, dienlich zur Sittenlehre*. New Market, Va.: n.p., 1812. 3rd ed. In the Sheeleigh Collection, Gettysburg Theological Seminary.

EC22 Hergert, Elias. *Das Köstliche Schatz*. 11th ed. Portland, Ore.: n.p., n.d. 422p. Songs of the Germans from Russia.

EC23 Hess, Albert. "Deutsche Bräuche und Volkslieder in Maryhill (Waterloo County, Ontario)." *German-Canad. Yearbook*, vol. 3 (1976), 220–24.

EC24 Homan, Wayne F. "The Sorrow Song of Susanna Cox." *Pa. Folklife*, vol. 20, no. 4 (1971), 14–16.

EC25 Jackson, George P. "'Frog Went Accourting' and Two German Kindred Songs." *Southern Folklore Quar.*, vol. 13, no. 2 (1949), 133–35.

EC26 Kloberdanz, Timothy J. "'We Sing Our History': Oral Tradition and the Germans from Russia." In: *Germans from Russia in Colorado*. Ed. Sidney Haitman. Ann Arbor, Mich.: University Microfilms, 1978, p.145–59.

EC27 Long, Amos, Jr. "Dutch Country Scarecrows." *Pa. Folklife*, vol. 12, no. 3 (Fall 1961), 54–59. Songs, verses and tales about the scarecrow.

EC28 Mattson, Jeremy. "The Comic Song in the American Midwest, 1825–1875." *Mid-America* (Mich. State), vol. 4 (1977), 30–55. Incl. songs on ethnic subjects and songs that "express a sense of comic wonder at the newness of the country."

EC29 "A New Mournful Song Containing the History of Susanna Cox, Who Was Hanged in Reading for Infanticide, In the Year 1809, from the German." "'S Pennsylfawnisch Deitsch Eck," Allentown *Morning Call*, 22 July 1944. With the original German text.

EC30 Owens, William A. *Texas Folk Songs*. Publs. of the Texas Folklore Soc., no. 23. Austin: 1950.

EC31 *Pennsylvania Folk Songs and Ballads for School, Camp, and Playground*. Lewisburg, Pa.: Folk Festival at Bucknell Univ., 1937. Forew. by George Korson. Arrangements for voice and piano.

EC32 Pfannenstiel, Nick J., and Lawrence A. Weigel. "German Folk Songs from Ellis County [Kans.]." *Heritage of Kans.*, vol. 9, nos. 2–3 (1976), 17–30.

EC33 Rubin, Ruth. "Nineteenth Century History in Yiddish Folksong." *N.Y. Folklore Quar.*, vol. 15 (1959), 220–28.

EC34 Rubin, Ruth. *Voices of a People: The Story of Yiddish Folk Song*. New York: T. Yoseloff, 1963. Rev. by E. Richmond, *Jour. of Amer. Folklore*, vol. 79, (1966), 489–90.

EC35 Rubin, Ruth. "Yiddish Folksongs of Immigration and the Melting Pot." *N.Y. Folklore Quar.*, vol. 17 (1961), 173–82. Also in: *Recall*, vol. 2 (1961), 4–12. Texts, translations, and brief histories of songs.

EC36 Recktenwald, Lester N. "A Pioneer Woman's Songs and Proverbs." *Minn. Hist.*, vol. 30, no. 2 (1949), 135–37. Were originally sung in German, Dutch, or English.

EC37 Schroeder, Adolf E. "Nineteenth Century Folksong Collectors." *Semasia. Beiträge zur germanisch-romanischen Sprachforshung*, vol. 2 (1975).

EC38 Schroeder, Adolf E. "Traditional Song Current in the Midwest." In: *Proceedings of the In-*

ternational Centenary Conference of the Folklore Society. Ed. Venetia Newall. London: n.p., 1981, p.384–90.

EC39 Shaw, Gaylord. "Hays: America's Fertile Heritage." *Los Angeles Times*, 4 July 1975. On folksong collecting in Kansas.

EC40 *Sing Schticker*. Shillington, Pa.: Baerricks Kounty Fersommlinge. Addr.: John H. Schrack, 353 Pennsylvania Ave., Shillington, Pa. 19607. Songbook for use in Berks County meetings.

EC41 Ullman, Christianne. "German Folksongs of Lunenburg County, Nova Scotia." *German-Canad. Yearbook*, vol. 5 (1979), 143–53.

EC42 Weigel, Lawrence A. "The History of the Germans from Russia Expressed in Song." *Work Papers, Amer. Hist. Soc. of Germans from Russia*, no. 18 (1975), 21–26.

EC43 Weigel, Lawrence A. "The Songs and Music of the Volga-Germans of Ellis County, Kansas." In: *Germanica-Americana 1976: German-American Literature and Culture*. Ed. E. A. Albrecht and J. Anthony Burzle. Lawrence, Kans.: Max Kade Document and Research Center, Univ. of Kansas, 1977, p.121–25.

EC44 Weigel, Lawrence A. "We Sing Our History." *Jour. of the Amer. Hist. Soc. of Germans from Russia*, no. 20 (1976), 63–65; *ibid.*, no. 23 (1977), 65–67; *ibid.*, vol. 2, *ibid.*, no. 1 (1979), 59; *ibid.*, vol. 3, no. 1 (1980), 54–56.

EC45 Weigel, Lawrence A., producer. *Volga German Music*. LP Record. Heritage Savings Assoc., Hays, Kansas, ca. 1976.

EC46 Weigel, Lawrence A., and Nick J. Pfannenstiel. *A Collection of German-Russian Folk Songs*. Hays, Kans.: Privately printed, 1962. 300 songs of the Volga Germans in Ellis Co. Tape recording included.

EC47 Wiebolt–Rosenwald Collection of German Folklore. Ca. 150,000 songs. In Univ. of Chicago Library (MS 64-179). From originals in the Deutsche Volksliederarchiv, Freiburg and elsewhere.

EC48 Wolf, Edwin. *American Song Sheets*. Philadelphia: The Library Company of Philadelphia, 1963. 205p. Rev. by G. M. Laws, *Jour. of Amer. Folklore*, vol. 77, no. 306 (October-December 1964), 366–67. Dialect songs from various ethnic groups, including the German.

EC49 Yoder, Don H. "Hegins Valley in Song and Story." "'S Pennsylfawnisch Deitsch Eck," Allentown *Morning Call*, 11, 26 January, 1, 8 February 1947.

EC50 Yoder, Don H. "Pennsylvania German Folklore Research: A Historical Analysis." In: *The German Language in America: A Symposium*. Ed. G. G. Gilbert. Austin: Univ. of Texas Pr., 1971, p.70–105. See esp. "Folksong Research," p.86–95.

EC51 Yoder, Don H. "Die Volkslieder der Pennsylvanien-Deutschen." In: *Handbuch des Deutschen Volksliedes*. Lutz Röhrich and Rolf W. Brednich. Vol. 2. Freiburg i. B.: Deutsches Volksliedarchiv, 1972.

EC52 Yoder, Don H. "Willy Brown of Mahantongo: Our Foremost Folksinger." *The Pa. Dutchman*, vol. 4, no. 2 (1952–1953), 1–3.

Dance / Folk Music

EC53 Barrick, Mac E. "Dancing in the Pig Trough." *Western Folklore*, vol. 37 (1978), 56–57.

EC54 Hartmann, Joseph E. "Folk Festival Music." *Pa. Folklife*, vol. 29, no. 4 (1979–1980), 6–7. At the Kutztown Folk Festival.

EC55 Hausman, Ruth L. *Sing and Dance with the Pennsylvania Dutch*. New York: E. B. Marks, 1953. 112p. Rev. by J. William Frey, *The Pa. Dutchman*, vol. 5, no. 7 (1953), 15; P. A. Barba, "'S Pennsylfawnisch Deitsch Eck," Allentown *Morning Call*, 3 April 1954; J. A. Hostetler, *Mennonite Quar. Rev.*, vol. 29, no. 2 (1955), 167–68. Compiled and copied from printed sources, in most cases without permission or acknowledgment.

EC56 Martens, Helen. "The Music of Some Religious Minorities in Canada." *Ethnomusicology*, vol. 16 (1972), 360–71. On the Mennonites and Hutterites.

EC57 Merrill, Peter C. "Volga German Music is Alive in Schoenchen." *Newsletter of the Soc. for*

Dance / Folk Music *(cont.)*

German-Amer. Studies, vol. 2, no. 5 (1980–1981), 7.

EC58 Murray, Sterling E. "Weeping and Mourning: Funeral Dirges in Honor of General Washington." *Jour. of the Musicological Soc.*, vol. 31 (1978), 282–308. Incl. mention of the Moravian memorial services.

EC59 Nettl, Bruno, and Helen Myers. *Folk Music in the United States: An Introduction*. Detroit: Wayne State Univ. Pr., 1976. Rev. by E. Klusen, *Zeitschrift für Volkskunde*, vol. 74 (1978), 260–61.

EC60 Shaner, Richard H. "The Amish Barn Dance." *Pa. Folklife*, vol. 13, no. 2 (Winter 1962–1963), 24–16. The Amish dance has undergone fewer changes than that of the "Gay" Dutch.

EC61 Wetzel, Richard D. *Frontier Musicians on the Connoquenessing, Wabash, and Ohio: A History of the Music and Musicians of George Rapp's Harmony Society (1805–1906)*. Athens, Ohio: Ohio Univ. Pr., 1976. 294p. Rev. by R. L. Davis, *Amer.-Heritage*, vol. 64, no. 1 (June 1977), 144–45; K. Arndt, *Monatshefte*, vol. 71, no. 1 (Spring 1979), 57–58.

EC62 Yoder, Don. "The 'Strauss Dance' of the Dutch Country—A Lost German Dance of our Forefathers?" *The Pa. Dutchman*, vol. 5, no. 11 (1954), 6–7. Known in Pennsylvania in the first half of the 19th century.

Fiddle and Dulcimer

EC63 Allen, R. Raymond. "The Fiddle Tradition in Pennsylvania." *Pa. Folklife*, vol. 31 (1981–1982), 50–55.

EC64 Feintuch, Bert H. "Pop Ziegler, Fiddler: A Study of Folkloric Performance." Diss., Univ. of Pennsylvania, 1975.

EC65 Sackett, S. J. "Hammered Dulcimer." *Sing Out* (New York), vol. 15, no. 6 (January 1966), 49–51. German-Russians in Kansas.

EC66 Sackett, S. J. "The Hammered Dulcimer in Ellis County, Kansas." *Jour. of the Internat. Folk Music Council* (London), vol. 14 (1962), 61–64. An instrument constructed by decendants of the Germans from Russia.

ED
Folklore

Folk Customs—General

ED1 "April 1—Moving Day." *Pa. Dutch News and Views*, vol. 4, no. 1 (1972), 6–7.

ED2 Bechtel, Ernest W. "The Bautz." *Der Reggeboge*, vol. 14, no. 2 (April 1980), 1–2. "The Tramp," a bogey called on to discipline children.

ED3 Brungardt, Barnard J., Phyllis A. Dinkel, and John B. Terbovich. "Volga German Customs." *Heritage of Kans.*, vol. 9, nos. 2–3 (1976), 62–71.

ED4 Craigie, Carter Walker. "A Movable Feast: The Picnic as a Folklife Custom in Chester County, Pennsylvania, 1870–1925." Diss., Univ. of Pennsylvania, 1976.

ED5 Currie, Raymond, Leo Driedger, and Rick Linder. "Abstinence and Moderation: Mixing Mennonite Drinking Norms." *Mennonite Quar. Rev.*, vol. 53, no. 4 (1979), 263–81.

ED6 DeChant, Alliene S. *Seed Time to Harvest.* Kutztown: Kutztown Publ., 1957. 159p. Rev. in *Amer.-German Rev.*, vol. 25, no. 2 (1958), 38; by D. R. Shenton, *Hist. Rev. of Berks Co.*, vol. 22, no. 3 (1958), 87–88. Customs and practices of everyday life related by an 86-year-old informant, John Z. Harner.

ED7 Estill, Julia. "Customs Among the German Descendants of Gillespie County (in 1923)." In: *The Folklore of Texan Cultures.* Ed. F. E. Abernethy. Publs. of the Texas Folklore Soc., vol. 38. Austin: Encino Pr., 1974, p.145–51. German-Texan folklife in Fredericksburg.

ED8 Gilbert, Russell W. "The Pennsylvania German in His Will." *Amer.-German Rev.*, vol. 17, no. 3 (1951), 24–26. Samples of wills from 1773 to 1836.

ED9 Gilbert, Russell W. *Pennsylvania German Wills.* Publs., Pa. German Folklore Soc., no. 15. Allentown: Schlechter's, 1951. 139p. Rev. by F. C. Rosenberger, *Pa. Hist.*, vol. 20, no. 2 (1953), 207–08.

ED10 Gilbert, Russell W. "Some Characteristics of Pennsylvania German Wills." "'S Pennsylfawnisch Deitsch Eck," Allentown *Morning Call*, 18, 25 September 1951.

ED11 Gougler, Richard C. "Amish Barn-Raising." *Pa. Folklife*, vol. 21 (1972), Folk Festival Supplement, 14–18.

ED12 Hand, Wayland D. "A German House-Raising Ceremony in California." *Western Folklore*, vol. 13 (1954), 199–202.

ED13 Hoffmann, Klaus D. "'Sewing is for Women; Horses Are for Men': The Role of German Russian Women." In: *Germans from Russia in Colorado.* Ed. S. Heitman. Ann Arbor: Univ. Microfilms, 1978, p.131–44.

ED14 Hollenbach, Raymond E. "The Blue Dyer—Der blo Farrewer." "'S Pennsylfawnisch Deitsch Eck," Allentown *Morning Call*, 22 June 1968.

ED15 Kaufman, David B. "A Minister's Son Attends a Frolic (A Description and a Condemnation)." "'S Pennsylfawnisch Deitsch Eck," Allentown *Morning Call*, 2 March 1968.

ED16 Kehr, Kurt. "Jagdmethoden und Jagdwortschatz der 'Pennsylvania Germans' im Shenandoah Valley / Virginia." In: *Et multum et multa. Beiträge zur Literatur, Geschichte und Kultur der Jagd. Festgabe für Kurt Lindner zum 27. November 1971.* Ed. Sigrid Schwen, Gunnar Tilander and Carl Arnold Willemsen. New York & Berlin: de Gruyter, 1971, p.147–63.

ED17 Reichmann, Felix. "Bread of Our Forefathers." "'S Pennsylfawnisch Deitsch Eck," Allentown *Morning Call*, 22 October 1955. Also in: *Hist. Rev. of Berks Co.*, vol. 9 (1943–1944), 11–13. Folk customs associated with the use of bread.

ED18 Shoemaker, Alfred L. "Barring Out the Schoolmaster." *The Pa. Dutchman*, vol. 7, no. 3 (1956), 14–17. On Christmas or Shrove Tuesday it was the custom to bar out the schoolmaster.

ED19 Shoemaker, Alfred L. "The 'Glingelsock'." *Pa. Folklife*, vol. 12, no. 2 (Summer 1961), 53–55. On a device used for collecting church offerings.

ED20 Smith, Edward C., and Virginia van H. Thompson. *Traditionally Pennsylvania Dutch.* New York: Hastings House, 1947. 81p. On Amish customs and dress.

ED21 Smith, Elmer L., and Leon Milchunas. *Bundling among the Amish.* Akron, Pa.: Applied Arts Pr., 1961. Rev. in *Hist. Rev. of Berks Co.*, vol. 26, no. 4 (1961), 104.

ED22 "So Hen die Alte Leit Geduh." *Der Reggeboge.* See esp. vol. 14, no. 1, 16; no. 2, 20; no. 3, 16. Continued feature on folk customs of the Pennsylvania Germans.

ED23 Stoltzfus, G. M. "Cooperation Builds a Barn in a Day." *Amer.-German Rev.*, vol. 16, no. 6 (1950), 18–19.

ED24 Tortora, Vincent R. "Amish Barn Raising." *Pa. Folklife*, vol. 12, no. 3 (Fall 1961), 14–19.

Superstitions, Beliefs, the Occult

ED25 Aurand, A. Monroe, Jr. *The Realness of Witchcraft in America. With Special Reference to the Pennsylvania Germans and the Conflict of Sci-*

Superstitions, Beliefs, the Occult *(cont.)*

ence vs. *Old Time Beliefs and Customs*. Harrisburg: Aurand Pr., 1942. 32p.

ED26 Byington, Robert H. "Popular Beliefs and Superstitions from Pennsylvania." *Keystone Folklore Quar.*, vol. 9, no. 1 (Spring 1964), 3–12. On W. D. Hand's projected dictionary of American popular beliefs and superstitions, with the cooperation of the Pennsylvania German Folklore Society.

ED27 Capuzzo, Make. "A Grave Affair: Horrors of an Old Halloween." *Miami Herald*, 25 October 1981, Tropic Sunday Supplement, 37–46. On Karl Tanzler von Cosel.

ED28 Frey, J. William. "'God's Time' and 'Devil's Time'." *Amer. Speech*, vol. 17, no. 4 (1942), 281–82.

ED29 Gandee, Lee R. *Strange Experience: The Autobiography of a Hexenmeister*. Philadelphia: n.p., 1975.

ED30 Gerhard, Elmer Schultz. "Pennsylvania Germans not Alone Superstitious." "'S Pennsylfawnisch Deitsch Eck," Allentown *Morning Call*, 25 November 1950.

ED31 Hand, Wayland D. "Dairy Witchcraft and the Ash." *Western Folklore*, vol. 18, no. 2 (1959), 176. Use of ash switches for driving cows.

ED32 Hering, Irwin M. "Folklore and Superstitions among the Pennsylvania Germans." "'S Pennsylfawnisch Deitsch Eck," Allentown *Morning Call*, 7–28 September, 5–19 October 1968. From a TS in the Muhlenberg College library, consisting of excerpts from "Boyhood Memoirs. A Retrospective after Sixty Years of a Farmer's Lad in Pennsylvania German Land in the 1880's and 90's."

ED33 Hertzog, Phares H. "Snakes and Snakelore of Pennsylvania." *Pa. Folklife*, vol. 17, no. 1 (Autumn 1967), 14–17; "Snakelore in Pennsylvania German Folk Medicine." *Ibid*., no. 2 (1967–1968), 24–26; "Pennsylvania German Snakelore." *Ibid*., no. 4 (1968), 16–19. Incl. the Pennsylvania German names for snakes.

ED34 Jones, Louis C. "The Evil Eye among European-Americans." *Western Folklore*, vol. 10, no. 1 (1951), 11–25. Various European immigrant groups believe in the "evil eye." The Germans look with suspicion on those with red eyes.

ED35 Klinefelter, Walter. "The Peter Cox Robbery." *Der Reggeboge*, vol. 13, no. 4 (1979), 1–4. On witchmongering.

ED36 Kozumplik, William A. "Seven and Nine Holes in Man." *Southern Folklore Quar.*, vol. 5, no. 1 (1941), 1–24. Doctrine of holes in the body; citations from German literature.

ED37 Kring, Hilda Adam. "The Cult of St. Walburga in Pennsylvania." *Pa. Folklife*, vol. 24, no. 2 (1974–1975), 2–7.

ED38 Kring, Hilda Adam. "Mary Goes over the Mountain." *Pa. Folklife*, vol. 19, no. 4 (1969), 54–60.

ED39 Loomis, Grant. "German Witchcraft." *Western Folklore*, vol. 17, no. 2 (1958), 131. Quoted from the Berkeley *Daily Gazette*, 5 July 1957.

ED40 Millspaw, Yvonne J. "Witchcraft Belief in a Pennsylvania German Family." *Pa. Folklife*, vol. 27, no. 4 (1978), 14–24.

ED41 Roberts, Kenneth. *Henry Gross and His Dowsing Rod*. Garden City: Doubleday, 1951. 310p.

ED42 Rosenberger, Homer T. "The Hex Doctor and the Witch of Farrandsville." *Keystone Folklore Quar.*, vol. 3 (1958), 42–45. A witch story.

ED43 Schroeder, Johann G. "Exorcism—1789: 'The Noteworthy Story of a Man Who Entered a Pact with the Devil for Eighteen Years and Was Released Again through Christ!'" *Der Reggeboge*, vol. 9, no. 2 (1975), 2–17. Trans. by Larry M. Neff. Concerns Thomas Solvon.

ED44 Shaner, Richard H. "Living Occult Practices in Dutch Pennsylvania Country." *Pa. Folklife*, vol. 12, no. 3 (Fall 1961), 62–63.

ED45 Shoemaker, Alfred L. "Water Witching." *Pa. Folklife*, vol. 12, no. 3 (Fall 1961), 25–27.

ED46 Smith, Elmer L., and John G. Stewart. "The Black Walnut." "'S Pennsylfawnisch Deitsch Eck," Allentown *Morning Call*, 19 December 1964. Lore associated with the black walnut.

ED47 Smith, Elmer Lewis. "Conjuring Rats." "'S Pennsylfawnisch Deitsch Eck," Allentown *Morning Call*, 23 October 1965.

ED48 Smith, Elmer Lewis. "Shenandoah Valley Folklore. The Elusive Elbedrich." "'S Pennsylfawnisch Deitsch Eck," Allentown *Morning Call*, 25 January 1969.

ED49 Smith, Elmer Lewis. "Water Witching: Wish or Wisdom?" "'S Pennsylfawnisch Deitsch Eck," Allentown *Morning Call*, 31 July 1965.

ED50 Stephenson, Peter H. "Pshrien: Hutterite Belief in 'Evil Eye' and Concepts of Child-Abuse." In: *Canadian Ethnology Society: Papers from the Fifth Annual Congress 1978*. Ed. Joan Ryan. Ottawa: National Museum of Canada, 1980, p.113–27.

ED51 Swetnam, George. "Sex—The Missing Fascicle." *Keystone Folklore Quar.*, vol. 10, no. 4 (Winter 1965), 155–71. Repr. and commentary on the fascicle on sex omitted from E. M. Fogel's *Beliefs and Superstitions of the Pennsylvania Germans*. Philadelphia, 1915.

ED52 Troxell, William S. "The First Grundsow Lodge." *The Pa. Dutchman*, vol. 4, no. 12 (1953), 4. The groundhog belief.

ED53 Vogt, Evon Z., and Ray Hyman. *Water Witching U.S.A.* Chicago: Univ. of Chicago Pr., 1959. 259p. Dowsing was first practiced in Germany in the 15th century.

Folk Medicine and Healing

ED54 Aurand, A. Monroe, Jr. *Popular Home Remedies and Superstitions of the Pennsylvania Germans*. Forew. by Logan Clendening. Harrisburg: Aurand Pr., 1941. 32p.

ED55 Baker, Holly Cutting. "Patent Medicine in Pennsylvania before 1906: A History through Advertising." *Pa. Folklife*, vol. 27, no. 2 (1977–1978), 21–33.

ED56 Banks, Betty F. "Local Powwow Rituals." *Hist. Rev. of Berks Co.*, vol. 33 (Winter 1967–1968), 15–17, 28–32. Rituals to relieve pain and effect cures.

ED57 Barrick, Mac E. "Folk-Beliefs of a Pennsylvania Preacher." *Keystone Folklore Quar.*, vol. 10, no. 4 (Winter 1965), 191–96. Beliefs concerning healing and harvesting held by the Rev. Daniel Stock, Lutheran minister near Carlisle, 1850–1867.

ED58 Baver, Russell S. "Strange Deaths." *Pa. Dutch News and Views*, vol. 3, no. 2 (1971), 4–9. Accounts of peculiar deaths from the 19th century.

ED59 Boot, Christine. "Home and Farm Remedies and Charms in a German Manuscript from a Texas Ranch." In: *Ethnic Medicine in the Southwest*. Ed. Edward H. Spicer. Tucson: Univ. of Arizona Pr., 1977, p.273–81. Also in *Publs., Texas Folklore Soc.*, vol. 41 (1978), 111–32.

ED60 Brendle, Thomas R., and Claude W. Unger. "Witchcraft in Cow and Horse." *The Pa. Dutchman*, vol. 8, no. 1 (1956), 28–31. Cures for cows and horses.

ED61 Byington, Robert H. "Powwowing in Pennsylvania." *Keystone Folklore Quar.*, vol. 9, no. 3 (1964), 111–17. An account largely excerpted from Hohman.

ED62 Colbert, Lisa. "Amish Attitudes and Treatment of Illness." *Pa. Folklife*, vol. 30 (1980–81), 9–15.

ED63 DeBoeser, Charles J. "Medicinal Remedies and the Healing Arts Used by the Pennsylvania Dutch and Delaware Indians." *Hist. Rev. of Berks Co.*, vol. 45 (1979), 8–11, 26–27.

ED64 Estep, Glenn, and William Pietchke. "A Study of Certain Aspects of Spiritualism and Powwow in Regard to the Folklore of Lancaster County." *The Pa. Dutchman*, vol. 5, no. 13 (1954), 10–11, 15.

ED65 Gebhard, Bruno. "The Interrelationships of Scientific and Folk Medicine in the United States of America since 1850." In: *American Folk Medicine: A Symposium*. Ed. Wayland D. Hand. Berkeley, Calif.: Univ. of Calif. Pr., 1976, p.87–98.

ED66 Gourley, Norma M. "About Powwowing." *The Pa. Dutchman*, vol. 5, no. 14 (1954), 7–8. From a Master's thesis on "Some Phases of Witchcraft among the Pennsylvania Germans."

ED67 Grabner, Elfriede. "Verlorenes Mass und heilkräftiges Messen: Krankheitserforschung und Heilhandlung in der Volksmedizin." *Zeitschrift für*

Folk Medicine and Healing *(cont.)*

Volkskunde, vol. 60, Erster Halbjahresband 1964, 23–34. On the practice of "measuring" for ailments; some information from Karl Knortz's investigations into American practices.

ED68 Graeff, Arthur D. "Stoy's Remedy." "'S Pennsylfawnisch Deitsch Eck," Allentown *Morning Call*, 22 February 1969. Anecdotes centering on the Rev. William Stoy, Reformed clergyman of Colonial times, in Lebanon, Pa.

ED69 Hand, Wayland D. "The Folk Healer: Calling and Endowment." *Jour. of the Hist. of Medicine and Allied Sciences*, vol. 26 (July 1971), 263–75.

ED70 Hand, Wayland D. *"Padepissers* and *Wekschissers*: A Folk Medical Inquiry into the Cause of Styes." In: *Folklore Studies in Honor of Herbert Halpert. A Festschrift*. Ed. Kenneth Goldstein et al. St. John's, Newfoundland: Memorial Univ. of Newfoundland, 1980, p.211–23.

ED71 Hand, Wayland D., ed. *American Folk Medicine: A Symposium*. Publs. of the UCLA Center for the Study of Comparative Folklore and Mythology. Berkeley: Univ. of California Pr., 1976. 347p. Rev. by William M. Clements, *Jour. of Amer. Folklore*, vol. 92 (1979), 86–87.

ED72 Hirte, Tobias. *Warnung, vor falschen Seneca-Oel. Indianisch–French–Crieck–Seneca-Oel. Ein vortreffliches...Medicament, ist zu haben in Philadelphia bei T. Hirte...Kurze Nachricht über dessen Nutzen und Gebrauch....* [Philadelphia: 1794?] Broadside 36 x 23 cm.

ED73 Hoffman, Francis Arnold ("Hans Buschbauer," "Junghans Buschbauer"), ed. *Der Familienschatz...Sammlung werthvoller Rezepte und Rathschläge für den Familienkreis, Hauswirtschaft, den Ackerbau...* Milwaukee: G. Brumder, ca. 1888. 376p.

ED74 ["Hohmann, Johann George."] In: *Grundriss zur Geschichte der Deutschen Dichtung aus den Quellen.* Ed. Karl Goedeke. Dresden: Ehlermann, 1964, Ausland IV, p.575–78. Bio-bibliography of Hohmann (or Homan), artist of birth and baptismal certificates, folk healer, writer of pious instructional literature. Came to Philadelphia in 1802 as a redemptioner; lived in New Jersey and Pennsylvania.

ED75 Horne, Abraham Reeser. "Zeeche Glawwe un Braucherei." "'S Pennsylfawnisch Deitsch Eck," Allentown *Morning Call*, 12 January 1963. Excerpted from *'M Horn sei Pennsylvawnisch Deitsch Buch*. Allentown, 1910. Continued in: "Zeecheglaawe un Braucherei. Was der Mond dutt, was die Zeeche bedeite, un wie mer Krahkeete los watt." *Ibid.*, 25 June 1966. Lore of moon phases and signs in folk medicine. Repr. from the *Pennsylvania-German Calendar* of 1905.

ED76 Hostetler, John A. "Folk and Scientific Medicine in Amish Society." *Human Organization*, vol. 22, no. 4 (Winter 1963–1964).

ED77 Hostetler, John A. "Folk Medicine and Sympathy Healing among the Amish." In: *American Folk Medicine*. Ed. Wayland W. Hand. Berkeley: Univ. of California Pr., 1976, p.249–58.

ED78 Hyde, Louise, and Cyrus Hyde. "Herbs at Kutztown." *Pa. Folklife*, vol. 30 (1979), Folk Festival Supplement, 8–11. At the Kutztown Folk Festival.

ED79 Kemble, Howard R., and Harry B. Weiss. "The Forgotten Water-Cures of Brattleboro, Vermont." *Vt. Hist.*, vol. 37 (1969), 165–76. Origins found in Graefenberg, Austrian Silesia.

ED80 *Eine kurtzgefasste neue Sammlung, in sich haltend mehrenteils wunderseltsamen, auserlesenen, nützlichen und bewährten Recepten und Kunst-Stücke...Auf Kosten des Liebhabers herausgegeben.* N.p.: n.p., 1815. 30p. Noted in Ralph Shaw. *American Bibliography 1801–19*.

ED81 Leib, Isaac. *Wohlerfahrner Pferde-Arzt; enthaltend Mittel für die Heilung aller bekannten und verschiedenartigen Krankheiten und Seuchen der Pferde...* Lebanon, Pa.: n.p., 1842. 184p.

ED82 Loewen, Solomon L. "The Art of Bloodletting as Practised by My Father." *Jour. of the Amer. Hist. Soc. of Germans from Russia*, vol. 3, no. 2 (1980), 13–17.

ED83 Neff, Larry M., and Frederick S. Weiser, trans. "Manuscript 'Pow-Wow' Formulas." *Der Reggeboge*, vol. 13, no. 1 (1979), 1–7, 20–21.

ED84 Oda, Wilbur H. "John Georg Hohman." *Hist. Rev. of Berks Co.*, vol. 13, no. 3 (April 1948), 66–71. On the author of a powwow manual.

ED85 Pocius, Gerald L. "Veterinary Folk Medicine in Susquehanna County, Pennsylvania." *Pa. Folklife*, vol. 25, no. 4 (1976), 2–15.

ED86 Reimensnyder, Barbara. "Annotated Bibliography of Pennsylvania Folk Medicine." *Pa. Folklife*, vol. 27, no. 1 (1977), 40–48.

ED87 Robacker, Earl F. "Search for a Long-Lost Friend." "'S Pennsylfawnisch Deitsch Eck," Allentown *Morning Call*, 9 June 1956. On J. G. Hohman's "Long-Lost Friend" and the persistence of "Braucherei" among the Pennsylvania Germans.

ED88 Safrit, Gary Lee. "An Investigation of Folk-Medicine Practices in North and South Carolina." B.D. thesis, Lutheran Theological Southern Seminary, Columbia, 1964.

ED89 Shaner, Richard H. "Powwow Doctors." *Pa. Folklife*, vol. 12, no. 2 (Summer 1961), 72.

ED90 Smith, Elmer L. "Aawaxe (Contracting a Liver Ailment)." "'S Pennsylfawnisch Deitsch Eck," Allentown *Morning Call*, 30 October 1965.

ED91 Smith, Elmer L. "The Mill as a Preventative and Cure of Whooping Cough." *Jour. of Amer. Folklore*, vol. 77, no. 303 (January–March 1964), 76–77. Pennsylvania-German superstition.

ED92 Smith, Elmer L. "Wild Fire [Erysipelas]." "'S Pennsylfawnisch Deitsch Eck," Allentown *Morning Call*, 23 April 1966. Lore and superstitions about treatment.

ED93 Smith, Elmer L., and John G. Stewart. "Hydrophobia and the Madstone." "'S Pennsylfawnisch Deitsch Eck," Allentown *Morning Call*, 17 July 1965.

ED94 Smith, Elmer L., and John G. Stewart. "The f All Evil: The Master Root." "'S Penn-ch Deitsch Eck," Allentown *Morning Call*, 12 November 1966. Lore of medicinal herbs.

ED95 Smith, Elmer L., and John G. Stewart. "Measuring." "'S Pennsylfawnisch Deitsch Eck," Allentown *Morning Call* 22 January 1966. Medical lore and superstitions of physical measuring.

ED96 Smith, Elmer L., and John G. Stewart. "The Old Mill as a Medicine." "'S Pennsylfawnisch Deitsch Eck," Allentown *Morning Call*, 5 March 1966.

ED97 Smith, Elmer L., and John G. Stewart. "Warts." "'S Pennsylfawnisch Deitsch Eck," Allentown *Morning Call*, 15 May 1965.

ED98 Speck, Frank G. et al. *Rappahannock Herbals, Folklore and Science of Cures*. Media, Pa.: Delaware Co. Institute of Science, 1942. 55p.

ED99 Stewart, John, and Elmer L. Smith. "An Occult Remedy Manuscript from Pendleton County, West Virginia." *Bull., Madison College*, vol. 22 (1964), 77–85. Trans. and evaluation of a MS volume in German describing occult cures.

ED100 Stewart, Susan. "Rational Powwowing: An Examination of Choice among Medical Alternatives in Rural York County, Pennsylvania." *Pa. Folklife*, vol. 26, no. 1 (1976), 12–17.

ED101 "Veterinary and Household Recipes from West Calico." *Pa. Folklife*, vol. 16, no. 2 (Winter 1966–1967), 28–29. A nineteenth-century English language MS of home remedies from the Pennsylvania-German country.

ED102 *Ein vortrefliches Kräuter-Buch für Haus-Väter- und Mütter, nebst etlichen auserlesenen Recepten, Wie auch eine Anweisung zur Färbe-Kunst, blau, roth, gelb...zu färben*. [Ephrata, Pa.: J. Baumann?] 1803. 32p. Household recipes and directions for dyeing.

ED103 Weiser, Daniel. "Braucherei." *The Pa. Dutchman*, vol. 5, no. 14 (1954), 6, 14. Repr. from the *Guardian*, 1868.

ED104 Weiss, Harry B., and Howard R. Kemble. *The Great American Water-Cure Craze. A History of Hydropathy in the United States*. Trenton: The Post Times Pr., 1967. 236p.

ED105 Westkott, Marcia. "Powwowing in Berks County." *Pa. Folklife*, vol. 19, no. 2 (1969–1970), 2–9.

ED106 Yoder, Don. "Hohman and Romanus: Origins and Diffusion of the Pennsylvania German Powwow Manual." In: *American Folk Medicine: A Symposium*. Ed. Wayland D. Hand. Berkeley: Univ. of California Pr., 1976, p.235–48.

Religious Lore

ED107 Barba, Preston A. "Himmelsbriefe or Talismanic Letters." "'S Pennsylfawnisch Deitsch Eck," Allentown *Morning Call*, 13 August 1949.

ED108 Boudreaux, Florence. "German Customs Still Retained in Robert's Cove." *Attakapas Gazette* (St. Martinsville, La.), vol. 3, no. 2 (June 1968), 16–23. Article in German and English describing religious feasts and other practices observed by Catholic people in Roberts Cove, La.

ED109 Buffington, Albert F. "A Pennsylvania German Goddesdienscht." *Der Reggeboge*, vol. 13, no. 2 (1979), 1–10. A worship service described.

ED110 Durnbaugh, Donald F. "The German Journalist and the Dunker Love-Feast." *Pa. Folklife*, vol. 18, no. 2 (Winter 1968–1969), 40–48.

ED111 Hand, Wayland D. "A North Carolina Himmelsbrief." In: *Middle Ages—Reformation—"Volkskunde." Festschrift for John G. Kunstmann*. Chapel Hill: Univ. of N. Car. Pr., 1959, p.201–07.

ED112 Hostetler, Beulah S. "An Old Order River Brethren Love Feast." *Pa. Folklife*, vol. 24, no. 2 (1974–1975), 8–20.

ED113 Kemp, A. F. "The Pennsylvania German Versammlinge." *Publs., Pa. German Folklore Soc.*, no. 9 (1944), 187–218.

ED114 Marchand, James W. "A Note on the Sunday Letter." *Tenn. Folklore Soc. Bull.*, vol. 29, no. 1 (1963), 4–9. American variants of the *Himmelsbrief* or Letter from Heaven.

ED115 Terbovich, John B. "Religious Folklore among the German-Russians in Ellis County, Kansas." *Western Folklore*, vol. 22, no. 2 (1963), 79–88.

ED116 Yoder, Don. "Love Feasts." *The Pa. Dutchman*, vol. 7, no. 4 (1956), 34–37. "Love feasts" still held in the Pennsylvania German area by Brethren, Moravians, Methodists, Evangelical United Brethren and related groups.

ED117 Yoder, Don. "Trance-Preaching in the United States." *Pa. Folklife*, vol. 18, no. 2 (1968–1969), 12–18.

Weather, Nature, and Calendar Lore

ED118 Barba, P. A. "Elbedritschelcher." "'S Pennsylfawnisch Deitsch Eck," Allentown *Morning Call*, 26 February, 12 March 1966. Folklore of mythical birds or beasts hunted in the nights of February.

ED119 Barba, P. A. "Fastnacht." "'S Pennsylfawnisch Deitsch Eck," Allentown *Morning Call*, 23 February 1963. Article and poems about *Fastnacht* (Shrove Tuesday) customs.

ED120 Barba, P. A. "Groundhog or Bear?" "'S Pennsylfawnisch Deitsch Eck," Allentown *Morning Call*, 29 January 1955. Why early German settlers in Pennsylvania chose the groundhog as weather prophet and also why his prognostications occur on 2 February.

ED121 Barba, P. A. "Lichtmess." "'S Pennsylfawnisch Deitsch Eck," Allentown *Morning Call*, 2 February 1957. The lore of candlemas and how the groundhog became its weather prophet.

ED122 Barba, P. A. "Notes on Mattheis Daag." "'S Pennsylfawnisch Deitsch Eck," Allentown *Morning Call*, 5 April 1947. Pennsylvania German folklore of St. Matthew's Day.

ED123 Baver, Mrs. Russell. "Washday Lore." *The Pa. Dutchman*, vol. 5, no. 1 (1953), 6–7, 15.

ED124 Berky, Andrew S. "Bread and Apple-Butter Day." *Pa. Folklife*, vol. 12, no. 3 (Fall 1961), 42–43. A festival of thanksgiving, celebrated with meager food.

ED125 Best, Martha S. "Christmas Customs in the Lehigh Valley." *Pa. Folklife*, vol. 22, no. 2 (1972/1973), 15–24.

ED126 Brendle, Thomas R. "Customs of the Year in the Dutch Country." *The Pa. Dutchman*, vol. 2 (15 November 1951).

ED127 Dieffenbach, Victor C. "Weather Signs and Calendar Lore from the 'Dumb Quarter'." *Pa. Folklife*, vol. 17, no. 1 (Autumn 1967), 26–30. Sayings in the Dutch dialect with English translations.

ED128 Gerhard, Elmer S. "Lorenz Ibach, The Stargazing Blacksmith." *Hist. Rev. of Berks Co.*, vol. 14, no. 2 (1949), 45–47. Pennsylvania almanac maker and calculator of eclipses.

ED129 Gerhard, Elmer S. "Pennsylvania German Weather Lore." *Hist. Rev. of Berks Co.*, vol. 18, no. 1 (1952), 2–7. Also in "'S Pennsylfawnisch Deitsch Eck," Allentown *Morning Call*, 22, 29 January, 5 February 1955.

ED130 Love, K. M. "German Winter Festivals in Fredericksburg, Texas." *Amer.-German Rev.*, vol. 16, no. 2 (1949), 17–20.

ED131 Mook, Maurice. "Halloween in Central Pennsylvania." *Keystone Folklore Quar.*, vol. 14 (1969), 124–29.

ED132 Moyer, Earl H., and Kay M. Krick. *Almanac Lore of the Pennsylvania Germans*. Collegeville: Institute on Pennsylvania Dutch Studies, 1975. 24p.

ED133 Reichard, Harry H. "Die Wedderberichte." "'S Pennsylfawnisch Deitsch Eck," Allentown *Morning Call*, 2 February 1951. Weather reports.

ED134 Shoemaker, Alfred L. "February Lore." *The Pa. Dutchman*, vol. 5, no. 11 (1954), 11. "Harning," Groundhog Day, and other lore.

ED135 Shoemaker, Alfred L. "Folklore on Snow." *The Pa. Dutchman*, vol. 5, no. 12 (1954), 5.

ED136 Shoemaker, Alfred L. "March Lore." *The Pa. Dutchman*, vol. 5, no. 13 (1954), 9.

ED137 Shoemaker, Alfred L. "Shrove Tuesday Lore." *The Pa. Dutchman*, vol. 5, no. 11 (1954), 5.

ED138 Shoemaker, Alfred L. "Whit-Monday—Dutch Fourth of July." *The Pa. Dutchman*, vol. 5, no. 1 (1953), 5, 12.

ED139 Smith, Elmer L., and John G. Stewart. "Grundsau Dag." "'S Pennsylfawnisch Deitsch Eck," Allentown *Morning Call*, 30 January 1965.

ED140 "So Hen Die Alde Leit Geduh." *Der Reggeboge*, vol. 15, nos. 3–4 (July–October 1981), 25–27. On the signs of the zodiac and the related tradition of the "vein man" illustrations in old almanacs. The latter indicated the signs which governed the parts of the human body for bleeding and cupping.

ED141 Sutton, David. "Helvetian Fastnacht." *Tygart Valley Press* (Elkins, W. Va.), 13 February 1980. Shrove Tuesday customs in a Swiss-American community.

ED142 Winkler, Louis. "Astronomical Contributions of Carl Friedrich Egelmann." *Hist. Rev. of Berks Co.*, vol. 38 (Fall 1973), 120–24.

ED143 Winkler, Louis. [Series on Pennsylvania German Astronomy and Astrology.] "Almanacs." *Pa. Folklife*, vol. 21, no. 3 (1972). "The Moon." *Ibid.*, vol. 21, no. 4. "Comets and Meteors." *Ibid.*, vol. 22, no. 1 (1972–1973). "Tombstones." *Ibid.*, vol. 22, no. 2. "Religion and Astronomy." *Ibid.*, vol. 22, no. 3. "Astrological Philosophy." *Ibid.*, vol. 22, no. 4. "Pennsylvania German Astronomy and Astronomy: Carl Friedrich Egelmann." *Ibid.*, vol. 23, no. 1 (1973). "Pennsylvania German Astronomy and Astrology: Johann Friedrich Schmidt." *Ibid.*, vol. 24 (Fall 1974). "Christopher Saur's Almanacs." *Ibid.*, vol. 24, no. 3 (1975). "Christopher Witt's Device." *Ibid.*, vol. 24, no. 2. "Contemporary Almanacs," *Ibid.*, vol. 24, no. 4. "Conjunctions of 1683, 1694 and 1743." *Ibid.*, vol. 25, no. 1 (1975). "Benjamin Franklin's Almanacs." *Ibid.*, vol. 26, no. 4 (1977). "Health and the Heavens." *Ibid.*, vol. 26, no. 1 (1976). "Pennsylvania German Astronomy and Astrology: The Gruber–Baer Era." *Ibid.*, vol. 27, no. 3 (1978). "Pennsylvania German Astronomy and Astrology: German Language Almanacs." *Ibid.*, vol. 28, no. 2 (1978–1979).

ED144 Yoder, Don. "Harvest Home." *Pa. Folklife*, vol. 9, no. 4 (1958), 2–11. Festival celebrated in the Pennsylvania German area.

Weddings and Marriage Customs

ED145 Bauman, Richard. "Belsnickling in a Nova Scotia Island Community." *Western Folklore*, vol. 31 (1972), 229–43.

ED146 Beckel, Clarence E. "Early Marriage Customs of the Moravian Congregation in Bethlehem, Pa.: The Use of the Lot in Relation to Marriage Rites and Description of Some Notable Ceremonies." *Publs., Pa. German Folklore Soc.*, vol. 3 (1938), 1–32.

ED147 Brednich, Rolf W. "Die russlanddeutschen Mennoniten in Saskatchewan (Kanada) und ihre Hochzeitsbräuche." *Jahrbuch für Ostdeutsche Volkskunde*, vol. 20 (1977), 61–98.

ED148 Brendel, John Binkley. "Recollections of Belsnickeling in Northern Lancaster County, Pennsylvania." *Goschenhoppen Region*, vol. 1, no. 2 (Aller Heil 1968), 7–11.

ED149 Cline, Ruth H. "Belsnickles and Shanghais." *Jour. of Amer. Folklore*, vol. 71 (1958), 164–65.

ED150 Gapp, Samuel H. "The Moravian Use of the Lot in Marriage." *Publs., Pa. German Folklore Soc.*, vol. 22 (1958), 151–54.

ED151 Goertz, Reuben. "Wedding Bells Ringing, Skeletons in Closets Jingling." *Work Papers, Amer. Hist. Soc. of Germans from Russia*, vol. 17 (1975), 3–7.

ED152 Gougler, Richard C. "Amish Weddings." *Pa. Folklife*, vol. 22 (1972–1973), Folk Festival Supplement (1973), 12–13. *See also* his article "The Amish Wedding." *Ibid.*, vol. 30 (1980–1981), 158–60.

ED153 Hollenbach, Raymond E. "Ausschteir." "'S Pennsylfawnisch Deitsch Eck," Allentown *Morning Call*, 5 December 1964. Lore and customs of dowries and dower chests. *See also* his "Aussteuer—Dowries." *Ibid.*, 23 March–6 April 1968.

ED154 Kloberdanz, Timothy J., ed. "Folklore Forum: Marriage Beliefs and Customs of the Germans from Russia." *Work Papers, Amer. Hist. Soc. of the Germans from Russia*, vol. 23 (1977), 37–64.

ED155 Korson, George. "Courtship and Marriage Customs among the Hard Coal Region Pennsylvania Dutch." *Keystone Folklore Quar.*, vol. 6, no. 2 (Summer 1961), 2–16.

ED156 Martin, Aaron. "Courtship and Marriage Practices of Lancaster Mennonites." *Mennonite Life*, vol. 17 (January 1962), 31–35.

ED157 Pfeifer, Leona W. "Marriage Traditions of the Ellis County Volga-Germans." In: *Germanica Americana 1976: Symposium on German-Amer. Literature and Culture*. Ed. E. A. Albrecht and J. Anthony Burzle. Lawrence: Max Kade Document and Research Center, Univ. of Kansas, 1977, p. 113–16.

ED158 Rowland, Florence W. *Amish Wedding*. New York: Putnam's Sons, 1971.

ED159 Schreiber, William I. "Amish Wedding Days." *Jour. of Amer. Folklore*, vol. 73 (1960), 12–17. *See also* "'S Pennsylfawnisch Deitsch Eck," 25 June, 2 July 1960, and *Mennonite Life*, vol. 17, no. 2 (1962), 96. Tuesday and Thursday are the only wedding days for the Amish people.

ED160 Shoemaker, Alfred L. "Barricading the Road." *The Pa. Dutchman*, vol. 5, no. 8 (1954), 2. The old custom of barring the road to newlyweds.

ED161 Shoemaker, Alfred L. "Belsnickel Lore." *The Pa. Dutchman*, vol. 6, no. 3 (1954), 34–38.

ED162 Smith, Elmer L. "The Amish Wedding Season." "'S Pennsylfawnisch Deitsch Eck," Allentown *Morning Call*, 17 January 1959. November and December have been the preferred months for Amish weddings.

ED163 Smith, Elmer L. "Family Harvest, the Amish Wedding." *Hist. Rev. of Berks Co.*, vol. 26, no. 1 (1960), 6–12.

ED164 Smith, Elmer L., and John G. Stewart. "Belling." "'S Pennsylfawnisch Deitsch Eck," Allentown *Morning Call*, 23 January 1965. Visiting the newly married couple on the wedding night.

ED165 Stewart, John G. "Shanghaiing in the Valley of Virginia." *Bull.*, Madison College, vol. 24, no. 2 (1966), 97–105. A folk custom similar to belsnickling.

ED166 Tortora, Vincent R. "The Courtship and Wedding Practices of the Old Order Amish." *Pa. Folklife*, vol. 9, no. 2 (1958), 12–21.

Death and Funeral Lore

ED167 Barrick, Mac E. "Cumberland County Death Lore." *Pa. Folklife*, vol. 28, no. 4 (1978–1979), 37–46.

ED168 Bixler, Miriam Eyde. "Early Lancaster County Funeral Customs." *Jour. of the Lancaster Co. Hist. Soc.*, vol. 77 (Michaelmas 1973), 163–70.

ED169 Brumbach, Paul D. "Funerals in My Childhood Days." *Pa. Folklife*, vol. 16, no. 1 (1964), 30–34. Incl. attitudes toward the minister and his role in the community.

ED170 Bryer, K. B. "The Amish Way of Death." *Amer. Psychologist*, vol. 34 (1979), 225–61.

ED171 Gilbert, Russell W. "Funerals and the Undertaker." *Der Reggeboge*, vol. 11, no. 2 (1977), 7–8.

ED172 Kaufman, David B. "Funerals in the Early Days." *Procs., Lehigh Co. Hist. Soc.*, vol. 29 (1972), 50–55.

ED173 Stucky, Gary. "Funeral Practices at Pretty Prairie." *Mennonite Life*, vol. 17, no. 4 (1962), 184–87. Mennonite funeral practices.

ED174 Tortora, Vincent R. "Amish Funerals." *Pa. Folklife*, vol. 12, no. 3 (1961), 8–13.

Games and Amusements

ED175 Brewster, Paul G. "Some Games from Other Lands." *Southern Folklore Quar.*, vol. 7, no. 2 (1943), 109–17. Incl. games of German origin.

ED176 Brown, Waln K. "Cultural Learning through Game Structure. A Study of Pennsylvania German Children's Games." *Pa. Folklife*, vol. 23, no. 4 (1974), 2–11.

ED177 Grey, Sara. "Children's Games among Lancaster County Mennonites." *Pa. Folklife*, vol. 16, no. 4 (Summer 1967), 46–47.

ED178 Hale, Leon. "A Lesson on Playing Mühle." In: *Some Still Do: Essays on Texas Customs*. Ed. F. E. Abernethy. Publs. of the Texas Folklore Soc., no. 39. Austin: Encino, 1975, p.74–76. A German beer drinkers' game played with buttons or corn kernels.

ED179 Keyser, Alan G. "Nineteenth Century Shooting Matches." *Pa. Folklife*, vol. 12, no. 1 (1961), 8–9.

ED180 Mehl, Erwin. "Notes to 'Baseball in the Stone Age'." *Western Folklore*, vol. 8, no. 2 (1949), 152–56. Supplement to the author's "Baseball in the Stone Age," publ. in *Western Folklore*, vol. 7, no. 2 (1948), 145–61. Incl. several accounts of the 17th-century "Schlagball."

ED181 Patterson, Ward. "Two Volga German Games." *Heritage of Kans.*, vol. 9, nos. 2–3 (1976), 60.

ED182 *Skat: The German Game of Cards*. New York: B. Westermann & Co., 1885. 24p.

ED183 Waddington, Anna Jane. "Early Childhood Toys and Pastimes." *The Goschenhoppen Region*, vol. 1 (Aller Heil, 1969), 4.

ED184 Wieand, Paul R. *Outdoor Games of the Pennsylvania Germans*. Keyser Home Craft Course Series, no. 28. Plymouth Meeting, Pa.: Mrs. C. Naaman Keyser, 1950. 34p.

ED185 Winter, Jack W. "'S Pennsylfawnisch Deitsch Liegner Match." *The Pa. Dutchman*, vol. 1, no. 19 (1949), 4. Competition of liars.

ED186 Tortora, Vincent R. "The Amish at Play." *The Pa. Dutchman*, vol. 8, no. 4 (1957), 14–34.

ED187 Tortora, Vincent R. "The Get-Togethers of the Young Amish Folk." *Pa. Folklife*, vol. 11, no. 1 (1960), 17–21.

Christmas Customs / Christmas Lore

ED188 Arndt, Helen. "The Christmas House." *Pa. Folklife*, vol. 24 (1975), Folk Festival Supplement, 48–49.

ED189 Barba, Preston A. "Bethlehem in Pennsylvanien: Amerikas Weihnachtsstadt." *Die Weihnachts Krippe*. Köln: Landesgemeinschaft der Krippenfreunde, 1967. Account of the founding of Bethlehem and its Christmas festivities.

ED190 Bauer, Theodor. "Celebration of Christmas by the Black Sea Germans in Dakota." *Heritage Rev.*, vol. 12 (1975), 6–9.

ED191 Baur, John E. *Christmas on the American Frontier 1880–1900*. Illus. by Charles McLaughlin. Caldwell, Idaho: Caxton Printers, 1961. 320p. Rev. by K. W. Clarke, *Midwest Folklore*, vol. 12, no. 2 (1962), 114. Some eyewitness accounts; Christmas customs of various ethnic groups.

ED192 Benton, Elbert J. *Cultural Story of an American City*, Part III. Cleveland: n.p., 1946. On the introduction of the Christmas tree.

ED193 Berky, Andrew S. "Christmas Customs of the Perkiomen Valley." *The Pa. Dutchman*, vol. 4, no. 8 (1952), 1–2, 7.

ED194 Best, Martha S. "Christmas Customs in the Lehigh Valley." *Pa. Folklife*, vol. 22, no. 2 (1972–1973), 15–24.

ED195 Caldwell, Dorothy J. "Christmas in Early Missouri." *Mo. Hist. Rev.*, vol. 65 (January 1971), 125–38.

ED196 Christ, Katherine D. "Christmas in Pennsylvania." *Hist. Rev. of Berks Co.*, vol. 26, no. 1 (1960), 21–29.

ED197 "Christmas in Lancaster in 1874." *Jour. of the Lancaster Co. Hist. Soc.*, vol. 71, no. 4 (Michaelmas 1967), 209–15.

ED198 "Christmas Lore." "'S Pennsylfawnisch Deitsch Eck," Allentown *Morning Call*, 21 December 1968.

ED199 "The Christmas Tree Legend." *Amer.-German Rev.*, vol. 15, no. 2 (1948), 8.

ED200 Creighton, Helen. "Old Christmas Customs in Nova Scotia." *Canad. Geographic Journal*, vol. 63, no. 6 (December 1961), 218–21.

ED201 "Der erste Weihnachtsbaum in Jersey City, New Jersey." *New Yorker Staats-Zeitung und Herold*, vol. 146, no. 2 (1980), Sec. A, 9.

ED202 Finckh, Alice H. "In the Candle's Glow." *Amer.-German Rev.*, vol. 14, no. 2 (1947), 4–6. The Christmas tree and its earliest records in the United States.

ED203 Friend, Neita O. "How They Celebrated Christmas: The Christmas-Keeping Germans." *Wis. Tales and Trails*, vol. 6, no. 4 (Winter 1956), 20–22.

ED204 Froehlich, Christine. *Zwei weihnachtliche Spiele für Schulbühnen*. Toronto: German-Canad. Hist. Assoc., ca. 1979. 63p.

ED205 Goulder, Grace. "Amish Send Santa Packing: Christmas among the Plain People is Simple Observance of Christ's Birthday." *Cleveland Plain Dealer Pictorial Mag.*, 11 December 1954.

ED206 Gröber, Karl. "Christkind, Krippe und Christbaum." *Amer.-German Rev.*, vol. 14, no. 2 (1947), 15–21. The Christmas tree and the creche.

ED207 James, Henry. "Christmas with the Moravians." *Amer.-German Rev.*, vol. 27, no. 2 (1960), 4–7.

ED208 Hutchison, Ruth. *Christmas in Bethlehem*. New York: Oxford Univ. Pr., 1958. 32p. Limited ed. for the Typophiles. On the Moravian Brethren of Bethlehem, Pa., and their Christmas customs.

ED209 Kiehlbauch, Rosina. "Christmas in the New World." *Jour. of the Amer. Hist. Soc. of Germans from Russia*, vol. 3, no. 3 (1980), 19–22. See also her "Christmas on the Homestead in 1884." *Ibid.*, vol. 4, no. 3 (1981), 1–4.

ED210 Klees, Fredric Spang. "The Christmas Present and the Pennsylvania Dutch." *Hist. Rev. of Berks Co.*, vol. 18 (1953), 34–36. Did the early Germans in Pennsylvania introduce the custom of gift-giving at Christmas time? See also "'S Pennsylfawnisch Deitsch Eck," Allentown *Morning Call*, 4 December 1954.

ED211 Kulp, Isaac Clarence, Jr. "Christmas Customs of the Goschenhoppen Region." *The Goschenhoppen Region*, vol. 1, no 2 (Aller Heil 1968), 4–11.

ED212 Laurence, June C. "A Shining Heritage." *Hist. Rev. of Berks Co.*, vol. 34, no. 1 (Winter 1968–1969), 9–10, 24. On the Christmas star.

ED213 Mertz, Beata. "The Memorable 'Weihnachten' Season in Western North Dakota." *Heritage Rev.*, vol. 9 (1974), 7–10.

ED214 Myers, Richmond E. "The Moravian Christmas Putz." *Pa. German Folklore Soc. Publs.*, vol. 6 (1941). 10p.

ED215 Nelson, Kay Shaw. Photos by Jon Riley. "A Moravian Christmas." *Americana*, vol. 7, no. 5 (November–December 1979), 54–61. Christmas traditions of food and festivities at Old Salem, N. Car., and Bethlehem, Pa.

ED216 Nettl, Paul. "O Tannenbaum." *Amer.-German Rev.*, vol. 15, no. 2 (1948), 6–7, 9.

ED217 Nitzsche, George E. "The Christmas Putz of the Pennsylvania Germans." *Pa. German Folklore Soc. Publs.*, no. 6 (1941), 1–29. *See also* Richmond E. Myers. "The Moravian Christmas Putz of the Pennsylvania Germans." *Ibid.*, 1–10.

ED218 "An Old-Fashioned Christmas, Told by a Pennsylvania German Housewife." "'S Pennsylfawnisch Deitsch Eck," Allentown *Morning Call*, 13 January 1968.

ED219 Pauli, Hertha E. *The Story of the Christmas Tree*. Boston: Houghton-Mifflin, 1944. 69p.

ED220 "Pennsylvania German Christmas." *Antiques*, vol. 52, no. 6 (December 1947), 426. Featuring the Geesey Collection, Philadelphia Museum of Art.

ED221 Reichard, Harry Hess. "The Christmas Poetry of the Pennsylvania Dutch." *Pa. German Folklore Soc. Publs.*, no. 6 (1941), 1–87.

ED222 Robacker, Earl F. "Christmas—Back Along." *Pa. Folklife*, vol. 16, no. 2 (Winter 1966–1967), 2–13.

ED223 Robbins, Walter L. "Christmas Shooting Rounds in America and Their Background." *Jour. of Amer. Folklore*, vol. 86, no. 339 (1973), 48–52.

ED224 Rominger, Charles H. "Early Christmases in Bethlehem, Pennsylvania (1742–1756), with Translations by Dr. William N. Schwarze..." *Pa. German Folklore Soc. Publs.*, vol. 6 (1941), 1–35.

ED225 Schreiber, William I. "The First American Christmas Tree." *Amer.-German Rev.*, vol. 10, no. 2 (December 1943), 4–5.

ED226 Schreiber, William I. "First Christmas Trees in America." *Jour. of German-Amer. Studies*, vol. 15, no. 1 (March 1980), 25.

ED227 Schreiber, William I. "Virginia's 'German' Tree." *Va. Cavalcade*, vol. 6, no. 3 (1956), 4–7. First Christmas tree in Virginia, 1842.

ED228 Schreiber, William I. "Wie der Weihnachtsbaum nach Amerika kam." *Christ Unterwegs*, vol. 11, no. 12 (1957), 2–4.

ED229 Schwarze, William N., trans. "Early Christmases in Bethlehem, Pennsylvania (1742–1956). Transcription of items from the Bethlehem Diary Relating to Early Celebrations of Christmas in Bethlehem, Pennsylvania." *Pa. German Folklore Soc., Publs.*, vol. 6 (1941), 1–35.

ED230 Shoemaker, Alfred L. *Christmas in Pennsylvania: A Folk-Cultural Study*. Introd. by Don Yoder. Kutztown: Pa. Folklore Soc., 1959. 116p. Lg. Quarto. Rev. in *Amer.-German Rev.*, vol. 25, no. 3 (1959), 39; by W. E. Boyer, *Jour. of Amer. Folklore*, vol. 73 (1960), 160–62; J. F. McDermott, *Western Folklore*, vol. 21, no. 1 (1962), 51–53; A. D. Sanders, *Hist. Rev. of Berks Co.*, vol. 25, no. 1 (1959), 33; J. J. Stoudt, "'S Pennsylfawnisch Deitsch Eck," Allentown *Morning Call*, 14 February 1959.

ED231 Snyder, Philip. *The Christmas Tree Book. The History of the American Christmas Tree and Antique Christmas Tree Ornaments*. New York: Viking Pr., ca. 1976.

ED232 Sowers, Betty. "Christmas Customs from the Germans." *N. Car. Folklore*, vol. 20, no. 4 (November 1972), 171–73.

ED233 Tennant, Eugenia L. *American Christmases: From the Puritans to the Victorians*. Hicksville, N.Y.: Exposition Pr., 1975. 126p.

ED234 Webb, Walter Prescott. "Christmas and New Year in Texas." *Southwestern Hist. Quar.*, vol. 44 (1940–1941), 357–79. With emphasis on the Texas German farmers.

ED235 Wust, Klaus G. "Deutsches Christfest und der Weihnachtsbaum in Virginia." *Washington Jour.*, 9, 16, 23 December 1960.

ED236 Yoder, Don. "Christmas Fraktur, Christmas Broadsides." *Pa. Folklife*, vol. 14, no. 2 (1964), 2–9. Bookplates, Madonnas, sketches, Christmas greeting cards, etc.; all richly illustrated.

ED237 Zehner, Olive G. "Christmas in the Dutch Country." *Amer.-German Rev.*, vol. 20, no. 2 (1953), 7–9. Tree decorations, cookies, and food among the Pennsylvania Germans.

ED245 Robbins, Walter L. "Wishing In and Shooting In the New Year among the Germans in the Carolinas." In: *American Folklife*. Ed. Don Yoder. Austin: Univ. of Texas Pr., 1976, p.257–79.

ED246 Soldner, Dora M. "Serenading on the New Year's Eve." *Amer.-German Rev.*, vol. 18, no. 2 (1951), 26–28. A folk custom observed in Ohio, Indiana and Missouri.

ED247 Troxell, William S. *Alta Neiyohrs-Winscha*. Allentown, Pa.: n.p., 1933. New Year's wishes in the dialect.

New Year's Lore

ED238 Barba, Preston A. "Es Neiyaahr Aaschiesse." "'S Pennsylfawnisch Deitsch Eck," Allentown *Morning Call*, 31 December 1949. Repr., *ibid.*, 2, 16 January 1965.

ED239 Boyer, Walter E. "The New Year Wish of the Pennsylvania Dutch Broadside." *Pa. Folklife*, vol. 10, no. 2 (1959), 45–49.

ED240 Leh, Leonard L. "Shooting In the New Year." *The Pa. Dutchman*, vol. 4, no. 9 (January 1953), 3f.

ED241 Neff, Larry M. "Annie German's New Year's Wish." *Der Reggeboge*, vol. 7, nos. 3–4 (1973), 7–13.

ED242 Robbins, Walter L. "The German-American Custom of Wishing in and Shooting in the New Year." Diss., Univ. of North Carolina, 1969. 436p.

ED243 Robbins, Walter L. "The North Carolina New Year's Shoot." "'S Pennsylfawnisch Deitsch Eck," Allentown *Morning Call*, 3 January 1959. German settlers brought to this country the custom of "shooting in" and "wishing in" the New Year.

ED244 Robbins, Walter L. "Pastor Thomas R. Brendle's Remarks on Wishing in and Shooting in the New Year." *Historic Schaefferstown Record*, vol. 6, no. 5 (1972). Whole issue.

Easter

ED248 Best, Martha. "Easter Customs in the Lehigh Valley." *Pa. Folklife*, vol. 17, no. 3 (Spring 1968), 2–13.

ED249 Jordan, Terry G. "The Old World Antecedent of the Fredericksburg Easter Fires." In: *The Folklore of Texan Cultures*. Ed. F. E. Abernethy. Publs. of the Texas Folklore Soc., no. 38. Austin: Encino, 1974, p.151–54.

ED250 Kulp, Isaac Clarence, Jr. [Lenten and Eastertide Folk Customs.] *The Goschenhoppen Region*, vol. 1, no. 3 (Lichtmess 1969), 7–11.

ED251 "Oster-Baum im Metropolitan Museum of Art." *New Yorker Staats-Zeitung und Herold*, vol. 146, no. 14 (1980), Sec. A, 3. A Pennsylvania-German "Easter Tree."

ED252 Shoemaker, Alfred L. *Eastertide in Pennsylvania: A Folk-Cultural Study*. Kutztown: Pa. Folklife Soc., 1959. 96p. Rev. in *Amer.-German Rev.*, vol. 26, no. 4 (1960), 40.

ED253 Shoemaker, Alfred L. "Good Friday and Easter Lore." *The Pa. Dutchman*, vol. 4, no. 15 (1953), 2–3, 5, 11.

ED254 Shoemaker, Alfred L. "Scratch-Carved Easter Eggs." *The Dutchman*, vol. 6, no. 4 (1955), 20–23. Cites mentions of the custom appearing in newspapers from 1874 to 1883. On the Fred Wichmann Collection.

EE
Folk Arts / Material Culture

General

EE1 Adams, Ruth. *Pennsylvania Dutch Art.* Cleveland/New York: World Publ. Co., 1950. 64p. Rev. by P. A. Barba, "'S Pennsylfawnisch Deitsch Eck," Allentown *Morning Call*, 27 January 1951; G. O. Bird, *Hist. Rev. of Berks Co.*, vol. 16, no. 2 (1951), 57.

EE2 Allen, George. "A Note on Pennsylvania Dutch Art." "'S Pennsylfawnisch Deitsch Eck," Allentown *Morning Call*, 19 March 1949.

EE3 Barton, J. R. *Rural Artists of Wisconsin.* Madison: n.p., 1948.

EE4 Bird, Michael. "A Germanic Plenitude." *Canad. Antiques and Art Rev.*, October 1981, 34–37.

EE5 Bird, Michael, and Terry Kobayashi. *A Splendid Harvest: Germanic Folk and Decorative Arts in Canada.* New York: Van Nostrand Reinhold, ca. 1981. 240p. A general survey from architecture to Frakturs through the whole of Canada.

EE6 Bishop, Robert, and Patricia Coblentz. *American Decorative Arts. 360 Years of Creative Design.* New York: Abrams, ca. 1980. 406p.

EE7 Bixler, Miriam E. "David Bixler, Folk Artist." *Jour. of the Lancaster Co. Hist. Soc.*, vol. 81 (Hilarymas 1977), 30–38.

EE8 Bridenbaugh, Carl. *The Colonial Craftsman.* New York: N.Y. Univ. Pr., 1950. 214p. Rev. by P. Rouse, *Va. Mag. of Hist. and Biog.*, vol. 58, 526–27; L. P. Stavisky, *Amer. Hist. Rev.*, vol. 56 (1950), 112–13; E. C. Kirkland, *William and Mary Quar.*, vol. 7 (1950), 614–16.

EE9 "Carl Ned Foltz: A Multiply Talented Craftsman in the Pennsylvania German Tradition." *Newsletter of the Soc. for German-Amer. Studies,* vol. 2, no. 2 (1980–1981), 14. Craftsman in pottery and baskets, Reinholds, Pa.

EE10 Coffman, Barbara F. "Early Pennsylvania German Arts and Crafts in Canada." "'S Pennsylfawnisch Deitsch Eck," Allentown *Morning Call*, 7, 14 August 1954.

EE11 "Crafts Today and Tomorrow." *Amer.-German Rev.*, vol. 15, no. 1 (1948), 15–16. Report on an exhibit by the Carl Schurz Memorial Foundation.

EE12 Douglas, Paul H. "The Material Culture of the Harmony Society." Diss., George Washington Univ., 1973. Publ. in *Pa. Folklife*, vol. 24, no. 3 (1975), 2–14.

EE13 Dow, James R. "Amana Folk Art: Tradition and Creativity among the True Inspirationists of Iowa." In: *Papers from the St. Olaf Symposium on German-Americana.* Ed. L. J. Rippley and S. M. Benjamin. Occasional Papers of the Society for German-American Studies, no. 10. Morgantown, W. Va.: Department of Foreign Languages, West Virginia University, 1980, p.19–30.

EE14 Dow, James R., and Madeline Roemig. "Amana Folk Art and Craftsmanship." *The Palimpsest*, vol. 58, no. 2 (March–April 1977), 54–63.

EE15 Downs, Joseph. *Pennsylvania German Arts and Crafts. A Picture Book.* New York: Metropolitan Museum of Art, 1942, 1943, 1946, 1949. 4p. and 30 plates. Frakturs.

EE16 Drepperd, Carl. *American Pioneer Arts and Artists.* Springfield, Mass.: The Pond-Ekberg Co., 1942. 172p.

EE17 Ford, Alice. *Pictorial Folk Art, New England to California.* New York: The Studio Publs., Inc., 1949. 172p.

EE18 Gerhard, Elmer Schultz, ed. "Schwenkfelder Craftsmen, Inventors and Surveyors." *Schwenkfeldiana* (Norristown, Pa.), vol. 1, no. 5 (1945).

EE19 Gusler, Wallace B. "The Arts of Shenandoah County, Virginia 1770–1825." *Jour. of Early Southern Decorative Arts*, vol. 5, no. 2 (November 1979), 6–35.

EE20 Hansen, Hans Jürgen, ed. *Europas Volkskunst und die europäisch beeinflußte Volkskunst Amerikas*. Forew. by Robert Wildhaber. Zürich: Neue Sehweizer Bibliothek; Oldenburg: Stalling, 1967. 288p. Issued in English.: London: Thames & Hudson, 1968; New York: McGraw Hill, 1968. 288p.

EE21 Hershberger, Abner, ed. *Mennonite Artists Contemporary 1975*. Goshen, Ind.: n.p., 1975.

EE22 Hirschl and Adler Galleries, New York. *Plain and Fancy. A Survey of American Folk Art*. New York, 1970. 72p. Catalogue of an exhibit shown 30 April–23 May 1970.

EE23 Horst, Mel, photographer. *The Folk Art of Pennsylvania Dutchland*. Lebanon: Applied Arts Publ., 1966. 4th printing, 1973. 33p.

EE24 Jensen, Dana O. "The Decorative Art of Jacob Keller." *Bull., Mo. Hist. Soc.*, vol. 23 (1967), 234–35.

EE25 Johnson, Kathleen E. "19th-Century Moravian Schoolgirl Art." *Art and Antiques*, vol. 3, no. 6 (1980), 78–83.

EE26 Kauffman, Henry. *Pennsylvania Dutch American Folk Art*. American Studio Books. New York: Holme Pr., 1946. 136p. Repr. New York: Dover Publs., 1964. Rev. by J. W. Frey, *Jour. of Amer. Folklore*, vol. 62, no. 245 (1949), 335–36.

EE27 Keyser, Mrs. C. Naaman. *Home Craft Course Series*. Plymouth Meeting, Pa.: Mrs. C. Naaman Keyser, 1943–1950. A series of 28 booklets on Pennsylvania arts and folk culture.

EE28 Lichten, Frances. *The Folk Art of Rural Pennsylvania*. New York: Scribner's Sons, 1946. 276p. Reissued in 1963. Rev. by J. W. Frey, *Jour. of Amer. Folklore*, vol. 62, no. 245 (1949), 335–36; in *William and Mary Quar.*, vol. 4, no. 3 (1947), 371–73.

EE29 Lichten, Frances. "Pennsylvania German Folk Art." In: *The Concise Encyclopedia of American Antiques*, vol. 2. New York: Hawthorn Books, Inc., 1958, p.401–12; plates 249–56.

EE30 Lipman, Jean. *American Folk Art in Wood, Metal, and Stone*. New York: Pantheon Pr., 1948. 193p.

EE31 Lipman, Jean. *The Flowering of American Folk Art, 1776–1876*. New York: Viking Pr., 1974. For Pennsylvania Germans, see p.104–17.

EE32 Loserth, Johann. "Crafts of the Hutterian Brethren." *Mennonite Encyclopedia* (1956–1969). Vol. 1, 728–30.

EE33 Lutz, Gladys. "Upper Lehigh Pennsylvania German Folk Arts and Crafts." *Procs., Lehigh Co. Hist. Soc.*, vol. 34 (1980), 165–88.

EE34 Patterson, Nancy-Lou. "Mennonite Folk Art of Waterloo County." *Ontario Hist.*, vol. 60, no. 3 (September 1968), 81–104.

EE35 Patterson, Nancy-Lou. "Mennonite Traditional Arts." *Canad. Antiques*, vol. 6, no. 5 (1971), 78–79.

EE36 Patterson, Nancy-Lou. *Mennonite Traditional Arts of the Waterloo Region and Southern Ontario*. Kitchener: Kitchener–Waterloo Art Gallery, 1974.

EE37 Patterson, Nancy-Lou. *Swiss-German and Dutch-German Mennonite Traditional Art in the Waterloo Region, Ontario*. Ottawa: National Museum of Canada, 1979. 216p.

EE38 "Pennsylvania Dutch Influence." *House and Garden*, vol. 79, no. 6 (1941), 21–41. Notes on language, art, cookery, etc.

EE39 "Pennsylvania German Arts." *Antiques*, vol. 75 (March 1959), 264–71.

EE40 Pieske, Christa. "Volkskundliche Aktivitäten in Pennsylvanien." *Zeitschrift für Volkskunde*, vol. 76 (1980), 89–92.

EE41 Prime, Alfred Coxe. *The Arts and Crafts in Philadelphia, Maryland and South Carolina. Gleanings from Newspapers*. [Topsfield, Mass.]: n.p., 1929. 323p. Also his *The Arts and Crafts in Philadelphia Maryland and South Carolina 1786–1800. Ser. Two. Gleanings from Newspapers*, 1932. 331p.

EE42 Ramsay, John. "Pioneer Arts and Crafts in Ohio." *Amer.-German Rev.*, vol. 9, no. 3 (1943), 25–27, 35.

EE43 Reichmann, Felix. "On American Folk Art." *Amer.-German Rev.*, vol. 9, no. 6 (August 1943), 34–36. Rev. of Carl W. Drepperd's *American Pioneer Arts and Artists*.

EE44 Riccardi, Saro John. *Pennsylvania Dutch Folk Art and Architecture: A Selective Annotated Bibliography*. New York: New York Public Library, 1942. 15p. Cf. *Bull. of the N.Y. Public Library*, vol. 46 (June 1942), 473–88.

EE45 Richman, Irwin. *Pennsylvania's Decorative Arts in the Age of Handcraft*. Harrisburg: Pa. Hist. and Museum Commission, 1978.

EE46 Robacker, Earl F. *Arts of the Pennsylvania Dutch*. New York: Castle Books, 1965. 240p. Discusses certain specialties: spatterware, tin, redware, chalkware, butter molds, and book collecting.

EE47 Robacker, Earl F. *Touch of the Dutchland*. New York: A. S. Barnes, 1965. 240p. Illus.

EE48 Shelley, Donald A. *The Fraktur-Writings...of the Pennsylvania Germans*. Allentown, 1961, Sec. A, p.187–89. Bibliography of writings on the European backgrounds of Pennsylvania German folk arts (to 1968).

EE49 Smith, Elmer L. *Arts and Crafts of the Shenandoah Valley, A Pictorial Presentation*. Publ. for the Shenandoah Valley Folklore Soc. Witmer, Pa.: Applied Arts, 1968. 43p. Rev. in "'S Pennsylfawnisch Deitsch Eck," Allentown *Morning Call*, 15 February 1969.

EE50 Steinmetz, Rollin C., and Charles S. Rice. *Vanishing Crafts and Their Craftsmen*. New Brunswick, N.J.: Rutgers Univ. Pr., 1959. 160p. Rev. by A. J. Wall, *Pa. Mag. of Hist. and Biog.*, vol. 84, no. 2 (1960), 260.

EE51 Stoudt, John Joseph. *Early Pennsylvania Arts and Crafts*. New York: A. S. Barnes, 1964. 360p. Rev. by E. DeJonge, *Pa. Hist.*, vol. 33, no. 2 (April 1966), 245–47; V. E. Lewis, *Western Pa. Hist. Mag.*, vol. 49, no. 2 (April 1966), 165–69; I. M. Quimby, *Pa. Mag. of Hist. and Biog.*, vol. 89, no. 4 (1965), 493–95.

EE52 Stoudt, John Joseph. *Pennsylvania German Folk Art*. Allentown: Schlechter's, 1948. 403p. Rev. by R. W. Albright, "'S Pennsylfawnisch Deitsch Eck," Allentown *Morning Call*, 19 February 1949; A. L. Shoemaker, *William and Mary Quar.*, vol. 7 (1950), 158.

EE53 Stoudt, John Joseph. *Sunbonnets and Shoofly Pies. A Pennsylvania Dutch Cultural History*. New York: Castle Books, 1973. 272p. See esp. Chap. 6: "Problems of Pennsylvania Folk Art," p.139–66.

EE54 Swisher, Bob. "German Folk Art in Harmony Cemetery." *Appalachian Jour.*, vol. 5 (1978), 313–17.

EE55 Taylor, Lonn W. "Fachwerk und Brettstuhl: The Rejection of Traditional Folk Culture." In: *Perspectives in American Folk Art*. Eds. Ian M. G. Quimby and Scott T. Swank. New York: Norton, for the Winterthur Museum, 1978, p.162–76.

EE56 Van Ravenswaay, Charles. *The Arts and Architecture of German Settlements in Missouri: A Vanishing Culture*. Columbia, Mo.: Univ. of Missouri Pr., 1977. 536p. Rev. by B. L. Hermann, *Jour. of the Soc. of Architectural Historians*, vol. 37 (1978), 211–12; O. Overby, *Mo. Hist. Rev.*, vol. 72 (1978), 351–53; R. W. Perrin, *Jour. of Amer. Hist.*, vol. 66 (1979), 681–82; D. E. Pitzer, *Amer. Hist. Rev.*, vol. 83 (1978), 536–37; J. Tager, *South Atlantic Quar.*, vol. 77 (1978), 383–84; R. E. Taggart, *Antiques*, vol. 113 (1978), 1311; D. H. Tolzmann, *Jour. of German-Amer. Studies*, vol. 13 (1978), 122–23. Survey and analysis of log and frame construction; buildings in stone and brick, barns, furniture, and their decorative features.

EE57 Van Ravenswaay, Charles. "Missouri River German Settlements. Part 1. The Buildings, 1831–1870. Part 2. The Decorative Arts, 1831–1900." *Antiques*, vol. 113 (1978), 178–91, 394–409.

EE58 Weiser, Frederick S. "Baptismal Certificate and Gravemarker: Pennsylvania German Folk Art at the Beginning and End of Life." In: *Perspectives on American Folk Art*. Eds. Ian M. G. Quimby and Scott T. Swank. New York: Norton, for the Winterthur Museum, 1978, p.134–61.

EE59 Weiser, Frederick S. "Pennsylvania German Folk Art." In: *How to Know American Folk Art: Eleven Experts Discuss Many Aspects of the Field*. Ed. Ruth Andrews. New York: Dutton, 1977, p.135–52.

EE60 Weygandt, Cornelius. "Dutch Folk Art." *The Pa. Dutchman*, vol. 5, no. 15 (1954), 12–15.

EE61 Whitemore, Eleanor M. "Origins of Pennsylvania Folk Art." *Antiques*, vol. 39, no. 9 (1940), 106–10. Reply to a statement by Carl Drepperd.

EE62 Wismer, Helen. "Folk Art of the Pennsylvania Dutch." *Pa. German Folklore Soc. of Ontario*, vol. 7 (1979), 137–44.

Exhibitions / Museums / Collections

See also Museums / Restorations / Festivals / Tour Guides *under* Section BH: The Pennsylvania Germans.

GENERAL

EE63 Allentown Art Museum. *Pennsylvania Folk Art*. Allentown, 1974. 99p. Catalogue of an exhibition, 20 October–1 December 1974.

EE64 Downs, Joseph. *A Handbook of the Pennsylvania German Galleries in the American Wing*. New York: Metropolitan Museum of Art. American Wing, 1934. 22p. Describes a collection that "has come to the museum in the generous gift of Mrs. Robert W. de Forest." See also *Publs. of the Pa. German Folklore Soc.*, vol. 1 (1936), 91–100.

EE65 *The Folk Art and Crafts of the Susquehanna and Chenango River Valleys. Catalogue*. Exhibit at the Roberson Center for the Arts and Sciences, Binghamton, N.Y., 26 February–11 June 1978.

EE66 Garvan, Beatrice B. *The Pennsylvania German Collection* [in the Philadelphia Museum of Art]. Handbooks in American Art, no. 2. Philadelphia: Philadelphia Museum of Art, ca. 1982. 416p. 1128 illus. Descriptions of objects; name of artist with date and place of manufacture; translations of inscriptions.

EE67 Handley, Mimi. "Heart of America." *Early Amer. Life*, vol. 10 (February 1979), 22. On the exhibit "The Heart of American Life," an exhibit of folk art at Museum of American Folk Art, New York, 26 June–15 October 1978. Incl. many Pennsylvania German pieces.

EE68 "The Henry F. duPont Winterthur Museum." *Antiques*, vol. 60, no. 5 (November 1951), 443–46.

EE69 "In the Museums. (Fraktur at the Brussels World's Fair)." *Antiques*, vol. 73, no. 5 (May 1958), 476.

EE70 Kauffman, Henry J. "Himmelreich Collection." *The Dutchman*, vol. 7, no. 3 (Winter 1956), 18–29. Walter Himmelreich Collection.

EE71 "The Pennsylvania Folklife Society Archives Collection." *Pa. Folklife*, vol. 28 (Autumn 1978), 49. Prof. W. T. Parsons is archivist of this collection of MSS., prints, books, cassettes, slides, etc.

EE72 "Pennsylvania German Arts." *Antiques*, vol. 75, no. 3 (March 1959), 264–71. On the Decorative Arts Wing at the Philadelphia Museum of Art.

EE73 "Sale of Wetzel Collection Brings to Light Masterpieces of German-American Art." *Newsletter, Soc. for German-Amer. Studies*, vol. 2, no. 3 (1980–1981), 18.

EE74 Utterback, Martha. *Early Texas Art in the Witte Museum*. San Antonio: San Antonio Museum Association, 1968.

EE75 Weiser, Frederick S. "Two Folk Art Exhibits." *Der Reggeboge*, vol. 9, no. 1 (1975), 25–26. At Allentown, Pa., and Stuttgart, Germany.

EE76 Zehner, Olive G. "High Folk Art Collection." *The Dutchman*, vol. 6, no. 1 (June 1954), 16–19. On the Harry S. High Collection.

EE77 Zehner, Olive G. "Trump Collection." *The Dutchman*, vol. 6, no. 3 (Winter 1954–1955), 10–13. Pennsylvania German arts and crafts.

GEESEY COLLECTION, PHILADELPHIA MUSEUM OF ART

EE78 "Folklore." *Hist. Rev. of Berks Co.*, vol. 17, no. 3 (April–June 1952) 66–74.

EE79 Lichten, Frances. *Pennsylvania Dutch Folk Arts from the Titus C. Geesey Collection*. Philadelphia: Philadelphia Museum of Art, 1958. 33p. 63 illus.

EE80 "Titus C. Geesey Collection." *Antiques*, vol. 52, no. 4 (October 1947), 255–59.

EE81 Wolfe, Beatrice B. "The Geesey Collection." *Amer.-German Rev.*, vol. 20, no. 6 (1954), 14–17. On a collection of furniture presented to the museum.

WILLIAMSBURG, VIRGINIA

EE82 Colonial Williamsburg, Inc. *American Folk Art.* Williamsburg: Colonial Williamsburg, Inc., 1940. 50p. Catalogue.

EE83 Little, Nina Fletcher. *The Abby Aldrich Rockefeller Folk Art Collection.* Williamsburg: Colonial Williamsburg, Inc., 1957. 402p. With 165 color plates.

Antiques / Collecting / Auctions

EE84 Asher, J., Jr. *The Collector's Art A and Z.* Keyser Home Craft Course Series, no. 26. Kutztown: The Kutztown Publ. Co., 1948.

EE85 Asher, J., Jr. "The Odenwelder Collection." *Antiques*, vol. 51, no. 4 (April 1947), 246–49. Illus.

EE86 Aurand, Ammon Monroe. *Where to Dine in the Pennsylvania Dutch Region: A Guide to Travel Information, Historic Places, Points of Interest, Antique Dealers, Card and Gift Shops, Rare Book Dealers.* Rev. ed. N.p.: the author, 1946. 32p.

EE87 Breininger, Lester P. "Country Auctions: Going, Going, but not Gone." *Pa. Folklife*, vol. 28 (1978–1979), Folk Festival Supplement, 25–27.

EE88 "Brinton '1704' House." *Antiques*, vol. 71, no. 1 (January 1957), 64–65. Pennsylvania German arts and crafts.

EE89 *Catalogue of the Mr. and Mrs. Richard Quigley Sale.* Kenhorst, Pa.: Pennypacker Auction Center, 1947.

EE90 Kessler, Merrill M. "Altfaeschend." *Der Reggeboge*, vol. 6, no. 1 (1972), 3.

EE91 Krahn, Cornelius. *Antiques, Auctions, and Pottage.* North Newton, Kans.: Mennonite Library and Archives, 1969.

EE92 Lefèvre, Edwin. "The Meaning of Pennsylvania Dutch Antiques." *Saturday Evening Post*, vol. 207, 20, 27 April 1935.

EE93 Robacker, Ada F., and Earl F. Robacker. "...Three Times—and Sold!" *Pa. Folklife*, vol. 24 (1975), Folk Festival Supplement, 35–43.

EE94 Robacker, Earl F. "Antiques for Fancy and for Fun." *The Pa. Dutchman*, vol. 6, no. 5 (1955), 2–6. Early Pennsylvania German toys and ornamental objects.

EE95 Robacker, Earl F. *Old Stuff in Up-Country Pennsylvania.* Photography by Stephen A. Karas and Bryden Taylor. South Brunswick, Pa.: A. S. Barnes, 1973. 283p.

EE96 Robacker, Earl F. *Pennsylvania Dutch Stuff. A Guide to Country Antiques.* Philadelphia: Univ. of Pennsylvania Pr., 1944. 163p. Rev. by H. S. Bornemann, *Pa. Mag. of Hist. and Biog.*, vol. 69, no. 2 (1945), 179–80; G. E. Brumbaugh, *Pa. Hist.*, vol. 12, no. 2 (1945), 175–76; W. G. Dooley, *N.Y. Times Book Rev.*, 7 January 1945, 19; G.E.P., *Hist. Rev. of Berks Co.*, vol. 10, no. 3 (1945), 90; A. W. Rutledge, *Md. Hist. Mag.*, vol. 40, no. 2 (1945), 167; C. Weygandt, *William and Mary Quar.*, vol. 2, no. 3 (1945), 327–29.

EE97 Robacker, Earl F. "The Rise of Interest in Pennsylvania Dutch Antiques." *The Pa. Dutchman*, vol. 8, no. 1 (1956), 18–22. "The Rise of Interest in Folk Art." *Ibid.*, vol. 10, no. 1 (Spring 1959), 20–29.

EE98 Robacker, Earl F., and Ada F. Robacker. "Ancient of Days—Plus Tax!" *Pa. Folklife*, vol. 16, no. 4 (Summer 1967), 2–9. Pennsylvania German household objects.

EE99 Robacker, Earl F., and Ada F. Robacker. "Antiques in Dutchland." *Pa. Folklife*, vol. 12, no. 3 (Fall 1961), 2–7.

EE100 Robacker, Earl F., and Ada F. Robacker. "Like the One Grandma Had!" *Pa. Folklife*, vol. 14, no. 4 (1965), 14–20. Antiques and artifacts.

EE101 Sussel, Arthur J. *Auction Catalogue*. Part 1. *Arts and Crafts of Pennsylvania and Other Notable Americana*. New York: n.p., 1958. Illus.

EE102 Weygandt, Cornelius. "From a Haycock Garret." In: *The Dutch Country*. New York: Appleton-Century, 1939, p.92–101. On the collecting of early examples of German printing in Pennsylvania.

EE103 Wright, Louis B. *The American Heritage History of Colonial Antiques*. New York: American Heritage Publ. Co., ca. 1966. Rev. in *N. Y. Folklore Quar.*, vol. 23, no. 4 (December 1967), 309. With extensive treatment of Pennsylvania German craftsmanship.

EE104 Zehner, Olive G. "Hardly Bigger than a Peanut." *The Dutchman*, vol. 6, no. 2 (Fall 1954), 34–36. Antique miniatures.

EF
Motifs and Symbols in Folk Art

General

EF1 Barba, Preston A. "Symbols and Stones." *Pa. History*, vol. 23, no. 2 (1956), 241–47. Folk art motifs on 18th-century tombstones in Pennsylvania.

EF2 Boyer, Walter E. "The Meaning of Human Figures in Pennsylvania Dutch Folk Art." *Pa. Folklife*, vol. 11, no. 2 (Fall 1960), 5–23.

EF3 Breitenbach, Edgar. "Des Kaysers Abschied: Das Totentanzmotiv unter den Deutschen Pennsylvaniens." *Philobiblon*, vol. 22 (ca. 1978), 42–49. Also in: *Der Reggeboge*, vol. 12, no. 1 (1978), 4–9. Refers to a Christopher Sauer broadside of 1745.

EF4 Bronner, Simon J. "Investigating Identity and Expression in Folk Art." *Winterthur Portfolio*, vol. 16 (1981), 65–83.

EF5 Christensen, Erwin O. *The Index of American Design*. New York: Macmillan, 950. 229p., with 378 plates. Rev. by Keith K. Cunningham, *Jour. of Amer. Folklore*, vol. 92 (1979), 373–74. Publ. for the National Gallery of Art, Washington, D.C.

EF6 Day, Jo Anne C. *Pennsylvania Dutch Cut and Use Stencils*. New York: Dover Publs., n.d. 64p. 43 authentic working stencils, 4 in 2-part designs.

EF7 Drachman, Albert I. "Tracking the Elusive Distelfink." *The Pa. Dutchman*, vol. 6, no. 5 (1955), 28–35.

EF8 "The Eagle in Americana." *Antiques*, vol. 44 (July 1943), 34–35.

EF9 Ferris, Edythe. "Some Origins of Pennsylvania-Dutch Art." *Amer.-German Rev.*, vol. 10, no. 2 (December 1943), 14–16.

EF10 *Folk Art in Rural Pennsylvania—A Portfolio of 15 Plates*. Presented by the Pennsylvania Art Project. N.p.: privately printed, 1941. Rev. in "'S Pennsylfawnisch Deitsch Eck," *Allentown Morning Call*, 8 March 1941.

EF11 Friedman, Herbert. *The Symbolic Goldfinch: Its History and Significance in European and Devotional Art*. Washington, D.C.: n.p., 1946. 254p.

EF12 Gehret, Ellen J. "O Noble Heart . . . : An Examination of a Motif of Design from Pennsylvania German Embroidered Hand Towels." *Der Reggeboge*, vol. 14, no. 3 (1980), 1–14.

EF13 Heckscher, William S. "Renaissance Emblems: Observations Suggested by Some Emblem-

Books in the Princeton University Library." *Princeton Univ. Library Chronicle*, vol. 15, no. 2 (Winter 1954), 55–68. On frakturs.

EF14 Hurwitz, Elizabeth A. "Decorative Elements in the Domestic Architecture of Eastern Pennsylvania." *The Pa. Dutchman*, vol. 7, no. 2 (1955), 6–29. Motifs used in domestic architecture.

EF15 Knotts, Benjamin. *Pennsylvania German Designs. A Fortfolio of Silk Screen Prints.* New York: Metropolitan Museum of Art, 1943. 20 plates in color, printed on heavy board, with text on verso. From the Index of American Design, National Gallery of Art; research by the Pennsylvania Works Project Administration.

EF16 Krick, Richard D. *Examples of Pennsylvania Dutch (German) Folk Art.* Philadelphia: Carl Schurz Memorial Foundation, 1942, 14 pages of ornamental motifs. See also this Krick's *Portfolio of Pennsylvania Dutch Art.* Philadelphia; CSMF, 1941.

EF17 Lichten, Frances. *Folk Art Motifs of Pennsylvania.* New York: Hastings House, 1954. Repr. Dover Publ., 1954. 80p. Rev. by P. A. Barba, "'S Pennsylfawnisch Deitsch Eck," Allentown *Morning Call*, 4 December 1954; A. D. Graeff, *Pa. Mag. of Hist. and Biog.*, vol. 79 (1955), 266–67; O. G. Newcomer, *Hist. Rev. of Berks Co.*, vol. 20, no. 2 (1955), 53.

EF18 Lipman, Jean, and Eve Meulendyke. *American Folk Decoration.* New York: Oxford Univ. Pr., 1951. 163p. Rev. by P. A. Barba, "'S Pennsylfawnisch Deitsch Eck," Allentown *Morning Call*, 5 January 1952.

EF19 *Pennsylvania Dutch Designs.* A Portfolio of Ten Plates in Full Color. Plymouth Meeting, Pa.: Mrs. C. Naaman Keyser, 1946. The first of a series of silk screen prints by the Folk Art Press.

EF20 Robacker, Earl F. "The Peacock in Pennsylvania." *Pa. Folklife*, vol. 11, no. 1 (1960), 10–16.

EF21 Robacker, Earl F., and Ada F. Robacker. "The Far-From-Lonely-Heart." *Pa. Folklife*, vol. 17 (1967–1968), no. 2, 2–11. The heart motif in Pennsylvania German ornament.

EF22 Robacker, Earl F., and Ada F. Robacker. "Flight of the *Distelfink*." *Pa. Folklife*, vol. 20, no. 4 (1970–1971), 2–8. Goldfinch imagery in Pennsylvania German folk art.

EF23 Robacker, Earl F., and Ada F. Robacker. "Floral Motifs in Dutchland's Art." *Pa. Folklife*, vol. 17, no. 4 (1968), 2–7.

EF24 Stoudt, John Joseph. *Pennsylvania German Folk Art: An Interpretation.* Pa. German Folklore Soc., vol. 28. Allentown: Schlechter's, 1948. 386p. Revised ed. 1966. Rev. by H. Glassie, *Pa. Hist.*, vol. 35, no. 1 (January 1968), 95–97; D. Yoder, *Pa. Mag. of Hist. and Biog.*, vol. 92, no. 3 (1968), 413–15. Revision and amplification of his *Consider the Lilies* (1937).

EF25 Weygandt, Cornelius. "Beasts in Dutchland." *The Pa. Dutchman*, vol. 6, no. 5 (1955), 10–15. Domesticated and wild animals in the Pennsylvania area and their representation in folk art.

EF26 Weygandt, Cornelius. "Birds in Dutchland." *The Pa. Dutchman*, vol. 6, no. 2 (1954), 8–11.

EF27 Weygandt, Cornelius. "Consider the Rose." In: *The Dutch Country.* New York: Appleton-Century, 1939, p.37–70. On the decorative motif of the rose in Pennsylvania German art.

EF28 Wood, T. Kenneth. "Medieval Art among the Pennsylvania Germans." *Antiques*, vol. 7, no. 5 (May 1925), 263–66.

The "Hex Sign" as Barn Symbol

EF29 Alderfer, Harold F. "On the Trail of the 'Hex Signs'." *Amer.-German Rev.*, vol. 19, no. 6 (1953), 4–8. Reports discovery of hex signs on the walls of a thousand-year-old Byzantine church in Athens.

EF30 Clarke, Kenneth W. "Pennsylvania Hex Signs." *Western Folklore*, vol. 22, no. 1 (1963), 47. Repr. from an AP dispatch from Lenhartsville, Pa., to the Salt Lake *Tribune*, 4 December 1961.

EF31 Heizmann, Louis J. "Are Barn Signs Hex Marks?" *Hist. Rev. of Berks Co.*, vol. 12, no. 1 (October 1946), 11–14.

EF32 "It's Good Luck By Hex!" *Holiday Inn Mag.* (Memphis). April 1968, 8–10. On Pennsylvania Dutch barn signs.

EF33 Johnston, Ames. "The Barn Signs of the Dutch." In: *Yearbook, German Society of Pennsylvania.* Vol. 2. Philadelphia: The Soc., 1951

EF34 Kauffman, Harry H. *Golden Stars on the Barn.* Illus. by Hermann E. Wright. Allentown: n.p., 1965. Repr. in "'S Pennsylfawnisch Deitsch Eck," Allentown *Morning Call*, 13 February 1965.

EF35 Landis, Henry K. "Hex Marks as Talismans." *Antiques*, vol. 30 (October 1936), 156–57, 178.

EF36 Lerch, Lila. "Hex Signs or Fire Marks?" "'S Pennsylfawnisch Deitsch Eck," Allentown *Morning Call*, 10 December 1949. A new approach to the interpretation of hex signs.

EF37 Mahr, August C. "Origin and Significance of Pennsylvania Dutch Barn Symbols." *Ohio State Archaeological and Hist. Quar.*, vol. 54, no. 1 (1945), 1–32. Traces origins to German and general European sources. Full bibliography.

EF38 Shaner, Richard. "Hex Signs: A Living Tradition." *Pa. Folklife*, vol. 27 (1977–1978), Folk Festival Supplement, 2–5.

EF39 Shoemaker, Alfred L. *Pennsylvania Dutch Hex Marks.* Lancaster: The Pa. Dutch Folklore Center, Inc., Franklin and Marshall College, 1950. 32p.

EF40 Stoudt, John Joseph. *The Decorated Barns of Eastern Pennsylvania.* Keyser Home Craft Course Series, no. 15. Allentown: Schlechter's, 1945; Plymouth Meeting, Pa.: Mrs. C. Naaman Keyser, 1945. 16p.

EG

Fraktur—Illuminated Writing

Collections and Exhibits

EG1 Bornemann, Henry S. "Exhibition of Pennsylvania German Fraktur." *Amer.-German Rev.*, vol. 9, no. 4 (April 1943), 33–34.

EG2 [Bornemann, Henry S.] *Pennsylvania German Fraktur. Catalogue.* Philadelphia: Carl Schurz Memorial Foundation, 1943. Catalogue of exhibition, 1 April–1 September 1943.

EG3 Eckhardt, George H. "The Henry S. Bornemann Collection of Pennsylvania-German Fracturs." *Antiques*, vol. 71, no. 6 (June 1957), 538–40.

EG4 Evans, Nancy G. "Documented Fraktur in the Winterthur Collection." *Antiques*, vol. 103 (1973), 307–18, 539–49.

EG5 German Fraktur collection, 1738–1930. 1 ft. In Lancaster County Hist. Soc. collections (MS 66-1657). Hand-drawn and colored baptismal, birth, and marriage certificates.

EG6 Landis Valley Museum. Frakturs, 1793–1873. Ca. 350 items. In the Pennsylvania Farm Museum of Landis Valley, Lancaster (MS 69-1735).

EG7 Lichten, Frances. "Fractur from the Hostetter Collection." *The Pa. Dutchman*, vol. 6, no. 1 (1954), 10–13.

EG8 "New Rooms at The Winterthur Museum (the Fractur Room)." *Antiques*, vol. 67, no. 2 (February 1955), 135. See also: Sweeney, John A. H. "New Pennsylvania Rooms at the Henry F. duPont Winterthur Museum." *Ibid.*, vol. 75, no. 1 (January 1959), 88–90.

EG9 *Pennsylvania German Fraktur and Color Drawing....* Introd. by Don Yoder. Lancaster: Landis Valley Associates, ca. 1969. Exhibited at the Pennsylvania Farm Museum, Landis Valley, Lancaster, Pa., 19 May-30 June 1969.

EG10 Philadelphia, Free Library of Philadelphia. Frakturs, ca. 1750-ca. 1850. In Pennsylvania German Fraktur Collection (*see* MS 60-1142).

EG11 Shaffer, Ellen. "Illuminators, Scribes and Printers: A Glimpse of the Free Library's Pennsylvania Dutch Collection." *Pa. Folklife*, vol. 9, no. 4 (Fall 1958), 18-27.

EG12 Shelley, Donald A. *Catalogue of Pennsylvania German Fraktur-Schriften.* New York: n.p., 1945. 8p. Exhibit January 1945 at Harry Shaw Newman Gallery.

EG13 Sommer, Frank H. *Pennsylvania German Prints, Drawings, and Paintings. A Selection from the Winterthur Collection.* Winterthur, Del.: The Henry Francis duPont Winterthur Museum, 1965. Unpaged. Rev. by J. J. Stoudt, "'S Pennsylfawnisch Deitsch Eck," Allentown *Morning Call*, 24 July 1965. Text and filmstrip of color reproductions.

EG14 Wehmann, Howard H., and Monroe H. Fabian. "Pennsylvania German Fraktur: Folk Art in the National Archives." *Prologue: Jour. of the National Archives*, vol. 2 (Fall 1970), 96-97.

EG15 Weiser, Frederick S., and Howell J. Heaney, comps. *The Pennsylvania German Fraktur of the Free Library of Philadelphia: An Illustrated Catalogue.* Publs. of the Pa. German Soc., nos. 10-11. Philadelphia: The Pa. German Soc., 1976. 2 vols. Rev. in *Choice*, December 1977; by Nancy G. Evans, *Antiques*, vol. 113 (1978), 642-54; Mrs. A. N. B. Garvan, *Pa. Mag. of Hist. and Biog.*, vol. 102 (1978), 115-16; in *Publisher's Weekly*, with remarks by Paul Doebler in columns on book design and manufacturing: vol. 214, no. 6 (7 August 1978), 57-58.

EG16 Western Reserve Historical Society, Cleveland, Ohio. Frakturs. In the oversize MSS. collection (MS 75-1665).

EG17 Wust, Klaus. *American Fraktur: Graphic Folk Art 1745-1855.* New York: Pratt Institute, 1976. 16p. Catalogue of exhibit in the Pratt Graphics Center Gallery.

Frakturs—General

EG18 Abrahams, Ethel E. "The Art of 'Frakturschriften' among the Dutch-German Mennonites." M.A. thesis, Wichita State Univ., 1975.

EG19 Abrahams, Ethel E. "Fraktur by Germans from Russia." *Work Papers of the Amer. Hist. Soc. of Germans from Russia*, vol. 21 (1976), 12-16.

EG20 Abrahams, Ethel E. "Learning Arithmetic with the Help of Fraktur." *Festival Quar.*, May-July 1981, 34.

EG21 Adams, E. Bryding. "The Fraktur Artist Henry Young." *Der Reggeboge*, vol. 11, nos. 3-4 (1977), 1-24.

EG22 Allis, Mary. "The Last of the American Folk Arts." *Amer. Collector*, vol. 9, no. 12 (January 1941), 10-11, 14. On fraktur.

EG23 Bird, Michael S. *Ontario Fraktur. A Pennsylvania-German Folk Tradition in Early Canada.* Toronto: M. F. Feheley Publs., Ltd, 1977. 144p. Rev. by F. S. Weiser, *Antiques*, vol. 114 (1978), 118; in *Der Reggeboge*, vol. 12, no. 1 (1978), 14-15.

EG24 Bird, Michael S. "Ontario Fraktur Art: A Decorative Tradition in Three Germanic Settlements." *Ontario Hist.*, vol. 68, no. 4 (December 1976), 247-72.

EG25 Bivins, John, Jr. "Fraktur in the South: An Itinerant Artist." *Jour. of Early Southern Decorative Arts*, vol. 1, no. 2 (November 1975).

EG26 Bornemann, Henry S. "On the Illuminated Writings (Fraktur Schriften) of the Pennsylvania Germans." *Amer.-German Rev.*, vol. 9, no. 5 (June 1943), 32-35.

EG27 Bornemann, Henry S. *Pennsylvania German Bookplates.* Publs., Pa. German Soc., vol. 54. Philadelphia: the Soc., 1953. 169p. Rev. by P. A. Barba, "'S Pennsylfawnisch Deitsch Eck," Allentown *Morning Call*, 9 January 1954; F. S. Klein, *Pa. Hist.*, vol. 21, no. 2 (1954), 187; I. A. Shave-

Frakturs—General *(cont.)*

lenko, *Pa. Mag. of Hist. and Biog.*, vol. 78 (1954), 387–89.

EG28 Bornemann, Henry S. *Pennsylvania German Illuminated Manuscripts: A Classification of Fraktur-Schriften and an Inquiry into Their History and Art.* Norristown: n.p., 1937. Repr. New York: Dover, 1973. 60p.

EG29 Brenner, Scott F. "Pennsylvania German Bookplates." *Hist. Rev. of Berks Co.*, vol. 9, no. 3 (1944), 66–69.

EG30 Brigham, Clarence S. *History and Bibliography of American Newspapers, 1690–1820.* 2 vols. Worcester: Amer. Antiquarian Soc., 1947. Incl. treatment of printed frakturs.

EG31 Eyde, M. Louise. *Pennsylvania German Illuminated Manuscripts.* Keyser Home Craft Course Series, no. 7. Plymouth Meeting, Pa.: Mrs. C. Naaman Keyser, 1945.

EG32 Fabian, Monroe H. "The Easton Bible Artist Identified." *Pa. Folklife*, vol. 22, no. 3 (1972–1973), 2–14.

EG33 Fabian, Monroe H. "John Daniel Eisenbrown, Frakturist." *Pa. Folklife*, vol. 24, no. 2 (1974–1975), 31–35.

EG34 Fabian, Monroe H. "Margareta Schwartz's Taufschein." *Prologue: Jour. of the National Archives*, vol. 4 (Winter 1972), 224–26.

EG35 Friedrich, Gerhard. "The Seven Rules of Wisdom." *Amer.-German Rev.*, vol. 11, no. 2 (1944), 15–16. A specimen of *Fraktur-Schrift* in the Cassel Collection, Juniata College.

EG36 Good, E. Reginald. *Anna's Art: The Fraktur Art of Anna Weber, a Waterloo County Mennonite Artist, 1814–1888.* Kitchener, Ont.: Pochauna, 1976. 48p.; New York: Van Nostrand, 1976.

EG37 Good, E. Reginald. "Isaac Ziegler Hunsicker: Ontario Schoolmaster and Fraktur Artist." *Pa. Folklife*, vol. 26, no. 4 (1977), 2–8.

EG38 Good, E. Reginald. "Ontario Fraktur Artist Joseph Bauman (1815–1890)." *Canad. Collector*, vol. 11, no. 4 (1976), 35–37.

EG39 Hollyday, Guy Tilghman. "The Ephrata Codex: Relationships between Text and Illustration." *Pa. Folklife*, vol. 20 (Autumn 1970), 28–43.

EG40 Hollyday, Guy Tilghman. "The Ephrata Wall-Charts and Their Inscriptions." *Pa. Folklife*, vol. 19 (1969–1970), 34–46. Discussion of the fraktur work at this Pennsylvania cloister.

EG41 Hommel, Rudolf. "Tavern Inscriptions." *Amer.-German Rev.*, vol. 9, no. 1 (October 1942), 31–32. 2 illus. with fraktur lettering.

EG42 Hopf, Carroll. "Calligraphic Drawings and Pennsylvania German Fraktur." *Pa. Folklife*, vol. 22, no. 1 (1972), 2–9.

EG43 Johnson, David R. "Christian Strenge, Fraktur Artist." *Der Reggeboge*, vol. 13, no. 3 (1979), 1–24.

EG44 Johnson, J. A. *Type Designs, Their History and Development.* London: n.p., 1934. On the development of fraktur lettering.

EG45 Jones, Leslie Webber, "Pricking Manuscripts: The Instruments and Their Significance." *Speculum. A Jour. of Medieval Studies*, vol. 21, no. 4 (October 1946), 389–403.

EG46 Kieffer, Elizabeth C. "Penmanship, The Art of the Scrivener." *The Pa. Dutchman*, vol. 5, no. 13 (1 March 1954), 3, 12, 15.

EG47 Kolbe, Christian, and Brent Holcomb. "Fraktur in the 'Dutch Fork' Area of South Carolina." *Jour. of Early Southern Decorative Arts*, vol. 5, no. 2 (November 1979), 36–51.

EG48 Kriebel, Lester K. "A Brief History and Interpretation of Pennsylvania-Geman Illuminated Writings ('Fraktur-Schriften')." *Bull., Hist. Soc. of Montgomery Co.*, vol. 3 (October 1941), 20–31. Motifs, types, historical influences, symbolism, and use.

EG49 Kriebel, Lester K. "Irwin Peter Mensch—Last of the Pennsylvania Dutch Fraktur Artists." *Hist. Rev. of Berks Co.*, vol. 18, no. 2 (1953), 40–46.

EG50 Leeds, Wendy. "Fraktur: An Annotated Bibliography." *Pa. Folklife*, vol. 25, no. 4 (1976), 35–46.

EG51 Lichten, Frances. *Fraktur: The Illuminated Manuscripts of the Pennsylvania Dutch.* Philadelphia: Free Library of Philadelphia, 1958. 26p.

EG52 "The Lost Art of Fractur Painting: Pennsylvania German Design." *Design*, vol. 61 (1959), 72.

EG53 McClinton, Katharine Morrison. "Pennsylvania Dutch and Other Illuminated Manuscripts and Cutwork." In: *A Handbook of Popular Antiques.* New York: Random House, 1945 and 1946, p. 160–66.

EG54 Merrill, Elizabeth L. "Fraktur: A Pennsylvania Dutch Folk Art." *Jour. of the Alleghenies*, vol. 8 (1972), 16–18.

EG55 Nash, Ray. *Some Early American Writing Books and Masters.* Hanover, N.H.: n.p., 1942. 25p. On fraktur type faces.

EG56 Nazareth School. *Manuscript Examination Book*, Nazareth, Pa., 1793. Ca. 200 leaves. Made by the Scholars in Nazareth School for the Autumnal Examination, October 1793. In various hands, all done in meticulous care, mostly English, with some in German and French. Listed in catalogue no. 675, 11 October 1978 of Argosy Book Stores, New York. The book incl. fine drawings, poetry, prayers, mathematical figures, landscape scenes, dialogues, architecture, etc.

EG57 Nesbitt, Alexander. *Decorating Alphabets and Initials.* New York: Dover, 1959. Fraktur type faces.

EG58 "North Carolina Fraktur." *Der Reggeboge*, vol. 6, nos. 2–3 (1972), 3–5.

EG59 Patterson, Nancy-Lou. "Anna Weber hat das gemacht: Anna Weber (1814–1888), a Fraktur Painter of Waterloo County, Ontario." *Work Papers of the Amer. Hist. Soc. of Germans from Russia*, vol. 20 (1976), 50–54.

EG60 Paul, Velma Mackay. "Geburts und Taufschein (sic)." *Amer. Antiques Jour.*, vol. 3, no. 1 (January 1948), 8–11.

EG61 *Pennsylvania German Fraktur and Color Drawing.* Introd. by Don Yoder. Lancaster, Pa.: n.p., 1969.

EG62 "A Pennsylvania Illuminated Manuscript 1801." *Antiques*, vol. 41, no. 2 (February 1942), 117.

EG63 Robacker, Earl F. "The Fraktur of Monroe County [Pa.]." *Pa. Folklife*, vol. 21, no. 1 (1971–1972), 2–15.

EG64 Robacker, Earl F. "Major and Minor in Fractur." *The Pa. Dutchman*, vol. 7, no. 3 (1956), 2–7. Analysis of kinds of frakturs.

EG65 Robacker, Earl F., and Ada Robacker. "Fraktur: An Enduring Art Form." *Pa. Folklife*, vol. 26 (1977), Supplement, 48–55.

EG66 Schwartz, Esther I. "New Jersey Water Colors." *Antiques*, vol. 74, no. 4 (October 1958), 333. Frakturs from New Jersey.

EG67 Scott, Kenneth. "Pennsylvania-German Taufscheine." *National Genealogical Soc. Quar.*, vol. 65 (1977), 114–22.

EG68 Shelley, Donald A. "American Primitive Paintings: Illuminated Manuscript." *Art in America*, vol. 42, no. 2 (May 1954), 139–46, 165.

EG69 Shelley, Donald A. *The Fraktur-Writings or Illuminated Manuscripts of the Pennsylvania Germans.* Publs., Pa. German Folklore Soc., vol. 23. Allentown: The Soc., 1958–1959. 373p. Rev. by P. A. Barba, "'S Pennsylfawnisch Deitsch Eck," Allentown *Morning Call*, 26 August 1961; J. J. Stoudt, *Amer.-German Rev.*, vol. 28, no. 1 (1961), 35–36; C. Scoon, *N.Y. Hist. Soc. Quar.*, vol. 46, no. 4 (1962), 466–67.

EG70 Shelley, Donald A. "Illuminated Birth Certificates, Regional Examples of an Early American Folk Art." *The N.Y. Hist. Soc. Quar.*, vol. 29, no. 2 (April 1945), 92–105.

EG71 Shelley, Donald A. "An Unusual Valentine." *The N.Y. Hist. Soc. Quar.*, vol. 27, no. 3 (July 1943), 62–67.

EG72 Shoemaker, Alfred L. *Check List of Pennsylvania Dutch Printer Taufscheins.* Lancaster: The Pa. Dutch Folklore Center, Inc., 1952. 48p.

EG73 Shoemaker, Alfred L. "First Reference to Pennsylvania Dutch Fractur." *The Pa. Dutchman*, vol. 5, no. 10 (15 January 1954), 16. Excerpted from the *Lancaster Examiner* for 16 April 1835.

EG74 Shoemaker, Alfred L. "Johann Valentin Schuller: Fraktur Artist and Author." *The Pa. Dutchman*, vol. 3, no. 10 (1951–1952), 1.

EG75 Shoemaker, Alfred L. "More *Taufschein* Scriveners." *The Pa. Dutchman*, vol. 3, no. 22 (15 April 1952), 7.

EG76 Shoemaker, Alfred L. "Notes on Frederick Krebs, The Noted Fractur Artist." *The Pa. Dutchman*, vol. 3, no. 11 (1 November 1951), 3.

EG77 Shoemaker, Alfred L. "*Taufschein* Scriveners." *The Pa. Dutchman*, vol. 3, no. 19 (1 March 1952), 6.

EG78 Shoemaker, Alfred L. "Taufscheins." *The Pa. Dutchman*, vol. 4, no. 7 (November 1952), 14.

EG79 Smith, Elmer L., and John Stewart. "Peter Bernhart: Fraktur Artist." "'S Pennsylfawnisch Deitsch Eck," Allentown *Morning Call*, 7 May 1966.

EG80 Sommer, Roger L. "Old German and English Baptismal Certificates." *Concordia Hist. Inst. Quar.*, vol. 31 (1958), 89–92.

EG81 Stoudt, John Joseph. "From *Patenbrief* to *Taufschein*." *Hist. Rev. of Berks Co.*, vol. 31, no. 1 (1965), 80–81.

EG82 Tschichold, Jan. *Schatzkammer der Schreibkunst, Meisterwerke der Kalligraphie aus vier Jahrhunderten, auf zweihundert Tafeln.* Basel: Verlag Birkhäuser, 1945. Fraktur type faces.

EG83 Unger, Claude W. "Reading Dated Taufscheins Printed before the Year 1800." *The Pa. Dutchman*, vol. 3, no. 12 (15 November 1951), 3.

EG84 "A Valentine in Fractur." *Antiques*, vol. 41, no. 2 (February 1942), 144.

EG85 "Virginia Fraktur." *The Pa. Dutchman*, vol. 4, no. 9 (1 January 1953). Description of an example of illuminated writing in the possession of the Ohio Historical Society; dated 1788–1789.

EG86 Walters, Donald R. "Jacob Stricker: Shenandoah County Virginia Fraktur Artist." *Antiques*, vol. 112 (September 1976), 536–43.

EG87 Weiser, Frederick S. *Fraktur, Pennsylvania German Folk Art.* Ephrata, Pa.: Science Pr., 1973. Rev. by J. Bevins, *Der Reggeboge*, vol. 9, no. 1 (1975), 22–23.

EG88 Weiser, Frederick S. "His Deed Followed Him: The Fraktur of John Conrad Gilbert." *Der Reggeboge*, vol. 16, no. 2 (1982), 33–45.

EG89 Weiser, Frederick S. "I A E S D: The Story of Johann Adam Eyer (1755–1837), Schoolmaster and Fraktur Artist with a Translation of His Roster Book, 1779–1787." In: *Ebbes fer Alle—Ebber Ebbes fer Dich. Essays in Memoriam Albert Franklin Buffington.* Publs., Pa. German Soc., vol. 14. Breinigsville: The Soc., 1980, p.435–506.

EG90 Weiser, Frederick S. "Piety and Protocol in Folk Art: Pennsylvania German Birth and Baptismal Certificates." *Winterthur Portfolio*, vol. 8 (1973), 19–43.

EG91 Weiser, Frederick S. "The Place of Fraktur among the Mennonites: An Introduction to the Fraktur Collection of the Lancaster Mennonite Historical Society." *Pa. Mennonite Heritage*, vol. 4, no. 1 (1981), 2–9.

EG92 Wust, Klaus. *Virginia Fraktur. Penmanship as a Folk Art.* Edinburg, Va.: Shenandoah History Publs., 1972. 28p.

EG93 Yoder, Don. "Fraktur in Mennonite Culture." *Mennonite Quar. Rev.*, vol. 48 (1974), 305–42.

EG94 Zehner, Olive. "Ohio Fractur." *The Pa. Dutchman*, vol. 6, no. 3 (1954–1955), 13–15.

EH
Folk Traditions in Building

EH1 Abernethy, Francis E., ed. *Built in Texas*. Publs. of the Texas Folklore Soc., no. 42 (1979). Austin: Encino Pr., 1979. Waco: E-Heart Pr., 1979. 276p.

EH2 Apps, Jerry. *The Barns of Wisconsin*. Illustrations by Allen Strang. Foreword by Glenn S. Pound. Madison: Tamarack Pr., 1977. 143p.

EH3 Arthur, Eric. *The Barn*. Toronto: McClelland & Stewart, 1972.

EH4 Bailey, Rosalie Fellows. *Pre-Revolutionary Dutch Houses and Families in Northern New Jersey and Southern New York*, 1936. Repr. New York: Dover Publs., 1968.

EH5 Baker, T. Lindsay. "Silesian Polish Folk Architecture in Texas." In: *Built in Texas*. Ed. F. E. Abernethy. Dallas: E-Heart Pr., 1979, p.130-35.

EH6 Ball, Bernice. *Barns of Chester County, Pennsylvania*. West Chester: Chester Co. Day Committee, 1974. Rev. by Claudia J. Hopf, *Pa. Hist.*, vol. 43 (1976), 190-91.

EH7 Barba, Preston A. "Unser Scheiere." "'S Pennsylfawnisch Deitsch Eck," Allentown *Morning Call*, 6 August 1949. Pennsylvania barns.

EH8 Bastian, Robert W. "Southeastern Pennsylvania and Central Wisconsin Barns: Examples of Independent Parallel Development?" *Professional Geographer*, vol. 27 (1975), 200-04.

EH9 Becker, Carl M., and William H. Daily. "Some Architectural Aspects of German-American Life in Nineteenth-Century Cincinnati." *Bulletin, Hist. & Philos. Soc. of Ohio*, vol. 20, no. 1 (1962), 75-88.

EH10 Blair, Don. *Harmonist Construction, Principally as Found in the Two-Story Houses Built in Harmonie, Indiana, 1814-1824*. Indiana Hist. Soc. Publs., vol. 23, no. 2. Indianapolis: Indiana Hist. Soc., 1964.

EH11 Brumbaugh, G. Edwin. "Continental Influence on Early American Architecture." *Amer.-German Rev.*, vol. 9, no. 3 (February 1943), 7-9, 37.

EH12 Brumbauch, G. Edwin. "Early Middle-Western Buildings; Drawings by Kenneth Becker." *Amer.-German Rev.*, vol. 14, no. 5 (1948), 42-43.

EH13 Bucher, Robert C. "The Cultural Backgrounds of Our Pennsylvania Homesteads." *Hist. Soc. of Montgomery Co., Publs.*, vol. 15, no. 3 (Fall 1966), 22-26. On Swiss origins of the style of construction.

EH14 Bucher, Robert C. "The Swiss Bank House in Pennsylvania." *Pa. Folklife*, vol. 18, no. 2 (1968-1969), 3-11.

EH15 Bucher, Robert C., and Isaac Clarence Kulp, Jr. "Bau-Typen in Goschenhoppen." *The Goschenhoppen Region (Peterkett)*, vol. 2 (1969), 4-7. Log houses, stone houses, Swiss bank houses with gable fireplace, gambrel roofs, French kitchens, etc.

EH16 Cadzow, Donald A. "Pennsbury: Pennsylvania Restores the Manor House of Its Founder, William Penn." *Amer. Heritage*, vol. 1, no. 4 (Summer 1950), 50-51, 66-67.

EH17 Chappell, Edward A. "Acculturation in the Shenandoah Valley: Rhenish Houses of the Massanutten Settlement." *Procs., Amer. Philosophical Soc.*, vol. 124 (29 February 1980), 55-89. In Page Co., Va.

EH18 Collier, G. Loyd. "The Cultural Geography of Folk Building Forms in Texas." In: *Built in Texas*. Ed. F. E. Abernethy. Austin: Encino Pr., 1979, p.20-43.

EH19 Davis, Mary Lee P. "The History of the Hain Houses." *Hist. Rev. of Berks Co.*, vol. 33 (Autumn 1968), 122-24, 137, 146. Nineteenth-century houses built by members of a family of German descent.

EH20 Dickson, Harold E. *A Hundred Pennsylvania Buildings*. State College, Pa.: Bald Eagle Pr., 1954.

EH21 Dieffenbach, Victor C. "Building a Pennsylvania Barn." *Pa. Folklife*, vol. 12, no. 3 (Fall 1961), 20–24.

EH22 Dornbusch, Charles H. *Pennsylvania German Barns*. Introd. and text by John K. Heyl. Publs., Pa. German Folklore Soc., vol. 21. Allentown: The Soc., 1956. 312p. 150 illus. Rev. by J. Cummings, *Amer.-German Rev.*, vol. 25, no. 1 (1950), 37; A. D. Graeff, "'S Pennsylfawnisch Deitsch Eck," Allentown *Morning Call*, 22 November 1958; and G. M. Stoltzfus, *Hist. Rev. of Berks Co.*, vol. 23, no. 4 (1958), 110.

EH23 Driedger, Leo. "Nomos—Building on the Prairies. Construction of Indian, Hutterite, and Jewish Sacred Canopies." *Canad. Jour. of Sociology*, vol. 5, no. 4 (1980), 341–56.

EH24 Durand, Loyal. "Dairy Barns of Southeastern Wisconsin." *Economic Geography*, vol. 19 (1943), 37–44.

EH25 Eighmy, Jeffrey Lynn. "Mennonite Architecture: Diachronic Evidence for Rapid Diffusion in Rural Communities." Diss., Univ. of Arizona, 1977. 231p.

EH26 Emsminger, Robert F. "A Search for the Origin of the Pennsylvania Barn." *Pa. Folklife*, vol. 30 (1980–1981), 50–70.

EH27 Ennals, Peter M. "Nineteenth-Century Barns in Southern Ontario." *Canad. Geographer*, vol. 16 (1972), 256–70.

EH28 Fitchen, John. *The New World Dutch Barn*. Syracuse, N.Y.: Syracuse Univ. Pr., 1968.

EH29 Gillon, Edmund V., Jr. *Pennsylvania Dutch Farm: To Cut Out and Assemble*. New York: Scribners, 1979. A paper model with instructions and text, incl. a history of German immigrants who came to southeastern Pennsylvania.

EH30 Glass, Joseph W. "The Pennsylvania Culture Region: A Geographic Interpretation of Barns and Farmhouses." Diss., Pennsylvania State, 1971.

EH31 Glass, Joseph W. "The Pennsylvania Culture Region: A Geographic Interpretation of Barns and Farmhouses." Diss., Pennsylvania State, 1971.

EH32 Glassie, Henry. "A Central Chimney Continental Log House from Cumberland County." TS. Deposited in the Winterthur Museum libraries.

EH33 Glassie, Henry. *Pattern in the Material Folk Culture of the Eastern United States*. Monographs in Folklore and Folklife, no. 1. Philadelphia: Univ. of Pennsylvania, 1969. 316p. Rev. by P. O. Wacker, *Jour. of Amer. Folklore*, vol. 83, no. 327 (January–March 1970), 92–93. Study of folk housetypes and other elements of the cultural landscape.

EH34 Glassie, Henry. "The Pennsylvania Barn in the South." *Pa. Folklife*, vol. 15, no. 2 (1965–1966), 8–19; vol. 15, no. 4 (1965–1966), 15–25.

EH35 Glassie, Henry H. "The Types of the Southern Mountain Cabin." In: *The Study of American Folklore*. Ed. Jan Brunvand. New York: W. W. Norton & Co., 1968. Appendix C, p. 338–70.

EH36 Hall, Connie. "The Old Koch House." In: *Built in Texas*. Ed. F. E. Abernethy. Publ. of the Texas Folklore Society. Waco: The Soc., 1979, p. 106–19.

EH37 Hansen, Hans Jürgen, ed. *Architecture in Wood: A History of Wood Building and Its Techniques in Europe and North America*. Trans. by Janet Seligman. London: Faber & Faber, 1971.

EH38 Heimsath, Clovis. *Pioneer Texas Buildings*. Photos by Maryann Heimsath. Forew. by Louis Kahn. Austin: Univ. of Texas Pr., 1968.

EH39 Heyl, John K. "The Peter Steckel House." "'S Pennsylfawnisch Deitsch Eck," Allentown *Morning Call*, 28 August 1943.

EH40 Herzog, Lynda V. "The Early Architecture of New Bern, North Carolina, 1750–1850." Diss., Univ. of California, Los Angeles, 1977.

EH41 *Historical American Buildings Survey. Wisconsin Architecture. A Catalog of Buildings Represented in the Library of Congress, with Illustrations from Measured Drawings*. Narrative by Richard W. E. Perrin. U.S. Dept. of the Interior National Park Service. Washington, D.C.: Government Printing Office, 1965.

EH42 Horst, Melville, and Elmer L. Smith. *Covered Bridges of Pennsylvania Dutchland*. Akron, Pa.: Applied Arts, 1960. 42p. Rev. by P. A. Barba, "'S Pennsylfawnisch Deitsch Eck," Allentown *Morning Call*, 3 December 1860.

EH43 Howland, Garth A. "An Architectural History of the Moravian Church, Bethlehem, Pa." *Transactions, Moravian Hist. Soc.*, vol. 14 (1947), 51–132.

EH44 Howland, Garth A. "Reconstructional Problems Associated with the Moravian Buildings in Bethlehem." *Transactions, Moravian Hist. Soc.*, vol. 13, no. 6, parts 3–4 (1944), 174–280. Careful, well illus. analysis of Moravian architecture.

EH45 Hurwitz, Elizabeth A. "Decorative Elements in the Domestic Architecture of Eastern Pennsylvania." *The Pa. Dutchman*, vol. 7, no. 2 (1955), 6–29.

EH46 Johnson, Francis Benjamin, and Thomas T. Waterman. *The Early Architecture of North Carolina*. Chapel Hill: Univ. of N. Car. Pr., 1941.

EH47 Johnson, Hildegard Binder. "Immigrant Traditions and Rural Middle Western Architecture." *Amer.-German Rev.*, vol. 9, no. 5 (June 1943), 17–20.

EH48 Jordan, Albert F. "Some Early Moravian Builders in America." *Pa. Folklife*, vol. 24, no. 1 (1974), 2–17.

EH49 Jordan, Terry G. "Alpine Alemannic and American Log Architecture." *Annals of the Assoc. of Amer. Geographers*, vol. 70 (1980).

EH50 Jordan, Terry G. "A Forebay Bank Barn in Texas." *Pa. Folklife*, vol. 30 (1980–1981), 72–77.

EH51 Jordan, Terry G. "German Folk Houses in the Texas Hill Country." In: *German Culture in Texas, A Free Earth: Essays from the 1978 Southwest Symposium*. Ed. Glen E. Lich and Dona B. Reeves. Boston: Twayne, 1980, p.103–20.

EH52 Jordan, Terry G. "German Houses in Texas." *Landscape*, vol. 14, no. 2 (September 1964), 24–26.

EH53 Jordan, Terry G. "Log Corner Notching in Texas." In: Ed. F. E. Abernethy. Publs., Texas Folklore Soc., no. 42. *Built In Texas*. Waco: E-Heart Pr., 1979, p. 78–83.

EH54 Jordan, Terry G. "Log Corner Timbering in Texas." *Pioneer America*, vol. 8 (1976), 8–18.

EH55 Jordan, Terry G. "A Russian-German Folk House in North Texas." In: *Built in Texas*. Ed. F. E. Abernethy. Publs., Texas Folklore Soc., no. 42. Waco: E-Heart Pr., 1979, p.136–38.

EH56 Jordan, Terry G. *Texas Log Buildings: A Folk Architecture*. Austin: Univ. of Texas Pr., 1978. 230p. Rev. by Fred B. Kniffen, *Annals of the Assoc. of Amer. Geographers*, vol. 69 (1979), 330–31; Glen E. Lich, *Jour. of German-Amer. Studies*, vol. 13 (1978), 126–27. Traces influences of this indigenous architecture from Texas Germans, among others.

EH57 Kauffman, Henry J. "Church Architecture in Lancaster Co." *The Dutchman*, vol. 6, no. 5 (1955), 16–27.

EH58 Kauffman, Henry J. "Literature on Log Architecture." *The Dutchman*, vol. 7, no. 2 (Fall 1955), 30–34.

EH59 Kauffman, Henry J. "Moravian Architecture in Bethlehem." *The Pa. Dutchman*, vol. 6, no. 4 (1955), 12–19.

EH60 Kauffman, Henry J. "Of Bells and Bell Towers." *The Dutchman*, vol. 6, no. 1 (1954), 24–25.

EH61 Kauffman, Henry J. "The Riddle of Two Front Doors." *The Dutchman*, vol. 6, no. 3 (Winter 1954–1955), 27.

EH62 Kauffman, Henry J. "The Summer House." *The Pa. Dutchman*, vol. 8, no. 1 (1956), 2–7. Functions and architectural forms of "summer houses" found in rural Pennsylvania.

EH63 Kerkhoff, Jennie Ann. *Old Homes of Page County, Virginia*. Luray: Lauk & Co., 1962. 212p. Rev. by E. J. Wilhlem, Jr., *Keystone Folklore Quar.*, vol. 12 (1967), 143–44. Reflecting a Pennsylvania-German architectural tradition.

EH64 Keyser, Alan G., and William P. Stein. "The Pennsylvania German Tri-Level Barn." *Der Reggeboge*, vol. 9, nos. 3–4 (1975), 1–25.

EH65 Kiebach, Raymond E. "Fences in Pennsylvania German Land." "'S Pennsylfawnisch Deitsch Eck," Allentown *Morning Call*, 18 September 1954.

EH66 Kniffen, Fred, and Henry Glassie. "Building in Wood in the Eastern United States (A Time–Place Perspective)." *Geographical Rev.*, vol. 56, no. 1 (January 1966), 40–66. Half-timbering brought in from Gemany; Pennsylvania German log construction.

EH67 Kowert, Elise. *Old Homes and Buildings of Fredericksburg* [Texas]. Fredericksburg: Fredericksburg Publ., 1977.

EH68 Krahn, Cornelius. "Developments and Trends: Mennonite Church Architecture." *Mennonite Life*, vol. 12 (1957), 19–27, 34.

EH69 Larimore, Ann. "The Cultural Geography of St. Charles, Missouri: House Types." M.A. thesis, Univ. of Chicago, 1955.

EH70 Lawton, Arthur J. "The Pre-Metric Foot and Its Use in Pennsylvania German Architecture." *Pa. Folklife*, vol. 19, no. 1 (Autumn 1969), 37–45.

EH71 Lewis, Arnold. "A European Profile of American Architecture." *Jour. of the Soc. of Architectural Historians*, vol. 37 (1978), 265–82.

EH72 Lich, Glen, and Lera Tyler. "When the Creeks Run Dry: Water Milling in the German Hill Country." In: *Built in Texas*. Ed. F. E. Abernethy. Austin: Encine Pr., 1979, p.236–45.

EH73 Lippold, John W. "Early Lancaster Architecture." *Jour. of the Lancaster Co. Hist. Soc.*, vol. 75 (Michaelmas 1971), 145–78.

EH74 Long, Amos, Jr. "Architectural Survivals in Berks." *Hist. Rev. of Berks Co.*, vol. 31, no. 1 (1964), 13–18. Houses and farm buildings.

EH75 Long, Amos, Jr. "Bank [Multi-Level] Structures in Rural Pennsylvania." *Pa. Folklife*, vol. 20, no. 2 (Winter 1970–1971), 31–39.

EH76 Long, Amos, Jr. "Farmstead Arches in Berks." *Hist. Rev. of Berks Co.*, vol. 30 (Autumn 1965), 116–17, 124–25.

EH77 Long, Amos, Jr. "Fences in Rural Pennsylvania." *Pa. Folklife*, vol. 12, no. 2 (Summer 1961), 30–35.

EH78 Long, Amos, Jr. "Outbuildings on the Early Pennsylvania German Farmstead." *Amer.-German Rev.*, vol. 29, no. 3 (1963), 18–21.

EH79 Long, Amos, Jr. "Outdoor Privies in the Dutch Country." *Pa. Folklife*, vol. 13, no. 3 (1963), 33–38.

EH80 Long, Amos, Jr. *The Pennsylvania German Family Farm: A Regional Architectural and Folk Cultural Study of an American Agricultural Community*. Pa. German Soc. Publs., no. 6. Breinigsville: The Soc., 1972. 518p.

EH81 Long, Amos, Jr. "Springs and Springhouses." *Pa. Folklife*, vol. 11, no. 1 (Spring 1960), 40–43.

EH82 Long, Amos, Jr. "The Woodshed." *Pa. Folklife*, vol. 16 (Winter 1966–1967), 38–45. Pennsylvania-German nomenclature.

EH83 Lord, Arthur C. "Barns of Lancaster County: 1798." *Jour. of the Lancaster Co. Hist. Soc.*, vol. 77 (Hilarymas 1973), 26–40.

EH84 McKee, Harley J. *Introduction to Early American Masonry: Stone, Brick, Mortar and Plaster*. Washington, D.C.: The National Trust for Historic Preservation and Columbia University, 1973.

EH85 Maresch, Franz, and Gerhard Maresch. "Das Dürrhäusel im oberen Pielachtal." *Österreichische Zeitschrift für Volkskunde*, vol. 17, no. 1 (1963), 17–22. Information on the European "dry house."

EH86 Merritt, Olive. "Recessed Porches of Southeastern Pennsylvania." *Hist. Rev. of Berks Co.*, vol. 45 (1980), 100–04, 108, 111, 114–15, 118.

EH87 Miller, Hope R. "Heurich Mansion Reflects Age of Opulence." *Antique Monthly*, vol. 14, no. 11 (1981), 2C, 13C.

EH88 Milner, John D. "Germanic Architecture in the New World." *Jour. of the Soc. of Architectural Historians*, vol. 34 (1975), 29. Abstract of a paper presented at the annual meeting of the society.

EH89 Montgomery, Richard S. *Home Craft Course in Pennsylvania German Architecture*. Keyser Home Craft Course Series, no. 19. Allentown: Schlechter's; Plymouth Meeting, Pa.: Mrs. C. Naaman Keyser, 1945. 30p. Rev. by G.E.P., *Hist. Rev. of Berks Co.*, vol. 10, no. 4 (1945), 120.

EH90 Montgomery, Richard S. "Houses of the Oley Valley." *The Pa. Dutchman*, vol. 6, no. 3 (Winter 1954–1955), 16–26.

EH91 Morrison, Hugh. *Early American Architecture, From the First Colonial Settlements to the National Period.* New York: Oxford Univ. Pr., 1952. See esp.: "Pennsylvania Dutch Architecture," p.541–49.

EH92 Murtagh, William J. "Half-Timbering in American Architecture." *Pa. Folklife*, vol. 19, no. 1 (Winter 1957–1958), 2–11. As used by the first generation of immigrants from the Rhineland area.

EH93 Murtagh, William J. *Moravian Architecture and Town Planning: Bethlehem, Pennsylvania and Other Eighteenth Century American Settlements.* Chapel Hill: Univ. of N. Car. Pr., 1967. 145p. Rev. by Lee H. Nelson, *Pa. Hist.*, vol. 35, no. 3 (July 1968), 319–20; G. E. Brumbaugh, *Pa. Mag. of Hist. and Biog.*, vol. 92, no. 2 (1968), 259–60; K. G. Hamilton, *N. Car. Hist. Rev.*, vol. 45, no. 2 (Spring 1968), 222–23; J. K. Heyl, "'S Pennsylfawnisch Deitsch Eck," Allentown *Morning Call*, 30 December 1967; in *Ind. Mag. of Hist.*, vol. 44, no. 2 (March 1968), 157; F. D. Nichols, *William and Mary Quar.*, vol. 26, no. 1 (January 1969), 141–42. See also his dissertation on Moravian architecture and city planning submitted at the Univ. of Pennsylvania, 1963.

EH94 Noble, Allen G. "Barns and Square Silos in Northeast Ohio." *Pioneer America*, vol. 6, no. 2 (July 1974), 12–21. Incl. remarks on the German-style barn.

EH95 Noble, Allen G. "Barns as Elements in the Settlement of the Landscape of Ohio." *Pioneer America*, vol. 9, no. 1 (1977), 62–79.

EH96 Perrin, Richard W. E. *The Architecture of Wisconsin.* Madison: State Hist. Soc. of Wisconsin, 1965. 208p. Rev. by B. Bunting, *Jour. of Amer. Hist.*, vol. 55, no. 1 (1968), 135–36.

EH97 Perrin, Richard W. E. "Boulders, Cobblestones, and Pebbles: Wisconsin's Fieldstone Architecture." *Wis. Mag. of Hist.*, vol. 47, no. 2 (1964), 136–45. North European influences on early Wisconsin building.

EH98 Perrin, Richard W. E. "A Fachwerk Church in Wisconsin." *Wis. Mag. of Hist.*, vol. 43, no. 4 (Summer 1960), 239–44. The former Trinity Ev. Lutheran Church at Freistadt, Ozaukee Co., built in 1844.

EH99 Perrin, Richard W. E. "German Timber Farm Houses in Wisconsin: Terminal Examples of a Thousand-Year Building Tradition." *Wis. Mag. of Hist.*, vol. 44, no. 3 (1961), 199–202.

EH100 Perrin, Richard W. E. *Historic Wisconsin Buildings, A Survey of Pioneer Architecture, 1835–1870.* Milwaukee: Milwaukee Public Museum, 1962. 96p. 2nd ed., 1981. 123p.

EH101 Perrin, Richard W. E. "Pointed Arches and Buttressed Walls: Gothic Stylism in Wisconsin Architecture." *Wis. Mag. of Hist.*, vol. 47, no. 3 (1964), 238–48. Churches designed for German congregations and built by immigrants in the Gothic style.

EH102 Peterson, Albert J. "The German-Russian House in Kansas: A Study in Persistence of Form." *Pioneer America*, vol. 8 (January 1976), 19–27.

EH103 Pillsbury, Richard. "The Construction Materials of the Rural Folk Housing of the Pennsylvania Culture Region." *Pioneer America*, vol. 8 (1976), 98–106.

EH104 Pillsbury, Richard, and Andrew Kardos. *A Field Guide to the Folk Architecture of the Northeastern United States.* Geography Publications at Dartmouth, no. 8. Hanover, N.H.: Dartmouth College, 1970.

EH105 Prudhon, Theodore H. "The Dutch Barn in America: Survival of a Medieval Structural Frame." *N.Y. Folklore Quar.*, vol. 2, nos. 3/4 (1976), 122–42.

EH106 Raymond, Eleanor. *Early Domestic Architecture of Pennsylvania: Photographs and Measured Drawings.* New York/Exton, Pa.: Helburn & Schiffer, Ltd., 1977. 98p.

EH107 Ridlen, Susanne S. "Bank Barns in Lass County, Indiana." *Pioneer America*, vol. 4, no. 2 (1972), 25–43.

EH108 Rivinus, Willis M. *Old Stone Work in Bucks County.* Doylestown: Bucks Co. Hist. Soc., 1972.

EH109 Rose, Harold Wickliffe. *The Colonial Houses of Worship in America.* New York: Hastings House, 1963. 589p. Histories and photos of Colonial churches that have survived.

EH110 Ross, Terri. "Alsatian Architecture in Medina County." In: *Built in Texas*. Ed. F. E. Abernethy. Dallas: E-Heart Pr., 1979, p.120–29.

EH111 Schmidt, Mildred, and Joseph Schmidt. "German Influences on Hermann (Missouri) Houses." *Amer.-German Rev.*, vol. 20, no. 4 (1954), 13–17.

EH112 "Schneider Home a Living Museum: It Illustrates How the Well-Off Lived More than a Century Ago." *Toronto Daily Star*, 11 November 1981. Repr. *Canadiana Germanica*, vol. 32 (1981), 13.

EH113 Schreiber, William I. "The Pennsylvania Dutch Bank Barn in Ohio." *Jour. of the Ohio Folklore Soc.*, vol. 2 (Spring 1968), 5–30. Two contributions of the Germans to the cultural scene of Ohio were the narrow rectangular three-story house and the bank barn.

EH114 Schweigert, Kurt. "Hutmacher Complex, Dunn County." *N. Dak. Hist.*, vol. 46, no. 4 (1979), 3. Stone slab houses built by Ukrainian and German-Russian immigrants.

EH115 Schweigert, Kurt. "Winter House, Sheridan County." *N. Dak. Hist.*, vol. 47, no. 3 (1980), 3. Description of a winter house, a tradition among German-Russian immigrants.

EH116 Shoemaker, Alfred L. "Barracks." *Pa. Folklife*, vol. 9, no. 2 (1958), 2–11. The "barrack" or "Schottscheier," a structure consisting of four posts with holes for pegging, so as to support a roof that can be raised or lowered.

EH117 Shoemaker, Alfred L. "Dry House." *Pa. Folklife*, vol. 9, no. 4 (Fall 1958), inside front cover; illus.

EH118 Shoemaker, Alfred L. "Pennsylvania German Barns." *Mennonite Life*, vol. 6, no. 4 (1951), 6–11.

EH119 Shoemaker, Alfred L. "Somerset County Decorated Barns." *The Dutchman*, vol. 6, no. 1 (June 1954), 4–5.

EH120 Shoemaker, Alfred L., et al., eds. *The Pennsylvania Barn*. Kutztown: Pa. Folklife Soc., 1955; Lancaster: Pa. Dutch Folklore Center, 1956. Rev. by P. A. Barba, "'S Pennsylfawnisch Deitsch Eck," Allentown *Morning Call*, 17 March 1956.

EH121 Solms-Braunfels, Karl von. "Building in Texas, 1844–45." In: *Built in Texas*. Ed. F. E. Abernethy. Dallas: E-Heart Press., 1979, p. 46–51. Reprinted from Solms' *Texas* (1844–1845).

EH122 Stair, J. William. "Brick-End Barns." *The Pa. Dutchman*, vol. 6, no. 2 (1954), 14–33. 35 illus.

EH123 Stauffer, Elmer C. "The Trail of the Stone Arched Bridges in Berks County." *The Pa. Dutchman*, vol. 8, no. 3 (Spring 1957), 20–31. 38 illus.

EH124 Stevens, Bryan J. "The Swiss Bank House Revisited: The Messerschmidt-Dietz Cabin." *Pa. Folklife*, vol. 30 (1980–1981), 78–86. In York Co., Pa.

EH125 Stotz, Charles Morse. *The Architectural Heritage of Early Western Pennsylvania: A Record of Building Before 1860*. Pittsburgh: Univ. of Pittsburgh Pr., 1966. 497p. Reissue. Rev. by J. D. V. Trump, *Western Pa. Hist. Mag.*, vol. 50, no. 1 (January 1967), 68–71; G. B. Tatum, *Pa. Mag. of Hist. and Biog.*, vol. 91 (1967), 369–70. Incl. a chapter on the architecture of Harmony and Economy in Pennsylvania.

EH126 Tappert, Theodore G. "Colonial Lutheran Churches." *Amer.-German Rev.*, vol. 9, no. 1 (October 1942), 18–22.

EH127 "A Visit at the Hottensteins." *Der Reggeboge*, vol. 8, no. 1 (1974), 1–3. Discussion of architecture.

EH128 Wacker, Peter O. "Traditional House and Barn Types in New Jersey: Keys to Acculturation, Past Cultureographic Regions, and Settlement History." *Geoscience and Man*, vol. 5 (1974), 163–76.

EH129 Wacker, Peter O., and Roger T. Trindell. "The Log House in New Jersey: Origins and Diffusion." *Keystone Folklore Quar.*, vol. 13 (Winter 1969), 248–68. Swedish-Finnish and German-Swiss log traditions considered in "the philosophical and methodological framework of cultural-historical geography." Also as TS. (by Peter O. Wacker) in the libraries of the Winterthur Museum.

EH130 Waterman, Thomas Tileston. *The Dwellings of Colonial America*. Chapel Hill, N. Car.: Univ. of N. Car. Pr., 1950. See esp. Chap. 2, "The Delaware Valley and Pennsylvania," p. 115–157.

EH131 Weaver, William W. "A Blacksmith's 'Summerkich'." *Pa. Folklife*, vol. 22, no. 4 (1973), 22–26.

EH132 Weaver, William W. "Pennsylvania German Architecture: Bibliography in European

Backgrounds." *Pa. Folklife*, vol. 24, no. 3 (1975), 36–40.

EH133 Weaver, William W. "Weizenthal and the Early Architecture of New-Strassburg: Swiss Plantations in the Province of Pennsylvania—An Illustrated Thesis Abstract." *Historic Schaefferstown Rec.*, vol. 7, no. 1 (1973), 2–11.

EH134 Weslager, C. A. *The Log Cabin in America: From Pioneer Days to the Present*. New Brunswick N.J.: Rutgers Univ. Pr., 1969.

EH135 Wilhelm, Hubert G. H. "The Pennsylvania-Dutch Barn in Southeastern Ohio." In: *Man and Cultural Heritage: Papers in Honor of Fred B. Kniffen*. Ed. H. J. Walker and W. G. Haag. Baton Rouge: La. State Univ. Pr., 1974, p.155–62. See also *Geoscience and Man*, vol. 5 (1974), 155–62.

EH136 Wilhelm, Hubert G. H., and Michael Miller. "Half-Timber Construction: A Relic Building Method in Ohio." *Pioneer America*, vol. 6 (July 1974), 43–51.

EH137 Willis, Stanley. "Log Houses in Southwest Virginia." *Va. Cavalcade*, vol. 21 (1972), 36–44.

EH138 Wright, Martin. "The Antecedents of the Double-Pen House Type." *Annals of the Assoc. of Amer. Geographers*, vol. 48 (1958), 109–17.

EH139 Zeidler, Eberhard A. "Architecture in Our Time. Necessities and Possibilities." *German-Canad. Yearbook*, vol. 4 (1978), 168–79.

EH140 Zelinsky, Wilbur. "The Log House in Georgia." *Geographical Rev.*, vol. 43 (1953), 173–93.

EI
Other Folk Arts

Furniture

EI1 Albers, Marjorie K. *Old Amana Furniture*. Shenandoah, Iowa: Locust House, ca. 1970. Rev. by K. D. Barron, *Antiques*, vol. 66 (June 1971), 908, 918. Illus. of chair once owned by Christian Metz (1794–1867), leader of the Inspirationists and a cabinetmaker.

EI2 Bird, Michael S. "Perpetuation and Adaptation: The Furniture and Craftsmanship of John Gemeinhart, 1826–1912." *Canad. Antiques and Art Rev.*, March 1981, 19–34.

EI3 Bramm, Otto. "Truhentypen." *Volkswerk. Jahrbuch des Staat-Museums für deutsche Volkskunde*. Jena: Eugen Diederichs Vlg., 1941. Chests.

EI4 Brazer, Clarence W. "Primitive Hall and Its Furniture." *Antiques*, vol. 53, no. 1 (January 1948), 55–57.

EI5 "Cabinets and Chests from the Middle Atlantic States." *Antiques*, vol. 52, no. 1 (July 1947), 34–35. Kernodle Collection.

EI6 Cummings, John. "Painted Chests from Bucks County." *Pa. Folklife*, vol. 9, no. 3 (1958), 20–23.

EI7 Cummings, John, and Martha S. Cummings. "John Drissel and His Boxes." *Pa. Folklife*, vol. 9, no. 4 (Fall 1958), 28–31.

EI8 Deneke, Bernward. *Bauernmöbel. Ein Handbuch für Sammler und Liebhaber*. München: Keysersche Verlagbuchhandlung, 1969.

EI9 Dundore, Roy H. *Pennsylvania German Painted Furniture*. Keyser Home Craft Course Series, no. 6. Allentown: Schlechter's, 1944.

EI10 Fabian, Monroe H. "An Immigrant's Inventory." *Pa. Folklife*, vol. 25, no. 4 (Summer 1976), 47–48. Refers to furniture.

EI11 Fabian, Monroe H. "The Pennsylvania-German Decorated Chest." *Antiques*, vol. 113 (1978), 1032, 1044–51.

EI12 Fabian, Monroe H. *The Pennsylvania-German Decorated Chest*. Publs., Pa. German Soc., vol. 12 (1979). Forew. by Frederick S. Weiser. New York: Universe Books, 1978. Rev. by Donald A. Shelley, *Pa. Mag. of Hist. and Biog.*, vol. 103 (January 1979), 132–33.

EI13 Fabian, Monroe H. "Research on the Pennsylvania German Kist." *Der Reggeboge*, vol. 6, no. 4 (1972), 3–6.

EI14 Fabian, Monroe H. "Sulfur Inlay in Pennsylvania German Furniture." *Pa. Folklife*, vol. 27, no. 1 (1977–1978), 2–9.

EI15 Fales, Dean A., Jr. *American Painted Furniture, 1660–1880*. New York: Dutton, 1972.

EI16 Fritsch, Mabel. "The Chaff Bag and Its Preparation." *Pa. Folklife*, vol. 16, no. 4 (Summer 1967), 42–43. How the farmers prepared beds for sleeping.

EI17 Gottschall, Marie. "Band Boxes." *Pa. Folklife*, vol. 28 (1979), Folk Festival Supplement, 8–9. Small hand-made containers as fashioned by the Pennsylvania Germans.

EI18 Hoech, Annie E. "German Music Boxes in America." *Amer.-German Rev.*, vol. 9, no. 2 (1942), 15–17.

EI19 Hollenbach, Raymond E. "Peter Wotring—Sein Schreib Buch—1799." "'S Pennsylfawnisch Deitsch Eck," Allentown *Morning Call*, 7 March 1964. Business account book of a carpenter-cabinetmaker.

EI20 Hopf, Carroll. "Decorated Folk Furniture." *Pa. Folkife*, vol. 20, no. 2 (Winter 1970–1971), 2–8.

EI21 Keyser, Alan G. "Beds, Bedding, Bedsteads and Sleep." *Der Reggeboge*, vol. 12, no. 4 (1978), 1–28.

EI22 Keyser, Alan G., Larry M. Neff, and Frederick S. Weiser, trans. *The Account Books of Two Pennsylvania German Furniture Makers*. Breinigsville, Pa.: The Pa. German Soc., 1979. Abraham Overholt, Bucks Co., 1790–1833, and Peter Ranck, Lebanon Co., 1794–1817.

EI23 Lee-Whiting, Brenda B. "Furniture Maker from Germany: Renfrew County's J. Albert Zadow." *Canad. Collector*, vol. 16, no. 5 (1981), 37–41.

EI24 Lerch, Lila. "Berks County Box Chests." *Hist. Rev. of Berks Co.*, vol. 28, no. 4 (Fall 1963).

EI25 Lichten, Frances. *Pennsylvania German Chests*. Keyser Home Craft Course Series, no. 11. Allentown: Schlechter's, n.d.

EI26 Locke, Louis G. "Antique Furniture of the Shenandoah Valley." *Va. Cavalcade*, vol. 24 (1975), 109–15.

EI27 McFarland, Barry. "The Furniture-Makers at the Kutztown Folk Festival." *Pa. Folklife*, vol. 27 (1977–1978), Folk Festival Supplement, 35–39.

EI28 Morse, John D., ed. *Winterthur Conference Report 1969: Country Cabinetwork and Simple City Furniture*. Charlottesville: Univ. Pr. of Va., 1970.

EI29 Nykor, Lynda M., and Patricia D. Musson. *Mennonite Furniture: The Ontario Tradition in York County*. Toronto: Lorimer, 1977. 95p.

EI30 Poole, Earl L. "Joseph Lehn, Driven to Design." *Amer.-German Rev.*, vol. 15, no. 1 (1948), 12–14. Cabinetware made by Lehn in Clay, Lancaster Co.

EI31 Reichmann, Felix. "Pennsylvania-Dutch Furniture." *Bull., Hist. Soc. of Montgomery Co.*, vol. 3, no. 2 (April 1942), 84–97. Assimilation of Anglo-American influences; derivation and significance of decorative elements.

EI32 Ritz, Gislind M. *The Art of Painted Furniture*. New York: Van Nostrand Reinhold Co., 1971.

EI33 Ritz, Gislind M. *Alte geschnitzte Bauernmöbel*. München: Callwey, 1974. Carved peasant-style furniture. See also *Alte bemalte Bauernmöbel*. München: Callwey, 1975. Painted peasant furniture.

EI34 Robacker, Earl F. "The Paint-Decorated Furniture of the Pennsylvania Dutch." *Pa. Folklife*, vol. 13, no. 1 (1962), 2–8.

EI35 Robacker, Earl F. "Such Fancy Boxes, Yet." *The Pa. Dutchman*, vol. 8, no. 4 (1957), 3–8. Decorated wooden boxes of the Pennsylvania-German area.

EI36 Robacker, Earl F. "Wooden Boxes of German Pennsylvania." *Antiques*, vol. 61, no. 2 (February 1952), 171–73.

EI37 Robacker, Earl F., and Ada F. Robacker. "Decorative Painting." *Pa. Folklife*, vol. 28 (1979), Folk Festival Supplement, 34–39.

EI38 Schmidt, Leopold. *Bauernmöbel aus Süddeutschland, Österreich und der Schweiz.* Wien: Forum Vlg., 1967.

EI39 Schwarze, Wolfgang. *Antike deutsche Möbel. Bürgerliche und rustikale Möbel in Deutschland 1700 bis 1840.* Wuppertal: Dr. Wolfgang Schwarze Vlg., 1975.

EI40 Scott, G. W., Jr. "Lancaster and Other Pennsylvania Furniture." *Antiques*, vol. 115, no. 5 (May 1979), 984–93. Cupboards, dressers, clocks, etc. of Pennsylvania German provenience.

EI41 Seitz, Albert Fletcher. "Furniture Making by the Slaugh Family of Lancaster." *Jour. of the Lancaster Co. Hist. Soc.*, vol. 73, no. 1 (Hilarymas 1969), 1–25. John Slaugh emigrated from Germany to Philadelphia in 1847.

EI42 Shackleton, Philip. *The Furniture of Old Ontario.* Toronto: Macmillan, 1983.

EI43 Shea, John. *The Pennsylvania Dutch and Their Furniture.* New York: Van Nostrand Reinhold, 1980. 226p. Dutch furnishings; patterns and procedures for painting designs; measured drawings of chairs, tables, cupboards, etc.

EI44 Sieber, Friedrich. *Bunte Möbel der Oberlausitz.* Berlin (DDR): Akademie Vlg., 1955. On the furniture of the Herrnhuter colony.

EI45 Snyder, Tricia, Gil Snyder, and Paul A. Goody. *Zoar Furniture 1817–1898: A Preliminary Study.* New Philadelphia, Ohio: Tuscarawas Co. Hist. Soc., 1978. 128p.

EI46 Steinfeldt, Cecilia, and Donald L. Stover. *Early Texas Furniture and Decorative Arts.* San Antonio: San Antonio Museum Assoc., 1973.

EI47 Walter, Donald. "Johannes Spitler, Shenandoah County Furniture Decorator." *Antiques*, vol. 108 (October 1975), 730–35.

EI48 Walzer, Albert. "Baden-Württembergische Bauernmöbel, Teil II." *Der Museumsfreund*, vol. 10/11 (1969), 17, 20.

EI49 Weiser, F. S., and Mary Hammond Sullivan. "Decorated Furniture of the Mahantango Valley." *Antiques*, vol. 103 (May 1973), 932–39.

EI50 Weiser, Frederick S., and Mary H. Sullivan. "Decorated Furniture of the Schwaben Creek Valley." In: *Ebbes fer Alle—Ebber Ebbes fer Dich: Essays in Memoriam, Albert Franklin Buffington.* Publs. of the Pa. German Soc., vol. 14 (1980), p.331–94. Furniture from Schuylkill and Northumberland counties.

EI51 Zook, Jacob Gustavus, and Jane Zook. *How to Paint and Decorate Furniture and Tinware.* N.p.: n.p., n.d. 32p. On the art of painting and stencilling.

Pottery

EI52 Barber, Edwin A. *Tulip Ware of the Pennsylvania-German Potters.* Repr. New York: Dover, 1970. 233p.

EI53 Bivins, John, Jr. *The Moravian Potters in North Carolina.* Photography by Bradford L. Rauschenberg. Chapel Hill: Univ. of N. Car. Pr., 1972. 303p. Rev. by E. P. Alexander, *Jour. of Southern Hist.*, vol. 39 (1973), 105–06; M. Menapace, *South Atlantic Quar.*, vol. 72 (1973), 166–67; S. Ragan, *N. Car. Hist. Rev.*, vol. 50 (1973), Publ. for Old Salem, Inc., Winston-Salem. Glossary of Moravian terms, bibliography. Moravians established potteries in the Wachovia tract in North Carolina in the mid-eighteenth century.

EI54 Breininger, Lester, and Barbara Breininger. "Potters of Robesonia, Pennsylvania." *Newsletter of the Soc. for German-Amer. Studies*, vol. 1, no. 3 (1979–1980), 2.

EI55 Breininger, Lester P., Jr. *Potters of the Tulpehocken.* Robesonia, Pa.: privately printed, 1979. A Taylor Mansion Publ. Address: the author, 476 Church St., Robesonia, Pa. 19551.

EI56 Bridges, Daisy W. "Catawba Valley Pottery has Unique Beauty." *Antiques Monthly*, vol. 13, no. 7 (1980), 13B. A pottery founded by Germans in North Carolina in the early 19th century.

EI57 Bridges, Daisy W. *Potters of the Catawba Valley, North Carolina*. Journal of Studies: Ceramic Circle of Charlotte, vol. 4. Charlotte: Mint Museum, 1980. 96p.

EI58 Cardinalli, Wayne F. "The Festival Potters." *Pa. Folklife*, vol. 21 (1972), Folk Festival Supplement, 44–47. At the Kutztown Festival.

EI59 Dieter, Gerald W., and John Cummings. *The Bible in Tile. The Story of the Mercer Biblical Tile in the Sanctuary of Salem Church [Doylestown, Pa.]*. Doylestown: Consistory, Salem United Church of Christ, 1957. 36p.

EI60 Fox, Claire Gilbride. "Henry Chapman Mercer, Tilemaker, Collector, and Builder Extraordinary." *Antiques*, vol. 104 (October 1973), 678–85.

EI61 Greaser, Arlene, and Paul H. Greaser. *Homespun Ceramics*. Allentown, Pa.: n.p., 1964.

EI62 Greer, Georgeanna H., and Harding Black. *The Meyer Family: Master Potters of Texas*. San Antonio: Trinity Univ. Pr., 1971. Repr. San Antonio: Witte Memorial Museum, ca. 1979. Rev. by S. L. Myres, *Southwestern Hist. Quar.*, vol. 76 (1972), 115.

EI63 Guilland, Harold F. *Early American Folk Pottery*. Philadelphia: Chilton Book Co., 1971.

EI64 Haddon, Rawson W. "Early Slip Decorated Canister." *Antiques*, vol. 9, no. 3 (March 1926), 166. Canister by Joseph Smith of Wrightstown, Bucks Co., dated 1767.

EI65 Hettinger, E. L. "Early Pennsylvania Potters." *Amer.-German Rev.*, vol. 9, no. 2 (1942), 23–26.

EI66 Hume, Ivor Noel. "Rhenish Gray Stonewares in Colonial America." *Antiques*, September 1967, 349–53.

EI67 Jack, Phil R., and Ronald L. Michael. "Stoneware from New Geneva and Greensboro, Pennsylvania." *Pa. Folklife*, vol. 22, no. 4 (1973), 33–42.

EI68 James, Arthur E. *The Potters and Potteries of Chester County, Pennsylvania*. West Chester: Chester Co. Hist. Soc., 1945. Repr. Exton, Pa.: Schiffer Publ. Co., 1978. 116p.

EI69 Jegglin Pottery, Boonville, Missouri. Records. Unpublished. For information apply to Charles Van Ravenswaay, at the pottery.

EI70 Kaufman, Stanley A. *Heatwole and Suter Pottery*. Harrisonburg, Va.: Good Printers, 1978. 48p. Catalogue of the February 1978 Exhibit at Eastern Mennonite College. On the work of two nineteenth-century workers in redware and stoneware: John D. Heatwole and Emanuel Suter, Rockingham Co., Virginia.

EI71 Kaufman, Gerhard. *North German Folk Pottery of the 17th to the 20th Centuries*. Richmond: Internat. Exhibitions Organized and Circulated by the International Exhibits Foundation, 1979–1980.

EI72 Keyser, Mrs. C. Naaman. *Pottery*. Keyser Home Craft Course Series, nos. 1 and 2. Plymouth Meeting, Pa.: n.p., 1943.

EI73 Kramer, Lester. "The Making of a 'Brenmist'." *Heritage Rev.*, vol. 8 (1974), 14–16. German-Russian fire brick.

EI74 Lasansky, Jeannette. *Central Pennsylvania Redware Pottery, 1780–1904*. Lewisburg, Pa.: Union County Oral Traditions Project, 1979.

EI75 Merrill, Peter C. "Lester and Barbara Breininger: Master Potters of Robesonia, Pennsylvania." *Newsletter, Soc. for German-Amer. Studies*, vol. 1, no. 3 (1979–1980), 2.

EI76 Miller, Warren E., and Mrs. Warren E. Miller. "Stahls of Powder Valley / Potters." *Goschenhoppen Region*, vol. 1, no. 3 (Lichtmess 1969), 4–6. A business established by Charles Ludwig Stahl for the production of sgraffito ware and thrown pieces. Emig. from Germany ca. 1843; ceased operation after 1948.

EI77 Newlands, David L. *The New Hamburg Pottery, New Hamburg, Ontario, 1954–1916*. Waterloo: Wilfred Laurier Univ. Pr., 1978.

EI78 Oakley, Raymond W. "Remmey Family: American Potters." *Antiques*, June and September 1937. John Remmey, b. 1706 in Neuwied, emigrated to New York City in 1735.

EI79 Oakley, Raymond W. "Unmarked New York Pottery: Crolius and Remmey." *The Antiquarian*, January 1930, 54f.

EI80 Postle, Kathleen R. *Chronicle of Overbeck Pottery*. Indianapolis: Ind. Hist. Soc., 1978. Rev. by K. Martz, *Ind. Mag. of Hist.*, vol. 75 (1979), 211–12.

EI81 *Potters of the Catawba Valley*. Charlotte: Mint Museum, 1980. Catalogue of the Mint Museum, 1980. Incl. the work of Seagle, Hartsoc (Hartsock), the Reinhardts, Probsts and Havners, ca. 1820, producers of utilitarian stoneware.

EI82 Powell, Elizabeth A. *Pennsylvania Pottery: Tools and Processes*. Doylestown: Bucks Co. Hist. Soc., 1972.

EI83 Quimby, Ian M. G., ed. "The Moravian Potters in North Carolina, 1756–1821." In: *Ceramics in America*. Ed. I.M.G. Quimby. Charlottesville: Univ. of Va. Pr., 1973. 374p. A technical treatise publ. for the Henry Francis duPont Winterthur Museum.

EI84 "Redware—The Germanic Influence [in American Pottery]". In: *The Art of the Potter*. Ed. Diana and J. Garrison Stradling. New York: Main Street/Universe Books, 1977, p.22–47. A collection of articles from *Antiques* magazine published between 1925 and 1965. Incl. "Ceramics in the South," by Arthur W. Clement, "Pottery at Old Salem [N. Car.]" and "Early North Carolina Pottery," by Joe Kindig, Jr., "Henry McQuate, Pennsylvania Potter," by Rhea M. Knittle, "A Maker of Pennsylvania Redware," by Cornelius Weygandt, "Early Pottery Lighting Devices of Pennsylvania," by William J. Truax, "American Pottery Lamps," by Lura Woodside Watkins, "Mehwaldt [Charles Augustus, b. 1808 Berlin, Germany; Resident of Bergholtz] a Pioneer American Potter," by Ada Walker Camehl, and "The Roof Tiles of Zoar," by E. J. Bognar.

EI85 Reinert, Guy F., and Sherwood J. Weber. "Isaac Stahl: One of the Last Pennsylvania Dutch Potters." *Hist. Rev. of Berks Co.*, vol. 15, no. 4 (1950), 242f.

EI86 Robacker, Earl F. "Pennsylvania Gaudyware." *The Dutchman*, vol. 7, no. 4 (Spring 1956), 2–7.

EI87 Robacker, Earl F. "Pennsylvania Redware." *The Pa. Dutchman*, vol. 8, no. 2 (1957), 2–7.

EI88 Robacker, Earl F. "Spatterware." *The Dutchman*, vol. 6, no. 2 (Fall 1954), 2–4.

EI89 Robacker, Earl F. *Spatterware and Sponge: Hardy Perennials of Ceramics*. South Brunswick, N.J.: Barnes, 1978. 167p.

EI90 Robacker, Earl F. "Stick-Spatter Ware." *Antiques*, vol. 99 (February 1971), 245–51. An English import made between 1820 and 1860 and popular in America first with the Pennsylvania Germans. A brightly decorated earthenware for household use.

EI91 Robacker, Earl F., and Ada F. Robacker. "The Art of the Potter." *Pa. Folklife*, vol. 27 (1977–1978), Folk Festival Supplement, 48–55. Pennsylvania-German potters exhibiting at the Kutztown festival.

EI92 Smith, Elmer L. "Shenandoah Pottery." "'S Pennsylfawnisch Deitsch Eck," Allentown *Morning Call*, 15 February 1969.

EI93 Smith, Elmer L. "The Strasburg [Virginia] Pottery." "'S Pennsylfawnisch Deitsch Eck, Allentown *Morning Call*, 1 March 1969.

EI94 Smith, G. Hubert. "Minnesota Potteries." *Minn. Hist.*, vol. 33 (1953), 229–35. Many were operated by German craftsmen.

EI95 Solon, M. L. *The Ancient Art of Stoneware of the Low Countries and Germany*. 2 vols. London, 1892.

EI96 Thompson, Clara Belle, and Margaret Lukes Wise. "She Makes the Potter's Wheel Hum." *Woman's Day*, vol. 5, no. 7 (April 1942), 12–13, 49–51. Mrs. C. Naaman Keyser and her pottery.

EI97 Van Ravenswaay, Charles. "Missouri Potters and Their Wares, 1780–1924." *Bull. of the Mo. Hist. Soc.*, vol. 7 (1951), 453–572.

EI98 Webster, Donald B. *Decorated Stoneware Pottery of North America*. Rutland, Vt.: Charles E. Tuttle, 1971. 232p.

EI99 Weygandt, Cornelius. "The Last of the Potters." In: *The Dutch Country*. New York: Apple-

Pottery *(cont.)*

ton-Century, 1939, p.19–30. Essay on Jacob Medinger of Neiffer, Pa.

EI100 Weygandt, Cornelius. "A Maker of Pennsylvania Redware." *Antiques*, vol. 49, no. 6 (June 1946), 372–73. Jacob Medinger and assistant William J. McAlister.

EI101 Wiltshire, William E., III. *Folk Pottery of the Shenandoah Valley*. New York: Dutton, 1975. 127p. German potters of the area included the Bell family (from Wiesbaden, prior to 1767), Anthony W. Baecher (from Falkenberg, Oberfalk, Bayern, 1824), Jeremiah and Amos Keister, W. H. Christman, W. B. Kenner, George W. Miller, and L. D. Funkhouser. The pottery shows traits and designs derived in part from German precedents.

EI102 Zug, Charles G., III. "Pursuing Pots: On Writing a History of North Carolina Folk Pottery." *N. Car. Folklore Jour.*, vol. 27 (1979), 35–55.

Glass

EI103 *Amelung Glass. An Exhibition...* Baltimore: Md. Hist. Soc., 1952. 20p. John Frederick Amelung, native of Bremen; 18th-century glass manufacturer.

EI104 Amelung, John Frederick. "Remarks on Manufactures, Principally on the New Established Glass-House near Frederick-Town, in the State of Maryland." Frederick, Md.: n.p., 1787. 13p. Repr. *Procs., Amer. Antiquarian Soc.*, vol. 60, no. 1 (1950), 101. Brief note on an American work of the 18th century on glass manufacture.

EI105 Atkinson, Robert. "The Kreutz Brothers: Craftsmen in Glass." *N.Y. Folklore*, vol. 25 (June 1969), 100–18. Processes, tools and lore associated with the craft.

EI106 Brill, Robert H., and Victor F. Hanson. "Chemical Analyses of Amelung Glasses." *Jour. of Glass Studies*, vol. 18 (1976), 215–37.

EI107 Cheesman, George. "Frederick County's Forgotten Glassmaker." *Md.*, vol. 9 (Summer 1977), 27–31. On John Frederick Amelung.

EI108 Cunz, Dieter. "Amelung's Old Frederick Glass." *Amer.-German Rev.*, vol. 12, no. 5 (1946), 16–19.

EI109 Elkinton, Howard W. "The Wandering Glass-Makers of Gablonz." *Amer.-German Rev.*, vol. 15, no. 4 (1949), 20–21.

EI110 "Famous Firsts." *Antiques*, vol. 62 (December 1952), 488–89. On a goblet made at Amelung's factory, New Bremen, Md., 1793.

EI111 Fry, George. "Henry C. Fry and the H. C. Fry Glass Company." *Western Pa. Hist. Mag.*, vol. 57 (July 1974).

EI112 Hubbard, Daniel, Lillie B. Jenkins, and Elizabeth M. Krumrine. "Amelung Glasses and Modern Commercial Glasses." *The Scientific Monthly*, vol. 75, no. 6 (1952), 327–38. Discussion of technical processes; excellent illus.

EI113 Kaufman, Ralph. "Glass Blowing: America's First Industry." *Pa. Folklife*, vol. 29, no. 4 (1979–1980), 25–27.

EI114 Lanmon, Dwight P., and Arlene M. Palmer. "John Frederick Amelung and the New Bremen Glassmanufactory." *Jour. of Glass Studies*, vol. 18 (1976), 13–136.

EI115 McKearin, Helen A., and George S. McKearin. *Two Hundred Years of American Blown Glass*. Garden City: Doubleday, 1950. 382p. See also *American Glass* by the same authors, 1941.

EI116 Manchee, Kathryn Hait Dorflinger. "Dorflinger Glass." *Antiques*, vol. 101, no. 4 (April 1972), 710–15; no. 5 (June 1972), 1006–1011; no. 6 (July 1972), 96–99. Christian Dorflinger, glassmaker of Brooklyn, N.Y. B. in Alsace in 1828; studied in France. Emig. with widowed mother to America and established a glass factory in Camden ca. 1852.

EI117 Milford, Harriet N. "Amelung and His New Bremen Glass Wares." *Md. Hist. Mag.*, vol. 47 (1952), 1–10.

EI118 Oland, Dwight D. "The New Bremen Glass Manufactory." *Md. Hist. Mag.*, vol. 68, no. 2 (Summer 1973), 255–72. On Amelung's and A. Kohlenberg's new glass works, from 1797.

EI119 Plaut, James S. *Steuben Glass, A Monograph*. New York: H. Bittner and Co., 1948. 30p. Rev. by E. Poole, *Amer.-German Rev.*, vol. 14, no. 5 (1948), 39.

EI120 Palmer, Arlene. "Glass Production in Eighteenth-Century America: The Wistarburgh Enterprise." *Winterthur Portfolio*, vol. 11 (1976), 75–101. Works founded in Salem Co., N.J., by Caspar Wistar, son of Hans Caspar and Anna Catharina Wistar, natives of Hilspach, Germany, who came to America in 1717. This work traces the history of the Wistar factory and its German workmen. Based on an M.A. thesis submitted at the Univ. of Delaware, 1973.

EI121 Quynn, Dorothy Mackay. "Johann Friedrich Amelung at New Bremen." *Md. Hist. Mag.*, vol. 43, no. 3 (1948), 155–79. A history of the Western Maryland glass industry, 1785–1804.

EI122 Steuben Glass, Inc. *The Story of Steuben Glass*. New York: Steuben Glass, Inc., ca. 1942. 24p.

EI123 *The Steuben Glass Collection of Antique Glass*. New York: Steuben Glass, Inc. Catalogues issued in 1941, 1943, 1944, 1945.

EI124 Suydam, F. D. *Christian Dorflinger, A Miracle of Glass*. White Mills, Pa.: n.p., 1950. Rev. by J. W. Oliver, *Pa. Hist.*, vol. 18, no. 4 (1951), 351–52.

EI125 Watkins, Lura Woodside. *American Glass and Glassmaking*. New York: Chanticleer Pr., 1950. 104p. Rev. by A. Winchester, *William and Mary Quar.*, vol. 8 (1951), 160–61.

EI126 Watkins, Lura Woodside. *Development of American Glassmaking. Account of the 4th Exhibition of the National Early American Glass Club*. Boston: n.p., 1935. 39p.

EI127 White, Margaret E. "Germanic Glass." *Amer.-German Rev.*, vol. 21, no. 6 (1955), 11–15. Examples of the products of Caspar Wistar, Henry W. Stiegel, and John Frederick Amelung as exhibited in the Newark, N.J., Museum.

EI128 Wood, Thomas. "'Mt. Vina,' the Quynns and Johann Frederick Amelung. Part III." *Now and Then* (Muncy, Pa.), vol. 10, no. 2 (1951), 50–53. On the manufacture of glass in the United States.

EI129 Wust, Klaus G. "German Craftsmen in Jamestown." *Amer.-German Rev.*, vol. 23, no. 4 (1957), 10–11. German glassblowers and shipbuilders in Virginia in the 17th century.

EI130 Ziegler, Elsie Reif. *The Blowing-Wand. A Story of Bohemian Glassmaking in Ohio*. Illus. by Jacob Landau. Philadelphia: Winston, 1955. 212p.

Wrought and Cast Iron

EI131 Bivins, John, Jr. "Decorative Cast Iron on the Virginia Frontier." *Antiques*, vol. 101, no. 3 (March 1972), 535–39. Products of the Winchester area and Marlboro Furnace; traces parallels and kinship with Pennsylvania German stove plates.

EI132 Gamon, Albert T. "Story of a Stove." *Pa. Folklife*, vol. 28, no. 4 (1978–1979), 12–16. "Plate" stoves.

EI133 Gunnion, Vernon S., and Carroll J. Hopf, eds. *The Blacksmith: Artisan within the Early Community*. Harrisburg, Pa.: Pa. Hist. and Museum Commission, 1976.

EI134 Kauffman, Henry J. *Early American Ironware: Cast and Wrought*. Rutland, Vt.: Tuttle, 1966. 166p. Rev. by J. W. Fawcett, *Western Pa. Hist. Mag.*, vol. 50, no. 2 (April 1967), 152–54; R. T. Trump, *Pa. Mag. of Hist. and Biog.*, vol. 91 (1967), 108–09. Incl. some Pennsylvania German ironware.

EI135 Kelly, James J. "Metal Casting in Sand at the Festival." *Pa. Folklife*, vol. 24 (1975), Folk Festival Supplement, 52–55. Kutztown Festival.

EI136 Loose, Thomas. "Blacksmiths and Whitesmiths." *Pa. Folklife*, vol. 29, no. 4 (1979–1980), 10–13.

EI137 Peirce, Josephine H. *Fire on the Hearth*. Springfield, Mass.: The Pond-Ekberg Co., 1951. Iron furnaces.

EI138 Reagan, William A. "The Blacksmith and His Tools." *Pa. Folklife*, vol. 17, no. 2 (Winter 1967–1968), 27–29. Pennsylvania-German nomenclature; illus.

EI139 Reid, Jo, and John Peck. *Stove Book*. New York: St. Martin's Press, 1977. 107p.

EI140 Reinert, Guy F. "Henry Dreihaus—Wrought Iron Craftsman." *Amer.-Geman Rev.*, vol. 12, no. 6 (1946), 7–11.

EI141 Robacker, Earl F. "The Dutch Touch in Iron." *The Pa. Dutchman*, vol. 8, no. 3 (Spring 1957), 2–6. Hand-wrought iron work.

EI142 Savage, Robert H. *Pennsylvania German Wrought Ironwork*. Home Craft Course Series, no. 10. Plymouth Meeting. Pa.: Mrs. C. Naaman Keyser, 1947. 33p.

EI143 Souders, Paul D., ed. "The Iron Furnaces of Union County. *Procs., Northumberland Co. Hist. Soc.*, vol. 26 (1974), 95–108. Several Germans built and operated furnaces.

EI44 Streeter, Donald. "Early American Wrought Iron Hardware: Cross Garnet, Side, and Dovetail Hinges." *Bull. of the Assoc. for Preservation Technology*, vol. 6 (1974), 7–31.

Basketry

EI145 Foltz, Carl Ned. "Basketmaking at the [Kutztown] Festival." *Pa. Folklife*, vol. 24 (1975), Folk Festival Supplement, 44–47.

EI146 Gould, Mary Earle. "Early American Splint Work." *Antiques Jour.*, vol. 17 (1962), 14–15.

EI147 Lasansky, Jeannette. *Willow, Oak, and Rye: Basket Traditions in Pennsylvania*. Lewisburg, Pa.: Union County Oral Traditions Projects, 1978. Rev. in *Der Reggeboge*, vol. 12, no. 3 (1978), 9.

EI148 Reinert, Guy F. *Pennsylvania German Splint and Straw Baskets*. Keyser Home Craft Course Series, no. 22. Kutztown: The Kutztown Publ. Co., 1946. 16p.

EI149 Robacker, Earl F. "Basketry: A Pennsylvania Dutch Art." *The Dutchman*, vol. 7, no. 2 (Fall 1955), 2–5.

EI150 Shaner, Richard H. "The Oley Valley (Berks Co.) Basketmaker." *Pa. Folklife*, vol. 14, no. 1 (1964), 2–9. The work of Freddie Bieber, well-known Dutch personality.

EI151 Weygandt, Cornelius. "Of Basketry and Basketing." In: *The Dutch Country*. New York: Appleton-Century, 1939, p.213–33.

Stonecutting

EI152 Alderson, Jo, Jim Alderson, and Kaye Alderson. "The Deathless Art." *Wis. Trails*, vol. 13, no. 3 (1972), 22–27. Gravestones in New Glarus, Wisconsin; some German and Swiss in style.

EI153 Barba, Preston A. "Folk Art on Pennsylvania German Tombstones." *Hist. Rev. of Berks Co.*, vol. 20, no. 2 (1954), 42–47. Also in *Amer.-German Rev.*, vol. 20, no. 6 (1954), 24–28.

EI154 Barba, Preston A. "Pennsylvania German Tombstones—A Study in Folk Art." *Publs., Pa. German Folklore Soc.*, no. 18 (1954), 1–228. Rev. by F. Lichten, *Amer.-German Rev.*, vol. 21, no. 5 (1955), 36; P. R. Jack, *Pa. Hist.*, vol. 22 (1955), 394; R. W. Gilbert, *Hist. Rev. of Berks Co.*, vol. 20, no. 2 (1955), 85–87.

EI155 Bronner, Simon J. "The Durlauf Family: Three Generations of Stonecarvers in Southern Indiana." *Pioneer America*, vol. 13 (1981), 17–26.

EI156 Klein, Frank A. "Vanguard Master." *Amer.-German Rev.*, vol. 9, no. 3 (February 1943), 15–17, 37. German artisans in the Quincy, Mass., granite and stone-cutting industry.

EI157 McDonald, Frank E. "Pennsylvania German Tombstone Art of Lebanon County, Pennsylvania." *Pa. Folklife*, vol. 25, no. 2 (1975), 2–19.

EI158 Rafferty, Milton D. "The Limestone Fenceposts of the Smokey Hill Region of Kansas." *Pioneer America*, vol. 6, no. 1 (1974), 40–45.

EI159 Swisher, Bob. "German Folk Art in Harmony Cemetery." *Appalachian Jour.*, vol. 5, no. 3 (Spring 1978), 313–17. The art of stonecutting displayed in the Jane Lew Methodist Church cemetery, with work dating from 1827 to 1855.

EI160 Swope, Martha R. "Lebanon Valley Date Stones." *The Pa. Dutchman*, vol. 6, no. 1 (1954), 20–22.

EI161 Wust, Klaus. *Folk Art in Stone—Southwest Virginia*. Edinburg, Va.: Shenandoah History, 1970. 26p. Early stone workers; study of principal motifs on gravestones.

Metal Work—Copper, Brass, Tin, Pewter

EI162 Breininger, Lester P., Jr. "The Lure of Tinsmithing." *Pa. Folklife*, vol. 22 (1973), Folk Festival Supplement, 36–37.

EI163 Clark, Roger W. "Cincinnati Coppersmiths." *Bull. of the Cincinnati Hist. Soc.*, vol. 23 (1965), 257–72. Incl. brief biographies of J. Kierstad and Henry Deckebach.

EI164 Craigie, Carter W. "The Tinsmith of Kutztown." *Pa. Folklife*, vol. 16, no. 4 (Summer 1967), 38–41. Charles Wagenhurst—"fourth-generation Pennsylvania German tinsmith."

EI165 Hoke, Elizabeth S. *The Painted Tray and Free Hand Bronzing*. Keyser Home Craft Course Series, no. 29. Plymouth Meeting, Pa.: Mrs. C. Naaman Keyser, 1949.

EI166 Hoke, Elizabeth S. *Pennsylvania German Painted Tin*. Home Craft Course Series, no. 5. Plymouth Meeting, Pa.: Mrs. C. Naaman Keyser, 1943. 32p. Repr. 1946.

EI167 Hollenbach, Raymond E. "Der Blechschmidt [Tinsmith]." "'S Pennsylfawnisch Deitsch Eck," Allentown *Morning Call*, 8 May 1964.

EI168 Jacobs, Carl. *Guide to American Pewter*. New York: The McBride Co., 1957.

EI169 Kauffman, Henry J. *American Copper and Brass*. Camden / Toronto: Th. Nelson & Sons, 1968.

EI170 Kauffman, Henry J. "Coppersmithing in Pennsylvania." *Publs., Pa. German Folklore Soc.*, vol. 11 (1946), 82–153.

EI171 Kauffman, Henry J. *Early American Copper, Tin, and Brass*. New York: McBride, 1950. 112p.

EI172 Kauffman, Henry J. *Pennsylvania German Pewter*. Keyser Home Craft Course Series, no. 8. Allentown: Schlechter's, 1944.

EI173 Kauffman, Henry J. "Punched Tinware." *The Pa. Dutchman*, vol. 5, no. 10 (15 January 1954), 3.

EI174 Kauffman, Henry J., and Zoe Elizabeth Kauffman. *Pennsylvania German Copper and Brass*. Home Craft Course Series, no. 25. Plymouth Meeting, Pa.: Mrs. C. Naaman Keyser, 1947. 32p.

EI175 Lipman, Jean. In: *American Folk Art in Wood, Metal and Stone*. New York: Pantheon, 1948., p.120–21. On Wilhelm Schimmel.

EI176 Robacker, Earl F. "The Case for Pennsylvania German Painted Tin." *Antiques*, vol. 52, no. 4 (October 1947), 263–65.

EI177 Robacker, Earl F. "Painted Tin or 'Tole'." *The Dutchman*, vol. 6, no. 4 (1955), 2–7. Submits evidence to show that some of the painted tin or "tole" was a Pennsylvania German product.

EI178 Robacker, Earl F. "The Painted Toleware of Pennsylvania." Early American Industries Assoc. *Chronicle*, vol. 2, no. 24 (September 1943), 209.

EI179 Robacker, Earl F. "Pennsylvania Pewter and Pewterers." *Pa. Folklife*, vol. 13, no. 2 (Winter 1962–1963), 2–6. Incl. discussion of "Dutch Country" artisans.

EI180 Robacker, Earl F. "Tin—With Holes In." *Pa. Folklife*, vol. 12, no. 1 (Spring 1961), 2–7. Punched tinware.

EI181 Robacker, Earl F., and Ada F. Robacker. "Metalcrafting at the Festival." *Pa. Folklife*, vol. 23 (1974), Folk Festival Supplement, 48–55.

EI182 Weygandt, Cornelius. "Provinciality and Painted Tin." In: *The Dutch Country*. New York: Appleton-Century, p.181–93.

Woodcarving

EI183 Flower, M. E. "Schimmel the Woodcarver." *Antiques*, vol. 44 (October 1943), 164–66. Wilhelm Schimmel (1817–1890), was a German-born itinerant whittler who lived in an almshouse in Carlisle, Pa. He produced polychrome toys, animals, eagles, and human figures.

EI184 Fried, Frederick. *Artists in Wood: American Carvers of Cigar Store Indians, Show Figures and Circus Wagons*. New York: n.p., ca. 1978. 297p.

EI185 Grier, Katherine C. "The Wandering Whittler." *Antique World*, vol. 3, no. 3 (1981), 36–40. William Schimmel of Pennsylvania.

EI186 Herricht, Fred. *The Putz, Carved Wood Figures*. Keyser Home Craft Course Series, no. 17. Kutztown: Kutztown Publ. Co., 1946.

EI187 Lichten, Frances. "'Tramp Work': Penknife Plus Cigar Boxes." *Pa. Folklife*, vol. 10, no. 1 (Spring 1959), 2–7.

EI188 Lowe, David G. "Wooden Delights. An Obscure Pennsylvania German Carpenter Named John Scholl Left the World a Legacy of Charming Toys and Beautiful Fantasies." *Amer. Heritage*, vol. 20, no. 1 (December 1968), 19–23. B. in Württemberg in 1827, Scholl emigrated to America in 1853; d. 1916. Produced intricately carved toys and decorations.

EI189 McAllister, William J. *Pennsylvania German Wood Carving*. Keyser Home Craft Course Series, no. 13. Plymouth Meeting, Pa.: Mrs. C. Naaman Keyser, 1945.

EI190 Robacker, Earl F., and Ada F. Robacker. "Folk Whittling in Pennsylvania." *Pa. Folklife*, vol. 22 (1973), Folk Festival Supplement, 38–48.

Clock Making

EI191 Albright, Frank P. *Johann Ludwig Eberhardt and His Salem Clocks*. Chapel Hill: Univ. of N. Car., 1978. 160p.

EI192 Church, R. A. "Nineteenth-Century Clock Technology in Britain, the United States, and Switzerland." *Economic Hist. Rev.*, vol. 28 (November 1975).

EI193 "Clock and Watchmakers of Lancaster County, 1750–1850." *Jour. of the Lancaster Co. Hist. Soc.*, vol. 77 (1973), 173–82.

EI194 Conrad, John. "Pennsylvania Clockmakers." *Bull. of the Hist. Soc. of Montgomery Co.*, vol. 3 (1942), 260–61.

EI195 Drepperd, Carl W. *American Clocks and Clockmakers*. Garden City: Doubleday, 1947.

EI196 Eckhardt, George H. *Pennsylvania Clocks and Clockmakers: An Epic of Early American Science, Industry, and Craftsmanship*. New York: Devin-Adair, 1955. 247p.

EI197 Hommel, Rudolf P. "Jacob Godschalk of Towamencin and Philadelphia, Clockmaker." *Bull., Hist. Soc. of Montgomery Co.*, vol. 5, no. 1 (1945), 3–6.

EI198 James, Arthur E. *Chester County Clocks and Their Makers*. West Chester: Chester Co. Hist. Soc., 1947. 205p.

EI199 Landes, David S. "Watchmaking: A Case Study in Enterprise and Change." *Business Hist. Rev.*, vol. 53 (1979), 1–40. Brief mention of German-American watchmakers.

EI200 Lerch, Lila. "Early [Pennsylvania German] Clocks." "'S Pennsylfawnisch Deitsch Eck," Allentown *Morning Call*, 21, 28 August 1965.

EI201 Nolan, J. Bennett. "The Governor's Clock." "'S Pennsylfawnisch Deitsch Eck," Allentown *Morning Call*, 23 January 1943.

EI202 Palmer, Brooks. *The Book of American Clocks.* New York: Macmillan, 1950. 318p.

EI203 Robacker, Earl F. "Tick-Tock Time in Old Pennsylvania." *Pa. Folklife*, vol. 9, no. 4 (1958), 32–37. Suggestions for the collector of Pennsylvania German clocks.

EI204 Stephens, W. Barclay. "Hermann Wenzel and His Air Clock." *Calif. Hist. Soc. Quar.*, vol. 27 (1948), 1–8. Famous clockmaker born in Saxony.

EI205 Sweinhart, Fred C. "Early Pennsylvania Clocks and Their Makers." *Bull., Hist. Soc. of Montgomery Co.*, vol. 3 (1942), 42–52.

EI206 Wood, Stacy B. "The Hoff Family: Master Clockmakers of Lancaster County." *Jour. of the Lancaster Co. Hist. Soc.*, vol. 81 (1977), 169–225.

EI207 Wood, Stacy B. "Rudy Stoner, 1728–1769: Early Lancaster, Pennsylvania, Clockmaker." *Jour. of the Lancaster Co. Hist. Soc.*, vol. 80 (1976), 112–27.

EI208 Wood, Stacy B. C., Jr., and Stephen E. Kramer III. *Clockmakers of Lancaster County and Their Clocks, 1750–1850. With a Study of Lancaster County Clock Cases, by John J. Snyder, Jr.* Introd. by John W. W. Loose. New York: Van Nostrand Reinhold, 1978. 224p. Rev. by Edwin A. Battiston, *Antiques*, vol. 113 (1978), 1312.

Gunsmithing

EI209 Abels, Robert. *Early American Firearms.* Cleveland/New York: World Publ. Co., 1950. 63p.

EI210 Dyke, Samuel E. "The Beck Family of Gunsmiths, Lancaster County, Pennsylvania." *Jour. of the Lancaster Co. Hist. Soc.*, vol. 72, no. 1 (Hilarymas 1968), 28–49.

EI211 Dyke, Samuel E., comp.; C. B. Grove, revisor. "List of Gunsmiths of Lancaster County, Pennsylvania: Period 1728–1863." *Jour. of the Lancaster Co. Hist. Soc.*, vol. 72, no. 1 (Hilarymas 1968), 50–60.

EI212 Gill, Harold B., Jr. *The Gunsmith in Colonial Virginia.* Williamsburg: Colonial Williamsburg Foundation, 1974. 139p. Rev. by E. A. Battison, *Jour. of Amer. Hist.*, vol. 63, no. 3 (December 1976), 687–88. "Evidence of rifled guns, usually attributed to the German immigration beginning in the late seventeenth century, was discovered prior to 1640...."

EI213 Gluckman, Arcadi, and L. D. Satterlee. *American Gun Makers.* Harrisburg: Stackpole, 1953. 243p. Rev. by W. A. Albaugh, *Va. Mag. of Hist. and Biog.*, vol. 61, no. 3 (1953), 339–40.

EI214 Huyett, Harvey T. "A 'Lost Chapter' of American History: An Interview with Harvey T. Huyett." *Hist. Rev. of Berks Co.*, vol. 7 (1941–1942), 116–18. The Schnader family gun shop and the Kentucky rifle. Berks Co. munitions were important in the Revolutionary and the Civil War.

EI215 Kauffman, Henry J. *Early American Gunsmiths, 1650–1850.* Harrisburg: Stackpole, 1952. 94p. Rev. by J. E. Jordan, *N. Car. Hist. Rev.*, vol. 30 (1953), 135–36.

EI216 Kauffman, Henry J. *The Pennsylvania Kentucky Rifle.* Harrisburg: Stackpole, 1960. 376p. Rev. by W. White, *Pa. Mag. of Hist. and Biog.*, vol. 86, no. 2 (1962), 211–13.

EI217 Kauffman, Henry J. "Rifles in Berks County." *Hist. Rev. of Berks Co.*, vol. 31, no. 1 (Winter 1965–1966), 12–13.

EI218 Keim Co., Glen Mills, Pa. Records, 1848–1855. In the Eleutherian Mills Historical Library, Greenville, Del. (MS 72-101). Records of the W. & J. H. Keim Co., manufacturers of rifles and gun barrels: letter book, accounts, correspondence.

EI219 "The Kentucky Rifle as Art." *Amer. Heritage*, vol. 24 (1973), 70–73.

EI220 Kindig, Joe, Jr. *Thoughts on the Kentucky Rifle in Its Golden Age.* Wilmington: George N. Hyatt, 1960. 561p. 856 plates.

EI221 Klinefelter, Walter. "The Gunsmiths of York County, Pennsylvania." In: *Ebbes fer Alle—Ebber Ebbes fer Dich....* Publs. of the Pa. German Soc., vol. 14 (1980), p.131–81.

EI222 Landis, Henry Kinzer, and George Diller Landis. "Lancaster Rifle Accessories." *Pa. German Folklore Soc. Publs.*, vol. 9 (1944), 113–84.

EI223 Landis, Henry Kinzer, and George Diller Landis. "Lancaster Rifles." *Pa. German Folklore Soc. Publs.*, vol. 7 (1942), 107–57.

EI224 Lindsay, Merrill. *The Kentucky Rifle*. New York: Arma Press and Hist. Soc. of York Co., 1972. 101p.

EI225 *Memorial of Sundry Gun Manufacturers of the Borough of Lancaster, in the State of Pennsylvania. 4th February, 1802...* Washington City, Pa.: William Duane & Son, 1803. 6p. Signed by Jacob Dickert, Peter Gonter, Abram Henry, and others.

EI226 Nolt, Samuel K. "Henry Eichholtz Leman and His Production of the Pennsylvania Rifle." *Jour. of the Lancaster Co. Hist. Soc.*, vol. 71 (Michaelmas, 1967), 185–97.

EI227 Parsons, John E. *Henry Deringer's Pocket Pistol*. New York: William Morrow & Co., 1952. Rev. by H. W. Shoemaker, *Pa. Hist.*, vol. 20, no. 1 (1953), 110–11.

EI228 Reichmann, Felix. "The Pennsylvania Rifle: A Social Interpretation of Changing Military Techniques." *Pa. Mag. of Hist. and Biog.*, vol. 69, no. 1 (1945), 3–14.

EI229 Shumway, George. *Longrifles of Note, Pennsylvania*. York, Pa.: The Author, 1968. 74p.

EI230 Smith, Ray. "The Kentucky Rifle and Its Snyder County Makers." "'S Pennsylfawnisch Deitsch Eck," Allentown *Morning Call*, 13, 20 July 1946.

EI231 Teasdale, Jerald T. "The Gunmaking Industry in Wisconsin." *Wis. Mag. of Hist.*, vol. 32, no. 3 (1949), 302–11. The majority of gunsmiths were German and Swiss. Their guns were preferred for use in *Schützenfeste*.

EI232 Walck, Lee A. "Reuben Strauss: Allentown Gunsmith." *Procs., Lehigh Co. Hist. Soc.*, vol. 31 (1976), 163–65.

EI233 Wilson, R. L. *L. D. Nimschke, Firearms Engraver*. Teaneck, N. J.: John J. Malloy, 1965. 107p. A German-born artist (1832–1904) who worked in Brooklyn as an engraver of embellishments for sporting guns.

Wagon Building

EI234 Benson, Evelyn A. "The Earliest Use of the Term 'Conestoga Wagon'." *The Pa. Dutchman*, vol. 4, no. 14 (1953), 6–8. The origin of the wagon and its name.

EI235 Brown, Waln K. "The Pennsylvania Dutch Carriage Trade." *Pa. Folklife*, vol. 22, no. 3 (1973), 22–26.

EI236 Drachman, Albert I. "The Conestoga Horse." *The Pa. Dutchman*, vol. 6, no. 4 (1955), 24–29.

EI237 Dunham, B. Mabel. *The Trail of the Conestoga*. Toronto: McClelland & Stewart, 1942. Rev. by G. Graber, *Mennonite Hist. Bull.*, vol. 4, no. 1 (March 1943), 4.

EI238 Espenschied, Lloyd. "Louis Espenschied and His Family." *Bull., Mo. Hist. Soc.*, vol. 18, no. 2 (1962), 87–103. Early wagon builder of St. Louis.

EI239 Frey, H. C. "The Conestoga Wagon." *Procs., Lancaster Co. Hist. Soc.*, vol. 51, no. 3 (1947), 62–91.

EI240 Frey, J. William, and H. C. Frey. *The Conestoga Wagon—A Pennsylvania Dutch Product*. Lancaster: n.p., 1947. 42p.

EI241 Hafer, Ermine S. *A Century of Vehicle Craftsmanship*. Boyertown: Hafer Foundation, ca. 1972.

EI242 Herrick, Michael J. "The Conestoga Wagon of Pennsylvania." *Western Pa. Hist. Mag.*, vol. 51, no. 2 (April 1968), 155–63. A sketch of its history, 1750 to ca. 1800.

EI243 Hollenbach, Raymond E. "Solomon Fisler, der Wagner." "'S Pennsylfawnisch Deitsch Eck," Allentown *Morning Call*, 22 March 1947. The account book of a Pennsylvania German wainwright.

EI244 Hollenbach, Raymond E. "Wagons and Carriages." "'S Pennsylfawnisch Deitsch Eck," Allentown *Morning Call*, 8 March 1947. Wagon building in the nineteenth century.

EI245 Jentsch, Theodore W. "Whoa There Nellie...." *Pa. Folklife*, vol. 29, no. 4 (1979–1980), 8–9. Horsedrawn vehicles at the Kutztown Folk Festival.

EI246 Scott, Stephen E. *Plain Buggies: Amish, Mennonite, and Brethren Horse-Drawn Transportation.* Lancaster: Good Books, 1981.

EI247 Shaner, Richard H. "Conestoga Wagons of Berks County." *Hist. Rev. of Berks Co.*, vol. 36 (Autumn 1971), 128–33.

EI248 Shumway, George, Edward Durell, and Howard C. Frey. *Conestoga Wagon, 1750–1850: Freight Carrier for 100 Years of America's Westward Expansion.* York, Pa.: The Early Amer. Industrial Assoc., and G. Shumway, 1964. 206p. 2nd ed., 1966. Rev. by P. A. Barba, "'S Pennsylfawnisch Deitsch Eck," Allentown *Morning Call*, 29 May 1965; E. A. Benson, *Pa. Folklife*, vol. 14, no. 4 (1965), 56–59; P. Perry, *N. Car. Hist. Rev.*, vol. 42, no. 1 (Winter 1965), 116–17; W. N. Richards, *Pa. Mag. of Hist. and Biog.*, vol. 91 (1967), 477–79; O. O. Winther, *Amer. Hist. Rev.*, vol. 70, no. 2 (1965), 567. Wagons and horses developed in the Conestoga River Valley, Lancaster Co., by German and English settlers.

Weaving / Stitchery / Embroidery

EI249 Aid, C. Toney. "Missouri Handweavers of the 19th Century." Paper prep. for a course in American Decorative Arts, Univ. of Missouri, December 1973. TS.

EI250 Bishop, Robert, and Elizabeth Safanda. *A Gallery of Amish Quilts: Design Diversity from a Plain People.* New York: Dutton, 1976. 96p. Incl. photos of the Amish people and their land.

EI251 Bixel, Phyllis. "Pennsylvania German Coverlets." *Mennonite Life*, vol. 5, no. 4 (1950), 34, 39.

EI252 Burnham, Harold B., and Dorothy K. Burnham. *Jacquard Coverlets, "Keep Me Warm One Night."* Toronto: Univ. of Toronto Pr., 1972, p.317–78. History of the introduction of the Jacquard weaving process into Canada and the United States by William Horstmann of Philadelphia (1824); its subsequent development in Canada among German-speaking settlers, incl. the Mennonites.

EI253 Davison, Marguerite P. *Home Craft Course in Pennsylvania Dutch Home Weaving Patterns...* Photographs by E. Fletcher Brown. Home Craft Courses, vol. 4. Allentown: Schlechter's, 1943. Rev. by P. A. Barba, "'S Pennsylfawnisch Deitsch Eck," Allentown *Morning Call*, 4 December 1943.

EI254 Foust, Barbara K. "Vegetable Dyeing at the Kutztown Folk Festival." *Pa. Folklife*, vol. 25 (1976), Folk Festival Supplement, 20–22.

EI255 Galvin, Nellie L., ed. *A German Weaver's Pattern Book.* N.p.: n.p., 1961. Pattern book from Canada.

EI256 Gehret, Ellen J., and Alan G. Keyser. *The Homespun Textile Tradition of the Pennsylvania Germans.* Harrisburg: Pa. Hist. and Museum Commission, 1976.

EI257 Gilberg, Laura S., and Barbara B. Buchholz. *Needlepoint: Designs for Amish Quilts.* New York: Scribner's, 1977.

EI258 Graeff, Marie Knorr. *Pennsylvania German Quilts.* Keyser Home Craft Course Series, no. 14. Kutztown: Kutztown Publ. Co., 1946. 32p.

EI259 Haders, Phyllis. *Amish Quilts. A Universe Calendar for 1977.* New York: Main Street/Universe Books, ca. 1976.

EI260 Haders, Phyllis. *Sunshine and Shadow: The Amish and Their Quilts.* New York: Main Street/Universe Books, 1976. 71p. Rev. by S. Terry, *Christian Science Monitor*, 26 April 1977, p.27.

EI261 Harrison, Eliza Cope. *Decorative Needlework of the Pennsylvania Germans.* Hershey, Pa.: Hershey Museum of American Life, 1979. 15p. Catalogue.

EI262 Hartmann, Gail M. "Fifteen Years of Quilting at the Festival." *Pa. Folklife*, vol. 28 (1978–1979), Folk Festival Supplement, 2–5. Kutztown Folk Festival.

EI263 Hartmann, Gail M. "Quilts, Quilts, Quilts." *Pa. Folklife*, vol. 25 (1976), Supplement, 2–9.

EI264 Heisey, John W., Gail C. Andrews, and Donald R. Walters. *A Checklist of American Coverlet Weavers.* Williamsburg, Va.: Abby Aldrich Rockefeller Folk Art Center, 1978. Rev. by D. K. Burnham, *Der Reggeboge*, vol. 13, no. 1 (1979), 15–17.

EI265 Hollenbach, Raymond E. "Gottschalk Gottschalk, An Old-Time Weaver." "'S Pennsylfawnisch Deitsch Eck," Allentown *Morning Call*, 16 March 1968.

EI266 Hommel, Rudolf. "About Spinning Wheels." *Amer.-German Rev.*, vol. 9, no. 6 (August 1943), 4–7.

EI267 *Jacob Angstadt. His Weavers Patron Book.* Replica of an 18th-century MS. owned and reproduced by Ruth N. Holroyd. N.p.: n.p., copyright 1976. 96p. Incl. a genealogy of the Angstadt family of weavers, 1727–1912.

EI268 *Jacob Angstadt Designs Drawn from His Weavers Patron Book.* Trans. from the German by Ulrike L. Beck. N.p.: privately printed, 1976. Address: Ruth N. Holroyd, 20 Old Farm Circle, Pittsford, N.Y. 14534. A pattern book with 252 "figures."

EI269 *Jacob Snavely Personal Account Book, Lebanon Co., 1727.* MS. in the library of Lebanon Valley College, Annville. From this work Isabel I. Abel has reproduced Snavely's multiple harness weaving patterns. Publ. in paperback by the author, R.D. No. 4, Bix 44, Altoona, Pa. 16601.

EI270 Kelley, Hazel Reeder. *The ABC of Rug Making.* Keyser Home Craft Course Series, no. 24. Kutztown: Kutztown Publ. Co., 1947.

EI271 King, Gail. "The Christian Decker Collection: Embroidery Stamping Blocks Still in Use." *Americana*, January–February 1980, 60–66. Immigrant from Germany, Christian Decker (d. 1894) carved embroidery stamping blocks. His business has been revived by his descendants.

EI272 Lichten, Frances. "Pennsylvania Dutch Needlework: Where Did the Worker Find her Patterns?" *The Dutchman*, vol. 7, no. 4 (Spring 1956), 18–21.

EI273 Osburn, Bernice B. *Pennsylvania German Spinning and Dyeing.* Keyser Home Craft Course Series, no. 16. Allentown: Schlechter's, 1945; Plymouth Meeting: Mrs. C. Naaman Keyser, 1945.

EI274 "Pennsylvania-German Needlework." *Amer.-German Rev.*, vol. 7, no. 6 (June 1941).

EI275 Reardon, Philip H. "Philip Schum: Carpet and Coverlet Weaver." *Jour. of the Lancaster Co. Hist. Soc.*, vol. 82 (1978), 160–64.

EI276 Reinert, Guy F. "Coverlets of the Pennsylvania Germans." *Publs., Pa. German Folklore Soc.*, vol. 13 (1948), 1–215. Rev. by A. D. Graeff, "'S Pennsylfawnisch Deitsch Eck," Allentown *Morning Call*, 15 October 1949.

EI277 Reinert, Guy F. *Pennsylvania German Coverlets.* Keyser Home Craft Course Series, no. 9. Kutztown: Kutztown Publ. Co., 1947.

EI278 Robacker, Earl F. "Piece-Patch Artistry." *Pa. Folklife*, vol. 13, no. 3 (1963), 2–10. Quilt patterns.

EI279 Robacker, Earl F. "Stitching for Pretty." *Pa. Folklife*, vol. 15, no. 3 (Spring 1966), 2–9. Pennsylvania German stitchery.

EI280 Robacker, Earl F. "The Townshi[p] Weavers of Pennsylvania." *Pa. Folklife*, vol. 12, no. 2 (Summer 1961), 3–7. Coverlets and traditional weaving.

EI281 Robacker, Earl F., and Ada F. Robacker. "Quilting Traditions of the Dutch Country." *Pa. Folklife*, vol. 21 (1972), Folk Festival Supplement, 31–38.

EI282 Robacker, Earl F., and Ada F. Robacker. "Quilts and Quilting: Picking the Winners." *Pa. Folklife*, vol. 30 (1980–1981), 169–73.

EI283 Robertson, Elizabeth Wells. *American Quilts.* New York: The Studio Publications, Inc., 1948.

EI284 Rogers, Grace L. "Peter Stauffer." *Handweaver and Craftsman*, vol. 7, no. 1 (1955–1956), 12–14.

EI285 Safanda, Elizabeth. "Design Origins of Amish Quilts." *Clarion*, Spring 1979, 32–37, 59.

EI286 Schiffer, Margaret B. *Historical Needlework of Pennsylvania.* New York: Scribner's Sons, 1968. Samplers, crewel, canvas, and Berlin work, incl. Moravian and Pennsylvania Dutch. Rev. by F. M. Montgomery, *Pa. Mag. of Hist. and Biog.*, vol. 93, no. 2 (April 1969), 269–71.

EI287 Stewart, Susan. "Sociological Aspects of Quilting in Three Brethren Churches of Southeastern Pennsylvania." *Pa. Folklife*, vol. 23, no. 3 (1974), 15–29.

EI288 Walker, Sandra Rambo. *Country Cloth to Coverlets: Textile Traditions in 19th Century Pennsylvania*. Lewisburg: Folk Textiles, Oral Traditions Project, n.d. 64p.

Clothing

EI289 Baldwin, Sioux. "Amish Plain Costume: A Matter of Choice." *Pa. Folklife*, vol. 19, no. 4 (1968–1969), 10–17.

EI290 Berky, Andrew S. "Buckskin or Sackcloth?—A Glance at the Clothing Once Worn by the Schwenkfelders in Pennsylvania." *Pa. Folklife*, vol. 9, no. 2 (1958), 50–52.

EI291 Enninger, Werner. "Nonverbal Performatives: The Function of a Grooming and Garment Grammar in the Organization of Noverbal Role-Taking and Role-Making in One Specific Trilingual Social Isolate." In: *Understanding Bilingualism: Life, Learning and Language in Bilingual Situations*. Ed. Werner Hüllen. Frankfurt: Peter Lang, 1980, p.25–65. A study of the Old Order Amish in Delaware.

EI292 Gehret, Ellen J. *Rural Pennsylvania Clothing*. York, Pa.: Liberty Cap Books, George Shumway Publ., 1976. 309p. Rev. by J. M. Coram, *Md. Hist. Mag.*, vol. 73, no. 1 (Spring 1978), 103–04; S. B. Swan, *Der Reggeboge*, vol. 13, no. 1 (January 1979), 12–15. Incl. instructions for making clothes in the manner of the early German immigrants.

EI293 Gingerich, Melvin. *Mennonite Attire Through Four Centuries*. Breinigsville: Publs. of the Pennsylvania German Society, vol. 4 (1970). 192p. Rev. by I. Richman, *Pa. Hist.*, vol. 39 (1972), 299–301; M. H. Schrag, *Church Hist.*, vol. 40 (December 1971), 500; J. J. Stoudt, *Pa. Mag. of Hist. and Biog.*, vol. 95, no. 3 (July 1971), 426–27; E. K. Ziegler, *Brethren Life and Thought*, vol. 16 (1971), 245–46.

EI294 Hostetler, John A. "Amish Costume: Its European Origins." *Amer.-German Rev.*, vol. 22, no. 6 (1956), 11–14. Tracing the dress of the Amish to Alsace and the Palatinate.

EI295 Huyett, Laura. "Straw Hat Making among the Old Order Amish." *Pa. Folklife*, vol. 12, no. 3 (1962), 40–41.

EI296 Nolan, J. Bennett. "Pennsylvania Sunday Best." *Amer. Heritage*, vol. 8, no. 3 (1957), 48–51. Dress of the early nineteenth century as revealed in portraits.

EI297 Yoder, Don. "The Costumes of the... 'Plain People'." *The Pa. Dutchman*, vol. 4, no. 13 (1953), 6–7. On the origins of the costumes.

EI298 Yoder, Don. "Men's Costumes among the Plain People." *The Pa. Dutchman*, vol. 4, no. 15 (1953), 6–9.

Paper Cutting

EI299 *American Folk Art Calendar 1980*. Wichita, Kans.: Hammond Publ. Example of work of Claudia Diehl Hopf, self-taught artist of papercutting, "Scherenschnitte." Native of Cincinnati; student of Pennsylvania German crafts; writer on crafts subjects. See sketch in the *Newsletter, Soc. for German-Amer. Studies*, vol. 1, no. 4 (1979–1980), 18.

EI300 Andrews, Katherine. "Walter von Gunten—Scherenschnitte Artist." *Wis. Tales and Trails*, vol. 7, no. 4 (1966), 23–25. Swiss-born artist who came to Madison, Wisconsin in 1962.

EI301 Dreis, Hazel. "Lancaster, Pennsylvania, Bookbindings. An Historical Study." *Publs., Bibliographic Soc. of Amer.*, vol. 42 (1948), 119–28. Printing and bindings in the Lancaster region, especially at the Ephrata Cloister.

EI302 Hopf, Claudia. *Scherenschnitte: The Folk Art of Scissors Cutting. A History and Patterns Including Instructions*. Lancaster: John Baer's Sons, 1971. Rev. in *Der Reggeboge*, vol. 5, nos. 3–4 (1971), 8.

EI303 Hopf, Claudia. *Scherenschnitte; Traditional Papercutting*. Lebanon, Pa.: Applied Arts Pr., 1977. 32p.

EI304 Merrill, Peter C. "The Paper-Cutting Art of Claudia Hopf." *Newsletter, Soc. for German-Amer. Studies*, vol. 1, no. 4 (1978–1980), 18. Pennsylvania-German *Scherenschnitte*.

EI305 Schaffer, Sharon A. "*Scherenschnitte* of the Pennsylvania Dutch." *Pa. Folklife*, vol. 29, no. 4 (1979–1980), 14–16. The art of paper-cutting.

EI306 Weygandt, Cornelius. "Cut-Outs of Yesterday." In: *The Dutch Country*. New York: Appleton-Century, 1939, p.77–83. The art of *Scherenschnitte*.

Other

EI307 Allis, Mary. "The Last of the American Folk Arts [Chalkware and Painted Plaster Objects]." *Amer. Collector*, vol. 9 (January 1941), 10–11, 14.

EI308 Barrick, Mac E. "Central Pennsylvania Fishing Spears." *Pa. Folklife*, vol. 21, no. 3 (1971–1972), 32–35.

EI309 Barrick, Mac E. "An Esoteric Doughtray Scraper." *Jour. of Amer. Folklore*, vol. 92 (1979), 215–19. Pennsylvania-German folk art.

EI310 Barrick, Mac E. "Folk Toys." *Pa. Folklife*, vol. 29, no. 1 (1979–1980), 27–34.

EI311 Benson, Evelyn A. "A Pennsylvania Dutch Colonial Button Mold." *The Pa. Dutchman*, vol. 8, no. 4 (Summer-Fall 1957), 34–48.

EI312 Breininger, Lester. "Just a Bone." *Pa. Folklife*, vol. 21, no. 3 (Spring 1970), 21–23. Articles of bone, and the "gnochemann" who bought bones after the butchering season.

EI313 Davis, Thomas M., and Franz R. Beinke. "Franz Schwarzer, Missouri Zither Maker." *Mo. Hist. Rev.*, vol. 60 (1965), 1–30.

EI314 Hoke, Elizabeth S. *Pennsylvania German Reverse Painting on Glass*. Keyser Home Craft Course Series, no. 12. Kutztown: The Kutztown Publ. Co., 1946.

EI315 Jungwirth, Joachim, & Co. Records, 1904–1916. In the Burton Historical Collection, Detroit Public Library (MS 69-712). Records of the sculpting, modelling, and carving firm of Joachim Jungwirth & Co.

EI316 Kettermann, Marie. *Two Hundred Years of Pennsylvania Dolls*. Plymouth Meeting, Pa.: n.p., 1949. 36p.

EI317 McClintock, Inez, and Marshall McClintock. *Toys in America*. Washington: Public Affairs Pr., 1961. 480p. The history of importation of toys from Germany, as well as the native crafts of carving and toy manufacture.

EI318 Marquardt, Lewis R. "Metal Grave Markers in Geman-Russian Cemeteries of Emmons County, North Dakota." *Jour. of the Amer. Hist. Soc. of Germans from Russia*, vol. 2, no. 1 (1979), 18–26.

EI319 Merrill, Peter C. "Pennsylvania German Easter Eggs: The Art of Evelyn Althouse." *Newsletter of the Soc. for German-Amer. Studies*, vol. 1, no. 4 (1979–1980), 5.

EI320 Osburn, Burl N. *Bookbinding*. Keyser Home Craft Course Series, no. 21. Allentown: Schlechter's, 1945.

EI321 "Pens and Penmanship. Henkel's Instructions. (So Henn Die Alde Leit Geduh.)" *Der Reggeboge*, vol. 16, no. 2 (1982), 46–48.

EI322 Robacker, Earl F. "Books Not for Burning." *Pa. Folklife*, vol. 9, no. 1 (Winter 1957–1958), 44–52.

EI323 Robacker, Earl F. "Butter Molds." *The Pa. Dutchman*, vol. 6, no. 1 (1954), 6–8. Designs and dates of Pennsylvania German molds.

EI324 Robacker, Earl F. "Knife, Fork and Spoon: A Collector's Problem." *Pa. Folklife*, vol. 9, no. 2 (1958), 28–33.

EI325 Robacker, Earl F. "Let's Talk about Slate." *Pa. Folklife*, vol. 22, no. 4 (1973), 2–10.

EI326 Robacker, Earl F. "Paper for Fancy." *Antiques*, vol. 72, no. 6 (December 1957), 543–45.

EI327 Robacker, Earl F. "Pennsylvania Chalkware." *Pa. Folklife*, vol. 9, no. 3 (1958), 2–7.

EI328 Robacker, Earl F., and Ada F. Robacker. "Decorative Painting." *Pa. Folklife*, vol. 28 (1978–1979), Folk Festival Supplement, 34–39.

EI329 Robacker, Earl F., and Ada F. Robacker. "How Far that Little Candle Throws...." *Pa. Folklife*, vol. 29, no. 4 (1979–1980), 34–40. On candleholders and lamps.

EI330 Thwing, Leroy. *Flickering Flames. A History of Domestic Lighting Through the Ages*. Rutland, Vt.: Charles E. Tuttle Co., 1958.

EI331 Weygandt, Cornelius. "Bone, Horn and 'Ivory'." In: *The Dutch Country*. New York: Appleton-Century, 1939, p. 267–88.

EJ
Cookery and Food

EJ1 American Historical Society of Germans from Russia. *Küche, Kochen: The AHSGR Cookbook*. Greeley, Colo.: The Soc., 1973.

EJ2 Barba, Preston A. "Cherry Bounce." "'S Pennsylfawnisch Deitsch Eck," Allentown *Morning Call*, 15 March 1969. A beverage.

EJ3 Barba, Preston A. "Distilleries, Cider Presses, etc. among Our Early German Settlers." "'S Pennsylfawnisch Deitsch Eck," Allentown *Morning Call*, 28 September 1957.

EJ4 Barba, Preston A. "Greens." "'S Pennsylfawnisch Deitsch Eck," Allentown *Morning Call*, 27 March 1954. Dandelions and other wild plants; the lore of the wild greens.

EJ5 Barba, Preston A. "Old-Time Christmas Baking." "'S Pennsylfawnisch Deitsch Eck," Allentown *Morning Call*, 8 December 1956.

EJ6 Barba, Preston A. "Pie and the Pennsylvania Germans." "'S Pennsylfawnisch Deitsch Eck," Allentown *Morning Call*, 24 February 1951.

EJ7 Beck, James N. "Apple-Butter Boiling in Solomon's Temple." *The Pa. Dutchman*, vol. 2 (1 October 1951). From the Philadelphia *Evening Bulletin*, 1858.

EJ8 Best, Martha S. "Food Varieties at the Festival." *Pa. Folklife*, vol. 22 (1973), Folk Festival Supplement, 14–18.

EJ9 Best, Martha S. "Leaving the Festival with Thoughts of Food." *Pa. Folklife*, vol. 20, no. 4 (1971), 37–41. Kutztown Festival.

EJ10 *Best Loved Pennsylvania Dutch Recipes*. N.p.: Photo Arts Pr., 1977.

EJ11 Boyertown Area Historical Society. *Boyer Area Cookery, the Boyertown Housewife and Kitchen Efficiency Guide and Companion*. Boyertown: n.p., n.d. Rev. by W. W. Weaver, *Pa. Mag. of Hist. Biog.*, vol. 109 (1979), 408–09.

EJ12 Bucher, Robert C., and Alan G. Keyser. "Some Pennsylvania Dutch Cheese." *Der Reggeboge*, vol. 11, no. 2 (1977), 1–6.

EJ13 *Canadian Mennonite Cookbook*. Altona, Man.: D. W. Friesen, 1971. 14th Printing.

EJ14 *Carillon Centennial Cookbook*. Steinbach, Man.: D. W. Derksen, 1974.

EJ15 Dieffenbach, Victor C. "Cabbage in the Folk-Culture of My Pennsylvania Dutch Elders." *The Pa. Dutchman*, vol. 3, no. 22 (1952), 1–2.

EJ16 Ellis, Susan J. "Traditional Food on the Commercial Market: The History of Pennsylvania Scrapple." *Pa. Folklife*, vol. 22, no. 3 (1973), 10–21.

EJ17 Engelman, E. M. "Mr. Jahrling's Christmas Dinner." *Amer.-German Rev.*, vol. 15, no. 2 (1948), 39. Immigrant restaurateur and hotel chain founder.

EJ18 *Das Essen unsrer Leute. A Collection of Folk Recipes from the Six Original German Communities in Ellis and Rush Counties* [Kansas]. N.p.: n.p., n.d. 248p. Incl. recipes for traditional beverages.

EJ19 *Favorite Recipes from Eastern Mennonite College*. Harrisonburg, Va.: Faculty Ladies of Eastern Mennonite College, 1972.

EJ20 "German Cook Uses 'Handful' and a 'Pinch'." *Windsor (Colo.) Beacon*, 23 December 1976, p. 16, 17.

EJ21 Graeff, Arthur D. "Cake Baking Recipes from Pennsylvania German Almanacs." *Amer.-German Rev.*, vol., 7, no. 2 (December 1940), 25–29. Also in: *Hist. Rev. of Berks Co.*, vol. 29, no. 1 (1964), 149–52, 154–55.

EJ22 Groff, Betty. *Betty Groff's Country Goodness Cookbook*. Illus. by Laurence Jarrett. Garden City: Doubleday, 1981. 320p.

EJ23 Groff, Betty, and Jose Wilson. *Good Earth and Country Cooking*. Harrisburg, Pa.: Stackpole Books, 1974. 253p.

EJ24 Gross, Michael C. "Volga German Food Customs." *Heritage of Kans.*, vol. 9, nos. 2–3 (1976), 31–37.

EJ25 Hark, Ann, and Preston A. Barba. *Pennsylvania German Cookery. A Regional Cookbook*. Allentown: Schlechter's, 1949. 2nd ed., 1957. 258p. Rev. by H. W. Elkinton, *Amer.-German Rev.*, vol. 19, no. 5 (1953), 35–36; M. Jordan, *Hist. Rev. of Berks Co.*, vol. 15, no. 4 (1950), 245–47; F. Klees, "'S Pennsylfawnisch Deitsch Eck," Allentown *Morning Call*, 24 Feb. 1951; J. A. Meredith, *Pa. Hist.*, vol. 18, no. 3 (1951), 258–59.

EJ26 Hasson, Nancy. "The Christmas Dinner." *The Goschenhoppen Region*, vol. 1, no. 2 (Aller Heil 1968), 12–16. Incl. recipes for cakes and cookies.

EJ27 Hasson, Nancy. "'Ei, Ei, Ei! Pei!' Pies of the Goschenhoppen Region." *The Goschenhoppen Region*, vol. 2, no. 2 (Aller Heil 1969), 8–10.

EJ28 Hasson, Nancy. "Foods of Butchering." *The Goschenhoppen Region*, vol. 1, no. 3 (Lichtmess 1969), 14–19. Scrappel, sausage, liver pudding, bacon, lard, etc.; recipes and instructions.

EJ29 Hasson, Nancy. "Hearth Baked Rye Bread." *The Goschenhoppen Region*, vol. 1, no. 1 (Peterkett 1968), 19–22. Incl. the recipe.

EJ30 Heller, Edna E. *The Art of Pennsylvania Dutch Cooking*. Garden City: Doubleday, ca. 1968. 243p.

EJ31 Heller, Edna E. "Candy Making in the Dutch Country." *Pa. Folklife*, vol. 20, no. 4 (1970–1971), 44–46.

EJ32 Heller, Edna E. "Cookies Just for Nice." *The Dutchman*, vol. 6, no. 3 (Winter 1954–1955), 8–9.

EJ33 Heller, Edna E. "Drinks in Dutchland." *The Pa. Dutchman*, vol. 8, no. 1 (1956), 8–9. Certain drinking habits of the Pennsylvania Germans.

EJ34 Heller, Edna E. "Pennsylvania Dutch Cooking Today and Yesterday." *Pa. Folklife*, vol. 17, no. 4 (1968), 38–39.

EJ35 Heller, Edna E. "Pies in Dutchland." *Pa. Folklife*, vol. 9, no. 2 (1958), 44–45.

EJ36 Heller, Edna E. "Restaurants, Too, Go Dutch." *The Pa. Dutchman*, vol. 6, no. 1 (1954), 9, 23.

EJ37 Heller, Edna E. "Rye Bread: Lehigh County Style." *Pa. Folklife*, vol. 12, no. 1 (Spring 1961), 38–39.

EJ38 Heller, Edna E. "We Waste Not." *Pa. Folklife*, vol. 21 (1971–1972), Supplement, 12–13. Utilization of food among the Pennsylvania Dutch.

EJ39 *Heritage of Cooking. A Collection of Recipes from East Perry County, Saxon Lutheran Memorial*. St. Louis: Concordia Memorial Institute, 1966.

EJ40 Hollenbach, Raymond E. "Buckweetze Kuche." "'S Pennsylfawnisch Deitsch Eck," Allentown *Morning Call*, 20 February 1954. Buckwheat cakes.

EJ41 Hollenbach, Raymond E. "Fasenacht Kuche." *The Pa. Dutchman*, vol. 5, no. 11 (1954), 5.

EJ42 Hollenbach, Raymond E. "Grumbiere." "'S Pennsylfawnisch Deitsch Eck," Allentown *Morning Call*, 21 August 1948. The potato.

EJ43 Hollenbach, Raymond E. "Gwidde." "'S Pennsylfawnisch Deitsch Eck," Allentown *Morning Call*, 9 October 1954. Use and lore of the quince.

EJ44 Hollenbach, Raymond E. "Hockelbeere Roppe. A Summer Outing." "'S Pennsylfawnisch Deitsch Eck," Allentown *Morning Call*, 16 July 1966. Lore of the huckleberry; nomenclature and recipes.

EJ45 Hollenbach, Raymond E. "Hollerbeere-Elderberries." "'S Pennsylfawnisch Deitsch Eck," Allentown *Morning Call*, 10 July 1965.

EJ46 Hollenbach, Raymond E. "Mer gehne fische." "'S Pennsylfawnisch Deitsch Eck," Allentown *Morning Call*, 2, 4 May 1959. Fish and fishing.

EJ47 Hollenbach, Raymond E. "Mush." "'S Pennsylfawnisch Deitsch Eck," Allentown *Morning Call*, 18 April 1964.

EJ48 Hollenbach, Raymond E. "Neinuhrschdick un Fieruhrschdick." "'S Pennsylfawnisch Deitsch Eck," Allentown *Morning Call*, 29 June 1957. Nine and four o'clock snacks of the early Pennsylvania German farmer.

EJ49 Hollenbach, Raymond E. "Welschkarn." "'S Pennsylfawnisch Deitsch Eck," Allentown *Morning Call*, 28 April, 5 May 1951. History and folklore of the raising and harvesting of corn.

EJ50 Hostetter, Adele, and Ruth Hershey Irion. *Pennsylvania Dutch Recipe Frakturs*. Allentown: Schlechter's, ca. 1947. 8 leaves.

EJ51 Hottenstein, Mary DeTurk. "Traditional Pennsylvania German Christmas Cookies." *Hist. Rev. of Berks Co.*, vol. 36, no. 1 (Winter 1970–1971), 14–16.

EJ52 Hutchison, Ruth. *Cooking "Dutch" with Caloric: The New Pennsylvania Dutch Cookbook*. New York: Benjamin, 1975. 240p.

EJ53 Hutchison, Ruth. *The New Pennsylvania Dutch Cookbook*. New York: Harper, 1958. 240p.

EJ54 Hutchison, Ruth. *Pennsylvania Dutch Cook Book*. New York: Harper, 1948. 213p. Repr. Bethlehem: The Moravian Book Shop, 1977. 240p.

EJ55 *Inglenook Cook Book*. N.p.: Brethren Press and Pyramid Publications, ca. 1974. Recipes from women of the Church of the Brethren.

EJ56 Irion, Ruth Hershey. *The Christmas Cookie (sic) Tree*. Philadelphia: Westminster Press, ca. 1976. 56p. Rev. by Mary A. Minderhout, *Der Reggeboge*, vol. 11, no. 1 (1977), 23. A Pennsylvania-Dutch Christmas story.

EJ57 Jentsch, Theodore W. "Cooking for the Lord." *Pa. Folklife*, vol. 28 (1978–1979), Folk Festival Supplement, 10–11. Dutch specialties served at the Kutztown Folk Festival.

EJ58 K. "So Hen Die Alte Leit Geduh—That's the Way the Old Folks Did It. Saffron (Crocus Sativus): Saffran, Saffrich." *Der Reggeboge*, vol. 14, no. 1 (January 1980), 16.

EJ59 Kauffman, Henry J. "The Pennsylvania Copper Tea Kettle." *Pa. Folklife*, vol. 31 (1981–1982), 2–7.

EJ60 Kauffman, Henry J. "Philadelphia Butter." *The Pa. Dutchman*, vol. 8, no. 2 (Fall-Winter 1956–1957), 8–13.

EJ61 Kaufman, Alice, Ruby Stucky, and Harley J. Stucky. *The Centennial Treasury of Recipes*. North Newton, Kans.: Mennonite Press, 1973.

EJ62 Kaufman, Edna R., and the Bethel College Women's Association. *Melting Pot of Mennonite Cookery, 1874–1974*. Newton, Kans.: n.p., 1974.

EJ63 Kohler, Karl. *Das algemeine Kochbuch für die algemeine (sic) deutsche und deutsch-amerikanische Küche. Ein lehreiches (sic) und klares Anweisungsbuch für Hausfrauen und Köchinnen nebst aller Art praktischen Rath für das Speisezimmer Verfast (sic) und verbessert*. Chicago: Merchants Specialty Co., 1891. 400p.

EJ64 *The Lancaster County Farm Cook Book: A Collection of Nearly Two Hundred Popular Recipes Gathered from Amish, Mennonite and German Pennsylvania Farm Families of Lancaster County*. Lebanon: Applied Arts, 1972.

EJ65 Livingood, Charles Jacob. "Recollections of Food and Drink in Berks County." *Hist. Rev. of Berks Co.*, vol. 8 (1942–1943), 43–45.

EJ66 Long, Amos, Jr. "Bakeovens in the Pennsylvania Folk-Culture." *Pa. Folklife*, vol. 14, no. 2 (1964), 16–29.

EJ67 Long, Amos, Jr. "Dryhouses in the Pennsylvania Folk-Culture." *Pa. Folklife*, vol. 13, no. 2 (Winter 1962–1963), 16–23. Preservation of fruits and vegetables by drying.

EJ68 Long, Amos, Jr. "The Ice-House in Pennsylvania." *Pa. Folklife*, vol. 14, no. 4 (1965), 46–55.

EJ69 Long, Amos, Jr. "Pennsylvania Cave and Ground Cellars." *Pa. Folklife*, vol. 11, no. 2 (Fall 1960), 36–41.

EJ70 Longacre, Doris. *More-With-Less Cookbook*. Scottdale, Pa.: Herald Press, 1976.

EJ71 Lynch, Charles O., and John W. W. Loose. "A History of Brewing in Lancaster County, Legal and Otherwise." *Jour. of the Lancaster Co. Hist. Soc.*, vol. 70, no. 1 (Hilarymas 1966), 1–100.

EJ72 Marshall, Howard W. "Meat Preservation on the Farm in Missouri's 'Little Dixie'." *Jour. of Amer. Folklore*, vol. 92 (1979), 400–17.

EJ73 Mertz, Beata. *Food'n Folklore*. Bismarck, N.D.: N. Dak. Hist. Soc. of Germans from Russia, 1976.

EJ74 Mitchell, Leonard Jan. *Lüchow's German Cookbook: The Story and the Favorite Dishes of America's Most Famous German Restaurant*. Introd. and illus. by Ludwig Bemelmans. Garden City: Doubleday, 1952. 224p.

EJ75 Mook, Maurice A. "Bread Baking in Mifflin County, Pennsylvania: Commentary for the Documentary Film in the 'Encyclopaedia Cinematographica'." *Pa. Folklife*, vol. 21, no. 1 (1971–1972), 42–45.

EJ76 Mook, Maurice A. "Old-Fashioned Bread Baking in Rural Pennsylvania." "'S Pennsylfawnish Deitsch Eck," Allentown *Morning Call*, 19 February 1966.

EJ77 Muenscher, Minne Worthen. *Minnie Muenscher's Herb Cookbook*. Woodcuts by Elfrieda Abbe. Ithaca: Cornell Univ. Pr., 1980. 241p.

EJ78 Muenscher, Walter C., and Myron A. Rice. *Garden Spice and Wild Pot-Herbs*. Woodcuts by Elfriede Abbe. Ithaca: Cornell Univ. Pr., 1978. 212p.

EJ79 Newcomb, Thomas L. *Hometown Recipes of Pilgrim Mennonite Church*. Garrettsville, Ohio: n.p., 1981.

EJ80 *Our Swiss Pantry*. Berne, Ind.: Women's Missionary Society, First Mennonite Church, 1968. 236p.

EJ81 Peachy, Joseph N., and Sylvia Peachy. *Favorite Amish Family Recipes. A Cookbook from the Kishacoquillas Valley*. Aylmer, Ont.: Pathway Publ. Corp., 1965. 253p. Rev. ed. 1969.

EJ82 *The Pennsylvania Dutch Cook Book*. Reading, Pa.: The Culinary Arts Pr., 1936. 48p. Rev. by Ann Williams, *Western Folklore*, vol. 8, no. 2 (1949), 186–87.

EJ83 "Pennsylvania Dutch Cookery." In: *Woman's Day Encyclopedia of Cookery*. Vol. 9. New York: Fawcett Publs., Inc., 1966, p.1349–57.

EJ84 Plaat, Martha. MS. of German Cookbook. 1 vol. In New York Public Library. Recorded in the late 19th or early 20th century. See Manuscript Catalogue, NYPL.

EJ85 Rahn, Bell Farrand. "Traditional Recipes." *Amer.-German Rev.*, vol. 9, no. 2 (1942), 9–11.

EJ86 Randle, Bill. *Plain Cooking: Low-Cost, Good-Tasting Amish Recipes*. New York: Quadrangle Pr., 1974. 270p.

EJ87 Reaman, G. Elmore. "Folk Art and Characteristic Foods of the Province of Ontario." *German-Canad. Yearbook*, vol. 1 (1973), 77–80.

EJ88 Roan, Nancy. *Boyertown Cookery*. Boyertown, Pa.: Boyertown Area Hist. Soc., 1978.

EJ89 Roan, Nancy. "Recipes from the 1830's." *Der Reggeboge*, vol. 15, nos. 1–2 (January–April 1980), 1–9. Analysis and interpretation of old recipes for *Lebkuchen* and *Zuckerkuchen*.

EJ90 Robacker, Earl F. "Art in Christmas Cookies." *The Pa. Dutchman*, vol. 6, no. 3 (Winter 1954–1955), 2–7. Cookie cutters.

EJ91 Robacker, Earl F. "Butter Molds." *The Pa. Dutchman*, vol. 6, no. 1 (June 1954), 6–8.

EJ92 Robacker, Earl F. *Christmas Cookies and Cutters*. Keyser Home Craft Course Series, no. 18. Kutztown: Kutztown Publs., 1946.

EJ93 Robacker, Earl F. "Folk Art in Pennsylvania Dutch Cooky Cutters." *Amer. Collector*, vol. 10, no. 12 (January 1942), 10–11.

EJ94 Robacker, Earl F. "Of Cookies and Cooky Cutters." *The Pa. Dutchman*, vol. 4, no. 8 (December 1952), 4–5.

EJ95 Robacker, Earl F. *Pennsylvania German Cooky Cutters and Cookies. Decorated Cookies and Recipes by Mrs. Ada F. Robacker and Miss Bessie E. Gower*. Keyser Home Craft Series, vol. 18. Kutztown: Kutztown Publ. Co., 1946; Plymouth Meeting, Pa.: Mrs. C. N. Keyser, 1946.

EJ96 Robacker, Earl F. "The Shape of the Food That Was." *Pa. Folklife*, vol. 14, no. 2 (1964), 10–15. Molds for cakes, breads, butter and the like.

EJ97 Robbins, R. L. *Pennsylvania Dutchland in Stamp and Story*. N.p.: Culinary Arts Pr., 1948. 32p.

EJ98 Robertson, Archie. "'Fill Yourself Up, Clean Your Plate'." *Amer. Heritage*, vol. 15, no. 3 (1964), 56–65, 80–82. Pennsylvania German cookery, food arts, and utensils.

EJ99 Sackett, Marjorie. "Meatless Dishes among the Volga Germans of Ellis County, Kansas." *Work Papers of the Amer. Hist. Soc. of Germans from Russia*, vol. 21 (1976), 24–26.

EJ100 Sackett, Marjorie. "Volga German Recipes." *Heritage of Kans.*, vol. 9, nos. 2/3 (1976), 39–46.

EJ101 Sauers, W. Ray. "Fruit Harvesting and Preservation in Early Pennsylvania." *Pa. Folklife*, vol. 23, no. 3 (1974), 38–43.

EJ102 Schoor, G., and F. Schoor. *Lüchow's German Festival Cookbook*. N.p.: n.p., 1976. Two hundred seasonal specialties, with the history of each festival.

EJ103 Schrock, Johnny, ed. *"Wonderful Good Cooking" from Amish Country Kitchens*. Scottdale, Pa.: Herald Pr., 1974.

EJ104 Schultz, George W. "Kitchen Utensils of the Provinces." *Amer.-German Rev.*, vol. 9, no. 4 (April 1943), 11–12.

EJ105 Seybold, Carol F. "White Summer Beer." *Der Reggeboge*, vol. 10, no. 2 (1976), 24. A Pennsylvania German recipe.

EJ106 Shaner, Richard H. "Distillation and Distilleries among the Dutch." *Pa. Folklife*, vol. 13, no. 3 (1963), 39–42.

EJ107 Shaner, Richard H. "Outdoor Ovens in the Dutch Country." *Pa. Folklife*, vol. 30 (1980–1981), 150–51.

EJ108 Shoemaker, Alfred L. "About Apees." *The Pa. Dutchman*, vol. 5, no. 8 (1954), 5. Origin of the word "Apees," a cooky from southeastern Pennsylvania.

EJ109 Showalter, Mary Emma. "Christmas Cookery and Customs from Greatgrandmother's Day." *Amer.-German Rev.*, vol. 17, no. 2 (1950), 7–9.

EJ110 Showalter, Mary Emma. *Favorite Recipes from the Mennonite Community*. Scottdale, Pa.: Herald Pr., 1972.

EJ111 Showalter, Mary Emma. *Mennonite Community Cookbook. Favorite Family Recipes*. Scottdale, Pa.: Herald Pr., n.d. 494p.; Philadelphia: John C. Winston Co., 1950; Kitchener, Ont., n.d. Illus. by Naomi Nissley. 2nd ed.: Philadelphia: Winston, 1957. Rev. by J. S. Weber, *Hist. Rev. of Berks Co.*, vol. 15, no. 4 (1950), 244–45; H. M. Elkinton, *Amer.-German Rev.*, vol. 16, no. 6 (1950), 39.

EJ112 Simms, Brigitte S. *German-American Cookery: A Bilingual Guide*. Rutland, Vt.: Charles E. Tuttle, 1967. In English and German.

EJ113 Sise, Mary E. "The Old Country Kitchen Where Food Preparation Was an Art." *Pa. Folklife*, vol. 27 (1977–1978), Folk Festival Supplement, 12–15.

EJ114 Staebler, Edna. *Food That Really Schmecks. Mennonite Country Cooking as Prepared by a Mennonite Friend, Bevvy Martin, My Mother, and Other Fine Cooks*. Chicago: Follett Publ. Co., 1968. 297p.

EJ115 Stauffer, Eva. "Pennsylvania German Cooking." "'S Pennsylfawnisch Deitsch Eck," Allentown *Morning Call*, 20 March 1948.

EJ116 Steffy, Muriel K. "The Humble Pretzel." *Amer.-German Rev.*, vol. 16, no. 2 (1949), 27–29.

EJ117 Stinsmen, Jane Ann. "The Foods of the Kutztown Folk Festival." *Pa. Folklife*, vol. 29, no. 4 (1979–1980), 2–5.

EJ118 Weaver, William Woys. "Food Acculturation and the First Pennsylvania-German Cookbook." *Jour. of Amer. Culture*, vol. 2 (Fall 1979).

EJ119 Weaver, William Woys. "Swiss Foods and Foodways in Early Pennsylvania." *Swiss-Amer. Hist. Soc. Newsletter*, vol. 16, no. 2 (1980), 4–17. On folk dishes, cheese, cookbooks, distilling and viticulture in nineteenth-century Pennsylvania.

EJ120 Weiser, Frederick S. "Ganns-Shenkel." *Pa. Dutch News and Views*, vol. 3, no. 1 (1971), 13. Recipe for turnovers.

EJ121 Wilson, Fred J., Johnny Schrock, and Larry Rogers. *Wonderful Good Cooking*. Scottdale, Pa.: Herald Pr., n.d. Amish cooking from rural Ohio.

EJ122 Wilson, Marian W. "Present Day Food Habits of the Pennsylvania Dutch." *Pa. Folklife*, vol. 9, no. 4 (1958), 38–39.

EJ123 Woys, W. "Swiss Foods and Foodways in Early Pennsylvania." *Swiss-Amer. Hist. Soc. Newsletter*, vol. 16 (June 1980), 4–17.

EJ124 Yeich, Edwin B. "Essen, oder Fressen." *Hist. Rev. of Berks Co.*, vol. 21, no. 3 (1956), 91–93. Discussion of the eating habits of the Pennsylvania Germans.

EJ125 Yoder, Don. "Historical Sources for American Traditional Cookery: Examples from the Pennsylvania German Culture." *Pa. Folklife*, vol. 20, no. 3 (Spring 1971), 16–29.

EJ126 Yoder, Don. "Pennsylvanians Call It Mush." *Pa. Folklife*, vol. 13, no. 2 (Winter 1962–1963), 27–49. Treatise on history, nomenclature, recipes, lore.

EJ127 Yoder, Don. "Sauerkraut in the Pennsylvania Folk-Culture." *Pa. Folklife*, vol. 12, no. 3 (1961), 56–69.

EJ128 Yoder, Don. "Schnitz in the Pennsylvania Folk-Culture." *Pa. Folklife*, vol. 12, no. 2 (1961), 44–53.

EJ129 Zecher, Paul E. "In the Country Kitchen: Pennsylvania Dutch Dishes Are Created by Instinct." *Pa. Folklife*, vol. 24 (1975), Folk Festival Supplement, 16–19.

EJ130 Zeller, Susanna. "Applebutter Yesterday." "'S Pennsylfawnisch Deitsch Eck," Allentown *Morning Call*, 16 October 1954. Also in *Hist. Rev. of Berks Co.*, vol. 16 (October–December 1950), 8–11.

EJ131 Zimmermann, Thomas C. "A Pig-Roast Under the Trees." *Hist. Rev. of Berks Co.*, vol. 34, no. 3 (Summer 1969), 96–98, 109.

EK

Gardening / Husbandry / Horticulture

EK1 Baver, Russell S. "Corn Culture in Pennsylvania." *Pa. Folklife*, vol. 12, no. 1 (1961), 32–37. The growing of corn; associated verses and games.

EK2 Bixler, Leo H. "Pine Tar and Its Uses." *Pa. Folklife*, vol. 13, no. 3 (1963), 18–23. Pine tar burning, a Pennsylvania Dutch art; notes on Geirmon Straub, tar burner.

EK3 Breininger, Lester. "Beekeeping and Bee Lore in Pennsylvania." *Pa. Folklife*, vol. 16, no. 1 (Autumn 1966), 34–39.

EK4 Brendle, Thomas R., and Claude W. Unger. "Illness and Cure of Domestic Animals among the Pennsylvania Dutch." *The Pa. Dutchman*, vol. 8, no. 4 (1957), 36–47.

EK5 Buschbauer, Junghans (pseud.), ed. *Der Familienschatz . . . Sammlung werthvoller Rezepte und Rathschläge für den Familienkreis, Hauswirtschaft, den Ackerbau . . .* Milwaukee: G. Brumder, ca. 1888. 376p.

Gardening / Husbandry / Horticulture

EK6 Geiser, Samuel Wood. *Horticulture and Horticulturists in Early Texas*. Dallas: Southern Methodist Univ. Pr., 1945. 100p.

EK7 Hedrick, Ulysses. *A History of Horticulture in America to 1860*. New York: Oxford Univ. Pr., 1950. 551p.

EK8 Hoffman, Francis Arnold ("Hans Buschbauer"). *Amerikanische Bienenzucht*. Milwaukee: Brumer, ca. 1886. 138p.

EK9 Hoffman, Francis Arnold ("Hans Buschbauer"). *Das Pferdebuch des amerikanischen Farmers*... Milwaukee: Brumder, ca. 1917.

EK10 Hollenbach, Raymond E. "Falliwalder." "'S Pennsylfawnisch Deitsch Eck," Allentown *Morning Call*, 13 November 1948. The favorite apple of the Pennsylvania Germans.

EK11 Hollenbach, Raymond E. "The Harness-Maker—Der Saddeler." "'S Pennsylfawnisch Deitsch Eck," Allentown *Morning Call*, 9 February 1957. On the importance of the "Saddeler" in early Pennsylvania German rural life.

EK12 Hollenbach, Raymond E. "In der Schmid—1836-1840." "'S Pennsylfawnisch Deitsch Eck," Allentown *Morning Call*, 5, 12 October 1957. Record of the daily work and transactions of an early German blacksmith.

EK13 Hollenbach, Raymond E. "The Old Tannery—Die alt Garwerei." "'S Pennsylfawnisch Deitsch Eck," Allentown *Morning Call*, 23 February, 2 March 1957.

EK14 Hollenbach, Raymond E. "The Pennsylvania Germans and Grape Culture." "'S Pennsylfawnisch Deitsch Eck," Allentown *Morning Call*, 3, 10, 17 February 1951.

EK15 Hollenbach, Raymond E. "Riewe." "'S Pennsylfawnisch Deitsch Eck," Allentown *Morning Call*, 13 March 1954. Origin, cultivation, and lore of the turnip.

EK16 "Horticulturists, North American." In: *The Standard Cyclopedia of Horticulture*. Liberty Hyde Bailey. New York: Macmillan, 1935. Vol. 2, p.1563-1603. Brief biographical sketches written by various authorities. Incl. George C. Butz (of Swiss parentage), Alfred Fellenberg Conard (desc. of German Quakers), Frederick Dorner (b. Baden, 1837), George Ellwanger (b. in Germany, 1876), Andrew H. Ernst (native of Germany, 1796), Thomas Andrew Garey (b. in Cincinnati of German stock, 1830), Frederick M. Hexamer, b. in Heidelberg, 1833, Gabriel Hiester, Pennsylvania-German, b. 1850, Herman Jaeger, b. in Switzerland, 1844, Samuel Miller, b. in Lancaster, Pa., 1820, John Rock (b. Johann Fels), native of Germany, 1836, Frederick Christian Roeding, b. in Hamburg, 1824, and Adolph Strauch, b. in Prussia, 1822.

EK17 Hyde, Cyrus. "An Early Pennsylvania Dutch Garden Revisited." *Pa. Folklife*, vol. 30 (1980-1981), 156-57.

EK18 Imschwiller, P. *The Family Dyer, Containing: a Number of Excellent Dies (sic). Carefully Selected for the Use of Private Families; in the English and German Language. Der Familien Färber, enthaltend: eine Anzahl vortreffliche Farben*... York, Pa.: n.p., 1826. 70p.

EK19 Jones, Dorothy Bovee. *The Herb Garden*. Keyser Home Craft Course Series, no. 23. Plymouth Meeting, Pa.: Mrs. C. Naaman Keyser, 1947.

EK20 Kecht, J. S. *Der verbesserte praktische Weinbau in Gärten und vorzüglich auf Weinbergen. Mit einer Anweisung den Wein ohne Presse zu keltern...Den amerikanischen Weinbauern gewidmet von Heinrich B. Sage*. Reading: G. Adolph Sage, 1828. 84p. The editor, H. B. Sage, had become acquainted with the author on a trip through Germany; he recommends the introduction of viticulture in America.

EK21 Kermes, Constantine. "Farm Animals at the Kutztown Folk Festival." *Pa. Folklife*, vol. 30 (1980-1981), 146-49.

EK22 Keyser, Alan G. "Gardens and Gardening among the Pennsylvania Germans." *Pa. Folklife*, vol. 20, no. 3 (1971), 2-15.

EK23 Kramb, Christian, ed. *Auf Erfahrung gegründete Vorschriften, um Wolle, Leinen und Baumwolle zu farben (sic)*... Libanon [Pa.]: Henrich B. Safe, 1809. 52p.

EK24 Krauss, Johann. *Oeconomisches Haus- und Kunst-Buch, oder Sammlung ausgesuchter Vorschriften, zum Nutzen und Gebrauch für Land- und Hauswirthe, Handwerker, Künstler und Kunst-Liebhaber*. Allentown: Henrich Ebner, 1819. 452p. Selections from English and German Sources.

EK25 Long, Amos, Jr. "Chickens and Chicken Houses in Rural Pennsylvania." *Pa. Folklife*, vol.

18, no. 3 (Spring 1969), 34–43. Architecture, lore, sayings, and jokes.

EK26 Long, Amos, Jr. "Pennsylvania Corncribs." *Pa. Folklife*, vol. 14, no. 1 (1964), 17–23. Incl. corn-shelling machines, husking bees, and the uses of husks.

EK27 Long, Amos, Jr. "Pumps, Rams, Windmills and Waterwheels in Rural Pennsylvania." *Pa. Folklife*, vol. 17, no. 3 (Spring 1968), 28–39.

EK28 Long, Amos, Jr. "The Rural Village." *Pa. Folklife*, vol. 29, no. 3 (Spring 1980), 124–32. European and American styles of villages compared and contrasted.

EK29 Rauch, John. *John Rauch's Receipts on Dyeing Cotton and Woollen Goods: Containing Correct and Exact Copies of All His Best Receipts on Dyeing, Obtained and Improved by Him, during Twelve Years Practice, in the Best Manufactories in Switzerland, France, Germany and America....* New York: Printed for John S. Ermantinger (sic), 1815. 97p.

EK30 Reinert, Guy F. "Wooden Pumps and Pipes." *Amer.-German Rev.*, vol. 11, no. 4 (1945), 14–16. Pennsylvania German products.

EK31 Smith, George M. "The Trade and Mysterie of Farming." *Historic Preservation*, vol. 20, nos. 3–4 (1968), 40–49. German farming practices in the Shenandoah Valley, Virginia.

EK32 Snyder, Mabel. "How I Make Soap." *Pa. Folklife*, vol. 17, no. 4 (1968), 12–15.

EK33 Souder, David. *The Rural Economist's Assistant in the Management of Bees, Principally Taken from the German....* Lancaster: William Greear, 1807. 55p.

EK34 *Die wahre Brantwein-Brennerey: oder, Brantwein-, Gin- und Cordialmacher-Kunst, wie auch die ächte Färbe-Kunst, wie man alle Couleuren auf Seide, Leinen und Wolle färben kan*. York, Pa.: Salomon Mayer, 1797. 2 vols. in 1. 40, 30p. Vol. 2 bears the title: *Besondere Kunst, auf eine leichte und wohlfeile Art zu färben; allerley Farbe, so wohl auf Wolle, Halbwolle, Leinen und Seide. ...* By Henrich Hartmann.

EK35 Wiestling, John S. *Der vollständige Bienen-Wärter; oder, Nützliche Anweisungen zur Bienen-Zucht...* Harrisburg: John S. Wiestling, 1819. 50p.

EK36 Willich, Anthony Florian Madinger. *The Domestic Encyclopedia; or, A Dictionary of Facts, and Useful Knowledge...the Latest Discoveries, Inventions, and Improvements*. 1st American ed., with additions... by James Mease. 5 vols. Philadelphia: n.p., 1803–1804. Publ. in London, 1802.

F

Fine Arts, Architecture, and Decorative Arts

FA
Arts in America: Background

General

FA1 B., L. "Swiss Painters of the American Indians." *Swiss-Amer. Hist. Soc. Newsletter*, vol. 1, no. 3 (1965), 7–9. On Bodmer, Kurz, and Rindisbacher.

FA2 Barton, J. R. *Rural Artists of Wisconsin.* Madison: n.p., 1948.

FA3 Bayer, Herbert, Walter Gropius, and Ilse Gropius, eds. *Bauhaus, 1919–1928.* New York: Museum of Modern Art; Boston: New York Graphics Soc., 1975. Orig. edition was publ. in 1938.

FA4 Becker, Stephen. *Comic Art in America. A Social History of the Funnies, the Political Cartoons....* Introd. by Rube Goldberg. New York: Simon & Schuster, 1960. 387p.

FA5 Born, Wolfgang. *American Landscape Painting: An Interpretation.* New Haven, Yale Univ. Pr., 1948. 228p.

FA6 Brackenridge, H. M. *Recollections of Persons and Places in the West.* 2nd ed. Philadelphia: n.p., 1868.

FA7 Burnet, Mary Q. *Art and Artists of Indiana...* New York: n.p., 1921.

FA8 Butts, Porter. *Art in Wisconsin.* Madison: Univ. of Wisconsin Pr., 1936.

FA9 *Catalogue of the Winterthur Museum Libraries: Printed Books and Periodicals.* Introd. by Frank H. Sommer. 10 vols. Wilmington: Scholarly Resources, Inc., 1973.

FA10 Chew, Paul A. *Two Hundred and Fifty Years of Art in Pennsylvania.* Greensburg, Pa.: The Westmoreland Co. Museum of Art, 1959. 105p. See esp. plates 148–151, 153–161.

FA11 Cist, Charles. *Cincinnati in 1841: Its Early Annals and Future Prospects.* Cincinnati: by the author, 1841. ca. 300p.

FA12 Cist, Charles. *Sketches and Statistics of Cincinnati in 1851.* Cincinnati: W. H. Moore, 1851. ca. 363p.

FA13 Cist, Charles. *Sketches and Statistics of Cincinnati in 1859.* Cincinnati: n.p., 1859. ca. 367p.

FA14 Clark, Edna Maria. *Ohio Art and Artists.* Richmond, Va.: Garrett and Massie, c. 1932. 509p.

FA15 Clarke, Thomas Wood. *Émigrés in the Wilderness.* New York: Macmillan, 1941. 247p.

FA16 Cline, Isaac M. "Art and Artists in New Orleans since Colonial Times." In: *Louisiana State Museum, Biennial Report of the Board of Curators for 1920–21*, vol. 9 (1922), 32–42.

FA17 Cowdrey, Mary Bartlett. *National Academy of Design Exhibition Record, 1826–1860.* New York, n.p., 1943. *Cited in this Bibliography as* Cowdrey NAD).

FA18 *The Crayon: A Journal Devoted to the Graphic Arts and the Literature Related to Them.* 1855–1861. Monthly journal publ. in New York.

FA19 Dawdy, Doris Ostrander. *Artists of the American West.* Chicago: Swallow Press, 1974.

FA20 DeFrancesco, I. L. *Art of the Pennsylvania Germans.* N.p.: American Crayon Co., 1947.

FA21 *A Descriptive Key to Kaulbach's Grand Cartoon of the Era of the Reformation with a Biographical Sketch of the Artist.* New York: Sackett & MacKay, 1868. 31p.

FA22 De Voto, Bernard. *Across the Wide Missouri.* Boston: Houghton Mifflin Co., 1947. 451p. This account of the crucial years of westward expansion in 1833–1838 is illus. with reproductions from Alfred Jacob Miller, Charles Bodmer, and others. (*Cited in this Bibliography as* De Voto.)

FA23 Dickson, Harold E. *Pennsylvania Painters.* Univ. Park: Pennsylvania State Univ., 1955.

FA24 Dickson, Harold E. *A Working Bibliography of Art in Pennsylvania.* Harrisburg: Pa. Hist. and Museum Commission, 1948.

FA25 Dresser, Louisa. "The Background of Colonial American Portraiture: Some Pages from a European Notebook." *Procs. of the Amer. Antiquarian Assoc.*, vol. 76 (1966), no. 1, 19–58. Incl. the works of Justus Engelhardt Kühn and Jeremiah Theüs.

FA26 Dunlap, William. *History of the Rise and Progress of the Arts of Design in the United States.* New York: 1834. Repr. Boston, 1918. Ed. Frank W. Bayley and Charles E. Goodspeed.

FA27 Ewers, John C. *Artists of the Old West.* Garden City: Doubleday, 1965. 240p. Incl. discussion of Rindisbacher, Bodmer, Alfred J. Miller, Rudolf F. Kurz, Gustavus Sohon, Bierstadt, Neagle, and others.

FA28 Fairman, Charles E. *Art and Artists of the Capitol of the United States of America.* Washington, D.C.: n.p., 1927.

FA29 Fielding, Mantle. *American Engravers upon Copper and Steel...A Supplement to...Stauffer's American Engravers.* Philadelphia: n.p., 1917.

FA30 Fielding, Mantle. *Dictionary of American Painters, Sculptors, and Engravers.* Philadelphia: for the subscribers, 1926.

FA31 Fisk, Frances B. *A History of Texas Artists and Sculptors.* Abilene: n.p., 1928.

FA32 Frankenstein, John. *American Art: Its Awful Altitude.* Cincinnati: n.p., 1964.

FA33 French, Henry W. *Art and Artists in Connecticut.* Boston: n.p., 1879.

FA34 Gardner, Albert T. E. *Yankee Stonecutters: The First American School of Sculpture 1800–1850.* New York: n.p., 1944.

FA35 Gideon, Samuel E. "Two Pioneer Artists in Texas." *Amer. Mag. of Art*, vol. 9 (September 1918), 452–56.

FA36 Goetzmann, William H. *Exploration and Empire: the Explorer and the Scientist in the Winning of the American West.* New York: n.p., 1966. 700p. Illus. with plates by Bodmer and Alfred Jacob Miller, among others.

FA37 Goss, Charles F. *Cincinnati, the Queen City, 1788–1912.* Chicago/Cincinnati: n.p., 1912.

FA38 Greve, Charles. *Centennial History of Cincinnati and Representative Citizens.* Chicago: n.p., 1904.

FA39 Groce, George C., and David Wallace, eds. *The New York Historical Society's Dictionary of Artists in America, 1564–1860.* New Haven: Yale Univ. Pr., 1957. (*Cited in this Bibliography as Groce-Wallace.*)

FA40 Heilbron, Bertha L. "With Pencils, Paints, and Palettes: Early Artists Portrayed the Upper Mississippi Valley." *Wis. Trails*, vol. 13, no. 1 (1972), 31–35. Cites the Austrians Johann-Baptist Wengler and Franz Hölzlhuber and the German Adolf Hoeffler.

FA41 Hocker, Edward W. *Germantown 1683–1933...* Germantown, Pa.: n.p., 1933.

FA42 Horton, Loren N. "Through the Eyes of Artists. Iowa Towns in the Nineteenth Century." *Palimpsest*, vol. 59, no. 5 (1978), 133–47. Descriptions and reproductions incl. works by Henry Lewis (*Das Illustrierte Mississippi-Thal*), painter John Casper Wild, native of Zürich; engravers Alfred Anradeas, Henry Wellge, Albert Ruger, E. C. Gnahn, and William Momberger, and painter A. Hageboeck.

FA43 Howat, John K. *The Hudson River and Its Painters.* New York: n.p., 1972. 207p.

FA44 Isham, Samuel. *The History of American Painting.* New York: Macmillan, 1927.

FA45 Jarves, James J. *The Art Idea: Sculpture, Painting and Architecture in America.* Cambridge: Harvard Univ. Pr., 1960.

FA46 Kouwenhoven, John A. *The Columbia Historical Portrait of New York.* Icon Editions. New York: Harper & Row, 1972.

FA47 Lancaster County Historical Society. *Loan Exhibition of Historical and Contemporary Portraits Illustrating the Evolution of Portraiture in Lancaster County...November 23 to December 13, 1912.* Lancaster: n.p., 1912.

FA48 Levering, Joseph M. *A History of Bethlehem, Pa. 1741–1892*... Bethlehem: n.p., 1903.

FA49 Lipman, Jean, and Tom Armstrong, eds. *American Folk Painters of Three Centuries*. New York: Hudson Hills Pr., in Assoc. with the Whitney Museum of American Art, 1980. 233p.

FA50 Lipman, Jean, and Alice Winchester. *Primitive Painters in America*. New York: Dodd Mead, 1950. 182p.

FA51 McCracken, Harold. *Portrait of the Old West. With a Biographical Check List of Western Artists*. New York: McGraw-Hill. 1952. 232p.

FA52 McDermott, John Francis. *The Lost Panoramas of the Mississippi*. Chicago: Univ. of Chicago Pr., 1958. 211p.

FA53 McGuire, James P. "Views of Texas: German Artists on the Frontier in the Mid-Nineteenth Century." In: *German Culture in Texas, a Free Earth: Essays from the 1978 Southwest Symposium*. Ed. Glen E. Lich and Dona B. Reeves. Boston: Twayne, 1980.

FA54 Maximilian Alexander Philipp, Prince of Wied-Neuwied. *Maximilian, Prince of Wied's Travels in the Interior of North America, 1832–1834*. Vols. 22–25 of R. G. Thwaites. *Early Western Travels*. Cleveland: Arthur C. Clark Co., 1906.

FA55 Moras, Ferdinand. "Der deutsche Künstlerverein 'Die Namenlosen'." *Deutsch-Amerikanisches Mag.*, vol. 1 (1887), 434–47. A club which originated in Philadelphia in 1857. Among the members whose biographies are presented are: Alexander Finkeldey, Karl E. Schnabel, Karl Harnisch, Christian Schüssele, Ernst Strakloff, Theodore Leonhardt, August Wegener, Anton Hohenstein, Konstantin Kaiser, Eduward Stauch, Karl Heinrich Schmolze.

FA56 Olbrich, Harald. "Antifaschistische Kunst in der Emigration." *Wissenschaftliche Zeitschrift der Univ. Greifswald*, 1966. Gesellschafts- und Sprachwissenschaftl. Reihe, no. 4.

FA57 Peat, Wilbur D. *Pioneer Painters of Indiana*. Indianapolis: Art Assoc. of Indianapolis, 1954. 254p.

FA58 Peters, Harry T. *America on Stone* ....Garden City: Doubleday, 1931. 415p.

FA59 Peters, Harry T. *California on Stone*. Garden City: Doubleday, 1935. 227p.

FA60 Phelps, I. N., and Daniel C. Haskell. *American Historical Prints; Early Views of American Cities, etc., from the Phelps Stokes and Other Collections*. New York: New York Public Library, 1933.

FA61 Pinckney, Pauline A. *Painting in Texas: The Nineteenth Century*. Austin: Univ. of Texas Pr., 1967. 232p. Rev. by W. E. Hollon, *Amer. Hist. Rev.*, vol. 74, no. 2 (December 1968), 715–16. Publ. for the Carter Museum of Western Art, Fort Worth. Incl. artists who emigrated from Europe and Americans who studied abroad.

FA62 Pleasants, J. Hall. *Two Hundred and Fifty Years of Painting in Maryland*. Baltimore: The Baltimore Museum of Art, 1945.

FA63 Poole, Earl L. "Artists and Painters of Reading." *Hist. Rev. of Berks Co.*, vol. 9, no. 2 (January 1944), 34–38.

FA64 *Portraits in Delaware, 1700–1850, a Check List*. Wilmington, 1951. (*Cited in this Bibliography as Portraits.*)

FA65 Powell, Mary M. "Three Artists of the Frontier." *Bull. of the Mo. Hist. Soc.*, vol. 5 (October 1948), 34–43.

FA66 Richardson, E. P. "Romanticism: The Second Generation, 1825–1850," and "The Closing Phase of Romanticism: The Generation of 1850. Luminism, Naturalism, and Sentimentalism." In: *A Short History of Painting in America*. New York: Harper & Row, 1963, p.121–84.

FA67 Schutz, Géza. "Old New York in Switzerland." *Antiques*, vol. 33 (May 1938), 260–61.

FA68 Smith, Ophia D. "A Survey of Artists in Cincinnati: 1789–1830." *Bull. of the Cincinnati Hist. Soc.*, vol. 25 (1967), 3–20. Mention of Frederick Frank and Johann and Frederick Eckstein.

FA69 Steinfeldt, Cecilia. "The Folk Art of Frontier Texas." *Antiques*, vol. 114 (1978), 1280–89. Julius Ploetz of New Braunfels; Rudolph Mueller of Castroville; Louis Hoppe, Fayette and Colorado counties; Theodor Gentilz, Richard Petri, Hermann Lungkwitz, C. G. von Iwonski, and John Henry Sievers—potters, silversmiths, carvers, and carpenters.

FA70 Sweet, Frederick A. *The Hudson River School and the Early American Landscape Tradition.* Chicago: n.p., 1945. Catalogue of exhibition at the Art Institute of Chicago and Whitney Museum of American Art, New York.

FA71 Taft, Robert. *Artists and Illustrators of the Old West, 1850–1900.* New York: Scribners, 1953.

FA72 "Texas in Pictures." *Antiques,* vol. 53 (June 1948), 453–59.

FA73 Thieme, Ulrich, and Felix Becker. *Allgemeines Lexikon der bildenden Künstler von der Antike bis zur Gegenwart; under Mitwirkung von etwa 400 Fachgelehrten des In- und Auslandes.* Liepzig: Seemann, 1907–1950. 37 vols. Vols. 16–37 ed. by Hans Vollmer. (*Cited in this Bibliography as* Thieme-Becker.)

FA74 Vitz, Robert C. "Seventy Years of Cincinnati Art: 1790–1860." *Bull. of the Cincinnati Hist. Soc.,* vol. 25, no. 1 (1967), 50–69. Cincinnati, an oasis of intellectual and creative talent west of the Appalachians; a period of significant Germanic influence.

FA75 Washington Art Association, Washington, D.C. *Catalogue of the 1st to 4th Annual Exhibitions of the Washington Art Association, 1857–60.* Washington, D.C.: The Association, 1856–1860. 4 vols.

FA76 Weller, Allen W. *Art U.S.A. Now.* Ed. Lee Nordness. 2 vols. New York: Viking Pr., 1963.

FA77 Wilkie, Franc B. *Davenport, Past and Present....* Davenport, Iowa: n.p., 1858.

FA78 Writers' Program. California. *Introduction to California Art Research, I and II.* Works Projects Administration. San Francisco: n.p., 1936–1937.

FA79 Writers' Program. Missouri. *Missouri, A Guide to the "Show Me" State.* American Guide Series, Works Projects Administration. New York: Duell, Sloan and Pearce, 1941. 652p.

FA80 Zieglschmid, A.J.F. "[Richard] Petri and [Hermann] Lungkwitz, Pioneer Artists in Texas." *Amer.-German-Rev.,* vol. 9, no. 1 (1942), 4–6.

Reception of German Art and Artists in America

FA81 Bier, Justus. "A Forgotten Work by Ferdinand von Miller the Younger. A Contribution to the History of Confederate Monuments." *Ky. Hist. Soc. Register,* vol. 54 (1956), 125–33. A German sculptor who was active in Munich 1843–1929.

FA82 Caumann, Samuel. *The Living Museum. Experiences of an Art Historian—Alexander Dorner.* New York: New York Univ. Pr., 1957. 216p. On the impact of the Dessau Bauhaus on American architecture and art. Dorner was one of its members until 1933. Rev. by M. S. Young, *Ohio Hist. Quar.,* vol. 67 (1958), 394–95.

FA83 Edenbaum, Robert I. "Dada and Surrealism in the United States." *Arts in Society,* vol. 5 (Spring-Summer 1968), 114–25. Why surrealism was relatively slow in achieving a reputation in America.

FA84 Essers, Volkmar. "Werke Berliner Bildhauer in Philadelphia: das Washington-Denkmal von Rudolf Siemering." *Jahrbuch für Preussischen Kulturbesitz,* vol. 10 (1972), 110–37.

FA85 Huebner, H. M., and V. Pearce Delgado. *Die Maler der Romantik in Amerika.* Bonn: Vink, 1953. 62p.

FA86 Kaes, Anton. *Expressionismus in Amerika. Rezeption und Innovation.* Tübingen: Niemeyer, 1975. 162p. Rev. by B. Zimmermann, *German Quar.,* vol. 51, no. 4 (November 1978), 555–56.

FA87 Levin, Sandra G. "Wassily Kandinsky and the American Avant-Garde, 1912–1950." Diss., Rutgers University, 1976.

FA88 Motherwell, Robert, ed. *Dada: the Dada Painters and Poets.* Texts by Arp [and others.] Illus. by Arp [and others.] New York: George Wittenborn, [1967, ca. 1951]. 403p. An anthology.

FA89 Newton, Robert P. "Dada, Expressionism, and Some Modern Modes." In: *Studies in German: In Memory of Andrew Louis.* Ed. Robert L. Kahn. Rice Univ. Studies, vol. 55, no. 3. Houston, Texas: Rice Univ., 1969, p.163–84.

FA90 Pevsner, Nikolaus. *Pioneers of Modern Design from William Morris to Walter Gropius.* New York: Museum of Modern Art, 1936. 151p. Repr. New York, 1949. On the development of the modern tradition from Loos, Wagner, the Bauhaus, Mies, Wright and Gropius.

FA91 Remak, Joachim. "The Bauhaus' Long Shadow: Some Thoughts about Weimar and Us." *Pacific Northwest Quar.*, vol. 61 (1970), 201–11.

FA92 Talbot, Charles W., Gaillard F. Ravenel, and Jay A. Levenson. *Dürer in America.* New York: Macmillan, 1971.

FA93 Tashjian, Dickran. "The Influence of European Dada on American Visual Arts and Letters: 1913–1925." Diss., Brown Univ., 1968. Cites influences on M. Crowley, E. E. Cummings, M. Josephson, William Carlos Williams, and others.

FA94 Weisstein, Ulrich, comp. "Expressionism as an International Phenomenon: An Annotated Bibliography." In: *Expressionism as an International Literary Phenomenon: 21 Essays and a Bibliography.* Ed. U. Weisstein. Paris: Didier; Budapest Akad. Kradó, p.329–49.

Holdings of German and German-American Art in America

FA95 *American Folk Art; A Collection of Paintings and Sculpture...The Gift of Mrs. John D. Rockefeller, Jr., to Colonial Williamsburg....* Williamsburg: n.p., 1940.

FA96 Bisanz, Rudolf M. *The René von Schleinitz Collection of the Milwaukee Art Center. Major Schools of German Nineteenth-Century Popular Painting.* Madison: Univ. of Wisconsin Pr., 1979, 256p. Catalogue; works include the painters Oehme, Grützner, Lenbach, Spitzweg, Waldmüller, Defregger, Knaus, and Vautier.

FA97 Deresiewicz, Bogdan. "California Schedeliana; or, the Nuremberg Chronicle in California." *Soundings: Collections of the University Library, Univ. of California, Santa Barbara*, vol. 6, no. 1 (1974), 35–40.

FA98 Feinberg, Charles E. Charles E. Feinberg Autograph Collection, ca. 1800–1930. Ca. 300 items. In Archives of American Art (MS 67-263). Holdings include cartoons by Thomas Nast, letters of Albert Bierstadt, autographs, etc.

FA99 Finckh, Alice H. "Medieval Knights in Cleveland." *Amer.-German Rev.*, vol. 14 no. 3 (1948), 8–11. Medieval armor—Severance Collection, Cleveland Museum of Art.

FA100 Francis, Henry S. "Early German Paintings in the Cleveland Museum of Art." *Amer. German Rev.*, vol. 21, no. 2 (1954), 4–9.

FA101 Gardner, Albert Ten Eyck, and Stuart Feld. *American Paintings—A Catalogue of the Collections of the Metropolitan Museum of Art.* Greenwich: New York Graphic Society, 1965.

FA102 Goff, Frederick R. "Johann Gutenberg and the Scheide Library." *Princeton Univ. Library Chronicle*, vol. 37, no. 2 (Winter 1976), 72–84.

FA103 Harding, Anneliese. *German Sculpture in New England Museums.* Boston: The Goethe Institute, German Cultural Center for New England, ca. 1978. Catalog.

FA104 Harding, Anneliese, Charles W. Haxthausen, Lucie B. Beebe, and Ilse M. Fang. "Collections. German Art in Boston Museums. A Treasure Trove of German Culture in the Boston Public Library." In: *Germans in Boston.* Boston: Goethe Society of New England, 1981, p.47–67.

FA105 Kuhn, Charles L. "The Busch-Reisinger Museum: Three Years of Collecting." *Amer.-German Rev.*, vol. 22, no. 6 (1956), 19–23.

FA106 Kuhn, Charles L. *German and Netherlandish Sculpture, 1280–1800. The Harvard Collections.* Cambridge: Harvard Univ. Pr., 1965. 146p. Catalogue of 93 items in the collections of the Fogg and Busch-Reisinger Museums.

FA107 Kuhn, Charles L. *German Expressionism and Abstract Art: The Harvard Collections—A Supplement to the 1957 Catalogue of Twentieth Century German Art at Harvard.* Cambridge: Harvard Univ. Pr. for the Busch-Reisinger Museum, 1967. 33p. 34 plates. A list of works of modern German art acquired by the University between 1957 and 1967, apart from the Feininger Archive and the Houghton Library collection.

FA108 Kuhn, Charles L. "Recent Acquisitions of the Busch-Reisinger Museum." *Amer.-German Rev.*, vol. 19, no. 2 (1952), 14–21. German and Austrian art objects, mainly of the 16th century.

FA109 Leloux, Herman. "Eine mittelniederdeutsche Gebethandschrift aus nordamerikanischem Besitz. (Ms. 76 der Pierpont Morgan Library." *Niederdeutsches Wort: Kleine Beiträge zur niederdeutschen Mundart und Namenkunde*, vol. 16 (1976), 108–25.

FA110 *Max Beckmann. Gemälde und Aquarelle der Sammlung Stephen Lackner, U.S.A., und Druckgraphie aus dem Besitz der Kunsthalle Bremen.* Auction 22 March–7 May 1967. Sale catalogue of the Lackner Collection.

FA111 Milliken, William M. "The Guelph Treasure in Cleveland." *Amer.-German Rev.*, vol. 22, no. 2 (1955), 5–10. Medieval art objects acquired by the Cleveland Museum in 1930.

FA112 Museum of Fine Arts, Boston. *M. and M. Karolik Collection of American Painting, 1815–1865.* Cambridge: Harvard Univ. Pr., for the Museum of Fine Arts, 1949.

FA113 Needham, Paul. "Incunabula, Bibles, and Early Americana in the Scheide Library." *Princeton Univ. Library Chronicle*, vol. 37, no. 2 (Winter 1976), 85–108.

FA114 Richter, F. "The Art of Miniature." *Amer.-German Rev.*, vol. 16, No. 6 (1950), 20–22. The collection of miniatures of Magda Heuermann, Chicago.

FA115 Russell, Haide. "Lehmbruck's Sculpture Moves into the New Met." *Amer.-German Rev.*, vol. 33, no. 1 (1966), 27. Placing of "Die Knieende" commemorates the gift of the Federal Republic of Germany toward construction of the new Metropolitan Opera house.

FA116 Rutledge, Anna W. "Hand-List of Miniatures in the Collections of the Maryland Historical Society." *Md. Hist. Mag.*, vol. 40 (1945), 119–36. Cites works by well known Germans of Baltimore: Sol. Etting, Miriam Etting Myers, George H. Repold, Baron von Hartman, and Bernard von Kapff.

FA117 Rutledge, Anna W. "Portraits in Varied Media in the Collections of the Maryland Historical Society." *Md. Hist. Mag.*, vol. 41 (1946), 282–326. Works by Etting, Mayer, Volck, and others are cited.

FA118 Rutledge, Anna W. "Portraits Painted before 1900 in the Collection of the Maryland Historical Society." *Md. Hist. Mag.*, vol. 41 (1946), 11–50.

FA119 "Sale of Wetzel Collection Brings to Light Masterpieces of German-American Art." *Newsletter of the Soc. for German-Amer. Studies*, vol. 2, no. 3 (1980–1981), 18.

FA120 Scheyer, Galka E. Blue Four Archives. Ca. 1200 items. In the Pasadena (Calif.) Art Museum collections (MS 65-2000). Relating to Lyonel Feininger, Alexei Jawlensky, Kandinsky, and Klee, consisting primarily of letters from the four artists, 1924–1945; clippings and reviews.

FA121 Schreiber, Theodore. "German Art in the City Art Museum of St. Louis." *Amer.-German Rev.*, vol. 13, no. 3 (1947), 19–23.

FA122 Utterback, Martha. *Early Texas Art in the Witte Museum.* San Antonio: San Antonio Museum Assoc., 1968.

FA123 Wainwright, Nicholas B. *Paintings and Miniatures at the Historical Society of Pennsylvania.* Philadelphia: Hist. Soc. of Pennsylvania, 1974.

FA124 White, Margaret E. "Styles of German Beverage Vessels." *Amer.-German Rev.*, vol. 20, no. 2 (1953), 10–16. A collection mainly from the 16th to 18th centuries at the Museum in Newark, N.J.

FA125 Zieglschmid, A.J.F. "Unpublished Richter Sketches in the United States." *Amer.-German Rev.*, vol. 9, no. 3 (1943), 18–21. On Adrian Ludwig Richter.

Exhibitions of German and German-American Art

See also Appendix.

FA126 Armstrong, Thomas N., III. *Pennsylvania Almshouse Painters.* Williamsburg: Colonial Williamsburg, 1968. Exhibit Brochure. The painters Hofmann, Rasmussen, and Mader.

FA127 Bier, Justus. "German Expressionism." *Amer.-German Rev.*, vol. 18, no. 5 (1952), 28–30. Exhibition of works by Kirchner, Otto Müller, Nolde, Pechstein, Schmidt-Rottluf and others, by the Museum of Modern Art, New York.

FA128 Champa, Kermit S., and Kate Champa. *German Painting of the Nineteenth Century.* New Haven: Yale Univ. Art Gallery, 1970. 239p. Exhibition Catalogue.

FA129 City Art Museum, St. Louis. *A Tribute to Curt Valentin; An Exhibition of Twentieth Century Art Selected from St. Louis Collections.* St. Louis: City Art Museum, 1955. 20p. See *Bull. City Art Museum of St. Louis*, vol. 39, nos. 2 and 3. Curt Valentin (1902–1954); 14 January–14 February 1955.

FA130 Coen, Rena Neumann. *Painting and Sculpture in Minnesota, 1830–1914.* Minneapolis: Univ. of Minnesota Pr., 1976. Issued in Connection with a Bicentennial Exhibit of Minnesota Art. Showing the contributions of explorers, tourists, and settlers toward the evolution of diverse modes of painting in the Old Northwest.

FA131 "Deutschamerikanische Kunstgegenstände gesucht." *New Yorker Staats-Zeitung und Herold*, vol. 145, no. 43 (1979), A–2. For a planned exhibition "Die Deutschen von New Jersey."

FA132 *From Colony to Nation: An Exhibition of American Painting, Silver and Architecture from 1650 to the War of 1812.* Chicago: The Art Institute of Chicago, 1949.

FA133 Garvan, Beatrice B., and Charles F. Hummel. *The Pennsylvania Germans: A Celebration of Their Arts 1683–1850.* Philadelphia: Philadelphia Museum of Art, 1982. 196p. Catalogue of the exhibition shown in Philadelphia, Houston, San Francisco and Chicago 1982–1983.

FA134 *German and Austrian Expressionism: Art in a Turbulent Era: An Exhibition.* Essay by Peter Selz. Chicago: Museum of Contemporary Art, 1978. 36p. Catalogue of exhibit, 10 March–30 April 1978.

FA135 *German and Austrian Painting of the Eighteenth Century: Exhibition.* Chicago: The David and Alfred Smart Gallery, the University of Chicago, 1978. 56p. Catalogue of Exhibit, 20 April–11 June 1978. Cosponsored by the Department of Germanic Languages, University of Chicago, the Goethe Institute, German Cultural Center, and the Austrian Institute, New York.

FA136 *German Master Drawings of the Nineteenth Century.* Cambridge: Busch-Reisinger Museum, Harvard Univ., 1972. 93p.

FA137 Guenther, Peter. *Deutscher Expressionismus, German Expressionism, Toward a New Humanism. Catalogue of an Exhibition at Blaffer Gallery, University of Houston.* Houston: Blaffer Gallery, 1977.

FA138 Harding, Anneliese. *America Through the Eyes of Immigrant Painters.* Boston, 1975–1976. 72p. Catalogue of Exhibit at Boston's City Hall and elsewhere, 1975–1976, organized by Goethe Institute, Boston. A survey of eras, styles. Biographical sketches of 44 artists; bibliography. Artists represented incl. Bierstadt, Bodmer, Leutze, Haidt, Rindisbacher, Nast and many others.

FA139 Hugelshofer, Walter. *Swiss Drawings: Masterpieces of Five Centuries.* Washington, D.C.: Smithsonian Institution Pr., ca. 1967. 176p. Catalogue of an exhibiton displaying Swiss drawing from the work of Hans Holbein in the 16th century to that of Alberto Giacometti in the 20th.

FA140 McCabe, Cynthia. *The Golden Door: Artist–Immigrants of the United States, 1876–1976.* Washington, D.C.: Smithsonian Institution Pr., 1976. 432p. Catalogue of a major Bicentennial exhibit at the Hirschhorn Museum and Sculpture Garden, Washington, D.C.

FA141 Mayor, A. Hyatt. *Life in America.* New York: The Metropolitan Museum of Art, 1939.

FA142 Merrill, Peter C. "Retrospective Exhibition Recalls German-American Contributions to Art in Cincinnati." *Newsletter of the Society for German-American Studies*, vol. 2, No. 5 (1980–81), 3.

FA143 Metropolitan Museum of Art. New York. *Masterpieces from the Berlin Museums Exhibited in Cooperation with the United States Army, 1948–1949.* N.p.: n.p., n.d. 112p. Catalogue. 52 plates. Showing of works of art recovered by the U.S. Third Army under Gen. Patton in 1945.

FA144 Metropolitan Museum of Art. New York. *Nineteenth Century American Paintings and Sculptures.* New York: New York Graphics Soc. Ltd., 1970.

FA145 Milwaukee Art Center. *Paintings from the Von Schleinitz Collection. German Genre Paintings of the Nineteenth Century.* Milwaukee: Mil-

German-American Art *(cont.)*

waukee Art Center, 1968. Milwaukee Art Center, 13 September–19 October 1968. Catalogue incl. the essay "Die Genremalerei im neunzehnten Jahrhundert. Genre Painting in the Nineteenth Century," by Siegfried Wichmann; "The Von Schleinitz Collection."

FA146 Museum of Fine Arts. Boston. *Frontier America: The Far West*. Boston: The Museum, 1975. 233p. Catalogue of exhibit.

FA147 Museum of Fine Arts. Montreal. *The Painter and the New World. Le Peintre et le Nouveau Monde. A Survey of Painting from 1584 to 1867*. Montreal: Museum of Fine Arts, 1967. 346p. Exhibited from 9 June to 30 July 1967. Incl. works by William von Moll Berczy, A. Bierstadt, Karl Bodmer, Ludwig Choris, J. V. Haidt, O. R. Jacobi, J. E. Kühn, R. F. Kurz, P. Rindisbacher, Severin Roesen, Johann Moritz Rugendas, Louis Augustin Wolff, and A. L. von Wittkamp.

FA148 Sandweiss, Martha. *Pictures from an Expedition. Early Views of the American West*. New Haven: Yale University Center for American Art and Material Culture and the Yale Univ. Art Gallery, 1978. 63p. Catalogue to accompany the exhibition, 29 September 1978–6 January 1979. Features 30 items by Karl Bodmer, 22 by Alfred Jacob Miller, along with others by J. J. Audubon, G. Catlin, Samuel Seymour, and Titian Ramsay Peale.

FA149 Seattle Art Museum. *Lewis and Clark's America*. 2 vols. Seattle: Seattle Art Museum, 1976. Vol. 1: *A Voyage of Discovery*. 95p. Incl. works by Bierstadt, Geo. Caleb Bingham, Karl Bodmer (22 items), Rudolf F. Kurz, Alfred Jacob Miller, Peter Rindisbacher, and Karl Wimar. Exhibit shown 15 July–26 September 1976.

FA150 *The Splendor of Dresden: Five Centuries of Art Collecting*. An exhibition from the State Art Collections of Dresden, German Democratic Republic. Shown at the National Gallery, Washington, D.C., Metropolitan Museum of Art, New York, and the Fine Arts Museum of San Francisco, Sept. 1978 to May 26, 1979. Catalogue: New York: Braziller, 1978. 229p.

FA151 Thompson, Lawrence S. "Exhibit of Modern German Bookbinding." *Amer.-German Rev.*, vol. 19, no. 6 (1953), 20–23. Opened in April 1953 at the Univ. of Kentucky's annual Foreign Language Conference.

The Düsseldorf Academy and Its Influence in America

ANDREWS, ELIPHALET FRAZER

FA152 Groce-Wallace, p.10. A. (1835–1915) studied at the Düsseldorf Academy. Portraitist of Steubenville, Ohio and Washington, D.C.

BINGHAM, GEORGE CALEB

FA153 Bloch, E. M. *George Caleb Bingham. A Catalogue Raisonne*. Berkeley/Los Angeles: Univ. of California Pr., 1967.

FA154 Bloch, E. M. *George Caleb Bingham. The Evolution of an Artist*. Berkeley/Los Angeles: Univ. of California Pr., 1967. 2 vols. B. (1811–1879) studied at the Düsseldorf Academy.

FA155 Christ-Janer, Albert. *George Caleb Bingham—Frontier Painter of Missouri*. New York: n.p., 1975. See also his *George Caleb Bingham of Missouri*. New York: Dodd Mead & Co., 1940.

FA156 Ehrlich, George. "George Caleb Bingham as Ethnographer: A Variant View of His Genre Works." *Amer. Studies*, vol. 19, no. 2 (Fall 1978), 41–45.

FA157 *George Caleb Bingham. The Missouri Artist*. New York: Museum of Modern Art, 1935.

FA158 McDermott, George F. *George Caleb Bingham, River Portraitist*. Norman: Univ. of Oklahoma Pr., 1959.

CHASE, WILLIAM MERRITT

FA159 *Centennial Exhibition*. Indianapolis: John Herron Art Museum, 1949. In 1872 C. (1849–1916) was a student in Munich. He had been sent to Europe by a group of St. Louis businessmen. Returned to America in 1878.

FA160 *The First West Coast Retrospective Exhibition of Paintings by William Merritt Chase (1849–1916)*. Santa Barbara: The Art Gallery, Univ. of California, Santa Barbara, 1964.

FA161 Roof, Katherine Metcalf. *The Life and Art of William Merritt Chase.* New York: n.p., 1917.

FA162 Wickenden, Robert J. "William Merritt Chase." *Dictionary of American Biography*, vol. IV, 38–9.

DÜSSELDORF ACADEMY AND MUSEUM

FA163 *The Düsseldorf Academy and the Americans. An Exhibition of Drawings and Watercolors.* Atlanta: The High Museum of Art, 1972; Utica, N.Y.: The Munson-Williams Proctor Institute, 1973; Washington, D.C.: National Collection of Fine Arts, Smithsonian Institution, 1973. Exhibition Catalogue.

FA164 *Handzeichnungen und Aquarelle 1800–1850.* Bildhefte des Kunstmuseums Düsseldorf, no. 8. Ed. Dieter Graf. Düsseldorf: Kunstmuseum, 1971.

FA165 *The Hudson and the Rhine. Die amerikanische Malerkolonie in Düsseldorf im 19. Jahrhundert.* Düsseldorf: Kunstmuseum, 1976. 218p. Catalogue of exhibit, 4 April–16 May 1976. With essays on the history of the Düsseldorf school by Wend von Kalnein, Donelson Hooper, R. L. Stehle, and Worthington Whittredge. Embraces the work of German, German-American, and American artists associated with the Düsseldorf academy. See "Amerikanische Kunststudenten in Düsseldorf," p.97–101.

FA166 Hütt, W. *Die Düsseldorfer Malerschule 1819–1869.* Leipzig: n.p., 1964.

FA167 Luhrs, Kathleen. "Düsseldorf Artists." *New-York Hist. Soc. Quar.*, vol. 58 (October 1974).

FA168 Markowitz, I., and E. Schaar. *Ausstellungskatalog Handzeichnungen und Aquarelle des 19. Jahrhunderts aus den Beständen des Kupferstichkabinetts im Kunstmuseum Düsseldorf.* Düsseldorf: Kunstmuseum, 1965–1966.

FA169 Stehle, R. L. "The Düsseldorf Gallery of New York." *N.Y. Hist. Soc. Quar.*, vol. 58, no. 4 (1974), 305–14. The owner of the gallery was John Boker (Johannes Böcker).

FA170 Trier, E., ed. *200 Jahre Kunstakademie Düsseldorf.* Düsseldorf: n.p., 1973.

ELDER, JOHN ADAMS

FA171 Groce-Wallace, p.209. E. (1833–1895) was a native of Virginia; went to Düsseldorf Academy with Emanuel Leutze; spent five years abroad.

FEWSMITH, HENRY

FA172 Cramer, Maurice B. "Henry FewSmith, Philadelphia Artist, 1821–1846." *Pa. Mag. of Hist. and Biog.*, vol. 65 (1941), 31–55. F. studied in Düsseldorf from 1842 to 1845.

FA173 Sokol, David M. "Henry FewSmith and the Düsseldorf Academy." *Antiques*, vol. 104 (November 1973), 867–71.

JOHNSON, EASTMAN

FA174 Baur, John I. H. *An American Genre Painter: Eastman Johnson (1824–1906).* Brooklyn: The Brooklyn Museum, 1940. Exhibition Catalogue. J. (1824–1906) was luminist American painter; b. in Lowell, Maine. Studied with E. Leutze at Düsseldorf for two years. After 1855 established a career in Wisconsin, Cincinnati, Washington and New York.

FA175 *Eastman Johnson; Retrospective Exhibition by Patricia Hills.* New York: Whitney Museum of American Art, 1972. Catalogue of traveling exhibition shown in the Detroit Inst. of Fine Arts, Cincinnati Art Museum, and Milwaukee Art Center, 1972.

RICHARDS, WILLIAM TROST

FA176 *William Trost Richards.* Brooklyn: The Brooklyn Museum; Philadelphia: Pennsylvania Academy of Fine Arts, 1973. Catalogue for an exhibition shown at the museums in 1973.

WHITTREDGE, WORTHINGTON

FA177 Baur, John I. H. ed. *The Autobiography of Worthington Whittredge.* In: The *Brooklyn Museum Journal*, 1942, 7–68. W. (1820–1910) studied at the Düsseldorf Academy, ca. 1850, with the German painter Andreas Achenbach.

FA178 Dwight, Edward H. *Worthington Whittredge: Retrospective.* Utica: Munson-Williams-Proctor Institute, 1969. 70p. Catalogue.

WOODVILLE, RICHARD CATON

FA179 Cowdrey, Mary B. "Richard Caton Woodville, An American Genre Painter." *Amer. Collector*, vol. 13 (April 1944), 14, 20. W. Studied at Düsseldorf Academy.

FA180 *Exhibition Catalogue Richard Caton Woodville, An Early American Genre Painter*. Washington: The Corcoran Gallery of Art, 1967.

FB

German-American Painters

Individual Artists

Sources: America Through the Eyes . . . , see entry FA138; Dunlap, *see* entry FA26; Fairman, *Art and Artists of the Capitol, see* entry FA28; French, *Art and Artists in Connecticut, see* entry FA33; Gardner, *see* entry FA34; Levering, *History of Bethlehem, see* entry FA48; Nordness, *Art U.S.A., see* entry FA76; Peat, *Pioneer Painters, see* entry FA57; Peters, *America on Stone, see* entry FA58; Peters, *California on Stone, see* entry FA59; Pleasants, *Two Hundred and Fifty Years . . . , see* entry FA62; *Portraits in Delaware, see* entry FA64; Prime, *see* entry EE41; Taft, *see* entry FA71; Writer's Program, *California, see* entry FA78; Writers' Program, *Missouri, see* entry FA79.

ALBERS, JOSEF

FB1 Finkelstein, Irving L. "The Life and Art of Josef Albers." Diss., New York Univ., 1968. 485p.

FB2 Gomringer, Eugen. *Josef Albers—Das Werk des Malers und Bauhausmeisters als Beitrag zur visuellen Gestaltung im 20. Jahrhundert*. Starnberg: Jos. Keller Vlg., 1967. 200p.

FB3 *Josef Albers at the Metropolitan Museum of Art*. New York: Metropolitan Museum, 1971. An exhibit, "50 Works and Albers' Commentary. A Memorial Exhibit," ran at the N.Y. Public Library, 19 July–30 September 1976.

FB4 Kuh, Katherine. *The Artist's Voice*. New York: Harper & Row, 1960.

BAHR, C. O.

FB5 Phelps, I. N., and Daniel C. Haskell. *American Historical Prints . . . .* New York: New York Public Library, 1933, pl. 91-b. Executed a drawing of Galveston, Tex., ca. 1955.

BAUMGARTEN, GUSTAVUS E.

FB6 Groce-Wallace, p.37. B. (1837–1910) was a physician and amateur artist. Born in Clausthal, Germany; emigrated to St. Louis, ca. 1846.

BAUMGRAS/BAUMGRASS, PETER

FB7 Pratt, Waldo. *A Forgotten American Painter: Peter Baumgras*. N.p., n.d.

FB8 Washington Art Assoc. *Catalogue* 1859. See also *Art Annual*, vol. 5 (1905–1906), 118. An obituary for B. (1827–1904), portraitist b. in Bavaria. Emigrated to Washington, D.C., in 1853; later a professor at the Univ. of Illinois.

BAYER, HERBERT

FB9 Dorner, Alexander. *Way Beyond Art*. New York: Wittenborn-Schulz, 1947. Painter, architect, and designer. B. 1900 in Haag, Austria. U.S. citizen. Associated with the Bauhaus. (See also Wingler, Hans M. *The Bauhaus*.)

FB10 Roters, Eberhard. *Painters of the Bauhaus*. New York: Praeger, 1969.

FB11 Van der Marck, Jan. *Herbert Bayer: From Type to Landscape-Designs; Projects and Proposals 1923–1973*. Univ. Pr. of New England, 1977. 55p.

BECKER, AUGUST

FB12 "Charles Wimar." *Catalogue, Charles Wimar*. St. Louis: City Art Museum of St. Louis,

1946. Born in 1840 in Germany, Becker came to St. Louis at an early age. Assisted his half-brother Charles Wimar in painting the dome in the St. Louis courthouse.

BELLER, AUGUSTUS G.

FB13 "Special Acquisitions of the Society." *Mo. Hist. Rev.*, vol. 44 (January 1950), 109–12. B. (b. 1830) was an amateur artist of Weston, Mo. Born in Baden; emigrated to Missouri ca. 1841. Only one painting is known: "View of Weston, Mo."

BENZIGER, AUGUST

FB14 Benziger, Marieli, and Rita Benziger. *August Benziger, Portrait Painter*. Glendale, Calif.: Arthur H. Clark Co., 1958. Portrait painter. Born in Einsiedeln, Switzerland; worked in New York City. Painted presidents, the Popes, and the famous.

FB15 Braungart, Richard. *August Benziger, His Life and Work*. München: F. Bruckmann, 1922. 59p.

BERCZY, WILLIAM VON MOLL

FB16 Betcherman, Lita-Rose. "Genesis of an Early Canadian Painter: William von Moll Berczy." *Ontario Hist.*, vol. 57, no. 2 (1965), 57–68. Berczy was born in Saxony in 1748.

BERGER, ANTON

FB17 Thieme-Becker, vol. 3, p.394. Genre painter of New York; exhibited in the National Academy 1860. Probably a native of Passau. (Cowdrey; NAD Cat.)

BERSCH, CARL

FB18 Faust, Albert B. "Carl Bersch—Artist and Portrait Painter." *Amer.-German Rev.*, vol. 10, no. 6 (1944), 4–7.

BEYER, EDWARD

FB19 Wright, Lewis R. "Edward Beyer in America: A German Painter Looks at Virginia." *Art and Antiques*, vol. 3, no. 6 (1980), 72–77. B. (1820–1985) was a landscape and panorama painter; born in the Rhineland; worked in America from 1848 to 1857. (Groce-Wallace; Thieme-Becker). See *Portfolio*, June 1945, 234–45; *Antiques*, September 1951, 1–2.

BIERSTADT, ALBERT

FB20 Albert Bierstadt. A Retrospective Exhibition. Santa Barbara, Calif.: The Santa Barbara Museum of Art, 1964. B. 1830 in Solingen; painter of landscapes, animals, and Indians. Reared in New Bedford, Mass.; studied in Düsseldorf from 1853 to 1857; joined the expedition of Col. F. W. Landers, 1858. D. 1902.

FB21 Baigell, Matthew. *Albert Bierstadt*. New York: Watson-Guptil, 1981. 84p. 32 color plates.

FB22 Hendricks, Gordon. *Albert Bierstadt, 1830–1902. Painter of the American West*. New York: Abrams, 1973. 360p. New edns., 1974, 1975. Publ. in assoc. with the Amon Carter Museum of Western Art, Fort Worth, TX.

FB23 Hendricks, Gordon. "The First Three Western Journeys of Albert Bierstadt." *Art Bull.*, vol. 46, no. 3 (September 1964), 333–65.

FB24 Hendricks, Gordon. "Roaming the West with Albert Bierstadt." *Amer. West*, vol. 12 (January 1975), 22–29.

FB25 Lewisohn, Florence. "The Uniqueness of Albert Bierstadt." *Amer. Artist*, September 1964, 28–33f.

FB26 Spieler, Gerhard G. "A Noted Artist in Early Colorado. The Story of Albert Bierstadt." *Amer.-German Rev.*, vol. 11, no. 5 (1945), 13–17, 27.

FB27 Thomas, Phillip Drennon. "Bierstadt of Düsseldorf: Painter of America's Western Vision." *Montana, the Mag. of Western Hist.*, vol. 26, no.2 (April 1976), 2–17.

FB28 Trump, Richard S. "The Life and Works of Albert Bierstadt." Diss., Ohio State, 1963.

BIESTER, ANTHONY

FB29 Groce-Wallace, p.48. B. (1840–1917) was a portrait painter and landscapist; b. in Cleves, Germany, d. Madisonville, Ohio. Resident of Cincinnati in 1905.

BISCHOFF, FRANZ A.

FB30 Stern, Jean. "California Impressionist Franz A. Bischoff." *Art and Antiques*, vol. 4, no. 3 (1981), 82–89. B. (1864–1929) was an Austrian-born painter who died in California.

FB31 Stern, Jean. *The Paintings of Franz A. Bischoff* (1864–1929). Los Angeles: Peterson Publ., 1980. Catalogue of an exhibition of B.'s paintings.

BISCHOFF, FREDERICK CHRISTOPHER

FB32 Shoemaker, Alfred L. "Reading's First Artist, A Painter of Butterflies." *Hist. Rev. of Berks Co.*, vol. 13, no. 3 (April 1948), 89–90. B. (1771–1834) was a portrait painter, miniaturist, known as the painter of butterflies. A native of Stadtilm, Germany; emigrated to America before 1800 and resided in Reading, Pa. (Groce-Wallace).

BIXLER, DAVID

FB33 Bixler, Miriam E. "David Bixler, Folk Artist." *Jour. of the Lancaster Co. Hist. Soc.*, vol. 81 (1979), 30–38.

BODMER, KARL

FB34 "Bodmer-Millet Bonanza Comes to Omaha's Joslyn Art Museum." *Mont. Mag. of Hist.*, vol. 12 (1962), 75. The museum holds 427 original drawings, paintings, and engravings of American scenes depicted by Bodmer. B. (1809–1893) was a painter and engraver of France and Germany. Accompanied Maximilian of Wied-Neuwied as artist-recorder on his tour of the West 1832–34. Native of Riesbach, Switzerland; d. Barbizon, France. (Thieme-Becker; De Voto).

FB35 Bodmer, Karl, and George Catlin. *Die schönsten Indianerbilder.* München: Droemer Knaur, 1981. 96p. With 31 color plates.

FB36 Davidson, Marshall. *Life in America.* 2 vols. Boston, 1951. See vol. 1, p.168, 194, 196, 208–09; vol. 2, p.241.

FB37 Davidson, Marshall B. "Carl Bodmer's Unspoiled West." *Amer. Heritage*, vol. 14, no. 3 (1963), 43.

FB38 Draper, Benjamin P. "American Indians, Barbizon Style: The Collaborative Paintings of Millet and Bodmer." *Antiques*, vol. 44 (September 1943), 108–10; and "Karl Bodmer, An Artist among the Indians." *Ibid.*, vol. 45 (May 1944), 242–44.

FB39 Engel, Lorenz. *Among the Plains Indians.* Photos by Heinz Binder. Trans. into English by Susan W. Dickinson. Minneapolis: Lerner, 1970; ca. 1967. Children's Picture Book. Illus. with paintings of Bodmer and George Catlin. From the German original entitled *Unter Indianern.* Stuttgart: Deutsche Verlagsanstalt, 1967.

FB40 "Karl Bodmer: Earliest Painter in Montana." *Montana. Mag. of Western Hist.*, vol. 20, no. 3 (1970), 36–41.

FB41 Läng, Hans. *Indianer waren meine Freunde: Leben und Werk Karl Bodmers.* Bern/Stuttgart: Hallwag, 1976. Rev. by J. Christadler, *Amerikastudien*, vol. 24 (1979), 168–71.

FB42 Läng-Hembd, H. "Der Schweizer Indianermaler Carl Bodmer." In: *Ethnologische Zeitschrift Zürich*, 1974, no. 1 (*Festschrift Otto Zerries*). Bern: Lang, 1974. 407p.

FB43 Lepley, John. "The Prince and the Artist on the Upper Missouri." *Montana. Mag. of Western Hist.*, vol. 20, no. 3 (1970), 42–54.

FB44 *Maximilian Expedition Commemorative Calendar 1833–1983. Prinz Maximilian Expedition Gedenkkalender 1833–1983.* Chicago: Newberry Library, 1982. 17 leaves. The Newberry Library Calendar for 1983 with Illustrations from the Library's Karl Bodmer Collection. Co-sponsored by the University of Nebraska, Center for Great Plains Studies; Joslyn Art Museum, Center for Western Studies; and Historic New Harmony, Inc.

FB45 Röder, Joseph. "The Prince and the Painter." *Natural Hist.*, vol. 64, no. 6 (June 1955), 326–29.

FB46 Smithsonian Institution. *Carl Bodmer Paints the Indian Frontier; A Traveling Exhibition...* Washington, 1954.

FB47 Thomas, David, and Karin Ronnefeldt, eds. *People of the First Man. Life among the Plains Indians in Their Final Days of Glory. The Firsthand Account of Prince Maximilian's Expedition up the Missouri River, 1833–34.* Text by Prince Maximilian zu Wied. Watercolors by Karl Bodmer. New York: Dutton, 1976. 256p.

FB48 Weitenkampf, Frank. "A Swiss Artist among the Indians." *Bull. of the N.Y. Public Library*, vol. 52 (November 1948), 554–56.

BRANDT, CARL LUDWIG

FB49 Thieme-Becker, vol. 4, p.535. B. (1831–1905) was a portrait, landscape and historical painter, b. in Hamburg; emigrated to New York in 1852.

BRANDTNER, FRITZ

FB50 *Fritz Brandtner, 1896–1969. A Retrospective Exhibition.* Montreal: Sir George Williams University, 1969. Catalogue of works by B. (1896–1969).

BREHME, CLAIRE EICHBAUM

FB51 "Claire Eichbaum Brehme." *Amer.-German Rev.*, vol. 22, no. 6 (1956), 29. German-born artist of Philadelphia.

BRENNER, CARL

FB52 Bier, Justus. "Carl C. Brenner, a German American Landscapist." *Amer.-German Rev.*, vol. 17, no. 4 (1951), 20–25, 33. A Kentucky artist, b. 1838 in Lauterecken, Pfalz; d. 1888.

FB53 Weisert, John J. "Carl Brenner's Polimosorama." *Filson Club Hist. Quar.*, vol. 30 (1956), 315–18. On Brenner's gigantic panorama of the Civil War.

BUCHSER, FRANK

FB54 Erlanger, Liselotte. "Frank Buchser: A Swiss Artist in the American West." *Amer. West*, vol. 15 (March/April 1978).

BUSCH, JULIUS THEODORE

FB55 French, H. W. *Art and Artists in Connecticut.* Boston: n.p., 1879. p. 184–89. A native of Dresden, B. (1821–1858) came to Hartford ca. 1848 and worked there as teacher of drawing.

COPMANN, (PIERCE OR PATER)

FB56 Groce-Wallace, p. 148. Danish or North German portrait and landscape painter who emigrated to America after 1832. Worked in Brooklyn, Charleston, New Orleans, Louisville.

DANNER, ADAM (OR J. A.)

FB57 "Portraiture in Lancaster County." *Publs., Lancaster Hist. Soc.*, 1912, p. 118. Portraitist of Lancaster Co., Pa., ca. 1836–1837.

DASSEL, (MRS.) HERMINIA BORCHARD

FB58 Groce-Wallace, p. 166. D. (d. 1857) was a genre and portrait painter, native of Koenigsberg. Studied at the Düsseldorf Academy and emig. to New York in 1849. Known for paintings of children and Italian genre scenes.

DE BEET, CORNELIUS

FB59 Thieme-Becker, vol. 3, p. 173. De B. (b. ca. 1772) was a landscape and still life artist, b. ca. 1772 in Germany; worked in Baltimore and Philadelphia.

DEGERSDORFF, ERNEST BRUNO VON

FB60 *Essex Institute Hist. Collections*, vol. 79 (April 1943), 134–52. Illustrated letters and humorous pen sketches of an amateur artist and physician, native of Germany, who came to Salem, Mass. before 1849.

DEMUTH, JOHN

FB61 "Portraiture in Lancaster Co." *Lancaster Co. Hist. Soc. Publs.*, 1912, P. 119. D. (ca. 1770–1820) was a portrait and miniature painter and wood carver of Lancaster, Pa.

DRACH, S.

FB62 Thieme-Becker, vol. 9, p. 534. German miniaturist and portrait painter of New York City, ca. 1820.

DREXEL, FRANCIS MARTIN

FB63 Groce-Wallace, p. 189. D. (1792–1863), a native of the Tyrol who came to Pennsylvania in 1817. Portraitist, Louisville and Philadelphia. The same who later opened the brokerage office of Drexel and Co. (*Portraits in Delaware 1700–1850*).

DUDENSING, RICHARD

FB64 Thieme-Becker, vol. 10, p. 50. D. (d. 1899), portrait and landscape painter, engraver and book publisher. Emigrated to America ca. 1857.

ECKSTEIN, JOHANN (JOHN)

FB65 Beynroth, Charles E. Papers. In the collections of the Filson Club, Louisville (MS 68-927). Incl. a group of religious drawings by Eckstein. E. (ca. 1736–1817) was a portrait and historical painter, sculptor and engraver. Probably born in Mecklenburg; worked as painter at the Prussian court from 1772 to 1794. Emigrated in 1794.

EICHHOLTZ, JACOB

FB66 Beal, Rebecca J. "Five Portraits on Panel by Jacob Eichholtz, 1776–1842." *Jour. of the Lancaster Co. Hist. Soc.*, vol. 80 (Easter 1976), 61–76. Pennsylvania-born German-American craftsman and portrait painter, who produced "over 900 faithful and sometimes handsome likenesses of his Lancaster neighbors."

FB67 Beal, Rebecca J. *Jacob Eichholtz 1776–1842: Portrait Painter of Pennsylvania.* Philadelphia: Hist. Soc. of Pa., 1969. 401p. Rev. by C. H. Bohner, *Pa. Hist.*, vol. 37, no. 4 (October 1970), 431–32; L. B. Miller, *Jour. of Amer. Hist.*, vol. 57, no.

Individual Artists (cont.)

2 (September 1970), 419-20; Eugenia Holland, *Md. Hist. Mag.*, vol. 67, no. 1 (Spring 1972), 87-88.

FB68 Henderson, Helen W. "Jacob Eichholtz—His Life and Paintings." *Procs. of the Lancaster Hist. Soc.*, vol. 49, no. 1 (1945), 18-27.

FB69 Hensel, William Uhler. "Jacob Eichholtz... Paper read before the Lancaster Co. Hist. Soc, December 6, 1912." *Procs., Lanc. Co. Hist. Soc.*, vol. 16, no. 10, Supplement, 1912. 39p.

FB70 Impink, Mary Dives. "Jacob Eichholtz—Portrait Painter." *Hist. Rev. of Berks Co.*, vol. 7 (1941-1942), 66-69.

FB71 Newton, Earle. "Jacob Eichholtz." *Pa. History*, vol. 26, no. 2 (April 1959), 103-18.

FB72 Weygandt, Cornelius. "Jacob Eichholtz Points the Way." In: *The Dutch Country. Folks and Treasures in the Red Hills of Pennsylvania.* New York: D. Appleton-Century Company, 1939, p.1-11. An appreciation of the painter.

ELLINGER, DAVID

FB73 Ferris, Edythe. "The Hymn of the Fruitful Heart." *Amer.-German Rev.*, vol. 10, no. 6 (1944), 17-19.

ENZING-MÜLLER, JOHANN MICHAEL

FB74 Thieme-Becker, vol. 10, p.572. E.-M. (1804-1888) was a religious painter, designer, engraver; native of Nürnberg who came to America ca. 1848.

ERNST, MAX

FB75 Ernst, Jimmy, and Francine du Plessix. "The Artist Speaks: My Father, Max Ernst." *Art in America*, November-December 1968, 54-61. Reminiscences of E. (1891-1976), his life in Arizona and in France.

FB76 Spies, Werner. *Max Ernst*. Trans. by Joseph M. Bernstein. New York: H. N. Abrams, 1968. 50p.

EULER, CHARLES (KARL)

FB77 Thieme-Becker, vol. 11, p.75; Groce-Wallace, p.215. E. (b. 1815), landscape painter and lithographer, b. at Kassel. Emig. in the late 1850's.

FABER, HARMAN

FB78 [Obituary.] *Art Annual*, vol. 11 (1913). Portrait painter and medical illustrator, F. (1832-1913) was born in Germany and emigrated to America in 1854. Worked as illustrator for the Surgeon General's medical record of the Civil War. (Groce-Wallace).

FASEL, GEORGE WILHELM

FB79 Thieme-Becker, vol. 11, p.282; Groce-Wallace, p.221. Portrait, historical and religious painter and lithographer. B. in Germany; in New York City in 1850. Had started his career in Germany ca. 1829.

FEININGER, LYONEL

FB80 Feininger, T. Lux. "Lyonel Feininger's Heritage." *Amer.-German Rev.*, vol. 32, no. 5 (1966), 9-12. American painter (1871-1956) who resided for 50 years in Europe. His paternal grandfather was a Forty-Eighter who settled in South Carolina.

FB81 The Museum of Modern Art. *Lyonel Feininger, Marsden Hartley.* Ed. by Dorothy C. Miller. New York: Museum of Modern Art, 1944.

FB82 Schreyer, Ernst. *Lyonel Feininger: Caricature and Fantasy.* Detroit: Wayne St. Univ. Pr., 1964. 196p.

FB83 Wight, Frederick S. "Lyonel Feininger." *Amer. German Rev.*, vol. 20, no. 6 (1954), 18-19.

FETTER, GEORGE

FB84 Levering, *History of Bethlehem*, p. 654, 709. Landscape artist and portrait painter. "View of Bethlehem" (1797).

FEUCHTER, LOUIS J.

FB85 Burgess, Robert H. *Louis J. Feuchter, Chesapeake Bay Artist.* Newport News, Va.: Mariner's Museum, 1976.

FISCHER, ERNST (ERNEST) GEORG

FB86 Thieme-Becker, vol. 12, p.19; Groce-Wallace, p.227. F. (1815-1874) was a portrait and genre painter, native of Coburg. Stayed briefly in the United States after 1848 and returned to Germany.

FLEISCHBEIN, FRANÇOIS

FB87 Fielding, Mantle. *F. Fleischbein, Portrait Painter.* New Orleans: n.p. 1936. Portrait painter,

b. in Germany ca. 1804; resident of New Orleans from 1833–1856. (Groce-Wallace).

FOERSTER, EMIL

FB88 Groce-Wallace, p.232. F. (1822–1906) was a native of Giessen; a portrait, genre and church subject painter. Resided in the 1850's in Pittsburgh.

FRANKENSTEIN, GEORGE L.

FB89 Groce-Wallace, p.238. Portrait and landscape artist; probably a native of Germany; grew up in Cincinnati. Assisted his brother Godfrey in painting the panorama of Niagara Falls. In 1875 he moved to New York City.

FRANKENSTEIN, GODFREY N.

FB90 Arrington, Joseph E. "Godfrey N. Frankenstein's Moving Panorama of Niagara Falls." *N.Y. Hist.* vol. 49, no. 2 (1968), 169–99. A painting 1600 feet in length; it has disappeared. F. (1820–1873) was a portrait and landscape painter, presumed to have been a native of Darmstadt, who arrived with his parents in the United States in 1831. Painted the panorama of Niagara Falls in 1844; became the first president of the Cincinnati Academy of Arts.

FB91 Martin, Oscar T. *The City of Springfield* [Ohio]. In: *The History of Clark County, Ohio.* Chicago: n.p., 1881, p.489–96.

FRANKENSTEIN, JOHN P.

FB92 Coyle, William. *The Frankenstein Family in Springfield.* Springfield, Ohio: Clark County Historical Society, 1967.

FB93 Dwight, Edward H. "John P. Frankenstein." *Museum Echoes*, 27 July 1954, 51–53.

FUCHS, OTTO

FB94 Groce-Wallace, p.245. F. (1839–1906), a teacher of drawing and design in New York City, subsequently professor at the U.S. Naval Academy. Native of Germany who emigrated in 1851.

FUECHSEL, HERMANN

FB95 Thieme-Becker, vol. 12, p.552; Groce-Wallace, p.245. F. (1833–1915) was a landscape artist, native of Braunschweig; studied at the Düsseldorf academy. In New York City from 1858.

GERHARD, GEORGE

FB96 Thieme-Becker, vol. 13, p.451. G. (1830–1902), portrait painter, b. in Hanau; came to the U.S. before 1860.

GERKE, JOHANN (JOHN) PHILIP

FB97 Thieme-Becker, vol. 13, p. 468. G. (1811–1847) came to the U.S. with his mother in 1834 from Kassel. In New York City in 1837; died in St. Louis in 1847. Portrait and historical painter.

GILDEMEISTER, KARL (CHARLES)

FB98 Thieme-Becker, vol. 14, p.29. G. (1820–1869), painter, lithographer, and architect, native of Bremen who studied in Italy. He came to America before 1850; returned to Bremen before 1860. (Known also as Gildermeister or Geldmeister).

GOLDBERG, ERIC

FB99 Pfund, Harry W. "The Canada of Eric Goldberg, Artist." *Amer.-German Rev.*, vol. 19, no. 5 (1953), 10–13. Born in Berlin, Germany; in Canada since 1936.

GOLLMANN, JULIUS

FB100 Thieme-Becker, vol. 14, p.346. G. (d. 1898), portrait painter, born in Hamburg, who came to the U.S. before 1852. Returned to Germany in later life.

GRAFFENRIED, CHRISTOPH VON

FB101 Phelps, I. N., and D. C. Haskell. *American Historic Prints....* New York: New York Public Library, 1933, p.12

FB102 Schutz, G. "Old New York in Switzerland," *Antiques*, vol. 33 (May 1938), 260–61. With a reproduction of a view of New York City of 1713; amateur painter (1661–1743), founder of the New Bern settlement in North Carolina (Groce-Wallace).

GRIDER, RUFUS ALEXANDER

FB103 Dickinson, Thomas A. "Rufus A. Grider." *Proc., Worcester Soc. of Antiquity*, vol. 17 (March–April 1900), 110–13.

FB104 Levering, J. M. *History of Bethlehem, Pa. 1741–1892....* Bethlehem, 1903, p.710, 714–15. Landscape, flower and still life painter of Lititz, Pa. G. (1817–1900); see sketches and watercolors

Individual Artists *(cont.)*

in the Moravian Archives, Bethlehem; in 1883 he was teacher of art in Canojoharie, N.Y.

GROENLAND, HERMANN

FB105 Cist, C. *Sketches and Statistics of Cincinnati in 1851.* Cincinnati: n.p. 1851. Portrait and landscape painter, Cincinnati, working from 1844 to 1860.

GROSZ, GEORGE

FB106 Baur, John I. H. *George Grosz.* New York: Macmillan, 1954. On G. (1893–1959), illustrator-satirist-cartoonist who came to America to teach in 1932.

FB107 Bittner, Hubert. *George Grosz.* New York: Arts, Inc., 1959.

FB108 Grosz, George. *A Little Yes and a Big No.* New York: Dial Pr., 1946. 343p. Autobiography.

GRUNEWALD (GREENWALD), GUSTAVUS

FB109 Peters, Harry T. *America on Stone*; Garden City: Doubleday, 1935. (Thieme-Becker). G. (1805–1878) was a landscape and portrait artist and lithographer, teacher. A native of Gnadau, Germany, and resident of Bethlehem, Pa. who arrived in America before 1831.

GSCHWINDT (GESCHWINDT OR SCHWINDT), ROBERT

FB110 Thieme-Becker, vol. 15, p.157. Austrian portrait painter; studied in Paris and Rome. Came to New Orleans by 1854 but returned to Europe.

GUMPERT, GUNTHER

FB111 Huppert, Willy. *Gunther Gumpert.* Kunst und Kunstgewerbe-Verein, Pforzheim, 1964. Artist, born in 1919, in Krefeld, Germany; resident of Washington, D.C.

FB112 Summa, Victor. *Gumpert and the Evolution of His Art.* Educational TV Assoc., 1963.

HABICHER, SEBASTIAN

FB113 Thieme-Becker, vol. 15, p.403. H. (b. 1805) was a portrait and genre painter, native of the Tyrol, who came to America in 1848.

HAGEDORN, HERMANN(?) CONRAD(?)

FB114 Thieme-Becker, vol. 15, p.453. Portrait painter and architect who resided in New Orleans in 1842. Probably had worked in Berlin 1828–1838.

HAHN, GUSTAV

FB115 Weissenborn, George K. "Gustav Hahn: Beloved Teacher and Art Nouveau Pioneer, 1886–1962." *Canad.-German Yearbook*, vol. 6 (1981), 238–40.

HAIDT, JOHN VALENTINE (JOHANN VALENTIN)

FB116 Nelson, Vernon H. *John Valentine Haidt.* Williamsburg, Va.: The Abby Aldrich Rockefeller Folk Art Collection, 1966. H. (1700–1780) was a portrait and religious painter, born in Danzig of an Augsburg family; member of the Moravian community in Bethlehem, Pa. H.'s father had been court goldsmith in Berlin. In 1754 he emigrated from London to Bethlehem, Pa.

FB117 Norman, John F. "The Painting Preacher: John Valentine Haidt." *Pa. Hist.*, vol. 20, no. 2 (1953), 180–86.

HANSEN, H. W.

FB118 "The Pictorial Record of the Old West. Part VIII: The End of a Century." *Ky. Hist. Quar.*, vol. 19 (1951), 225–53. Native of Dittmarschen, b. 1854; arrived in the U.S. in 1877. Hansen recorded frontier life in watercolors.

HEGLER, JOHN JACOB

FB119 Peat, *Pioneer Painters of Indiana*, p.232. Portrait artist, native of Bertzville, Switzerland; came to America in 1831 and worked in Indiana.

HEINE, PETER BERNARD WILLIAM (WILHELM HEINE)

FB120 Vagts, Alfred. "Wilhelm Heine, Traveler Artist." *Amer.-German Rev.*, vol. 22, no. 1 (1955), 9–13. H. (1827–1885) was the artist with Perry's expedition to Japan 1852–1854. A native of Dresden, he resided in the U. S. from 1849 to 1859. This Saxon Forty-Eighter also was illustrator of the archaeologist Squier's Central-American explorations. (Thieme-Becker; Groce-Wallace).

HEINRICH, FRANCIS H.

FB121 *Antiques* (August 1946), 91. Portrait of the Fiedler family. H. was landscape and portrait painter, in New York City in 1848. Had studied in Italy and Germany.

HEKKING, J. ANTONIO

FB122 French, *Art and Artists in Connecticut*, 162. German landscape painter of Connecticut and Cherry Valley, N.Y.

HERSHBERG, ISRAEL

FB123 *Who's Who in American Art*. New York: Bowker, 1980, p.327. Artist of Baltimore; native of Linz, Austria (b. 1948).

HESS, B.

FB124 Groce-Wallace, p.312. Landscape painter; thought to have been born in Switzerland.

HETZEL, GEORGE

FB125 Kantner, Dorothy. "George Hetzel: Mountain Artist." *Jour. of the Alleghanies*, vol. 8 (1972), 14–16. H. (1826–1899) was a painter of landscapes, still lifes, portraits and figures. A native of Alsace who came to America before 1855 and resided in Pittsburgh. (Thieme-Becker; Groce-Wallace).

HEYD, CONRAD

FB126 Butts, Porter. *Art in Wisconsin*. Madison: Univ. of Wisconsin Pr., 1936, p.97–98. H. (1837–1912) was a portrait and miniature painter. A native of Germany, Heyd came to New York ca. 1860 and later worked in Milwaukee and Prairie du Chien. Became one of Wisconsin's foremost artists.

HILMER, GEORGE H.

FB127 "George H. Hilmer. A Painter of Saxon Immigration Scenes." *Concordia Hist. Inst. Quar.*, vol. 28 (1955), 27–34. Native of Germany.

HOEFFLER, ADOLF

FB128 Hoeffler, Adolf, and John Francis McDermott. "Minnesota 100 Years Ago." *Minn. Hist.*, vol. 33 (1952), 112–25. Reproductions of H.'s paintings of Minnesota. H. (1825–1898) was a landscape and portrait artist, native of Frankfurt am Main. Came to America via New Orleans in 1848, but returned to Europe in 1853. Painted and sketched extensively along the Mississippi.

HÖLZLHUBER, FRANZ

FB129 Gröger, Hilde. "Amerikas Pionierzeit: Bilder des oberösterreichischen malers Franz Hölzlhuber." *Alte und Moderne Kunst*, vol. 9 (March–April 1964), 31–34. H. did sketches of Western life and Indians; his woodcuts were used as illustrations in *Harper's* and *Frank Leslie's Illustrated Weekly*. An exhibit of watercolor sketches, *The American Sketchooks of Franz Hölzlhuber. An Austrian Visits America in 1856–1860*, was held at the Univ. of Kansas Museum of Art, 15 November–18 December 1959.

FB130 Hölzlhuber, Franz. "Sketches from Northwestern America and Canada—Skizzen aus dem Nordwesten von Amerika und Canada aufgenommen in den Jahren 1856 bis 1860 von Franz Hölzlhuber." *Amer. Heritage*, vol. 16, no. 4 (1965), 49–64. Scenes of Indians, the frontier and the West done in watercolors by this Austrian artist.

HOERMAN, CARL

FB131 "Chalet studio—A Lifetime of Art." *The Commercial Record* (Saugatuck), 7 July 1970. Carl Hoerman of Babenhausen, Germany, came to Chicago in 1904; resided in Saugatuck, Michigan.

FB132 Merrill, Peter C. "From Babenhausen to Saugatuck: The Art and Architecture of Carl Hoerman." *Jour. of German-Amer. Studies*, vol. 13 (1978), 52–62.

HOFMANN, CHARLES

FB133 Armstrong, Thomas. "God Bless the Home of the Poor." *Hist. Rev. of Berks Co.*, vol. 35, no. 3 (Summer 1970), 86–90, 103–09, 116. B. in Germany. H. lived and painted in the Berks County Almshouse, Reading; d. 1882.

HOFMANN, HANS

FB134 Hofmann, Hans. *Hans Hofmann*. 2nd ed. New York: Harry N. Abrams, Inc., 1964. Bavarian-born modernist painter living in the U.S. since 1931. (Nordness, *Art U.S.A.*).

FB135 Hofmann, Hans. *Search for the Real and Other Essays.*, Ed. by Sara T. Weeks and Bartlett H. Hayes, Jr. Cambridge: MIT Pr., 1967. (Nordness: *Art U.S.A.*).

FB136 Rosenberg, Harold. "Homage to Hans Hofmann." *Art News*, vol. 66 (1949), 72–73.

FB137 Wight, Frederick S. *Hans Hofmann*. Berkeley/Los Angeles: Univ. of California Pr., 1957. 66p.

HÜCK, FERDINAND

FB138 *Lancaster Co. Hist. Soc., Papers and Addrs.*, vol. 17 (1913), 92–93. Portrait and reli-

Individual Artists *(cont.)*

gious painter from Mainz who emigrated to Lancaster, Pa., in 1729.

HUGE, JÜRGEN FREDERICK

FB139 Lipman, Jean. *Rediscovery: Jurgen Frederick Huge*. New York: Archives of American Art, Smithsonian Institution, 1973. Native of Hamburg, H. (1809–1878) painted large watercolor marine scenes from 1838 to 1878.

FB140 "When Bridgeport was Beautiful: A Portfolio of Paintings by J. F. Huge." *Amer. Heritage*, vol. 25, no. 4 (June 1974), 16–31.

ISENBURGER, ERIC

FB141 Rox, Henry. "Eric Isenburger's Paintings." *Amer. German Rev.*, vol. 13, no. 1 (1946), 14–17.

JACOBI, OTTO REINHOLD

FB142 Weissenborn, George K. "Otto Reinhold Jacobi: The Landscape Painter from Königsberg 1812–1901." *Canad.-German Yearbook*, vol. 6 (1981), 248–50.

JACOBS, EMIL

FB143 Thieme-Becker, vol. 18, p.248–49; Groce-Wallace, p.344. Portrait and historical painter, (1802/1812?–1866), a resident of Gotha. This German artist may have visited Philadelphia in 1850.

JANSCHKA, FRITZ

FB144 Grafly, Dorothy. "Fritz Janschka." *Amer.-German Rev.*, vol. 20, no. 1 (1953), 6–8. A young Viennese painter, in 1953 artist-in-residence at Bryn Mawr and Haverford colleges.

JAUSS, ANNE MARIE

FB145 Gürster, Eugen. "Anne Marie Jauss, an American German Painter." *Amer.-German Rev.*, vol. 17, no. 5 (1951), 8–12.

KATZ, LEO

FB146 Katz, Leo. Papers. In the Archives of American Art, Washington, D.C. (MS 72-1409). Autobiographical MS. notes describing K.'s life in an Austro-Hungarian Jewish community, cultural life in Vienna, and studies in Munich (1924–1960). K. was born in 1877.

KAUFMAN, ENIT

FB147 "Enit Kaufman." *Amer.-German Rev.*, vol. 23, no. 4 (1957), 27. Austrian-born painter; in the U.S. since 1939.

KAUFMANN, ARTHUR

FB148 Kaufmann, Arthur. Papers, ca. 1928–1968. 2 boxes and 1 package. In New York Public Library (MS 79-1859). Play scripts, memoirs, notes of K. (born 1888). Excerpts from the memoirs were privately printed in *Old Canvas New Varnish* (1963).

KAUFMANN, THEODOR

FB149 Zucker, Adolf E. "Theodor Kaufmann, Forty-Eighter Artist." *Amer.-German Rev.*, vol. 17, no. 1 (1950), 17–24. K. (b. 1814) was a historical painter, born near Hannover. A Forty-Eighter, Kaufmann came to America in 1850 and worked in New York and Boston.

KEMPF, STARR

FB150 "An American Artist." *Amer.-German Rev.*, vol. 16, no. 4 (1950), 28. An artist of Colorado Springs, born in the Swiss-German community of Bluffton, Ohio.

KIRCHBAUM, JOSEPH

FB151 Arrington, J. Earl. "Nauvoo Temple," Unpubl. MS., chap. 8. K. (ca. 1831–1926) was an amateur artist from Germany who emigrated to Nauvoo, Illinois after 1846.

KLASSEN, JOHN P.

FB152 Kehler, Larry. "John P. Klassen—Artist and Teacher." *Mennonite Life*, vol. 24, no. 4 (October 1969), 147–50. Artist of German-Russian background who has taught at Bluffton College, Bluffton, Ohio since 1925.

KNATHS, KARL

FB153 Mocsanyi, Paul. *Karl Knaths*. Washington: Phillips Gallery; New York: G. Wittenborn, 1957. 101p. Contemporary painter, son of German immigrants.

KOEHLER, KARL

FB154 Koehler, Karl. *Briefe aus Amerika*. Darmstadt: n.p., 1854. Illustrated with drawings by this amateur artist, who recounts his visit to America in the 1850's.

KÖHNER, WILLIAM

FB155 French, Henry W. *Art and Artists in Connecticut.* Boston, 1879, p.90. K. (1816–1876) was a portrait painter, native of Berlin. Worked in Hartford and Warehouse Point, Connecticut.

KÖLLNER, AUGUST(US)

FB156 Peters, *America on Stone*, p.254–55. K. (1813–1906) was born in Düsseldorf, Germany and was in Philadelphia in 1839. Prepared watercolor views of American cities and scenes and military prints for the *U.S. Military Mag.* Worked as lithographer, engraver, landscape painter, and book illustrator. His work was exhibited at the Free Library of Philadelphia in February 1947.

FB157 Wainwright, Nicholas B. "Augustus Köllner, Artist." *Pa. Mag. of Hist. and Biog.*, vol. 84 (1960), 325–35. States that K. was born in Württemberg. Resided in Washington, Baltimore and Philadelphia until his death in 1906.

KOERNER, W.H.D.

FB158 Hutchinson, W. H. *The World, the Work and the West of W. H. D. Koerner.* Norman: Univ. of Oklahoma Pr., 1967. 243p. K. (b. 1878) emigrated with parents to Iowa in 1888. Became prominent newspaper artist in Chicago and prolific magazine illustrator of the Western genre type, producing some 2400 magazine illustrations from 1905 to 1938.

FB159 Kennedy, Michael S. "W. H. D. Koerner, Portrayer of Pioneers." Montana. *The Mag. of Western Hist.*, vol. 15, no. 1 (January 1965), 52–65.

KRANICH, EDWARD

FB160 Gerdts, William H. "Edward Kranich, 1826–1891." *N.J. Hist. Soc.*, vol. 79 (1961), 16–20. German-born artist who lived in New Jersey.

KRIEGHOFF, CORNELIUS

FB161 *Minn. Hist.*, vol. 40, no. 4 (Winter 1966), cover illustration. K. (1812–1872) was a German-born itinerant artist; emigrated 1837. Portrayer of American Indians; lived in Canada in later life.

KRIMMEL, JOHN LEWIS

FB162 Groce-Wallace, p.377; Thieme-Becker, vol. 21, p.541. K. (1789–1821) was a portrait and genre painter, b. in Ebingen, Württemberg; came to Philadelphia in 1810. In 1821 elected president of the Association of American Artists. His painting "Election Scene, State House in Pennsylvania" (1815) hangs in the Winterthur Museum. (Dunlap; *America Through the Eyes of German Immigrant Painters.*)

FB163 Jackson, Joseph. "Krimmel, 'The American Hogarth'." *Internat. Studio*, vol. 93 (June 1929), 33–36, 86, 88.

KÜHN, JUSTUS ENGELHARDT

FB164 Dresser, Louisa. "The Background of Colonial American Portraiture: Some Pages from a European Notebook." *Procs. Amer. Antiquarian Soc.*, vol. 76, no. 1 (1966), 19–58. On K. (d. 1717) and Jeremiah Theüs.

FB165 Pleasants, J. Hall. "Justus Engelhardt Kühn, an Early Eighteenth Century Portrait Painter." *Procs., Amer. Antiquarian Soc.*, vol. 46 (1936), 243–80. K. was a German native who settled in Annapolis before 1708; portrait painter.

KUMMER, JULIUS HERMANN

FB166 Powell, Mary M. "Three Artists of the Frontier," *Bull. of the Mo. Hist. Soc.*, vol. 5 (October 1948), 35, 41–43. Landscape painter and lithographer; K. (1817-post 1869) was a native of Dresden who emigrated to New York City in 1849.

KURZ, FRIEDRICH (RUDOLPH FRIEDRICH)

FB167 Bushnell, David I., Jr. "Friedrich Kurz, Artist-Explorer." In: Smithsonian Institution *Annual Report* 1927. Washington, D.C.: Smithsonian Institution, 1928, p. 507–27. K. (1818–1871) was a portrait, animal and landscape painter and teacher; native of Bern, Switzerland. He was in the United States from 1846 to 1852 sketching along the Mississippi and upper Missouri Rivers. He returned to his native Switzerland after 1852. His sketchbooks are now in the Historical Museum, Bern. (Thieme-Becker; Groce-Wallace; *Museum Graphic* for Summer 1952).

FB168 Kurz, Rudolph Friedrich. *Journal of Rudolph Friedrich Kurz.* Trans. by Myrtis Jarrell; ed. J. N. B. Hewitt. Lincoln: Univ. of Nebraska Pr., 1970. Rev. by H. S. Marks, *Jour. of the West*, vol. 10 (1971), 386.

Individual Artists (cont.)

LAER, FERDINAND VON

FB169 Peters, *America on Stone*. Painter and lithographer of Berlin, who emigrated to Cincinnati in 1850. (Thieme-Becker).

LANG, LOUIS

FB170 Argosy Book Store, *Catalogue no. 671*. New York, 19–. Offered an original sketchbook of Louis Lang's. This comprised about 30 sheets of thin paper mounted on heavier stock, containing signed pencil sketches: figure studies, portraits, etc., dated Paris, 1834. L. (1814–1893) was a portrait, miniature and genre painter, native of Wurttemberg. Came to America in 1838; later settled in New York City. Became National Academician in 1852. (Thieme-Becker; Groce-Wallace).

LANG, PHILIP

FB171 Goss, Charles F. *Cincinnati, The Queen City, 1788–1912*. Chicago/Indianapolis, 1912.

FB172 Peat, Wilbur D. *Pioneer Painters of Indiana*, Indianapolis, 1954. German portrait painter who worked in Cincinnati and Rockport, Ind., from the late 1840s.

LEMOYNE, JACQUES DEMORGNES

FB173 Thieme-Becker, vol. 23, p.31–32; Groce-Wallace, p. 392–93. L. (d. 1588) was the first artist to visit the continental North America. His views were publ. in Frankfurt a.M. by Theodore de Bry, together with his narrative of an expedition.

LESSING, CARL FRIEDRICH

FB174 Jenderko-Sichelschmidt, I. "Die Historienbilder Carl Friedrich Lessings." Diss., Köln Univ. 1973.

LEUTZE, EMANUEL GOTTLIEB

FB175 *Ausstellungskatalog. Emanuel Leutze, 1816–1868*. Museum Schwäbisch-Gmünd, 1968. A native of Gmünd, Württemberg, L. (1816–1868) was brought to the United States as a child. He studied painting in Philadelphia and went abroad to Düsseldorf for further study. In 1859 he returned to America to carry out a commission in Washington.

FB176 Champlin and Perkins, "Portraiture in Lancaster County" *Publs. Lanc. Co. Hist. Soc*.

FB177 Groseclose, Barbara S. *Emanuel Leutze, 1816–1868: Freedom is the Only King*. Washington, D.C.: National Collection of Fine Arts, 1976. 160p. 169 illus. Catalogue raisonné.

FB178 Groseclose, Barbara S. "Emanuel Leutze, 1816–1868: A German-American History Painter." Diss., Univ. of Wisconsin, 1974.

FB179 Howat, J. K. "Washington Crossing the Delaware." *The Metropolitan Museum Bull*., March 1968.

FB180 Kratz, E. "Emanuel Leutze zum 100. Todestag." *Malkastenblätter*, vol. 13, no. 9 (September 1968).

FB181 Nirenberg, Morton. "Emanuel Leutze and the Hester Prynne Hoax." *Amer.-German Rev*., vol. 36, no. 4 (April–May 1970), 20–22. Leutze's discovery concerning Hawthorne's *Scarlet Letter*.

FB182 Scheer, George F. "Why Washington Stood Up in the Boat." *Amer. Heritage*, vol. 16, no. 1 (1964), 17–19.

FB183 Schreyer, E. "Leutze und Lessing, Düsseldorf und Amerika." In: *Aurora/Eichendorff-Almanach*, vol. 26 (1966).

FB184 Stehle, Raymond L. "Emanuel Leutze, 1816–1868." *Records of the Columbia Hist. Soc. of Washington* (1969–70), 306–31.

FB185 Stehle, Raymond L. "Emanuel Leutze's Three Masks of Washington." *Pa. Hist*., vol. 38, no. 3 (1971), 297–301. L. obtained a copy of Houdon's life mask from the sculptor Ferdinand Pettrich in 1840.

FB186 Stehle, Raymond L. *The Life and Works of Emanuel Leutze*. 2 vols. MS, 1972.

FB187 Stehle, Raymond L. "Virginia Episodes in the Life of Emanuel Leutze." *Va. Mag. of Hist. and Biography*., vol. 75 (1967), 3–10.

FB188 Stehle, Raymond L. "Washington Crossing the Delaware." *Pa. Hist*., vol. 31 (1964), 269–94. Full account of Leutze and his famous painting.

FB189 Sweet, Frederick A. *The Hudson River School and the Early American Landscape Tradition*. Chicago, 1945.

FB190 Taylor, David. *Lights Across the Delaware*. Philadelphia: Lippincott's, 1954. 367p. On L.'s painting of Washington's crossing.

LEWIS, ALBERT

FB191 Allen, Oliver E. "The Lewis Albums." *Amer. Heritage*, vol. 14 (1962), no. 2, 65-80. Albums of family history through 3 generations from 1775 compiled by L. (b. 1829). Emphasis on the history of grandfather Johann Andreas Philipp Ludwig, "Hessian" soldier with the Anspach regiment, who married Anna Maria Klingemann of Pennsylvania and remained in the United States. Charmingly illustrated with paintings, text, mementoes, portraits.

LEWIS, HENRY

FB192 Arrington, Joseph Earl. "Henry Lewis' Moving Panorama of the Mississippi River." *La Hist.*, vol. 6 (1965), 239-72. See also: Arrington's *Nauvoo Temple*; Butts, Porter. *Art in Wisconsin*. Madison: Univ. of Wisconsin Pr., 1936, p.59-63; Groce-Wallace.

FB193 Heilbron, Bertha L. "Documentary Panorama." *Minn. Hist.*, vol. 30 (March 1949), 14-23.

FB194 Heilbron, Bertha L. "Henry Lewis in English." *Publs. of the Bibliographical Soc. of America*, vol. 45 (1952), 359-62. An incomplete copy, the first to be discovered, of an English version of Lewis's book.

FB195 Heilbron, Bertha L. "Henry Lewis' Das illustrierte Mississippithal: A Contemporary Advertisement." *Papers of the Bibliographical Soc. of America*, vol. 43 (1950), 344-45. On the book, now rare, published by Arnz in Düsseldorf, 1854.

FB196 Heilbron, Bertha L. "Lewis' Mississippithal in English." *Minn. Hist.*, vol. 32 (1951), 202-13. (With reproduction of the German title page.)

FB197 Heilbron, Bertha L. "Making a Motion Picture in 1848; Henry Lewis on the Upper Mississippi," *ibid.*, vol. 17 (1936), 131-58, 280-301, 421-36.

FB198 Heilbron, Bertha L. "Where to Settle? A Brother's Advice." *Minn. Hist.*, vol. 39 (1965), 286-89. Henry Lewis visited Minnesota and described it to his brother in 1862.

FB199 Lewis, Henry. Papers. In the Minnesota Hist. Soc. Collections, St. Paul. (MS 76-2059). Copied from originals in various centers. Incl. correspondence, clippings, sketches, etc. as collected by Bertha L. Heilbron, 1895-1973. The author of *Das Illustrierte Mississippi-Thal* was born in England in 1819. He came to St. Louis in 1836 and in his later years resided in Düsseldorf (d. 1904). His great work on the scenes along the upper Mississippi was published in German.

FB200 Lewis, Henry. *The Valley of the Mississippi Illustrated*. Ed. Bertha L. Heilbron. Trans. by Hermina Poatgieter. St. Paul: Minn. Hist. Soc., 1968. 600p. 78 color plates. Lim. ed. The first complete translation of the work as compiled and illustrated by Lewis in the 1950's. Rev. by C. F. Hinds, *Papers of the Bibliographical Soc. of America*, vol. 62, no. 4 (1968), 632-33; J. E. Sander, *Jour. of Amer. Hist.*, vol. 55, no. 3 (December 1968), 401.

FB201 McDermott, John Francis. "Henry Lewis' Das Illustrierte Mississippithal." *Papers of the Bibliographical Soc. of America*, vol. 45 (1951), 152-55. On the question of the English and German editions.

LIBHART, JOHN JAY

FB202 Libhart, Henry Miller. "John Jay Libhart, Nineteenth-Century American Eclectic." *Antiques*, vol. 100, no. 5 (November 1971), 778. L. (1806-1883), a self-taught artist and ornithologist; native of Marietta, Lancaster Co., Pennsylvania. See also: I. D. Rupp, *History of Lancaster Co.* (1844), chap. 14.

LINKE, CONRAD J.

FB203 "Conrad J. Linke." *Amer.-German Rev.*, vol. 22, no. 3 (1956), 20-21. Philadelphia artist born of German-Czech parents.

LOECHER, ALBERT

FB204 Spawn, William. "To Many Lands." *Amer.-German Rev.*, vol. 14, no. 1 (1947), 25-28. Biographical sketch; illustrated.

LOTICHIUS, ERNEST

FB205 Thieme-Becker, vol. 23, p.407; Groce-Wallace, p.404. Animal, landscape and genre painter. Worked at Düsseldorf and Munich, ca. 1841. In 1858 was in New York City.

LUCKENBACH, REUBEN O.

FB206 Levering, *History of Bethlehem*, p.595, 690, 710. L. (1818-1880) was a landscape painter and teacher of drawing. Native of Bethlehem, Pa.

Individual Artists *(cont.)*

LUNGKWITZ, HERMAN

FB207 Zieglschmid, A. J. F. "(Richard) Petri and (Herman) Lungkwitz, Pioneer Artists in Texas." *Amer.-German Rev.*, vol. 9, no. 1 (1942), 4–6; "Texas in Pictures," *ibid.*, 456, 458. L. (1813–1891) was a landscape artist, b. in Halle, studied in Dresden. In 1848 emigrated to Fredericksburg, Texas. Set up photographer's shop in San Antonio with Carl G. von Iwonski. (Thieme-Becker; Groce-Wallace).

MAENTEL (MAENTLE?), JACOB

FB208 Black, Mary C. "A Folk Art Whodunit." *Art in America*, vol. 53, no. 3 (June 1965), 96–105. M. (1763–1863) was a portrait painter, native of Kassel. A physician, he came to New Harmony, Ind. in the 1830's.

FB209 Peat, Wilbur D. *Pioneer Painters of Indiana*, Indianapolis, 1954, p.36–37.

MARSCHALL, NICOLA

FB210 Hume, Edgar Erskine: "Nicola Marschall—The German Artist who Designed the Confederate Flag and Uniform." *Amer.-German Rev.* vol. 6, no. 6 (1940), 6–9. M. (1829–1917) was a portrait painter and teacher. B. in Prussia, he emigrated to New Orleans.

MAYR, CHRISTIAN

FB211 Groce-Wallace, p.435. M. (ca. 1805–1851) was a German native who appeared in New York City about 1834. Portrait and genre painter, designer and daguerreotypist. Afterwards in Boston, Charleston, and New Orleans.

MENG, JOHN

FB212 Groce-Wallace, p.438. M. (1734–1754) was a portrait painter, b. at Germantown, Pa. Died in the West Indies.

MEYER, CHRISTIAN

FB213 [Obituary.] *Art Annual*, vol. 6 (1907). M. (1838–1907) was a landscape painter who emigrated from Germany as a young man. (Groce-Wallace; Fielding).

MILLER, ALFRED JACOB

FB214 Brunet, Pierre. *Descriptive Catalogue of a Collection of Water-Colour Drawings by Alfred J. Miller (1810–1874) in the Public Archives of Canada*. Ottawa, 1951. 39p. M. (1810–1874) was a Baltimore native; studied with Sully in Baltimore and in Europe in 1833–34. He served as artist with a Western expedition. (De Voto, Groce-Wallace).

FB215 Hunter, Wilbur H., Jr. *Alfred Jacob Miller, Artist of Baltimore and the West*. Baltimore: n.p. 1950.

FB216 Randall, Richard H., Jr. "A Gallery for Alfred Jacob Miller." *Antiques*, vol. 106 (November 1974), 836–43. The Walters Art Gallery.

FB217 Ross, Marvin C., ed. *The West of Alfred Jacob Miller. From the Notes and Water Colors in the Walters Art Gallery, With an Account of the Artist*. Norman: Univ. of Oklahoma Pr., 1952. 200p. Enlarged ed., with Miller's Notes and Comments. Norman, 1967. 488p. 200 pl.

MILLER, LEWIS

FB218 Barba, P. A. "'S Pennsylfawnisch Deitsch Eck," Allentown *Morning Call*, 15 March 1969. M. (1795–1882) was a carpenter and amateur artist; native of York, Pa. His diaries and sketchbooks are held in the York, Pa., Hist. Soc. (Groce-Wallace).

FB219 Bishop, Robert. "Lewis Miller's 'Guide to Central Park'." *The Herald* (Greenfield Village and Henry Ford Museum, Dearborn, Michigan), vol. 6, no. 2 (Spring 1977), 1–57.

FB220 "Lewis Miller, Folk Artist." *Journal of the Roanoke Hist. Soc.*, vol. 6, no. 1 (Summer 1969), 1–7.

FB221 Rinker, Harry L., and Richard M. Kain. "Lewis Miller's Virginia Sketchbook: A Record of Rural Life." *Antiques*, vol. 119 (1981), 386–401.

FB222 Turner, Robert P., ed. *Lewis Miller, Sketches and Chronicles: The Reflections of a Nineteenth Century Pennsylvania German Folk Artist*. Introd. by Donald S. Shelley. York: Hist. Soc. of York Co., 1967. Rev. by F. C. Rosenberger, *Va. Mag. of Hist. and Biog.*, vol. 77, no. 3 (July 1969), 372–74; R. Butterfield, *N.Y. Times Book Rev.*, 4 February 1968, 6–7; J. J. Stoudt, *Pa. Mag. of Hist. and Biog.*, vol. 92 (1968), 268; M. A. Mook, *Jour. of Amer. Folklore*, vol. 81, no. 321 (July–September 1968), 266–67. Selections from the annotated drawings and written jottings on local affairs and current history in York, Pa.

MILLER, WILLIAM

FB223 Clark, Edna M. *Ohio Art and Artists*: Richmond, Va., 1932, p.479. M. was the son of Gerhardt Mueller, who came to Cincinnati ca. 1840. Miniaturist in Cincinnati, Indianapolis, and New York. See Burnet, Mary Q. *Art and Artists of Indian*: New York, 1921. Peat, Wilbur D. *Pioneer Painters of Indian*: Indianapolis, 1954. (Groce-Wallace).

MOELLER, LOUIS

FB224 *New York Times*, Art Section, 16 April 1967. Nineteenth-century artist.

MÖLLHAUSEN, HEINRICH BALDUIN

FB225 Hartman, Horst. *George Catlin und Balduin Möllhausen. Zwei Interpreten der Indianer und des alten Westen*. Berlin: Reimer, 1963. 156p. M. (1825–1905) was born in Germany near Bonn; made trips to America in 1849, 1853, 1857, on which occasions he served as topographical artist. Some of his sketches were lithographed for the official expedition reports; more were incorporated into his writings, *Diary of a Journey from the Mississippi to the Coast of the Pacific* (London, 1858) and *Reisen in die Felsengebirge Nord-Amerikas* (Leipzig, 1861).

FB226 Taft, Robert. "Heinrich Balduin Möllhausen." In: *Artists and Illustrators of the Old West 1850–1900*. New York: Scribner's, 1953, p.22–35.

FB227 Taft, Robert. "The Pictorial Record of the Old West: Heinrich Balduin Möllhausen." *Kans. Hist. Quar.*, vol. 16, no. 3 (August 1948), 225–44. Evaluation of the sketches made by M. on his expeditions in the West.

FB228 United States War Department. *Reports of Explorations and Surveys 1855–1860*. Vol. III. Ives. Report on the Colorado River.

MOHOLY-NAGY, LASZLO

FB229 Moholy-Nagy, Dorothea M.P.A. Sibylle (Pietzsch). *Moholy-Nagy, Experiment in Totality*. Intro. by Walter Gropius. New York: Harper, 1950. 253p. Biography of the Hungarian-born artist associated with the Bauhaus and refugee in America from 1937 to his death in 1946.

MOMBERGER, WILLIAM

FB230 Peat, Wilbur D. *Pioneer Painters of Indiana*. Indianapolis, 1954. M. (b. 1829) was a landscape painter, lithographer and illustrator, born in Frankfurt/Main. Came to New York City in 1848.

MUELLER, JOHN JACOB

FB231 Levering, Joseph M. *History of Bethlehem, Pa., 1741–1892*... Bethlehem, 1903. M. (d. 1781) was a portrait painter of Nürnberg who joined the Moravian Church in 1740. Served as secretary to Count Zinzendorf on his visit to America, 1741–43. (Groce-Wallace).

NAHL, CHARLES CHRISTIAN

FB232 Gudde, Erwin. "Carl Nahl, California's Pioneer of Painting." *Amer.-German Rev.*, vol. 7 (1940), 18–20. N. (1818–1878) was a portrait, historical, genre and animal painter, engraver and lithographer; born in Kassel in 1818. Nahl came to America in 1849 and worked with his half-brother Hugo Nahl in the California gold fields, later setting up a studio for photography and commercial art in San Francisco. (Groce-Wallce; Peters; *America on Stone*).

NAHL, HUGO WILHELM ARTHUR

FB233 Writers' Program. California. *Introduction to California Art Research, I*. San Francisco, 1936. N. was a painter, illustrator, designer, engraver. Native of Kassel, Forty-Eighter. (Groce-Wallace).

NAST, THOMAS

FB234 Glover, William, comp. *The Christmas Drawings of Thomas Nast*. New York: World Publ. Co., ca. 1970. Reissue of 28 favorite Christmas drawings by N. Illustrator, cartoonist, caricaturist, N. (1840–1902) was born in Landau (Pfalz); came to America at an early age and was raised in New York City. Studied with Theodor Kaufmann and Alfred Fredericks. Drew cartoons for *Frank Leslie's Illustrated Newspaper*, the *New York Illustrated News*, and *Harper's Weekly*. An exhibit, 75 Wood Engravings by Cartoonist Thomas Nast (1840–1902), was held at Los Angeles County Museum of Art, 1979–1980.

FB235 Hobbs, Franklin Warren. "Thomas Nast, Caricaturist of His Age." Honors thesis, Harvard Univ., 1970.

FB236 Hornung, Clarence, P., ed. *An Old-Fashioned Christmas*. New York: Dover Publ., ca. 1977. 128p. Contains the complete Thomas Nast Santa Claus series and other Christmas prints.

FB237 Keller, Morton. *The Art and Politics of Thomas Nast*. New York: Oxford Univ. Pr., 1968. 350p. 245 illus. On Nast's involvement with the principal issues of the latter half of the nineteenth century. His caricatures of Boss Tweed provided

Individual Artists (cont.)

the foundation of his reputation. Rev. by J. C. Vinson, *N.Y. Hist. Soc. Quar.*, vol. 53, no. 2 (April 1969), 193–94.; D. Montgomery, *Pa. Mag. of Hist. and Biog.*, vol. 93, no. 1 (January 1969), 138–39.

FB238 Nast, Thomas. Papers, sketches, notebooks, MSS., and accounts, 1860–1902. 6 boxes. In the Rutherford B. Hayes Library, Fremont, Ohio (MS 61-2114). Letters to Mrs. Nast, 1851–1916. In the Henry E. Huntington Library, San Marino, Cal. (MS 68-380). *See also* Nast cartoons and autographs in the Charles E. Feinberg collection, Archives of American Art (MS 67-263).

FB239 Nast, Thomas. *Thomas Nast's Christmas Drawings for the Human Race.* New York: Harper & Row, 1971. Reissue of a collection published in 1890.

FB240 Paine, Albert Bigelow. *Thomas Nast; his Period and His Pictures.* New York: Peter Smith, 1967. Repr. of a work publ. by Harper in 1904.

FB241 *Thomas Nast, Freiheitskämpfer mit dem Zeichen-stift.* Frankfurt a.M.: U.S. Information Service, 1957. 31p. Rev. in *Amer.-German Rev.*, vol. 23, no. 3 (1957), 39.

FB242 Vinson, J. Chalmers. "Thomas Nast and the American Political Scene." *Amer. Quar.*, vol. 9 (1957), 337–44.

FB243 Vinson, J. Chalmers. *Thomas Nast 1840–1912: Political Cartoonist.* Athens: Univ. of Georgia Pr., 1967. 46p. 154 illus. Rev. in *N.Y. Folklore Quar.*, vol. 24 (March 1968), 74–75; by S. Hamilton, *N.Y. Hist. Soc. Quar.*, vol. 52, no. 3 (July 1968), 295–96. A reprinting of cartoons with a biographical sketch.

NEAGLE, JOHN

FB244 Patrick, Ransom R. "The Early Life of John Neagle, Philadelphia Portrait Painter." Diss., Princeton Univ., 1958.

NEYNABOR, AUGUSTUS

FB245 Andes, Martin L. "Augustus Neynabor (Neunaber), Chester County Folk Artist." *Chester Co. Collections*, no. 9 (January 1938), 335–36. On N. (d. 1887).

NEWSWANGER, KIEHL AND CHRISTIAN

FB246 Gomersall, R. "A Father and Son Paint." *Amer. German Rev.*, vol. 17, no. 1 (1950), 10–13. Evaluation of the work of Kiehl and Christian Newswanger, Lancaster County, Pa.

NIEMEYER, JOHN HENRY

FB247 Burnet, Mary Q. *Art and Artists of Indiana*: New York, 1921, p.385. N. (1839–1932) was a portrait and figure painter, teacher of art. Came to Cincinnati from Bremen in 1843, Worked in Indianapolis in 1858 as sign painter. In 1871–1908 was professor of drawing at Yale University and teacher of Saint-Gaudens and Frederick Remington.

FB248 Peat, Wilbur D. *Pioneer Painters of Indiana.* Indianapolis, 1954, p.169.

OELSCHLAGER, GUSTAVUS

FB249 Groce-Wallace, p.476. Native of Canada, son of James C. Oelschlager (professor of languages from Hamburg, Germany, who emigrated to Newfoundland before 1830). Gustavus resided in Philadelphia in 1860.

OERTEL, JOHANNES ADAM SIMON

FB250 Oertel, J. F. *A Vision Realized: A Life Story of Rev. J. A. Oertel, Artist, Priest, Missionary.* Milwaukee: n.p. 1917. O. (1823–1909) was a religious and portrait painter, engraver; b. in Fürth, Bavaria, he came to New York in 1848. Designed ceiling decorations for the House of Representatives, Washington.

PETER, GEORGE

FB251 Heinrich Herbatschek, "George Peter—ein deutsch-amerikanischer Maler." *Amer.-German Rev.*, vol. 13, no. 1 (1946), 32. Austrian-American artist of Milwaukee.

PETERS, J., Sr.

FB252 Born, *Landscape Painting*, p.126 (fig. 84). Painter of a landscape with Mennonite figures, probably at the Delaware Water Gap, early 19th century.

PETRI, RICHARD

FB253 Newcomb, William W. "German Artist on the Pedernales." *Southwestern Hist. Quar.*, vol. 82 (October 1978), 149–72. N. (1824–1857) was a portrait and figure painter, native of Dresden. After the Revolution of 1848 he and his brother-in-law Hermann Lungkwitz emigrated to Texas. *See: Texas in Pictures*, p.456; Gideon, "Two Pioneer Artists of Texas."

FB254 Newcomb, William W., and May S. Carnahan. *German Artist on the Texas Frontier: Friedrich Richard Petri.* Austin: Univ. of Texas Pr., 1978. 256p. Rev. by G. E. Lich, *Jour. of German-Amer. Studies*, vol. 14, no. 3 (1979), 146–47; E. C. Parry, *Amer. Art and Antiques*, vol. 2, no. 6 (1979), 24–25; D. L. Smith, *Jour. of Southern Hist.*, vol. 45 (1979), 280–81; E. N. Thompson, *Amer. West*, vol. 16, no. 3 (1979), 58.

PFAU, GUSTAV

FB255 Alderfer, William K. "The Artist Gustav Pfau." *Jour. of the Ill. State Hist. Soc.*, vol. 60 (Winter 1967). P. (1808–1884) was a native of Leipzig, lived in Springfield, Ill. Worked as topographic artist for lithographers.

FB256 Wyneken, H. "A Memorial to Gustav Pfau, Artist." *Concordia Hist. Inst. Quar.*, vol. 21 (1948), 149–51.

PFETSCH (OR FETSCH), CARL P.

FB257 Peat: *Pioneer Painters of Indiana.* P. (1817–1898) was a portrait and genre painter; native of Blankenburg, Germany. Arrived in America shortly after 1848. Worked in New York, Cincinnati, and New Albany, Ind. (Groce-Wallace).

POMAREDE, LEON

FB258 Arrington, J. Earl. "Leon D. Pomarede's Original Panorama of the Mississippi River." *Mo. Hist. Soc. Bull.*, vol. 9 (April 1953), 261–73.

FB259 McDermott, John F. "Leon Pomarede, Our Parisian Knight of the Easel." *Bull. of the City Art Museum of St. Louis*, vol. 34 (Winter 1949), 8–18.

POST, EDWARD C.

FB260 Groce-Wallace, p.512. Landscape painter; exhibited at the National and Pennsylvania academies before 1860. In New York City in 1853. In 1860 was at Düsseldorf.

RACKELMANN, GEORGE

FB261 Wagner, William J. "George Rackelmann, Iowa Artist." *Annals of Iowa*, vol. 37 (1966), 275–91. Native of Nürnberg (b. 1887); emigrated in 1910.

REICHEL, WILLIAM CORNELIUS

FB262 Levering, Joseph M. *History of Bethlehem, Pa., 1741–1892....* Bethlehem, 1903 R. (1824–1876) was a native of Salem, N. Car.; a Moravian minister and teacher-naturalist. He studied art at Bethlehem under Grunewald.

REINBERGER, JOSEPH

FB263 Groce-Wallace, p.530. German artist who settled at Nauvoo, Ill., in 1850. Made a drawing of the ruined city.

REINKE, AMADEUS ABRAHAM

FB264 Rice, William H. *In Memoriam Amadeus Abraham Reinke*: New York, 1889. R. (1822–1889) was an amateur artist, son of Samuel R. B. at Lancaster, attended and taught at Moravian schools in Nazareth and Bethlehem. (Levering, *History of Bethlehem.* p.648, 700, 710).

REISS, WINOLD

FB265 Finckh, Alice H. "Friend of the Blackfeet." *Amer.-German Rev.*, vol. 17, no. 6 (1951), 12–13. R. was a German-born painter; in the U.S. since 1913. Taught art in the U.S. from 1919.

FB266 Reiss, W. Tjark, and George Schriever. "Winold Reiss: Painter of Plains Indians." *Amer. West*, vol. 18 no. 5 (1981), 28–37.

RICHTER, FRITZ

FB267 "Water Colors by Fritz Richter." *Amer. German Rev.*, vol. 17, no. 4 (1951), 18–19.

RIMPRECHT, JOHN (JOHANN) BAPTIST

FB268 Groce-Wallace, p.537. R. (1801–1877) was a genre and portrait painter, b. in Triberg, Germany. Emigrated to America in 1843; returned to Germany after the Civil War. (Thieme-Becker).

RINDISBACHER, PETER

FB269 Arndt, Karl J. R. "The Peter Rindisbacher Family on the Red River in Rupert's Land: Their Hardships and Call for Help from Rapp's Harmony Society." *Canad.-German Yearbook*, vol. 1 (1973), 95–106. R. (1806–1834) was a genre, landscape, animal and miniature painter. B. in Upper Emmenthal, Canton Bern, Switzerland; in 1821 R. was brought with his family to the Earl of Selkirk's Red River colony in western Canada. R. moved to Wisconsin in 1826 and thence to St. Louis.

FB270 Benisovich, Michael, and Anna M. Heilmaier. "Peter Rindisbacher, Swiss Artist." *Minn. Hist.*, vol. 32, no. 3 (1951), 155–62.

FB271 Clifford, Wilson. "Peter Rindisbacher, First Western Artist." *Canad. Art*, vol. 20, no. 1 (1963),

Individual Artists (cont.)

50–53. R.'s Indian paintings made at the Red River in 1821.

FB272 Josephy, Alvin M., Jr. "The Boy Artist of Red River." *Amer. Heritage*, vol. 21, no. 2 (February 1970), 30–49. With reproductions of 16 paintings of American Indian subjects in color.

FB273 McDermott, John F. "Peter Rindisbacher: Frontier Reporter." *Art Quar.*, vol. 12 (1949), 129–45.

FB274 Meuli, Karl. "Peter Rindisbacher, der Indianermaler aus dem Emmental." In: *Beiträge zur Volkskunde*, by Karl Meuli. Basel: n.p., 1960.

FB275 Nute, Grace Lee. "Peter Rindisbacher, Artist." *Minn. Hist.*, vol. 14 (September 1933), 283–87; also her article "Rindisbacher's Minnesota Water Colors," *ibid.*, vol. 20 (March 1939), 54–57.

FB276 Smith, Alice Elizabeth. "Peter Rindisbacher: A Communication." *Minn. Hist.*, vol. 20 (1939), 173–75.

ROEHNER, WILHELM

FB277 Thieme-Becker, vol. 28, p.486; Groce-Wallace, p.543. Portrait and genre painter, New York City in 1854; at Newark in 1859. Possibly the same Wilhelm Roehner who worked in Vienna and Berlin from 1839 to 1846.

ROESEN, SEVERIN

FB278 Mook, Maurice A. *Lycoming College Mag.*, vol. 25, no. 6 (1972), 33–42; vol. 26, no. 6 (1973), 13–16, 23–30; vol. 7 (Spring 1974). "Severin Roesen and His Family." *Jour. of the Lycoming Co. Hist. Soc.*, vol. 8, no. 2 (1972), 8–13. "Severin Roesen, 'The Williamsport Painter'." "'S Pennsylfawnisch Deitsch Eck," Allentown *Morning Call*, 3 December 1955. Still life and porcelain enamel painter; native of Köln who emig. in 1848 to Williamsport, Pa. Said to have died ca. 1871 in a Philadelphia almshouse. Eighty known paintings by R. exist. (Thieme-Becker; Groce-Wallace).

ROESSLER, HERMANN

FB279 "An American German Primitive Painter." *Amer.-German Review*, vol. 26 (1960), no. 4, 29.

ROETTER, PAULUS

FB280 Powell, *Three Artists of the Frontier*, p.38–41. Landscape and botanical painter, b. in Nürnberg, Germany or Thun, Switzerland. Studied art in Düsseldorf and Munich. Emigrated in 1845 with plan to found a communal society. Settled in St. Louis and taught at Washington University. George Engelmann's *Cactaceae of the Boundary* in the *Report of the U.S. and Mexican Boundary Survey* (1859) was illustrated by Roetter. Became an associate of Agassiz at Harvard University. (Thieme-Becker; Groce-Wallace; Writers' Program, *Missouri*.)

ROSENTHAL, TOBY EDWARD

FB281 Kramer, William N., and Norton B. Stern, eds. "The Great Elaine Robbery: The Crime Against Civilization." *Jour. of the West*, vol. 10 (1971), 585–609. Deals with the Prussian-born San Francisco painter T. E. Rosenthal.

ROTHERMEL, PETER FREDERICK

FB282 Rothermel, P. F. Papers, 1863–1872. In the Pennsylvania Hist. and Museum Commission (MS 60-2868). Relate to the painting "The Battle of Gettysburg" in the Pennsylvania State Museum. R. (1817–1895).

RUNGIUS, KARL

FB283 Ferris, Edythe. "Karl Rungius, Artist." *Amer.-German Rev.*, vol. 18, no. 4 (1952), 9–10.

FB284 Fulda, Elizabeth (Rungius). Papers, 1879–1968. 1 reel. In the Archives of American Art (MS 71-1454). Correspondence in German and English of Carl Rungius, wildlife painter of Calgary, Canada.

SATTLER, HUBERT

FB285 Thieme-Becker, vol. 29, p.486–87. S. (1817–1904), panorama and landscape painter, a Viennese artist who visited Boston and New York in 1850–1851. (Groce-Wallace).

SCHAMES, SAMSON

FB286 "Samson Schames." *Amer.-German Rev.*, vol. 22, no. 4 (1956), 28–29. New York City painter, native of Frankfurt a. M.

SCHMIDT, PETER

FB287 Cline, Isaac M. "Art and Artists in New Orleans since Colonial Times." In: Louisiana State Museum, *Biennial Report of the Board of Curators for 1920–21*, p.32–42. S. (1822–1867) was a portrait painter, native of Germany, at New Orleans in 1859–1867.

SCHMOLZE, KARL HEINRICH (OR HERMANN)

FB288 Thieme-Becker, vol. 30, p.179. S. (1823–1861), portrait, genre, historical painter and engraver; born at Zweibrücken, Germany; came to Philadelphia in 1849.

SCHREYVOGEL, CHARLES

FB289 Horan, James D. *The Life and Art of Charles Schreyvogel, Painter-Historian of the Indian-Fighting Army of the American West.* New York: Crown Publs., 1969. 62p. 36 color plates. Native of New York, descendant of immigrant grandparents who came to America in the 1840's. Grew up in a German-American milieu, in New York and Hoboken.

SCHUSSELE (SCHÜSSELE), CHRISTIAN

FB290 *Antiques*, vol. 114, no. 6 (December 1978). His "Skating at Kelley's Dam, Germantown" is shown as frontispiece. S. (1824/1826–1879) was a historical, genre, portrait and landscape painter, lithographer and teacher. B. in Alsace; studied art in Strasbourg and Paris. Emigrated to Philadelphia in 1848. (Thieme-Becker; Groce-Wallace).

FB291 Johnston, Rev. George H. *A Sermon Memorial to Christian Schussele, for Eleven Years of Drawings and Paintings in the Pennsylvania Academy of Fine Arts.* Philadelphia: n.p. 1879. 24p.

FB292 Onorato, Ronald. "The Context of the Pennsylvania Academy: Thomas Eakins' Assistantship to Christian Schuessele." *Arts Magazine*, vol. 53, no. 9 (May 1979), 121–30. Schuessele, professor of fine arts at the academy, established the terms of practice and pedagogy that became the matrix of Thomas Easkins' teaching of art.

SCHUSTER (SHUSTER), ARNAULD

FB293 Groce-Wallace, p.565. Portrait painter of New York City in 1852. Had previously studied at the Academy of Munich.

SCHUSTER (SHUSTER), SIGISMUND

FB294 Schuster, Sigismund. *Practical Drawing Book.* New York: n.p., 1851. S. was a miniature pastellist, lithographer, landscape painter and teacher. Came to New York from his native Germany ca. 1851. (Thieme-Becker; Groce-Wallace).

SCHWARTZE, JOHAN GEORG

FB295 Groce-Wallace, p.565. S. (1814/15–1874), portrait and religious painter. Exhibited in Philadelphia in 1837–1858. In 1844–1847 was in Düsseldorf, and later in Amsterdam.

SCHWITTERS, KURT

FB296 Steinitz, Kate T. *Kurt Schwitters: A Portrait from Life.* Berkeley: Univ. of Calif. Pr., 1969. Modern artist, native of Hanover, who worked for many years in America.

SEIDEL, CHARLES FREDERICK

FB297 Levering; *History of Bethlehem, Pa., 1741–1892.* ... Bethlehem, 1903. Amateur artist and Moravian minister. Emigrated to Bethlehem, Pa., in 1806 and served as pastor at Salem, N. Car., to 1809.

SEIFERT, PAUL A.

FB298 Huff, Richard L. "Paul Seifert. A Wisconsin Pioneer Artist." *Wis. Tales and Trails*, vol. 8 (1967), no. 4, 16–19. S. (1840–1926) was a Dresden-born artist, itinerant painter and farmer of Richland Center who painted water-colors of Wisconsin farms, villages, shops and mills.

FB299 Lipman, Jean. "Paul Seifert." In: *Primitive Painters in America, 1750–1950.* Ed. Jean Lipman and Alice Winchester. New York: Dodd, Mead, 1950, p.160–64.

SELINGER, JOHN PAUL ("JEAN PAUL")

FB300 Vogel, Charles, and Gloria Vogel. "Jean Paul and Emily Selinger." *Hist. N.H.*, vol. 34, no. 2, 125–42. S. (1850–1909) was a well-known New England portraitist and landscape artist. Native of Boston, son of a woodcarver who emig. from Bavaria. S. studied art in Stuttgart and München; he was a pupil of Wilhelm Leibl. In later years he maintained his studio at Crawford House, N.H.

SHEUE, ———

FB301 Brackenridge, H. M. *Recollections of Persons and Places in the West*, Philadelphia, 1868, p.96–97, 233. Miniature and landscape painter, native of Prussia. Taught German and worked as a painter in Pittsburgh and St. Louis. (Groce-Wallace).

SHINDLER, A. ZENO

FB302 Groce-Wallace, p.576–77. S. (b. ca. 1813), German pastell portraitist and landscape painter. Worked as a teacher in Philadelphia in 1850.

Individual Artists *(cont.)*

SIEBNER, HERBERT

FB303 Riedel, Walter E. "Der deutschkanadische Expressionist Herbert Siebner." *German-Canad. Yearbook*, vol. 6, 172-77.

STECHER, KARL

FB304 [Obituary.] *Art Annual*, vol. 21 (1924). S. (1832?-1924) was a German portrait painter and craftsman who came to New York at an early age. (Groce-Wallace).

STETTINIUS, SAMUEL E.

FB305 Millar, Bruce. "Stettinius: Pennsylvania Primitive Portrait Painter," *Amer. Collector*, vol. 8 (May 1939), 5. S. (1768-1815) was a portrait painter in watercolors and oils, native of Friedrichgratz, German Silesia, who came to America in 1791. Lived in Hanover, Pa., and Baltimore. (Groce-Wallace).

STUCKEN, FERDINAND

FB306 Thieme-Becker, vol. 32, p.233; Groce-Wallace, p.613. S. (d. 1878) was a portrait and historical painter at Düsseldorf in 1848. Resided in New York City 1856 and after.

TAYLOR, BAYARD

FB307 *Art in America* (April 1940), p.76. Native of Kennet Square, Pa.; traveler, author, ambassador, famous translator of *Faust*. (*Yesterday in Chester County (Pa.) Art*, West Chester, 1936; Perry, *Expedition to Japan*).

THEUS, JEREMIAH

FB308 Middleton, Margaret S. *Jeremiah Theus, Colonial Artist of Charles Town*. Columbia: Univ. of S. Car. Pr., 1953. 162p. T. (ca. 1719-1774) was a limner and decorative painter, b. in Graubunden, Switzerland. Came to South Carolina with his parents in 1735.

FB309 Middleton, Margaret Simons. "Jeremiah Theus." *Amer.-German Rev.*, vol. 19, no. 2 (1952), 11-13.

THOLEY, AUGUSTUS

FB310 Peters, *America on Stone*. Painter, pastel artist, engraver and lithographer. Came to Philadelphia from Alsace-Lorraine in 1848.

THOMPSON, BENJAMIN (COUNT RUMFORD)

FB311 Brown, Sanborn C. *Benjamin Thompson, Count Rumford*. Cambridge: MIT Pr., ca. 1979.

376p. American expatriot inventor and scientist; was an amateur artist. B. in Boston, he resided in later life in Munich and Auteuil, France.

TILESIUS VON TILENAU, WILHELM GOTTLIEB

FB312 Groce-Wallace, p.631. Von T. (1769-1857), an artist and naturalist, b. at Mulhouse, Alsace. Accompanied Czar Alexander I's expedition to the North Pacific in 1803. His sketches of this voyage incl. some of the California scenes used in Langsdorff's *Bemerkungen auf einer Reise um die Welt* (1812).

ULKE, HENRY

FB313 Fairman, *Art and Artists of the Capital*, p.356. U. (1821-1910) was a portrait painter and naturalist, b. at Frankenstein, Germany. Studied art in Berlin. A Forty-Eighter, he emigrated to America in 1849, coming to New York City and Washington, D.C.

FB314 Ulke, Titus. "Henry Ulke, Painter and Naturalist." *Amer.-German Rev.*, vol. 11, no. 1 (1944), 12-14.

UNGER, LEOPOLD PAUL

FB315 Allen, Anna F. "Leopold Paul Unger: Allentown Artist." *Procs. of the Lehigh Co. Hist. Soc.*, vol. 31 (1976), 43-52.

VIANDEN, HEINRICH

FB316 Butts, *Art in Wisconsin*, p.109-13. V. (1814-1899) was a landscape painter, b. at Poppelsdorf, Germany; trained in engraving and lithography. In 1849 he moved from Cologne to Wisconsin, where he became a leading landscape painter for almost 50 years. (Thieme-Becker, Groce-Wallace).

VISCHER, EDWARD

FB317 Farquhar, F. P. *Edward Vischer: His Pictorial Art of California*. San Francisco: n.p. 1932. V. (1809-1870) was a landscape painter, b. in Bavaria; emigrated to Mexico at the age of 19, thence to California in 1849 as merchant and agent. Started sketching about 1852. (Peters, *California on Stone*).

VOGT, FRITZ G.

FB318 Lamont, Karen W. "Fritz G. Vogt: Itinerant Artist." *N.Y. Folklore Quar.*, vol. 31, nos. 1/2 (1975), 45-55.

FB319 Scheuttle, Frank A. "Fritz G. Vogt: The Bookman's Corners Drawings." *Ibid.*, vol. 31, nos. 1/2 (1975), 57-74.

VOLCK, ADALBERT JOHN

FB320 Anderson, McC. George. *The Work of Adalbert Johann Volck, 1828-1912, Who Chose For His Name the Anagram V. Blada*. Baltimore: n.p., 1970. Available at the Maryland Historical Society.

FB321 Catton, Bruce. "A Southern Artist on the Civil War." *Amer. Heritage*, vol. 9, no. 6 (1958), 117-20. Southern patriotism and Northern cruelty portrayed in V.'s engravings.

FB322 Foley, Gardner P. H. "Adalbert Volck, Dentist and Artist." *Md.*, vol. 19 (March 1948), 4f.

FB323 Pleasants, *Two Hundred and Fifty Years of Painting in Maryland*, p.62. Caricaturist, painter, and worker in bronze and silver. A native of Augsburg, came to America as a Forty-Eighter. Became a dentist in Baltimore. As a skillful cartoonist he published sketches of the Civil War from the Confederate point of view. (Metropolitan Museum of Art. *Life in America*, and *Mag of Hist*. Extra no. 60, (1917).

VORST, JOSEPH P.

FB324 "Joseph P. Vorst." *Mo. Hist. Rev.*, vol. 42 (1948), 198. Obituary of the artist; b. 1897 in Essen, d. 1947 in St. Louis.

WEBER, PAUL

FB325 Davis, W.W.H. *Doylestown Old and New*. Doylestown: n.p. 1905. W. (1823-1916) was a landscape and portrait painter, born in Darmstadt, came to Philadelphia in 1848. After 1860 he returned to his birthplace as court painter. He frequently collaborated with the painter Christian Schüssele. *Philadelphia: Three Centuries of American Art*. Philadelphia: Museum of Art, 1976, p.343.

WEHNER, WILLIAM

FB326 Kurtz, Wilbur G. *The Atlanta Cyclorama*. Atlanta: The City of Atlanta, 1954. Kurtz, Wilbur G. "How the Cyclorama was Painted." *Amer. Heritage*, vol. 7, no. 2 (1956), 45. Creation of the Atlanta cyclorama. Executed by twelve imported German artists under the direction of William Wehner. W. was painter from Munich who directed a team of painters during the 1880's. The studio offices were in Milwaukee. After painting battles scenes of the Franco-Prussian War in Europe, the team produced cycloramas of famous Civil War battles in America. See also "Scraps of Panorama." *Wis. Then and Now*, vol. 15, no. 8 (March 1969), 2-3.

WEIAND, PAUL R.

FB327 Fetterman, William B. "Paul R. Weiand: Lehigh County Folk Artist." *Pa. Folklife*, vol. 30 (1980-1981), 87-93.

WEINGARTNER, (GOTTFRIED) WALLRATH

FB328 Pitzer, Don E. "Harmonist Folk Art Discovered." *Historic Preservation*, October-December 1977, 11-12. Reference to the bird paintings of (Gottfried) Wallrath Weingartner (b. 1793 in Württemberg; in Harmony, Pa., 1803).

WENDEROTH, AUGUST

FB329 Peters, *America on Stone*; Peters, *California on Stone*. W. (b. 1825) worked in San Francisco and in the East; was a historical, animal, landscape and portrait painter and lithographer. Born at Kassel, the son of the painter Carl W. Wenderoth. Emigrated to America ca. 1848.

WENGLER, JOHN B.

FB330 Butts, *Art in Wisconsin*, p.63-64. An Austrian landscape painter who visited Wisconsin ca. 1850-51.

WIECZOREK, MAX

FB331 E. C. Maxwell. "Max Wieczorek." *Amer.-German Rev.*, vol. 18, no. 4 (1952), 15-18. A painter, native of Breslau; in California from 1911.

WILD, JOHN CASPAR

FB332 McDermott, John F. "J. C. Wild and Fort Snelling." *Minn. Hist.*, vol. 32 (Spring 1951), 12-14. W. (ca. 1804-1846) was a landscape painter and lithographer, a native of Zurich who came to America ca. 1830. Published views of St. Louis in 1840 and *The Valley of the Mississippi Illustrated in a Series of Views*, 1841.

FB333 McDermott, John F. "J. C. Wild, Western Painter and Lithographer." *Ohio St. Archaeological and Hist. Quar.*, vol. 60 (April 1951), 111-25.

FB334 Wilkie, Franc B. *Davenport, Past and Present....* Davenport, Iowa, 1858. p.307-10.

Individual Artists (cont.)

WIMAR, CHARLES

FB335 Matthey, Horst. "Indianermaler und posthumer Botschafter: Charles Wimar." *Zeitschrift für Kulturaustausch*, vol. 19, no. 3 (1969), 250–52. W. (1828–1862) was a well-known painter of Western Indians and buffalo; b. at Siegburg, near Bonn. Emigrated with parents to St. Louis. In 1851 went to Düsseldorf for study with Leutze. On three trips to the headwaters of the Mississippi he sketched life in the Great Plains. He executed murals in the rotunda of the St. Louis Court House.

FB336 Rathbone, Perry T. *Charles Wimar, Painter of the Indian*. St. Louis: City Art Museum of St. Louis, 1946. Catalogue of an exhibition at the City Art Museum.

FB337 Rathbone, Perry T., ed. *Westward the Way*. St. Louis: n.p., 1954.

FB338 Spiess, Lincoln Bunce. "Some Little-Known—and Unkown—Portraits by Carl Wimar." *Missouri Hist. Soc. Bulletin*, vol. 34 (January 1978).

FB339 [Wimar, Charles.] Exhibition Catalogue. *Charles Wimar*. City Art Museum of St. Louis, 1946.

WUNDER, ADALBERT

FB340 French, *Art and Artists in Connecticut*, p.136. W. (b. 1827), a native of Berlin, came to Hartford in 1855. Made portraits in crayon and ink.

WYNEKEN, F.D.C.

FB341 W. G. P(ollock). "Wyneken Paintings." *Concordia Hist. Inst. Quar.*, vol. 20, no. 1 (1947), 2. Reproductions of paintings by the Lutheran missionary and minister; biographical notes.

Artists of German Origin Listed in the Censuses of 1850 and 1860

FB342 United States. Bureau of the Census. *Seventh Census of the United States* (1850). Washington, D.C., 1854. *Eighth Census of the United States* (1860). Washington, D.C., 1864. (Cited in Groce-Wallace.) Provides the following information on laborers who listed themselves as artists:

Backofen, Charles. Portraitist. In New York in 1850. B. in Germany ca. 1801.

Bayer, Justin, portrait painter. In New York 1850, age 38.

Becher, George T., professor of drawing at Girard College, Philadelphia, 1860. Native of Bavaria, ca. 1817. Arrived in Pennsylvania before 1840.

Beckh, Frederick, artist in Baltimore and New York, ca. 1842. Born in Württemberg, ca. 1814.

Borgman, John, artist of Baltimore, 1860. Native of Germany.

Botts, George, German artist, born ca. 1829. In Philadelphia 1860.

Braun, John, German artist. In New York in 1850, age 26.

Buckner, Henry, German portrait painter. In New York in 1850, age 28.

Christ, Henry, fresco painter, b. in Nassau, Germany, ca. 1824. In Philadelphia in 1860.

Curtis, Robert J., portrait painter, born in Germany, ca. 1816. Came to America in childhood and resided in Charleston, S. C.

Eckhart, Otto, Prussian-born portrait painter. In New York City in 1860, age 32.

Exner, Carl, fresco painter of Washington. Age 38 in 1850. Born in Germany.

Fahrenberg, Albert, portrait painter, b. in Cologne. Came to New York City ca. 1850. Later resided in Louisville and New Orleans.

Fischer, Frederick, artist from Sachsen. At New York in 1860, age 50.

Fischer, Lewis, German-born fresco painter, 25 years of age in 1850. Lived in Boston.

Gebhard, Charles E., portrait painter, b. in Leipzig *ca*. 1810–1815. Lived in Baltimore 1840–1860.

Geisler, Joseph, Austrian artist. In New York 1860, age 44.

Gendhart, John W., German artist of Baltimore in 1850, age 49.

Giesecke, Ferdinand, German artist of New York 1860, age 35.

Graeff, Celestine, Swiss artist in Philadelphia, 1860, age 30.

Hanton, Andrew, German artist in New York, 1860, age 30.

Hedinger, John H., German artist in Philadelphia, 1860, age 34.

Heill, Carl, German artist, New Orleans in 1850, age 21.

Heill, George, German artist, New Orleans in 1850, age 27.

Heill, Philip, German artist, New Orleans in 1850, age 30.

Hohenstein, Anton, portrait painter from Bayern, b. ca. 1823. Came to America in the 1850's. Also listed as Anthony Hochstein(?) See Peters: *America on Stone.*

Holste, or Holtze, Peter Caspar, German artist, b. *ca.* 1775. Operated drawing and painting academy in Baltimore, 1819–1850.

John, Augustus. Landscape painter, teacher of drawing in Baltimore 1849–1850. Native of Prussia, b. ca. 1821.

Johnson, Henry, drawing master from Hamburg. At San Francisco in 1860, age 30.

Johnson, John, artist from Baden, Germany. In Boston 1860, age 28.

Kerder, August, artist from Prussia, at New York City in 1860, age 36.

Kett, Emil, landscape painter, b. Bayern, ca. 1828. Came to Baltimore ca. 1850.

Keyser, Constantine, artist from Baden. In 1860 resided in Philadelphia, age 38. Listed in the 1860 directory as commission merchant.

Kohler, Robert. Artist from Sachsen. In New York in 1850, age 48. Also listed as "Kohelar."

Krause, Henry, portrait painter of New York in 1860. Native of Hamburg, ca. 1820.

Kuchel, Jacob, German artist in Philadelphia in 1850, age 32.

Kurtz, Henry, engraver, portrait and landscape painter in 1850. Son of German baker in Boston; b. ca. 1822.

Lamor, Antony, portrait and decorative painter; in Philadelphia 1856–1860; native of Hungary, ca. 1824. Arrived in America before 1847.

Lessen, Ferdinand, German artist in Philadelphia. Age 27 in 1850.

Levly, Morris. German artist in Philadelphia, 1850.

Lindenmeyr, Philip, artist. Native of Hesse-Kassel. In New York City in 1860.

Lorenz, Alexander, portrait painter b. in Prussia ca. 1808. Resided in Baden 1842–1843; in New York 1852–1863.

Lotz, Frederick, German fresco painter. In Pittsburgh in 1850, age 31.

Luceck, G. Hungarian artist, at New Orleans in 1860, age 44.

Meister, Fred, Prussian artist. At Baltimore in 1860, age 60.

Merving, Christopher, German-born artist. In New Orleans 1850, age 27.

Metz, A. F., portrait painter. From Sachsen. In New York 1860, age 45.

Miler, Gottfried, portrait and miniature painter in New York 1841–1887. Listed in the census of 1850 as Godfrey Miller, age 30; listed as "Guthrie Miller," native of Germany, age 46, in the 1860 census.

Miller, C. G., artist from Germany, b. ca. 1800. In Louisville in the early 1850's.

Miller, Emil, artist from Germany. New York City 1850, age 31.

Müller, Frederick, German artist. In Philadelphia in 1850, age 42.

Nolte, Emil F., Boston artist. Age 25 in 1860. Emigrated from Germany.

Peters, John E., fresco painter. Native of Osnabruck. In Washington, D.C., 1860, age 33.

Poldeman, William F. Artist from Baden. In New York 1860, age 33.

Rauch, William, artist from Bayern. New York, 1860, age 43.

Rebole, Henry, German fresco painter. Pittsburgh in 1850, age 29.

Recoley(?), Julius, German artist. Philadelphia 1850, age 24.

Reen, Charles, German artist and lithographer, b. ca. 1827. In Philadelphia in 1850.

Rehn, Michael, German artist. In New Orleans, 1850, age 30.

Reisner/Reissner, Martin, landscape, panorama and scenery painter. Emig. to America ca. 1848. Had worked at the Imperial Theatre of St. Petersburg, Russia.

Remecke, Adolphe, German artist. In Philadelphia 1850, age 27.

Riffinburg, William, German artist. In Philadelphia in 1850, age 30.

Runge, John, artist from Bremen. In New York, 1860, age 39.

Schonberg, James, artist from Hanover. In Philadelphia in 1860, age 28.

Schwan, Philip, German artist; in New Orleans in 1850, age 26.

Schwebel, Lewis, Jr., portrait painter; native of Germany. In Cincinnati in 1850, age 17. Associated with his father Lewis Schwebel, also a portrait painter.

Schwode, Andrea, portrait painter. In New Orleans in 1860, age 35. Emig. from Bayern to New Orleans.

Sheets, John, Prussian-born artist, age 48 in Philadelphia, 1860.

Shepheart, Frederick, artist in Philadelphia in 1850, age 37. His wife and children were born in Germany.

Shrank, William, German artist. Inmate of the Philadelphia Alms House 1850, age 43.

Sietz, Lewis, artist from Württemberg. In New York 1860, age 33.

Artists of German Origin Listed *(cont.)*

Simon, August, artist. In New York in 1860, age 35. Place of birth "Wittenberg" or "Württemberg."

Singer, John, German artist. In New York in 1850, age 30.

Spangenberg, Ferdinand T., portrait painter; b. ca. 1820 in Prussia. In New York City in the 1850's and Richmond in 1859. By 1866 had returned to Germany.

Statfeld, Moritz, artist; native of Germany. In New York City 1860, age 30, as photographer.

Stein, A., landscape painter from Munich. After 1850 had a Philadelphia address.

Trung, F., German artist. In New York, 1850, age 23.

Vaerrick/Verrick, Prussian-born artist. In San Francisco in 1860, age 34.

Valentine, Julius, portrait painter in Baltimore in 1850, age 33. B. in Germany.

Vinckleback, William, German artist. In New York 1850, age 26.

Volkmar, Charles, portrait and landscape painter from Germany. B. ca. 1809. Came to Baltimore ca. 1842.

Vollmering, Joseph (1810–1887). Portrait and landscape painter. B. at Anhalt, Germany. Came to New York in 1847.

Wachter, Mileus, artist; b. in Sachsen. In New York in 1860, age 70.

Walther, Henry, Prussian-born fresco painter. In Washington in 1860, age 30.

Weiss, Rudolph, landscape painter. B. ca. 1826 in Hesse-Kassel. In Philadelphia from 1855.

Welcher, F., German-born artist in St. Louis in 1834. Assisted E. Robyn in painting of panorama.

Werner, Ernest, fresco painter from Sachsen. In Philadelphia in 1860, age 39.

Weyl, Max (1837–1914). Landscape painter; b. in Mühlen-on-Neckar. Came to America in 1853 and worked in Washington. See obit., *Art Annual*, vol. 11.

Whetting, John, German-born artist. In Cincinnati in 1850, age 38.

Wilder, Emil, German portrait painter. In Boston 1850, age 30.

Winter, T. or J., German-born portrait painter. In New Orleans 1850, age 29.

Zahner, Ralph, artist from Prussia. In New York City in 1850, age 25.

FC
Sculptors

Individual Sculptors

For information on abbreviated sources cited, see Section FB: German-American Painters.

BAERER, HENRY

FC1 [Obituary] *Art Annual*, vol. 8 (1908) p.397. Native of Kirchheim, Hesse-Kassel (1837–1908) Portrait sculptor who came to the U.S. in 1854. (Thieme-Becker; Groce-Wallace).

BERGER, HENRY

FC2 Gardner, *Yankee Stonecutters*. Sculptor in New York City, ca. 1858. Patented his designs for busts of Lincoln (1865) and von Humboldt (1867). (Groce-Wallace).

BITTER, KARL

FC3 Dennis, James Munn. *Karl Bitter, Architectural Sculptor, 1867–1915*. Madison: Univ. of Wisconsin Pr., 1967. 316p. Austrian-born sculptor (1867–1915) who came to America in 1889. Known for statues of Jefferson, Marshall, Hamilton, Sigel and Schurz.

FC4 *Proceedings at the Meeting in Memory of Karl Bitter Held at the Ethical Culture Hall on Wednesday, May 5, 1915.* New York: The Nation Press, 1915. 23p. Eulogies and addresses by various parties.

FC5 Villard, Oswald Garrison. "Karl Bitter, Sculptor." *Common Ground*, vol. 5, no. 3 (1945), 40–44.

FC6 Weinman, R. A., and L. I. Sharp. "Guide to Gotham's Statues." *Nat. Sculpture Rev.*, vol. 25, no. 2 (Summer 1976), 24–25. Illus. with two views of Bitter's "Abundance."

BUBERI (BUBERL), CASPAR

FC7 Groce-Wallace, p.93. B. (1834–1899), a native of Bohemia, Buberl was a sculptor who came to America in 1854.

ECKSTEIN, FREDERICK

FC8 Smith, Ophia D. "Fred Eckstein, the Father of Cincinnati Art." *Bull., Hist. and Philosophical Soc. of Ohio*, vol. 9 (Oct. 1951), 266–82. E. (ca. 1775–1852) was sculptor and drawing master; son of Johann Eckstein. Probably born in Berlin; came to America with his father in 1794. In Philadelphia was instrumental in founding the Pennsylvania Academy.

EHRICH, WILLIAM

FC9 "William Ehrich," *Amer.-German Rev.*, vol. 17, no. 4 (1951), 10. American sculptor, native of Königsberg, Prussia.

FLAESCHNER, JULIUS

FC10 Thieme-Becker, vol. 12, p.65. German sculptor of Berlin. Resided in New York City ca. 1854–1857.

GRAUEL, ANTON

FC11 Weiner, Egon. "Anton Grauel, the Sculptor." *Amer.-German Rev.*, vol. 20, no. 5 (1954), 19, 31. Native of Hesse (b. 1897); teacher at Beloit College from 1951.

GRESSEL, MICHAEL L.

FC12 "Michael L. Gressels Erfolge." *New York Staats-Zeitung und Herold*, vol. 145, no. 48 (1979), A 3. German-American sculptor and woodcarver. Exhibited in 1979.

HAHN, EMANUEL OTTO

FC13 L., A. "Emanuel Otto Hahn." *German-Canad. Rev.*, vol. 10, no. 1 (1957), 14. Obituary of German-born Canadian sculptor (1881–1957).

FC14 Weissenborn, Georg K. "Emanuel Otto Hahn: Teacher and Sculptor, 1881–1957." *German-Canad. Yearbook*, vol. 6 (1981), 241–44.

HITZBERGER, OTTO GEORG

FC15 Koenig, Karl F. "Otto Georg Hitzberger." *Amer. German Rev.*, vol. 19, no. 5 (1953), 24–26. Sculptor and woodcarver; in the U.S. since 1949.

KIRCHMAYER, JOHANNES

FC16 Tucci, Douglas Shand. "Johannes Kirchmayer. A Carver of Saints." In: *Germans in Boston*. Boston: Goethe Society of New England, 1981, p.30–36. Architectural woodcarver working in the Gothic Revival style; native of Oberammergau (b. 1860) who came to the U.S. in 1880.

KUNTZE, EDWARD J.

FC17 Groce-Wallace, p.378. Sculptor and etcher (1826–1870); native of Pomerania who came to America in 1852. Associate of the National Academy 1869–1870.

LANGENBAHN, AUGUST A.

FC18 [Obituary.] *Art Annual*, vol. 6 (1907), 111. German sculptor (1831–1907) who emigrated to Buffalo, N.Y., in 1852 (Groce-Wallace).

LAUNITZ, ROBERT EBERHARD SCHMIDT VON DER

FC19 Groce-Wallace, p. 386–87. von der L. (1806–1870), native of Riga; a sculptor who studied in Rome and emigrated to New York City in 1828. Assoc. of the National Academy. Known for his mantels and gravestones.

LAUTZ, WILLIAM

FC20 Groce-Wallace, p.387. L. (1838–1915), a native of Unstadt, Germany; sculptor and actor who came to America in 1854. Resided in Buffalo.

MELCHERS, JULIUS THEODORE

FC21 Groce-Wallace, p.438. M. (1830–1903), Woodcarver and sculptor; native of Soest, Westfalia, who emigrated after 1848. In later life a teacher of art in Detroit.

NEY, ELISABET

FC22 Barba, Preston A. "Elisabet Ney: The Singular Destiny of a German Woman." *Ameri.-German Rev.*, vol. 3, no. 2 (1936–1937), 16–21. Born in Münster in 1833, the daughter of a famous sculptor; emigrated to Texas in 1873.

FC23 Dielmann, Henry B. "Elisabeth Ney, Sculptor." *Southwestern Hist. Quar.*, vol. 65 (1961), 157–83.

FC24 Fortune, Jan (Isbelle), and Jean Burton. *Elisabet Ney.* New York: Knopf, 1943. 300p

FC25 Loggins, Vernon. *Two Romantics and Their Ideal Life.* New York: Odyssey Pr., 1947. Biography of Elisabet Ney.

FC26 Merrill, Peter C. "Texas Remembers Elisabet Ney." *Newsletter of the Soc. for German-Amer. Studies*, vol. 2, no. 5 (1980–1981), 11.

PETTRICH, FERDINAND

FC27 Fairman, *Art and Artists of the Capitol . . .*, p.76. P. (1798–1872), a German sculptor present in the U.S. from 1835 to 1845; native of Dresden. See also *Antiques*, August 1948; Thieme Becker, vol. 26, p.509.

FC28 Stehle, R. L. "Ferdinand Pettrich in America." *Pa. Hist.*, vol. 33 (1966), 389–411.

PLASSMAN, ERNST

FC29 Plassman, Ernst. *Modern Gothic Ornaments.* 1875. Sculptor and woodcarver (1823–1877), b. in Sondern, Westfalia. Emigrated to New York in 1853 and established an art school. See also his *Designs for Furniture* (1877). Groce-Wallace.

REUTHER, RICHARD GOTTLIEB

FC30 Reuther, Richard Gottlieb. Papers, 1848–1914. In the Archives of American Art, Detroit (MS 67-1128) Sculptor and designer (1859–1913) who lived in Detroit: correspondence business papers, journals, and letters in German exchanged among members of his family in the United States and Germany.

RINEHART, WILLIAM HENRY

FC31 Rusk, William S. *William Henry Rinehart, Sculptor.* Baltimore: n.p., 1939.

ROX, HENRY

FC32 Maass, Joachim. "The Work of the Sculptor—Henry Rox." *Amer.-German Rev.*, vol. 12, no. 3 (1946), 23–27.

SCHWEIZER, J. OTTO

FC33 "An Artist at Ninety." *Amer.-German Rev.*, vol. 19, no. 3 (1953), 20. Congratulatory tribute to J. Otto Schweizer, Swiss-born sculptor, in Philadelphia from 1894.

FC34 Jockers, Ernst. *J. Otto Schweizer. The Man and His Work.* Philadelphia, 1953. 164p. Rev. by G. Hanstein, *Amer.-German Rev.*, vol. 19, no. 5 (1953), 32–33.

FC35 Jockers, Ernst. "Tribute to J. Otto Schweizer." In *Yearbook, German Soc. of Pa.* Vol. 1 (1950). Philadelphia: The Society.

SIEMERING, RUDOLF

FC36 Essers, Volkmar. "Werke Berliner Bildhauer in Philadelphia: Das Washington-Denkmal von Rudolf Siemering." *Jahrbuch Preussischer Kulturbesitz*, vol. 10 (1972), 110–37.

STAUCH, ALFRED

FC37 Groce-Wallace, p.600. Philadelphia sculptor, native of Saxe-Coburg (b. ca. 1836). In the United States in 1860.

TAUCH, WALDINE

FC38 Hutson, Alice. *From Chalk to Bronze: A Biography of Waldine Tauch.* Austin, Tex.: Shoal Creek Pr., 1978. 172p. Rev. by G. E. Lich, *Jour. of German-Amer. Studies*, vol. 14, no. 3 (1979), 147–48.

UMLAUF, CHARLES

FC39 Goodall, Donald B. *Charles Umlauf, Sculptor.* Introd. by Gibson A. Danes. Austin: Univ. of Texas Pr., 1967. 124p.

VAN LOEN, ALFRED

FC40 "Alfred Van Loen." *Amer.-German Rev.*, vol. 26 (1960), no. 3, 28. German-born sculptor of New York City.

FD

Graphic Artists/Printmakers and Engravers

For information on abbreviated sources cited, see Section FB: German-American Artists.

General

FD1 Albers, Anni. *On Drawing.* Middletown: Wesleyan Univ. Pr., 1962. A. (b. 1899), a native of Berlin; studied at the Bauhaus; assitant professor of Art at Black Mountain College, 1937–1949; designer and graphic artist. *See also* her *On Weaving.* Middletown, 1965.

FD2 Benson, Evelyn. "Gilbert and Mason—Pennsylvania Wood Engravers." *The Pa. Dutchman*, vol. 7, no. 3 (1956), 8–13. 22 illus.

FD3 Chamberlain, Georgia S. "John Reich, Assistant Engraver to the United States Mint." *The Numismatist*, vol. 68 (March 1955), 242–49.

FD4 *Characteristic Work of Fritz Eichenberg, Whose Technique in the Art of Wood Engraving has Given Added Charm and Vitality to the Printed Page.* Camden: Haddon Craftsmen, n.d. 16p.

FD5 *Cincinnati Directories,* 1853–1860. Information on engraver and die sinker named Autenrieth. B. ca. 1832 in Germany; arrived in the U.S. in 1843 or later. Active in Cincinnati from 1850 to 1860.

FD6 Drepperd, Carl W. "New Delvings in Old Fields; Found: A New Early American Engraver [Gabriel Miesse.]" *Antiques*, vol. 42, no. 4 (October 1942), 204–05.

FD7 Ebert, John, and Katherine Ebert. *Old American Prints for Collectors.* New York: Scribner's, 1974.

FD8 Eichenberg, Fritz. *Art and Faith. Wood Engravings by the Author.* Wallingford, Pa.: Pendle Hill, 1952. 32p. E.b. in Cologne, 1901.

FD9 ["Frederic Girsch."] *Dictionary of Amer. Biography.* Engraver, etcher, and portrait artist. B. at Büdingen (Darmstadt); studied in Paris. Worked in New York since 1849.

FD10 Gottesman; *Arts and Crafts in New York,* vol. 1, p.13–14. On Joseph Simons, heraldic engraver on stone, steel, silver, and other metals. Advertised in New York, May 1763. Native of Berlin.

FD11 Hamilton; *Early American Book Illustrators and Wood Engravers,* p.71,440. On F. (or J. F.) Reiche, wood engraver in Philadelphia, 1794–1804. His cuts were used chiefly in German books of the Pennsylvania-Maryland area. Known also as "Frederick Richie (Reiche / Reicke / Francis Reiche)."

FD12 Hankammer, O. A., and F. C. Lampe. *The Art of Block Cutting....* Chicago: Lampe, 1930.

FD13 Heintzelman, Arthur W. "Woodcuts by Karl Friedrich Zähringer." *Boston Public Library Quar.,* vol. 8 (1956), 204–08. On the discovery of a collection of Z.'s woodcuts in Northfield, Mass.

FD14 Hofer, Philip. "Rudolph Ruzicka." *Procs., Mass. Hist. Soc.,* vol. 90 (1978), 143–45. R. (1883–1978) was a native of Bohemia; emigrated to Chicago in 1894. Graphic artist, designer, engraver, designer of types.

FD15 Hommel, Rudolf P. "Gabriel Miesse, Copyist." *Antiques*, vol. 43, no. 5 (May 1943), 325. Illus. of two *Haus-Segen.*

FD16 Kent, Alan E. "Early Commercial Lithography in Wisconsin," *Wis. Mag. of Hist.,* vol. 36 (1953), 247–51. On Henry Gugler, Sr. (1816–1880), banknote and portrait engraver, lithographer. Emigrated to the U.S. in 1853, worked in Washington and New York and founded a lithographic firm in Milwaukee.

FD17 Lambton, Gunda. "Contributions of German Graphic Artists in the History of Canadian Printmaking." *German-Canad. Yearbook*, vol. 4 (1978), 180–204.

FD18 Loubat, Joseph F. *Medallic History of the United States*, New York: n.p., 1878, pl. 70, 72–73, 75–76. Work of Anthony C. Paquet (1814–1882), engraver on wood, copper, and steel. Native of Hamburg; emigrated in 1848. Worked in Philadelphia and New York; was assistant engraver at the U.S. Mint. (Thieme-Becker).

FD19 Oda, Wilbur H. "Gabriel Miesse—Doctor and Engraver." *The Pa. Dutchman*, vol. 3, no. 2 (1 November 1951), 1.

FD20 Prime, vol. 2, p.69. On John David Hechstetter, engraver on wood, stone, and ivory. Came to America from Germany in 1796; worked in Philadelphia.

FD21 *Prints from the Drawings Appearing in "The Catholic Worker."* New York: Thistle Pr., 1955. Drawings by Fritz Eichenberg.

FD22 Purnell, M. A. "Fritz Eichenberg." *Amer.-German Rev.*, vol. 16, no. 3 (1950), 7–12, 26.

FD23 Stauffer, David McN. *American Engravers upon Copper and Steel.* New York, 1907.

Engravers of German Origin Listed in the Censuses of 1850 and 1860

FD24 United States. Bureau of the Census. *Seventh Census of the United States* (1850). Washington, D.C., 1854. *Eighth Census of the United States* (1860). Washington, D.C., 1864. (Cited in Groce-Wallace.) Provides the following information on laborers who listed themselves as engravers:

Ahrens, Hermann, in New York City, 1850, age 28. Also spelled "Ahrenz."
Edward Bauchman. Switzerland native. In New York City, 1860, age 53.
Baumgarten, Julius. b. ca. 1835 in Germany; emig. to Washington in 1860.
Bechler, Christian, present in Philadelphia in July 1860, with William Bracher. B., ca. 1828, in Saxony.
Beyer, Frederick. German engraver, in New York in 1850, age 30.
Bloome, Robert. German engraver. In New York in 1850, age 29.
Bloss, Michael. Wood engraver from Bavaria, in New York in 1860, age 31.
Boesser H., wood engraver, b. in Germany ca. 1820. In Louisville, 1850.
Bollet, Charles, Swiss. In Philadelphia, 1860, age 40.
Bracher, William, engraver and lithographer, native of Württemberg. B. ca. 1828; emig. to America ca. 1857.
Brotze, Rudolph, German engraver, b. ca. 1820. In Philadelphia 1850.
Busse, Herman, wood engraver. In New York, 1860, age 25.
Christiana, Joseph, Switzerland native. In New York in 1850, age 29.
Comgmacker (sic), August, b. ca. 1825 in Germany. In Philadelphia 1850.
Conrad, Augustus, b. Brunswick, ca. 1842. In Philadelphia in 1860.
Doll, Charles W., from Württemberg. In New York in 1860, age 38.
Doll, Frederick W., in New York in 1850, age 25.
Dreka, Louis, steel engraver. B. in Pennsylvania, ca. 1839; son of a German piano-maker.
Dutzer, Frederick. In New York City in 1860, age 32.
Eck, William, engraver and die sinker. Came to New York in 1856. Born in Prussia ca. 1824.
Eichberg, Solomon. In New York City in 1850, age 45.
Ernst, Thomas J., wood engraver and designer. Born in Ohio of German parents. Worked in Cincinnati 1850–1857.
Falker, Fletiss(?), native of Germany; in New Orleans in 1850, age 20.
Fassilat, Henry. Swiss engraver; in Philadelphia in 1850, age 26.
Fest, Adam, age 15. In Philadelphia 1850.
Fey, Charles, age 19. In Cleveland in 1850.
Gaul, Frederick. In Philadelphia in 1850, age 19.
Gebhard, Louis, b. ca. 1826 in Hanover; in Philadelphia 1860.
Geiershofer, Maurice (Moritz). In Philadelphia in 1850, age 32. Listed as button manufacturer, 1859–1872. Also "Gairshofer."
Ginenback, John V., at Philadelphia in 1850, age 18.
Goll, Frederick P., Jr. Engraver, die sinker and daguerreotype case maker; in New York, 1840–1860.

Gratz, John, Bavarian born. In Philadelphia in 1860, age 22.

Haplacher (also Hasslacher), George I. In New York, 1850, age 32.

Hassen, Wilhelm. In New York in 1860, age 36; came to New York ca. 1854.

Hausman, E. C. Prussian-born. In New York in 1860, age 25.

Hentzelmann, A. In New York, 1860, age 23.

Huffman, Frederick W., from Hesse-Kassel. In New York, 1860, age 33.

Ibelshauser, John. Wood engraver from Hesse. In New York in 1860, age 26.

Jacobs, Hiram, Swiss engineer. In New York, 1860, age 45.

Keinley, Augustus. At Philadelphia, 1850, age 25.

Kesler (Kessler), Frederick, of Saxony. In Philadelphia, 1860, age 30.

Kiesling, Charles. Bavarian-born; in New York, 1860, age 45.

Klumpp, William, b. ca. 1828 in Württemberg. In San Francisco 1852–1860.

Kollmer, Huber, in Cincinnati 1850, age 22.

Korn, Joseph, in New York 1860, age 30. With German-born wife and two children.

Kreel, John, from Hesse. In Philadelphia 1860, age 36.

Küner, Albert (1819–1906), engraver and die sinker. A George Ferdinand Albert Küner, b. 1819 in Lindau, Bavaria, emig. to California in 1848. (Thieme-Becker).

Leichtweis, Louis. B. in Germany ca. 1824. In New York City 1850–60.

Leiser, Christian, engraver from Württemberg. In Philadelphia 1860, age 30.

Lutz, Conrad, wood engraver; from Hesse-Darmstadt. In New York City in 1860, age 24.

Mahl, Max. In New York City in 1850, age 22.

Margraff, Francis, in New York City in 1850, age 32.

Matel, Adolph. In Washington in 1860, age 53.

Menker, Samuel, born ca. 1820; lived in New York from about 1853.

Miller, Hammond, from Baden. In Philadelphia in 1860, with Prussian wife. Was age 33 in 1860.

Miller, Thomas, Jr. Native of Germany; was in Philadelphia in 1850 with father. Age 30 in 1850.

Mitzscherling (sic), Gustave, from Württemberg; b. *ca*. 1823. In San Francisco from 1856.

Nessig, Peter, b. in Hanover; in New York in 1860, age 44.

Numyer (sic), Frederick; in Baltimore in 1850 age 32.

Rau, Jacob, b. in Holstein ca. 1821. In New York from ca. 1851.

Riekarts (sic), Frederick; in Philadelphia in 1850, age 19.

Rolle, Albert, Prussian-born. In Washington in 1860, age 44.

Rosse, Christ; in Philadelphia in 1860, age 21.

Rost, Christian. In 1860 employed by the American Bank Note Company. German native; studied in Paris and London.

Rudiger, August E., engraver and die sinker; b. in Germany ca. 1818. In New York in 1850.

Sachse (*also* "Sase"), August. In Baltimore in 1860, age 50. With wife and son born in Germany.

Scandberger, August; in Philadelphia 1860, age 19.

Scheron, William; in Philadelphia in 1850, age 23.

Schmidt, Solomon, b. in Baden ca. 1806; emig. to New Orleans ca. 1840. Also known as "Henry Schmidt."

Scholl, Gustave, of Hamburg. In New York 1860, age 41.

Schultz, Frederick; in New York 1860, age 37.

Sebald, Hobarth; in Philadelphia 1860, age 34.

Seitz, John; in Philadelphia 1850, age 42.

Serz, John, b. in Bavaria, 1810; emig. to America ca. 1848. Lived in New York and Philadelphia.

Shoemaker, Andrew; Bavarian. In Philadelphia in 1860, age 32.

Siebert, Selmar (1808–?); copper engraver born at Lehnin, Prussia. Emig. between 1840 and 1843. Lived in Washington.

Steffan, Eugene, from Switzerland. In New York in 1860, age 21.

Stern, Gerson, Bavarian. In New York 1860, age 36.

Stifft, M. B. in Poland; in New Orleans in 1860, age 38; with wife Bertha from Prussia.

Stiner, Louis. Inmate of the New York City penitentiary in July 1860 (for petit larceny). Age 36.

Stote, Theodore. In New York in 1860, age 54. With wife and three children born in Germany.

Thomas, George; b. in Germany 1815. In New Orleans 1844, in Philadelphia 1844–1850. Worked as wood engraver and managed a lithographic firm.

Truist, Sigmund. In Philadelphia 1850, age 28.

Weaver, Lewis. In Philadelphia with German-born wife in 1860, age 30.

West, Frederick; in Washington 1860, with wife from Pennsylvania; age 35 in 1860.

Wider, Charles, b. in Prussia. In New York City 1860, age 32.

Wilhelm, August. Wood engraver from Hesse, in Philadelphia in 1860, age 23.

Engravers of German Origin *(cont.)*

Wirth, Colvert, and Robert Wirth. Prussian-born engravers in New York City 1860.

Wissler, Jacques (James) (1803–1887). Engraver, lithographer and portrait painter; native of Strasbourg; emigrated in 1849.

Wurms, Gottlieb, from Württemberg. In Philadelphia 1860, age 34. With German-born wife.

Young, J.H.A., native of Prussia. In Washington 1860, age 30.

FE
Lithographers

General

FE1 Eckhardt, George H. "Early Lithography in Philadelphia." *Antiques*, vol. 28 (December 1935), 249–52.

FE2 Halbmeier, Carl. *Senefelder: The History of Lithography*. New York: Senefelder Publ., 1926. 216p.

FE3 Krummel, D.W. "The 'Schinderhannes Variations.' ca. 1805: The First Lithographs Published in the United States." *Papers of the Bibliographic Soc. of America*, vol. 67 (1973), 306–309. Finds stylistic grounds for stating that the lithographed sheet of piano music dated ca. 1805 was produced in Europe and sold in America by Philip B. Sadtler of Baltimore.

FE4 Marzio, Peter Cort. "The Art Crusade; A Study of American Drawing Books and Lithographs 1830–1860." Diss., Univ. of Chicago, 1969. 242p.

FE5 Marzio, Peter C. *The Democratic Art: An Exhibit on the History of Chromolithography in America, 1840–1900*. Fort Worth: Amon Carter Museum of Western Art, 1979. 112p. Catalogue.

FE6 Marzio, Peter C. *The Democratic Art; Pictures for a 19th-Century America: Chromolithography, 1840–1900*. Boston: D.R. Godine; Fort Worth: Amon Carter Museum of Western Art, 1979. 357p.

FE7 Senefelder, Alois. *A Complete Course of Lithography*. Introd. by A. Hyatt Mayor. New York: n.p., 1977. 370p. 31 pl. A facsimile of the first English ed. of S.'s own account of the development of the lithographic process; a technical manual.

FE8 Wainwright, Nicholas B. *Philadelphia in the Romantic Age of Lithography, An Illustrated History of Early Lithography in Philadelphia... Lithographers before 1866*. Philadelphia: n.p., 1958.

FE9 Wiesendanger, Martin W. "Lithographic Lives." *Amer.-German Rev.*, vol. 9, no. 4 (1943), 4–6; vol. 9, no. 5 (1943), 7–10. On German lithographers in the United States.

Individual Lithographers

For information on abbreviated sources cited, see Section FB: German-American Painters.

ACKERMAN, EMIL

FE10 Peters; *America on Stone*. A. was native of Dresden; came to the U.S. with his father in 1848.

CAMP, JOHN HENRY

FE11 Peters, *America on Stone*. C. (1822–1881), lithographer. Native of Prussia; emigrated to Philadelphia before the 1840's.

DRESEL (DRESSEL), EMIL

FE12 Peters, *California on Stone*. Lithographer. In San Francisco 1953–1959. Partner in Kuchel and Dresel.

DUBOIS, GEORGE

FE13 Peters, *America on Stone*. Lithographer, native of Germany; son of Albert DuBois. Came to Philadelphia in 1850.

FENDERICH, CHARLES

FE14 Miller, Lillian B., ed. *Charles Fenderich: Lithographer of American Statesmen*. Introd. by Alice Lee Parker and Milton Kaplan. Chicago: Univ. of Chicago Pr., 1977. 78p. text; three black-and-white microfiches embracing 229 photographs. Portrait painter and lithographer; b. 1866 in Switzerland. Worked in Philadelphia and Washington, D.C. and San Francisco. Well known for his portraits of political figures. After emigrating to the U.S. in 1838 he worked in Philadelphia with John Caspar Wild. (Peters, *America on Stone*.)

FINKELDEY, JOHN FREDERICK

FE15 Peters, *America on Stone*. Lithographer. Native of Hesse; active in Philadelphia 1850–1860.

HARNISCH, CARL (1800–1883)

FE16 Thieme-Becker, vol. 16, p.47–48. H. (1800–1883), lithographer, painter of literary and genre pieces. Native of Altenburg who came to Philadelphia before 1843. Known for his paintings of scenes from Shakespeare and Goethe. Genre sculptures.

HOEN, AUGUST

FE17 Peters, *America on Stone*. Lithographer. A native of Germany (b. ca. 1825); came to the U.S. as a youth. Worked in Baltimore with his brothers Ernest and Henry Hoen.

KETTERLINUS, PAUL, EUGENE, AND LOUIS

FE18 Landenberger, J. Louis. "Ketterlinus, Lithographer." *Amer.-German Rev.*, vol. 14, no. 4 (1948), 26–28.

KLAUPRECHT & MENZEL

FE19 Peters, *America on Stone*. Lithographers of Cincinnati, 1840–1859. Senior partner in the firm Emil Klauprecht was editor of the *Cincinnati German Republican*. Adolphus Menzel was chief lithographer.

KNIRSCH, OTTO

FE20 Peters, *America on Stone*. Lithographer. Resided ca. 1853 in Hoboken, working for Currier & Ives of New York. Said to have been a native of Germany.

KRAMER, PETER (KRAEMER)

FE21 Peters, *America on Stone*. K. (1823–1907), painter and lithographer; native of Zweibrücken, Germany. Came to the United States in 1848. Employed by P. S. Duval in Philadelphia. (Thieme-Becker).

KUCHEL, CHARLES CONRAD

FE22 Peters, *America on Stone*. Native (b. 1820) of Zweibrücken, Switzerland. In 1846 at Philadelphia, employed by P. S. Duval. Later moved to San Francisco. *See also* Peters, *California on Stone*.

KURZ, LOUIS

FE23 *Battles of the Civil War: The Complete Kurz and Allison Prints, 1861–1865*. Birmingham: Oxmoor, 1976. 95p. K. (1833–1921), lithographer, mural and scene painter. A native of Austria and Forty-Eighter, he settled in Chicago in 1852. Founder of the Lithographic Co. (1863–1871) and the American Oleograph Co., Milwaukee, in the 1870's. (Peters, *America on Stone*; Thieme-Becker).

FE24 Kent, Alan E. "Early Commercial Lithography in Wisconsin." *Wis. Mag. of Hist.*, vol. 36 (1933), 249–50.

LEONHARDT, THEODORE

FE25 Peters, *America on Stone*. L. (1818–1877), lithographer and engraver. Born in Bautzen, Saxony; came to New York in 1849.

MAURER, LOUIS

FE26 Peters, *Currier & Ives*. M. (1832–1932), lithographer and printer. From Biebrich-on-the-Rhine. Emigrated in 1851 with parents. Employed by Currier and Ives for eight years.

MORAS, FERDINAND

FE27 Peters, *America on Stone*. M. (1821–1908), lithographer from Rhenish Prussia; came to Philadelphia in 1853 and conducted a lithographic business there to the 1890's.

NAGEL, LOUIS

FE28 Peters, *America on Stone*. N. (ca. 1817–ca. 1872), lithographer. Born in Germany; in New York City in 1844. Nagel was partner in business of Adam Weingaertner (Weingartner), active in San

Individual Lithographers *(cont.)*

Francisco in the 1850's. Was employed to assist in the preparation of Audubon's *Quadrupeds*.

PRANG, LOUIS

FE29 Breen, Robert V. "Merry Christmas, Happy New Year!" *Amer.-German Rev.*, vol. 20, no. 2 (1953), 22–23. Exhibit of old Christmas cards, dating mainly from 1870–1900, incl. those of the most popular designer, Breslau-born Louis Prang (1824–1909). P. was a lithographer, maker of chromolithographs and wood engraver. Son of a calico printer. Fled with the Forty-Eighters to Bohemia, thence to Switzerland and finally New York City in 1850, but settled in Boston. Self-taught lithographer; set up in business with Julius Mayer. In the 1870's the firm introduced the Christmas card and began to issue color reproductions of famous paintings, drawing books, toy prints for children, and the like. Rushford, "Lewis Prang"; Peters: *America on Stone; Dictionary of Amer. Biography*, vol. 15, 165–66).

FE30 Brooks, Ken. "The Twenty Year Madness. German Picture Postcards." *Rundschau* (NCSF), vol. 4, no. 9 December 1974, 2–3. On the flood of cards "Printed in Germany" in the early years of the 20th century; ubiquity and popularity in America.

FE31 Buday, György. *History of the Christmas Card*. Rockliff (London), n.p., 1954.

FE32 Chase, Ernest Dudley. *The Romance of the Greeting Card*. Cambridge, Mass.: n.p., 1956.

FE33 Cheney, Lynne. "You Can Thank Louis Prang for All Those Cards." *Smithsonian*, vol. 8, no. 9 (December 1977), 120–25.

FE34 Freeman, Larry. *Louis Prang: Color Lithographer. Giant of a Man*. Watkins Glen, N.Y.: n.p., 1971. 150 illus. Description of the printing process and catalog of prints.

FE35 McClinton, Katharine Morrison. *The Chromolithographs of Louis Prang*. New York: Clarkson N. Potter, 1973. 246p.

ROBYN, EDWARD

FE36 *Mo. Hist. Soc. Bull.*, vol. 3 (October 1946), 27; *ibid.*, vol. 4 (January 1948), 103; vol. 6 (October 1949), 102; vol. 7 (April 1951), 382–83. Lithographer, engraver, portrait and landscape painter (1820–1862). Native of Emmerich, Prussia. Was in Philadelphia as lithographer in 1848–1850; went to St. Louis, 1850. Resided on a farm near Hermann, Mo. from 1856.

ROSENTHAL, L. N.

FE37 Webber, C. W. *Wild Scenes and Song-Birds*. New York: Riker, Thorne & Co., 1855. 347p. Chromolithographs for this book prepared by R. Said to be "the first chromolithographs of consequence to be utilized as book illustrations. Earlier used in Webber's *The Hunter Naturalist* (1852).

SACHSE, EDWARD

FE38 Pleasants, *Two Hundred and Fifty Years of Painting*.... Lithographer and painter (1804–1873). Born in Görlitz; emig. to America in the late 1840's with his family. *See also* Peters, *America on Stone*.

SACHSE, THEODORE

FE39 Pleasants, *Two Hundred and Fifty Years of Painting in Maryland*. S. (b. 1815), lithographer. Came to America after 1847. Worked in Baltimore with his brother Edward S.

SEIFERT, HENRY

FE40 Kent, Alan E. "Early Commercial Lithography in Wisconsin." *Wis. Mag. of Hist.*, vol. 36 (1953), 247–51. Lithographer (1824–1911). Emigrated from Saxony to Milwaukee in 1852.

THURWANGER, MARTIN

FE41 Lithographer (ca. 1850–1890). Native of Mulhausen, Alsace. Brought to America by the Smithsonian Institution to carry out a commission of 18 months. Returned to Paris.

WEBER, EDWARD

FE42 Peters, *America on Stone*. Lithographer. Probably a native of Germany. Worked in Baltimore ca. 1835–1851. The brothers Hoen were his nephews.

WICHT, JOHN VON

FE43 Moschzisker, Bertha von. "Order is the First Law: John von Wicht." *Amer.-German Rev.*, vol. 20, no. 3 (1954), 15–17. German-born lithographer; in the United States since 1934.

WOLF, GUSTAV

FE44 *Germans in Boston*. Boston: German Society of New England, 1981, p.36–43. Woodcut artist, lithographer, etcher, maker of drawings and watercolors (b. 1887). B. at Oestringen, near Karlsruhe; emigrated in 1933 and came to New York in 1937. Later resided in Cummington, Mass. His papers and literary remains are deposited in the Boston Public Library.

Lithographers of German Origin Listed in the Censuses of 1850 and 1860

FE45 United States. Bureau of the Census. *Seventh Census of the United States* (1850). Washington, D.C., 1854. *Eighth Census of the United States* (1860). Washington, D.C., 1864. (Cited in Groce-Wallace.) Provides the following information on laborers who listed themselves as lithographers:

Adelung, Ernst; native of Württemberg, b. ca. 1824. In Philadelphia in 1860.

Alschuch, Martin, b. ca. 1832. In Philadelphia in 1860.

Amey, Henry, b. 1831 in Baden. In Baltimore in 1860.

Berendsohn, Sigmond; b. Hamburg ca. 1831. In America before 1859.

Blicker, George, b. ca. 1833 in Hannover. Came to Philadelphia before 1855.

Boehler, John E., b. ca. 1811 in Baden. In New Orleans 1841–1870.

Bohurd (Bohhurd), G. A., b. Baden, ca. 1810. Emig. between 1840 and 1844. In New Orleans, ca. 1844–46.

Brian, Julius, German-born lithographer. In New York in 1860, age 34.

Bromstead, Henry, b. ca. 1806. In Washington in 1850.

Bruder, Charles, b. ca. 1811 in Baden. Louisville 1848–1852.

Buckman, Henry and John, aged 27 and 26; New York 1850.

Dietz, August, Prussian-born. New York City 1860, age 24.

"Douritch" (possibly Danrith or Denrith), Francis. B. ca. 1825 in Germany. In Pittsburgh in 1850.

Dreser, William, b. 1820 in Germany. In Philadelphia 1847–1860.

Eckhart, Francis, German-born lithographer. New York 1850, age 30.

Ehret, Adolph. In New York City in 1860, age 29.

Ehrgott, Peter. In Cincinnati in 1850, age 24.

Eiseman, Paul. In New York City in 1850, age 31.

Engleken, Jacob. In Philadelphia in 1850, age 46.

Ernest/Ernst, Julius, b. Darmstadt 1831. In New York City 1854–60.

Fabronius, Christian, b. ca. 1804 in Germany. In New York in 1850 and in Cincinnati 1858 to 1873.

Falk, Frederick. B. in Bavaria. In Philadelphia 1860, age 29.

Fischer, John G. Native of Baden. In Philadelphia 1860, age 29.

Fleischman, E., b. in Saxony. In New York 1860, age 24.

Flicon, Henry, b. in Baden. In New Orleans 1860, age 18.

Frederick, Charles. In New York in 1850, age 32.

Freudenberg, E. G. In New York in 1860, age 27.

Fromme, Frederick W. In Baltimore in 1850 and 1858. Age 36 in 1850.

Goble, Conrad, b. in Hesse. In New York 1860, age 32.

Goldbacker, Barbara; native of Baden, b. ca. 1826. In Philadelphia 1860.

Goldbacker, Isaac; native of Baden, b. ca. 1834. In Philadelphia 1860.

Gotbut, Edward. Prussian-born lithographer. In New York City 1850, age 37.

Graff,—. German native. In New York City 1860, age 28.

Grambay, E. German native. In New York 1860, age 35.

Gunter, Frederick, b. in Bremen. Came to America ca. 1832. In Louisville 1850, age 49. Also known as "Daniel Ganter."

Halder, Rudolph, b. in Switzerland. In Charity Hospital, New Orleans, December 1850, age 52.

Hanly, George, German-born lithographer. In Pittsburgh in 1850, age 28.

Hartman, Martin. German lithographer. In Baltimore, res. with August Hoen, 1850, age 19.

Heit, Benjamin, b. in Frankfurt. In New York 1860, age 33.

Herlin, August, b. in Württemberg. In Philadelphia 1860, age 22.

Herline (or Herrlein/Harline). In Philadelphia 1850, age 24.

Herr, George, from Hesse-Kassel. In Philadelphia 1860, age 17.

Herrlein, Gustave. In Cincinnati 1850, age 23.

Hermandt, Ph., b. in Darmstadt. In New Orleans 1860, age 35. It is possible that the name Philip Amendt was confused with Hermandt.

Hessels, Louis, b. in Prussia. New York 1860, age 48.

Hohl, August, German native. In Philadelphia 1860, age 16. Later became a pharmacist and salesman.

Johnson, William, German native. In New York 1850, age 40.

Kalber, Edward. In New York City 1860, age 50.

Lithographers of German Origin (cont.)

Kann, Alexander and Moritz Kann, b. in Prussia, ca. 1826, 1828. In New York City 1860.

Kayflick, Henry. Prussian-born lithographer. In New York City 1860, age 22.

Kealy, Minrath, b. in Switzerland. In New York 1860, age 43.

Kemb, Charles. In New York 1850, age 25.

Kimmel, Christopher, engraver, lithographer and painter. B. in Germany in 1830. In New York 1850–1876.

Kling, Philip, age 25. In Louisville in 1850.

Konger, Henry. In New York City 1850, age 22.

Kraft, Lewis. In Philadelphia 1850, age 39. Came to America between 1845 and 1849.

Kramm, Gustavus. In Philadelphia 1843–1854. Age 42 in 1850. Also known as Gustavus Krim.

Lang, Charles, b. in Bavaria. New York 1860, age 28.

Leitz, Louis, from Hannover. In Philadelphia 1860, age 36.

Lenhard, Augustus. In New York 1860, age 21.

Leonard, Anton, Prussian-born. In New York 1860, age 38.

Lewinhoff, Theodore. In Philadelphia 1850, age 32.

Limburg, Francis, Prussian-born. In New York 1860, age 40.

Liper, John. In New York 1850, age 19.

Loghuer, Henry, b. in Switzerland. New York 1850, age 36.

Lorio, Peter, b. in Austria. Philadelphia 1860, age 40.

Ludwig, William, b. in Brunswick. In Philadelphia in 1860, age 26.

Lutz, Jacob, b. in Germany, ca. 1831. In New York City in 1850, age 19. See Peters: *America on Stone*.

Martin, Ferdinand. In Baltimore 1860, age 23.

Mayer (or Meyer), Ferdinand. In New York 1845–1877. B. in Germany ca. 1817.

Meckel, Max. In New York 1850, age 34.

Menzel, Charles. B. ca. 1822 in Germany. In Cincinnati 1842–1850.

Merkle, Augustus. In New York City 1850, age 22.

Meyer, Gottlieb, b. in Württemberg. In Philadelphia 1860, age 24.

Miller, Charles F., b. in Baden. In Philadelphia 1860 age 18.

Miller, Edward. Prussian-born. In Philadelphia 1860, age 29.

Miller, George. In Baltimore 1860, age 25.

Muchlen, Thomas. In Philadelphia 1850, age 35.

Myer, Felix. In New York City Lunatic Asylum, 1850, age 27.

Myer, Henry, b. in Württemberg. In New York 1860, age 27.

Nott, Charles. B. in Bavaria. In New York 1860, age 31.

Onken, Otto. B. in Germany ca. 1815. In Cincinnati 1848–1860.

Power, John, Prussian-born. In Baltimore 1860, age 30.

Probst, John, b. ca. 1805 in Germany. In New York ca. 1838–1850.

Raab, Francis, b. 1813. In New York City, 1848–1854.

Reitman, Joseph. Native of Bavaria. In Philadelphia 1860, age 30.

Rickner, Louis. In Pittsburgh 1850, age 24.

Ruen ("Reen"), Charles. Swiss-born. In Philadelphia 1860, age 37.

Sachs, Frederick. In Philadelphia in 1850, age 33. Sachs, his wife, and three children were b. in Germany.

Schieffer, Paul. In New York 1850, age 30.

Schmidt, Frederick. In New York 1856–60 and after. He and his wife had come from Saxony.

Schmitt, Julius. In Baltimore 1850, age 29.

Schnabel, Edward. In Philadelphia 1850, age 31. Listed in Peters: *America on Stone*.

Schuckman, George, and William Schuckman. In Pittsburgh 1850, age 14 and 26.

Seybold, Henry, of Frankfurt. In New York 1860, age 28.

Shoemaker, Gottlieb. In Philadelphia 1850, age 30.

Shrader, Alfred, b. in Darmstadt. In Philadelphia 1860, age 37.

Shultz, Charles, b. in Württemberg. Lived in Philadelphia in 1860 with parents. Age 19.

Simon, Dennis or Dionis, b. in Baden. New Orleans 1857–70. Born ca. 1830.

Smith, E. P. In New York 1860, age 38.

Snyder, George. In New York 1850, age 48.

Stacker, Antoine. In Boston 1850, age 36.

Steel or Steels, John. In New York 1850–60, B. in Germany ca. 1825.

Steinegger, Henry. B. in Switzerland, ca. 1831. In San Francisco 1859–1880. See Peters: *California on Stone*.

Stevens, William, b. in Hamburg. In New York 1860, age 28.

Stewel, or Steivel, Gustav. In Baltimore 1850, age 18.

Stiebel, Augustus. In Baltimore 1860, age 28.

Stocker, Frank Anthony, b. ca. 1812. In Boston ca. 1846–1860. S. and his wife were natives of Prussia.

Stoper, Frank, b. in Austria. In Philadelphia 1860, age 40. S.'s wife and three children were b. in Austria before 1853.

Trapp, August. In New York 1860, age 20.

Traubel, M (orris or Martin) H. (1820–1897). Native of Frankfurt; trained in Germany. Emig. to Philadelphia ca. 1850. See Peters: *America on Stone.*

Wagner, Philip, b. ca. 1811. In New York, ca. 1843–49. In Boston 1850–1853.

Wagner, Rudolph. Prussian-born. In Philadelphia 1860, age 24.

Wagoner, Charles. In Pittsburgh 1850, age 26. Assoc. with the firm of Wegner & Buechner.

Wartz, Michael, b. in Darmstadt. In Philadelphia 1860, age 30.

Weil, Alexander, b. in Baden ca. 1818. In New York City from ca. 1854.

Werner, Otto, b. Prussia. In Baltimore with his wife Dora, a native of Hannover, in 1860. W. was age 27 in 1860.

Wild, Alexander. In New York City in 1860, age 46.

FF

Architecture and Architects

General

FF1 Brumbaugh, G. Edwin. "Continental Influence on Early American Architecture." *Amer.-German Rev.*, vol. 9, no. 3 (February 1943), 7–9, 37.

FF2 Burchard, J., and A. Bush-Brown. *The Architecture of America.* Boston: n.p., 1961. European (German and Austrian) backgrounds of American building.

FF3 "Chicago: Metropole der Architecktur." *Der Milwaukee Herold*, 13 September 1973. On German architects in Chicago.

FF4 Darnall, Margaretta J. "From the Chicago Fair to Walter Gropius: Changing Ideals in American Architecture." Diss., Cornell Univ., 1975.

FF5 Eaton, Leonard K. *American Architecture Comes of Age: European Reaction to H. H. Richardson and Louis Sullivan.* Cambridge: M.I.T. Pr., 1972. 256p. The Germans were "surprisingly well aware of American developments...."

FF6 Ebe, C. M. *Canadian Architecture 1960/70.* Toronto: Burns & MacEachern, 1971.

FF7 Hertz, Richard. "American Churches and the Principle of Originality (in Architecture)." *Amer.-German Rev.*, vol. 10, no. 1 (October 1943), 4–7.

FF8 Heuck, Theodor Christopher. Papers, 1850–1874. Ca. 600 items. In the Hawaii Public Archives (MS 70-540). Letters (in German), journals, plans, clippings, etc.

FF9 Jordy, William H. "The Aftermath of the Bauhaus in America: Gropius, Mies, and Breuer." In: *The Intellectual Migration; Europe and America 1830–60.* Ed. Donald Fleming and Bernard Bailyn. Cambridge: Harvard Univ. Pr., 1969, p.485–544.

FF10 Junker, Wolfgang. "Kunstler und Architeckt in vollendeter Zusammenarbeit." *Manitoba-Courier* (Winnipeg), 2 June 1966. On Toni Bisig, Swiss sculptor, and J. M. Schmidt, architect, as they collaborate in church design.

FF11 Kuhn, Charles L. "America and the Bauhaus." *Amer.-German Rev.*, vol. 15, no. 2 (1948), 16–22.

FF12 Pommer, Richard. "The Architecture of Urban Housing in the United States during the Early 1930's." *Jour. of the Soc. of Architectural Historians*, vol. 37 (1978), 235–64. The work of German architects Alfred Kastner (1900–1975) and Oskar Stonorov (1905–1970).

FF13 Roger, Dieter. "From Pioneer Building to 'Bauhaus' and Beyond." *German-Canad. Yearbook*, vol. 4 (1978), 135–67. Inquiry into the historical trends and conditions of pioneer building in Canada.

FF14 Rose, Harold Wickliffe. *The Colonial Houses of Worship in America.* New York: Hastings House,

General *(cont.)*

1963. 589p. Rev. by F. B. Tolles, *Quaker Hist.*, vol. 53, no. 2 (1964), 115–16. Histories and photographs of Colonial churches that have survived.

FF15 Swendon, Alfred, and Pao-Chi Chang. *Architectural Education at IIT (Illinois Institute of Technology) 1938–1978.* Chicago: n.p., 1980. 200p. Pioneering influence of instructors Ludwig Mies van der Rohe, Ludwig Hilberseimer, and Walter Peterhans.

Individual Architects

BREUER, MARCEL

FF16 Breuer, Marcel. Papers, 1934–1953. 30 ft. In the Syracuse University Library (MS 68-1714). Correspondence, documents, miscellaneous papers.

CLUSS, ADOLPH

FF17 Beauchamp, Tanya Edwards. "Adolph Cluss: An Architect in Washington during the Civil War and Reconstruction." *Records of the Columbia Hist. Soc. of Washington, D.C., 1971–72*, vol. 48 (1973), 338–58.

GRAFF, FREDERICK

FF18 Graff, Frederick. Architectural and technical drawings. 50 items dated ca. 1825. In the Franklin Institute Library, Philadelphia (MS 64-1373). G. (1774–1847) was an engineer of Philadelphia.

GROPIUS, WALTER

FF19 Giedion, S. *Walter Gropius, Work and Teamwork.* New York: Reinhold, 1954. 249p.

FF20 Gropius, Ilse, and William B. O'Neal. "A Supplement to the Bibliography of Walter Gropius." *Amer. Assoc. of Architectural Bibliographers, Papers*, vol. 9 (1972).

FF21 Gropius, Walter A. G. *New Architecture and the Bauhaus.* Trans. by P. Morton Shand. London: Faber & Faber, 1955. 112p.

FF22 Harding, Anneliese. "Walter Gropius." In: *Germans in Boston.* Boston: Goethe Society of New England, 1981, p.44–46.

FF23 O'Neal, William B., ed. *The American Association of Architectural Bibliographers Papers*, vol. 3 (1966). Charlottesville: Univ. of Virginia Pr., 1966. 113p. Bibliography of writings by and about Gropius.

GRUEN, VICTOR

FF24 Guzzardi, Walter, Jr. "Victor Gruen." *Fortune Mag.*, January, 1962, 77f. Los Angeles architectural firm founded by the Austrian-born Victor Gruen, well known for his construction of stores and shopping centers.

HEIMAN, ADOLPHUS

FF25 Frank, John G. "Adolphus Heiman: Architect and Soldier." *Tenn. Hist. Quar.*, vol. 5 (1946), 35–57. Leading Nashville architect, b. 1809 in Potsdam, Prussia; encouraged by Humboldt to emigrate to America. Served as colonel in the Confederate forces.

FF26 Parrent, H. Clinton. "Adolphus Heiman and the Building Methods of Two Centuries." *Tenn. Hist. Quar.*, vol. 12, no. 3 (1953), 204–12.

FF27 Patrick, James. "The Architecture of Adolphus Heiman." *Tenn. Hist. Quar.*, vol. 38 (1979), 167–87, 277–95.

HINCKELDEYN, KARL

FF28 Lewis, Arnold. "Hinckeldeyn, Vogel, and American Architecture." *Jour. of the Soc. of Architectural Historians*, vol. 31 (1972), 276–90. Well-known German architect who interpreted American architecture of 1850–1900 to his colleagues.

FF29 Lewis, Arnold. "Karl Hinckeldeyn: Critic of American Architecture." *Amer.-German Rev.*, vol. 27, no. 2 (1960), 10–13, 37.

KESSLER, GEORGE

FF30 Wilson, William H. *The City Beautiful Movement in Kansas.* Columbia: Univ. of Missouri Pr., 1965. Role of the German-born George Kessler in association with editor William Melson and the architect Jarvis Hunt.

KIESLER, FREDERICK

FF31 "Design's Bad Boy." *Architectural Forum*, vol. 86, no. 2 (February 1947), 88–91, 138, 140.

Viennese architect, designer, and raconteur, who taught at the Columbia Univ. School of Architecture. Came to the U.S. in 1926.

FF32 Held, Roger. "Endless Innovation: The Theories and Scenic Design of Frederick Kiesler." Diss., Bowling Green State Univ., 1977, 466p.

FF33 Kiesler, Frederick. *Inside the Endless House. Art, People and Architecture: A Journal.* New York: Simon & Schuster, ca. 1966. 573p. Rev. by J. M. Fitch, *N.Y. Times Book Rev.*, 15 January 1967, 30.

FF34 Creighton, T.H. "Kiesler's Pursuit of an Idea: Interview." *Progressive Architecture*, vol 42, no. 7 (July 1961), 104=23.

KUTZBOCK, AUGUST

FF35 Kutzbock, August. Papers, 1855–1868. 1 Package. In the State Hist. Soc. of Wisconsin (MS 68-2250). Architect involved in the construction of the Wisconsin State Capitol. Many papers in German, on the building of the capitol and miscellaneous subjects.

LIENAU, DETLEF

FF36 Kramer, Ellen W. "The Domestic Architecture of Detlef Lienau, a Conservative Victorian." Diss., New York Univ., 1958. L., a German-Dane, came to America in 1848.

FF37 Lienau, Detlef. Papers, ca. 1850–1900. In the Detlef Lienau collection in the Columbia Univ. Library, New York (MS 62-1216). Biographical materials and memorabilia.

MAYBECK, BERNARD

FF38 Cardwell, Kenneth H. *Bernard Maybeck: Artisan, Architect, Artist.* Santa Barbara: Peregrine Smith, 1977. 255p. M. (1862–1957) was an architect in Berkeley, Calif.; son of a German-born woodcarver. Maybeck developed the Bay Area shingle style.

MIES VAN DER ROHE, LUDWIG

FF39 Mies Van der Rohe, Ludwig. Papers, 1921–1969. Ca. 22,000 pieces. In the MS. Div., Library of Congress (MS 76-169). Correspondence, memoranda, misc. papers and writings, incl. the correspondence on van der Rohe (1886–1967) with leading architects of his time.

NEUTRA, RICHARD J.

FF40 Neutra, Richard J. *Auftrag für Morgen. Rückblick auf ein Leben für die Architektur.* Trans. from the English by Werner von Grünau. Hamburg: Claasen, 1962. 406p. In part printed as the series "Als ich in die Staaten ging," in *Die Zeit*, beginning 30 March 1962.

FF41 "Richard Neutra to be Honored by AIA." *Austrian Institute. New and Events*, May 1977. Gold Medal of the American Institute of Architects bestowed on the late Richard Neutra at the Convention in San Diego, 5–8 June 1977.

PELZ, PAUL JOHANNES

FF42 Pelz, Paul Johannes. Papers, 1873–1931. In the Ms. Div., Library of Congress (MS 64-776). P. (1841–1918) was an Architect of Washington, D.C., son of Baron and Baroness Henriette Helfensreider von Pelz.

PFEIFFENBERGER, LUCAS

FF43 Jensen, Dano O. "Lucas Pfeiffenberger, Architect." *Mo. Hist. Soc. Bull.*, vol. 24 (1967), 47–49.

SCHWARZMANN, HERMAN JOSEPH

FF44 Maass, John. *The Glorious Enterprise: The Centennial Exhibition of 1876 and H.J. Schwarzmann, Architect-in-Chief.* Watkins Glen, N.Y.: Amer. Life Foundation, 1973. 156p. Munich-born architect who came to Philadelphia in 1868. He was author of great Victorian designs for the Centennial Exhibition of 1876. Rev. by D. Glidden, *Md. Hist. Mag.*, vol. 69, no. 4 (Winter 1974), 436–48.

STRECKER, HERMAN

FF45 Strecker, Herman. Papers, 1866–1900. 653 items. In the Natural History Museum, Chicago (MS 66-764). S. (1836–1901) was an architect, sculptor and lepidopterist.

SULLIVAN, LOUIS

FF46 Menocal, Narciso G. *Architect as Nature. The Transcendentalist Idea of Louis Sullivan.* Madison: Univ. of Wisconsin Pr., 1981. 264p. Analysis of the thought of Louis Sullivan in relation to the development of his architectural style.

FF47 Paul, Sherman. *Louis Sullivan: An Architect in American Thought.* Englewood Cliffs, N.J.: Prentice-Hall, 1966. 176p.

FG
Other Arts

For information on abbreviated sources cited, see Section FB: German-American Painters.

Book Arts

FG1 Hammer, C. R. "A Victor Hammer Bibliography (1930–1955)." *The Amer. Book Collector*, vol. 6 (January 1956), 3–12 passim.

FG2 Kent, Norman. "The Art of Victor Hammer." *Amer. Artist*, vol. 20 (June 1956), 44–49 passim.

FG3 "Kunst-Gewerbe. Die Buchbinderkunst in Amerika (i.e., die Arbeit von den Firmen Ringer und Hertzberg, Chicago." *Die Glocke*, vol. 1 (1906), 40.

FG4 Larremore, Thomas A. "An American Typographic Tragedy—The Imprints of Frederick Conrad Bursch." *Papers of the Bibliographical Soc. of America*, vol. 43 (1950), 1–38, 111–72, 425f. Geman-American art printer and book designer of the early 20th century.

FG5 Loring, Rosemond B. *Decorated Book Papers. Being an Account of Their Designs and Fashions.* Cambridge, Mass.: Harvard College Library, Dept. of Printing and Graphic Arts, 1942.

FG6 Reading, Carolyn. *A Hammer Bibliography 1930–1952.* Occasional Contributions, no. 45. Lexington, Ky.: Margaret I. King Library, Univ. of Kentucky, 1952.

FG7 Standard, Paul. "Hermann Zapf in Amerika." *Börsenblatt für den deutschen Buchhandel*, vol. 17, no. 4 (1961), 49–51. German-born book designer of Pittsburgh.

FG8 Thompson, Lawrence S. "Victor Hammer of Kentucky." *Amer.-German Rev.*, vol. 20, no. 5 (1954), 13–15. Typographic designer, printer and painter. B. in Vienna; in the U.S. since 1939.

Cartography and Topographical Drafting

For information on abbreviated sources cited, see Section FB: German-American Painters.

EGLOFFSTEIN, F. W. VON

FG9 Taft, *Artists and Illustrators ...*, p. 264. Topographical draftsman (ca. 1824–1898); native of Prussia who emigrated to America before 1853. Was engaged as artist to Western expeditions, including Frémont's last trip to the Rockies.

HASSLER, FERDINAND RUDOLPH

FG10 See: *Papers on Various Subjects Connected With the Survey of the Coast of the United States.* Extracted from the American Philosophical Transaction, vol. 2, N.S. Philadelphia: A. Small, 1824. 200p. H. (1770–1843) was a surveyor and topographer.

JENNY (YENNI), JOHANN HEINRICH

FG11 Thieme-Becker, vol. 18, p. 512. Topographical draftsman from Switzerland. In New York City in 1820. Known for his views of the city of New York.

PAUL-FRÉDÉRIC-WILLIAM, DUKE OF WÜRTTEMBERG

FG12 Groce-Wallace, p. 490. Topographical artist; natural historian and traveler. Made four visits to the Western Hemisphere, 1822–1857. Publ. an account of his first voyage (Stuttgart 1835).

PREUSS, CHARLES

FG13 Wilford, John Noble. *The Mapmakers.* New York: Knopf, ca. 1981. 414p. Artist and mapmaker.

On Frémont's expedition of the 1840's. His were "the first important maps of the West;" they pointed the way while Frémont's words inspired people to head west. See also Frémont's *Report*.

SCHOTT, ARTHUR

FG14 Emory, William H. *United States and Mexican Boundary Survey, Report of William H. Emory* .... Washington, D.C.: n.p., 1857–1859. S. (ca. 1813–1875) was a topographic artist with the U.S.–Mexican Boundary Survey expedition of 1849–1855. Resided in Washington where he worked as professor of German and music. Also a naturalist, engineer, and physician. See Taft, *Artists and Illustrators of the Old West*, p.277.

SCHUCHARD, CARL

FG15 Taft, *Artists and Illustrators* ..., p.269. Topographic artist, b. 1827 in Germany. Came to California in 1849 as engineer. Worked as surveyor and draftsman.

SOHON, GUSTAVUS

FG16 Ewers, John C. "Gustavus Sohon's Portraits of Flathead and Pend d'Oreille Indians, 1854." *Smithsonian Miscellaneous Collections*, vol. 90, no. 7 (November 1948). S. (1825–1903) was a topographic draftsman and portrait artist. Native of Tilsit, East Prussia; came to Brooklyn at the age of 17. In the U.S. Army in 1852. Artist on Western expeditions and a military road-building expedition in the Northwest. See Taft, *Artists and Illustrators of the Old West*, p.276.

STANLEY, JOHN MIX

FG17 Draper, Benjamin P. "John Mix Stanley, Pioneer Painter." *Antiques*, vol. 41 (March 1942), 180–82.

Ceramics/Art Pottery

GENERAL

FG18 Clark, Garth, and Margie Hughto. *A Century of Ceramics in the United States 1878–1978*. New York: Dutton, 1979. Notes and data presented in this work trace the study of ceramics in Vienna by American artists. Biographies of artist potters and decorators of German-Austrian heritage, 1880–1915.

FG19 Clark, Garth R. "George E. Ohr—Clay Prophet." *Craft Horizons*, vol. 38 (October 1978). An exhibit of the Biloxi Art Pottery of Ohr was shown at the Mississippi State Hist. Museum, Jackson, in 1978.

FG20 Stradling, Diana, and J. Garrison Stradling, eds. *The Art of the Potter. Redware and Stoneware Antiques* Magazine Library. New York: Universe Books, 1977. 160p. *See* Chap. II: "Redware—the Germanic Influence." Collection of articles by various contributors to *Antiques*, p.22–47.

AUST, GOTTFRIED

FG21 Bivins, John, Jr. "Gottfried Aust," In: *The Moravian Potters in North Carolina*. Chapel Hill: Univ. of N. Car. Pr., 1972, p.16–30. A. (1722–1788) was a native of Heidersdorf, Silesia, who moved to Herrnhut in 1742. Member of the Moravian community in North Carolina; arrived in America 1754.

FG22 South, Stanley. "The Ceramic Forms of the Potter Gottfried Aust at Betharaba, North Carolina, 1755 to 1771." In: *The Conference on Historic Site Archaeology and Anthropology Papers, 1965–1966*. Ed. Stanley South. Columbia, S. Car.: Conference on Historic Site Archaeology, 1967. Mimeogr.

BILLHARDT, HUGO

FG23 Franco, Barbara. "Stoneware Made by the White Family in Utica, New York." *Antiques*, vol. 99 (6 June 1971), 872–76. A German who worked as designer for the White Family potters, Utica, New York, 1894–1901.

CHRIST, RUDOLF

FG24 Bivins, John, Jr. *The Moravian Potters in North Carolina*. Chapel Hill: Univ. of N. Car. Pr., 1972, p.30–38. C. (1750–1833), master potter in N. Carolina, 1789–1821.

DZUBAS, FRIEDEL

FG25 Hughto, Margie. *New Works in Clay by Contemporary Painters and Sculptors*. Syracuse: Everson Museum of Art, 1976. B. 1915 in Berlin; left Germany for the United States in 1939. Expressionist, later abstract painter and sculptor in clay.

HAUBRICH, ALBERT

FG26 Coleman, Duke. "The Art of Albert Haubrich." *American Art Pottery*, vol. 48 (May 1980), 1, 4–5. Native of Biersdorf, Germany, H. (1875–1931) was associated with the Weller Pottery, Zanesville, Ohio.

MERCER, HENRY CHAPMAN

FG27 Blasberg, Robert. "Moravian Tiles: Fairy Tales in Colored Clay." *Spinning Wheel*, vol. 27 (June 1971), 16–19. The Moravian Pottery and Tile Works were founded by M. in Doylestown, Pa.

FG28 Clark, Garth, and Margie Hughto. *A Century of Ceramics in the United States 1878–1978*. New York: E. P. Dutton, in Assoc. with the Everson Museum of Art, 1979., p.308–09. Biographical sketch of M.

FG29 Dunning, Jennifer. "Historic Pottery: A Craft Endures." *N.Y. Times*, 12 May 1977. On Moravian Tiles.

FG30 Ellis, Elsa R. "Records from the Moravian Tile Works." *Jour. of the Bucks Co. Hist. Soc.*, vol. 1 (Spring 1973), 12–17.

FG31 Mercer, Henry C. *The Tiled Pavement in the Capitol of Pennsylvania*. Rev. and ed. by Ginger Duemler. Illus. by Linda Brown. State College, Pa.: The Pennsylvania Guild of Craftsmen, 1975. 83p.

MUELLER, HERMAN C.

FG32 Taft, Lita L. "Herman Carl Mueller (1854–1941): Innovator in the Field of Ceramics." Diss., Ohio State, 1979. M. (1854–1941) was an artist-designer at the Rookwood Pottery, Cincinnati. Educated in Nürnberg and Munich; came to Cincinnati at the age of 20, in 1878. Later went to Indiana to work on ornaments for the state capital.

NATZLER, OTTO AND GERTRUDE

FG33 Andreson, Laura. "The Natzlers." *Calif. Arts and Architecture*, vol. 58 (July 1941). Artist potters; natives of Austria.

FG34 *Form and Fire—Natzler Ceramics 1939–1972*. Washington, D.C.: Renwick Gallery, Smithsonian Institution, 1973. Exhibition catalogue.

FG35 Henderson, R. "Gertrud and Otto Natzler." *Design*, vol. 49 (January 1948).

FG36 Henderson, R. "Natzler Ceramics." *The Studio*, no. 1, vol. 57.

FG37 Natzler, Otto. *Gertrud and Otto Natzler: Ceramics*. Catalog of the collection of Mrs. Leonard M. Sperry, and a monograph by Otto Natzler. Los Angeles: Los Angeles County Museum of Art, 1968. 80p.

FG38 Penney, E. *The Ceramic Art of the Natzlers*. Film Associates, Los Angeles, 1967.

FG39 Penny, Janice. "The Natzlers, Masters of Ceramic Art." *Amer. Artist*, vol. 14 (March 1950), 48–51.

OHR, GEORGE E.

FG40 Blasberg, Robert W. *George E. Ohr and His Biloxi Pottery*. Port Jervis, N.Y.: Carpenter, 1972. O. (1857–1918) was born in Biloxi, Miss., the son of a blacksmith and a German mother from Württemberg; apprenticed to the potter Joseph Fortune Meyer at an early age; established a pottery of his own in Biloxi. He was innovative and an aesthetic loner, anticipating Funk styles and the "verbal visual" cartoon-strip Pop approach of a later time.

FG41 Ohr, George E. "Some Facts in the History of a Unique Personality." *Crockery and Glass Jour.*, vol. 54 (December 1901).

SINGER, SUSI

FG42 Neuwirth, Waltraud. *Wiener Keramik*. Braunschweig: Klingkhardt & Biermann, 1975. S. (1895–1949) was a native of Austria; studied at the Kunstgewerbeschule, Vienna, under Professor Michael Powolny. Produced ceramics for the Wiener Werkstätte studio at Grunbach. In the late 1930's transferred to Pasadena, California. See also: *A Century of Ceramics in the United States 1878–1978*, by Garth Clark and Margie Hughto. New York: Dutton, 1979, p.329.

VOLKMAR, CHARLES

FG43 Walton, William. "Charles Volkmar, Potter." *Internat. Studio*, vol. 36 (January 1909). B. in Baltimore, s. of a German portrait painter and restorer. Studied in Paris and established a career in Paris as painter, graphic artist and potter. Returned to the United States after 1879. Teacher of pottery in New York and Philadelphia.

FG44 Whiting, Margaret C. "Charles Volkmar's Crown Point Pottery." *The House Beautiful*, vol. 42 (October 1900).

WIESELTHIER, VALERIE ("VALLIE")

FG45 Canfield, Ruth. "The Pottery of Valerie Wieselthier." *Design*, vol. 31, no. 6. (November 1929).

FG46 Neuwirth, Waltraud. *Wiener Keramik*. Braunschweig: Klinkhardt & Bierman, 1975. W. (1895–1945) was a native of Austria. Studied at the Kunstgewerbeschule, Vienna, and worked at the Wiener Werkstätte. Work exhibited in 1928 at the International Exhibition of Ceramic Art, Metropolitan Museum of Art, New York. Came to the U.S. in 1929 as designer. (See: American Federation of Arts, 1928).

WILDENHAIN, FRANS

FG47 Johnston, R. H. *Frans Wildenhain*. New York: Rochester Institute of Technology, 1975.

WILDENHAIN, MARGUERITE

FG48 Petterson, Richard B. "Marguerite Wildenhain." *Ceramics Monthly*, vol. 25 (March 1977). Prominent European potter, daughter of a German father; student at the Bauhaus; emigrated to the U.S. in 1941.

FG49 Prothro, Hunt. "Marguerite Wildenhain: Sustained Presence." *Amer. Craft*, vol. 4, no. 4 (August/September 1980), 28–31, 76, 81. With photographs by Bruce Miller. On a retrospective exhibit of the potter's work organized by the Herbert F. Johnson Museum of Art, Cornell University. The exhibit premiered at Ithaca, April 27–June 8, 1980; traveled to the Oakland Museum, Oakland, California, and the Mint Museum, Charlotte, N.C.

FG50 Wildenhain, Marguerite. *The Invisible Core. A Potter's Life and Thoughts*. Palo Alto, Calif.: Pacific Books Publishers, 1973. 207p.

Furniture Design

GENERAL

FG51 *Early Texas Furniture and Decorative Arts*. San Antonio: San Antonio Museum Association, 1973. Based on an exhibit.

FG52 Himmelheber, Georg. *Biedermeier Furniture*. Trans. and ed. by Simon Jervis. London: Faber & Faber, 1974.

FG53 Lichten, Frances. "A Masterpiece of Pennsylvania-German Furniture." *Antiques*, vol. 77 (February 1960), 176–78. Sulfur inlay decoration on wooden furniture.

FG54 Quimby, Ian M., ed. *American Furniture and Its Makers*. Winterthur Portfolio, no. 13. Chicago: Univ. of Chicago Pr., 1979. 244p.

FG55 Schiffer, Margaret B. *Furniture and Its Makers of Chester County, Pennsylvania*. Philadelphia: Univ. of Pa. Pr., 1966.

FG56 Sikes, Jane E. *The Furniture Makers of Cincinnati, 1790 to 1849*. Cincinnati: n.p., 1978.

FG57 Streifthau, Donna. "Cincinnati Cabinet- and Chairmakers, 1819–1830." *Antiques*, vol. 88 (June 1971), 896–905. Only a few of the several hundred craftsmen here listed have German names: Geyer, Hoffman, Charles Lehman, Pittinger, Reiniger, John Urwiller, John Vinshonhaller.

FG58 Swan, Mabel M. "Moravian Cabinetmakers of a Piedmont Craft Center." *Antiques*, vol. 59 (June 1951), 456–59.

FG59 Taylor, Lonn, and David B. Warren. *Texas Furniture: The Cabinetmakers and Their Work, 1840–1880*. Austin: Univ. of Texas Pr., 1975. 387p. Examination of the heritage of locally made furniture, much of it produced by German immigrant craftsmen; detailed introduction to the art of cabinetmaking.

BACHMAN FAMILY

FG60 Dyke, Samuel E. "The Bachman Family of Cabinetmakers, 1766–1894." *Jour. of the Lancaster Co. Hist. Soc.*, vol. 69 (Trinity 1965), 168–80. John B., native of Switzerland, emigrated with his father in 1766.

BARTELS, WILLIAM

FG61 *The Craftsman in America*. Washington, D.C.: National Geographic Soc., ca. 1975, p.40. Illus. of work of German-born Illinois farmer who took up woodworking while recovering from a bout of illness. His masterpiece, a hand-carved inlaid dolphin-legged oak table, was shown in the Victorian room of the Illinois State Museum, Springfield.

BELTER, JOHN HENRY

FG62 Douglas, Edward P. "The Rococo Revival Furniture of John Henry Belter." *Art and Antiques*, July–August 1980, nos. 3–4, 34–43. B. (1804–1863) was a German-born cabinetmaker and furniture manufacturer of New York City, after 1844. This master of the carved neo-Rococo style was born in Württemberg and emig. to the U.S. in 1840. A major exhibition of B.'s work toured American museums in 1980–1981. See *Newsletter of the Soc. for German-Amer. Studies*, vol. 2, no. 2 (1980–1981), 3.

FG63 Hogrebe, Jeffrey. "Belter and Rococo." *Americana*, vol. 9, no. 1 (1981), 22–27.

FG64 Reif, Rita A. "A Museum Focuses on Belter's Furniture." *N.Y. Times*, 8 March 1981. A rev. of the exhibition "John Henry Belter and the Rococo Revival," shown 10 March–24 May at the Cooper-Hewitt Museum, New York.

FG65 Schwartz, Marvin D. "The Manney Collection of Belter Furniture." *Antiques*, vol. 119 (1981), 1165–73.

FG66 Schwartz, Marvin D. "New Exhibition Defines Belter's Individuality." *Antique Monthly*, vol. 13, no. 7 (1980), Sec. A, 1, 9.

FG67 Schwartz, Marvin D., Edward L. Stanek, and Douglas K. True. *The Furniture of John Henry Belter and the Rococo Revival: An Inquiry into Nineteenth-Century Furniture Design through a Study of the Gloria and Richard Manney Collection.* New York: Dutton, 1981. 88p.

FOLTZ, CARL NED

FG68 "Carl Ned Foltz: A Multiply Talented Craftsman in the Pennsylvania German Tradition." *Newsletter of the Soc. for German-Amer. Studies*, vol. 2, no. 2 (1980–1981), 14.

HAHN, SYLVIA

FG69 Weissenborn, George K. "Sylvia Hahn: The Many-Faceted Design Artist." *German-Canad. Yearbook*, vol. 6 (1981), 245–47.

HERRMANN, HENRY

FG70 Landis, Mary A. "Henry Herrmann: An American Manufacturer in the London Furniture Trade." *Antiques*, vol. 119 (1981), 1174–77.

FG71 Reif, Rita. "Echoes of the Japanomania of the 1860's." *N.Y. Times*, 11 May 1980. Rev. of the exhibit at the Washburn Gallery.

HUNZINGER, GEORGE

FG72 Flint, Richard W. "George Hunzinger, Patent Furniture Maker." *Arts and Antiques*, vol. 3, no. 1 (1980), 116–23. H. (b. 1835), furniture designer and manufacturer, a native of Tuttlingen, Württemberg.

JAHN, JOHANN

FG73 Stover, Donald L. *Tischlermeister Jahn.* San Antonio: Witte Memorial Museum, ca. 1977. J. settled in New Braunfels, Texas, in 1845.

LAPP, HENRY

FG74 Lapp, Henry. *A Craftsman's Handbook.* Introd. and Notes by Beatrice B. Garven. Philadelphia: Philadelphia Museum of Art, in Assoc. with the Tinicum Pr., 1975. A collection of designs, with 48 colored plates. Pennsylvanian of the Amish faith, born deaf; operated his business of carpentry and cabinetmaking at Bird-in-Hand, Pa.

LEHN, JOSEPH

FG75 Poole, Earl L. "Joseph Lehn, Driven to Design." *Amer.-German Rev.*, vol. 15, no. 1 (October 1948), 12–14.

PABST, DANIEL

FG76 Hanks, David A. "Daniel Pabst, Philadelphia Cabinetmaker." *Art and Antiques*, vol. 3, no. 1 (1980), 94–101. Also in: *Bull. of the Phila. Museum of Art*, vol. 73, no. 316 (1977), 3–24. A native of Hesse-Darmstadt who settled in Philadelphia in 1849.

PLOETHNER, FRIEDRICH K.

FG77 Bird, Michael S. "Cabinetmaker and Weaver Friedrich K. Ploethner." *Canad. Collector*, vol. 15, no. 3 (1980), 28–32.

STICKLEY, GUSTAV

FG78 Bavaro, Joseph J., and Thomas L. Mossman. *The Furniture of Gustav Stickley: History, Techniques, Projects.* New York: Van Nostrand Reinhold, 1982. Native of Osceola, Wisconsin.

Trained in chair making by an uncle in Brandt, Pennsylvania. Became a leading designer of furniture in the era of the Arts and Crafts Movement in America.

FG79 Freeman, J. *Forgotten Rebel: Mission Furniture.* New York: Century House, 1966.

FG80 "Gustav Stickley." In: *The Arts and Crafts Movement in America 1876–1916. An Exhibition Organized by the Art Museum, Princeton University, and the Art Institute of Chicago.* Ed. Robert J. Clark. Princeton: Princeton Univ. Pr., ca. 1972, p.38–44.

FG81 Stickley, Gustav. *Craftsman Homes: Architecture and Furnishings of the American Arts and Crafts Movement.* New York: Peter Smith, n.d.

Photography

HESTER, WILHELM

FG82 "The Wilhelm Hester Maritime Photographs." *Pacific Northwest Quar.*, vol. 67, no.2 (April 1976), 69–75.

HOHENBERGER, FRANK M.

FG83 Hohenberger, Frank M. Diary. In the Hohenberger Collection, Lilly Library, Indiana Univ. Bloomington, H. came to Brown County in 1917 after working in various print shops in the Midwest.

SEIGEL, ARTHUR

FG84 Viskochil, Larry A. "Arthur Seigel: A Life in Photography, 1913–1978." *Chicago Hist.*, vol. 10 (1981), 66–73. On S. (1913–1978).

ZERBE, JEROME

FG85 Gill, Brendan. "Profiles [Jerome Zerbe]. Happy Times." *New York*, 9 June 1973, 39–68. Sketch, incl. the German-American background and family history, of the photographer Zerbe. B. 1904 in Euclid, Ohio.

Goldsmithing, Jewelry, and Silver

GENERAL

FG86 Drepperd, Carl W. "Silversmiths of Lancaster." *Procs., Lancaster Hist. Soc.*, vol. 49, no. 1 (1945), 1–7.

FG87 Gerstell, Vivian S. *Silversmiths of Lancaster, Pennsylvania, 1730–1850.* Lancaster: Lancaster Co. Hist. Soc., 1972. Rev. by L. C. Madeira, *Pa. Mag. of Hist. and Biography*, vol. (1973), 255–56.

FG88 Knittle, Rhea Mansfield. *Early Ohio Silversmiths and Pewterers, 1787–1847.* Ohio Frontier Series, no. 2, Ashland, Ohio: n.p., 1943. 63p.

FG89 Pearsall, John. "Gold and Silversmithing at the Kutztown Folk Festival: A Look at the Craftsmen and Their Techniques." *Pa. Folklife*, vol. 30 (1980–1981), 152–55.

FG90 Roach, Ruth Hunter. *St. Louis Silversmiths.* St. Louis: n.p., 1967.

HIMMEL, ADOLPHE

FG91 Mackie, Charles L. "New Orleans' Answer to Tiffany."*Antiques World*, vol. 3, no. 2 (1980), 54–57. German-born silversmith of New Orleans, ca. 1850.

NICKEL, LUDWIG

FG92 "Der Kunsthandwerker ist einer der letzten Pioniere." *Der Nordwesten* (Winnipeg), 22 November 1966, 3. German goldsmith of Winnipeg.

PARISEN, OTTO

FG93 Kelby, *Notes on American Artists, 1754–1820...* New York: n.p., 1922; Gottesman, *Arts and Crafts in New York*, vols. 1–2; Dunlap, *History*, vol. 1, p.160. On P. (1723–1811), miniaturist, goldsmith, ornamental hairworker. A native of Berlin, Parisen came to New York in the early 1760's.

SEELER, MARGARET

FG94 Baker, Adelaide N. "The Work of Margaret Seeler." *Amer.-German Rev.*, vol. 28, no. 5 (1962), 10–12. German-born artist in fine metal, jewelry, and enamel.

Medals/Die Sinking

FURST, MORITZ

FG95 Chamberlain, Georgia S. "Medals Made in America by Moritz Furst." *The Numismatist*, vol. 67 (September 1954), 937–43; (October 1954), 1075–80. Medallist, engraver, and die sinker. B. ca. 1782 near Pressburg, Hungary; studied in Vienna. In 1807 became engraver for the United States Mint (Thieme-Becker).

FG96 Chamberlain, Georgia S. "Moritz Furst, Die-Sinker and Artist." *The Numismatist*, vol. 67, (June 1954), 588–92.

GOBRECHT, CHRISTIAN

FG97 Darrach, Charles G. "Christian Gobrecht, Artist and Inventor." *Pa. Mag. of Hist and Biography*, (July 1906), vol. 30, 355–58. Clockmaker, engraver, die-sinker, and seal engraver. Worked in Hanover, Pa., and Philadelphia. In 1840 was named head of the engraving department, U.S. Mint.

KOEHLER, FRANCIS X.

FG98 Thieme-Becker, vol. 21, p.119. K. (1818–1886), medallist, engraver, die sinker, jeweler. B. in Gmünd (Württemberg), coming to Baltimore in 1850.

REICH, JOHN (JOHANN) MATHIAS

FG99 Chamberlain, Georgia S. "John Reich, Assistant Engraver to the United States Mint." *The Numismatist*, vol. 68 (March 1958), 242–49. R. (1768–1833) was a die sinker and medallist; a native of Furth, Bavaria. Came to Philadelphia ca. 1800. Assistant engraver, U.S. Mint. See also: *Medallic History of the U.S.*, by Joseph F. Loubat. New York: n.p., 1878, pl. 22–25.

Pewter

GENERAL

FG100 Carter, John H. "A Checklist of the Extant Pewter of Johann Christoph Heyne." *Pewter Collectors Club of Amer. Bull.*, vol.7, no. 1 (December 1974), 26–33.

FG101 Downs, Joseph. *American Pewterers and Their Marks*. New York: The Metropolitan Museum of Art, 1942.

FG102 Evans, John J., Jr. "Lovebirds and Lions: A Pewter Mystery Solved." *Antiques*, vol. 76, no. 2 (August 1959), 142–43.

FG103 Graham, John M., II. *American Pewter*. Brooklyn: The Brooklyn Museum Pr., 1949. 36p.

FG104 Kerfoot, J. B. *American Pewter*. New York: Scribner's, 1924. New ed.: Crown Publs., 1942.

FG105 Nichols, Melville T. "'Trade Marks' on American Pewter." *Antiques*, vol. 51, no. 6 (June 1947), 394–96.

WILL, WILLIAM

FG106 Auman, Paul M. "New Finds in Old Pewter by William Will: The Aaronsburg Communion Service." *Antiques*, vol. 57, no. 4 (April 1950), 274–75.

FG107 Evans, John J., Jr. "Some Pewter by William Will." *Antiques*, vol. 61, no. 2 (February 1952), 178–79.

FG108 Hamilton, Suzanne. "The Pewter of William Will: A Checklist." *Winterthur Portfolio* (Charlottesville), vol. 7 (1972). A German-born artist of Philadelphia.

Glass/Porcelain/Silhouettes/Wax Portraiture

FG109 Andre, John, and Hartmut Froeschle. "The American Expedition of Emperor Joseph II and Bernhard Moll's Silhouettes." In: *The German Contribution to the Building of the Americas: Studies in Honor of Karl J. R. Arndt.* Ed. Gerhard K. Friesen and Walter Schatzberg. Hanover, N.H.: Clark Univ. Pr., and University Press of New England, 1977, p.135–72.

FG110 Bolton, Ethel Stanwood. *American Wax Portraits.* Boston: n.p., 1929. See also: *Wax Portraits and Silhouettes.* Boston, 1914.

FG111 Grafly, Dorothy. "Paula Himmelsbach Balano." *Amer.-German Rev.*, vol. 22, no. 1 (1955), 26–28. German-born designer of stained glass windows.

FG112 Saldera, Axel von. *German Enamelled Glass: The Edwin J. Beinecke Collection and Related Pieces.* Corning, N.Y.: Corning Museum of Glass, 1965.

FG113 Sellers, Charles Coleman. "Joseph Sansom, Philadelphia Silhouettist." *Pa. Mag. of Hist. and Biography*, vol. 88, no. 4 (October 1964), 395–438.

FG114 Swan, Mabel M. "Moravian Cabinetmakers of a Piedmont Craft Center," *Antiques*, vol. 59 (June 1951), 456–59. See p.458 for discussion of John Vogler (1783–1881), silhouettist, cabinetmaker, clockmaker and silversmith of Salem, N. Car. See Vogler Room in the Wachovia Museum.

G

Music and the Performing Arts

GA
Music

Bibliography and Sources

GA1 American Liszt Society. Papers. In Isidore Philipp Archive and Memorial Library, Univ. of Louisville Music Library.

GA2 American Society of Composers, Authors and Publishers. *ASCAP Biographical Dictionary of Composers, Authors, and Publishers*. Ed. Daniel I. McNamara. 2nd ed. New York: Crowell, 1952. 636p.

GA3 *Bach. The Quarterly Journal of the Riemenschneider Bach Institute*. Vol. 1, no. 1. Winter, 1970–. Ed. Elinore L. Barber, Baldwin-Wallace College, Berea, Ohio.

GA4 Baldwin-Wallace College, Berea, Ohio. *Emilie and Karl Riemenschneider Memorial Bach Library. Catalog*. Ed. Sylvia W. Kenney. New York: Columbia Univ. Pr. for Baldwin-Wallace College, 1960. 295p. Scores, MSS. and Bach memorabilia collected by Albert Riemenschneider and given to the college in memory of his parents.

GA5 *Bio-Bibliographical Index of Musicians in the United States of America from Colonial Times*. Washington, D.C.: Pan-American Union, 1941. 462p.

GA6 *Boston Symphony Orchestra Program Notes 1881–1975. Microfilms*. Millwood, N.Y.: Kraus-Thomson Organization, 1978–1979. 41 reels microfilm (35mm). Complete collection including alphabetical listings of works performed, conductors, soloists, and dates of performance.

GA7 Cincinnati Musical Festival Association. Records, 1874–1967. 7 ft. In Cincinnati Hist. Soc. (MS 71-1523). Papers, correspondence, notes.

GA8 Dunn, Julia Elizabeth. Papers. 1 box. In New York Public Library. Letters of Julia Dunn (1851–1987) from German musicians and American critics; MSS. from Clara Schumann, C. T. Brooks, Ellen Frothingham, etc. (*See* New York Public Library Manuscript Catalogue.

GA9 German Theater (in Germany). Papers, 1853–1917. 1 box. In the New York Public Library (MS 72-1031). Correspondence of persons associated with the theater in Germany.

GA10 Institute for Studies in American Music. *American Music before 1865 in Print and on Records: A Biblio-Discography*. Brooklyn: Dept. of Music, School of Performing Arts, Brooklyn College, CUNY, 1976.

GA11 Lockwood, Lewis. "The Beethoven Sketchbook in the Scheide Library." *Princeton Univ. Library Chronicles*, vol. 37, no. 2 (Winter 1976) 137–53.

GA12 Mouson, Katherine B. "A Bibliography of Articles and Books in English about Mozart." *Bull. of Bibliography*, vol. 19 (1949), 259–67.

GA13 Showalter, Grace I. *The Music Books of Ruebush and Kieffer, 1866–1942: A Bibliography*. Charlottesville: Univ. Pr. of Virginia, 1975. 40p.

GA14 Sonneck, Oscar G., and William T. Upton. *A Bibliography of Early Secular Music: 18th Century*. New York: Da Capo, 1964. Repr. of 1945 ed.

GA15 Wagner, Richard. Papers. 866 items. In the Burrell Collection, 1800–1900, Curtis Inst. of Music Library, Philadelphia (MS 66-1052). (1813–1883). Correspondence, MSS. diaries, and portraits.

GA16 Weichlein, William J. *A Checklist of American Music Periodicals, 1850–1900*. Detroit Studies in Music Bibliography, no. 16. Detroit: Information Coordinators, 1970. 103p. Rev. by D. J. Epstein, *Notes*, vol. 27, no. 3 (March 1971), 489. With bibliography and index of editors and publishers.

GA17 Wolfe, Richard J. *Secular Music in America 1801–1825. A Bibliography*. Introd. by C. S. Smith. N.Y.: N.Y. Pub. Lib., 1964. 3 vols. 1238p. Rev. by D. W. Krummel, *Library Quar.*, vol. 35, no. 3 (1965), 187–88; *Publs. of the Bibliographic Soc. of America*, vol. 59, no. 2 (1965): 225.

GA18 Wunderlich, Charles E. "A History and Bibliography of Early American Musical Periodicals, 1782–1852." Diss., Michigan, 1962. 796p. A list of 66 items; many editors were European-born.

German Music in American Life—General

GA19 Adler, Samuel H. "Music in the American Snyagogue." *Amer. Choral Rev.*, vol. 6 (April and July 1964), 7–9, 3–6. Capsule history on the European backgrounds of over a century of synagogue music.

GA20 Ascher-Nash, Franzi. "Millersville—and Vienna—Leo Ascher." In: *Papers from the Conference on German-Americana in the Eastern United States, Millersville State College, Nov. 9–10, 1979*. Ed. Steven M. Benjamin. Occasional Papers of the Soc. for German-Amer. Studies, no. 8. Morgantown, W. Va.: Dept. of Foreign Langs., W. Va. Univ., 1980, p.12–20. Establishment of the annual Leo Ascher Award (1977–) at Millersville State College for the best composition on a theme by Ascher, Viennese operetta composer.

GA21 Bakken, Howard Norman. "The Development of Organ Playing in Boston and New York, 1700–1900." Diss., Illinois at Urbana–Champaign, 1975. 166p. Organ playing was "consistently dominated by French and German styles, due primarily to European musical training."

GA22 Benton, Rita. "Early Musical Scholarship in the United States." *Fontes Artis Musicae*, vol. 9 (January–April 1964), 12–21. A survey of the field from the mid-19th century to the 1930's.

GA23 Berges, Ruth. "Mahler in America." *Amer.-German Rev.*, vol. 26, no. 4 (1960): 12–13. On Mahler's visits to the United States.

GA24 Binder, Abraham Wolf. "Synagogue Music in America." *Jour. of Church Music*, vol. 6 (January 1964), 2–4. Summary sketch.

GA25 Brown, Margaret L. "David Blakely, Manager of the First American Tour of Eduard Strauss." *Bull. of the N.Y. Public Library*, vol. 64, no. 4 (1962), 215–38; no. 5, 316–39. Eduard, brother of Johann S. the younger, toured the United States in 1890 with an orchestra.

GA26 Camus, Raoul F. *Military Music of the American Revolution*. Chapel Hill: Univ. of N. Car. Pr., 1976. 218p. Rev. by J. W. Molnar, *William and Mary Quar.*, vol. 34, no. 3 (1977), 503–04. The fife and drum and bands indicate English and Prussian influences.

GA27 Carson, Gerald. "The Piano in the Parlor." *Amer. Heritage*, vol. 17, no. 1 (1965), 54–63. The vogue of the piano in connection with music study at German conservatories.

GA28 Chase, Gilbert. *America's Music: From thePilgrims to the Present*. New York: McGraw Hill, 1955. Revised and expanded version of a standard work.

GA29 Covey, Cyclone. "Puritanism and Music in Colonial America." *William and Mary Quar.*, vol. 8 (1951), 378–88.

GA30 Davis, Ronald L. *The Gilded Years, 1865–1920*. Vol. II of *A History of Music in American Life*. Huntington, N.Y.: Krieger, 1980. 268p.

GA31 De Fries, Stanley. "An Analysis of Performance Patterns in Choral Programs of the United States of America 1900–1958." Diss., Indiana, 1966. 127p. The dominance of the Austrian-German repertory is demonstrated in this tabulation of some 66,000 items.

GA32 Downs, Lynwood G. "The German Music Journal," *Amer.-German Rev.*, vol. 22, no. 5 (1956), 8–9, 35. On the *Deutsche Musik-Zeitung*, ed. by P.M. Wolsieffer in Philadelphia, 1856–1861.

GA33 Downs, Philip George. "The Development of the Great Repertoire in the Nineteenth Century. Two vols." Diss., Toronto, 1964. 346p. This investigation focuses on the difficulties of putting new compositions into the repertory.

GA34 Eberlein, Harold, and Cortland Van D. Hubbard. "Music in the Early Federal Era." *Pa. Mag. of Hist. and Biography*, vol. 69 (1945), 103–27.

GA35 Ehmann, Wilhelm. *Alte Musik in der Neuen Welt: Berichte und Gedanken über eine Konzertreise der Westfälischen Kantorei durch die USA.* Darmstadt: Merseburger, 1961. 63p.

GA36 Elkinton, Howard. "From Bach to Gershwin—The Eitel Musical Calendar." *Amer.-German Rev.*, vol. 12, no. 1 (1945), 26–27.

GA37 Ervin, Horace. "Notes on Franklin's Armonica and the Music Mozart Wrote for It." *Jour. of the Franklin Institute*, vol. 262 (1956), 329–48.

GA38 Ewen, David. "America Becomes Musical." *Common Ground*, vol. 2, no. 2 (1942): 79–83. Sketch of the German influence on musical life in America from the Bethlehem *Singstunde* of 1742 to the present.

GA39 Ewen, David. "German Music in America—and the First World War." *Decision*, vol. 3, no. 1 (1942), 47–53. On the attitude of Americans toward German music during the first war, with a report on the famous case of the conductor Karl Muck.

GA40 Fisher, William A. *One Hundred and Fifty Years of Music Publishing in the United States. An Historical Sketch with special Reference to the Pioneer Publisher, Oliver Ditson Co., 1783–1933.* Boston: n.p. 1933.

GA41 Forbes, Elliot, ed. *Thayer's Life of Beethoven.* 2 vols. Princeton Univ. Pr., 1964. 1136p. Rev. by A. M. Garrett, *Catholic Hist. Rev.*, vol. 51, no. 2 (1965), 271–72. Revision of the standard biography last re-edited and augmented in 1921.

GA42 Gehrkens, Karl W. "A Philosophy of Universal Music Education." *Jour. of Research in Music Education*, vol. 16 (Fall 1968), 278–81. On the Pestalozzian principles of education as applied by Lowell Mason in this country.

GA43 Goodman, Alfred. *Die amerikanischen Schüler Franz Liszts.* Veröffentl. zur Musikforschung, no. 1. Wilhelmshaven: Heinrichshofen Vlg., 1973. 172p. Incl. music.

GA44 Graf, Max. "Anton Bruckner and Gustav Mahler in America." *Musical Courier*, vol. 147, no. 4 (15 February 1953), 4.

GA45 Greer, Thomas Henry. "Music and Its Relation to Futurism, Cubism, Dadaism, and Surrealism, 1905 to 1950." Diss., North Texas State Univ., 1969. 501p.

GA46 Gross, Harvey. "Gustav Mahler: Fad, or Fullness of Time?" *Amer. Scholar*, vol. 42 (Summer 1973), 484–88.

GA47 *Die Hamburgische Staatsoper in Amerika. Montreal, June, 1967 anlässlich der Weltausstellung New York, June–July 1967 im Rahmen der "Lincoln Center Festival".* Hamburg: Christian, 1968. 164p.

GA48 Harris, William Torrey. "Thoughts on the Music of Beethoven (As Illustrated in the F Major Sonata for Violin and Piano" and "On Beethoven's Sixth Symphony." *The Western* (St. Louis), N.S., vol. 1 (April 1875), 218–23; (June), 381–89.

GA49 Hart, Philip. *Orpheus in the New World: The Symphony Orchestra as an American Cultural Institution.* New York: Norton, 1973. 562p. Rev. by Alan Rich, *N.Y. Times Book Rev.*, 5 August 1973, 7. On the history and present state of the symphony from the work of Theodore Thomas as founder of several orchestras; personnel derived from German immigration in the 19th century.

GA50 Hatch, Christopher. "Music for America: A Critical Controversy of the 1850s." *Amer. Quar.*, vol. 4, no. 4 (1962): 578–86. On John S. Dwight and other pro-German theorists in their clash with the "Young Americanists" led by William H. Fry.

GA51 Herzfeld, Friedrich. "Musik und Musikleben in Amerika." In: *Amerikakunde. Dreizehn Beiträge von N. Altwicker u.a.* 4th ed. Frankfurt/Berlin, 1966, p.510–45.

GA52 Hitchcock, H. Wiley. *Music in the United States: A Historical Introduction.* Englewood Cliffs, N.J.: Prentice-Hall, 1969. 270p. Rev. by R. L. Davis, *Jour. of Amer. Hist.*, vol. 56, no. 4 (March 1970), 890–91.

GA53 Howard, John Tasker. *Our American Music. Three Hundred Years of It.* New York: n.p., ca. 1934; 3rd rev. ed., New York: Crowell, 1946.

German Music in American *(cont.)*

The section entitled "Foreign Invasion of 1848," p.211–25, deals with the Germania Society of New York.

GA54 Howard, John Tasker, and George K. Bellows. *A Short History of Music in America*. New York: n.p., 1957. 470p.

GA55 Johnson, H. Earle. *First Performances in America to 1900*. Detroit: Publ. for the College Music Society by Information Coordinators, ca. 1979. Rev. by Harold C. Schonberg. *N.Y. Times*, 2 September 1979, Sec. D, 15, 23. A compilation and statistical study of orchestral performances which constitutes a review of American musical taste through 200 years.

GA56 Kallmann, Helmut. "Beethoven and Canada: A Miscellany." In: *German-Canad. Yearbook*. Vol. IV. Ed. Hartmut Froeschle. Toronto: Hist. Soc. of Mecklenburg Upper Canada, Inc., 1978. p.286–94. Also in: *The Canada Music Book* (Spring-Summer 1971).

GA57 Kallmann, Helmut. "Der deutsche Beitrag zum Musikleben." *Mitteilungen des Instituts für Auslandsbeziehungen*, vol. 7 (1957), 200–04. Historical survey of German contributions to the musical life of Canada.

GA58 Kallmann, Helmut. "The German Contribution to Music in Canada." *German-Canad. Yearbook*, vol. II. Toronto: Hist. Soc. of Mecklenburg Upper Canada, 1975.

GA59 Kallmann, Helmut. *A History of Music in Canada, 1534–1914*. Toronto: Univ. of Toronto Pr., 1960. 311p.; repr. Toronto: Canadian Univ. Paperbooks, no. 90, 1969. Rev. by E. C. Krohn, *Manuscripta*, vol. 6, no. 3 (1962), 185–87. Treats performances, composers, folk music, and the development of taste and institutions.

GA60 Lang, Paul Henry. *One Hundred Years of Music in America*. New York: n.p., 1961.

GA61 Lenhart, Charmenz S. *Musical Influence on American Poetry*. Athens: Univ. of Georgia Pr., 1956. 337p. Rev. by C. Simpson, *Jour. of Engl. and Germanic Philology*, vol. 56 (1957), 649–51; B. Q. Morgan, *Compar. Lit.*, vol. 9 (1957), 264–65.

GA62 Lerner, Laurence. "The Organization and Promotion of Musical Performance and Taste in the Later 19th Century." Diss., Univ. of Wisconsin, 1967.

GA63 Lowens, Irving. *Music and Musicians in Early America*. New York: Norton, 1964. 328p. Rev. in *N.Y. Times Book Rev.*, 17 January 1965. Includes essays on "Music and American Transcendentalism" and "The American Tradition of Church Song;" and "A Checklist of Writings about Music in the Periodicals of American Transcendentalism (1835–50)."

GA64 Lowens, Irving. "Music in American Civilization, 1770–1820." Diss., Univ. of Maryland, 1961.

GA65 McCue, George, ed. *Music in American Society, 1776–1976: From Puritan Hymn to Synthesizer*. New Brunswick: Transaction Books, ca. 1976.

GA66 Mason, Lowell. *Musical Letters from Abroad*. Introd. by Elwyn A. Wienandt. New York: DaCapo Pr., 1967. 312p. These letters were originally published in 1854. Mason was a leading musical authority and teacher of the 19th century.

GA67 [Mencken, H. L.] *H. L. Mencken on Music*. Selected by Louis Cheslock. New York: Macmillan, ca. 1975.

GA68 Mortimer, Frank H. "Music in American Literary History: A Survey of the Significance of Music in the Writings of Eight American Literary Figures." Diss., New York Univ., 1968. 301p. Esp. chaps. 4 and 5 on Mark Twain, James Huneker, and H. L. Mencken.

GA69 Mueller, John H. *The American Symphony Orchestra: A Social History of Musical Taste*. Bloomington, Ind.: n.p., 1951.

GA70 Mueller, Kate. *Twenty-Seven Major American Symphony Orchestras: A History and Analysis of Their Repertories, Seasons 1842 through 1969–70*. Bloomington: Indiana Univ. Pr., 1973. 398p.

GA71 Mussulman, Joseph Agee. "Mendelssohnism in America." *Musical Quar.*, vol. 53, no. 3 (July 1962), 335–46. His musical image from the 1830's to 1900.

GA72 Mussulman, Joseph Agee. *Music in the Cultured Generation: A Social History of Music in America, 1870–1900*. Pi Kappa Lambda Studies in Amer. Music. Evanston: Northwestern Univ. Pr., 1971. 298p.

GA73 Mussulman, Joseph Agee. "Music in the Literary Magazines: 1870–1900." Diss., Syracuse, 1966. 384p. Analysis of 600 articles in the *Atlantic, Harper's, Century,* and *Scribner's* magazines; thus a survey of the vogue and reception of "classical composers" in the Genteel Era.

GA74 Nettl, Paul. "Abt and Strauss in the United States." *Amer.-German Rev.,* vol. 9, no. 6 (August 1943), 21–23, 27.

GA75 Nettl, Paul. "Beethoven's Grandnephew in America." *Amer.-German Rev.,* vol. 23, no. 5 (1957), 14–16. Ludwig, son of Beethoven's nephew Karl, lived in the U.S. from 1871 to the middle eighties. (Also printed in *Music and Letters,* July 1957).

GA76 Nettl, Paul. "The Classical Composers and America." *Amer.-German Rev.,* vol. 8, no. 5 (1942), 4–6, 35.

GA77 Nettl, Paul. "Immigration and American Music." *Amer.-German Rev.,* vol. 9, no. 2 (1942), 6–8, 34.

GA78 Nettl, Paul. "Two Hundred Years British National Anthem." *Amer.-German Rev.,* vol. 11, no. 1 (1944), 7–9. On the German derivation of "God Save the King."

GA79 Noth, Elena F. "MacDowell and Germany." *Amer.-German Rev.,* vol. 24, no. 5 (1958), 9–11. On the influence of German musicians and German poets on the work of Edward MacDowell.

GA80 "Observations on the Music of Handel." *Portfolio* (Philadelphia and New York), N.S., vol. 3 (1810), 472–76.

GA81 Oursler, Robert Dale. "The Effect of Pestalozzian Theory and Practice on Music Education in the United States between 1850 and 1900." Diss., Northwestern, 1966. On the influence of William Maclure, Joseph Neef, William C. Woodbridge, Elan Ives, Thomas Hastings, and Lowell Mason.

GA82 Overvold, Lieselotte Z. "Wagner's American Centennial March: Genesis and Reception." *Monatshefte,* vol. 68 (1976), 179–87.

GA83 Randel, William. "Frederick Delius in America." *Va. Mag. of Hist. and Biography,* vol. 79 (1971), 349–66. Delius' sojourn in America and its impact on his work.

GA84 Rattermann, Henry A. "Karl Maria von Weber. Gedenkrede." *Deutsch-Amerikanisches Magazin,* vol. 1 (1887), 290–304.

GA85 Reutter, Hermann. "Konzert- und Vortragsreisen in USA." *Zeitschrift für Kulturaustausch,* vol. 17 (1967), 208–13.

GA86 Smith, Carleton Sprague. "America in 1801–1825: The Musicians and the Music." *Bull. of the N.Y. Public Library,* vol. 68, no. 8 (1964), 483–92. This is the "Introduction" to R. J. Wolfe's *Secular Music in America 1801–1825,* q.v.

GA87 Spaulding, E. Wilder. "Contemporary Music." In: *The Quiet Invaders. The Story of the Austrian Impact upon America.* Wien: Österr. Bundesvlg für Unterr., Wissenschaft und Kunst, 1968, p.129–49.

GA88 Spaulding, E. Wilder. "The Discovery of Austrian Music." In: *The Quiet Invaders. The Story of the Austrian Impact upon America.* Wien: Österr. Bundesverlag für Unterricht, Wissenschaft und Kunst, 1968, p.104–28.

GA89 Thompson, James William. "Music and Musical Activities in New England, 1800–1838." Diss., George Peabody College for Teachers, 1962. 685p.

GA90 Van Camp, Leonard. "Nineteenth-Century Choral Music in America: A German Legacy." *Amer. Choral Rev.,* vol. 23, no. 4 (1981), 5–12.

GA91 Waters, Edward N. "Liszt and Longfellow." *Musical Quar.,* vol. 41 (1955), 1–25.

GA92 Wolverton, Byron A. "Keyboard Music and Musicians in the Colonies and the United States of America before 1830." Diss., Indiana, 1966. 503p. Includes among others: A. Reinagle, G. Graupner, C. Meineke, J. Eckhard, Jr., and A. F. Heinrich.

Reception of German Musical Culture in the Cities and Regions

GA93 Aldrich, Richard. *Concert Life in New York 1902–1923.* New York: Putnam's, 1941. 795p. A record of concert performances in New York, with reviews, articles, and index.

GA94 Babow, Irving. "The Singing Societies of European Immigrant Groups in San Francisco: 1851–1953." *Jour. of the Hist. of the Behavioral Sciences*, vol. 5 (January 1969).

GA95 Bardell, Eunice B. "The Music in the Air When Milwaukee was Young." *Hist. Messenger of the Milwaukee Co. Hist. Soc.*, vol. 30, no. 4 (1974), 94–105.

GA96 "Beethoven and Quebec." In: *The Lawrence Lande Foundation for Canadian Historical Research*, no. 2. Montreal: Redpath Library, McGill Univ., 1966.

GA97 Bellinger, Martha F. "Music in Indianapolis, 1900–1944." *Ind. Mag. of Hist.*, vol. 42, no. 1 (1946), 47–65. Strongly influenced by the *Musikvereine* of German membership.

GA98 Betterton, William F. "Music in Early Davenport (Iowa)—Bands and Orchestras." *Palimpsest*, vol. 45, no. 7 (1964), 273–82.

GA99 Broueck, Jack Wolf. "Eighteenth Century Music in Savannah, Georgia." Diss., Florida State, 1963. 256p.

GA100 Carlson, Joyce Elen Mangler. "Early Music in Rhode Island. Part V: Oliver Shaw and the Psallonian Society." *R.I. Hist.*, vol. 23, no. 2 (1964), 35–50. A record of performances of works of German composers.

GA101 Carlson, Joyce Ellen Mangler. *Rhode Island Music and Musicians, 1733–1850.* Detroit Studies in Music Bibliog., no. 7. Detroit: Information Service, Inc., 1965. 90p.

GA102 Cassiday, Clara. "The Years of Splendor: Chicago's Music and Theater." *Chicago Hist.*, Spring 1972, 4–13.

GA103 Crews, Emma Katherine. "A History of Music in Knoxville, Tennessee, 1791 to 1910." Diss., The Florida State Univ., 1961.

GA104 Draegert, Eva. "Cultural History of Indianapolis: Music, 1875–1890." *Ind. Mag. of Hist.*, vol. 53 (1957), 265–304.

GA105 Drummond, Robert R. *Early German Music in Philadelphia.* New York: Appleton, 1910. 88p. Repr. New York: AMS Pr., 1972. 88p.

GA106 Dunn, James Taylor. "St. Paul's Schubert Club: Musical Mentor of the Northwest." *Minn. Hist.*, vol. 38 (June 1964).

GA107 Engler, Martha C., Klaus Goetze and Anneliese M. Henderson. "Boston's Era of German Music 1800 to 1918." "After World War I." "Ballet." In: *Germans in Boston.* Boston: Goethe Soc. of New England, 1981, p.23–29.

GA108 Fisher, James Long. "The Origin and Development of Public School Music in Baltimore to 1870." Diss., Maryland, 1970.

GA109 Franke, O. H. "Ludwig O. Teach In Memoriam." *Report of the Soc. for the Hist. of Germans in Md.*, vol. 32 (1966), 71–72. Organizer of Baltimore's Bach Club.

GA110 Gifford, Robert T. "Cincinnati's Music Hall: A Century of Continuity and Change." *Cincinnati Hist. Soc. Bull.*, vol. 36 (1978), 79–104.

GA111 Grater, Fred. "Music in Pennsylvania to 1800: A Selective Discography." *Hist. Rev. of Berks Co.*, vol. 37 (Winter 1971–1972), 18–22.

GA112 Holliday, Joseph. "The Cincinnati Philharmonic and Hopkins Hull Orchestras, 1865–68." *Bull. of the Cincinnati Hist. Soc.*, vol. 26 (1968), 158–73.

GA113 Hoxie, Frances Alida. "Five Decades of Concerts in Hartford, 1800–1850." *Conn. Hist. Soc. Bull.*, vol. 41 (October 1976), 119–28.

GA114 Joan of Arc, Sister. *Catholic Music and Musicians in Texas.* San Antonio: Our Lady of the Lake College, 1936.

GA115 John, Theodore. "Singing Societies in Texas." Diss., Texas State, 1975. 501p. Founding and support of singing societies and *Liedertafel* in Texas; growth of German musical influence from the 1880's to 1900.

GA116 Johnson, Harold E. *Musical Interludes in Boston, 1795–1830.* New York: Columbia Univ. Pr., 1943. 366p.

GA117 Jordan, John W. "Gedenkblätter an Jedidiah Weiss, Karl F. Beckel und Jacob C. Till, Posaunisten." *Deutsch-Amerikanisches Mag.*, vol. 1 (1887), 108–112. Members of the trombone choir of Bethlehem, Pennsylvania.

GA118 Kendall, John S. "New Orleans' Musicians of Long Ago." *La. Hist. Quar.*, vol. 31, no. 1 (1948), 130–49. Cites a number of German-American musicians and teachers.

GA119 Klinzing, Ernestine M. "Music in Rochester: A Century of Musical Progress: 1825–1925." *Rochester Hist.*, vol. 29, no. 1 (1967), 1–24. Cites the role of the Forty-Eighters in the local musical development.

GA120 Kmen, Henry A. *Music in New Orleans: The Formative Years, 1791–1841.* Baton Rouge: Louisiana State Univ. Pr., 1966. 314p. Includes discussion of concerts and opera.

GA121 Krohn, Ernst C. "A Beethoven 'First' in St. Louis." *Bull., Mo. Hist. Soc.*, vol. 23, no. 1 (October 1966), 59–64.

GA122 Krohn, Ernst C. "Some Notes on the Philharmonic Orchestra and Related Amateur Orchestras in St. Louis." *Bull. of the Mo. Hist. Soc.*, vol. 4, no. 3 (April 1948), 169–73.

GA123 Kuhl, Carl, ed. *Fest-Zeitung für das 18. National Sängerfest, 21.–26. Juni, 1897 in Philadelphia.* N.p.: n.p., 1897.

GA124 Mahan, Katherine Hines. "History of Music in Columbus, Georgia, 1828–1928." Diss., Florida State, 1967. 398p. Shows influence of the German element from 1840 to 1860.

GA125 Miller, Richard. "The Liederkranz in Louisville, 1848–1877." *Filson Club Hist. Quar.*, vol. 49 (July 1975).

GA126 Olson, Ivan. "Music and Germans in Nineteenth Century Richmond, Va." *Jour. of Research in Music Educ.*, vol. 14 (Spring 1966), 27–32. Compares the "indigenous" activity before 1855 with the "immigrant" stimulus thereafter.

GA127 Petersen, William J. "Music in Early Davenport (Iowa), Land of Music and Song." *Palimpsest*, vol. 45, no. 7 (1964), 301–04.

GA128 Osburn, M. H. *Ohio Composers and Musical Authors.* Columbus: n.p., 1942.

GA129 Philadelphia, Pa. Germania Orchestra. Records, 1856–1896. 7 vols. In Dickinson College Library, Carlisle, Pa. (MS 73-441). Papers include constitution and minutes, and membership records.

GA130 Raddin, George G. "The Music of New York City 1797–1804." *N.-Y. Hist. Soc. Quar.*, vol. 38 (October 1954), 478–99. A picture of the flourishing state of musical interest: societies and performances.

GA131 Rogers, Delmer Dalzell. "Nineteenth Century Music in New York City as Reflected in the Career of George Frederick Bristow." Diss., Univ. of Michigan, 1967. 216p. New Yorkers' tastes were cosmopolitan and English-centered.

GA132 St. Paul, Minn. Schubert Club. Records, 1885–1944. 56 vols. and 2 boxes. In Minnesota Hist. Soc. collections (MS 60-856.) Minutes, programs and misc. records of the club.

GA133 Schlicher, J. J. "The Milwaukee Musical Society in Time of Stress." *Wis. Mag. of Hist.*, vol. 27, no. 2 (December 1943), 178–93.

GA134 Shanet, Howard. *Philharmonic. A History of New York's Orchestra.* Garden City: Doubleday, 1974. Reviews the effect of the heavy Germanic influence on the orchestra's development.

GA135 Spell, Lota M. "The Early German Contributions to Music in Texas." *Amer.-German Rev.*, vol. 12, no. 4 (1946), 8–10.

GA136 Stoutamire, Albert Lucian. "A History of Music in Richmond, Virginia, from 1742 to 1865." Diss., Florida State Univ., 1959.

GA137 Taricani, Jo Ann. "Music in Colonial Philadelphia: Some New Documents." *Musical Quar.*, vol. 65 (1979), 185–99.

GA138 Tyler, Merle. "Evenings of Song. Amateur Musical Societies Drew Large Audiences in Postwar Richmond." *Va. Cavalcade*, vol. 17, no. 2 (1967), 42–47. The Gesang-Verein Virginia, Mozart Academy, and other organizations.

GA139 Wetzel, Richard D. "Frontier Music Makers." *Carnegie Mag.*, December 1968, 343–47. Reference to Old Economy.

GA140 Wetzel, Richard D. "The Music Collection of George Rapp's 'Harmonie Gesellschaft' (1805–1906)." *Monatshefte*, vol. 68 (1976), 167–70.

GA141 Wetzel, Richard D. "The Music of George Rapp's Harmony Society, 1805–1906." Diss., Pittsburgh, 1971.

GA142 Wolz, Larry. "The College of Music of Cincinnati: A Centennial Tribute." *Bull., Cincinnati Hist. Soc.*, vol. 36 (1978), 105–16.

GA143 Yerbury, Grace H. "Concert Music in Early New Orleans." *La. Hist. Quar.*, vol. 40, no. 2 (April 1957), 95–109.

Performers/Virtuosi/Teachers of Music

ANSCHÜTZ, KARL

GA144 Rattermann, Henry A. "Deutsch-Amerikanische Pioniere der Musik: Karl Anschütz." *Deutsch-Amerikanisches Mag.*, vol. 1 (1887), 515–24.

ANTES, JOHN

GA145 McCorkle, Donald M. "John Antes, American Dilletante." *Musical Quar.*, vol. 42 (October 1956), 486–99. On a strange and intriguing figure of the eighteenth century—inventor, instrument maker, composer, and Moravian minister.

ANTHEIL, GEORGE

GA146 Antheil, George. *Bad Boy of Music.* Garden City: Doubleday, 1945. 368p. American composer.

ARON, PAUL

GA147 Poladian, Sirvart. "Paul Aron and the New Music in Dresden." *Bull., N.Y. Public Library*, vol. 66, no. 5 (1962), 297–315. New York pianist and conductor, b. 1886 in Dresden, was in correspondence with leading composers of his time.

BALATKA, HANS

GA148 Schlicher, J. J. "Hans Balatka and the Milwaukee Musical Society." *Wis. Mag. of Hist.*, vol. 27, no. 1 (September 1943), 40–55. A Forty-Eighter, Balatka was a leading figure in the musical life of Milwaukee and Chicago.

BEIDERBECKE, BIX

GA149 Perhonis, John P. "The Bix Beiderbecke Story: The Jazz Musician in Legend, Fiction, and Fact—A Study of the Images of Jazz in the National Culture." Diss., Minnesota, 1978. On B. (1903–1931). The first Beiderbecke to come to Davenport, Iowa, was Bix's great-grandfather, a professional organist and leader of the Deutsch-Amerikanische Choral Society in the 1890's.

GA150 Sudhalter, Richard M., and Philip R. Evans. *Bix: Man and Legend.* London: Quartet Books: New Rochelle: Arlington House, 1974. 512p.

BLOCH, ERNEST

GA151 "Ernest Bloch as a Teacher." *Music Jour.*, vol. 35 (1977), 26–27.

GA152 *Ernest Bloch, Biography and Comment.* San Francisco: n.p., 1925. 42p.

GA153 Rafael, Ruth. "Ernest Bloch at the San Francisco Conservatory of Music." *Western States Jewish Hist. Quar.*, vol. 9 (April 1977).

BORNSCHEIN, FRANZ CARL

GA154 Music MSS. and printed scores, 1897–1948. 2300 items. In the Maryland Hist. Survey Library (MS 78-772). B. (1879–1948) was composer and teacher at the Peabody Conservatory, Baltimore.

BÜLOW, HANS VON

GA155 Levarie, Siegmund. "Hans von Bülow in America." *Newsletter of the Institute for Studies in Amer. Music*, vol. 11 (November 1981), 8–10.

CLAUDER FAMILY

GA156 Grant, Marilyn. "Father, Son, and Grandson Create Music for 100 Years in Wisconsin." *Wis. Then and Now*, vol. 25, no. 5 (December 1978), 2–3. Joseph, Walter, and Joseph Clauder, Jr. were associated with musical activity in Milwaukee from 1855. The father was a second-generation German-American musician born in New York.

DAMROSCH FAMILY

GA157 Frantz, Edna Vee. "One Man's Musical Family." *Amer.-German Rev.*, vol. 12, no. 3 (1946), 417.

DAMROSCH, WALTER

GA158 Ewen, David. *Dictators of the Baton*. New York Chicago: Alliance Book Corp., 1943. 305p. Rev. ed. 1948. See p.119-31 for discussion of the conductor Walter Damrosch.

GA159 Finletter, Gretchen. *From the Top of the Stairs*. Boston: Little, Brown, 1946. Account of life with her father, Walter Damrosch.

ENGEL, CARL

GA160 Bedford, William. "A Musical Apprentice: Amy Lowell to Carl Engel." *Musical Quar.*, vol. 58, no. 4 (1972), 519-42. Correspondence of Carl Engel (1883-1944) in connection with his post as music editor and president of G. Schirmer. A native of Germany, he came to America in 1905.

GA161 Engel, Carl. Papers. In the Music Div., Library of Congress (MS 67-643; 69-2058). E. was a musicologist, librarian and editor.

FALK, LOUIS

GA162 Miller, Francesca Falk. "Dr. Louis Falk." *Amer.-German Rev.*, vol. 10, no. 6 (1944), 30-31, 39. F. (1846-1925) was a prominent musician and music teacher of Chicago.

FINGER, OTTO J.

GA163 "Otto J. Finger in Memoriam." *Report of the Soc. for the Hist. of Germans in Md.*, vol. 32 (1966), 70. Music teacher of Baltimore.

FROMM, HERBERT

GA164 Fromm, Herbert. *The Key of See. Travel Journals of a Composer*. Boston: Plowshare Pr., 1967. 191p. German-born composer who came to the United States in 1937 and served with the Temple Beth Zion in Buffalo, 1937-1941.

FUNK, JOSEPH

GA165 Showalter, Samuel. "Musical Heritage of the Shenandoah Valley." *Mennonite Life*, vol. 18, no. 1 (1963), 38-40. On the life and work of Joseph Funk.

FURTWÄNGLER, WILHELM

GA166 Gillis, Daniel. *Furtwangler and America*. New York: Basic Books, 1971. 148p. Rev. by Ainslee Cox, *Music Jour.*, vol. 29, no. 2 (1971), 78. Emphasis on the attitudes of the American press toward this conductor.

GEHRKENS, KARL WILSON

GA167 Lendrim, Frank Torbet. "Music for Every Child. The Story of Karl Wilson Gehrkens." Diss., Michigan, 1962. 339p. Editor of music periodicals, teacher, and supervisor of musical training in the Oberlin, Ohio, public schools.

GRAM, HANS

GA168 King, Rolf. "The Significance of Hans Gram for Early American Musical Development." *Amer.-German Rev.*, vol. 12, no. 3 (1946), 17-22.

GRAUPNER, GOTTLIEB

GA169 King, Rolf. "Gottlieb Graupner, Musical Pioneer." *Amer.-German Rev.*, vol. 11, no. 1 (1944), 19-22. Graupner formed the first instrumental group in Boston, 1798. A German who had played in Haydn's orchestra in London, he formed a Philharmonic Society in 1810.

GROFE FAMILY

GA170 "Nature in Art: the Grofes." *Amer.-German Rev.*, vol. 13, no. 4 (1947), 24-28.

GYRING, ELIZABETH

GA171 Tauber, Violetta. "Elizabeth Gyring: Profile in Music." *Amer.-German Rev.*, vol. 28, no. 6 (1963), 30-32. Sketch of the Viennese-born composer.

HAGEN, OSKAR FRANK LEONARD

GA172 Hagen, Oskar Frank Leonard. *Choral Rhapsody*. Words by Samuel Rogers after Schiller's poem "The Sun." Madison, Wis., 1943. 52 1. Reproduced from MS. copy, score chorus SATB and orchestral parts. H. was professor of Art History at the Univ. of Wisconsin.

HAGEN, PETER ALBRECHT VON

GA173 Johnson, H. Earle. "The Musical von Hagens." *New England Quar.*, vol. 16, no. 1 (1943), 110-17. On a musical family of Boston.

GA174 King, Rolf. "Peter Albrecht von Hagen." *Amer.-German Rev.*, vol. 12, no. 2 (1945), 23. German-American musician of the late 18th and early 19th century.

HAHN, JACOB H.

GA175 Hahn, Jacob H. Papers and music mss. 1 box. In the Burton Hist. Collection, Detroit Public Library (MS 70-1167). H. (1847-1902) was a composer and music teacher.

HEINRICH, ANTHONY PHILIP

GA176 Bruce, Neely. *The Dawning of Music in Kentucky*. Vanguard Records, SRV 349 SD. 1975. Music by H. (1781–1861), German-American Composer, native of Bohemia.

GA177 Chase, Gilbert. "A. P. Heinrich's 'Condor'." *Stereo Rev.*, vol. 42, no. 4 (April 1979): 134.

GA178 Merrill, Peter C. "Anthony Philip Heinrich: The 'Log-House Composer from Kentucky'." *Newsletter of the Soc. for German-Amer. Studies*, vol. 1, no. 4 (1979–1980), 19.

GA179 Paratore, Anthony, and Joseph Paratore, pianists. *The Ornithological Combat of Kings, or the Condor of the Andes and the Eagle of the Cordilleras*. New World Records, NW-208, ca. 1979. Music by Anthony Philip Heinrich.

GA180 Upton, William T. *Anthony Philip Heinrich*. New York: Columbia Univ. Pr., 1939. 337p. Repr. New York: AMS Pr., 1967.

HINDEMITH, PAUL

GA181 Boatwright, Howard. "Paul Hindemith as a Teacher." *Musical Quar.*, vol. 50 (July 1964), 279–89. Recollections of his classes at Yale University.

GA182 Breuer, Robert. "Hindemith dirigiert seine letzte Oper in New York." *Melos*, vol. 30 (1963), 172–73.

HIRCHLEITNER, GEORG

GA183 Werner, Heinz. "Die Opa Hirchleitner Story." *Schlagzeug*, vol. 3, no. 13 (1958), 24–26; no. 14, 25–26; no. 15, 25–27; no. 16, 26–29. Life story of the Nestor of German jazz musicians who lived for some time in Milenburg, La.

HOFFMAN, RICHARD

GA184 Hoffman, Richard. *Some Musical Recollections of 50 Years*. New York: n.p., 1910. With a biographical sketch by his wife.

KALBECK, MAX

GA185 Kalbeck, Max. Papers, 1873–1920. 201 items. In the Music Div., Library of Congress (MS 67-648). K. (1850–1921) was a German music historian, critic and poet.

KNEISEL, FRANZ

GA186 Kneisel, Franz. Correspondence, 1895–1926. 49 items. In the Music Div., Library of Congress (MS 67-649). Letters to Kneisel and his family relating to musical life in Boston and New York. K. (1865–1926) was a violinist and musician.

KORNGOLD, ERICH WOLFGANG

GA187 Korngold, Erich Wolfgang. Papers and music, 1915–1928. In the Leo Baeck Institute collections, New York (MS 78-1234). Letters and scores, incl. 25 letters from Korngold's father, Julius Korngold, to Max Kalbeck. In German. K. (1897–1957) was an Austrian composer, conductor and critic.

KUNKEL, CHARLES

GA188 Krohn, Ernst C. "Charles Kunkel and Louis Moreau Gottschalk." *Bull., Mo. Hist. Soc.*, vol. 21 (July 1965). K. (1840–1923), native of the Palatinate, was pianist and music publisher in St. Louis from 1868.

LUENING, OTTO

GA189 "An Influential Musician at 80." *N.Y. Times*. 15 June 1980. Sec. D, 27, 30.

MERZ, KARL

GA190 Schreiber, William I. "Karl Merz—German-American Musician." *Amer.-German Rev.*, vol. 7, no. 3 (1941), 4–7, 33; no. 5, 24–27.

GA191 Schreiber, William I. "Karl Merz Memorial." *Amer.-German Rev.*, vol. 9, no. 2 (1942), 37–38.

MEYEROWITZ, JAN

GA192 Berges, Ruth. "The Glory around His Head." *Amer.-German Rev.*, vol. 23, no. 4 (1957), 4–7. On a cantata composed by Jan Meyerowitz, native of Breslau, who came to America in 1946.

MOLLER, JOHN CHRISTOPHER

GA193 Stezel, Ronald D. "John Christopher Moller (1755–1803) and His Role in Early American Music." Diss., St. Univ. of Iowa, 1965. 2 vols. 581p. On M., native of Germany, active in Philadelphia.

OBERHOFFER, EMIL

GA194 Oberhoffer, Emil. Correspondence, 1895–1922. 53 items. In the Minnesota Hist. Soc. (MS

60-944). O. (1867–1933) was an orchestra conductor; a Bavarian who came to St. Paul in the early 1890's and founded the Minneapolis Symphony.

GA195 Sherman, John K. "The Birth of a Symphony Orchestra." *Minn. Hist.*, vol. 33, no. 3 (1952), 93–104.

OLDBERG, ARNE AND OSCAR

GA196 Oldberg, Arne and Oscar Oldberg. Papers, 1974–1969. 23 ft. and ca. 1500 items. In the Library of Congress Music Div. (MS 72-1787). Correspondence, scores, MSS. Arne O. (1874–1962) had studied in Munich and Vienna in the late nineties; composer and dean at Northwestern Univ. Oscar O. (1846–1913) was dean of the school of pharmacy.

PHILLIP, ADOLF

GA197 Marx, Henry. "Adolf Phillip: German-American Playwright, Singer, Composer." In: *Germanica-Americana 1976. Symposium on German-American Literature and Culture.* Ed. Erich A. Albrecht and J. Anthony Burzle. Lawrence, Kans.: Max Kade Document and Research Center, 1977, p.43–47.

RUDEL, JULIUS

GA198 Kolodin, Irving. "Rudel of City Center." *Saturday Rev.*, 13 February 1960. Conductor and director at the New York City Opera.

GA199 Sargeant, Winthrop. "Portraits." Profile of Julius Rudel. *New Yorker*, 20 October 1962, 57–82.

SCHAAF, EDWARD OSWALD

GA200 Schaaf, Edward Oswald. Papers. 61 items. In the Newark Public Library (MS 62-3608). Scores and literary works. S. (1869–1939) was a composer and author.

SCHATZ, ALBERT

GA201 Schatz, Albert. Papers, 1877–1927. 30 ft. (100,000 items). In the Music Div., Library of Congress (MS 67-656). Notes and papers, scores and librettos. S. (1839–1910) was a music dealer and historian of opera.

SCHILLING, ERNEST

GA202 Hill, Thomas H. "Ernest Schilling (1876–1939): His Life and Contributions to Music Education through Educational Concerts." Diss., Catholic Univ., 1970. 456p. Native of Belvidere, N.J., son of a Swiss-born father; conductor and lecturer for the Philharmonic Soc. of New York.

SCHLESINGER, SIGMUND AND JACOB

GA203 Tuckman, William. "Sigmund and Jacob Schlesinger and Joseph Block: Civil War Composer and Musicians." *Amer. Jewish Hist. Quar.*, vol. 53 (1963), 70–75. German-born musicians who emigrated to Mobile, Ala.

SCHNABEL, ARTUR

GA204 Saerchinger, César. *Artur Schnabel; A Biography.* New York: Dodd, Mead, 1957. 354p.

SCHOEN-RENÉ, ANNA EUGÉNIE

GA205 Schoen-René, Anna Eugénie. *America's Musical Inheritance....* New York: Putnam, 1941. 244p. Memoirs of a voice teacher.

SCHOENBERG, ARNOLD

GA206 Schoenberg, Arnold. Papers, 1912–1950. 182 items. In the Univ. of Michigan Library, Department of Rare Books and Special Collections (MS 78-535). Correspondence of the Austrian composer with A. Schnabel, Alfred Wallenstein, Heinrich Jalowetz, Klaus and Monika Mann, W. Furtwängler.

GA207 Schoenberg, Arnold. Papers. Ca. 1890–1951. 50 ft. and 31 reels. In the Arnold Schoenberg Archives at the Univ. of Southern Calif. (MS 78-1162). Notebooks, diaries, scores, MSS., etc.; microfilm negatives from originals in the Library of Congress. See: *Journal of the Arnold Schoenberg Inst.*, for 1976 and subsequently for information on the collection.

SCHIRMER, GUSTAV

GA208 Schirmer, Gustav. Papers, 1903–1939. 122 items. In the Music Div., Library of Congress (MS 67-657). Letters to figures in the world of music. S. (1864–1907) was a music publisher of New York and Boston.

SCHREKER, FRANZ

GA209 Schreker, Franz. Papers. 92 items. In the Music Div., Library of Congress (MS 67-658). Letters and miscellaneous papers of the composer, S. (1878–1954).

SEIDEL, ANTON

GA210 Seidel, Anton. Papers, 1870–1898. 4 boxes. In Columbia Univ. Libraries (MS 62-82). Scores, correspondence. S. (1850–1898).

SONNECK, OSCAR GEORGE THEODORE

GA211 Sonneck, Oscar. Papers, 1894–1928. 6 ft. In the Music Div., Library of Congress (MS 67-662). Personal and literary correspondence with well-known figures in music and the performing arts. S. (1873–1928) was a musicologist and librarian.

STEINBACH, FRITZ

GA212 Steinbach, Fritz. Correspondence, 1885–1912, 1946. 125 letters. In the Music Div., Library of Congress (MS 67-664). Letters from prominent composers (Mahler, Strauss, Joachim, etc.) S. (1855–1916) was a conductor.

STEINBERG, WILLIAM

GA213 Tennenbaum, Silvia. "William Steinberg: A Very Personal Memoir." *Music Jour.*, vol. 3 no. 10 (1978), 16–19. German-American composer.

STEINMANN, ADOLF GUSTAV

GA214 Zucker, Adolf E. "Adolf Gustav Steinmann." *Report of the Soc. for the Hist. of Germans in Md.*, vol. 30 (1959), 29–35. S. (1851–1923), a German immigrant to Baltimore, was active in the musical life of the city.

STOECKEL, GUSTAVE

GA215 Browne, Robert B. "Musical Genesis at Yale." *Music Jour.*, vol. 29, no. 10 (1971), 33–42. On the influence of S. (1819–1907).

STOESSEL, ALBERT

GA216 Stoessel, Albert. Correspondence, 1931–1943. In Amer. Academy of Arts and Sciences Library (MS 61-2590). S. (1894–1943) was a conductor and violinist.

STRUBE, GUSTAV

GA217 Franke, Otto H. "Gustav Strube." *Report of the Soc. for the Hist. of Germans in Md.*, vol. 29 (1956), 75–77. S. (1867–1953) was a composer and musician, native of Ballenstedt, Harz.

GA218 Klemm, Gustav. "Gustav Strube: The Man and the Musician." *Musical Quar.*, vol. 28, no. 3 (1942), 288–301.

THOMAS, THEODORE

GA219 Holliday, Joseph E. "The Musical Legacy of Theodore Thomas." *Cincinnati Hist. Soc. Bull.*, vol. 27, no. 3 (Fall 1969), 191–205. Famous German-American composer and director.

ULLMAN, BERNARD

GA220 Lerner, Laurence M. "The Rise of the Impresario: Bernard Ullman and the Transformation of Musical Culture in Nineteenth Century America." Diss., Wisconsin, 1970. 313p.

VOEGELI, HENRY EDWARD

GA221 Voegeli, Henry Edward. Correspondence, 1909–1953. 200 items. In Chicago Hist. Soc. Library (MS 61-411). V. (1876–1943) served as business manager of the Chicago Symphony Orchestra.

WEBER, MILTON F.

GA222 Dugan, Jo Curtis. "Waukesha's Amazing Austrian." *Wis. Tales and Trails*, vol. 5, no. 4 (Winter 1964), 12–14. Conductor of the Waukesha Symphony.

WEILL, KURT

GA223 Sanders, Ronald. *The Days Grow Short. The Life and Music of Kurt Weill.* New York: Holt, Rinehart & Winston, n.d. 469p.

WELK, LAWRENCE

GA224 Welk, Lawrence. *My America, Your America.* By Lawrence Welk with Bernice McGeehan. Boston: G. K. Hall, ca. 1976. 296p. Autobiography of W. (b. 1903).

ZEISL, ERIC

GA225 Cole, Malcolm S. "Eric Zeisl: The Rediscovery of an Emigré Composer." *Musical Quar.*, vol. 64 (1978), 237–44.

Instruments

GA226 Armstrong, William H. *Organs for America. The Life and Work of David Tannenberg.* Philadelphia: Univ. of Pennsylvania Pr., 1967. 154p. Colonial German-American organ builder.

GA227 Barr, John Gladden. "A Tonal History of Pipe Organs Built by M. P. Möller, Inc." Diss., Union Theological Seminary, New York City, 1977. 483p. On the family firm of M. P. Möller of Hagerstown, Md.

GA228 Bleyle, Carl Otto. "Georg Andreas Sorge's Influence on David Tannenberg and Organ Building in America During the Eighteenth Century." Diss., Minnesota, 1969. 374p.

GA229 C., G. W. "The Dieffenbach Organ." *Hist. Rev. of Berks Co.*, vol. 11, no. 1 (1945), 19–21.

GA230 Eader, Thomas S. "Baltimore Organs and Organ Building." *Md. Hist. Mag.*, vol. 65 (Fall 1970), 263–82.

GA231 Gemünder, George. *George Gemünder's Progress in Violin-Making, with Interesting Facts Concerning the Art and Its Critics in General.* Astoria, N.Y.: n.p., 1881. Autobiographical account. Also publ. in a German-language version: Astoria: n.p., 1880. 94p.

GA232 Hanstein, George. "John Jacob Diffenbach, Wheelwright and Organ Builder." *Amer. German Rev.*, vol. 11, no. 4 (1945), 4–6, 23.

GA233 Hart, Kenneth W. "Cincinnati Organ Builders of the Nineteenth Century." *Cincinnati Hist. Soc. Bull.*, vol. 31 (1973), 79–103. With a chronological listing of organs built in Cincinnati, 1808–1900.

GA234 Hoech, Annie E. "German Music Boxes in America." *Amer.-German Rev.*, vol. 9, no. 2 (1942), 15–17.

GA235 Holmquist, Donald C. "Pride of the Pioneer's Parlor. Pianos in Early Minnesota." *Minn. Hist.*, vol. 39, no. 8 (Winter 1965), 312–26. Comprehensive study on the building, history, playing and selling of the piano on the American frontier.

GA236 Kass, Philip, and Michael Olmert. "Violin-Making as American Art." *The Smithsonian*, vol. 8, no. 6 (September 1977), 106–10. Mainly on the work of August M. L. Gemünder, August Gemünder, Jr., and George Gemünder of New York. The elder Gemünder was trained in Germany.

GA237 Lenehan, Michael. "The Quality of the Instrument. Building Steinway Grand Piano K2571." *Atlantic Monthy*, August 1982, 32–58. On the Steinway family and family history; their enterprises; how a concert grand piano is built.

GA238 *Lob und Anbetung des Gottmenschen, am Tage der Einweihung der neuen Orgel in der Deutschen Evang. Lutherischen Zions Kirche in Philadelphia, den 10. Oktober 1790.* Germantown: Michael Billmeyer, 1790. Dedication of an organ in the Zions Kirche of Philadelphia.

GA239 McCorkle, Donald M. "Prelude to a History of American Moravian Organs." *Amer. Guild of Organists Quar.*, vol. 3, no. 4 (October 1958), 142–48.

GA240 McManis, Charles W. "David Tannenberg and the Old Salem Restoration." *The Amer. Organist*, vol. 48, no. 5 (May 1965, 15–20.

GA241 Ochse, Orpha Carolina. *History of the Organ in the United States.* Bloomington: Indiana Univ. Pr., 1975. 494p. Rev. by E. Wolf, *Musical Quar.*, vol. 61, no. 4 (1975), 618–22.

GA242 Ogasapian, John K. "Organ Building in New York City: 1700 to 1900." Diss., Boston Univ., 1977.

GA243 *The Organ in America.* Performed by E. Power Biggs. Columbia Records ML 5496, MS 6161. Substantial portions of this record are performed on the 1804 Tannenberg Organ in York, Pa.

GA244 "The Organ in Central Moravian Church." *Amer. Organist*, vol. 41, no. 11 (November 1958). In Bethlehem, Pa.

GA245 Raichelson, Richard. "The Social Context of Musical Instruments within the Pennsylvania German Culture." *Pa. Folklife*, vol. 25, no. 1 (1975), 35–44.

GA246 Schmauk, Theodore E. *The Church Organ and Its History.* Lebanon, Pa.: n.p., n.d. MS. in the Archives of the Ministerium of Pennsylvania at the Lutheran Theological Seminary, Philadelphia; On the work of David Tannenberg.

GA247 Singer, Aaron. "Labor-Management Relations at Steinway and Sons 1853–1896." Diss., Columbia Univ., 1977. 220p.

GA248 Spillane, Daniel. *History of the American Pianoforte.* New York: n.p., 1890. Repr. with new introd. by Rita Benton: New York: DaCapo Pr., 1969. 383p.

GA249 Steinway, Theodore E. *People and Piano, A Century of Service to Music, Steinway and Sons, New York, 1853–1953*. New York: n.p., 1953. 122p.

GA250 Steinway and Sons. *Steinway Yesterday, Today, Tomorrow*. Illus. and designed by Susanne Suba. New York: n.p., 1948. 29p.

GA251 Webber, F. R. "Gemshorn and Klingel." *Concordia Hist. Inst. Quar.*, vol. 29 (1956), 41–47. On German organs imported into America and on native builders: Tannenberg of Lititz, Pa., Johann Geib, New York City, and John G. Pfeffer, St. Louis.

GA252 Webber, F. R. "Worship by Machinery." *Concordia Hist. Inst. Quar.*, vol. 33 (January 1961), 97f. Organ builders, incl. Tannenberg, Snetzler, Erben, Johnson, Hook and others.

GA253 Wechsberg, Joseph. "Trustee in Fiddledale—Profile of Emil Herrmann." *The New Yorker*, vol. 29, nos. 35 and 36 (1953), 38–59; 39–55. Herrmann is the leading expert on old musical instruments.

GA254 Weygandt, Cornelius. "Zitters and Hymns." In: *The Dutch Country*. New York: Appleton-Century, 1939, p.300–05. Description of the instrument called the zitter used for the accompaniment of hymns sung in the home.

GA255 Whiting, Robert B. "John Ziegler: Montgomery County (Pa.) Organ Builder." *Bull., Hist. Soc. of Montgomery Co.*, vol. 19 (1973), 46–53.

GA256 Wolf, Edward C. "The Tannenberg Organ at Old Zion Church Philadelphia." *Jour. of Church Music*, vol. 3, no. 4 (April 1961), 2–5.

GB
Secular Song

See also Section EC: Folk Music.

GB1 Arndt, Karl J. R. "The First Wabash Song." *Ind. Mag. of Hist.*, vol. 38 no. 1 (1942), 80–82. Publication of a German song sung by the Harmonists.

GB2 Arndt, Karl J. R., and Richard D. Wetzel. "Harmonist Music and Pittsburgh Musicians in Early Economy." *Western Pa. Hist. Mag.*, vol. 54 (April 1971), 125–27; (July 1971), 284–311; (October 1971), 391–413.

GB3 *Catalogue*, the Max Kade German-American Document and Research Center. Lawrence: Univ. of Kansas, 1976, p.79–80. Nineteen examples of German-American secular songbooks are listed.

GB4 Corry, Mary Jane. "The Role of German Singing Societies in the Music of Philadelphia in the Nineteenth Century." In: *Papers from the Conference on German-Americana in the Eastern United States*. Occasional Papers of the Soc. for German-Amer. Studies, no. 8. Ed. Steven M. Benjamin. Morgantown, W. Va.: Dept. of Foreign Lang., W. Va. Univ., 1980, p.82–90.

GB5 Cortinovis, Irene E. "The Golden Age of German Song." *Mo. Hist. Rev.*, vol. 68 (July 1974), 437–42.

GB6 Fornell, Martha, and Earl W. Fornell. "A Century of German Song in Texas." *Amer.-German Rev.*, vol. 24, no. 1 (1957), 29–31. The first *Gesangverein* was established in 1850 in New Braunfels.

GB7 *Frisch, fröhlich, frei; deutsch-amerikanisches Turn-Liederbuch mit Weisen*. New York: New Yorker Turnverein, 1864.

GB8 Goleeke, Wallace John. "A History of the Male Chorus Singing Movement in Seattle." Portion of a dissertation project, Univ. of Washington, 1969.

GB9 Hall, Alvin L. "Charles Chaky de Nordendorf: Soldier-Songster of the Confederacy." *Va. Cavalcade*, vol. 24 (Summer 1974), 41–47. Emigrated from Austria in 1863.

GB10 Haas, Oscar. *A Chronological History of the Singers of German Songs in Texas*. New Braunfels: by the author, 1948. 73p.

GB11 Kiesewalter, Dietrich P. "Deutscher Gesang in Kanada." *New Yorker Staats-Zeitung und Herold*, vol. 146, no. 9 (1980). Sec. A, 11. Treats the Deutsch-Kanadischer Sängerbund.

GB12 Matthews, Stanley. "Aftermath of a Golden Jubilee." *Bull. of the Hist. and Philosophical Soc. of Ohio*, vol. 16 (1958), 143–50. The great Cincinnati *Sängerfest* of 1899 and its financial problems.

GB13 Most, Johann, comp. *Neuestes Proletarier-Liederbuch von verschiedenen Arbeiterdichtern.* 3rd rev. ed. Chemnitz: n.p., 1873.

GB14 Nau, John F. "The History of German Song in New Orleans." In: *The 43rd National Saengerfest of the North-American Singers Union.* New Orleans: Deutsches Haus, 1958, p.13–17.

GB15 Nettl, Paul. "First of the Song Hits." *Amer.-German Rev.*, vol. 14, no. 4 (1948), 17–19. With incidental references to Pennsylvania German traditions.

GB16 Nettl, Paul. "German Melodies in American College Songs." *Amer.-German Rev.*, vol. 13, nos. 5–6 (1947), 21–23.

GB17 Redding, Earl William. "Vocal and Musical Problems Found in Selected Solo Songs of Various Periods with Specific Consideration of the German Lied in English." D.M.A. thesis, Univ. of Missouri at Kansas City, 1965. 71p. Contends that the fusion of words and music is not lost when using English translations.

GB18 Rodda, Anne E. "Translation and the German Art of Song: Some Problems." In: *Translation in the Humanities.* Ed. Marilyn Gaddis Rose. Binghamton: State Univ. of New York, 1977, p.67–76. Concerning the trans. of "Das Veilchen" by Mildred Guntlett.

GB19 *Saenger Zeitung. Journal for Singers.* 1924–. German- and English-language monthly. Ed. Walter Hoops. 1832 Hillsdale Ave., Dayton, Ohio 45414. Published by Federation of Workers' Singing Societies of the United States; reports of affiliated singing societies and their song festivals.

GB20 Schaper, F. "Der deutsch-kanadische Sängerbund." *Torontoer Zeitung*, 28 March 1969.

GB21 Stebbins, Lucy Poate, and Richard Poate. *Frank Damrosch. Let the People Sing.* Forew. by Frank Damrosch, ed. Durham, N. Car.: Duke Univ. Pr., 1945. A songbook.

GB22 Tawa, Nicholas E. *Sweet Songs for Gentle Americans: The Parlor Song in America, 1790–1860.* Bowling Green, Ohio: n.p., 1980. 273p.

GB23 *Texanische Lieder. Aus mündlicher und schriftlicher Mitteilung deutscher Texaner. Mit Singweisen.* San Felipe de Austin: n.p., 18–?.

GB24 Thomas, Arnold R. "The Development of Male Glee Clubs in American Colleges and Universities." Diss., Columbia, 1962. 165p. The movement is found to be an outgrowth of "singing groups in England and on the Continent, especially the German *Männerchöre.*"

GB25 Wetzel, Richard D. "The Music Collection of Georg Rapp's *Harmonie Gesellschaft* (1805–1906)." *Monatshefte*, vol. 68 (1976), 167–70.

GB26 Wetzel, Richard Dean. "The Music of George Rapp's Harmony Society: 1805–1906." Diss., Pittsburgh, 1970. 569p.

GB27 Yerbury, Grace H. *Song in America, From Early Times to About 1850.* Metuchen: Scarecrow Pr., 1971. 305p.

GB28 Yerbury, Grace Helen. "Styles and Schools of Art-Song in America 1720–1850." Diss., Univ. of Indiana, 1953. 423p.

GB29 Zucker, Adolf E. "One Hundred and Ten Years of German Song." *Amer.-German Rev.*, vol. 26, no. 6 (1960), 10–11, 18. History of the Washington, D.C. Sängerbund.

GC
Sacred Music

General

GC1 Begemann, Renate. *Die Lieder der Pennsylvaniadeutschen in ihrem sozialen Kontext: Eine Analyse der Brendelschen Sammlung 1935–1950.* Marburg: n.p., 1973. 335p. Diss., Marburg.

GC2 Brown, Robert Benaway, and Frank X. Braun. "The Tunebook of Conrad Doll." *Papers of the Bibliogrophical Soc. of America*, vol. 42, no. 3 (1948), 229–38. Contents and sources of *Sammlung, Geistlicher Lieder nebst Melodien, von Verschiedenen Dichtern und Componisten.* Ed. Conrad Doll. Lancaster: n.p., 1798.

GC3 Eskew, Harold. "Joseph Funk's 'Allgemein Nützliche Choral-Music' (1816)." *Report of the Soc. for the Hist. of the Germans in Md.*, vol. 32 (1966), 38–46.

GC4 Farlee, Lloyd Winfield. "A History of the Church Music of the Amana Society, the Community of True Inspiration." Diss., Iowa, 1966. 929p.

GC5 Gould, Nathaniel D. *History of Church Music in America.* . . . Boston: n.p., 1853. 240p.

GC6 Hall, James W. "The Role of the Tune-Book in American Culture: 1800–1820." Diss., Univ. of Pennsylvania, 1967.

GC7 Hartzell, Lawrence. "Music and the Mystics of the Wissahickon." *Jour. of German-Amer. Studies*, vol. 13 (1978), 81–86.

GC8 Kerr, Phil. *Music in Evangelism and Stories of Famous Christian Songs.* Rev. ed. Glendale, Calif.: n.p., ca. 1944.

GC9 *Kinder-Lieder zum Gebrauch für Schulen, Sonntagsschulen und Familien.* . . . Comp. and trans. by Sunday school staff, Somerset County, Pa. Aylmer, Ont.: Pathway Publ. Corp., 1967. 56p.

GC10 Lindsley, Charles Edward. "Early Nineteenth Century American Collections of Sacred Choral Music, 1800–1810: Part I. A Historical Survey of Tune-Book Production to 1810. Part II. An Annotated Bibliography of Tune-Books, 1800–1810." Diss., Univ. of Iowa, 1968. 283p.

GC11 Lumpkin, Ben Gray. "Der Traum des Baume [sic],—A Religious Song from the Middle Ages." *Jour. of Amer. Folklore*, vol. 78, no. 307 (January–March 1965), 66–68. Comment on a recording made by Mrs. Fred Ehrlich, who came to Windsor, Colorado in the 1920's. Text of the song is included. See commentary by J. Szöverffy, *ibid.*, no. 310 (October–December 1965), 349; and by E. S. Dick, *ibid.*, no. 310 (October–December 1965), 346–48.

GC12 Martens, Helen. "The Music of Some Religious Minorities in Canada." *Ethnomusicology*, vol. 16 (1972), 360–71. Music of the Old Order Amish, Old Colony Mennonites, Hutterites, and others. Words and music reproduced.

GC13 Pennsylvania Society of the Colonial Dames of America. *Church Music and Musical Life in Pennsylvania in the Eighteenth Century*, Philadelphia: n.p., 1926, 1927. 3 vols. in 4. Repr. New York: AMS Pr., 1972.

GC14 Rosewall, Richard Byron. "Singing Schools of Pennsylvania, 1800–1900." Diss., Univ. of Minnesota, 1969. 439p. Functioned at first (to 1840) as part of parochial education by and for the Germans; served to teach the hymns of the church and keep the German language alive.

GC15 Saltzman, Herbert Royce. "A Historical Study of the Function of Music among the Brethren in Christ." D.M.A. thesis, Univ. of Southern California, 1964. 346p.

GC16 Seip, Oswell J. "Pennsylvania German Choral Books." *Lehigh Co. Hist. Soc., Procs.*, (1944), 39–43.

GC17 Stevenson, Robert M. *Patterns of Protestant Church Music.* Durham, N. Car.: n.p., 1953.

GC18 Stevenson, Robert M. *Protestant Church Music in America*. New York: Norton, 1966. 168p. Survey of men and movements from 1564 to the present.

GC19 Whitaker, Pauline L. "Musical History of Lancaster County." *Procs., Lancaster Co. Hist. Soc.*, vol. 46 (1942), 128–31. History since 1837 of Amish and Mennonite singing; Trinity Lutheran Church; etc.

GC20 Wolkan, Rudolf. *Die Lieder der Wiedertäufer*. Berlin: n.p., 1913.

Spirituals and Hymns

GC21 Anderson, Verlyn D. "Acculturation of an Immigrant Church's Hymnals." Diss., Minnesota, 1968.

GC22 Bittinger, Emmert F. "More on Brethren Hymnology." *Brethren Life and Thought*, vol. 8, no. 3 (1963), 11–16. Examination of *Die kleine Lieder Sammlung*. Hagerstown, 1826; and *A Choice Selection of Hymns from Various Authors*. Canton, Ohio, 1830.

GC23 Brightbill, Alvin F. *German Hymns of the Brethren*. 3 mimeogr. leaves, with music and text of German *Kernlieder*, plus *Kommt, Brüder, kommt, wir eilen fort*, as sung by the Brethren at the Second Annual Pa. Dutch Folk Festival, Kutztown, 1951.

GC24 Buffington, Albert F. *Dutchified German Spirituals*. Procs, Pa. German Soc., vol. 62. Lancaster. n.p., 1966. 239p. Rev. by R. W. Schlosser, *Hist. Rev. of Berks Co.*, vol. 31, no. 4 (Autumn 1966), 144; C. R. Beam, "'S Pennsylfawnish Deitsch Eck," Allentown *Morning Call*, 3 September 1966.

GC25 England, Martha Winburn. "The First Wesley Hymn Book." *Bull., N.Y. Public Library*, vol. 68. no. 4 (1965), 225–38. John Wesley's *A Collection of Psalms and Hymns* compiled during his stay in Georgia and publ. in Charleston in 1737.

GC26 Fisher, Nevin W. *The History of Brethren Hymnbooks*. Bridgewater, Va.: Beacon Publs., 1950. Early German hymnbooks of the German Baptist Brethren.

GC27 Frey, J. William. "Amish Hymns as Folk Music." In: *Pennsylvania Songs and Legends*. Ed George Korson. Philadelphia: n.p., 1949, p.129–62.

GC28 *Gemeinschaftliches Gesangbuch. Herausgegeben zum Gebrauch an der Vereinigten Lager-Versammlung der deutschen erweckten Gemeinden von Baltimore*. Baltimore: n.p., 1871. 400p. For the use of German Methodist, Evangelical Association and United Brethren members.

GC29 Gilman, Sander L. "German Hymnals in the Harris Hymnal Collection: A Short-Title Checklist." *Cornell Library Jour.*, vol. 10 (1970), 40–48.

GC30 Haeussler, Armin G. *The Story of Our Hymns*. St. Louis: n.p., 1952.

GC31 Hamm, Charles. "Folk Hymns of the Shenandoah Valley." *Va. Cavalcade*, vol. 6, no. 2 (1956), 14–19. Hymnbooks and song collections publ. by Lawrence Wartmann, Joseph Funk and the Ruebush-Kieffer Company in Rockingham Co., Va.

GC32 Hewitt, Theodore B. "German Hymns in American Hymnals." *German Quar.*, vol. 21, no. 1 (1948), 37–50.

GC33 Hohmann, Rupert K. "The Beginning of Protestant Hymn Melodies." *Mennonite Life*, vol. 19, no. 4 (1964), 174–76. Their derivation from German tunes.

GC34 Horn, Dorothy. "Tune Detecting in 19th Century Hymnals." *Tenn. Folklore Soc. Bull.*, vol. 26, no. 4 (1960), 99–109. Influence of the German chorale in American hymns published from 1793 to 1864.

GC35 Hudson, Arthur Palmer. "The Singstunde in Old Wachovia [Salem, N. Car.]." *N. Car. Folklore*, vol. 14 (November 1966), 4–11. A distinctive musical service used mainly between 1753 and 1783. See also *Abstracts of Folklore Studies*, no. 148: Vol. 6, no. 1 (Spring 1968), 32.

GC36 *Hymn Book of the United Evangelical Church*. Harrisburg: n.p., 1897. 396, 415p. United Evangelical Church hymnal.

GC37 Jackson, George Pullen. *Another Sheaf of White Spirituals*. Gainesville, Fla.: Univ. of Fla. Pr., 1952.

GC38 Jackson, George Pullen. *Down-East Spirituals and Others*. New York: n.p., 1939.

GC39 Jackson, George Pullen. "Pennsylvania Dutch Spirituals." *The Musical Quar.*, vol. 38 (1952), 80–84.

GC40 Jackson, George Pullen. *Spiritual Folk Songs of Early America*. 2nd ed. Locust Valley, N.Y.: n.p., 1953.

GC41 Julian, John. *Dictionary of Hymnology*. London: n.p., 1892.

GC42 Kadelbach, Ada. "The German-American Evangelical Hymns up to 1880." Diss., Mainz, 1967.

GC43 Kemmerer, J. F., and D. Kemmerer. *Hymns, Temperance Odes &c. Sung at the Juvenile Concerts*. Taught by J. F. and D. Kemmerer. Philadelphia: n.p., 1849. 401p.

GC44 *Der köstliche Schatz, die neuesten Lieder für den Brüderkreis*. 14th ed. Yankton, S. Dak.: The Pioneer Pr., 1943. 359p.

GC45 Kurzenknabe, J. H. *Gates Ajar*. Harrisburg, Pa.: n.p., 1885. 429p. Gospel songbook.

GC46 Long, Edwin M. *Illustrated History of Hymns and Their Authors*. Philadelphia: n.p., ca. 1882.

GC47 Morgan, Catharine. "Sacred Folk Song in America." *Amer. Guild of Organists Quar.*, vol. 12 (April 1967), 54–60.

GC48 Ninde, Edward S. *The Story of the American Hymn*. New York: n.p., 1921. 429p.

GC49 Rauch, John. "The History of the Evangelical United Brethren Hymnal." Diss., Pittsburgh, 1961.

GC50 Rauschenbusch, Walter, trans. *Evangeliums-Lieder*. Cincinnati: n.p., ca. 1891. 424p. Gospel hymns.

GC51 Rodeheaver, Homer A. *Hymnal Handbook for Standard Hymns and Gospel Songs*. Chicago: n.p., 1931.

GC52 Routley, Erik. *The Musical Wesleys*. London: Jenkins, 1968 (i.e., 1969). New York: Oxford Univ. Pr., 1968. 272p.

GC53 Schaeffer, Aaron. "Historical Evolution of the Hymnal of the Evangelical United Brethren Church." M.A. Thesis, United Seminary, Dayton, Ohio.

GC54 Seipt, Allen A. *Schwenkfelder Hymnology and the Sources of the First Schwenkfelder Hymnbook Printed in America*. Repr. New York: AMS Pr., 1971. 112p.

GC55 Stoll, Jacob. "Four Hymns (Verse)"; "Four Hymns"; "Six Hymns." Trans. by Ora W. Graber. *Brethren Life and Thought*, vol. 16 (1971), 227–32; vol. 18 (1973), 71–76; vol. 19 (1974). Selections from the *Geistliches Gewürz-Gärtlein Heilsuchender Seelen* (1806).

GC56 Weinand, Peter. *Gemeinschafts-Lieder*. Chicago: n.p., 1917. 422p. Songs of the Germans from Russia.

GC57 Weinbrenner, Johannes. *Das Christliche Gesangbuch*. Harrisburg: n.p., 1833. 399p. Hymnal of the Church of God.

GC58 Weishampel, John F. *The Prayer Meeting Hymn Book*. Baltimore: n.p., 1858. 398p. Hymnal of the Church of God.

GC59 Winebrenner, John. *A Prayer Meeting and Revival Hymn Book*. Harrisburg: n.p., 1825. 397p. Hymnal of the Church of God.

GC60 Winebrenner, John. *The Church Hymn Book*. Harrisburg, 1859. 397p. Hymnal of the Church of God.

GC61 *Wolga Gesangbuch*. 1st Amer. edition. Chicago: n.p., 1928. 422p. Songs of the Germans from Russia.

GC62 Wright, Elisha C. *The Union Songster*. Circleville, Ohio: n.p., 1835. 408p. United Brethren hymnal.

GC63 Y., S. T. *"Bald Watt's Besser Gee*—A Pennsylvania Dutch Spiritual." *The Pa. Dutchman*, 16 June 1949.

GC64 Yeakel, I. C. *Hymns and Choruses Compiled for Distribution at the Yorkana Campmeeting*. York, Pa.: n.p., n.d. 411p.

GC65 Yoder, Don. "German Spirituals." *The Pa. Dutchman*, vol. 1 (19 May 1949).

GC66 Yoder, Don H. "Pennsylvania Dutch Spirituals: Folk-Hymns of the Bush Meeting." *The Pa. Dutchman*, vol. 1, no. 23 (1949–1950), 1f.

GC67 Yoder, Don. *Pennsylvania Spirituals*. Lancaster, Pa.: Pa. Folk Life Soc., 1961. 528p. Rev. by E. A. Benson, *Jour. of the Lancaster Co. Hist. Soc.*, vol. 69, no. 4 (Michaelmas, 1965), 240–41; G. Swetnam, *Western Pa. Hist. Mag.*, vol. 46 (1963), 292–94; P. H. Kennedy, *Southern Folklore Quar.*, vol. 28 (1964), 229–31.

GC68 Yoder, Don. "Spirituals from the Pennsylvania Dutch Country." *Bull. of Franklin and Marshall College*. Institute of Religion Number, 1951. Rev. ed. in *The Pa. Dutchman*, vol. 8, no.2 (Fall-Winter 1956–1957), 22–23.

GC69 Yoder, Don. "The Themes of the Pennsylvania Dutch Spiritual." *The Pa. Dutchman*, vol. 3, no. 7 (1951–1952), 1, 5.

GC70 *Zions-Loblieder. Eine Sammlung guter geistlicher Lieder*. York, Neb.: Christian Unity Pr., 1943. 424p.

Music of the Moravian Church

GC71 Albertini, Johan B. von. *Jubel-Psalm zum 4ten May 1830 in Salem in Erinnerung an den 4ten May, 1730*. N.p.: n.p., n.d. At Salem, N. Car., Congregation of Moravian Church.

GC72 *Alter und Neuer Brüdergesang*. London: Moravian Publications Office, 1953–1954. 2 Parts.

GC73 Anderson, Thomas J. "The *Collegium Musicum Salem*, 1780–1790: Origins and Repertoire." Diss., Florida State Univ., 1976.

GC74 Antes, John. *Three Trios: The Birth of Chamber Music in America*. Vol. 3: *Music of the American Moravians*. Fine Arts Quartet. Columbia Records. ML 6141, MS 6741.

GC75 Cumnock, Frances. *Catalogue of the Salem Congregation Music*. Chapel Hill: Univ. of N. Car. Pr., 1980. 682p. Music of the community of Old Salem, N. Car.

GC76 David, Hans T. *Musical Life in the Pennsylvania Settlement of the Unitas Fratrum*. Forew. by Donald M. McCorkle. *Transactions, Moravian. Hist. Soc.*, 1942. Repr. 1959. 44p. Rev. in *Amer.-German Rev.*, vol. 25, no. 6 (1959), 39.

GC77 [Early American Moravian Music Festival and Seminar. 20–26 June 1976. Bethlehem, Pa.] *New York Times*, 20 June 1976. Performance of "A Poem of Joy," composed by Johann Friedrich Peter (1746–1813) for what is believed to have been the first official celebration of Independence Day in the United States, at Salem, N.C., 1783. Also, the "Water Music" by David Mority Michael (1751–1827).

GC78 Falconer, John. "The Second Berlin Song School in America." *Musical Quar.*, vol. 59, no. 3 (1973), 411–40. Johannes Herbst (1735–1812) called his group of singers "Die Zweite Berliner Liederschule."

GC79 Gombosi, Marilyn. *A Day of Solemn Thanksgiving. Moravian Music for the Fourth of July, 1783, in Salem, North Carolina*. Chapel Hill: Univ. of N. Car. Pr., ca. 1977. 215p. Reconstruction of scores used in celebrating the first anniversary of the Declaration of Independence after peace was declared.

GC80 Gombosi, Marilyn, comp. *Catalog of the Johannes Herbst Collection*. Ed. M. Gombosi. Chapel Hill: Univ. of N. Car. Pr., 1970. 255p. Thematic catalogue of Moravian church music copied by Johannes Herbst.

GC81 Hall, Harry Hobart. "The Moravian Wind Ensemble: Distinctive Chapter in America's Music." Diss., George Peabody College for Teachers, 1967. 2 vols. 568p. Traces a tradition established in 1731 at Herrnhut, Saxony, and transplanted to Bethlehem, Pa.

GC82 Hamilton, Kenneth G. "The Bethlehem Christmas Hymn." *Transactions, Moravian Hist. Soc.*, vol. 14, nos. 1 and 2 (1947), 11–23.

GC83 Hark, Ann. "Mr. Dynamo." *Amer.-German Rev.*, vol. 28, no. 2 (1962), 23–24. The Moravian

Music of the Moravian Church *(cont.)*

Symphony in Brass and Reeds, Bethlehem, Pa., and its founder-director, Charles W. Noll.

GC84 Hoople, Donald G. "Moravian Music Education and the American Moravian Music Tradition." Diss., Columbia Teachers College, 1976.

GC85 Lawson, Charles Truman. "Musical Life in the Unitas Fratrum Mission at Springplace, Georgia, 1800–1936." Diss., Florida State, 1970. 180p. A mission to the Cherokees; their music in school and church, love feasts, hymns, sacred and secular orchestral music.

GC86 McCorkle, Donald M. "The *Collegium Musicum Salem*: Its Music, Musicians, and Importance." *N. Car. Hist. Rev.*, vol. 33 (1956), 483–98. Moravian music and musicians in the Wachovia region from 1786 into the 1840's.

GC87 McCorkle, Donald M. "The Moravian Contribution to American Music." *Music Library Assoc. Notes*, vol. 13, no. 4 (September 1956), 597–606. Stresses the value and importance of the Moravian archives.

GC88 McCorkle, Donald M. "Musical Instruments of the Moravians in North Carolina." *Amer.-German Rev.*, vol. 21, no. 3 (February–March 1955), 12–17.

GC89 McCorkle, Donald M. "Musical Life in Salem [N. Car.]." *Antiques*, vol. 88, (July 1965), 65–68.

GC90 Maurer, Joseph A. "America's Heritage of Moravian Music." "'S Pennsylfawnisch Deitsch Eck," Allentown *Morning Call*, 21, 28 May 1955.

GC91 Maurer, Joseph A. "America's Heritage of Moravian Music—Contributions of Early Pennsylvania Composers." *Hist. Rev. of Berks Co.*, vol. 18, no. 3 (1953), 66–70, 87–91.

GC92 Maurer, Joseph A. "Central Moravian Church: Center of Moravian Music." *Amer. Organist*, vol. 41, no. 2 (November 1958), 407–12.

GC93 Maurer, Joseph A. "The Moravian Trombone Choir." *Hist. Rev. of Berks Co.*, vol. 20, no. 1 (1954), 2–8. Also in "'S Pennsylfawnisch Deitsch Eck, 20, 27 November 1954.

GC94 Maurer, Joseph A. "Music in Wachovia, 1753–1800." *William and Mary Quar.*, vol. 8, (1951), 214–27.

GC95 Moravian Church. *The Liturgy and Hymns of the American Province of the Unitas Fratrum, or the Moravian Church*. Bethlehem: Moravian Publ. Office, 1876.

GC96 Moravian Festival Chorus and Orchestra. *Arias, Anthems and Chorals of the American Moravians*. Conducted by Thor Johnson. 2 vols. Columbia Records MR ML 5427, MS 6102; ML 5688, MS 6288.

GC97 Moravian Festival Chorus and Orchestra. *Music of The American Moravians*. Conducted by Thor Johnson. Odyssey Stereo, 32–160340. Reissued with compositions by John Antes. Performed by the Moravian Festival and the Fine Arts Quartet.

GC98 Müller, Joseph T. *Hymnologisches Handbuch zum Gesangbuch der Brüdergemeine*. Herrnhut: n.p., 1916.

GC99 Pfatteicher, Carl F. "The Hymns of the Bohemian Brethren." *Amer.-German Rev.*, vol. 21, no. 3 (1955), 35. Music at Bethlehem, Pa.

GC100 Pfatteicher, Carl F., trans. *Oh, Man, Behold Thou Thy Master*. The Words and Melody from the Bohemian Brethren. Harmonization by Friedrich Riegel. New York: Carl Fischer Inc., 1929. 2p. A capella anthem of Moravian Church for mixed voices. English text.

GC101 Poole, Franklin P. "The Moravian Musical Heritage: Johann Christian Geisler's Music in America." Diss., George Peabody College for Teachers, 1971.

GC102 Pruett, James W. "Francis P. Hagen: American Moravian Musician." *Amer.-German Rev.*, vol. 24, no. 2 (1957), 15–17. Hagen (1815–1907) was a Moravian preacher and composer.

GC103 Rau, Albert G. *A Catalogue of Music by American Moravians, 1742–1842 from the Archives of the Moravian Church at Bethlehem, Pa.* Comp. by A. G. Rau and Hans T. David. Bethlehem: Moravian Seminary and College for Women, 1938.

GC104 Roberts, Dale A. "The Sacred Music of David Moritz Michael: An American Moravian Composer." Diss., Kentucky, 1978.

GC105 Runner, David C. "Music in the Moravian Community of Lititz." Diss., Eastman School of Music, Univ. of Rochester, 1976.

GC106 Schwarze, W. N. "Early Hymnals of the Bohemian Brethren." *Transactions of the Moravian Hist. Soc.*, vol. 13, nos. 3-4 (1944), 163-73.

GC107 Sparrow, John. "George Herbert and John Donne among the Moravians." *Bull., N.Y. Public Library*, vol. 68, no. 10 (1964), 625-53. The Moravian Hymnbook of 1754 attempted to popularize a considerable body of English religious poetry of the 17th century.

GC108 Spice, Gordon P. "Johann Gottfried Gebhard: Moravian Musician." Diss., N. Car., 1975.

GC109 Stoudt, John Joseph. "The Pennsylvania Christmas Hymn of 1742." *Pa. Hist.*, vol. 22, no. 1 (1955), 69-73. On an extemporized chain of 37 strophes composed by Zinzendorf in the *Gemein Haus* at Bethlehem, Pa.

GC110 Weckman, George, organist. *The Chorale Prelude*. With the Choir of the Lutheran Theological Seminary, Philadelphia. Ken-Del Productions, Inc., Wilmington, Del., 1963. Monophonic MA 6. In part recorded on the 1791 Tannenberg organ at Zion Lutheran Church, Spring City, Pa.

GC111 Williams, H. L. "The Development of the Moravian Hymnal." *Transactions, Moravian Hist. Soc.*, vol. 18, Part 2 (1962), 239-66.

Music of the Ephrata Community

GC112 Blakely, Lloyd. "John Conrad Beissel and the Music of the Ephrata Cloister." *Jour. of Research in Music Education*, vol. 15 (Summer 1967), 120-38. Music developed from 1732 to 1768.

GC113 Carlson, Charles Howard. "The Ephrata Cloister's Music of Yesteryear." *Music Jour.*, vol. 22 (January 1964), 52, 118-20. On Conrad Beissel and his unique musical culture in the 1740's.

GC114 David, Hans T. "Hymns and Music of the Pennsylvania Seventh-Day Baptists." *Amer.-German Rev.*, vol. 9 no. 5 (June 1943), 4-6, 36.

GC115 David, Hans T. "Musical Composition at Ephrata." *Amer.-German rev.*, vol. 10, no. 5 (June 1944), 4-5.

GC116 Henry, Thomas L. "The Singing School at the Ephrata Cloister." *Keystone Folklore Quar.*, vol. 11, no. 3 (Fall 1966), 203-06.

GC117 Miller, Elizabeth K. "An Ephrata Hymnal." *Antiques*, vol. 52, no. 4 (October 1947), 260-62.

GC118 Viehmeyer, L. Allen. "Anna of Ephrata." *Hist. Schaefferstown Record*, vol. 8 (1974), 22-31. Writer of hymns.

Hutterite Music

GC119 Brednich, Rolf W. "Beharrung und Wandel im Liedgut der hutterischen Brüder in Amerika: Ein Beitrag zur empirischen Hymnologie." *Jahrbuch für Volksliedforschung*, vol. 26 (1981), 44-60.

GC120 Martens, Helen. "Hutterite Melodies from the Strassburg Psalter." *Mennonite Quar. Rev.*, vol. 48 (1974), 201-14.

GC121 Martens, Helen. "Hutterite Songs: Aural Transmission from the Sixteenth Century." *Ares Nova* (Pretoria), vol. 6 (1974), 5-15.

GC122 Martens, Helen. "Hutterite Songs: The Origins and Aural Transmission of Their Melodies from the Sixteenth Century." Diss., Columbia, 1968. 306p. Traces Hutterite and Amish melodies to 16th-century sources.

GC123 Schilling, Arnold J. "The Music of the Hutterites of Tschetter Colony." M.A. Thesis, South Dakota, 1955; diss., Univ. of S. Dakota, 1965.

Lutheran and Reformed Hymnology

GC124 Anders, Charles R. "The Search for New Song: Developments in Contemporary Hymnody in the American Lutheran Churches." In: *Vita Laudande. Essays in Memory of Ulrich S. Leupold.* Ed. Erich R. W. Schultz. Waterloo, Ont.: Wilfried Laurier Univ. Pr., 1976. p.101–15.

GC125 Bruening, H. D. "Professor Martin Lochner, M. Mus." *Concordia Hist. Inst. Quar.*, vol. 18, no. 3 (1945), 67–71.

GC126 [Henkel, Paul.] *Kurzer Zeitvertreib, Bestehend in einigen Liedern, dienlich zur Sittenlehre.* New Market, Va.: n.p., 1812. 3rd ed. See Sheeleigh Collection, Gettysburg Theological Seminary.

GC127 Jennings, Robert Lee. "A Study of the Historical Development of Choral Ensembles in Selected Lutheran Liberal Arts Colleges in the United States." Diss., Michigan St., 1969. 470p. Ensembles of Augustana, Concordia, Luther, and St. Olaf colleges.

GC128 Koriath, Kirby L. "Walter E. Buszin: Lutheran Hymnologist, Church Musician, Editor." Diss., Eastman School of Music, Univ. of Rochester, 1977.

GC129 Kunze, J. C. *A Hymn and Prayer Book for the Use of Lutheran Churches as Use the English Language.* New York: J. Tiebout, 1795.

GC130 Lehmann, Arnold Otto. "The Music of the Lutheran Church Synodical Conference, Chiefly the Areas Missouri, Illinois, Wisconsin, and Neighboring States, 1839–1941." Diss., Western Reserve, 1967. 442p.

GC131 Monroe, Fabian, and Larry Neff. "Fasting and Penitence, July 20, 1775: Text of a Hymn by Muhlenberg." *Der Reggeboge*, vol. 9, no. 2 (1975), 1.

GC132 "Music in Old Zion, Philadelphia, 1750–1850." *Musical Quar.*, vol. 58, no. 4 (1972), 622–52. Musicians, programs, pastors at St. Michael's and Zion German Lutheran Church.

GC133 Nettl, Paul. *Luther and Music.* Philadelphia: Muhlenberg Pr., 1948. 174p.

GC134 Neve, Paul Edmund. "The Contribution of the Lutheran College Choirs to Music in America." S.M.D. Diss., Union Theological Seminary, New York City, 1967. Points out the strong influence of the St. Olaf a cappella choir.

GC135 Schmucker, Samuel S. *Hymns, Selected and Original, For Public and Private Worship.* Gettysburg: n.p., ca. 1830. Low church Lutheran hymnal.

GC136 Sillivan, Peter M. "The Jacob Leiser Family's German Hymnal and Its Inscriptions: A Note on an Unbound Lutheran Hymnal." *Proc., Lehigh Co. Hist. Soc.*, vol. 30 (1974), 59–62.

GC137 S[ingmaster], J. A. *"Gospel Hymns," verdeutschet zum Gebrauch der Betstunde.* Macungie, Pa.: n.p., 1884. 424p. A low church Lutheran hymnal.

GC138 W., D. "German Psalmody and Singing." *Messenger of the German Reformed Church*, 30 May 1849.

GC139 Williams, George W. *Jacob Eckhard's Choirmaster's Book of 1809.* Columbia, S. Car.: Univ. of S. Car. Pr., 1971. Rev. by E. Robinson, *S. Car. Hist. Mag.*, vol. 73 (1972), 102. Eckhard, an erstwhile Hessian mercenary, served as organist in Charleston after the Revolution.

GC140 Wolf, Edward C. "America's First Lutheran Chorale Book." *Concordia Hist. Inst. Quar.*, vol. 46 (Spring 1973), 5–17.

GC141 Wolf, Edward C. "Justus Henry Christian Helmuth: Hymnodist." *German-Amer. Studies*, vol. 5 (1972), 117–47. Incl. a list of Helmuth imprints—hymn, anthem, and cantata texts as preserved in the Krauth Memorial Library, Lutheran Theological Seminary, Mt. Airy, Philadelphia.

GC142 Wolf, Edward C. "Lutheran Hymnody and Music Published in America, 1700–1850: A Descriptive Bibliography." *Concordia Hist. Inst. Quar.*, vol. 50 (1977), 164–85.

Mennonite and Amish Mennonite Hymnology

GC143 Burkhart, C. "The Church Music of the Old Order Amish and the Old Colony Mennonites." *Mennonite Quar. Rev.*, vol. 27 (1953), 34–54. Also: M.A. thesis, Colorado State, 1952

GC144 Classen, Johann P. "Editions of *Ein schön Gesangbüchlein*." *Mennonite Life*, vol. 12, (1957), 47–48, 96.

GC145 Duerksen, Rosella R. "Early German Anabaptist Hymn Books." *Mennonite Life*, vol. 12 (1957), 61–63, 96.

GC146 Erb, Paul. "Mennonite Hymnbooks." *Gospel Herald*, 4 March 1952.

GC147 Hohman, Rupert K. "The Church Music of the Old Order Amish of the United States." Diss., Northwestern Univ., 1959.

GC148 Hohmann, W. H. *Outlines in Hymnology with Emphasis on Mennonite Hymnology*. North Newton, Kans.: n.p. 1941.

GC149 Jackson, George Pullen. "The American Amish Sing Medieval Folk Tunes Today." *Southern Folklore Quar.*, vol. 10, no. 2 (1946), 151–57.

GC150 Jackson, George Pullen. "The Strange Music of the Old Order Amish." *Musical Quar.*, vol. 31 (1945), 275–88.

GC151 Jost, Walter James. "The Hymn Tune Tradition of the General Conference Mennonite Church." Diss., Univ. of Southern California, *ca.* 1966. An historical study of hymns; the major hymnals and the sources in the German chorale.

GC152 Jost, Walter. "A Mennonite Hymn Tradition." *Mennonite Life*, vol. 21, no. 3 (1966), 126–28.

GC153 Kadelbach, Ada. *Die Hymnodie der Mennoniten in Nordamerika (1742–1860): Eine Studie zur Verpflanzung, Bewahrung und Umformung europäischer Kirchentradition*. Mainz: n.p., 1971. Also Diss., Mainz, 1971. 285p. With Bibliography, p.242–70.

GC154 Kadelbach, Ada, and Elizabeth Bender, trans. "Hymns Written by American Mennonites." *Mennonite Quar. Rev.*, vol. 48 (July 1974), 343–70.

GC155 *Die kleine geistliche Harfe der Kinder Zions*. Germantown, Pa.: n.p., 1803. 390p. The first hymnal of the Mennonites of the Franconia Conference.

GC156 Luthy, David. "Four Centuries with the Ausbund." *Family Life*, June 1971, 21–22. On the well known Amish hymnal.

GC157 Maust, Earl Marion. "The History and Development of Music in Mennonite-Controlled Liberal Arts Colleges in the United States." Diss., George Peabody College for Teachers, 1968. 313p.

GC158 Nettl, Bruno. "The Hymns of the Amish: An Example of Marginal Survival." *Journal of Amer. Folklore*, vol. 70 (1957), 323–28.

GC159 Ressler, Martin E. *Bibliography of Mennonite Hymnals and Songbooks, 1742–1972*. Mimeogr. Ganser Library, Millersville State College, Pa.

GC160 Schreiber, William I. "The Hymns of the Amish Ausbund in Philological and Literary Perspective." *Mennonite Quar. Rev.*, vol. 36, no. 1 (1962), 36–60.

GC161 Wenger, Martin D. *The Philharmonia*. Elkhart, Ind.: n.p., 1875. Mennonite tunebook.

GC162 Yoder, Joseph W. *Amische Lieder*. Huntington, Pa.: Yoder Publ. Co., 1942. Rev. in *Mennonite Quar. Rev.*, vol. 24, no. 1 (1950), 97–98.

GC163 Yoder, Paul M., Elizabeth Bender, Harvey Graber, and Nelson P. Springer. *Four Hundred Years with the Ausbund*. Scottdale: Herald Press, 1964. 48p.

GC164 Yoder, Paul Marvin. "Nineteenth Century Sacred Music of the Mennonite Church in the United States." Diss., Florida State Univ., 1961. 188p. Abstr. in *Mennonite Quar. Rev.*, vol. 38, no. 3 (July 1964), 304–05.

Music of the Evangelical Church and Evangelical Association

GC165 *A Collection of Hymns, Selected from Various Authors for the Use of the Evangelical Association, And All Lovers of Pious Devotion.* New Berlin, Pa.: n.p., 1835.

GC166 *Evangelisches Gesangbuch.* Cleveland: n.p., 1850. 393p. Successor to the *Geistliches Saitenspiel.*

GC167 Hoffman, Elisha A. *Glaubens-Lieder.* Cleveland: n.p., 1876. 424p. Evangelical gospel songbook.

GC168 Hoffman, Elisha A. *Liederperlen.* Chicago: n.p., *ca*. 1890. Evangelical gospel songbook.

GC169 Horn, W. *Hosianna.* Cleveland: n.p., 1891. Evangelical gospel songbook.

GC170 Jäckel, R., and E. A. Hoffman. *Jubeltöne.* Cleveland: n.p., *ca*. 1871. 422p. Evangelical gospel songbook.

GC171 Kanaga, J. B. "Our Evangelical Hymn-Book." *Evangelical Messenger*, 13 March 1895.

GC172 Walter, Johannes. *Eine kleine Sammlung alter und neuer Geistreicher Lieder.* Reading: n.p., 1810. 391p. Evangelical Association hymnal.

GC173 Weiss, Alvin. *German Choruses and Hymns.* Slatedale, Pa.: n.p., ca. 1932. 417p. Evangelical hymnal.

GD

Theater and Stage

German and German-American Theater in the United States

GD1 "Die Armut der deutsch-amerikanischen Bühne." *Der deut. Pionier*, vol. 14 (1882–1883), 104–06. Repr. from the New York *Figaro*.

GD2 Ballet, Arthur H. "Brecht in Minnesota: A Director's Note." *Drama Survey*, vol. 3 (1964), 145–51.

GD3 Bauland, Peter. "Expressionism in Modern American Drama." In: *Amerikanisches Drama und Theater im 20. Jahrhundert.* Ed. Alfred Weber and Siegfried Neuweiler. Göttingen: Vandenhoeck & Ruprecht, ca.1970, p.15–35.

GD4 Bauland, Peter Max. "German Drama on the American Stage, 1894–1961." Diss., Pennsylvania, 1964. 444p.

GD5 Bauland, Peter Max. *The Hooded Eagle: Modern German Drama on the New York Stage.* Syracuse Univ. Pr., 1968. 299p. Rev. by M. Y. Himelstein, *Amer. Quar.*, vol. 21, no. 2, part 2 (Summer 1969), 354–55; by J. W. Thomas, *Amer. Lit.* vol. 40, no. 4 (January 1969), 478–79, On German drama performed in translations, 1894–1965; study of American attitudes, with extensive lists of German plays on the New York stage.

GD6 Baurn, Egon. "Das deutsche Theater in New York." *Deutsch-Amerikanische Dichtung*, vol. 1, nos. 7–8 (1888), 72–73.

GD7 Behrmann, Alfred. "Kotzebue on the American Stage." *Arcadia. Zeits. für vergleich. Literaturwissenschaft*, vol. 4, no. 3 (October 1969), 274–84.

GD8 Binder, Wolfgang. *Europäisches Drama und amerikanische Kritik: skandinavische, deutschsprachige und russische Dramatiker in der nordamerikanischen Kritik 1890–1914.* Nürnberg: Carl, 1974. 490p.

GD9 Bowen, Elbert R. "The German Theatre of Early Rural Missouri." *Mo. Hist. Rev.*, vol. 46 (1952), 157-61.

GD10 Bowen, Elbert R. *Theatrical Entertainments in Rural Missouri before the Civil War.* Univ. of Missouri Studies, no. 32. Columbia: Univ. of Missouri Pr., 1959. 144p. Includes the German theater and the *Turnverein*.

GD11 Bruce, William G. "The German Theatre." In: *History of Milwaukee.* Chicago: S. J. Clarke, 1922, Vol. I, p.774-75.

GD12 Brüning, Eberhard. "Relations between Progressive American and German Drama in the Twenties and Thirties." *Zeitschrift für Anglistik und Amerikanistik*, vol. 25 (September 1977), 221-26.

GD13 Bryson, Artemisia B. "German Theater Methods and Theory in Texas." *Amer.-German, Rev.*, vol. 28 no. 5 (1961-1962), 26-29. On Walther R. Volbach at the Little Theater, Texas Christian Univ.

GD14 "The Burnside Mystery—Checklist of the Burnside-Frohman Collection." *Bull., N.Y. Public Library*, vol. 75 (1971), 371-409. See esp. p.380-83 for biographical notes on Charles Frohman, "The Napoleon of the Theatre."

GD15 Byer, Jay Warren. "The History of Eric Bentley's Contribution to the American Theatre." Diss., Carnegie Mellon Univ., 1967.

GD16 Carle, Barbara L. "Modern German Plays on the New York Professional Stage." M.A. Thesis, Univ. of Washington, 1949.

GD17 Carvajal, Christa L. "German Theaters in Central Texas, 1850-1915." Diss., Texas, 1977.

GD18 Clifton, Lucille. "The Early German Theater in Columbus, Ohio, 1820-1840." *Ohio State Archaeological and Hist. Quar.*, vol. 62 (1953), 234-46.

GD19 Cortez, Jerry Vincent. "Fanny Janauschek: America's Last Queen of Tragedy." Diss., Univ. of Illinois, Urbana–Champaign, 1973.

GD20 Costas, Carlos J. "De Viena a Broadway (La opereta cambia de nombre)." *Cuadernos Hispanoamericanos* (Madrid), no. 283 (1974), 75-87.

GD21 Cronau, Rudolf. "German Drama and Opera in the United States." In: *German Achievements in America....* New York: n.p., 1916, p.178-82.

GD22 Deuss, Edmund. "Das verflossene Bühnenjahr." *Die Glocke*, vol. 7, no. 1 (1906), 103-04. On German theater in Chicago.

GD23 Deuss, Edmund. "Die Welt der Bretter." *Die Glocke*, vol. 1, no. 1 (1906), 21-22.

GD24 *Dem deutschen Stadttheater 1846-96.* Milwaukee: Milwaukee Herold, n.d. In Milwaukee.

GD25 De Vries, Jenny B. "August von Kotzebue: His Popularity on the Early American Stage." *Schatzkammer*, vol. 2 (1976), 33-42.

GD26 De Vries, Jenny B. "Kotzebue on the American Stage, 1798-1840." Diss., Virginia, 1971-1972.

GD27 Dew, Deborah S. "Expressionism in the American Theatre, 1922-1936." Diss., Yale, 1968. 352p.

GD28 Downer, Alan S., ed. *The Memoir of John Durang, American Actor, 1785-1816.* Univ. of Pittsburgh Publs. for the Hist. Soc. of York Co. (Pa.) and the Amer. Soc. for Theatre Research. Pittsburgh: n.p., 1966. 176p. Rev. by P. M. Ryan, *Jour. of Amer. Hist.*, vol. 54, no. 2 (1967), 393-94. Durang's father, a native of Strasbourg, came to Pennsylvania in 1767.

GD29 Dürrenmatt, Friedrich. "Amerikanisches und europäisches Drama." In: *Theater-Schriften und Reden.* Zürich: im Verlag der Arche, 1966, p.159-64. Lecture given in New York City, 1960.

GD30 Ehrenberg, Adolf von. "Saisonschluß in Cleveland und Cincinnati." *Die Glocke*, vol. 3, no. 2 (1908), 83-85.

GD31 "Eine morsche 'Brücke' zu deutscher Kultur. Sendboten unseres Theaters in America." *Frankfurter Rundschau*, no. 265, 14 November 1970. On the theater in exile in Los Angeles.

GD32 Elfe, Wolfgang, James Hardin, and Günther Holst, eds. *Deutsches Exildrama und Exiltheater: Akten des Exilliteratur-Symposiums der University of South Carolina 1976.* Frankfurt: Lang, 1977.

GD33 Ellwood, William R. "Early Manifestations of German Expressionism in New York Productions of American Drama." Diss., Oregon, 1966. 350p.

GD34 Ellwood, William R. "Preliminary Notes on the German *Dramaturg* and the American Theater." *Mod. Drama*, vol. 13, no. 3 (December 1970), 254–58. Argues the need for dramaturges in theater departments.

GD35 Evans, Thomas G. "Piscator in the American Theatre: New York, 1939–1951. Diss., Wisconsin, 1968.

GD36 Felheim, Marvin. *The Theatre of Augustin Daly: An Account of the Late Nineteenth Century American Stage*. Cambridge, Mass.: n.p., 1956.

GD37 Fiedler, Leonnard M. "Max Reinhardt's American Experience." In: *Actes du VIIe congrès de l'Association Internationale de Littérature Comparée/Proceedings of the 7th Congress of the Internat. Comp. Literature Assoc. I. Littératures américaines...* Ed. Milan V. Dimić and Juan Ferraté. Stuttgart: Bieber, 1979, p.179–84.

GD38 Ford, James L. "The German Stage in America." *Munsey's Mag.*, (1898), 232–45.

GD39 Freedman, Morris. "Bertolt Brecht and American Social Drama." In: *The Moral Impulse. Modern Drama from Ibsen to the Present*. Carbondale: South. Ill. Univ. Pr.; London: Feffer and Simons, 1967, p.99–114.

GD40 Frenz, Horst. "Edwin Booth in Polyglot Shakespeare Performances." *Germanic Rev.*, vol. 18 (1943), 280–85.

GD41 Frenz, Horst. "The German Drama in the Middle West." *Amer.-German Rev.*, vol. 8, no. 5 (1942), 15–17, 37.

GD42 Friedman, Daniel H. "The Prolet-Bühne: America's First Agit-Prop Theatre." Diss., Wisconsin, 1979. 820p.

GD43 Frohman, Gustave. "America's Oberammergau." *Overland Monthly*, N.S. vol. 56 (1910), 215–21.

GD44 Fuhrich-Leisler, Edda, and Gisela Prossnitz. *Max Reinhardt in Europa und Amerika: Ausstellung der Max-Reinhardt-Forschungs- und Gedenkstätte, Salzburg, 1976*. Salzburg: Otto Müller, 1976. 456p. A chronological documentation of the work and the man in relation to America.

GD45 Fulda, Ludwig. "Über das deutsche Theater." In: *Jahrbuch der Deutschen in Chicago für das Jahr 1915*. Chicago: n.p., 1915, p.40–44.

GD46 Gaiser, Gerhard W. "The History of the Cleveland Theatre from the Beginning until 1854." Diss., Iowa State, 1953.

GD47 Gallagher, Kent Grey. "The Foreigner in American Drama to 1830: A Study in Attitudes." Diss., Indiana Univ., 1962. 302p.

GD48 Garten, H. F. *Modern German Drama*. Fairlawn, N.J.: Essential Books, 1959. 272p. With a bibliography of drama in translation.

GD49 German Stock Company, Milwaukee. Pabst German Theater collection, 1865–1935. Ca. 3,000 items. In Milwaukee Public Library (MS 63-230). Scripts, scores, and papers.

GD50 "German Theatre in Milwaukee." *Theatre Arts*, vol. 28 (1944), 465–74.

GD51 "Geschichte der Deutschen Bühne." In: *Baltimore: Seine Vergangenheit und Gegenwart*. Baltimore: n.p., 1887, p.135–42. In Baltimore.

GD52 *Geschichte des Washington Turnvereins in der dramatischen Sektion*. Washington, Missouri: n.p., 1900.

GD53 G[ittler], L[ewis] F. "Piscator's Years in New York." *Amer.-German Rev.*, vol. 32, no. 5 (June–July 1966), 19. For the years 1939 to 1951.

GD54 Gohdes, Clarence. *Literature and Theater of the States and Regions of the U.S.A.: An Historical Bibliography*. Durham, N. Car.: Duke Univ. Pr., 1967. 276p.

GD55 Grandstaff, Russell J. "A History of the Professional Theatre in Cincinnati, Ohio, 1861–1886." Diss., Michigan, 1963. 2 vols.

GD56 Grzybowski, Paul. "Deutschamerikanisches Theater und deutschamerikanisches Schriftstellertum." In: *Jahrbuch des Verbandes deutscher Schriftsteller in Amerika*. Ed. Friedrich Michel. New York: n.p., 1911, p.131f.

GD57 Guertler, Siegfried. *Der Turm: Eine Schrift des Deutschen Theaters des Kulturkreises Salt Lake City*. Salt Lake City: German Theater, 1959. 20p.

GD58 Hampton, Charles C., Jr. "Verfremcluhanseffekt." *Mod. Drama*, vol. 14 (1971), 340–54.

GD59 Hart, Moss. *Lady in the Dark. A Musical Play.* Lyrics by Ira Gershwin and Music by Kurt Weill. New York: Random House, ca. 1941.

GD60 Herbatschek, Heinrich. "Die Anfänge des deutschen Theaters in Milwaukee." *Amer.-German Rev.*, vol. 13, no. 3 (1947), 17–18.

GD61 Higham, Charles. *Ziegfeld.* Chicago: H. Regnery, 1972. 245p. On Florenz Ziegfeld (1869–1932), American theatrical impresario. A native of Chicago, he went to Europe at the age of 23 to arrange appearances of European artists in this country.

GD62 Hill, Claude, and Ralph Ley. *The Drama of German Expressionism. A German-English Bibliography.* Univ. of N. Car. Studies in the Germanic Langs. and Literatures, no. 28. Chapel Hill: Univ. of N. Car. Pr., 1960.

GD63 Himmelfarb, Morgan Y. *Drama Was a Weapon: The Left Wing Theatre in New York 1929–1941.* New Brunswick N.J.: Rutgers Univ. Pr., 1963.

GD64 Hodge, Francis. "German Drama and the American Stage." In: *The German Theater Today. A Symposium.* Ed. Leroy R. Shaw. Austin: Univ. of Texas Pr., 1963, p.69–88.

GD65 Huder, Walter, et al., eds. *Theater im Exil: 1933–1945.* Berlin: Akademie der Künste, 1973. 200p.

GD66 Ingle, Patricia. "Departures from Realism on the New York Stage." Diss., Univ. of Arkansas, 1965. 1011p. Treats the influence of the European Expressionists.

GD67 Isaacs, Edith J. R., and Rosamond Gilder. "The German Theatre in Milwaukee." *Theatre Arts*, vol. 28 (1944), 465–74.

GD68 Jackson, Allan S. "The Max Reinhardt Archive, Binghamton, New York." *Theatre Studies*, vol. 20 (1974), 50–56.

GD69 Jacoby, Philo. "Das deutsche Theater in San Francisco." *Californischer Staats-Kalender*, (1868), p.33–38.

GD70 Jessen, K. D. "Das deutsche Theater in New York." *Die Glocke*, vol. 2, no. 11 (1908), 487–88.

GD71 Jones, Robert Alston. "German Drama on the American Stage: The Case of Georg Kaiser." *German Quar.*, vol. 37, no. 1 (1964), 17–25.

GD72 Kaufman, George Simon, and Moss Hart. *The American Way.* Drama. New York: Random House, ca. 1939. A first- and second-generation German family in America confronts the rise of the Bund and the appeal to rally to the Nazi side.

GD73 King, Rolf. "Sketches of Early German Influence on Rochester's Theatrical and Musical Life." *Amer.-German Rev.*, vol. 8, no. 2 (1941), 13–15.

GD74 Kistler, Mark O. "The German Theater in Detroit." *Mich. Hist.*, vol. 47, no. 7 (1963), 289–300. German theater from 1850 to 1900.

GD75 Knust, Herbert. "Piscator and Brecht: Affinity and Alienation." In: *Theater and Politics.* Ed. S. Mews and H. Knust. Chapel Hill: Univ. of N. Car. Pr., 1974, p.44–70. Piscator's career in America and Brecht's sojourns in New York and Hollywood.

GD76 Koeppler, Paul. "Max Reinhardt auf der Probe: Im Spiegel der zeitgenössischen Autobiographie." *Maske und Kothurn*, vol. 19 (1973), 95–183.

GD77 Kopp, W. LaMarr. "Das klassische deutsche Drama an den New Yorker Bühnen seit dem Zweiten Weltkrieg." *Zeitschrift für Kulturaustausch.* (Inst. für Auslandsbeziehungen, Stuttgart), vol. 20 (1970), 289–96.

GD78 Kopp, W. LaMarr. "Popular Reception of Classical German Drama in New York 1945–1965." *Mod. Lang. Jour.*, vol. 55 (1971), 510–14.

GD79 Kremling, Helmut. "The Beginnings of Cleveland's German Language Theater, 1820–1860." In: *Papers from the St. Olaf Symposium on German-Americana.* Ed. L. J. Rippley and S. M. Benjamin. Morgantown: Dept. of Foreign Langs., W. Va. Univ., 1980, p.79–86.

GD80 Kremling, Helmut. "German Drama on the Cleveland Stage: Performances in German and English from 1850 to the Present." Diss., Ohio State, 1975–1976.

GD81 Krich, John F. "The Amiable Lady Charms the Iron City: Adah Isaacs Menken in Pittsburgh [1859–1862]." *Western Pa. Hist. Quar.*, vol. 51 (July 1968), 259–78.

GD82 Leuchs, Frederick A. H. "Die Anfänge des deutschen Theaters in der Stadt Neu-York." *Mitteilungen der deutschen Akademie von München*, vol. 14 (1939), 66–76.

GD83 Ley-Piscator, Maria (von Czada). *The Piscator Experiment: The Political Theater*. New York: Heinemann, 1967. 336p.

GD84 Loeffler, Michael P. *Friedrich Dürrenmatts "Besuch der alten Dame" in New York: Ein Kapitel aus der Rezeptionsgeschichte der neueren Schweizer Dramatik*. Basel: Birkhäuser, 1976. 122p.

GD85 Londré, Felicia Mae (Hardison). "A Guide to the Production of Plays in Foreign Languages in American Colleges and Universities." Diss., Wisconsin, 1969. 289p. Data based on a questionnaire. Arthur Schnitzler is found to have been most frequently performed of all German playwrights.

GD86 Loomis, C. Grant. "The German Theater in San Francisco, 1861–1864." In: *In Honorem Lawrence Marsden Price*. Univ. of Calif. Publs. in Mod. Philology, no. 37. Berkeley: Univ. of Calif. Pr., 1952, p.193–242. Rev. by L. M. Price, *Amer.-German Rev.*, vol. 19, no. 4 (1953), 32–33; E. Feise, *Mod. Lang. Notes*, vol. 69 (1954), 616–18; A. Gillies, *German Quar.*, vol. 27 (1954), 69–71.

GD87 McDermott, Douglas. "The Odyssey of John Bonn: A Note on German Theatre in America." *German Quar.*, vol. 38, no. 3 (May 1965), 325–34. Bonn directed the WPA-sponsored "German Theatre" in New York.

GD88 Madden, C. Stuart. "The Oberammergau of California." *Catholic World*, vol. 98 (1913), 183–91. At San Gabriel, Calif.

GD89 Marx, Henry. "The Players from Abroad, 1946–1949." In: *Deutsches Exildrama und Exiltheater: Akten des Exilliteratur Symposiums der University of South Carolina 1976*. Ed. W. Elfe, J. Hardin and Günther Holst. Frankfurt: Lang, 1977, p.272–75. On the drama in New York City.

GD90 "Max Reinhardt, 1873–1943." *Theater Arts*, vol. 28, no. 1 (1944), 36–52.

GD91 Meersman, Roger. "The Meininger in America." *Speech Monographs*, no. 32 (1966), 40–49. Many of the original Meiningen actors toured the United States in 1891 and 1892 with authentic Meininger productions.

GD92 Mennemeier, Franz Norbert. "Zur deutschsprachigen Exildramatik." In: *Handbuch des deutschen Dramas*. Ed. Walter Hinck. Düsseldorf: Bagel, 1980, p.431–39.

GD93 Mennemeier, Franz Norbert and Frithjof Trapp, *Deutsche Exildramatik 1933 bis 1950*. München: Fink, 1980p.

GD94 Merrill, Peter C. "Ernst Anton Zündt and the Theater." South Central Mod. Lang. Assoc., 31 October, 1980, Summarized in *South Central Bull*. (Fall 1980).

GD95 Merrill, Peter C. "The German-American Theater in the Nineteenth Century." South Atlantic Mod. Lang. Assoc., 6 November 1976. Summarized in the *South Atlantic Bull.*, vol. 42, no. 1 (1977), 95–96.

GD96 Mierendorff, Marta. "Deutsches Theater im Exil. Das Schicksal der 'Freien Bühne' in Los Angeles." *Die deutsche Bühne*, vol. 5, no. 1 (January 1961), 6–7.

GD97 Mierendorff, Marta. *First West Coast Exhibition. German Language Theater in Exile: Hollywood 1933–1950*. Los Angeles: Univ. of Southern Calif. German Department, 1974. 110p. Held 1 November–15 December 1973.

GD98 Miller, Karina L. "The Popular Acceptance of German Drama on the New York Stage After World War II: 1945–1965." Diss., Vanderbilt, 1974.

GD99 *Milwaukee Theater Kalender*. Milwaukee: n.p., 1864.

GD100 *Mitteilungen des Deutschen Theater-Verbandes von New York*. New York: n.p., 1928–1929?

GD101 Moehlenbrock, Arthur H. "The German Drama on the Charleston Stage." *Furman Studies (Furman Univ. Bull.)*, N.S., vol. 1 (Spring 1954), 32–39.

GD102 Moehlenbrock, Arthur H. "The German Drama on the New Orleans Stage." *La. Hist. Quar.*, vol. 26, no. 2 (1943), 361–627. See also the dissertation at Iowa Univ., 1942, with the same title.

GD103 Moehlenbrock, Arthur H. "Kotzebue on the Charleston Stage." *Furman Studies*, vol. 34 (1951), 22–31.

GD104 Morrill, Reed, and Joanne Morrill. "Deutsches Theater Salt Lake City." *Amer.-German Rev.*, vol. 24, no. 2 (1957), 26–27. Siegfried and Lotte Guertler founded the *Kulturkreis* in 1952.

GD105 Neff (Knef), Hildegard. *Der geschenkte Gaul. Bericht aus einem Leben*. Berlin: Ullstein, 1972. 472p. Stage and movie actress who worked both on the Continent and in New York; includes accounts of her experiences on the stage and with many refugee Germans in the U.S.

GD106 Obkirchen, Wilhelm. MSS. In Columbia University Libraries (MS 67-804). 74 musical scores and scripts of 4 plays. In German.

GD107 Parish, Fraeda. "Max Reinhardt's American Tour 1927–28: A Legacy Understood or Misunderstood?" *Mod. Austrian Lit.*, vol. 10, no. 1 (1977), 55–67.

GD108 Paetel, Karl O. "Deutsches Theater in Amerika." *Deutsche Rundschau*, vol. 81 (1955), 271–75.

GD109 Peacock, Ronald. *The Poet in the Theatre*, New York: Hill and Wang, 1946. Some consideration of German verse drama in the English-speaking world, notably Hebbel and Grillparzer.

GD110 Prudhoe, John. "On Translating Goethe and Schiller for the English-Speaking Stage." *Theater Research/Recherches Théâtrales*, vol. 2 (1976), 28–33.

GD111 Puknat, E. M., and S. B. Puknat. "An American Critic and a German Vogue: The Theatrical Pioneering of Robert Treat Paine." *Transactions, Colonial Soc. of Mass.*, vol. 43 for 1956–1963 (1966), 203–89.

GD112 Reiter, Wilhelm. "Deutschsprachige Dramen auf Bühnen der USA." *IFA-Korrespondenz* (Stuttgart), vol. 3, no. 12 (1963), 1–3.

GD113 Richardson, Horst F. "German Play Productions in U.S. and Canadian Colleges and Universities since 1945." *Die Unterrichtspraxis*, vol. 7, no. 1 (1974), 142–47.

GD114 Richter, August P. "Das deutsche Theater in Davenport." In: *Die Geschichte von der Stadt Davenport....* August P. Richter. Davenport: n.p., 1917, p.618–51.

GD115 Richter, August P. "Thalia im Goldenen Kranz. Fünfzig Jahre deutschen Theaters in Davenport." *Der Demokrat*, 9 December 1905. See also: *Der Tägliche Demokrat*, 10 December 1905 and *Wochenausgaben* 14 and 21 December 1905.

GD116 Rippley, La Vern J. "German Theater in Columbus, Ohio." *German-Amer. Studies*, vol. 1, no. 2 (1970), 78–101.

GD117 Rothfuss, Hermann E. "The Beginnings of the German-American Stage." *German Quar.*, vol. 24, no. 2 (1951), 93–102.

GD118 Rothfuss, Hermann E. "Criticism of the German-American Theater in Minnesota." *Germanic Rev.*, vol. 27, no. 2 (1952), 124–30. Repertory and critics—Samuel Ludvigh, Albert Wolff, Ludwig Bogen—between 1860 and 1880.

GD119 Rothfuss, Hermann E. "The Early German Theater in Minnesota." *Minn. Hist.*, vol. 32, no. 2 (1951), 100–05; no. 3, p. 164–73. Dramatic performances in St. Paul, St. Anthony, Minneapolis, and New Ulm.

GD120 Rothfuss, Hermann E. "The German-American Theatre in Minnesota." *Germanic Rev.*, vol. 27 (1952), no. 2 (April 1952), 124–30.

GD121 Rothfuss, Hermann E. "German Plays in American Colleges, 1947–1950." *Monatshefte*, vol. 43, nos. 4–5 (1951), 237–39.

GD122 Rothfuss, Hermann E. "German Plays in American Colleges, 1951–1954." *Monatshefte*, vol. 47 (1955), 400–03.

GD123 Rothfuss, Hermann E. "German Plays in American Colleges, 1955–1958." *Monatshefte*, vol. 51 (1959), 351–54.

GD124 Rothfuss, Hermann E. "The German Theater in Minnesota from Its Beginnings to 1890." Diss. Minnesota, ca. 1951.

GD125 Rothfuss, Hermann E. "Gustav Amberg, German-American Theater Promoter." *Monats-*

German and German-American Theater *(cont.)*

hefte, vol. 44, no. 7 (1952), 357–65. Amberg's service in the great period of the German theater of New York 1879–1892.

GD126 Rothfuss, Hermann E. "Plays for Pioneers: German Drama in Rural Minnesota." *Minn. Hist.*, vol. 34 (1955), 239–42.

GD127 Rothfuss, Hermann E. "Theodor Steidle, German Theater Pioneer." *Amer.-German Rev.*, vol. 17, no. 3 (1951), 17–19, 33. German theater in Minnesota in the sixties.

GD128 Schechner, Richard, and John Fuegi. "Gespräch mit Richard Schechner über seine New Yorker Aufführung der *Mutter Courage*." Trans. by Jost Hermand. *Brecht-Jahrbuch* 1976, p.166–76.

GD129 Schildkraut, Joseph. *My Father and I. As Told to Leo Lania.* New York: Viking, 1959. 246p. Born in Vienna, Joseph Schildkraut was naturalized in 1926 and became prominent in Hollywood and on the American stage.

GD130 Schreiber, Earl G. "*Everyman* in America." *Compar. Drama*, vol. 9 (1975), 99–115. Production history and influence of the Middle English *Everyman* and Hugo von Hofmannsthal's *Jedermann* in the United States.

GD131 Schreiber, Theodore. "Berthold Kraus, Prairie Actor and Writer." *Amer.-German Rev.*, vol. 19, no. 5 (1953), 14–15. In the 1890's this Middle-Western actor was manager of the German theater in Davenport, Iowa.

GD132 Schulz-Behrend, George. "German Theater at the University of Texas, 1947–1957." *Amer.-German Rev.*, vol. 23, no. 5 (1956–1957), 9–11.

GD133 Seman, Philip L. "America's Oberammergau." *Recreation*, vol. 43 (1949), 254–55. At San Jacinto, Calif.

GD134 Shaw, Leroy R. "Modern Austrian Dramatists on the New York Stage." In: *Österreich und die angelsächsische Welt. Kulturbegegnungen und Berichte.* Ed. O. Hietzsch. Wien: Braumüller, Vol. II, 1968, p.547–63.

GD135 Singer, Michael. "Deutsches Bühnenleben in Amerika [1917, 1918]." In: *Jahrbuch der Deutschamerikaner für das Jahr 1917.* Chicago: n.p., 1917, p.221–28; *Jahrbuch...1918.* Ed. Michael Singer. Chicago: n.p., 1918, p.273–312.

GD136 Stadelmann, Egon. "Deutsches Theater in New York." *New Yorker Staats-Zeitung und Herold. Sonderbeilage zum 135. Jubiläum*, 28 December 1969, 4, 18.

GD137 Steg, Mary M. "Aspects of German Expressionism in Theatre and Art." M.A. thesis, Tulane, 1967.

GD138 Sturm, Ellen. "Toronto und das deutsche Theaterleben in den Nachkriegsjahren." *German-Canadian Yearbook*, vol. 3 (1976), 225–33.

GD139 Taylor, Harley U., Jr. "The Dramas of August von Kotzebue on the New York and Philadelphia Stages from 1798 to 1805." *W. Va. Univ. Philological Papers*, vol. 23 (1977), 47–58. Including consideration of William Dunlap's involvement.

GD140 Taylor, Robin. "Elements of German Expressionism in American Drama, 1920–1940." Diss., New York Univ., 1974.

GD141 "Die Theater der Waldstadt—ihre Entwicklung." Cleveland *Wächter und Anzeiger* (50. Jubiläumsausgabe) 9 August 1902. In Cleveland.

GD142 Utz, Kathryn E. "Columbus, Ohio, Theatre Seasons 1840–1841 to 1860–61." Diss., Ohio State, 1952.

GD143 Valgamae, Mardi. *Accelerated Grimace: Expressionism in the American Drama of the 1920's.* Pref. by Harry T. Moore. Crosscurrents/Modern Critiques. Carbondale: Southern Illinois Univ. Press, 1972. 145p.

GD144 Valgemae, Mardi. "Expressionism in American Drama." Diss., Univ. of California, Los Angeles, 1964. 239p.

GD145 Valgamae, Mardi. "Expressionism in the American Theatre." In: *Expressionism as an International Literary Phenomenon: 21 Essays and a Bibliography.* Ed. U. Weisstein. Paris: Didier, 1973, p.193–203.

GD146 Wächter, Hans-Christof. *Theater im Exil: Sozialgeschichte des deutschen Exiltheaters 1933–1945.* München: Hanser, 1973. 798p.

GD147 Walk, Cynthia. "Hofmannsthal und Reinhardt. Das amerikanische Debüt: Zwei Briefe über eine geplante Aufführung des *Salzburger Grossen Welttheaters* in New York." *Hofmannsthal Blätter*, vol. 12 (1974), 428-38.

GD148 Walton, Luverne. "*Anatol* on the New York Stage." *Mod. Austrian Lit.*, vol. 2 (ca. 1968), 30-44.

GD149 Ward, Robert E. "Deutsches Bühnenwesen in Amerika." *German-Amer. Studies*, vol. 5 (1972), 53-54.

GD150 Weber, Betty Nance. "*Mauser* in Austin, Texas." *New German Critique*, vol. 8 (1976), 150-56. Play by Heiner Müller.

GD151 Weisert, John J. "Beginnings of German Theatricals in Louisville." *Filson Club Hist. Quar.*, vol. 26, no. 4 (1952), 347-59. Establishes the connections of the Louisville theater with Cincinnati in the years 1850-1854.

GD152 Weisert, John J. "Some Characters of the German-American Stage." *Amer.-German Rev.*, vol. 24, no. 4 (1958), 12-15.

GD153 Weisert, John J. "A *Trinkspruch* from Louisville's Bohemia." *Amer.-German Rev.*, vol. 18, no. 3 (1952), 16-17, 35. Theatrical activities of Julius Boetzow in Louisville and Cincinnati in the 1850's.

GD154 Weitenkampf, Frank. "German Theatre in New York City." *Seven Arts*, vol. 1 (1917), 676-77.

GD155 West, William Francis. "The Legitimate Theater in Rural Missouri from the Beginning of the Civil War through 1872." Diss., Univ. of Missouri, 1964.

GD156 Weyr, Thomas. "Theater: A German [Heinar Kipphardt] Looks at the U.S. In the Matter of J. Robert Oppenheimer at Lincoln Center." *Amer.-German Rev.*, vol. 35, no. 5 (June-July 1969), 20-21.

GD157 Wilk, Gerard H. "Austausch über den Atlantik, deutsches und amerikanisches Theater." *Amerikanische Rundschau*, vol. 5 (1949), 86-92.

GD158 Wittmann, A. "Das erste deutsche Theater in Manitowoc." In: *Prämien Buch des "Nord-Westen für das Jahr 1882*. N.p.: n.p., 1882.

GD159 Youngerman, Henry C. "Theatre Buildings in Madison, Wisconsin, 1836-1900." *Wis. Mag. of Hist.*, vol. 30, no. 3 (1947), 273-88. Madison's Turner Hall lasted longest, from 1858 to 1885, and constituted the link for German theatre between Milwaukee and the West.

GD160 Zeller, Emmy. "Bayrische Volksbühne Newark, New Jersey 1937-1975." *German-Amer. Studies*, vol. 9 (Spring 1975), 79-80.

GD161 Zipes, Jack. "Dunlap, Kotzebue, and the Shaping of American Theater: A Reevaluation from a Marxist Perspective." *Early Amer. Lit.*, vol. 8 (Winter 1974), 272-84.

GD162 Zucker, Adolf E. "Bibliographical Notes on the German Language Theater in the United States." *Monatshefte*, vol. 35 (1943), 255-64.

GD163 Zucker, Adolf E. "The History of the German Theatre in Baltimore." *Germanic Rev.*, vol. 18, no. 2 (April 1943), 123-35.

Opera and the Musical Stage

GD164 Barbee, David Rankin. "The Musical Mr. Lincoln." *Abraham Lincoln Quar.*, vol. 5 (1949), 435-54. Comments on German operas in Washington, D.C.

GD165 Bardell, Eunice R. "A New National American Opera." *Hist. Messenger of the Milwaukee Co. Hist. Soc.*, vol. 32, no. 1 (1976), 10-22. On Eduard de Sobolewski and his musical activities in Milwaukee in 1859.

GD166 Berges, Ruth. "Offenbach Comes to New York." *Amer.-German Rev.*, vol. 30, no. 4 (1964), 31-33. Conducted opéra bouffe in New York in 1875.

GD167 Blumenthal, George. *My Sixty Years in Show Business. A Chronicle of the American Theater, 1874-1934, as Told by George Blumenthal to Arthur H. Menkin.* New York: Fred. Osberg, 1936. 336p. B. (1862-1943) was associated for many years with Oscar Hammerstein.

GD168 Briggs, John. *Requiem for a Yellow Brick Brewery. A History of the Metropolitan Opera*. Boston: n.p., 1969.

GD169 Brubaker, Robert. "130 Years of Opera in Chicago." *Chicago Hist.*, vol. 8 (1979), 156–69. On French, Italian, and German opera companies.

GD170 Cone, John Frederick. *Oscar Hammerstein's Manhattan Opera Co.* Norman: Univ. of Okla. Pr., 1966. 399p. Rev. by T.D.S. Bassett, *Jour. of Amer. Hist.*, vol. 53, no. 4 (1967), 840–41. H. emigrated to America at the time of the Civil War and financed an opera company to rival the Metropolitan.

GD171 Davis, Ronald Leroy. "A History of Resident Opera in the American West." Diss., Texas, 1961. 517p.

GD172 Graf, H. *Producing Opera for America*. Zürich: n.p., 1961. 212p.

GD173 Holliday, Joseph. "Cincinnati Opera Festivals in the Gilded Age." *Bull., Cincinnati Hist. Soc.*, vol. 24, no. 2 (April 1966) 131–49. A large repertory of German opera under the direction of Theodore Thomas.

GD174 Holliday, Joseph E. "Notes on Samuel N. Pike and His Opera House." *Bull., Cincinnati Hist. Soc.*, vol. 25 (1967), 165–83. The impresario is thought to have been born in Germany and brought to America at an early age. The *Männerchor* and Grover's Grand German Opera Company of Philadelphia performed in Pike's Opera House.

GD175 Huneker, Erik Hinton. "The Big Four." *Opera News*, vol. 30 (18 December 1965), 8–13. On the music criticism of James G. Huneker, Henry E. Krehbiel, Henry T. Finck, and William J. Henderson.

GD176 Hurst, P. G. *The Operatic Age of Jean de Reszke; 40 Years of Opera 1874–1914*. New York: n.p., 1959.

GD177 Jelen, Walter. "Herman Geiger-Torel, Canada's Mr. Opera." *Amer.-German Rev.*, vol. 28, no. 4 (1962), 18–19. Director of the Canad. Opera Co., Toronto; a native of Frankfurt who had been active in South and North America since the 1930's.

GD178 Jeritza, Maria. *Sunlight and Song*. New York/London: n.p., 1924.

GD179 Kolodin, Irving. *The Musical Life*. New York: n.p., 1958.

GD180 Kolodin, Irving. *The Story of the Metropolitan Opera 1883–1950; A Candid Story*. New York: n.p., 1953.

GD181 Lehmann, Liza [Elizabeth Nina Mary Frederica (Lehmann) Bedford] *The Life of Liza Lehmann, By Herself*.... London: Unwin, 1919. 232p. L. (1862–1918) was an Austrian-born composer and operatic singer.

GD182 Leiser, Clara. *Jean de Reszke and the Great Days of Opera*. New York: n.p., 1934.

GD183 Mueller, Lillian. "Mohega, The Flower of the Forest." *Amer.-German Rev.*, vol. 11, no. 1 (1944), 14–16. Concerning Edward de Sobolewski's German opera, performed in Milwaukee in 1859.

GD184 Pleasants, Henry. "The Golden Era. When the 'Met' was a German Opera House." *Amer.-German Rev.*, vol. 33, no. 2 (December 1966–January 1967), 18–20. From 1884–1985 through 1890–1891 it housed a resident German company under Leopold Damrosch.

GD185 Schnoor, Hans. [Karl Maria von] *Weber auf dem Welttheater*. 2nd. rev. ed. Hamburg: Deutscher-Literatur-Vlg., 1963. 248p.

GD186 Schonberg, Harold C. "The Don Quixote of Opera [Max Maretzek, impresario.]" *Amer. Heritage*, vol. 27 (February 1976), 48–56, 97. M. dominated the New York City opera scene in the mid-19th century.

GD187 Sheean, Vincent. *The Amazing Oscar Hammerstein. The Life and Exploits of an Impresario*. Pref. by Oscar Hammerstein II. New York: Simon & Schuster, 1956. 363p.

GD188 Slezak, Walter. *What Time's the Next Swan?* Garden City: Doubleday, 1962. Biographical memoirs of the Austrian tenor well known as a Metropolitan Opera and movie star.

GD189 Sonneck, Oscar G. T. *Early Opera in America*. New York: Benj. Blom, 1963. 230p. Reissue of study orig. publ. in 1915.

GD190 Spelman, Franz. "American Opera Singers—Made in Germany." *Amer.-German Rev.*, vol. 36, no. 2 (December 1969–January 1970), 10–13.

George London, James King, Claire Watson, Jean Cox, Keith Engen, Grace Bumbry, etc.

GD191 Steigman, B. M. "Precursor to Lincoln Center." *Amer. Quar.*, vol. 13, no. 3 (Fall 1961), 376–86. Touches on the anti-German agitation in the field of music and opera in New York City, 1919.

GD192 Tucker, Edward L. "James Fox, Jr.: Bon Vivant and Mountain Chronicler." *Va. Cavalcade*, vol. 21, no. 4 (1972), 18–29. See p.26–27, 29 on his marriage to the German-American opera star Fritzi Scheff.

GD193 Weisert, John. "The First Decade at Sam Drake's Louisville Theater." *Filson Club Hist. Quar.*, vol. 39 (October 1965), 287–310. On musical history, 1815 to 1830.

GD194 Zuckermann, Elliott. *The First Hundred Years of Wagner's "Tristan."* Berkeley: Univ. of Calif. Press, 1964. Vogue of *Tristan* in all countries.

Other Stage Entertainments

GD195 Arrington, Joseph E. "John Maelzel, Master Showman of Automata and Panoramas." *Pa. Mag. of Hist. and Biography*, vol. 84 (1960), 56–92. Johann Nepomuk M., 1772–1838, native of Regensburg, brought his exhibit to New York in 1825.

GD196 Blitz, Signor. *Life and Adventures of Signor Blitz by Himself*. Hartford, Conn.: n.p., 1872. A magician who visited St. Louis in 1837.

GD197 Bowen, Elbert R. "The Circus in Early Rural Missouri." *Mo. Hist. Rev.*, vol. 47, no. 1 (1952), 1–17. Some information about the performer and owner Driesbach, p.6–7.

GD198 Burlingame, H. J. *Herrmann the Magician. His Life, His Secrets*. Chicago: Laird & Lee, 1897. The magician dynasty of the Herrmanns originated in Hannover: Carl, the first of the line, Alexander, and Leon, nephew of Carl.

GD199 Callahan, John M. "Fritz Emmett: St. Louis's Favorite German." *Mo. Hist. Soc. Bull.*, vol. 35 (1979), 69–82. Late 19th-century German-dialect comedian of Irish descent.

GD200 Chindahl, George L. *A History of the Circus in America*. Caldwell, Idaho: Caxton, 1959. 295p.

GD201 Christopher, Milbourne. "Around the World with Kellar." In: *Illustrated History of Magic*. New York: Crowell, 1973, p.198–221. Harry Kellar, born Heinrich Keller in Erie, Pa., 1849. Active in the magician's trade from boyhood, he became a dominant figure, a "globe-circling illusionist" after the demise of Herrmann.

GD202 David, John R. "Joseph K. Emmett as *Fritz, Our German Cousin*: The Stage Immigrant and the American Dream." *Mo. Hist. Rev.*, vol. 73, no. 2 (January 1979), 198–217.

GD203 Gollmar Bros. Circus. Records, 1891–1916. 12 ft. In Circus World Museum, Baraboo, Wis. (MS 79-291). Papers, accounts, receipts.

GD204 Guest, Ivor. *Fanny Elssler*. Middletown: Wesleyan Univ. Pr., 1970. 284p. Biography of the Viennese-born star of the Paris ballet (1830–1870); her triumphant American tour.

GD205 [Jones, Thomas P.] *Observations upon the Automaton Chess Player of von Kempelen, and upon other Automata and Androides, Now Exhibiting in the United States, by Mr. Maelzel....* Philadelphia: J. Dobson, 1827. 12p.

GD206 Kieffer, Elizabeth C. "John Durang—the First Native American Dancer." *The Pa. Dutchman*, vol. 6, no. 1 (1954), 26–38.

GD207 Maelzel, Johann Nepomuk. *Maelzel's Exhibition... Automaton Chess Player. Automaton Trumpeter. Automaton Rope Dancers*. [Boston: W. W. Clapp, 1826.] Broadside.

GD208 McPharlin, Paul. "German Puppetry in America." In: *The Puppet Theatre in America. A History*. New York: n.p., 1949, p.221–38.

GD209 Morrish, Ray Sells. "Sells Brothers Circus." *Amer.-German Rev.*, vol. 21, no. 5 (1955), 25–26. Sells brothers, of German ancestry, opened a circus in 1872; sold to Ringling Bros. & Bailey ca. 1904.

GD210 North, Henry Ringling, and Alden Hatch. *The Circus Kings—Our Ringling Family Story*. Garden City: n.p., 1960. Rev. by M. Murray, *Fla. Hist. Quar.*, vol. 39, no. 2 (1960) 191–93.

GD211 Richardson, Alice I. "Mummers Plays in the Americas." Diss., New York Univ., 1976.

GD212 Ringling Brothers Barnum and Bailey Combined Shows. Business records, 1919–1967. 630 ft. and 300 vols. In the Circus World Museum, Baraboo, Wis. (MS 79-294). On loan by the circus.

GD213 Steinitz, Hans. "Ein Kabarett-Abend mit Wolfgang Roth." *Aufbau*, 19 October 1973.

GD214 Trapp, (Mrs.) Maria Augusta. *Around the Year with the Trapp Family*. Music Arranged by Franz Wasner. Illus. by Rosemary Trapp and Nikolaus E. Wolff. New York: Pantheon, 1955. 251p.

GD215 Trapp, (Mrs.) Maria Augusta. *The Story of the Trapp Family Singers*. Philadelphia: Lippincott, 1949. 309p.

GD216 Trapp, (Mrs.) Maria Augusta. *Yesterday, Today, and Forever*. Philadelphia: Lippincott, 1952. 220p.

GD217 Trapp, (Mrs.) Maria Augusta and Ruth T. Murdoch. *A Family on Wheels. Further Adventures of the Trapp Family Singers*. Philadelphia: Lippincott, ca. 1959. 222p.

GD218 *Trapp Family Book of Christmas Songs*. Ed. F. Wasner. New York: Pantheon, n.d.

GD219 Yoder, Don. "The Tradition of the Dutch-English Comedian." *Pa. Folklife*, vol. 21 (1972), Folk Festival Supplement, 7–11.

GE

Cinema and Film

GE1 Bitzer, G. W. *Billy Bitzer*. New York: Farrar Straus & Giroux, 1973. 266p. Rev. by S. Stern, *N.Y. Times Book Rev.*, 16 December 1973, 25. A "purported autobiography" of Johann Gottlob Wilhelm Bitzer (1872–1944), famous cameraman with D. W. Griffith.

GE2 Bogdanovich, Peter. "Ernst Lubitsch." In: *Picture Shows: Peter Bogdanovich on the Movies*. London: Allen & Unwin, 1975.

GE3 Bogdanovich, Peter. *Fritz Lang in America*. London: Studio Vista, ca. 1967; New York: Praeger, 1969. 144p.

GE4 Desiletto, Elliot M. "F. W. Murnau's *Sunrise*: A Critical Study." Diss., Columbia, 1979.

GE5 Dieterle, William. "Max Reinhardt in Hollywood." In: *Max Reinhardt, 1873–1973: A Centennial Festschrift of Memorial Essays and Interviews on the One Hundredth Anniversary of His Birthday*. Ed. George E. Wellwarth, Alfred G. Brooks and Fraeda Parrish. Binghamton: Max Reinhardt Archiv, SUNY-Binghamton, 1974, p.39–45.

GE6 Eisner, Lotte H. *Fritz Lang*. New York: Oxford Univ. Pr., 1977. 416p. Rev. by R. C. Figge, *Die Unterrichtspraxis*, vol. 12, no. 2 (1979), 97–98.

GE7 Finler, Joel. *Stroheim*. Berkeley: Univ. of California Pr., 1968. 144p. Biographical-critical study of a pioneering German-born actor-director (1885–1957).

GE8 Higham, Charles. *Marlene: The Life of Marlene Dietrich*. New York: Norton, 1977. 319p.

GE9 "Klieg-Light Kliegl," *New Yorker*, vol. 33, no. 21 (13 July 1957), 20f. Anton and John Kliegl, inventors of the arc light, were natives of Bavaria.

GE10 Koszarski, Richard. "The Unknown Cinema of Erich von Stroheim: Reconstruction and Analysis of 'The Devil's Passkey,' 'Queen Kelly' and 'Walking Down Broadway'." Diss., New York Univ., 1977.

GE11 Kracauer, Siegfried. *Von Caligari bis Hitler. Ein Beitrag zur Geschichte des deutschen Films*. Hamburg: Rowohlt, 1958. 200p. German trans. of *From Caligari to Hitler. A Psychological History of the German Film*. New York, 1948. Includes many references to refugees in America.

GE12 Krupa, Catharine. "The House of Krupa: A History of the Motion Picture Industry in Lancaster, Pa." *Jour. of the Lancaster Co. Hist. Soc.*, vol. 69 (Michaelmas, 1965), 187–214.

GE13 Lang, Fritz. "The Freedom of the Screen." *Theatre Arts*, vol. 31, no. 12 (1947), 52–55. Views on censorship.

GE14 Manvell, R., and H. Frankel. *German Cinema*. New York: Praeger, 1971. Historical survey incl. the work of Max Reinhardt.

GE15 Sakall, S. Z. *The Story of Cuddles. My Life under the Emperor Francis Joseph, Adolf Hitler and the Warner Brothers*. Trans. by Paul Tabori. London: Cassell, 1954. 231p. Screen actor.

GE16 Sandeen, Eric G. "Anti-Nazi Sentiment in Film: *Confessions of a Nazi Spy* and the German-American Bund." *Amer. Studies*, vol. 20 (Fall 1979), 69–81.

GE17 Tuch, Ronald. "Themes and Structures in the Cinema of Fritz Lang." Diss., New York Univ., 1977.

GE18 Weinberg, Herman G. *The Complete "Greed" of Erich von Stroheim*. Comp. and annotated by H. G. Weinberg. New York: Arno Pr., 1972.

GE19 Weinberg, Herman G. *The Complete "Wedding March" of Erich von Stroheim*. New York: Arno Press, ca. 1972. 261 movie stills. With action synopsis, excerpts from the script.

GE20 Weinberg, Herman G. *An Index to the Creative Work of Erich von Stroheim (1885–1957)*. London: Sight and Sound, 1943. 7p.

GE21 Weinberg, Herman G. *Josef von Sternberg: A Critical Study*. New York: Dutton, 1967. 254p.

GE22 Weinberg, Herman G. *The Lubitsch Touch; A Critical Study*. New York: Dutton, 1968. 344p. On director Ernst Lubitsch.

GE23 Wellwarth, George E., and Alfred G. Brooks, eds., Fraeda Parrish, assoc. ed. *Max Reinhardt, 1873–1973: A Centennial Festival of Memorial Essays and Interviews on the One Hundredth Anniversary of His Birth*. Binghamton, N.Y.: Max Reinhardt Archive, SUNY at Binghamton., 1974. 132p. Memorials by Stella Adler, Fritz Feld, Otto Klemperer, Francis Lederer, Otto Preminger, Jack Warner, and others.